The Rebirth of the West

The Rebirth of the West

The *Americanization* of the Democratic World, *1945–1958*

PETER DUIGNAN AND L. H. GANN

BLACKWELL

Copyright © Peter Duignan and L. H. Gann 1992

First published 1992

Blackwell Publishers
3 Cambridge Center
Cambridge, Massachusetts 02142, USA

108 Cowley Road, Oxford, OX4 1JF, UK

Library of Congress Cataloging in Publication Data

Duignan, Peter.
    The rebirth of the West: the Americanization of the democratic world,
1945–1958/Peter Duignan and L. H. Gann.
    p.   cm.
    ISBN 1-55786-089-0
    1. Civilization, Occidental—History—20th century. 2. Europe—
Civilization—1945– 3. United States—Civilization—1945– 4.
Canada—Civilization—1945– 5. Political culture—History—20th
century. I. Gann, Lewis H., 1924– II. Title.
CB245.D76 1992   90–417
909.82—dc20   CIP

British Library Cataloguing in Publication Data

A CIP catalogue record for this book is available from the British Library.

Typeset in 10/11 pt Garamond
by Butler & Tanner Ltd, Frome and London
Printed in Great Britain by Butler & Tanner Ltd, Frome and London

Contents

Acknowledgements

The authors gratefully acknowledge permission from *New Statesman and Society* to reprint the following poems. "A Eurocrat" by David Thompson, "The British 'U'" by J. M. Crook, "Left Book Club" by John Strachey.

Preface

The story of the revival of the West and the creation of the Atlantic Community has been told in part in masterful works by Sir Richard Mayne, Alan S. Milward, Maurice Crouzet, Walter Laqueur, Derek W. Unwin, Paul Johnson, and many others. Most of these books are, however, now out of date or did not cover all the subjects we discuss. We ourselves sought to go into greater detail, cover more topics, and place greater stress on trans-Atlantic links and reciprocal relations. We propose to examine the extent of the West's achievement in various spheres – political, economic, social, scientific and technical, cultural, and military. Our approach is multi-disciplinary and comparative in nature. Our aim is an interpretative synthesis. Given the enormous extent of the literature available in many languages, we have mainly relied on monographs, secondary works and articles, as well as on a number of private interviews, and our own experiences.

We have tried to blend the thematic and the chronological approach. This method has necessarily entailed some repetition. We have moreover sought to introduce some comparative material and have in a somewhat discursive fashion strayed into more general fields than history, politics, and economics. Sociologists will not find in this book one single model, nor philosophers of history an all-embracing system. But we do have two great themes, inextricably linked, the great postwar recovery, and the special role therein of the United States in creating an Atlantic Community – an extraordinary achievement in the face of extraordinary difficulties. The period from 1945 to 1958 witnessed the acceptance of global responsibilities by the United States, the recovery of Europe, and the partial Americanization of Europe. In this narration, we hope to make some contribution both to the semi-popular history of the contemporary world, and to ongoing debates concerning the Western world at large.

The task of precisely designating the areas to be covered in this book has proved difficult. We deal with the US (to a much lesser extent with Canada) and with Western Europe. But what precisely is Western Europe? The Iron Curtain that divided Western from Eastern Europe was arbitrarily drawn. Poland prides itself on being a Western country. Mecklenburg in East Germany has immensely more in common with Schleswig-Holstein in West Germany than either Mecklenburg or Schleswig-Holstein have, say, with Andalusia in Spain. The Eastern and Central European countries now stress their common European heritage; their peoples look toward the West. In 1989 the Iron Curtain suddenly disintegrated. So, in a wider sense, did the settlement arrived at between the great powers in 1945 – having lasted 44 years, as long as the European settlement effected after the Napoleonic wars in 1815. Nevertheless, the countries of East and Central Europe remain distinct, marked as they all are by their separate historical and national traditions, and also by the long experience of communist rule. Likewise, of course, the countries of Western Europe, as defined by the EEC, NATO, and Warsaw Pact planners, remain diverse in character; their respective citizens' political loyalty primarily continues to center on the nation state. Western Europe lacks a central government or a beloved flag. Membership of trans-national organizations is based on individual states. There are other differences. Western Europe includes members of NATO, and also neutrals such as Sweden, Austria, and Switzerland. Turkey and Greece, by contrast, belong to NATO, but we have not included them on the grounds that they remain linked in many ways to the Middle East or the Balkans, and that they face peculiar problems of their own, as does Israel. We have neglected the British dominions. We have concentrated instead on the US and on the countries that in 1958 united in the European Economic Community and are part of the Atlantic Community.

Our task then has been to fashion a synthesis based on the best scholarship. On the one hand, we are impressed by the many features that these countries have in common, as well as by their differences. We are equally struck by their mutual interdependence and their many links with the US. On the other hand, we are concerned by the relative ignorance that continues to prevail on both sides of the Atlantic concerning the various partners whose safety and well-being remains so inextricably connected. Inadequate interest in particular has been shown by US academics toward the US role in Europe and toward trans-national Western European institutions such as the European Community. Western European studies received little enough attention in the US during the 1950s and the early 1960s, and interest subsequently suffered a further decline. This was caused in part by the diminution in European language teaching from the late 1950s on, and was linked to growing US cultural and political isolationism after the Vietnam war, and earlier to the rise of "area studies." While far more US tourists visited foreign countries than ever before, the number of US students majoring in European languages diminished; hence fewer scholars chose to go into fields where a knowledge of foreign tongues was essential but where there were no funds for study. While African and Asian studies prospered after 1955, European studies declined.

Later on, during the 1980s, many scholars of the first postwar generation retired from academia, including major figures such as Gordon Wright and Gordon Craig at Stanford University. Regional interest among many political scientists and historians increasingly centered on areas such as the Middle East or the Pacific Rim – at the expense of Western Europe, whost stability by now had come to be taken for granted. Demographic shifts in the US away from the East Coast toward the South and West also influenced the trend away from Western Europe; so did more general disenchantment in the US regarding trans-national organizations such as NATO and the UN. There was also disenchantment in Western Europe – albeit for different reasons. Outside Great Britain, European study of the US had always lagged far behind the work done by Americans on Europe, and the position did not improve much during the 1980s. To the growing generation of students, moreover, the trials and successes of the postwar years appeared increasingly to be ancient history – little honored and mostly forgotten.

We hope that our work will in part counteract these trends, and reinvigorate US interest in Europe and vice versa – as well as reporting on a success story. In this respect, our interpretation runs counter to that of so many other academic studies which are marked by a sense of cultural dismay. Neither do we share the widespread dislike of capitalism and the bourgeoisie, and even more of the petty bourgeoisie, found in many lecture halls and Senior Common Rooms. Though intended as a self-contained book, this work will form part of a larger series that will bring the story of the Atlantic Community up to the present. This project will be backed by a number of collaborative works on specific aspects such as the military, politics, economics, society, and culture in Western Europe. The present study will go from 1945 to 1958, the year which saw the start of the European Economic Community (EEC); the completion of Western Europe's economic recovery, following major events such as the granting of independence to Ghana (ushering in the decolonization of Africa), and the launching of *Sputnik* in the USSR. Depending on the context, we shall sometimes, however, look beyond 1958.

We should like to take this opportunity to thank all those at Stanford who have read parts of the manuscript, including Agnes Peterson, Richard Gunther, Wolfgang-Uwe Friedrich, William Ratliff, Robert Deutsch, John Dunlop, Donald Abenheim, Kurt Leube, Ronald I. McKinnon, S. Dorfman, David Marquand, Mikhail Bernstam, William Johnson, Robert Lasorda, Michael Zoellers, David B. Tyack and Sam Barnes while a visiting scholar at the Hoover Institution. We thank St Antony's College, Oxford, for successively giving the two of us the opportunity of doing research there. We would also like to pay tribute to Peter Paret, Macgregor Knox, and Felix Gilbert of the School of Historical Studies at the Institute for Advanced Study, Princeton, who so generously gave of their time to discuss the manuscript with Peter Duignan during his term there in the fall of 1988. We should also like to express our gratitude to our secretary, research assistant and friend, Theory Berger, for her unwearying help and to Terrel Hale who also typed many chapters and brought us hundreds of books.

The authors take full responsibility for any errors that remain, and the opinions and judgements expressed here are theirs alone.

Peter Duignan
L. H. Gann

Introduction

In 1945 much of Western Europe lay prostrate. Whole cities had been reduced to rubble. Millions of people had lost their lives on the battlefields, in bombed towns, and in concentration camps. Millions more had been expelled from their homes. There was the psychological legacy of defeat suffered by all European countries except Britain, the Soviet Union, and a handful of neutral states. There was the legacy of mass murders, conducted in the twentieth century on a scale that would have sickened Genghis Khan. The Germans' very language had been debased. (Old Germany had enriched foreign languages with friendly words such as *Lieder* and *Kindergarten*. Nazi Germany, by contrast, exported words such as *Panzer, Blitzkrieg, Gestapo*, and *Endlösung*.) In the formerly German-occupied countries, resistance and collaboration alike had entailed countless moral dilemmas. Innumerable accounts had been left to settle with real or assumed traitors and criminals. Children had grown up in a world where the grandmotherly concierge next door might well be a police informer with blood on her hands. Forgery and assassination had become for many a patriotic duty. The future looked grim. The Hitler cult might well revive in Germany: the Soviet threat, to many, looked irresistible. Recovery was a prospect uncertain and remote.

Pessimists could draw on an extensive philosophical legacy to justify their forebodings. There were the heirs of Oswald Spengler who, after World War I, had predicted the inevitable decline of the West as part of an immutable, quasi-biological process leading to decadence. There were historians like Arnold Toynbee, who was convinced that Western civilization had exhausted its spiritual vitality. According to Marxist-Leninists, capitalism had reached a point where its internal contradictions had become irresolvable, and no further progress – material or spiritual – might be expected in the capitalist countries.

Gloomier still were the technological pessimists. These included men as different as Winston Churchill, a Tory in love with empire and the glories of war, and H. G. Wells, a self-styled progressive. Long before the outbreak of World War II, Churchill had asked "Shall we all commit suicide?" He had looked to the application of nuclear energy in peace and war alike, to the construction of "a bomb not bigger than an orange," guided without the aid of a human pilot, capable of annihilating an entire township.[1] With terrifying prescience, Churchill anticipated a world in which some pinched, bespectacled bureaucrat might, by remote control, cause entire communities to be wiped out with the same efficiency and unconcern as his gardener might destroy a nest of wasps. In Churchill's view the new power would bring "dangers out of proportion to the growth of man's intellect, to the strength of his character or to the efficacy of his institutions." H. G. Wells, by 1945, had abandoned former optimism; the title of his book *Mind at the End of its Tether* delivered its own message. Worse still was George Orwell's vision in *Nineteen Eighty-Four* which pictured a dreadful totalitarian counter-utopia to come.

> *According to the Marxist historian Eric Hobsbawm, the period since 1945 has been the most revolutionary era in recorded history. Western society, in particular, was structurally transformed in a few decades. Ten times as many students went to university as previously. The young came to dominate society and to revolutionize it. The number of peasant farmers declined by two-thirds, ending drudgery, hard labor and poverty on the West's farms.*
>
> *There was an explosion of knowledge and knowledge industries; the industrial working class declined (though less than the peasants). Industrialization spread through much of the world. Yet as Hobsbawm notes, we who lived through this revolutionary period, especially the intellectuals, seem not to have been wholly aware of it and, therefore, largely failed to understand it.*

Western democracy had emerged triumphant in 1945; but it is difficult to remember how precarious democracy's future had seemed to many just a few years before. From 1933 to 1941 the German National Socialists (the Nazis) had marched from victory to victory, convinced that theirs was the flag of youth, the flag of the future. Judah would perish; a Greater Germanic Empire would rule the world. As late as 1942, the Nazi sway had extended from the Pyrenees to the Volga, from the North Cape to the Libyan desert. It was not only thugs who had placed their faith in the swastika. A generation of German-speaking intellecturals had initially backed the Nazi cause – Carl Jung, Martin Heidegger, Gottfried Benn. So had many gifted admirers abroad – Robert Brasillach, Louis-Ferdinand Céline. Even greater was the number of poets, novelists, and scientists who had regarded, or continued to regard, Soviet communism as the wave of the future, and Stalin as an enlightened overlord – Pablo Neruda, J. D. Bernal, Beatrice and Sidney Webb, Lion Feuchtwanger, Heinrich Mann – the list would fill a telephone directory.

Pessimism about the future of Western democracy was heightened by the fears of a nuclear Armageddon. This strong apprehension remained rooted among many intellectuals thereafter. It would continue during the 1960s and the 1970s when the New Left went on to berate Western civilization for its greed, soullessness, and manipulative cunning. Indeed many Western intel-

---

[1] Winston Churchill, "Shall we all commit suicide?", and "Fifty years hence," in his *Amid These Storms: Thoughts and Adventures*. New York, Scribner, 1932, pp. 250, 274, 280.

lectuals gloried in their alienation and despair. For their patron, they might have chosen Thersites, the archetypal scoffer in Homer's *Iliad*, who railed at the mighty and the brave in the Greek army besieging Troy.

This melancholic mood among intellectuals of many kinds bore, however, no relation to what actually happened. After 1945, the Western world experienced an unparalleled and unanticipated prosperity – thirty golden years. War was followed by an age of achievement that would have seemed incredible during the Great Depression, and even more so during World War II and its immediate aftermath. Islands of poverty were to remain, but overall Western Europe experienced the most rapid recovery in its history. Unemployment – the scourge of the interwar years – strikingly declined. Living standards rose throughout the Atlantic Community. Health improved; street drugs as yet were little used. Families remained reasonably stable, compared to subsequent decades. Western Europe (especially France) achieved a rapid demographic rejuvenation, notwithstanding the numerous gloomy forecasts made on the subject during the interwar period.

The North American economy grew at an equally impressive rate. Women flooded into the work place; education for both men and women expanded enormously. New industries spread to the Southwest and West. Suburbs grew and grew; new transcontinental highways and air routes linked America ever more closely. In all these respects, the Western European countries followed suit in a process correctly described as partial Americanization.

The US took a major part in rebuilding the polities and economies of Western Europe and Japan – with a degree of foresight and generosity unparalleled in world history. The US achieved a predominant position in science and technology; its example profoundly influenced Europe with regard to education, scientific research, technology, business methods, managerial practices, agriculture, and marketing. America's constitutional democracy and consumer culture spread to Europe and Japan. American radio and television, movies, musicals, and print media made a profound impression on popular culture in Europe. English turned into a world-wide language, the new *koine* (the popular Greek during the Hellenistic era) of the Western world. At the same time, the technology and dollar gap between the US and Western Europe began to close, in part through American help.

Even more astounding were the political achievements of the Western world. Democracy revived. Democratic institutions took root in West Germany and Italy. Despite many pessimistic predictions, Nazism failed to revive; the specter of the Third Reich was laid – there would be no Fourth. In part under US influence, the Western European countries developed new forms of political association; former enemies were reconciled. The Western European states developed into liberal democracies; their example later also prevailed in Spain and Portugal where authoritarian governments had held sway. The legitimacy of parliamentary governance and the peaceful relations that came to prevail between the states contrasted most favorably with a long record of domestic instability and foreign wars. National sentiments toward each other improved: the Franco-German rapprochement in particular would have appeared incredible to previous generations brought up to think in terms of a "hereditary enemy" on the wrong side of the Rhine. And there would be no more of the chauvinist tomfoolery that, in England during World War I, had turned the German Shepherd dog into an Alsatian, and the noble British house of Battenberg into Mountbatten.

The architects of this new order all derived from the center – Christian Democrats (Catholics), Social Democrats, and liberals on the European Continent; reformist Tories and Labour people in Britain; progressive-minded Republicans and Democrats in the US. The Western democracies at the time produced an astonishing array of political talent, with luminaries such as Churchill, de Gaulle, Adenauer, de Gasperi, Spaak, Truman, and Eisenhower. Acting in opposition to one another, the moderate parties yet acted in informal concert on major issues. Between them, they strove for the reconciliation of social classes (through welfarism), and for economic productivity (through private enterprise modified by various forms of state intervention). The European Coal and Steel Community (formed 1951) and the European Economic Community (set up in Rome, 1957) were the moderates' achievements. It was the moderates who prevailed in politics.

The US and its allies obtained equal success in defense and foreign policy, the former abandoning its traditional isolationism. The Marshall Plan (developed by the US, and proclaimed in 1947), was designed to shore up the faltering economies of Western Europe, reduce trade barriers, lower unemployment, and ensure political and economic stability. Led by the US, the Western powers mastered the perils of the Cold War. As we see it, this conflict was the inevitable concomitant of then prevailing Soviet doctrines concerning mankind's future. Peaceful coexistence, argued the Soviet theoreticians and their allies in the West, could work only among contending state systems. But there could be no such permanent coexistence of contending social classes. Peaceful coexistence was merely one of many devices to allow the intensification of the international class struggle until such time as socialism would emerge victorious. This doctrine was backed by the mightiest military force in existence, a force committed to a series of sustained offensives, aided by diplomacy, propaganda, and subversion.

> "No peaceful international organization is possible." (Stalin)

But NATO (formed in 1949), with its associated agencies, turned out to be very much more successful than its makers could have anticipated. Despite numerous strains and stresses, the NATO alliance endured longer than any in history, even though it was based on voluntary cooperation among its members rather than on imperial dictation imposed from without. The US avoided the temptations of a preventive war, though by 1949 the Americans held in their arsenal some 200 nuclear bombs – at a time when the Soviet Union was only just ready for its first atomic bomb test. Long-standing national animosities diminished in Western Europe. The various Western European countries under American pressure increasingly opened up towards one another, and also towards North America. However tentatively and imperfectly, a new Atlantic system came into being.[2] The Soviets lost the battle for European and US public opinion which they had won in World War II. Within Western Europe itself the communist challenge proved ineffective even in France and Italy, where the communists after the end of World War II had commanded widespread support among workers and intellectuals alike.

The late 1940s and the 1950s were also years of cultural creativity, in literature, the arts, architecture, and the study of society. Despite numerous forecasts to the contrary, religion failed to decline. Instead religious minorities, such as the Catholics in Britain, West Germany and the US, improved their political, social, and economic position; anti-semitism ceased to be a major force in Western politics and society.

Many dark patches of course remained in the tapestry. As cities grew in size, so did traffic snarls and pollution. Horse-drawn plows gave way to tractors, old-fashioned peasant holdings to rationalized farms. Agricultural production grew, but so did surplus mountains of butter and lakes of wine. In politics, inherent problems remained between the European Economic Community on the one hand and the US on the other; between the member states of the European Economic Community themselves; and between national and European loyalties. The new European institutions, designated by impersonal acronyms, created burgeoning bureaucracies that kept growing in size, scope, and officiousness. (Bureaucrats would end by attempting to standardize tractor seats and to banish swallows' nests from cow sheds.) Poverty diminished, but did not disappear. Growing wealth, heightened physical and social mobility were sometimes paid for by a sense of social disorientation. In the desperate race to rebuild the European economies, ecological problems were largely (though not wholly) ignored. The Europeans did wonders in reviving basic industries such as agriculture, coal, iron, and steel. But they all too readily shaped their policies to confront the problems of the past instead of the future.

The US became a global power with global responsibilities and a greatly expanded foreign policy establishment. The economy kept growing and a consumer revolution brought goods and services to the great majority. Women kept flowing into the workplace; more men and women graduated from high school and college, and the American worker became the most productive and highest paid in history. The US had specific troubles of its own, however. At the end of World War II, the American economy stood supreme. The "American century" supposedly would last forever. But as Western Europe and Japan recovered, the trade gap, the "dollar gap", and the technology gap between the US and its allies naturally began to close – partly because of American aid. In the US as in Western Europe, spending on social welfare and entitlements increased. The US progressively started to tax its citizens

---

[2]We have borrowed the phrase from Forrest Davis, *The Atlantic System: The Story of Anglo-American Control of the Seas.* Westport, Conn., Greenwood Press, 1941, reprinted 1973.

more, to invest proportionately less, and to spend less on research and development. Hence its predominance slowly diminished, though it remained the world's leading economic and scientific power. The US also had to contend with the ugliness of McCarthyism. Racial discrimination did weaken, and compared with multinational countries such as the Soviet Union or Yugoslavia, the US was indeed a paradise for ethnic minorities. Nevertheless the pace of racial reform in the US was excruciatingly slow.

There were unexpected difficulties for the Atlantic Community at large. Yesterday's solutions all too easily turned into tomorrow's predicaments. At the end of World War II, the interventionist state and the welfare state, with Keynesianism modified and vulgarized, commanded widespread, though not universal, public approval. Solid popular support for the welfare state went with an almost instinctive trust for a new class of diploma-bearing "experts". Planners were assumed to know the secret of making mankind wealthy, and educators of making mankind wise. But the ever-expanding state, with its burgeoning bureaucracies and their collective arrogance, in turn created new problems that the architects of the welfare state failed to anticipate.

Overall, the history of the postwar years turned out to be a great success story. There was not merely a German *Wirtschaftswunder*; there were corresponding miracles in the other countries of Western Europe. The West, especially the US, remained the main source of artistic, technological, scientific, industrial, and agricultural innovation in the world at large. In every respect, Western democracy proved more successful than the dictatorship over the proletariat of the *nomenclatura* within the Soviet bloc. The West remained inviolate from invasion, and the world free of global war. It was an age of achievement. Who at the war's end could have foreseen this outcome? And who could have asked for more?

PART I

The State of Europe: 1945

The Tread of War

TRIAL BY COMBAT

Even in defeat, Hitler's impact on Europe was immense. His victories shattered the existing order in Europe – East and West. Defeat at German hands discredited the Third Republic in France. Defeat also discredited for a time those smaller democracies, Norway, Denmark, Belgium, and Holland, that had placed their trust in social progress at home and an under-armed neutrality in their dealings abroad. (Norway, for instance, was completely unprepared for war, and mobilized no more than 25,000 men; Switzerland, a country only slightly more populous than Norway, by contrast, stood ready to put 400,000 men into the field.) Even Great Britain in 1940 held on only by a narrow margin. British belief in ultimate victory at the time rested on nothing more than faith, a faith not shared either by the bulk of public opinion on the European Continent, or in Britain by the remnant of the appeasers and a minority of craven politicians who, like Dick Stokes and Lloyd George, looked for a negotiated peace.

The *Wehrmacht* and the *Waffen SS*, by contrast, for a time were held in awe all over the world. Their military victories were paralleled by what was probably the last invasion of German words into the English language, military terms such as *Panzer, Blitzkrieg,* and *Schwerpunkt*; and words derived from the vocabulary of genocide including *Endlösung,* (Final Solution), *Untermenschen,* and *Gestapo.* For a time, the German soldier seemed – and often felt himself – invincible. So great was the impact of German victories that even 40 years after Germany's surrender, books continued to come out in great numbers from popular and academic printing presses in praise of Germany's military achievements. Many of these conclude that the Germans had "a genius for war," that made them superior to all their opponents.[1]

The German military certainly earned their reputation. The Germans were the first to develop the *Blitzkrieg* doctrine in a theoretical as well as practical

---

[1]Colonel T. N. Dupuy, *A Genius for War: The German Army and General Staff: 1807–1947.* London, MacDonald and Jane's, 1977.

fashion. They were past masters in the art of coordinating tanks, infantry, and artillery; they stood out in their willingness to launch immediate counterattacks to regain lost ground; in their capacity of improvising and reforming broken divisions into *Kampfgruppen* (combat teams); in the initiative and dash possessed by junior leaders; in the skill involved in operating in the face of overwhelming Allied airpower; in their infantry training that made the best possible use of infiltration and small unit tactics. The Germans rarely tired of fighting, and when matters came to a crunch, even cooks, clerks, and mechanics readily served as combat troops. The German reserve officers (who commanded the bulk of the troops actually in combat), and the German noncommissioned officers proved superb by any standards. The *Wehrmacht,* and also the *Waffen SS,* formed one of the best fighting machines in the history of war. Their exploits for a time enormously added to the political reputation of the Nazi regime for which the *Landser* (the German equivalent of the GI) had fought with such misplaced dedication.

Fortunately for Europe and the world at large, the German military also suffered from distinct weaknesses. Cyril Falls, a doyen of British military historians dryly put it:

> When we admire ... German skill in strategy, tactics, administration, and design in equipment, we ought to make the qualification that the state which embarks upon two wars, entirely on its initiative and with every reasonable means of assessing the risks, within a single generation, and is routed hip and thigh in both, must be held to fall short of supreme military capacity and genius.[2]

For all its stunning successes, the *Wehrmacht* was in fact in no wise as effective as the *Kaiserheer*, led in World War I by those reactionaries whom Hitler heartily despised. The Kaiser's armies had utterly defeated Russia – a feat that the *Wehrmacht* could never achieve. In 1917, a year before World War I actually ended, Imperial Germany could in all probability still have secured a negotiated peace, had the general staff been willing to relinquish the Western front conquests and the *Reichsland* Alsace-Lorraine. Hitler, by contrast, was beaten by 1944, and no Allied power then would have considered negotiation with the Reich.

The *Wehrmacht,* for one thing, lacked a sense for grand, as opposed to minor, strategy. No such sense could have developed, given the manner in which the German military, like the civilian, administration broke into a collection of ill-coordinated military fiefdoms – Navy, Army, *Luftwaffe, Waffen SS* (the latter with its own ill-fated field divisions), and finally the *Volkssturm* (Home Guard, under the Nazi Party's control). German science, depleted by racial and political prosecution, began to lag – this at a time when war had begun to speed up the rate of technological and scientific innovation in many fields.

Whereas Germany in World War I had been one of the world's undisputed

[2]Cyril Falls, *A Hundred Years of War 1850-1950*. New York, Collier Books, 1962, p. 351.

leaders in science, Germany in World War II dropped behind in the race. The Germans still led in rocketry and the design of jet engines, for instance; but the major breakthroughs in medicine, and also in military technology (including RADAR, ASDIC, SONAR), the proximity fuse, the "Norden" bomb sight, the long-range fighter plane, the first rudimentary computer (built by the British to decipher German codes), and ultimately, the atomic bomb derived neither from Germany nor from the Soviet Union but from the Western allies.

In 1942, the German High Command was dumbfounded when they realized that Germany ranked behind the Soviet Union in tank technology. *Blitzkrieg* practitioners such as Guderian could not get their ideas fully accepted. The German army remained essentially wedded to the ideas of World War I, when strategists such as Alfred von Schlieffen had planned for massive battles of encirclement fought in the traditional manner. As Matthew Cooper, a British historian, explains, "The Germans developed substantial *panzer* formations in the years preceding the outbreak of World War II. But these forces were not built according to the specifications of the armor enthusiasts. The most influential generals distrusted the *Blitzkrieg* concept, and were reluctant to use armored forces in the independent manner that Guderian and his colleagues had anticipated."[3]

Neither did Hitler prove quite up to the mark of an inspired military revolutionary. For all his imagination, his mind remained bounded by his experience in the trenches in World War I. He could not therefore conceive of an elastic defense dependent on quick withdrawals and rapid armored thrusts. He could not consider strategy in terms other than the extent of ground captured or the sheer number of divisions employed, without regard to their varying composition, tasks, and quality. Above all, the *Führer* mistakenly believed that leadership in the end rested on sheer willpower, on the willingness to throw men recklessly into battle and to accept limitless casualties – concepts applied with equally disastrous effects by Karl Dönitz, Hitler's Grand Admiral and final successor, in German naval warfare.[4]

The German armed forces accordingly began to suffer from numerous disabilities of a kind not usually associated with Germany. They began to lag behind the Allies in many (though by no means all) technical areas, and encountered a problem popularly associated only with Western armies, an excessively low ratio of combat to administrative troops – a state of affairs brought about largely by Hitler's preoccupation with increasing the number of divisions, even though the newly formed units were much below strength and customary competence. Notwithstanding Germany's reputation for efficiency, long-range planning was ill-conceived. Military intelligence, especially intelligence regarding the Soviet Union and the USA, was quite inadequate. This was inexcusable. For the price of a few dollars or francs, the

[3]Matthew Cooper, *The German Army 1933–1945: Its Political and Military Failure*. New York, Bonanza Books, 1984.
[4]Peter Padfield, *Dönitz, The Last Führer, Portrait of a Nazi War Leader*. New York, Harper and Row, 1984.

"Foreign Armies" branch of German staff intelligence could have purchased just before the war – among other publications – a comparative assessment of the various European powers' military capability written by Max Werner (Alexander Schiffrin), an expatriate German officer of left-wing persuasion.[5] Writing on his own, without the resources of a huge and expensive intelligence organization, Werner produced a striking balance sheet from whose perusal the *Wehrmacht* could only have profited.

Instead the German High Command entered the greatest campaign in world history, code-named "Barbarossa," the campaign against the Soviet Union, with a degree of carelessness that exceeded even the much-derided British in the Crimean War and the Boer War. The German – like the British – High Command knew little about the Soviet Union, its enormous military potential, industrial strength, and capacity for recuperation. The Germans' lack of adequate planning was all the more astounding since, during the days of the Weimar Republic, the *Reichswehr* had cooperated with the Red Army; German officers had trained with Soviet forces; Germans had bought Soviet equipment. But during World War II, they had insufficient intelligence concerning the location of Soviet industries, the morale of the Red Army, or its equipment. The Germans entered the war without adequate preparations for a winter campaign, and were without proper maps and clothing. They consistently underestimated the ability of Soviet military leaders to learn from their mistakes. In the end, the Soviets proved superior not just in terms of numbers, but also in the high degree of operational and tactical skill practiced in the conduct of individual battles.[6]

Worse still was the German generals' inability to preserve their professional independence from the ever-accelerating intrusion of Nazi political leadership. The generals forsook their military duty, and abandoned their responsibility toward the men whom they led. They allowed the *Führer,* a gifted amateur, to direct even minor military operations; they permitted a dangerous civilian arrogation of technical military leadership. Both from the standpoint of its narrow class interests and of Germany's as a whole, the *Wehrmacht* should have stuck to its original claim to be the sole arms-bearing corporation in the *Reich.* Instead, the *Waffen SS* grew into a powerful political army as well as into an efficient military force. The *Wehrmacht,* an army that took pride in

---

[5]Max Werner, *The Military Strength of the Powers.* New York, Modern Age Books, 1939, originally published as *Der Aufmarsch zum Zweiten Weltkrieg,* Strasbourg, Stefan Brandt Verlag, 1938. Werner predicted that there was a very real danger that, despite their superior economic potential, Great Britain and France might receive a fatal blow before they were ready to raise mass armies and place their industries on a war footing. He stressed Germany's vulnerability to air assaults and, while overestimating the extent of the Soviets' immediate superiority over the Germans, correctly insisted that the Soviet Union's resources would prove superior to Germany's. Italy's real strength, by contrast, in no wise – according to Werner – corresponded to Mussolini's boasts. For a more recent assessment concerning deficiencies in German planning and intelligence, see Louis Rotundo, "The creation of Soviet reserves, and the 1941 Campaign," *Military Affairs,* vol. 50, no. 1, January 1986, pp. 21–8.

[6]For a detailed analysis of one particular engagement, see for instance, Major R. McMichael, "The Battle of Jassy-Kishinev, (1944)," *Military Review,* July 1985, pp. 52–65.

honor and comradeship, yielded in 1936 almost without a struggle on the so-called race question. Parts of the *Wehrmacht* were thus implicated in the political crimes of the Nazis, the murder campaign against the Jews, the barbarous treatment of Soviet and other supposedly inferior prisoners of war. In the attempted coup of July 1944, part of the old officer corps did try to restore traditional values and concepts of honor – much to its credit. But by then it was too late. The generals had been demoralized by Hitler's brutality; above all, the German generals had missed too many moral *Schwerpunkte* (axes of assault in German military parlance), with consequences that ultimately deprived the *Wehrmacht* leaders of all power and true self-respect.

Under the impact of war, especially in the East, the German army changed its character. The *Wehrmacht* began its career smartly, with a high sense of formal discipline. Thereafter, it became increasingly egalitarian, with a great sense of comradeship between field officers and men. The smart uniforms were transformed into British-style battledress and camouflage coats, and these in turn all too often into assorted rags. The German army in the East widely came to suffer from an extreme sense of alienation.[7] The soldiers felt themselves misunderstood by the "home front" where a man due to be posted to the East was likely to become an object of pity. The soldiers were shocked by Germany's initial unwillingness to wage total war, by the privileges claimed by the *Goldfasanen* (the "golden pheasants," meaning the Nazi Party's senior functionaries); the *Landser* widely came to believe that the "true Germany" was to be found in the weapon pits of the Eastern Front (just as many a patriotic German Jew exiled in Britain or the US felt convinced that he and his kind alone represented the "true Germany").

As the war dragged on, fewer and fewer combat officers could respond to the apparently ever more senseless orders that came from above. The *Landser* became dispirited, at Allied superiority in numbers and airpower, at the Reich's apparent inability to produce a sufficient quantity of weapons on a par with the Soviet T34 or the *Katyusha* rocket, and at the *Luftwaffe's* failure to resist Western airpower. The soldiers kept on fighting. But they began to lose trust in their generals, as did the *Führer* himself. The German high command became emasculated through the execution or degradation of so many of its senior leaders; there was a disastrous disintegration of structure and widespread lack of moral courage at the top. (It was not insignificant that many a German officer translated the acronym OKW *Oberkommando der Wehrmacht* as *oben kein Widerstand*, "no backbone at the top.")

By the end of the war, much of the *Wehrmacht* had turned into a crazy quilt of disparate formations, many of them hastily raised and ill-equipped. Most, however, continued to fight stubbornly. (The defenders of Berlin, for instance, were sustained in many cases by the military equivalent of the "Cargo Cult," a cult among South Sea islanders who expected imminent redemption through

---

[7]James Lucas, *War on the Eastern Front: 1941–1945. The German Soldier in Russia.* New York, Stein and Day, 1979. Alan Clark, *Barbarossa: The Russian German Conflict 1941–45.* New York, Quill, 1985, pp. 192–4.

cargoes brought by mysterious white strangers – the soldiers hoped for deliverance through new wonder weapons, or a mythical "Army Group Wenck," or even US paratroopers who would somehow relieve the beleaguered city.) But faith in the Nazi system by that time had largely waned. The men who had seen the initial successes of Nazism had mostly perished; the younger age cohorts in the *Wehrmacht* associated the swastika with retreat and defeat.

The denazification of the German army had begun in the fox holes. The Hitler movement had proclaimed a millenarian creed, with Hitler as Messiah and the Jews as Satan. The New Order, according to its prophets and profiteers, would create a "New Man", steely and hard, icy-cold, a worker-warrior whose imagined characteristics strikingly resembled "Soviet Man" as envisaged by Stalin's literary hacks. But the new Aryan man had failed to materialize. The once-proud *Wehrmacht* became an army of war prisoners. The survivors became part of a generation which was for the most part sceptical of militant ideologies and distrustful of generals and of traditional authority.

The very enormity of defeat put an end to all those dreams of German hegemony that had sustained the two "German wars."[8] There was no more room for "stab-in-the-back" legends of the kind created after World War I. Given German's all-prevailing misery, the kinds of grievance that had inspired Free Corps volunteers after World War I seemed petty and insubstantial in 1945. Hitler's grisly end, and the ignominious conduct of his surviving paladins left no room for the German equivalent of a Napoleonic legend. The romantic sentiments, mirrored in those German soldiers' songs that echoed the sound of tramping boots, and that interminably rhymed *Mut* with *Blut* and *rot* with *tot,* had waned in the trenches. There was much less appeal than formerly in the thumpety-thump music that had enjoined little Erika or little Annemarie to wait for the return of their menfolk from hiking, hunting, or war. Such sentiments no longer corresponded to the realities of a grey world where women cleared rubble in the street, cut firewood, earned money by fair means and foul, and cared for wounded veterans. The only tune of those years to survive was "Lilli Marlene" meeting her lover underneath the lamp post by the barrrack gate – a song that the Germans came to share with their enemies.

Then came the end, das *Ende mit Schrecken* (the terrible end) that so many had feared. The experience of defeat proved particularly devastating in East Germany where Russian violence and rapes continued for two years until 1947, as shown by professor Norman Naimark in his ongoing research. Relations between the Germans and the Soviet victors, of course, varied enormously. Some elite units were highly disciplined, and impressed the Germans who had been taught to regard the Russians as *Untermenschen*. There was no attempt at racial extermination. But mass rape nevertheless had an enormous political and emotional impact on the Germans, making the Red Army appear as a terrible specter. Rapes were not merely the result of indis-

[8]The phrase derives from Lt Col D. J. Goodspeed, *The German Wars: 1914–1945.* New York, Bonanza Books, 1985.

cipline on the part of Soviet troops, but also sprang from a Soviet desire to humiliate the Germans, as the Russians themselves had previously been humiliated. Soviet political officers tried to prevent rape, understanding the disastrous political impact, but usually failed in their endeavor. The subject still remains largely taboo in Germany and the Soviet Union, rapes at the time passing under the euphemism of "stolen bicycles."

To the worn-out, ragged survivors of the *Wehrmacht* there remained nothing but the silent conviction that they had fought better than their opponents, and the unspoken fraternity of the defeated, that fellow feeling that animated those "poor front swine" who had shared the hell of Kursk or of the Falaise Gap. In a sense they felt themselves victims; whereas demobilized British and American soldiers were usually willing enough to indicate their war service and decoration in their curriculum vitae, or in potted autobiographies for *Who's Who*, *Wehrmacht* veterans would rarely do so – not to speak of former members of the *Waffen SS*. The bulk of the *Landsers* – like demobilized soldiers in the Allied armies – were determined henceforth to rebuild their lives, to make up for the lost years. The most stunningly successful film in the immediate postwar years was the American movie, *The Best Years of Our Lives,* which showed how demobilized GIs adjusted to a civilian existence. Germany had reached the "hour of zero." As a German veteran and an ex-Nazi put it, "much has been made of German *Wirtschaftswunder,* the economic miracle of the later years, fueled by the generosity of the Marshall Plan. I believe its roots were firmly anchored in the utter despair of our defeat. There was no way to go but up or to perish as a people."[9]

Defeat put an end to those who had collaborated with the Nazis in the occupied territories. The collaborators had distinguished themselves, not only by their lack of patriotism, but commonly also by their cowardice in defeat. (For instance, on "Mad Tuesday", in September 1944, thousands of Dutch NSB (*National-Socialistische Beweging*) members – gripped by mass hysteria – suddenly fled from their homes, leaving everything behind. Their leaders, sworn to die to the last man, were the first to go. Their fear-psychosis and flight discredited the movement forever.)[10]

Fascism in Italy fared no better. Fascism, for all its brutality, had been more benign, less totalitarian in its claims than Nazism; neither the monarchy nor the church had been eliminated as powers within the body politic, thereby allowing an opportunity for Italy's peaceful reconstruction after the disasters brought about by Mussolini's German alliance. The Fascists had turned out to be good at building public works. But they failed in what they had exalted the most – the enterprise of war. Italy's military performance in World War I had been much more impressive than in World War II, when Fascist leadership had failed to match the excellent qualities of the much-derided Italian soldier.

[9]Alfons Heck, *A Child of Hitler: Germany in the Days When God Wore a Swastika.* Frederick, Col., Renaissance House, 1985, p. 204.

[10]Henry A. van der Zee, *The Hunger Winter: Occupied Holland, 1944–5.* London, Jill Norman and Hobhouse, 1982, p. 23.

As General Siegfried Westphal, Field Marshal Rommel's chief of staff, explained, the Italian army was ill-prepared for war; its armor, artillery, communications system, and air force were all antiquated; supplies were quite inadequate; the soldiers were poorly fed. The splendid dash of individual units (especially those drawn from the old cavalry regiments), of specialist formations, and small units in the navy (for instance the motor torpedo boats) could not make up for Fascist inefficiency and for the lack of popular support for a war waged on the side of Germany.[11] When Italy capitulated, Fascism was both dead and damned. For the defeated Italians, as for the Germans, there was henceforth no way but "up or out" in a mood of sturdy self-reliance.

By contrast, war vindicated Western democracy: in the English-speaking countries democracy proved itself supremely capable of surmounting the ultimate challenge. The Westerners' astounding success has of late been tarnished by a spate of revisionist works that find fault with both the British and the American soldier. British defense, according to Correlli Barnett, a distinguished British historian, was flawed by the defects of British society. Even the Eighth Army that smashed Rommel's forces at El Alamein was "a cumbersome and inferior fighting instrument capable of winning against German troops only in a carefully rehearsed, tightly controlled setpiece operation with ample margins of numerical and material superiority."[12]

Barnett was not alone, nor the first to make such a harsh judgement. Discouraged by continued defeats, there were high-placed Britons during the early 1940s who mourned that the soldier of World War II was no longer the equal of his father in World War I, a belief that failed to explain why British marines, airmen, and sailors – drawn from the same manpower pool – had everywhere done as well as their opposite numbers in German and Japan. The US Army (as distinct from the Marines, Navy and Air Force) fared, if anything, even worse in the assessment of academicians. The performance of the German Army had always exceeded that of the US forces, argues Martin L. van Crefeld, a gifted Israeli student of strategy,[13] and according to Colonel Dupuy, the Germans consistently outfought the far more numerous Allied armies that eventually defeated the Third Reich.

The Allied armies indeed had many initial weaknesses. During the interwar years, the British and American armies had long been under-manned and under-funded. Shortages of funds and promotion prospects, and lack of opportunities for realistic large-scale maneuvers had discouraged recruitment of able and ambitious men. The British army had faced two incompatible tasks – to serve as a constabulary of empire, thin on the ground in every British possession overseas, and to wage conventional campaigns in Europe. The regimental spirit, while commendable in itself, was so strong that infantry and cavalry

[11]Siegfried Westphal, *Heer in Fesseln: Aus den Papieren des Stabschefs von Rommel, Kesselring und Rundstedt*. Bonn, Athenäum Verlag, 1950, pp. 197–200.

[12]Correlli Barnett, *The Desert Generals*. London, Pan Books, 1962, p. 313.

[13]Martin L. van Creveld, *Fighting Power: German and US Army Performance, 1939–1945*, Westport, Conn., Greenwood Press, 1982.

regiments at first seemed like military confederations, parochial in their loyalties, wedded more to good form than to technical efficiency. (By contrast, the engineers, the tank corps (as distinct from the aristocratic cavalry regiments), the supply services, the Royal Air Force and the artillery formed unified corps without regional loyalties; they valued functional more than gentlemanly virtues, and they did uniformly well.)

The Americans had troubles of their own. They were much less beset than the British by problems of social class. But starved of funds and public support for many years, their land forces were at first minuscule in numbers. The US Army in 1939, numbering 507,150 men, including regulars, National Guard, and reserves, was inferior to a host of minor powers such as Switzerland. Many of the original cadres were lost in the first disastrous campaigns against the Japanese. Having mobilized for war, the Americans tended to be seduced by what Werner more than 40 years before had called their "intoxication with technics at the expense of intrinsic military criteria; one-sided industrial-statistical estimates, and the substitution of technology for strategy."[14]

There was a striking inequality of sacrifice within the US armed forces – enhanced by a huge administrative superstructure needed to maintain the GI's relatively high living standards. As Robert Leckie points out in his fine history, rotation was not introduced until late in the war; hence the same men were again and again thrown into battle. There was even greater disparity between the armed forces and the civilians for whom war widely entailed a rise, rather than a fall in living standards. (By 1944, the US produced 45 percent of the arms of *all* belligerents; but even this was only half of the national output; the other half went to consumer goods.) The quip "you never had it so good" derived from the armed services to chide those well-fed, well-clothed, and well-paid noncombatants who had come from underprivileged homes, and benefited from the country's newfound prosperity.[15] The specialist consistently took precedence over the ordinary soldier, especially the infantryman, who bore the main burden of combat. Seduced by their incurable diploma-worship, the Americans mistakenly put the most intelligent men into specialist units instead of the infantry – the most versatile yet in a sense the most specialized arm on the battlefield.

There were also psychological problems. The Americans did not hate the Germans as they detested the Japanese, whose atrocities against Allied prisoners and civilian internees almost paralleled the horrors of Belsen. The war in Europe seemed infinitely remote to the bulk of Americans – save for those engaged in battle, and their friends and relatives. Except in elite units, there was little enthusiasm. As Leckie puts it, the draftee's "self-imposed nickname of GI was an abbreviation of the phrase 'Government Issue,' and that was what he thought of the Army and the war."[16]

[14]Max Werner, *The Great Offensive: The Strategy of Coalition Warfare.* New York, Viking Press, 1942, p. 322.

[15]Robert Leckie, *The Wars of America,* New York, Harper and Row, 1981, pp. 781–2.

[16]Ibid., p. 787.

And yet the Anglo-Saxon democracies' capacity for war enormously outweighed their weaknesses. Their strength derived not merely from their enormous economic potential, great as it was, but from the structure of democratic society. Democratic governance – unlike that of its enemies – proved legitimate. Unlike Hitler, Mussolini, and Stalin, neither Roosevelt nor Churchill feared plots from their generals. American society – based on the free enterprise principle – created a productive miracle that would have appeared improbable even to writers of science fiction. (Between July 1940 and August 1945, the US turned out 86,000 tanks and 207,000 aircraft of all kinds.) The British and Americans had a credible record of maintaining civil liberty. (The internment of Japanese Americans in the US and of many German Jewish refugees in Great Britain was a regrettable departure from the Allies high standards; all the same, civilian prisoners in every other belligerent country – Germany, Japan, France, the Soviet Union – would have given their eye teeth to trade places with those in Anglo-Saxon hands.)

American society, though ethnically mixed, displayed its accustomed cohesion. German-Americans, Italian-Americans, Japanese-Americans overwhelmingly proved loyal, as did the great mass of African and Asian soldiers in the British empire forces. The Germans never managed to raise the equivalent of the Vlassov Army (recruited from Russian prisoners-of-war) among British or American troops. The American way of life made a strong appeal even to German prisoners-of-war in the US. There were about 400,000 of them (as against only 50,000 Italians). Of a selected sample returning to Germany, 74 percent left with friendly feelings toward the US.[17] (They included men of subsequent prominence in the Federal Republic of Germany such as Baron Rüdiger von Wechmar, later West German Ambassador in Washington.)

Democratic society also produced superior morale. The soldiers of the English-speaking nations never envisaged ultimate defeat – not even the British in the worst days of their war. As Siegfried Westphal later testified, the British soldiers may have lacked enthusiasm, but they possessed a much more valuable quality, an unshakable equanimity. Even at times of disastrous defeat, they remained sturdily convinced that they would win in the end. The divisions drawn from the United Kingdom were the toughest; tenacious in assault and steady in defense. They were remarkably consistent in quality; they were distinguished not so much by dash, as by steadiness.[18]

British society moreover produced a great array of outstanding military leaders. Perhaps the greatest of these was Sir William (later Viscount) Slim, the very model of a democratic general. Blending humanity with discipline and leadership, profoundly aware how morale, training, and health interrelated as military factors, Slim rebuilt the British Fourteenth Army in Burma. He turned a dispirited and defeated army, ethnically heterogeneous, feeling

[17]Arnold Kammer, *Nazi Prisoners of War in America*. New York, Stein and Day, 1979.
[18]Westphal, *Heer in Fesseln*, p. 200.

itself forgotten, into a powerful force that inflicted on the formidable Japanese the greatest defeat they had ever suffered on land.[19]

After the initial euphoria following World War II, British military leadership was bitterly challenged by academic writers – just as it was during the aftermath of World War I. Many of them questioned the British class system that produced these leaders – especially the public (that is to say private boarding) schools that, in the censors' view embodied the system's archaic values. For instance, Norman Dixon, a military psychologist, considers that the public schools had a deleterious effect on British generalship by helping to shape authoritarian personalities, casting men into conventional and inflexible molds ill-suited to the needs of high command. Correlli Barnett's criticism goes further. The public schools, Oxford, and Cambridge, he argues, artificially separated youngsters from aristocratic and upper-middle-class backgrounds from the bulk of the nation. The public schools taught nothing about technology, business, economics, military strategy, or the realities of power in general. Not surprisingly, British technology and British military leadership became increasingly obsolete, and military performance suffered accordingly. All in all, the public schools came to be held responsible for a variety of ills, ranging from the inefficiency of British factories and the incompetence of British generals, to an acquired taste for sodomy. Public school values, the critics add, moreover seeped down into the elitist grammar schools, whose graduates aped the social values of their betters – much to the nation's disadvantage.[20]

We are not convinced by these charges, for the overwhelming majority of successful British generals and military thinkers who made their marks before and during World War II all came from these derided institutions. (Basil Liddell Hart, Sir Richard O'Connor, Earl Wavell, Viscount Montgomery, Orde Wingate had attended great public schools; Slim graduated from King Edward's School, Birmingham, a member of the exclusive "headmasters' conference" group of educational establishments.)

American society proved equally capable of turning out great leaders (a substantial proportion of whom – ironically enough – bore Teutonic names such as Nimitz, Eisenhower, Wedemeyer, Kruger, Eichelberger). Once fully trained and led with dash and imagination by a general such as George Patton, "the Americans proved fantastically good in a manner that neither Japanese nor German planners had anticipated. In the Pacific, the Americans pioneered 'island hopping' and new amphibious techniques; they could also take immense casualties without flinching. (In the assault units at Iwo Jima, the average loss was 60 per cent.)"[21] In Northwestern Europe, the US Third Army's record was unmatched. Hubert Essame, a British major-general not wont to give

---

[19]Major General E. K. G. Sixsmith, *British Generalship in the Twentieth Century*. London, Arms and Armour Press, 1970, esp. pp. 280–1.

[20]See Norman Dixon, *On the Psychology of Military Incompetence*. London, Cape, 1976. Correlli Barnett, *The Swordbearers: Studies in Supreme Command in the First World War*. London, Eyre and Spottiswood, 1963. Correlli Barnett, *The Collapse of British Power*. New York, Morrow, 1972.

[21]For details, see Bill D. Ross, *Iwo Jima: Legacy of Valor*. New York, Vanguard Press, 1985.

unnecessary praise to foreigners, said that the Third Army's record was "peerless by any measure and in the strictest sense of the term." In statistics alone, it outclassed "anything achieved by any other Allied Army."[22] The Third Army had suffered 136,856 casualties and had accounted for 1,486,700 of the enemy by May 8, 1945.

Overall, the Allied victory in Normandy proved even more crushing than the spectacular success of the Soviets who at the time shattered the German "Army Group Center" in a great disaster inflicted on the *Wehrmacht*. The "West Wall" on the Atlantic had failed, as had the Maginot line, and many other famed fortifications. (The Western forces engaged in Normandy were considerably smaller than the massive Soviet armies thrown into battle against the Army Group Center. Nevertheless, the Allies between them annihilated 27 infantry and 11 armored divisions; 500,000 German soldiers were put out of action or killed, as against 28 German divisions, and 300,000 soldiers written off through the catastrophe suffered by the Army Group Center.) In Normandy, an entire OKW "theatre" was simply obliterated. It was the most shattering blow suffered by the *Wehrmacht* in its history.[23]

The Allies performed miracles of mobilization. Scholars wont to praise German and Japanese over British and American performances are apt to forget the time-lag involved in getting armies into a combat-worthy condition. Japan had been at war in China since the early 1930s; the soldiers who faced the Americans in 1941 were battle-hardened men. The Germans had at first enjoyed similar advantages, having introduced conscription in 1935. Hastily raised, the new *Wehrmacht* had as many teething troubles as the Anglo-American mass armies in the first stages of their formation. It was initially riddled with inefficiency, impeded by military conservatism, beset by intrigues and dissensions. As Kurt von Tippleskirch, a German general not noted as a detractor of the *Wehrmacht*, put it, "the army that entered the war in 1939 still had substantial weaknesses; it was certainly not ready from the standpoint of top level military performance."[24] Thereafter, the *Wehrmacht* enjoyed all those advantages prayed for by the manager of a first-class football team – a series of trials in ascending order of severity. It steadily improved its performance – first in the large-scale, but unbloody maneuvers involved in the successive occupations of Austria and Czechoslovakia, and thereafter by the relatively easy Polish campaign. By 1940, the *Wehrmacht* was a magnificently professional force.

The Western Allies, by contrast, were given little time. They had to build their massive land forces in a hurry. The British only introduced conscription in 1939, the Americans in 1940. Not surprisingly, the US troops first engaged in North Africa in 1942 still had much to learn;. they performed no better

[22] John Keegan, *Six Armies in Normandy: From D-Day to the Liberation of Paris*. Harmondsworth, Penguin Books, 1982, p. 425.

[23] Ibid., p. 424–6.

[24] General Kurt von Tippelskirch, *Geschichte des Zweiten Weltkriegs*, Bonn, Athenäum Verlag, 1959, p. 7.

than the *Wehrmacht* would probably have done in 1936. But the speed of Allied mobilization was breathtaking. The British by 1943 had 4,841,000 men under arms; in the US, no less than 16,000,000 – an achievement unparalleled in history.

The Americans' record deserves special consideration, given the extent of the criticism to which the GIs have since been subjected in comparison with their Japanese and German opponents. During the war, the British and French had all too often explained their initial failures in terms of the Germans' "special genius" for war. Once the war ended, the sources available to historians created a new bias. German material available to English-speaking authors was dominated by official records and, later, by memoirs of captured German officers. American sources were much broader, and featured large bodies of correspondence, anecdotes, interviews from soldiers of all ranks, and the findings of psychologists and behavioral scientists, findings widely infused by anti-military and anti-establishment predilections. American débâcles, such as those suffered at Kasserine in North Africa, specially engaged the attention of historians, journalists, and professional humorists.

American soldiers did not come out well from this scholarly and media-centered ordeal. They became subject to far-reaching criticism of the kind put forward by Colonel Dupuy, mentioned above, who proved to his own satisfaction that German soldiers consistently had a higher "score effectiveness" than the Americans. As John Sloan Brown, an American soldier-scholar points out, Dupuy's calculations, however, leave much to be desired. (For instance, Dupuy erred in comparing oranges with apples, by disproportionately over-representing in his samples German panzer and panzer grenadier divisions, the most potent of their units.) As Brown demonstrates with a wealth of statistics, "the effectiveness of American armor and German panzers and the effectiveness of American infantry and panzer grenadiers were roughly equivalent. American divisions, armor and infantry, outclassed German infantry divisions by a wide margin, and American infantry was not at its best when faced by German panzers."[25] In the end, Americans developed "a qualitative edge," as well as quantitative superiority. Overall, the English-speaking countries for a brief time created the most formidable fighting force the world had ever seen. By doing so, they retrieved the power and prestige of Western democracy that appeasers and pacifists had threatened forever to destroy.

This enormous aggregation of military power, however, was soon allowed to dissipate. Between August 1945 and June 1946, the US Army declined from 8 million to 1.5 million men, the British Army from 3 million to 400,000. Only the French proved an exception. Starting with a small nucleus of expatriate French soldiers, General Charles de Gaulle creditably rebuilt the armed forces during and after the liberation of his country, determined to win back for France her accustomed role among the powers by the time-honored method

[25] John Sloan Brown, "Colonel Trevor N. Dupuy and the mythos of *Wehrmacht* superiority: a reconsideration," *Military Affairs,* vol 50. no. 1, January 1986, pp. 16–20.

of displaying military strength. He employed a French army of 500,000 men in southwestern Germany, studiously ignoring American battle plans in a display of stubborn independence that threatened an early Franco–American clash. But de Gaulle's sweeping plans for an army of 20 divisions (drawn up in 1945) came to nothing. The French soon shipped most of their regulars to Indo-China in a vain attempt to maintain their empire.[26] By 1946, the Allied army of occupation in Germany numbered three weak French divisions, two British divisions, and for a time no more than one US division. The Soviet Union by that time had also demobilized some of its armed forces; nevertheless, the "Group of Soviet Forces Germany" by that time stood at 20 divisions; theirs was now the giant among the allied forces of occupation. Military imbalance in Central Europe henceforth became an accepted fact of life – with far-reaching consequences for the future.

THE PHYSICAL DAMAGE

World War I had been the first of the great disasters that struck Western Europe in the twentieth century. It had occasioned immense physical damage, but most of this had been limited to certain regions in Belgium and northeastern France, where positional warfare had raged with bitter ferocity. World War II, by contrast, spread wide the effects of conflict through the development of mobile armies and air war. The total extent of physical destruction occasioned by operations during World War II is hard to measure – the contrasts were too great. Among the capitals of the belligerent powers, Copenhagen and Oslo, Paris, Brussels and Rome escaped extensive damage. (The German command in France had refused to carry out Hitler's order to destroy Paris before abandoning the city.) Allied soldiers who came to liberate these cities could still use the prewar guide books to find their way and see the sights. In many other European towns, such guide books in 1945 served little or no purpose.

After World War I, novelists such as H. G. Wells had predicted that the next war would bring about the end of the world. This was far from the truth. Even in heavily bombed Germany, not more than about one quarter of the habitable dwellings of 1939 were lost through military action.[27] Indeed the contrasts were astounding. In cities such as Cambridge or Carlisle in England, Heidelberg in Germany there was little or no damage. Many parts of London remained unscarred. Yet the citizens of many towns throughout Europe went through a local apocalypse, whose date was indelibly imprinted in their minds, remembered in phrases such as *die Katastrophe* by survivors of the Hamburg

---

[26]F. Roy Willis, *The French Paradox: Understanding Contemporary France*. Stanford, Hoover Institution, 1982, p. 2, and Colloque Organisé par l'Institut d'Histoire du Temps Présent de l'Institut Charles de Gaulle, *De Gaulle et la Nation Face aux Problèmes de Défense 1945–1946*, Paris, Plon, c. 1983.

[27]J. Frederic Dewhurst et al. *Europe's Needs and Resources: Trends and Prospects in Eighteen Countries*. New York, Twentieth Century Fund, 1961, p. 214.

inferno, or "the hungry winter" by the people of Amsterdam. "Catastrophe" was an apt term, as the managers of modern war had learned, by this time, how to create disasters resembling natural events like floods, fires, and earthquakes.

In Holland the center of Rotterdam had been laid low by the Luftwaffe, as had Belgrade and Warsaw in Eastern Europe. In France and the Netherlands, something like one-fifth of the available housing had disappeared. Such gener alized statistics, however, meant little to people in these towns actually involved in the war. The land battle around Dunkirk in May 1940, for instance, resulted in the destruction of four-fifths of all dwellings in the city. Then came intensive British air attacks on ports that the Germans might use for their projected invasion of Britain; such assaults devastated Brest and Le Havre. The Allied invasion of Northern France in 1944 occasioned further damage; the old town of Caen was almost totally destroyed. Italy had likewise been heavily bombed by Allied air forces; during the last 18 months of the war, the country had not only been a battlefield but had also been occupied at either end by opposing forces – the ex-enemy Allies in the South, and the ex-Ally Germans in the north. The country had seen bitter partisan warfare. Milan and Turin had suffered badly, as had Florence, Pisa, Verona, and other beautiful cities.

Britain also sustained severe damage. By the end of the war, German bombs and rockets had destroyed or damaged something like 3.5 million houses. Part of London's commercial core and the East End, Coventry, and many provincial towns lay in ruins; by the end of the war, much of the rubble had been removed, but the empty spaces looked almost as eery as the wrecked buildings. Before the outbreak of World War I, modernist architects, some of them Cubist in inspiration, had called for the planned destruction of old cities so that new creations might take their place. Such dreamers now had their wish granted in an unlooked-for manner. (Overall, the British had lost an estimated $18.1 billion of capital assets as a result of the war; bomb damage to buildings and machinery amounted to $9.9 billion of this total.)[28]

More devastating still had been the effects of Allied air raids on Germany, the main target of the air war. (Between them, the British and US air forces had dropped 2,690,000 tons of bombs over Europe – of this tonnage, half hit Germany; 27.7 percent France; 13.7 percent Italy; 6.7 percent Austria and the Balkans; the remainder was dropped over other parts of Europe.) In many German cities, life had become a matter of sheer survival amidst

> craters, caves, mountains of rubble, debris-covered fields, ruins that hardly allowed one to imagine that they had once been houses, cables and water pipes projecting from the ground like the mangled bowels of antediluvian monsters, no fuel, no light, every little garden a graveyard and, above all this, like an immovable cloud, the stink of putrefaction. In this no-man's land lived human beings. Their life was a daily struggle

[28]Robert A. Brady, *Crisis in Britain. Plans and Achievements of the Labour Government.* Berkeley, University of California Press, 1950, pp. 5–8.

for a handful of potatoes, a loaf of bread, a few lumps of coal, some cigarettes.[29]

In Germany about half the available housing space was damaged or destroyed; 13 million people lost their homes during these air raids, many of which affected medium and small towns to an even greater extent than the great metropolitan centers. (In Berlin, an estimated 37 percent of all houses were ruins; in Hamburg 53.5 percent; in Kassell 63 percent; in small towns such as Worms 60 percent; in Pforzheim 62 percent; in Siegen 75 percent, and in Hanau 87 percent. Worse still 97 percent of Jülich was wiped out, and Düren was annihilated, only six houses were left standing.)[30] The horrors of Hiroshima had been presaged in Europe.

An exile returning to his native town would no longer recognize the streets where he had played as a child. The familiar landmarks had disappeared. Even without the employment of nuclear weapons, military technology had developed to such a point that centuries of art and enterprise could now be destroyed within a few minutes. Overall, the destruction occasioned by World War II was much greater than the ravages of World War I. Devastation was also much more wide-spread geographically, thereby oddly giving something in common to belligerents of all nations in bomb-damaged cities, towns, and villages. An estimated 20 percent of the houses in France and 30 percent in Great Britain were destroyed or damaged.

The raids killed great numbers of people – a subject to which we shall return. (In the two great raids on Dresden alone, carried out in 1945, an estimated 30,000 people died, and many more injured.) The bombers left in their wake damaged sewage pipes, wrecked water purification plants, broken gas mains and electrical supplies – the entire machinery of modern urban living was impaired, though it never ceased entirely to operate for long. The bomber squadrons pounded architectural diversity into a terrible uniformity. Baroque palaces, Gothic churches, department stores in sober *Bauhaus* style, rich men's villages in fake Tudor, apartment blocs jerry-built for the poor in the nineteenth century, all turned into rubble, and all rubble looked much the same. This rubble piled up in unimaginable quantities. In Berlin alone, it amounted to 55,000,000 cubic meters, in Hamburg 35,800 cubic meters, that is to say respectively 12.7 cubic meters and 20.9 cubic meters per inhabitant. The mass of shattered masonry was so immense that recovery, for that reason alone, seemed out of the question. According to the calculations made by Gustav Stolper, an economic historian, the problems of merely removing the rubble

---

[29]See Gordon Craig, *The Germans*. New York, New American Library, 1982, p. 35, citing Willy Brandt's memories of wartime.

[30]For a statistical summary, see Hans Rumpf, *Das war der Bombenkrieg: Deutsche Städte im Feuersturm*. Oldenburg, Gerhard Stalling Verlag, 1961, pp. 191–200. *The United States Strategic Bombing Survey. Over-all Report. (European War)*. Washington, DC, US Government Printing Office, 1945–7. Charles Webster and Noble Frankland, *The Strategic Air Offensive Against Germany*. London, HM Stationery Office, 4 vols, 1961.

from Germany's shattered towns was such that 30 years would be required to complete the task.[31]

Life, of course, continued. Men, women, and children huddled in cellars and sheds – often displaying extraordinary ingenuity in giving to this miserable makeshift accommodation some degree of comfort notwithstanding the hunger and cold, the stench and overcrowding. This is how Victor Gollancz, a British humanitarian, described one of these habitations in Germany:

> The place was a cellar under rubble in one of the huge devastated areas. For light (during the day) and air there was one tiny window. On a table was a sort of open lamp with a naked flame – some sort of kerosene affair. There was one bed about the size of mine at home, in which the wife and husband were sleeping; on a sort of couch was the son, crippled in the war, and I should say in his twenties; and on the floor, on an indescribably filthy "mattress" which was all broken open with the sawdust spilling out, was the daughter. She looked fifty, but I suspect she was about twenty-five ... There was no free space in the cellar at all – and again they lived, ate, and slept here. Nobody could work – the young man couldn't because he was crippled, and the father because he was too weak.[32]

Theirs was a new pan-European life style, the life style of the bombed-out – identical from Caen to Warsaw. Work continued, and so did entertainment. Only a short time after the fighting had ended in Berlin, for example, an enterprising operatic group put on a performance of Offenbach's *Parisian Life* on one of those few stages that had somehow survived the bombing and the final battle for Berlin. No surrealist artist could have done full justice to the incredible contrast between the brilliance, the color, the melody of Offenbach's masterpiece, and the scene of utter devastation that once more hit the audience as they emerged into the night when the performance was over.

Men and women adjusted with extraordinary resilience, compounded of toughness and of opportunism – the latter symbolized in Berlin by the red flags put out by the defeated Germans to pacify the Russian conquerors. On closer inspection these flags mostly bore in the middle a round, red patch, sewn in to replace the black swastika on a white globe that had graced these flags at the time when the *Führer*'s sway stood supreme. But the price of war had nevertheless been terrible in terms of civic culture, infrastructure, health, wealth, and lives shattered or lost.

The effects of bombing were multiplied by damage done to communications. Postwar analyses of Allied air strategy clearly indicate that the mass destruction of cities could not by itself have shattered the German war economy. The transportation system, by contrast, formed the Achilles heel of German defense. Between them, attacks on railways, bridges, viaducts, canals, ports, and oil refineries had a much more devastating effect on an enemy's ability to

---

[31]Gustav Stolper, *German Realities*. New York, Reynal and Hitchcock, 1948, p. 162.
[32]Victor Gollancz, *In Darkest Germany*. Hinsdale, Ill., Henry Regnery, 1947, pp. 90–1.

wage war than the area bombing of cities. The full extent of this destruction is hard to estimate for all belligerents developed considerable skill in repairing stricken targets. (The Germans thus repeatedly put the Leuna works back into commission; Allied engineers performed marvels in getting damaged ports back into working order.) Nevertheless, postwar Europe had to make do with a gravely damaged transport system, whose deficiencies were made worse by the inability to replace aging equipment or to carry out normal maintenance.

In Italy, for example, 60 percent of the major highways and 20 percent of the minor highways had been damaged or put out of commission; so had 2,968 large bridges and 5,269 minor bridges; so had 90 percent of the electrified railway lines.[33] Private cars, taxis, and buses had largely disappeared from the roads. In Belgium, the total number of vehicles on the roads had, by 1942, declined to 12.8 percent of the 1938 figure.[34] In France, only 17 percent of the railways remained usable after the end of the war; 340,000 trucks had been destroyed out of a prewar total of 520,000.[35] Much of Europe's prewar prosperity had depended on its waterways. These were largely out of commission, with their barges sunk, their locks damaged, their skilled staff gone. (Out of over 8,000 kilometers of French canals, only about 500 kilometers were still usable.)

War retarded the motorization of Europe – a process that had been well under way by the late 1930s. (Between 1937 and 1948, the number of private automobiles diminished in France from 2,020,000 to 1,519,000; in Germany from 1,108,000 to 283,000; in Italy from 270,000 to 219,000; only the British figures increased – from 1,833,000 to 2,020,000.) The German, Italian, and Japanese merchant marines had largely been wiped out; the British lost half their merchant fleet; by the end of the war, more than 23 million tons of Allied shipping had been sunk. The loss of seaborne transport intensified the effects occasioned by the destruction of land transport; worsening the enormous difficulties of supplying food to stricken cities, repairing factories and houses, and returning displaced men and women to their respective homes. Transport itself became what it had been at the start of the industrial revolution – a rare and treasured service. In many parts of Europe passengers, after a long and indeterminate wait in a bombed-out railway station, would count themselves lucky just to be aboard a train – even if it meant having to climb on the roof of a carriage and clinging on for dear life as it clattered along the track.

The damage to transport and distribution systems greatly added to the food shortages experienced in Europe and was perhaps their principal cause. Before World War II, most European farmers had still relied on draft animals to pull wagons and plows. It was only in Great Britain that farming had been highly mechanized. Horses continued to play an important part in the European

---

[33]Epicarmo Corbino, "L'Economia" in A. Battaglia et al., ed., *Dieci Anni Dopo 1945–1955*. Bari, Editizione Laterza, 1955, pp. 409–58.

[34]Fernand Baudhuin, *L'Economie Belge Sous L'Occupation Allemande*. Brussels, Etablissement Bruylant, 1945, p. 396–7.

[35]Charles Bettelheim, *Bilan de L'Économie Français, 1919–1946*. Paris, Presse universitaires de France, 1957, pp. 265–6.

economies, even in war. The *Blitzkrieg* image notwithstanding, the German, like the Soviet, armies in Russia had still greatly relied on horses to move their supplies and many of their men, just as they had in World War I. Germans and Russians alike had dealt with the farmers as soldiers had from times immemorial; the soldiers bought or commandeered horses from the villagers – at the cultivator's expense.

Shortage of draft animals was, however, only one of the farmer's many troubles. Huge areas had become flooded (especially in Holland where nearly 500,000 acres stood under water). Livestock had been looted, slaughtered, or had perished from disease. There were ever-present shortages of pesticides, seeds and artificial manure. Fields in battle zones had been disfigured by pill boxes and barbed wire entanglements, cut by trenches and fox holes, strewn with mines – so much so that years after the war's end, a child at play or a stray animal might be blown up by an unlocated mine. Skilled farm workers had been called up into the various forces; many of them had come back as cripples or not at all, and their skills could not be replaced. Farming also suffered from the destruction of timber, lack of spare parts for machinery; neglected dams; broken-down water pumps.

In a wider sense, war and its aftermath cut off Western from Eastern Europe with its supplies of food and timber. It occasioned population shifts in Eastern and Central Europe unequalled in modern history. This demographic displacement further reduced agricultural production, as fields remained untended after their owners' enforced departure, machinery rusted, and cattle was looted or left to perish. Overall, German statisticians estimate that during the war the European wheat and rye harvest diminished by 45 percent (from 61.5 million tons, 1934–8 to 34 million tons in 1945). Fodder crops such as maize, oats, and barley, declined by 38 percent (from 54.9 million tons to 34.3 million tons).

Conditions of course differed widely from country to country, and from region to region. The soldiers who landed in Normandy discovered to their surprise that the local people were much better fed than Allied propaganda had led the invaders to believe. Yet overall France was in desperate straits. The country had been looted by the invader.[36] The production index had dropped to about half of the 1938 level. Agriculture outputs had declined since the start of the war in every European country, bar Great Britain, Sweden, and Switzerland.[37] There were widespread shortages and a great deal of hunger.

War had likewise gravely interfered with industrial production. As an official report put the matter soberly, the industrial structure of Western Europe was mainly based on coal, steel, chemicals, whose output before the war had been slightly higher than that of the US. The most efficient producers had made the most use of imported supplies. European industries had developed a high

[36]Claude Paillat, *L'Occupation. Le Pillage de la France, Juin 1940–Novembre 1942*. Paris, Laffont, 1987.
[37]United Nations, Department of Economic Affairs, *A Survey of the Economic Situation and Prospects of Europe*. Geneva, 1948, p. 17.

degree of specialization and interdependence, made possible by a complex network of international trade. The war had greatly injured this system. The German occupation in France entailed astronomical costs through outright spoliation, through the deportation of 776,000 workers to Germany, and through the occupiers' enormous levies, equivalent in 1940 to 10.9 percent of the estimated French national income and rising to 36.6 percent in 1943. Not surprisingly, French industrial production by 1944 had dropped by more than one half.[38] In many parts of Europe war had occasioned a great amount of damage to factories and workshops, made worse by shortages of spare parts, raw materials, and epecially fuel and power.[39] Coal production in Europe outside the USSR was down by three-fifths of its prewar production, with pits flooded and workmen short of pit props and machinery. Rebuilding at first proceeded at a snail's pace. (In the first quarter of 1946, the level of building and construction stood at no more than 14 percent of the 1938 level in Western Germany, 49 percent in Italy, 55 percent in Great Britain, and 67 percent in Italy and Belgium; only France had already picked up with 112 percent of the 1938 figure.)

The outlook seemed equally grim for industry. In Italy, in 1945, industrial production had fallen to less than a quarter of the prewar level, in France, Belgium and Holland to one-fifth.[40] Germany by the end of the war was in an even more desperate condition. German war production had continued to rise until 1944, despite the Allied bombing offensive. Thereafter, the bombers had obtained the upper hand, and the German industrial economy began to disintegrate. By the end of 1945, the output of the Ruhr, Germany's industrial heart, had been reduced by 80 percent; bridges, railway marshalling yards, canal installations were wrecked; coal supplies had been exhausted, and the country faced total economic collapse.[41] Whole cities were depopulated. (Cologne had 120,000 people left out of a former 780,000, Frankfurt 35,000 out of 500,000.) The clear skies over the Ruhr region, Germany's industrial heart, were a terrible sight that symbolized cold, misery, hunger and closed factories. The first palls of smoke that at long last emerged from factory funnels, by contrast, turned into a symbol of hope, of returning life; at a time when the physical damage alone was so extensive that full recovery seemed impossible.

Overall then, the outlook in 1945 seemed desperate. According even to a conservative such as Geoffrey Crowther, editor of the British *Economist,* writing three years after the war when conditions were much better, Europe was in grim shape, and would remain so. Whereas the US still had an expanding economic frontier, Europe would mainly have to concern herself with prob-

---

[38] Arthur Marwick, *War and Social Change in the Twentieth Century: A Comparative Study of Britain, France, Germany, Russia.* New York, St Martin's Press, 1974, p. 186.

[39] Committee of European Economic Cooperation. *General Report,* vol. 1. London, Her Majesty's Stationery Office, 1947, pp. 3–8.

[40] Sir Richard Mayne, *The Recovery of Europe.* New York, Harper and Row, 1970, p. 32.

[41] S. B. Clough, T. Moodie, C. Moodie, eds, *Economic History of Europe.* London, Macmillan, 1969, pp. 314–24.

lems of allocation, adjustment, and transfer of resources.[42] Germany, where the physical damage had, on the average, been even greater than in the remainder of Western Europe, was supposedly out of the race forever. Wrote Gustav Stolper, an economist and an international expert, "Germany as a nation ... has been destroyed and cannot be resurrected ... the German nation is ruined. It is fatally weakened in its biological substance, in its cultural and technical environment, in its moral fibre ..."[43] A European renaissance was out of the question, most observers agreed. To many Europeans – and not only to adherents of the discredited Nazi regime – a world had ended. "The sun of Rome is set! Our day is gone; clouds, dews and dangers come; our deeds are done."[44] Disheartened and ravaged, Europe seemed burnt out. But time would show that there was still fire in the ashes.

THE BLOOD TOLL

World War II was one of the greatest killers in history; but no one can know for sure how many people perished or what were the long-range demographic effects of the war. Men, women and children died in combat, in burning cities, in concentration camps. Their lives ended through disease, through the hardships endured in flight, through forced labor, through cold, sickness, hunger, mental grief and suicide. War also had indirect demographic consequences, as the number of births declined, and infantile mortality rates increased in many stricken regions. Overall, something between 30,000,000 to 60,000,000 people may have met their end as the result of war, perhaps 3 percent of the world's estimated 2.346 billion people in 1940 alone.

While the effects of war might be likened to those of a man-made disease, the impact on the global population in purely demographic terms was not catastrophic. It is all too easy to romanticize the past – including those supposedly more humanitarian epochs of "limited wars" fought by European monarchs for dynastic reasons in the age of absolutism. Louis XIV had devastated the Palatinate in one of his periodic wars against the Holy Roman Empire, with incalculable loss of life. Prussia's loss in wealth and blood was in all likelihood proportionately much greater in the Seven Years' War (1756–63) than the whole of Germany's during World War II. Even in the immediate past, the influenza pandemic that hit the world in 1918 proportionately took more lives than World War II. Discoveries in medicine such as the use of sulfa drugs, DDT, improvements in the techniques of blood transfusion, more efficient ways of storing and distributing food, and of getting the wounded to hospitals, helped to keep down the death rate in Western countries, including the death rates of men wounded in battle. (During the American Civil War,

[42]Geoffrey Crowther, *The Economic Reconstruction of Europe*. Claremont College, Claremont, Cal., 1948, p. 38.
[43]Stolper, *German Realities*, p. 22.
[44]William Shakespeare, *Julius Caesar*, V. iii. 63–4.

something like one in seven wounded had perished; by the Korean War, the rate dropped to one in 50, and by the Vietnam War to one in 400.)[45] After World War II, moreover, because of better public health facilities, the world was spared a reputation of anything like the influenza pandemic, that would have borne heavily on populations weakened by malnutrition and physical displacement.

World War II did not delay in the long run the steady decline in the death rates of Western Europe, that had begun in the nineteenth century and thereafter accelerated as a result of improved standards in diet, sanitary practices, public health administration, medical knowledge, and personal hygiene. (In 1900 the death rate, per thousand, in Western Europe amounted to 20.2; in 1939, 13.7; and in 1955, 10.6.)[46] In terms of human reproduction, World War II made but a minor impact. The war years actually witnessed an

TABLE 1.1   *Crude birthrate (per 1,000 inhabitants)*

Weighted average rates	1935–9	1940–4	1945–8
Northern Europe (UK, Sweden, Denmark, Norway, Ireland)	15.8	16.9	19.3
Western Europe (Germany "Federal Republic only after 1945", France, Netherlands, Belgium, Austria, Switzerland)	17.3	17.2	18.8
Southern Europe (Italy, Spain, Yugoslavia, Greece)	24.3	21.4	23.1
Eastern Europe (Poland, Romania, Czechoslovakia, Hungary, Yugoslavia)	24.1	21.5	25.1
USA	17.2	19.9	23.4

Source: *Encyclopaedia Britannica*, 1968 edn, vol. 23, p. 81.

expansion of the crude birthrate in various parts of Europe. Astonishingly, these included France, a country long plagued by a low birthrate, a country that also suffered from the enforced absence of 1.5 million young men in German factories and prisoner-of-war camps. As Colin Dyer, an Australian demographer put it, absence might make the heart grow fonder, but not necessarily toward the husband or lover in a German prisoner-of-war camp.[47]

[45] James M. McPherson, *Battle Cry of Freedom: The Civil War Era*. New York, Oxford University Press, 1988, p. 485.

[46] Detailed figures for these three respective years stood as follows: Austria: 22.3; 15.3; 12.2. Belgium: 17.7; 13.9; 12.3. Denmark: 15.4; 10.1; 8.7. France: 20.2; 15.6; 12.2. Germany: 20.6; 12.3; 11.0. Italy: 22.6; 13.4; 9.3. Netherlands: 16.8; 8.6; 7.6. Norway: 14.9; 10.1; 8.5. Spain: 27.0; 18.5; 9.4. United Kingdom: 16.9; 12.2; 11.7. Dewhurst, *Europe's Needs and Resources*, p. 36.

[47] See Colin Dyer, *Population and Society in Twentieth Century France*, London, Hodden and Stoughton, 1978.

The war years moreover were everywhere followed by a startling population increase that more than made up for the demographic losses.

Nevertheless, the toll of war was grim, for the conflict extended over a larger area, and was fought with technological resources immensely more sophisticated, than any previous conflict in history. Its impact was also most uneven in a geographic sense. The statistics of death are necessarily incomplete

TABLE 1.2(a)   *Crude death rate (per 1,000 inhabitants)*

	1935–9	*1940–4*	*1945–9*
Northern Europe	12.1	13.0	11.4
Western Europe	13.2	14.4	14.9
Southern Europe	15.5	15.2	11.9
Eastern Europe	15.1	16.1	14.8
USA	11.0	10.6	10.0

(b)   *Rate of natural increase (per 1,000 inhabitants)*

Northern Europe	3.7	3.8	8.0
Western Europe	4.1	2.8	3.9
Southern Europe	8.8	6.2	11.1
Eastern Europe	9.0	6.2	10.3
USA	6.2	9.3	13.4

Source: *Encyclopaedia Britannica*, 1968 edn, vol. 23, p. 81.

and sometimes conflict; but overall, the picture is clear. In terms of absolute numbers, the USSR experienced the greatest loss of all – estimates of Soviet dead, both military and civilian, vary from 12,000,000 to 19,000,000; Poland may have lost 5,800,000 people (including the bulk of its Jewish population), and Yugoslavia about 1,500,000. The Germans suffered comparably. Whereas in World War I, 2,050,000 German soldiers had perished, World War II entailed a loss of something like 6,000,000 people, of whom an estimated 3,712,000 were servicemen, killed or missing in action, victims of disease, suicide, execution squads, or of hardships suffered in Soviet prisoner-of-war camps (1.5 million German soldiers were imprisoned in the Soviet Union; only a fraction returned).[48]

[48]For country-by-country figures, see Gregory Frumkin, *Population Changes in Europe Since 1939: A Study of Population Changes During and Since World War II as Shown by the Balance Sheets of Twenty-Four European Countries*. New York, Augustus M. Kelley, 1951. See also Dyer, *Population and Society in Twentieth Century France, passim*; Martin K. Sorge, *The Other Price of Hitler's War: German Civilian and Military Losses Resulting from World War II*. New York, Greenwood Press, 1986.

Military losses

In the Western countries, by contrast, the demographic effects were nothing like as serious as in World War I. In France, about 250,000 servicemen died in the armed forces, in the French underground, as prisoners of war, or even more tragically, as volunteers or conscripts in the *Wehrmacht*. This was a heavy toll, but nothing like as bad as the sacrifices made during World War I, when 1,224,500 French fighting men had failed to return from the trenches. Italy lost 233,000 military personnel in battles fought as far afield as Ethiopia and Russia – as against 680,000 dead in World War I. Great Britain lost 264,443 soldiers, sailors, and airmen, as against over 800,000 in World War I.

In terms of purely military losses, the smaller belligerents in Western Europe escaped relatively lightly – if such a word can ever be used in referring to the statistics of death. In the course of brief campaigns, Belgium lost 12,000 servicemen; the Netherlands 11,600; Norway 6,600. The US sustained over 1,000,000 casualties, including over 393,000 dead out of 15,130,000 mobilized (as against 130,000 in World War I, out of the 4,619,000 who had put on uniform). But no one on the American mainland died by direct military action.

Statistical summaries tell of course only a very small part of the story. Total casualty percentages are meaningless to a sailor drifting in a lifeboat, the driver of a tank caught in a burning vehicle, or an air raid warden trapped in the cellar of a house shattered by a blockbuster. Statistics can, however, serve as a signpost. They can provide some indication of the loss of life entailed by modern war, and of the way in which the changing manner of war risks attenuated older distinctions between front and rear, soldiers and civilians.

In World War II – as in all the wars ever fought – the military death toll was of course selective, not merely in a geographical but also in a generational and a social sense. Certain age cohorts of men suffered disproportionately. A German or a Russian born, say in 1922, and called to the colors at the age of 18 in 1940, would have to survive – or somehow avoid – five years of fighting to make it to the end of the war unscathed. Many did not do so, nor did their juniors. In Germany, for instance, 31 percent of those born in 1924 were dead or missing by the year 1945, 31 percent had sustained wounds of varying severity.

Fighting also took a special toll of specific occupational and social groups, groups unevenly represented in the various arms of the fighting services. According to Max Hastings, a British military historian, there existed in all belligerent countries a "brutally self-evident hierarchy of risk among the armies" – lowest among lines-of-communication troops, staff services, and heavy artillery, rising through field artillery, armored units, and engineers, to reach a pinnacle in the infantry, especially the riflemen. To give just two examples, of the 100,000 US casualties suffered in Normandy in June 1944: 85 percent were infantrymen and 63 percent were riflemen. Overall, the infantry, while only accounting for 10 percent of the US army, accounted for 70 percent of all battle casualties in World War II.[49] British figures were comparable; so were figures for the German army.[50]

These differential losses had social as well as military significance, for infantrymen are always likely to be drawn disproportionately from the ranks of the young unskilled and semi-skilled working class, from those deemed to lack special aptitude – a most inappropriate criterion for the selection of the most versatile fighting men on any battlefield. War also took a heavy toll from selected groups of qualified technicians, mechanics, and skilled workers, from those most likely to seek service in military high-risk occupations of a technological kind. Submariners, a chosen naval elite in every maritime country, stood a particularly poor chance of making it through the war. (The Germans, for instance, lost 90 percent of their submarine crews.) Flying personnel of all nations experienced heavy casualties. The US Air Force had 52,172 fatalities; its losses exceeded those in all branches of the army, except the infantry. Death also struck heavily in elite forces such as commandos, paratroopers, rangers – men specially chosen for their physical fitness and intelligence. Three-quarters of the British First Airborne Division perished in the Arnheim battle in ten days. The US Tenth Mountain Division, a picked body of men in terms of intelligence, fitness, and training, suffered a heavier rate of casualties in training and combat than any other US division in the Italian campaign.[51]

Among officers, lieutenants and other field officers suffered by far the heaviest casualties, especially in the infantry and elite formations. (A study of four US infantry divisions fighting in Italy showed that second lieutenants in the infantry constituted 0.9 percent of the total strength while contributing 2.7 percent of all battle casualties.) Not that generals stayed out of harm's way. Brilliant leaders such as Erwin Rommel or Richard O'Connor (a British "desert general") led their formations from the front – exposed, like fighting admirals, to the same risks as their men. Particularly in the German Army, the privilege of being a general entailed membership in a high-risk occupation whose members were decimated under a tyrannical regime by death in battle, suicide, or execution after a rigged court-martial or the murderous proceedings of a "people's court."[52]

By and large, the burden fell heaviest on commanders of sections, platoons, and companies; men who were expected to suffer the greatest exposure under enemy fire, and who took greater casualties than the enlisted men. Such junior officers derived from many different backgrounds, though certain strata contributed disproportionate numbers. They included members of ruling groups whose collective values exalted a military career – the Ulster gentry,

[49]Max Hastings, *Overlord: D-Day and the Battle for Normandy*. New York, Simon and Schuster, 1984, p. 210. Samuel A. Stouffer et al., *The American Soldier: Adjustment During Army Life*. Princeton, Princeton University Press, 1949, v. 2, p. 101, v. 1, p. 330.

[50]James Lucas, *War on the Eastern Front 1941–1945. The German Soldier in Russia*. New York, Bonanza Books, 1979, p. 19.

[51]Roger A. Beaumont, *Military Elites*. Indianapolis, Bobbs-Merrill, 1974, p. 177.

[52]For statistics see Albert Seaton, *The German Army 1933–1945*. New York, St Martin's Press, 1982, p. 250.

Prussian noblemen, white Rhodesian settlers, and members of military families from the American South. But the overwhelming number of junior officers were young men who had switched to the military services from civilian jobs – students, lawyers, junior bank managers or business executives, and also many schoolteachers – accustomed through their experience in the classroom to such militarily useful skills as enforcing discipline, lecturing, and imparting information to unwilling listeners.

In all totalitarian states, both in the Soviet Union and in Nazi Germany, war also exacted a particularly high price from the ideologically dedicated among the young, the future elites. The best divisions of the *Waffen SS* – as against second-line SS units raised at the end of the war – performed superbly well in battle and with striking consistency. These formations all paid for their brief glory with enormously high casualty rates. So did the most enthusiastic members of the Hitler Youth, those who had advanced in its ranks, and then took pride in joining the *Waffen SS* and other top-notch fighting units. A high proportion of true believers perished in battle – perhaps helping to diminish the chances of a Nazi revival in postwar Germany.

Men without such commitment, and also men with superior academic qualifications, well established in specialized occupations, stood a better chance of surviving the war – being relegated to "reserved occupations" or to specialist jobs in the armed forces. Unusual skills of course did not always keep their possessors out of harm's way. A German-language interpreter in the British Army, unlucky enough to be drafted into an unarmored radio van in order to call on surrounded but still combat-worthy Germans to surrender, was likely to have a brief life. But overall, a qualified interpreter, a meteorologist, or a physician was less likely to be hit than a rifleman.

The same applied to members of assorted political groups. Conscientious objectors in the English-speaking countries, whether motivated by religious beliefs such as the Old Amish and the Mennonites in the US or by secular humanist convictions, escaped most of the perils of war, unless they chose to enlist in civilian ambulance units. Matters went very differently for conscientious objectors in Germany, where many of them (especially Jehovah's Witnesses) suffered martyrdom in concentration camps. For very different reasons, the functionaries in the Nazi Party likewise widely failed those heroic precepts that they proclaimed in public. Such men commonly stayed out of the armed services or, if drafted, kept out of combat, effectively helping to delegitimize their privileged position in the eyes of the German public.[53]

Civilian losses in all the combatant countries were much higher than they had been in World War I – a fact that reflected alike the impact of airpower, the increased willingness of all sides to use airpower against civilians, and above all the rise of the totalitarian state, with its perfected technique of mass deportation and mass murder. Modern techniques of communication, the telephone and the cable, and modern techniques of storing and retrieving

[53]Michael H. Kater, *The Nazi Party: A Social Profile of Members and Leaders 1919–1945*. Cambridge, Mass., Harvard University Press, 1983, p. 214.

information, gave to the state an enormously increased capacity for doing evil as well as good.

Death camps

The most potent instrument for human destruction in the twentieth century was the death camp – infinitely more devastating in its effects than the atomic bomb. Of camps there were many, forced labor camps in the Soviet Union, concentration camps in Nazi Germany; their impact varied. The Japanese imprisoned captured Allied soldiers and civilians under conditions that beggar description. There was indeed an unimaginable contrast between the mild and generous treatment meted out to the inmates of American internment camps for Japanese, and the sadistic perversions practiced by Japanese against allied captives. A large proportion of German prisoners of war held in Soviet camps likewise perished miserably, but it was not the Soviet leadership's intention to liquidate all German military prisoners, let alone all Germans. The Nazis, in contrast, widely practiced what amounted to genocide against Soviet prisoners of war, intending them to starve. "Let them eat each other" – Hermann Goering observed. Overall, more than 3,000,000 Soviet military prisoners may have gone to their death.[54]

In addition, the Nazis and Soviets alike set up "civilian" camps. Between them, these formed a separate universe, with its own language (*Lagerdeutsch* in Nazi camps), its own ranking system, and its own terrors. Under the rule of the swastika, inmates comprised men and women of every European nation, men and women of every condition. Hitler's hatreds were insatiable. He tried to exterminate Polish intellectuals, gypsies, homosexual men, real or assumed lunatics. He murdered communists, socialists, and practicing Christians who considered Nazism a despicable creed. The chief, though not the only, objects of Hitler's wrath were the Jews, whom he considered a diabolical people. They perished in another war, one that Hitler almost won in Europe – the war against the Jews.[55] The Jewish catastrophe in subsequent years was misnamed a "holocaust" (literally: a burnt offering or a wholesale sacrifice). The memory of the dead was further degraded when, in more recent years, some would-be reformers began to liken the victims of lesser kinds of oppression, ethnic or social, to those of mass murder. The Jews were not martyrs in the sense of having voluntarily chosen suffering and death. They were sacrificed to a millennial creed that believed in a form of total predestination, one that assumed that members of certain ethnic communities lacked the divine gift of Free Will, and were fated inevitably to do evil.

[54]Alan Clark, *Barbarossa: The Russian German Conflict 1941–1945*. New York, Quill, 1985, p. 207.

[55]Martin Gilbert, *The Holocaust: A History of the Jews of Europe During the Second World War*. New York, Holt, Rhinehart and Winston, 1985. Lucy Dawidowicz, *The War Against the Jews, 1933–1945*. New York, Holt, Rinehart and Winston, 1975. Raul Hilberg, *The Destruction of the European Jews*, Revised edn. New York, Holmes and Meyer, 1985, 3 v. Michael Marrus, "The history of the holocaust: a survey of recent literature," *Journal of Modern History*, v. 59, no. 1, March 1987, pp. 114–60.

The death camps, set up from 1941 onward, differed qualitatively from other horrors with which they have since been mistakenly compared. Air raids on cities, however awesome, promised to end upon the enemy's capitulation. The misery of a refugee trek would also end, once "resettlement" had been accomplished. The death camps were an end unto themselves, serving only to kill. They fundamentally challenged all accepted notions of what human beings might do to others, and of what the victims might endure. They destroyed the last remnants of an optimistic view concerning man and his assumed natural goodness. The death camps stood for murder organized on lines of supreme industrial efficiency, sustained by hard work, punctuality, attention to minute detail – conventional virtues used in the service of a satanic Utopia.

The Nazi murder campaign brought about the greatest catastrophe that had ever befallen the Jewish people, with an estimated loss of 5,800,000 overall. Of these, 4,565,000 perished in Poland and the German occupied parts of the Soviet Union, with further heavy loss of life in Romania, Hungary and Czechoslovakia. An entire national culture, based on the Yiddish language and the Jewish religion, almost vanished. In Western Europe Jews largely disappeared from the Low Countries (with about 106,000 dead in Holland, and 24,000 in Belgium). Substantial Jewish communities survived only in Great Britain, and also in France where about three-quarters of the resident Jews managed to live through the war (as against 83,000 dead).[56] In Germany and Austria about 190,000 perished; and these losses, added to those incurred by previous emigration, put an end to the cultural symbiosis that had previously been created through the fusion of German and Jewish elements. The former intellectual supremacy of German-speaking Jewry within the Jewish world at large became a matter of history and American Jewry henceforth assumed that leading position.

As regards Jewry as a whole, the camps failed in their professed object of breaking a people's mind and soul. Millions died, but some survived. Their health was damaged. Memories of terror remained. Nightmares continued to stalk their sleep. But the bulk of survivors neither descended into permanent insanity nor committed suicide. They mostly rebuilt their existence as far as they could. They found new homes in countries as far afield as the US and Palestine. The Zionist movement gained enormously in strength – with far-reaching consequences for Jewish self-perception and for the future of the Middle East. Overall, human resilience proved very much greater than the hell-makers had anticipated.

In the end, the Nazis undoubtedly weakened German national feeling by a legacy of guilt. In more immediate terms, the persecution of the Jews affected German war-making capacity through the expulsion or murder of many talented scientists, physicians, entrepreneurs, technicians, and trained soldiers of Jewish descent.[57] Nazi propaganda notwithstanding, the destruction of

---

[56]For a summary of losses, see *Encyclopedia Judaica*. New York, Leon Amiel Publishers, 1974, p. 266.

[57]Bert Engelmann, *Germany Without Jews*. New York, Bantam Books, 1984.

the Yiddish-speaking Jews annihilated great communities that were in some measure *artsverwandt* (akin) to Germany. The Yiddish-speakers' tongue mainly derived from medieval German (*Mittlehochdeutsch*). It would have been infinitely more intelligible to those great medieval German troubadors prized by the Nazis than the Nazis' own jargon. Eastern European Jewish intellectuals and businessmen had traditionally been pro-German; they had commonly looked to Germany as a source of secular enlightenment and technological innovation. The Eastern European Jews' destruction – ironically enough – thus delivered a shattering blow to German cultural influence in Eastern Europe – as did the subsequent expulsion of most German ethnic communities of Eastern Europe.

The war against the Jews (and also the persecution of dissident intellectuals not of Jewish descent) had other unintended effects. Jewish people had traditionally played an important role in the metropolitan culture of Berlin, Vienna, Prague, and Budapest. Their loss helped to turn these cities into intellectual backwaters. Above all, German-speaking Europe lost its former scientific supremacy (as expressed, for instance, in the large number of Nobel prizes that had gone to Germany and Austria respectively). Henceforth, this hegemony passed to the US.

Other less-publicized victims of ethno-terror comprised the Gypsies, a people whom a contributor to a respected British encyclopedia could still unblushingly describe 16 years after the end of the Third Reich as "slovenly in their habits," dirty, and characterized by "great moral defects."[58] Estimates concerning the total number of Gypsies who fell victim to the Third Reich vary from 250,000 to 500,000, with 80,000 slain in Central Europe. Had the war continued, or had Nazi rule actually survived, the machinery of terror would certainly have continued to grind on; the Nazis might even have outdone Stalin and his henchmen in the art of mass murder, an achievement that in fact eluded them in the 12-year period in which they held sway. Prospective Nazi victims would almost certainly also have included men and women of partially Jewish origin (who were mostly spared during the war), Catholic priests, and those styled "incurably insane" by Nazi psychiatrists, that is to say those who had managed to survive the previous Nazi "euthanasia" campaign designed to "purify" the Aryan race and to provide a trial run for killing techniques later employed against Jews.

How far did Nazi and Soviet horrors resemble one another? The question has been complicated by the fact that far more has been written about the former than the latter. The Soviets moreover had found more defenders in the West than the Nazis on the grounds that the Soviet aim – the creation of a classless society – is intrinsically nobler in concept than the Nazis' professed objective – a world ruled by Aryan supermen. Advocates of a "totalitarian" interpretation, such as Hannah Arendt, have stressed similarities. But Arendt herself met with strong opposition on the grounds that she had simplified the

---

[58]*Everyman's Encyclopaedia*. London: Reader's Union, 1961, v. 6, p. 252. For Gypsy persecution in general, see H-J. Döring, *Die Zigeuner im nationalsozialistischen Staat*. Hamburg, Kriminalistik Verland, 1964.

issue. During the 1980s the question led once more to a bitter confrontation, the so-called *Historikerstreit* in West Germany. This battle pitted conservatively minded scholars such as Andreas Hillgruber and Ernst Nolte against liberals such as Jürgen Habermas, a distinguished sociologist. Hillgruber, Nolte, and their supporters did not in any way attempt to exculpate the Nazis, as did a handful of charlatans who tried to prove that the holocaust never happened, or that it had been accomplished without Hitler's knowledge. Rather they argued that the "Final Solution" had formed part of a greater tide of totalitarian terror, that during the twentieth century had engulfed countless others – Armenians slaughtered by the Turks in World War I, Kulaks done to death by Stalin, real or alleged counter-revolutionaries murdered by Mao Tse-tung and Pol Pot. The German conservatives also wished to defend the German heritage in general, and believed that history should call to account those guilty of having inflicted crimes on the German people.[59]

The liberals, by contrast, regarded as intolerable what they saw as the relativization of Auschwitz, and the *tu quoque* (you also) arguments used by Hillgruber and others against the Allies of World War II. Habermas also objected to what he stigmatized as the drift to the right in German scholarship, the so-called *Tendenzwende* of the 1980s. Habermas was himself a Social Democrat; many of his opponents backed the CDU (Chritian Democratic Union); hence the struggle hinged as much on contemporary German politics as it did on Germany's past. We ourselves occupy a midway position in the debate. The "Final Solution" was unique in that the Nazis considered Jews in the nature of bacilli, to be destroyed once and for all. Not even the Turks, by contrast, had planned to annihilate every Armenian on earth. Not even Stalin had intended to wipe out every person ever descended from Kulaks, their children and children's children. But Hitler shared with Stalin and Pol Pot and Mao Tse-tung the idea that a brave new world could only be created by the mass liquidation of millions. In demographic terms, the casualties inflicted by Stalin and his coadjutors greatly exceeded even those of the Hitler terror. Still, forced labor and the concentration camps turned out to be the greatest killers in history.

The Western Allies – to their discredit – contributed to the death toll of Soviet camps by forcibly repatriating huge numbers of Soviet nationals who had fallen into Allied hands during the liberation of Western and Central Europe. These men and women included not merely Soviet citizens who had volunteered for, or more often been impressed into the *Wehrmacht* or its auxiliary formations, but also civilian refugees who had sought safety from Stalin's terror abroad. For the Western allies, good relations with the Soviets mattered more than the fate of displaced persons, especially as long as the war with Japan continued. In any case, what was to be done with them? No

---

[59]For a general discussion, see for instance Richard J. Evans, "New nationalism and old history: perspectives on the West German *Historikerstreit*," *Journal of Modern History*, v. 59, no. 4, December 1987, p. 761. Charles S. Maier, *The Unmastered Past: History, Holocaust and German National Identity*. Cambridge, Mass., Harvard University Press, 1988.

country in the world wanted alien paupers by the millions. Some had apparently collaborated willingly with the Nazis. Let them go back to where they bloody well came from! – a never to be forgotten phrase imprinted on the minds of refugees then and thereafter. It was only in 1947, after riots and suicides in many camps, and after further deterioration in East–West relations, that enforced repatriations ended altogether. By that time, millions of people had been sent to their deaths, a fact that Westerners unacquainted with Soviet realities failed to grasp. A former American soldier and an eye witness later remembered one of these scenes.

> [Having been handed over] many were taken behind some building or over some hill and executed out of hand. You could hear the machine-gun fire. There was a young girl, maybe 18 or 19 years old, who sat huddled with her companions in the back of one of our six-by-six artillery trucks. Pitifully, she tried to catch the eye of her soldier-escorts, displaying her charms as though flirtatiously. It was not flirting, it was an appeal for help, for she knew, as did her companions, what return to Russian control meant. The young American soldiers did not know. How could one believe that the gallant Red Army, our brothers-in-arms, who had helped to rid Europe of the Nazi barbarians, could be no less barbaric, treating helpless refugees like enemies. That poor girl, trying so hopelessly to barter her body for survival to young men too innocent to grasp the significance of her gesture and ignorant of what lay ahead for those they had been given to safeguard on the journey east.[60]

Other political exiles were sent back to Yugoslavia where they fell victim to Tito's vengeance. Sweden, though on an infinitely smaller scale, acted no better by forcibly repatriating a number of Baltic refugees to the Soviet Union. Only the tiny, unarmed principality of Liechtenstein preserved the spirit and letter of international law in this matter. Its sovereign, Prince Franz Josef II, a David without a sling, steadfastly resisted all Soviet threats, and protected those Russian refugees who had sought safety on his territory.

Overall, both Hitler and Stalin created hells whose darkness was illuminated by individual flashes of kindness, courage, and unbelievable resilience. (The most moving monument to human resolution in the face of death examined by one of the co-authors was a card-catalogue, surreptitiously and methodically compiled in the face of ever-present peril in Belsen by a German-Jewish accountant who had resolved to leave a record of his fellow German-Jewish inmates, so that their fate, whereabouts, and relatives' addresses abroad might be traced in the seemingly improbable event of liberation.)

[60]Nicholas Bethell. *The Last Secret: The Delivery to Stalin of Over Two Million Russians by Britain and the United States.* New York, Basic Books, 1974. Julius Epstein, *Operation Keelhaul, The Story of Forced Repatriation from 1944 to the Present.* Old Greenwich, Conn., Devin-Adair, 1973. Henning von Vogelsang, *Kriegsende in Liechtenstein. Das Schicksal der Ersten Russischen Nationalarmee der Deutschen Wehrmacht.* Freiburg i. Br., Herder Taschenbuch, 1985. The description cited in the text derives from Harold W. Rood, "Win a few: lose a few; World War II remembered,' *Claremont Review of Books,* Summer 1985, p. 3.

When liberation came, an insurmountable wall seemed to separate the surviving victims from the liberators, who all too often failed to comprehend that the starving scarecrows behind barbed wire were people like themselves – nurses, stockbrokers, shoemakers, professors. These camps have since been described innumerable times – in proceedings of war-crimes courts, in reminiscences written by survivors (or in some cases even by perpetrators such as the commandant of Auschwitz while awaiting execution).[61] More recently the camps have become the subject of thrillers that trivialize the collective tragedies of which they deal. The camps nevertheless deserve to be remembered, as their ghosts continue to stalk the consciousness of the postwar world.

Enforced migrations

Labor camps, concentration camps, re-education camps – whatever names were applied to them – between them, killed many more people than were slain in air raids employing either conventional or nuclear explosives. But the civilian toll of war extended far beyond these death camps. Again, the statistics defy human comprehension. Between 1939 and the end of 1945, at least 60,000,000 Europeans – not counting servicemen and prisoners of war – had been uprooted from their homes in the greatest population shifts that Europe had experienced since the Dark Ages. Of these, 27,000,000 had left their homelands, few of their own free will. Something like 4.5 million had been deported by the Nazis for forced labor, many more millions were sent to Soviet forced labor camps or Central Asia. In addition to these, there were by 1945 7,000,000 prisoners of war in Allied hands in Western Europe. To be specific, by the end of World War II, there were in the Western zones of occupied Germany between 6 and 7 million displaced persons. (This figure includes forced laborers and prisoners of war held by the Nazis, but excludes German refugees from the East and Germans who had fled from their native cities to escape allied bombing raids.)[62] A small number of these displaced persons turned to violence or crime, thereby spoiling the reputation of all "DPs" in the minds of many Germans and Allied soldiers alike. The overwhelming majority were, of course, respectable people. The Western Europeans among them, as distinct from the Eastern Europeans, were only too anxious to go home. So most did, helped in part by UNRRA (United Nations Relief and Rehabilitation Organization) and the International Refugee Organization, but more often they relied on their own ingenuity.

Great as their hardships were, the Western European DPs were the lucky ones. Many more civilians never managed to return, or lost their lives. The demographic and social impact of these human catastrophes, like the impact of battle, was uneven and for its victims entirely fortuitous. In France, some-

[61]Rudolf Höss, *Commandant of Auschwitz: Autobiograph.* Cleveland, World Publishing Co., 1960.

[62]Richard Mayne, *The Recovery of Europe: From Devastation to Unity.* New York, Harper and Row, 1970, p. 35. Wolfgang Jacobmeyer, *Vom Zwangsarbeiter zum Heimatlosen Ausländer: The Displaced Persons im Westdeutschland, 1945–1951,* Göttingen, Vandenhoeck and Ruprecht, 1985.

thing like 350,000 civilians may have died (including 60,000 killed in air bombardments, an equally large nunber in fighting on land, 30,000 through executions and massacres, 60,000 among political deportees, 40,000 workers who died in Germany, in addition to Jewish Frenchmen slain). Italy may have lost 80,000 people (half of them among deportees and workers in Germany, half of them direct victims of battle and air assaults). An estimated 49,100 died in Belgium, and 94,450 in the Netherlands – a figure that excludes Jews, but includes 20,400 killed in warfare, 16,000 victims of famine; the rest were done to death in concentration camps, executed, or died in Germany as compulsory workers (27,000). In Great Britain, 60,595 people were killed by bombs, long-range rockets, and long-range artillery.

But no Central or Western European country suffered as much as Germany. The number of people killed by air raids in Germany is estimated at 300,000; the total may even have exceeded this. Nearly 160,000 British and American aircrews (79,265 Americans and 79,281 Britons to be exact) perished in the assaults that inflicted these civilian losses – a profoundly stupid misuse of the elite of trained manpower. Even without the employment of nuclear weapons, the technology of air terror by the end of World War II had reached the degree of perfection predicted in the 1930s by science fiction writers such as H. G. Wells, and also by Winston Churchill who foresaw "wars not of armies but of whole populations" in which "men, women, and children, old and feeble, soldiers and civilians, sick and wounded" would suffer annihilation.[63]

The air offensive created no sense of guilt. On the contrary, the thousand-bomber raids at the time had seemed fit punishment for an enemy who had preached total war and who had never tired of jeering at "humanitarian drivel" (*Humanitätsduselei*). The air offensive, according to its proponents, for the first time brought home to the German civilians the realities of war; the air offensive tied down German productive resources and military manpower now engaged in air defense. But for the Allied air offensive, German military production might have expanded at a faster rate. Aerial bombing seemed an easy way to solve the strategic dilemma at a time when Britain stood alone. But the air offensive, in the final accounting, had twisted Britain's productive capacity out of shape, wasted men and materials, weakened the army's front line fighting ability, and lengthened the Allied casualty list.[64] Above all, the air offensive against civilian objectives – whether carried out by British, Germans, or Americans – further contributed to that barbarization of war that came to characterize the global conflicts of the twentieth century.

Terror took many other forms – including enforced population transfers. The twentieth century stands out in world history as the century of the refugee. Refugees, like other travelers, divide into different classses. The first consists of people, not necessarily distinguished by great wealth, but by their ability

[63]Winston Churchill, *Amid These Storms, Thoughts and Adventures*. New York, Scribner, 1932, p. 264.
[64]John Terraine, *The Right of the Line: The Royal Air Force in the European War 1939–45*. London, Hodder and Stoughton, 1985.

to foresee trouble a long time ahead, and by their command of unusual skills or of moveable wealth. In emigration, they travel first class by plane, ship, or rail. Upon arrival in the new country, they may find a favorable reception, so long as they are well-behaved, well-qualified, and few in numbers. Below them in the hierarchy rank those men and women who are lucky enough to leave just in time, find a country willing to take them, and a job to enable them to survive. These two classes comprised the bulk of the refugees who had been forced to leave Central Europe before World War II. The third class embraces evacuees, sent away in wartime from their homes by their own government's decree, to ecape from air raids or other threats. They do not travel in style at all, but at least they go by some recognized means of public conveyance.

The fourth class stands at the bottom at the hierarchy of misery. They must suddenly depart in a dire emergency; they go perhaps in a wagon, if they are lucky, more likely they travel on foot; they carry their few belongings in a rucksack, or push them on a bicycle or in a pram. They are the victims of war; as long as the fighting continues they may be machine-gunned from the air, or pushed aside or run over by tanks. They may also fall victim to every kind of personal violence, from robbery to rape. They are the defeated, and to them applies the Roman curse *vae victis*, woe to the vanquished. They counted among their ranks the French refugees who had fled from the German invaders in 1940. Five years later, it was the Germans' turn.

At the end of World War II and the years immediately following, a substantial numbr of minority groups in Eastern Europe also experienced what might be called a modified form of ethno-terror, one distinct from the atrocities that the Nazis had previously inflicted on their enemies. The chief – but not the only – sufferers were those Germans who lived in what had formerly constituted Eastern Germany, or who had formed part of scattered German communities in other parts of Eastern Europe. As the Soviet armies approached, German civilians frequently fled – and with good reason. Germany therefore suffered the amputation of about one-third of the Reich's prewar territory. According to the new rules of war, annexation entailed, so to speak, vacant possession. The postwar settlement in Eastern and Central Europe, accomplished under the aegis of the Soviet Union and the "People's Democracies," thereby involved a new gigantic *Völkerwanderung*.

Something like 4.5 million Poles migrated from the eastern parts of Poland, annexed to the Soviet Union, into the formerly German regions joined to Poland. All in all, about 12,000,000 Germans were expelled from East Germany and the Sudetenland. (Translated into contemporary American terms, this enforced population movement would have equalled the obligatory displacement from their accustomed homes of well over 40,000,000 Americans.) Other ethnic groups who shifted without their consent included Hungarians in Czechoslovakia; Italians expelled from territories taken over by Yugoslavia; the Volga Germans and other suspect national groups who lost their traditional homes in the Soviet Union. In theory, the new rulers in Eastrn Europe after World War II believed in the class struggle, one that would transcend national barrier. In practice, the Soviet Union and its satellite governments in Czechoslovakia and Poland used ethnic, not class affiliation as the criterion for expulsion – so much so that the handful of German Jews who had survived the death camps and returned to their homes in Breslau, were then driven out as undesirable Germans by the new Polish authorities.[65]

Methods of expulsion varied, from relatively "orderly transfers" to brutal drives in which untold numbers were robbed, beaten, tortured, killed, or died of exposure in horror-numbing treks. The total number of people who lost their homes in these population shifts may have been around 30,000,000. According to official German calculations, over 7,800,000 refugees from the eastern territories were living in the German Federal Republic. Figures for the total loss of human life incurred in these enforced migrations vary between 1,000,000 and 2,000,000 – but no one can be certain.[66]

Largely ignored in Western literature of the time, this gigantic movement of people gravely disrupted both farming and industrial production in the affected regions, and completely changed their demographic and cultural character.[67] The forced migrations annihilated a broad range of regional subcultures – Pomeranian, Silesian, East Prussian – that henceforth lived on only in the migrants' memories. Expulsions created a gigantic refugee problem, one that for the time being seemed insoluble in the recipient regions, especially in the Western occupation zones of Germany. The Germans' traditional stake in Eastern Europe, already weakened by war and its aftermath, further diminished in importance – Germany's *Drang nach Osten*, the drive toward the East, had become a matter of history.

The survivors' memories varied – from those of a German woman forcibly consigned to a privately set up Polish brothel before being released,[68] to the cheerful tale of a compatriot who could only recall, many years after, that her most memorable experience during the trek had been the joy of playing hide-and-seek with other small children in a graveyard where they had encamped at night. No storyteller or poet has as yet plumbed to the full the turmoil of those days when – to many sufferers – it seemed that Apocalypse had come to them, that death and hell had descended, "and . . . power was given unto them over the fourth part of the earth, to kill with sword, and with hunger, and with death, and with the beasts of the earth."[69]

---

[65]Theodor Schieder et al., eds, *The Expulsion of the German Population from the Territories East of the Oder-Neisse-Line.* Bonn, Federal Ministry for Expellees, Refugees and War Victims, c. 1954, vol. 1, p. 1–41, p. 233. For a general review, see Rainer Schulze, Doris von Der Brelie-Lewien, Helga Grebing, *Flüchtlinge und Vertriebene in der westdeutschen Nachkriegsgeschichte: Bilanzierung der Forschung und Perspektiven für die zukünftige Forschungsarbeit.* Hildesheim, Verlag August Lax, 1987.

[66]See for instance Presse und Informationsdiesnt der Bundesregierung. *Deutschland Heute.* Wiesbaden, Graphische Anstalt, 1955, pp. 153–5. Roy H. H. Mellor, *The Two Germanies: A Modern Geography.* London, Harper and Row, 1978, p. 153.

[67]For one of many nostalgic German accounts, see for instance Wolf Jobst Siedler, *Weder Maas noch Memel: Ansichten vom beschädigten Deutschland.* Munich, Deutscher Taschenbuchverlag, 1982, pp. 13–30.

[68]Schieder, *The Expulsion of the German Population,* p. 268.

[69]Revelations. 6:8.

THE WAR OF THE CIVILIAN

> During the nineteenth century, our cities increasingly began to lose their character as centers of culture; instead they came to be degraded into human beehives. The proletarians of a great metropolis have ceased to be rooted in their temporary residence where the individual city dweller's location has become a matter of chance. *Adolf Hitler*[70]

Hitler's contempt for the people of big cities has been shared by countless others – and by poets, philosophers, and artists. Disdain for metropolitan populations indeed runs deep in the Western tradition and goes back to antiquity. Concerns with the "health" of big cities made sense, say in sixteenth-century London where conditions were more insanitary and the death rate higher than in the countryside.[71] Industrialization made cities far more healthful places than they had been in former days, but romantic writers were apt to idealize the rural past; some even became convinced, as a German proverb would have it, that God had made the countryside, but the devil had fashioned the metropolis. In their detractors' eyes, city dwellers are soft and materialistic; they lack psychic wholeness. They are the children of sterile asphalt rather than of the fertile soil. They are in want of both physical and spiritual health. They succumb to mob psychology. They do meaningless jobs; they are slaves to social, economic, or psychological forces beyond their comprehension, hence they are unfit to guide their own destiny, and faced by catastrophe they will seek refuge in unreason or panic.

In the military sphere, such assessments of crowd psychology widely found reflection in theories that, from the end of World War I, had begun to advocate the massive use of airpower against urban centers. The city folk were thought to lack staying power. Confronted by shock and terror, they would soon waver and morale would give way, thereby forcing their stricken country to capitulate. Thus argued general Giulio Douhet, an Italian and an early theoretician of airpower, and his view was shared by British "bomber barons," and the designers of German long-range rockets in World War II.

None of these theories worked in practice. In Germany Dr Goebbels's *Durchaltepropaganda* (stick-it-out propaganda) met with a striking response. The German city folk's endurance and ingenuity exceeded all expectations. (On the other hand, the availability of cheap radios, known as *Volksempfänger* and diffused by the Nazis for propaganda purposes, also enabled ordinary Germans to listen to Allied, particularly British broadcasts.) Britain's successful resistance to the Blitz in 1940 and the rocket attacks at the end of the war was equally impressive; British resilience in a certain sense helped to rehabilitate the reputation of democracy in those now far-off days when France had been

---

[70]Adolf Hitler, *Mein Kampf*. Munich, Zentralverlag der NSDAP, 1944 edn, p. 288.

[71]For an early, and a brilliant critique of these romantic ideas, see Lord Macaulay, "Southey's colloquies of society" in *Critical and Historical Essays*. New York, A. C. Armstrong and Son, c. 1888, p. 98–121.

beaten in the field, when smaller democracies such as Holland, Denmark and Norway had failed adequately to prepare themselves for battle, and when Nazi Germany alone seemed strong, dynamic, and efficient. The British moreover maintained their democratic institutions intact under fire. Despite forecasts to the contrary, the experience of war did not cause them to become like their enemies; their morale failed to give way. The British initially responded to the threat of air warfare by a massive evacuation from supposed danger zones of schoolchildren, complete with their teachers, and of mothers with young boys and girls. When initially no bombs fell, many of the evacuees returned to the London they loved, with its pubs, fish-and-chip shops, its neighborhood ties and powerful local loyalties.

The massive air assaults of 1940 produced a second evacuation, much of it unplanned, but fraught like its predecessor with far-reaching social consequences. Many city people got to know the countryside for the first time, and had to adjust to different social mores. Countryfolk, to some extent even the well-to-do, learned for the first time how the poor lived in the big cities. Evacuation to some extent became a disguised social welfare scheme, as the authorities raised the standards of school meals, and introduced inexpensive milk, vitamins, and cod liver oil for children and expectant mothers. As A. J. P. Taylor, the British historian, put it, "the Luftwaffe became a powerful missionary of the welfare state."[72]

The toll of air war was heavy – not merely in terms of casualties, but also indirectly through the effects of sleepless nights, sudden mental trauma, and physical hardship. But far fewer people needed psychiatric attention than the planners had anticipated. Air raids in fact brought some psychological compensations. City-bred men and women proved their courage and initiative as ambulance drivers, air raid wardens, fire watchers – all services started by voluntary recruitment. Ordinary men and women under fire, both in Britain and on the Continent, displayed a high degree of rationality and common sense – qualities that a host of psychologists and literary people had been inclined to play down. Panic might break out for short, terrible spells in enclosed spaces, say in a large air raid shelter underneath a stricken building. But no bombed city ever succumbed to wholesale panic. Admittedly, morale was by no means uniformly good – British wartime propaganda notwithstanding. By the time rockets began to hit London in 1944, the people had become weary; long years of rationing, blackout, and interruption of ordinary life had caused Londoners to become depressed. Yet neither bombs nor rockets ever occasioned a popular demand for peace.

For some, enemy assaults even brought excitement and color. War turned into a drama in which ordinary people became at the same time both spectators and participants, a drama commented upon at regular times by radio newscasters. Most Londoners felt a sense of exhilaration when, for the first time, noisy cannonades opened from massed batteries against enemy bombers. There

[72]A. J. P. Taylor, *English History, 1914–1945*. Oxford, Oxford University Press, 1965, pp. 455, 503–4.

was terror, but even for otherwise timid souls, a strange thrill in watching a VI flying bomb approach its target area, cut its engine and circle crazily for a time in the air, before shattering a house or building. There was for many an ordinary householder a sense of achievement when he managed to put out an incendiary bomb; many a policeman, an ambulance driver, or an air raid warden enjoyed a responsibility and even a brief authority unthinkable in times of peace.

In Britain as well as abroad, air assaults had other unintended consequences. Embattled Cockneys – or, for that matter, Berliners – no longer seemed soft. On the contrary, they had faced dangers that seemed to render insignificant the perils that had confronted once romanticized empire builders along India's northeast frontier or in the African bush. Newspapers, newsreels, feature films, and paintings by officially commissioned war artists made much of the bravery and the achievements of the home front. Performing artists tried to support the people through their work (such as pianist Dame Myra Hess's "lunchtime" concerts). The BBC (British Broadcasting Corporation) played an enormously important part at a time when sporting events and theater performances were few, and when the radio formed the main source of entertainment during the long blackouts. Long hours at night were brightened by programs both popular and intelligent, such as commonsensical talks on health by the "Radio Doctor" (Charles Hill, later Lord Hill and a chairman of the BBC) or by the "Brains Trust," a popular colloquium in which scientist Julian Huxley, Commander Campbell, and philosopher C. E. M. Joad confidently answered questions on every topic under the sun.

Overall, the air war in Britain, linked to war experience in general, helped to heighten rather than depress popular expectations for the postwar years. Britain was quite unlike the continental countries in that the war gave the British the experience of victory rather than defeat. The very contrasts between the dire forecasts made before World War II concerning total annihilation in wartime and the realities of wartime experience heightened British confidence in the state. Public services worked efficiently, given the strain to which they were exposed. Rationing seemed to work fairly and effectively; there was a black market, but its activities were marginal; the stricken cities did not produce a pervasive underground economy at least during wartime. War gave to the British a sense of national solidarity rarely equalled abroad. Whereas the *Führer* never visited the stricken German cities, British VIPs from the Prime Minister downward willingly made their way to bombed cities. The king stayed in London, though even Buckingham Palace suffered damage.

Not that the British experienced universal social concord. War in fact created new social disparities of its own. There was the obvious inequality between those who had lost their homes and those whose houses remained standing. Rationing created new kinds of subservience; housewives suddenly learned how to be polite to their grocers, butchers, and bakers, as tradesmen had the power of doing favors for favorite customers. Officialdom increased its power and standing in a highly regulated community. The enemy bombs rained down on rich and poor alike. But East London (especially the docks) was struck harder than middle-class and upper-middle-class districts. Many a working man and working woman came to curse an establishment that had failed to provide adequate air defenses and sufficient shelter space – forgetting that the British prewar electorate would never have countenanced sufficient expenditure for such purposes.

The experience of war, on the other hand, was also capable of acting as a solvent of class hostilities by providing common bonds of new experience. In Britain, as later in Germany and the US, more women moved into the labor force – into factories, into the "Women's Land Army," into the military. Rationing helped to diminish former inequalities in food consumption and clothing standards, and the black market was probably less pervasive in Great Britain than in any other belligerent country in Europe. Air raids also diminished the lack of comprehension that had divided civil soldiers in World War I. Not even the most arrogant of Guards imagined that ambulance drivers or firemen in the London Blitz were stay-at-homes unwilling to risk their skins. Even more hazardous was the lot of merchant seamen, British, Danish, German, or Italian. For them it remained true in the twentieth century, as it had done three and a half centuries before, that "no kinde of men of any profession in the common wear their yeres in so great and continual hazard of life ... of so many grow so gray haires."[73]

> Civilians suffered greatly in World War II – they made up about 50 percent of the dead in Europe, compared to only 5 percent in World War I. (Gordon Wright, The Ordeal of Total War, 1939–1945)

Air assaults also promoted plans for the reconstruction of cities (for instance Coventry), and legislation such as the Town and Planning Act, 1944. Sir William Beveridge's plan for social services attained the distinction, unusual among government reports, of becoming a national best-seller, turning its author into a national figure. Beveridge's underlying assumptions were not new; the phrase "security from the cradle to the grave" was actually Churchill's. As the conflict increasingly appeared a people's war, the hardships suffered and the exertions of the people seemed to merit improved living standards and greater equality in times of peace.[74]

The impact of air war on Germany strikingly resembled the impact on Britain – except that the Allied air offensive in the end turned out immensely more destructive. In the first two years of war, the bombing accomplished relatively little. Hermann Goering, Reich Marshal, Coordinator of the Four Year Plan, Grand Master of the Germanic Hunt, went so far as to promise his

[73]Richard Hakluyt, cited by David S. Landes, *Revolution in Time: Clocks and the Making of the Modern World*. Cambridge, Mass., Belknap Press, 1983, p. 110.

[74]For the effects of war in general, see for instance, Angus Calder, *The People's War, 1939–1945*. New York, Pantheon Books, 1969. Henry Pelling, *Britain and the Second World War*. Glasgow, Collins, 1970. Arthur Marwick, *Britain in the Century of Total War ...* London, Bodley Head, 1968. John Stevenson, *British Society 1914–1945*. Harmondsworth, Penguin Books, 1984. Gordon Wright, *The Ordeal of Total War, 1939–1945*.

countrymen that if the British ever bombed the German capital, he would change his name to Meier. The British did bomb Berlin; air raid sirens henceforth became known to Berliners as "Meier's hunting horn." The raids continued with ever-increasing severity; their results beggar description. Cities such as Hamburg, Kassel, and Dresden were consumed by apocalyptic fire storms. Dresden's civil defense chief described their effects after the annihilation of his city:

> Never would I have thought that death could come to so many people in so many different ways. Never had I expected to see people ... burnt, cremated, torn and crushed to death; sometimes the victims looked like ordinary people apparently peacefully sleeping; the faces of others were racked with pain, the bodies stripped almost naked by the tornado; there were wretched refugees from the East clad only in rags, and people from the Opera in all their finery; here the victim was a shapeless slab, there a layer of ashes shovelled into a zinc tub. Across the city, along the streets wafted the unmistakable stench of decaying flesh.[75]

Four years earlier, such devastation would have aroused massive indignation in every Western country. By the end of the war, it had become commonplace. Even the *New Statesman*, a socialist British weekly with a long humanitarian tradition, while censuring attacks that unnecessarily destroyed great European art treasures, insisted that "in total war there is no place for emotional squeamishness. If heavy damage and casualties are essential for victory, the price must be paid."[76] The strategy of area bombing left no room for niceties, and turned into a doctrine of unlimited war in which destruction became an end unto itself, without consideration for the problems of postwar recovery. The consequences were shattering. In terms of morale, the effects of air raids on Germany were heightened by steadily mounting military casualties, and by ever-worsening news from the front – with 1943 as the watershed in Germany's military fortune.[77]

These devastating raids weakened the bonds of society, bonds already relaxed by dint of wartime conscription. Parents might lose their children, and children their parents. Men and women anxious to go underground or escape from accustomed ties by assuming new names found their task easier, as records of births, death, and residence went up in flames. When it came to fighting fires or conducting rescue operations, a man's or a woman's social origins no longer mattered; a courageous *Ostarbeiter* (a workman or labor conscript from Eastern Europe) turned out as good or better than an Aryan. The raids were apt also to encourage a spirit of *carpe diem,* "live for the day." As a local Gestapo chief reported with displeasure, "women and girls in

---

[75]Cited in David Irving, *The Destruction of Dresden.* London, Wiliam Kimber, 1963, p. 198. Earl R. Beck, *Under the Bombs, The German Home Front 1942–1945.* Lexington, University Press of Kentucky, 186.

[76]*New Statesman and Nation,* 29 April 1944, p. 1.

[77]Matthew Cooper, *The German Army 1939–1945. Its Political and Military Failure.* New York, Bonanza Books, 1984 edn., pp. 457–9.

bombed cities now enjoy themselves to the full, convinced that they are just as much entitled to the few remaining pleasures of life as the soldiers at the front, seeing that they might be rendered homeless or killed the very same night.'[78] Carl Zuckmeyer, a distinguished writer and a convinced anti-Nazi, was even more shaken when he returned to his native city just after the war had ended and looked at sights that had become all too commonplace in many parts of Europe:

> I walked, half stunned, through the ruins of Mainz, my birth place. I gazed at the pile of rubble that had once been our house. I could no longer recognize my former way to school. I looked at the walls of train stations, linked to the very ceiling with scrawled messages asking for the whereabouts of friends and kin. These train stations had become eery places, crowded with the expectant, the hopeful, and the hopeless, with monsters and murderers, cripples, refugees; with worn out and broken German soldiers returning from prisoner-of-war camps; with black marketeers and starvelings; with youthful prostitutes – both male and female; and with Allied soldiers in search for, or sought after by such prey.[79]

In Mainz as in so many other historic cities an entire way of life perished, as the *Altstadt*, with its narrow, picturesque (though insanitary) lanes and alleys vanished into rubble; a way of life sustained by close links of neighborhood and kin, with a naive enjoyment of food and drink – *Weck, Worscht un' Woi* (bread roll, sausage, and wine) – and crude jokes at carnival time. In its place came a profound mood of sadness and loss that took many years to disappear.

The air war also created all manner of cleavages in society. In German and Italy there was a widespread breakdown of communications. Travel became difficult, sometimes almost impossible; railway journeys turned into nightmares, with passengers clinging even to carriage roofs. Neighbors increasingly turned toward one another for help. Churchmen, trade unionists, and party functionaries faced great difficulties in rebuilding their organizations on a national basis. There was the rift between those cities which had been bombed and those which had not. There was an even wider gulf between city folk and farmers. During Holland's "hunger winter" in 1944, for instance, when 18,000 people died of starvation, and during the period immediately following World War II in Germany, the ordinary network of trade largely collapsed, as towns had little to sell, inflation was rampant, and communications often broke down. Black markets became institutionalized. Thousands, tens of thousands, hundred of thousands of hungry townsmen then descended on farmers to get food by barter, begging, or theft. Cold, rain, worn-out shoes, road blocks,

[78]Chief of Security Police, Darmstadt, 13 April 1944, reporting from Mainz, cited in Heinz Leiwig, *Mainz, 1933–1948: Von der Machtergreifung bis zur Währungsreform*. Mainz. Schmidt, 1987, p. 108.

[79]Carl Zuckmeyer, *Als wär's ein Stück von mir: Horen der Freundschaft*. Vienna, S. Fischer Verlag, 1969, p. 552.

lack of cash – nothing could put an end to the interminable tide of people searching for food. The farmer became a king – or so it seemed to starving city dwellers whose furniture, clothes, jewelry ended up in farmhouses, in exchange for milk, potatoes, and even turnips. "I never felt more humiliated," wrote an out-of-work Dutch journalist, "than when I was waiting, with 60 other men, for the farmer ... We stood there, just like a pack of beaten dogs, with pale faces and empty bags, until we realized that he was not going to sell."[80] But farmers also suffered, as their unbidden guests might take the chickens from the farmyard, milk the cows, or even steal the horses. It was a bad time to be hungry.

Still, Dutch and German civilian morale no more collapsed under the bombing than British or French morale did. In Germany as in the rest of Europe ordinary men and women proved a good deal more resilient than the bulk of literati, psychologists and air war planners had ever dreamt. The great majority of bombed-out people somehow went on with their lives. They went back to work each morning; their recuperative power proved immense. Even during the final months of the war, by which time Berlin had largely been reduced to a gigantic rubble field, more than 65 percent of the factories continued to operate after a fashion. It was hard to go to work: traffic was clogged; there were slowdowns, detours, breakdowns; but every morning Berliners got up from their shelters, basements, cellars, and make-do sheds. As historian Cornelius Ryan put it, those who had survived another night were determined to live another day.[81] Extremes of terror might reduce victims to a temporary state of apathy. But most recovered, aided often enough by that spirit of solidarity, even of mutual kindness that common afflictions are apt to produce.

Recovery came most easily to those able to do active work, especially in civil defense. The German, like the British, home front produced countless unknown heroes who put out incendiary bombs, extinguished fires, participated in rescue operations, and cleared rubble.[82] Organized civil defense everywhere made an immense difference to a stricken people's capacity to resist. But even the best organization would have proved useless without an extraordinary and unplanned display of private initiative and improvisation, qualities without which no belligerent country would have survived. In Berlin, as in London and Coventry, men and women learned new skills and shouldered new responsibilities of a kind that they had never dreamt of in times of peace.

Air raids, in theory, should have produced ferocious hatred of the enemy, and it is true that they did bring about widespread demands for retaliation. But they occasioned remarkably little in the way of personal hostility. Few

[80]Henri A. van der Zee, *The Hunger Winter: Occupied Holland 1944–1945*, London, Jill Norman and Hobhouse, 1982, pp. 146–58.

[81]Cornelius Ryan, *The Last Battle*. New York, Simon and Schuster, 1966, pp. 16–17.

[82]For details, see for instance Hans Rumpf, *Das war der Bombenkrieg: Deutsche Städte im Feuersturm: Ein Dokumentarbericht*. Oldenburg, Gerhard Stalling Verlag, 1961. Sir Charles Webster and Noble Frankland, *The Strategic Air Offensive Against Germany 1939–1945*. Official History: UK Military Series, London, HM Stationery Office, 1961, 4 vols, V. II, pp. 238–41.

bomber crews forced to parachute over enemy country were harmed. Air raids, for all their terrors, had an impersonal quality. Sirens wailed; searchlights pierced the evening sky; flack thundered; planes droned overhead; bombs whistled their crescendo; walls shook; houses collapsed. But enemy fliers remained hidden in a fog of anonymity; air raids appeared like natural catastrophes.

Infinitely more dreadful, by contrast, was the fear of personal violence, of rape or mutilation at the hands of enemy soldiers. Such had been the experience of many Russian or Polish civilians under Nazi rule. Such was the experience of many Eastern Europeans and Germans when it was the Red Army's turn to enjoy the fruits of victory. To many Berliners, for example, the brief battle for Berlin against the Red Army appeared in retrospect far more terrifying than years of air raids. For Italian refugees from Zara (Zadar) on the Adriatic coast, their city's occupation by Tito's troops – accompanied by countless outrages – proved the most dreadful days they had ever experienced. And so the sorry list continued.

The survivors' adjustment was made no easier by the incomprehension shown by the world at large to their ordeal (an experience shared by the victims of mass expulsion, or incarceration under gruesome conditions suffered by civilians and soldiers in Soviet, Nazi, or Japanese camps). In a sense, this lack of comprehension was not surprising. Men and women who were themselves under heavy pressure were more preoccupied with their own troubles than those endured by strangers. There was an equally understandable inclination for those spared even temporary catastrophe to assume that the sufferers might, at least in part, have deserved their fate. A half-facetious jingle circulating in the Ruhr region of Western Germany thus enjoined the British to bomb Berlin, rather than the Ruhr:

> British fliers, please stay clear,
> We are only miners here.
> It's in Berlin where "heil" they yell,
> Better bomb Berlin to hell.[83]

Human disasters on the scale endured in World War II simply proved too great for understanding on the part of those who did not experience them. As a Belsen survivor tried to explain soon after the end of the war, "when my neighbour dies, it is a tragedy; when a city is wiped out, it is an act of God; when a nation dies, it is a statistic." Hence catastrophes of such a scale were apt to be displaced in public memory, to emerge into public consciousness only many years later. Enquiries into the cause of the relative indifference shown by Western countries concerning the Jews in wartime Europe thus

[83]Original in Gordon Craig, *Germany 1866–1945*. Oxford, Oxford University Press, 1978, p. 758.

only got under way many years after the end of the war.[84] There was a similar time-lag with regard to academic enquiries concerning the effect of massive city bombing. The tragedy involved in the enormous population shifts affecting Central and Eastern Europe has still as yet failed to strike the sympathy of the Western world.

Overall, historians cannot easily arrive at general conclusions concerning the civilian experience. War upset accustomed ways. War put men and women on their mettle in a way rarely achieved in peace, and placed a premium on the person who could cope with impossible situations, the *macher* in Yiddish, the *débrouillard* in French, the *kombinator* in Polish, the "fixer" in American. War begat new skills, as students turned into tank drivers, and scholars into spies. War broke accustomed ethnic moulds in industry. In the United States, new jobs opened in factories and ship yards to skilled and unskilled blacks. Ethnic discrimination against some European minorities also diminished. Jewish Americans, for example, had previously faced severe restrictions in a great variety of jobs. The needs of wartime largely did away with the old reluctance of major corporations to employ Jews as industrial chemists or engineers. Above all war profoundly changed the condition of women. It turned them into welders, riveters, and truck drivers. The British, alone among the Western belligerents, extended compulsory war service to women – at a time when unemployment had given way to an all-pervading labor shortage, and when governmental direction had become both acceptable and popular. (By 1941, Great Britain had 49 per cent of her total population engaged on war work.) The US relied on voluntary recruitment (but with pressure to get women to work in war industries). In the US, as everywhere else, many men resisted the drift of women into factories, lest returning soldiers should find themselves without jobs. Nevertheless, millions of women took work of a kind they had never done before. They put on uniforms; they worked on assembly lines, in offices, and workshops. Even those who stayed at home found themselves saddled with a wide range of new responsibilities, forced to cope with both emotional and financial difficulties entailed in separation from husbands in the armed services.

During the war, with so many men in the services and millions of women in the workplace, traditional sexual morals declined. Juvenile crime rates doubled, teenage prostitution was a major problem (New York City had to set up a Wayward Minors' Court), the divorce rate rose, and infidelity became commonplace. Churches, schools and government all became convinced that there had been a moral breakdown in society – broken homes, illegitimacy and venereal diseases increased because of wartime pleasure seeking. (There was a strong postwar reaction to all this, and marriage and birthrates went up

[84]See for instance, Alfred Hasler, *The Lifeboat is Full: Switzerland and the Refugees, 1939–1945*. New York, Funk and Wagnall, 1969. Bernard Wasserstein, *Britain and the Jews of Europe, 1939– 1945*. Oxford, Clarendon Press, Institute for Jewish Affairs, 1979. Irving Abella and Harold Troper, *None Is Too Many: Canada and the Jews of Europe, 1933–1948*. Totonto, L. and O. Dennis, 1982. David S. Wyman, *The Abandonment of the Jews: America and the Holocaust, 1941–1945*. New York, Pantheon Books, 1984.

and divorce and illegitimacy went down. In France the new morality succeeded in closing the brothels in 1946.)

The seeds of the sexual revolution of the 1960s may have been sown in wartime permissiveness and family dislocations. Certainly, many prewar taboos fell; girls and women did men's work and earned their own money; they could go into bars and pubs alone, buy their own drinks and share costs for a date often for the first time. All these practices continued after the war. True enough, many young married women still preferred to remain home-makers. But, as D'Ann Campbell, a feminist historian, suggests, returned women war workers began to reinterpret their role in the family. "Rosie the Riveter" (a patriotic propaganda figure of World War II) and WAAC "mop commandos" may have passed on new aspirations to their daughters and, indirectly, inspired the new feminism of the 1960s.[85]

Perhaps the most important social consequence of World War II was this change in the workplace. Traditional gender roles were overturned – more women went to work in World War II than at any time in history and more remained in the workplace after the war than had been employed in 1940. New jobs opened to women, some of which remained available after the war. Although the government and employers assumed women would return to the home once "Johnny came marching home," many women (60 to 85 per cent) did not want to give up their jobs. Admittedly, large numbers were summarily fired in 1945, others were encouraged or pressured into spending more time at home with their children or to get married. But the number of working married women grew slowly but steadily in the years after 1945 until, by 1970, over 60 percent were employed.

Even Nazi Germany, firmly committed by its ideology to the propositions that the Aryan woman's place was in the home, could not hold back the tide. After an initial time-lag, German women too began to do war work. They also enormously increased their share of the student population in universities and technical colleges at a time when most men were at war. (Between 1939 and 1944 the percentage of women in German universities increased from 11.2 to 49.3 percent, and at technical colleges from 1.9 to 18.0 percent.)

Increased areas of work opened to women in industry and government, and stirred women to seek more independence and more opportunities The gains were probably greatest for Italian women during World War II when 2,000,000 soldiers were away fighting, according to Meriam Mafi. Fascist Italy wanted women to be passive and cheerful, chaste before marriage and productive in child-bearing after. There were only 15,000 women at university in Italy in 1940 and women could not vote. The economic recovery brought thousands of women back into the workplace, and schools were more open to women matriculants.

World War II then was in this respect a boon to many women. It brought millions into the labor market for the first time; it eliminated barriers to women

[85]For the US, see D'Ann Campbell, *Women at War with America: Private Lives in a Patriotic Era.* Cambridge, Mass., Harvard University Press, 1984.

working and opened new opportunities of work and second vocations for older married women. Before 1940 married women rarely had paid employment, but during the war over 6.5 million women entered the workforce, three-quarters of whom were married. In America, structural and behavioral changes induced by World War II continued to reshape society in peacetime. War thus accelerated the drive for equality, revived feminism and may have contributed to a sexual revolution.[86]

War destroyed many peoples' links with their traditional homeland. Persecution, migrations, and expulsions created an army of people who looked back with regret to an often idealized past, and thereby aroused their new neighbors' derision: the *chez nous*, of the German refugees in France during the 1930s; the *tuves* (I had), of Cuban exiles among fellow-Hispanics in the US; the "when-wes", of white Rhodesians of a later generation in South Africa. Refugees and "expellees" responded to the shock of expatriation in many different ways. There were those who continued to suffer from a sense of deprivation; some lived by the motto *patriam mecum porto* (I take my homeland with me wherever I go); others tried to forget and pushed homesickness into the unconscious. But overwhelmingly, the expatriates learned how to function in several cultures and how to adjust.

War loosened what had seemed permanent links of allegiance. There were far-reaching shifts in self-identification. A middle-aged German-Jewish lady, herself an ex-officer's wife, explained this well when she recalled in exile her grief at the defeat of the Kaiser's army in 1918. "We watched our soldiers marching back across the Rhine bridge. They were ragged and worn. But they still held themselves proudly as they sang 'The Watch on the Rhine.' But then, of course, *we* were still *them*." War at the same time created new bonds between those who had gone through comparable hardships and psychological traumas.

War gave increased scope for every human quality from the vile to the splendid. Later generations found something unnerving in seeing a bent and white-haired lady, in appearance everybody's grandmother, convicted for war crimes committed 30 years earlier, crimes that shocked the most hardened. At the same time there were acts of heroism that went far beyond the most imaginative in Hollywood fiction, deeds that seem incredible in retrospect. And yet it was true that the kindly emeritus professor reading a paper at a conference, a quiet scholarly man, dignified, with a little paunch, still speaking English with a Polish trace, had once parachuted into German-occupied Europe, organized a network of underground fighters and, at unbelievable risk to himself, saved numerous Jewish lives.[87]

[86]William Henry Chafe, *The American Woman: Her Changing Social, Economic and Political Roles, 1920–1970*. Oxford, Oxford University Press, 1972, pp. 143–6. For the role of German women at the universities, see Jacques R. Pauwels, *Women, Nazis, and Universities: Female University Students in the Third Reich, 1933–1945*. Westport, Conn., Greenwood Press, 1984, and for a general work see Dorothea Kinksiek, *Die Frau im NS Staat*. Stuttgart, 1982. For Britain, Penny Sumerfield, *Women Workers in the Second World War*. London, Croom Helm, 1984.

[87]We refer with respect to our friend George Lerski, Professor Emeritus at the University of San Francisco who in 1985 was honored by the Yad Vashem with the designation of a "Righteous Among the Nations" for his work in saving Jewish lives during World War II. According to

The heroes, however, could not make up for the disasters of war and their consequences – death, destruction, injuries, the loss of trust, the broken families, the shattered friendships, the violence, the hatreds, the thirst for vengeance. Great as the physical costs of war had been, they could not compare with the human costs. Even the most tenacious optimist in 1945 might have been forgiven for looking into the future with gloom. Albrecht Haushofer, a resistance fighter and a poet spoke for many of his countrymen, when he foresaw, shortly before his execution in a Berlin prison, how hubris would bring about an end with horror:

> A thunderstorm arises in the Western sea
> Great fires come from distant Eastern steppes.
> Their searing flames consume the land.
> And none are left to stem the doom . . .
> A splendid past sinks into dust,
> And only rubble shall bear witness
> To long-lost splendors of the past.[88]

THE MILITARY WAR EXPERIENCE

World War II was the greatest conflict in history. In Europe and North America alone, more than 50,000,000 people put on uniform. The exact total will never be known because auxiliaries (such as the German *Volkssturm* or the *Forces Françaises de l'Intérieur*) fluctuated in size and composition, and because statistical services broke down for the defeated. The fighting men served in every conceivable circumstance, on the seas, in the air, on land – in the jungle, on the tundra, in marshland, on alpine ranges, in the desert, in city blocks. They were plagued by dysentery, frostbite, ulcers, malaria, lice, mosquitoes, hunger, thirst, heat, cold, fear and boredom. For all too many, war turned out to be an incomprehensible tragedy

> Of carnal, bloody, and unnatural acts;
> Of accidental judgments, casual slaughters;
> Of deaths put on by cunning and forc'd cause;
> And, in this upshot, purposes mistook
> Fall'n on the inventors' heads . . .[89]

For better and for worse, war reshaped the modern world. World War II once again destroyed many illusions – including those idealistic assumptions to the effect that in a new military conflict, the masses would no longer risk their lives in wars between nation states, or that the outcome of such conflicts was a matter of indifference to the common people. World War II certainly

---

Professor Lerski's estimate, something like 100,000 Jews in Poland owed their survival to the assistance of Polish Christians.

[88] Albrecht Haushofer, "Verhängnis," *Moabiter Sonette*, Berlin, Blanvalet, 1946, p. 49.

[89] William Shakespeare, *Hamlet, Prince of Denmark*, V. iii. 380–4.

witnessed some striking breakdowns in military morale. These struck at armies that had been poorly prepared and trained for the exigencies of mobile operations (the Dutch, the French in Western Europe, the Italians in North Africa in 1940, parts of the Red Army in the initial phase of the German invasion in 1941). But no army anywhere experienced any of those great mutinies that had shaken the French and Russian armed forces in 1917 and those of Imperial Germany in 1918. Once the war had gotten into its stride, the opposing armies of the major powers in fact all proved astonishingly resistant to enemy propaganda. The bulk of British and American, German, and Soviet soldiers seemed to live in fact in different ideological worlds, little affected by enemy broadcasts, a fact apparent to interpreters charged with interrogating prisoners. If anything, the English-speaking democracies proved even more cohesive than the Soviet and Nazi dictatorships. The Nazis in the end thus found themselves compelled to use terror against their own soldiers as well as against the enemy. During the last stages of fighting, the sight of *Wehrmacht* deserters, or supposed deserters, dangling from trees with warning placards around their necks became a common sight in Germany. The British and Americans, by contrast, rarely executed those who went AWOL (absent without leave). Nonetheless, their armies sustained the will to fight, despite the numerous defeats they endured in the earlier stages of the war. None of the major industrialized powers developed a powerful peace movement.

On the face of it, this may seem surprising, for none of the belligerents had entered World War II with the enthusiasm that had been evident in all the major capitals in 1914, when generals, poets, and mobs had all expected that war would be brief, glorious, and not too bloody. The mood in 1939, on the contrary, had been grim and apprehensive – in Berlin as much as in Paris and London. World War II did not occasion the literary cult of the *Fronterlebnis,* the supposedly searing and cathartic experience, that had inspired, or pretended to inspire so many German war books in the past. Neither did it produce that cult of the "unknown soldier" that had become part of Europe's civic religion after the first war. Outside the Soviet Union, few war memorials went up following World War II. German soldiers after the capitulation widely sold their hard-earned medals for cigarettes, or put their decorations into a dustbin, unconsciously following in this respect the example of German-Jewish veterans from World War I who, during the 1930s, had disgustedly consigned their World War I decorations to the garbage dump. Relatively few British soldiers after the end of the war even bothered to claim the campaign medals to which they were entitled. But neither did World War II bring about that mood of disillusionment that had struck the victors after 1918. For these winners, war turned out to be supremely worthwhile.

How did World War II affect the enormous number of its participants? Generalizations are hard, given the immense extent of the war and its operations, the diverse make up and organizations of the various armies, the enormous differences experienced in the many theaters of operation. Members of base units had a different war from that endured by members of combat formations, subjected to long spells of boredom and briefer spells of intense fear. War was different for those who won and those who lost; those who languished in an American, a Japanese, or a Soviet prisoner-of-war camp; those who were but briefly under fire, and those whose units were burnt out, *verheizt* (consumed as fuel) in the German combat soldiers' phraseology.

All soldiers, however, had certain experiences in common. Soldiers – unlike most civilians, even most civilians under fire – wore uniform. They found themselves subject to a discipline harsher and more all-embracing than the sternest of foremen could enforce in a factory or workshop. War created new bonds of loyalty and of shared experiences. War took men (and many women) away from their families and neighbors. Combat produced that particular allegiance to small units under heavy stress, the soldier's own "mob" (in British) or *Haufen* (in German parlance).

War also proved an exacting teacher, at every level of command. Tactics and technology kept changing to a degree unknown in previous conflicts. Established skills in fields such as radar needed constant revision. A particular type of tank would quickly become outmoded and turn into a steel-clad coffin. The exigencies of war both required and created an immense number of new organizations and skills, in the civilian and military spheres. Workers at home learned new trades in war-related industries; civil defense crews acquired new kinds of expertise to cope with emergencies. So did soldiers, sailors, and airmen. Mobile warfare in particular made greater demands on the individual soldier's skills and on the versatility of small units than trench warfare had done in World War I. World War I had seen the culmination of a lengthy development in which the defensive had temporarily become supreme. As Karl Marx had already put it (with regard to the siege of Sebastopol, in 1854), "in the same proportion as the *materiel* of warfare has by industrial progress advanced during the long peace, in the same proportion has the *art* of war degenerated."[90]

Having been called to the colors, millions of men became proficient in a wide range of new skills. They learned how to drive a truck, fire a mortar, understand the workings of a car engine, fly a plane, build a bridge, read a map, find directions in the bush, repair a tank, cook a meal, evaluate intelligence, give first aid – the list extends almost indefinitely. War also taught less desirable skills – how to fiddle accounts and "organize" supplies by illicit as well as licit means. Conflict produced a new lingua franca intelligible to victors, neutrals, and vanquished, with made-up words such as *nix, kaputt,* and *jig jig,* the latter, a reference to sexual activity, drawn from Britain's imperial vocabulary.

War created some of the most awesome spectacles ever witnessed by mankind. These might be exhilarating to one's own side, such as the sight of the Allied armada that darkened the south of England at the time of the Normandy invasion. For those on the receiving end such impressions were numbing, blinding, ear- and earth-shattering, and would remain forever etched

---

[90]Karl Marx, *The Eastern Question: A Reprint of Letters Written 1853–1856 Dealing with the Events of the Crimean War.* Ed. Eleanor Marx Aveling and Edward Aveling, London, Swan Sonnenschein and Co., 1897, p. 493.

in the consciousness of those who had survived. Such experiences brought home the terrors of mutilation and sudden death – the sight of a tank "brewed up" or a friend suddenly dismembered. War created a large number of psychological as well as physical casualties. (In the US Army, in the European theater in 1944, the ratio of psychological casualties to ordinary wounded was 20 percent, though the figures varied greatly between different units.)[91]

On the other hand, war also gave to many a new confidence in their own abilities under stress. To some came brief moments of incredible achievement – an American with a bazooka, an Englishman with a PIAT, a German with a *Panzerfaust* who had managed to knock out an enemy tank. Despite all literary conventions to the contrary, the great majority of soldiers did not return from the wars as broken men. For some, war in fact became a special experience that set them apart from other men. As a good many German veterans oddly concluded in interrogations concerning their terrible experiences in Russia: *schön war's doch* – "all the same, it was great."

War also placed many a young man in a position of great authority. Eighteenth-century officers in the British army used to hope for "a sickly season and a bloody war" to speed promotion. World War II provided these advantages. The enormous expansion of all belligerent armies created a huge demand for commissioned officers, and often made for rapid advancement. A young university student might rise to command a company, a battalion, or a regiment; he might find himself in charge of an entire city as a newly appointed civil affairs officer. War did away with snobberies of a traditional kind, simply because they interfered with the efficient prosecution of the war. In the British army, to give just one example, Sir Brian Horrocks assumed a senior command in North Africa, despite complaints from aristocratic cavalry officers that Horrocks had come from a very humble regiment, the Middlesex.[92] Social levelling went even further in Germany. Hitler, intensely distrustful of the old nobility, largely replaced the top leadership with people of humble birth, men such as Wilhelm Keitel, Alfred Jodl, Sepp Dietrich, Eduard Dietl, whose ancestors had never been able to boast of the coveted "von" before their surnames. There was, too, more ethnic mobility within the armed forces, even in Nazi Germany, the country dedicated to ideas of racial purity. The *Waffen SS,* originally designed as a Nordic elite, ended by recruiting large numbers of Croatians, Ukrainians, Hungarians, Bosnians, Albanians, and other assorted Eastern Europeans of dubious Nordic credentials, as well as Belgians, Frenchmen, Scandinavians and Dutchmen, acceptable from Himmler's racist standpoint.[93] In the US, black soldiers as yet remained in segregated units, but other little-favored ethnic groups, such as the Italian-Americans, Mexican-

---

[91]For details, see Brian Chermoni, "Wounds without scars: treatment of battle fatigue in the US armed forces in the Second World War," *Military Affairs,* January 1985, pp. 9–12. For the British experience, see Major-General F. M. Richardson, *Fighting Spirit: A Study of Psychological Factors in War.* London, Leo Cooper, 1978.

[92]Nigel Hamilton, *Monty: Portrait of a General.* New York, McGraw Hill, 1981, p. 89.

[93]For their order of battle, see John Keegan, *Waffen SS: The Asphalt Soldiers.* New York, Ballantyne Books, 1971, pp. 158–9.

Americans and Japanese-Americans, served with distinction in combat formations, earning the highest military honors that their country was able to give.[94]

War entailed at the same time the disruption of ordinary life. In German-occupied countries, foreign rule produced violence; illegality became an expected way of life. Thereafter, there was an intense desire for revenge against real or alleged collaborators. (In France alone, an estimated 50,000 people were killed after liberation, most of them by communist resistance forces.) At the same time, the power of the state increased in an extraordinary fashion – to cope with evacuees, to regulate industry, to direct labor, to influence public opinion by fair means or foul. World War I in this respect had been a trial run; World War II perfected existing techniques. Even in the US, a country that took pride as no other in the free enterprise system, official agencies had multiplied both for the purpose of increasing production and for directing production from peaceful to warlike objectives. Federal power had come to tough peoples' lives in innumerable ways – through rationing, increased taxation, through a new Fair Employment Practices Commission designed to prevent racial discrimination in firms given military contracts, and so on. The Office of Scientific Research Development spent huge sums in university-based scientific research, and solidified the new partnership between academics and the state. All over the Western world, war cemented a form of "managed state capitalism," one that operated quite smoothly from the start in Great Britain, and one that Albert Speer struggled hard to establish in Germany .

War entailed moreover the greatest travel scheme known to history, compulsory, publicly funded, but effective. This was obligatory tourism on a gigantic scale – at a time when mass tourism had not yet become as affordable and widespread as it did in the 1950s. The military migration vastly spread the use of English, which became the lingua franca of the world (further promoted after the end of hostilities though technical variants such as "air speak", the idiom of aviators and airport controllers, "sea speak," and "NATO English"). Compulsory travel abroad profoundly influenced the soldiers' image of foreigners, and equally the image that foreigners received of their more or less unwelcome guests.

British servicemen, for example, went as far as Ethiopia and Egypt, Libya and Tunisia, Italy and France, Holland and Germany. Many of them held pre-existing imperial stereotypes concerning Middle Easterners and Indians. Some returned with more respect for the Germans, with their formidable fighting qualities, than for Britain's colonial subjects. British wartime commitment to social welfare began to spill over into the colonies in that parliament voted for funds for colonial development (including the generously framed Colonial Development and Welfare Act of 1945, which made £120 million available for improvement in the colonies during the coming decade).

But British decolonization owed little or nothing to the ordinary soldier's

[94]See for example Raul Morin: *Among the Valiant: Mexican-Americans in World War II and Korea.* Los Angeles, Borden Publishing Co., 1966.

impression of the colonies in wartime. Overall, British, like American, veterans returned from the war with a sense of national achievement. Their country alone had withstood Germany from the start of the war in 1939. They had retrieved every defeat, in the North African desert, in the Burmese jungle. They had no idea of how much their country had, by the end of the war, become militarily reliant on the enormous productive capacities of the US.

Americans went overseas in even larger numbers; theirs was a military migration unequalled in history. (By 1943, they had deployed 1.8 million men against Germany, and an equal number against Japan.) Some Americans were impressed by aspects of foreign cultures. But overall, they felt their belief almost universally confirmed in their own country's superior institutions and material well-being. The US – prosperous, strong, infused with a sense of normality, safe in its constitutional liberty, free from the obvious class snobberies that beset so many foreign countries – seemed to be the world's best country. It was a land that refugees and war brides from many nations longed to call their own, and one to which practically every American veteran desperately wanted to return.

The Americans overseas roused both admiration and envy in foreign eyes. The GIs on the average were taller than Europeans; they were better equipped – with a plethora of trucks and jeeps – better clad, better fed. They displayed a personal generosity and a sense of nonchalance that Europeans rarely equalled. Theirs was, it seemed to Europeans, a mass consumer society in uniform, a society that produced a potent demonstration effect. A British sergeant temporarily assigned to an American mess would find himself in a different world. Among the Americans, noncommissioned officers and enlisted men dined together; there was none of the social separation entailed in the institution of a separate sergeants' mess with its intense commitment to regimental pride. Among the Americans, every ordinary soldier owned, or expected to own, a car in peacetime – an extraordinary ambition for the ordinary British or French private at the time. Americans were strikingly good at organization, not just in major matters such as building bridges, but in small matters. Instead of plates, easy to break and laborious to clean, they used a strange implement, a bakelite tray, with special indentations for putting in different kinds of foods – an innovation then unknown to the British army. The Americans thus aroused both admiration and resentment, and countless jokes circulated at their expense. They were "overpaid, oversexed, overdressed, and over here," said the British. "You British are underpaid, undersexed, underdressed, and under Eisenhower," replied the Americans.

The American influence was pervasive, as John Keegan, a British military historian, noted, thinking back to his childhood in the West of England with American encampments, "the feudal West would never be quite the same again, and a good thing too thought many, particularly the young." [95] The Americans made an equal impression on their German foes. The GIs lacked

---

[95] John Keegan, *Six Armies in Normandy: From D-Day to the Liberation of Paris*. Harmondsworth, Penguin Books, 1982, p. 13.

the *Wehrmacht*'s long-practiced battle skills, but once bloodied in battle and well led, the Americans could face the toughest opponents. They, like the British, were moreover infinitely preferred as conquerors to the Red Army, with its grim reputation for rape and violence — so much so that during the final months of the war, the Germans, especially the women, prayed that American and British troops would march in before the Russians arrived.[96]

Participants in the war found many striking distinctions between different theaters, for example, between those that entailed garrison duty and those that meant combat. A German soldier assigned to occupied Norway or France would consider himself a fortunate man. He might meet hatred from the civilians, but he also encountered a good deal of acceptance — ranging from the opportunistic friendship of political collaborators to those many *horizontales* who slept with, and sometimes married their German lovers.[97]

The presence of foreign soldiers in foreign countries, and their desire for sexual liaisons, everywhere created new tensions and new anxieties. (In British barracks these oddly found expression in tales about Polish soldiers stationed there, whose sexual prowess was such that an English girl, having slept with a Pole, would never again have an Englishman.) Moralists complained about the soldiers' real or supposed sexual escapades. Social scientists pontificated. (Margaret Meade, a doyenne of American anthropology sent to England by the US government to investigate relations between GIs and Englishwomen, contributed to public disinformation by mistakenly suggesting the English girls looked to boys to impose restraints; American boys by contrast, expected the girl to say "no." The clash of opposing expectations, according to Meade's erudite silliness, led each side to regard the other as immoral.)[98] Amorous associations, temporary or permanent, in fact played a real part in breaking down national stereotypes, as did real life experiences with foreigners in all countries, at work in factories or in farms.

Service in Russia for the Germans (and also for Italian soldiers mobilized for the Eastern front) was altogether different. Conflict in the East was total in a manner not witnessed in Europe since the war of religion in the seventeenth century. The fault was, above all, the Nazis'. When the *Wehrmacht* first invaded the Soviet Union, the Germans were often treated as liberators in regions such as the Ukraine and the Baltic states. Germans in Russia also established personal relations with the indigenous people, contacts that taught the German soldiers that Russians were very different from Dr Goebbels's propaganda image of bestial *Untermenschen*. (A popular German soldiers' ditty in fact praised the charms of "black Natasha," a legendary Russian girl.) Something like 1,000,000 Soviet citizens served the Germans in some capacity or other, as auxiliaries. But once the conquered found that they had merely exchanged Soviet com-

---

[96]See, for instance, Cornelius Ryan, *The Last Battle*. New York, York, Simon and Schuster, 1966, pp. 23–33.

[97]See Richard Cobb, *French and Germans; Germans and French: A Personal Interpretation of France under Two Occupations, 1914–1918/1940–1944*. Hanover, University Press of New England, 1983.

[98]Jane Howard, *Margaret Meade: A Life*. New York, Simon and Schuster, 1984, p. 239.

missars for Nazi ones, the character of war changed. There was widespread partisan warfare on a scale unequalled in Western Europe. These guerrilla actions engendered the inevitable chain of atrocities and counter-atrocities.

Warfare became ever more bitter due to the theory and practice of two struggling totalitarian systems. Both contenders mercilessly sent to penal battalions, or executed, real or alleged slackers and deserters. Both combatants were wont to use extreme cruelty against their opponents – the Soviets because they regarded the Fascist invaders as enemies of humanity, whose very graves should be plowed under so as to wipe out each and every memory of the enemy occupation. Both sides, in addition, tended to deal with prisoners in the grimmest possible way, instilling in the ordinary fighting man on both sides the fear that surrender meant death – *wer sich ergibt ist verloren*, according to German military lore on the Eastern front. (In fact, a much higher proportion of German prisoners returned alive from the Soviet Union than Soviet prisoners survived in German camps. The German prisoners suffered from cruelty and neglect; Soviet captives were widely exposed to starvation of the genocidal kind.)[99]

There were other terrors in Russia. The USSR was an incredibly alien country, cornfields of unimaginable size; immense tangled forests; marshes greater than many a German principality; there was unbanked rivers prone to flood across the flat monotonous landscape; there was heat and dust in summer, mud in autumn, snow and subarctic temperatures in winter. The railways were inadequate. Roads were likely to turn into mud traps; maps turned out to be useless. The people mostly lived in a state of primitiveness that appeared inconceivable even to the hardiest of German soldiers brought up in a remote village in Pomerania or the March of Brandenburg. The Soviet was an opponent incomprehensible in his apparent willingness to accept limitless casualties. Then there was the loneliness, the melancholy of a land whose horizons seemed to stretch into infinity.[100] The experience of war on the Eastern front dispelled the illusions that even the most committed of German communists had held about Russia. Few believers preserved their faith; the bulk of German prisoners in Russian hands proved immune to the propaganda efforts of those German intellectuals who had sided with the Soviets and thereafter tried to spread communist doctrine among German prisoners of war.[101] Overall, the experience of war in the East decisively turned German veterans toward the West, at least those lucky enough to return from Soviet camps.

[99]Omer Bartov, *The Eastern Front, 1941–45: German Troops and the Barbarisation of Warfare*. New York, St Martin's Press, 1986. Christian Streit, *Keine Kameraden: Die Wehrmacht und die sowjetischen Kriegsgefangenen 1941–1945*. Stuttgart, Deutsche Verlagsanstalt, 1978.

[100]See for instance, James Lucas, *War on the Eastern Front 1941–1945: The German Soldier in Russia, New York, Bonanza Books, 1979*. For the reminiscences of a thoughtful German prisoner of war, see for instance *Helmut Gollwitzer, ... Und Führen Wohin Du Nicht Willst, Bericht einer Gefangenschaft*. München, Kaiser, 1954.

[101]David Pike, *German Writers in Soviet Exile, 1933–1945*. Chapel Hill, University of North Carolina Press, 1982.

In a wider sense, the social experience of war did away with its glorification. In the nineteenth and the first half of the twentieth century, aristocratic Guards officers and middle-class professors of rightist persuasion used to exalt armed conflict for its supposed ability to mobilize the best in man. So had Karl Marx. Marx had detested "the peace-mongering bourgeoisie, represented in the Government by the oligarchy, who surrender Europe to Russia." Europe, Marx had insisted "may be rotten," but at least "a war should have roused the sound elements, a war should have brought forth some latent energies ... ar least one decent struggle might be got up wherein both parties could reap some honour, such as force and spirit can carry off from the field of battle." [102]

By 1945, such sentiments had almost disappeared in Europe. This was not because war in itself had become so much more destructive than in the past. For all Western Europeans excepting soldiers, Jews and Gypsies, World War II had been relatively benign in terms of demographic loss. Earlier conflicts had been worse. During medieval times, the Renaissance period, and the seventeenth century, even fairly minor clashes had been liable to produce catastrophic consequences through famine, plague, the destruction of livestock and draft animals, seed grain and crops, the atrocities committed by marauding armies obliged to live off the land, and the inordinate burden of taxation.[103] Whereas the Thirty Years' War (1618–48) may have destroyed one third of Germany's population, World War II had, relatively speaking, imposed a much smaller blood toll.[104]

By the middle of the twentieth century, however, the attitude of the mass of people toward the sudden and terrible human losses and fall in living standards brought about by total war had altered. Expectations of life on the part of industrial populations had become infinitely higher than those of their rural ancestors, who had been wont to accept plagues, hunger, or war as natural impositions, or evidence of divine wrath. The Nazis' ignominious conduct had discredited those who called upon others to live by the sword for the sake of a higher morality. From then on, even the warmongers claimed to stand for peace.

COLLABORATION AND RESISTANCE

Between 1939 and 1942, Hitler's armies conquered the bulk of Europe. For a few years, the Nazis established an empire without parallel, a tyranny whose writ ran from the North Cape to the Libyan desert, from the Volga to the Pyrenees. Historians, knowing that this empire soon collapsed, are all too apt to endow contemporaries with foreknowledge. But to the bulk of Germans,

[102]Karl Marx, *The Eastern Question*, pp. 132 amd 452.

[103]See, for instance, J. R. Hale, *War and Society in Renaissance Europe*. Leicester, Leicester University Press, 1985.

[104]See Henri A. van der Zee, *The Hunger Winter: Occupied Holland 1944–45*. London, Jill Norman and Hobhouse, 1982.

Frenchmen, Poles, Dutchmen, and Norwegians alive in 1940, the future appeared in a very different light. Nazi domination seemed firmly established; Great Britain was in no position to reconquer Europe; Hitler's new subjects somehow had to learn to live under the swastika. This was an experience common to nearly all Continental Europeans – all of whom saw their respective homelands at various times either reduced to defeat or exalted in victory, in a manner unknown to Britons or Americans.[105]

How far did the resistance extend? In the first flush of liberation, almost every adult citizen in the formerly occupied country claimed to have opposed the Nazis by force or stealth. France, according to Gaullist hagiography, had been a nation of resisters. Appearances notwithstanding, few Austrians had ever wanted the *Anschluss*. (As a German jibe put it, the Austrians persuaded themselves and the world that Hitler had been a German, and Beethoven an Austrian.) These myths were later subjected to bitter re-examination. Films such as *The Sorrow and the Pity* and *Lacombe Lucien*, for instance, showed occupied France in a sorry light. There were unending scholarly confrontations in which the realities of yesterday's resistance were linked to the facts of present-day politics. Throughout the Western (albeit not in the Soviet-dominated) world the resistance debate began to resemble the German game of *Schwarze Peter*, a contest in which a participant tries to land an opponent with "Black Peter," the dud card, in this case overt or covert collaboration with the enemy. No one escaped censure – not even Britain or the US, neither of which had ever been occupied. (The US was indicted on the grounds that there had been influential American pro-Nazis during the war, while after the war the US had collaborated with Nazi rocket experts such as Wernher von Braun, German intelligence specialists such as Bernhard Gehlen, and even more despicable characters.)[106]

The realities were more complicated. First of all, resistance was genuine and widespread. No reader of John F. Sweet's book on *Choices in Vichy France* will repeat the old chestnut that France was predominantly a nation of collaborators, or that the resistance drew only on 2 percent of the population. But faced with the brute fact of foreign domination, the majority of Europeans turned out to be neither avowed collaborators nor dedicated resistants. The tale of these ordinary men and women is not often told. Unlike surviving

[105]For general works see for instance Stephen Hawes and Ralph White, *Resistance in Europe, 1939–1945*. London, A. Lane, 1975. Kenneth Macksey, *Partisans of Europe in the Second World War*. New York, Stein and Day, 1975. Jørgen Haestrup, *European Resistance Movements, 1939–1945: A Complete History*. Westport, Conn., Meckler Publishing Co., 1981. Werner Rings, *Leben mit dem Feind: Anpassung und Widerstand in Hitler's Europe 1939–45*. Munich, Kindler Verlag, 1979. M. R. D. Foot, *Resistance: An Analysis of European Resistance to Nazism, 1940–1945*. London, Eyre Methuen, 1976. Peter Hoffman, *Widerstand, Staatsstreich, Attentat: Der Kampf der Opposition gegen Hitler*. Berlin, Ullstein Verlag, 1970. Jürgen Schmädke and Peter Steinbach, eds, *Der Widerstand gegen den Nationalsozialismus: Die deutsche Gesellschaft und der Widerstand gegen Hitler*. Munich, R. Piper Verlag, 1986. Jørgen Haestrup, *Secret Alliance: A Study of the Danish Resistance Movement 1940–1945*. New York University Press, 3 vols, 1976.

[106]Charles Higham, *American Swastika: The Shocking Story of Nazi collaborators in our Midst from 1933 to the Present Day*. New York, Doubleday, 1985.

collaborators, resistance leaders or committed intellectuals, the man or woman in the street rarely wrote books – either in self-exculpation, self-revelation, and self-discovery, or to glorify a cause. The overwhelming mass of Europeans did not like the German occupiers, but nevertheless tried to get on with their lives, earn their bread, look after their respective families, stay out of trouble, and remain aloof from the New Order as well as they might.

Even this turned out to be a difficult assignment. There was no escape from being involved. Merely by delivering the mail, or by keeping a train running, a postman or an engine driver might indirectly assist the Nazis' extermination campaign against the Jews. By the efficient running of a plant making trucks, or by doing good work at an assembly line, a manager or an auto worker would contribute to the Nazi war effort. Conversely, conduct normally regarded as anti-social might harm the enemy cause – black market deals, poor workmanship, lack of punctuality would interfere with war production. The man who forged a ration coupon or an identity card could become a hero. In a certain sense, collaboration and resistance alike turned out to be almost everybody's experience in a manner that is hard to disentangle in retrospect.

Who then was a collaborator and who a *résistant*? We apply the term collaborator only to non-Germans. For Germans, after all, the Hitler government enjoyed legal, if not moral legitimacy, having received diplomatic recognition from every country around the globe. A collaborator was a person who, for whatever reason, chose to further the cause of the Third Reich, a country not his or her own. We regard as a *résistant* a person of any nationality who, as a matter of personal choice, decided to do his or her best to overthrow Hitler's rule. Either choice, deliberately to back or to oppose Hitler's tyranny, was apt to set an individual apart from fellow citizens. Such a decision might involve all kinds of motives – from the exalted to the despicable. Angry or idealistic men and women might suddenly find the means for settling personal as well as political scores. A janitor, after a lifetime of obscure subservience, could find a new power in his position, suddenly able to intimidate wealthy residents. A wronged husband might unexpectedly acquire an opportunity of doing away with his wife's lover in what passed for an act of patriotic resistance.

A small number of Hitler's new subjects turned out to be enthusiastic collaborators, either because they believed in the New Order, or because they were opportunists, or because they hated their foreign overlords less than their foes at home. Hitler's New Order initially enjoyed the prestige of victory. Its appeal went far beyond the borders of Germany. It attracted those who identified a democratic form of government with the miseries of the Great Depression, domestic corruption, or the real and alleged evils of urban life.

The New Order also made sense to many of those who hated Jews. August Bebel, the nineteenth-century German Social Democrat, had once stigmatized anti-semitism as the socialism of fools, because only simpletons would identify Jewry with capitalism. (Bebel might, with equal justice, have styled Judeophobia as the anti-socialism of fools, on the grounds that only simpletons would identify Jewry with socialism.) The New Order also found support among a good number of smaller nationalities: Estonians, Latvians, Lithuanians, Slovaks, Ukrainians, Croats, Georgians, and others who hoped to achieve statehood, or to restore independence to their respective countries by riding the Nazi tiger. Italy, Hungary, Bulgaria, Finland, Romania were all allies, albeit rather shaky, of the Third Reich, hoping thereby to make territorial gains.

Without these collaborators, Nazi rule could not have functioned. Only about 2,000 German officials of various ranks administered the Protectorates of Bohemia and Moravia. In all of France there were no more than three battalions of German police engaged in rounding up Jews and similar tasks. Isolated, distrusted by the people, unable to communicate easily with the local population, unfamiliar with the country where they were stationed, they could not by their own efforts have performed those horrendous tasks assigned to them by their superiors in Berlin.[107] The entire network of the *Reichssicherheitshauptamt*, the Main Office for Reich Security primarily responsible for exterminating the Jews, comprised fewer than 70,000 people. Collaborators thus played a crucial role.

The collaborators derived from every social group, from bankers to beggars. There were members of the establishment, fearful of social revolution. There were corporatists, racists, jingoists, who maintained that defeat, however painful, was preferable to the continuation of a corrupt parliamentary regime. The New Order also attracted the loyalty of many malcontents. They resembled those ancient Hebrew dissidents who had joined the young David in the Cave of Adullam where, according to the Book of Samuel in the Old Testament, "everyone that was in distress, and everyone that was in debt, and everyone that was discontented, gathered themselves unto him, and he became a captain over them."[108] The New Order was, in a sense, a Cave of Adullam gone public.

Contrary to legend, Nazi sympathizers included many intellectuals and professional people, men and women disgusted with the real or supposed weaknesses of democracy, fearful of the spread of communism, resentful at Jewish competition, or fascinated by a mythical past or a millennial future. In Germany, Hitler had enjoyed support – at least for a time – from luminaries such as Carl Jung, the psychiatrist; the poet Gottfried Benn; the philosopher Martin Heidegger; and Carl Schmitt, a legal scholar. At least one-third of the leaders commanding the German *Einsatzgruppen* (murder squads) employed in killing Jews held doctoral degrees.[109] In France there were intellectuals such as Robert Brasillach, the "critical *Wunderkind* of Parisian letters in the 1930s";[110] in Norway there was Knut Hamsun, a Nobel laureate in literature, and so the sorry list continued. There were politicians of every stripe: Marcel Déat, a

---

[107]Theodore S. Hamerow, "The hidden holocaust," *Commentary,* September 1983, pp. 32–42, esp. p. 37.

[108]1 Samuel 22. 2.

[109]Omer Bartov, *The Eastern Front, 1941–45. German Troops and the Barbarisation of Warfare.* New York, St Martin's Press, 1986, p. 50.

[110]Michael R. Marrus and Robert O. Paxton, *Vichy France and the Jews.* New York, Schocken Books, 1983, p. 38.

former socialist, Jacques Doriot, a renegade communist, as well as unrepentant rightists such as Joseph Darnand, a highly decorated soldier turned thug.

A substantial number of Western Europeans, drawn from every social class, enlisted in the *Waffen SS*. According to John Keegan's figures, these included an estimated 50,000 from Holland, 40,000 from Belgium, 20,000 from France, 12,000 from Denmark and Norway between them.[111] More Dutchmen fought and died wearing the Germans' field-grey uniform than the Allies' khaki. French soldiers of the *Charlemagne* division helped to defend Berlin with the same tenacity as Free French soldiers serving with the British Eighth Army in North Africa had held out at Bir Hakheim. Overall, the Western European volunteers to the German armed forces heavily outnumbered those who had joined the International Brigades in Spain, a grim testimony to the extent of Hitler's appeal.

But the collaborators left no honorable legacy. A handful of fanatics may have continued to dream of Hitler's glory when the Third Reich had collapsed. There were obscure networks assisting those who had gone into hiding, fled abroad, or – more likely – changed their story and claimed that they had really done their best to impede the Third Reich. Hitler bequeathed no colorful legend to posterity, as Napoleon had done. An ideology that exalted the mighty and despised the weak did not know how to cope with defeat. The Nazis' exploitation of Europe had been too patent to make palatable their propaganda for a new European Order. The extermination campaign against the Jews discredited anti-semitism even for most anti-semites. The Nazis' heroic pretensions in no wise conformed to the actual conduct of Nazis and collaborators when the war was over. All but a small minority looked for whitewash or obscurity.

Collaboration contrasted with resistance. Resistance, like collaboration, became a pan-European experience; its extent and scope widened as the war dragged on. As the promises of victory receded beyond the horizon, Nazi rule became visibly more oppressive, and increasingly impinged on people's private lives (for instance when the Nazis began to conscript foreign laborers for war work in Germany). Resistance assumed many forms. There was symbolic resistance, expressed in songs or in gestures of defiance, or modes of dress. There was polemical resistance through underground broadsheets or underground schools. There was "defensive resistance" in the way in which Europeans helped Allied prisoners on the run, deserters from forced labor assignments, Jews in hiding, or other victims of persecution. There was religious resistance. There was resistance through espionage and sabotage, resistance in jails, ghettos, and concentration camps, and in some cases there was outright guerrilla war.

Historians have continued to debate the extent and effect of the resistance with an acrimony that has lost none of its bite as the surviving combatants age and die. According to James D. Wilkinson, resistance entailed a reassertion of "hope, reason, and firm ethical standards; that splendidly contrasted with

[111] John Keegan, *Waffen SS: The Asphalt Soldiers.* New York, Ballantine Books, 1970, p. 99.

the despair, skepticism, or moral relativism" so widely associated with the European intelligentsia during the first part of this century. The resistance spirit was "a blend of defiance and idealism." To the intellectuals especially, resistance "gave to politics a moral dimension that led many to sacrifice their own safety and self interest in unequal combat."[112] Other accounts are less complimentary. "Between you and me," de Gaulle later said to an acquaintance, "the resistance was a bluff that worked."[113]

Who was right? A balance sheet is hard to draw up, for resistance divided into two basic kinds, diffuse and informal, or organized. The former was immensely widespread, lacking in glamour, and therefore little documented in retrospect. At home and abroad, the Third Reich established an immense number of controls as part of a coercive economy designed for domination and conquest. In every country of Europe, ordinary people tried to slip through the net. The black market itself formed a huge and uncoordinated network of resistance that depended on private initiative. Farmers sold meat without authorization. Labor conscripts absconded. Housewives fiddled their ration cards. "Beating the system" became a way of life.

Even in Germany, long subjected to Nazi propaganda,

> it was precisely the "little people" who were not prepared to comprehend the full implications of the controls, and had no inclination to make them work ... The war ... brought shortages, queues and constraints which generated widespread discontent. The truth was that housewives expected to obtain fresh fruit in summer, war or no war; farmers expected the logic of the market place to prevail when their products were in great demand, and deeply resented price controls ... these irritations gave rise to a variety of violations of the war economy regulations, but – even more disturbingly, for the authorities – they also erupted at times into scenes of outright disorder ... the practical effect of price controls was to make goods actually less widely available, because of the resistance of producers to their application. The producer, after all, had little incentive to maintain, let alone raise, production of a crop if his returns were meagre. The requirement that he distribute his produce through state-controlled collection depots was an added irritant ... Barter thus became widespread, and barter interfered with Nazi planning, all the more so as the prevailing manpower shortage also rendered impossible the high level of policing necessary to ensure that the controls were fully applied.[114]

Personal and unorganized resistance also took numerous other forms. A German farmer who treated a Ukrainian prisoner laboring on his land as a

---

[112]James D. Wilkinson, *The Intellectual Resistance in Europe*, Cambridge, Mass., Harvard University Press, 1981, p. 278.

[113]André Gillois (Maurice Diamant-Bert), *Histoire secrète des Français à Londres de 1940 à 1944*. Paris, Hachette, 1973, p. 164.

[114]Jill Stephenson, "War and society in Würtemberg, 1939–1945," *German Studies Review*, v. 8, no. 1, 1985, pp. 89–105, esp. p. 96.

colleague rather than as an *Untermensch,* offended against Nazi doctrine; so did a German farm girl, who, at great risk to both, slept with a Polish worker, another supposed *Untermensch.* Even more admirable was the courage, say, of a Dutch socialist who at peril to himself and his family, hid a Jewish neighbor in the attic, and after the war refused a decoration, and would not even permit his name to be publicized, on the grounds that such conduct represented no more than a civic duty not requiring special notice. There were similar examples of heroism in Germany, especially in Berlin where several thousand Jews managed to survive through the aid of non-Jewish sympathizers. The Danes played an honorable role in resisting anti-Jewish persecution. So, for the most part, did the Italians, always inclined – despite Fascism – to distrust the motives and power of officialdom. Such conduct maintained the standards of humanity at a time when humane behavior had turned into an indictable offense.

Then there was formalized resistance. Its precise extent again is hard to assess, for the resisters lacked central coordination, much less central direction. They were fragmented from country to country, region to region, city to city. Their problems differed enormously. In Germany, the resisters opposed an incumbent government, and to many Germans – not necessarily Jew baiters or xenophobes – resistance appeared treasonous in the face of the enemy. Again there were great disparities between countries such as Holland and Norway, whose legitimate governments had simply gone into exile; Italy which switched alliances halfway, and France, divided since 1940 between the adherents of Pétain and those of General de Gaulle (condemned to death for his activities by those very *maréchalistes* who later cavilled with scant justification at the treatment meted out to them at the end of the war).

The resisters were split by class, and occupation. There were striking disparities between those who simply wanted to throw out the Germans and restore traditional liberties (the object of most Norwegian, Danish, and Dutch resisters) and those who strove for a new social order (desired by the bulk of French and Italian underground fighters). The resisters comprised liberals, trade unionists, socialists, communists, anarchists, and nationalists. They included not only honest men, but also a contingent of opportunists, crooks, and gangsters. Resistance, like collaboration, came in many shades, and all too often these merged in a bewildering fashion.

Only a few generalizations apply to all the resistance movements, which developed in every occupied country. Resistance, again like collaboration, represented a departure from established norms, a flight from daily routine, an escape into risk and adventure. The resisters overwhelmingly drew their inspiration from patriotic motives, rather than from those trans-national loyalties of class that Marxists had emphasized. Resistance rehabilitated traditional virtues. As Paul Reynaud, the French statesman, had put it in 1940, "the idea of the fatherland and of military valor had been too long neglected."[115] But formal resistance involved only a small part of the population – something

---

[115]Cited in John Lukacs, *The Last European War, September 1939–December 1941.* New York, Garden City, Anchor Press, 1976, p. 289.

between 1 and 2 percent of the total. In Holland, for instance, a country justly proud of its stand against the *Moffen* (Germans), the total number of activists in the resistance amounted to no more than 76,000 out of a total population of 9,100,000 in 1939. (Of the resisters, 5,000 belonged to the fighting units; 4,000 worked as spies. More than 25,000 were involved in the illegal press, or helped Allied pilots escape, or forged official documents, while 40,000 or so gave help to the men and women who had gone underground for political, religious, or racial reasons.)[116]

The resistance suffered from other limitations. The individual resister's record was not always as glorious as was later claimed. Jean-Paul Sartre, for instance, a doyen of the intellectual resistance, staged his well-known play *Les Mouches* ("The Flies") in a perfectly legal fashion under the German occupiers' watchful eyes. The resistance depended on outside, especially British, support. Even given such backing, the resisters could nowhere endanger, much less overthrow German rule without foreign aid. Churchill and the organizers of the British Special Operations Executive (SOE) had thought in terms of the Irish guerrilla struggle against British rule. They had hoped to "set Europe ablaze." They overlooked, however, the enormous difference between British constitutional rule and a totalitarian regime unrestrained by criticism in the press, in parliament, or by constraints operating through the law courts or within the army and the civil service itself. For all the resisters' heroism, the liberation of Western Europe derived in the main from the might of American and, to a lesser extent, of British arms.

The resisters' military achievement is hard to document, given its diversity. (The standard bibliography concerning the armed resistance movement in Belgium, a small country geographically not well suited to guerrilla actions, contains over 300 items.)[117] For all its limitations, that achievement was nevertheless impressive. The largest partisan movement in Western Europe centered in Italy where some 200,000 men and women took up arms. The *Resistenza Armata* substantially contributed to the liberation of central and northern Italy. In France, the *Forces Françaises de l'Intérieur* likewise played a valuable though less prominent part in guerrilla warfare. After liberation, volunteers from the *Forces Françaises de l'Intérieur* helped to swell the ranks of the French regular forces that were being rapidly expanded under de Gaulle's command. Colonial rather than metropolitan in experience, the new military leaders did not always trust these recruits. The regulars were apt to misconstrue the aims of the resistance fighters (who would have preferred a revolutionary mass levy, and who were later kept out of the higher echelons of the regular forces).[118]

---

[116]Henri A. van der Zee, *The Hunger Winter: Occupied Holland 1944–45*. London, Jill Norman and Hobhouse, 1982, p. 109.

[117]M. Goossens, J. L. Charles, J. J. Herwegh, E. Cleenwerck de Crayencour, eds, *Le Résistance Armée en Belgique, 1940–1944, Guide Bibliographique*. Brussels, Ecole Militaire, 1977. The standard work thereafter is Jacques Willequet, *La Belgique sous la Botte: Résistance et Collaboration, 1940–45*. Paris, Editions Universitaires, 1986.

[118]George Armstrong Kelly, *Lost Soldiers: The French Army and the Empire in Crisis 1947–1962*. Cambridge, Mass., MIT Press, 1965, pp. 19–20.

In the smaller countries of Western Europe, the military resistance, properly speaking, played but a negligible role. All over Western Europe, however, the underground assisted the allies by sabotage, and by collecting intelligence, and by propaganda. The resisters also comprised men and women from every way of life. The urban working class provided untold numbers of recruits – especially railwaymen, "the solitary instance of a subclass devoted as such, in many areas, to resistance on grounds of class interest and class solidarity."[119] The resisters also included clerks, unobtrusive men and women, with access to news or documents. There were professional men with special skills and connections, physicians, pastors, priests, engineers, newspapermen, and others. There were farmers and forest rangers, familiar with the countryside. Most important were regular soldiers, especially those with unconventional ideas or unconventional backgrounds – men such as Col Draza Mihailovic, who even before World War II had pondered over the need to fight a guerrilla war, or Henri Koot, a Colonel of mixed Indonesian, Chinese, and Dutch blood, who took charge of the Dutch Forces of the Interior (BS, *Binnenlandse Strijdkrachten*). Between them, the guerrillas and saboteurs represented a great social coalition, especially of former soldiers (known as *sbandati* in Italy) and youths seeking to evade compulsory service, or seeking adventure.

What of their politics? The resisters, like the collaborators, included men and women representing a broad range of opinion. Initially, they mainly derived from the ranks of conservatives. As John Lukacs, an American historian put it, "the principal struggle in the politics of Europe during the [years] 1939–41 and in many ways even afterward, was not so much between Right and Left as it was, rather, a struggle between two Rights," those who saw Nazism as a greater evil than communism, and those who feared communism more than Nazism.[120] The first head of government to have actively resisted the Nazis after their takeover in Germany had been Engelbert Dollfuss, the Austrian Chancellor, a Catholic of the most reactionary kind, who was murdered by Nazi gunmen in 1934. Other foes of the Third Reich were former generals turned conservative politicians – Edward Smigly-Ridz in Poland, Jan Smuts in South Africa, John Metaxas in Greece, and above all, Charles de Gaulle in France. Reigning monarchs took an honorable part in opposing the Third Reich. These included Queen Wilhelmina of the Nether lands, and King Haakon VII of Norway, exiled in London after their respective countries' defeat, as well as King Christian X of Denmark who stayed on in Denmark, where he conducted himself with princely courage. In Italy, King Victor Emmanuel III made up for his inglorious part in installing Mussolini as head of government in 1922 by helping to break him in 1943. Even King Boris of Bulgaria, one of Hitler's allies, resisted the deportation of Bulgarian Jews.

In Germany itself, resistance followed a similar pattern. The German-

[119]Foot, *Resistance: An Analysis of European Resistance to Nazism, 1940–1945*, p. 13.
[120]John Lukacs, *The Last European War, September 1939–December 1941*, Garden City, NY, Anchor Press and Doubleday, 1976, pp. 289–90.

speaking opponents taken most seriously by the Nazis after they came to power were not the Reds (*Rotfront*) but the *Reaktion*, the reactionaries. Both factions were lampooned in the Nazi party anthem. Resistance in Germany was especially strong among senior *Wehrmacht* officers, including disillusioned former Nazi supporters such as Colonel Count Claus von Stauffenberg whose bomb – with better luck – might have killed the *Führer* in 1944. But even had the conspirators succeeded in their assassination attempt, it is hard to know whether the *Wehrmacht* would have followed them, given the extent of the conspirators' social isolation within Nazi Germany. (The *Wehrmacht* putsch, it is true, was briefly successful in Paris; but had it spread further, it might conceivably have given rise to a new "stab in the back" legend.)

In addition there was religious resistance. Its extent is hard to evaluate, for the impact of the churches differed widely, not merely from country to country, but within each European nation. When war broke out, the overwhelming majority of Europeans were baptised members of the Christian faith, but only a minority were regular churchgoers, while even regular churchgoers overwhelmingly regarded themselves as Germans, Englishmen, or Frenchmen first, Catholics or Protestants second. Church leaders and unbelievers alike tended to overestimate the Churches' ability to influence their parishioners' political conduct. The churches' part in the resistance was not, moreover, particularly glorious. In Germany, for instance, numerous Lutherans and Catholics alike had initially done their best to collaborate with the Nazis. The believers did so partly from a justifiable fear of communism, partly from a desire to safeguard their own patriotic credentials, partly from the clerical conservatives' mistaken proclivity to see parallels between communism and liberalism with its free market doctrines, and partly from a fear of not offending Nazi voters and sympathizers within their own ranks. The churches, moreover, were internally split. (The Protestant resistance found expression in the *Bekennende Kirche*, the "Confessional Church." The Catholics contained prominent anti-Nazis such as Cardinal von Galen at Münster; the Catholic Church in no wise corresponded to its opponents' stereotype of a unified hierarchy ready to follow papal orders at the drop of a hat.)

Speaking in general, churchmen all too often failed to recognize the ideological implications of Nazism, a creed that stood committed to a form of biological predestination, and hence denied the divine gift of Free Will to the Jews. Hence the churches widely failed to see that there was a natural solidarity between Church and Synagogue, that in attacking the Jews, the Nazis also attacked the Church. The churches also widely failed to perceive the totalitarian, indeed the Gnostic nature of Nazism. (Alfred Rosenberg, the chief Nazi theoretician, had identified in his book *Der Mythos des 20 Jahrhunderts* the heretical Albigensians, Waldensians, Cathars of the Middle Ages with the racial spirit of German heroism.)[121]

The churches suffered from other disadvantages. They were linked to the

---

[121] Alfred Rosenberg, *Der Mythos des 20. Jahrhunderts: Eine Wertung der seelischgeistigen Gestalterkämpfe unserer Zeit*. Munich, Hoheneichen Verlag, 1930, p. 87 ff.

machinery of the state in a great many ways, for instance through the *Kirchensteuer*, a church tax raised through the German inland revenue. Lutherans in particular suffered from their traditional ties with the Reich's establishment, in contrast to the Catholics who had always formed a minority within the Reich, and who had created their own party, the *Zentrum*, to defend Catholic interests. Overall, the Catholic resistance record in Germany was better than the Lutheran. But the Catholic Church also had serious leadership problems. It had sustained a grievious blow through the death of Pius XI (Achille Ratti) in 1939. Pius XI had protested, in 1931, against the Fascists's pagan state worship (through his letter *Non abbiamo bisogno*). In an even more famous epistle *Mit brennender Sorge*, the Pope had attacked violations of natural law and justice in Germany (1937). Pius XI's successor Pius XII (Eugenio Pacelli), by contrast, was inclined to temporize. Pius XII was a master of personal honor who did not deserve the strictures of men such as Rolf Hochhut, the Swiss playwright, who later depicted Pius XII on stage as a Pontius Pilate washing his hands of the Jewish tragedy. But he was a Germanophile, at the wrong time and in the wrong place. He feared the hammer and sickle even more than the swastika. He therefore failed to give to the Church the leadership it required over grave issues such as Nazi oppression of Catholics, and atrocities committed by Catholic fanatics in Croatia against Serbs, as well as the murder campaign against Jews and Gypsies.

The churches could not stem the tide in a secular age, but they did not wholly fail. In Germany alone, there were many modern martyrs, including divines such as the Catholic Bernhard Lichtenberg, who died for their faith with a stoic courage that would have aroused the admiration of a Spartan. Some smaller sects displayed equal, or even greater fortitude, especially the Jehovah's Witnesses. The Witnesses considered all forms of government and all political parties as irredeemably depraved, hence they refused to serve in the armed forces. Ironically, the Witnesses' bizarre theology provided them with a most realistic assessment of the Nazi system. Their faith also inspired them with a degree of heroism in concentration camps that aroused the reluctant but sincere admiration of that expert killer Rudolf Höss, the commandant of Auschwitz.

In the German-occupied countries, the churches' position was even more complex. In France, for instance, the overwhelming majority of churchgoers initially welcomed Vichy's assumption of power in 1940. Subsequent disillusionment affected the churches as much as the laity. The French episcopate itself split between the advocates of resistance and those of collaboration. But the collaborators themselves were not necessarily pro-Nazi. For instance, Cardinal Pierre Gerlier, archbishop of Lyon, a leading Pétain supporter, also opposed the deportation of the Jews, as did Jules-Gerard Saliège, archbishop of Toulouse, one of Vichy's firm critics from the very start. The clerical resisters' position grew ever stronger as they identified their cause with their congregations' national aspirations and their social grievances. The perils of war moreover encouraged men and women to turn to religion. (More pragmatically, so did the decline in secular entertainment.) In countries such as Holland, the churches filled with worshippers as attending divine service became a legitimate means of expressing opposition to the conqueror. War increased the churches' social consciousness. (For instance, French priests returning home from forced labor in Germany became all the more determined to spread Catholicism in France, by then regarded by many churchmen as a partially de-Christianized country and a new field of missionary endeavor.) War and resistance strengthened those Catholics who stood for social reform and for the conviction that public authority should intervene in the economy for the purpose of benefiting the poor, a philosophy that had been shared alike by medieval schoolmen and by Catholic social thinkers of the nineteenth century. Socially committed Catholics thereby helped to lay the foundations of great Christian Democratic parties, mass organizations with broad support among workers as well as middle-class people, bodies that played a major role in Italy, France, and West Germany after the war. It had not counted for nothing that Hitler had grimly vowed to settle with the churches, once he had won.

The militant left initially had done no better than the churches. At the beginning of the war, the left all over Western Europe was dispirited and fragmented. In Germany, the left had declared public bankruptcy when, in 1933, communist *Rotfrontkämpferbund* and the Social Democrats' *Reichsbanner*, powerful only on paper, had been dissolved without a struggle. There was some underground opposition, but there was a tragic element of futility about leftist resistance cells such as the *Gruppe Baum* (made up of young Jewish Berliners, all dedicated communists) who were wiped out, having made a sacrificial attempt to bomb an anti-Soviet exhibition.[122] The left had fought bravely in Spain, but they had suffered a disastrous defeat; this in turn had created a sense of pessimism so widespread that even as dedicated an anti-Fascist as George Orwell became convinced that Fascism might win, unless the left could quickly eradicate its crankishness, machine-worship, and stupid cult of Russia.[123] Disarray within the left-wingers' ranks worsened as a result of the Nazi–Soviet non-aggression pact of 1939, and by reason of the Comintern's subsequent commitment to "revolutionary defeatism."

The communists were saved from their predicament by Hitler's invasion of the Soviet Union. They now benefited equally from the Red Army's splendid resistance to the invaders, from popular ignorance concerning the Soviet Union's own *Gulag* Archipelago, and from the communists' new emphasis on patriotic rather than revolutionary motives. All over Europe, the resistance, including non-communist resistance, shifted to the left, and the resisters hoped for a new order in society as well as for the end of foreign domination. The communists had an added advantage: they represented the only political movement prepared in peacetime for underground, as well as legal activities. They now used their organizational talent to fuse the struggle to defend the

---

[122]Margot Pikarski, *Jugend im Berliner Widerstand: Herbert Baum and Kampfgefährten*. East Berlin, Militärverlag der Deutschen Demokratischen Republik, 1984.
[123]George Orwell, *The Road to Wigan Pier*, London, Gollancz, 1937, pp. 246, 248.

Soviet Union, the "workers' true fatherland," with the battle to liberate their own countries. In this they managed to draw on mass support formed into fronts in countries where they had already been strong in peacetime, especially Italy and France, where communism relied on wide backing from the industrial workers and, to a lesser extent, the intellectuals.

The French communists conducted themselves with particular ability. They had the advantage of a long tradition going back to the Jacobins during the French Revolution and the *Communards* during the Franco–German War (1870–1), who had combined patriotic with revolutionary endeavor. The communists built up their own armed forces, the *Francs Tireurs et Partisans Français*; they built up their own *Front National de Lutte pour l'Indépendance de la France*. They played a conspicuous part within the *Conseil National de la Résistance* (CNR), the coordinating body of the resistance; in 1944 they joined de Gaulle's provisional government, and by the time Paris was liberated the PCF (*Parti Communiste Français*) had become "the best organized political party in France, both politically and militarily."[124]

The communists played an equally important part in Italy. Italian contingents had fought on both sides in Spain, whose civil war therefore also turned into an inter-Italian confrontation, in which Palmiro Togliatti (later an Italian Cabinet minister) represented the Comintern in the Iberian Peninsula. Working originally from exile, the Italian communists organized an extensive underground movement within Italy, collaborated with the Italian crown after Italy's break with Germany, and built up the largest armed contingent within the armed Italian resistance movement, as well as a massive civilian organization with a wide appeal to the electorate. The communists also took a major share in the various *Comitati da Liberazione Nazionale* (CLN), composed of political parties rather than resistance bodies (as in the French *Conseil National de la Résistance*). In Italy, as in France, the communists managed to gain a foothold in many major institutions – trades unions, cooperatives, local and national governments – they built a network of clients, not necessarily committed to the principles of Marxism-Leninism, but beholden to the party for a variety of favors.

Liberals and moderate socialists, by contrast, lacked any kind of international coordination. After the demise of the German Social Democratic Party, the British Labour Party became foremost among the moderate workers' parties of Europe. Labour gained immense prestige in Great Britain, but failed to develop a socialist internationale during the war, either in Europe or even within the British empire. In France, the socialists had an honorable, but not a leading share in the resistance. The non-communist left in Italy was divided. The *Partito d'Azione*, for example, mainly appealed to intellectuals. The socialists allowed themselves to be enmeshed within a communist-led alliance (1941) that robbed them of effective independence. In Norway, Holland, and Denmark, where the moderate parties had predominated before the war, they

---

[124]Claude Harmel, "France," in Witold S. Sworakowski, *World Communism: A Handbook, 1918–1965.* Stanford Hoover Institution, 1973, p. 141.

also predominated in the resistance; activists in these countries mainly engaged in sabotage and intelligence, rather than in military operation.[125]

How much did the resistance achieve? In military terms its impact came to be considerably exaggerated – and for a variety of reasons. During World War II, especially during the disastrous first three years, the Allies bolstered their own morale by magnifying the extent of effective popular unrest in occupied Europe. After the Third Reich had collapsed, Frenchmen, Italians, Dutchmen, and Norwegians alike found solace for earlier defeats in their own country's resistance record, whose glory lost nothing in the telling. During the 1960s, revolutionary romantics throughout the Western world tended to exaggerate the role played by guerrilla warfare in history, ancient and modern.[126]

These enthusiasts also tended to take insufficient account of the heavy price exacted by guerrilla warfare. German reprisals were usually savage, entailing heavy losses for the civilian population at large. Guerrilla warfare, in a more general sense, engendered habits of illegality and violence, and sowed a legacy of distrust and lawlessness that continued into peacetime. Innocent as well as guilty people were murdered by vigilantes, especially in Italy and France. In France, some estimates go as high as 40,000 to 50,000 victims, and elsewhere too there were many who found good reason to adopt the Frenchmen's bitter tag, *un pur trouve toujours un plus pur qui l'épure* (a pure man will always find an even purer man to purge him). Guerrilla warfare engendered distrust for civil power – not surprising in countrues such as Italy and France where upon liberation guerrilla bands widely competed for local power against their respective rivals, and where brigands joined the game, as well as legitimate partisans. War became even more barbarous, as legitimate governments embarked on guerrilla diplomacy and planned to assassinate their enemies in a manner previously practiced only by Balkan underground organizations such as IMRO (the International Macedonian Revolutionary Organization, a scourge of post-World War I politics in Bulgaria).

In purely military terms, the resisters' sacrifices paid but limited dividends. Overall, the resistance forces on their own, unsupported by conventional formations, proved no more than an expensive nuisance to the occupying power. This was not their fault; it was due to geography. Western Europe lacks those mountain massifs, those huge roadless forests and swamp lands that afforded hideouts for guerrillas in Yugoslavia and in many parts of Russia. There were, of course, exceptions. In France, for example, the Vercors Massif, a natural fortress between the Rhône and Isère rivers, became a bastion for the French *maquis*. When the time came to alert the resistance in support of the Allied invasion, bands of Vercors responded with audacity. For ten weeks, the *maquisards* stood their ground. But they lacked artillery and air support;

---

[125] Jeremy Bennett, "The Resistance against the German occupation of Denmark 1940–5," and Magne Skodvin, "Norwegian non-violent resistance during the German occupation," in Adam Roberts, ed., *Civilian Resistance as a Defence*. Baltimore, Penguin Books, 1969, pp. 182–203, pp. 162–81.

[126] For a critique, see L. H. Gann, *Guerrillas in History,* Stanford, Hoover Institution, 1971, *passim*.

they were heavily outnumbered; and they were divided politically. The civilian side was directed by an ardent communist; the military formations were mainly led by right-wing officers who themselves disagreed over questions of strategy and tactics. They were soon crushed, with heavy losses.[127]

By contrast, the partisans achieved much greater results when acting in direct coordination with regular military forces. For example, the *Forces Françaises de l'Intérieur* mobilized in Brittany; the partisans cooperated with airborne Free French elite troops, and achieved considerable diversionary effects by forcing the Germans to keep entire regiments away from Normandy while defending Bretagne against a landing that never materialized.[128] Even more effective were the guerrilla attacks on railway communications that helped to slow down German reinforcements going to Normandy. Equally successful was industrial sabotage. This was a skilled worker's, technician's, and planner's war – potent only when pursued with consistency, technological expertise, and when fully integrated into a wider industrial strategy, rather than left to spontaneous and spasmodic endeavor.[129]

Guerrilla warfare was even more important in psychological terms. For many, partisan warfare gave intense personal satisfaction. The defeated found a way of striking back at the enemy and restoring their national self-respect. Partisan warfare was intensely risky, the guerrillas depended on their own resources even more than conventional soldiers, who were able to draw on the organization and resources of great armies, and provided with leave, rations, clothing, pay. If captured, the guerrilla was likely to be tortured or shot; while at large, he was concerned even more than a conventional soldier with those elementary needs of remaining warm, dry, and fed. Guerrilla war, even more than regular operations, provided a stern test in which combatants were forced to judge people by standards more fundamental than those applicable in ordinary life – by a combatant's willingness or otherwise to help a wounded companion, or to keep silent when interrogated by the enemy. Overall, the underground fighter had to develop immense versatility and initiative, as journalists were turned into editors, printers, and publishers of underground newspapers and taxi drivers became experts in logistics.[130]

The resistance movement had other, unanticipated consequences. In large and variegated countries such as Italy and France, the fragmented and localized nature of the resistance was apt to strengthened local concerns at the expense of the central state. At the same time the movement gave to those comparatively

[127]Michael Pearson, *Tears of Glory: The Betrayal of Vercors 1944*. London, Macmillan, 1978, passim.

[128]Blake Ehrlich, *Resistance France; 1940–1945*. Boston, Little Brown and Company, 1965, pp. 192–3. John F. Sweet, *Choices in Vichy France: The French Under Nazi Occupation*, Oxford, Oxford University Press, 1986.

[129]Alan S. Milward, "The economic and strategic effectiveness of resistance," in Stephen Hawes and Ralph White, eds, *Resistance in Europe, 1939–1945: Based on the Proceedings of a Symposium Held at the University of Salford, March 1973*. London, Allen Lane, 1975, pp. 186–203.

[130]Winston Churchill, *Amid These Storms: Thoughts and Adventures*. New York, Scribner, 1932, pp. 255–66.

few intellectuals associated with it a sense of community with the people at large. As Emmanuel d'Astier de la Vigerie put it, the resistance years were "the only period in my life when I lived in a truly classless society."[131] The resistance also provided a pan-European experience of a novel kind. In World War II it was much more broadly based and less parochial than those local and dispersed resistance movements that had developed in some of the German-occupied areas in World War I. Resistance work during World War II led activists to think in wider European, as well as national terms. Pan-European sentiments in the prewar days had mainly been associated with upper-class people, noblemen such as Counts Hermann Keyserling and Richard Coudenhove-Kalergi, who had been among the principal spokesmen for a European union. The resistance movements helped to democratize such views, so that they were no longer linked to a world of society hostesses and cranks.

The resistance, in a subtle fashion, also contributed to the incipient Americanization of Europe. American influence had already become potent around the turn of the century. Unlike Anglophilia, a sentiment largely confined to the European upper classes, pro-American sentiments transcended the boundaries of social class, and American influence operated on many levels. Countless Europeans had emigrated to the US. Letters from friends and relatives who had settled in the New World provided a source of information far more reliable than any amount of official propaganda. The "rich uncle in America" had entered folklore as a *deus ex machina*, ready to assist an erring nephew, or to lead back a fallen maiden to the path of virtue. American jazz and American movies had become widely popular; Mickey Mouse and the Western cowboy had become established characters of modern folk tale. American methods of mass production and management had come to be widely admired even by Soviet communists. Their scientific and literary achievements had begun to be treated with some respect. The migration of European intellectuals to the US during the 1930s created new bonds between the Old World and the New, though all too many of these newcomers, like their colleagues at home, tended to look on their adopted country with a cultivated lack of comprehension – convinced that Europeans were culturally superior to the Americans (and intellectuals to the rest of mankind).

The collapse of France made America's reputation more resplendent than before, even among intellectuals. So much so, that Sartre later recalled "the black market for American books" in Paris during the war, when "the reading of Faulkner and Hemingway became for some a symbol of resistance."[132] The US also exerted a minor influence through the experience gained by German prisoners of war. (For instance, Hans Werner Richter and Alfred Andersch, two German writers who later joined Group 47, a German literary group set up after World War II, had been prisoners of war in the US where Richter

---

[131]Cited in Wilkinson, *The Intellectual Resistance*, p. 49.
[132]Henry Pachter, "On being an exile," in Robert Boyers, ed., *The Legacy of the German Refugee Intellectuals*. New York, Schocken, 1972, *passim*.

edited a camp paper, *Die Lagerstimme* that opposed secret Nazi terror in the camps.)

The resistance, above all, succeeded splendidly in a more diffuse sense. Nazi doctrines failed to convert Europe. The literary intellectuals within the resistance could claim a modest share in occasioning the Nazis' propagandistic defeats, but intellectuals in retrospect grossly exaggerated the intelligentsia's modest role in the resistance. There were many exceptions, such as Georges Bidault and Marc Bloch, both of them history professors. (Bloch, a French-Jew, an ex-officer, and one of the leading medievalists of the century, was tortured and murdered by the Gestapo for his role in the resistance. Georges Bidault, a Catholic, editor of the prestigious journal *L'Aube*, advanced to be head of the French resistance council and later Prime Minister (1946).) But overall, the universities and research institutes in occupied Europe turned out to be tractable and conformist. Intellectuals were to be found on every side, left, center and right, among the collaborators and the *résistants*.

The bulk of the credit goes to the common people, who only half believed what they heard over the radio and read in the papers, or did not believe it at all. Marxist and right-wing intellectuals alike had widely assumed before World War II that the "masses" would turn out to be infinitely malleable, likely to be guided by a vanguard's well-ordered propaganda. This assumption proved unfounded. Even in Germany itself, where Nazis appealed to patriotic sentiments, official propaganda was weakened by dint of steady repetition, through the ageing of the party cadres, through the effects of official corruption, and, above all, through the Nazis' inability to create the "New Man" of Hitler's imagination. Outside Germany, the effects of official propaganda were negligible, so much so that in Holland, for example, the German-directed papers were bought mainly by Dutch readers for the list of ration coupons announced for the coming week. Once the Third Reich collapsed, the Nazi creed vanished with it among all but a few fanatics. All Europe had cause to adopt for itself the Dutch province of Zeeland's proud motto *luctor et emergo*, "I struggle and rise again." [133]

---

[133]For a detailed study of the effects of Nazi propaganda, see Marlis G. Steinert, *Hitlers Krieg und die Deutschen: Stimmung und Haltung der Deutschen Bevölkerung im Zweiten Weltkrieg*. Düsseldorf, Econ Verlag, 1970.

Politics and Economic Conditions

On April 25, 1945, during the last stages of the war in Europe, the first advanced detachments of the US and the Red armies met on the River Elbe. The press photographers' cameras clicked; there was friendly posing; toasts were drunk. But the initial mood of euphoria did not last, and within a year the two allies had begun to denounce one another in public. Not surprisingly, the causes and origins of the Cold War became, and remain, a matter of bitter dispute.

THE COLD WAR BEGINS

How did the Cold War start? In the Soviet Union, there are no available records of any debate. In the West, where scholars had access to records and could publish what they thought, there was no unanimity. But there were distinct shifts and trends of opinion, influenced by changes in domestic politics, as well as by scholarly considerations. During the aftermath of World War II and the Korean War, hard-line anti-Sovietism remained respectable in academia. Later on, in the turmoil occasioned by the Vietnam War, blame for the Cold War was laid at Washington's door. The US incurred bitter censure for its supposed belligerence – attributed to the supposed tendency of mature capitalism to seek imperial expansion abroad. Thereafter, academics became more inclined to criticize both contenders in the Cold War, or even to regard the conflict as an unfortunate misunderstanding between two muscle-bound bullies unable to communicate.[1]

[1]The most recent standard work is Hugh Thomas, *Armed Truce: The Beginnings of the Cold War 1945–1946*. New York, Atheneum, 1987, a magisterial study. Others are John Lewis Gaddis, *The Long Peace: Inquiries into the History of the Cold War*. Oxford, Oxford University Press, 1987. Richard M. Freeland, *The Truman Doctrine and the Origins of McCarthyism*. New York, Knopf, 1970. Thomas T. Hammond, ed., *Witnesses to the Origins of the Cold War*. Seattle, University of Washington Press, 1982. Robert A. Pollard. *Economic Security and the Origins of the Cold War 1945–1950*. New York, Columbia University Press, 1985. For Anglo-American relations and the Cold War, see, for instance, Ritchie Ovendale, *The English-Speaking Alliance: Britain, The United States, the Dominions, and the Cold War, 1945–1951;* London, Allen and Unwin, 1985. Fraser J. Harbutt, *The Iron Curtain:*

The setting

The details of analysis varied in an equally striking fashion. Some critics of the Soviet Union, rather than simply blaming communism as such, adhered to what might be called the "Eternal Russia" school of thought. Its advocates linked the Cold War to an ancient tradition of Russian expansionism, a force said to be deeply rooted in the past, and in traditions of personal despotism going back to the Czars. This explanation has historical antecedents. In the nineteenth century scholars as different as Karl Marx, the German revolutionary, and Constantin Frantz, a German reactionary, had agreed on one issue: Russia was a threat to Europe. Unless the European powers cooperated, they foresaw that Russia would expand westward until her influence stretched all the way from Danzig to Trieste.

A second school of thought regarded the Cold War as no more than a normal rivalry between two great powers. As John Gaddis, a US historian, puts it, "the external situation – circumstances beyond the control of either power – left Americans and Russians facing one another across prostrated Europe... Leaders of both super powers sought peace, but in doing so, yielded to considerations which ... made a resolution of differences impossible."[2] The Soviet Union, according to this interpretation, was not culpable in any particular degree, for its aims were limited and defensive in character.[3] The US's only escape from this confrontation must therefore come through "the hard and often frustrating search for an accommodation with the Communist states."[4]

Soviet, or pro-Soviet, historians have placed the fault for the Cold War with the US or – more properly speaking – with those contradictory elements of international capitalism, of which the US had come to form the chief exponent during and after World War II. Some academic propagandists suggested that the Western powers had plotted from the start to dismember Germany and to crush an imperialist rival. Others argued that the West had banked on a German–Soviet conflict that would lead to a compromise and an anti-Soviet peace.[5] In any case, the West was always wrong. This was the line, repeated

---

Churchill, *America and the Origins of the Cold War*. Oxford, Oxford University Press, 1986. Henry B. Ryan, *The Vision of Anglo-America. The US-UK Alliance and the Emerging Cold War, 1943–1946.* Cambridge, Cambridge University Press, 1987. Terry L. Deibel and John Lewis Gaddis, eds, *Containing the Soviet Union*, Washington DC, Pergamon-Brassey's International Defense Publishers, 1987. A full bibliography would entail an article of its own. For a review of works written up to 1970, see for instance, Geoffrey Warner "The United States and the origins of the Cold War," *International Affairs*, July 1970, pp. 522–44. For a recent bibliographical account see Bernard Weisberger, *Cold War, Cold Peace: The United Stated and Russia Since 1945*. New York, American Heritage Publishing Co., 1984, pp. 322–8.

[2] John Lewis Gaddis, *The United States and the Origins of the Cold War, 1941–1947*. New York, Columbia University Press, 1972, p. 361.

[3] Louis Halle, *The Cold War as History*. London, Chatto and Windus, 1967.

[4] Adam B. Ulam, *The Rivals: America and Russia Since World War II*. New York, Viking Press, 1971, p. 395.

[5] Lionel Kochan, *The Struggle for Germany 1914–1945*. New York, Harper and Row, 1963, p. 79.

with countless tactical shifts according to prevailing political expedients, by the CPSU (Communist Party of the Soviet Union) and its allies and associated organizations throughout the world.[6]

US revisionist historians arrived at similar conclusions, albeit for somewhat different reasons. These scholars were rarely trained Marxist-Leninists, but rather moralists who widely detested Middle America's presumed bigotry and greed. They were also "America Firsters" in a negative sense – holding their own country primarily responsible for most of the ills on earth. According to the revisionists, the US had shown not the slightest regard to the Soviet Union's vital interests during or after World War II; it had ignored Soviet sufferings and achievements; it had tried to hinder the Soviet Union's peaceful reconstruction, and to intimidate the Soviet Union. US threats included the employment of nuclear weapons against Japan in 1945, weapons designed to blackmail Moscow at a time when Japan already stood ready to surrender. The Cold War strategy pursued by the US according to this interpretation, represents domestic McCarthyism raised to global dimensions.[7]

The revisionists reached the height of their influence during the 1960s and early 1970s, the years shaped by the disillusionment of the Vietnam War. Thereafter, the extreme critics of US foreign policy lost some of their popularity. But a substantial number of American scholars continued to hold the US responsible, at least in part, for the Cold War and its consequences. Louis Rene Beres, for instance, spoke for many academics when, in a more recent work, he decried US foreign policy, and castigated those who employed President Reagan's "evil empire imagery." To Beres, "the alleged contrast between the forces of evil and the forces of good represents little more than childlike caricature." The world can only be saved if the US puts an end to a misplaced *realpolitik,* and embarks instead on a "revolution of consciousness" entailing an "expanded awareness of global interdependence."[8]

A fourth school of thought stressed instead the Soviets' ideology as a source of international tension. Some adherents of this school therefore called for a policy of containment – demanded in 1947 for example by George Kennan.[9]

---

[6]For interpretations written from the pro-Soviet standpoint, see for instance, Nikolai V. Sivachev and Nikolai N. Yakovlev, *Russia and the United States.* Chicago, University of Chicago Press, 1979. Karl Drechsler, *Die USA Zwischen Antihitlerkoalition und Kaltem Krieg.* East Berlin, Akademie-Verlag, 1986. The current official position of the various communist parties throughout the world annually appears in the *Yearbook on International Communist Affairs* (Stanford, Hoover Institution Press, annual, 1966 – with the years before 1966 being covered by a volume edited by Witold S. Sworakowski, *World Communism: A Handbook 1918–1965.* Stanford, Hoover Institution Press, 1973).

[7]See for instance, Denna Frank Fleming, *The Cold War and Its Origins, 1917–1960.* Garden City, NY, Doubleday, 1961, 2 vols. Joyce and Gabriel Kolko, *The Limits of Power: The World and the United States Foreign Policy 1945–54.* New York, Harper and Row, 1972. Richard M. Freeland, *The Truman Doctrine and the Origins of McCarthyism.*

[8]Louis Rene Beres, *Reason and Realpolitik: US Foreign Policy and World Order.* Lexington, Mass., Lexington Books, 1984, p. 127.

[9]George F. Kennan (using the pseudonym "X." "The sources of Soviet conduct," *Foreign Affairs* n. 25, July 1947, pp. 566–82. For a revision of his own views, see George F. Kennan, *American Diplomacy.* Chicago, University of Chicago Press, 1984. David Mayers, *George Kennan and*

Others went further and like John Foster Dulles demanded that the West should work for a "roll back of Soviet power." But all agreed that the Soviet system had its own inherent dynamic, that party directives issued by the CPSU and its allies, party resolutions and such like, could not simply be dismissed as "rhetoric." As this school saw it, the dialectic of Soviet foreign policy must be understood within its own terms. The "Cold War" is not therefore just a Western policy but a process, a state of affairs. It results from a basic Soviet assumption, "that regards cold war and peaceful co-existence as exactly the same thing."[10] The Cold War could not be avoided as long as the Soviet Union strove for world revolution and global hegemony.

The final judgment in this debate must wait until those distant days when Soviet archives are opened, just as most Western records have already been made available to historians. Until scholars can use Soviet material, their accounts must necessarily be distorted. At worst, their analyses, in Walter Laqueur's telling analogy, resemble a boxing match in which only one of the two fighters is visible. The audience watches him punch, feint, and counter punch; but since his opponent remains unseen, such efforts seem aggressive and ludicrous.[11]

Despite these obvious difficulties, Cold War studies have considerably advanced over the last two decades, and historians have unearthed a great deal of new information.[12] Students interested in the underlying motives of Soviet policy makers can moreover benefit from the frankness that CPSU theoreticians and its foreign supporters have always shown regarding their long-term, as opposed to their short-term, objectives. Given the extent to which so many studies of the Cold War have ignored or underplayed these objectives, we shall recapitulate the communists' ideological assumptions. During the crucial wartime and postwar years, these derived from Stalin's leadership and Lenin's legacy. Lenin ranked as the Moses of the communist movement, and Stalin as his heir and as a superman. Both stressed the importance of ideology; both deserve to be taken at their word. In discussing the communists' assumptions, we are not unaware that there were some differences of opinion. But overall, unity prevailed among those parties that followed Moscow. In referring to "communists," we allude to those who determine the CPSU's general line and to those who – for good reasons and bad – follow its dictates in politics.

Mikhail Gorbachev's accession to power will certainly mark a revolutionary departure in Soviet intellectual, as well as political, history. But

the Dilemmas of US Foreign Policy. Oxford, Oxford University Press, 1988. George F. Kennan, Memoirs 1925–1950. New York, Pantheon Books, 1967.

[10]Hugh Seton-Watson, Neither War nor Peace: The Struggle for Power in the Post-War World. London, Methuen, 1960. p. 256. Robert Conquest, Power and Policy in the USSR: The Study of Soviet Dynastics. New York, St Martin's Press, 1961. Robert Conquest: Present Danger: Towards a Foreign Policy. Stanford, Cal., Hoover Institution Press, 1979.

[11]Walter Laqueur, "Visions and revisions," Times Literary Supplement, 5 March 1983, p. 9.

[12]See for instance Vojtech Mastny, Russia's Road to the Cold War: Diplomacy, Warfare, and the Politics of Communism, 1941–1945. New York, Columbia University Press, 1979.

before he attained office, there was structured uniformity in official – as opposed to *samizdat* – Soviet history. Interpretations of current and past events might fluctuate slightly. But as communist theoreticians saw it, twentieth-century conflicts, cold, lukewarm and hot, ultimately derive from the very nature of world capitalism in its advanced, indeed its terminal stage. The patient is bound to die, but it is the communist's task to speed him on his way to the grave. Capitalism's demise will be brought about by a series of revolutions that will assure a socialist transformation of society. The revolution, according to Lenin, must depend on a party of a new type made up of professional revolutionaries dedicated to a rigid discipline in the name of "democratic centralism." The party serves as a vanguard to lead the workers who – left to their own devices – would develop but a mere "trade union consciousness." Only the communist vanguard can lead the backward masses on the long trek toward a classless society. The revolutionary struggles required to propel humanity forward cannot be confined to a single country; combat must be worldwide, given that capitalism has become internationalized in a way that Marx and Engels could not have foreseen.[13] Final victory for the proletariat can only be achieved on a global scale. Communists cannot afford to adhere to outworn notions of "bourgeois" morality or legalism. Deception, terror, the physical liquidation of opposing social classes form essential components of the revolutionary struggle. The end justifies the means, for the end is glorious beyond description – the redemption of mankind through the "dictatorship of the proletariat."

Lenin, and later Stalin, in their ambitions thus went infinitely further than the most despotic of Czars. Once installed as rulers in Moscow, the CPSU did not look merely to ruling in one country, or even to making territorial conquest, but to victory worldwide. The communist party exacted a blood toll infinitely greater than that taken by any other religious or political movement in world history.[14] The party created instruments of coercion more powerful than any dreamt of by Ivan the Terrible or his Romanov successors. In the Soviet Union – as in all communist states built on the Soviet model – it was the party that guided the state, with each party organ superior to each corresponding state agency.

Was this a totalitarian system? According to scholars such as Leonard Schapiro, Richard Pipes, and Adam Ulam, the Soviet system was indeed a tyranny, distinguished by a unique concentration of power at the top, and by a unique commitment to the maintenance and extension of its own might. Historians such as Stephen Cohen, by contrast, dismissed the very term "totalitarian" as a part of the Cold War vocabulary. The Soviet Union remains,

---

[13]The literature on the subject is enormous. For the origins of the revolution, see for instance, Bertram D. Wolfe, *Three Who Made a Revolution*. New York, Dial Press, 1948. Perhaps the most important single document of the many key documents produced by Lenin was *What Is To Be Done*; in V. I. Lenin, *Burning Questions of our Movement*. Moscow, Foreign Languages Publishing House, 1952.

[14]See, for instance, Robert Conquest, *The Great Terror: Stalin's Purge of the Thirties*. New York, Collier's Books, 1973.

as it has always been, riddled by dissent. Indeed, it had only been Stalin's evil genius that had so grossly distorted Soviet history. As Cohen sees it, communism's corruption was not, however, inevitable. All roads need not have led to the Gulag Archipelago. There was no inner totalitarian logic that inevitably resulted in terror.[15] Had power fallen to a "right oppositionist" such as Nikolai Bukharin (liquidated during Stalin's "Great Purge") Soviet communism might have developed a humane and progressive society. (Unfortunately Cohen cannot find a single example of such a communist society; all communist parties that have come to power have followed Lenin's and Stalin's path.) To some degree Soviet society, the argument continues, may be oppressive. But "the growth of Soviet military power, however formidable, is the result of a whole complex of reasons, in part reactive to the external situation, in part driven by internal processes; but in general the Soviet Union is ... aspiring to maintain its status rather than aiming at world hegemony."[16] What is more, the communist system is not uniform. By the 1980s, communist governance in Hungary or in Poland strikingly differed from communist rule in the Soviet Union, or in Albania, or in Cuba. Communism everywhere came to be modified by local factors that did not fit tidily into the framework of Marxist-Leninist philosophy. In a more fundamental sense, the argument sums up, the totalitarian model caricatures the essentials of human nature. Kindness, compassion, moral integrity did not disappear in the Soviet Union – any more than sloth, pride, and disobedience. Even during the worst days of Stalin, the party bosses had not all been slave drivers, nor the ordinary people willing serfs.

These criticisms carry some weight. Communism did not indeed create a society of robots although it enslaved tens of millions. The communist system had numerous inner tensions. There were moreover considerable differences between countries such as Hungary and Poland, where communist rule had been imposed by foreign conquest, and countries where communist governance had derived from internal revolution. Not all communist countries had experienced terror to the same extent. Walter Ulbricht in East Germany, for example, had not been an exemplar of moral rectitude. But he did not use the axe as Stalin had done, or as did Stalin-like strong-men such as Ho Chi Minh, Kim Il Sung, Pol Pot, or Mao Tse-tung. Nevertheless, these arguments, in our view, should not be carried too far. Terror had in fact been widespread and effective, no matter what label political scientists choose to affix. Right from the start, Lenin and his coadjutors had been committed to terror; it had made sense to them as part of a worldwide assault on the capitalist system which they hoped to destroy by first striking at its weakest links. This grand design, in Lenin's view, could not be accomplished without rigid censorship and mass terror. Hence Lenin and his friends had created, for instance, the *Cheka* with its arsenal of murderous devices – torture, the imprisonment of

[15]Stephen F. Cohen, *Rethinking the Soviet Experience: Politics and History Since 1917*. Oxford, Oxford University Press, 1985.

[16]Michael Howard, *The Causes of War*. Cambridge, Mass., Harvard University Press, 1984.

"class hostages," forced labor camps, mass executions – instruments of repression unknown to the *Okhrana,* the secret police that had served Emperor Nicholas II.[17] (The *Okhrana* had served only as an investigative and domestic intelligence agency, but had exercised no penal functions, and had not administered prisons or punitive camps.) Thereafter, countries as varied as North Korea, China, Vietnam, Ethiopia, and Cambodia all came to experience a regime of terror of the most horrendous kind under Stalin.

In this respect, there was certainly a likeness between communism of the Stalinist kind and Nazism. There were other parallels. Both owed a great debt to the growth of state power during World War I. Both combined terror with mendacity. (As Muscovite wits put it, "they lie even when they lie.") From their very inception, both systems considered themselves at war with Western democracy. Each meant to expand its domination by propaganda and force of arms. Each took pride in styling itself "socialist." Both created a nether-world of concentration camps, designed not merely to destroy the real or assumed enemies of the regime, but to persuade them of their own utter depravity. Both systems employed forced labor on a large scale – in a manner that occasioned the most profligate use of manpower imaginable, wretchedly low levels of productivity, and enormous loss of life.[18]

The similarities went even deeper. In a philosophical sense, each system professed a gnostic faith that called for a total break with an evil past, and looked toward a radiant future that would transcend existing reality and create a "New Man." It was these underlying ideals and assumptions that shaped the terrorist practices of these regimes, more so than so-called pragmatic considerations. Not that these were forgotten. Both the Soviet Union and Nazi Germany acted as great powers, in pursuit of traditional power objectives. Both looked to economic, as well as political gains. But ideological considerations prevailed above all others, especially as these meshed with the rulers' own self-interest and with the concern of the elite to maintain power.

In the Soviet Union, the "new class" of party functionaries formally identified itself through the *nomenklatura* (the secret table of ranks).[19] All Marxist-Leninist states that have since come into existence replicated the *nomenklatura* in some shape or another; all created, a "new class" of party functionaries and ideologues on the public payroll. Their fortunes depended, and continue to depend, on an everlasting struggle for power within the party and the operation of interlocking systems of clientage. The "new claims" did not own the means of production as individuals; instead it collectively directed the means of production by virtue of its monopoly over the means of coercion. The new

[17]George Leggett, *The Cheka Lenin's Political Police.* Oxford, Oxford University Press, 1981.

[18]In Ernst Nolte's definition "fascism is anti-Marxism which seeks to destroy the enemy by the involvement of a radically opposed and yet related ideology by the use of almost identical and yet typically modified methods, always, however, within the unyielding framework of national self-assertion and autonomy." Ernst Nolte, *Three Faces of Fascism: Action Française, Italian Fascism, National Socialism.* New York, Mentor Books, 1963, p. 40.

[19]For a brilliant study of the *nomenklatura,* see Michael Voslensky, *Nomenklatura: The Soviet Ruling Class.* New York, Doubleday, 1985.

class's governance created a new order of privilege – special housing, special shops, special consumption patterns, special powers and respect. The system achieved considerable success in expanding the Soviet Union's industrial production; but the system's ultimate aim was the maximization of its own power and the militarization of society. It therefore had an inbuilt bias for expansion. Victories abroad would help to legitimize the *nomenklatura*'s position at home, multiply positions of leadership, and eliminate actual or potential opposition beyond the borders of the Soviet Union. Ultimately, expansion would do away with the international "demonstration effect" provided by those foreign countries that offered to their own workers better conditions than the Soviets could provide. As historian Jiri Hochman put it, the main motivation of Soviet foreign policy derived from "the concern of the elite to maintain power."[20]

In a more immediate sense, both Nazism and Stalinism demanded total and uncritical obedience on the part of the population, and endowed the supreme leadership with virtues beyond the scope of ordinary humanity. It was Stalin with whom Western statesmen had to deal – a tyrant feared by his friends as much as by his enemies. It was Stalin who wielded unlimited power in the Soviet Union. It was he whom Western statesmen should have trusted, according to revisionist orthodoxy. In fact, Stalin's system, like Hitler's, rested on the dictatorship of a single party (supported by a separate political army); both ruling parties in some ways functioned like a secular church – with its martyrs, processions, ceremonies, hymns, and more or less obligatory rallies. Both systems depended on a secret police and a nationwide network of internal espionage. Both, in a way, resembled a ship whose captain and chief officers take credit alike for having built the craft and for maintaining total discipline over the passengers, and sharing responsibility alike for navigation and for the vessel's ultimate destination – a paradise of their own definition.[21] According to a statement by Lenin, thereafter repeated and elaborated innumerable times by communist theoreticians, "we live not in one country but in a system of countries, and for the Soviet Republic to exist for long side by side with imperialist nations is impossible. One of the two systems will ultimately triumph over the other. But before that happens, there is bound to be a series of terrible conflicts between them."[22] The "two-camp" theory was reiterated in 1947 by Andrei Zhdanov, Stalin's loyal associate. It was only after the dictator's death in 1953 that there was a temporary thaw, and in 1956 the doctrines of "capitalist encirclement" and the "inevitability of war" were repudiated at the CPSU's Twentieth Party Congress.[23]

[20]Jiri Hochman, *The Soviet Union and the Failure of Collective Security, 1934–1938*. Ithaca, Cornell University Press, 1984, p. 172.

[21]For a brilliant dissection of the millenial temperament, see Norman Cohn, *The Pursuit of the Millenium: Revolutionary Messianism in Medieval and Reformation Europe and Its Bearing on Modern Totalitarian Movements*. New York, Harper and Row, 1961.

[22]Cited in Branko Lazitch and Milorad M. Drachkovitch, *Lenin and the Comintern*. Stanford, Cal., Hoover Institution, 1972, p. 127.

[23]For Zhdanov's statement, see Vernon V. Aspaturian, "The Soviet Union," in Roy C. Macridis

In the pursuit of their respective struggles, Stalin possessed many advantages over both the Nazis and the democracies. He did not profess an avowedly racist religion. His system of governance was more effectively unified than Hitler's system of competing fiefs, held together by the *Führer's* will. The communists also displayed much greater flexibility. They perfected the art of forming temporary alliances with assorted friends and enemies (fronts), alliances that would utilize the dissensions that existed abroad between different classes, between competing groups within the same social class, and between rival countries.

Stalin, unlike Hitler, was prepared to proceed with guile and caution, ready to use trade, propaganda, loan agreements, cultural exchanges, espionage, diplomacy, and war as instruments for strengthening Soviet power. From the very beginning the communists, for instance, did not disdain to accept humanitarian aid, provided to them on a large scale by Herbert Hoover's relief agency after World War I, during a period of Soviet famines (1922–5). (In 1923, the Council of People's Commissars of the USSR indeed passed a formal resolution, "in the name of the millions who have been rescued," thanking Hoover and his colleagues for their help.)[24]

More importantly, the Soviets from the 1920s onwards secured for themselves a massive and indispensable transfer of Western technology, capital, and managerial skills through deals with US, German, British, and other foreign businessmen. In theory, capitalists as a class should have sabotaged Soviet industrialization. In practice, commissars and corporations often collaborated successfully; Western capitalists provided the Soviet Union with the bulk of all industrial and technical innovations during the first half century of Soviet rule; giants such as Ford, Vickers-Armstrong, General Motors, RCA, Union Carbide, and Imperial Chemical Industries played a major part in the creation of a socialist economy.[25]

The Soviets likewise gained the sympathy of scores of public servants, academics, and other opinion leaders in the US and elsewhere. These comprised men such as labor leader Harry Bridges, US Ambassador Joseph E. Davis (a loyal defender of Stalin and his show trials), Alger Hiss, and Harry Dexter White (Assistant Secretary of the US Treasury under President Roosevelt, and a bitter Germanophobe). The Soviets likewise benefitted from the way in which many liberal and left-wing journalists (such as Walter Lippmann) defended Moscow's cause in the Western press, and also from the extensive spy networks that had managed to infiltrate agents and sympathizers into Western intelligence organizations and the research establishments – men such as the German-born physicist Klaus Fuchs, or Guy Burgess, a British civil servant.

---

and Robert E. Ward, eds, *Modern Political Systems: Europe*. Englewood Cliffs, NJ, Prentice-Hall, 1963, p. 451.

[24]Benjamin M. Weissman, *Herbert Hoover and Famine Relief to Soviet Russia: 1921–1923*. Stanford, Cal., Hoover Institution Press, 1974, pp. 177–8. In Stalin's last days the Soviets wanted this resolution returned to them by the Hoover Library and condemned Hoover's relief activities.

[25]For a detailed account, see Antony C. Sutton, *Western Technology and Soviet Economic Development, 1917–1965*. Stanford, Hoover Institution Press, 1968–1973, 3 vols.

But above all, the Soviet Union could count on the good will of an enormous number of men and women, trade unionists, intellectuals and professional people, loyal to their respective countries, and some averse to communism, yet somehow convinced that Stalin's Russia stood for a noble experiment, and therefore deserved at least the benefit of the doubt. Moreover, the Great Depression, the supposed lessons of the Civil War in Spain during the 1930s, as well as the rise of Hitler, convinced many non-communists that the Soviet Union somehow remained mankind's last hope.

The new American Ambassador Joseph E. Davis, upon first meeting Stalin told him that he (Davis) had praised the Red Army and defended it before President Roosevelt. Stalin turned to his interpreter and said "What is this fool saying; our army was terrible; it lost every battle with the Germans at first."

WALTER LIPPMANN (1889–1974)

Star journalists had already made their names in the English-speaking world during the Crimean War, the US Civil War and the partitioning of Africa. But it was only during World War II and its aftermath that the profession reached its apogee. By that time there was a whole crop of outstanding non-academic public intellectuals and journalists – well-connected, well-educated, highly literate, able to make their names both as newspaper writers and authors. They spoke out boldly on political and social issues. They included journalist-historians such as Alan Moorehead, Edward Murrow, Chester Wilmot (author of The Struggle for Europe *1952), and William L. Shirer (author of* The Rise and Fall of the Third Reich, *1960, an even more influential book). There were many others: Daniel Bell, William F. Buckley, Jon Jacobs, Bernard De Voto, Reinhold Niebuhr (called by one scholar "the last intellectual"), and so on.*

Perhaps the most powerful of all was Walter Lippmann. Lippmann began his career as a brilliant young man at Harvard; he ended as a power in the land, his work read by all and sundry. When he traveled, he traveled in style; doors opened. Heads of state would seek him out for the privilege of being interviewed. To his readers, he represented what many of them would have liked to have been themselves – an omniscient insider, oracular moralist, and a stylish man-of-the-world. His political judgement was often open to doubt. (During World War II, he did not write about the death camps, even though he was of Jewish origin.) At the end of the war, he felt convinced that a settlement with Stalin was not hard to attain, provided only that the West would accept, in good faith, Soviet supremacy in Eastern Europe. He saw no need for NATO or for West German rearmament. Later on, he became an impassioned critic of the Vietnam War. But right or wrong, his syndicated columns appeared year in and year out in all the leading newspapers for nearly four decades. Lippmann was, at the time, a charter member of the establishment and one of its chartered critics. As Ronald Steel put it, in Walter Lippmann and the American Century *(1980), when Lippmann went into semi-retirement in 1967, "it was as though an institution had suddenly ceased to exist." Every newspaper columnist in the US would thereafter have liked to step into Lippmann's shoes but none managed to do so.*

In pursuing their strategy, Stalin and his successors made successful use of all those communist parties, fronts (coalitions), and fellow travellers and liberals in the rest of the world that looked to Moscow's leadership. It was indeed one of Stalin's unique achievements to have standardized these parties, uniting them in a common allegiance to Moscow, a common terminology, methods of organization, and strategy. These parties maintained, or cooperated with, a complex network of front organizations. Their names would fill a small encyclopedia. They included a plethora of bodies inspired by the genius of Willie Münzenberg, a veteran Comintern agent during the 1930s. Their number expanded during and after World War II with the formation, among others, of the World Federation of Democratic Youth (1941); the Women's International Democratic Federation, and the World Federation of Trade Unions (1945). These bodies collaborated in a fashion infinitely more effective than the loose association of fascists, collaborators, anti-semites, reactionary conservatives, and thugs who, in Hitler's heyday, had supported the Nazi movement.

The communist parties of Moscow orientation received worldwide direction through the Comintern (the Russian abbreviated title of the Communist Internationale formed in 1919). In 1943, the Comintern was formally dissolved as a gesture of goodwill toward Stalin's Western allies; but effective coordination from Moscow of the pro-Soviet parties continued through a variety of devices, including the Cominform (Communist Information Bureau, set up in 1947). Overall, Stalin had extraordinary success in forcing not only his own, but also the bulk of the foreign parties to submit to his leadership, and to purge them of real or alleged dissidents.[26]

The Communist Party of the United States (CPUSA) was no exception; it faithfully followed every shift and turn of the Moscow line, so that the Cold War proceeded within the USA's own boundaries long before the term "Cold War" had passed into the political currency. In 1929, for instance, Jay Lovestone and his followers were expelled from the CPUSA as part of a purge that imposed the Stalinist line on communist parties throughout the world.[27] At home, the CPUSA had initially denounced Roosevelt as a "social fascist," using the same epithet that German communists had bestowed on the German Social Democrats in the communists' struggle to overthrow the Weimar Republic. In 1935, the CPUSA adopted the "popular front" policy, together with the other communist parties throughout the world, and Roosevelt turned from an enemy to a friend. The CPUSA's line changed again after the conclusion of the Nazi-Soviet pact in 1939; the party thereafter opposed the "imperialist" war, called for a militantly anti-capitalist stand, and for the sabotage of the Anglo-French war effort.

After the German assault on the Soviet Union in 1941, the CPUSA, like

[26]Milorad Drachkovitch and Branko Lazitch, "The communist internationals," in Milorad M. Drachkovitch, ed., *The Revolutionary Internationals*. Stanford, Cal., Hoover Institution Press, 1966, pp. 159–202. Paolo Spriano, *Stalin and the European Communists*. New York, Schocken, 1985.

[27]For a history of the CPUSA and a detailed account of the manner in which it was controlled by Stalin, see Theodore Draper, *American Communism and Soviet Russia: The Formative Period*. New York, Viking Press, 1960.

its sister parties everywhere, immediately became a militant supporter of the war, and strongly backed Roosevelt. Earl Browder, the party's leader, however, went too far on this course, and for too long a time. In a major policy statement in 1944 Browder interpreted the US–British–Soviet alliance as a guarantee for peaceful coexistence and collaboration, with far-reaching consequences for the future relations between capitalism and communism. Had Moscow backed Browder's line, effective cooperation between East and West could have perhaps become a practical proposition; the two social systems might conceivably have worked side by side peacefully. Such an arrangement, however, would have been totally incompatible with Lenin's heritage. Moscow's condemnation of Browder's views initially came through an indirect route – as remained the Soviet style. In April 1945, at the very time when Nazi Germany was about to collapse and when the American press continued to praise US–Soviet friendship, Jacques Duclos, a member of the French Communist Party's Politbureau, published a major article in *Cahiers du communisme*, a theoretical journal for the French communist's intellectual elite. This strongly criticized Browder's conciliatory approach, and insisted that communists should not renounce their objective of seizing power because peaceful coexistence between capitalism and communism was impossible.[28]

The significance of this article remains in dispute. Duclos – hardly an unbiased witness – later explained that the article was timed merely to warn the West against a possible reversal of alliances.[29] What is not in dispute is the communists' reaction both at home and abroad. The American communists believed that Duclos's views represented Stalin's own, and acted accordingly. In fact Browder and his views on peaceful coexistence between competing social systems incurred opprobrium throughout the communist world. The CPUSA's line swung from measured support of US foreign policy to an unconditional opposition that echoed the USSR's own animosity. The Cold War thereafter intensified.[30]

[28]For a brief summary of these events, see Theodore Draper, "The United States of America," in Sworakowski, *World Communism: A Handbook*, pp. 462–71.

[29]Mastny, *Russia's Road to the Cold War: Diplomacy, Warfare, and the Politics of Communism, 1941–1945*. p. 272. Peter L. Steinberg, *The Great "Red Menace:" United States Prosecution of American Communists, 1947–1952*. Westport, Conn., Greenwood Press, 1984, p. 64. Sternberg's general interpretation, however, differs from our own.

[30]See for instance Morton Kaplan, ed., The *Many Faces of Communism*. New York, Free Press, 1978. Adam B. Ulam, *The New Face of Soviet Totalitarianism*. New York, Frederick A. Praeger, 1963. R. Judson Mitchell, *Ideology of a Superpower: Contemporary Soviet Doctrine on International Relations*. Stanford, Hoover Institution Press, 1982. For a shattering critique of communist and *Marxisant* influence at US universities, see Sidney Hook, "Communists, McCarthy and American Universities," *Minerva: A Review of Science, Learning and Policy*, v, xxv, no. 3, Autumn 1987, pp. 331–48, and his discussion of Ellen Schrecker, *No Ivory Tower: McCarthyism and the Universities*. Oxford, Oxford University Press, 1986.

Teheran, Yalta, and Potsdam

Polemics in print went with struggles at the conference table. As long as the Third Reich remained under arms, the Grand Alliance held after a fashion. In November 1943, Churchill, Roosevelt, and Stalin met at Teheran, a conference even more important than the subsequent meetings at Yalta and Potsdam. It was at Teheran that the Allies agreed that the Soviet border should move westward into Poland, and Poland would be compensated by the annexation of east German territory. The Baltic States were recognized as Soviet territory. Discussions began regarding Allied military zones for the future of occupied Germany. Teheran gave Stalin a demonstration of the ease with which he could play off the Americans against the British – given Roosevelt's hostility to the British empire, and his determination at the time to conciliate Stalin. The conference resulted, among other things, in a one-sided flow of military information from the Western powers to the Soviet Union, including plans and preparations for *Overlord,* the invasion of Western Europe. The Soviets, for their part, failed to reciprocate and remained quite unwilling to furnish the West with details concerning their own plans or the German order of battle. Teheran presaged the bipolar world of the future, and demonstrated also the manner in which British power had rapidly declined.[31]

> *Churchill was taken in by Stalin for a time and cared little for Poland and free elections because he cared more for Britain protecting its empire in the postwar period. He refused at first to believe the stories about Soviet brutality in its march toward the West – not even the massacre of Polish officers at Katyn alerted him to Soviet treachery and evil. By agreeing with Stalin over spheres of interest in Eastern Europe, he may have encouraged the Soviet leader to take over Romania and Bulgaria, knowing he need not worry about what was said in Western parliaments.*
>
> *Churchill awakened to the realities of Soviet aims after Yalta and the misuse by Stalin of the Yalta Declaration on Liberated Europe. Until his speech at Fulton, Churchill's egotism made him believe he could win over "Uncle Joe." When he finally realized the communist threat he helped to awaken the still politically naive Americans.*

Churchill, in his own words, did all he could to prevent the British donkey from being squeezed between the American buffalo and the Russian bear. In October 1944 Stalin and Churchill at a private meeting worked out a rough and ready agreement according to which the USSR would have 90 percent predominance in Romania, the British 10 percent. In Bulgaria, Soviet influence would amount to 75 percent. In Yugoslavia and Hungary, the Soviets and British (in cooperation with the Americans) would split their power equally. In Greece, the British (in concert with the Americans) would enjoy 90 percent predominance, and the Soviets 10 percent.[32]

[31]Keith Eubank, *Summit at Teheran: The Untold Story.* New York, William Morrow, 1985. Keith Sainsbury, *The Turning Point.* Oxford, Oxford University Press, 1985. For the British side, see Elisabeth Barker, *The British Between the Superpowers, 1945–1950.* London, Macmillan, 1983, pp. 1–25.

[32]Herbert Feis, *Churchill, Roosevelt, Stalin: The War They Waged and the Peace They Sought.* Princeton, Princeton University Press, 1957, pp. 447–50.

In practice, this casual arrangement did not work. As long as their archives remain closed Soviet strategy can never be fully fathomed. It seems possible, however, that the Soviets might actually have ended the war in 1944, by which time Germany stood in disarray. However, a direct Soviet march on Berlin, before the Balkans had been overrun, would have entailed serious political disadvantages for Moscow. The war would have ended with a large area of Eastern Europe still under nominal German occupation. A sudden German collapse would leave in power "bourgeois" governments in Hungary, Romania, and Bulgaria that might appeal to the Western Allies for support. In Autumn 1944, the Soviets therefore shifted their main efforts to the Balkans; their military power thereafter became supreme in southeastern, as well as Eastern, Europe. Only Greece escaped occupation. And possession, for the Soviets, was to prove ten-tenths of the law.

No matter what Moscow said or did, the Grand Alliance held firm so long as the Third Reich stood. Western aid to the Soviet Union reached impressive figures.[33] For a brief moment the Yalta Conference, held February 4–11, 1945, seemingly marked "The high tide of Big Three Unity."[34] The contracting parties agreed, among other points, to eliminate or control all German industries that could be used for war production and that major war criminals should be tried. The conference issued a "Declaration on Liberated Europe" that affirmed the rights of all peoples to choose their own form of government and called for free elections. The conference, however, failed to resolve inter-allied disagreements on Poland where the Western Allies backed the expatriate Polish Government in London, and the Soviets their own committee of national liberation, a communist-dominated body with its temporary seat in Lublin. The conference could do no more than suggest a provisional government in which both groups would collaborate, but pledged support to free and unfettered elections. The conference discussed the United Nations Charter, and once more committed the Soviet Union to enter the war against Japan after Germany's surrender.

Above all, the conference confirmed existing agreements on the *de facto* partition of Germany into allied zones, (finalized earlier by the London Protocol of September 12, 1944, a key document arrived at in a curiously ill-planned fashion by ad hoc arrangements).[35] France received an occupation zone of her own, carved out of the previously agreed American zone; this arrangement marked both France's re-emergence as a European power and

[33]From 1 October 1941 to April 1944 alone, the USA shipped to the Soviet Union 8,500,000 tons of armaments, raw material, food and equipment valued at $5,357,000,000. British shipments amounted to 1,150,000 tons worth £83,700,000. Keesing's *Contemporary Archives*. London, Keesings Publications, June–September 1944, p. 6511. For a more detailed history, see George C. Herring, *Aid to Russia 1941–1946. Strategy Diplomacy, and The Origins of Cold War*. New York, Columbia University Press, 1973.

[34]The title of a chapter heading in a book by James F. Byrnes, *Speaking Frankly*. London, Heinemann, 1947.

[35]Reprinted in full in *Gesamtdeutsches Institut, Bundesanstalt für Gesamt-Deutsche Aufgaben. Materialien zur deutschen Frage*. Bonn, Gesamtdeutsches Institut, 1985.

symbolized her indebtedness to the US for her revival. Without having originally meant to do so, the Allies in fact – though not in theory – committed themselves to the partition of Germany, an object for which none of the belligerents had originally gone to war. This partition was linked to an arrangement that left the Western Allies in control of West Berlin, but without giving them a Western controlled access route to their sector, leaving West Berlin a hostage to future Soviet interferences.[36]

The Western Allies were thus left at a severe disadvantage. But the Soviets too may have erred as regards their long-term objective. Having secured a part of east Prussia for themselves, and having allotted to Poland a considerable portion of East Germany, the Soviets put their money on the Polish card. They thereby denied themselves the possibility of creating a large East German state under their own control, a state that might have covered nearly half of the former German Reich. Such a state might in future have served as a Red Prussia, the nucleus around which communists might later have reassembled a Red Reich. The resultant Soviet zone of occupation turned out to be relatively small, much less significant in terms of population, resources, and area than the Western zones of occupation ($108,333 \text{ km}^2$ against $248,630 \text{ km}^2$).

Even this gain might have been denied to the Soviets, had the Western powers at the time pursued that deliberate Cold War strategy later imputed to them by their revisionist critics. General Eisenhower, for instance, could certainly have captured Berlin, Prague, and Vienna had he chosen to do so albeit at a high cost in casualties and in Soviet ill-will, as Theodore Draper has shown. Instead, Eisenhower insisted that Berlin at this point had become no more than a point on a map, of no strategic significance.[37] A commander with more imagination might have seen the political advantage to be gained from seizing the German capital, an advantage that had not been lost earlier on in General Mark Clark's dash to Rome in 1944. By the end of the war the bulk of the *Wehrmacht* had become very anxious to surrender to American and British rather than Russian forces and the majority of German civilians felt the same way.

The Allies, however, took little account of changing political and military realities, and failed to plan for the long-term future. Throughout 1944, at a critical time in inter-Allied negotiations, American dignitaries, from the President downward, repeatedly warned the British that US forces would not stay long in Europe after the war had ended. In Britain itself, the Foreign Office was horrified at the very thought that military planners might make provision

---

[36]Daniel J. Nelson, *Wartime Origins of the Berlin Dilemma*. Tuscalusa, University of Alabama Press, 1978. Avi Shlaim, *The United States and the Berlin Blockade 1948–1949: A Study in Crisis Decision-Making*. Berkeley, University of California Press, 1983.

[37]See David Eisenhower, *Eisenhower at War, 1943–1945*. New York, Random House, 1986, and for an extensive review of the literature see Theodore Draper, *New York, Review of Books*, v, xxx, no. 15, 9 October 1986, pp. 34–41; and no. 16, 23 October, 1986, pp. 61–7. Eric Larrabee, *Commander in Chief: Franklin Delano Roosevelt. His Lieutenants, and Their War*. New York, Simon and Schuster, 1987, esp. p. 506.

for a worst case scenario in which the Soviet Union would appear as a possible future enemy.[38]

Far from planning a Cold War against the Soviet Union, the US and the British remained mesmerized by the German peril – at the moment when the Third Reich was about to collapse – and sent an army off to see if Hitler was hiding in his Berchtesgaden retreat. (The US Treasury, to mention just one other example, elaborated a plan to strip Germany of her most basic industries, to transform the Ruhr and the Kiel Canal into an international zone that would not be allowed to trade with the Reich.)[39] The Allies' circumscribed thinking at the time went with a continuation of the bomber offensive against the most insignificant German targets – again, at a time when German's logistic and economic infrastructure had already been shattered.

The Allies also denied themselves other potential advantages. The Americans, for instance, could have captured Prague and Vienna, but failed to do so. Worse still from their point of view, the allies after Yalta voluntarily vacated strategic key areas that they had occupied. By May 7, 1945, Allied forces had advanced well beyond their agreed occupation zones. Western troops had reached the Elbe; they had occupied the whole of Thuringia and much of Saxony in Eastern Germany, including the cities of Leipzig and Chemnitz. The Western Allies could have held on to these valuable provinces on the legal grounds that the Soviets were violating the Yalta engagements, especially over Poland, and that one-sided compliance with existing agreements would therefore be to the Western Allies disadvantage. Instead, Western forces retreated into their zones of occupation. This decision made permanent a frontier that might have been drawn in a manner more favorable to the West politically, and more defensible militarily.

As it was, the Allied decision to withdraw left the Soviets with enough German territory to make possible the construction of a German communist state. Such a task would hardly have been feasible had the Soviets been forced to create a satellite out of the narrow land belt, stretching roughly from Rostock ro Dresden, with Berlin in the center – all the land that would have been left to them had the Allies acted in enlightened self-interest. Admittedly, such action would not have been without its costs. Demobilization would have had to be delayed. The Cold War would have taken a more overt form somewhat earlier than it did; the Soviets would probably have held on to part of northern Persia, occupied by them during World War II by agreement with the British. The Soviets might or might not have abstained from entering the war against Japan during the last stages of this conflict. But overall, the global balance of power would have improved in the Allies' favor.

In the end, the Yalta Conference merely papered over the cracks in the wartime alliance. The fundamental dissensions, left unresolved at Yalta, became more evident during the Potsdam Conference of July–August 1945,

---

[38]Graham Ross, ed., *The Foreign Office and the Kremlin: British Documents on Anglo-Soviet Relations, 1941–45.* Cambridge, Cambridge University Press, 1984, pp. 51 and 67.
[39]Gaddis, *The United States and the Origins of the Cold War, 1941–1947.* pp. 65–6.

and fittingly code-named "Terminal." Roosevelt, by this time, had been replaced by Harry S. Truman; Clement Attlee stepped into Winston Churchill's shoes after the Conservative Party had been voted out of office in a British general election. Nazi rule had disintegrated, and inter-Allied disagreements had become more bitter than before. The most important issues facing the conference were either deferred or only came out in the open later. Stalin's demand for territorial concessions from Turkey proved unacceptable to the Allies. The US and the Americans protested against the treatment accorded to their representatives in the Balkan area and the way in which the Soviets imposed their hegemony. The extension of Poland's western boundary beyond the previously agreed line was presented to the Western Allies as a *fait accompli*; in the end the conference could only approve Polish administration of the entire region, pending a final peace treaty with Germany. But such a document was never signed. A genuine settlement, such as was achieved by the great powers at the Congress of Vienna in 1815, after the Napoleonic Wars, proved unattainable. The signatories at Vienna had bitterly clashed, but they all had seen themselves as members of a European concert, however vaguely defined. The signatories of the Teheran, Yalta, and Potsdam agreements had no such common bond. Nevertheless, the Yalta settlement would continue after a fashion for nearly half a century, until shattered by the Gorbachev reforms in the Soviet Union, and the free elections held in Eastern Europe in 1990.

Clash of opinion

Could the Western powers have avoided the Cold War? According to the revisionists, the answer is clear: Western policy had been flawed from the beginning. The West had erred by failing to cement an alliance with the Soviet Union during the 1930s when the Soviet Union had proved the stoutest opponent of Nazism, both before and after Hitler came to power. During World War II, the Western powers – the revisionist argument continues – had delayed the "Second Front" for the purpose of deliberately weakening the Soviet Union, leaving the main burden to be borne by the Soviet peoples. As John Lewis Gaddis puts it, the delay in creating a Second Front convinced the Russians that their capitalist comrades had decided to let them carry the main burden of the war. The resulting atmosphere of suspicion was hardly conducive to Roosevelt's "grand design" for putting Soviet–American relations on a firm basis of mutual understanding. So the war's main burden came to be shouldered by the Soviet Union.[40] The US and, less obviously, Great Britain opposed any extension of Soviet influence in Eastern Europe, including the most reasonable demands made by Stalin for the purpose of safeguarding Soviet security against renewed aggression. President Roosevelt,

---

[40]For a detailed discussion, see Alan J. Levine, "Some revisionist theses on the Cold War, 1943–1946: a study of a modern mythology," *Continuity*, no. 1, Fall, 1980, pp. 75–97. Philip J. Jaffe, "The Cold War revisionists and what they omit," *Survey*, Autumn, 1973, v. 19, no. 4, pp. 123–43.

had he lived, might have been more sensible in this regard than Churchill and other assorted Cold Warriors. But Roosevelt's untimely demise, followed by Truman's succession to the presidential office, wrecked any chance for a statesmanlike settlement. The Western Allies were guilty of many other acts of commission or omission. These included the Western failure to accommodate the Soviets over issues such as foreign aid, nuclear cooperation, and the payment of German reparations. Above all, the Americans attempted indirectly to blackmail the Soviet Union by using nuclear weapons against Japan, and thus committed one of the supreme crimes of the present century. Western acts of provocation, the revisionists conclude, made the Cold War inevitable.[41]

We do not concur with this indictment. For a start, the relations between communism and Nazism were far more ambivalent than the revisionists assumed. For instance, the German communists, backed by the Comintern, had played their part before 1933 in weakening the Weimar Republic, they held that even if the Nazis were to seize power, the new Nazi regime would be short-lived and act as the "ice-breaker" for revolution. The "popular front" policy, adopted between 1933 and 1939, did not endure for long; it was followed by an anti-Western entente between the two totalitarian powers, an understanding aimed against the West, and broken, not by Soviet action, but by the Nazis' ill-considered attack on the Soviet Union in 1941.[42] Having for long engaged in intense vituperation against the Western powers, and having attempted to sabotage their war effort, prior to the German invasion of the Soviet Union, the Soviets and their communist allies in the West were hardly in a position to moralize thereafter.

Nevertheless they did. Moscow insisted, in and out of season, that the Western powers should start "a Second Front now." Revisionists such as Gabriel Kolko found a sinister significance in Allied delay. In framing their indictment, the revisionists downplayed the contribution made by Great Britain and (from 1941 onward) the US to the war at sea, a vital theater in which the British might easily have lost. The revisionists' plea equally underestimated the part played by the Western air forces; one of their achievements was to prevent the *Luftwaffe* from throwing its entire weight against the Soviet Union. The revisionists likewise gave all too little credit to the US and, to a lesser extent, to Great Britain for tying down Japan's armed might in the Pacific struggle, whereby they relieved pressure on the Soviet Union, and permitted the Soviets to deploy the bulk of their Far Eastern divisions against the *Wehrmacht* at a critical juncture of the war.

[41]See for instance, Alan J. Levine, "Communist anti-fascism," *Continuity*, no. 6, Spring, pp. 35–53.

[42]Gabriel Kolko, *Politics of War: The World and United States Foreign Policy, 1943–1945*. New York, Random House, 1968, *passim*.

> *Wedemeyer drafted the so-called Victory Plan in July–September 1941, stressing a global strategy that assumed "Hitler first," and calling for a direct strategy in Europe as opposed to the indirect one of attrition favored by the British. His scheme called for a huge build-up in Britain; a massive assault on the French northern coast in 1943, then a quick drive eastward to seize the industrial heart of Germany. The other theaters would fall easily once Germany was conquered. Chief of Staff Marshall, Secretary of War Stinson, and Roosevelt, at times approved Wedemeyer's plans. But Churchill's "periphery-pecking" prevailed: attacks were launched in North Africa and Italy in 1943 and no attack could be launched against Europe.*
>
> *When the Soviets started advancing into Eastern Europe, Wedemeyer again pushed for an early attack across the Channel so that allied troops could get to Central Europe before the Russians. Wedemeyer argued, according to his biographer Keith Eiler, that the relative balance of forces favored the Allies. The Germans were deeply involved in the East; the defenses of the Atlantic Wall were primitive and the Germans could not withdraw forces quickly enough to counter a cross channel landing. Landing craft and material had been foolishly wasted in peripheral attacks, with the consequence that the Russians took Central as well as Eastern Europe.*

As regards the "Second Front," military historians still debate whether the invasion of Western Europe could have taken place earlier than 1944.[43] Some authorities such as General Wedemeyer believed that the Western Allies could have successfully landed in France in 1943, thereby shortening the war, and making sure that the Western Allies reached Central Europe well ahead of the Red Army. On the other hand, an Allied invasion at an earlier date might well have failed. Even by 1944, by which time the Allies had built up a great superiority, the venture still seemed so much of a gamble that General Eisenhower, prior to the Normandy landings, had prepared a statement – fortunately never needed – announcing to the world that the invasion had foundered. At best, an earlier invasion might have incurred even heavier loss of life than was suffered in 1944. Roosevelt, as historian Alan J. Levine puts it, has been the target of many strange attacks; but the argument that he should have adopted a strategy that would have cost *more* of his people's lives may well be the weirdest charge ever levelled at a national leader.[44]

Soviet conduct thereafter hardly inspired confidence or trust, especially with regard to East-Central Europe. The Soviet Union likewise annexed the three Baltic republics of Lithuania, Estonia, and Latvia, whose independence Moscow had formally recognized in 1920, and which had become viable states recognized by the international community. Most revisionists accept such action as a legitimate defense of Soviet interests, but do not accord similar legitimacy to Western interests. Other revisionists take a somewhat different line, and argue that the "percentage agreement," concluded between Churchill and Stalin might have laid the basis for a realistic settlement. Such an accord

[43]The argument that the Allies could have won in 1943 is set out in John Grigg, *1943: The Victory that Never Was*. London, Eyre Methuen, 1980. General Albert C. Wedemeyer, the German-trained American strategist, still held this view in 1988.

[44]See for instance, Alan J. Levine, "Communist anti-fascism," *Continuity*, no. 6, Spring, p. 52.

would have corresponded with the facts of power, and would have conformed to those "spheres of influence" accords that great powers had traditionally made to solve outstanding differences. The Anglo-Soviet agreement, however, was never clarified; neither was it binding on the Americans who were not informed of these conversations at the time. And with good reason. To the Americans, such secret covenants smacked too much of the Old World power diplomacy that humanitarian opinion in the US had condemned. The US public at the time paid far more attention to the birth of the United Nations than to great power rivalry. Roosevelt and Wendell Willkie, the Republican candidate in 1940, had one thing in common – they both looked toward the peaceful dissolution of the Western colonial (including the British) empires as the sovereign means of preserving world peace, rather than to restraining Soviet power in Eastern Europe.

The Soviet Union, for its part, had no intention of accepting the implications of the Churchill–Stalin accord. To do so would have implied abandoning the World Revolution, to which Stalin stood firmly committed; it had been fervently proclaimed once more by the Seventh Congress of the Communist International, at the height of the "popular front" era in 1935 – even before the Great Purge of 1937, with its mass arrests and show trials had gotten under way.[45]

The British certainly derived little benefit from the Stalin–Churchill accord. They were never given any say, much less the promised half share, in the determination of Hungary's and Yugoslavia's future, even though Tito had heavily relied on British assistance. There was no share for the West in Bulgaria either. In the Fall of 1945, when the Red Army approached Bulgaria's Northern border, Bulgaria made peace with the US and Great Britain, and simultaneously declared war against Nazi Germany. A Fatherland Front, composed of liberals, agrarians, socialists and communists took power, only to be faced by a Soviet declaration of war and the Soviet invasion of a country hardly on the direct road to Berlin. In Bulgaria, as in Poland and Romania, there was widespread domestic opposition to the imposition of communist rule. The Western powers made some attempts at diplomatic resistance. But eventually, the Soviets overrode all obstacles and Bulgaria became a communist preserve, even though communist indigenous strength in the past had been negligible.[46]

Greece had been placed in the British sphere by the Churchill–Stalin accord. This did not prevent the Greek communists from attempting a coup against

---

[45]Sworakowski, "The communist international," in Sworakowski, ed., *World Communism: A Handbook 1918–1965.*

[46]See Michael M. Boll, *Cold War in the Balkans: American Foreign Policy and the Emergence of Communist Bulgaria, 1943–1947.* Lexington, University Press of Kentucky, 1984. Boll's interpretation differs from our own in that he does not see a preconceived Soviet plan for the Sovietization of Bulgaria. For a recent study of Soviet policy in Poland, see Jan Karski, *The Great Power and Poland 1919–1945: From Versailles to Yalta.* Lanham, University Press of America, 1985. For Hungary, Stephen Kertesz, *Between Russia and the West: Hungary and the Illusions of Peacemaking, 1945–1947.* Notre Dame, Ind., University of Notre Dame Press, 1984. Audrey Kurth Cronin, *Great Power Politics and the Struggle over Austria 1945–1955.* Ithaca, NY, Cornell University Press, 1986.

the Greek exile government shortly after its return in October 1944. Historians will again have to wait until the Soviet Union opens its archives to determine the extent of Soviet involvement in this venture. Only one thing is certain, the Greek communists never incurred censure for the sin of "adventurism" on the part of CPSU, an organization never loathe to criticize real or alleged deviations on the part of other foreigners, such as Earl Browder in the US. The communist insurrection was suppressed with British aid; Greece therefore escaped being drawn into the Soviet sphere. However, the communists resumed hostilities in 1946, and bitter fighting continued until August 1949, as the Greek communists received essential support from privileged sanctuaries in Soviet-dominated Bulgaria, and in Yugoslavia (loyal to Moscow until 1948). The Soviets – far from conceding predominance to the British in Greece – insisted on the withdrawal of British troops from the country, and condemned them for supporting "reactionary forces."[47]

In a cautious and conditional defense of Stalin, Peter J. Stavrakis argues that Stalin did not in fact lose sight of British interests. Stalin's help to the Communist Party of Greece (KKE) was slow and intermittent. Had Stalin failed to render assistance, he would have risked losing his influence on the KKE to Tito.[48] We are not convinced. To a Soviet statesman genuinely intent on peaceful coexistence with the West, good relations with Great Britain would have been more valuable than good relations with either the KKE or Yugoslavia. Stavrakis, in our opinion, also underestimates the extent of the Soviet bloc's support to the KKE. But fortunately the Soviet ploy came to nothing.

This was not the end of the British achievement. Between 1940 and 1942 the British had already performed an inestimable service to the West by preventing the eastern Mediterranean and the Middle East from falling under Nazi domination. Between 1945 and 1947 they played an equally important role in helping to defend the region against Soviet advances. At the Council of Foreign Ministers' meeting in London in 1945, the British, for instance, successfully resisted Soviet demands for a ten-year trusteeship in Tripolitania (part of Libya).[49] They likewise helped to sustain Turkey against Soviet pressure. The British thus played a crucial role in restricting the Soviet Union, for whom spheres of influence agreements, however informal, were meant to work only in Soviet interests.

The Soviet Union proved equally unyielding in Poland. Great Britain and France had gone to war in 1939 in order to preserve Poland's inviolacy. In this regard, they lost the war. The Western Allies, at the Teheran and Yalta Conferences yielded to Stalin's demand for recognition of the 1941 frontiers. In July 1945 the United States recognized the Communist-dominated Lublin

[47]D. George Kousoulas, *Revolution and Defeat: The Story of the Greek Communist Party*. Oxford, Oxford University Press, 1965, p. 231.

[48]Peter J. Stavrakis, *Moscow and Greek Communism 1944–1949*. Ithaca, NY, Cornell University Press, 1989, *passim*.

[49]Kenneth O. Morgan, *Labour in Power 1945–1951*. Oxford, Oxford University Press, 1985, pp. 240–2.

government, even though the overwhelming majority of the country's huge underground movement had consisted of non-communists. The puppet government had no intention of implementing the free elections promised at Yalta. The reason is not hard to find. As the US Ambassador in Poland, Arthur Bliss Lane, reported in October "if free elections were held now, Gvt. [the government] would receive no more than 10 to 15 percent of votes."[50]

The US was, however, by no means unmindful of Soviet interests – this applied even to US military planners. According to Melvyn P. Leffler, a critic of US policy, defense officials at the end of the war desired to create for the US an extended security zone that would comprise the Pacific and Atlantic Oceans; they also wished to prevent the domination of the Eurasian land mass by a single power. But these experts tended to dismiss the role of ideology in Soviet foreign policy; they emphasized Russian distrust toward foreigners, Soviet strategic imperatives, historical ambitions, and reactions to British and US moves. Defense officials in the US, though distrustful of the Soviet Union, were not at first eager to sever the wartime coalition. (When members of the Joint Postwar Committee met their colleagues on the Joint Planning Staff in 1945, Major General G. V. Strong, for instance, strongly argued against using US installations in Alaska for staging expeditionary forces, lest such a project should exacerbate Russo–US tensions.) During the same year, Eisenhower and other officers advised against creating a central economic authority for Western Europe that might appear to be an anti-Soviet bloc. By aggravating Soviet fears, the US (in the experts' opinion) might foster what it would avoid. While acknowledging doubts about ultimate Soviet intentions, US planners believed in the possibility of accommodation. At the time, they feared above all the prospect of anarchy, famine, disease, and revolutions that would promote the spread of Soviet influence by indirect means.[51]

US diplomats took a similar line. At a meeting of the Council of Foreign Ministers in September 1945, the US vainly sought to convince the Soviets that Washington had no desire to see the formation of governments hostile to the Soviet Union in countries such as Poland, Romania, and Hungary. They met with Soviet scepticism.[52] According to revisionists, the Soviets could hardly be blamed for this. The Italian armistice agreement, for example, had made Italy a closed preserve for the West; the Soviets naturally responded by treating their own conquests in similar fashion. This argument, however, will not do. At Potsdam, the Western powers had proposed joint supervision of elections in Italy, the former Axis satellites, and Greece (about which the Soviets were complaining). The Soviets refused the offer.[53]

[50]Cited in Geoffrey Warner, "The United States and the Cold War," *International Affairs,* July 1970, p. 532.

[51]Melvyn P. Leffler, "The American conception of national security and the beginnings of the Cold War, 1945–48," *American Historical Review,* 89, no. 2, April 1984, pp. 346–400, esp. pp. 357 and 363.

[52]For the continuity between Roosevelt's and Truman's policies, see Robert J. Maddox, "Roosevelt and Stalin: the final days," *Continuity,* Spring 1983, no. 6, pp. 113–22.

[53]Alan J. Levine, "Some revisionist theses on the Cold War, 1943–1946," p. 84. For a more

Another revisionist argument asserts that Stalin permitted free elections in Finland, in the Soviet zone, in Austria, and, initially, in Czechoslovakia and Hungary, thereby indicating his good faith. Finland, however, was never occupied by the Soviet Union; the Finns, able to rely on a substantial army, switched their alliance in 1944; they submitted to a harsh peace treaty but kept their independence – an arrangement that may also have helped to persuade Sweden to stick to its accustomed neutrality. Soviet-occupied Austria was too small to serve as a separate communist entity. Free elections were held in Hungary in November 1945, but the Soviets soon took action to undo the results, as they did in East Berlin.

The fate of Czechoslovakia also serves to discredit the revisionists' case. Czechoslovakia, at the end of World War II briefly continued as a "bourgeois democracy." The Czech leaders sympathized with the Soviet Union, feared a German revival, and were resentful of the West because of Munich. Nevertheless, in 1948 Czechoslovakia was taken over by the communists, acting with Soviet assistance – this in a country where the communists in the 1946 elections had secured no more than 114 deputies in a 300-seat parliament. Had the Soviets been concerned merely to serve their security interests, they could have chosen to impose a Finnish-style option on their remaining neighbors. "Bourgeois" leaders such as Eduard Benes and Thomas Masaryk in Czechoslovakia were only too anxious to maintain good relations with Moscow, but this policy availed them nothing. They were thrown out of power, and within a few years some 100,000 Czechs had been sentenced for political crimes.[54]

The Soviets' aim went far beyond their security needs. Delays in imposing communist regimes did not depend on moderation, but more on diplomatic considerations, on the initial shortage of qualified cadres to impose full-fledged regimes in one move, and on the communists' commitment to reach power in stages, through temporary alliances with what they regarded as members of the bourgeoisie. Had the Western allies from the start desired to take up the challenge of the Cold War, they could at least have refused to maintain diplomatic relations with the new satellite regimes of Eastern Europe – as the Soviet Union later refused with regard to Israel and South Africa.

Stalin wanted a buffer zone of friendly communist states between him and the West, but he also planned to reap economic benefits from the area as well as to lay the foundations for further political gains in Western Europe. And he believed the victor in a war had a right to impose his own social system in the conquered region. He was aided in his plans by American and British officials, who kept deferring the negotiation of postwar political agreements and who then conceded too much at Teheran and Yalta. Stalin may well have come to believe that the West would do nothing to stop him controlling Eastern Europe through the Red Army. Nothing that he did seemed to lead

---

detailed discussion, see Robert Maddox, *The new Left and the Origins of the Cold War*. Princeton, Princeton University Press, 1973.

[54]Karel Kaplan, *Die Politischen Prozesse in der Tschechoslowakei 1948–1954*. Munich, Oldenbourg, 1986.

to a break with his allies. Take for example, the Warsaw uprising in August, 1944. The Soviets refused to aid the resistance; they did not even attack for two months after the resistance leaders had surrendered and been shot, thus effectively ending the problem of what to do with non-communist Polish leaders. The Allies also had not strongly protested against the Russian refusal to let them fly relief supplies to the Warsaw fighters, thereby ensuring their defeat and murder, according to Hugh Thomas in *The Beginning of the Cold War* (1987).

The question of wartime and postwar assistance to the USSR has occasioned controversy among historians. According to many of its critics, the US mistakenly used economic aid as an instrument for bringing pressure on the Soviet Union. Alternatively, the US has been indicted for failing to give assistance to the Soviet Union in its postwar reconstruction, thereby missing an opportunity for improving US–Soviet relations. George C. Herring, in his standard book on the subject, however, finds no evidence for either contention. US wartime aid served for both the Roosevelt and the Truman administrations primarily as a means of war, and only secondarily – if at all – as an instrument for promoting postwar objectives. The US may or may not have erred in cutting off Lend Lease aid as soon as it did. But policy regarding Lend Lease was not mainly determined by Cold War considerations but by pressure from Congress. Lend Lease was also terminated for Great Britain, the most loyal of US Allies. Indeed, the British received Lend Lease on terms far more restrictive than those extended to the Soviet Union. (The British were required by an agreement signed in 1942 to reduce their trade barriers and to eliminate customs discrimination after the war. No corresponding conditions were imposed on the Soviet Union.)[55]

> *Speaker of the House John McCormack had opposed Lend Lease – he claimed it was a bill to save Catholicism.*

Lend Lease in fact constituted the greatest voluntary transfer of resources effected in world history up to that time. (Under Lend Lease, the Soviets had received a total of $2.6 billion in nonmilitary goods, as well as $8.5 billion in military hardware, and including $1.25 billion of the latest American industrial equipment.[56] Expressed in comparative terms, the total amount of aid given by the US to the Soviet Union under Lend Lease amounted to about three times the value of all US exports to the world at large (worth $4.021 billion in 1940). Conceivably, of course, the continuation of Lend Lease after the victory over Japan, the provision of transitional assistance and a postwar loan might have improved Soviet–US relations. But, as Herring puts it, "it is naive to assume that postwar American generosity would have provoked deep

---

[55]A. J. P. Taylor, *English History, 1914–1945*. Oxford, Oxford University Press, 1965, p. 533.
[56]Carl Gershman, "Selling them the rope," *Commentary*, v. 67, no. 4, April 1979, p. 38.

gratitude and good will in the Soviet Union."[57] If aid given in wartime had not cemented Soviet–American relations, why should peacetime assistance have been more effective? The Soviets certainly did not think so, for they later refused to let their Eastern European satellites accept Marshall aid after the end of the war. Neither would relations have improved by enhanced trade between East and West. (In 1946, for instance, the British agreed to supply the Soviet Union with advanced jet engines, and to promote their production under licence. The resultant benefits to the Soviet aeronautical industry were enormous. But there was no reciprocal gratitude on Moscow's part.)

Revisionists have also used the US decision to drop atomic bombs on Japan as part of their case against America's conduct of the Cold War.[58] In their view, Japan had already been reduced to desperation before Hiroshima and Nagasaki were destroyed, and Truman was more concerned to intimidate the Soviet Union than to defeat Japan, by using nuclear weapons. It is true that Japan was at that time in fact seeking Soviet mediation to get out of the war on favorable terms. But the Japanese leaders were in no mood for unconditional surrender. It was only after the assault on Hiroshima (on August 6, 1945) and Nagasaki (on August 9) that Japan announced its willingness to capitulate. Even afterwards, the out-and-out militarists still attempted to continue the struggle – fortunately in vain.[59]

It may be true – as physicist Edward Teller later suggested – that the US used the atomic bomb in a mistaken manner; in his opinion the US should have organized a nuclear explosion at 30,000 feet over Tokyo Bay, thereby staging a terrible demonstration visible to millions of Japanese.[60] But whatever the case, the nuclear bomb did shorten the war. Without its use, US troops would have had to land in Japan. No military analyst can now be certain of the number of both American and Japanese soldiers who would have perished in the ensuing struggle. Given the performance of the Japanese army hitherto, especially on Iwo Jima and Okinawa, the fighting would have been fierce and bloody, every step of the way. Americans (and also British soldiers) at the time can hardly be blamed for universally welcoming the decision to use nuclear weapons against the island empire, which would shorten their own casualty list. It is certainly inappropriate for an academic writing in the safety of his study to style the American decision a "blunder," on the grounds that –

[57]George Herring, *Aid to Russia, 1941–1946. Strategy, Diplomacy: The Origins of the Cold War,* New York, Columbia University Press, 1973, pp. 292–3.

[58]For details, see Robert C. Butow, *Japan's Decision to Surrender.* Stanford, Cal., Stanford University Press, 1954. For the revisionist interpretation, see Gar Alperovitz, *Atomic Diplomacy: Hiroshima and Potsdam; the Use of the Atomic Bomb and the American Confrontation with Soviet Power.* New York, Penguin Books, 1985. By contrast, the book by Gaddis Smith, *American Diplomacy During the Second World War, 1941–1945.* New York, Knopf, 1985, considers that the atomic bomb would have been used even had US–Soviet relations been unclouded.

[59]Rufus E. Miles, Jr, "Hiroshima: the strange myth of half a million American lives saved," *International Security,* v. 10, no. 2, Fall, 1985, pp. 121–40.

[60]See also letters by Edward Teller in *Policy Review,* no. 34, Fall 1985, p. 7, and Robert H. Wheatley in the *Times Literary Supplement,* September 1965, p. 975, the latter regarding the Japanese casualties argument.

while the use of nuclear weapons undoubtedly saved American lives – the employment of atom bombs may have failed to prevent more Japanese casualties.

An alternative explanation, put forward by Rufus E. Miles, suggests that Truman dropped the nuclear bombs partly in order to keep the Soviet Union from occupying Japan.[61] Given the nature of Soviet governance in South Sakhalin and the Kurile Islands, conceded to the Soviets under the terms of the Yalta agreement, guarding Japan from the Soviets would indeed have been a legitimate object. (The Soviets expelled 400,000 Japanese from southern Sakhalin.) But with the enormous superiority of US seapower, no nuclear threats were needed at the time to keep the Japanese islands in their preserve.

The Truman Administration might of course have accepted something less than Japan's unconditional surrender. Considering, however, the experience of Germany after World War I, and the rise of the disastrous "stab-in-the-back" legend in that country thereafter, prospects for a permanent peace between the US and the Japanese warlords hardly seem to have been favorable. But assuming that a compromise peace would have been concluded and would have endured, the revisionists would merely have shifted their ground. They would then surely have complained of collusion between US monopoly capitalists and Japanese militarists, of betrayal, and of anti-Soviet encirclement. Such considerations must of course remain speculative. What are not speculative are the results of US policy. The speedy surrender of Japan was followed by what was the most constructive military occupation in history – and all the more admirable considering the vilification of the US by imperial Japanese propaganda, and the horrors endured by US (and other Allied) prisoners in Japanese camps and by civilians wherever Japan conquered. The country's economy was quickly rebuilt with US help, and soon it experienced a beneficent political and social revolution and a growth in prosperity unimaginable at the time. Comparing the options that seemed available, America's "first use" of nuclear weapons still appears to us the best of several bad alternatives.

Neither are we impressed by the argument that the US promoted Soviet suspicions by failing to communicate to the Soviet Union details concerning US nuclear weapons' development. The Soviets themselves were immensely secretive concerning their research, including their own work on nuclear arms. Stalin himself did not reproach the US for its policy of secrecy – one of the few charges that the Soviet leader did *not* make, perhaps because Moscow was well informed through its own espionage network in the West. We ourselves are impressed rather by the moderation of US diplomacy during the immediate postwar years, when the Western powers held a nuclear monopoly.[62]

---

[61]Rufus E. Miles, Jr, ibid.

[62]According to Professor P. M. S. Blackett, reported estimates of the cumulative stocks of bombs by January each year stood as follows: 1946, US: 40; UK: 0; USSR: 0. 1949, US: 280; UK: 40; USSR: 0. 1951, US: 400; UK: 120; USSR: 0. 1952, US: 520; UK: 160; USSR: 40.

> *Hugh Thomas has put it best in his monumental volume* The Beginning of the Cold
> War, 1945–46: *"There is no sign that Stalin wanted to remain on friendly terms with
> the Western allies in peace as he had done in war; or indeed could have done, given his
> loyalties, career and personality … Stalin and communism needed an enemy; Capitalism
> had to be 'menacing,' imperialism had to be 'on the march'; a 'Cold War' was in short
> not so much inevitable as essential."*

In conclusion, we therefore feel justified in rejecting the revisionist case in
its entirety. Our confidence springs in part from the intellectual reassessment
that has begun within the Soviet Union itself since Mikhail Gorbachev's
accession to power. Soviet scholars such as Alla Latynina now say openly what
used to be said only behind locked doors or in *samizdat*.[63] Stalin was a
monstrous despot, guilty of genocide, one of many communist tyrants steeped
in "social utopianism." Soviet policy abroad was based on appeals for class
struggles, class hatred, and Soviet "hegemony." (In private, visiting Soviet
academicians in the US go even further – as one senior scholar put it to us off
the record "communism was worse than the Tartar yoke.")

The Cold War, as we see it, did not start when Winston Churchill, in his
much quoted speech at Fulton, Missouri, in 1946 deplored the manner in
which an "iron curtain" had "descended across the Continent."[64] Neither did
the Cold War begin with President Truman's call for the Marshall Plan
to restore Europe. The Cold War was inherent in Soviet ideology, in the
Sovietization of Eastern Europe, and in Soviet activities concerned with
supporting and dominating communist parties around the world. Far from
sharing the responsibility for the Cold War the US tried desperately to avoid
it. If the US had truly wished to stop the Soviet advance in Europe, it would
have kept land it had occupied in East Germany and also seized Berlin and
Prague and large areas of Central Europe. In May of 1945, the US Army in
Central Europe numbered 3,500,000; by March 1946 only 400,000 troops
remained, and even after the Truman Doctrine and the policy of containment
were in place, troop strength in Europe was reduced even further until it
numbered 81,000 in 1950 – hardly the kind of force an aggressive, anti-
communist power would have deployed. As we see it, the Cold War was
indeed made in Moscow. Henceforth – as "Vercors" (Jean Bruller, a French
resistance fighter) put it, Europe passed into "a strange era … [when] we
[were] neither at war nor at peace."[65]

---

[63] John B. Dunlop, "Alla Latynina: a self-proclaimed centrist …," *Report on the USSR*, Munich,
23 June 1989, pp. 26–9.

[64] Winston S. Churchill, *Memoirs of the Second World War*. New York, Bonanza Books, 1959,
pp. 996–9.

[65] Cited in James D. Wilkinson, *The Intellectual Resistance in Europe*. Cambridge, Mass., Harvard
University Press, 1981, p. 79.

Winston Churchill said in his famous speech in Fulton, Missouri, March 5, 1946:

"From Stettin on the Baltic to Trieste on the Adriatic, an iron curtain has descended across the continent. Behind that line lie all the capitals of the ancient states of central and eastern Europe – Warsaw, Berlin, Prague, Vienna, Budapest, Belgrade, Bucharest and Sofia ... From what I have seen of our Russian friends and allies during the war I am convinced that there is nothing they admire so much as strength, and nothing for which they have less respect than military weakness."

Churchill was seriously criticized at the time for stating the obvious. Had he not advocated intervention against the Soviets as early as 1918? Was he not inconsistent in praising the Soviets during World War II and condemning them after? Why should Churchill, an ardent imperialist unwilling, in his own words, to preside over the liquidation of the British empire, blame Stalin for acting as he did? The Boston Globe, *the* Chicago Sun *and the* Washington Post *condemned the speech. Republicans like Senator Taft opposed the alliance, or, like the young Richard Nixon, thought Churchill might have gone too far. But as Paul Johnson, the British historian, has pointed out, Churchill's speech came at exactly the right time. By May, US polls showed that 83 percent of the US favored his idea of a permanent military alliance, as against a withdrawal into isolationism. The communist takeover in Prague, the Berlin blockade in 1948, and the excommunication of Tito by Moscow thereafter further justified Churchill's fears.*

George Kennan's "Long Telegram" written from the US Embassy in Moscow in early 1946 outlined the prospects for Soviet foreign policy in the postwar period. Later, Kennan prepared a paper for Secretary of the Navy James Forrestal in December of 1946. This became the basis for the *Foreign Affairs* article under the pseudonym "X" in July 1947, which brilliantly set forth the American policy of containment. Previous events had made such a policy necessary. Kennan's July article provided a cogent rationale for the Truman Doctrine, the Marshall Plan and the policy of containment. In spite of Soviet behavior and threats the US had not rearmed or attempted to project its power other than by building bases around the Soviet Union, and that really happened more under Eisenhower than Truman after the Cold War became formalized. It took the Korean War planned by Stalin, Mao Tse-tung, and Kim Il Sung for the US to rearm. Between 1945 and 1950 the US had disarmed even in the face of Soviet military might and its aggressive behavior.

Later, Kennan came to oppose the worldwide military containment of the Soviets, saying he only wanted to limit their ideological-political threat. Yet his 1947 article in *Foreign Affairs* rightly showed the Soviets as a militarized system, threatening a weakened, dazed Western Europe overrun with refugees and vulnerable to disruption by well-organized communist parties. Kennan was under no illusion about Stalin and his gang of thugs ruling the Kremlin – he called them sinister, cruel, devious and cynical, full of contempt for the US. (Unfortunately, liberals in Washington, D.C. and the military in West Germany had to learn from experience about the Soviets.)

Soviet contempt for the US was especially galling, given the vast amount of aid the US had sent to them during the war and the extensive concessions made to Stalin, trying to win his confidence and good will. Neither Roosevelt's charm and concessions, nor Churchill's realpolitik succeeded in winning over

Stalin. Containment became necessary. Kennan therefore approved of US efforts to stabilize Western Europe and to stop "any more unnecessary con cessions to these people." From the American perspective, the Cold War had just begun.

Although Kennan was the author of the policy of containment and a major drafter of the Marshall Plan, he took to warning Washington against seeing containment primarily in military terms and as a global effort to thwart communism everywhere, rather than a means of protecting vital American interests and treaty obligations to Europe and Japan, and to Latin America through the Monroe Doctrine. Kennan did not want America to waste its resources in doing what he felt it could not do – save the world from communism.

COUNTRY PROFILES

The US and Canada

"America stands at this moment at the summit of the world," said Winston Churchill in 1945. After a brief effort to pull out of Europe during 1945 to 1946, the US indeed became the most internationalist of all major powers, and the global leader of a democratic alliance. The Americans lavishly spread their resources throughout the world, altruism and self-interest playing about equal roles in this "consensual hegemony." The Americans determined to save the world from hunger, poverty, illiteracy, disease, trade restrictions, monopolies, and communism. They extolled with fervor the benefits of democracy and productivity alike. They played a vital part in the recovery of Italy, Germany, and Japan, their erstwhile enemies. American popular culture spread through-out the world; American science and technology assumed a dominant role. The US, somewhat reluctantly, became a superpower, and returned to Europe to help in rebuilding and defending the countries from which most Americans were descended.

The US in 1945 was rich and powerful; the bulk of its people were well-fed and ready to spend their savings on cars, refrigerators, and houses. While war had cut back Europe's productive capacity, it had stimulated America's. Billions of bushels of wheat harvested in 1944 and 1945 allowed US farmers to feed both their allies and former enemies, and their fellow Americans as well. Industrial production expanded further, but factories henceforth turned out automobiles instead of tanks, houses instead of landing craft. Corporate profits stood at their highest at the end of the war, and workers had twice as much money to spend as they had had in 1940. Trade unions increased their membership from 8.7 million in 1940 to 14.3 million in 1945. The US had the highest growth rate of output per employee, the highest average income per person (in 1949, in US dollars, incomes stood at 320 for West Germany, 482 for France, 773 for Great Britain, 1,453 for the US), and the highest growth rate of the gross national product as a whole (1.6 percent for Great Britain, 1.9 percent for West Germany, 2.9 percent for the US, for the period 1929 to

1950).[66] Overall, the US had become a giant on the world scene, a country both hated and envied by the Soviet Union's rulers. Between 1935 and 1945, the gross national product of the United States had doubled (in 1929 prices, from 91.4 billion dollars to 180.9 billion dollars); in terms of total output, per capita incomes had risen from 718 dollars to 1,293 dollars during the same decade. The United States led the world in the production of basic commodities such as iron ore, pig iron, crude steel, and hard coal, and in the output of electricity. Western Europe as a whole, ranked a poor second. The Soviet Union – ravaged by war and many years of domestic terror – could only claim superpower status by courtesy, in so far as economic output in many key commodities was concerned (see table 2.1).

TABLE 2.1   *Production of key primary products: 1946*

Iron ore (*million tons*)		Crude steel (*million tons*)	
World	154.8	World	111.5
US	72.0	US	60.4
USSR	22.4	USSR	13.3
W. Europe	43.2	W. Europe	27.4
Pig iron (*million tons*)		Hard coal (*1,000 tons*)	
World	78.7	World	1,166,700
US	41.9	US	571,417
USSR	10.2	USSR	108,000
W. Europe	19.3	W. Europe	291,706

Source: J. Frederick Dewhurst, John O. Coppock, P. Lamartine Yates, *Europe's Needs and Resources: Trends and Prospects in Eighteen Countries*. New York, Twentieth Century Fund, 1961, appendices, *passim*.

The US also led in most other economic fields. For example, it dominated the world's communications industry in terms of privately owned radios, telephones, television sets, and similar devices. The productivity of its workers exceeded the productivity of workers abroad in almost every industry. (To give just one example, American miners in 1948 turned out 5.9 tonnes of coal per man shift, as compared to 1.5 in the United Kingdom, and 1.3 in the Ruhr region of Western Germany.)[67] Americans' private savings between 1935 and 1945 had quintupled (from 8.37 billion dollars in current prices to 44.25 billion dollars in 1945).[68] America had pioneered the art of mass production, the

[66]Stanley Rothman, *European Society and Politics*. New York, Bobb-Merrill Co., 1970, pp. 167, 137, 78.

[67]Norman Luxenburg, *Europe Since World War II: The Big Change*. Carbondale, Southern Illinois University Press, 1979, p. 132.

[68]US Department of Commerce, *Historical Statistics of the United States: Colonial Times to 1957*. Washington DC, US Government Printing Office 1947, p. 153.

utilization of the conveyor belt, the standardization of industrial products, department stores, credit sales, and the art of conveniently packaging an enormous number of consumer products. Americans took out more patents than anyone else, and subsequently enriched Europe's technology by massive technological transfers, (including the transfer of patents). American farmers produced more crops per acre than almost any other country. Americans were, and remained, by far the world's richest and most generous people, donating more for good causes than the rest of the world put together.

The people of America, at this time, had also come to own more cars than the rest of the world put together. The automobile seemed a symbol of American civilization. Hitler had promised the Germans a "people's car," and boosted his reputation by building *Autobahnen* (freeways). But the American highway system came to dwarf Europe's. (The system was extended through the construction of interstate highways, begun in 1956.) Freeways added enormously to the mobility that had always distinguished life in America, and gave a boost to the trucking industry, with its own life style, its own camaraderie, even its own vocabulary. Freeways expanded existing service industries – including chains of motels and diners where travelers could find meals and lodging to agreeable, predictable, standards. The automobile became the conveyance of the common people in the US long before it did in Europe. The tractor and the automobile revolutionized America's way of life, at a time when the horse still dominated farming in every European country bar Great Britain, and when European travelers as yet relied mainly on the tram and the railway train. Cars provided a new sense of independence for all: young lovers, job-seekers making for the West, farmers in the backwoods, criminals, urban commuters, people intent on buying a house and yard of their own. The automobile helped speed urbanization and migration and altered the shape of neighborhoods, cities, and indeed conventional concepts of geographical distance.

Intellectuals might despise the American car culture – complete with freeways, "diners" and drive-ins along the road, junk yards, and bill boards on the horizon. But ordinary people all the world over did not. When John Ford's film *The Grapes of Wrath,* based on John Steinbeck's novel of impoverished migrant laborers, was shown in the Soviet Union, the authorities discovered to their dismay that Russian viewers were impressed by a country where even some of the most abject of poor people wore shoes and owned cars.[69] American wage levels indeed generally exceeded their competitors; hence American workers could buy cars and houses at a higher rate than any others in the world. Achievements of industrial development that later appeared commonplace still had the power to amaze even a critical foreign traveler such as Ernest Bevin who had visited the US before World War II.[70] The US continued to be a haven for immigrants from the Old World.

[69]Kenneth T. Jackson, *Crabgrass Frontier: The Suburbanization of the United States.* Oxford, Oxford University Press, 1985, p. 188.
[70]Alan Bullock, *The Life and Times of Ernest Bevin.* London, Heinemann, 1960, v. 1, p. 357.

Wartime production did more than end unemployment; it brought over 6.5 million women into the work place, and most did not want to return to the home when it ended. During the war over 8 million women participated in a labor force of 18.5 million, whereas up to 1940 only one in five women had worked. Many, though not all, continued in employment after the war, as paid labor became an accepted part of middle-class life, and as better wages and opportunities continued to attract women to the workplace. (By 1952 over 10.4 million held jobs and by 1985 three women in five worked outside the home, a revolutionary social development which affected marriage, the birthrate, child rearing, and relations between the sexes.)

War weakened existing occupational restraints on all minorities. As qualified labor became scarce, black workmen increasingly gained advancement into skilled positions. Higher up on the technological level, Jews found jobs as engineers or industrial chemists in firms that had hitherto employed only Gentiles. War also accelerated wider occupational shifts; the number of white collar workers increased by 20 percent, manual and service employees by 7 percent; white farm laborers declined in number from 9 million to 7 million. These trends continued as employees in the service industries and white collar workers grew in number more than any other group, while the number of farm workers declined. The figures for women in employment continued to rise for the next 40 years (mostly because more married women worked than hitherto).

The northwestern states and the Great Lakes area remained the most populated areas; but the war also brought prosperity and an influx of population to many parts of the West and South West; thereby accelerating a long-term shift into what later became known as the "Sun Belt." The South experienced heavy emigration, as black and white Southerners left the country for the big cities. At the same time, the South underwent industrial expansion and agricultural modernization, in part through numerous defense contracts. The Californian economy, to give another example, grew in striking fashion, as commercial agriculture prospered, and as manufacturing industries obtained a boost through burgeoning war demands. Before World War II the West had played a subordinate role, dependent to a considerable extent on Eastern money, and occupied mainly in the production of raw materials. World War II accelerated economic diversification, and raised the West to a dominant position within the US national economy. This transformation went with a massive population shift toward the West.[71] (Between 1930 and 1950, the Californian population nearly doubled, from 4,408,260 to 9,915,173, a shift of resources that no European country could remotely match.) The Federal Government enormously helped this process through defense contracts, and the Defense Plant Corporation (DPC), the greatest investing and producing agency in history. The DPC increased manufacturing in the West by some 250 percent. It also helped to create the industrial base – aluminum, aviation,

[71]Gerald D. Nash, *The American West Transformed: The Impact of the Second World War*. Bloomington, University of Indiana Press, 1985, p. 23.

electronics, shipbuilding, steel – that promoted the postwar boom. The West became the most rapidly growing area in the country; California's economy turned into the largest, weathiest, the most diversified, and productive in the US. At the same time, talented newcomers (many of them Jewish refugees from Europe) transformed southern California's cultural and scientific life, and broke down western provincialism. After 1945, California became a major cultural center, even though few easterners would recognize the shift.

Overall, the war hastened urbanization and the application of new techniques in many fields. Especially in the US, health care improved dramatically during the war; life expectancy increased from 62.9 years in 1940 to 69.5 in 1945, and continued to grow thereafter.[72] America also grew in demographic terms. Its people were replenished both by immigration and a high natural growth rate. (In 1945, the annual birthrate per thousand of population stood at 20.4 and thereafter rose to 25.0 in 1955.) The population increased from 131.6 million in 1940 to 139.9 in 1945, and 159.6 million in 1953. As the veterans returned and started families, the "baby boom" got under way. A youthful country spent money on baby buggies and playpens, on schools and medical care. The divorce rate remained low, and actually dropped after the war ended (from 3.5 per thousand in 1945 to 2.3 in 1955). Illegitimacy rates too, remained low for whites and blacks alike. "Motherhood and apple pie" commanded universal respect, instead of becoming – as they did in the following generation – the subject of gibes by *littérateurs* and entertainers.

America, without a doubt, continued to face an immense array of social problems. Racial and religious discrimination remained rife. Crime was widespread in a way that shocked European newcomers. The continuing migration of poverty-stricken rural folk (including over 700,000 black southerners, and hundreds of thousands of white Appalachians) into the industrial cities of the North produced new social tensions. Their extent, however, should not be overestimated. Ethnic hostility did not threaten to rend the social fabric, as it did in countries such as Cyprus, the Lebanon, and Northern Ireland. Crime, to give another example, was nothing like as pervasive as it became a generation later. Big city parks for instance, had not as yet turned into "no-go" areas for peaceful citizens at night, and even in Harlem, men and women could sleep in the streets on a hot summer's night without being robbed or raped.

The US likewise had become the world's leading power in terms of industrial and scientific innovation (as reflected for instance in the number of Nobel Prizes awarded to its native-born and naturalized citizens). Crude numbers of course can serve only for illustrative purposes, given the international

[72]For a description of the US in 1945 see Donald R. McCoy, *The Presidency of Harry S. Truman.* Lawrence, Kansas, University Press of Kansas, 1984, pp. 8–13. Popular works include: William Manchester, *The Glory and the Dream: A Narrative History of America 1932–1972,* New York, Bantam Books, 1975. William L. O'Neill, *American High: The Years of Confidence 1945–1960.* New York, Free Press, 1986. Godfrey Hodgson, *America In Our Time.* New York, Vintage Books, 1976. William H. Chafe, *The Unfinished Journey: America Since World War II.* Oxford, Oxford University Press, 1986. Michael Barone, *Our Country: The shaping of America from Roosevelt to Reagan.* New York, Free Press, 1990.

connections of science, and the difficulty of comparing achievements in different fields. But numbers do indicate general trends. Between 1901 and 1932, just before Hitler's coming to power, Germany had enjoyed a decisive lead in Nobel prizes. In physics, chemistry, physiology, and medicine (fields in which awards occasioned much less controversy than for literature or "peace"), Germany easily came first, with 29 prizes (about a quarter of which had gone to Germans wholly or partly of Jewish descent). Great Britain came second (17 prizes), France third (12 prizes), and the US fourth (9 prizes). During the next three decades, the balance of power in the sciences swung decisively toward the New World; this shift was accelerated, but not caused by, the trans-Atlantic migration of European scholars. Between 1933 and 1963, the US won 61 prizes, attaining a lead much greater even than Germany's during its golden age of science; Great Britain continued to occupy an impressive second position (32 prizes). Germany had fallen to third place with 17 prizes, and France secured no more than 2 prizes.[73]

American scientific and industrial leadership went with an astonishing confidence in the real or assumed abilities of the academically qualified expert to improve the world, or to predict the future through a variety of techniques drawn from technology, economics, and the social sciences. There was no sense of cynicism when statesmen vowed in the Atlantic Charter, issued by Churchill and Roosevelt in 1941 to ensure for mankind freedom from want and freedom from fear – freedoms that earlier generations might have left to the Second Coming of Christ.

> *The Declaration of the United Nations was signed on January 1, 1942 in Washington D.C. Twenty-six nations agreed to abide by the Atlantic Charter and resist the Axis powers – there was to be no separate peace. This declaration brought unity in war and built the foundation for the United Nations organization. It also ended the American tradition of nonentanglement with any form of military alliance. Isolationism was defeated, and the US was bound to Britain and Western Europe, at least until the war was over.*

Social scientists predicted none of the radical changes of the postwar world, and many of their explanations or predictions proved wrong. No one predicted the baby boom or the greatest economic growth in global history. Many of the liberal-left not only did not predict the economic revival; they argued that it had not happened.

The American historical perspective changed the most, and the US saw itself as playing the major role in world history. It assigned to itself the political, economic, moral, and military responsibility of reviving the world economy and of turning back world communism and preventing its further expansion. There was no isolationism in those years.

[73]For a full listing, see *Encyclopaedia Britannica*. Chicago, Encyclopaedia Britannica, 1968 edn, v. 16, pp. 545–51.

> *Secretaries of State were seldom popular in the postwar era. Dean Acheson recalled that one time when he got into a cab, the driver said "Aren't you Dean Acheson?" The Secretary of State replied "Yes I am, do you want me to get out?"*

American politics of the period had ceased to be parochial, and instead profoundly affected the world at large. US politics of that time conjure up in retrospect the overused term "establishment." This supposedly consisted of an inner ring of East Coasters: bankers with names like Harriman and Rockefeller; victorious generals such as Marshall and Eisenhower; senior State Department officials; corporation presidents; heads and trustees of great universities and foundations. All were allegedly educated at places such as Groton and Choate, Yale and Harvard and Princeton, or perhaps West Point. They supposedly shared membership in the same clubs; their ancestors had all come from northwestern Europe; their surnames never ended in a vowel. Patrician in manner, they spoke with similar accents. They were Anglophiles, internationalists, subjects to the same social prejudices, and Episcopalians to boot. They might be praised as "wise men" or censured as members of a selfish cabal. But, for better or for worse, they held the strings of real power. (It was "wise men" such as Acheson, Bohlen, Harriman, Kennan, Lovett, and McCloy who saved Europe and contained the Soviets.)[74]

The stereotype only holds a modicum of truth. Political and social influence in the US was more widely distributed than the legend suggests. The tyranny of accents did not prevail in the US to the same extent as in Britain. (General Eisenhower, for instance, spoke to his dying day with the flat accent of his native Kansas.) During and after World War II, moreover, the social basis of the "power elite" expanded. (For example, the Foreign Service Act of 1947 extended the social and geographical reservoir of recruitment to the State Department.) The US elites moreover were far from unanmous in political orientation. Power swayed to and fro; America's course was far from certain. All the same, the elections of 1944 had formed a watershed in American history. Had the Republicans won in 1944, the drift toward state intervention would have slowed, though not ended. Thomas Dewey, the Republican candidate in 1944, opposed Roosevelt's domestic, rather than his foreign, policy. Dewey, a well-informed critic of the "New Deal," made much of its failings. In his electoral campaign, Dewey thus promised to labor great freedom of bargaining, he criticized the existing machinery of economic control; he condemned the real or supposed inefficiencies of government agencies with their profuse acronyms, wasteful government expenditure, what Dewey

---

[74]For biographical details on major "establishment" figures, see for instance Walter Isaacson and Evan Thomas, *The Wise Men: Six Friends and the World They Made: Acheson, Bohlen, Harriman, Kennan, Lovett, McCloy*. New York, Simon and Schuster, 1986. Forrest C. Pogue, *George C. Marshall. Statesman: 1945–1959*. New York, Viking, 1987. Stephen E. Ambrose, *Eisenhower: The President*. New York, Simon and Schuster, 1984. David Eisenhower, *Eisenhower*. New York, Random House, 1986. For a more general interpretation, see, for example, Arthur M. Schlesinger Jr, *The Cycles of American History*. Boston, Houghton, Mifflin Co., 1986.

described as the untoward influence of communists and the domination of corrupt big city machines.[75]

Dewey's cause was far from hopeless. Whilst Roosevelt in the 1944 elections gained an overwhelming majority of the electoral votes, Dewey obtained some 22,000,000 popular votes, as against Roosevelt's 25,500,000. The Republicans enjoyed much support both on Wall Street and Main Street. The Republicans, however, were divided. They also lacked intellectual defenders of their cause. Not that conservatives went unrepresented in US academia, which boasted of names such as Leo Strauss and John Lucacs (the former a philosopher, the latter a historian). But overall, conservative writers were few and far between. "Those who are well trained are often pedantic. Those who are exciting are often uninformed ... Some are barely literate." As Richard Whalen, a life-long conservative put it with some exaggeration, "real conservatives do not write."[76] Roosevelt, by contrast, had the backing of most intellectuals, and of the liberals. Roosevelt also had the backing of the communists who, for a time, attacked in the columns of *Pravda* and the American *Daily Worker* "irresponsible" elements among their liberal allies, while courting Wall Street and the National Association of Manufacturers. The communists' pro-Roosevelt stand seemed so strident that Dewey's predecessor, Wendell Willkie, had privately regarded himself as opposing in Roosevelt "the favourite candidate of both the Kremlin and Number 10 Downing Street."[77]

But Roosevelt once more prevailed. Not only could he rely on the mass of industrial workers and the bulk of Polish, Italian, Irish, Mexican, and other ethnic voters, from Europe, and Latin America, but also the Jews, blacks, and the South – a coalition which would hold until 1968. The majority of these people felt themselves at a disadvantage owing to real or perceived economic, ethnic, or racial grievances. Such people looked askance at Dewey, overly dapper, too much the "man on the wedding cake," too much the representative of Country Club America. Roosevelt, by contrast, commanded a personal loyalty that no Republican leader could rival. As a Yiddish pun put it, there were three worlds, *diese velt, jene velt, un 'Roosevelt* (this world, the other world, and Roosevelt). Not even the most faithful Republican farmer, tradesman, business executive, would ever have spoken in similar terms of Dewey. Overall, "it was the vote of the great cities, the great industrial areas, the less privileged classes that, for the fourth time, chose Franklin D. Roosevelt. It was a victory for a great national leader, but it was a class victory too."[78]

The presidential election of 1944 entailed another major decision. The election set strict limits to the leftward drift of the US politics. Henry A. Wallace, Roosevelt's Secretary of Agriculture between 1933 and 1940, had

[75]"Mr Dewey's Campaign," Keesing's Contemporary Archives, 24 February to 3 March 1945, p. 7031. London, 1945.

[76]Ralph E. Ellsworth and Sarah M. Harris, *The American Right Wing: A Report to the Fund for the Republic*. Washington DC, Public Affairs Press, 1962, p. 8.

[77]Lord Halifax, "Political Review for the First Quarter of 1944," in Hachey, pp. 168–9.

[78]Denis W. Brogan, *The Era of Franklin D. Roosevelt: A Chronicle of the New Deal and Global War*. New Haven, Yale University Press, 1950, p. 354.

played a major part in shaping the "New Deal." In 1944, however, Wallace was passed over as vice-presidential candidate in favor of Harry S. Truman, a momentous shift. Had Wallace been chosen in Truman's stead, Wallace would have assumed the presidency on Roosevelt's death in 1945. No one of course can be sure how Wallace would have acted, had he been required to confront Stalin in a presidential capacity. Strict, straitlaced, honest, Wallace might have reacted at Potsdam in a manner similar to Truman, a man as yet unschooled in foreign affairs but quick to learn. But given Wallace's subsequent opinions, he might well have responded to Soviet pressure by further concessions, disguised as acts of statesmanship. As it was, Wallace served as Truman's Secretary of Commerce for a time, but disagreed with his chief's "get-tough" policy toward Moscow. Wallace instead insisted that the Soviet Union had as much cause to fear the US as the US had reason to dread the Soviet Union. The US, Wallace declared, should prepare "even at the expense of risking epithets of appeasement, to agree to reasonable Russian guarantees of security."[79]

Wallace left Truman's cabinet in 1946. He subsequently became the new Progressive Party's candidate for the presidency, emphasizing closer cooperation with the USSR, and a new commitment to civil rights, arms reduction, and UN administration of all foreign aid – the standard program thereafter of the moderate left in US politics. Wallace's "Third Party" was a harbinger of things to come, a prototype, in some respects, of the "Green" parties that came into being in Western Europe a generation later. Wallace was also the candidate of the pacifists, the "One Worlders," the self-styled progressives. His party, like the Greens of the later generation, lacked a mass base among the industrial workers and farmers, but instead appealed mainly to the well-educated, to artists, teachers, professors, to many members of the diploma-bearing salariat that manned the growing public sector and had a vested interest in its expansion.

The Democrats' choice of Truman for its vice-presidential candidate, by contrast, turned out to be an unanticipated defeat for the pro-Soviet Left, who, for many years thereafter, became politically marginalized. Truman, trim and bespectacled, of average height, had no college education and little wealth, but possessed many personal qualities of vitality, strength of character, loyalty to his friends, decisiveness, a passion for orderly procedure, and an understanding of how to get his way.[80] He was also a man of considerable culture, with a thorough grounding in the classics, music, and history, qualities unappreciated by those who snobbishly disdained him as an ex-haberdasher. Truman – like Bevin in Great Britain – quickly acquired an understanding of Soviet realities. The decision to elevate Truman to the vice-presidential candidacy thus constituted a major event, one that helped to shape the fate of a generation.

---

[79]McCoy, *The Presidency of Harry S. Truman,* p. 86.

[80]For an excellent appreciation, see for instance Dean Acheson, *Present at the Creation: My Years in the State Department.* New York, W. W. Norton, 1969.

> *Roosevelt in 1944 informed the State Department that the US should not bear the expenses of reconstructing Europe but should leave it to the British.*

Americans after 1945 wanted security and prosperity. But the war-born spirit of internationalism almost failed to survive the first years of peace.[81] On the contrary, isolationism revived between 1944 and 1945. Congress inclined toward a "fortress America" mentality, toward stinginess regarding the US Allies, and toward a resolve to ensure US economic predominance in the postwar world. Relief for Europe was acceptable as a stopgap; but there was little commitment toward the long-term European reconstruction – much less the development of the Third World. Neither was the US willing to cede any part of its sovereignty to the newly formed United Nations. US military power, nuclear weapons, and advanced technology were not to be shared with the Allies – much less with neutral countries, or potential enemies. The long-existing fear of once again playing "Uncle Sucker" drove Congress to pressure an unsure President Truman to end Lend Lease in August 1945, and to do so suddenly and without consultation with US Allies. Britain had been promised at least one year of aid following the end of the war, and had also counted on Lend Lease to ease her adjustment in peacetime. Instead the British met with bitter disappointment.

> *American politicians had a keen memory of the unpaid war debts of World War I, so Roosevelt had to invent the term Lend Lease – an analogy is the lending to one's neighbor of a fire hose to save his burning house, but expecting the hose back when the fire is out. Nevertheless opposition to Lend Lease was fierce – "no blank check!" "Kill bill 1776" "Not our boys" – but the bill passed on November 11, 1941. It meant the end of neutrality and an unofficial declaration of war – eventually $50 billion was spent. It was a momentous act and helped to save Britain and the Soviet Union.*

The Americans were equally reluctant to continue the large-scale deployment of their military overseas. American servicemen wanted to go home, and never put on a uniform again. Between October 1945 and June 1946, 12,807,000 men and women were demobilized – this at a time when the Soviets continued to maintain a great army in Eastern Europe, and when the strength of the US nuclear deterrent, was widely overestimated. The United States had vaguely hoped that Britain would sustain the balance of power in Europe and the Middle East, while the United States would dominate the Pacific Basin. Instead, US sought to dominate the postwar world in a financial sense through the 1944 Bretton Wood Agreement which established the International Bank for Reconstruction and Development, and the International Monetary Fund. Congress, moreover, failed to recognize the precarious position of the Euro-

[81]See John Morton Blum, *V Was For Victory: Politics and American Culture During World War II*. New York, Harcourt Brace, 1976, *passim*.

pean economies, or the strength of the Soviet challenge. The US began to revert to isolationism.

> *The postwar era saw the partial Americanization of Europe through US military presence, the Marshall Plan, NATO and the push for the economic integration of Western Europe. American popular culture spread rapidly as did US consumerism, science and technology, business and production methods, and, above all, marketing technologies – distribution, marketing strategies, and advertising.*

The British, by contrast, wanted to continue the Anglo-American defense cooperation after the war in order to prevent Soviet domination of Europe. The Americans at first would have preferred to leave the responsibility of policing Europe to the British, while the US looked to the Pacific Rim and the western hemisphere. But events in 1946–7, added to British advice, convinced some American officials that the Soviet threat to British influence in the eastern Mediterranean (especially Greece) involved American security as well. The British initiative persuaded Truman and Marshall that the US had to keep a strong ground force in Western Europe and a commitment to the governments there. This commitment reversed the reliance on strategic bombing from advanced bases as America's main defense. Thus was reborn the Anglo-American Alliance, with the renewal of the wartime alliance and the beginning of NATO (founded 1949).[82]

In part, the US was linked to Western Europe through Canada, a country known to many Americans, but understood by few. English-speaking, as distinct from French-speaking, Canada was in many ways just like the US. Canadians talked with almost the same accent as Americans. They built the same freeways and the same skyscrapers; they inhabited a country physically larger and even more thinly populated than the US. Canada was one of the world's breadbaskets, but also had a substantial mining industry, great resources of oil, and massive manufacturing skills. Like the US, Canada was a country of immigrants – indeed its population grew in an even more startling fashion (between 1941 and 1961 the Canadian population rose from 11,506,655 to 18,238,247; the US population between 1940 and 1960 increased from 131,699,275 to 179,323,175). Both countries were parliamentary democracies; their economies were inextricably intertwined. There were massive US (as well as British) investments in Canada; tourists and permanent settlers crossed and recrossed an undefended and unguarded frontier without hindrance. Canadians and Americans watched the same movies and read the same comics. They played baseball instead of cricket, and when they spoke of football, they did not mean soccer. There was constant interchange between Canadian and US universities, colleges, orchestras, newspapers. Many distinguished Canadians made their mark in the US, no matter what their political orientation. (John Kenneth Galbraith, a spokesman for US liberalism, was an

[82]See Richard A. Best Jr, *Co-operation with Like-Minded Peoples: British Influence on American Security Policy, 1945–49.* Westport, Conn., Greenwood Press, 1985, *passim.*

economist of Canadian birth, as was W. Glenn Campbell, a conservative.)

But there were also striking differences. Divided into French-speaking Quebec and the English-speaking provinces, Canada was a bilingual state. In this respect, it resembled South Africa and Belgium. There was a further likeness to these countries in that the Franco-Canadians, like Flemings and Afrikaners at the time, were more often rural people than their Anglophone (or in the case of Belgium, Francophone) neighbors. Quebec people tended to be regular churchgoers with traditional values. Hence linguistic divisions went with cultural, as well as social and political divisions. (In Canada, however, this division may not have gone quite as deep as in Belgium. Canadians at least could look up important personages within their country in one single *Who's Who in Canada*. A Belgian would need to consult two separate reference books *Qui est qui en Belgique* and *Wie is wie in Vlaanderen*.) Canadians, lacking one accepted national pattern, were less inclined than Americans to look upon their own country as a melting pot. They were more restrictive in their attitude toward foreign immigrants. (For instance, only a handful of Jewish academic refugees from Europe gained admittance as teachers at Canadian universities; the overwhelming number of emigré Nobel Prize laureates went to US universities.)

> *For Canada, the US was the biggest foreign policy consideration. Canada was dominated politically, economically, and culturally by its neighbor, which had ten times as great a population and consumed 70 percent of Canadian exports. The US, on the other hand, tended to neglect if not ignore Canadian interests and views.*

Canadians differed from Americans in their attitude toward the state. British Canada had initially been created by British-American loyalists, those "good Americans" who had refused to accept the revolution. To Canadians, the Anglo–American War of 1812 had been a war of defense against the Yankees and their kind of democracy. French Canadians, Catholic to the core, had stood aloof from the French Revolution. Canadians prized the Commonwealth connection; they honored their Governor-General as the representative of the British Crown. They were more willing than Americans to accept state intervention as a desirable good rather than as a necessary (or perhaps unnecessary) evil. Canadians (especially the intellectuals) often displayed in their attitude toward the US, an ambivalent defensiveness, one that might remind a European of the Austrians' attitude toward Germany. Americans had their own culture – unselfconscious, unmistakable. The "St Louis Blues" were American; so was the splendid razzle-dazzle of an American football marching band. But what was Canadian? Canadian academics found the question as hard to answer, though they battled mightily for a reply.

Canada was divided by great regional differences, not merely between French-speaking Quebec and the rest, but also between the English-speaking eastern provinces and the West. Its people believed themselves to be more "laid back," more civic-minded, more willing to compromise, more law abiding, but also less pushing, less ambitious than Americans. Canadians also took pride – not without reason – in their country's ability to serve as a bridge-builder between North America on the one hand, Great Britain, the British Commonwealth, and Continental Europe on the other. Canada, of course, was a latecomer on the stage of global diplomacy; at the outbreak of World War II, she had few diplomatic representatives abroad. Inward-looking, her leading politicians were concerned above all to assert their country's independence from Britain, and separateness from the US.[83] Canadian diplomats did display considerable skill as mediators, and the "Canadian factor" played an important, though often unrecognized part in the stability of the Anglo-American Alliance of World War II, and later in the creation of NATO.

Great Britain

All around us the world is convulsed by the agonies of great nations. Governments ... have been of a sudden shaken and overthrown. The proudest capitals of Western Europe have streamed with civil blood. All evil passions, the thirst of gain and the thirst of vengeance, the antipathy of class to class, the antipathy of race to race, have broken loose from the control of divine and human law. Fear and anxiety have clouded the faces and depressed the hearts of millions ... Doctrines hostile to all sciences, to all arts, to all industry, to all domestic charities, doctrines which, if carried into effect, would in thirty years, undo all that centuries have done for mankind ... have been avowed from the tribune and defended by the sword. Europe has been threatened with subjugation by barbarians, compared with whom the barbarians who marched under Attila and Alboin were enlightened and humane ... Meanwhile in our island the regular course of government has never for a day been interrupted.[84]

Lord Macaulay's lines, penned during the 1848 revolutions on the European continent, marvelously express the state of Europe and the British mood of confidence during World War II and its aftermath. In 1940 the British had apparently faced certain defeat: by 1945 Britain had emerged triumphant. Her economic condition might be grim; the country was beset by coal shortages and electricity failures. Wartime rationing not only continued, but became even more severe during the early years of peace. (Bread and coal rationing in Britain, for example, was introduced to help feed the British Occupation Zone in Germany. Food was rationed until 1954; coal was still rationed in 1958.) Cities remained bomb-scarred; trains were overcrowded; shoppers stood in line, their clothes dowdy, their patience tested by the scarcity of consumer

---

[83]Denis Smith, *Diplomacy of Fear: Canada and the Cold War 1941–1948*. Toronto, University of Toronto Press, 1988.

[84]Thomas Babington Macaulay, *The History of England from the Accession of James II*. Chicago, Belford, Clarke and Co., 1867, v. 2, pp. 224–55, referring to the 1848 revolutions on the European Continent.

goods, fuel, and by delays. Yet Britain in 1945 was a confident country, the most powerful state in Europe outside the USSR.

Britain, to start with, was the most populous state of Western Europe (49.22 million inhabitants, as against 45.29 million in Italy, 43.32 million in West Germany, 40.32 million in France; 27.01 million in Spain). Britain, like most Western European countries, but unlike Germany and Italy, experienced a striking rise in the birthrate after the war – the much discussed "baby boom." (Between 1939 and 1947, the number of live births per 1,000 persons increased in Britain from 15 to 21; in France at exactly the same rate; in the Netherlands from 21 to 28; in Belgium from 16 to 18. By contrast there was a decline in Germany from 20 to 17; in Italy from 24 to 22; in Austria from 21 to 19.)[85]

For several years after the initial recovery, Britain's gross domestic product was by far the highest in Western Europe (in million US dollars, at factor cost, in 1950: 39,704, as against 27,286 for France, 22,640 for West Germany, 13,820 for Italy). Britain was one of the world's healthiest countries (with an infant mortality in 1946 of 42.7 per thousand as against 45.8 in Denmark, 71.9 in France, 86.7 in Italy, and 90.2 in West Germany). Despite rationing, the British were relatively well fed (with an average daily per capita supply of calories and proteins, in 1947–50, of 3,250 as against 2,660 for France, 2,550 for West Germany, 2,320 for Italy). They owned more cars than the citizens of any other European country (46.0 cars per thousand inhabitants in 1950, as against 36.4 in France; 12.8 in West Germany, 7.3 in Italy). They were also better supplied with trucks than their competitors (905,000 compared with 563,000 in France; 382,600 in West Germany, 225,900 in Italy, in 1950). Production of primary energy stood higher in Britain than in the rest of Europe (213.21 million tons (coal equivalent) in 1948, compared to 122.56 million in West Germany; 51.69 in France; 6.6 million in Italy). Overall, the British produced nearly half the primary energy turned out in Western Europe as a whole (472.25 million in 1948). They led in the production of pig iron (with 7.9 million tons in 1947, as against 4.9 million in France, 3.0 million in West Germany). Overall, the British turned out nearly half of all Western Europe's steel (22.8 million tons) in 1947.[86]

The British had mobilized their economy for war in a more effective fashion than any other country. Their agriculture, having recovered its prosperity during and after the war, stood out as one of the most efficient farming systems in the world. British industry was famed for the quality of its products – ships, textiles, bicycles, motor-bicycles, and the like. At the end of the war, Britain excelled too in the skills and international connections of her bankers. The country enjoyed for a short time an exceptionally powerful position in international trade, as one of the two major exporters of manufactured goods (Britain and the US each accounted for about a quarter of the world's total

[85] J. Frederick Dewhurst, John O Coppock, P. Lamartine Yates and Associates. *Europe's Needs and Resources: Trends and Prospects in Eighteen Countries.* New York, Twentieth Century Fund, 1961, p. 40.

[86] Ibid., pp. 916, 945, 978, 1012, 1014, 1097, 1027.

exports of manufactured merchandise).[87] Her immediate postwar recovery was impressive (productivity in 1948 was higher than before the war, and exports had grown by nearly 50 percent). Nothing would have appeared less likely to the ordinary British voter in 1945 than the prospect of seeing Britain regarded 20 years later as the "sick man of Europe" in economic terms.

Militarily, Britain and the empire as yet remained a formidable power. At the end of the war with Germany, British forces in Europe, the Mediterranean, and the Far East amounted to 5,100,000 men and women, with 3,900,000 men and women producing military equipment. (Alone among the Western Allies, Britain in 1941 had introduced conscription for women, who accordingly went to work in munitions factories, labored on the land in the "Women's Land Army," or served in women's auxiliary branches of the armed forces in innumerable capacities, as clerks, technicians, and even as anti-aircraft gunners.) The British Army was the second largest in Europe; Britain's Royal Air Force exceeded the Soviet Union's in strike power. The Royal Navy was easily the world's second in size, at a time when the Red Fleet was as yet Moscow's military stepchild, and when the Japanese and German navies had disappeared from the world's oceans.

But the British, like the Americans, rapidly demobilized, as the British Defence Committee in 1946 decided to reduce the three services to a total of 1,100,000 men, and the total number of workers in defense industries to 500,000. Even so, British armed power continued to count in the calculations of strategists. The British had equal pride in their military technology. They and the Americans had admittedly neglected rocketry during the war, a field in which the Germans took a decisive lead. Also, the quality of British tanks left much to be desired in comparison with German and Soviet models. But the British turned out superb ships and planes (like the wartime Spitfire fighter and Lancaster bomber), had helped to pioneer radar and the jet aircraft, and had played an important initial part in the construction of the atom bomb. British scientists and technologists were accounted among the best in the world.

Great Britain still headed the greatest empire the world had seen. Winston Churchill later earned some derision for himself when he proclaimed (in a "Report on the war situation" to the House of Commons, 11 November 1942) that he had not become the King's First Minister to preside over the liquidation of the British Empire. Churchill proved as good as his word. In 1945, the extent of Britain's territorial influence was even greater than it had been in 1939. The British occupied the former Italian colonies, including Ethiopia and Libya. They occupied northwest Germany, some of whose citizens even suggested in a tentative fashion that the British-occupied zone would be better off as a British dominion. They were the predominant power in Southeast Asia and also dominated the Middle East, where British troops were stationed in Egypt, Palestine, in the "Fertile Crescent," the Persian Gulf, and Iran.

[87]Central Statistical Office (UK) Ken Mansel, "UK visible trade in the post war years CSOI," *Economic Trends,* London, October 1980, pp. 1–14.

Independence for India and Pakistan was not to come for another two years. Independence for any of the African colonies was not advocated by any but a few militant African expatriates.

According to an Irish witticism the sun never set on the British empire because the good Lord could not trust an Englishman in the dark. In fact, the empire depended on moral zeal, conciliation, and diplomacy rather than on force. (To give just one example, Northern Rhodesia, a territory larger than Great Britain, West Germany, Denmark, Switzerland, Holland, and Belgium combined, in peacetime depended for its domestic defense between 1900 and 1950 on only one Aftican battalion, some 800 men with a handful of white officers and NCOs.) The empire still enjoyed international legitimacy. Roosevelt and his New Dealers might look askance, and hope for its eventual liquidation by peaceful means in order to gain a new "open door" policy for US trade, but at Yalta, the trusteeship principle was limited to former enemy and mandated territories. Far from planning to dismantle their African empire, the British hoped both to humanize and consolidate their rule through rapid economic development, through developing new institutions for local self-government, and through measured constitutional advance. "No territory had been ceded in the interwar years; no cession was on the immediate agenda after 1945."[88] The British dominions – Canada, Australia, New Zealand, South Africa had all rallied to the king's cause in 1939; white-skinned, brown-skinned, and black-skinned troops from the empire had fought with distinction in theaters of war far from home.

The British had other, less tangible assets – a firm commitment to monarchical principles and a parliamentary system that commanded the electorate's absolute allegiance. Britain had the most cohesive ruling class in Europe – unified not in the sense of holding common political opinions, but culturally. This feeling of unity came partly from the links established through the Anglican Church, clubs, universities, the great public and grammar schools. There was a common language of discourse, strangely blended from the King James Bible, the *Book of Common Prayer, Alice in Wonderland,* Shakespeare, and Gilbert and Sullivan. This literary heritage provided common reference points for all – those who subscribed to the conservative *Times* or to the leftist *New Statesman*. This tradition was not confined only to those who had enjoyed an academic education. Before the war, there were only about 50,000 students at the various British universities. By 1961 their number had increased to 106,000, but the great expansion of British universities only began afterwards. However, a great literary legacy had previously been widely transfused through the BBC, through hymn books, through the reading of the daily "lesson" at compulsory divine services at school, through amateur dramatics, and through the earnest labors of bodies such as the Workers' Educational Association.

In addressing the British public, Churchill – like Gladstone and Disraeli before him – felt no need to descend to labored folksiness. He assumed as a

[88]Elisabeth Barker, *The British Between the Superpowers, 1945–1950.* London, Macmillan, 1983, p. 56.

matter of course that every truck driver, barber, and shop assistant in the kingdom would understand highflown literary oratory – and so they did. Interelite conflicts might be fierce; but there was nothing like the bitterness and contempt with which soldiers had disdained civilian politicians in Wilhelminian Germany, or the loathing that had traditionally split clericals and anti-clericals in France – not to speak of the savagery that disfigured relations, even between so-called friends, in totalitarian countries. The British establishment, unlike the French, had not lost prestige through collaboration, or assumed collaboration, with the enemy – a feature that Britain shared with the US. No senior British civil servant, no industrialist, no highly placed politician had worked for a German victory. David Low's cartoon character "Colonel Blimp" (representing an aged, unrepentant reactionary) appeared as a club bore and a fool – but nevertheless a patriot.

> *The Klaus Fuchs confession in 1950 that he had been passing on atomic secrets to the Soviets since 1942 harmed the "special relationship" between the US and the UK. The incident ended work on Anglo-American weapons; it convinced the Americans that British security was not to be trusted. Scientific cooperation was not fully resumed for years.*

Britain indeed remained a class-ridden country; the U (Upper Class) against the Non-U. Social divisions found expression, for instance, in British "social humor," that is to say in those folk stories that gave licensed expression to hidden tensions in society. In Great Britain, such jokes centered on class (except for tales about the Irish); by contrast social jokes in the US hinged on ethnicity, and in Nazi Germany and the Soviet Union on politics. But British class consciousness was also a source of strength. This was displayed in the workers' sense of solidarity, commitment to fair play, mutual aid, good manners, and social discipline. (The British army at the time was probably unique in the way in which, say, a member of a sergeants' mess could – by a spontaneous collective decision – be "sent to Coventry," that is to be subjected to a social boycott, for speaking ill of a fellow-sergeant in that man's absence, until such time as the offender had made a public apology.)

THE BRITISH "U" (UPPER CLASS) VERSUS "NON-U"

> *When bicycles stand by the gate,*
> *And Jack the Rocker whets his knife*
> *And Mum wears curlers in the hall,*
> *And Dad's been put away for life.*
> *When housing's on "Slum Clearance" lists,*
> *Then cry the sociologists: Non U!*
> *To you, Non U! To us, Grade E*
> *How unlike us these people be.*
>
> *When mini cars stand by the gate,*

And Bill the budgie pecks his corn,
And Mum puts doyleys on the plate,
And plastic gnomes are on the lawn.
When housing's on the "Des. Res." lists,
Then cry the sociologists: Non U!
To you, Non U! To us, Grade C;
How unlike them we hope to be.

When all around the Jags do roar
And whisky drowns the coq au vin,
And Marion's seat is saddle-sore;
And "birds" are bronzed from trips to Cannes;
When housing's on "Historic" lists
Then cry the sociologists: How U
To you, how U! To us, Grade A,
How much we'd like to live as they.

Contributed to the weekly competition by J. M. Crooks, New Statesman, *8, November 1968, p. 645.*

("Doyley," in British English, is a small, paper serviette. "Des. Res." is a British realtor's abbreviation for "desirable residence".)

Britain's stern sense of civic culture entailed many other benefits. The crime rate was one of the lowest in the Western world (and it actually dropped after the war). There was probably less political and administrative corruption in Britain at the time than anywhere else in the world. The British of course had their "spivs" and "wide boys" adept at "fiddles" (cheating). But the "Second Economy," or underground economy based on the systematic evasion of taxes and of public regulations, in all likelihood played a much lesser role than it did in any other country. It was only in Britain, through the 1940s, that the Chancellor of the Exchequer would habitually thank in the columns of *The Times* those donors who had forwarded "conscience money" to the Treasury, that is anonymous remittances of various sizes, designed to assuage the donor's sense of guilt for having successfully avoided past tax obligations.

The British, by 1945, had ceased to be a nation of churchgoers. But there still persisted a mood of moral earnestness, a commitment to "fair shares for all," respect for controls imposed for the country's real or assumed benefit, a sense of rectitude Victorian in its intensity. With all her assets, Great Britain therefore seemed in 1945 the one European state that might provide leadership to Western Europe as a whole.[89] Given a different political constellation,

[89]See for instance, Kenneth O. Morgan, *Labour in Power, 1945–1951*. Oxford, Oxford University Press, 1985, and A. J. P. Taylor, *English History, 1914–1945*. Oxford, Oxford University Press, 1985, both as brilliant as they are readable. See also Alan Sked and Chris Cook, *Post-War Britain, a Political History*. Harmondsworth, Penguin Books, 1979. Arthur Marwick, *British Society Since 1945*. Harmondsworth, Penguin Books, 1982. Sir Daniel Norman Chester, *The Nationalization of British Industry 1945–1951*. London, HMSO, 1975. J. C. R. Dow, *The Management of the British Economy, 1945–1960*. Cambridge, Cambridge University Press, 1964. T. E. B. Howarth, *Prospect and Reality, Great Britain, 1945–1955*. London, Collins, 1985. Alec Cairncross, *Years of Recovery. British Economic Policy, 1945–1951*. London, Methuen, 1985. Michael Sissons and Philip French, eds, *Age of Austerity, 1945–1951*. Baltimore, Penguin Books, 1964.

London at the time could well have become the capital of a Western European association. Such an association might have seemed even more probable, given the outcome of the 1945 election. The 1945 general election seemed to vindicate all those who said that Great Britain could create her own style of democratic socialism, a socialism that would avoid alike the evils of Soviet communism and those of US capitalism. For the first time in British history, the Labour Party gained a decisive majority.

Great Britain and West Germany – for very different reasons – stood out in 1945 as the two major countries in Western Europe where the communists had failed to make much headway among the industrial workers. British left-wing intellectuals were rarely communists; those who were had been forced on the ideological defensive, in part owing to the efforts of writers such as George Orwell (whose classics *Animal Farm* and *Nineteen Eighty-Four* were published in 1945 and 1949 respectively), and Arthur Koestler (whose novel *Darkness at Noon* appeared in print in 1940).

The new Labour government wielded great prestige. The party also enjoyed the advantage of having played a major part in the wartime government – domestic affairs having largely been run by Labour men. They fielded a first-rate team in the House of Commons. It had the backing of a well-organized and dynamic trades-union movement, now recognized, for all practical purposes, as yet another estate of the realm. Labour also dominated the political debate in intellectual terms. A free enterprise economist such as Friedrich von Hayek (who had published his *Road to Serfdom* a year before the election) carried no weight in public discourse. The educated general reader was more likely to derive his opinions from the titles chosen by the Left Book Club (formed in 1935 by the left-wing publisher Victor Gollancz). As a London bookseller explained in doggerel verse

Forced to make the choice themselves
Our rude forefathers loaded shelves
With Tennyson and Walter Scott
and Meredith, and Lord knows what!
But we don't have to hum and ha,
Nous avons changé tout cela –
Our books are chosen for us – Thanks
To Strachey, Laski, and Gollancz.[90]

The Labour government moreover had plenty of political courage. For instance, inflation rates were kept low; domestic consumption was kept down so as to favor exports and state industrial investment. The Labour years "appear in retrospect, and rightly so, as years when the government knew where it wanted to go ... with an understanding of what was at stake."[91]

Many of the Labour voters' underlying assumptions were shared even by Conservatives who disliked Labour's program. Tory paternalism had deep

[90]Stuart Samuels, "The left book club," *Journal of Contemporary History*, v. 1, no. 2, 1966, p. 65.
[91]Cairncross, *Years of Recovery*. p. 509.

roots, and Tory squires had long been wont to do good works on their estates, subsidized often from profits made through industrial investments in the City. Tory Guards officers, trained at Sandhurst, or Tory civil servants educated at Oxford or Cambridge, had for long shared with socialist intellectuals the conviction that public service was more honorable than trade or commerce in the "cut-throat" competition of the free market.

The Conservative Party in 1945 was in no sense a free enterprise party; the bulk of the Conservatives had accepted the need for controls and restrictions, for major improvements in the social services, and for public planning to put an end to old-style unemployment. Tory MP David Eccles noted in 1945 that no sensible party would oppose nationalization on principle. The Tories themselves had created public bodies such as the General Electricity Board and the BBC (British Broadcasting Corporation). Coal mining had been strictly controlled by a series of Mine Acts passed in the 1930s, and so had the railways.[92] Given such scanty political opposition to the principles of an economy regulated in the real or supposed public interest, Labour's prospects seemed excellent. If ever there was a land where democratic socialism might succeed, Great Britain in 1945 seemed to be that country.

Unfortunately, the new Labour government faced a host of problems whose gravity few British voters fully understood. Britain's remarkable war effort had increasingly become dependent on US production. In financing the war, postwar armaments, colonial development, and the massive expansion of social services, the British had gone far beyond their means. (By 1944 tax revenue amounted to 50.1 percent of public expenditure; the national debt had grown from £8,401 million to £20,858 million.) Whereas Britain had to liquidate overseas assets to the tune of 15 percent of her wealth, during World War I, World War II brought a loss of 28 percent. The foreign investments that had served to render tolerably comfortable the relative long-term decline of her manufacturing industries had thus largely gone. Britain henceforth depended on exports. But exports during the war had declined by about two-thirds as part of the war effort. Manufacturing plants had worn out; factories needed to be repaired and modernized; the entire economy had been distorted for the sake of maximizing war production; a substantial part of the merchant navy and shipping fleet had been sunk; the purchasing power of the pound had gravely declined. British expenditure on consumer goods and services diminished by 16 percent between 1938 and 1944 – compared with an equivalent increase over prewar figures in the US.

The British also faced grave difficulties in their relations with the US. To Europeans, the British, Australians, New Zealanders, Canadians, and Americans, all seemed almost the same people, *les Anglo-Saxons, die Anglo-Amerikaner*. The British public's attitude was not all that dissimilar. The average Briton might consider Americans and Australians to be brash and *nouveau riche*; but he considered himself more akin to these English-speakers from overseas than to foreigners from Europe. (This attitude found expression

[92]Godfrey Hodgson, "The steel debates," Sissons and French, eds, *The Age of Austerity 1945–1951*, pp. 297–316.

even in the very layout of such a standard British reference work as the *Statesman's Yearbook,* which grouped the world in a descending hierarchy of esteem: "The Commonwealth" (headed by the United Kingdom), "The United States of America", and "Other Countries"). A senior officer in SHAPE (Supreme Headquarters Atlantic Powers Europe) might justifiably have shared this viewpoint. A highly-placed British civil servant in Whitehall, by contrast, could be excused for regarding the Americans as allies of the most capricious kind, helpful at their best, and at their worst apt to mingle sanctimoniousness with effrontery.

Roosevelt and his coadjutors had looked upon the British empire as a strategic asset, an anachronism in politics, a moral liability, and a rival in trade. American policy regarding Britain tended towards inconsistency. The US during World War II created the Atlantic Alliance and had greatly assisted Britain through Lend Lease, but at the same time imposed strict controls on the use of Lend Lease items, limited the extent of Britain's dollar reserve, and restricted British exports in a variety of ways.[93] (Help to the Soviet Union, as we have seen, was given without strings of any kind.) In 1945 Congress forced President Truman abruptly to cancel Lend Lease. The Americans thereafter granted to Great Britain a loan of $3.75 billion at 2 percent interest – but only on condition that sterling would, within a designated period, become freely convertible for purposes of international trading, and that Britain would abandon imperial preferences regarding tariffs. But the severe winter of 1947 cut down coal exports and slowed factories because of coal shortages. All Europe suffered but Britain's economy suffered the most because it depended on exports and also had the responsibility of feeding and supplying its zone of occupation in Germany. The overly rapid ending of Lend Lease and the overly rapid use of the loan weakened Britain's economic recovery; the struggle in Greece was the final blow to economic recovery. Yet the US herself would neither promise to reduce her own high customs duties nor envisage any reduction in the huge US export surplus. The Americans proved equally uncooperative in other spheres. For instance, the US during the war had greatly benefited from British cooperation in the making of the atomic bomb, but Britain was abruptly excluded from further nuclear cooperation by the US McMahon Act of 1946.

> *The Atlantic Alliance evolved from the Atlantic Charter drawn up by Churchill and Roosevelt in secret meetings between 9 and 19 August, 1941, aboard the US Cruiser* Augusta *and the battleship* Prince of Wales *off Newfoundland. The meetings laid down the postwar aims of the US and Great Britain. The document called for freedom from want and fear, freedom of the seas, opposition to territorial aggrandizement and support for self-determination. Later (24 September) Washington announced that 15 anti-Axis nations had endorsed the charter, but the Churchill–Roosevelt talks were more important than that. These sessions planned Lend Lease and the common defense of Europe and meant that isolationism was defeated and that the US agreed to help defeat Hitler.*

[93] Alan P. Dobson, *US Wartime Aid to Britain, 1940–1946.* London, Croom Helm, 1986.

The British dominions proved somewhat more sympathetic. With the exception of Canada, they all belonged to the Sterling Area whose members during the war had "pooled" their vital dollar requirements, an arrangement that continued into peacetime. Nevertheless, the dominions increasingly distanced themselves from Britain and retreated into political and military isolationism or sought new patrons; for example, New Zealand and Australia became dependent on US military might through the ANZUS Pact of 1951. The British connection was thus weakened by a series of blows. Especially dramatic were the withdrawal from India (1947), and the fall from power of General Jan Smuts (1948), an old and tried friend of Great Britain's, and his replacement as prime minister of South Africa by Daniel François Malan, an Afrikaner nationalist. (In a sense, the Afrikaners' takeover initiated the long British retreat from Africa.)

To make matters worse, the world economy as a whole had changed to Britain's disfavor. There was a strict division between "hard currency" areas that had done well out of the war (especially the US), and "soft currency" areas that had not. It was in these latter areas that Britain found her major export markets, with receipts in non-convertible currencies. Most British imports, however, came largely from countries that required payments in gold and dollars. Britain's deficit with America was of long standing; henceforth, however, a surplus derived from exports to the Sterling Area could no longer provide the wherewithal to finance dollar imports.[94] The "dollar gap," in the experts' opinion had become a permanent feature in the economic landscape of both Great Britain and Western Europe.

The British economy also suffered from a variety of long-term problems that had plagued the kingdom long before Hitler had come into power. Many industries were antiquated. The British steel industry, for example, had for many decades failed to keep up with its German and US competitors. As a contemporary observer put it, there were too many works which "sprawl ... which are a tangled riddle of gaps, corners, adjacent shops alternatively empty and overcrowded, illogical separation, unbalanced and tortuous routes and methods in the handling of materials. The works ... are old and have too much past history incorporated in their layout."[95] Overall, the British worker in 1939 had worked on the average 27 percent more hours in 32 selected sample industries, but the US worker's average output per man hour was much higher – a process that had accelerated during World War II. The British, even before World War I, had fallen behind Germany in the development of modern scientific industries, especially such as chemicals, electrical, and optics.

Critics of the British economy had many other complaints, some of them dating from the decades preceding World War I. American and German managers were, on the whole, more professionally trained than their British

[94]See, for instance, the major review article by Peter Clarke, "Guessing at the future," *Times Literary Supplement*, 21 June 1985, pp. 683–6.

[95]Cited by Robert A. Brady, *Crisis in Britain: Plans and Achievements of the Labour Government*. Berkeley, University of California Press, 1950, p. 209.

colleagues. The British supposedly were held back by the dead hand of class, and by an antiquated system of education that taught Greek and Latin to the academic elite, rather than engineering and sociology. Many industrial innovators had been foreigners, men such as Ludwig Mond, Charles Dreyfus, William Siemens. Marketing and technical experts suffered from inadequate social esteem. As Lord Rothschild put it, there were three roads to ruin – women, gambling, and engineering: the first two were more agreeable, but the last was the surest.[96] The British worker, the charge sheet continued, was on the whole less hard working and less well trained than his opposite number in Germany and the US, especially as regards the "noncommissioned" ranks of industry. They had experienced difficulties in switching to mass production methods as readily as the Germans and the Americans; British workmen were more traditional in their outlook than their competitors, more trade union minded, more willing to strike over grievances connected with status rather than cash. The British, above all, failed to develop technical education. At a critical juncture in their economic history, they did not put themselves out to build institutions comparable to MIT in the United States, or to the *Technische Hochschulen* and *Fachschulen* in Germany: they were deficient in the teaching of industrial design and advanced managerial techniques.

The "lazy" British worker figures as a bête noire *in many Tory tracts. The image is exaggerated. Nevertheless, even casual observers from abroad were often struck by the cult of amateurism among British students, blue collar workers, white collar workers, and managers – a tendency not to work too hard, learn too much, or appear an eager beaver. (Emigrant British bricklayers in Rhodesia, for instance, had a much higher output than their colleagues at home, where productivity was restrained by trade union restrictions, and by social pressure to conform to an informally agreed working norm.) Britain's relative decline in Europe may be linked in part to the cult of the "all rounder" as opposed to the specialist, contempt for the "swot" (or "grind" in American student parlance) and by inadequate facilities for technical education.*

There is some merit in these criticisms, but the picture is overdrawn. The British economy in 1945 was not decadent. The British GNP and average incomes had grown steadily since the 1870s, albeit at a slower rate than the USA's and Germany's. After World War I British industries had moved progressively into science-based industries, and were responsible for much of the world's finest industrial research.[97] The British had not lost the art of organization. Alone among Western armies, the British armed forces after 1945 – with the possible exception of Northern Ireland – would uniformly win every conventional and unconventional war in which they engaged, in places as far afield as Malaya, Cyprus, Kenya, and the Falkland Islands.

In a more general sense, a classical education, a taste for great literature,

[96]Cited by G. C. Allen, *The British Disease*. London, Institute of Economic Affairs, 1976, p. 49.
[97]Arthur Shenfield, *The Failure of Socialism: Learning from the Swedes and English*. Washington DC, The Heritage Foundation, 1980, pp. 29–30.

and a developed sense of social snobbery has never prevented anyone from making a great deal of money, or from successfully running an industrial economy. In Wilhelminian Germany, a country known for its economic dynamism, senior civil servants, and many a wealthy *Kommerzienrat* had been nurtured on Greek and Latin in traditional *Gymnasien*. These men had tended to pursue legal rather than economic or technological studies at university; they had valued a reserve officer's commission more highly than the best of technical diplomas; they had prided themselves on being able to recite long passages of Schiller's, Goethe's, and Heine's poetry over the dinner table. Yet they had successfully helped to run an economically dynamic Reich. By the same token, Wilhelminian Germany had been intensely preoccupied with the realities or supposed realities of Germany's past. At its best, this sense of history had found expression in fine scholarship, at its worst in countless monuments of heavy-bosomed, sword-yielding *Germanias* cast in bronze. This taste for pseudo-history and *kitsch,* however, had not prevented the Kaiser's Germany from making rapid industrial progress.

As we see it, the causes of Britain's relative decline derived in part from the successes, rather than the failures, of the past. The British had planned well in war, but the needs of war differed from those of peace. In wartime, resources had been squandered. In peacetime, Britain had to prepare for a competitive future in which they would need to hold their own against a resurgent Europe where professionalism was prized more than gifted amateurism. Naturally, such difficulties were not apparent to the average British elector. On the contrary, the average voter had high expectations for a better future soon. An electoral cartoon published in 1945 showed a returning soldier and his young wife banging on the counter of the Tory Peace Stores. Under the counter were hidden "Jobs", "Good Homes," "Proper Medical Attention," "Decent Schools," all marked "reserved for the rich and privileged." Said the young veteran to the store keeper "What do you mean, you are out of stock? I've paid twice for these goods, once in 1914 and again in 1939!"[98] No returning *Wehrmacht* soldier, trudging home in his tattered uniform, would have expressed similar sentiments.

The British during wartime had acquired a profound faith in the virtues of planning and government control; Labour's magic words. But Labour came into office without having seriously thought out a new strategy for the industries that it intended to nationalize. Labour stood prepared to fight the battles of the past, when the British had apparently faced problems of overproduction and under-consumption. In 1945, Britain confronted the difficulties occasioned by underproduction and growing demand; there was more money than goods, more jobs than men and women to fill them, more demands on the economy than the economy could supply.

The 1944 White Paper on Employment Policy was, according to the British political historian Keith Middlemas, a key document that set out the postwar doctrine of reciprocal obligations of labor, industry, and finance in order to

[98]The *Daily Mirror,* June 1945.

get the state to guarantee full employment and high wages. A British kind of corporatism would continue well into the postwar era, and the "political contract" held for over 30 years.

All therefore came to depend on the quality of British industrial planning. Unfortunately, the machinery left much to be desired for the purpose of peacetime reconstruction. The planners had mistakenly become accustomed to thinking in military metaphors. The machinery worked better at the top than at the bottom of the pyramid. During the war, the Whitehall mechanism had come to consist of some 30 departments, with many branches throughout the kingdom. The whole was directed by a small number of ministers and civil servants, both permanent and temporary (including some distinguished businessmen and academics called in for administrative tasks). These men kept in touch by breakfasting, lunching, and dining together; they developed thereby a corporate consciousness. Collectively, they wielded enormous power. "In the sphere of general economic policy there were probably 20 to 50 people at Whitehall who, if their views coincided, could do almost anything."[99] But the increasing power of central departments made government increasingly remote, as the top officials lost touch with the people whose lives they affected to such an extraordinary extent.

Planning necessarily rested on sound statistics. But statistical services were flawed. The greatest source of weakness lay in imperfect information, as too many civil servants depended too much on hearsay when dealing with problems of production. There was excessive reliance on licences and other restrictive devices; there was a flood of forms to be filled in for the benefit of civil servants who instinctively assumed that the time spent by citizens in completing this copious documentation had no cost. There was the eternal conflict between central staff and field officers, and between the central departments themselves. Economies were often obtained through quantitative restrictions that ignored price differentials. Above all, there was the widespread conviction that economic progress in future would hinge on distributing existing wealth in a fair and equitable fashion rather than by creating new wealth. None of the giants of British socialism – G. D. H. Cole, Richard Tawney, the Webbs – had even considered the problem of how publicly owned enterprises would be made more efficient and productive than private firms. British theoreticians of whatever political persuasion were interested more in the problem of how to share out existing wealth in a fairer and more equitable fashion than before. As Geoffrey Crowther, editor of the *Economist,* wrote a few years after the war ended, Europe – unlike the US – had nearly reached its economic limits. "Increasingly ... the problems they [the Europeans] have to face are not those of growth or construction, or of producing for a mighty future, but the problems of allocation, of adjustment, of transfer of resources."[100] Instead of permitting new industries to grow in regions best suited to their respective

[99]D. N. Chester, ed., *Lessons of the British War Economy.* Cambridge, Cambridge University Press, 1951, pp. 5–33.
[100]Geoffrey Crowther, *The Economic Reconstruction of Europe,* Claremont, Cal., 1948, p. 73.

needs, without bureaucratic interference, the British committed themselves to an industrial strategy of shoring up decaying industries in decaying areas. Instead of giving priority to the modernization of industry, the British gave first priority to an impressive program of social services, including a National Health Service, and a huge housing program. (By 1951, capital investment in British industry had risen to no more than 5 percent of the gross national product, as compared to West Germany's 15 percent.)[101] For Britain's current and future ills, it turned out to be the wrong prescription.

> *The British disease, according to the* Economist, *was made up of: a second-rate managerial class, adversarial industrial relations, second-rate schooling for the masses, poor marketing, too little investment in research and development, and a "a disdain for business and a liking for tea breaks." "There is nothing wrong with British managers except poor training, poor schooling and poor leadership. A bit sweeping? Yes, but the same is true for workers too." (the* Economist, *May 20, 1989.)*

Germany and Austria

We are for our sins, most utterly destroyed.
The insolent men-at-arms, the savage clarion call,
The sword that reeks with blood, the mighty
    cannon's roar
Have wrecked whatever sweat and work have built.
The town hall smashed, the strong men dead
    in battle.
The women raped, the gutters dyed with blood
    – at every turn
We see but fire, pestilence, and death that numb
    the heart.
For fully eighteen years, the slain have filled
    our rivers.
But worse than pestilence, or fire, famine,
    death –
The fate of those who lost the treasure of their
    souls.

Andreas Gryphius, 1636
(during the Thirty Years' War).[102]

In 1945 Germany was a shattered nation, physically and spiritually. *Die Stunde Null,* the hour of zero had arrived. Though World War I had left Germany defeated, she had remained a great power. World War II had broken the Reich

---

[101]Correlli Barnett, *The Audit of War: The Illusion and Reality of Britain as a Great Nation.* London, Macmillan, 1986, p. 264.
[102]Translated from Andreas Gryphius, "Tränen des Vaterlands, anno 1686," in E. L. Stahl, ed., *The Oxford Book of German Verse.* Oxford, Clarendon Press, 1967, p. 48.

asunder and *de facto,* though not *de jure,* eliminated Germany as a political entity. Government and army had disintegrated and so had national morale, amid scenes both terrible and bizarre. For generations the carillon bells of the famed Potsdam garrison church had rung Mozart's melody *üb' immer Treu und Redlichkeit ...,* "Forever be faithful and honorable until your cold grave, and do not stray one finger's breadth from the path of God." In April 1945, British bombers attacked Potsdam at night. Bombs struck the church and damaged the carillon mechanism. For hours afterwards the bells incessantly played the tune amid a madhouse of crumbling masonry and raging fires, until the spire collapsed, and the music stopped.[103]

Germany's economic collapse in 1945 also seemed total; the country had no future – or so the experts claimed. "The mass of Germans and foreigners imported to work inside Germany," editorialized the *New Statesman and Nation,* a great British weekly, "is not capable of political attitudes, nor indeed understanding the world in which, by accident, it continues to exist. Those who have no homes, no food, no clothes, no personal possessions of any sort, and often no relations left, belong to a great new 'Internationale of the Dispossessed,' menaced by hunger. disease, and final decay,"[104] Germany had become a vacuum in the middle of Europe, wrote Geoffrey Crowther, editor of the British *Economist.*[105] "Germany ... as it was known to the world throughout its history, has been destroyed and cannot be resurrected ... The German nation is ruined." "It is fatally weakened in its biological substance, in its cultural and technical environment, in its moral fiber," argued Gustav Stolper, another economist. Reconstruction would have to be undertaken by a rapidly shrinking population, Stolper noted, a task without precedent since the start of the industrial age – this in a country beset by a shortage of skills, and worse, by a sense of impotence and helplessness.[106] Germany's condition, to the historically-minded, seemed to equal the misery and destruction of the Thirty Years' War three centuries ago. Nothing but bare survival seemed possible.

The experts had good reason for pessimism, as did the mass of ordinary Germans. Hunger pervaded the land, with rations down sometimes to the starvation level of 700 to 800 calories a day. Everything was scarce – food, fuel, clothes, shoes, medicine, tools, machinery, spare parts, vehicles for transportation. Civil administration had largely collapsed. Many cities lay in ruins, bridges were down, railway marshalling yards out of commission, sea ports and river ports wrecked. Germany, a country used for over a century to spectacular economic growth, had suffered a decline in its agricultural and industrial output unparalleled in the preceding two centuries (illustrated in table 2.2).

[103]Eye witness reports cited by Donald Abenheim, *Reforging the Iron Cross: The Search for West German Armed Forces.* Princeton, Princeton University Press, 1988.

[104]*New Statesman and Nation,* 6 January 1946, p. 1.

[105]Geoffrey Crowther, *The Economic Reconstruction of Europe.* Claremont, Cal., 1948, p. 27.

[106]Gustav Stolper, *German Realities.* New York, Reynal and Hitchcock, 1948, pp. 22, 64.

TABLE 2.2   *Key indices of production: 1939–1946*

	1939 (Reich)	1946 (The four zones of occupation)
National income (in billion marks, at 1936 prices)	76	32
Index of industrial production (1936 = 100)	116	27
Wheat and rye harvested (in million tons)	10.3	5.5
Potatoes (million tons)	50	22
Food consumption (calories per day)	3,113	1,729

Note: The loss to Germany was even greater than the table indicates, since the 1946 figures take no account of the agrarian production in that part of East Germany annexed by Poland.
Source: Gustav Stolper et al., *The German Economy, 1870 to the Present*, London, Weidenfeld and Nicolson, 1967, p. 205.

The greatest and most irreparable loss derived from the territorial resettlement of East Central Europe. German history books in the past had extolled Germany's *Drang nach Osten,* the drive to the East. German specialists in many fields had traditionally looked for jobs in Eastern Europe. Her scholars had been wont to devote far more attention to Eastern Europe (including Russia) than to the United States (where many more Germans had settled than in Eastern Europe). Germans tended to look at Eastern Europeans with a sense of superiority, whereas they had widely been accustomed to regard Western Europe, especially France and Britain, in an ambiguous fashion that mingled censoriousness with sentiments of inferiority. World War II caused the pendulum to swing, as the resultant West German rump state forcibly turned to the West as the only alternative. World War I had reduced the area of the former Reich from 208,803 square miles to 181,714 square miles. After the end of World War II, Germany's much disputed *Lebensraum* (living space) diminished in an even more dramatic fashion, leaving to the four Allied occupation zones no more than 137,117 square miles (95,737 square miles to the British, US, and French zones, 41,380 square miles to the Soviet zone).

The loss of Germany's eastern provinces to Poland (with Königsberg going to the Soviet Union) was indeed a desperately serious matter. During World War II, Germany had not starved because it had looted Europe when food supplies became low. The amputation of Pomerania, Silesia, and East Prussia from the Reich, however, deprived Germany of her former "breadbasket," as well as of the Silesian industrial complex. The lost provinces had accounted for about 48 percent of Germany's acres suitable for arable or pastoral farming, for many raw materials (75 percent of German lead production and 40 percent of zinc production) as well as many industrial centers such as the shipbuilding industry at Stettin. The German economy suffered further impairment from artificial barriers set up between the Allied occupation zones, lowered agricultural productivity brought about in part by shortages of fuel and fertilizers, lack of transport (horses, cars, trucks, trains), and the collapse of the currency. Between them, these disabilities produced serious food shortages, especially in the British zone (where such shortages continued until the Fall of 1948).[107]

Hunger went with the human tragedy brought about by the expulsion of the German population from the areas ceded to Poland, and from the Sudet enland. Some 2,000,000 people may have perished in these terrible treks or as a result of hardships in flight. By 1950, the total number of exiles in West Germany amounted to 7,876,000. By 1960, the number had grown to 9,697,000 (including people who had fled to West Germany from what had by then become the German Democratic Republic). The refugees mainly settled in agrarian regions where there were fewer jobs, but more space, rather than in industrial areas. Schleswig-Holstein, Lower Saxony, and Bavaria, by 1950, accounted for about 59 percent of the refugees in West Germany.[108] By that year, about 16.6 percent of the population consisted of refugees, most of whom had arrived at their destination with no more than the clothes on their backs and what they might carry in a suitcase or rucksack. (Some 33 percent of Schleswig-Holstein's and 27.2 percent of Lower Saxony's people by that time consisted of refugees.) No earlier century in European history had witnessed enforced migrations on such a scale. Equally grim was the psychological burden of loss, displacement, and alienation. (*Aber die eigenen Deutschen waren die Schlimmsten*; "but our own Germans were the worst," was a harsh refrain that constantly recurred in conversation.)

The movement of people into Germany coincided with an exodus from Germany of forced laborers, refugees, prisoners and displaced persons who had been coerced into or had volunteered for work there and those who had fled from the Soviets. When the Western Allies entered Germany, they had to cope with more than 11,000,000 refugees – a staggering number. (Of these, about 5,000,000 made their own way home in 1945; another 5,000,000 were repatriated, leaving more than 1,000,000 in "displaced persons'" camps – hapless and homeless, unwanted and subject to unmerited contempt.[109] As regards German nationals, the bulk of the *Wehrmacht* had become prisoners of war, some of them under the harshest circumstances in the Soviet Union, and years passed until the last survivors returned from captivity. (A higher percentage of Germans survived Stalin's camps than Soviet prisoners captured by the Germans – about 3.3 million died.)

Germany's economic problems were worsened by the burden of reparations, by the dismantling of many industrial installations, and by restrictions placed by the Allies on manufacturers for the purpose of destroying German war-making capacities. Until May 1946, the Western Allies' policy toward Germany

---

[107]Gabriele Stüber, *Der Kampf gegen den Hunger, 1945–1950. Die Ernährungslage in der Britischen Zone Deutschlands, insbesonders in Schleswig-Holstein und Hamburg.* Neumünster, Karl Wachholtz, 1984.

[108]Wolfgang Köllmann, "*Die Bevölkerungsentwicklung der Bundesrepublik: Beiträge zum Kontinuitätsproblem.* Stuttgart, Ernst Klett, 1983, pp. 70–1.

[109]Wolfgang Jacobmeyer, *Vom Zwangsarbeiter zum Heimatlosen Ausländer: Die Displaced Persons in Westdeutschland 1945–1951.* Göttingen, Vandenhoeck und Rupprecht, 1985.

was punitive. Initially Germany could only manufacture strictly limited quantities of steel, aluminum, and copper. She was forbidden to produce a vast range of intricate machinery, to build planes, synthesize rubber, or gasoline. In the Ruhr, workmen stood in sullen silence as they watched the French take coal and the dismantlers survey a plant for the removal of generators and rolling mills. At the Bochumer Verein, where submarines had been assembled the newest shops were dismantled. But Bochumer Verein engineers explored new markets with extraordinary ingenuity. For instance, the firm added two musicians to its staff and learned how to cast enormous bells of alloy – Protestant bells with one particular pitch, and Catholic bells with another, all molded with the words "God is Love" in them.[110]

In theory, Germany should have remained a permanently distressed area. In practice, matters turned very differently. Stripped of industrial equipment, the Germans were forced to invest in the most modern machinery. The host of refugees became an unexpected economic asset. Uprooted from home, severed from accustomed links of neighborhood, tradition, and family, the migrants suddenly had to make immense psychological readjustments in order to adapt; find housing, food, new jobs, and learn new skills or perish – most went to work with a passion. Their presence weakened the position of established trades unionists by providing employers with a plentiful supply of willing workers. In a more general sense they became reluctant pioneers, with the sole advantage of not having to learn a new language in the land of their destination. Private initiative was now at a premium – in a country that had previously prided itself on an ability to organize and regulate on a national scale.

Above all, war had not destroyed Germany's (or indeed Europe's) great human potential, its social capital. As we have indicated, Germany suffered enormous casualties in World War II. (Overall, something like 6,000,000 people may have perished including an estimated 3,712,000 servicemen whose demise left a demographic imbalance between men and women of marriageable age.) But augmented by refugees Germany remained a populous country (an estimated 43,694,041 people were resident in West Germany in 1946). Despite the hardships suffered by the mass of Germans during and after the war, the crude death rate did not increase nor did the crude birth rate fall to anything like the extent contemporary observers imagined. (In 1937, the crude birth rate for the entire Reich had stood at 18.8 per thousand, as opposed to 16.4 in West Germany in 1946. The crude death rate in 1937, at a time of relative prosperity, had amounted to 11.7 per thousand for the Reich; in 1946 it numbered 12.3 for Western Germany.[111] There remained a vast reservoir of highly skilled, educated, and hardworking, disciplined people, familiar with running modern industries and modern agriculture, and determined to improve

[110]Theodore H. White, *Fire in the Ashes: Europe in Mid-Century*. New York, William Sloane Associates, 1953, p. 136.

[111]United Nations, *Demographic Yearbook*. New York, Statistical Office of the United Nations, 1952, pp. 115, 228–9, 270–1.

their material well being. This social capital formed the true foundation of West Germany's and Western Europe's recovery.

At first the Allies had tried to punish and break up German cartels: later they needed a stronger German economy and pursued different policies in the four zones of a divided Germany. The chemical industry revived – the chemical giant I.G. Farben and its management had been charged with war crimes but by 1950 such firms were prospering. Reasons for the revival included continuity of organization, managerial acumen, new technology, plant, and expert personnel. But the US emphasis on free trade and export industries was also important.

In addition, Germany retained a powerful industrial foundation, with great investments in modern, export-oriented industries based on the production of machinery, chemical and electrical products, cars, tractors, and the like – the greatest manufacturing complex in Europe at the time. In theory, this manufacturing capacity should have been wiped out by the combined effects of Allied bombing, Hitler's insane "scorched earth policy" designed to deprive the advancing Allies of German industrial production, and Allied plans for dismantling many German factories after World War II. In practice, this did not happen. Factories indeed suffered heavy damage. But an effective policy of dispersal and skilful improvisation had preserved much of Germany's industrial capacity. (According to contemporary estimates, only 10 percent of the iron industry, 10 to 15 percent of the chemical industries, and 15 to 20 percent of the textile industries had been destroyed.) The "scorched earth" policy had not been enforced at the end of the war, and dismantling mainly occurred in the Soviet-occupied zone. Postwar German estimates said 45 percent of the available industrial capacity was removed in the Soviet zone, 8 percent in the Western zones. Overall, Germany's dismantling bill amounted to DM 5.66 billion, at 1936 prices.[112] Despite these heavy losses, Germany, the major provider of capital goods to Western Europe markets since 1890, remained Europe's major and most modern industrial power, once the heavy damage to her infrastructure had been repaired and new factories had risen from the ashes of the old.

The Western Allies' record in Germany was ambiguous. From the start, the Allied forces played an honorable part in helping to rebuild bridges and railway marshalling yards, in restoring essential services, and providing aid. However, they began with a punitive program; from 1946 onward the emphasis shifted to speeding recovery, and from 1948, to helping an ally.[113] Allied policy makers

[112]Alfred Grosser, *Geschichte Deutschlands seit 1945: Eine Bilanz*. Munich, Deutscher Taschenbuch Verlag, 1984, p. 94.
[113]The literature on the Western, particularly the US occupation of Western Germany, is vast. See, for instance: Edward N. Peterson, *The American Occupation of Germany: Retreat to Victory*. Wayne State University Press, 1978. Wolfgang Benz, *Von der Besatzungsherrschaft zur Bundesrepublik: Stationen einer Staatsgründung, 1946–1949*. Frankfurt, Fischer, 1984. Eugene Davidson, *The Death and Life of Germany: An Account of the American Occupation*. London, Jonathan Cape, 1960. James F. Tent, *Mission on the Rhine: Reeducation and Denazification in American-Occupied Germany*. Chicago, University of Chicago Press, 1982. Robert Wolfe, ed., *Americans as Proconsuls: United States Military*

were, however, far from united in how best to achieve this object. American bankers and the military, schooled in the tradition of the New Deal but not Keynesianism, and British advisers, steeped in the ideals of the British Labour Party, were not agreed on the desirability of a planned economy – whatever its shape. Within the traditional German economy the state had enjoyed immense power and respect. The Nazis had only continued an existing process of regimenting the German economy; they had substantially increased the extent of publicly-owned industries. (By 1939, 42.4 percent of the gross national product was already going into the coffers of the state.)[114] Using influence, blackmail, and confiscation, party potentates had built economic fiefdoms; their internecine struggles, privileges, and exploitative labor practices might ultimately have led to industrial decadence, had the Third Reich won the war. The Nazis also created a rigid system of wage and price controls, of licencing and resource allocation.

The British did not like asking for reparations from Germany, but did so in spite of their bad experience in this respect after World War I. Since they opposed reparation payments from current production, they therefore had to dismantle plants – a nasty, complicated business that brought little or no profit, as Alex Cairncross has shown in The Price of War: British Policy on German Reparations, 1941–1949; *1986. Allied reparations policies did not start the Cold War or ensure the division of Germany, but they did put many senseless burdens on relations with the Soviets, Cairncross believes. The Americans and the British asked the Soviets to deliver agricultural goods to the Germans before exporting industrial products; in effect making the Soviets pay for goods not received as reparations. Then the American Military Governor Lucius D. Clay stopped dismantling in the US zone and the delivery of reparations to the Soviets on May 4, 1946. Four-power cooperation collapsed soon after.*

Reparations, Cairncross argues, slowed the German recovery and hurt Allied cooperation. The Americans and the British could not stop the Soviet reparation program but limited it to the Soviet-controlled Eastern zone. The French, however, had some success in their reparations program; they took a share of the Ruhr's coal output. This hurt German industrial production and affected British reparations. The British unfortunately then resumed dismantling in 1949, further delaying German recovery and integration into Western Europe.

The Western Allies at first tried to keep this system intact on the regional

---

Government in Germany and Japan, 1944–1952. Carbondale, Ill., Southern Illinois University Press, 1984. Theodore Eschenburg, *Jahre der Besatzung 1945–1949*. Stanford, Cal., Stanford University Press, 1986. John H. Backer, *Winds of History: The German Years of Lucius DuBignon Clay*. New York, Van Nostrand, Reinhold, 1983. Wolfgang Krieger, *General Lucius D. Clay und die Amerikanische Deutschlandpolitik 1945–1949*. Stuttgart, Klett-Cotta, 1987. Roy Willis, *The French in Germany, 1945–1949*. Stanford, Cal., Stanford University Press, 1962. Claus Scharf and Hans-Jürgen Schröder, eds, *Die Deutschlandpolitik Frankreichs und die Französische Zone, 1945–1949*. Wiesbaden, Steiner, 1983. Raymond Ebsworth, *Restoring Democracy in Germany: The British Contribution*. New York, Praeger, 1960. Arthur Hearnden, ed., *The British in Germany*. London, Hamish Hamilton, 1978. Udo Wetzlaugh, *Die Alliierten in Berlin*. Berlin, Berlin Verlag Arno Spitz, 1988.

[114]Hermann Kellenbenz, *Deutsche Wirtschaftsgeschichte*. Munich, Verlag C. H. Beck, 1981, v. 2, p. 473.

and local level (especially in agriculture). They instituted rigid rationing. (The official clothes ration in the British zone, according to the regulations published in 1946–7, would have enabled each citizen to buy a pair of socks every four years, a shirt every ten years, and a suit every 40 years.) But in practice, the system broke down. There was no longer a central guiding authority to make it effective. The Allies moreover were neither able nor willing to use those methods of terror employed under the Nazis; no German went to a concentration camp for "profiteering," as he might have done under Hitler's regime. The black market helped to save the country. Thereafter the Marshall Plan and the currency reform put underway in 1948 speeded the recovery by increasing production, providing at long last a sound currency, and by ending the unofficial coinage based on cigarettes. The West Germans then rapidly dismantled much of the system of controls and regulations inherited from the Nazis and the occupation regimes – a striking and beneficent reform that mightily contributed to the *Wirtschaftswunder*. Then American Keynesian advisers could not dominate economic planning as they attempted to do in France and Italy, for the military were supreme in occupied Germany.

> *Reinhard Mohn, head of the largest media company in the world, the Bertelsmann Group, is a good example of how America helped produce the German economic miracle. He had been a prisoner of war in Kansas and returned empty-handed to Germany in 1946, only to find his family publishing business destroyed. While a prisoner, he had studied American society and was impressed with its openness, compared to Germany's patriarchal business and social traditions. He read about, and adopted, General Motor's Alfred Sloan's decentralization technique, came back to the US often to see how businesses were run there, and introduced American methods and philosophy to his Bertelsmann Group (Reported in the* Economist, April 9, 1988).

Defeat had equally far reaching effects on German politics. War had irretrievably smashed the Prussian-dominated Reich founded by Bismarck in 1871. According to conventional Prussophile historiography, Germany's unification under Prussian leadership had possessed an element of the inevitable. The collapse of the Third Reich and the formal dissolution of Prussia (proclaimed by the Allies in 1947) led, however, to a profound and unexpected change in German opinion. A new generation of outstanding German scholars from the 1960s re-evaluated the processes that had led to the formation of the Reich. (According to a public opinion poll taken in 1965, 20 years after the defeat, only 11 percent of the respondents regarded the era of the *Kaiserreich* as the greatest epoch in German history.)[115] This change was greatly influenced by the Allied occupation. Allied armies – not German resistance – had shattered the Nazi regime. The Western occupation helped to end Germany's previous intellectual isolation under the Third Reich. (For instance, the British had

[115]See M. Koch-Hillebrecht, *Das Deutschenbild: Gegenwart, Geschichte, Psychologie*. Munich, C. H. Beck, 1977, p. 40. Major works of reinterpretation include Heinrich Lutz, *Zwischen Habsburg und Preussen: Deutschland 1815–1866*. Berlin, Siedler Verlag, 1985. Thomas Nipperdey, *Deutsche Geschichte 1800–1866*. Munich, C. H. Beck, 1983.

some influence on the evolution of local government in West Germany, the Americans on constitutional thought and education.) In a political sense, proconsuls such as US General Lucius Clay had a reasonable claim to be counted among the initially unwitting architects of the German Federal Republic founded in 1949.

But above all, German public opinion had changed of itself. Defeat, so overwhelming and palpable, left little room for the "stab-in-the-back" legend that had plagued the Weimar Republic after World War I. Defeat also rendered impossible any attempts at a Nazi revival. Contemporary Allied misconceptions concerning the supposed strength of Nazi sentiment in 1945 in fact oddly mirrored Dr Goebbels's views on the subject. The Allied commanders therefore initially imposed "non-fraternization" directives on their troops, orders as ill-conceived as unenforceable. British soldiers off duty were also under order to go about armed, lest they be murdered by "werewolves" (Nazi guerrillas). Allied political officers kept looking for signs of a Nazi revival. Historians such as A. J. P. Taylor, in *The Course of German History,* an otherwise stimulating book, unwittingly followed Nazi propaganda in linking personages as disparate as Luther, Frederick the Great, and Adolf Hitler, in an unbroken line of destructive succession.

For many years afer the end of the war, political pundits continued to predict a Nazi revival on German soil. Thriller writers went on composing lurid tales about Nazi villains, prevented by ingenious sleuths from restoring the *Führer's* vanished glory through imagined conspiracies financed by hidden Nazi gold. But in fact there were no "werewolves" in 1945. There was no underground war, no Nazi renaissance. The mass of the German people, far from trying to drive out the Western Allies, regarded them at worst as a lesser evil – preferable to the Soviets. The bulk of former Nazis, rather than dying in the last ditch, only thought of disappearing into decent obscurity.

Their caution should occasion no surprise. The party bosses had incurred bitter hostility even before the end of the war when most of them had failed to live up to their heroic words. Disillusionment had begun to spread before the war ended, especially among many youngsters who had become bored by the party's incessant propaganda, and to whom the *Bewegung,* the "movement," no longer represented a daring venture, but a degraded establishment.[116] Nazism moreover was not a doctrine that could cope well with defeat. The *Führer* had exalted armed might, victory, and success; he had despised the weak; his quasi-Messianic creed lacked the transcendental qualities that could interpret earthly disasters as divine trials. Politically the surviving Nazis in 1945 knew themselves to be on the defensive; the accusers had become the accused. In this respect, the Allied denazification campaign, however ill-conceived and poorly carried out, surely played a positive part. Few Nazis had any thought of reviving the party. Ex-members of the SS, *Waffen SS,* and the SD (the SS security service) initially fell under the "automatic arrest"

[116]Marlis Steinert, *Hitlers Krieg und die Deutschen, Stimmung and Haltung der Deutschen Bevölkerung im Zweiten Weltkrieg.* Düsseldorf, Econ Verlag, 1970.

category. A few of the chief evildoers committed suicide; a handful were jailed or hanged by the Allies. A large proportion of the real criminals never got their just deserts, in part owing to the leniency of so many West German courts.

In this, as in all other regards bearing on the occupation, the Allies had made no effective preparation; their policies vacillated; they lacked information, and lacked qualified personnel, including interpreters. (The British, unwilling to allow war criminals an honorable death by firing squad, also suffered from a shortage of qualified hangmen.) Those Nazis who feared punishment at first kept on the move; they provided support to one another; they left Germany when they could. But "no evidence was ever found that ODESSA [an ex-SS veterans' organization] was anything like a coherent network," much less that there was a great Nazi conspiracy to set up a "Fourth Reich."[117] Nazis and Nazi sympathizers there were still aplenty in 1945, both inside and outside Germany. The virus mutated instead of dying; but to the great majority of Germans, even former party comrades, Hitler was, to use Arthur Koestler's phrase in a different context, "the God that failed."

Neither could anti-semitism provide a political rallying point, not withstanding numerous contemporary forecasts to the contrary. The German Jews have since become the subject of an enormous literature and bitter debate despite their small numbers – less than 1 percent of the Reich's population in 1933. Interest was stimulated both by the extent of their contribution to German culture and their nightmare fate. The German Jew was also cast in the role of the archetypal outsider, a role once deemed discreditable by the Nazis, but later regarded as praiseworthy by those leftist intellectuals who gloried in their own alienation. The German Jew was identified likewise with the Weimar culture, which itself later became a role model for the radicals of the 1960s. The German Jews of historical fact, as opposed to those of fiction, had not been particularly left wing; few of them had read Marx or Freud, or had listened to Schönberg's music. Hardly any of them – even the university-educated – had ever heard of the Frankfurt School of Social Research. The typical German Jew had made his living as a lawyer, a businessman, a shop-keeper, a white-collar worker, a journalist, a technician, or an artisan – not as a rabbi, professor, or psychoanalyst. To the Nazis anti-semitism had indeed served as the core of a millenarian creed that considered Jewry as the source of all evil. This creed had nothing to do with the real Jews whom Germans met in daily life – physicians, lawyers, accountants, upholsterers, cabinet makers, tailors. These men and women had indeed experienced anti-semitism of sorts in pre-Nazi Germany – as evidenced by the proverb Jews whispered among themselves, *Stiefkinder müssen doppelt artig sein* (stepchildren must be

---

[117]Magnus Linklater, Isabel Hilton, and Neal Ascherson, *The Fourth Reich: Klaus Barbie and the Neo-Fascist Connection*. London, Hodder and Stoughton, 1984, p. 137. Tom Bower, *Blind Eye to Murder: Britain, America and the Purging of Nazi Germany*. London, Granada, 1983. For a most pessimistic assessment, see Anne Huhn and Alwin Meyer, *"Einst kommt der Tag der Rache": Die Rechtsextreme Herausforderung, 1945 bis Heute*. Freiburg, Dreisam Verlag, 1986.

twice as good), an injunction likely to bring financial success to those who harkened to the message. (The economic success of German Jews was a major source of anti-semitism among the German middle classes, who resisted competition.) But overall, German Jews had been relatively well integrated into society, as evinced by their combat record in successive wars (an important consideration in a country where the army had always played a major part in socializing young men), and by the high rate of German–Jewish intermarriage.[118] In a cultural sense, the German Jews had widely internalized the values of those liberal German bureaucrats who had taken the lead in emancipating them in the first half of the nineteenth century. (The *Yekke* jokes, told in Israel at the German Jews' expense, depicted them as well-educated, hard working, obedient to constituted authority, conscientious, and without the slightest touch of common sense – the same qualities Germans attributed to civil servants.)

Neither had Hitler's extermination campaign against the Jews enjoyed mass support. Atrocities had derived not from the "people's rage" postulated by Dr Goebbels, nor from spontaneous outbursts, but from the organized action of the state. Hatred for the Jews had played but a minor role in mobilizing German voters for the Nazi cause before 1933 (there had in fact existed almost an inverse relationship between the strength of the Nazi vote in any given German city and the number of Jews residing therein). Hitler, far from publicizing his atrocities, in fact did all he could to keep them a state secret (*Geheime Reichssache*). Few of the most fervent party members who had voted for Hitler in 1933 would have approved of his "Final Solution." If anything, the horrors of Nazi persecutions had perhaps discredited anti-semitism even among many anti-semites in Western Europe and the US. Anti-semitism had ceased to count for much in German politics by 1945.[119]

"Why do you want to leave Poland, your native land, and go to Palestine?" a Pole asked his Jewish friend. "I hear the Party wants to liquidate the Jews and the barbers," replied the Jew. "Why the barbers?" "You see," came the Jew's answer, "everybody asks that very same question. That is why I want to emigrate."

The German collapse had also shattered the Prussocentric German Reich. According to Prussophile historiography, German unification under Prussian leadership had been the culmination of a historically inevitable process that had given expression to the German's inborn desire for national unity. But in terms of German history, the Reich created by Bismarck had not lasted long – 74 years to be exact, the lifetime of a grandparent. The Bismarckian Reich had

---

[118]For their military service, see Rolf Vogel, *Ein Stück von Uns: Deutsche Juden in den Deutschen Armeen, 1813–1976, Eine Dokumentation*. Mainz, von Hase and Koehler, 1977. For their occupational structure, see *Philo-Lexicon Handbuch des Jüdischen Wissens*. Berlin, Philo Verlag, 1937, p. 809. For mixed marriages, see the entry therein under *Mischehen*. Also see, L. H. Gann, "German Jews", in *Commentary,* 1984, pp. 64–5.

[119]For a more detailed discussion, see Sarah Gordon, *Hitler, Germans, and the "Jewish Question"*. Princeton, Princeton University Press, 1984.

been only one of many states in German history. Even German national sentiment had been of a more complex character than the old-time historians had assumed. (One of the authors remembers, as a member of the British occupation force, listening in 1946 to a debate among German farmers near Monschau, on the Belgo-German border, conducted in the local *patois*. The discussion concerned the desirability of joining the region to Belgium. The arguments for and against hinged on the price of coffee and other commodities that might be expected if Monschau were to become Belgian.)

What of the social effects brought about by Nazi governance and the resultant collapse? In 1945 Germany was stripped of its eastern territories. East Prussia, Pomerania, and Silesia were lost. The ruling East German SED (*Sozialistische Einheitspartei*) later tried to develop a separate nationality, founded on socialist principles. But try as it might, the SED's attempts all failed. No ordinary German would look at Saxons, Brandenburgers, and Thuringians as members of a separate nation – unlike Swiss, Austrians, and Luxemburgers.[120] As a German politician put it, the reunification question would remain open as long as the Brandenburg Gate remained closed. (A precedent for reunification was unwittingly provided by the Saar territory. In 1945 this was totally integrated into France in an economic sense. But in 1957 it returned to West Germany as *Saarland*, a separate *Land*.)

As regards West Germany as a whole, scholars usually assumed at the end of the war that the Nazi defeat had ushered in a complete transformation. The old order had collapsed. The *Junkers* had gone. Germany had learned from her defeat. During the 1960s and later this interpretation aroused bitter challenges. For instance, Fritz Fischer, a leading German historian, argues that Germany from Bismarck to Hitler had remained subject to an "alliance of elites." This establishment had consisted of landed magnates, great industrialists, military officers, and bureaucrats. Between them, they had relied on repression at home, and conquest abroad.[121] In West Germany, as opposed to the East, these elites managed to hold on to power, even though social mobility overall did slightly increase during the twentieth century.[122]

Equally restricted in their effect, the argument continues, were the changes regarding the position of women. During World War II, German women had

---

[120]In 1987, nearly 40 years after the creation of the Federal German Republic, a poll taken in West Germany indicated that 93 percent of the respondents characterized the East Germans as Germans, and declined to look upon the GDR as just another foreign state. Among respondents under 29, the total was 90 percent. See Gerald R. Kleinfeld, "Holes in the wall: German-German relations," in James A. Cooney, Wolfgang-Uwe Friedrich, Gerald R. Kleinfeld, eds, *German-American Relations Yearbook*, New York, Campus, 1989, p. 233.

[121]For details on the position in the US during the 1930s, see Charles E. Silberman, *A Certain People: American Jews and Their Lives Today*. New York, Summit Books, 1985, esp. pp. 47–57. According to Silberman, a series of polls taken between 1940 and 1945 indicated that a high proportion of the American public would have sympathized with or participated in an anti-semitic political campaign and no more than 30 percent would have opposed it. Thereafter US anti-semitism strikingly declined, as indicated by successive public opinion polls.

[122]Fritz Fischer, *Bündnis der Eliten: Zur Kontinuität der Machtstrukturen in Deutschland 1871–1945*. Düsseldorf, Droste Verlag, 1979.

indeed found new kinds of employment, in academic jobs, in the administration, and as *Wehrmacht* auxiliaries.[123] The shift was, however, much smaller
than in the Allied countries. The Nazis had been committed to keeping women
at home. Even in 1943, when the Reich belatedly turned to "total war" on the
production front, the number of women in employment did not substantially
increase (though there was a slight shift from farm and domestic labor to office
work during the war). The overall employment statistics altered little. (In May
1939, there were 14,262,000 women in employment, as against 14,897,000 in
September 1944.)[124] German women did not have to work in vast numbers
perhaps because forced labor from the occupied territories made this unnecessary. Change came immediately after the war, when women had to step in to
take the place of millions of men left crippled or consigned to prisoner of war
camps. Women did the heaviest labor, from plowing fields to clearing rubble
in city streets (the so-called *Trümmerfrauen*). But the decisive transformation
in the labor market for women only occurred during the 1960s, as a result of
postwar economic development. Only then did German women begin to
approach the percentage of American or British women in the workforce.

Arguments in favor of the essential continuity within German society have
some merit. They especially appeal to those who remain critical of West
German society today. We, however, are impressed more by what appear to
us to be the shattering discontinuities in modern German history. We cannot
agree, for example, with those who regard Nazism as no more than the ultimate
stage of German capitalism. This is a thesis of old standing. During the 1930s
and 1940s, socialist and communist alike had considered Hitler a mere puppet
of Germany's great industrial magnates. This assumption also played an
important part in shaping the initial occupation policies adopted by the Western
Allies, and for a time became part of a well-established orthodoxy. It will not,
however, bear detailed examination. As Henry A. Turner showed in his classic
work on the subject, the great corporations had at first remained bitterly
suspicious of the Nazis.[125]   Even after their remarkable success in the early
1930s, the financial aid given to the Nazis by big business had been small by
comparison with their income from other sources. It was only from 1933, after
Franz von Papen had agreed to serve under Hitler, that industry switched its
support – by now mistakenly convinced that Hitler's conservative allies would
both constrain and "domesticate" the *Führer*.

But Hitler's conservative allies understood as little about the realities of
power as his Marxist opponents. The industrialists could not control the
monster they had helped to create. Once Hitler was firmly in office, he was
free from control by any specific social class. The workers could not constrain
him – but neither could the capitalists. For instance, once in power Hitler

---

[123]Hartmut Kaelble, "Social mobility in Germany, 1900–1960," *Journal of Modern History*, v. 50,
no. 1, March 1978, p. 445.
[124]Dörte Winkler, *Frauenarbeit im "Dritten Reich"*. Hamburg, Hoffman and Campe, 1977, p. 201.
[125]Henry Ashby Turner, *German Big Business and the Rise of Hitler*. Oxford, Oxford University
Press, 1985.

increased corporate taxes, and enforced a sweeping reduction of interest on mortgages, municipal and Reich bonds. He introduced strict controls on wages, prices, and foreign currency transactions. Titled profiteers, such as Hermann Goering, learned the art of transmuting political control over the means of production into ownership of the means of production; thus they built for their own benefit great state enterprises that spread their control over the whole of Europe, with interests in steel, arms of every kind, oil, machinery, transport equipment, and so on.[126]

Nazi rule had changed Germany in other ways. The Nazis had given new scope to ambitious newcomers to the officer corps, to proliferating party offices and state agencies. (Nazism appealed to many students and intellectuals because an expanding bureaucracy offered jobs and promotion.) Moreover the Nazis borrowed older German concepts such as "public weal before private profit" (*Gemeinnutz geht vor Eigennutz*), and *Volksgemeinschaft* (a classless national society) however fraudulent, had exercised considerable appeal, not merely among young middle-class and upper-middle-class voters, but also many workers, especially the formerly unemployed. (Workers accounted for 34.6 percent of the Nazi Party members, in 1937, as against 57.4 percent of lower-middle-class and middle-class people, and 8 percent from the so-called elites.)[127] The "Third Reich" had created a new class of privileged beneficiaries of the "New Order." But thereafter the social disruption brought about by massive bombing raids and enforced migrations profoundly altered the social landscape of postwar Germany – all the more so as the refugees from the East were largely proletarianized.[128]

Politically, Germany was a land divided, without a capital, without a government, with a patriotism ambiguous and full of self-questioning. The best German artists and writers had gone abroad (like Thomas Mann), or had chosen "inner emigration" (like Ricarda Huch, a distinguished novelist and historian). *Wo ist des Deutschen Vaterland?* (where is the Germans' fatherland?) a nineteenth-century poet had asked. In 1945, the answer seemed unclear. The bulk of Germans by that time were concerned, not with Germany's identity, but with the most pressing problems of survival – jobs, food, shelter, clothing. They were inclined, like so many other Europeans then, to push into the darkest recesses of memory their miseries and humiliations, and to concentrate on improving their immediate condition.

Postwar Germany developed a large middle class and saw a decline in the old aristocratic element. Society became less hierarchical, more open, less formal and differential – in fact, more like the US than Weimar Germany. Much of the change was due to the loss of Protestant and Prussian-dominated

---

[126]R. J. Overy, *Goering: The "Iron Man"*. London, Kegan Paul, 1984.

[127]Michael H. Kater, *The Nazi Party: A Social Profile of Members and Leaders, 1919–1945*. Cambridge, Mass., Harvard University Press, 1983, p. 252. Another major work is Richard Hamilton, *Who Voted For Hitler?* Princeton, Princeton University Press, 1982.

[128]In 1939, 37 percent of the refugees from the East in employment had been self-employed or run their own farms; by 1949 92 percent of the refugees were wage workers. Grosser, *Geschichte Deutschlands Seit 1945*. p. 273.

East Germany and to the rise in influence of Catholic Germany. The Catholic Adenauer dominated the political scene and Erhard guided the economy. The large, developing middle class and non-political unionized workers moderated German society. Civil competence increased as ideological differences and inter-party hostility declined. There was more social trust and less inequality between classes and between Protestants and Catholics; there was also greater voter participation as trust in government increased.

Austria by 1946 had resumed its separate path, and today Austrian sovereignty seems beyond doubt. It was by no means evident during World War II when the Allies were still considering plans to make Austria part of a larger political unit.[129] Austria's independence was occasioned by sheer pragmatic considerations, rather than a definitive program. But in the end, having been briefly united with the Reich between 1938 and 1945, Austria went back to a separate existence under a four-power regime, made harsher by extensive reparation payments to the Soviet Union. Austria, by that time, had had enough of the *Anschluss*; henceforth the Austrian Republic for the first time in its brief history attained full legitimacy for nearly all its people. They had suffered heavy casualties on every front, and the country was subject to successive brain-drains. First Hitler drove out or murdered the Jews and "Judaized" Gentiles.[130] Once Western Germany recovered after World War II, more Austrians departed – this time to find jobs in Germany. During the war, moreover, Austria had served the Third Reich as a giant air raid shelter; many Germans had been evacuated there. (By the end of the war, the country's population had risen from around 6,000,000 to about 10,000,000.) Austria by then suffered from serious shortages of housing and food for which the *Piefkes*, the Germans from the "Old Reich," were widely held responsible. The "Third Reich" lost its glamor, as Austrian farmers during the war largely circumvented the German-imposed system of economic controls, and left-wing opposition had continued among many factory workers, just as it did in Germany.

> *To defend their industry and banks from being confiscated as German assets, the Austrian government nationalized them. By opting for neutrality, the Austrians got rid of the Russians and the Allies. The economy did well until the crisis of 1974, but corruption and inefficiency plagued the state-run concerns and an imperial-sized bureaucracy consumed much and slowed down economic growth.*

Nevertheless, it is probably true that the Austrians in 1945 retained greater respect than the Germans for the power of the state – hallowed as it was by both Austro-Marxism and by the prestige of the Habsburg bureaucratic tradition. (Senior officials of the Austrian Republic continued to take pride in

[129]Fritz Fellner, "The problem of the Austrian nation after 1945," *Journal of Modern History*, v. 60, no. 2, June 1988, pp. 264–89. Also see Barbara Jelavich, *Modern Austria: Empire and Republic 1815–1986.* Cambridge, Cambridge University Press, 1987.
[130]Paul Hofmann, *The Viennese: Splendor, Twilight, and Exile.* New York, Anchor Press, 1988.

being awarded the title of *Hofrat* (Court Councillor) created by a long-departed monarchy.) Elections after the war in 1945 returned the (Catholic) People's Party with a majority. In contrast to the bitter struggles of the past, the Catholics in practice closely cooperated with the Social Democrats. (Karl Renner, a veteran Social Democrat, became president.) Austria was to be ruled between 1946 and 1966 by this socialist–conservative alliance – the red–black coalition. The new government carried out the most far-reaching nationalization program initiated in any Western country. Most heavy industries, the major banks, and numerous other enterprises passed under public ownership. Catholics and Social Democrats, once unforgiving enemies, entered into a close alliance cemented by the *Proporzsystem* (according to which jobs in public enterprises were shared out in a proportionate fashion between members of the two parties). *Protektion* (personal patronage, common in the imperial days) was transmuted into party-centered nepotism. Labor unrest strikingly diminished through the *Paritätsprinzip* (according to which organized labor, employers, and government departments settled wages in an informal fashion). Whether efficient or not in a purely functional sense, the Austrian compromise did much to heal the bitter wounds remaining from former strife.

Austrians, at the same time, evolved a new set of usable myths about their national identity. There were lengthy debates among scholars and politicians about whether Austria was simply a German state, or a separate and distinct nation. The claim to nationhood derived from a strange medley of misconceptions, which included memories of Austria's supposed mission to bring culture to south-eastern Europe; exaggerated (though not wholly mistaken) references to the tolerance displayed towards Jews and other minorities by the long departed Emperor Franz Josef; the splendors of Austrian baroque and rococo; the glitter of Strauss's and Lehar's operas; and also the erroneous assumption that Austria was particularly suited as a bridge between East and West. Equally important was the fairy-tale that Austria, Hitler's homeland, had in 1938 been the reluctant victim of enforced annexation to the Reich. (A cabaret show, produced amid the ruins of Berlin in 1945, satirized this misconception by putting on stage a sweet *Dirndl* (young woman) in Austrian peasant costume, wearing a sash inscribed "Austria." Hair tousled, blouse half-undone, she smilingly sang a current hit "I didn't want to do it; he made me do it.") Austria's experiences in the Third Reich had in fact been ambivalent. While Austrians had suffered heavily, they had also given the SS some of its most infamous malefactors. On the other hand, the Third Reich had also encouraged the creating of new industries, thereby unintentionally facilitating Austria's future as an independent nation. Unwittingly, Hitler had succeeded where Dollfuss had failed. Pan-Germanism (a creed calling for the political unification of all German-speaking lands) was henceforth deemed both dead and damned.

France

France emerged from World War II both defeated and victorious. The Allies had hoped that French recovery would hasten a general European recovery and stabilize the political life of the Continent at a time when Germany was disarmed, but still regarded by her neighbors as a potential threat, to be hamstrung by restrictions on her productive capacity. But France had suffered serious damage; the German occupation had divided society, and diminished respect for governmental institutions; initial recovery was slow and US policy makers instead made West Germany the main engine of recovery.[131]

Despite her misfortunes, France once again claimed the status of a great power, with her own zone of occupation in Germany as a token of international importance. French rule in Indochina was already under attack, but French possessions in Africa remained intact. Far from desiring to abandon them, the French meant both to reform and strengthen their colonial empire which, in part, had served as a territorial base for the Free French at a time when the Germans had occupied their French homeland. The French had begun to rebuild their armed forces; there were 284,000 men of all arms by 1947. Charles de Gaulle had become a statesman of international stature, and France, after many years, had acquired a decisive and charismatic leader.

Nevertheless, France was in deep economic trouble. During World War II, she had served as Germany's principal milch cow, having supplied probably as much as 42 percent of all the contributions extracted by the Third Reich from the occupied countries. (By 1943, French payments of all kinds to Germany amounted to 9.1 percent of Germany's gross national product.)[132] Equally shattering was the impact of sabotage and battle. (The estimated loss by 1945 of capital equipment brought about through bombing, shelling, looting, and sabotage was estimated at twice the French gross national product of 1938.) By 1945 industrial production amounted to no more than 20 percent of the prewar figures and was up to only 75 percent by 1946.[133] Nothing could be done until wrecked transportation and communication systems were restored. (For instance, French river traffic by 1946 had fallen to 40 percent of the 1938 level. The merchant fleet had been reduced to no more than 32 percent of the prewar figures. By September 1944, only 18,000 kilometers of the railway system remained in operation out of some 40,000 kilometers.) A

---

[131]Alan S. Milward, *The New Order and the French Economy*. Oxford, Clarendon Press, 1970, pp. 268–97. Other works on the French economy and French society include the following: Stanley Hoffman, *Decline or Renewal? France Since the 1930s*. New York, Viking Press, 1974. John Ardagh, *France in the 1980s*. Harmondsworth, Penguin Books, 1982; (update of an earlier version). François Caron, *An Economic History of Modern France*. New York, Columbia University Press, 1979. Jean-Pierre Rioux, *The Fourth Republic 1944–1958*. Cambridge, Cambridge University Press, 1987. André de Lattre, *Politique Économique de la France*. Paris, Cours de droit, 1969, 3 v. E. H. Lacombe, *Les Changements de la Société Française*. Paris, Editions Economie et Humanisme, 1971.

[132]Norman Luxenburg, *Europe Since World War II: The Big Change*. Rev. edn., Carbondale, Southern Illinois University Press, 1979.

[133]Warren C. Baum, *The French Economy and the State*. Princeton, Princeton University Press, 1958, pp. 16–17.

railway journey from Paris to Marseille, once a routine undertaking, had turned into a dreary and sometimes dangerous chore. A modest recovery began thanks to the political stability brought by de Gaulle and his allies.

Many Frenchmen, like their German neighbors, went hungry. (French official rations at the beginning of 1945 were down to between 45 percent and 55 percent of the minimum calorific intake.) As all over Europe, townsmen suffered the most, because only about 55 to 60 percent of the meat produced in the country went through official channels, and because the peasants were more inclined than in the past to keep for themselves and their families the food they had grown. Many homesteads lay in ruins. Much farmland had been withdrawn from use by reason of flood damage, uncleared minefields, or temporary fortifications. Much livestock had been slaughtered – no one knew exactly how many beasts. The number of horses, still the main source of draft power all over Continental Europe, was halved. Fertilizers and spare parts for worn out agricultural machinery were in short supply and trained manpower was scarce. Not surprisingly, French agricultural production had slumped to perhaps 50 percent of prewar output – food was scarce everywhere and the US had to help feed Europe.

> *The effects of war on agriculture varied. The US, Britain, and the neutral countries increased production. Even on the Continent some farmers did well as demand for their produce increased. On the other hand, there was also much destruction. Men and draft animals were diverted to the armies; spare parts for agricultural machinery and artificial fertilizers were hard to get. Governments tried to control the situation by directives, rationing, and subsidies; but the black market dominated much of Europe. Above all it was the US that came out of the war with increased agricultural production and an agricultural surplus for export to its hungry allies and former enemies. Europe's overall agricultural production had fallen and did not regain prewar levels until 1951.*
>
> *Eventually the war proved to have been a blessing in disguise for agricultural productivity, permitting revitalizing structural changes (land reforms, mechanization after 1945).*
> *See Bernd Marten and Alan S. Milward,* Agriculture and Food Supply in the Second World War, *1985.*

French foreign trade had also gravely diminished. (By March 1944, French imports from other nations had fallen to 12.2 percent of the 1938 level and exports to 53.3 percent.)[134] By 1945 France, like Great Britain, faced grave trade and budgetary deficits. (In 1945 French imports stood at 54,839,000 francs, as against exports worth only 34,041,646,000 francs.) American food imports helped somewhat to retrieve the situation. (During the first two years after liberation, American food imports amounted to between 4 and 6 percent of the normal production in France.) But overall the French economy remained in a desperate state. The black market, so strong during the war, continued and affected recovery; colonial wars drained the treasury. Then came the disastrous winter of 1947 and the loss of bumper crops. But the Marshall Plan

[134]Charles Bettelheim, *Bilan de L'Économie Française 1919–1946.* Paris, Presses Universitaires, 1947, p. 270.

was to shore up Western Europe and increase productivity.

The French did an efficient job in repairing the immediate damage of war. But there were greater difficulties ahead. For many years, the French economy had suffered from pervasive weaknesses, and was thought to be perpetually stalled. During the preceding two generations, France had been the world's first industrial country to have experienced a long period of relative (though certainly not absolute) decline. In 1870, France had been a great power in every sense, more or less equal in industrial output to Great Britain and Germany.[135] Seventy years later, the French national income had fallen to less than half of Great Britain's, and little over one third of Germany's. There was also a long-standing and serious demographic problem. In 1870 the French population had exceeded Britain's and Italy's, and nearly equalled Germany's. By 1945 the French ranked below them all (with a total population of only 40,517,923) due to a declining birth rate.[136] France had paid a heavy toll in two world wars as well. (Adding the losses incurred through migration, higher death rate and reduced birth rate brought about by the war, to the number of persons killed in combat, or who died in concentration camps and prisoner-of-war camps, France may have lost 1,428,000 people in World War II.)

In addition, the Germans had deliberately retained something like 2,000,000 Frenchmen in prisoner-of-war camps. But for reasons that are hard to explain, France from 1942 started a remarkable demographic recovery, and the birth rate began to rise in a striking fashion. (By 1946, the birth rate had reached 20.9 per thousand, as against 15 per thousand in 1939.) For whatever reason, the French nation had decided not to die out, and they set themselves the task of rejuvenating their country with remarkable energy.

France had many assets or social capital in spite of war damages and losses. For all its economic weaknesses, it had not been a stagnant country. After World War I, the French had rapidly reconstructed the devastated areas of the Northeast. Thereafter, they modernized many of their mines. Electrification made great strides, as had oil refineries, rubber and aluminum industries, iron and steel, and various branches of chemical and electrical engineering. (During the 1920s, the French industrial growth rate had actually exceeded that of the other European countries.)[137] The French had shown a great deal of initiative, for instance, in the motor car industry. It was not for nothing that French loan words such as "automobile" and "garage" had enriched English and many other languages. There were plenty of Frenchmen famed for their entrepreneurial skill – not merely in traditional industries such as *haute couture* but in modern manufactures too. French publishers and film makers, aca-

---

[135]Baum, *The French Economy and the State,* p. 16. Between 1870 and 1879 the real national income of France in billions of international units stood at 7.66; corresponding figures for Germany (1876) were 7.69 and for Britain 8.14. By 1938, corresponding figures respectively amounted to 12.38; 35.7; and 27.55.

[136]Colin Dyer, *Population and Society in Twentieth Century France.* London, Hodder and Stoughton, 1978, a brilliant assessment.

[137]François Caron, *An Economic History of Modern France.* New York, Columbia University Press, 1979, p. 179.

demicians and scientists were renowned the world over. Other prewar assets had included a substantial hoard of gold, a slow fall in agricultural prices that benefited consumers, and an apparently low unemployment rate (occasioned in part by misleading statistics, and in part by the French social structure, characterized by a large farming sector that enabled jobless workers to return from the city to the family farm).

These real or apparent strengths, had not, however, sufficed to balance the country's economic weaknesses. Defensively minded in the economic field as well as in foreign policy, the French during the interwar period had surrounded their country with a "Chinese wall" of customs barriers that had paralleled the Maginot line in the military sphere, sheltering French farmers and manufacturers from competition. Rent controls discouraged housing construction that had stagnated since the 1930s. There was a widespread spirit of pessimism and self-pity, as all too many turned to blaming *les affameurs et les accapareurs* (the famine-makers and monopolists), those mythical miscreants variously defined as corrupt politicians, speculators, communists, "the Two Hundred Families," Jews, and foreigners, or just circumstances in general – "C'est la crise," as many French were wont to say with a shrug. The *douce France,* the France of small farms, village cafés, and family shops, romanticized in innumerable novels and movies, had not been so sweet as might have appeared in retrospect.

France during the interwar period had experienced what amounted almost to a strike on the private investors' part. (Between 1921 and 1936, private investments through the stock exchange had diminished in volume by four-fifths of their value, measured in 1928 francs.) The state, by contrast, had taken an increasingly important share in the economy. (Before World War I, the ratio between private and public investment had stood at 80 percent to 20 percent; by 1938, this had reversed to 12 percent against 88 percent.)[138] *Autofinancement* on the part of large companies, though increasingly in fashion, had not sufficed, for undistributed profits in the major companies had seriously diminished (from 21 percent in 1929 to 6 percent in 1939) – at a time when Popular Front politicians used to declaim against the French capitalists' supposedly huge gains. Industrial productivity overall had failed to keep pace with the increase in productivity registered by France's major competitors. By 1937, French industrial production amounted to no more than 12.9 percent of the USA's, and 45.7 percent of Germany's, though France had helped to pioneer the industrial revolution.

French agriculture likewise had long-term problems. By 1946, farming still employed 36 percent of the French working population. Generalizations with regard to their methods and living conditions are hard to make, given the enormous disparities that existed between the well-run wheat and cattle farms of the Paris region and the Northeast, compared to the poverty-stricken little holdings in the Massif Central, Britanny, and the extreme Southwest. But French agriculture was as a whole beset by archaic methods and marketing

---

[138]Bettelheim, *Bilan de Économie Française,* pp. 113–15.

systems, by widespread rural discontent, and by the burden of having to maintain too many people on small and uneconomic freeholds. Indeed one of the main impediments to general economic advance was the peculiar backwardness that characterized so many small farms.[139] Neither the Third Republic nor the Pétain regime had been able to cure these ills – all of which were made worse by the ravages of occupation and war. The Marshall Plan did what the Third Republic could not – it helped to change agriculture and increase production.

> *Paris dominated France in a way not found in any other European country. Government and industry were centered in the capital, as was the cultural and intellectual life of France; the regions suffered from unintentional neglect.*

France, by 1945, appeared a house divided, split not only by politics, but riven also in the economic sense, the prosperity of the industrialized North and Northeast contrasting with the relative poverty of Corsica and the Southwest, where scoffers inclined to deride refugees from Paris or Lille as *les boches du nord*. Even though production increased after 1945 in France, and elsewhere, it did not at first restore the material well-being of the population to even the prewar level. Replacement of goods and services destroyed by the war came first. The standard of living in France and Western Europe rose slowly because of this and because of the shortage of coal – the main source of energy for heat and power. Frenchmen did not want to return to the mines and Polish and German labor had been sent home. (Britain and Germany also suffered from a dearth of workers.) Lack of incentives and worn-out mines further crippled coal production. The fierce winter of 1947 caused great suffering; widespread strikes, in part motivated by political reasons by communist-dominated unions caused additional damage. The result: coal production in France, Britain, and Germany was below prewar figures even by 1948.

The political problems facing France in 1945 seemed perhaps even more intractable than her economic predicament. The Third Republic had ended in failure, just as the Bismarckian Reich had. In a certain sense, they had been twin children born of the defeat of Napoleon III's "Second Empire" in 1870. Both had come to rest on a social alliance that found its embodiment in heavy import duties on the products of agriculture and on those of heavy industry; both regimes had exalted the army as the true repository of national virtue; both had delighted in honors and decorations. Both had lacked the legitimacy needed to survive disastrous defeats on the battlefield.

[139]Gordon Wright, *Rural Revolution in France: The Peasantry in the Twentieth Century*. Oxford, Oxford University Press, 1964.

> *France was a badly fragmented, over-administered society; there was little social or political consensus; there were deep regional splits; secularists attacked clericalists; and political legitimacy was still not deeply ingrained. The Fourth Republic (1946–58) was marred by a high level of cabinet instability and ministerial rotation. The party system was strongly ideological, and less practical and programmatic than in Great Britain and the US. Divisiveness had long created political stress and instability in France, and this resulted in social turmoil. Partisanship was high; modernism and tradition clashed fiercely and caused more conflict in French society than in most other states in Western Europe.*

The causes of the Third Republic's political troubles were many: an interminable series of political shifts and expedients; a serious economic crisis during the 1930s when French overall productivity fell, investment declined, and inflation worsened. By the end of the 1930s the government was too feeble for firm decisions – unable either to impose a socialist plan of taxation and investment or to rely on an untrammeled market economy. The political climate had become poisonous. As Eugen Weber puts it in a classic work, *Action Française,* "myths of pervading evil turned superficial disagreements into haunting fears and political differences into vendettas, and the French body politic became incapable of any kind of unity because all foundations for mutual trust had been shattered during these ruthless and bitter fights, which no one carried on with more envenomed shrillness than the Right.[140] The French tragedy had become all the greater, given the intellectual brilliance that had distinguished French literati such as Robert Brasillach and Charles Maurras above Nazi scribblers such as Alfred Rosenberg.

Germany's defeat at last discredited the Vichy regime, most of whose former supporters now claimed to have been *résistants* at heart. A great many customary fads ceased to be fashionable: the cult of the soil and the dead; praise of a mythical peasantry shaped in the imagination of *boulevardiers*; sophisticated abuse of big city folk, Jews, and other supposed undesirables; the crankiness that had turned the beret into a national headgear and physical fitness programs into a means for promoting national recovery. Pétain's *Etat Français* was consigned to the political attic, together with so many other discards – two empires, two royal monarchies, and three republics that had served France since the fall of the Bourbon dynasty.

By 1945 then, France was politically disorganized, economically shattered, and staggered under the burden of inflation and heavy state expenditure. As French wits put it, her troubles sprang from having to pay for three wars all at once – yesterday's, today's, and tomorrow's. France had to pay for two former wars in pensions and annuities to veterans, cripples, and orphans; she also had to spend money on the reconstruction of her industries and for damaged or ruined houses. She had to cope with a bitter legacy of violence, lawlessness, and hatred that divided families and former friends. On the face of it, the country seemed ready to come apart at the seams.

France, however, was fortunate in the leadership of Charles de Gaulle, a general who, for all his failings, turned out to be a statesman. Bismarck had

---

[140] Eugen Weber, *Action Française: Royalism and Reaction in Twentieth Century France.* Stanford, Stanford University Press, 1962, p. 402.

once praised Paul Kruger, President of the Transvaal Republic, as a much more outstanding figure than himself. "I had all the resources of a great nation behind me," said the "Iron Chancellor," "Kruger had nothing." He might have eulogized de Gaulle in similar terms. Tall, regal in bearing, endowed with a caustic wit, completely self-centered, yet feeling himself the embodiment of living France, de Gaulle performed wonders. An unknown general in exile, de Gaulle for a time turned into an uncrowned king, with all the departed monarchs' gift for dignified showmanship. He created both a rallying point for French patriotism and a political alternative to Vichy and all its works.

During the war, de Gaulle first sought to represent France from London. Despite American hostility, he finally secured Allied recognition of his *Comité Français de la Libération Nationale* at Algiers in 1943, and a year later this body became the French Provisional Government. De Gaulle saw himself as a man standing above parties, both a conservative and a reformer. He meant at the same time to improve the workers' lot, resist alike the encroachment of "Anglo-Saxons" and Soviets, refashion French glory, rebuild France as a great power, and conciliate his country's warring factions.

In 1944, de Gaulle took a historic step and enfranchised the women of France (who, in their majority for many years voted for the more conservatively inclined parties). De Gaulle would have no truck with anti-semitism, and drew on the abilities of Frenchmen of whatever descent or previous political conviction, as long as they had acquired an honorable record in the resistance, and in supporting de Gaulle. At the same time, he stood for the traditional virtues. During the miserable years of the occupation, Free French broadcasts from London had invariably prefaced their news bulletins with the stirring line: "Honneur et patrie, c'est la France Libre qui vous parle," thereby exalting those patriotic values that the "soft left" had consistently denigrated.

One of de Gaulle's most immediate tasks was to rebuild the armed forces. The navy, a stronghold of pro-Vichy sentiments, had been largely destroyed. The army's defeat in 1940 had shocked the French, as evinced in books later written by patriots as different in outlook as Jean Dutourd and Marc Bloch.[141] Rebuilding the forces was a difficult task, entailing the amalgamation of regulars and recruits and the Communist *Francs Tireurs-Partisans*. (The communists had tried to merge all resistance groups under their own leadership but de Gaulle and the socialists defeated them, thus denying the communists a military force for a coup.) Given the existing disabilities, the army performed well enough; a French armored division liberated Paris, thereby confronting the communists in the capital with a *fait accompli*. The enlarged army (broadened by fusing regulars, the original Free French volunteers, and the *Forces Françaises de l'Intérieur,* the guerrillas) also fought creditably in the last stages of the war, even though many of its members felt that the nation had not fully supported them.

The army also had its share of troubles. The military establishment experienced a series of purges of those who had not joined the resistance by the time

[141] Jean Dutourd, *Les Taxis de la Marne*. Paris, Gallimard, 1962; Marc Bloch, *L'Etrange Défaite, témoignage Écrit en 1940 Suivi d'Écrits Clandestins 1942–44*. Paris, A. Michel, 1957.

of the Normandy invasion. (By 1947, 12,000 officers had been retired from the army.) Many middle-class and upper-class families henceforth proved reluctant to send their sons to the army. There was a striking decline in the officers' pay relative to senior academics and civil servants, and made worse by inflation; there was discontent over the army's antiquated equipment, and over the creeping and inconclusive guerrilla war that broke out in Indochina.[142] Nevertheless, the army's loyalty to de Gaulle held, and provided the general with an indispensable power base.

The civil machinery of the state – like the army – experienced a series of purges, but essentially stayed in place. The high hopes of the *résistants,* by and large, were disappointed. Though many former resistance people gained official positions, they did not build a *république pure et dure. Epuration* (the purge) in France, like *epurazione* in Italy, *zuivering* in Holland, *Entnazifizierung* in Germany, inevitably left in place many time-servers who profited from personal connections, and sheer luck. In the end, the Fourth Republic set up after the war did not prove all that different from the Third Republic. The administration was rebuilt in the traditional manner perfected by Napoleon Bonaparte.

De Gaulle, to his supreme credit, did not attempt to become a military dictator. Neither did he try to create a constitution that simply sought to perpetuate his own personal power, as Bismarck had done in Germany. In fact, he trod warily. A new constitution was promulgated in 1945 and a National Constituent Assembly was convened, followed by a new constitution adopted by a national referendum in 1946. (The National Constituent Assembly contained 136 members of the *Mouvement Républicain Populaire,* 129 socialists, 121 members of minor groups, and 136 communists of the *Parti Communiste Français (PCF)* – 522 deputies in all.)

Within the assembly, the communists occupied a powerful position, unique in French politics, with a strength quite out of proportion to their numerical representation. The French Communist Party (PCF) was the most Stalinist party in Western Europe, rigidly organized in a hierarchical order, and a counter-state within the French body politic. During the war it spent much of the time killing its enemies (much as Tito did in Yugoslavia or as the communists had done in the Spanish Civil War). The party had massive support among the industrial workers, among many intellectuals, and also some middle-class people. It also benefited from the Soviet Union's military prestige, from the discipline of its cadres, and from its striking record in the resistance.

Yet for all their skill and tactical expertise, the communists were outmaneuvered at every turn. De Gaulle proved a masterful political campaigner; he and his supporters were as determined as the communists and just as skilled in underground warfare. De Gaulle had the army ready, in case the communists staged open insurrection. The majority of French civilians would also have

---

[142]John Stewart Ambler, *The French Army in Politics 1945–1962.* Columbus, Ohio State University Press, 1966, pp. 93–8.

opposed them, backed, if necessary, by the Allied forces in Western Europe. The communists led violent labor strikes and street riots. But de Gaulle disarmed the resistance (including the communist militias) and set up his own administration. While admitting the communists to a coalition government, he fobbed them off with a number of ministries. These afforded to the party a considerable amount of patronage but not the means of seizing power. According to a German proverb, he who sups with the devil needs a long spoon. De Gaulle's was the longest.

The Mediterranean countries

The Mediterranean lands (including Portugal, an Atlantic state) possess certain features in common. They share a similar climate – harsh for farmers, though not for the tourist enjoying a vacation by the seaside. The Mediterranean countries all formed part of the Roman Empire; their people spoke Latin languages, and each had a splendid literary heritage. They took a similar pride in family, and enjoyed a similar sense of honor. They were nearly all Catholic countries; yet they had also been for centuries in touch with the Muslim world that had left an imprint on Mediterranean art, music, architecture, and even language. (*Ojalá* – Oh Allah, meaning "may God grant" – remains a customary Spanish interjection.) All these countries had experienced a decline from a nostalgically remembered "golden age" and from former great power status (the Iberian countries in the sixteenth, and Italy in the twentieth century). Overall, the southern states were less developed than the northern democracies. The southern states were less industrialized, and they employed a larger proportion of their people in farming. There were, however, striking regional disparities (say, between developed Catalonia on the one hand, and relatively backward Castile on the other); these differences heightened political tensions derived from ethnic and other problems. Generally speaking, the South had higher rates of illiteracy, higher birth rates, higher rates of emigration. After World War I, the Mediterranean states had all gone through cycles of political instability, violence, and personality cults.[143] In the South the Catholic Church remained powerful; Protestantism by contrast was insignificant. But the Church had never served as national champion during long periods of alien domination, as it had done in Poland and Ireland. Mediterranean countries – unlike Ireland and Poland – had long witnessed bitter strife between the Church and anti-clericals. The Mediterranean countries had experienced, to a greater or lesser extent, long-standing struggles that pitted region against region, cities against the countryside, royalists against republicans, rich against poor.

Of Europe's Mediterranean lands, Italy was by far the most important and populous. But Italy, by the end of 1945, had paid a grim price for Mussolini's

---

[143]Roy C. Macrides, ed., *Modern Political Systems: Europe.* Englewood Cliffs, N J, Prentice-Hall, 1983, pp. 437–44. Also see Don Sassoon, *Contemporary Italy: Politics, Economy and Society Since 1945.* New York, Longman, 1987.

delusions of grandeur and for the lack of that Machiavellian realism in which the Duce had taken pride. Defeat cost Italy her African empire (though she managed to keep two disputed areas in Europe – Trieste, coveted by the Yugoslavs, and South Tyrol, to which the Austrians had put forward tentative claims). Her economy was shattered. The full extent of the damage was hard to measure, given the difficulty of securing precise statistics; but Italy had suffered heavy losses on the battlefield (perhaps as many as 700,000). At home, many cities had been bombed; much housing lay in ruins, even though industrial plants had escaped relatively lightly. Her merchant ships were mostly sunk; her farming industry stricken – and so the sorry catalogue continued.[144]

In Italy, as in the rest of Europe, reconstruction was made worse by inflation, and also by the widespread demoralization of youth, aggravated by the physical destruction of schools, the partial breakdown of the educational system, by hunger, and privation. Illiteracy had risen during the war, and in 1945 stood perhaps at near 7,000,000; the 1931 figure. By the end of 1945, Italy's gross national product had supposedly reverted to the 1911 level, and had diminished by about 40 percent in real terms, as compared with 1938. With her physical wealth much reduced, her colonial investments wiped out, Italy had to support a much larger population than before (45,645,000 in 1945), a population enhanced by a high birth rate, by the cessation of prewar emigration to the US, Brazil, and the Argentine, and by the return of Italy's uprooted settlers from the lost African colonies. Without US aid, and without the black market, many Italians would have starved.[145]

War, moreover, had magnified Italy's deep-seated structural weaknesses, for instance the enormous disparities between the North and the South. Italians differed from one another in customs, life style, and dialects. The North was wealthier, more urbanized, and more industrialized than the South. Cities such as Turin and Milan were famed for their manufacturing enterprise. They had always looked across the Alps rather than toward the Mediterranean. Italy's first industrial revolution had indeed centered on Milan, encouraged by capital investment from Britain and Germany. Turin had represented a tradition of governmental efficiency and centralization with the former kingdom of Piedmont. Piedmont, in a sense, had been Italy's Prussia; but its legacy was widely disliked in the South. Traditional divisions were augmented by the experience of war. For something like 20 months, Italy had been divided into two separate parts, the German-held North, and the South under Allied occupation. The worst damage had been inflicted on the regions between Naples and Rome, and between Florence and Bologna. Even before the Allies had landed, the combined effects of Allied bombing, together with administrative inefficiency and political dissent, had gravely weakened the

[144]Epicarmo Corbino, "L'Economia," in A. Battaglia et al., eds, *Dieci Anni Dopo, 1945–1955.* Bari, Edizione Laterza, 1955, pp. 409–58.
[145]Sergio Ricossa, "Italy: 1920–1970," in Carlo M. Cipolla, ed., *The Fontana Economic History of Europe: Contemporary Economies,* Part 2. London, Collins, Fontana Books, 1978, pp. 290–1. George H. Hildebrand, *Growth and Structure in the Economy of Modern Italy.* Cambridge, Mass., Harvard University Press, 1965.

central government. After Mussolini's fall from power in 1943, Italy in effect had two governments, neither of them truly capable of governing.

> *Fascism and Nazism shared many common features: both came to power legally in modern, industrial states and cooperated with the existing elites and institutions. Both regimes pursued foreign conquest to glorify their rule, but also to give them a mandate to transform their societies internally by means of social engineering. Policies of* spazio vitale *and* Lebensraum, *as Macgregor Knox shows* (Journal of Modern History, March 1984), *were intertwined, and produced first violence, then defeat for both systems.*

The South (*il mezzogiorno*), traditionally Italy's most poverty-stricken region, found itself in a particularly parlous condition. As long as Italy remained divided by armed conflict, jobless people could neither seek work in the industrialized North nor overseas, a serious matter for a region perennially subject to rural underemployment. Inflation had specially hit the South, whose people had been particularly accustomed to put their savings into treasury bonds and other investments with a fixed rate of return. There were the more deep-seated problems of an area where *latifundia* (large estates) were widespread, and agricultural productivity was low.

The condition of the South had created a widespread debate concerning the causes of southern misery, a debate that presaged wider disagreements within the scholarly community regarding the cause of misery in the Third World. According to romantics, such as the novelist Carlo Levi, the South suffered from its status as an economic dependency. According to this school of thought, the political unification of Italy had benefited only the progressive North, leaving the South neglected and exploited. The South had therefore turned into a gigantic labor reservoir. The southern labor migrant, stranded in the North, became a rootless and alienated person – defamed into the bargain as a *mangiasapone* (a soap eater, who used soap for filling his stomach rather than for washing his face). This interpretation went with peculiar views concerning southern national psychology – mirrored later in Third World doctrines concerning *négritude* (in West Africa) or Chicanismo (in the US). Southern villagers supposedly remained wedded to magic concepts from antiquity, that juxtaposed woman and cow, man and wolf, baron and lion, goat and devil – and other such fancies.

There was widespread lawlessness, especially in Sicily, where civil servants and policemen were looked upon with disdain as *Piemontesi,* people from Piedmont, northerners, hardly better than foreigners. In western Sicily, the Mafia, reduced almost to insignificance by Mussolini's brutal police methods, had once more become a powerful body (some critics claim because of links to the OSS), wedded to a strict though perverted sense of loyalty, involved in local politics and a great variety of extortion rackets that had not as yet been supplanted by the international drug trade with its immensely greater profits.

Other critics blamed the southerners, rather than the North, for southern ills. These had derived from the southerners' assumed ignorance, clerical superstition, from Bourbon misgovernment during the nineteenth century, from native southern indolence, and from a knack for corruption, that had combined to turn southerners from private entrepreneurship toward bureau cratic advancement in the service of the state. According to this interpretation, industrialized Milan constituted Italy's moral capital: "What Italy had to fear was the *meridionalizzazione* (the 'southernization') of Italy."[146] "Southernization," according to its critics, entailed a continuous, massive influx of expatriate southerners into the civil service that had been going on since the 1870s. Many of them advanced to the highest posts, unrestrained by anything like the administrative elitism fashioned by the *grandes écoles* in France. How was the southern sickness to be cured? By massive public planning and investment (*Riforma Agraria*) – a conclusion that once again presaged subsequent prescriptions concerning foreign aid to the Third World. The *Cassa del Mezzogiorno* provided capital to develop and to industrialize the South.

In fact, poverty was not, and never had been, confined to the South. Southerners were not necessarily devoid of entrepreneurial ability, as evinced by a variety of southern industries, and the success attained by southern emigrants in cities as far afield as Milan, Buenos Aires, São Paulo, and New York. Southern ills derived in part from the heritage of seigneurial privilege, from excessive centralization of the Italian state, from relative geographical isolation, and – in good measure – from the cures adopted to cure the disease. These included, among others, those adopted for Italy as a whole by Mussolini's tyranny.

Mussolini, though later censured by many opponents as a capitalist tool, had begun his career as a socialist, and in a certain sense remained a socialist – even after he had turned from internationalism to chauvinism. Mussolini's Fascist Party had appealed to a broad cross section of voters (including a minority of the workers, the middle class, and many intellectuals). Fascism, like Soviet communism, had its chosen clique among foreign literati: these included men such as Ezra Pound, the American poet and traitor who, after World War II, escaped trial by the US by faking insanity with the connivance of his hospital psychiatrist.[147]

Far from embodying Roman virtues of the kind praised by Pound, the Italian Fascist Party had in fact become a huge patronage machine, with the *tessera,* the party card, a passport maintained for advancement. The Fascists

---

[146]For a good summary see Fabio Luca Cavazza and Stephen R. Graubard, eds, *Il Casa Italiano.* Milan, Garzanti, 1974, specially Robert N. Bellah, "Le cinque regioni dell'Italia moderna," pp. 433–46, Gabriele de Rosa "La 'meridionalizzazione' dello stato," pp. 231–9. Also see Epicarno Corbino, *Cinquant'Anni di Vita Económica Italiana, 1914–1965,* v. 2. Naples, Edizioni Scientifiche Italiane, 1966. Carlo Levi, *Christo si é Fermato a Eboli.* Milan, Montadori, 1968, pp. 103–5. For the impact of the US on Italy, see James Edward Miller, *The United States and Italy 1940–1950.* Chapel Hill University of North Carolina Press, 1986. John Lamberton Harper, *America and the Reconstruction of Italy, 1945–1948.* Cambridge, Cambridge University Press, 1986. Frederic Spotts and Theodor Wieser, *Italy: A Difficult Democracy.* Cambridge, Cambridge University Press, 1986. Joseph La Polombara, *Democracy Italian Style.* New Haven, Yale University Press, 1967.

[147]E. Fuller Torrey, "The protection of Ezra Pound," *Psychology Today,* November 1981, pp. 47–65.

had regulated the economy in minute detail, instituted a rigid regime of tariff protection and nationalized numerous enterprises. (After 1936 the Italian state owned a proportionately greater share of industry than any other European state outside the Soviet Union.) State-owned enterprises included the railways, most of the iron and steel industry, numerous electrical and engineering works, and shipyards. Under the Fascists, labor mobility and entrepreneurial initiative were seriously restricted in a manner that militated against growth. Fortunately the Italians had learned over many generations the art of dealing with oppressive overlords; Fascist rule – like Habsburg monarchical governance – functioned as an autocracy tempered by inefficiency and socially accepted disobedience to the law. Nevertheless a number of new industries developed during the interwar period, and even though real wages declined after the Fascist takeover, there was an increase in real per capita income.[148]

Mussolini, for all his ambitions, moreover, had not managed to create a truly totalitarian state. Much to the *Führer*'s distaste, Italian prisons did not compare in severity of regime with German or Soviet concentration camps. (Confined to a Fascist jail, Antonio Gramsci, a founding father of the Italian Communist Party, had been able to fill prison note books with philosophical and political reflections, a privilege not accorded to the inmates of Belsen or Vorutka.) In Italy, moreover, the *ancien régime,* though pushed to the political periphery, remained in existence. The traditional establishment comprised the monarchy, the Church, (traditionally critical of the Italian state that had absorbed the Papal dominions in the nineteenth century), and the army (royalist rather than Fascist in sympathy and bound to a traditional morality that assured relative safety for persecuted Jews in areas occupied by Italian forces, as opposed to the *Wehrmacht*). The Fascists met with a widespread resistance movement (especially after the region's fall in 1943), one far more impressive than its German equivalent. The resistance comprised communists, Christian Democrats, socialists, and adherents of minor parties. The opposition united in the *Comitato di Liberazione Nazionale* (CLN). The CLN differed from the French *Comité National de la Résistance,* in that the CLN's sole participants were the political parties; by contrast, the French Resistance council only tolerated party representatives, looking upon the prewar parties with disdain.

On their own, the CLN groups could not have overthrown the Fascist state. It was the king who, with the support of the army and the Church, ended the Fascist era by appointing Marshal Pietro Badoglio as Prime Minister. Badoglio and the monarchy, however, failed to hold on to power. The Allies insisted on recognizing all the anti-Fascists (six) of the CLN as the sole legitimate political forces in Italy; the captured towns in Italy were handed over to local CLN committees, and the CLN parties thereby attained a political monopoly.

Under their new dispensation, only political parties could take part in

---

[148]Given 1913 as 100, real wages went down from 123.6 in 1922 to 105.5 in 1939. Real per capita incomes rose (with 96.8 for 1913) from 105.7 to 132.3. See Sergio Ricossa, "Italy: 1920–1970," p. 274.

elections; only the central directorate of such parties could approve of candidates; the monarchy was eliminated, and a new regime came into being that in effect divided the Fascist legacy of influence and patronage among all the political parties, even the smallest. Parties now turned into clientage machines. The principal parties were the Christian Democrats (who won 35.2 percent of the popular vote and 205 seats in the elections held in 1946 to choose a Constituent Assembly) and the Communist Party, with its Socialist allies (who obtained 39.6 percent of the vote and 229 seats for the Socialist-Communist bloc).

For a time, odds seemed to favor the Italian communists. They were well organized; they controlled numerous subsidiary organizations, they were – and remained – more adept at the patronage game than their opponents; they directed the main labor unions; they were loyal to the Soviet Union (where Palmiro Togliatti, the party's leader, had resided in exile until 1944). The bourgeoisie was dispirited and divided. For a brief period, Italy was perhaps closer toward coming under communist predominance, with a constitutional façade, than at any time in her history. The political equation only decisively altered in 1947, when 65 Socialist deputies defected from the alliance, thereby enabling Alcide de Gasperi, the Christian Democratic leader, to put an end to the ruling coalition of Christian Democrats, Socialists, and Communists. The stage was set for a long era of Christian Democratic rule, marked by an old Italian tradition of bargaining between the various parties for patronage exercised through a complex system of local contracts, favors, promotion in the civil service and burgeoning public enterprises – a system that helped to finance the parties, turning them into the true beneficiaries of the anti-Fascist victory.

> Trasformismo – *politics without principles or ideals, for materialism, power, and honors. Since the beginning of the Italian state, the spoils system has dominated politics.*

Italian democracy, developed during and after World War II, thus faced an extraordinarily large number of problems.[149] These included factionalism, corruption, and ministerial instability (between 1945 and 1988, there were 47 different cabinets). Italian politics were further troubled by church–state relations, the Southern Question, disputes over the role of the state in the economy, social issues concerned with abortion and divorce, and the communist challenge. Nevertheless, the Christian Democratic Party continued to dominate the state, and the Republican form of government, adopted after a referendum in 1946, thereafter remained secure.

[149]We are indebted to Angelo Codevilla who has shown us his as yet unpublished manuscript on the Italian political system.

> *Italian politics tends to be all* spettacolo *– all flash – yet its citizens are conservative.*
> *Joseph la Polombara, an American political scientist, explains this "democracy Italian*
> *style" when he states that although Italians constantly denounce* la classa politica *they*
> *vote at a higher rate than other European countries (90 percent to 60 percent). But, of*
> *course voting is compulsory! Italy is a much divided nation, with many subcultures each*
> *with fierce loyalty to their group. The three major subcultures are Catholics, Marxists,*
> *and secularists.*

Spain, in 1945, remained in an even sorrier condition, still stricken by the
effects of civil strife. The civil war that had devastated the country during the
1930s had been many wars rolled into one. It had been at the same time a class
struggle and a conflict that pitted particular regions – Catalonia and the Basque
lands – against central control from Castile. The war had also been a religious
confrontation, with anti-clericals set against the Church. Having avoided a
religious war during the sixteenth and seventeenth centuries, the Spaniards
now fought theirs in the twentieth. In addition to being a Spanish affair,
revolving on traditional national issues, the civil war provided a trial ground
for foreign ideologues, and military tactics. To countless foreigners the Spanish
civil war became a crusade that, for the first time in centuries, brought tens of
thousands of foreign volunteers to fight on both sides, a war clouded by
propaganda, of dreams and idealistic posters in which young men and maidens,
their eyes fixed on the horizon, were forever marched uphill, holding upraised
banners against a shining sun. Finally, war had involved strife within differing
leftist factions, civil wars within a larger one in which communists, supported
by the Comintern, tried to dominate the coalition of the left. Even had the
army failed to rise in 1936, Spain would probably have experienced armed
struggles of the kind that later arrayed the communists and their supporters
against dissident leftists, including anarchists and the "Trotskyite" POUM
(*Partido Oberero de Unificación Marxista*) in Catalonia.[150]

Franco's forces, better led, better disciplined, more unified, sustained by
German and Italian help, won after terrible sacrifices. Spain lost some 600,000
people through battle, massacres, and reprisals; another 200,000 had been
driven into exile – a devastating toll for a country then numbering 26,750,000
(1944 estimate). As late as 1941, 233,375 Spaniards still languished in jail. The
country's gold reserve had disappeared (mostly to the Soviet Union), and
foreign trade had suffered severely. Without the resources required to obtain
the essential equipment, fuel, and fertilizers required to rebuild the economy,
without foreign aid, with her political reputation besmirched all over the
Western world, Spain's reconstruction dragged on over many years. Slow
recovery began after 1945, but it was not until the 1950s that Spain once more
regained pre-1936 production levels.[151] Overall, Spain stayed a backwater, half

---

[150]Standard works on the civil war in English include Burnett Bolloten, *The Grand Camouflage:*
The Spanish Civil War and Revolution, 1936–1939. New York, Praeger, 1968, and Hugh Thomas,
The Spanish Civil War. New York, Harper, 1961.

[151]Josep Fontana and Jordi Nadal "Spain 1914–1970," in Carlo M. Cipolla, ed., *The Fontana*
Economic History of Europe: Contemporary Economies, Part 2. London, Collins, 1976, p. 504ff. Stanley
G. Payne, *The Franco Regime 1936–1975.* University of Wisconsin Press, 1987.

isolated from the rest of the world, beset by shortages, the inadequacy of investment capital, rigid regulation of industry, backward methods of agriculture, a legacy of bitter internecine hatreds, and a host of other ills.

The Spanish civil war of the 1930s had seen the end of an epoch. The quarrels that had led to war had turned into a battle for survival at any cost. All combatants – even the apparent victors – turned into losers. The causes of liberalism and socialism seemed lost. Anarcho-syndicalism, with its millenarian aspirations, had ceased to be a political force. Basque and Catalonian aspirations of a national kind had been repressed. Even the Church was relatively power-less. More than 8,000 priests, nuns, and monks had suffered martyrdom during the war; countless churches and convents had been razed in passionate outbreaks among a people as ready to burn as to build them. The victorious Nationalists took pride in their commitment to the Church. But once the war had been won, the Spanish Church stood almost isolated within the Catholic Church at large, by now generally committed to Christian democracy. None of the various partners in the Franco coalition had been able to impose their will on the *caudillo*. The Church extended its power slowly through *Opus Dei* and Catholic technocrats. But the pro-Fascist Falange's social aspirations in turn had vanished almost as completely as the anarchists'. Neither monarchists nor Carlists had secured their aims. A generation of intellectuals had perished. The armed forces, in which the *caudillo* took so much pride, remained over-officered and under-equipped, a military anachronism. The passion of old had gone from Spanish politics; the equivalents of Caesar and Pompey, Brutus and Mark Antony, Cato and Cicero had been slain; duller and grayer men had survived, represented by Franco, "the Octavius of Spain."[152]

Nevertheless, Spain, under General Francisco Franco, had achieved a stab-ility of sorts. The Republic, divided by internal quarrels, had been unable to govern. Franco, by contrast, was firmly in control, and harshly repressed communist attempts at guerrilla warfare after the end of World War II. The Spanish Communist Party (*PCE, Partido Comunista Español*), powerful during the civil war when the party had formed part of the Popular Front, had been reduced to insignificance. Franco was hated by the bulk of urban workers, but he commanded the loyalty both of smallholders and of large proprietors in the countryside. Whereas the workers experienced a decline in real wages, the food producers' income rose. This redistribution of income between city and countryside reversed a long-standing trend, and sharply differentiated Spain from most Third World countries of a subsequent generation. The same generalization applied to Franco's fiscal policy; the Spanish budget was made to balance, and by 1946, annual revenue actually exceeded annual expenditure.

> *The political cultures of Spain and Portugal were remarkably alike: authoritarian, bureaucratic, conservative, corporatist, nationalist, Catholic, anti-socialist, communist-liberal, and one party rule, with each party operating a patronage system.*

Franco's foreign policy turned out to be equally cautious, bearing no

[152]Thomas, *The Spanish Civil War*. P. 609.

resemblance to what the left had feared and Nazi Germany had expected. Franco maintained Spain's neutrality during World War II; this position reflected both Franco's steely realism, and the hostility borne towards Nazi Germany by Spain's traditional upper class and by conservative churchmen such as Cardinals Emanuel Cerejeira and Pedro Segura. Their sentiments prevailed over the pro-Nazi leanings of Franco's allies in the Falange (a pro-Fascist party of plebeian character) and Spain, like Portugal, did not participate in the persecution of the Jews. Far from turning Spain into a Fascist country, Franco provided for the ultimate transformation of his regime into a monarchy (through the so-called "Law of Succession," overwhelmingly approved by popular vote in 1947). Spain finally emerged from international isolation in 1953. In that year Franco signed an agreement according bases to US military forces; at the same time he concluded a concordat with the Pope. Tourism, foreign trade, and financial investments thereafter began to grow, and Spain ceased to be a pariah state, though still much hated by the left.

Portugal, in contrast, had by and large escaped international censure. It remained, however, one of the poorest countries of Europe, dependent largely on the production of primary products, and later on, the massive migration of workers to France and West Germany. According to critics such as the left-wing historian Vitoriano Magelhães Godinho, Portugal lacked "social efficiency," owing to the backward nature of her economy and social structure.[153] Beset by the cult of *papel selado* ("sealed paper," like "red tape" signifying bureaucratic sloth and incompetence), suspicious of foreign capital and with her own African white settlers suspected of *separatismo,* Portugal remained incapable of effectively exploiting the enormous African empire to which the Portuguese as yet laid unchallenged claim.

The dictator António de Oliviera Salazar was profoundly anti-American and fought US efforts to unite Europe. He tried to get the British and French to exclude the United States from Europe and to regain their strength by developing their African empires. He feared the US was trying to take over Europe's colonial empires.

Nevertheless Portugal's dictatorship was moderate and relatively benevolent – for instance, this was one of the world's few countries whose statutes made no provision for the death penalty. António de Oliviera Salazar, the country's virtual ruler since 1932, had proven that a professor of economics could effectively govern a country. Since 1933, the budget had been balanced, the foreign debt remained small. Portugal, like Spain, maintained her neutrality in World War II, but had leaned toward the West by making arrangements with Great Britain for the naval use of the Azores in the Atlantic. Economic progress remained slow and unspectacular until the 1950s, when restrictions relaxed on foreign investments at home and in the colonies, and secondary industries started to expand (as evidenced by the first six-year development

---

[153]Vitoriano Magelhães Godinho, *A Estratura na Antiga Sociedade Portuguesa.* Lisbon, 1971. See also Richard Gunther, "Spain and Portugal," in Gerald A. Dorfman and Peter J. Duignan, *Politics in Western Europe,* Stanford, Cal. Hoover Institution Press, 1988, ch. 7.

plan inaugurated in 1953). All the same, even during the immediate postwar period Portugal remained a peaceful country, and seemed to foreign visitors an island of stability.

The smaller northern democracies

In 1942, E. H. Carr, a British historian, published a political best-seller *Conditions of Peace*; this explained that small nations on their own had not much of a future – a sentiment widely shared by self-styled progressives. In fact, the small democracies had all done well, and continued to do well after the war. Belgium, the Netherlands, and Luxemburg (later known as the Benelux countries), the Scandinavian states, and Switzerland all maintained pacific, democratic governments – so did Ireland after the initial upheaval following its independence after World War I, contrary to British expectations.

All these states tried to maintain their neutrality, but only Sweden, Switzerland, and Ireland succeeded – the first two, in part, because of their willingness to maintain relatively large and well-equipped military forces, and Ireland owing to British naval strength. Later, these countries played a role disproportionate to their physical power in the European arena. With the exception of Ireland, economically the most backward of the group, the smaller democracies had built up specialized industries reliant on a great deal of skill; they had acquired a substantial stake in international commerce and finance, and in all endeavors connected with postwar international cooperation. Their schools were good at teaching foreign languages. Men such as Paul-Henri Spaak, prime minister for a time in postwar Belgium, played a distinguished part in the European unification movement. Neither was it by accident that Belgians and Dutch played a disproportionately important part in transnational bodies set up in Western Europe after World War II.

Of the smaller states, the Benelux countries shared certain characteristics: high population densities; a high degree of urbanization; a striking degree of interdependence between city and countryside; a superb system of roads, railways, rivers, and canals; easy access to their respective neighbors; impressive foreign trade statistics; a highly skilled labor force; widespread technical, managerial, and linguistic skills; stern habits of work; a long tradition of capitalist enterprise (mistakenly associated by Protestant professors with the so-called Protestant ethos); a splendid system of education; an impressive record of industrial skill (Belgium had been a pioneer of the Industrial Revolution on the Continent); and long experience in soil reclamation, and intensive usage of the land. (Visitors from more spacious lands such as the US could not but admire the love and care with which Belgians and Dutch would cultivate even small patches of land outside factories.) Holland and Belgium also shared an excellent record in banking and other forms of financial enterprise, marked by the extent of their international connections, the importance attained by their foreign investments, and great financial resources controlled by a few firms.

The Benelux countries also shared a long tradition of constitutional monarchy, and in addition, Belgium and Holland in 1945 still counted among the colonial powers, with Belgium's hold on the Belgian Congo as yet unshaken, though Holland's empire in Southeast Asia – occupied by the Japanese in World War II – was already slipping from its grasp. All three countries, lastly, had unsuccessfully attempted in the years preceding World War II to follow a policy of neutrality, ill supported by military power. Well armed and united, they might have stood. (Belgium, in 1947, had a population of 8,345,000, Holland of 9,290,000.) Divided they quickly fell to German domination. Both thereafter went through the same sorry experience of oppression, internal strife, hunger, the conscription of labor, and eventual devastation.

There were, however, some striking differences between the Benelux states. Luxemburg was a Germanic country with its own *patois*. It had highly developed heavy industries, and its economic history had given the lie to those German nationalist and Marxist theoreticians who argued that the small, traditional German principalities could not experience rapid economic development and prosperity without German unification. (During the war, the small Grand Duchy had been placed under a *Gauleiter,* with the intention of permanently absorbing the country into the Reich as *Gau Moselland.*) Luxemburgers thereafter remained more convinced than ever of the advantages to be derived from being subjects in the world's last Grand Duchy. (Luxemburg not only took an important role in developing heavy industry but, during the 1970s, became one of the world's most successful countries in making the new shift from heavy industries to services – this with a minimum of unemployment.)

EURO-DUCHY LUXEMBURG

The Grand Duchy of Luxemburg, with an area of 999 square miles and a population (1960) of 307,000, is one of Europe's mini-states. It is the last survivor of that congerie of principalities that once made up a considerable part of the long-defunct "Holy Roman Empire of the German Nation." Foreigners made fun of Luxemburg. (In his musical Call Me Madam, *Irving Berlin presented it as a sleepy little land where peasant maids with names like Wilhelmina danced to the tune of the ocarina.) But in a certain sense, it was to turn into a microcosm of the new Europe. Luxemburg was multilingual, with three official languages; French, German, and* Letzeburgesch *(a West German patois, with its own literature, considered by its speakers to be the true national tongue). In addition, Luxemburg attracted numerous outsiders – so much so that by 1988 one in three Luxemburg residents was a foreigner, and something like 10 percent of the population spoke Italian. It attracted these newcomers because of its own remarkable success in economic adaptation. In former days, Luxemburg had depended on agriculture and transit trade; later the country turned to heavy industry; then to light and service industries (including tourism, banking, and insurance). Luxemburg boasted a balanced budget, an excellent system of education, and a broad range of social services. The capital (also named Luxemburg) became the home of numerous international bodies (including the headquarters of the European Coal and Steel Community, and the* Institut Universitaire International de Luxembourg*).*

> *Luxemburg's social structure thus changed in the postwar era – not necessarily to the liking of indigenous Luxemburgers. Broadly speaking, the foreigners fell into two main groups, both almost isolated social enclaves. At the top stood Eurocrats, bankers, and businessmen who patronized the best restaurants and most expensive golf courses. At the bottom were road-menders, waiters, and garbage workers – many of them Italian or Portuguese. Native-born Luxemburgers of course attended the Grand Ducal Court, and ran the duchy. But most Luxemburgers were middle class – hardworking, inconspicuous, sometimes fearful that they might ultimately be outnumbered by foreigners. Being dependent, as no other state, on other European countries for trade, labor, markets, and employment, Luxemburg embodied many of the new Western Europe's problems in miniature.*

Holland, by contrast, had once been one of the world's great powers, but – unlike Spain and possibly Great Britain – had managed to slip into a secondary position on the international stage without damage to her national morale, wealth, or creativity. Holland (unlike Belgium) had only one language; the Dutch enjoyed a striking measure of social peace, even though their society was divided by religious and other differences so irreconcilable that Dutch sociologists were wont to speak of *verzuiling* (likening the structure of their society to several separate pillars, *zuilen*). Catholics, Protestants, socialists, and liberals (the latter mainly non-religious middle-class people) acted almost as separate communities, each with its own schools, welfare associations, and social clubs – a system that went with a multiplicity of parties. It was only at the end of the 1950s that the pillars began to crumble, a process speeded by a sharp rise in the population, the growing demand for social services provided directly by the state, and declining deference for traditional hierarchies.[154] Holland's prosperity had depended more on agriculture (an important export industry in its own right), together with commerce, shipping, and banking, than on industry. After World War I, manufacturing had increasingly expanded and diversified; the Dutch, like the Swedes and Swiss, had gained a reputation for manufactures requiring a high degree of skill. Economic diversification in Holland had been assisted by the country's liberal economic traditions and also by an overall wage level lower than neighboring Belgium's.

Holland had been heavily stricken by the war, especially in the North, where the *Wehrmacht* had held out longest. Physical damage had been heavy – caused by bombing (which had destroyed a large part of Rotterdam), by inundation when the Germans broke canals to flood the advancing Allies, and other calamities. War interrupted the country's industrial progress, and it was only in the 1950s and 1960s that Holland became truly industrialized. But postwar reconstruction benefited from many advantages, not least the Dutchman's proverbial knack for hard work, plus financial skills and the rapid reconstruction of the currency, directed by Professor P. Lieftink, a Laborite and a

---

[154]M. P. C. M. Van Schendeln, "Politics and social science in the Netherlands," *PS*, Summer 1987, pp. 790–9. Arend Lijphart, *The Politics of Accommodation*. Berkeley, University of California Press, 1968. Johan de Vries, *The Netherlands Economy in the Twentieth Century: An Examination of the Most Characteristic Features in the Period 1900–1970*. Assen, Van Gorcum, 1978.

brilliant Minister of Finance. The port of Rotterdam was quickly rebuilt, and played a major part in the Dutch recovery. The Dutch system of planning depended on peaceful labor relations. (The port of Rotterdam, just like the port of Antwerp in Belgium, thus successfully competed with London, where trade unionists engaged in bitter demarcation disputes, and resisted modernization in a way inconceivable to Dutch and Belgian longshoremen.)

Planning, Dutch fashion, left wide scope to private enterprise. (In 1945, the Dutch set up a *Centraal Planbureau* that turned into an economic research body, publishing economic prognoses and advising the government, while a *Sociaal-Economische Raad* gave counsel on labor matters.) The Dutch Queen Wilhelmina and her government, who had sought refuge in London during the war, enjoyed almost unquestioned legitimacy. Dutch postwar politics were dominated by moderate coalitions, which included Catholics, Socialists, and the new Party of Labor (founded 1946, and comprising former Socialists, left-wing liberals, progressive Catholics and Calvinists). Churchmen, politicians, and voters by this time gradually became convinced that party and religious denomination need not necessarily coincide, and the customary division between religious and non-religious parties slowly began to blur.

Belgium found herself both in a more fortunate and a more difficult position than Holland. Modern Belgium (which had broken away from the United Kingdom of the Netherlands in 1830) had been shaped in the image of the French-speaking urban bourgeoisie, inclined toward free trade and anti-clerical politics. French had long been the language of the court, polite conversation, big business, scholarship, and government. French-speakers remained ignorant of Flemish, and had little notion of the brilliant literary revival that enriched the language during the nineteenth and early twentieth centuries; they tended to despise Flemish as a jargon fit for cab drivers and housemaids. The French-speaking bourgeoisie had taken the main part in pioneering Belgium's industrial revolution; it was they who built the new railways, steel mills, and coal mines, creating a country hard and bracing, kind to self-made men, utterly different from the old *Pays Bas,* with a transport system based on canals, and beautiful but staid cities like Bruges.

The Flemings were originally largely a rural people, with a high birth rate and relatively low living standards. (In Dutch ethnic humor, the "stupid Belgian" had been wont to take the place of the "dumb Pole" in the US, the "foolish Portuguese" in Brazil, and the "gullible Friesian" in Germany.) The Flemings in Belgium, however, grew in numbers, advanced into urban occupations, and augmented their stake in politics, a process that accelerated after World War II. (It was, however, only in 1967 that the Flemish gross national product for the first time exceeded French-speaking Wallonia's.)[155] Belgian politics became even further complicated by the fact that each ethnic group in turn was split into clericals and anti-clericals – a division that made *verzuiling,* Belgian style, even harder for foreigners to understand.

Despite these ethno-religious problems, despite wartime losses and the

[155] John de Vries, "Benelux," in Cipolla, ed., *The Fontana Economic History of Europe,* pp. 1–71.

exactions of the German occupation, and despite roaring inflation, Belgium recovered even more speedily than Holland. Reconstruction owed a great deal to the course of the war. Belgium was liberated quickly; hence the country's productive machinery survived the war in relatively sound condition. Thanks to the revenue from Congolese uranium sold to the US during World War II to sustain the "Manhattan Project," thanks also to the military use made by the Allies of Antwerp's vital port, Belgium at the end of the war found herself in possession of substantial reserves – a unique position in Western Europe at the time. In the Europe of 1946, only Belgium's coal production almost equalled prewar figures; arrivals and departures on Belgian waterways had actually increased.

Belgium's speedy recovery was all the more impressive, given the political and ethnic divisions. Belgian politics, unlike Holland's were envenomed by linguistic quarrels, and by disputes over the monarchy (the king having capitulated at the head of his army in 1940 instead of setting up an exile government in London). After the war, the country was governed by a series of coalitions, headed from 1947 for a time by Spaak, who included both Socialists and Christian Socialists in his cabinet, and turned out to be Belgium's greatest postwar statesman. Despite her linguistic disputes and unstable coalitions, despite many forecasts to the contrary, Belgium retained her cohesion as a state.

Scandinavia (Sweden, Denmark, and Norway) has been marked by long periods of stability and well-entrenched democratic institutions. The Scandinavian lands were multi-party states with proportional representational systems, but they had avoided the instability and *immobilisme* of the Mediterranean states. Scandinavia, Ireland, and Switzerland also had escaped the physical destruction brought about by World War II; Norway and Denmark had been occupied and exploited by the Germans, but there had been little fighting on the Danish and Norwegian territories; their blood toll was small and industry and agriculture escaped with little damage (with the exception of their merchant fleets).

The Scandinavian countries, however, benefited from good management as well as good fortune. According to an economic orthodoxy widespread during the 1960s, small agricultural countries, dependent on primary products, devoid of heavy industry, reliant on trade with great manufacturing countries, would be bound to stay backward, locked in an inescapable poverty cycle. Instead of taking what was in effect an Anglo-centric viewpoint, Third World planners would have gone well to study the small northern countries whose history belied such generalizations. Ireland, Switzerland, and the Scandinavian countries all labored under natural difficulties. They suffered from difficult climatic conditions, with much of their soil ill-suited for arable farming. Except for Sweden (a major producer of iron ore for many centuries), they lacked mineral wealth. For long periods, they all depended heavily on the sale of primary products to a few heavily industrialized countries. Even after attaining independence, Ireland continued to look to Great Britain as a customer for Irish beef, butter, and pork, and as an employer of emigrant labor (including military labor, as a large contingent of Irish volunteers continued to serve in the British forces both before and during World Wars I and II). Ireland experienced slow but real growth. Its pace, however, accelerated only from the late 1950s, occasioning thereby a rapid tilt from West to East, from farm to factory, from village to city.

The Scandinavian example is even more striking. Overall, the sale of raw materials had formed the foundation for northern prosperity. (Between 1936 and 1939, 72 percent of Danish exports had consisted of agricultural products, Denmark, like Ireland, having, in a certain sense, formed part of Great Britain's agricultural circumference.) Forty one percent of Norway's exports in 1935 had been made up of primary produce – food, timber, fish products, ores, and so on; 58 percent of Sweden's exports between 1934 and 1938 had been composed of timber, wood pulp, iron ores, and so on.[156] This commerce in turn helped to provide the base for agricultural processing industries and specialized manufactures requiring high engineering skills.

Politically and culturally the northern states shared a tradition of unitary government; a Lutheran heritage with its inherent respect for constituted authority; a similar sense of rectitude; and an agreeable absence of those ethnic minority problems upon which many Scandinavian intellectuals felt qualified to instruct more benighted nations. In the realm of foreign policy, the Nordic states were sundered by a long history of conflict, by the survival of mutual prejudice, and by differences in their respective geopolitical situation. (The Danes had been wont to favor Britain but regarded Germany with suspicion, whereas the Swedes had been more inclined to look on Germany with favor, and on Russia with apprehension.)

The northern countries, however, also had experiences in common; all had been shaped in large measure by the experience of the Great Depression of the 1930s, which resulted in heavy unemployment for the industrial workers and hard times for the farmers. In all the Scandinavian countries, the agriculturists had secured state intervention to lighten their lot. In addition, the state everywhere began to intervene heavily in industry, a trend promoted by the Stockholm School of political economists, which included Bertil Ohlin and Gunnar Myrdal. Farmers accepted aid for unemployed workers in exchange for extensive assistance for farming – the Swedish formula. In the Scandinavian countries, as elsewhere, war accelerated the growth of state power. While expanding social services, the state, however, made no attempt to transfer factories to public ownership. Overall, the Social Democratic governments of Sweden, Norway, and Denmark went for a socialization of consumption, not of production.[157]

In this policy, the Scandinavian states were remarkably successful. Limited

---

[156]See table 12 "Percentual distribution of exports by commodities," in Lennart Jörberg and Olle Krantz, "Scandinavia: 1914–1970," in Cipolla, ed., *The Fontana Economic History of Europe,* pp. 406–7.

[157]Diane Sainsbury, *Swedish Social Democratic Ideology and Electoral Politics, 1944–1948: A Study of the Functions of Party Ideology.* Stockholm, Almquist and Wiksell International, 1980.

in resources, small in population (Sweden in 1947 had 6,763,685 inhabitants; Norway 3,123,338; Denmark 4,078,000), all made a rapid recovery after World War II, without major political disturbances. In Norway, King Haakon returned from exile; the collaborators were brought to justice, and the most prominent traitors were executed. The Labor Party, already the largest in the assembly, increased its representation in parliament, gaining a majority over all others. In Denmark, a coalition government took power, made up of representatives drawn from the resistance movement and political parties. A new election, in 1945, temporarily put in power a government formed by Liberals (mainly farmers), replaced in 1947 by the Social Democrats. Sweden followed a similar pattern with a wartime coalition later replaced by a Social Democratic government – honest, solid, and convinced of its ability to ameliorate the ills of society.

The system worked, in part because the three Scandinavian countries were ethnically homogenous, because they lacked rigid distinctions of social class, with its attendant social resentments, and because of their small populations. In each of these three states a relatively large proportion of the people lived in the capital; hence politicians of whatever persuasion tended to know one another, so that the social consensus required for the creation of an effective welfare state developed much more easily than in any of Europe's larger countries. Sweden especially became an idealized paradigm for Social Democrats all over Europe. The Swedes felt themselves to be the world's moral leaders. Indeed their system worked well until the 1960s and the 1970s, when demands made on the welfare state increased, the trend toward statism accelerated, and the tax burden rose with untoward rapidity.

Switzerland provided a different model for successful neutrality. Switzerland was both the least European, and the most European, of European states. This was the only Central European country not involved in warfare during the twentieth century. European travelers lucky enough to visit Switzerland during and after the war felt amazement, not merely at the peacetime luxuries of Berne and Basel, but at a sense of being transported into the past, as if by some Wellsian time machine. But Switzerland was also Europe in microcosm, a confederation in which people of differing religions and cultures, speaking four languages – German, Italian, French, and Rhaeto-Romance – had successfully joined in a single state.

Swiss democracy rested on several pillars – none of them easy to replicate elsewhere. These included the ability to provide each linguistic group with at least one canton of its own; a long tradition of local self-government based on more than 3,000 communes; a striking measure of political decentralization, leaving a great deal of autonomy to the 22 cantons; a military system that turned each male citizen into a militiaman who kept his rifle at home;[158]

---

[158]L. H. K. Fuhrer "The Swiss and Austrian military systems," in L. H. Gann, ed., *The Defense of Western Europe*. London, Croom Helm, 1987. For a general survey see James Murray Luck, *A History of Switzerland*. Palo Alto, Society for the Promotion of Science and Scholarship, 1985, ch. 11. *Laurent Duvanel, Politique en Rase: Mottes, Movements et Contestrations Suisses, 1945–1978*. Lausanne,

reliance on a market-oriented economy; and an addiction to hard work, sound organization, and punctuality that put even Prussians to shame. The Swiss also had a fiscal system based on federal and local laws requiring voters' approval and were spared political personality cults. (The federal power was exercised by a federal council, elected by the federal parliament; the council's president and vice-president were in office only for a single year. Outside Switzerland, there are few who would be able to name the Swiss president at any one time.)

Despite a small population (4,345,000 people in 1945), and the scanty range of her natural resources, Switzerland developed a balanced economy, with efficient farms, highly specialized industries reliant on diversified skills, and extensive service and banking sectors that became a wonder of the financial world. At the same time she had responded to the Great Depression by a policy deliberately designed to favor small firms, and to avoid both massive taxation and massive federal intervention in the economy. German right-wing academics in the past had been wont to allude with horror to the threatened *Verschweizerung* ("Swissification") of Germany and Europe. If only their fears had come true!

Editions Réalités Sociales, 1984. André Eisele, *La Neutralité dans La Guerre Froide, 1948–1950.* Lausanne, André Eisele, 1984.

PART II

Politics in the Atlantic Community

3

Political Cultures

As long as people have argued about politics, they have thought about political culture. Hebrew prophets, Greek philosophers, Roman historians all commented on the political character, behavior, and values of their friends and enemies. Systematic analyses of a comparative kind are of more recent origin; in the US they have owed much to the work of scholars such as Gabriel Almond, Sidney Verba, Sam Barnes, and Lucian Pye, who used a variety of empirical techniques and a comparative, cross-national, and cross-disciplinary approach to illuminate their subject.[1] These scholars were particularly interested in democratic stability, an issue of deep concern in postwar Europe.[2]

By and large, the Western democratic states after 1945 all followed similar paths. Coalition politics came to dominate many (though not Great Britain), although there were many cultural, historical and institutional constraints on coalition building. Europeans were less inclined than in prewar days to exalt traditional patriotism. The Germans dropped *Deutschland Über Alles* (Germany above all) from their national anthem. The French no longer sang with the old conviction the *Marseillaise* which prayed for the furrows of France to be stained by her enemies' impure blood. The English forgot those lines in *God Save the Queen* that called on God to confound the foe's politics, frustrate their knavish tricks, and make them fall. Patriotism henceforth was widely merged with welfarism. The public weal would be assured through state intervention by

[1]Gabriel A. Almond and Sidney Verba, *The Civic Culture: Political Attitudes and Democracy in Five Nations*. Princeton, Princeton University Press, 1963. Lucian W. Pye and Sidney Verba, eds, *Political Culture and Political Development*. Princeton University Press, 1972. Studies concerning particular countries include David P. Conradt, *The German Polity*. New York, Longman, 1986. J. M. W. Bean, ed., *The Political Culture of Modern Britain*. London, Hamilton, 1987. Donald John Devine, *The Political Culture of the United States: The Influence of Member Values on Regime Maintenance*. Boston, Little Brown, 1972. Recent publications comprise the Scott, Foresman, Little, Brown Series in Political Science (Glenview, Ill.), Gabriel A. Almond and Lucian W. Pye, eds., including Russell J. Dalton, *Politics in West Germany*, 1989. Richard Rose, *Politics in England,* 1986. Henry W. Ehrmann, *Politics in France,* 1976. Samuel Barnes, Politics and Culture. Ann Arbor: CPS-ISR, 1989.

[2]Gabriel A. Almond and Sidney Verba, eds, *The Civic Culture Revisited*. Boston, Little Brown, 1980.

way of public ownership or by public control of key industries and key services, and by the extension of social security programs. Widespread disillusionment with these assumptions only set in during the late 1970s and the early 1980s – marked by voters' revolts in politics, and critiques of state power in academe.

> *Postwar Europe saw the development of new state and society relations, the development of the welfare state and increased social mobility. Citizens had greater access to, and participation in, power and politics. The development of the consumer society and mass consumption resulted from the economic recovery of Europe and America's great wealth and productivity.*

The immediate postwar years, in contrast to developments in the 1960s and 1970s, saw a political consensus in Western Europe, and to a lesser extent in the United States. There was widespread agreement regarding the merits both of a mixed economy guided by Keynesian principles, and of the social service state. This did not mean that private saving, private insurance schemes, and private health care declined – on the contrary. But there was trust in the beneficence of public authority. Overall the state's share of the budget kept increasing; so did state ownership in industry and regulation of the economy and of society. Parties of the right, center, and left widely supported health schemes, social security programs, transfer payments, welfare and unemployment benefits. As a rule, state bureaucracies multiplied in Europe, Canada, and the US.

No party or government foresaw the full impact of enormously expanding the power of government, both local and national. Governments stepped in with sublime confidence. Pressures increased for new social and political rights, for sensitivity and understanding towards the formerly underprivileged. But the new liberalism failed in several ways. It did not develop a new public philosophy that satisfactorily explained how the benefits and burdens should be allocated for the public good in the fairest and most efficient fashion. The new liberalism (in North American parlance) did not create a sense of obligation or a moral commitment toward public enterprise; employees in publicly-owned corporations did not regard these bodies as truly their own, any more than workers laboring for private firms. The reallocation of resources and national planning did not necessarily improve economic productivity; on the contrary, many businesses and many private citizens after the mid-1960s felt increasingly trapped in onerous regulations framed by ever-expanding bureaucracies.

THE UNITED STATES

To the great majority of Americans, Europe was the "mother continent" from which they traced their ancestry. As US historian Daniel J. Boorstin put it, "our roots were European; we got our religion, common-law, constitutionalism and political ideals of liberty, justice and equality from Europe." Americans equally derived from Europe their fears of aristocrats, feudalism, and monopoly. The vast size and wealth of their continent and their pioneering history, tended to make them more confident, self-reliant, and individualistic than Europeans. European travelers traditionally stressed the Americans' untoward bumptiousness. But at the same time they had a sense of insecurity and of cultural inferiority in their feelings toward Europe. The achievements of World War I and even more so of World War II brought about a major attitudinal change; Americans thereafter were more confident in their experiment; they wanted to export the blessings of their own system to the world at large, and increasingly believed in the worth, even the superiority of US culture, political and economic systems, science, and technology.

America, Alexis de Tocqueville had written admiringly nearly a century and a half before, may justly boast of "a marvellous combination ... the spirit of religion and the spirit of freedom." Religion supplies to freedom "the divine source of its right." Freedom also stands indebted to those many newcomers "who came in waves to plant themselves on the shores of the New World ... When the immigrants left their motherland, they had no idea of any superiority of some over others. It is not the happy or the powerful who go into exile, and poverty with misfortune is the best-known guarantee of equality among men."[3]

Tocqueville may have romanticized America. But he was rarely wrong. Religion affected American political culture in a direct and even more in an indirect way. Pastors and church elders left their imprint, both in promoting moral idealism and, often, in giving to American politics a peculiar touch of self-righteousness. Equally important, as Tocqueville had stressed, was the role of the immigrants. These men and women had come to the US for economic, political, or racial reasons; they had crossed the ocean to escape from the authority of noblemen, kings, landlords, and, more recently, commissars. (Anti-communism in America was strengthened by successive waves of refugees from Eastern Europe, China, Cuba, and Vietnam.) Generally speaking, these newcomers were ambivalent in their attitude toward their respective countries of origin; but they were self-consciously patriotic toward the land of their adoption. Americans – on the whole – were accustomed to self-help, and more respectful toward the self-made man or woman than most Europeans. Not that there was full social equality in the United States: Americans were used to striking differences of wealth, and familiar with ethnic and religious prejudice. But the country was too vast and varied to permit the emergence of a nationally recognized upper class. An old family in Boston counted for nothing in Los Angeles, where its very name might be unknown. The higher ranks in the civil service and the armed forces did not carry the same prestige as they did in Europe. The average Texan or Nevadan might not even

[3]Alexis de Tocqueville, *Democracy in America,* ed. J. P. Mayer. Garden City, NY, Doubleday and Co., 1969, p. 33. Daniel J. Boorstin, *American and the Image of Europe.* New York, World Publishing Co., 1964.

recognize the names of eastern prestige schools such as Philips Exeter Academy in New Hampshire, or Hotchkiss School, Connecticut.

The US has enjoyed a higher level in its civil culture – interest in politics, media attention to political affairs, patriotic feeling, sense of civic duty, and sense of being able to effect political change and to trust political solutions – than any other Western nation. Yet the US voters' turnout in the postwar world puts it in last place compared to other democracies. The turnout of voters, then, is not always a good indicator of civil culture, according to political scientists such as Mary R. and Robert Jackman.

Historically, Americans have displayed more confidence in their system of government than most Continental Europeans, notable exceptions being the Scandinavians, Swiss, British, and Dutch. Roosevelt, like Churchill, had political apprehensions. But these did not include a dread of plots that might be hatched by discontented generals – the nightmare of Hitler, Mussolini, and Stalin. Americans, for all their country's political chicanery, are more inclined to take one another on trust than Europeans are. US political culture was dominated by respect, indeed veneration, for the constitution. This constitutionalism helped unify wave after wave of immigrants into American politics. Up to the late 1960s, US citizens had a higher opinion about their political systems, displayed a more participatory and supportive attitude (85 percent of respondents expressing approval of their system) than in Great Britain (46 percent), West Germany (7 percent), or Italy (3 percent). Americans also felt more certain of their ability to influence government attitudes than most Western Europeans.

The US constitution of 1787 is the oldest written constitution in the world and has helped to make this one of the most politically stable countries. The system of separation of powers and checks and balances has been modified, but has endured and remains a strength of the system. A stronger presidency was developed under Franklin Roosevelt. The federal courts, once thought to be the weakest branch of government, became a powerful force after World War II, making public policy while they interpreted the laws.

It was a system that made for a surprising degree of stability – given the enormous disparities that divided US society. Americans voted more often, in national, state, and local elections, than the citizens of any other country. There was a great army of unpaid activists. (During the 1960 presidential elections, for instance, some 4,000,000 volunteers were busy organizing rallies, ringing doorbells, mailing envelopes, and so on.) Each presidential, each gubernatorial candidate had to create or rebuild a personal organization – in a country where people moved often, and over enormous distances. The American system accommodated flux in a way which no European system could rival. It gave temporary places of prominence to an extraordinarily large number of people, and provided for political alliances of the strangest kind, even alliances that might cut across ideological divisions.

But there are problems: divided governments have been common. Since 1955 Congress has commonly been controlled by one party and the executive

PLATE 1   *Path of appeasement.*
(*Credit: Library of Congress*)

PLATE 2   *Roosevelt and Churchill formulating the Atlantic Charter, August 1941, off Newfoundland.*
Admirals King and Stark behind them.
(*Credit: The National Archives*)

PLATE 3   *B-24 "Liberator."*
(*Credit: Library of Congress*)

PLATE 4 *US Tanks for Europe.*
(*Credit: Library of Congress*)

PLATE 5   *Destruction of a German bridge.*
(*Credit: The National Archives*)

PLATE 11   *The Liberation of Paris, August 24, 1944.*
(Credit: The National Archives)

PLATE 12   *King Vittorio Emanuele III.*
(Credit: Italian Cultural Institute)

PLATE 9 *Normandy landing at the end of the battle.*
(Credit: The National Archives)

PLATE 10 *Americans capture a French town.*
(Credit: The National Archives)

PLATE 8   *Berlin, July 1945,* Trümmerfrauen, *women clearing rubble.*
(Credit: Landesarchiv Berlin)

PLATE 6   *Berlin* Stadtschloss (*City Palace*) *destroyed in February 1945. This was the home of Prussian kings and German Kaisers.*

PLATE 7   *Surburg, France.*
(*Credit: Hoover Archives*)

PLATE 13 *Bomb attack on Hitler, July 20, 1944. Goering and Bormann inspect the Wolf's Lair.*
(*Credit: GIC*)

PLATE 14 *Mussolini and Hitler.*
(*Credit: Italian Cultural Institute*)

PLATE 15   *Potsdam Conference: July–August 1945, Churchill, Truman, and Stalin.*

PLATE 16   *Potsdam Conference: Attlee (replaced Churchill), Truman, and Stalin.*

PLATE 17   *Field Marshal Wilhelm Keitel signing the capitulation in Berlin, May 8, 1948.*
(Credit: GIC)

PLATE 18   *Allied council meeting for Germany.*
(*Credit:* Hoover *Archives*)

PLATE 19   *Marshal G. K. Zhukov and Allied Control Council, Berlin, reviewing troops.*
(*Credit:* Hoover *Archives*)

PLATES 20–21   *May 1945, starting anew in West Germany.*
(*Credit: GIC*)

PLATES 22–23   *Refugees from East Germany in Berlin.*
(*Credit: GIC*)

PLATE 24   *Disabled German POWs returning to Frankfurt.*
(*Credit: GIC*)

PLATE 25   *Returning serviceman with his grandson, 1947.*
(*Credit: GIC*)

PLATE 26   *Millions of refugees left East Europe with only what they could carry.*
(*Credit: GIC*)

PLATE 27 *Nuremberg Trial in 1946 againt Nazi leaders.*
(*Credit: The National Archives*)

PLATE 28 Trümmerfrauen, *1946, helped rebuild Germany.*
(*Credit: GIC*)

branch by another. For many reasons, coherence, consistency, and clarity have often been lacking in US foreign policy. Too often the US government appears to be indecisive, gridlocked, unable to move quickly. Periodically a crisis of confidence develops, unless there is strong presidential leadership. Observers such as James MacGregor Burns (*The Power to Lead*) have commented on the resultant political disarray, of stalemates between executives and Congress, and governmental ineptitude. Reformers have made many suggestions: a parliamentary system of rule by the majority party; strengthening party control; lengthening terms of office, campaign financing, reforming congress. But in spite of changes, things remain much the same.

Under the US constitutional system, the president is responsible for the directing of foreign policy. Not Congress nor the courts, but the executive branch is supposed to handle all relations with the external world. However, as Cecil Crabbe and Kevin Mulcahy show in *Presidents and Foreign Policy Making: From FDR to Reagan* (1986), since World War II a host of other agencies, as well as the legislature, has intruded into the foreign policy process, even though their normal domain is domestic affairs. This intrusion has deflated the state department's role in foreign affairs. Hence dissension, diffusion, and confusion have all too often become the norm in the American foreign policy process. Disunity and lack of clarity, coherence and consistency have damaged the effectiveness of American diplomacy, especially after the Eisenhower presidency and the Vietnam imbroglio.

In the postwar world, however, Truman and Acheson worked well together, and so did Eisenhower and Dulles, in formulating sound foreign policy. The United States has long felt that its institutions (especially its constitution) and ideology were the best in the world. (America was regarded by some as the new Jerusalem; Europe the burnt-out Babylon.) Since its beginnings the United States has distrusted monarchies, balance-of-power politics, the Papacy and the Catholic Church. The prevailing attitude, at least among WASPS, was: if only other nations would adopt our ways, the world would be peaceful and moral.

The number of foreign students in the US grew from 34,232 in 1953–4 to 48,486 in 1959–60, and kept expanding thereafter. Sister-city programs grew steadily after the war (from 60 in 1956 to 165 in 1961). Fulbright scholarships 1949–85 brought 99,414 foreigners to the US and sent 52,957 Americans abroad. The US Information Agency brought America to the world from 1953 on, and the Voice of America broadcasted to over 100 million Eastern Europeans. Time and Newsweek were widely read by Europe's intellectuals and university students and teachers. America's best-sellers were often Europe's also. In the 1950s, Europe was awash with American servicemen, bureaucrats, students, scholars, Coca-Cola, jazz, baseball and I Love Lucy.

The Americanization of Europe increased during the Marshall Plan years, as US statesmen sought to create a neo-liberal political economy in Europe such as had developed in Washington during the New Deal's period of Keynesianism, and to remake Europe in America's image. Free trade and multilateral trade, it was believed, could reduce political rivalry and ensure peace. The introduction of American technology, production and marketing methods could revise the economy, increase the material comfort of Europeans and thereby make them less vulnerable to communism.

Americanization proceeded in everyday matters too, in the introduction of air conditioners, car ownership, all kinds of electrical equipment (refrigerators, washing machines etc.), IBM, snack bars, American-style cafeterias, food vending machines, eating and drinking habits (Canada Dry, Coca-Cola, milk shakes, sundaes, and so on). There was more open discussion of sex in popular magazines and newspapers. Movies and records spread the American vision. The US provided the Europeans with military equipment, industrial machines, business techniques, advertising, and public relations. Suburbs, tract housing, and supermarkets all came from the US and English spread everywhere in diplomacy, science, technology, and the social sciences. As Rome and Latin once dominated European life so America and English did after World War II.

Americans have preferred to operate on their own when gaining international cooperation proved difficult. While internationalism dominated US relations with Western Europe, NATO, and the EEC, these soon became self-centered institutions. NATO was not intended to operate beyond Europe. It was the US that formed the main obstacle to communist expansionism and militarism around the world. After 1960, the EEC increasingly became narrow and restrictionist. By contrast, the US saw itself as more globally minded, more virtuous. The Europeans, for their part, prided themselves on their allegedly greater aptitude for *realpolitik*, against the Americans' supposed taste for the politics of sanctimony. As the French prime minister Georges Clemenceau scathingly commented on President Wilson's Fourteen Points for reordering Europe in World War I: "Fourteen Points – bah – ten were enough for the Almighty!"

The Americans' faith in their country was, however, well founded. The late 1940s and the 1950s were indeed "years of confidence."[4] Historian William O'Neill's assessment runs counter to the now more conventional views – expressed by scholars such as Michael Harrington, or novelists such as Norman Mailer. According to these and other critics of "Middle America," the late 1940s and the 1950s were an age of conformity, philistinism, and repression – a time when the crude and the bland triumphed. It was supposedly an age of suburban boredom and banal consumerism, when sexism and racism ruled supreme, when would-be social climbers took foolish delight in chasing dollar bills, performing meaningless labor, and building ticky-tacky little houses that all looked the same.

[4]William L. O'Neill, *American High: The Years of Confidence, 1945–1960*. New York, Free Press, 1987.

From 1948 to 1961 the most admired women and men in the world were mainly Americans, according to annual Gallup polls of that period. Eleanor Roosevelt, Mamie Eisenhower and Madam Chiang Kai Shek made the list often, as did Claire Booth Luce and Helen Keller.

The most admired man tended to be the President of the United States, although military men such as Eisenhower or MacArthur were often chosen before 1952. Eisenhower reigned from 1952 to 1960; but Churchill, Marshall, and Herbert Hoover also made the list.

In fact, these were years of stability and achievement. Hyphenated Americans, especially Italian- and Irish-Americans, acquired equality and made great social progress during this period. Americans made up for the neglect of long-enduring depression and war by building new churches, schools, bridges, and highways. The housing shortage turned into a boom, thanks to suburban real-estate developers such as William Levitt. Real wages between 1945 and 1960 went up by about half; the median family income doubled. The proportion of those living below the poverty line slumped. American science, medicine, and technology maintained a world lead. The armed forces were desegregated. The Supreme Court considerably reduced restrictions on black people. Between 1946 and 1958, the divorce rate declined by nearly half; the rate of illegitimacy remained low for whites and blacks alike, as did drug usage. It was a good time to raise children – a fact reflected in the statistics of the "baby boom."

A 1942 survey showed that more than half of the white population felt that blacks were less intelligent than whites; 54 percent opposed integration of public transportation and 64 percent wanted segregated schools. The postwar period, especially the 1960s, saw significant attitudinal changes, but not always effective implementation of them.

Not surprisingly, Americans – on the whole – had greater faith in humanity than Europeans. They were more optimistic, and on the average more willing to go to church and to spend time and money on good causes. John Wesley's injunction "gain all you can, save all you can, give all you can" struck an answering chord in all the multifarious congregations in America. They tended to cooperate more easily than Europeans, and were more prepared to accept a neighbor on his or her own valuation. Politics were not all-embracing in their demands and there were greater difficulties in registering voters compared with other countries; hence Americans widely lagged behind citizens of many other countries in their willingness to vote in local or national elections. There was indeed a class bias and a racial bias in politics, but there were no mass-membership parties or parties that claimed to speak exclusively for one particular class or ethnic group.[5] Americans, above all, believed in equality of opportunity. Theory indeed widely belied practice, given the strength of

[5]See Alan L. Abramowitz, "The United States: political culture under stress," in Gabriel A. Almond and Sidney Verba, *The Civic Culture Revisited*. ch. 6.

ethnic, racial, and religious prejudice. But during World War II and its aftermath, barriers weakened; economic growth and diversification, and a growing commitment to civil rights, brought new job opportunities in areas in which minorities had previously encountered severe restrictions.

> *America was the haven for refugee intellectuals such as Albert Einstein, Hannah Arendt, and Paul Tillich. The 1950s then were a good time to be American. Gone was the depression and the war, prosperity was here, not around the corner, and Vietnam was in the future. America was best portrayed by Jacques Barzun, a history professor at Columbia, who wrote* God's Country and Mine *(1954). While the* New Republic *and the* New York Times *criticized the US, Barzun praised it (although not without severe criticism of medicine, science, urban discomforts, and the weakness of higher education in the US). He liked the US, with its ethnic melting pot, its vitality and size, generosity and equality, and yes, even US culture and scholarship. (From Jeffrey Hart,* When the Going Was Good.*)*

Americans, generally, had long been disinclined to pay deference to persons of higher rank, station, or educational attainments – as evidenced early on by de Tocqueville's testimony. Other Europeans such as Sir Charles Dilke (a British radical who had visited the United States during the early 1860s) had likewise been struck by US social characteristics later thought to be the product of the industrial revolution or of "post-industrial" society. These distinctive traits included the Americans' proclivity for permissive education; the apparent leniency and excessive legalism of courts; high status and independence accorded to women; religiosity and the proliferation of strange sects and stranger saints; commitment to standards of living and creature comforts for the common people; willingness to make and break laws; a high crime rate; naive trust in education as an instrument for creating good citizens and levelling social differences; a pragmatic bent; commitment to building institutions of higher learning on the very frontiers of settlement; and generosity in giving to good causes.[6] According to a 1988 Gallup poll, seven out of ten Americans donate to charitable causes (a much higher proportion than in Europe).[7] Americans of moderate and modest incomes on average give far more of their time and money than the rich. In this, as in so many other respects, it is Middle America that leads in the civic virtues. Also Americans traditionally spend more on education than Western Europeans, but less on pensions, health, and other services, thereby emphasizing a different set of social priorities.

> *For American conservatives, but not only conservatives, the US was a new and a free land where there was religious freedom, economic opportunity, and a chance to start over and to rise in status. They created a society, for whites, built on individualism and equal*

---

[6]Sir Charles Dilke, *Greater Britain: A Record of Travel in the English-Speaking Countries During 1866–7*. Philadelphia, J. B. Lippincott, 1869, v. 1, *passim*.

[7]For a summary, see *San Francisco Chronicle*, 29 October 1988. Also see Stuart M. Butler, *Philanthropy in America: The Need for Action*, Washington, DC, Heritage Foundation, 1980.

opportunity. Americans have a tradition of being a reforming and a self-improving society, a restless and a mobile one – since 1945 half the population have changed their residence every five years.

Americans honor athletes, entrepreneurs, scientists, engineers, and technological progress. They are optimistic, given to "problem-solving." The US has always seemed a land of opportunity to foreigners and immigrants seeking the "American dream." It was the first great nation to achieve modernization: economic freedom, partial elimination of class barriers, social mobility, and equal opportunity. There has been widespread political participation in the US. Equal justice for all took a while, however; it was not until the Civil Rights Act of 1964 that blacks shared more fully in the American dream.

Political power is more widely fragmented in the US than in any European country. (Newcomers from Europe remain bewildered, for instance, at a country where the estimated number of separate police forces in the early 1970s stood at 40,000.) Power is divided between the federal establishment, the states, cities, and counties; between a multiplicity of agencies; between the executive, the judiciary and the legislature; between and within the two major parties that dominate the American political system. The two-party system is in good working order only during a presidential election year.

During the twentieth century, the Republicans widely came to be looked upon as the representatives of wealth, privilege, and Protestantism. The Democrats, by contrast, claimed the votes of immigrants ("hyphenated Americans") brown people and black, Catholics, Southerners, and other outsiders. Self-defined outsiders also included intellectuals – especially those in institutions such as the New School for Social Research in New York, or who contributed to journals such as *The New Republic* or *Partisan Review*. They formed a new group in US political culture. Their outlook on life was similar to the old-time minister's; but their faith was secular. Some intellectuals were convinced that social scientists had a duty to promote social reform; they believed in economic planning, and intervention into the economy and society on the part of the federal government; they stood for enlightenment and education. In economic terms, they formed a diploma-bearing salariat, with a stake in the expansion of public services. In ideological terms, they considered themselves as members of a moral and intellectual vanguard, and of a reference group for the country at large.

Such generalizations, of course, can never be absolute. There were intellectuals in the Republican as well as the Democratic Party; there were rich Democrats and poor Republicans. There was a considerable shift to Republicanism among Catholics. Both parties had participated in social reform; both parties constituted heterogeneous coalitions of a regional, occupational, and ethnic kind. The Republicans won the great majority of presidential elections after World War II. But the Democrats usually controlled Congress – at least the House of Representatives, and the majority of state political offices. Democrats had remained the majority party ever since Franklin Roosevelt's victory in 1932. from the early 1950s, however, the United States (as most of Western Europe) experienced a gradual decline in party loyalty, a dealignment rather than a realignment. Politics became more volatile during the 1960s, both in the United States and Western Europe, partly as a result of a decline of confidence in the government, partly because of changes in class structure, and partly as a result of the electorate's increasing youthfulness.

Overall, labor and worker-dominated parties grew stronger all over the Western world from 1945 to the 1960s; thereafter class consciousness, political and union solidarity began to fall off among the working class. Nevertheless, the American trades unions among them formed in numerical terms the largest free labor movement in the world. They especially drew on workers in mining, steel, and the traditional manufacturing industries, large-scale enterprises where men and women could easily be organized. Some unions suffered from corruption; nevertheless, they widely commanded intense loyalty from their members. American unions had grown rapidly since the 1930s. They derived support from intellectuals, from progressive legislators, and in part even from employers, who preferred to negotiate with solid organizations rather than deal with wildcat strikers. Unions benefited from the National Labor Relations Board (formed 1935), and from the National War Labor Board set up in World War II. Labor's strength was to some extent diminished by the operation of the Taft-Hartley Act (1947), and by the split between the CIO and the AFL (1930 to 1955). Nevertheless, workers, especially union workers, enjoyed unparalleled prosperity during the 1950s and 1960s. After 1947, the AFL and the CIO became fiercely anti-communist. (Many union members traced their ancestry to countries under communist domination.) The AFL and CIO helped non-communist unions in Western Europe to defeat communist takeovers in local unions. They also helped to split the Soviet-dominated World Federation of Trade Unions (WFTU). The anti-communist International Confederation of Free Trade Unions (ICFTU, set up in 1949) owed much to American inspiration.

WALTER REUTHER (1907–1970)

Walter Reuther was one of the most powerful but also controversial union leaders of his day. John L. Lewis, president of the United Mine Workers Union, described Reuther as a "pseudo-intellectual nitwit." Governor George Romney of Michigan, former president of the American Motors Corporation, called Reuther "the most dangerous man in Detroit." James R. Hoffa, president of the International Brotherhood of Teamsters, used much stronger language still – and so did Reuther's communist rivals in the union movement. Reuther was not one of the run-of-the-mill organizers. German-American by descent, brought up on a blend of Lutheranism and high-minded socialist principles, Reuther frowned on many things – tuxedos, poker, and all other kinds of gambling. He did not drink and did not smoke. He disliked back-slapping and frivolous jests; he always wore his wedding ring. Unionism was for Reuther more than just a means for extracting larger paychecks from employers (at which he excelled), it was also a means of creating a richer culture for the working man.

In 1946 Reuther helped to bring about the merger of the CIO and AFL (Congress of Industrial Organizations and the American Federation of Labor). He had a reputation as an astute strike strategist. For instance, he evolved the "one-at-a-time" approach based on the assumption that competition between the auto industry's Big Three – Ford, Chrysler, and General Motors – was stronger than their distrust of the unions. He believed in technological advance to better the workers' lot – not to depress it. He put forward the slogan "look-at-the-books" which shocked not merely industry, but also some union leaders who considered that it was the unions' job to win money, and management's job to decide how increases were to be met. Later, in 1953, he introduced the "living document" principle. This assumed a living contract obligating both parties to work out any new problems that might develop during the terms of that contract – that is to say an ongoing partnership between capitalism and unionists.

Communists within the union movement had good cause to hate him. During the 1930s, Reuther actually worked as a foreman for two years in a Ford-built plant in Gorky in the Soviet Union, for him a disillusioning experience. From 1947 on, he removed communists from leadership positions within the CIO (which his own union, the United Auto Workers had joined in 1939). In 1949 Reuther served as chairman of a CIO delegation that went to London and helped to found the anti-communist International Confederation of Free Trade Unions. He was a man whom it was unwise to cross.

The US unions represented a relatively affluent working class, satisfied with the political status quo.[8] No labor party developed in the US comparable to the SPD in Germany or the Labour Party in Britain. US labor was integrated into an individualistic system based on free enterprise and welfare capitalism. Collective bargaining with employers helped to achieve major improvements in wages, hours, benefits, and conditions in the workplace. In return, unions had to forego direct (as opposed to indirect) intervention in politics; they relinquished the right to strike during contract periods; they also lost control over plant grievance procedures to labor experts. Unions, however, played a leading role in the Democratic coalition, and helped the Democratic Party to win control over Congress during the 1950s, and the presidency. The American example also influenced many European unions – up to a point. (In the US, the principle of worker management control to reshape industry, advocated by Philip Murray and Walter Reuther, was dropped. In West Germany, by contrast, unions gained a measure of control through the "co-determination" procedure.)

Thereafter, the US union movement had passed its zenith. Membership in the United States declined from its high point in 1958–9 (one-third of all workers) to only one sixth in 1985, thereby weakening the left–liberal wing of the Democratic Party. At the same time, US voting habits changed from the 1950s; participation had then amounted to almost 66 percent, but thereafter diminished, as did the strength of the voters' party allegiance. (Up to World War II, the Democrats had invariably won the South. Realignment for presidential elections began in the South; from the 1950s, the Democrats lost the South, except for President Carter's victory in 1976.) Generally speaking, the state of the economy probably affected voting habits more than party loyalty or family tradition. Political scientists use a "misery index" (i.e. the extent of unemployment plus the inflation rate) to account for loss of elections by

[8]Robert H. Ziegler, *American Workers, American Unions, 1920–1985*. Baltimore, Johns Hopkins Press, 1986.

incumbents. (The "misery index" also helps to explain voting behavior in Western Europe, as a prospering economy usually produces electoral satisfaction for voters and victory to the party in power.)

By the end of the war, three major issues dominated US politics. The first concerned isolationism; the second revolved on the role of the state in the economy; the third hinged on the struggle for civil rights and entitlements. Of these issues, the shift from isolationism was the most important from the standpoint of both Europe and the world at large. Isolationism had been strong before World War II, and corresponded to the US's secondary position in world trade. Even at the end of the war the US remained largely self-sufficient. In 1945, exports and re-exports formed no more than 4.9 percent of its gross national product, imports only 1.9 percent – at a time when many left-wing and right-wing critics alike accused the US of shaping its foreign policy in accord with economic imperialism.[9] (By 1960, exports still amounted to no more than 4.2 percent of the gross national product, imports 4.7 percent. Comparative figures for France in 1960 stood at 14.2 and 12.5 percent; Great Britain 14.6 and 16.8 percent; West Germany 24.3 and 20.6 percent.) Isolationism also had a military dimension. But for Hitler's declaration of war against the US in 1941, the "Asia First" school of thought might have prevailed in shaping its wartime strategy, with far-reaching, and possibly irreversible consequences for Europe's future.

When the 1944 elections gave President Roosevelt his last term, isolationism seemed to be a dying cause. The isolationists formed a disparate group – old-style Anglophobes who blamed all the world's evils on the wiles of British diplomacy and the machinations of the City; anti-semites; a number (though by no means the bulk) of Irish and German-Americans; religious sectarians; most old-style pacifists; and also many intellectuals who had reached, or would later reach, leading positions in academia. (For instance, the "America First" committee included Robert Maynard Hutchins, president of the University of Chicago, and Kingman Brewster, Jr, a future president of Yale.) Pearl Harbor, however, inflicted as shattering a defeat on the isolationists as it had on the US Pacific fleet. Nazi atrocities had already disenchanted many ethnic minorities – Jews, Poles, Dutch, Scandinavians, and others – with previously isolationist sentiments. Wendell Willkie, himself a German-descended American, helped to wean the Republican Party from isolationist sentiments when selected as the Republican candidate for the presidency in 1940. As Lord Halifax, the British ambassador to Washington, put it in a confidential dispatch, "Republican foreign policy (by 1943) moved away from an isolationism modified to propitiate the Internationalist wing of the party towards a moderately Participationist platform modified to propitiate the Isolationists."[10]

---

[9]US Department of Commerce, *Historical Statistics of the United States*, p. 542. Ten years later, in 1955, the proportion still had hardly changed, with exports amounting to 3.9 percent of the gross national product, and imports at 2.9 percent.

[10]Lord Halifax, "Quarterly report, July–September, 1943," in Thomas E. Hachey, ed, *Confidential Dispatches: Analyses of America by the British Ambassador, 1939–1944*. Evanston, Ill., New University Press, 1973, p. 126.

At the end of the war, however, the pendulum swung back the other way, and the isolationist spirit revived for a time. The decisive reversal of US policy came only in 1947 when the civil war in Greece, the perceived menace from the communist parties in France and Italy, and Western Europe's economic troubles once more pulled the US into far-reaching and apparently permanent foreign commitments. The Atlantic alliance was born at a time when Americans rejected the concept of "Fortress America," and US advisers departed for Greece, and later for other European countries.

> *Washington replaced the maxim that he governs best who governs least with one that called for active government intervention in the economy. The New Deal, Keynesianism after 1938, and wartime planning ushered in the era of the activist, interventionist state. The 1946 Employment Act and the formation of the Council of Economic Advisers added to the president's role in the political economy.* Anthony S. Campagna, in US National Economic Policy, 1917–1985 *clearly details the efforts of each postwar administration to build a prosperous economy while limiting inflation and accepting deficits.*

The second great political controversy concerned the role of the state in the economy, and in public welfare. Roosevelt's New Deal had rested on an interventionist philosophy, especially from 1938 when Keynesians moved to Washington. Its proponents hoped both to humanize and preserve capitalism – if necessary at the capitalists' expense. The New Dealers continued to believe in progress as much as the Victorians, but in their estimation, capitalism needed to be bridled through the intervention of public-spirited legislators, judges, academic experts, and civil servants who would supply the required expertise and foresight. The New Dealers and Keynesians believed in a tri-partite alliance in which capital, labor, and the state would cooperate to restore prosperity. The interventionists had gained added strength during the war, when state regulation of industry had vastly increased and when the government had embarked on a wide program of wage and price fixing.

> *Contrary to their reputation, American elites, on the average, had higher educational levels and a higher social origin than their European counterparts. But, as Joel D. Aberbach, Robert D. Putnam, and Bert A. Rockman point out (in* Bureaucrats and Politicians in Western Democracies*) "American indexes of inequality generally are lower than most European indexes. The reason for this seeming paradox is that the educational and social profile of the American population is also skewed upwards in comparison with the European profiles. There are more sons of the middle class among the American elites, but at least in the previous generation, the American middle class was proportionately larger than the European middle classes." The German political elite was, however, an exception in being "unusually egalitarian both educationally and socially" – with a "surprising degree of intergenerational mobility."*

Following wartime trends, Congress increasingly delegated authority to administrative agencies; the judicature expanded its authority. The state (mainly the federal authorities) increasingly supervised conditions of work and the extent of permissible competition; it strengthened the labor unions' position in the market place; it strove with varying success to eliminate racial discrimination in hiring. The federal government especially embarked on a variety of major public enterprises (such as the Tennessee Valley Authority or the "Manhattan Project"); from 1935 onward, the US had laid the foundation of a nationwide social security system. With its peculiar mixture of welfare capitalism, high mindedness, and "One Worldism," the New Deal was also meant for export.

The democratic left in Europe had been widely disillusioned by the failure of the British Labour government in 1929, by the German Social Democrats' inability to resist Hitler, and by the troubles endured by Léon Blum's "Popular Front" government established in 1936. To moderate reformers in Europe, the New Deal was thus an inspiration – proof apparent that democracy could effect social reforms through the ballot box. After World War II, foreign aid programs, commitment to free trade, opposition to Western European colonialism, and projects for the "re-education" of Nazi Germany and Japan all owed a great debt to the Keynesians who came to administer the Marshall Plan in Europe (and also to the wartime legacy of Lend Lease).

War had contributed to an enormous expansion of the federal government's role in the life of Americans. "Big government" resulted more from war than the New Deal era. Every business, household, and factory had to comply with regulations concerning contracts, rationing, price control, and taxation. The Fair Employment Practices Committee sought to end job discrimination; the Office of Scientific Research and Development funneled millions of dollars into scientific research in the universities. A lasting, revolutionary partnership between government and higher education helped to speed the technological, scientific and economic advance of the post war era. America set about – at first reluctantly – to feed its friends and former foes, and to rebuild war-ravaged areas, both by private gifts and government aid. No victor in history ever proved more generous than the US in helping their ex-enemies toward political order and material well-being.

The extent of the changes brought about by the New Deal, the Keynesians, and the war should not be exaggerated. By the end of the war, government programs as yet did not amount to much, compared with those of later decades. Indeed the wartime machinery of price and wage fixing broke down. Wholesale and consumer prices shot up – so much so that the results might have been the same had controls never been introduced. Deficit financing did not last. (By 1945 there was a $15.9 billion budgetary deficit. By 1947 this had already turned into a $3.9 billion surplus.) The public debt for the US seems puny by comparison with the load carried 40 years later. (In 1940, the gross debt stood at $42.967 billion. By 1985, the debt had grown to over $2 trillion.)

Social expenditure was still strictly limited, both as regards the number of beneficiaries and the annual cash benefits they received. (In 1950 the number of beneficiaries was 3.5 million, as against 31.9 million in 1975. Annual cash benefits during the same period rose from $1 billion to $67.1 billion.)[11] The

[11]Rita Ricardo-Campbell, *Social Security: Promise and Reality*. Stanford, Hoover Institution, 1977, p. 20.

rules and regulations published in the *Federal Register*, by comparison with the flood of later years, amounted to a mere trickle. (In 1945, the total number of pages in the annual issue stood at 15,508, as against 60,221 in 1975.)[12] State regulation still operated on a limited scale. The wartime control machinery had worked imperfectly; as Lord Halifax noted, "the ill-organized Agriculture and Food Administration, still liable to recurrent fits of chaos ... together with the acknowledged inefficiencies of the Office of Price Administration ... form the two largest targets for the opposition. Anti-Roosevelt strength is, perhaps, fed more generously from these two springs of dissatisfaction than from any other source."[13]

Nevertheless, there was a great reform agenda, inherited by Truman from Roosevelt, to improve national health insurance, expand social security, provide federal aid for education and housing, ameliorate the condition of the cities, and so on. Not that liberal economic advisers had excessive influence with Truman. The president only pushed for a part of their program, and then only after the 1948 election, when the Fair Deal succeeded the New Deal. The Democrats continued to remain in a majority, even at a time when they were unable to elect a president.[14] The Democratic Party's social agenda prevailed. For many years to come, Americans would support an expanding role for the state in the economy, in society, and in the struggle for civil rights and entitlements. State intervention had come to be taken for granted as an instrument of domestic policy – just as interventions had become acceptable in the conduct of foreign affairs.

GREAT BRITAIN

Britain has always been seen as a land of deference. A century and a half ago, William Cobbett denounced his countrymen's overly willing subjection to the "Thing," the powerful ruling class with its pervasive institutions. More recently, Henry Fairlie, a conservative journalist, coined a new term "the establishment," a group of men, who, without formal authority, determined British politics and attitudes. "The establishment" was said to embrace the most senior politicians and civil servants; captains of industry; "Oxbridge" (Oxford and Cambridge universities); clubland; the peerage; the BBC. Members of the establishment spoke, or at least were supposed to speak, with

[12]Richard B. McKenzie, *Bound to be Free*. Stanford, Cal. Hoover Institution Press, 1982, p. 27.
[13]Lord Halifax, "Quarterly report, April, May, June, 1943," in Hachey, *Confidential Dispatches*, p. 100.
[14]By 1952 22 percent of the electorate considered themselves "strong" Democrats, 25 percent "weak" Democrats, 10 percent "independent" Democrats – 57 percent in all. By contrast only 13 percent described themselves as "strong" Republicans, 14 percent as "weak" Republicans, 7 per cent as "independent" Republicans, 5 percent as "pure independents," and 4 percent as "don't know". See Raymond E. Wolfinger, Martin Shapiro, and Fred L. Greenstein, *Dynamics of American Politics*. New York, Prentice Hall, 1980 edn, p. 159.

a "correct" accent. In England – as distinct from Germany, France, or Italy – a person's accent has traditionally denoted his or her social class, as well as their region of origin – a prejudice that also led to complications in intra-colonial relations. (Australians, according to their New Zealand critics, are endowed by God with a plebeian accent so that they may also be avoided in the dark.) Establishment persons, the image suggests, have held commissions in good regiments; they pretend to a knowledge of horses, dogs, and Georgian silver; they have uncles who have retired from governorships in the old empire. They willingly count among their ancestors brigands, madmen, and aliens – provided these are at least four generations removed from the living. In fact, the establishment was always harder to define than legend assumes. It was, and remains, open to outsiders. (By the early 1980s, the House of Lords contained three foreign-born economists, and Oxbridge scores of foreign academics.) Britain has indeed always been famed for a rich crop of dissenters and eccentrics who brightened the political scene; but they themselves frequently derived from, or intermarried with, "establishment" families.

Hence, there was a common culture that linked readers of the *New Statesman* with those of the *Economist* (the former a left-wing, the latter a more conservatively minded journal). This culture rested on shared literary and philosophical traditions – only in Britain could a publication such as the *New Statesman* run weekly competitions in which competitors parody with marvelous facility the rhymes of Chaucer and Kipling, or attempt to rival the witticisms of Shaw. This culture had created the BBC (British Broadcasting Corporation), high-minded in tone, and for long a radio and TV monopoly intent on avoiding that blatant competition which supposedly reigns in United States communication enterprises. In wartime and in postwar Britain, the BBC spoke for the establishment, with its belief in its moral mission, its dedication to "improving" the common people, and its commitment to "BBC English" as the recognized speech of the educated. This establishment culture in fact derived its main strength from London and southeastern England.

Until the 1960s, at least, the British had a strong belief in the superiority of their national institutions, their legacy of "fair play," "tolerance," "moderation," and political common sense. These qualities had not always been characteristic of Great Britain, given the bitterness of past religious strife. By the beginning of the present century, however, religion had ceased to play a major part in politics (except in Ireland, especially Northern Ireland). The tone of political discourse had become more courteous than in most other parts of the world, as evidenced by the mode of discussion that prevailed, not merely in parliament, clubs and senior common rooms of colleges, but also in the sergeants' mess and the public houses.

The British, moreover, had been the first Europeans to become aware of poverty as a problem to be solved, rather than as an affliction to be endured. Two hundred years ago, Benjamin Franklin had criticized the British for what he regarded as their excessive preoccupation with welfare. "There is no country in the world where there are so many provisions established for [the poor] . . . together with a solemn law made by the rich to subject their estates to a heavy tax for their support."[15] There was among Britons a striking commitment to social reform, and to shared political values. There was greater deference to established institutions, greater stability, more faithful adherence to the rules of the political game than among the French, West Germans, or Italians. As a professional group, politicians enjoyed greater prestige in Britain than they did on the European continent or in the United States. Until the re-emergence of the "Irish troubles" in Ulster during the 1960s, the British had faced no major crisis of political legitimacy since World War I.

Political symbols and political ritual had traditionally played a great part in British politics. The most important of these symbols was the monarch. The monarchy provided color, traditions, and glamor of a kind that democracies normally lack. The monarch represented traditional family virtues and the empire – irrespective of the monarch's own private life or absence of empire. The monarchy reigned but did not rule. It was linked to the Established (Anglican, or Episcopal) Church, whose splendid liturgical language still provided a common frame of reference, though much of its hold on the nation's faith had waned. The monarch, although *above* the entire aristocratic order, and apart from it, formed the apex of the aristocracy, who were recruited through a fusion of the hereditary and meritocratic principles. The king or queen continued to play a ceremonial role linking the various elements of the United Kingdom (England, Wales, Scotland, and Northern Ireland), and the empire and the Commonwealth. He or she expected to advise and to be advised by the prime minister, but did not interfere directly in political matters.

Parliament stood supreme in the British system, and in theory the majority party ran parliament through the cabinet and the prime minister. In practice, the winner of a general election was able to govern in a way that American presidents seldom could. Whereas the American president headed, but did not control his party and its nominees for office, the British prime minister wielded authority over both. The president's program was often amended or eliminated by congress; the prime minister, by contrast, normally had his or her way. If the prime minister suffered defeat in parliament, an election could be called. As a result, the prime minister could carry out the party's program to a much greater extent than a president could. Indeed the prime minister's power continued to expand, owing to the growth of patronage, the impact of "summit" diplomacy, the desire of governments to provide a coordinated response to criticism from the media, and the ever-growing involvement of government in technological and arms development. (Prime Minister Attlee, for instance, was able to develop an indepedent British nuclear deterrent while keeping most of his ministers in the dark about the details.)

[15]Cited in Gertrude Himmelfarb, *The Idea of Poverty: England in the Early Industrial Age.* New York, Vintage Books, 1985, p. 5.

British society is the most secretive in the Western world. Citizens have no "right to know" in Great Britain; the Official Secrets Act shields government from having to provide information. Waste, inefficiency, misuse of inside knowledge, corruption and treason can more easily be hidden than in the US where accountability is very strong. Even local water authorities meet in secret and refuse to reveal where hazardous waste sites are located.

Parliament is supreme; hence there is no supreme court to check or reform parliament. Whereas the US protects the First Amendment rights of free speech, Britain concentrates on the right to withhold information. There is no Freedom of Information Act in Britain as in the US. The British have a more elitist view of democracy than the Americans. They place more faith in the ability and public spirit of civil servants, elected officials, and academic experts than the Americans, who are overall less inclined to trust their supposed intellectual betters.

British politics have been profoundly influenced by pressure groups. (There were, by the late 1950s, something like 2,500 organizations in Britain that served the needs of commerce, agriculture, and industry – including the Institute of Directors, the British Employers' Confederation, and the Federation of British Industries.) These were balanced by the trade unions, represented by the powerful Trades Union Congress (TUC) with something like 8,000,000 members. There were also professional groups and civic groups, regional and cultural groups; between them they brought pressure to bear on parliament, provided administrators and legislators with technical information, and informed the public concerning controversial issues. The consumers, by contrast, remained badly organized as a lobby, a matter of importance in a country where for many years "austerity" continued to be regarded as a virtue rather than a failing, and where the workers' morale suffered as a result of inadequate incentives.

For all their veneration of political symbols, the British had no bill of rights or formal constitution. There were few legislative guarantees of personal freedom, though government remained low-key and rarely used its full powers. During the postwar years, the two-party system seemed part of an eternal "British" tradition. The party in power, whether Labour or Conservative, was preoccupied with the problems of employment and controlling income. The decline of empire, the Cold War, the defense of Europe stood out as basic issues in foreign affairs.

Britain staged a remarkable recovery after World War II; nevertheless the pace of economic expansion was the slowest among the major Western European states between 1945 and 1960. Industrial strife, poor management, outmoded methods of production, antiquated equipment, competition from Europe, Asia, and the US, all acted as brakes on output and productivity. The costs incurred in World War II, the loss of investments overseas and then the dissolution of the empire between 1947 and 1964 led to a further decline in Britain's power and profits. While the defeated (Germany, Italy, and Japan), and the conquered (Belgium, Holland, and France) recovered rapidly, Britain, the victor and the most powerful state in Western Europe at the end of the war, saw its influence slowly wane.

> Keynesians had dominated the British government during the 1930s and in the war. After the war, Sir Stafford Cripps, chancellor of the exchequer in the Labour Government, tried more detailed planning and controls than the Keynesians liked. But Cripps eventually had to return to the "macroeconomic demand control management" that Keynes preferred – he did not approve of coercive, physical control of the economy.

The issue of economic growth has therefore dominated British politics since 1945. The postwar period saw shifts of party popularity depending on the level of unemployment and inflation. By and large, however, the political scene remained stable and predictable – a two-party system and class-based parties; majority government exercised by a single party; parliamentary sovereignty; unchallenged unity of the United Kingdom; respect for the authority of government, trade unions, civil service, and other associated institutions. Labour sympathizers overwhelmingly considered the Labour Party as the party of the working class (although up to one-third of the latter voted for the Conservatives) and of the underdog, while the Conservatives were seen as the party of privilege and vested interest. Conservatives, on the other hand, mostly praised their party for its commitment to free enterprise, and opposition to overweening bureaucratic control – not altogether with good reason.

During the late 1950s and the early 1960s, party commitments weakened; British institutions and leaders came increasingly under attack at a time when the empire broke down, and Britain lost her former economic leadership in Western Europe. The economic and electoral contrast between northern and southern England widened. Feminism became a political force hostile to traditional values held alike by Labour and Tories. There was less deference toward authority – whether represented by trade union leaders, headteachers, parsons, or peers.

During the postwar period, Britain underwent striking social changes. Yet, in some respects, it remained a Victorian land, with Victorian values. Britain had won the war; Britons overwhelmingly felt that they deserved well of their country. There was deprivation, but there was also hope for the future, combined with a sense of stability. The crime rate remained surprisingly low; policemen continued to go about unarmed. Movie audiences watched without embarrassment films such as In Which We Serve (based on wartime life on a destroyer commanded by Lord Mountbatten) in which officers and men remained rigidly distinguished by accent, class, and demeanor, though this pattern had already been partially modified in the Royal Navy during World War II.

> Labour at its height in 1951 had 14 million voters and 48.8 percent of the poll, but declined thereafter.

Working-class deference for established institutions had, of course, never extended to employers. But strikes and walkouts were not nearly as frequent as they became during the 1960s. As long as it stayed out of labour negotiations, apparently neutral between workmen and industry, government in general continued to enjoy the workers' respect.[16] Working-class support for the Labour Party did not decline until the 1960s. After 1951 fewer working-class people came to be represented in Labour cabinets: whereas half of Clement Attlee's postwar cabinet had been former manual laborers, Harold Wilson had only one in his cabinet in 1970. Similarly, fewer and fewer Labour MPs derived from the working class after World War II. (In the interwar years, 72 percent of Labour MPs had come from the working class; in 1945 half did, but by 1978 only 28 percent.)[17]

BRITISH PARTY RITUAL

American elections seem much the same – no matter whether it is the Republicans or the Democrats who contest them. There are the same streamers, balloons, funny hats, and badges, the same rhetoric used by spokesmen to declaim on the splendid qualities of their respective candidates. The content of politics varies – but not the form. It is an all-American ritual, classless in appearance.

Not so for British party conferences. As Anthony Sampson points out in Anatomy of Britain Today, *the social contrast between the two parties is sharply in evidence at the annual conferences. These are held by both parties at seaside resorts in the off-season, when most tourists have gone, hotel bookings are cheap, and the rain begins to drizzle.*

At a Labour Party conference, the hotel lounge is traditionally full of hearty, comfortable men wearing braces, while the bar is packed with intellectuals. Speeches made in the hall contain a dual vocabulary, drawn in part from Marxist pamphlets, and in part from the stirring sermons once delivered in nonconformist chapels – with time-honored phrases such as "the commanding heights," and "the brotherhood of man." At the end of the conference delegates have customarily sung The Red Flag, *intellectuals showing visible embarrassment in rendering lines such as:*

> *The people's flag is deepest red*
> *It's shrouded oft our martyred dead*

Hotels during a Conservative conference are filled with elegant men in dinner jackets, trim men in well-tailored business suits and women with BBC accents wearing large hats. Speakers use a different idiom well caught by Sampson, "I must count myself fortunate," "We all know what that *means." Delegates do not squirm when they sing*

> *Land of hope and glory*
> *Mother of the free*

But the two parties have more in common than their rituals would indicate. Delegates are more extreme in their politics than members of parliament, members more extreme than the leaders – so much so that "the two sides sometimes nearly meet at the top."

---

[16]See Dennis Kavanagh, *British Politics: Continuities and Change.* Oxford, Oxford University Press, 1985, especially ch. 4 on "Political culture."

[17]See Dennis Kavanagh, "Political coalition in Great Britain: the decline of civic culture," in Gabriel A. Almond and Sidney Verba, *The Civic Culture Revisited.* Boston, Little Brown, 1980, pp. 143–4.

An increasing number of parliamentarians in fact had their origins in the middle class, especially from the professions and universities. There was also a steady decline in the voters' conviction that the parties strikingly differed from one another. (Whereas in 1951 71 percent of respondents in a major poll saw major differences, only 50 percent did so by 1970.) As partisanship diminished, so did class consciousness and the class basis of party support, and so did the old sense of national community. (The immigration after 1948 of tens of thousands of West Indians, Pakistanis, and Indians may have helped to disrupt the former sense of unity, as black and brown newcomers seemed neither to look nor act "British.")

During the 1940s and 1950s, the British believed that as voters they could influence their local and national government, and that government responded to the electorate's wishes. During the 1960s, they lost some of this confidence. Many more voters became convinced that government could neither satisfy the people's social aspirations nor cope with the country's economic problems. As the size and function of government expanded, trust in it contracted – all the more so since government had become ever more involved with the daily life of the nation and the economy. (For instance, in its capacity as a large employer, government had to step in between workers and bosses to secure what it regarded as the national interest. Labour especially came to question official policies concerning income, fair wages, strikes, and the like.)[18]

The civil service was more important and stable in Great Britain than in Italy or the United States. During the war, bureaucracy had grown in size, function, and importance. After 1945, the civil service continued to grow as the welfare state expanded, and as government came to control whole sectors of the economy. In its structure, the civil service continued to reflect Britain's stratified society; the "administrative class" derived from the ranks of the university-trained middle class, and consisted disproportionately of men with "Oxbridge" degrees in the liberal arts, rather than in technical or commercial subjects; below them came administrators in the "executive class," educated at grammar schools or "redbrick" universities, with the "clerical class" at the bottom of the hierarchy.

Parliamentarians and cabinet members usually shared a similar background, but whereas civil servants learned their trade and received promotion on the basis of experience, cabinet members were political appointees. British cabinet ministers were shifted from ministry to ministry, or replaced; they had the shortest average time in office (two years) of any Western democracy except the Italians. They usually made their career in parliament rather than business or academia; hence they often lacked specialist knowledge and managerial experience. Yet government kept shouldering more managerial tasks than ever before.

Writing in the early 1960s, Gabriel Almond and Sidney Verba, two leading political scientists in the US, assumed that Britain's existing political culture would continue to solidify. Socioeconomic "modernization" would continue;

[18]Ibid., pp. 145–57.

voters in future would become even more pragmatic and less ideologically committed than in the past. But the predictions proved wrong. Many citizens increasingly lost confidence in the problem-solving ability of the government and the bureaucracy; they began to criticize government both for regulating too much and, at the same time, for failing to reduce the "misery index," – a dilemma that remains to be resolved.

During the war years, according to Keith Middlemas, government, industry, and the trade unions had created an interdependent corporate system for ruling Great Britain in cooperation with the political parties and parliament. (Others strongly disagree. Despite the period of cooperation, Britain has not moved in a corporate direction, hence it is widely viewed as non-corporate. Today, the main reason is the unions' unwillingness to trade independence for representation and reassurances.) Labor's power had expanded to near parity with management. Thereafter a "corporate bias" dominated the relationship between government, labor, and capital in the postwar world. The resultant postwar settlement had grown out of wartime needs, Keynesian economics, and welfare planning of the kind advocated by Sir William Beveridge. A major White Paper in 1944 set out the road map for the next 20 years of British governance. Almost every interest group supported the program at least through the 1950s. Few thought the system would fail. The goal was steady, planned growth, the ends to be achieved were full employment, higher standards in education, better living conditions, and an expanding welfare state. The resultant political contract of the postwar period depending on high employment and industrial peace. After an initial spell of austerity (1945 to 1949) there was a prolonged period of relative prosperity. Planners and citizens alike tended to distrust the uncontrolled forces of the market, and looked to a corporate system that would speed economic recovery – aided by enlarged exports, sound budgeting and encouragement for both private and public investment.[19]

CLEMENT RICHARD ATTLEE (1883–1967)

"A modest man with much to be modest about," "a sheep in sheep's clothing," Churchill had joked about Attlee. Attlee indeed looked modest – a senior bank manager, perhaps, or a principal. But the man was much more than he seemed. According to his self-composed doggerel (cited by Kenneth O. Morgan, Labour People, Leaders and Lieutenants, Hardie to Kinnock, 1987):

> *Few thought he was even a starter*
> *There were many who thought themselves smarter*
> *But he ended PM [Prime Minister]*
> *CH and OM [Companion of Honour, Order of Merit]*
> *An earl and a Knight of the Garter.*

---

[19]Keith Middlemas, *Power, Competition and the State: vol. 1 Britain in Search of Balance, 1940–61*. London, Macmillan, 1986, *passim*.

Educated at Haileybury (a leading public school) and Oxford, a barrister, a former major with a distinguished record in World War I, Attlee served as deputy prime minister under Churchill in the British wartime coalition government. He gained an overwhelming victory in the general election of 1945. Thereafter he headed the first British Labour government with a clear House of Commons majority, from 1945 to 1951, Labour's most successful period in office. In 1955 he resigned from the House of Commons and the Labour Party leadership. He may have seemed colorless but he had a steely resolution, and successfully ran a government full of powerful personalities. A deeply conservative man in private life, he gave to his party what it badly needed in public, an image of honesty, reliability, and respectability. According to Morgan, an admirer, he thereby helped "to transform his beloved country into a welfare democracy and the old empire into a free, multiracial Commonwealth." (India achieved independence during his premiership.) Attlee had little understanding of economics, and not much interest in purely intellectual issues. But he was the greatest of all Labour prime ministers.

Despite economic crises (1947, 1949, 1951, and 1956), this political contract lasted until 1961. While Britain's external influence steadily declined, living standards rose after 1950. The Labour government had held back consumer demands from 1945 to 1950; but public discontent at wage and price restraints returned a Conservative government under Churchill and Sir Anthony Eden in 1951. Consumer spending grew faster than productivity and British industry failed to remain fully competitive. Unemployment increased in the 1950s; rising inflation and government welfare spending produced the crises of 1961. Both Labour and the Conservatives had failed to secure adequate industrial growth, promote competitiveness, or restrain wages. The relative decline of Britain had numerous other causes: growing cartels, aversion to risk taking, one of the lowest productivity rates in Western Europe, excessive dependence on domestic markets. But above all, the public and the corporate power elite alike had lost sight of the limits set to what the British government can accomplish. (The governments of a number of other European countries, especially Sweden, Austria, the Netherlands, and even West Germany, achieved a great deal that the British government could not achieve.)

GERMANY

Germany in 1945 was a country shattered. According to a black joke of the time, three Germans met in a pub. The first, a youngster, still proudly wore in memory of battles past the Knight's Cross of the Iron Cross; the second, a middle-aged man, the imperial order of *Pour le Mérite*; the third, an aged citizen, nothing but a Prussian campaign ribbon. "Stalingrad, 1943," proudly said the first, "Verdun, 1916," the second; "Sedan, 1870," feebly muttered the old man, "but then we won." Grandfather's memory of past glory by now seemed almost comic. Germany, in 1945, was a divided land, without a capital, without a government, with a patriotism ambiguous and full of self-questioning. The division of the country would last until 1990 – more than half a life-time.

The victors also faced innumerable problems in Germany: their extent is all too often forgotten by the Allies' *post facto* critics. The occupying powers had to govern a demoralized country, try war criminals, restore transport, repatriate displaced persons, prevent the spread of epidemics, feed starving people, reopen factories – the list was endless. Germany, for a time became a colonial territory, with zonal boundaries delineated in as arbitrary a fashion as those drawn across Africa during the later part of the nineteenth century. The borders between the Soviet zone and the Western zones later became rigid political frontiers. But even in West Germany, each Allied power initially ran its zone as a separate fief (particularly the French). The *Länder*, for the most part, were reconstituted as newly hyphenated entities: Nordrhein-Westfalen, Baden-Würtemberg, Rheinland-Pfalz. Bavaria, in the main, kept its old borders, as did Hamburg and Bremen. West Germany stayed a country without a true center, with Protestant Hamburg and Catholic Munich later vying for the status of West Germany's cultural and economic capital, and West Berlin an island in a communist sea.

The Allies had not originally intended permanently to divide Germany. But cooperation between the Soviet Union and the Western powers broke down almost from the beginning, and initially all the occupiers ruled like imperial overlords. Given, moreover, the political uncertainties inherent in the occupation, Allied governance lacked the positive aspects of colonialism at its best: a cohesive policy, and a reliable, well-qualified, and permanent service, whose members looked on their work as a mission and a life-long career. Instead there was administrative instability; offices rotated in a bewildering fashion, inviting derisory comments to the effect that the Allied government meant rule by interpreters and paramours. It is a wonder that the Allies achieved as much as they did.

Defeat and occupation had shattered the prestige of the Third Reich. As we have stressed before, there was no Nazi revival. Equally discredited were the former spokesmen of a "conservative revolution." Even had Colonel Count Klaus von Stauffenberg, hero of the attempted plot against Hitler in 1944, survived by some miracle, few Germans would have shared his romantic desire to rebuild a pseudo-traditional *Ständestaat* (hierarchical status society). The other right-wing parties of the Weimar era had likewise placed themselves beyond the political pale. For instance, the German nationalist party (*Deutschnationale Volkspartei*, a chauvinist group with monarchical leanings) had been put out of the running by their past association with the Nazis, and by the demise of loyalty to the defunct Hohenzollern dynasty. Not that the old right had disappeared. A number of former Nazis worked their way back into conventional party politics. Right-wing nationalist organizations, such as the National Democratic Party, continued to obtain some support (as much as 12 percent in some of the local elections, though only a maximum of about 2 percent in the federal election of 1965).[20] The "old right" only ceased to count

[20]This section is much indebted to Gabriel A. Almond and Sidney Verba, *The Civic Culture: Political Attitudes and Democracy in Five Nations*. Princeton, Princeton University Press, 1963. See

in German politics in the 1980s, by which time younger voters had come heavily to outnumber those aged Nazis who were still bemused by past glory and dreams of future revenge.

On the extreme left, the communists had managed to maintain a skeleton organization during the Third Reich. But the experience of the *Wehrmacht* in Russia, and those of the civilian population in the Soviet-occupied zone of Germany had gravely weakened the communist appeal. In the Soviet zone, the occupying force insisted on an enforced merger between communists and Social Democrats into the Socialist Unity Party (*Sozialistische Einheitspartei Deutschlands; SED*), accomplished with festivities to the strains of Beethoven's Ninth symphony (1946). In West Germany, the *KPD (Kommunistische Partei Deutschlands)* was reformed and licenced in 1945 as a separate party, but could not make much headway. (It was banned in 1956 and reformed in 1968 as the *Deutsche Kommunistische Partei.*)

This left the Social Democrats and the Catholics, the main supporters of the defunct Weimar Repubic, those men and women who, during the imperial era, had been stigmatized by right-wingers as *Vaterlandslose Gesellen* (rabble without a fatherland). It was these former outsiders who became the new insiders in West Germany. The transformation was aided by the electoral geography of prewar Germany. An electoral map showing voting patterns in 1933, at the time of the Nazi takeover, had in some ways ominously presaged Germany's partition line in 1945. The Nazi vote had been heaviest in those East German areas later lost to Poland (but also in Schleswig Holstein, later part of the West). Central Germany (much of it later included within the territory of the German Democratic Republic) had a somewhat lower Nazi vote, but still had yielded a majority to the Nazis and their right-wing allies. The bulk of West and southern Germany (and also Berlin), by contrast, had provided a majority to those parties opposing the Nazis, especially Catholics and Social Democrats.[21] It was these regions that later came to make up the greater part of the German Federal Republic.

The first of these two parties to reform their organization were the Social Democrats (SPD). They were the most traditional of the postwar parties. The Social Democrats looked back with pride to their past; they had been the pioneers of moderate socialism on the European continent. In their own eyes, history had proved them right. Having been vilified for so long for their alleged lack of patriotism, the Social Democrats were at first the most fervent advocates of German reunification. For the first time in their history, they

---

also Karl W. Deutsch and D. Brent Smith, "The German Federal Republic: Western Germany," in Roy C. Macridis, ed., *Modern Political Systems*. Englewood-Cliffs, Prentice Hall, 1983, and David P. Corrody, "Changing German political culture," in Gabriel A. Almond and Sidney Verba, eds, *The Civil Culture Revisited*. Boston, Little Brown, 1980, ch. 7. Dennis L. Bark and David R. Gress, *A History of West Germany*, vol. 1: *From Shadow to Substance 1945–1963*, vol. 2: *Democracy and Its Discontents, 1963–1988*. Oxford, Basil Blackwell, 1989.

[21]See map reproduced from *Neue Badische Landeszeitung*, March 9, 1933 in Günther Buchstaf, ed., *Keine Stimme dem Radikalismus: Christliche, Liberale, und Konservative Parteien in den Wahlen 1930–1933*. Berlin, Colloquium Verlag, 1984, p. 103.

became the German nationalist party *par excellence*. When their leader Kurt Schumacher censured his CDU rival Konrad Adenauer for serving as the "Chancellor of Allies," Schumacher was the first Social Democrat ever to have denounced a conservative for insufficient loyalty to the German national cause. From its rebirth, the SPD in West Germany moreover took the lead in formulating an anti-communist line – a policy partly explicable in terms of the Social Democrats' unhappy experiences with the KPD. The SPD instead looked for support to the Labour Party in Great Britain and to the socialist parties in Scandinavia (where many German socialist émigrés had sought refuge).

The Catholics were split into a liberal wing (strong especially in the Rhineland) and a conservative wing (powerful in Bavaria). It was not until 1950 that Catholic (as well as non-Catholic) conservatives founded, on the federal level, the *CDU* (*Christliche Demokratische Union*), associated with the *CSU* (*Christliche Soziale Union*), a Catholic Bavarian regional party. (The party had participated on the local level already in Lantag elections in 1946.) Making a virtue of inconsistency, the CDU called for a united Germany, but took the lead in founding a separate West German state. It drew on the "social Catholicism," elaborated by nineteenth-century thinkers such as Bishop Wilhelm Emmanuel von Ketteler, a Catholic spokesman for workers' rights. The CDU equally relied on the commitment to *soziale Marktwirtschaft* (free enterprise modified by social legislation). While claiming to be conservative, the CDU strikingly diverged from those conservative German traditions that had always been critical of the West; it was in fact a revolutionary party, within the historical context. Overall the party was pro-American, as befitted a country in which the US had gained enormous influence – not merely as the country's main ally, but also in the fields of industrial planning, advertising, labor relations, and the like. Equally pro-Western in orientation was the Free Democratic Party (FDP), a liberal party in the nineteenth-century sense of the word, less powerful in the electoral field than its opponents, but important as a coalition partner.

The new republic, sustained by these parties, was a child of defeat – unplanned, created in piecemeal fashion. Initially, the Allies' approach to Germany was an uneasy mixture between the pedagogic and the punitive. By 1947, the Western powers had altered course, and a *Wirtschaftsrat* (economic council) came into existence to serve the US and British zones of occupation. A year later, the *Bank Deutscher Länder* was set up at Frankfurt, and the German currency was reformed in all the Western occupation zones. In 1949, after the end of the Berlin blockade, the West Germans adopted the *Grundgesetz*, the Basic Law for the new Federal German Republic (*Bundesrepublik Deutschland* May 23, 1949).[22]

[22]The literature is extensive. It includes, among books not previously cited, Peter H. Merkl, *The Origins of the West German Republic*. Oxford, Oxford Unviersity Press, 1963, Dietrich Thränhardt, *Geschichte der Bundesrepublik Deutschland*. Stuttgart, Deutsche Verlagsanstalt, 1981–87, 5 vols. Richard Hiscocks, *Germany Revived: An Appraisal of the Adenauer Era*. London, Gollancz, 1966. Karl W. Deutsch and Lewis J. Edinger, *Germany Rejoins the Powers: Mass Opinion, Interest Groups,*

The Basic Law was developed under Allied pressure, especially American pressure. There was no popular participation or support and the document grew out of German precedents not American ones. Still, the Basic Law has acquired great symbolism and patriotic attachment for the German people, as the American Constitution has for Americans. The German Constitution, judicial review of the supreme court, and the Bill of Rights came to mediate between the state and society in a way unknown in German history since 1871. Legalism and a tendency to over-legislate developed in West Germany in the 1970s.

From its beginnings, the new republic labored under difficulties that in theory should have wrecked the state. The Germans credited themselves, and were credited by their neighbors, with the qualities of diligence, energy and thoroughness. These qualities were said to be vitiated by a proclivity toward arrogance, airy philosophizing, lack of civic courage, over-respect for authority, and militarism. These assumed attributes would prevent the Germans from making good democrats. (For instance, the Almond and Verba study in 1959–60 was by no means optimistic about democracy's chances in Germany.) German writers expressed similar forebodings, albeit for different reasons. There was freedom in West Germany – but freedom subject to recall.[23]

GERMAN POLITICAL CULTURE

The Germans after 1945 were intent on rebuilding their shattered society and economy. The American model was looked to for political development, since intellectuals and politicians held favorable views of the US up to the 1960s, when a resurgent German economy allowed the country to seek a different national identity.

The goodwill and trust the US had enjoyed with West Germany disappeared in part during the 1970s, but the American model left a deep impact on traditional German values and culture. American film, music, TV and dress dominated popular culture. American science and technology came to dominate German society as did their business and management techniques. More Germans studied in the US or came to do business there; more American businesses settled in Germany; and, of course, Germany housed the bulk of US military forces in Europe. But Germans never caught the American political optimism.

---

and Elites in Contemporary German Foreign Policy. Stanford, Cal., Stanford University Press, 1959. Henry Pachter, *Modern Germany: A Social, Cultural, and Political History*. Boulder, Col., Westview Press, 1978. Barbara Marshall, *The Origins of Post-War German Politics*. London, Croom Helm, 1988. Volker R. Berghahn, *Modern Germany: Society, Economy, and Politics in the Twentieth Century*. Cambridge, Cambridge University Press, 1987. Volker R. Berghahn, *The Americanisation of West German Industry. 1945–1973*. Cambridge, Cambridge University Press, 1987. Peter J. Katzenstein, *Policy and Politics in West Germany: The Growth of a Semi-Sovereign State*. Philadelphia, Temple University Press, 1987. Dietrich Tränhardt, *Geschichte der Bundesrepublik Deutschland*. Frankfurt, Suhrkamp Verlag, 1986.
[23]Winifried Martini, *Freiheit auf Abruf, Die Lebenserwartung der Bundesrepublik*. Berlin, Kiepenheuer und Witsch, 1960. Rüdiger Altmann, *Das Erbe Adenauers*, Stuttgart, Seewald Verlag, 1960.

There were also more tangible difficulties. The new constitution was a provisional arrangement. As the preamble put it, the new order would last for a "transitional period," until the entire German people had achieved "unity and freedom" through "free self-determination."[24] Hence the new republic, from the very start, bore a heavy mortgage – the pressure for a seemingly unachievable reunification. The Federal German Republic initially claimed to be the sole legitimate German government and the successor of the Reich. (In this capacity, for instance, West Germany paid reparations to Israel, whereas East Germany did not.) Despite numerous predictions to the contrary, the reunification issue failed, however, to dominate the politics of the new state. The West German parties, especially the SPD, continued to call for a freely united Germany. But as time went on, these appeals became increasingly ritualistic, for the West Germans were preoccupied with economic recovery and improving their standard of life.

The new state moreover was able to draw on powerful indigenous traditions that – unexpectedly – helped to strengthen German democracy. The country had a long and honorable history of local government. (Leading politicians during the reconstruction era, such as Konrad Adenauer and Ernst Reuter had gained their spurs there.) Germany had a great legacy of cultural, civic, ecclesiastical, and athletic associations, and trade unions, damaged, but not destroyed by Nazi tyranny. Germany had, too, its great traditions of religious reform and secular enlightenment. (Schiller and Lessing were among a few Gentile surnames consciously adopted by Eastern European Jews.) There were liberal traditions in German Catholic thought, represented in the nineteenth century by thinkers such as Bishop Wilhelm von Ketteler. There was the inheritance of what might be called ducal Germany – Saxe-Weimar, Hessen, and Baden. There was the Lutheran legacy of Prussian reformers such as von Stein and Hardenberg, with their austere commitment to honest government. And there was a constitutional tradition that emphasized the *Rechstaat* (state based on the rule of law).[25] The Nazis and their allies had downplayed these traditions: so had wartime critics of Germany such as the British historian A. J. P. Taylor, but they were real enough. Particularly influential among them at the end of World War II was the Freiburg School, represented by scholars such as Walter Eucken. Eucken and his coadjudators looked to a free society, free personal choice, and a *Rechtstaat* that would form the political counterpart to a free economic order. The West German constitution recognized the existence of fundamental human rights and an unwritten moral law superior to the laws of the state. This assumption, consonant with Catholic doctrine, strikingly departed from the positivist tradition of German jurisprudence.[26] Under the new dispensation, the citizen's rights were protected by a powerful

[24]Joachim Nawrocki; *Relations between the Two States in Germany: Trends, Prospects and Limitations.* Bonn, Verlag Aktuell, 1985, p. 17.

[25]Elmar M. Hocko, ed., *The Democratic Tradition: Four German Constitutions.* New York, St Martin's Press, 1988.

[26]G. Denton, M. Forsyth, and M. Maclennan, *Economic Planning and Policies in Britain, France and Germany.* London, Allen and Unwin, 1968, pp. 34–50.

court. In a profounder sense, defeat and its aftermath had shattered much of the Germans' traditional respect for the state – an authority once satirically personified by Thomas Mann (in our translation) as Fieldmarshal Doctor von State.

> The German constitutional court and its judicial review is more extensive than the US supreme court. The German court is more active in economic and federalist issues. The German supreme court regularly reviews the reasonableness of government laws and offers individuals more protection and economic liberties than does the US. The US protects against negative acts of government (shall not) whereas the German court has affirmative duties to protect people and provide benefits. Judicial review even checks foreign affairs and diplomacy.

The Basic Law (*Grundgesetz*) guaranteed human rights and democratic freedom. The *Grundgesetz* also outlawed parties dedicated to the destruction of the democratic order, a salutary provision, given the Weimar Republic's experiences. The new constitution also tried to rectify the procedural weaknesses that had beset the Weimar republic. The new republic was a federal state in which the *Länder* wielded considerable powers.[27] State power was decentralized; the *Länder* had their own police; they controlled education, radio, television, and a host of other services. Federal law, however, would overrule *Land* law, when the two conflicted. The *Länder* were represented in the federal council (*Bundesrat*) in which each *Land* had at least three votes. The federal assembly (*Bundestag*), by contrast, was elected for a term of four years by the voters as a whole. A federal president (*Bundespräsident*) served as the ceremonial head of state. Effective power rested with the federal government (*Bundesregierung*), which was headed by the *Bundeskanzler* (elected by the federal assembly), and the federal ministers (appointed and dismissed by the federal president on the federal chancellor's suggestion).

Whereas the Weimar parliament had been filled with a congerie of parties, the parliament at Bonn contained only three major groups – Christian Democrats, Social Democrats, and Free Democrats. While many of the Weimar parties had opposed the republic on principle, the three major parties at Bonn had all secured specific aims, and had a vested interest in the republic's survival. (The CDU won, for example, religious instruction in schools and strong power for the *Länder*; the Social Democrats gained a considerable amount of nationalization, welfare legislation, and extensive trade union rights; the Free Democrats worked within a state committed to the rights of private property and private enterprise.)

There were some unintentional similarities between the German Federal Republic and the US, despite the enormous disparities in their respective size.

---

[27]Powers reserved to the federal government included foreign policy; defense, federal citizenship; immigration etc.; currency, weights and measures; customs; federal airways, railways, airways, posts and telecommunications; the protection of the federal constitution; and a variety of other functions.

Both lacked a capital in the European sense. Bonn, like Washington DC, was no more than a political center, not a metropolis. Regional differences played a greater part in West Germany than they did in France or Britain. The German federal chancellor functioned in many respects like a US president – with the difference that the chancellor wielded much greater power within his party. Konrad Adenauer, a Catholic conservative, set the tone for the new *Kanzlerdemokratie*. Election campaigns turned out to be similar to those in the US – long and expensive. Unlike the US, West Germany tended to be ruled by coalitions – centrist in approach, and consensual in style (the CDU/CSU and the FDP dominated the first coalitions from 1949 to 1966; thereafter the SPD and FDP held power until 1980, when the CDU/CSU returned to office).

The German Federal Republic, like all the other Western countries, contained powerful pressure groups that worked in competitive cooperation. These included the churches, now thoroughly disillusioned with the Nazi experience, and no longer troubled moreover by the militant anti-clericalism that had been rife within the Nazi party, and within the SPD and KPD during the Weimar days. (Henceforth churches maintained their own offices in Bonn.) The main business groups (*Spitzenverbände*) consisted of the Federation of German Industries (BDI), the Diet of Germany Industry and Commerce (DIHT), and the Federal Union of German Employers Association (BDA). There were also many trade or specialized associations (for banking, insurance, shipping, and so on). These associations were linked through the Joint Committee of German Trades and Industries. Farmers and labor unions also constituted potent lobbies. These included three major labor unions; their members comprised about 50 percent of the blue-collar workers, 20 percent of the white-collar wage earners and 99 percent of the civil servants; these associations comprised a higher proportion of employees than did similar bodies in Britain, France, or the United States. The most important was the German Confederation of Trade Unions (DGB), followed by the German Employees' Union (DAG), and the German Federation of Civil Servants (DBB). Union strength increased steadily in postwar Germany, while membership diminished in the US (from a high of 34 percent in 1955 to less than 18 percent in 1986). German labor cooperated with government and business in the postwar decade; their collaboration assisted in the extraordinary growth of the economy, but wages did not increase significantly until after 1961.

The German trade union federation (*Deutscher Gewerkschaftsbund; DGB*) has 17 constituent unions and became, soon after its founding in 1947, one of the most powerful union movements in any Western industrial democracy. Over the years there were to be many clashes between activists and moderate union wings and between unions, government and political parties. The Metalworkers' Union was the most active and the largest noncommunist union in the world. In the 1950s unions won more and more concessions, one of the most important being the codeterminism law of 1952 which gave labor one-third of the seats on the boards of large companies. All kinds of laws favorable to labor were passed, but in the 1980s some of these had deleterious consequences for German capitalism and young job seekers. (Labor became expensive and hard to fire so the young were not hired; capital became expensive and taxes high as growth has slowed.)

GERMAN TRADE UNIONISM

The German labor movement was restricted in the postwar period. Most unions took an accommodating position (much like American trade unions) as opposed to a political activist role. Unions tended to be unaffiliated politically and to push for improved working conditions, as opposed to socialist ideals of state ownership. Federations of unions such as the Deutscher Gewerkschaftsbund *(DGB) developed to face employer associations. The DGB was a relatively new movement, compared to American or other European unions. It was marked by industrial unions – one for all workers in each industrial sector – and by its political neutrality. (Adenauer promised not to revive the Catholic-Christian labor movement if the DGB would remain neutral in politics.) Although the DGB leaders felt closer to the Social Democratic Party (SPD), neutrality continued into the 1980s. Codetermination was granted by Adenauer for firms in coal, iron, and steel. Union influence was further restricted by bureaucratic labor regulations that limited strike action until all peaceful means of conflict resolution had been tried. But the main problem for unions after 1957 was that many workers felt trade union activity was unnecessary, given the "economic miracle" of West Germany.*

Other pressure groups attempted to speak for the millions of refugees and expellees. In theory, these men and women should have created a powerful irredentist movement. In practice, they soon became integrated into the land of their adoption where their influence was limited by the very multiplicity of their organizations (24 in all). Much more powerful were the civil servants, traditionally members of a privileged group in Germany. During the Weimar Republic, judges and senior civil servants had widely (though not universally) rewarded an atmosphere of tolerance by disloyalty toward the state that paid their salaries and pensions. By means of denazification, internment, and dismissals, the Allies broke with the tradition that had given judges and senior bureaucrats almost complete security of tenure. Later on, the judges of the Third Reich tried to regain their position. They met salutary opposition from the new supreme court (*Bundesverfassungsgericht*), which denied their claims. This decision caused much bitterness in officials committed to the assumption *l'état c'est nous*, and was widely evaded. But at least the *Bundesverfassungsgericht* broke with the old *Obrigkeitsstaat* (the authoritarian state) and a discredited philosophy that placed civil service rights above all other considerations.[28]

Bonn also differed from Weimar in other respects. The communists had become almost completely discredited, given especially their poor record as rulers within the German Democratic Republic. The military ceased to be a major factor in politics. There were no more uniformed private armies of the kind that had brawled in the streets during the Weimar era. The cult of

---

[28]Richard Schmidt, "Rechtswirklichkeit in der Bundesrepublik," in Dietrich Bracher, ed., *Nach 25 Jahren: Eine Deutschland-Bilanz*. Munich, Kindler, 1970, pp. 127–50.

marching columns disappeared in a new Germany grown used to freeways and automobiles. The old rhetoric of marching and camp-fire songs became almost incomprehensible to the younger generation, who found the racist speechifying customary in the Third Reich almost a political curiosity. Whereas the anti-democratic parties (Nazis, German Nationalist, Communists) between them had successfully sabotaged the Weimar Republic, the extreme right and the extreme left both proved unsuccessful in Bonn. In 1951, something like 90 percent of German adults had still believed that Germany had been better off in 1939. By 1955, 60 percent had come to prefer the present to the past. By the 1970s, neither the Nazis, the Nazi sympathizers, nor the communists managed to secure more than 1 or 2 percent respectively in national elections (even though some 90 percent of eligible voters participated in elections).

Thereafter, Germans – especially the young – gained respect for their new institutions. As late as 1959, only 7 percent of West German respondents had expressed a pride in their political system (as compared to 85 percent of Americans). As this steadily increased, so did "civic competence," the belief that citizens can effectively influence their government. (Whereas the sense of powerlessness *vis à vis* the government had declined in West Germany during the 1950s and 1960s, this sentiment actually became more widespread in the US and Great Britain at that time.)

Not that the Federal German Republic lacked problems. According to its critics, the Bonn establishment depended on an unwritten contract; democracy within a separate West German state was acceptable only as long as it went with prosperity. For long, this prosperity seemed assured. (The West Germans' per capita income almost surpassed the Americans' during the 1970s.) Rising incomes affected all classes; many low-status and low-paid jobs passed to refugees and *Gastarbeiter* (foreign temporary workers) as in the US they widely did to Mexicans in California and Texas. Some wondered if democracy would continue to flourish, if prosperity were to recede.[29] But their pessimism in retrospect seems misplaced.

Prosperity created other difficulties. Growing wealth and rising living standards failed to reconcile the intelligentsia, many of whose members remained as critical of Bonn as their forebears had been of Weimar. West German prosperity was unevenly distributed, more so than in Britain or in the Scandinavian countries. The elite, delineated by rank, income, and especially by education, remained more clearly defined than in the US. (In the mid-1950s only 4 percent of West Germans graduated from academic high schools, roughly equivalent to two years in the average US college. Attendance figures thereafter rose, reaching 20 percent in 1980. The number of university students increased from 200,000 in 1957 to 1,000,000 in 1980.) A sense of grievance remained among those who compared the educational chances of young Germans with those of French or American youth. In the early 1960s, only 18

---

[29]See Deutsch and Smith, ch. 7. Also see for a fine interpretative survey, Gordon Craig, *The Germans*. New York, Putnam, 1982. Lewis J. Edinger, *West German Politics*. New York, Columbia University Press, 1986.

percent of German youngsters between the ages of 15 and 19 were full-time students, as opposed to 31 percent in France, and 66 percent in the United States – though this discrepancy was not reflected in the respective productivity of these countries.

But overall, West German society underwent profound and irreversible change. The rift between the young and their elders was probably greater there than in any other European country; the legacy of self-questioning and guilt would continue for decades to come. No other Western European country was faced with a similar refugee problem. West Germany became a new frontier, with something like one-fifth of the population consisting of mostly penniless refugees. Their speedy absorption turned out to be the country's greatest social achievement. In Germany, as in France, the division between city and countryside had traditionally been striking, much more so than in the US. During the postwar years, agriculture increasingly became mechanized; the peasantry declined in numbers; their ways of life changed. West Germany became mainly an urban, industrial or service-centered society (with about 5.5 percent of the work force in agriculture; 45 per cent in mining, construction, and crafts; 53.2 percent in commerce, transportation, or services). The blue-collar workers (about 42.3 percent of the population) ceased to be an alienated group within society; they continued to vote primarily for the SPD, but the old commitment to working-class solidarity weakened, especially as guest workers increased in numbers (reaching 2.5 million by the early 1960s).

Above all, religious divisions softened. These had always played an important part in German political culture, traditionally dominated by Protestants. With the loss of (mainly Lutheran) East Germany, Catholics ceased to be members of a separate minority and sub-culture, and increased in numbers. (Up to 1955, they constituted about 44 percent of West Germany's population; thereafter they almost attained parity.) The Catholics dominated the CDU, for long West Germany's governing party. They achieved greater representation in elite occupations than before; they significantly raised their level of education. In 1950, Catholics had comprised only 29 percent of those who had benefited from higher education; by the 1970s, their number had become proportionate to their population size. (West Germany's development in this respect matched Switzerland's, where the Catholics, during the 1980s, for the first time attained a small majority within the population.)

At the same time, West Germany decisively shifted toward the West, becoming a mainstay both of NATO and the Common Market. In this respect, the choice of Bonn as a capital of the new Federal German Republic was symbolic. It was selected for what, in retrospect, might appear petty reasons. Bonn had suffered relatively little war damage. The British liked the selection of a center located within their own zone of occupation. The Allies were willing to accept Bonn as an "extra-territorial" city that would not be occupied by Allied soldiers. Frankfurt, Bonn's strongest competitor had suffered much more severely. The Americans were not willing to withdraw all their troops from Frankfurt, and as a capital it seemed to its critics too "Americanized," overburdened with numerous Allied agencies. Adenauer favored Bonn,

Beethoven's birthplace, a neat, pleasant, unobtrusive city that could not possibly be associated with Germany's old reputation for arrogant display. Bonn was situated within a Catholic area, on the left bank of the Rhine; its very location symbolized the orientation that Adenauer wanted to give to the state. The choice of Bonn moreover reflected what was intended as the provisional character of the new state.[30]

But Bonn proved a durable capital and became associated with postwar prosperity, as the West Germany economy speedily recovered. Welfare state, educational and professional opportunities increased. Democracy became firmly established, and West Germans became more involved in their country's political life than at any previous time. By 1986, they had become more supportive of their political system, more trustful of their own government than the British or Dutch – traditionally among the foremost proponents of democracy. The reunification issue did not disappear – in fact it revived during the 1980s, having languished during the two preceding decades. All the same, the impermanent West German republic survived for forty years; its success seemed to justify the French proverb *il n'y a que le provisoire qui dure* (only the provisional lasts).

FRANCE

France is the oldest European nation state. It is a small country by US standards – Texas is bigger – but the area nevertheless is considerably larger than West Germany, Britain, or Italy. Historically, the French had first regarded their country as the eldest daughter of the church, and later as the home of liberty and the center of civilization. They had apostrophized Paris as *la ville lumière* (the city of light), and the French language as the tongue best fitted for logic, love, and war. (Even French callgirls enjoyed a reputation, merited or otherwise, for correcting their foreign clients' grammar while bargaining over the price of a rendezvous.) Unlike any other European country, France had sent hardly any emigrants to the US, although tens of thousands of French colonials came from Canada to settle in New England and Louisiana.

Instead, France herself had formed, during the interwar years, one of the world's great havens for immigrants. Like the US, she considered herself a model for the world to follow. The French also indulged in self-congratulation concerning their worldly realism in politics – as against the Anglo-Saxons blend of inept calculation and moralism. But in fact no other people were more romantic than the French when it came to extolling their country's grandeur and glory.

The French have reasons for their pride. France had for centuries overshadowed the European continent. Having lost her European primacy after

---

[30]Reiner Pommerin, "Entscheidung ueber die Bundeshauptstadt Bonn," in Bodo-Michael Baumunk and Gerhart Brunn, eds, *Haupstadt: Zentren, Residenzen, Metropolen in der Deutschen Geschichte*, Koeln, Verlag, 1989, pp. 400–4.

the Franco–German War (1870–1) France tried to rebuild greatness through a colonial empire that the French stood resolved to maintain after World War II. In a wider sense, the French had created the modern state, and exported its techniques of administration and governance to their Continental neighbors. This state centered on Paris. Within France, Paris occupied a position even more prominent than London did in Great Britain. Paris offered the most prestigious opportunities in politics, finance, administration, and academic life – as evidenced by that succession of great French novels in which young provincials depart for the capital to make their name or their fortune. (During the presidential campaign of 1985, François Mitterand, the socialist leader, was belittled by his opponent as a "Rastignac," the aristocratic but provincial parvenu of Balzac's novels, because Mitterand had come from Bordeaux.)

Whereas the universities of Oxford and Cambridge had always outshone London – at least in their own estimation – French intellectual and political life hinged on Paris, with its *Quartier Latin*, the Sorbonne, the *Grandes Écoles* (professional schools of outstanding attainment that train military officers, engineers, secondary school teachers, civil servants, archivists, and other specialists). While the British had for centuries prided themselves on a vigorous tradition of local government, even petty provincial matters were decided in Paris, enforced by a great administrative network that reached from the Ministry of the Interior down to the remotest *préfectures* and *mairies*.

The average citizen looked on this dominant state with ambivalence. France, *la patrie*, stands for the homeland. The state, by contrast, seems a huge, impersonal, and ever-intrusive organization, represented for the ordinary citizen by the clerk at the *préfecture*, the school teacher, and others like "officers in a meritocratic army."[31] The all-embracing state encountered respect, but also suspicion and distrust – Frenchmen readily served as conscripts in the army, but were notoriously more reluctant to make honest income tax declarations than British, Germans, or Americans. The very organization of the state and society was built on distrust – as reflected by the prestige of the *inspecteurs d'état*, members of an administrative elite, who reported on every major matter of administrative concern, and by the power of the *concierge* in every French hotel or apartment house who kept track of visitors and foreigners for the police.

A sense of distrust was not hard to explain in a country that for over two centuries had experienced more changes of government than any other of the great powers. Between 1789, the year of the Revolution, and 1958, France had seen three different monarchical systems (four, if Pétain's *Etat Français* is to be accounted as a bastard kingship), and five republics. French politics had a long tradition of violence sacralized by the "myth of revolution." Whereas the British had not experienced civil turmoil for three centuries, France had gone through successive outbreaks – 1789, 1830, 1848, 1871 – with barricades raised in Paris, and fierce street fighting. More recently, war and occupation had pitted *maréchalistes* against *résistants*. France, like Ireland, remained a land

---

[31] Angelo Codevilla, *Modern France*. La Salle, Ill., Open Court, 1974, p. 23.

where history ruled supreme. France was divided into 'ideological families' that derived their cohesion as much from the memories of the past as the disputes of the present. The French therefore had evolved a political culture that stressed the distinction between public and private life, a culture that valued an "isolated individualism," and that carried distrust to such lengths that many French were reluctant to reveal their true political convictions to friends – let alone neighbors.[32] (A Frenchman distrusts officialdom and feels insulted on being told that he has *la tête de fonctionnaire,* a bureaucrat's mind.)

And yet France was also a cohesive country – held together by a strong sense of patriotism, a great cultural tradition, and a powerful state machinery heavily indebted to the Napoleonic legacy. The civil service in particular served as a framework fashioned apparently of steel. By the end of the 1950s, it contained about 1,000,000 officials, directed by a small elite (about 6,000 to 8,000 top functionaries) recruited by competitive examinations from the *Grandes Écoles.* Most of their graduates derived from the upper-middle and middle class – but even a poor man's son could rise to the top by dint of scholastic ability. No political patron or party, however powerful, could tamper with those examination results that would thrust a successful student into a great career, or hurl a failed student into the obscurity of a provincial university!

Liberation left this system unchanged. Prefects – resplendent in their power, prestige, and, on gala occasions, their magnificent dress uniforms of blue and gold – resumed control over the respective *départements.* The *Grandes Écoles* continued as nurseries of the French technocratic and administrative elites. Indeed the new regime in 1945 added to their numger by forming the *École Nationale D'Administration (ENA),* whose curriculum henceforth emphasized Keynesian economics and planning. Its graduates, nicknamed *énarches,* formed a formidable freemasonry distinguished by intellectual ability and *esprit de corps,* and a sense of superiority over ordinary university graduates. Twenty-four-year-old graduates of ENA might immediately enter the *Inspectorat des Finances* where they would help to shape the French budget, whereas holders of ordinary university diplomas did not count for much. Between them, the *énarches* built up yet another old boys' network, whose members supposedly got their way within a highly centralized administration merely by ringing the right person and starting the conversation, "écoute, cher camarade" (listen, old buddy).

Far from diminishing, the power of the state and of the bureaucracy greatly expanded after liberation. Not merely socialists and communists, but also the Christian Democrats advocated a managed economy in which the state would hold the main levers of command. Between 1944 and 1945, the provisional government set up by de Gaulle placed under public ownership electricity and gas, and the coal mines of northern France, as well as various other enterprises whose owners had collaborated with the enemy (for instance the Renault

[32]Lowell G. Noonan, "France," in Peter H. Markl, ed., *Western European Party Systems: Trends and Prospects.* New York, Free Press, 1980, p. 87. Geoffrey Roberts and Jill Lovecy, *West European Politics Today.* Manchester, Manchester University Press, 1984, p. 33.

automobile plant). The Bank of France was nationalized, as well as several other major banks; so were the major insurance companies, a variety of utilities and Air France. A capital levy was imposed on large fortunes; the state provided large subsidies to the economy and the government instituted a comprehensive system of social security (old age insurance, unemployment and maternity benefits, medical care, family allowance, and national insurance).

French-style planning, however, also left a great deal of scope to private enterprise; far from evincing hostility to private business, the new-style civil servants actively promoted the interests of corporate endeavour. French civil servants were more independent of control by the legislature and cabinet than their British colleagues. On leaving the service French senior officials were more likely to find jobs in private business than their opposite numbers in Great Britain (a practice known as *pantouflage*, that is putting on another pair of slippers). The French were likely to be better trained in the technical sense and were given more responsibility for major projects than their British *confrères*. As Anthony Sampson, a student of comparative politics put it, "the forceful planners among the French *inspecteurs des finances* made their counterparts in Whitehall look timid and amateurish."[33]

When the war ended, French planners and politicians faced demands on the state that were so numerous and far-reaching as to seem incapable of fulfillment. The ravages of war had to be made good; the economy needed to be modernized. France faced a political situation that would have appeared inconceivable 20 years before. Much of the old right, the ultra-nationalists of yesterday, stood discredited by treason, whereas the communists, once internationalists *par excellence*, now boasted of their patriotic credentials. Between them, planners and politicians alike had, at the same time, to assimilate the resistance into civil life; cope with a legacy of suspicion and hatred inherited from the occupation; rebuild the state machinery; meet the new demands for social justices put forward by the resistance; reform the empire; regain the country's international prestige; and reconcile the latent differences between city and countryside (strong in France, where by the late 1950s, farmers, including proprietors, tenants, and farm workers, still formed 26 percent of those gainfully employed).

France also had to create for herself a new constitution and a new political consensus. De Gaulle himself laid the blame for French misfortunes on the institutions of the Third Republic, with its numerous parties and its ministerial instability. (Between 1870 and 1940, France had been governed by more than 100 successive cabinets.) To rebuild confidence in the political system and provide the country with effective government, de Gaulle called for two essential changes: a strong head of state with wide powers, elected by electoral college rather than by parliament, and the separation of the executive, the legislative, and the judicature. The General was ready enough to censure the US in theory, but profited from its experience in practice.

[33]Anthony Sampson, *The Changing Anatomy of Britain*. New York, Random House, 1982, pp. 182–3.

For all his prestige, de Gaulle could not at first get his way. Instead, the Fourth Republic began with a constitution very much like the Third Republic's. The new constitution (promulgated in 1946) provided for a head of state elected by the two houses of parliament – with the president of the republic a mere figurehead. Real power rested with the National Assembly. Ministerial instability continued. (Between 1945 and 1958, France had 17 prime ministers, and 20 cabinets.) Governments rested on shifting coalitions that unsuccessfully tried to paper over those ideological cracks that divided the country.

In France, as everywhere else in the West, it was the political parties that articulated the will of the electorate. All these parties formed class alliances of varying composition – including the communists. Within this political system, the communist party constituted a political enclave, a counter-society – comparable to some extent to the Protestants in sixteenth-century France – with the difference that the French communists looked to a foreign power, the Soviet Union, as the workers' true fatherland. The constitutional parties all formed political federations; they were numerous, and included the socialists (dedicated to a moderate program of reform); centrists such as the Radical socialist party (a party neither radical nor socialist); Liberals, and liberal-minded Catholics organized into the Christian Democratic *Mouvement Républicain Populaire*.

None of the parties possessed the communists' cohesion and ideological discipline. A deputy, once elected, was secure in his seat for the length of his or her term – no matter how he or she chose to vote on any given issue. A deputy could oppose the cabinet almost with impunity, even when the prime minister derived from the deputy's own party. Deputies in France, as in the US, remained strongly entrenched in their local constituencies, as mayors of important towns, or spokesmen for important lobbies. The nomination of candidates heavily depended on local factors; most parties formed by "loose affiliations of notables, political bosses, and leaders," often resembling "small detachments composed only of generals."[34]

Except for the communists, the parties remained internally divided to such an extent that virtually every issue confronting France was fought out within the parties as much as between them. Under such conditions effective leadership was hard to achieve. Altogether, the system aroused a great deal of distrust within the electorate. Each governing coalition was the product of parliamentary bargaining; no ruling coalition was ever itself approved by the electorate. Except for the communists, and to a lesser extent, the socialists, no party stood for a single, clear-cut program, as members of the same party would advocate different policies in different parts of the country.

France, moreover, was a land of lobbies, as numerous and powerful, and well-organized as those in the US. They comprised employers' organizations, for example the Conseil National du Patronat Français (CNPF), farmers' organ-

---

[34]Roy C. Macridis, "France," in Roy C. Macridis, *Modern Political Systems: Europe*. Englewood-Cliffs, Prentice Hall, 1963, p. 172.

izations, trade unions, teachers' unions, chambers of commerce, pressure groups designed to benefit welfare recipients, highway users, distillers – the list could extend over many pages. These lobbies acted in a manner similar to their US counterparts; they gave financial support to parliamentary candidates, placed their spokesmen in the legislature, swayed public opinion, and influenced civil servants. They secured for their members all kinds of favors – tax benefits, subsidies, tariff protection, price support, insurance against riots, and so on. These favors multiplied, as a succession of weak governments had trouble in saying no to any powerful group, and because governmental power was fragmented among many agencies.

Power was also divided in other ways. Whereas a British cabinet minister drew on the help of his permanent civil servants, every incoming French minister appointed his own personal staff, consisting of senior officials. Without any permanent position in their respective ministries, they were wont to look out for their own careers, determined to exploit their (usually brief) stay at the ministry to the best advantage. The ministerial cabinet therefore formed "an element of instability at the very heart of the administrative machinery."[35]

These weaknesses, however, were outweighed by strengths. Lobbies might be powerful; but they were so numerous and fragmented that none of them could prevail on their own, and they balanced one another's pretensions. The civil service provided its own checks and balances. For instance France possessed an institution that had no parallel in any of the Anglo-Saxon countries, but one that was widely copied on the Continent. This was the Council of State (*Conseil d'Etat*), composed of top-ranking civil servants who acted as watchdogs over the administration, investigated abuses, and defended the citizens' rights against the bureaucracy. The effects of cabinet instability, moreover, should not be overestimated. Though ministers changed places frequently, the same faces would reappear in cabinet after cabinet. Many ministers therefore developed a great deal of expertise – supported as they were by an experienced civil service.

The parties of the Fourth Republic, though much maligned in retrospect, had many virtues. They certainly promoted many newcomers, men and women schooled in the resistance, who were inspired by a mixture of patriotism and social concern, so that French politics were revitalized and infused with new energy. According to gloomy prognostications made at the time, France was beset, and would continue to be troubled by crises.[36] But for all its deficiencies the French political system turned out to be surprisingly successful. The politicians of the Fourth Republic did well for their country and France staged a remarkable, and wholly unanticipated, economic recovery. It also effectively maintained law and order at home – a remarkable and under-appreciated achievement after the violence engendered by war and resistance and communist-led strikes.

[35]Macridis, "France," p. 205.
[36]See Herbert Lüthy, *France Against Herself: A Perspective Study of France's Past, Her Politics, and Her Unending Crises.* New York, Praeger, 1955.

The Fourth Republic, however, could not cope with the violence brought about by the long guerrilla war overseas in Algeria. The festering Algerian sore proved an even more destructive malady than the Spanish ulcer had been to Napoleon's empire. In 1958 de Gaulle stepped into power, resolved to liquidate the empire that he had promised to defend. A new constitution was framed, and adopted by the electorate with a majority whose size reflected, not merely the general's personal popularity, but also the voters' dissatisfaction with the existing system.[37] The new constitution put de Gaulle's theories into practice. The constitution provided for a lower house (*Assemblée Nationale*), and upper house (*Sénat*), a prime minister, and a president of the republic endowed with far-reaching and well-defined powers. De Gaulle introduced single-member constituencies, a reform that weakened the communists. At the same time the constitution reduced the power both of parliament and political parties in order to diminish that ministerial instability that had bedevilled the coalition ministries of the Third Republic.[38] Under the new system, de Gaulle ruled almost as a king. When he died, there was nobody to fill his shoes, and in the long run the system partly reverted to older French traditions. But overall French political culture became more stable, less fragmented and ideological and less prone to suspicion and distrust.

France also changed in a profounder sense, more than any other Western European country. Before 1940, it had been primarily an agricultural country endowed with a number of major manufacturing industries, the economy backward compared with Germany's or Great Britain's. During the 1930s the economy had grown but little, and relative stagnation was worsened by large-scale destruction during World War II. Under the Fourth Republic, the French economy expanded at a rate equal to West Germany's. Agricultural productivity increased greatly from prewar levels, thanks in part to the Marshall Plan, and to far-reaching improvements with regard to the use of mechanical equipment, the application of agricultural science, rationalization of farm management, and consolidation of holdings. The peasantry declined in numbers; so did the traditional *rentier* class, with its traditional reluctance to take risks. By 1958 the national income was twice what it had been in 1939. French industrial production in all fields increased by two or three times over the 1938 figures.

In France, the state and its agencies took a leading part in modernizing the economy – much more so than in West Germany and the US. The French state from 1946 initiated new programs, expanded nationalized industries, and helped to develop agricultural enterprise in a variety of ways. Industrial policy emanated from the Ministry of Industry and its many committees, the most important of which was the Planning Committee for Strategic Industries. The

---

[37]In the referendum, 66.4 percent of the voters approved of de Gaulle's new constitution, 15.06 percent abstained; only 17.38 percent voted "no," presumably in preference to the old order.

[38]For a more detailed analysis, see D. L. Hanley, A. P. Kerr, and N. H. Waites, *Contemporary France: Politics and Society Since 1945*. London, Routledge and Kegan Paul, 1979, pp. 102–9.

JEAN MONNET (1888–1979)

Jean Monnet was both a conventional and an unconventional Frenchman. He was born in Cognac, a provincial town. His grandfather had been a farmer who had risen to the rank of major; his father was a well-to-do brandy manufacturer. Jean went to the local lycée *(without, however, completing his* bachot *– his first departure from convention). Thereafter Monnet made a great deal of money; he reached high office, acquired a string of decorations, and lived to the age of 91 – the very model of a provincial made good.*

In other ways, Monnet was as atypical a Frenchman as might be imagined, and in some ways the archetypal métèque *(biological or cultural halfbreed) so much detested by the French ultra-right. He eloped with another man's wife, and married her. The lady compounded the offense by being a foreigner, a painter, and by having secured her divorce in Moscow. Monnet spoke English with a perfect North American accent, an uncommon accomplishment among Frenchmen. (He had acquired this ability as a brandy salesman in the Canadian backwoods, and later as a successful entrepreneur in the US. At one stage he became vice-president of the Transamerica holding company, which then owned the Bank of America.) During World War I, Monnet entered French government service, and set up an Anglo-French supply commission to prevent the two countries from bidding against one another in purchasing scarce raw materials. When the war was over, he worked for a time for the League of Nations, convinced that the Allies had made a mistake in tying down the Germans. Thereafter he became an international consultant. (At the request of the Swedish government, for example, he wound up the bankrupt Kreuger match empire.)*

At the start of World War II, Monnet returned to government service as chairman of the Franco-British committee for Economic Coordination. Monnet realized, as few Europeans did at the time, the enormous economic potential of the US. He set his sights high in ordering airplanes and engines, a firm believer in planned economic expansion. But his designs went much further. During the dark days of 1940, when France faced disaster, it was Monnet who proposed to Churchill and de Gaulle an even more radical form of international pooling, a political union between France and Britain. The design failed. Had it succeeded, the Franco-British Union would have formed the foundation stone for a united Europe.

Monnet thereafter worked for the British Supply Council in Washington where he played an important part in devising Roosevelt's "Victory Program" of aircraft production. (He was credited with devising the slogan both of "arsenal of democracy" and of "Lend Lease.") Later he joined the French National Liberation Committee and proposed to de Gaulle what later became the Monnet Plan for the modernization of France. In 1946 he assumed office as France's first Commissaire au Plan. Aided by a small group of brilliant colleagues such as the engineer Etienne Hirsch, the economist Pierre Uri, and civil servant Paul Delouvrier, Monnet was the primary architect of the Schuman Plan. (Put forward in 1950, this plan was designed to pool European coal and steel resources under a supra-national authority in which France would share in the development and direction of West German industry.) Between 1952 and 1955 Monnet served as the president of the European Coal and Steel Community. He collected honorary doctorates from Columbia, Glasgow, Princeton, Yale, Cambridge and Oxford – not a bad record for a man who had never passed a university entrance examination. But above all Monnet was one of the most important advocates of the "European idea." Monnet died in 1979, and in 1988 his remains were transferred to the Panthéon – the highest posthumous honor that France can bestow on a citizen.

ministry gave subsidies and loans, and ran the atomic energy commission as well as the telecommunication industry. Partial ownership of companies was also used to control the economy. By the 1970s, the state had become a massive owner, part-owner, investor, and controller within the French economy.

From 1947 French governments became committed to economic planning in a way that neither Britain nor West Germany were. The first plan (1947–50), named after Jean Monnet, set the design for economic planning and modernization. The aim was to raise standards of living, to modernize the basic industries and agriculture, to make the state do the planning and financing of the economy both for domestic and export industries. By 1980, five successive plans had been in operation. (Over the years, these plans also influenced other Western countries, as they seemed to be working.) The plans were elaborated by civil servants. State administrators and technocrats also managed the nationalized industries, having been trained in the great state graduate schools, principally at ENA. Within three decades, the government became the greatest employer in France – one out of every four Frenchmen worked for the state by 1985. A vital private sector remained. But state ownership, control and planning, were taken to their limit, as far as was possible in a country that had not become fully socialist, or – as a disillusioned businessman put it in a phrase that would recur thereafter with growing frequency – *l'état, c'est le problème.*

Postwar modernization modified French society in every aspect. There ws a softening in the traditional differences between Paris and the provinces. The gap between city and countryside narrowed here, as it did elsewhere in Western Europe. The regions of France drew more closely together – despite separatist movements in Brittany and Corsica – and regional particularities weakened. Urbanization, the impact of the media, improvements in transportation, and a unified school system contributed to the development of a national society with similar views, dress, and habits. All classes found themselves better off than they had been in 1940; wages went up; material goods and state benefits became more easily available and more plentiful than in the past. Although France nominally remained a Catholic country, fewer than 25 percent stayed practicing Catholics, and almost as many so-called Catholics were anti-clerical, agnostic or atheistic. Many rural regions in the South found themselves without a priest or church.

Blue-collar workers continued to be relatively poorly paid by American or German standards; nevertheless their quality of life steadily improved since 1945. Even though a large number (two-thirds) voted communist or socialist, they mostly believed that reform, not revolution, would ameliorate their condition. Trade unions have remained powerful in France in contrast to the US. These include the *Confédération Générale du Travail* (*CGT*; controlled by the communists), which has been the largest union; the *Confédération Générale du Travail-Force Ouvrière* (*CFDT-FO*) under the socialists, second in rank; and the *Confédération Française Démocratique de Travail* (*CFDT*, formerly a Catholic trade union.) Although most workers voted for the left, the majority did not belong to unions.

Farmers have been declining in numbers throughout most of Western Europe and the US since 1945. The French rural population diminished at a fast rate. Government subsidies and technical support, however, helped to make French farmers more productive – by 1980 they provided half of all farm goods to the EEC and by their insistence on high protection, had become a financial burden on the community. The middle class became the largest of all the classes in France (40 percent of employed people), tending to support center groups. A new middle-class elite of technocrats (administrators, professionals, technicians, managers, intellectuals) increasingly replaced the old family-centered business elites. After the wounds inflicted by the colonial wars had healed, French political life became less divisive – so much so that henceforth a striking majority of the people expressed confidence in their political systems.[39]

ITALY

World War II improved the Italian image in the US; Italian-Americans won equality of esteem through service in the armed forces; tens of thousands of US soldiers who served in Italy eventually came to know, and many to love, its people and culture. After the war tourists rediscovered both the natural and man-made beauty of Italy – a country without many material resources, but blessed with an ancient and glorious history, ingenious and hard-working citizens. Within a few years, Italy would experience an industrial expansion and a new prosperity that would have seemed inconceivable in 1945.

> *Historically Italians have had a "distrust of government, indifference to politics, lack of belief in the honesty and capacity of bureaucrats and politicians, and, on the other hand, instrumental participation for personal benefit and gross pragmatism." (See Dante L. Germino, The Government and Politics of Contemporary Italy, 1968.)*

Italia di Minoranza is the title of a book in which the dean of Italian historians discusses the role of political mavericks in his country's modern history.[40] But in truth, Italy remains a country made up of regions. National legends notwithstanding, Italy had been unified in the nineteenth century by minorities, and run by minorities ever since. It owed its unification to Piedmont, a northern Italian state, efficient and centralized. Northern supremacy in the traditional, church-centred, poverty-stricken South had been immensely

---

[39]Macridis, "Politics of France," in his *Modern Political Systems: Europe*, pp. 137–268. Other general works include Douglas E. Ashford, *Policy and Politics in France*. Philadelphia, Temple University Press, 1982. Henry W. Ehrmann, *Politics in France*. Boston, Little Brown, 1983. Jean Marceau, *Class and Status in France*. Oxford, Oxford University Press, 1964. Theodore Zeldin, *France 1884–1945: Politics of Anger*. Oxford, Oxford University Press, 1979. David Thomson, *Democracy in France Since 1870*. Oxford, Oxford University Press, 1964.

[40]Giovanni Spadolini, *Italia di Minoranza: Lotta Politica e Culturale dal 1915 a Oggi*. Florence, F. Le Monnier, 1986.

unpopular – far more so, say, than Protestant Prussian rule over the Catholics in Prussia's Rhenish provinces, wealthy by comparison with Lutheran Brandenburg or Pomerania. In southern Italy, northern supremacy had been widely identified with anti-clericalism, and excessive centralization, as well as the burdens of conscription, and unfair taxation. Italy continued to be a country where government was regarded with suspicion, and a land split by social, and above all by regional, cleavages, made worse by striking economic disparities. (In 1953, the South, with about 41 percent of Italy's acreage and 37 percent of its population, accounted for no more than 21.2 percent of the country's national income – exact figures depend on the estimates used.)[41]

The Italian case was not unique. There were startling differences too between, say, Lisbon and the backward South in Portugal, Dublin and the Gaelic-speaking West in Ireland. But nowhere were these divergencies greater than between the Italian North and the poorest parts of Calabria and Sicily, whose real poverty shocked both northern Italians and the rest of Europe.[42]

In the postwar period, the Church in Italy was powerful and respected. However, it had not functioned so much as a national institution, but as the center of an ecclesiastical dominion that spanned the world, and gave Italian divines better opportunities for promotion in an international bureaucracy than other priests had. United Italy had always been divided politically. Pre-Fascist Italy had stumbled from crisis to crisis. Fascist attempts to unify the country by dint of state worship and violence had proved a dismal failure. Italians lacked confidence in the machinery of the state. All too many of them, in 1945, looked abroad with envy or hope, either to the USA or to the Soviet Union.

In theory, the miracle of a rapid Italian recovery should not have happened. Yet it did, for Italy had unseen assets of a kind that statisticians cannot measure – a strong sense of family, a capacity for work, a natural conservatism that made nonsense of facile generalizations according to which the Italians' private virtues contrasted with their public vices. Italians were not an anarchic people. The majority of them respected Catholicism, although there was considerable skepticism about the Church as an institution. They had a sense of public order. Even after Italy had been split in two by the Allied invasion, Italians continued to behave as if a unified state would be rebuilt; the *carabinieri,* the *sindaco,* and *pretore* maintained order; most taxpayers paid their dues. Private initiative took over after the Fascist collapse, even though much of the Fascists' legislation remained on the state's books. Italians practiced their old arts of *arrangiarsi* (getting by); they somehow fed and clothed themselves and their children in, what an Italian has called "a national community of suffering ... a common anxiety to rebuild."[43]

[41]Shepard B. Clough, *The Economic History of Modern Italy.* New York, Columbia University Press, 1964, p. 9.

[42]Elspeth Huxley, *Back Street New Worlds: A Look at Immigrants in Britain.* London, Chatto and Windus, 1964, p. 70.

[43]Eppicarmo Corbino, "Cinquant' anni di vita economica Italiana," v. 2, *L'Economia fra il 1945 e il 1955.* Naples, Edizione Scientifiche Italiane, 1966, p. 156.

The Italians were among the first Europeans to reconstruct their economy after the war, helped by the US. They also re-fashioned the state. Fascism, at the end of the war, was discredited – owing to acts of terror, the government's poor performance, military defeat and the antics of the so-called Fascist Social Republic (or Republic of Salò) in which Mussolini, at the end of his tether, had attempted to return to his socialist origins under the protection of German guns. Much more influential were the monarchists, particularly within the army and in the South. In 1946, the Allies pressured King Victor Emmanuel to retire. A subsequent referendum later on (1946) to decide on the future of the monarchy gave the Republicans a narrow majority (54 percent of the vote). The election had not been a model of fair play, as ballots had been counted by committees from which monarchists had been widely excluded. But the monarchy had itself become a party cause – a fatal handicap to legitimate kingship; and moreover the monarchists were divided, and the House of Savoy did not necessarily appeal even to conservatives. Monarchism faded into insignificance. (In the 1948 elections, the monarchists won no more than 4.8 percent of the vote. They combined with neo-Fascists, in about 1968, to form a radical right-wing group, the Italian Social Movement (MSI-DN).)

The Italian Liberals could have become an influential group. They had a long tradition in Italian history, and they comprised able men such as Eduardo Sogno and, particularly, Luigi Enaudi. After the war Enaudi served in a coalition government headed by Alcide de Gasperi, and, as Minister of the Budget, he played a major part in restoring the Italian currency. He subsequently served as president of the Italian Republic – one of those former economics professors who succeeded brilliantly in practical politics, as had António Salazar in Portugal, and Ludwig Ehrhard in West Germany. However the Liberals stood for a sound currency and fiscal prudence, even at the price of temporary unemployment – never a popular policy. Moreover they never attempted to appeal to the mass of those voters who found themselves excluded from patronage, and they failed to defend the so-called Second Economy with the slogan (increasingly popular from the 1970s onward) *meno stato, più mercato*, "less state, more market." From the 1950s onward the party went into what appeared to be irreversible decline, and defenders of free market economy found themselves a minority. Even the Christian Democrats (CD) supported the largest state-owned sector of any Western European economy.

After the fall of Mussolini all anti-Fascist parties, no matter how small, demanded to be heard. They created an electoral system which entrenched the power of parties, gave the maximum representation to all views, and brought parliamentary representation to even smaller parties through proportional representation. The result: governmental instability and inefficient government averse to using its full power. Critics such as Renzo de Felice claim that factional interests prevented a central mechanism from defending the common good, and encouraged union militance. Italian democracy therefore has not controlled unions even to protect essential public services. Nevertheless, Italy somehow "worked."

The CD under de Gasperi was to rule Italy throughout the postwar period. At the same time, Italo-American links tightened in a variety of ways – through US–Italian trade, US investment in Italy, Italian emigration to the US, private assistance given to Italians by their Italian-American relatives, links between US Catholics and the Church in Italy, military ties, and US cultural influence. Overall, the US beckoned as the land of modernity – far more so than the Soviet Union, which appealed to a smaller clientele found mainly among urban workers and intellectuals. The US made massive use of foreign aid and advisers, Keynesians all. Aid served as an instrument in the Cold War, a means of humanitarian endeavor, and a device for setting Italy on the path of social progress. (The Americans, for instance, strongly favored major land reform in the Italian South but this was never implemented.) The Americans' direct (as against indirect) impact was, however, small. By 1948, the United States had already largely "forfeited its already feeble control over the internal economy and politics" of Italy to the Italians themselves. As Pietro Quarone, an Italian ambassador, put it at the time, the Italians would have to make a show of putting up with the Americans' *bestialitá* (beastly behavior) – but in time even the Americans would get wise to their own foolishness.[44]

In *The United States and Italy, 1940–1950* ..., James Edward Miller deals with successful American efforts to integrate Italy into the Western Alliance after World War II. It was not an easy task – there were conflicts with Britain, and even within the various branches of the US government. There were struggles among the various Italian political parties, as well as between Italian-American groups who were working to restore Italy's legitimacy. The US aimed at the development of a middle-class democracy, and tried to use Keynesian economic levers. It wanted political stability, hence did not push too hard for economic and social reforms. American aid, money, and military presence helped the CD against the Italian left, and gave the Italians a chance to set up a stable democracy and integrate their country into the European community. The end justified the means, given the threat posed by the Italian Communist Party, and the tactics of disruption and strikes that they used. Less interference might have allowed the communists to take power. Alternatively, there might have been a civil war, as in Greece, and an end to parliamentary government. To get their way, the Americans meddled in Italy, as in Germany and Japan, and not always successfully. But the US did not undermine the legitimacy of the Italian government under the Christian Democrats – quite the contrary. Within a few years, Italian legitimacy was fully restored, democracy was working, albeit imperfectly, and Italy came to play a leading role in unifying Europe. The Christian Democrats could not have continued to win election after election for the next 30 years without the support of the electorate. Politics is the art of the possible, and an imperfect democracy was preferable to none at all.

What of the political culture of Italy – that is the sum of political values,

[44] John Lamberton Harper, *America and the Reconstruction of Italy 1945–1948*. Cambridge, Cambridge University Press, 1986, p. 160.

beliefs, perceptions, emotions, and institutional arrangements? It is hard to define, given the extent of Italian geographical and social divisions. According to H. Stuart Hughes, Italian attitudes alternated between resignation on the one hand, prowess and individualism on the other.[45] In the eyes of their critics, Italians love the dramatic and colorful *bel gesto*. A minor altercation is acted out in the spirit of grand opera. Italian party politics revolves around splinters and factions that are motivated less by ideology than by interests. Politicians must put together coalitions (*combinazioni*) and by adopting or co-opting opponents (*transformismo*) in order to stay in office, because no party has a majority. Bargains thus shape politics in a way that is perhaps unique to Italy. Politics are dominated by party patronage through the granting of jobs, directorships, contracts. Government ever since the unification of Italy in 1870 has been described as the rule of the millions by the thousands, for the benefit of a few hundred thousand.

THE ITALIAN CIVIL SERVICE

There was some truth in the negative picture drawn by Almond, Verba, and others. The civil service remained the Achilles heel of the Italian establishment. On the face of it, this seems surprising. Italians count among their numbers some of the world's most able administrators – as evinced by the record of Italian civil servants who serve the Catholic Church or aid the work of international agencies. Before World War I, the Italian bureaucracy had been known for efficiency and probity. Standards thereafter deteriorated because of the shocks administered by World War I, the Fascist dictatorship, and the disorders following World War II. The major parties thereafter used the bureaucracy for party ends, and filled agencies with deserving followers. Civil servants learned how to bend with the wind. Administrative standards declined at the very time when politicians kept expanding the functions of the state. Italians, in other words, had good reason for a general sense of distrust.

Almond and Verba, in their classic study *Civic Culture*, elaborate on this negative image. As they saw it, Italian political culture during the late 1950s continued to be marked by alienation, social isolation, and distrust. Italians were deficient in national pride, and partisan in politics. Italian voters supposedly were ill-informed and reluctant to participate in politics – much more so than was true of Britain or the United States. Italians, the critics said, lacked faith in their country's government and bureaucracy. Partisanship involved, not merely individual voters, but also primary groups, much as in Belgium (and the Netherlands) where religion widely dictated not only party affiliation, but also membership in sport, cultural, and professional associations – even

---

[45]For Italian politics see H. Stuart Hughes, *The United States and Italy,* revised edn. Cambridge, Mass. Harvard University Press, 1965, *passim*; Gabriel A. Almond and Sidney Verba, *The Civic Culture: Political Attitudes and Democracy in Five Nations.* Princeton, Princeton University Press, 1963, and *The Civic Culture Revisited.* Boston, Little Brown, 1980; and Norman Kogan, *A Political History of Italy: The Postwar Years.* New York, Praeger, 1983.

the choice of acquaintances, friends, and spouses. The division between secular and clerical groups continued to dominate Italian politics during the postwar period. The Christian Democrats defended the Church and religious values, and obtained popular votes in return. Fear of communism played a decisive part in Christian Democratic dominance – preventing many overdue reforms, especially with regard to the bureaucracy and state corporations.

Nevertheless, the negative picture of Italy was skewed. CD governance indeed contained many flaws. It did not achieve the expected success in improving conditions in the South. It used control of the public purse in expanding social and industrial projects, and thereby created new patronage networks. But the CD drew on the services of practical idealists as well as ward heelers. The bulk of Italians supported their constitution, respected civil rights, and supported the democratic system. Up to the 1960s, Italian politics did widely suffer from civic non-involvement. But as prosperity returned, and as educational standards improved, the civic institutions gained in strength. Having lost their colonial empire, Italians no longer wasted money and men on imperial glory. The economy expanded in a spectacular fashion. The communists remained excluded from power during a critical period of development (from 1947 to 1978). The Italians' social structure and political culture changed in a remarkable fashion. Traditionalism weakened, and the citizens' confidence in their political institutions increased – this was the true Italian miracle.[46]

[46]See Giacomo Sani, "The political culture of Italy: continuity and change," in Gabriel A. Almond and Sidney Verba, *The Civic Culture Revisted*, ch. 8.

4

Parties and Politicians

When the war in Europe ended, violence might have been expected to seep into politics. Millions of men had been taught how to use arms and to work underground. Countless arms caches remained hidden in cellars and haylofts; men and women alike had learned to live by deception and violence. Established authority had widely fallen into disrepute and many former resistance leaders turned to politics. Europeans had experienced bitter sufferings; and the hatred survived as a legacy of war. Yet the bulk of Europeans returned to peaceful habits with surprising readiness.

The reason is clear: they had had their fill of fighting. The cult of the uniform, of black shirts, green shirts, and brown shirts had ceased to appeal to men and women who had worn military dress for all too many years. Europeans had equally tired of that fervent worship of youth formerly expressed in Hitler Youth and Young Fascist songs. The most prominent statesmen consisted of middle-aged or aged people who expected to die in their beds. De Gaulle was 54 when, in 1944, he became president of the French Provisional Government. Adenauer was 73 when he accepted the chancellorship of the newly-founded German Federal Republic in 1949; Churchill was 66 when he was called to the prime ministership in 1940, and Clement Attlee was 66 on succeeding Churchill in 1945; Harry Truman was 61 when he stepped into the US presidency in 1945 – and so the list continues.

War had shattered the revolutionary prestige of the Nazi Party for which Hitler, in his own person, had combined the roles played for the contemporary communist parties by Marx, Lenin, and Stalin. But the communist parties in Western Europe still contained hard core contingents dedicated to the overthrow of the bourgeois order. They alone placed their hopes in a coordinated movement whose scope and political ambitions transcended the confines of the nation state in a manner not attained by the most multinational of multinational corporations. But the realities of Eastern Europe would gradually, over the next ten years, diminish the communists' appeal in Western Europe; the bulk of communist voters – as distinct from the cadres – wanted higher living standards rather than a Red October. Living standards slowly improved, as economic recovery accelerated. Above all, the workers in the Western Euro-

pean countries became more consumer-oriented and less committed to ideological ambitions, as they bettered their conditions through collective
bargaining, pension funds, publicly funded health and insurance schemes,
housing, and other amenities. Workers increasingly achieved their aims, not
merely by collective bargaining, but through party politics, so that they
enlarged their stake in the nation state. The politics of ethnic regionalism
played but a minor part at a time when many regionalists (such as the Flemings
in Belgium and Bretons in France) had compromised their cause by real or
alleged collaboration with the Third Reich. For all the challenges it faced, the
nation state remained the focus of politics throughout the Western world.

The chosen instrument of politics was the political party, once defined by
Disraeli as organized opinion. The political party tried both to educate the
electorate and to give voice to electoral opinion; it sought to win power
according to the rules of the parliamentary game. The party stood for – or at
least pretended to stand for – certain ideological principles. Parties, however,
varied to an extraordinary extent in composition and purpose. At one end of
the spectrum stood the "machine" party, represented by the great parties of
the US. The "machine" party was loosely organized; its purpose was to capture
votes and win office. At the other end of the spectrum was the "cradle-
to-grave" party, represented by the communists, some socialists, and to a
considerable extent, the Christian Democratic parties. The "cradle-to-grave"
party provided a great range of services designed to serve a member throughout
his or her lifetime. Thomas H. Reed, an American political scientist described
such a party structure in what became known to political scientists as a
"consociational democracy" (in this case Belgium) after World War I: A
Belgian socialist might, if he chose, live an almost exclusively socialist life. As
a child he would learn to sing and dance with the *enfants du peuple*. As a
youngster he would go on long hikes with the *jeunes gardes*. If he were inclined
to athletics, he would find a place on a socialist soccer team or he could play
in a socialist chess club. Once he began to work, he acquired membership in
a socialist union, read socialist newspapers, spent his evenings in a socialist
café or cinema, and found relief from illness in a socialist clinic where a socialist
doctor prescribed drugs compounded in a socialist pharmacy. When he died,
he might sink into oblivion in the blissful consciousness that his children
would be even more socialist than he had been.[1]

The remaining political parties in the Western world stood somewhere
between these two extremes. (In West Germany, for example, the major parties
maintained their own think tanks that held conferences and published work
of academic merit, for example the Friedrich Ebert Stiftung. In addition the
parties ran numerous subsidiary organizations of a social and even a convivial
kind. But the West German Christian Democrats and the Social Democrats
alike lacked the attributes of a political church (a statement much less true,
however, of Italy, Austria, and the Netherlands).) Over the long haul, all

---

[1]Thomas Harrison Reed, *Government and Politics of Belgium*. Yonkers-on-Hudson, NY, World
Book Company, 1924, *passim*.

the major Western parties increasingly became "catch-all" parties (in the phraseology of Otto Kircheimer), electoral machines that constantly improved their bureaucratic machinery. At the same time, the importance of political "cradle-to-grave" organizations declined, as the state expanded its social functions, and as the consumer revolution added to the range of private choice in leisure time. Political parties nevertheless continued to play the star role in Western politics.

SECULAR CONSERVATIVES

Introduction

Conservatism, during the postwar years, widely stood in disrepute among intellectuals. Yet it was the more conservatively minded parties that held the reins of government in the greater part of Western Europe (especially in Italy, France, and Germany). In Great Britain, the Labour government gave way to a Conservative government in 1951; in the US, a Republican administration attained office in 1953. Between them, the various conservative parties differed on many issues, especially on the role to be entrusted to the state in managing the economy. But outside the Iberian Peninsula, none of these parties fell subject to obscurantism; none of them were reactionary in the sense of calling for the restoration of an idealized rural past, with its imagined traditions, and ancestral pieties. None of the conservative parties rejected the world of power stations, factories, and laboratories. None were militaristic in the sense of believing that young men best learnt civic virtue on the rifle range or barrack square. None were simply bourgeois parties, on the contrary they all enjoyed at least some measure of working-class support. And none were anti-semitic; Hitler's legacy of anti-semitism survived mainly in the USSR (where Stalin developed his own form of national socialist paranoia, complete with Jewish doctors' plots), and in the Arab world (where anti-Zionism frequently merged into hatred of Jews in general).

The conservatives were far from united. There was little formal cooperation between the various parties, except for such bodies as the *Nouvelles Equipes Internationales* (*NEI*), formed in 1947 as a forum for discussion to serve Christian Democratic parties on the European Continent. The conservatives were also split internally. There were traditionalists who still looked to the gentry and the Church. But overall, these diehards increasingly lost out to businessmen who put their trust in banking, commerce, and industrial enterprise. Neither traditionalists nor businessmen were necessarily opposed to state intervention in the economy. Monarchs, enlightened or otherwise, had never been loathe to regulate business. And even merchants and industrialists rarely objected to state regulation, provided this served their own interests.

Much less influential were the heirs of Adam Smith, advocates of a minimal state, convinced that public authority should merely protect the citizens' person and property, while interfering as little as possible with his private life and economic pursuits. The free enterprise school commanded a number of brilliant thinkers, prominent among whom were Ludwig von Mises and Friedrich von Hayek, expatriates from Austria, a country – unlike neighboring Switzerland – more famed for its theoreticians than its practitioners of capitalism. But in Western Europe, their names were no more household words than those of the related "Freiburg School" in West Germany. Such free traders as existed widely gave their allegiance to self-styled liberal parties, whereas the Christian Democrats put their trust in the regulatory state. In the US, by contrast, the free traders primarily, though by no means exclusively, found their home in the Republican Party. European-style traditionalists hardly played a part in US practical politics during the twentieth century. Great Britain, as in so many other respects, remained an exception in that the Conservative Party embraced alike gentlefolk, businessmen, and intellectual free traders.

By and large, however, most conservatively minded men and women shared a general – though frequently disregarded – commitment to Christianity, Natural Law, historical continuity, the virtues of human variety, and the rights of private property, a belief in a general public interest transcending the bonds of class. Unlike the old defenders of seigneurial privilege, these parties believed that a self-made man who had earned money in business or the professions should be honored, rather than reviled as a parvenu. At the same time, most conservatives stood committed, at least in theory, to the assumption that inherited wealth required of its beneficiaries a sense of social responsibility. Conservative and reformist parties alike benefited from new widespread distaste for those radical parties committed to remaking the world according to "some plausible plan of reformation which" – in Adam Smith's caustic words – "will not only remove the inconveniencies and relieve the distresses immediately complained of, but will prevent in all times coming any return of the like inconveniencies and distresses."

The US Republican Party

Of all the Western nations, the US was both the most conservative country and the country most likely to welcome change. The US had been born of a revolution and took pride in the fact – unlike its northern neighbor Canada, where, as Seymour Martin Lipset points out, Frenchmen had cut themselves off from the French Revolution, and English-speaking Americans had elected to escape from the American Revolution. The US was huge and diverse. It lacked a feudal or aristocratic legacy, a truism ignored by those southern romantics who mistakenly identified Old South plantation owners with aristocrats. Both the major US parties lacked a program tied to a particular class or ideology. Both parties appealed to an electorate of which the majority described, and continued to describe itself as "middle-of-the-road", quite irrespective of the voter's income. Both parties contained within their ranks reformists who looked to the state to expand social services (though these were more numerous among the Democrats). Both parties embraced militant anti-communists, including many refugees from Eastern Europe and China, with first-hand experience of communist practice, as well as American intellectuals who had broken with the communist creed. Both parties included traditionalists who looked for a return to accustomed ethical, religious, and moral values. Both also had among their supporters liberals of the classic kind (more plentiful, by far, among Republicans) who dreaded what they regarded as America's drift to state planning. Both parties stood committed to the constitution. As Edward Greenberg, an American radical scholar, observed regretfully "nor do the parties differ except in details and rhetoric, over such givens as the primacy of private property, the beneficent nature of the free-enterprise system, and the maintenance of law and order in the face of dissent."[2]

From the late 1930s through the 1950s, the US enjoyed other political advantages. There was a widespread mood of confidence. This found expression in the arts, in such masterpieces as Irving Berlin's musical *Call Me Madam* whose gaiety mirrored the joyfulness in the operettas written by Gilbert and Sullivan at the height of Britain's imperial splendor. There was popular trust in government, a feeling that strikingly declined in the 1960s and 1970s. (In 1958, 74 percent of white and 78 percent of black respondents in a major poll believed that the people's elected representatives controlled the government for the common good. By 1970, by which time the governmental machine had vastly expanded, these percentages had declined to 31 percent and 34 percent respectively). There was no polarization between college-educated Republicans on the one hand and college-educated Democrats on the other – a state of affairs that changed during the 1960s and the 1970s when the college-educated Democrats became noticeably more liberal than their party's rank and file, while college-educated Republicans turned consistently more conservative than their fellow voters.[3] Both parties formed loose coalitions of groups with differing objectives – so much so that debates on major national and international issues were liable to be conducted with greater fervor within the two major parties, than between them.

Central party organizations remained weak, since party organizers would raise funds for candidates and campaigns on a local and regional, rather than on a national, basis except during a presidential election year. Both parties nevertheless maintained a surprising degree of continuity.[4] They kept their cohesion in part through great party conventions that made allowance for the size, diversity, and geographical dispersion of their respective electorates. For all their carnival atmosphere, for all their public hoopla and private deals, these conventions gave more influence to the party's rank and file than the general congresses of any major party in Europe. Neither of the two major US parties, by contrast, could rely on the tight bureaucracies of the European

[2]Edward S. Greenberg, *The American Political System: A Radical Approach*. Boston, Little Brown, 1983, p. 177.

[3]Everett Carl Ladd, Jr, "The American party system today," in Seymour Martin Lipset, ed., *The Third Century: America as a Post-Industrial Society*. Stanford, Hoover Institution Press, 1979, p. 169.

[4]Xandra Kayden and Eddie Mahe, Jr, *The Party Goes on: The Persistence of the Two-Party System in the United States*. New York, Basic Books, 1985, for a general discussion.

kind. (By the end of the 1950s, the permanent staff employed on the national level by each party numbered no more than 75 to 100 appointees for each of the two major parties.) Outsiders such as Willkie or General Dwight Eisenhower could secure a party's presidential nomination by moving into the seat of power in a "lateral" manner, from professions not directly related to electoral politics. This system gave to US politics an openness and a lively character not known to Europeans; at the same time America paid for this advantage by having to contend with an element of unpredictability and discontinuity greater than in any other major country in the West.

The two US parties also displayed distinctive differences. Of the two, the Republicans regarded themselves as the more conservative, and of all the world's conservative parties, the Republican Party was by far the most numerous in terms of votes. (In the presidential elections of 1952, for example, more than 33,000,000 people cast their vote for the Republicans – two and a half times the number who voted in favor of the Conservative Party in Great Britain.) The Republicans, according to their critics, represented wealth, privilege, and Protestantism. They stressed individual achievement, competition, and Americanism. The picture is overdrawn, for the Republican Party was by no means a free enterprise party pure and simple. But overall, Republicans were more likely than Democrats to consider the interests of the citizen from his position as a taxpayer, rather than as a recipient of tax-supported social services. Republicans contained within their ranks unionized workers, Catholics, and – until the 1960s, a substantial minority of blacks still loyal to the "party of Lincoln." But Republican voters were more likely than Democratic voters to be northerners, Protestants of North Western European descent, drawn from small towns and rural communities. Overall, income and class affiliation remained less important in determining a voter's party loyalty than his or her religious and regional background (see table 4.1).

TABLE 4.1   *Percentage of "party identifiers" from each major group: 1952–1960*

	Republicans	Democrats
Northern white Anglo-Saxon Protestants	56	19
Catholics	10	13
White northern union members	18	22
White southerners	11	31
Jews	1	5
Blacks	5	10

Source: Thomas Byrne Edsall, "Republican America" (reviewing Xandra Kayden and Eddie Mahe Jr, *The Party Goes On: The Persistence of the Two-Party System in the United States*. New York, Basic Books, 1985) in *New York Review of Books*, April 24, 1986.

Nevertheless, the Republican Party long faced serious trouble. Despite its mixed social composition, the party widely remained identified in the minds of many voters with industrialists, merchants, and farmers – and more seriously with the well-remembered misery of the Great Depression (widely, though inaccurately blamed on President Herbert Hoover). Ever since the 1930s the Republicans had been a minority party with a declining membership. A Democratic administration had led the country out of the slump and forward to victory in World War II. The country experienced unparalleled prosperity for which the incumbent administration took credit. This prosperity at first appeared to weaken the traditional bastions of Republicanism. Millions of people left the farm; small-town America declined, while the metropolitan areas, strongholds of the Democratic Party, grew apace.

Contrary to a persistent legend, the Republicans were by no means devoid of support among intellectuals. The University of Chicago, for instance, remained an exciting place for free enterprise economists willing to criticize Roosevelt's New Deal. But theoreticians such as Frank Knight remained totally unknown to the bulk of Americans; none of them reached popular fame of the kind attained by Lord Keynes, John Kenneth Galbraith, or (much later) Milton Friedman. Equally unreconciled to the existing order – albeit for very different reasons – were Catholic traditionalists, southern agrarian romantics, and Protestant fundamentalists. Catholic traditionalists included men such as William Buckley (whose *National Review* began publication in 1956). But their appeal remained limited, even among Catholic Americans at the time. Agrarian romantics believed their battle lost, and so did the adherents of Edmund Burke who looked with dismay on the uneducated masses. The fundamentalists had withdrawn from politics in what they regarded as a sinful world. It was only much later, under Ronald Reagan, that these disparate elements would fuse into a powerful political alliance. The real challenge to the existing order came from the liberal left, from intellectuals who remained unimpressed by the miracles of American technology, scientific achievements, and techniques of mass production. An army of professors now admonished their countrymen in the language of popular sociology, rather than the religious terminology employed by hellfire-and-brimstone preachers of an earlier generation. Americans were sheep lost in *The Lonely Crowd* (according to David Riesman); they submitted to *The Power Elite* (according to C. Wright Mills); they succumbed to the blatant materialism of *The Affluent Society* (according to John Kenneth Galbraith); or they were beguiled by *The Hidden Persuaders* of the advertising world (according to Vance Packard). Whereas capitalism had been denounced a generation earlier for creating poverty in the midst of plenty, it now appeared blameworthy for creating excessive comfort.

The Republican Party moreover had long wanted for outstanding personalities whose appeal went beyond the ranks of the party faithful. Robert Taft, foremost among old-style Republicans, was known for his integrity and knowledge of government. Taft predicted that US adherence to the UN, to the Bretton Woods Agreement, and similar exercises in "one worldism" would turn the country into an "international Santa Claus." But isolationism had ceased to be a popular cause; Taft was unable to secure nomination as a Republican candidate, and instead Eisenhower achieved another landslide victory at the party convention in 1952. In the following elections, the general again won an overwhelming victory, and was able to rely, moreover, on a small Republican majority in both Houses of Congress.[5]

Adlai Stevenson, Eisenhower's opponent, seemed too liberal and – despite his evident integrity – too partisan. Eisenhower had won a personal even more than a party victory. He obtained not merely the Republican, but also most of the independent and a substantial portion of the Democratic vote. His popularity derived not merely from his success as a soldier. (General Douglas MacArthur, even more impressive as a military leader, turned out quite unsuccessful in his attempt to secure the presidential nomination.) Eisenhower won precisely because he was more than a soldier, and more than a party politician. With considerable personal charm, "Ike" seemed, and was, a man of moderation, always drawn to the golden mean. He inspired trust; liberals voted for him because they thought he was at heart a liberal; conservatives regarded him as a fellow-conservative.[6] Eisenhower seemed a man capable of balancing the conflicting demands made by welfare planners, defense specialists, and taxpayers – at a time (in 1952) when the traditional functions of the state (including defense) still accounted for more than four-fifths of the budget – as opposed to less than half the budgetary appropriations 20 years later.[7]

DWIGHT D. EISENHOWER (1890–1969)

Political scientists have long been fascinated by the "man on horseback," the military man who makes himself dictator. But no general in postwar Western politics conformed to this model – not de Gaulle in France, Smuts in South Africa, or Eisenhower in the US. Neither did Eisenhower correspond to other stereotypes of military leaders. He came from a humble background (as did President Truman). He managed to get into West Point; but his meteoric rise in rank only began in World War II, when he came to the notice of George C. Marshall, army chief of staff, and rose to command the Allied armies in the invasion of France, 1944. Eisenhower was brilliantly successful in what was at the time a most difficult and risky operation. (Before the landing he prepared two public communiques, one announcing the failure of the invasion, the other its success.) Eisenhower

---

[5]Eisenhower obtained 33,043,529 popular votes, as against Stevenson's 26,600,076. Only nine states (all of them in the South) voted for the Democrats. In the Senate, the Republicans held 48 seats, as against 47 Democratic and one independent seat. In the House of Representatives, the Republicans commanded 221 seats, as against 213 Democratic and one independent seat. *Keesing's Contemporary Archives*, 8–15 November 1952, pp. 12, 533, 556.

[6]Herbert Hyman and Paul B. Sheatsley, "The political appeal of General Eisenhower," *Public Opinion Quarterly* no. 17, Winter 1954–5, pp. 443–6. Piers Brendon, *Ike: His Life and Times*. New York, Harper and Row, 1986.

[7]In 1952, the "traditional expenditure in fields such as defense, veterans' benefits, interest on the general debt, general and financial administration, etc. accounted for $58,097 million or 81 percent of the budget. All other expenditure, including all social services amounted to $13.471 million. By 1972, the respective figures stood at $114,865 million or 47 percent of the budget. All other expenditure stood at $127,321 million or 53 percent of the budget." Roger A. Freeman, *The Growth of American Government*. Stanford, Hoover Institution, 175, p. 111.

later incurred severe criticism for failing to capture Berlin, Vienna, and Prague ahead of the Soviets in 1945, at a time when he might well have done so. In fact he had no political awareness of the threat of Soviet communism, he admired the Red Army, prized his drinking companionship with Soviet General Zhukov, and initially believed that amicable relations could be maintained by a policy of wise accommodation – a view shared in 1945 by nearly all US generals, except George Patton. Eisenhower's popularity in the US transcended party affiliation. (His book Crusade in Europe, *published in 1948, was so popular as to turn him almost immediately from a poor to a rich man.) Indeed, when he became president in 1953, he preferred to take into his cabinet millionaires rather than military men. In office, he combined the new internationalism with a firm belief in private enterprise, and an apparent ability to transcend party affiliations in the style of a national father figure.*

Eisenhower, moreover possessed that supreme gift of being able to conceal his intellectual superiority. He gave the impression of being the amiable company chairman, fonder of golf than of business, addicted to pious generalities, such as the "nine priniciples" of American policy put forward during his inaugural address. The reality was of course quite different, as should have been obvious to anyone who had seen Eisenhower, in World War II, subordinate to his will men such as General George Patton and Field Marshal Lord Montgomery, equally able, arrogant, endowed with a gift of showmanship, and equally impatient of control. Eisenhower moreover was good at delegating authority. This skill had stood him in good stead as a military leader; he carried it over into the White House, where he filled key offices with capable people, and then allowed them to solve their problems in their own way. This leadership style was also applied to diplomacy, albeit with less success, with Secretary of State John Foster Dulles, and his brother CIA director Allen Dulles enjoying a good deal of independence. For all his well-cultivated image of a farm boy, Eisenhower worked extremely hard, adhered to highly efficient staffing principles, and maintained firm control over his team – all behind a screen of military gobbledegook that concealed his intentions. He was indeed "the most successful of America's twentieth-century presidents, and the decade when he ruled (1953–61) the most prosperous in American, and indeed world history."[8]

The British Conservative Party

During the first two decades following World War II, Great Britain appeared the very model of a modern democracy. The British economy staged a recovery – nowhere near as spectacular as West Germany's, but nonetheless solid. Full employment came to be taken for granted. Pay packets in industry kept growing; Britain was not as yet seriously plagued by industrial strikes. In 1955, it still had the highest gross national product of any country in Western

---

[8]Paul Johnson, *Modern Times: The World from the Twenties to the Eighties.* New York, Harper and Row, 1983, p. 461. For Eisenhower's career in politics, see for instance Stephen E. Ambrose, *Eisenhower, Volume 2. The President.* New York, Simon and Schuster, 1984.

Europe, both in terms of absolute size and per capita figures.[9] The expansion of the public sector, though extensive, had not as yet reached anything like the extent attained during the 1960s and the 1970s when expenditure increased in an unprecedented fashion, and institutional restraints on public spending steadily weakened.

The tone and noise of British political disputes as yet remained restrained. During the 1940s and 1950s, protest movements – whether concerned with nuclear power, ecological issues, race relations, immigration, or women's rights – had not acquired anything like the emotional impact, organizational skill, or political influence attained in later years. Private scandals there might be aplenty. But in public, British politicians insisted on standards of gravity and sobriety that occasioned smiles in later years. (As late as 1964, Lord Mountbatten, the most famous British admiral on the retired list, a peer, and related to the royal family into the bargain, received an official reprimand from the First Lord of the Admiralty about his "frivolity and vulgarity" in telling a few risqué stories at a naval chaplain's dinner.)[10] To foreign observers such as Samuel H. Beer, a Harvard professor, British politics still embodied a success story, set in a happy country, "in which concensus and conflict" were ordered in a manner making "the political arena at once a market of interests and a forum for debate of fundamental moral concern."[11]

The organization that most consciously identified itself with these traditions was the Conservative Party. It had indeed had a good claim to being the world's oldest conservative party; it looked upon itself as Britain's natural governing body (it had held office for more than 40 years between 1886 and 1945, and thereafter once more enjoyed a long incumbency, from 1951 to 1964). In the public mind, the Conservatives were associated with all those great institutions that had been created or had acquired their modern form during the Victorian era – the civil service, the major clubs, public schools, the universities of Oxford and Cambridge, cabinet government, the empire, and the Commonwealth. The Conservative Party, much more than Labour, was thus linked with the pomp and circumstance of British public life – the monarchy, the House of Lords, the Guards, whose ceremonial splendor none could rival in the West.

The Conservative Party also had traditional links with the Anglican Church (which was sometimes known as "the Tory party at prayer," whereas non-conformists were likely to vote Labour). Among the younger voters, religious

---

[9]Between 1946 and 1956, the percentage of jobless workers declined from 2.4 to 1.1 percent. The weekly wage of male industrial workers went up from £3.45 per week in 1938, to £7.52 in 1950, to £14.54 in 1960. Measured in thousands of working days lost each year through stoppages, the British figures were 1,334 in 1938; 1,389 in 1950, 3,024 in 1960, but 14,750 in 1974. Figures from *The Economist Diary*, London, 1980, p. 5–38.

[10]Philip Ziegler, *Mountbatten*. New York, Alfred Knopf, 1985, p. 646.

[11]Samuel H. Beer, *Modern British Politics: A Study of Parties and Pressure Groups*. London, Faber and Faber, 1965, p. 390. By 1982, Beer had completely changed his viewpoint, and spoke of "pluralistic stagnation" in his *Britain Against Itself: The Political Contradictions of Collectivism*. London, Faber and Faber, 1982.

affiliation, however, increasingly became irrelevant in determining political convictions – a change natural in a country whose people stopped going to church in ever larger numbers. The Conservative Party could claim to be the most "national" of British parties in terms of class composition. Whereas Labour mainly drew the working class, especially in Scotland and in the North of England, the Conservatives attracted voters from every social group, especially in the heavily populated Southeast; these included a substantial number (never less than about 30 percent) of workers (especially skilled operatives, foremen, and supervisors). With their help, the party staged an unexpected recovery during the 1950s, acquiring both a plurality of votes and a parliamentary majority.[12]

> *Postwar Conservative Party leaders were from aristocratic or upper-class families. Macmillan and Churchill were related to dukes, Eden and Home came from the landed gentry. This was a very different background both from earlier and later leadership. After 1965, Heath and Thatcher were more representative of the middle class, of managers and of suburbia.*
>
> *Conservative Party MPs from 1951 on came primarily from the middle class and above: 70–5 percent from public schools; 41–5 percent from the professions; 36–7 percent from business.*

The Conservative Party was also Winston Churchill's party. Having submitted his resignation to the King in 1945, Churchill's career seemed to have passed its zenith. Some thought that the ageing statesman had become an extinct volcano. Nothing could be further from the truth. Churchill – half American and half British by descent, a European as well as a Briton in outlook – stood for what might be called the outward-looking wing of his party. He was pro-American within a party that contained many anti-Americans. He played a leading part in the movement for a united Europe. (In 1948 he wrote a lengthy letter to Léon Blum, the French socialist leader so as to prevent a socialist boycott of the United Europe Movement.)[13] Churchill was an equally generous supporter of the Zionist cause. He was also determined that defeated Germany should rejoin Europe. Churchill in opposition played almost as important a part in world history as he had done as prime minister in World War II – and so did the party that he led.

The Conservative Party was never a monolithic organization. Its legacy was complex, with a long Tory tradition of a hierarchic, Christian society, rooted in hereditary privilege and reciprocal obligations. As Lady Mountbatten put

---

[12]In the 1945 election, the Conservatives won 213 parliamentary seats, against Labour's 393, with 39.8 percent of the votes. Corresponding figures for 1950 were 298 against 315 seats, and 43.5 percent of the vote. 1951: 321 against 295 seats, 48 percent of the vote. 1955: 344 seats against 277, 49.7 percent of the vote. 1959: 365 seats against 258, 49.4 percent of the vote. Source: Robert McKenzie, "Between two elections: a balance sheet of British politics, *Encounter*, January 1966, p. 12.

[13]Martin Gilbert *"Never Despair": Winston S. Churchill, 1945–1965*. New York, Houghton Mifflin, 1988.

it in a private letter to her son, Lord Louis Mountbatten, "we who come from an old stock of a privileged family, that has not had to worry over material existence, has inherited that sense of duty towards our fellow men, those specially whose nation we belong to, and who look to us instinctively for example and guidance ... Let us live and die honorably."[14] This was not an empty boast. The best of aristocrats were indeed patriotic, independent, courageous, and outspoken. Many who had been opponents of prewar appeasement – the Marquess of Salisbury, Winston Churchill, Sir Anthony Eden – had come from such backgrounds. (Churchill remained leader of the Conservative Party until 1955; he then resigned the Premiership to Eden, who was succeeded by Harold Macmillan in 1957.) By contrast, Neville Chamberlain, the principal proponent of appeasement, had started in business, made his early political reputation in the municipal affairs of Birmingham, and generally represented an outlook evinced by pacific, hardworking businessmen. Throughout their history, Tories had seen nothing wrong *per se* in state interference with the economy. For them the paternalistic, and if need be uneconomic, management of landed estates, subsidized for prestige purposes from profits made in the City, could easily be extended into paternalistic management of the nation's heritage.

More important than the aristocrats within the Conservative Party were the businessmen, who supplied the bulk of its funds. (Between 1950 and 1964, 67.4 percent of the revenue derived by the party's central office derived from firms, banks, and corporations, 16.9 percent from individual donations, 11.9 percent from local branches, and 3.9 percent from interest.)[15] In theory, the businessmen advocated a free market economy. In practice, they stood widely committed to the interventionist state; many businessmen had served in two world wars as temporary civil servants, many more had learned to work with the regulatory state in running their own firms.

In addition, the party enjoyed widespread support from shopkeepers, and artisans, as well as from Tory working men, especially in southeast England. The working-class Tories stood committed to state intervention and indeed pointed with pride to great Victorian Tory leaders such as Benjamin Disraeli (later Earl of Beaconsfield), who during the nineteenth century had enfranchised urban working-class men, and had initiated many social reforms. The interventionist tradition had gained additional strength through the Depression and the attendant unemployment that had struck both workers and professional people; state intervention in the economy came to be accepted as the sovereign remedy for unemployment.

[14]Ziegler, *Mountbatten*, pp. 123–4.
[15]Michael Pinto-Duschinsky, "Die Konservative Partei Grossbritanniens 1945–1980" in Hans-Joachim Venn, ed., *Christlich-Demokratische Parteien in Westeuropa*. Paderborn, Ferdinand Schoningh, 1983, p. 70. For a general survey, see for instance Joachim Raschke, ed., *Die Politischen Parteien in Westeuropa. Geschichte, Programm, Praxis. Ein Handbuch*. Hamburg, Rowohl, 1978. Richard Rose and Derek W. Urwin, "Persistence and change in Western party systems since 1945," *Political Studies*, v. XVIII, no. 3, 1970, pp. 287–319. Gerald Dorfman and Peter J. Duignan, eds, *Politics in Western Europe*. Stanford, Hoover Institution, 1988.

> *Keynesians laid the basis for the economics of growth in the 1950s and 1960s by using some of Keynes's ideas of the multiplier, the marginal efficiency of capital, and the propensity to save, according to Albert Hirschman. This made some economists believe they could plan economic growth. A new field of development economics was spawned in the postwar world, focusing on economic development in the colonial world and in Latin America.*

The economic theories developed by John Maynard Keynes, or the plans elaborated by William Henry Beveridge for full employment in a free society, merely expressed in print what the bulk of British voters felt in their bones to be true. (Keynes and Beveridge had come from similar stock, from the earnest, improving, professional, salary-earning upper-middle class, with a sense of mission. Keynes was the son of a registrar and lecturer in moral sciences at Cambridge; Beveridge's father had been a senior official in the Indian civil service.) Keynes and Beveridge were both raised to the peerage, showered with honors and secured popular esteem, including the good opinions of many Conservatives. (Few Conservatives, by contrast would have been able to identify the contemporary Austrian, much less the Freiburg school of economics, that stood committed to a free market economy.) Exponents of *laissez-faire* in Britain had been linked to the nineteenth-century Liberal Party and to a religious non-conformist ethos now in decline. Within the Conservative Party, advocates of a free market economy formed a minority that had long been opposed by outright protectionists or proponents of imperial preference. (F. A. Hayek's anti-protectionist *The Road to Serfdom*, published in Great Britain in 1944, made little impact in its country of origin, but a condensed version of the book appeared in the April 1945 issue of the *Reader's Digest* in the US, and thereafter found an enormous readership through over one million reprints by the Book of the Month Club.)[16] In Britain supporters of a market economy such as Enoch Powell failed to advance to the party's leadership; Powell himself was not even a businessman, but had made his name as a wartime soldier, and then as a classics professor. (It was only in 1957 that Arthur Seldon and Ralph Harris founded the Institute for Economic Affairs, a pro-free enterprise think-tank, followed in 1974 by the Centre for Policy Studies, initiated by Sir Keith Joseph, supported by intellectual luminaries such as Samuel Brittan of the *Financial Times*, and P. T. (later Lord) Bauer.)

The Tory party thus formed a loose coalition between divergent groups, held together in part by those habits of deference that swiftly weakened in British politics from the 1960s onward. According to a widespread assumption, the Conservative alliance derived its cohesion through an "old boy network" (the former pupils of expensive and prestigious private schools, such as Eton and Harrow). This elite was supposedly bound by links of friendship, family, common scholastic experience, and membership of exclusive clubs. This assumption is questionable. The presence of numerous Old Etonians and

---

[16]We are indebted for this information to Dr Kurt R. Leube, a Visiting Scholar at the Hoover Institution.

Harrovians in British cabinets and boardrooms did not necessarily signify that Eton and Harrow occupied a leading position, either within the Conservative Party or in Britain as a whole. The public school men's predominance merely demonstrated the truism that "the rich and powerful, whose children will do well anyway, tend to send them to the best and most fashionable academies."[17] The public schools were not all exactly the same by any means, and they did not transmit to their graduates a shared political philosophy. In fact, public school men took prominent positions in every political party, including Labour. The public schools, and also the great grammar schools (government-supported secondary day schools with common admission standards) did, however, provide a degree of uniformity regarding wider cultural values; this assisted in creating a special understanding between senior civil servants, soldiers, parliamentarians, bankers, and – to a much lesser extent – merchants and industrialists, a civic cultural consensus that gave both peculiar strengths and weaknesses to British society.

Far more important than the public schools were the numerous pressure groups that influenced the Conservative Party – the National Farmers' Union, the Institute of Directors, the British Employers' Confederation, the Federation of British Industries, the Association of British Chambers of Commerce, and many others. The task of reconciling these divergent lobbies was not easy. The party's tight credit policy, for example, was disliked by banks and finance companies; its refusal to set quotas to protect home textile industries against Hong Kong cottons (in line with the party's commitment to Commonwealth preference) upset British textile manufacturers and workers; the party's working-class supporters wanted more money spent on social services; middle-class backers, by contrast, wanted a reduction in personal taxation. The party therefore rarely pursued a preconceived and detailed program comparable to Labour's, but tended to shift and turn.[18]

The Tories' general course, however, was clear. After its disastrous defeat in 1945, the party increasingly committed itself to the welfare state, the consequent rise in public expenditure, and the resultant scramble between competing lobbies for increased benefits. The leading advocate of this postwar consensus within the Conservative Party was Winston Churchill himself – the wartime hero, and a major Tory electoral asset thereafter. Churchill made a deep impact. (He was one of the few twentieth-century politicians who enriched the English language through new phrases that passed into popular speech ("their finest hour," "a sheep in sheep's clothing"). Churchill's warm-hearted paternalism made him sympathetic toward social reform. So did his wartime collaboration with trade unionists such as Ernest Bevin. He looked to con-

---

[17]Paul Johnson, "The imbalance of power," review article on Anthony Sampson, *The Changing Anatomy of Britain*; London, Hodder and Stoughton, 1982, and Samuel H. Beer, *Britain Against Itself*, London, Faber and Faber, 1982, in the *Times Literary Supplement*, 8 October 1982, pp. 1093–4.

[18]Samuel H. Finer, "Great Britain," in Roy C. Macridis and Robert E. Ward, eds, *Modern Political Systems: Europe*. V. 1, Englewood Cliffs, NJ, Prentice-Hall, 1963, p. 60. John D. Hoffman, *The Conservative Party in Opposition 1945–1951*. London, MacGibbon and Kee, 1964.

tinued collaboration with the unions – as in wartime. He placed special stress on housing for returned soldiers and bombed-out civilians, the heroes and victims of war. Though ageing and ailing, Churchill was far from a spent force in postwar politics. It was Churchill who led the party to victory in 1951 on a program of moderate reform. (He was to resign because of ill health four years later.)[19]

The reformers, both Tory and Labour, justified the commitment to ever-growing social expenditure, and loss of treasury control over public spending, on the assumption that the British economy would continue to grow rapidly. Rising revenue would thus provide the wherewithal to satisfy every claimant – a dangerously mistaken forecast. Within the Conservative Party, reformist groups such as the "Bow Group" (formed in 1951, the conservative equivalent of the Fabian Society within the Labour Party), gained increasing importance, as against more conservatively minded bodies. Throughout the late 1950s and the 1960s, the Conservatives maintained much the same social priorities as those set by Labour. For a considerable time, the underlying assumptions held by Conservative and Labour policy makers alike regarding the merits of a managed economy and expanding social services converged into a shared philosophy jokingly described as "Butskellism" (derived from the names of two Chancellors of the Exchequer, the progressive Conservative R. A. Butler and Labour's Hugh Gaitskell).[20] "Butskellism", in one form or another ruled in Britain until the late 1970s and helped to determine the country's successes and failures during the crucial postwar years.

THE CHRISTIAN DEMOCRATS

Introduction

"Crown and altar" had always formed a natural alliance; kings and churchmen had ever marched hand in hand against the common people. Such was the commonly held liberal belief during the nineteenth century. But the historical reality had been different. The Catholic Church had widely represented peasant masses against alien rulers – Catholic Irish against the Anglo-Protestant estab-lishment; Catholic Poles against Protestant Prussians and Greek-Orthodox Russians; Catholics in the Vendée against French revolutionary armies; Cath-olic Spaniards against Napoleon's invading hosts. The growth of industrial cities thereafter provided for the Catholic Church a new challenge. Churchmen now found among their congregations Catholic workers and urban entre-

[19]Paul Addison, "Churchill in British politics: 1945–1955," in J. M. W. Bean, ed., *The Political Culture of Modern Britain*. London, Hamish Hamilton, 1987, pp. 243–61.

[20]R. A. Butler was Minister of Education 1941–5, Minister of Labour 1945, Chancellor of the Exchequer 1951–5, Hugh Gaitskell was Minister of Fuel and Power 1947–50, Minister of State for Economic Affairs 1950, Chancellor of the Exchequer, 1950–1. For Butler's career, see Anthony Howard, *Rab: The Life of R. A. Butler*. London, Cape, 1987; for Gaitskell's, Philip Maynard Williams, *Hugh Gaitskell: A Political Biography*. London, Cape, 1979.

preneurs. Hence a new school of Catholic thinkers called for "social" policies that would give the workers their due, while eschewing what the papacy regarded as the errors of liberalism, secularism, and ultra-nationalism. (In Wilhelminian Germany, for example, Bishop Wilhelm Emmanuel von Ketteler called for a quasi-socialist program. At the same time he opposed Bismarck, refused in 1874 to take part in celebrating the anniversary of the German victory over the French at Sedan, and proclaimed the Rhine a "Catholic river.")

After 1945 there was further shift in emphasis. The Church increasingly began to drop its former suspicions of liberalism, individualism and urban industry. Instead, it supported Christian middle-of-the-road parties that would harness the votes of all moderates (not necessarily Catholics). The new Christian Democrats would appeal to a broad coalition of farmers, workers, and businessmen. They would attempt to weaken social dissent through social reform. They would find a middle way between unrestricted private enterprise on the one hand, and socialism on the other.

Christian Democratic parties thus gained power, or at least gained substantial electoral strength, in much of Western Europe – a striking disappointment to those who had predicted that rising class consciousness, urbanization, and industrialization would reduce the religious factor in politics. The Christian Democratic parties appealed largely, though by no means exclusively, to Catholics, and played a leading part in West Germany, Italy, Holland, Belgium, and Austria. They were likewise influential in France (where the *Mouvement Républicain Populaire*, however, forbore to style itself "Christian"), in Switzerland, and in Luxemburg. These parties were eclectic in approach and doctrine, but shared a commitment to the ideals of an open society, and broadly speaking functioned as moderately conservative parties within the context of the countries in which they operated. To list them all would turn this chapter into an encyclopedic entry; we shall confine ourselves to outlining their development in the three largest countries of Western Europe.

The German CDU and Austrian ÖVP

When Allied troops fought their way into Germany in 1945, Germany seemed at the end of its tether, the people concerned with nothing more than bare survival. Millions of *Wehrmacht* survivors had become prisoners of war, and the country was divided into four occupation zones; Allied commanders ruled supreme in French, British, American and Soviet sectors. The economy lay in ruins; the currency wrecked. The very infrastructure required for political life seemed shattered beyond repair – meeting halls and office buildings were in ruins, newspaper presses halted, funds scarce, Allied licences required for all party work. For many years, democracy had ceased to be practiced; the organization of the Weimar parties had been smashed. Nazi propaganda had defamed parliamentary governance. Hitler's spell had been shattered among the bulk of Germans; but a minority of Nazi sympathizers remained (something between 7 and 15 percent of the population).[21]

Even at the best of times, moreover, German politics had been marked by regionalism and sectarian narrowness, by bureaucratic habits and centralized management, by a tradition according to which many parties had formed communities of the faithful, with "a hierarchy of party bishops headed by a charismatic pope."[22] Under these circumstances, nothing seemed more unlikely than the creation of stable parliamentary democracy, much less the emergence of a conservative party with mass support.

One of the few remaining pillars of German society was the Catholic Church. (Whereas Catholics had formed a permanent minority within the Bismarckian Reich and the Weimar Republic, they amounted to 44 percent of the population by 1955 and to nearly half the population in West Germany after 1980.) Of course the Catholics were far from united. In Bavaria, for instance, there was a rural and conservative legacy, with a strong regional loyalty to the Bavarian *Land*, a loyalty violated by the Nazis who had split the *Land* into several *Gaue* (regions). In the Rhineland, on the other hand, where there was a large Catholic working class, there was also a tradition of social Catholicism that went back to the nineteenth century, and to thinkers such as Wilhelm von Ketteler, a bishop in Mainz who had defended workers' rights and helped to lead the battle against Bismarck in the *Kulturkampf* (a conflict between Church and state in which Bismarck had been forced to yield).

The Catholics did manage to coalesce. They also resisted the temptation of retreating into a political ghetto of the kind that had existed in the Wilhelminian empire and the Weimar Republic, when most of them had voted for the center party as a Catholic lobby. When the war ended, many initially thought in terms of rebuilding this center – understandably, at a time when Catholics still found themselves at a social disadvantage compared with Protestants. (As late as 1960, Catholics were still relatively under-represented among senior civil servants, college teachers, the technical occupations, and captains of industry. By contrast, they were over-represented among farmers.) But instead, the Catholics decided to create a broadly based party – "German, Christian, democratic, and social."[23] Catholics no longer had to face militant atheists or *Kulturkampf* ideologists within the ranks of the SPD; they were also impressed by the success of Catholics in the American Republic.[24]

[21]Peter H. Merkl, "West Germany," in Peter H. Merkl, ed., *Western European Party Systems: Trends and Prospects*. New York, Free Press, 1980, pp. 21–60. Between 1950 and 1957, between 7 and 15 percent in successive polls stated that they liked Hitler, disliked Jews, or would welcome the return of a new National Socialist party to power.

[22]See Karl W. Deutsch and Lewis J. Edinger, *Germany Rejoins the Powers: Mass Opinion, Interest Groups, and Elites in Contemporary Germany Foreign Policy*. Stanford, Cal., Stanford University Press, 1959, pp. 40–1.

[23]Peter Haungs "Christlich Demokratische Union Deutschlands (CDU) und die Christlich Soziale Union in Bayern (CSU)," in Hans-Joachin Veen, ed., *Christlich-demokratische und Konservative Parteien in Westeuropa*. Paderborn, Ferdinand Schöning, 1983.

[24]Karl Othman von Aretin, "20 Jahre Katholizismus in Deutschland," in Karl-Dietrich Bracher, ed., *Nach 25 Jahren: Eine Deutschland-Bilanz*. Munich, Kindler, 1970, p. 337.

The first party conference took place in 1945, with participation from all occupational zones, except the French. Within the party, leadership fell to Konrad Adenauer, a Rhineland Catholic. An ex-mayor of Cologne, first discharged by the Nazis, later again dismissed from office for alleged incompetence by the British occupation authorities, Adenauer at first seemed but an ageing remnant of the Weimar era, laboring moreover under the special disability of appearing overly friendly toward the Western Allies. (He was reviled as *der Alliiertenkanzler*, the Allies' Chancellor.) Adenauer took charge of a party that was riddled by regionalism, and that lacked – until the 1960s – a strong central organization. The party was initially split moreover between proponents of *laissez-faire* and adherents of Christian socialism, between those who looked first and foremost toward reunification, and those willing to make do with a purely West German state for a long time to come. Adenauer was a difficult man, suspicious, sly, and domineering. But he knew his own mind and that of his countrymen; he exuded confidence at a time when his countrymen were in despair; he displayed drive when the mere mechanics of creating a great party seemed to raise insuperable problems. A grandfatherly figure, with a soft *Kölsch* (Cologne) accent, a quiet manner, and a steely will, he turned into a benevolent autocrat.

KONRAD ADENAUER (1878–1967)

Adenauer was a founding father and the first chancellor of the Federal German Republic. He began his career in the Weimar Republic as mayor of Cologne, and made his name as a municipal reformer, and as a center party politician willing and able to cooperate with the Social Democrats. He never compromised with the Nazis, and returned to politics after the collapse of the Third Reich, by then in his late sixties. He ran a tight ship as chancellor (1949–63), as he had done when mayor. He skillfully combined the roles of chairman of the Christian Democratic Party, leader of an interparty coalition, and chief of the federal government. Politically, he represented the Catholic Rhineland. (According to one of his half-facetious remarks, Germany had for too long been run by the schnapps drinkers of the North, and the beer drinkers of the South; the time had come for governance by the wine drinkers of the West.) He commonly made major policy decisions on his own, or in consultation with a small "kitchen cabinet" of trusted ministers, party lieutenants, and key civil servants. Adenauer spoke German to two other leading Christian Democrats and "Europeanists:" Robert Schuman (a major figure in French politics, and a Lorrainer who held a commission in the imperial German Army in World War I), and Alcide de Gasperi, (the Italian prime minister whose ancestors had been subjects of the Austro-Hungarian monarchy.) Adenauer got on equally well with David Ben-Gurion, first prime minister of Israel (1952), providing essential financial support for Israel at a critical period in its existence – at a time when the US was more concerned with Germany's future contribution to Western security. Golo Mann, the German historian, described Adenauer as a "cunning idealist;" others used less flattering phrases. (Adenauer confided to Dulles that he feared the German people and felt that when he died they would do a deal with the Soviets.) But, as Gordon Craig put it, Adenauer's "long tenure of office had provided the West Germans with a sense of continuity and stability and the necessary time to become used to democratic institutions and to learn to make them work."

Adenauer moreover was blessed with luck. When he stepped into power, *Schachtism* (the Nazi variety of the regulatory state), stood discredited; communism had ceased to be attractive owing to the Soviet presence in East Germany. The Nazi state apparatus had been smashed, and the landed nobility in East Germany had ceased to exist. The Marshall Plan assisted West Germany's economic and political recovery. Soon afterwards, the Korean war turned West Germany into a power to be courted. Adenauer at home, unlike the Weimar politicians, did not initially have to deal with German generals. When he did, he turned out to be the first German statesman to accord about as much respect to army leaders as to heads of fire departments. Within the CDU, Adenauer at first faced a major rival, Jakob Kaiser, head of the CDU in East Germany, an advocate of Christian socialism and of a policy designed to turn Germany into "a bridge between East and West." In 1945, the Soviets removed Kaiser from the CDU presidency, leaving the CDU a mere puppet for decorative purposes. The CDU proper became a purely West German organization, and for a time was almost Adenauer's personal instrument, with the Bavarian-based *Christlich Soziale Union* (*CSU*) as its permanent associate.

We shall return to Adenauer's role in founding the German Federal Republic, where he served as the first chancellor (1949–63), as well as the all-powerful chairman of the CDU. Suffice it to say that Adenauer backed the trans-Atlantic connection from a sense of conviction, rather than for merely tactical purposes. In return, the American occupation authorities supported him.[25] He, moreover, had always been a francophile and looked askance at Protestant Prussia. (After World War I, Adenauer had favored the separation of Prussia's Rhenish province from Prussia, and the creation of a separate Rhenish *Land* within the Reich). Adenauer firmly committed the CDU and West Germany as a whole to European unity, rearmament and integration into the Western alliance. Bonn, West Germany's new capital, was a quiet, dignified Rhenish city. It stood on the left side of the Rhine, geographically nearer to Paris and Brussels than to Berlin. Bonn's choice as a capital was of profound, symbolic significance – indeed a stroke of genius.

For Adenauer, there could be no return to Germany as the *Land der Mitte*, the land in the middle, precariously balancing East against West. West Germany, and ultimately perhaps the whole of Germany, should be integrated into Western Europe. Adenauer also remained determined, however, that West Germany should be the sole heir of the broken *Reich*, its only legitimate successor. In support of his position, Adenauer could draw on a wealth of historical, ethical, and legal arguments. West Germany – unlike East Germany and Austria – paid substantial restitution to Israel in partial expiation of Nazi

---

[25]For a discussion see Hans-Jürgen Grabbe, *Unionsparteien, Sozialdemokratie und Vereinigte Staaten von Amerika, 1945–1966*. Düsseldorf, Droste, 1983. The Adenauer literature is extensive. See, for instance, Richard Hiscocks, *The Adenauer Era*. Philadelphia, Lippincott, 1966. Peter Koch, *Konrad Adenauer: Eine Politische Biographie*. Reinbeck, Rowohlt, 1985.

crimes. Bonn thereby tried to strengthen both its international position and its claim to domestic legitimacy. But at the same time, it inherited a legacy of guilt, guilt for the atrocities of the Third Reich, and also for the real and alleged misdeeds committed by Germany since Bismarck – an inheritance from which Vienna and East Berlin considered themselves exempt.

Adenauer had no serious opposition between 1949 and 1963 because the SPD lost support by opposing German rearmament, and Germany's entrance into the EEC and NATO, while calling for the nationalization of industry. Communism was still declining as a force in West German politics. (Whereas the communists had averaged 13 percent of the popular vote between 1924 and 1933, they had less than 6 per cent in 1949 and only 2 percent by 1953. Between 1956 and 1968 the party was outlawed; when it was allowed to contest a national election in 1969, it attracted just 1 percent of the vote.) The reason for communists' electoral failure was not hard to find; living next door to a communist state, the West Germans knew they were better off than their neighbors in East Germany.

Adenauer had no personal interest in economics. He only gave wavering support to Ludwig Erhard, his minister of finance, a brilliant economist but a poor politician, a man strongly committed to the principles of a free market economy. Adenauer was more concerned with immediate electoral advantages than with economic principle. He frequently clashed with Erhard. Erhard's position became even more precarious when, in 1951, John McCloy, the US high commissioner in West Germany, called on Adenauer to return to a regulated economy, complete with price controls and long-term planning. But overall, the advocates of *Soziale Marktwirtschaft* (a free market modified by welfarism) generally prevailed within the CDU. They drew on the work of scholars such as Alfred Müller-Armack and Walter Eucken, members of the Freiburg school of economics. These men derived inspiration in part from the liberal resistance against Hitler during the Third Reich, from Catholic social doctrine, and from a moral code rooted in freedom of choice. All of them believed in the *Soziale Marktwirtschaft*. Overall, their work bore a relationship to postwar German economic development similar to Keynes's work and postwar British economic policy. (Others were Luigi Enaudi, a leading Italian economist and financial expert, and Reinhard Kamitz, the most successful minister of finance in postwar Austria.)

WALTER EUCKEN (1891–1950)

Eucken is not a household name – not even among professional economists. He did not publish much. He died comparatively young. But he was an original thinker, and one of the theoreticians of the German Wirtschaftswunder. A university lecturer's son, born in the university town of Jena, he also took up an academic career. In 1927 he received an appointment as professor of economics at the University of Freiburg where he founded the Freiburg School. Eucken tried to profit from the lessons taught by successive German disasters. The first of these, the hyper-inflation experienced by the Reich after World War

I, helped to inspire his Grundlagen der Nationalökonomie *(1939). Disgusted by the Nazis' totalitarian practices, Eucken developed his own theories concerning a free market economy and a moral order (in collaboration with Franz Böhm). In 1948, he began to publish* Ordo, *an influential Freiburg journal. The year 1952 saw the publication of his* Grundsätze der Wirtschaftspolitik. *According to Eucken, a free market economy not only provided for greater economic efficiency than a state-run economy, but would also help to safeguard human freedom against the excessive powers of both private monopolies and of the state. His ideas profoundly affected policy makers in the early years of the German Federal Republic, particularly Ludwig Erhard.*

The Adenauer era coincided with the German *Wirtschaftswunder*, and the German economy expanded more rapidly than any other in Western Europe.[26] The CDU turned into West Germany's majority party. (In the elections of 1949, the CDU obtained 31 percent of the popular vote; in 1953, 45.2 percent; in 1957, 50.2 per cent.)[27] In doing so, the CDU absorbed several other right-of-center parties (by offering their leaders cabinet positions), and gained a large percentage of the refugee vote, an astonishing achievement, given the danger that former Nazis and 12,000,000 refugees might have turned into discontented revisionists. The CDU grew strong especially among businessmen, self-employed farmers, civil servants, and independent employers. In addition, the CDU relied on a substantial working-class minority.[28] The party was successful in uniting diverse groups, and bringing about order, security and prosperity. Under Adenauer West Germany doubled its industrial and agricultural production; its currency became the strongest in Europe, and its standard of living increased faster than any other Western democracy.

The CDU continued to enjoy substantial support from Catholics, as bishops, clergy, the church press, and lay organizations urged the faithful not to vote for "irreligious parties." In addition, it extended its appeal to a substantial proportion of Protestants, including such well-known divines as Bishop Otto Dibelius of Berlin-Brandenburg. The major Churches remained linked in many ways to the machinery of the state. (The state for instance continued to raise a church tax, despite opposition from those who stood for "a free Church within a free state.")[29] The CDU also extended its influence through specialized organizations such as, the *Union der Vertriebenen und Flüchtlinge* (for refugees),

[26]The index of gross national product (at 1954 prices and exchange rates, 1950 = 100, had gone up by 1957 as follows: West Germany 172; Austria: 156; Italy 147; Netherland: 140; France 139; Belgium 123; Denmark: 120; United Kingdom 118. Source: Dewhurst *et al.*, *Europe's Needs and Resources: Trends and Prospects in Eighteen Countries*. New York, Twentieth Century Fund, 1961, p. 17.

[27]Merkl, "West Germany," in Merkl, ed., *Western European Party Systems*, p. 25.

[28]By 1958, party preference for the CDU stood as follows, according to three consecutive surveys: independent farmers: 59 per cent; civil servants: 43 percent; employers and self-employed: 40 percent; white collar employees: 37 percent; free professions: 33 percent; rural laborers: 31 percent; unskilled workers: 28 percent; skilled workers: 26 percent. Karl W. Deutsch and Rupert Breitling "The German Federal Republic," in Roy C. Macridis and Robert E. Ward, *Modern Political Systems, Europe*, 2nd edn. Englewood Cliffs, NJ, Prentice-Hall, 1988, p. 365.

[29]Peter Haungs, "Die Christlich Demokratische Union ...," in Venn, ed., *Christlich-demo-kratische und Konservative Parteien in Westeuropa*, p. 120.

the *Frauenvereinigung der CDU* (women), the *Junge Union* (young people), the *Sozialauschüsse der Christlich Demokratischen Arbeiternehmerschaft* (workers and middle-class people), the *Ring Christlich-Demokratischer Studenten* (students), the *Evanglischer Arbeitskreis* (Protestants), and other Catholic sports and cultural groups.

Bonn differed from Weimar in many ways. The Weimar Republic had lacked effective symbolism, and had been unable to enforce respect for its flag: the black, red and gold later taken over by Bonn. The Federal German Republic shared the same colors with the German Democratic Republic, whose flag also bore the state symbol of a hammer and a pair of compasses – as archaic a representation of the new means of production as the communists' customary hammer and sickle. German families at the seaside used to build elaborate sandcastles, under father's supervision. In the expensive resorts, these castles were bedecked by banners that generally displayed the former Kaiser's colors. Rare indeed was the upper middle-class family that courageously raised the Weimar colors – standing forlorn within an imperial sea of black, white, and red. During the 1940s, however, there was a striking change, and by the end of the decade, black, white and red (embodied also within the old Nazi flag) was ceasing to form part of German political symbolism.[30] This significant shift went with a new sense of well-being and also of political legitimacy that would have been unimaginable at the end of the war. This mood was largely ignored by literary artists and poets. But it was real enough – finding incontrovertible expression, for instance, in West Germany's falling suicide rate. (Suicide rates dropped below those of the *Kaiserreich*, the Weimar Republic, the Third Reich, and the German Democratic Republic.)[31] It was not for nothing that West Germany's first federal chancellor stamped his name on those years of reconstruction – the "Adenauer era."

Austria was both in a more, and in a less, fortunate position than West Germany when the war ended. It – like Germany – was split into four Allied occupation zones, with provisions for a four-power administration of Vienna. But the Soviet zone was too small to serve as the basis for a separate communist state. The Soviets and the Western Allies had a common interest in neutralizing Austria – the Soviets for the sake of driving a territorial wedge into the NATO block, the Westerners to ensure the retreat of the Soviet forces. In 1955, a State Treaty restored full sovereignty to Austria, ended the Allied occupation, and turned the country into a neutral state on the Swiss model.

The Austrian state faced grave difficulties. It was cut off by the iron curtain

---

[30]As late as 1955, as many as 43 per cent of respondents in a poll still wanted the imperial colors as against 38 percent who desired the colors black, red, and gold. By 1961, only 26 percent preferred the imperial colors, as against 53 percent who opted for black, red, and gold. Christoph Klessman, "Geschichts-bewusstsein nach 1945: Ein Neuer Anfang," in Werner Weidenfeld, ed., *Geschichtsbewusstsein der Deutschen: Materialien zur Spurensuche einer Nation*. Köln, Verlag Wissenschaft und Politik, 1987, p. 126.

[31]Germany's male suicides (per 10,000) amounted to 3.5 in 1893; 3.5 in 1924; 4.1 in 1934; 2.6 in the Federal Republic in 1955, and 3.5 in the German Democratic Republic. For more details see Deutsch and Breitling, "The German Federal Republic," in Macridis and Ward, *Modern Political Systems: Europe*, p. 312.

from its former hinterland in Eastern Europe. The Austrian Republic moreover bore a difficult legacy. The First Austrian Republic, set up in 1918, had commanded little public trust; most Austrians at the time would have preferred to join Germany. Austria had only enjoyed a brief period of democratic governance, followed first by a clerico-conservative dictatorship, and then by incorporation into the Third Reich (1938). Moreover, she had experienced a short but fierce civil war (1934) that had pitted Catholics against socialists, and neighbor against neighbor.

The Austrians resolved these problems on lines different from West Germany's. The ÖVP (*Östereichische Volkspartei*) – like the CDU – had its origins in 1945. It heavily relied on those social groups that, in the past, had backed the *Christlichsoziale Partei* – farmers, middle-class people, and white-collar workers. At the same time, it took over much of the corporatist tradition that was inherent in the *Christlichsoziale Partei*, as well as the bureaucratic legacy inherited from the Habsburgs. Structurally, the ÖVP consisted of a federation of special interest groups (including a workers' and employees' league, a farmers' association, and the so-called economic league). Within the ÖVP, advocates of a free market economy, such as Kamitz, carried much less influence than Erhard within the CDU. The Austrian school of economics might enjoy fame abroad, but it wielded no power at home. Right from the beginning, the ÖVP would rather accept a partnership with the SPÖ (*Sozialistische Partei Östereichs*, the Social Democratic Party), lest Austria should once more experience the conflict that had divided Catholics from Social Democrats in 1934. Austrian, like German, opponents of Hitler's dictatorship had moreover experienced common sufferings, and exchanged common ideas in concentration camps, jails, or in exile; hence intimate cooperation between the two parties now became an acceptable expedient.

The ÖVP therefore made no objection to the nationalization of several key industries during the 1940s (especially the steel industry). The ÖVP collaborated with the Social Democrats in a long-lasting "Grand Coalition" (1949–66).[32] This alliance was sustained by the so-called Proporz system, under which jobs in the federal administration, in the administration of the *Länder*, and in the nationalized industries were shared in fixed proportions between the ÖVP and the socialists. The system avoided the split that had marked Austrian society in the olden days and prevented internal strife. Both parties acquired an equal stake in the regulatory state, in a burgeoning bureaucracy, and a system that gave the major decision-making powers to leading party functionaries, who struck their bargains in smoke-filled rooms, rather than in parliament. In this manner Austria bought for herself social peace – though at a price that posed the danger of petrification into a bureaucratized Republic

[32]The ÖVP generally held a slight lead in the voting, with 49.80 percent as against the SPÖ's 44.60 percent in the 1945 elections, 44.03 percent as against 38.79 in 1949, 41.26 percent as against 42.11 in 1953; 45.96 percent as against 43.04 in 1956. See Anton Pelinka, "Die Östereichische Volkspartei," in Hans-Joachim Veen, ed., *Christlich-demokratische und Konservative Parteien in Westeuropa*, pp. 198–9. For an assessment of Kamitz, a much under-rated statesman, see Fritz Diwok and Hildegard Koller, *Reinhard Kamitz: Wegbereiter des Wohlstands*. Vienna, Fritz Molden, 1977.

of Court Councillors (*Hofräte*). Nevertheless, the "Austrian solution" – based on neutrality in international politics, and a fusion of *dirigisme* and free enterprise in the domestic sphere – remained an alternative model, one that would later begin to make an appeal to West and East German neutralists alike during the late 1980s.

France: the Mouvement Républicain Populaire *(MRP), and the Gaullists*

The French revolutionaries invented the practice of dividing political parties into those seated on the right, the center, and the left in parliament. But nowhere else in the world do historians face greater difficulties in grouping parties into such convenient categories. In France after World War II, the term "conservative" became suspect because of Vichy's sorry record, and because the mystique of the resistance had fused with the mystique of revolution. Revolution had in fact become part of the traditional order, and after the war Frenchmen and Frenchwomen wanted to regain what the French Revolution had achieved. They wanted France respected – not treated as a nullity at Yalta and at Potsdam. They looked to a return of order and effective government. They also wanted social reform but (except for the communists) wished to preserve property – this was a country where property, especially in rural areas, was widely diffused and universally desired.

These were difficult aims to achieve, as France faced a seemingly desperate situation: widespread physical destruction, a legacy of hatred, inflation, a huge and ill-documented "second economy," the threat of communist dissidence from within, and – later – the burden of colonial wars abroad. There was a long legacy of internal divisions that affected conservatives as much as socialists. Under these circumstances, de Gaulle achieved astonishing success. He restored French prestige. He disarmed the communists by taking them into a coalition (lasting until 1947). He also achieved internal reforms in the traditional manner, by extending the role of the centralized state. The post-war government nationalized a variety of enterprises (including gas, electricity, the major banks and insurance companies, the coal mines, etc.). In this, de Gaulle and his alliance partners were following the example of the Third Republic, which during the interwar period had greatly extended the role of the state in the economy.

In addition, de Gaulle set out to make a new constitution. In 1945 a constituent assembly convened, containing the three major resistance parties, of nearly equal strength – the *Mouvement Républicain Populaire* (MRP), the Socialists and the Communists. Between them, they produced a constitutional draft, but the electorate rejected it, and in 1946 a new constituent assembly convened to try again. Women now had the vote; proportional representation was enshrined, the second chamber reduced to a shadow of its former self. But in all essentials, the Fourth Republic continued in the ways of the Third Republic. As hitherto, power centered in the Assembly, but within it no single party could hold power unaided. Except for the communists, each party formed a loose coalition without a centralized party machinery, leaving much power to notables entrenched in local constituencies. (Deputies often served as mayors of important cities or towns, and commonly acted as spokesmen for locally influential lobbies. France continued to be ruled by unstable coalitions. By casting their vote for any particular party, electors could not support any specific government, or even necessarily take a stand on any given issue. The system functioned because the same faces reappeared in ministry after ministry, and because of the administrative expertise and prestige possessed by the all-intrusive state, *le pouvoir*, respected but unloved – unlike *la patrie*, the native land.

One of the keys to French postwar stability was the MRP (founded in 1944). For a short time, the moderate conservatives managed to cooperate within a party diverse in origins and ideals. The Christian Democratic movement in France had many roots. The MRP bore a great debt to nineteenth-century reformers such as Jean Baptiste Lacordaire, a priest who had sought to reconcile the Church to the republic, and also to commit the Church to social reform. In France, as in many other continental countries, Catholic reformers had tried to strengthen the faith by creating networks of Catholic trade unions, cooperative societies, welfare associations, educational bodies, and missionary societies – designed to spread the gospel among the poor and the heathen, and also to lighten their material lot. In addition, Catholics set up a great variety of newspapers, professional organizations, and professional journals (including even a special bulletin for French pharmacists). Catholics in various countries also founded new political parties.[33]

During World War II, the Catholics' resistance record was as proud as the communists'. Maurice Schumann, first president of the MRP, had served under de Gaulle. Born a Jew, and a Catholic convert since the 1930s, Schumann had a quality of enthusiasm that sometimes verged on fanaticism, and earned him nicknames such as "Savonarola" (a fifteenth-century monk who was burnt at the stake for his beliefs). Schumann was succeeded in the party presidency by Georges Bidault, a former history professor who had served as chairman of the resistance council inside France during World War II. (He finally broke wih the Christian Democrats over the Algerian question in 1958, fearful of what he regarded as an African "Munich" i.e., comparable to the Munich settlement that he had opposed before World War II.) Another asset for the MRP was Maurice Schumann's namesake, Robert Schuman, an Alsatian, culturally at home in Germany as well as in France, a Catholic, a moderate, and a convinced advocate of European integration.

Led by men of such caliber, the MRP for a time managed to draw its backers from a wide social spectrum, and to play an important part in preventing French politics from polarizing into mere class or religious factions. The MRP made an original contribution to French political life in a variety of ways, for instance by setting up specialized teams (*équipes*) to enquire into specific

[33]For more detailed accounts, see for instance, William Bosworth, *Catholicism and Crisis in Modern France: French Catholic Groups at the Threshold of the Fifth Republic*. Princeton, Princeton University Press, 1962; R.E.M. Irving, *Christian Democracy in France*. London, Allen and Unwin, 1973.

problems, such as housing, factory conditions, farming, and the problems of the young. The MRP had a major role in the movement toward European integration, a movement strengthened by the natural bonds of sympathy that existed between Christian Democrats in France, Germany, and Italy. The MRP opposed Gaullist foreign policy insofar as the General took an "anti-European" and an "anti-American" stance. Neither would the MRP have any truck with his penchant for *pouvoir personnel*, his autocratic ways. During the late 1940s, a "third force" held sway in the national assembly; parliament was composed of the MRP, the Socialists, and the Radicals (the latter, despite their name, a centrist party). By the early 1950s, the MRP had become only one out of six evenly divided groups within a deadlocked parliament.

For all its able activists, the MRP failed where the German CDU and the Italian Christian Democrats succeeded. As the years went on, the MRP's share in the popular vote declined, dropping to a mere 11.1 percent in 1956. The party divided over a great variety of issues – the role of the state in the economy, decolonization, and agricultural policy. Moreover the MRP was peculiarly a rural party. This was no great disadvantage during the immediate postwar period when food shortages were rife; country folk experienced a relative improvement in their condition, unlike urban workers and salaried employees who faced a constant lag between rising prices and their own incomes. The farmers' initial advantage, however, disappeared as France recovered, and as more and more country folk moved into the cities.

The MRP also suffered from dissensions between Catholic trade unionists and Catholic employers, between youthful activists, widely committed to Christian socialism, and the mass of its much more conservative voters. The MRP increasingly reverted to the status of a regional party; mainly confined to traditionally Catholic regions in the East and West – though it also acquired a sizeable working-class component in Alsace-Lorraine and the *Nord*. Enthusiasm among the young militants waned, as party hack work turned out to be less exciting than clandestine resistance, and the MRP increasingly became yet another humdrum "caucus party." The MRP also suffered from chronic financial troubles. Above all, it stayed a Catholic body, even though its founders had striven to avoid a "confessional" image. Yet in the end, it was practicing Catholic men who abandoned the MRP; by contrast, 66 percent of the women claimed to have voted for the MRP in 1950. (Women in France continued to cast their vote predominantly in favor of conservatively minded parties until the 1970s; in France, as in Italy, the enfranchisement of women initially benefited the right; women tended to go to Mass and to confession more than their menfolk.) In the end, the MRP became an elite corps with not enough troops on the ground.[34] Their force failed to conquer, and finally disintegrated.

[34]Irving, *Christian Democracy in France*, pp. 91, 99.

CHARLES DE GAULLE (1890–1970)

De Gaulle was a man of contradictions: a famous general who never won a major battle; a keen Catholic whose resistance movement comprised many Protestants and Jews; a conservative who would at his convenience cooperate with communists; a believer in empire who surrendered Algeria; a critic of the republic who rebuilt the republic. He was tall and majestic; he looked like a king, and acted like one. He had a ready wit. Winston Churchill, in labored French, tried to explain to de Gaulle that he, Churchill, was an Elder Brother of Trinity House (an English maritime corporation), but mistranslated Trinity House as the Trinity. "Let me congratulate you on your distinguished relatives," was de Gaulle's reply.

His admirers worshipped him; his enemies detested him. The OAS (the French Algerian army's military underground organization) would have liked him assassinated. The British, upset at his insistence on excluding the United Kingdom from the EEC, would not have been overly regretful had the OAS succeeded. In fact, de Gaulle's greatest skill was to use magnificent rhetoric to conceal his lack of resources. He had practiced this in wartime London when he persuaded the free world to accept him as the embodiment of France. He perfected his art in recreating the illusion of France as a great power. In many ways, he was strikingly successful. As Seymour Martin Lipset put it in Political Man, *"In advocating a strong executive he follows in a tradition which in France has been largely identified with monarchism and the Church." And yet, unlike the old right, "he never sought to win the backing of the middle class by suggesting that their interests were threatened by big business and banks or by trade unions. Rather de Gaulle identified himself with ... the growth of efficient large industry ... and the strengthening of state power."*

Its chief rival on the conservative side was the *Rassemblement pour la République* (RPR), de Gaulle's own party. Since the French Revolution, France had a long tradition of personal rule by military chiefs. In 1944, de Gaulle had his chance, as a conquering hero with an army. But fortunately for France, he was no Napoleon. While favoring strong presidential government, and a broad program of social welfare measures, he was not an enemy of the Republic. He objected merely to those weaknesses of the Fourth Republic that had beset the Third – a weak executive and a deadlocked parliament. To cure these disabilities, de Gaulle in 1947 formed the RPR, dedicated to giving France a new constitution and to asserting French independence *vis-à-vis* both the USA and the USSR. The RPR also called for stern measures against the communists whom de Gaulle regarded as an alien element loyal to Moscow rather than Paris.[35]

The RPR had some initial success. (By the end of 1947, the party reportedly had over 800,000 members.) In many ways it operated like its rivals, with communal and departmental sections and federations, its own "teams" in factories, and professional organizations. However, the RPR was highly

[35]See, for instance, Anthony Hartley, *Gaullism: The Rise and Fall of a Political Movement.* New York, Outerbridge and Dienstfrey, 1971; Robert Aron, *An Explanation of De Gaulle.* New York, Harper and Row, 1966. Jean Charlot, *The Gaullist Phenomenon.* New York, Praeger, 1971.

centralized, with all real power in de Gaulle's hands. Unlike the MRP, the RPR mainly drew its support from the industrialized northern part of the country. More urban than rural, it attracted both the traditional strongholds of the right – the West and East – and bastions of the left in the North, Paris, and the Lyon regions. The RPR received more working-class votes than the Socialists (16 as against 15 percent). It also appealed to women and conservative voters, thus competing with the MRP.

The RPR, however, could make no further headway. De Gaulle would not enter into any of those electoral alliances permitted by the law, but forbidden by his conscience. During the first half of the 1950s, the RPR operated in splendid isolation; time and again it combined with the communists in a "negative minority" that controlled 220 out of 617 seats in the Assembly, and thereby condemned France to prolonged parliamentary, though not economic or social, instability. A handful of RPR dissidents, headed by Antoine Pinay, refused to follow the Gaullist line, and some of them even joined the cabinet.[36] De Gaulle would not play this game, and for a time retired to write his memoirs, cultivate his garden, and bide his time. His moment came in 1958, when the unending war in Algeria had split France, and the Assembly could neither form a stable government nor exercise effective authority over the Army. De Gaulle was swept into power by the old appeal of Bonapartism, a latent force that appealed both to conservatives and leftist voters. The Fourth Republic gave way to the Fifth, and a new chapter opened in French politics.[37]

The Christian Democrats in Italy

Early in 1945 Italy, like France, appeared ripe for revolution. War and the resistance had helped to radicalize labor, and had strengthened the communists. The rich and the well-born had widely compromised themselves with the Fascists. But no revolution occurred – largely because of the strong political leadership provided by the Christian Democrats (CD). The CD became Italy's true governing party. The party, formed in 1944, was the successor of the *Partito Popolare* (banned by Mussolini). It united with other resistance parties in the CNL (Committee of National Liberation). By 1945, these parties had become so powerful that, in effect, they shared out the Fascist legacy of patronage between them. The CNL parties produced the 1948 constitution (which unlike the French constitutions, was never submitted to the electorate, and was designed to center power in the parties). Between them, these leading parties "colonized" through their respective patronage the civil service, the public corporations, welfare programs, and associations, as "the last

[36]Roy Macridis, "France," in Roy C. Macridis and Robert E. Ward, eds, *European Modern Political Systems*. Englewood Cliffs, NJ, Prentice-Hall, 1963, pp. 184–91.
[37]Jean-Pierre Rioux, *The Fourth Republic, 1944–1958*. Cambridge: Cambridge University Press, 1987. Rene Remond and Jean-François Sirinelli, *Note Siecle, 1918–1988*. Paris: Fayard, 1988. Both are major works of synthesis.

frontier."[38] The CD's patronage system further benefited from attempts to develop the South, *il mezzogiorno*, where public enterprise vastly strengthened private clientage. The CD attracted voters (especially southern voters) from a variety of social strata – women, the farmers, the middle classes, artisans, and a minority of industrial workers.

During the long era of CD governance, the communists (*PCI, Partito Comunista Italiano*) dominated the left, leaving moderate socialists in a minority. The CD suffered from numerous internal dissensions; from 1953, moreover, it was obliged to find coalition partners, and the resulting alliances remained unstable. The longest coalition government after 1953 ruled only for three years (1983–6). (Nevertheless, the CD's strength grew from 35.2 percent in the 1946 elections, to 48.5 percent in 1948, then dropped to 40 percent in 1953.) The Christian Democrats had to tread warily. Even after the 1948 elections, the communists and socialists between them retained command over 2,000 local governments; they controlled the greater part of the labor movement; they stood strongly entrenched in the universities; their clientage and precinct work rivalled that of the Christian Democrats. Nevertheless, the CD attained a measure of success that escaped the MPR in France.

The nature of this success is not easily explained. The CD only had one outstanding statesman in its ranks, Alcide de Gasperi, a longtime opponent of Mussolini's who had enjoyed the Church's protection during the years of tyranny as a librarian in the Vatican, and who later served as prime minister from 1945 to 1953. Initially, de Gasperi, like de Gaulle, worked in cooperation with the communists led by Palmiro Togliatti. But the communists made a serious tactical error when, in 1947, they called a general strike against US aid and the European Recovery Program. With US help, de Gasperi outmaneuvered alike the PCI on the left and the neo-Fascists on the right. In the 1948 elections the CD won 307 seats, and for five crucial years thereafter completely dominated Italian politics.

De Gasperi was no de Gaulle, either in appearance or personality. He was not a particularly good speaker – a grave disability in a country where rhetoric was respected as a form of art. Like Cavour, de Gasperi seemed half a foreigner, speaking Italian with a northern accent. He was indeed one of those "transnational" Europeans who contributed so much to European recovery. He was lean and short, physically unimpressive. But what he lacked in size, he made up for in ability. He dominated the Italian political scene because he was what he seemed – honest, austere, astute, and a master of political *combinazioni*. His strong will was masked by a gentle manner. His political finesse played a major part in keeping his party in power.[39]

[38]Angelo Codevilla, unpublished manuscript, "Italian Politics," p. 85, Hoover Institution Archives.

[39]Richard A. Webster, *The Cross and the Fasces: Christian Democracy and Fascism in Italy*. Stanford, Ca., Stanford University Press, 1960, p. 81, and H. Stuart Hughes, *The United States and Italy* revised edn, Cambridge, Mass., Harvard University Press, 1965, pp. 145–59. De Gasperi biographies include Elisa A. Carrillo, *Alcide de Gasperi, The Long Apprenticeship*. South Bend, Ind., University of Notre Dame Press, 1965. Giulio Andreotti, *De Gasperi e il suo Tempo*. Verona, A. Mondadori, 1964. Leo Valiani, *l'Italia di de Gasperi, 1945–54*. Florence, F. Le Monnier, 1982.

De Gasperi's system was supported by the Catholic hierarchy, and strengthened by prudent reforms, US economic aid, US diplomatic assistance, and the influence exercised on the American government by successful Italian-Americans. De Gasperi thus managed to hold at bay both the monarchists and the neo-Fascist right, as well as the revolutionary parties of the left. His was a balancing act worthy of earlier Italian statesmen such as Cavour and Giolitti. Instead of government by revolutionary committees and party militias, Italy returned to constitutional government – despite threats of armed violence from communist combat squads. De Gasperi frankly preferred democratic coalitions to a one-party confessional regime.[40] His party entered into *combinazioni* at every level of government – even communists were not excluded from such arrangements. (One of the most famous of postwar Italian movies was *The Little World of Don Camillo*; this film depicted life in a small town where the communist mayor and the priest worked together in a spirit of cheerful pragmatism. The movie comically romanticized reality, but was not so far from the truth in a country that lacked alike the passionate clericalism and anti-clericalism found in Spain.)

De Gasperi's success was remarkable. The CD was more of a patronage party than an ideological party; its cadres lacked the cohesion displayed by communists at the senior, though not necessarily at the junior, level of party organization. Italian Catholics (like Catholics everywhere else) were politically divided. There were Christian socialists, old-style corporatists, and advocates of a free market economy; there were also many without any political preference. Italian businessmen, industrialists, and large landowners – supposedly the party's mainstay – were uncertain supporters. As Henry Tasca, a senior US official involved in the Marshall Plan, put it with some contempt, the Italian bourgeoisie was not a confident ruling class, but a collection of individualists, incapable of combining as a group to meet a common threat. They tended to deal with the left either by preparing to escape abroad, or by making undercover deals for their own protection.[41] The CD also had many organizational problems. Formally, the party was grouped into local sections, provincial federations, and a national organization, with a national congress and council. In effect, it comprised a coalition of factions and sub-factions – leftist, centrist, and rightist – each with their own systems of clientage. Under de Gasperi, the party lacked an effective grass roots organization, and heavily depended on the Church's network of parishes and church societies, and on specialized groups such as the *Coltivatori Diretti* (a farmers' group), or civic committees of Catholic Action, to round up voters.

[40]Norman Kogan, *A Political History of Italy: The Postwar Years*. New York, Praeger, 1983, p. 83.
[41]John Lamberton Harper, *America and the Reconstruction of Italy, 1945–1948*. Cambridge, Cambridge University Press, 1986, p. 157.

ALCIDE DE GASPERI (1881–1954)

De Gasperi was as unlike the popular stereotype of the Italian politician as could possibly be imagined. He was neither handsome nor eloquent; he had no gift for grand gestures. He spoke Italian with a harsh northern accent, but his German was perfect (he had completed his education at the University of Vienna). He liked bowling. He regularly went to Mass. He wrote learned books with titles such as I Tempi e gli Uomini che Prepararono la Rerum Novarum. *("Rerum Novarum" was a papal encyclical issued in 1891 by Pope Leo XIII; to its admirers, it was known as the social Magna Carta of Catholicism, and profoundly influenced de Gasperi's outlook with regard to the working classes.) He received an honorary doctorate from the University of Oxford. He believed in sound money, thus he was hardly a run-of-the-mill parliamentarian at Rome.*

Yet de Gasperi in some ways represented in his career all the great struggles in modern Italian history. Born under foreign rule, a subject of the old Austro-Hungarian empire, he initially stood as an irredendist deputy for Trento in the defunct Austrian parliament. (After World War II, he continued to defend tenaciously Italy's ownership of South Tyrol and Trieste.) He courageously fought against tyranny from the right. (He was arrested by the Fascists, having aroused Il Duce's displeasure as secretary of the Partito Populare Italiano *until its suppression.) Shortly after the end of World War II, in 1945, he became the first prime minister of the new Italian republic, and guided its fortunes until 1953, right through the formative years of the new state. In doing so, he stood as firmly against attempted tyranny from the left, as he had from the right, at a time when the communists were trying to subvert Italy through a skillful blend of agitation, compromise, and measured violence. Utterly incorruptible himself, he was nevertheless a master of the honored art of* arrangiarsi. *He needed these skills as head of a party that appeared as unstable as the country itself – an uneasy coalition of leftist planners, technocrats, clericalists, economic liberals, conservative businessmen, and welfare advocates. He was also one of the pioneers of European integration. He presided over the beginnings of the Italian "economic miracle" that few had expected, planning a* risorgimento *(rebirth) to overcome economic decline, overpopulation and underdevelopment through industrial expansion. The Marshall Plan made much of this possible.*

When he died his funeral cortege had to make its way slowly through the streets of Rome, thronged with crowds making their last tribute to the greatest Italian statesman since Cavour. George H. Hildebrand (in Growth and Structure of the Economy of Modern Italy*) called de Gasperi "undoubtedly one of Italy's most distinguished premiers ... a man of the utmost principle and rectitude, tolerant in outlook but strong and wholly dedicated to the rebuilding of his country according to the tenents of liberty and democracy."*

In 1954, a center-left faction, the *Iniziativa Democratica*, became the most powerful body within the party and its head, Amintore Fanfani stepped into the general secretary's office. Fanfani worked to diminish the influence on the party of conservatively minded civic committees, and to strenghen the power of party functionaries. Within the CD, the power of the *partocrazia* rose; the party shifted increasingly toward the left, and extended its patronage into public bodies such as the IRI (Institute for Industrial Reconstruction), a public agency with holdings in many parts of the Italian economy, charged specially with economic development of the South. The CD and its rivals thereby strengthened a system of clientage impossible to operate in France, where the *grandes écoles* and a highly centralized civil service wielded a magisterial power that parties could influence but not appropriate. Nevertheless, Fanfani did not succeed in making his own following predominant; it became just another faction within the "shifting league of interests which composed the Christian Democratic Party."[42]

Neither de Gasperi as an individual nor the CD as an institution has ever received its full due from English-speaking scholarship. Italian was not a language widely known in academia. British and American academics were not much attracted by a party such as the CD, Catholic in background, pragmatic in its conduct. Even in Italy itself, the CD met with bitter criticism. According to Luigi Barzini, one of Italy's foremost journalists, CD rule demonstrated in effect that "Catholics (in the political and not the religious sense of the word) cannot govern well anywhere because of their peculiar ideas. They are guided by charity instead of justice, hold man-made laws in contempt and consider man an inveterate and incorrigible sinner." CD governance, Barzini's charge sheet continued, "reduced the forces of order to impotence, destroyed the school system, filled the law courts with subversive judges, brought all state-owned industries to the verge of bankruptcy,"[43] because public enterprises provided political jobs – from the presidencies of great state holding companies with ministerial status down to humble clerkships. In fact, Italy did very well. Her economy recovered and expanded. (Between 1948 and 1960 the real gross national product more than doubled, from 8,497,000,000 lire to 17,258,000,000 lire.) The "underground" economy continued to flourish side by side with nationalized enterprises and "above ground" private firms.

The CD's main failure was that it did not build an efficient and trustworthy administration – except for such islands of competence as the Bank of Italy (run as a Liberal fief), and the Carabinieri. There was corruption aplenty, as the CD played a leading part in a nationwide spoils system that put CD loyalists into jobs at every level of government and into the state owned corporations. There was widespread and long-established distrust of government, and suspicion with regard to the ability and competence of civil servants even where such suspicions were unfounded. The news media played up scandals, and invented them when none could readily be found. Nevertheless, the CD remained in power, and did so in part by appealing to the conservatism of one of the most innately conservative countries in Europe. (As late as 1970, a majority of Italian respondents in public opinion polls opposed divorce. The bikini, introduced to the world of fashion in 1946 by designer Louis Réard, was widely regarded at first as an affront to public propriety.) Above all, the great majority of the Italian electorate remained united in a negative sense. The bulk of Italian voters did not want to see Italy fall under the sway of a communist minority. The communists were the second largest party (repre-

[42]Kogan, *A Political History*, p. 83.
[43]Luigi Barzini, "Governing Italian Style," *Policy Review*, Spring 1980, no. 12. pp. 65–6.

senting about one-fifth of the electorate), still formidable through its resistance record, its discipline, its street fighters, and its organizational and financial links to the Soviet Union.[44]

Critics of the CD ascribed the Italian electorate's conservative proclivity to a variety of causes – to US interference in Italian affairs, or to papal intransigence regarding Marxist-Leninist doctrine. These factors played a part, but were not in themselves decisive. The CD was indeed widely perceived as corrupt and ineffective, in a country whose citizens traditionally like to make fun of *la classa politica*. *La classa politica* includes the leading entrepreneurs, politicians, professionals, and intellectuals. "Ask any Italian about the cause of any particular crisis, and the words *la classa politica* will appear in the reply."[45] CD's leadership was firmly integrated into *la classa politica*, and accordingly, received all the blame that conventionally went to "them – the big wheels, the bosses, *la razza padrona*. Nevertheless, the bulk of Italian voters preferred the CD to the communists – with their customary common sense.

The Italian electorate's hostility to communism was not surprising, given the prestige of the US, which had attracted so many Italian immigrants, and had great influence in Italy itself, and given the experiences of Italian soldiers who had served in Russia. There was also the powerful demonstration effect produced by communist rule in Albania and Yugoslavia (a country that made territorial claims to Trieste), the communist-inspired civil war in Greece, and later the rising in Hungary against the Soviets (1956). By contrast, the CD maintained order in Italy, protected property, safeguarded the Catholic Church, promoted agricultural reform, and at the same time maintained civil liberties. Above all, the CD presided over Italy's astonishing economic revival.

In addition, the CD government won for Italy readmission into the Western community – despite the country's extended alliance with Hitler. Count Carlo Sforza as foreign minister provided both the design and the drive. He was cosmopolitan and regarded himself as a good European. For all his outspoken and sometimes tactless manner, he had personal charm, and he successfully maneuvered Italy into the Atlantic community. He did so by first restoring good relations with France, and then leading the way toward closer European cooperation. De Gasperi and Sforza both realized that Italy on her own would never rank higher than fourth in Western Europe. They sought to strengthen her by gaining influence within the framework of a Western European alliance, and by depending on US assistance against communism. They succeeded – despite misgivings among those Italian socialists and others who preferred a neutral Italy, and an entente with the Soviet Union.[46]

---

[44] In 1946 the Italian Communist Party gained 18.9 percent of the vote as against 28.2 percent for the French Communist Party. In 1948, the Italian Communists, allied with the Socialists, briefly won 31.0 percent, in 1953 the Italian Communists gained 22.6 percent, as against the French Communist Party's 25.7 percent (1956). For a more detailed comparison see Fabio Luca Cavazza and Stephen R. Graubard, eds, *Il Caso Italiano*. Milan, Garzanti, 1974, p. 133.
[45] Joseph La Palombara, *Democracy, Italian Style*. New Haven, Yale University, 1987, p. 140.
[46] Hughes, pp. 251–3.

Introduction

Western Europe and North America between them created industrial capitalism. Industrial capitalism transformed the world and immensely bettered mankind's material condition – no philosopher indeed had ever praised its achievement with more eloquence than Karl Marx in his *Communist Manifesto*. But capitalism never had any emotive appeal; no politician ever thought of naming his following a capitalist party. Old-fashioned country gentlemen would respond to assaults from factory owners by castigating conditions in the factories. Intellectuals as different in outlook as Karl Marx, Benjamin Disraeli, and, later, Hilaire Belloc would join in critiques of the 'millocracy." All of them drew on what might be called the literature of capitalist self-criticism, and the bulky tomes produced by commissions of enquiry and scores of researchers who investigated particular evils.

Critics were divided into two major schools – those who would mend the existing system, and those would would end it by force of arms. Both drew on many intellectual sources: Christianity, the democratic legacy, and Marxism. Particularly influential was Marxism, a creed that (when unalloyed with Leninism) could be used for reformist as well as revolutionary purposes. (Much of the program put forward in Marx's *Communist Manifesto* – progressive taxation, the centralization of credit through a national bank, the centralization of transport through state-owned enterprises, nationalization of selected industries, free public education – was later enacted in many countries by governments far from socialist.)[47]

SOCIALISM IN WESTERN EUROPE

The socialist world view was rooted in the belief in a benign, interventionist state. State ownership or control of the essential modes of production was seen as the means to achieve the perfect society by creating a redistributive, welfare state. The socialists achieved considerable success in countries such as Sweden and the Netherlands. But their dream of regenerating society has proved illusory. From the 1950s on socialist parties have had to change or reject their principles. The socialist economic model was the first to go, at least in West Germany where, at the meeting at Bad Godesberg in 1959, the SPD accepted the market economy but pushed for more social welfare. The British Labour Party followed suit in 1959 when the executive agreed to modify the party on principles regarding common ownership of the means of production.

The reformists generally prided themselves on being humanitarian and pragmatic in their approach – not necessarily with good reason, as shown, say, by the approval given by Beatrice Webb, a British Fabian, to Stalinist Russia

---

[47]K. Marx and F. Engels, *Manifest der Kommunistischen Party*. Berlin, Verlag Neuer Weg, 1945, p. 24.

in 1932. Reformists were mostly optimistic in their view of human nature; they tended to reject openly or tacitly the doctrine of original sin; they were wont to believe that mankind could almost infinitely improve its physical and moral condition. Reformists would be more likely than conservatives to believe that the problems of distribution were more pressing than those of production; they were prone to distrust businessmen more than workers or intellectuals. Their confidence in meritocratic elites marched uneasily with commitment to democracy and trust in the benevolence of the mass of people. Reformist parties embraced both believers and non-believers, Catholics and Protestants; but secular reformists were more likely to succeed in predominantly Protestant, as opposed to Catholic, countries. The reformists' electoral support derived in the main from the urban working class, from white-collar workers, and from professional people. Overall, their influence grew, as their numbers and skills expanded, and as they acquired a collective stake in the means of production through the growth of pension and insurance funds, as well as savings. Reformists, at the same time, placed almost universal confidence in the power and beneficence of the existing state – an outcome that would have surprised nineteenth-century conservatives such as Friedrich Julius Stahl who, during the 1860s, had still castigated socialist and liberal parties alike as revolutionary organizations.

In the United States, socialism made little headway; American reformists in the main (by no means exclusively) gathered in the Democratic Party. The British Labour Party contained some Marxists and Trotskyites, but likewise eschewed the Marxist heritage so far as the party as a whole was concerned. In Continental Europe, the socialists split in the wake of World War I and the October Revolution in Russia. Thereafter, the term "socialist" ceased to be synonymous with Social Democracy. Social Democracy rejected "scientific socialism" and the dictatorship of the proletariat through a disciplined "vanguard" party, as understoood by the communists.[48] Between them, the reformists of the left and the reformists on the right shaped the fortunes of the Atlantic states in the wake of World War II.

The Democratic Party in the US

The literature on the Social Democratic parties in Europe is immense. Books on the Democratic Party in the US – as distinct from US party politics in general, or on particular issues such as the New Deal – are scanty by comparison. Yet the Democratic Party, to use the *Encyclopaedia Britannica*'s magisterial description, forms "the oldest continuously existing political instrumentality in the United States."[49]

The Democratic Party during the mid-nineteenth century had already been

---

[48]For recent discussions of Western European parties, see Klaus von Beyme, *Political Parties in Western Democracies*. Aldershot, Gower, 1985 and Gerald Dorfman and Peter Duignan, eds., *Politics in Western Europe*. Stanford, Cal., Hoover Institution Press, 1988.

[49]*Encyclopaedia Britannica*, v. 7, p. 185.

the party of those who did not fit well into Yankee society – Southern slave owners, "crackers" ("swede-bashers" in British English), as well as poverty-stricken Irish immigrants in northeastern cities. But it was Franklin Delano Roosevelt, patrician of patricians, who shaped the party in its modern form, and without changing its style. The Democratic Party, like the Republican Party, remained a loose alliance, weak at the center, strong on the periphery, especially through big city machines. (In 1953, the National Committee Staff of the Democratic Party had no more than 59 employees and spent no more than $814,915, as against 98 staffers and an expenditure of $1,312,817 for the Republicans.)[50] Democratic Party programs praised private business with the same fervor as did Republican Party platforms, taking pride in the manner in which "the free enterprise system has flourished and prospered in America during the long years of Democratic stewardship."[51] Democratic leaders expressed, if anything, even more loyalty to the American Constitution and even greater hostility towards the communist system than their opposite numbers, the Republicans. Democrats – unlike European Social Democrats – did not stand committed, however, to any particular philosophy. Democrats (again like Republicans) comprised churchgoers and atheists, protectionists and free traders, admirers of Adam Smith, John Maynard Keynes, and Karl Marx. More important still, Democrats and Republicans both met in local and national politics. American voters would split tickets with much greater readiness than Europeans. (The percentage of split-ticket ballots continued to grow after World War II, giving rise to reiterated, though mistaken, prophecies concerning the forthcoming demise of the American party system.)[52]

In a social sense, Americans mixed much more easily with members of opposing political parties than did Austrians, Italians, Belgians, French, or Germans.[53] Nevertheless, there were striking differences between Democrats and Republicans. The Republicans supposedly represented the establishment. The Democratic Party, by contrast, claimed to speak for the poor, the blacks, the workers, and the underprivileged. Roosevelt rebuilt the Democratic Party as a grand coalition composed of those who, for one reason or another, considered themselves at least partially left out of the American mainstream. Admittedly, not all groups with a grievance joined. (For instance, German-Americans, shocked at the hostility shown toward them in World War I, widely sought refuge in the Republican Party, and there were also wealthy

[50]Hugh A. Bone, *Party Committees and National Politics*. Seattle, University of Washington Press, 1958, p. 37.

[51]"The 1952 platform of the Democratic Party," reprinted in appendix to Hugh A. Bone, *American Politics and the Party System*. New York, McGraw-Hill, 1955, p. 638.

[52]See for instance Walter Dean Burnham, "The end of American party politics," in Jerome M. Mileur, ed., *The Liberal Tradition in Crisis: American Politics in the Sixties*. Lexington, Mass., D.C. Heath and Co., 1974, pp. 312–32.

[53]One of the authors remembers a conference organized by the British Foreign Office in 1948 at Wilton Park to acquaint German politicians with British methods of local government. According to one of the German participants, the most useful part of the conference was to enable Germans of different parties to meet socially and discuss politics in an informal manner – a boon he had not experienced in Germany.

Democrats – rich men with a conscience, or entrepreneurs who had secured contracts for building dams, roads, or electric power grids under New Deal programs. But above all, the Democratic Party compromised most of the odd-men out. These included religious outsiders – Catholics, and especially Jews; and racial outsiders – Puerto Ricans, Mexicans, and especially blacks (who remained the most loyal of Democratic voters for generations, irrespective of income or class). In addition, the Democrats embraced regional outsiders (the South), trade unionists, and intellectuals with social-reformist, socialist, or even Marxist-Leninist convictions.

Perhaps the most important of the intellectuals were the Keynesian economists who had become strongly established at universities such as Harvard and MIT, where luminaries such as Paul Samuelson, and later John Kenneth Galbraith took an active part both in academic research and public policy. Their confidence was immense, their enthusiasm infectious. "Bliss was it in that Keynesian day to be alive, but to be young was very Heaven."[54] The Democratic party also appealed to many businessmen (who widely favored regulations that worked in their own interest), as well as to workers. Generally speaking, income and class affiliation remained less important in determining a voter's party preference than his or her religious, ethnic, and regional background. But overall, the Democrats considered their cause to be that of the Common Man.

Despite the weakness of its central organization, despite its social and ethnic heterogeneity, the Democratic Party defeated all challenges from splinter groups, whether the Progressive Party on the left, or the States Rights Party on the racialist right. For 20 years, after Roosevelt's first victory in 1932, the Democrats won every presidential election, and at the same time maintained control over both Houses of Congress with only brief interruptions.[55] Eisenhower's presidential success in 1952 was the first break in a long series of Democratic triumphs. Nevertheless, Eisenhower would hardly have won, had the Democrats not decided to field Adlai Stevenson, all too evidently a liberal. Eisenhower was widely perceived as a general and statesman standing above party politics, and as the man most likely to end the Korean war. Even in defeat, however, the Democratic Party seemed the party of the majority, the natural party of government.[56]

The Democrats' success rested in part on their ability to give the US a series of remarkable leaders – Roosevelt, Truman, and John F. Kennedy. These

[54]Cited by Leonard Silk, *The Economists*, New York, Basic Books, 1976, p. 98.

[55]For a general summary see Wilfred E. Binkley, *American Political Parties: Their Natural History*. New York, A. Knopf, 1962, p. 405 ff. Arthur M. Schlesinger, *History of US Political Parties*. New York, Chelsea House Publishers, 1973.

[56]In 1932, the Democrats gained 22,809,638 votes in the presidential elections, as against 15,758,901 Republican votes. Corresponding figures in 1936 were 27,478,945 as against 16,674,665; 1940: 26,890,401 as against 22,321,018; 1944: 25,602,505 as against 22,006,278; 1948: 24,105,695, as against 21,969,170; 1952: 27,314,987 as against 33,824,351. Between 1933 and 1957, the Democrats had a majority in the House and Senate except in the years 1947–9 and 1953–5. See tables in H. A. Bone, *American Politics and the Party System*, pp. 251 and 252.

leaders played both a lesser and a greater role in party politics than did their opposite numbers in Western Europe. A president, whether Democrat or Republican, could neither control his respective party organization nor the legislature – unlike a British prime minister. On the other hand, the two great parties lacked a national bureaucracy; as national organizations they mainly functioned during presidential elections. Wielding enormous prestige, patronage, and publicity, presidents enjoyed great personal power, and their respective personalities played a vital part in US politics.

The greatest of these Democratic leaders was Roosevelt. A cripple confined to a wheelchair, he towered over American politics in life, and continued to overshadow it after his death. Once adored by the bulk of the US scholarly community, his luster has since dimmed. To cite just one of his many recent critics, Alonzo L. Hamby, Roosevelt failed in many of his immediate objectives; his approach to the country's problems lacked system and was eclectic; he and his colleagues tackled the Depression with a curious blend of halfway measures, irrelevant reforms, and inconsistent attitudes.[57] His anti-business attitude after 1935 inhibited economic expansion. Roosevelt moreover knew little about foreign countries. He disliked the Germans, distrusted the French, and disapproved of the British empire. At the same time, he mistakenly imagined that he might co-opt Stalin as he could co-opt a powerful, ruthless, and corrupt city boss within his own party. Many of Roosevelt's domestic reforms – the charge sheet continues – unwittingly injured the very poor whom Roosevelt had meant to help.

Nevertheless, Roosevelt was a giant to the American people.[58] He came into power in 1933 almost at the same time as Hitler took over in Germany, and António de Oliveira Salazar and Sir Godfrey Huggins assumed office in Portugal and Rhodesia respectively. Whereas Hitler created a bloody dictatorship, and Huggins a "New Deal" for whites only, Roosevelt responded to the slump in democratic terms; he achieved immense influence both on the national and international stage, and (without meaning to do so) rebuilt the Democratic Party into the equivalent of an American Social Democratic Party. Within this party, the AFL-CIO (American Federation of Labor, Congress of Industrial Organizations) played a powerful part, led by such men as Walter Reuther. Also important were liberal groups such as the ADA (Americans for Democratic Action); LID (League for Industrial Democracy); and COPE (Committee on Political Education), which collectively stood for the American equivalent of British Fabianism.

Roosevelt was succeeded in 1945 by Harry S. Truman who, in the words of his most recent biographer, "played Augustus to Roosevelt's Caesar."[59] In

---

[57]Alonzo L. Hamby, *Liberalism and Its Challengers: FDR to Reagan*. Oxford, Oxford University Press, 1985, p. 22.

[58]Arthur M. Schlesinger, *The Age of Roosevelt*. Boston, Houghton Mifflin, 1957–1960, 3 vols. Robert J. Donovan, *Conflict and Crisis: The Presidency of Harry S. Truman, 1945–1948*. New York, Norton, 1977. Ted Morgan, *FDR: A Biography*. New York, Simon and Schuster, 1985.

[59]Donald R. McCoy, *The Presidency of Harry S. Truman*. Lawrence, University of Kansas Press, 1984, p. 312.

1948 he won an unexpected victory against Thomas E. Dewey, the pollsters having forecast to the contrary. The Democrats' success was remarkable, since they had to face at the same time the Republican challenge, and opposition both from Henry Wallace's breakaway Progressive Party on the left, and from J. Strom Thurmond with his "Dixiecrats" on the right; both of these groups drew traditional Democratic voters away from Truman's cause. Nevertheless, Truman finished with 24,179,345 votes, well over Dewey's 21,991,291, Thurmond's 1,176,125 and Wallace's 1,157,326 – one of the Democratic Party's most astonishing achievements in its history, made possible by Truman's ability to appeal to workers, blacks, farmers, and many other middle-of-the-road voters, while ignoring alike left-wing intellectuals and racists.

HARRY TRUMAN (1884–1972)

Truman was "blind as a bat," a poor public speaker (although a good extemporaneous one), and had neither brilliance nor charm. He had little or no charisma, but he was honest, trustworthy and without guile – all attributes President Roosevelt lacked. He was a compromise choice for vice-president (he hurt the least, the politicians said). He succeeded (in 1945) at a bad time for the alliance and knew little about measures Roosevelt had promised or agreed to.

Truman had many misfortunes in office; Republicans joked "to err is Truman." His popularity rose and fell; he lost control of Congress; he split the party. The Democrats even talked of passing him over in 1948 and drafting Eisenhower. His 1948 campaign had little party support and almost no money. Pundits gave him no chance to beat Thomas Dewey who was a fine speaker, had a good organization and a well-funded campaign. Yet Truman won with a cross-country "Give 'em hell" campaign. His second term was taken up mostly with foreign policy matters: the Cold War, the Marshall and Truman plans, the Korean war, the defense of Europe and peace treaties with Germany and Japan. He will go down in history as the man who revived Europe, contained the Soviets and North Koreans, and helped to create peaceful democracies in Germany and Japan. One biographer called him the bravest, most honest and honorable man to have served as President of the United States.

Truman's task was not easy after 1945. His administration had to deal with the Soviet threat abroad, McCarthyism at home, and the problems of reconverting the economy from war to peace. In addition, the US was still suffering from a host of racial, ethnic, and religious tensions. Contrary to many forecasts at the time, however, these problems diminished. From the early 1950s on, restrictive quotas against Jews and Catholics at major universities ceased to be enforced; Jews rose in professions to which their access had previously been limited. The improvement in white attitudes towards black was perhaps mirrored in supreme court decisions during the 1950s that outlawed segregation in schools and other public institutions.[60] These beneficent

[60]Everett Carl Ladd, Jr. and Seymour Martin Lipset, "Public opinion and public policy," in Peter Duignan and Alvin Rabushka, eds, *The United States in the 1980s*. Stanford, Hoover Institution Press, 1980, pp. 55–7.

changes owed a great deal to postwar prosperity that provided more jobs across the board, but at the same time the Democrats could rightly take pride in the achievements of the coalition that Roosevelt created and Truman preserved.

Truman determined to consolidate the "New Deal" through his own "Fair Deal." He resolved to extend social services and public housing, increase minimum wages and social security benefits, broaden civil rights, and assure what he regarded as a fairer distribution of the nation's wealth through greater control of the economy in respect of prices, resources, business practices, and aid to education. He succeeded only partially, and in spite of Congressional opposition to his initiatives. Nevertheless, the New Deal programs remained in place; some were considerably extended; the huge federal government with its great powers was made permanent. Presidential power was augmented through the extension of the presidential staff, the growth of agencies, such as the Bureau of the Budget (in which Truman placed particular reliance), the Council of Economic Advisers, and the National Security Council. Most important of all, the changes came to be accepted also by Republicans. By the time the Republicans returned to control the White House in 1953, they were reconciled to these Democratic policies, and sought only to modify their scope and administration.

> *Presidential power has grown continuously since the Depression of 1929, especially during the war years. Congress was unable to cope with solving the economic and social problems of the time, so government by the president, together with commissions and agencies, developed. To reduce its dependency on the executive branch and to be able to initiate legislation the Congressional staff not only increased after World War II but also took steps to become more professional. This is why Nelson Polsby, an American political scientist, calls Congress "the only competent legislature in the world."*

As regards qualified personnel, the Democrats – like the Republicans – relied heavily on experts from the great foundations and from prestigious universities. (To give just one instance, Rexford G. Tugwell, an influential governor of Puerto Rico, and an early member of Roosevelt's Brain Trust, had started his career as a college professor.) As regards ideas, the reformers drew heavily from two essentially American springs. The first was the reformers' firm faith in their own unblemished virtue, their conviction that they represented the cause of righteousness against the philistines. The second source lay in the reformers' belief in the ability of enlightened academic qualified experts – political scientists, lawyers, judges, sociologists, town planners, psychologists, Keynesian economists, and pedagogues – to cure humanity's ills through the courts, public agencies, regulatory, and redistributive bodies, staffed by a new diploma-bearing salariat. (It was only during the 1960s that "public choice" economics began to come into their own, with their implied critique of public servants as yet another self-interested lobby.)

Overall, the impact of these changes was immense. Federal power grew enormously by dint of judicial decisions, the expansion of public services, and the delegation of law-making power to designated agencies. Without having intended to do so, the Democratic Party set the agenda for a Keynesian, state-interventionist program that essentially came to be accepted also by the Republicans. Overall, the Democrats (and, to a much lesser extent, the Republicans) in part accomplished what the old Socialist Party of the US had intended, but had been unable to achieve. (The Socialist Party, a moderate group led by Norman Thomas, had been at the height of its influence during the late 1920s and early 1930s, when its voting strength reached just under 1,000,000.)

Nobel Prize laureate Milton Friedman and his wife Rose Friedman have briefly summarized this remarkable transformation. The 1928 platform of the Socialist Party had called for "the nationalization of our natural resources, beginning with the coal mines and water sites, particularly the Boulder Dam and Muscle Shoals."[61] (Boulder Dam, renamed Hoover Dam, and Muscle Shoals ended as federal government projects.) The Socialist party had advocated "a publicly owned giant power system ..." (put into effect through the Tennessee Valley Authority). Other Socialist demands had included "national ownership and democratic management of railroads and other means of transportation and communication." (Railroad passenger service was nationalized through AMTRAK. Some freight services were placed under public ownership through CONRAIL. The FCC came to control communication by telephone, telegraph, radio and television.) "An adequate national program for flood control, flood relief, reforestation, irrigation and reclamation." (Government expenditures for these purposes later rose to billions of dollars.) "Immediate governmental relief of the unemployed by the extension of all public works and a program of long range planning of public works ..." (In the 1930s, WPA and PWA carried out these functions, later paralleled by a wide variety of other programs.) "All persons thus employed to be engaged at hours and wages fixed by bona-fide labor unions." (The Davis-Bacon and Walsh-Healey Acts required contractors with government contracts to pay "prevailing wages," generally interpreted as highest union wages.) "Loans to states and municipalities without interest for the purpose of carrying on public works and the taking of such other measures as will lessen widespread misery." (Federal grants in aid to states and local municipalities rose to tens of billions of dollars a year.)

The Socialist Party's program continued in other ways. For instance, "a system of unemployment insurance." (This turned into part of the social security system.) "The nationwide extension of public employment agencies in cooperation with city federations of labor." (US Employment Service and affiliated state employment services subsequently administered a network of about 2,500 local employment offices.) "A system of health and accident insurance and of old age pensions as well as unemployment insurance." (Later realized in part through the social security system.) "Shortening the workday"

---

[61]Milton and Rose Friedman, "The tide is turning," appendix A, in Duignan and Rabushka, eds, *The United States in the 1980s*, p. 27–8.

and "securing to every worker a rest period of no less than two days in each week," (enforced by wages and hours laws with elaborate provisions for overtime). "Increase of taxation on high income levels, of corporation taxes and inheritance taxes, the proceeds to be used for old age pensions and other forms of social insurance." (In 1928, the highest personal income tax rate stood at 25 percent; in 1978, at 70 percent; in 1928 the corporate tax rate amounted to 12 percent; in 1978, 48 percent; in 1928, the top federal estate tax rate was 20 percent; in 1978, 70 percent).

To sum up, the US had never accepted a Social Democratic program in the sense in which the British Labour Party or German Social Democrats would have understood the term. Neither of the two great American parties had ever called for a nationally planned economy, much less the public ownership of the means of production, distribution, and exchange. Nevertheless, the US embarked on the road toward a publicly regulated economy and an interventionist welfare state. This process had only gotten underway by 1938, was speeded up during World War II and continued slowly through the late 1950s, But for better or worse, the Democratic Party had set an agenda for a transformation of American society so vast that Theodore J. Lowi, an expert in American government, could thereafter describe the process in terms of founding "the Second Republic of the United States."[62]

The British Labour Party

The British Labour Party was among the youngest of the socialist parties of Western Europe. Labour's official formation only dates from 1900 – a quarter of a century after the creation of the German Social Democratic Party at its Gotha Congress (1874). For many decades, the German Social Democrats had been the unofficial leaders among moderate socialists. After Hitler's rise, the balance of power shifted; during and after World World II the Labour Party for a time became the most prestigious and powerful working-class party in Western Europe – and with good reason. Labour had played an important part in Churchill's wartime coalition, had shared in the honors of victory, and subsequently held office during one of the most crucial periods in recent British history (1945–51).

During these years, the party presided over Britain's slow economic recovery and shaped British social policies for a long time to come. Everything seemed to work in the party's favor. Its victory, in 1945, was overwhelming. (The party gained 11,995,152 votes, 48.3 percent of the entire vote. Labour commanded an absolute majority in the House of Commons, 393 seats out of 640, with 213 for the Conservatives, who gained 9,988,306 votes.)[63]

---

[62] Theodore J. Lowi, *The End of Liberalism: The Second Republic of the United States*. New York, W. W. Norton and Co., 1979.

[63] Alan Sked and Chris Cook, *Post-War Britain: A Political History*. Harmondsworth, Penguin Books, 1984, p. 15. The classic work for the period is Kenneth O. Morgan, *Labour in Power: 1945–1951*. Oxford, Oxford University Press, 1985. Henry Pelling, *The Labour Governments 1945–51*. London, Macmillan, 1984, looks at the party from a critical standpoint. Other important works

The party possessed a self-confidence and unity of purpose never shown before or afterwards. It relied on a team of outstanding leaders who enjoyed respect, not merely within party ranks, but throughout the kingdom at large – men such as Clement Attlee, Ernest Bevin, Herbert Morrison, Hugh Dalton. Labour, with its commitment to fair shares for all, set the national agenda, at a time when the British confidently looked to the creation of a new society. The party's power in parliament did not rest on unstable coalitions with other parties, but on its own strength. Membership continued to expand (from 3,038,697 in 1945 to 6,520,186 in 1958, its high point).[64] Overall, the Labour administration that held sway after World War II constituted "without doubt the most effective of all Labour governments, perhaps the most effective of any British government since the passage of the 1832 Reform Bill."[65]

Labour differed from other social democratic parties (especially the German SPD during the Weimar Republic) in that it avoided the Marxist label. Labour's outlook was eclectic. The party comprised both advocates and opponents of empire, internationalists and "Britain-firsters," pacifists and militant supporters of a strong British defense (by now in an overwhelming majority). Some Labour voters sympathized with the Soviet Union, but the great majority did not, especially after wartime enthusiasm for the Soviet ally had evaporated. Labour adherents did include some Marxists of various hues among intellectuals, and also Fabians who meant to introduce socialism in homeopathic doses (this attitude was influential among civil servants and teachers). There were Guild Socialists who believed in workers' control of their employers' industries; there was a contingent of eccentrics – nudists, vegetarians, folkdancers, and fanciers of the alpenhorn. More importantly, the party retained a potent legacy of religious nonconformity (particularly in northern England, Scotland and Wales), with a long tradition of earnest self-improvement, self-education, and a commitment to creating a just society that would eschew the class divisions and the economic injustices associated in the minds of many Labour voters with the profit motive and a competitive society. Compared to the Tories, Labour was more collectivist in orientation, more egalitarian in social attitude, more favourable towards state ownership. But both parties wanted a strong government and both were elitist in their leadership. Both parties accepted nationalization programs and paternalistic roles for government. In some ways, British Conservatives were more social-democratic in outlook than American Democrats.

on the period include Alex Cairncross, *Years of Recovery: British Economic Policy 1945–1951*. London. Methuen, 1984. T E B Howarth, *Prospect and Reality: Great Britain 1945–1955*. London, Collins, 1985. Carl F. Brand, *The British Labour Party: A Short History*. Stanford, Cal., Hoover Institution Press, 1974. Kenneth O. Morgan, *Labour People: Leaders and Lieutenants, Hardie to Kinnock*. Oxford, Oxford University Press, 1987.

[64]In 1945, the party had 730,224 individual members; 2,510,369 members through trade unions; 41,281 through socialist societies. Corresponding figures for 1958 were 888,955; 5,627,690; 25,541. Thereafter the party experienced a slow decline in all categories. See Samuel E. Finer, "Great Britain" in Roy C. Macridis and Robert E. Ward, eds, *Modern Political Systems: Europe*. Englewood Cliffs, N J, Prentice-Hall, 1963, p. 63.

[65]Morgan, *Labour in Power, 1945–1951*, p. 503.

The Labour Party almost totally lacked the anti-clericalism common among socialists in Latin countries; anti-clericalism would have offended Welsh Methodists, Scottish Calvinists, and Irish Catholics (the latter grateful to Labour for its stand during the Irish War of Independence after World War I). Labour's quasi-religious belief in its ability to build in England a new Jerusalem had somewhat diminished since the 1930s. Songs like "The Red Flag," "The Internationale," or traditional folk songs modified to suit left-wing themes ceased to make the old emotional appeal to a generation more attuned to jazz than hymns. But there was still widespread in Labour's ranks disdain for those "guilty men" who had allegedly mismanaged World War I, lost the peace, slithered into the world slump, appeased the Fascists, and who would still ruin Britain if they could.

More importantly, there remained a fervent belief in the virtues of national planning of a kind that had apparently worked so well in World War II. The Labour Party had originated as a party devoted to the interests of working people, especially trade unionists. Committed socialists had originally formed a small minority within the party's ranks. Socialism was adopted as a solution to Britain's problems; but it had never been the party's *raison d'être*. Labour rejected the use of violence, and instead prided itself on a pragmatic approach. By strategic planning, Labour would extend democracy from politics to economic affairs; use the machinery of democratic governance to distribute wealth in an equitable fashion; create comprehensive social welfare services; avoid unemployment; reduce, and then eliminate, traditional divisions of class and status; encourage international cooperation, and ultimately bring the means of production under some kind of public control. These principles were by no means confined to Labour. They found wide acceptance among the electorate at large – and so much so that in 1945 Labour expressed a national consensus, reflecting the egalitarian sentiments popular in World War II.

Labour's electoral support derived in the main from the working class, in a country where class divisions continued to be sharply drawn and strongly felt not merely between workers and middle class, but also within the working class itself.[66] But it was by no means a working-class party pure and simple. The Labour Party, during World War II, also gained support from farmers who benefited from wartime controls, and in addition enjoyed widespread backing from intellectuals, and from white-collar workers. Labour, in other words, formed a coalition of disparate elements. Hence, Samuel E. Finer, a distinguished political scientist, felt confident in identifying three separate "cultures" within the Labour Party, each distinct and separate.[67]

---

[66]Roughly 15 percent of the British people were described in 1956 as middle class – comprising successful professional people, managers, entrepreneurs; 20 per cent were lower-middle class – shopkeepers, school teachers, junior civil servants, white-collar employees. 30 percent were upper-working class, including skilled workers, shop assistants, and such like. 35 percent were lower-working class, unskilled laborers, agriculture workers (the latter in fact a highly skilled group), porters, and so on. See Mark Abrams, "Class distinctions in Britain," in *The Future of the Welfare State*. London, Conservative Political Centre, 1958, p. 67.

[67]Finer, "Great Britain," p. 68.

The first of these was the culture of the working class, mainly employed in manufacturing and the service industries, attached to their trade unions, committed to a class solidarity that sharply distinguished between "them" and "us." The Labour Party was unusual among social democratic parties in that many genuine workers actually represented the party in parliament. (Before World War II, 72 percent of Labour's parliamentarians had been manual workers. In 1945 50 percent of Labour MPs still came from the working class. Between 1955 and 1959, manual workers formed 33 percent of the parliamentary Labour Party, as against 31 percent from the professions – mainly teachers, university lecturers, lawyers – and 26 per cent from miscellaneous white-collar occupations.) The chief representative in the cabinet of this working-class culture was Ernest Bevin, elephantine in appearance, formidable as a trade union leader, and as fervent in his imperial and anti-communist convictions as any Tory. (In fact, Tories much preferred a genuine working-class politician such as Bevin to "renegades" of their own class. The most unpopular of these was Hugh Dalton, an Anglican canon's son, educated at Eton and Cambridge, one of the great strategists of Labour victory in 1945, a leading proponent of the welfare state at the treasury – but also given to proletarian posturing of a kind that offended even the most tolerant.)

But although workers largely supported the Labour Party, the party failed to motivate the working class to produce as effectively as German, Swedish, or Swiss workers. Old class hostilities remained; memories of the General Strike of 1926 soured industrial relations. Workers, especially the unskilled and semi-skilled, seldom felt that by working harder they could improve their material well being and social status. Rather, they tended to believe that increases in productivity benefited the owner, not the worker. Nationalization also failed in a psychological sense; workers did not feel that the publicly owned industries were their own. Union rules and work restrictions continued to impede efficient production, as did poor management. At a time when an increase in coal output would have enormously improved the British economy and helped European recovery, the miners went on strike (1947), and production did not regain prewar levels until 1950. While the mines needed labor, the miners at first refused to allow Italians to be hired. There was trouble in the docks; there were strikes on the nationalized railways. There was not the slightest recognition that Britain would face a lengthy period of relative decline. (In 1951 Britain overall produced more than West Germany and France combined. Thirty years later West German industrial output was nearly three times that of Britain.)

Nothing would be more mistaken than simply to blame the British workers, or the Labour government. During World War II, Britain had been forced to sell a large part of her foreign investments. Profits from holdings overseas thus ceased to cushion the economy from the effects of a long-term decline in industrial productivity. The British faced all manner of additional difficulties; they did comparatively well, given the extent of their military and overseas commitments. (Between 1946 and 1952 the gross domestic product went up in real terms by 15 percent.) But socialist planning failed to come up to the planners' expectations. And the British worker – lionized with tireless persistence by Labour intellectuals – must take some responsibility for Britain's relative decline. During the entire postwar period, the British workforce as a whole (as distinct from particular segments within it) never equalled the overall productivity of northern European labor. Not that the urge for material goods failed to operate among British workers. But overall, the British worker – with his Spartan heritage, his union ethic, and his reluctance to exceed accepted group norms – did not work as hard at the time, as, say, his West German colleague.

The British economy did grow, though at a slower pace than any of the Continental countries except for Spain and Portugal. "Make do," "not to worry," "down tools," "don't work harder than your mate," – these all too often remained the workers' unofficial slogans. Admittedly, Tory politicians were inclined to exaggerate the British workers' truculence; during the 1940s and 1950s, labor disputes in Britain, compared with those on the European Continent, were not particularly severe. Nevertheless, Britain's relative decline in the postwar years owed much to labor questions – to over-manning, to disputes within the trade union movement over the allocation of work, to hostility regarding technological innovation – all of them occasioned by long and painful memories of unemployment.

PLANNERS AND PATRIOTS – BRITISH STYLE

British planning during the postwar years owed a great debt to a group of young, left-wing economists from Oxford and Cambridge, influential at first in bodies such as the New Fabian Research Bureau. They included men such as Hugh Gaitskell, Evan Durban, Douglas Jay, and James Meade who later occupied high office. Their time came in World War II. Government enormously expanded its function; many dons moved into influential civil service jobs; Hugh Dalton, chairman of the Labour Party Finance and Trade Committee, and a patron of these young academics, headed the Board of Trade. These planners owed little or nothing to Marx. Indeed they had not much time for foreigners, be they French, Italian, or German. The only Continental country of serious interest to them was Sweden, a social democratic welfare state that, in their view, deserved serious study. In every other respect, Britain was best. In reviewing a book by F. A. Hayek, Durban thus expressed surprise that a continental émigré should suggest that the British were on "the road to serfdom" – better for Hayek to find out for himself the secret of British freedom. There clung to these planners some of the old confidence and morality of imperial days. (Durban's father had been a missionary in Ceylon, Gaitskell's an Indian civil servant.) As Kenneth O. Morgan puts it in a brilliant summary (Labour People, Leaders and Lieutenants, Hardie to Kinnock) "Their vision had imperial overtones, too. It was a progressive, domestic version of the model of colonial rule once offered to the young Attlee at Haileybury, and to the Wykehamists and others who joined him after 1945, a kind of social imperialism with the common touch ... The Victorian empire (much admired by Bevin, Morrison, and other ministers after 1945) had been Joseph Chamberlain's Birmingham writ large. The public boards, economic councils, and development agencies in Britain after 1945 were Chamberlain's empire writ small. Their chairman (sometimes retired industrialists or even generals) were cast as the Cromer or Lugard de nos jours."

Labour's second "culture" was linked to the university-educated who supplied most of the party's leadership. Many of them had gone to Oxford; memories of tutorials, high table, and the Oxford Union (a prestigious debating society) provided them with a common background that they shared with many Tories. This included both respect for letters and contempt for "trade" – the latter not always openly avowed, but held with all the sincerity of Jane Austen's minor gentry. Labour and Tory governments had other features in common – pervasive secrecy surrounding central government affairs in the cabinet and Whitehall, and a reluctance to provide information to the public, sustained by the conviction that "government knew best."[68]

Labour Oxonians brought up in this tradition included Clement Attlee (later Earl Attlee), the party's leader and postwar prime minister.

HERBERT STANLEY MORRISON (1888–1965)

Together with Attlee and Bevin, Morrison was one of the three main pillars of Britain's great Labour ministry, 1945–51. A cockney, and a policeman's son, one-time errand boy, shop assistant, and telephone operator, he had to put up with snobbish contempt from the Oxbridge set. Virtually the founder of the London Labour Party, and the country's chief municipal politician, Morrison was also derided as a British-style Tammany boss. But he was much more than that. Like Joseph Chamberlain, a former mayor of Birmingham, Morrison, a Londoner, knew how to translate municipal into national power. He was strong in his local roots and loyalties. He was outstanding for his administrative competence. For better or worse he committed his party to the corporate public board as a model for running nationalized industries. Under the Attlee government, he played a vital part as Leader of the House of Commons, as manager of the parliamentary Labour Party, as a leading member of its national executive, and as a planner. In some ways, he was as sturdy an advocate of imperial might as any Tory. (For instance, he later supported Eden's Suez venture in 1956.) But Morrison also believed in cooperation with the Western European states in matters of defense and economics; he likewise did his best to modify existing British suspicions of the Council of Europe.

As Kenneth O. Morgan, the Labour Party's historian, puts it, Morrison, "more than any other minister ... was the prime orchestrator, manager, mechanic; always quick to oil or repair defective parts in Labour's machinery of government." He was the quintessential manager in politics.

The third "culture" derived from the minor professions – welfare workers, local government officers, insurance agents, journalists, and professional party workers, educated in grammar schools and provincial universities, often with the aid of scholarships. Herbert Morrison (later Baron Morrison), represented this particular group in the cabinet; he had advanced from employment as a

---

[68]Dennis Kavanagh, *British Politics: Continuities and Change.* Oxford, Oxford University Press, 1985, p. 60.

telephone operator and a newspaper circulation manager to the mayoralty of Hackney (a London borough), and finally to the Lord Presidency of the Council and the leadership of the House of Commons. Left out of this coalition were the small entrepreneurs; while Labour looked to the state, and the Tories would side with large-scale industry, "both showed little interest in the small businessman, offering little encouragement to true private enterprise."[69]

The Labour Party was formally governed by its National Conference representing the trade unions and the constituency parties. Usually about 1,000 to 1,200 men and women attended these mammoth meetings where resolutions were introduced and discussed. The Conference elected the National Executive Committee which in effect ran the party. (The committee consisted of 12 members nominated by the unions, 7 members from the constituency parties, 5 women elected by the Conference, 1 member elected by Socialist and Co-operative Societies, the leader and deputy leader of the parliamentary Party – that is to say the Labour members of parliament – and the party treasurer.)

Before 1952, the National Executive Committee was effectively controlled by the parliamentary Labour Party, when the Labour cabinet enjoyed high prestige, and easily defeated all dissidents, including challengers from the left, and those who wanted to turn Britain into a "third force".[70] By 1950 however, the party's unity weakened, as much of its original program had been put in place. Labour lost the 1951 election, though by a small margin. (Labour actually gained more votes than the Conservatives, who received only 48.8 percent of the total votes cast.) The idiosyncrasies of the British "winner-takes-all" system for each constituency provided the Conservatives with a small majority in the House of Commons, with 295 seats going to Labour and 321 to the Tories. The Tories increased their majority in the 1955 elections (49.7 percent of the vote, 344 seats, as against 46.4 percent and 277 for Labour).

Thereafter, Labour's constituency parties became more assertive, and began to elect to the National Executive Committee an increasing number of leftist MPs, named "Bevanites" after Aneurin Bevan, a turbulent Welshman who combined radical zeal of the traditional kind with great administrative competence as Minister of Health. Later, there was also a shift to the left in the largest of the unions, the Transport and General Workers Union, Ernest Bevin's former stronghold, and the split widened between the parliamentary Party and the National Executive.

The Labour Party's impact in Britain was profound. It maintained conscription, and Britain remained for a time the European cornerstone in the Western alliance. The first Labour government granted independence to India, Pakistan, and Burma (1947), and withdrew from Palestine (1948). In its international relations, Labour, in theory, should have looked to the "fraternal" socialist parties of Western Europe. In practice it remained if anything even more committed to Great Britain's "special relationship" to the United States.

[69]Arthur Marwick, *British Society Since 1945*. Harmondsworth, Penguin Books, 1982, p. 111.

[70]Jonathan Schneer, "Hopes deferred or shattered: the British Labour left and the third force movement, 1945–1949," *Journal of Modern History*, v. 56, no. 2, June 1984, pp. 197–226.

Labour intellectuals might deride US monopoly capitalism and working men might snipe at the "Yank" soldiers for their real or alleged boastfulness, for their ability to offer tempting presents to British lady friends, and for getting bigger paypackets for having done the same job in wartime as British fighting men. But wartime resentments were mingled with admiration. The US appeared praiseworthy, not merely for its productive record, but also for the doctrine of fairness enshrined in the New Deal. Western Europe, by contrast, seemed to many Labour voters the homeland of Fascism, reaction, and Catholicism; atavistic memories of "no Popery, no wooden shoes," the eighteenth-century mob rioters' slogan, took a long time to die.

At home, the Labour Party stood committed to full employment – easy to achieve during the years of postwar reconstruction, when unemployment was no problem for any Western country. (In Britain, the unemployment rate ranged between 1 and 2 percent of the labor force, a revolutionary change from the harsh days of the 1930s that had helped shape Labour's outlook). The party greatly extended social services, especially education and health (the latter by instituting the National Health Service, one of its most popular achievements). It greatly augmented the public sector by nationalizing the Bank of England, iron and steel, railways, canals, long-distance trucking, and civil aviation. The government maintained control over the private sector of the economy by rationing consumer goods, licencing, controlling imports and exports, and by regulating the rate of capital investment in industry.

PLANNING AND STATE INTERVENTION

*The "British disease" slowed growth of the economy in the postwar period according to Peter Hall (*Governing the Economy, New York, Oxford University Press, 1986*). He argues that the market was inefficient, did not react quickly enough because of the historical experiences of imperialism and industrialization. London banks preferred to lend money overseas and wanted deflation not inflation. There were few large investment banks to spur industrial modernization of the economy; in contrast to West Germany. British trade unions restricted work output and employer associations and trade union officials could not control the branch unions. Corporatist agreements failed to make the market efficient. State agencies and bureaucrats, Hall notes, were tied into cumbersome relationships that impeded change. The Bank of England continued to worry more about inflation than about stimulating industry.*

The French did a little better in their "plan" because they propagandized the virtues of modernization and state intervention was more direct than in Great Britain. French planners also found more opportunities to intervene than did the British government – due to relatively weak unions, discredited business, and effective aid to industry. Yet the French economy did no better than the Italian or West German, who had neither planning nor state intervention. Overall, the economies of Western Europe grew, Hall concludes, but he cannot trace that process to state intervention.

Nationalization did not meet with much resistance from the Tories, except in the case of iron and steel. Both Labout and the Conservatives implicitly believed at the time that "big was beautiful," that Britain's industrial future would rest, as it had done in the past, on traditional Victorian industries such as shipbuilding, mining, iron and steel. Neither Labour nor Tory stalwarts – and least of all the advocates of national planning within the Labour Party – had any inkling of the way in which British pioneering efforts in fields such as penicillin, radar, or computers (the latter developed in a rudimentary form in Britain for the purpose of deciphering German wartime codes) would revolutionize the world economy. Though committed to planning, Labour had made little attempt to plan for public ownership, or to consider in advance the problems of nationalization. Neither were the Labour theoreticians much concerned with improving Britain's competitive edge in the world economy – an understandable omission at a time when the world was starved for consumer goods.

Nationalization in fact did not prove much of a political asset. Working morale in the nationalized industries did not generally improve. Nationalization did not redistribute the national income, as the previous owners received generous compensation. Control over the nationalized industries passed to public corporations, such as the gas and electricity boards, which proved hard to control through parliament. As socialists within the party were keen to point out, only about 20 percent of the economy was nationalized – including, in many instances, the most unprofitable parts of industry. Public accountability left much to be desired. In the cautious words of a leading British expert "if one asks what nationalization contributed to economic recovery or to the resolution of the many urgent problems of the postwar years, it is not easy to find a convincing answer."[71]

In economic as well as political affairs, Labour's outlook remained as Anglocentric as the Tories'. It is not surprising to find Attlee, in 1948, proudly emphasizing that "the Labour Party is a characteristically British production differing widely from Continental Socialist Parties."[72] Labour at the time might well have taken the lead in an association of moderate socialist parties in Western Europe: it not only missed its chance, but failed even to understand that the opportunity existed. The economic record was likewise mixed. Britain recovered, but relatively slowly. As late as 1950, British living standards were lower than in 1939 (except for health care); the average food intake, 1947–8, stayed at only 93 percent of the 1937–8 level. State ownership of basic industries did not add to their productivity; the cost of such regulation and of the welfare state consumed great resources at a time when, in many industries, British

---

[71] Alec Cairncross, *Years of Discovery: British Economic Policy 1945–51*. London, Methuen, 1985, p. 464.

[72] Cited in Sked and Cook, *Post-War Britain: A Political History*, p. 71. The period is well served by biographies of leading Labour men. These include Ben Pimlott, *Hugh Dalton*. London, Cape, 1985. Alan Bullock, *The Life and Times of Ernest Bevin*. London, Heinemann 1960–7, 2 vols, third to come. Kenneth Harris, *Attlee*. London, Weidenfeld and Nicolson, 1982. Trevor D. Burridge, *Clement Attlee: A Political Biography*. London, Cape, 1985. John Thomas Murphy, *Labour's Big Three, A Biographical Study of Clement Attlee, Herbert Morrison, and Ernest Bevin*, London, Bodley Head, 1948.

efficiency failed to keep abreast of her Western European rivals. The British tried to build their welfare state, and, for a time, to develop the remaining African empire with far fewer resources and a greater debt than in prewar years. Nevertheless Britain remained a well-governed country. Whatever mistakes there were, there was also a sense of purpose and national confidence that made the years of the postwar government appear in retrospect as Labour's golden age.

The German SPD and the Austrian SPÖ

The two generations now aged between 45 and 75 years will surely succeed in rebuilding a new party. Its future and probably Germany's as a whole, will depend on the manner in which we shall succeed in teaching our ideals to the coming generations and in organizing them under our leadership.[73]

Kurt Schumacher, author of this appeal, and the Social Democratic Party's first leader in West Germany after World War II, had good reasons for his confidence. The SPD could look to a splendid past. Before World War I, it had been the world's most prestigious socialist party in terms of numbers, organization, discipline, and thought. (Marx, a German, had pioneered revolutionary socialism; German theoreticians such as Eduard Bernstein had played an equally important part in framing a reformist alternative). The SPD had thereafter fallen on evil days; the Nazis had smashed the party, just as they had smashed all other opposition groups. But many sympathizers remained. Schumacher himself was one of those rare politicians to whom the overworked adjective "charismatic" could justly be applied. His resistance record under the Nazis had been exemplary. A former concentration camp internee, and also a World War I veteran, badly crippled at the front, he was a man of exceptional courage. He was single-minded, honest, and intense. He was also power hungry, and able to persuade others to do his bidding – yet unswervingly hostile to totalitarianism, whether from the right or the left. His hatred of the Nazis had become a political asset at a time when their glory had crumbled. His loathing for the communists proved an even greater asset during a period when the prestige of communism had suffered among German workers as a result of the *Wehrmacht*'s experience in Russia, the German civilians' experience with the Red Army in the Soviet zone, and the experiences of millions of refugees driven from their former homes in eastern Germany and the Sudetenland.

Schumacher's worst enemies could not criticize him for being the tool of foreigners. He was, in a sense, a Bismarckian, undeviating in his German patriotism and his commitment to the restoration of a unified *Reich*. Right from the start (at a conference held at Wennigsen near Hanover in October

[73]Kurt Schumacher, "Ein Wort an die Partei," reprinted in Kurt Schumacher, *Nach dem Zusammenbruch*. Hamburg, Phonix Verlag Christen und Co., 1948, p. 177.

1945), he resisted cooperation with the communists, convinced that any alliance with them would inevitably lead to communist domination and Soviet supremacy. Events proved him right. In 1946 the Social Democratic Party in East Germany under Otto Grotewohl merged with the communists; the new party (*Sozialistische Einheitspartei Deutschlands, SED*) henceforth became one more among the communist ruling parties of Eastern Europe. At the first official party congress held by the Social Democratic Party in the Western zones (*Sozialdemokratische Partei Deutschlands, SPD*), convened in Hanover in 1946, Schumacher was elected the SPD's first chairman, and thereafter ruled the party as his personal fief. Only Schumacher equalled Adenauer in his initial impact on the incipient German democracy.[74]

Schumacher was no more beholden to the Western Allies than to the Soviets. He neither liked nor understood the Americans. He did not get on well with the French who bitterly opposed, after the war, the re-emergence of a unified Reich. (According to a current French witticism, it was only Schumacher's inability to raise his crippled right arm above his shoulder that prevented him from being another Hitler.) The British might have appeared more natural allies, given the Labour Party's status, and given that Schumacher resided in the British occupation zone.

During the Nazi era moreover, many German Social Democratic leaders sought refuge in London. The British foreign office might have been expected to make political usage of these émigrés. But neither the Labour Party nor the foreign office showed any sympathy toward them. The British public in wartime was bitterly hostile toward the Germans. (A report produced by the British Institute of Public Opinion in 1943, stated that 65 percent of the respondents expressed hatred or dislike of the Germans, and only 15 percent indicated feelings of "friendliness or pity.") The foreign office feared to alienate the Soviet Union by untimely support for "good" Germans; the British did not wish to commit themselves in advance to what might later appear concessions to the Germans; no alternatives were considered to challenge Soviet plans for the future of German domestic politics – a policy influenced by ignorance, and possibly even by treachery, at a time when both the foreign office and the British secret services contained a handful of officials who secretly desired a communist triumph in postwar Europe.[75]

The British moreover considered the exiled Social Democratic leaders as being unrepresentative of German opinion, a reasonable assumption at a time when the very names of these expatriates were unknown to the bulk of German

---

[74]For a biography in English, see Lewis J. Edinger, *Kurt Schumacher: A Study in Personality and Political Behavior*. Stanford, Cal., Stanford University Press, 1965. The most recent biography is Günther Scholz, *Kurt Schumacher*. Düsseldorf, Econ Verlag, 1988. For a party history in English, see Harold Kent Schellenger, *The SPD in the Bonn Republic: A Socialist Party Modernizes*. The Hague, Martinus Nijhoff, 1968. For a critical account, written from the left-wing standpoint, see for instance Jutta von Freyberg, and Georg Fülbert, Jürgen Harrer et al., *Geschichte der Deutschen Sozialdemokratie 1863–1975*. Köln, Pahl-Rugenstein, 1975.

[75]Anthony Glees, *Exile Politics during the Second World War: The German Social Democrats in Britain*. Oxford, Clarendon Press, 1982, esp. pp. 202ff.

voters and for that matter, even to the rank and file of German refugees in Britain. The British remembered all too well Lord Macaulay's stricture concerning political exiles – they miss their country; hence they imagine mistakenly that their country misses them. Indeed the military authorities openly discouraged German refugees who had served in the British army during the war from returning to Germany, preferring to grant them British nationality.

Once the war ended, the bulk of the exiled German Social Democratic leaders returned (among them Erich Ollenhauer from London, and Willy Brandt from Norway, both of them destined to attain high office in the postwar SPD). British attitudes towards the SPD subsequently became much friendlier – especially among middle-ranking civilians in the Control Commission for Germany and among field officers in the British Army of the Rhine, men and women likely to have voted for Labour in the 1945 election. But the British made no attempt to build a pro-British faction within the SPD – and Schumacher was not the man who would have permitted such a strategy to work.

Schumacher enjoyed other advantages. His was the first of the German inter-zonal parties to function – well before the CDU. The German Social Democrats enjoyed considerable residual prestige – during the twilight days of the Weimar Republic, they alone had voted against the law designed to give dictatorial powers to Hitler; numerous comrades (especially older men and women) had remained loyal to the party's ideals. (The party congress of 1946 was supported by 710,000 members, half the party's former membership.) Some loyal party functionaries had survived, despite the Nazi terror, ready once more to try their luck in politics. Many of these soon gained administrative experience as ministers in *Land* governments, deputies in local assemblies, mayors, and local officials, and played a major part in providing essential administrative services, as well as food, shelter, and clothing for the hungry people.

The Social Democrats had other assets. They regained international prestige quickly. In 1947 the party joined the Socialist International – a step forward in Germany's rehabilitation abroad.[76] The SPD made sure that there would be no comeback for discredited Weimar politicians such as Carl Severing, just as Adenauer was resolved that there would be no political return for Heinrich Brüning. At home, the SPD committed itself to a studiously moderate program that repudiated much of the traditional Marxist heritage. SPD speakers stressed democracy more than socialism.

In this respect they were wise. A generation of radical historians in the 1960s and early 1970s rediscovered the immediate postwar years as an age of potential change, "aborted by a sinister alliance between unrepentant German capitalists and antisocialist occupation governments."[77] But in fact the German

[76]Rolf Steininger, *Deutschland und die Sozialistische Internationale nach dem Zweiten Weltkrieg: Darstellung und Dokumentation.* Bonn, Verlag Neue Gesellschaft, 1979, pp. 87–9.
[77]Diethelm Prowe, "Economic democracy in post-world war II Germany: corporatist crisis response, 1945–1948, *Journal of Modern History*, v. 57, no. 3, September 1985, pp. 451–82.

voters were disillusioned with controls. The plans formulated by political parties, labor and industrial organizations "were far less revolutionary and far more consensus-oriented than one might have expected. There was striking, nearly universal skepticism about all ideologies." The central concerns were for order; there was deep-seated fear of new violence, a profound longing for normality. Contrary to all expectations, war and tyranny had turned the Germans into moderates. Compromise would be the order of the day. (In fact, the SPD's call for a regulated economy did not seem radical at a time when a US directive had enjoined the occupation authorities to establish or maintain price and wage controls, to prohibit all cartels, and disperse the ownership and control of industries.)[78] The Social Democrats moreover could justly claim that they now constituted, not merely the German workers' party *par excellence* but also a national party with a social basis broader than had been available to the SPD in the days of Weimar. (By 1952, about 45 percent of the SPD's membership consisted of manual workers, as opposed to 60 percent in 1930; 17 percent were salaried employers, as against 10 percent in 1930; 38 percent were self-employed, pensioners, and housewives, compared to 31 percent in 1930.)[79]

But the SPD also faced grave difficulties. Though the party was initially the strongest in Germany, it had suffered heavy losses during the Nazi era when many of its hardiest activists had been executed, and many of its potential voters had died in battle. In addition, the SPD had lost half its membership and countless potential voters as a result of its forced amalgamation with the communists in the Soviet zone, where the SPD was then outlawed – unlike small, and tolerated "bourgeois" parties. The SPD had traditionally drawn much of its support from Protestant East Germany. It continued to be much more of an all-German party than the CDU (with 41 percent of the SPD's leadership in 1956 born in territories then under communist control.) The SPD had been the governing party of the old Prussian *Land* under the Weimar Republic. Nowhere had the old Prussian virtues – discipline, punctuality, honesty, industry – been practiced to better effect than within party ranks. The dissolution of Prussia (formalized in 1947) had been a blow to traditional Social Democrats as much as to Prussian conservatives. In appealing to German nationalism after World War II, Schumacher turned out to be like so many generals who fought the last war. Nationalist slogans that would have benefited the SPD in 1918 found much less of an echo in the West Germany of 1945, where regionalism remained strong, where harsh north German accents were apt to grate on Bavarians or Rhinelanders, and where Catholics formed a much larger part of the population than in the undivided Reich.

Schumacher was not an embittered enemy of the Church, but the party's traditional anti-clerical image injured its reputation among Catholics. So did the SPD's opposition to "confessional" schools in the educational system.

[78]US occupation directive, JCS 1067/6 April 26, 1945, part II, col. 38, in Gustav Stolper, *German Realities.* New York, Reynal and Hitchcock, 1948, p. 287.
[79]Edinger, *Kurt Schumacher,* p. 107.

Schumacher's economic policy calling for a planned economy, and for nationalization of banking, iron, steel, coal, and the chemical industries was similar to the British Labour Party's. Such a program would have gained wide support had elections been held in 1945. By 1949, however, when West Germany held its first national elections, the economy had begun to recover; and the SPD did not profit from its commitment to public ownership in the way Labour had done in Britain.

Schumacher also faced ideological problems. His insistence that the working class must lead the country, and that the bourgeois parties had failed Germany carried less conviction than it would have done in Weimar Germany where class divisions had been drawn more sharply than after the collapse of the Third Reich. Many of the SPD functionaries available to Schumacher were old-timers; some of them reported with traditional conscientiousness to the new party offices, bearing the old membership books, ready to pay the outstanding membership fees due since 1933. These veterans were ready to take over administrative responsibilities under the Allies, and willing to form local alliances with "bourgeois" politicians; they were much more anxious to rebuild Germany than to revolutionize society.

Schumacher's critics were many. According to his opponents on the left, the Social Democrats were now no more socialist than Adenauer's Christian Democrats were Christian. Schumacher, according to his censors, had gravely erred in failing to draw on the revolutionary "anti-Fascists" who in 1945 had supposedly been willing to seize power from the Nazis in many German cities, but were prevented by Allied interference. (The Allies in 1945 had put an end to anti-Fascist committees that had been formed in a number of towns, controlled by communist and socialist survivors of Nazi prisons; most of these had proclaimed revolutionary goals, and excluded political leaders from the Weimar era with moderate aims and without a record of militancy.)

We do not agree with this interpretation. The legend of the revolution betrayed dies hard among German left-wingers. It parallels the "stab-in-the-back" myth popular after World War I among German nationalists, who had blamed sundry villains – Jews, socialists, freemasons – for the defeat. But there never was a popular revolution in Germany. The Kaiser's regime had been smashed by defeat abroad; Hitler's dictatorship was broken by military catastrophe. The "anti-Fascists" of 1945 vintage had not constituted a revolutionary force. Not a single German warship, not a single regiment had mutinied in 1945. The anti-Fascists owed such influence as they possessed solely to the Allied victory. Having failed to build a truly effective resistance organization under the Nazis, the anti-Fascists lacked in 1945 an effective popular base, and could not have formed an effective government.

Following a reformist course, Schumacher's party in fact did not do badly in the 1949 national elections, the first to be held in West Germany – the result was better than for many years to come. (The SPD gained 6,932,272 votes, and 131 Bundestag seats, 32.58 percent of the total, as against 7,357,579 votes, 139 seats, with 34.58 percent of the Bundestag seats that went to the CDU. The Free Democrats, a liberal party, won 2,788,653 votes, and 52 seats, 12.93

percent of the total.)[80] The Social Democrats prevailed in Hamburg, Bremen, Hesse, and Lower Saxony, mainly Protestant *Länder* destined to remain Social Democratic strongholds.

Schumacher died in 1952, and the party lost a leader who had ruled the SPD "as if he were its Moses and its members the Children of Israel, Boss, High Priest, Theoretician, Tactician, Speech-maker."[81] His successor, Ollenhauer, was Schumacher's very opposite – conciliatory, pacific, a party functionary's functionary, a fox and not a lion, a man who had risen through the party's ranks, spent the war years in London, and later formed part of an influential group held together through common experience in the British capital. Overall, Ollenhauer represented a party impressive in its integrity. The SPD, like the British Labour Party, still had an element of that traditional earnestness, that commitment to self-improvement, and personal morality, reminiscent more of Samuel Smiles (a Scotsman whose books *Thrift, Duty,* and *Character,* became Victorian best-sellers) than Karl Marx. The party had an impressive anti-Nazi record (in 1956, 32 percent of the SPD deputies in the *Bundestag,* and 26 percent of its top functionaries were men and women who had been arrested or jailed by the Nazis).

Still, the SPD was a party led by cadres, rather than those workers it claimed to represent. (Of the party's 78 leading functionaries in 1950, only 4 percent were workers, 28 percent were civil servants, 22.7 percent party secretaries, and 25.3 subordinate salaried employees. The "free professions" furnished 5.3 percent. Of the 78 leading functionaries, 14 percent held office as *Land* ministers, 45 percent were *Bundestag* deputies, and 31 *Landtag* deputies.) The cadres dominated the party's executive, the *Parteivorstand* (which numbered 30 members, of whom a majority of 17 were salaried officials). The executive was responsible for "the party's leadership," and for the policy followed by the executive bodies. It provided guidelines for the territorial districts (*Bezirke*), and approved the election of party secretaries in the *Bezirke* and *Unterbezirke* (sub-districts). It also had the right to veto parliamentary candidates nominated by the *Bezirke*. The executive was elected by the biennial party congress (*Parteitag*). But the party conference was in effect run by the cadres, who formed a majority within the congress.[82]

Organizationally, the SPD was more centralized than the CDU, its regional leaders enjoying much less power. It also contained fewer distinct interest groups than the CDU. The main lobbies within the SPD were the labor unions and consumer cooperatives – both directly represented in the party's leadership and the SPD representatives (*Fraktion*) in the *Bundestag*. Another lobby consisted of the numerous SPD functionaries and deputies linked to municipal governments, mayors such as Wilhelm Kaisen in Bremen, Max

---

[80]*Keesing's Contemporary Archives*, August 20–7, 1949. London, Keesing's, 1949, p. 10177.
[81]Theodore White, *Fire in the Ashes: Europe in Mid-Century*. New York, William Sloane, 1953, p. 149.
[82]Walter Theimer, *Von Bebel zu Ollenhauer*. Bern, Franke Verlag, 1957, p. 122–7.

Brauer in Hamburg, or Ernst Reuter in West Berlin. These functionaries played an equally important role in the party's representation, in the *Bundestag* and the *Länder* parliaments; many SPD deputies also held paid positions within the party executive, or served as salaried employees of the SPD or of one of the organizations under its control.

Not that the party was homogenous. Delegates within the *Bundestag* were more likely to be drawn from the middle class than were members of the executive. (In 1956, 55 percent of *Bundestag* deputies described themselves as being of middle-class origin, as against only 28 percent of the party's top functionaries.) But overall, the SPD was a highly cohesive and disciplined party governed by managers and secretaries (*Geschäftsführer* and *Sekretäre*). It was also a party run by sceptics and Protestants, without one Catholic in its leadership. (In 1956, 65 percent of the party leaders had no religious affiliation, 35 were Protestants.)[83] It was a party that a traditional Prussian *Landrat* (a senior territorial official) would have understood.

Despite its discipline and cohesion, the SPD's electoral position actually declined during the 1950s. In part, the party's weaknesses were financial. The Nazis had seized its funds. The SPD heavily depended on membership dues for its income whereas the CDU enjoyed substantial support from big business – more so than comparable parties in the US and Great Britain. The CDU disbursed far more cash than the SPD in elections. (In the 1957 national election, the CDU outspent the SPD by more than 2 to 1 per vote.)

But the SPD's problems went far beyond those connected with finance. The party emphasized concessions to the Soviets for German reunification at a time when regional sentiments were strong, and when the new West German state had made a successful beginning. It represented the old tradition of Protestant supremacy in a country where Catholics were numerous, and where the Catholics' social and financial power was growing apace. The SPD stood for workers' rights during a period when the workers' conditions generally improved, and when workers became more interested in social security and a stable currency than in socialism. The party's commitment to a planned economy did not pay off in electoral terms during the years of the *Wirtschaftswunder*, whose success resounded to the credit of the CDU with its commitment to free enterprise.

Schumacher personally favored German rearmament; but true to their traditionally pacifist convictions, many of his party comrades stood opposed. The SPD as a party was much more reluctant than the CDU to back the Federal German Republic's integration into the Western alliance, a policy welcomed by the bulk of German voters at the time. During the 1950s, the SPD never succeeded in gaining even a full third of the popular vote. (In the 1953 elections to the *Bundestag*, the SPD won 7,937,774 votes, that is to say

[83]Karl W. Deutsch and Rupert Breitling, "The Federal German Republic," in Roy C. Macridis and Robert E. Ward, eds, *Modern Political Systems: Europe*. Englewood Cliffs, NJ, Prentice-Hall, 1963, pp. 370–3.

28.8 percent of the total, with 150 seats. In 1957 they gained 9,495,571 votes, 31.8 percent of the total, with 169 seats.)[84]

During the 1950s the SPD failed to emerge from its traditional electoral "ghetto"; it remained essentially an industrial workers' party, in a country where the middle classes were numerous, and where white-collar professions kept expanding. Despite its moderation, the SPD experienced great difficulty in shedding its reputation as a party of "reds" and of perpetual "nay-sayers" (a generalization not equally valid, however, for local *Landtag* elections). As a result, the SPD moved even closer to the center. The Godesberg program, adopted in 1959, dropped Marxism altogether; as the introduction to the program put it, "the Social Democratic Party has developed from a working class party to a party of the nation as a whole."[85] In theory, as well as in practice, the SPD had become the party of the welfare state; it stopped demanding the nationalization of industries and called only for economic regulation in the New Deal fashion. What is more, the SPD did what it should have done 40 years earlier, dropping the Marxist and anti-religious program which had fatally alienated so many Protestant clergymen from the Weimar Republic.[86] Thereafter, the SPD accepted the *Bundeswehr*, German membership in NATO, and the "social market economy." It was a far cry from the SPD as rebuilt after 1945 – a great caesura in German politics.

Equally startling was the success of the Austrian *Sozialistische Partei Östereichs* (*SPÖ*). Like the SPD, the SPÖ began its postwar career as a moderate party that would especially represent the workers' interest. From being a *Klassenpartei*, a "class party", each increasingly turned into a *Statspartei* a "party of the state", that is to say, a catch-all organization. (In programmatic terms this shift occurred in the SPÖ through the Vienna program of 1958, adopted a year earlier than the Bad Godesberg program of the SPD.) Both parties found this transformation relatively easy; Austrians, like Germans, had become disillusioned with communism as a result of the soldiers' experience in the Soviet Union, and the civilians' experience with the invading Soviet armies. Both parties had set out immediately after 1945 to use the federal systems of their respective countries to build regional strongholds (the SPD doing well in West Berlin, Hesse, Hamburg, and Lower Saxony, and the SPÖ making a great impact in Vienna and Carinthia). They each built a legacy of good will as heads of local *Land* and municipal governments, and each dropped their traditional anti-clericalism.

In many respects the SPÖ did even better than the SPD. Overall, it secured proportionately more votes. Its party membership was considerably higher, taken as a percentage of SPÖ voters. It stood out in fact as "one of the best organized parties in Europe, East or West." Indeed the SPÖ's "organ-

[84]*Keesing's Contemporary Archives*, 1957 October 19–26. London, Keesing's, 1957, p. 15818.
[85]Günter Struve, *Kampf um die Mehrheit*. Köln, Verlag Wissenschaft und Politik, 1971, pp. 49–50.
[86]Frank J. Gordon, "Protestantism and socialism in the Weimar Republic," *German Studies Review*, v. XI, no. 3, October 1988, pp. 423–4.

izational penetration and daily presence in Austrian society has been much more thorough and all-encompassing than the SPD's comparable efforts in the Federal Republic."[87] For example, the SPÖ's ties to the Austrian labor movement were even closer than the SPD's to its West German equivalent. Above all, the SPÖ (like the ÖVP) exerted enormous power of patronage. Austrian socialists and Catholics became partners in a corporatist state. It was not the best of all possible solutions. Nevertheless, Austria had come a long way from the evil 1930s, when Social Democrats and Catholics had fought a nasty little civil war.

THE COMMUNIST PARTIES

Introduction

Communist and "bourgeois" parties share the label "party." But as conceived by Lenin, communist parties should differ from rival organizations as Guards regiments differ from popular levies. From the start, the communists saw themselves as an enlightened vanguard, desgined to lead the proletariat in a series of revolutionary struggles. These were to culminate in the dictatorship of the working class, exercised by communist cadres in the workers' name. According to Lenin and Stalin, all means were moral for the purpose of ultimately creating a classless society in which man would emerge from the realm of necessity to the reign of freedom. In pursuit of this struggle, the communist parties would combine the flexibility of a conspiratorial cabal with the discipline of an army. They would not shy from deception – however base, nor from terror – however bloody. They would succeed, not by their unaided strength, but with the help of makeshift coalitions (fronts) with allies destined to be eliminated after the hour of victory. Men and women of every condition had their place in this grand design – the hardened cadre, the loyal follower, and the "useful idiot," compliant intellectuals and pragmatically minded businessmen.

During the immediate postwar period – before the disintegration of the international communist movement, and before the decline of Soviet influence with the "fraternal" communist parties abroad – the communist parties bore certain common characteristics. Whether trained in Moscow, London, or New York, a communist should be at home in a party office anywhere in the world; here he or she would find the same organization, read similar directives, use the same stilted terminology that described every endeavor in phrases replete with "battles," "campaigns," and "fronts." There was everywhere the same emphasis on training in party schools; the same stress on power, prestige, and privilege allotted to the leading functionaries. The senior cadres in the various

[87] Andrei S. Markovits and Anton Pelinka, "Social democracy in Austria and West Germany in the 1970s: a comparative assessment," *German Studies Review*, v. XII, no. 2, 1989, pp. 333–52.

parties saw themselves as part of an international brotherhood, an all-encompassing Old Boy's Network, club, and counter-church. This network was guided by an infallible genius, praised at the time of his death by British communist leader Harry Pollitt as a glorious figure who has "written golden pages in world history, whose lustre time can never efface."[88] In more concrete terms, the party provided the senior cadres with a personal income and a permanent job, with staggering possibilities for promotion in the event of victory. The party ruled both their public and private lives – to the extent of making or breaking marriages. Toward the outside world, trained communists displayed the same honesty about the party's ultimate aim, and used the same tactics of camouflage and deception with regard to immediate goals. There was the same conviction that the party could with justification lie about the past to create a better future.

The bulk of the communists saw themselves as a part of an international army. Allegiance to this host transcended allegiance to their respective countries. Initially, it was the Communist International that exercised central direction. The Comintern was founded by Lenin in 1919, and centered on Moscow. All parties desirous of joining had to meet the same "twenty-one conditions." These prescribed "democratic centralism" (that is to say a system of governance in which power flowed from top to bottom). Member parties had to eschew "bourgeois legality," and reject "social patriotism" or "the hypocrisy of social pacifism." Communists elected to "bourgeois" parliaments remained in all respects subordinate to the party's presidium; iron discipline must prevail within each party, assured by periodic "cleansing," so as to eliminate "petty bourgeois elements." The Communist International proclaimed a state of war against "the entire bourgeois world" and all "yellow social-democratic parties." The "twenty-one conditions" were a battle plan.[89]

The International was uniquely successful in coordinating the main communist parties all over the world. All followed the same line or shifts in the party line – attempts to foment revolutions after World War I, subordination to Stalin and "revolution in industry" during the late 1920s and early 1930s, formation of "popular fronts" during the 1930s. No rival communist organization succeeded in creating an international network of equal strength – not the Trotskyites, nor the Chinese communists. The Comintern lasted until 1943, when Stalin publicly dissolved it so as to facilitate cooperation with the Western Allies. It was replaced by the Communist Information Bureau (Cominform), created in 1947 as an instrument of coordination. This continued to be supported by an impressive network of international front organizations, greatly extended from 1945. These bodies were designed to appeal to particular occupational groups (such as the World Federation of Trade Unions, the International Organization of Journalists, the World Federation of Scientific

[88]Reprinted in Günther Nollau, *International Communism and World Revolution*. New York, Praeger, 1961, pp. 337–44.
[89]Cited in David Childs, "The Cold War and the 'British road,' 1946–53," from the *Daily Worker*, in *Journal of Contemporary History*, v. 23, no. 4, October 1988, p. 570.

Workers, and the International Association of Democratic Lawyers); in addition there were fronts deemed appropriate for particular age groups (the International Union of Students), or for men and women whose particular life experience might turn them into communist allies (e.g., the International Federation of Resistance Fighters). These fronts in turn were linked to a complex network of international commissions, conferences, congresses, friendship societies, and so on – supported by radio broadcasts, a flood of printed propaganda, and overt and covert subsidies from the Soviet Union and its allies.[90] The major communist parties continued to cooperate effectively, with the Soviet Union as the recognized "mother country," predominant by virtue of power and experience, direction and monetary support.

The communist parties also closely resembled one another in their organizational structure, designed both to seize, and hold, power. There was a central organization (with power concentrated in the secretary-general, the Politbureau or its equivalent, and the Secretariat), with a subordinate regional organization, and "mass organizations" designed to serve as "transmission belts" of the party's policies. In the more highly developed parties, the organization formed a counter-state, designed to take over power at any time and to direct society.

No communist party, nor any of its specialized bodies, by contrast, concerned itself with technological or economic innovation. In theory, the communists believed that taking the means of production away from private hands would create new prosperity, since only labor gave value to production. In practice, the communists never planned how to plan for prosperity. They acted according to the dictum of Kwame Nkrumah, an African socialist of the 1950s, who enjoined his followers to seek firstly the political kingdom, and that all other things would follow.

At the end of World War II, there were communist parties in every major country in the world. But only two had obtained a mass membership and major political influence in Western Europe – the French and the Italian Communist Parties.[91] The communists' strength was particularly impressive in so-called red belts, where workers lived in quasi-segregated suburbs, and where the communists supplied a great array of recreational organizations, and social services. The differential impact of the various parties remains to be explained. Catholic countries have been said to be particularly attracted to communism, given the supposed parallels between the Catholic Church and

[90]Robert Orth, *International Communist Front Organizations*. Pfaffenhofen, Ilm, Ilmgau Verslag, 1964, and Milorad M. Drachkovitch, ed., *Yearbook on International Communist Affairs, 1966*. Stanford, Cal., Hoover Institution, 1967, pp. 475–518. For their subsequent expansion, see Richard F. Staar, *USSR Foreign Policies after Detente*. Stanford, Cal., Hoover Institution, 1985, pp. 66–74.

[91]The estimated membership of the most important among the minor communist parties in Western Europe and at the beginning of the 1960s stood as follows (approximate figures): Great Britain: 33,000; West Germany: 6,000–20,000 – the West German Communist party (*Kommunistische Partei Deutschlands, KPD*) had been banned in 1956; Netherlands: 15,000; Spain: 5,000; US: 7,000; Portugal: 2,000. See Witold S. Sworakowski, *World Communism: A Handbook 1918–1965*. Stanford, Cal., Hoover Institution, 1973.

the communist party as a counter-church. This explanation will not do. Communism was indeed potent in Italy and France, but made no impact in Catholic countries such as Ireland or Bavaria; nor were the communists strong in Poland, until the Red Army put them in power. Communism supposedly fed on poverty. But southern Italy, the poorest part of the country, was the least communist, while the industrialized north, Italy's wealthiest area, contained the largest popular communist following in the country. Communism, according to its own theoreticians, would be strongest in countries with a large and developed industrial working class. Britain and the US met these conditions, but neither country developed an influential communist movement. Communism was thought to benefit from ethnic dissension. But Belgium, though torn by ethnic strife, lacked a strong communist party. Military defeat and destruction would surely help to engender strong communist movements? But West Germany after World War II proved inhospitable to communism.

The success or otherwise of communism in different countries depended on a great variety of conditions, including social disorganization, and on the presence of an alienated intelligentsia of almost entirely middle-class origin. Few of these intellectuals wished to turn their own countries into communist dictatorships. Few would accept for themselves the harsh discipline of communism. Fewer still had any contact with those popular masses that *Marxisant* thinkers were wont to eulogize. Initially the Soviet Union, later Cuba, and the People's Republic of China, appeared to most of them as dream lands from which ignorance, hunger, and fear had forever fled. (Even the mosquitoes were said to have vanished from China.) Driven by a sense of moral outrage and intellectual superiority, fellow travelers would deceive themselves before deceiving others. Marxism in its various guises appeared to most of them as a new Philospher's Stone. Armed with this talisman, they would comprehend the past, master the present, mold the future. In practice, Marxism did not fare well as an analytical or predictive tool. In vain did Marxists theoreticians modify or drop embarrassing points of doctrine such as the labor theory of value, or belief in the inevitable and absolute immiseration of the proletariat. "In none of its many varieties did Marxist thought anticipate ... the most decisive developments which occurred in Europe and elsewhere in our century."[92] Marxists were taken by complete surprise when the European workers in 1914 overwhelmingly rallied behind their respective national flags – the Union Jack, the French *tricolore*, the imperial banner of Wilhelminian Germany. Marxists had been equally unprepared for the rise of National Socialism in Germany. They did not foresee the holocaust (sensed perhaps with tremors of premonition by an "imperialist" poet such as Rudyard Kipling in his "Prayer of Miriam Cohen," and "The Rabbi's song"). Nowhere did Marxists predict the Gulag Archipelago, the mass famines, and the mass killings launched by Marxist leaders such as Stalin, Mao Tse-tung, and Pol Pot.

[92]John Gray, "Fashion, fantasy or fiasco," *Times Literary Supplement*, 24 March 1989, pp. 183–4.

Nor did they foresee the inability of centralized Marxist-Leninist economies to compete with market economies in efficiency, and innovative skills.

Nevertheless Marxism as a millenarian religion created a remarkable degree of intellectual commitment among its adherents. Marxist-Leninist, Marxist, or *Marxisant* intellectuals provided valuable, though often wavering and uncertain, support to the communist cause in their professional capacities as professors, publishers, journalists, novelists, film-makers, and sometimes clergymen, and so on. These *compagnons de route, compagni di strada, Sympathisierende auf dem Weg* facilitated the communist propaganda offensive in the West, ready always to see the mote in the eye of a capitalist, and to ignore the beam in the eye of a commissar. Western fellow-travellers on conducted tours in Eastern Europe and the Soviet Union also helped further to depress the spirits of dissidents in communist countries – so visitors from the Soviet Union now tell us. But what mattered above all to the communist leaders was their ability to use for their own purposes existing national traditions, and the quality of their organization and leadership. In some of these respects, the communists did well, especially in blackening the international reputation of the US.

The movement suffered from profound weaknesses. Communist atrocities could not permanently be disguised. The economies of Eastern Europe continued to lag behind those of Western Europe. The break between Yugoslavia and the Soviet Union (1948) occasioned early tremors. Soviet intervention in Hungary (1956) caused numerous defections. (For instance, most intellectuals who had joined the Communist Party of Great Britain left it.) The cause suffered further damage from the Sino–Soviet split, resulting in open polemics between the Chinese and the Soviet parties from the end of 1962, and serious fractures in communist parties throughout the world.

The communist counter-churches encountered other weaknesses from the intellectual viewpoint. None of them managed to endow their creeds with a new and splendid art of a kind needed to sustain belief. The enlightenment had produced great operas and dramas to transmit its message, and the Reformation great poetry and chorales. But the communists' philosophy, and public ritual remained uncreative, fixed in the nineteenth and early twentieth centuries, subject always to the cadres' command. Marxism-Leninism produced no historians to rival Macaulay or Gibbon, no subsequent economists to rival Marx. Propaganda slogans were apt to be repetitive, dulling with their steady drone the recipients' attention. The ever-repeating shifts in the party line turned yesterday's heroes into present villains, and vice versa. In the long run, these shifts would create a mood of cynicism – ill designed to cope with the new challenges of consumerism and new emerging youth cultures. In the end, faith in a Utopia would disintegrate in every country where Marxism-Leninism held sway – from Warsaw to Beijing. Contrary to the expectation of so many intellectuals, East and West, the mass of ordinary people never had faith in the ruling party's pretensions. To the man in the street there was something intolerable in the ruling party's dream land of posters and slogans, with their "illimitable and splendid vistas," "radiant paths," "mighty and epochal tasks," and "inexhaustible treasures of Marxist-Leninist thought," together with the reality of terror, Gulags and long lines for food. Commitment, real or feigned, soon changed to disillusionment, mingled with contempt for the privileges assumed by a self-appointed vanguard. The wave of the future turned into the backwash of the past.[93]

The French Communist Party

The French Communist Party (*Parti Français Communiste, PCF*) was formed in 1920. At its foundation, the party was little more than a socialist sect. Half a century later, it was one of the most powerful and dogmatic of communist parties in Western Europe. The PCF's great Parisian headquarters (2, place du Colonel Fabien) in glass and concrete seemed like the head office of a great multinational corporation. The party's wealth was impressive, and its sources of income as varied as those of a great trust. Under different names, the party had built an economic empire, with massive investments in real estate and urban properties, with holdings in import–export companies, agricultural enterprises, tourist agencies, contracting services for municipalities, publishing, newspapers, and a host of other firms. There were "mass organizations" for every major group – students, women, farmers, intellectuals, workers – staffed by devoted cadres who provide members with services of the most varied sort, from classical concerts to children's holiday camps. The party played a major part in national politics and local government; it commanded an interlocking network of commercial ventures, labor organizations, cultural bodies, electoral organizations. It served as a Freemasonry with a shared *argot*, shared loyalties, and shared memories. There was within its ranks a shared discipline – *les camarades nous disent* (the comrades tell us) – and it brooked no contradiction. The party was alike a hierarchical counter-church, a counter-state, and a counter-society that provided non-material as well as tangible benefits. It acted as a political lobby and a mafia, and constituted both a part of the establishment and a revolutionary organization. The PCF could command every conceivable skill. Georges Marchais, the party leader, did not idly boast when he declared, in 1970 that the party could at any time effectively run the state.[94]

[93]For a magisterial study of the history of Marxism as a whole see Leszek Kolakowski, *Main Currents of Marxism. Its Origin, Growth, and Dissolution.* V. 1, *The Founders,* V. 2, *The Golden Age.* V. 3, *The Breakdown.* Oxford, Clarendon Press, 1978. Peter Lange and Maurizio Vannicelli. *The Communist Parties of Italy, France and Spain.* London, Allen and Unwin, 1981. Michael Ledeen, *West European Communism and American Foreign Policy.* New Brunswick, NJ, Transaction Books, 1987.

[94]Angelo Codevilla, *Modern France.* La Salle, Ill., Open Court, 1974, p. 146. Irwin M. Wall, *French Communism in the Era of Stalin: The Quest for Unity and Integration: 1945–1962.* Westport, Conn., Greenwood Press, 1983, p. 146. For the party's history during this period, see for instance, Jacques Fauvet (with Alain Duhamel *Histoire du Parti Communiste Français,* vol. 1, *De la Guerre à la Guerre, 1917–1939.* Vol. 2, *Vingt Cinq Ans de Drames, 1939–1965.* Paris, Fayard, 1964–5. Walter Gérard, *Histoire du Parti communiste Français.* Paris, Somogy, 1948. Ronald Tiersky, *French Communism: 1920–1972.* New York, Columbia University Press, 1974. For a general review article

FRENCH COMMUNIST MINISTERS

There were five communist ministers under de Gaulle (1945–6), eight under his successor Félix Gouin (January 1946–June 1946), and ten sharing power under Georges Bidault (June–November 1946). At its height, the ministerial structure included the Minister of Armaments and his under-secretary, the Minister of Industrial Production and his under-secretary, the Minister of Reconstruction and Urbanism, the Minister of Labor and his under-secretary, the Minister of Health, and the Minister for War Veterans. (See *Wall*, French Communism, *p. 39.*)

Strong as the party seemed in 1970, it had been much more powerful at the end of World War II. (In the 1945 elections, the PCF secured the largest poll of any party − 5,004,112 votes, 26 percent of all votes cast.) The PCF formed part of a government coalition that provided the party with an extensive clientele both within and outside key ministries, and also within those local governments under PCF control. Communist-held cabinet posts afforded the party a unique opportunity to preside over the building of the modern welfare state; communist control over the Ministry of Armaments and the Ministry of Industrial Production also gave communists extensive patronage over favored capitalists.

Politically, the party had benefited both from the Soviet Union's military prestige and from the many monetary, political and propagandistic privileges entailed in the Soviet connection. Led by Maurice Thorez, the PCF looked to Moscow for counsel on every major strategy decision − for all the party's nationalist tone and anti-German rancor, the Soviet Union remained its true home. The party ran its own training schools that specialized in revolutionary techniques, from the manipulation of labor unions, to the tactics of riot and street battle. Party leaders enjoyed not merely power but personal luxuries, with automobiles, bodyguards, chauffeurs, and villas in pleasant suburbs. At any time, the party could call on well-drilled militants, the so-called *durs*, to do battle in the streets. The party controlled a shadowy underground organization, including experts in secret assassination. The communist party ran the French confederation of trade unions (*Confedération Générale du Travail*), and a large number of affiliated mass organizations.

The PCF drew on the support of many prominent French intellectuals who believed that the nobility of the party's goals permitted any infamy in their pursuit. For instance, when the leadership calmly faked an entire number of the illegal *Humanité* (the official party journal) in order to convince readers that in June 1940 the party had appealed for resistance to the Germans,

of works by French communists see Bernard H. Moss "The politics of history: French communists review their past," *International Labor and Working Class History*, no. 26, Fall 1984, pp. 65–74. For the workings of a cell, see Jane Jenson and George Ross, *The View from Inside: A French Communist Cell in Crisis.* Berkeley, University of California Press, 1984. M. Ardereth, *The French Communist Party: A Critical History (1920–1984): From Comintern to the "Colours of France."* Manchester, Manchester University Press, 1984.

communist and fellow-travelling intellectuals kept quiet – even though the communists had in fact opposed the "British" war, and fully joined the fray only when Germany invaded the Soviet Union. Leftist intellectuals in particular also accepted a host of other myths about the party's war time performance: "silence about its subordination of French to Soviet interests, brazenly dressed up as internationalism; its callous sacrifice of leading militants ordered to make contact with the Germans in 1940 and thus exposed to the Gestapo; and Thorez' own inglorious role as a wartime deserter compelled to sit out the whole war in Moscow, until de Gaulle in 1944 allowed him to come back as part of a deal with Stalin."[95]

What was its dynamic and the source of its strength? According to its own spokesmen, the PCF was as French as the *tricolore*. The party represented widespread grievances among French workers and intellectuals. These grievances were extensive and deeply felt, especially at a time of inflation when the value of personal savings declined, and a good Frenchman endeavored to seek security through patronage and privileges – perhaps as a *père de famille nombreuse*, the father of a numerous family, entitled to cheap fares, or as a miner given free coal, or the employees of a factory with a generous pension progam. The revolutionary mystique was deeply embedded in a country that had successively produced Jacobins, Blanquists, and Communards, all resolved to challenge with musket or rifle the rule of privilege, and to build a new world on the ruins of the old. The French communists – indeed communists all over the world – saw themselves as the heirs of the French Revolution. It had indeed been the Revolution that had created the vocabulary of modern revolutionary politics: "left" and "right," "bourgeoisie," "reaction," "*ancien régime*" and "terror." The communist party, said its defenders, was French in the PCF's commitment to centralized rule, French in its anti-clerical tradition, and in its appeal to France as a great nation. In fact the party was unique in French history – a foreign enclave that unswervingly followed Moscow's lead, whether over the Popular Front, the war against Germany, the so-called Jewish doctors' plot against Stalin, German rearmament, Tito's defections from the alliance of Moscow-led communist parties, or relations with the US. As General de Gaulle mordantly observed, the PCF was neither left, nor right, but East. Muscovite too were those many leftist intellectuals who refused to condemn the Gulag Archipelago on the grounds that the untimely exposure of Soviet realities would deprive French working men of hope for the future. (These sympathizers included Jean-Paul Sartre, whose admirers confused his shallow moralizing with profundity of thought.)

The party was also unique in its personality cult. Frenchmen and women had always been willing to honor leaders perceived as great, from Napoleon, and Pétain, to de Gaulle. But the homage paid during the Stalin era to Maurice

---

[95]George Lichtheim, "The stranded whale: on the French Communist Left," *Encounter*, November 1964, pp. 31–5, a review essay on the important book by David Caute, *Communism and the French Intellectuals, 1914–1960*. New York, Macmillan, 1964. Tony Judt, *Marxism and the French Left: Studies on Labour and Politics in France, 1930–1981*. Oxford, Clarendon Press, 1986.

Thorez (secretary-general of the PCF until 1964) went beyond anything the French had previously seen or heard. In a country whose intellectuals had always claimed clarity and wit for their heritage, writers such as Louis Aragon, apostrophized Thorez as the son of the people, the son of hope, whose presence spread joy in the hearts of proletarians, and whose superhuman struggles would guide France toward a radiant future.

The PCF approved of Soviet purges, and rigorously conducted its own – with the difference that it could not jail or shoot its dissidents. The details of these PCF purges make tedious reading, suffice it to say that they were varied. They included the expulsion of members who had expressed untimely opposition to the Nazi-Soviet pact of 1939, members who had opposed the PCF's pacifist line between 1939 and 1941, and many veterans of International Brigades in Spain. Above all, the party purged itself of many prominent activists in the former resistance. (Of the 29 members of the central committee not re-elected at the party congress held in 1950, 23 had held prominent posts in the underground movement.)[96] Equally spectacular among these "liquidations" were the "Guingouin affair" (1951–2), the "Marty-Tillon affair" (1952–3), and the "Lecoeur affair" (1954), all of which added to the ranks of disaffected ex-communists who later criticized the PCF in its own terminology.

What of the party's wider role within French society? Scholarly opinion divides into two main schools of thought. Irwin Wall, on whose account of the PCF we have drawn extensively, described it as a counter-society, but nevertheless as an organization that sought integration within the French body politic, while articulating the only meaningful opposition to it.[97] Sterner critics include Annie Kriegel, the PCF's historian, who enjoys the advantage of having been one of the party's leading cadres at the height of Stalinism. To her the PCF simply represents a sectarian faction that unswervingly sought, and continues to seek, totalitarian power – under whatever guise. It is this interpretation that, in our view, best does justice to the party's history.[98]

After its foundation, the PCF became affiliated with the Comintern, and subsequently underwent Stalinization. Its internal structure rested on "demo-cratic centralism," that is to say, a system based on hierarchy, discipline, and obedience. The cell formed the most subordinate unit in industrial enterprises (shop cells), in urban areas (local cells), and in rural areas (village cells). Cells were grouped into sections, sections into federations. Delegates of the federations joined in the national congress, nominally the supreme authority within the party. The congress, in theory, chose the central committee, which in turn elected the politbureau and the Secretariat. (According to party theory the former ran the party between sessions of the central committee; the

[96]Wall, *French Communism*, p. 105.
[97]Ibid., p. 239.
[98]See, for instance, Michelle Perrot and Annie Kriegel, *Le Socialisme Français et le Pouvoir*. Paris, Etudes et documentation internationale, 1966. Annie Kriegel, *Aux Origines du Communisme Français* ... Paris, Flammarion, 1969.

secretariat conducted current affairs). The central committee also elected a control commission entrusted with party discipline.

In fact, power in the PCF, as in all communist parties, operated from the top downward. Members of the politbureau, the secretariat, and the central committee formed the elite. Below them came the cadres, something like 10,000 men and women who carried out full-time salaried work in party organizations and subsidiary bodies. No other political parties had such large numbers of officials. They formed a devoted corps of men and women whose livelihood depended on the party, and whose loyalty to the PCF remained little affected by the endless shifts in the party line. It was these *permanents* who assured the party's continuity. It was this hierarchy of cadres that offered to its members *la carrière ouverte aux talents*, a career open to the talents of ordinary people, specially those from working-class backgrounds. (For example, Maurice Thorez had been born to a poverty-stricken coal-mining family, and Jacques Duclos, another leading member, had started life as a pastry cook.) A cadre could carry in his knapsack not merely a field marshal's baton, but, in the event of total victory, the key to the highest political office that a future French People's Republic might bestow.

Cadres were supported by an army of *militants*, men and women willing to devote a great deal of time and effort to party affairs. They were likely to work in one of the party's numerous front organizations (including the CGT), in the so-called Peace Movement, in professional organizations under communist control, or in party cells. The proportion of these activists among the party's dues-paying members is hard to assess. The PCF, like its fraternal parties in other countries, was no ordinary political organization; it also served as a sacral body with its own feast days, processions, martyrs, and saints. Men and women joined the party's ranks for a greater variety of motives, ranging from intense commitment comparable to a religious vocation, to the crudest self-interest of a political entrepreneur. The proportion of militants to ordinary members fluctuated; but overall the activists may have amounted to about one-quarter of the ordinary dues-paying members.

The cadres derived further support from numerous sympathizers who supported the PCF from without. These sympathizers were drawn from many walks of life. They were particularly influential among the intellectuals at a time when Marxism, or at least a *Marxisant* vocabulary had become fashionable in academic circles. The sympathizers were to the trained cadres what irregular cavalry was to an old-fashioned guards regiment – useful auxiliaries, but unreliable and likely to desert when the battle went awry. (It was not until the 1970s, however, that Marxism lost its magic in the imagination of the French intellectual elite. From then on dialectical materialism ceased to be *chic*.)

At the bottom of the pyramid stood the ordinary voters. Their number increased during the immediate postwar years (from 4,831,264 in 1945 to an impressive 5,475,955 in 1946), but thereafter the PCF vote diminished, dropping to 3,822,204 in the 1958 election, a loss of 1,650,427 votes from 1956.[99]

[99]Philippe Robrieux, *Histoire intérieure du parti communiste, 1945-72*, v. 2. *De la Libération à L'avènement de Georges Marchais*. Paris, Fayard, 1961, *passim*.

This decline has been explained in a variety of ways, for instance – in terms favored by social scientists – modernization, *embourgeoisement*, and the rest. More important perhaps was boredom, induced by the repetitive nature of the party's slogans, and the public's growing familiarity with the realities of repression in the Soviet Union and Eastern Europe. Party work, by the 1950s, had ceased to be as adventurous and exciting as under the German occupation, or during the immediate postwar years. There was a world of difference between serving as an underground courier in wartime and the humdrum routine of a party cell. Nevertheless, the PCF in 1958 still managed to gain 18.9 percent of the popular vote – an impressive achievement made possible by the party's ability to instil in its voters a very high degree of loyalty.

In its social composition, the PCF, like France's other major parties, formed a coalition of several groups. (According to a sample taken in 1954, 48 percent of party members were industrial workers, and 10 percent worked in nationalized industries such as railways, electricity, postal, and telephone services.)[100] Forty-five percent of its voters derived from the industrial working class; even so, the PCF could not claim to represent the French workers as a whole; at its strongest it only managed to mobilize just over one-third of the working-class vote. On the other hand it did gain substantial support from middle and lower-middle-class people.[101] In geographical terms, the PCF was strong in the Northeast (especially in Parisian working-class suburbs and mining districts), in many Mediterranean regions, and in the Southeast, where there was a tradition of social dissent. At the height of its power, the party drew more than 2,000,000 voters from the countryside. The Catholic West, on the other hand, proved resistant to the PCF recruiters, and so did a majority of women voters.

Despite its impressive showing, the long-term history of the PCF is one of gradual decline. The party maintained a powerful position as long as it participated in the French government. Membership of a "bourgeois" administration became more difficult however, as military operations began in Indochina (1946), and the Indochinese war forced the party to adopt an increasingly anti-imperialist posture. In 1947, the Soviet Union refused to be a beneficiary of the Marshall Plan, and also forbade its satellites to accept Marshall aid. At the founding meeting of the Cominform (successor to the Comintern) in 1947, the PCF received censure for its lack of revolutionary daring, and in November the PCF and CGT launched a long series of strikes, economic, political, and insurrectional in character. The government by this time had, however, reorganized the police; Pierre Bertaux, director of the *Sûreté Nationale*, a *normalien*, and a leftist into the bargain, proved a man of exceptional ability; the army stayed loyal and the strikes collapsed.[102] Above all the CGT split in

[100]Wall, *French Communism*, p. 123.
[101]Roy Macridis, "France," in Roy C. Macridis and Robert Ward, eds, *Modern Political Systems: Europe*. Englewood Cliffs, NJ, Prentice-Hall, 1963, p. 176.
[102]Theodore H. White, "The story of Pierre Bertaux," in *Fire in the Ashes*. New York, Sloane, 1953, pp. 120–9.

1947 as moderates broke away to form their own organization, *CGT Force Ouvrière*, and thereafter the party suffered from a disastrous decline in membership. The communists never succeeded in making up for this defeat.

For the following six years, the PCF conducted bitter campaigns against "imperialism," against US nuclear armaments, against the "American occupation of Europe," the "dirty war" in Indochina, and the "revanchists" in Bonn – always blending traditionally nationalist with pacifist slogans. The PCF's violent opposition to the French government interlocked with Stalin's stern doctrine concerning the inevitability of conflict between the "socialist camp" and the "capitalist camp" on the global field. This policy, however, failed to enhance the party's strength. Stalin's death in 1953 and the ensuing "thaw" in the Soviet Union caused the PCF to modify its strategy so as to break out of its isolation.

In 1953 the PCF offered to support Pierre Mendès-France as prime minister, provided he would make peace in Indochina. Thereafter the communists continued to favor joint action. The PCF faced further problems, when, at the twentieth congress of the CPSU, in 1956, Nikita Khrushchev pushed de-Stalinization – much to the PCF's dismay. Thorez, like Walter Ulbricht in East Germany, survived de-Stalinization, and the PCF remained loyal to the Soviet Union when the communists forcibly suppressed opposition in East Germany, Poland, and Hungary. These crises, however, led to new dissent within the party; there were more defections, especially among intellectuals and those on the fringe of the communist movement. In 1957, the PCF managed to rebuild some of its influence as the party intensified its opposition to the now bitterly unpopular war in Algeria. But the old power was gone. In 1958, the party failed in its endeavor to prevent Charles de Gaulle's advent to power. Six years later, in 1964, Thorez died – the first and last proletarian *roi soleil* in the PCF. His demise failed to halt the party's long-term decline and it became, in George Lichtheim's phrase, "a stranded whale."

The Italian Communist Party

If the PCF stood out as the most rigid communist party in Western Europe; the Italian Communist Party was the most adaptable. The Italian Communist Party (*Partito Comunista Italiano, PCI*) dates its foundation from 1921, when it broke away from the strife-torn Italian Socialist Party (*Partito Italiano Socialista, PSI*). Whereas the French Communist Party operated as a legal organization until 1939, the PCI suffered repression under Mussolini's regime. By the communists' own standards this persecution was not overly severe. Many of the PCI leaders escaped into exile (especially into France); the communists continued to maintain an underground organization in Italy, an experience that hardened the party's cadres, forged the underground groups into disciplined formations, and increased the party's prestige, especially among urban workers and intellectuals.

Overall, the Italian communists were more flexible than their French comrades in tactics and more imaginative in social analysis (as evidence, for instance, by the work of Antonio Gramsci, a leading theoretician, who died in jail in 1937). The PCI was not simply Moscow's vassal. In fact the Soviets encouraged the PCI to follow its own "Italian road to socialism." Nevertheless the party in all essentials, followed Moscow's lead. During the late 1920s and early 1930s, it suffered the customary purges. Later, it switched to the "popular front" strategy, and many of its exiled members fought bravely in the Spanish civil war. Between 1939 and 1941, the PCI – like communists everywhere – stood aloof from the struggle against Hitler, but once the Germans invaded the Soviet Union in 1941, the PCI joined with the PSI in a pact calling for "union of the Italian people." The PCI began to play a leading part in the resistance, a role for which it was particularly fitted by virtue of its experience in undergound operations, its discipline, and its members' zeal. The party's resistance role enabled it to build widespread support in a country where the German alliance had become bitterly unpopular, and Mussolini's campaigns had turned to disaster.

In addition, the PCI benefited from its strategic adaptability. Palmiro Togliatti, the party leader, had never seen the inside of a Fascist jail, having spent the greater part of World War II in Moscow as a Comintern leader. In 1944 Togliatti returned to Italy, just as Thorez went back to France, and Walter Ulbricht to East Germany. But Togliatti was determined to extend alliances right into the ranks of the bourgeoisie and to cooperate with the Christian Democrats in a show of equivocal moderation. During the immediate postwar years, the PCI thus occupied an extremely powerful position. The Allied armies withdrew. The country was in turmoil, the middle class divided and afraid. The PCI, by contrast, was wealthy, disciplined, and omnipresent. Participating in a government coalition until 1947, it infiltrated loyal men into key positions in the civil service, the armed forces, railways, communications, and many publicly owned industries. The rank and file pleaded with Togliatti *quando si smura?* – when do we smash? Togliatti, however, felt convinced that the moment had not arrived, that the British and Americans would not permit Italy to fall under communist domination. He was no hot-blooded revolutionary, but a thoughtful, subtle intellectual, nicknamed by Stalin "the professor." As Togliatti saw it, revolution in Italy had to wait; time was on the communists' side. The Italian communists' immediate task was to defend the interests of the Soviet Union. By doing so, the PCI would both help the cause of the international proletariat, and enhance its own prestige at home. Make haste slowly, he argued – and the PCI followed his course.[103]

Togliatti's strategy was well conceived. Whereas the party had secured no more than 304,719 votes in the 1921 elections, its vote rose to 4,342,722 in 1946, 18.9 percent of the total, with 104 seats in the chamber.[104] In numerical terms, the party only came in third in the national polls. But its influence was

[103]Luigi Barzini, "Letter from Italy: on the locomotive," *Encounter*, v. 23, no. 3, July 1969, pp. 79–80.
[104]Keesing's *Contemporary Archives*. 1946, June 22–9, London, Keesing's, 1946, p. 7971.

magnified by a temporary coalition with the PSI (which had secured 20.7 percent of the vote). The PSI was badly outmaneuvered by the PCI; in 1947 it split, and the PCI became the leading party on the left. While the French Communist Party suffered a long-term decline, the PCI went from strength to strength, increasing its share of the total vote from one-fifth in 1946 to more than one-third 30 years later. (In 1958, the PCI gained 6,704,454 votes, 27.7 percent of the total, and 140 seats in the chamber; by 1976, its share had risen to 34.4 percent.)[105]

Once the PCI had been maneuvered out of the government in 1947, the party, like the French Communist Party, engaged in numerous political strikes, and vigorously opposed the Marshall Plan, NATO, and – at first – German rearmament. None of these endeavours succeeded. Nevertheless, the PCI's influence continued to reach into the most unlikely parts of Italian society. The communists proved equally skilled as patrons, lobbyists, and tribunes giving voice to widespread and genuine grievances. The Italian communists, under the new Republic, never succeeded, however, in establishing "dual power," a condition held necessary by communist theoreticians to create a genuinely revolutionary situation. Togliatti eliminated the wild men from the party; he disbanded its underground army. His party really played a major part in shaping Italy's postwar future as a veto group, with a powerful position in the trade unions, local government, and parliament, able at any time to harry the government in the chamber and mobilize rioters in the streets. The mere necessity of preventing a communist take-over distorted Italian politics, contributed to the growth of *étatisme*, and impeded necessary structural reforms.

Not that all went well for the PCI. De-Stalinization, initiated by Nikita Khrushchev in 1956, occasioned troubles for the PCI, as for the whole communist movement. After all, PCI leaders had been among the most faithful of the Comintern and Cominform's *apparatchiki*. Togliatti had for many years served as secretary in the Comintern's head office in Moscow. He might take pride in his reiterated advocacy of the "Italian road to socialism;" he might emphasize that Khrushchev's new line had always corresponded to the PCI's. But Togliatti, like Khrushchev himself, had been one of Stalin's men. No one could have served in as high a position as Togliatti's without being apprised of Stalin's methods. When Khrushchev denounced Stalin's crimes, Togliatti faced new difficulties, but hardly new knowledge. Luigi Longo (who took over the PCI leadership after Togliatti's death in 1964) had served as a senior political officer in the International Brigades in Spain. In this post, he had been involved in the liquidation of real or suspected Trotskyites and other dissident leftists. Enrico Berlinguer, another leading official, had spent his entire adult life as a member of the communist apparatus. All these men were familiar with the Bolshevik practice of eliminating fellow revolutionaries as readily as their enemies. Willing enough to praise Garibaldi's tradition, the

---

[105]See table in Raphael Zariski, "Italy," in Peter H, Merkl, *Western European Party Systems: Trends and Prospects*. New York, Free Press, 1980, p. 130.

PCI leaders also had been trained in Stalin's.[106] Given such leadership, the PCI – not surprisingly – continued to follow a pro-Soviet course, and defended the Soviet invasion of Hungary in 1956 as a "painful necessity" imposed on Moscow by the wiles of counterrevolutionaries. (It was only during the last years of Leonid Brezhnev's rule that Berlinguer began to take a more independent course, criticizing the treatment of Soviet dissidents, and Moscow's ventures in Africa.)

The Italian communists faced other problems. The invasion of Hungary contributed to a heavy loss of the PCI's membership; the Sino–Soviet dispute introduced new divisions within the party ranks. The extent of Italy's "economic miracle" – predicted by no one – confounded those who had foreseen the Italian proletariat's progressive impoverishment. Catholicism continued to be a powerful religious and social force, especially in the South, and in Sardinia and Sicily. The PCI's anti-American propaganda carried less popular weight than the PCF's in France. Few Frenchmen had emigrated to the US; few Frenchmen had first-hand knowledge of the country. By contrast, millions of Italians had already settled in the US, and many more continued to seek new homes on the other side of the Atlantic. (Between 1941 and 1960, 243,152 Italians arrived in the US, and 214,111 more in the following decade.)[107] Their letters and return visits to friends and relatives in Italy provided ordinary Italians with information concerning wages, living conditions, and life styles in the US, more reliable than the counter-reality widely constructed in academic journals and seminars and communist newspapers.

In addition, the PCI fought with its socialist allies. From 1956 onward, the long-standing links between the PCI and the PSI weakened. In 1959, the "unity of action" pact between the two parties was formally abrogated, and the PSI moved to ingratiate itself with the ruling Christian Democratic Party. Togliatti continued to call for a union of all democratic elements – peasants, workers, intellectuals, farmers, small industrialists, and white-collar workers – and for a new majority of progressive Catholics and anti-Fascists. The "dictatorship of the proletariat" disappeared as a stated aim, replaced by the demand for a "hegemony of the working class' within the framework of a

---

[106]We are indebted to Angelo Codevilla who has made available to us his unpublished manuscript on Italian politics. Another work that merits publication is Richard Eric Coe, "The two faces of Italian communism ... ," doctoral dissertation. Naval Postgraduate School, Monterey, 1977. Published works on the Italian Communist Party include, among others, Charles F. Delzell, *Mussolini's Enemies: The Italian Anti-Fascist Resistance*. Princeton, Princeton University Press, 1961. Paolo Spriano, *Storia del Partito Comunista Italiano*, Turin, Enaudi, 1967–1970, 3 vols. Donald L. M. Blackmer and Annie Kriegel, *The International Role of the Communist Parties of Italy and France*. Cambridge, Harvard University Center for International Affairs, 1975. Paolo Robotti and Giovanni Germanetto, *Trent' Anni di Lotte dei Comunisti Italiani*. Rome, Edizioni di Cultura Sociale, 1952. For relations with the Soviet Unoin, see Joan Barth Urban, *Moscow and the Italian Communist Party: From Togliatti to Berlinguer*. Ithaca, NY, Cornell University Press, 1986. Alexander de Grand, *The Italian Left in the Twentieth Century: A History of the Socialist and Communist Parties*. Bloomington, Indiana University Press, 1989.

[107]Humbert Nelli, "Italians," in Stephan Thernstrom, ed, *Harvard Encyclopedia of American Ethnic Groups*. Cambridge, Mass., Harvard University Press, 1980, p. 547.

pluralist democracy. Togliatti's demise, like Thorez's, marked the end of long leadership by strong men trained in Stalin's school. Nevertheless, the majority of Italians remained convinced that if the PCI once seized the reins of power, it would never let go, even if it were defeated at a subsequent election.[108] "Hegemonial power" accordingly continued to elude the PCI.

The PCI continued to wield much power in a more limited and immediate sense, especially as a patronage machine. It was acknowledged as a powerful protector who knew how to look after its own on the principle of *do ut des* (I give so that you may give). The party's patronage proved valuable to all manner of people, not necessarily communists – academics on the lookout for a lectureship, authors searching for a publisher or a good review, merchants applying for a loan or licence, factory owners seeking orders, builders in need of a contract, tourist agencies canvassing for clients (especially as regarded any deals with Eastern European countries). The PCI controlled many local governments and most major cities, either through the party's own strength or through political alliances. It was a past master in the art of making local compromises and *combinazioni*, not merely with leftist parties, but also with the Christian Democrats.

Above all, the PCI was more centralized, better organized, and more extensively staffed than its rivals, a tremendous advantage for any organization locked into the Italian clientage system. It could draw on the aid of some 12,000 or so employees, men and women serving at the party's pleasure, without permanent contracts, and dependent on the party's good graces for promotion. The PCI's structure resembled that of all great communist parties. Its party congresses essentially served propagandistic, ceremonial, and informational purposes. Real power nominally rested in the central committee, the party's supreme organ, but the committee's functions were more honorific than executive. It was, however, divided into several permanent sections with specialized functions, such as foreign policy, parliamentary, economic and social affairs, and propaganda. The most important of the subordinate elements was the central control commission which served as the party's judge, policeman, and arbitrator. Ultimate power rested with the secretary-general, and the central committee's directorate. The latter, comparable to the CPSU's politbureau, controlled the central committee's agenda, and played a major part in policy decisions. It contained specialized departments, which corresponded to the departments in the Italian government, and formed a shadow administration capable of running the country at any time.

The party's regional organization was equally impressive. There was a great network of cells (organized in factories and other work places), sections (more akin to Italian political clubs and organized on a territorial base), zonal, communal, and city committees, ascending to regional and federal committees. In addition, the party controlled a great number of subsidiary organizations,

---

[108]In a poll taken much later, during an era of detente, 30.4 percent of Italian respondents believed that the PCI, once in power, would return to the opposition, if it were defeated at the pools. 45.8 percent thought that the PCI would not leave. Cited by Coe, p. 228.

such as the Union of Italian Women, the National Association of Italian Partisans, the Peace Partisans, sports and recreational bodies. There were special youth groups, professional organizations and, above all, the Italian Confederation of Labor. This huge network was well financed, with income from membership dues, from Soviet subsidies, from kickbacks paid by labor and industry, from brokerage commissions, from salaries of party members holding official positions, from sales, from party newspapers, especially *L'Unità*, the main daily, and from other sources. (Details are hard to get and subject to dispute; but by the early 1970s the party's true budget was estimated at nearly 1,290 billion lire).

In terms of geographical support, the PCI derived its main strength from the industrialized North and from central Italy, regions where it had been strong during the resistance era. (These included especially Lombardy, Tuscany, Umbria, Piedmont, and Liguria.) The number of card-carrying members was impressive. (The number rose from approximately 1,770,896 in 1945 to around 2,112,000 in 1951, and then declined to just over 1.5 million.)[109] This was an electoral army vast in numbers, greater than the PCF's, though less disciplined. As regards social composition, 42 percent of its members in 1952 consisted of urban workers, 10 percent agricultural workers, 11.8 percent peasants, 4.3 percent artisans, 3.5 percent small businessmen, 2.5 percent white-collar workers, 1.1 percent professional people and students, 11.4 percent housewives, and the rest were drawn from the rank of the retired and miscellaneous groups.[110]

The party's true elite consisted of a self-perpetuating group of *apparatchiki*. Below them came the organizers, trained in party schools – infinitely more knowledgeable than the mass of lower-class voters who knew little of Marxism-Leninism, but simply regarded the PCI as the poor man's natural home. The party functionaries were somewhat more varied in social origins than the rank and file (14 percent were of middle-class origin, 23 percent lower-middle class, and 63 percent lower class).[111] But overall, the PCI was justified in its claim that it primarily formed a worker's party.

At the end of the 1950s, the PCI's position remained impressive. It continued to enjoy widespread popular support among the workers – at a time when the proportion of self-employed people in Italy rapidly declined, and the share of wage and salary-earners in the labor force accordingly increased.[112] The PCI could help or hinder an entrepreneur, advance or retard a civil servant's career, magnify or besmirch an academic reputation. Many intellectuals supported the party, and so did internationally known publishers. The PCI maintained international contacts of the most extensive kind, and could secure for itself

[109]Coe, table on p. 259.
[110]Ibid, p. 191.
[111]Ibid, p. 206.
[112]Between 1951 and 1961, the proportion of "autonomous" workers in the labor force went down from 40.9 to 31.6 percent. The proportion of "dependent" workers went up from 59.1 to 68.4 percent. Aris Accornero and Fabrizio Carmignani, "La composizione della classe operaia Italiana," *Critica Marxista*, 1972, no. 2, p. 97.

the most confidential intelligence. This is not to say that the party lacked troubles. As living standards rose, as memories of the Spanish civil war and World War II resistance waned, as foreign travel became cheaper, the cult and culture of youth spread in Italy, complete with mopeds and rock music. The Beatles made Berlinguer look dated – a serious matter for the self-styled party of youth.[113] Thereafter, young people would drift away from the PCI in alarming numbers. Even the party workers' wives became less tolerant than before of their husbands' prolonged absences and tremendous work loads in the party's cause. Orthodoxy weakened, especially during the 1970s, when the party called for a new "historic compromise," supported coalition governments led by Christian Democrats, backed wage restraint, urged a hard line against terrorists, and even accepted Italy's membership of NATO. Faced with these dilemmas, the PCI ultimately failed.

[113] Giacomo Sani, "Italy," in Richard F. Staar, ed., *Yearbook on Communist International Affairs*, Stanford, Hoover Institution Press, 1985, p. 499.

PART III

External Relations and Defense

5

The Cold War Continues

The Cold War dominated the postwar history of the Atlantic Community. As we have argued in a previous chapter, the Cold War did not "begin" in 1946 or 1947 or "end" at any particular point. George Kennan's "long telegram" written from the US embassy in Moscow in early 1946 outlined the prospects for Soviet foreign policy in the postwar period. Kennan prepared a paper for the Secretary of the Navy, James Forrestal, in December 1946. This became the basis for the *Foreign Affairs* article under the pseudonym "X" in July 1947, which brilliantly set forth the American policy of containment. Kennan's article provided a cogent rationale for the Truman doctrine, the Marshall Plan and the policy of containment. But it took the Korean war, supported by Stalin, Mao and Kim Il Sung, to get the US to rearm.

Later, Kennan came to oppose the world-wide military containment of the Soviets, insisting that he only wanted to limit their ideological-political threat. Yet his article in *Foreign Affairs* had rightly shown the Soviet Union as a militarized system threatening a weakened, dazed Western Europe, overrun with refugees and vulnerable to disruption by well-organized communist parties. Kennan was under no illusions about Stalin and his gang of thugs – he referred to them as sinister, cruel, devious and cynical, and full of contempt for the US. (Unfortunately, liberals in Washington DC, and the military in West Germany, had to learn from experience about the Soviets.)

Soviet contempt for the US was especially galling given the vast amount of aid the Americans had given the Soviet Union during the war, and the extensive concessions it had made to Stalin in trying to win his confidence and goodwill. Neither Roosevelt's charms and concessions, nor Churchill's *realpolitik* won Stalin over. Containment became necessary. Kennan therefore approved of US efforts to stabilize Western Europe and to stop "any more unnecessary concessions to these people."

For the Americans, the Cold War began publicly with the Truman doctrine; but global conflict was inherent from the beginning in the Soviet philosophy that envisaged world history as a series of inevitable class struggles, and identified the Soviet Union's grandeur with mankind's future. The specific shape assumed by the Cold War was, however, set by individual actors. By far the most powerful and influential of these was Joseph Stalin, who held office much longer (1924–53) than any individual Western European or US leader, and who wielded far greater personal power. Stalin's attitude toward the world was shaped by the Soviet Union's historical experience, by a combination of Marxist-Leninist doctrine (to which he made a major contribution as a theoretician as well as a practitioner), by his place at the head of the Communist Party, the *nomenklatura*, and above all, by his own personality.

Stalin was a man of strong convictions – the most emphatic being commitment to his absolute power. He insisted on slavish adulation from all and sundry. He persecuted religion; He was implacably hostile to all opposition – real or imagined. He was willing to sacrifice untold millions on the altar of socialism. (His campaign against the kulaks in the Ukraine during the early 1930s destroyed more lives than Hitler's murder campaign against the Jews.)[1] He consistently falsified history and Soviet statistics, and even falsified Soviet maps. He promoted cranks and time servers to the highest academic offices. He extended terror to all, including the most senior officers in his party and army; his paladins trembled in his sight. Above all, he believed that conflict between the capitalist and socialist "camps" was inevitable. At the end of his life Stalin had apparently plotted another "great purge" which would have produced yet more murderous upheaval throughout the land. Such was the man whom revisionist scholars in the West later believed to have been susceptible to conciliation through fair words, political concessions, and economic aid.

Stalin's death in 1953 reversed the more extreme aspects of Soviet policy. The "cult of personality" was modified; terror softened though it did not end. The Korean war was terminated two months after Stalin died. Soviet leaders recognized that "bourgeois" regimes in the Third World deserved support, as long as they were not pro-Western, and their ambitions in the Third World grew apace. Their confidence grew too – so much so that by 1966 Soviet leaders for the first time came to regard world communist victory as a target that might be achieved in the foreseeable future.[2] At the same time, the party reasserted its customary supremacy, exercised through "an oligarchy formally defined by the Central Committee, although actually consisting of a bureaucratic interest group composed of the upper-stratum of party officials."[3] Collective leadership through Stalin's principal lieutenants continued up to 1957; it was replaced by Nikita Khrushchev's personal ascendancy (1958–64).

[1]Robert Conquest, *The Harvest of Sorrow: Soviet Collectivization and the Terror Famine*. London, Hutchinson, 1986. Robert Conquest, *The Great Terror: Stalin's Purge of the Thirties*. New York Macmillan, 1968.

[2]Mikhail Agursky, "The prospect of national Bolshevism," in Robert Conquest, ed., *The Last Empire: Nationality and the Soviet Future*. Stanford Hoover Institution Press, 1986, p. 94.

[3]John A. Armstrong, "The communist party as a ruler of Russia: Khrushchev's rise reexamined (1953–1955)," in Gerhard L. Weinberg, ed., *Transformation of a Continent: Europe in the Twentieth Century*. Minneapolis Burgess Publishing Company, 1975, p. 207.

THE WAR WITHIN THE WEST

Despite these ongoing changes, Soviet policy preserved a strong element of continuity. The first objective of Stalin and his successors had been to consolidate Soviet power in Eastern Europe, and strike down any resistance there (in East Germany 1953, in Hungary 1956). Their second purpose was to heighten the "irresolvable contradictions" within the world capitalist system, and divide the West. Given the chaotic conditions that prevailed in parts of Western Europe, given also the Americans' initial resolve to pull their troops out of Western Europe, prospects for communism probably appeared most favorable to the Kremlin in countries such as Greece, France, and Italy. The details will not be known until Soviet archives are thrown open in the same way as those of Western powers. Until then, as historian William McNeil puts it, many crucial topics "must be dealt with from without, treating officially published materials, speeches and the like as a sort of distorting mirror from which, if one is clever enough, one may guess what really happened by correcting for the deliberate distortions and propaganda of the published record."[4]

In the pursuit of their objectives, the Soviets derived encouragement from their military superiority on the European Continent. There is no evidence that they at any time planned for an immediate preventive war. Not for them the *Blitzkrieg* which they identified with bourgeois idealism. Soviet strategists, schooled by Clausewitz and Lenin, regarded military power as a handmaiden of revolutionary politics; military might would strengthen the revolution; the revolution in turn would sustain military might in a long-term process in which armaments, diplomacy, trade, and cultural relations would interact. Hence the Soviet Union embarked on a sustained drive to acquire balanced offensive and defensive forces designed to limit damage to the homeland, fight and eventually win a nuclear war, while maintaining superior ground and airpower for operations in the Eurasian theater.[5] Far from relying on a defensive strategy, the Soviets put their trust in sustained offensives designed to conquer the enemy and occupy his territory and to drive the US out of Europe. This, of course, was not an easy strategy to pursue. The US remained almost invulnerable from direct Soviet attack until the early 1950s, but Western Europe stayed a quasi-hostage, difficult to defend, a source of diplomatic weakness for the US. Stalin and his successors relied too, on a great army of

[4]William H. McNeil, "Modern European history," in Michael Kammen, ed., *The Past Before Us: Contemporary Historical Writing in the United States*. Ithaca, Cornell University Press, 1980, pp. 106–7. Histories based on open sources include Adam H. Ulam, *Expansion and Co-Existence: Soviet Foreign Policy, 1917–73*. New York, Praeger, 1974; Dan Caldwell, *American–Soviet Relations from 1947 to the Nixon-Kissinger Grand Design*. Westport, Conn., Greenwood Press, 1981; Alvin Z. Rubin, ed., *The Foreign Policy of the Soviet Union*. New York, Random House, 1960. For a detailed Cold War bibliography, see for instance Bernard A. Wasberg, *Cold War, Cold Peace: The United States and Russia Since 1945*. New York, American Heritage, 1984, pp. 232–328.
[5]William T. Lee and Richard F. Staar, *Soviet Military Policy Since World War II*. Stanford, Hoover Institution Press, 1986, p. 171.

sympathizers in the West, intellectuals beguiled by the assumed rationality and egalitarianism of socialism.[6] Above all, Soviet leaders continued to count on a great network of communist parties and on numerous front organizations abroad.

> *Liberal-left opinion, especially among academics in the postwar era, consistently refused to see the ambitions of Moscow or to admit Stalin's terror until Khrushchev's speech in 1956. The liberal-left found excuses for Soviet brutality and expansion, while condemning Western capitalism and "imperialism." Many intellectuals and members of the media continued to be excessively sensitive to Russian feelings and overly critical of the US.*

The constituents of this network were not necessarily of communist origin. The World Federation of Trade Unions (WFTU), for example, began with a world-wide conference called by the British Trades Union Congress (TUC), in London, in 1945. Sir Walter Citrine, the British TUC secretary, was elected president, but the post of secretary-general went to Louis Saillant, a French communist, and the direction of the WFTU's press and information service went to a Soviet nominee. In 1947 differences between communist members and their opponents became acute; two years later both the TUC and the American CIO (Congress of Industrial Organizations) withdrew from the WFTU, and set up their own organization, the International Confederation of Free Trade Unions (ICFTU), leaving the WFTU as a communist front. The Cold War thereafter spread to trade unionism. (By 1956 the WFTU claimed a membership of about 140,000,000, 90 percent of whom derived from communist countries.) The WFTU, like kindred bodies, pursued a line uniformly in accord with the Soviet Union's on every major question of foreign policy.[7] So did a host of other front organizations whose complete enumeration would be tedious, but who comprised, among others, the World Federation of Democratic Youth (established in London, 1945, as a non-political organization, but later taken over by the communists), the Women's International Democratic Federation (founded in Paris in 1945 through French communist initiative), the International Organization of Journalists (set up in Copenhagen, in 1946), The International Association of Democratic Lawyers (1946), the World Council of Peace (Wroclav, Poland, 1948), the International Federation of Resistance Fighters (Vienna, 1951).[8] These bodies acted as the international equivalent of "transmission belts" within national parties, and attracted fellow-travelers and assorted leftists.

At the same time the Soviets extended their espionage in the West. Their agents drew on the aid of some sympathizers and a few "moles" in Western academic, administrative, and scientific bodies. The careers of these infiltrators,

---

[6]See for instance, Paul Hollander, *Political Pilgrims: Travels of Western Intellectuals to the Soviet Union, China and Cuba, 1928–1978*. Oxford, Oxford University Press, 1981.

[7]Milorad Popov, "The world federation of trade unions," in Witold S. Sworakowski, ed., *World Communism: A Handbook, 1918–1965*. Stanford, Hoover Institution Press, 1973, pp. 498–503.

[8]See separate articles on these various bodies in Sworakowski, *World Communism, passim.*

(like those of their Western counterparts) often outdid spy thrillers in melodrama; so did the stories of Soviet defectors, men such as Igor Gouzenko, or Viktor Kravchenko, whose accounts seemed so outlandish that many Western readers shook their heads in disbelief. Between them, these intelligence networks provided Moscow with information to suppplement the knowledge gained through legitimate trade and investment. Espionage, disinformation campaigns, and communist tactics of concealment moreover added to a new climate of controversy and distrust that both helped and hindered the Kremlin's cause.[9]

The Cold War thus continued on many different fronts. We have briefly referred to the Western European dimensions of this struggle in our discussion on the main communist parties. Within the US, the situation was somewhat different. The CPUSA, though loyal to Moscow, remained numerically small, electorally insignificant, beset by a steep decline in membership and growing public distrust. The party responded to this challenge by perfecting its camouflage, and by showing a universal willingness to carry out those humdrum organizational tasks that its allies commonly shunned. One of the communists main targets was Henry Wallace's Progressive Party. According to one highly critical member, the communists and their allies became so influential in the Progressive Party that they were able to "guide the major policies and word the major pronouncements."[10]

Communist strategists also paid particular attention to the intellectual community, to men and women regarded as opinion leaders. And for a time, the communists did seem to be winning. The World Peace Conference, held in Paris in 1949, turned out to be a glittering success for the communist cause and the United Front tactics inherited from the Spanish civil war. Luminaries such as Aaron Copland and Pablo Picasso lent their prestige to the cause of peace, as interpreted by the far left. Paul Robeson moved the audience by his rendition of "Ol' Man River." The US stood in the dock, guilty supposedly of every mortal sin. The Soviet Union, by contrast, was a peaceful land, and Stalin a benevolent statesman. The Cold War continued to echo through Western lecture halls, engaging not so much right against left, as the democratic left against the pro-communist left.

For illustrative purposes, we shall merely mention one of many left-wing bodies, the National Council of Arts, Sciences, and Professions (NCASP) in the US. The NCASP, unlike many Soviet friendship societies throughout the world, owed nothing to Soviet financial or organizational help. Its members were distinguished, their purpose sincere. Its masthead read like an excerpt from a *Who's Who* – scientist Linus Pauling; actress Lillian Hellman; singer Paul Robeson; historian W. E. B. Du Bois; and astronomer Harlow Shapley.

---

[9]See for instance, Rebecca West, *The Meaning of Treason*. New York, Viking Press, 1947. Douglas Southerland, *The Fourth Man: The Story of Blunt, Philby, Burgess and Maclean*. London, Secker and Warburg, 1980.

[10]James Loeb, cited in Clifton Brock, *Americans for Democratic Action: Its Role in National Politics*. Westport, Conn., Greenwood Press, 1985 reprint, p. 77.

Disillusioned by Wallace's defeat at the polls, embittered by their inabiity to mobilize the American "masses" behind a progressive banner, the NCASP leaders organized the Waldorf Peace Conference in New York (1949). This meeting was used by Soviet and pro-Soviet delegates to attack the US.[11] The conference, like many others of its kind, turned into an arena in which democratic socialists, such as the philosopher Sidney Hook, fought the fellow-travelers. In the end, the NCASP, like the CPUSA, over-reached itself. Its all too overtly pro-Soviet stance discredited pro-Soviet intellectuals. The democratic left moved into even more adamant opposition to Moscow's imperative; organizations such as ADA (Americans for Democratic Action) played a major part in "countering the postwar Communist drive in America to capture the liberal intellectuals."[12]

The non-communist left created for itself a new forum through the Congress of Cultural Freedom, founded in West Berlin in 1950. Terror had intensified in Eastern Europe. North Korea had just invaded South Korea. Supporters of the congress included the most distinguished spokesmen of the anti-Stalinist left, many of them ex-communists. Backers included Sidney Hook, Arthur Koestler, James Burnham, Ignazio Silone, Raymond Aran, Irving Kristol, and Mary McCarthy. Between them, they knew more about Marx than the entire Soviet politbureau. They argued well, and they wrote well. At the height of its influence, the congress maintained a string of offices, and supported a variety of cultural magazines, such as *Encounter* in Britain, and *Preuves* in France. The congress denounced oppression in non-communist as well as communist countries. Its backers had a sense of dedication equal to the communists.[13]

The congress, however, was split by bitter personal and political quarrels – not surprising in an organization united only by a common enmity to Stalinism. In the 1960s it was discovered that the CIA had surreptitiously subsidized the congress – at a time when the state department would not have dared publicly to give money to left-wing intellectuals of assorted national backgrounds. The congress was clearly right about the evils of Stalinism and its critics wrong, as was borne out first by Khrushchev's, and later by Mikhail Gorbachev's revelations. But to take CIA money was a political error, and to keep these transactions secret a moral failing. The quarrels of the time bequeathed a legacy of hatred among Western, especially US intellectuals; the resultant insults and counter-charges were never fogotten as long as the combatants survived. This was itself one of Stalin's unacknowledged victories.

The split within the American intellectual community widened at the time of Senator Joe McCarthy's notorious campaign against real or alleged communist infiltrators. McCarthy's crusade coincided with the communist victory in

[11] John P. Rossi, "Farewell to fellow traveling: the Waldorf peace conference of March 1949," *Continuity*, no. 10, Spring, 1985, pp. 1–31.
[12] Brock, *Americans for Democratic Action*, p.v.
[13] Peter Coleman, *The Liberal Conspiracy: The Congress for Cultural Freedom and the Struggle for the Mind of Postwar Europe*. New York Free Press, 1988.

China (1949), with revelations about successful Soviet intelligence activities concerning nuclear weapon development in the US and Great Britain, with the Korean war, and also with the much publicized Alger Hiss trial (in which Hiss was found guilty of perjury in concealing his membership of the CPUSA). According to many of his critics, McCarthy conducted a witch-hunt that destroyed countless lives; the American public fell victim to a "red scare" that heated the Cold War, and gravely damaged American academic integrity.[14]

The reality was less melodramatic. McCarthy was a political adventurer who skillfully used popular suspicion of the "Eastern establishment" to further his career. But his impact was strictly circumscribed. McCarthy had no secret police, or concentration camps to enforce his threats; he lacked executive authority of any kind. The courts resisted him; so did presidents Truman and Eisenhower. There was no academic persecution of the kind suffered by many conservative college teachers during the 1960s and early 1970s – no interrupted classes, no incendiarism, no "trashings," no threats of personal violence on the part of student mobs. There was no de facto exclusion of the kind later experienced by conservatives from teaching posts at prestige universities in Black studies, African studies, Chicano studies, and women's studies. About 100 professors, an insignificant proportion of the total number employed in the US, lost their jobs because they were members of the communist party, or because they refused to sign loyalty oaths, or because they would not testify before investigating bodies. Some of these teachers later resumed their academic careers; some went into other occupations such as publishing or psychoanalysis. The communists among them – in our opinion – deserved no sympathy. Our lack of compassion in this regard does not derive from the communists' commitment to Marxism-Leninism, but from their tactics. The communists and their allies had themselves waged a ruthless war of defamation and professional discrimination against all those who opposed, or diverged from the party line. They could hardly complain on moral grounds if similar tactics were used against them. Communist academics moreover had deliberately concealed their membership of the CPUSA, a semi-conspiratorial organization that required certain members to hide their true political affiliation, and sought to impose a rigid party line incompatible with scholarly independence. Academia was neither purged of left-wingers nor reduced to soulless conformity. (On the contrary, teachers describing themselves as "very liberal" or "liberal" continued heavily to outnumber self-professed conservatives at US prestige universities.)[15] In the end, McCarthy was destroyed by his own

[14]For the communist impact on US intellectuals, see William L. O'Neill, A Better World: Stalinism and the American Intellectuals. New Brunswick, NJ, Transaction Publishers, 1989. For the McCarthy controversy, see for instance Ellen Schrecker, No Ivory Tower: McCarthyism and the Universities. Oxford, Oxford University Press, 1986, and the thoughtful reviews by Sidney Hook, "Communists, McCarthy and American universities," Minerva: A Review of Science, Learning and Policy, v. xxv, no. 3, Autumn, 1987, pp. 331–48.

[15]Seymour Martin Lipset and Everett Carll Ladd, Professors, Unions, and American Higher Education. Washington, DC. American Enterprise Institute, 1973, p. 29. "Liberal" and "very liberal" teachers amounted to 55 percent in 1969, conservatives 29 percent, "middle-of-the-roaders" 17 percent.

paranoia. Publicity, his own chosen weapon, turned against him, and ruined his career. But the McCarthy era remained deeply embedded in the American progressive consciousness as "scoundrel time" – a tragedy for Americans, wrongly assumed to have delegitimized US power, and the country's position in the Cold War.

BRITAIN HOLDS THE LINE

When World War II ended, Britain was the only major power left in Western Europe. The British defense establishment remained impressive; the country's prestige stood high. The Labour government commanded a good majority in the House of Commons, national confidence, and strong leadership. Ernest Bevin, the new foreign secretary, was a powerful personality, trained in the rough school of British labor union politics. Unlike his successors, Bevin was not a mere cabinet representative, but a policy-maker in his own right. He was "the last of the line of foreign secretaries in the tradition created by Castlereagh, Canning and Palmerston in the first half of the 19th century, with Salisbury, Grey and Austin Chamberlain as his predecessors in the 20th century and no successors."[16] Bevin's views on fighting the Cold War were sober and realistic. Neither he nor his defense advisers anticipated an immediate military attack. Instead he looked to a protracted political confrontation of a kind he had experienced with communists in British labor unions.

Bevin felt convinced moreover that economic progress was not enough, that the Western countries must also "organize the ethical and spiritual forces inherent in ... Western civilization of which we are the chief protagonists."[17] This assessment was shrewd, not merely in perennial terms, but also from the standpoint of *realpolitik*. Bevin understood, as many intellectuals did not, the intense hostility that the Soviets aroused by their atheist philosophy; abhorrence was especially marked in the US where the various churches enjoyed mass support of a kind that no socialist sect could equal.

Bevin's political task, however, was vastly more difficult than that of any of his predecessors at the foreign office. According to their treasury experts, Britain had been overly careless about her economic future in the conduct of the war, and had borne an excessive share of its cost. This underlying mistake greatly complicated British postwar recovery, when she was burdened by

[16]Alan Bullock, *Ernest Bevin: Foreign Secretary, 1945–1951*. New York, W. W. Norton and Co, 1984, p. 75.
[17]Elisabeth Barker, *The British Between the Superpowers 1945–50*. London, Macmillan, 1983, p. 104. For the immediate postwar period also see Terry H. Anderson, *The United States, Great Britain and the Cold War*. Columbia, University of Missouri Press, 1984. Sir Richard Clarke and Sir Alec Cairncross, eds, *Anglo-American Economic Collaboration in War and Peace: 1942–1949*. Oxford, Oxford University Press, 1982. William Roger Louis and Hedley Bull, eds, *The Special Relationship: Anglo-American Relations Since 1945*. Oxford, Clarendon Press, 1986. James L. Gormly, *The Collapse of the Grand Alliance 1945–1948*. Baton Rouge, Louisiana State University Press, 1987. Richard A. Best Jr, *"Co-Operation With Like-Minded Peoples": British Influences on American Security Policy 1945–1949*. Westport, Conn., Greenwood Press, 1986.

heavy debt and a continuing balance of payments problem. With her resources depleted, her economy dependent on US aid, Britain continued to shoulder world-wide responsibilities that she could neither avoid nor meet with her own resources. Willy-nilly, she conceded national sovereignty to the bulk of her Asian empire. (India and Pakistan achieved independence in 1947, Burma in 1948.) Withdrawal from the subcontinent deprived the British of valuable bases. Moreover Britain could no longer rely on the Indian army, as she had in two world wars. Neither would the "white" dominions continue to support Britain in Europe. At the same time, the Americans felt reluctant to sustain what they regarded as a superannuated empire with a tainted past and a dubious future.[18]

As regards Anglo-Soviet relations, the Labour victory itself may have worsened the British bargaining position. Communists had traditionally disliked conservatives less than social democrats, who challenged the communists' claim to monopolize working-class allegiance. Not surprisingly, British visitors to Moscow in 1945 were struck by the way in which Soviet intellectuals and military men would rather have dealt with Churchill than Bevin, with a Tory rather than a Labour government.[19] Bevin moreover was not fully master in his own house. The Labour Party's left wing continued to insist that Britain should act as a third force in world affairs; overall the Labour left showed more concern with the real or alleged evils of US capitalism than the less-publicized failings of the Soviet Union which, at least in theory, laid claim to being a workers' state.

Britain faced the new challenge by behaving at the same time as an international "bulldog" and a "bullfrog" – to use Elisabeth Barker's graphic phrases.[20] The bulldog tried to hold on to various parts of the world until Britain could leave behind reasonably stable states, preferably linked to the Commonwealth (India and Pakistan), or to a Western alliance (Greece), or at least neutral in the East–West struggle (Burma). The bullfrog noisily exaggerated its military strength, diplomatic expertise, and cultural *savoir faire* so as to impress both friends and enemies. The bullfrog croaked to warn the US of Soviet threats, and to secure from a reluctant US such military and financial backing as London perceived essential for British and wider Western interests.

In this context, Germany, the Mediterranean and the Middle East formed key positions. British attitudes towards Germany lacked consistency, as did those of their wartime allies. The British wanted most to safeguard their waning status as a great power; at the same time they were concerned to lighten the strain on their own tight budget by urging the restoration of German productive capacities and the resumption of traditional trade between the various regions of Germany. For the British, the Potsdam Conference was

---

[18]William Roger Louis, *Imperialism at Bay: The United States and the Decolonization of the British Empire, 1941–1945*. Oxford, Oxford University Press, 1978.

[19]Sir Isaiah Berlin's impressions from a visit to Moscow, cited by Elisabeth Barker, *The British Between the Superpowers, 1945–1950*, p. 19.

[20]Ibid., pp. 241–2.

a bitter experience that created a new sense of disillusionment and insecurity – they were disappointed by Soviet hostility on the one hand, and US inconsistency on the other, at a time when Britain's economic position continued to deteriorate.[21]

The situation seemed hardly more favorable in the Middle East. On the face of it, British power in this region seemed stronger than at any time – since the war, for the first time in history, Britain had been the dominant great power here. Britain had 60,000 troops in Greece, a newly concluded alliance with Turkey, and a military force in Southern Iran. The British had replaced the Italians in Libya and levered the French out of Syria and Lebanon. They maintained a mandate in Palestine, and also had pacts with Egypt, Iraq, and Jordan.[22]

Nevertheless, British effective strength in the region was weak, and it was here that the Soviet threat seemed most evident. Stalin, in 1945, made claims for Soviet bases in the Turkish straits, for trusteeship in the former Italian colony of Tripolitania, and for privileges in northern Iran. These claims were accompanied by an unremitting propaganda campaign against Britain. In the long run the campaign may have ill-served Soviet interests by discouraging actual or potential neutralists (including Tories and Labour right-wingers afraid of the American, as well as the Soviet, challenge to the British empire).

Given the paucity of their resources, the British were surprisingly successful. Bevin's diplomacy, together with US support, assisted the Turks in their effective resistance to Soviet demands. British combined with US endeavors succeeded in maneuvering the Soviets out of northern Iran (1946). British resolution helped in preventing the Soviets from establishing bases in the former Italian colony of Libya. And Britain's military presence in the disputed Trieste territory (Venetia Giulia) ˙prevented Trieste from being seized by communist Yugoslavia, and assured its status as an Italian city.

The British position seemed particularly vulnerable in Greece, a country considered vital to Britain's interests by defense planners. As we have pointed out in a previous chapter, the "percentage agreement" concluded between Churchill and Stalin had allotted Greece to the British Sphere of influence. Civil war had broken out in Greece in 1944, and had temporarily ended through the so-called Varkiza agreement. The Greek Communist Party (*KKE, Kommunistikon Komma Ellados*) used this pact to regroup its forces, then launched a new civil war in 1946. British support once again proved vital in enabling the Greeks successfully to counter the first communist attempt made after World War II to take over by force of arms a country outside the Soviet sphere in Eastern Europe.

According to their critics, then and later, the British acted reprehensibly in

[21] Josef Foschepoth, "British interest in the division of Germany after the Second World War," *Journal of Contemporary History*, v. 21, no. 3, July 1986, pp. 391–411.

[22] For a more recent study, see for instance, Bruce Robellet Kuniholm, *The Origins of the Cold War in the Near East: Great Power Conflict and Diplomacy in Iran, Turkey, and Greece*. Princeton, Princeton University Press, 1980.

opposing the Greek communists. Similar arguments recurred with monotonous regularity to censure Western intervention against communist-led
insurgencies elsewhere. The communists formed only one of several segments
within a broader democratic alliance, went the argument. The communists
supposedly represented the masses – especially the urban working class –
against a tyrannical cabal. The interventionists, in this case the British, interfered in a civil war that arose from local causes, and not from "a sinister
communist aggression devilishly premeditated in Moscow," a notion derived
from "Cold War propaganda."[23]

Similar arguments continued to be put forward by many leftist critics of US
policy makers from Truman to Reagan. These followed a consistent pattern.
They remained a recurrent theme in anti-US polemics even in the late 1980s –
at a time when Marxism-Leninism was in evident disarray from Warsaw to
Beijing, when Soviet scholars themselves had begun to question the role of
Soviet "hegemonism" in the Cold War. According to this interpretation,
Americans generally, and their leaders, indulged in an exaggerated form
of anti-communism. They did so because they were "notably ignorant and
indifferent about world affairs," because they substituted "gut feelings" for
close analysis, and because of their penchant for "stereotyping and paranoia."
As regards Greece, the communists were "strong nationalists." The US nevertheless intervened, thereby becoming responsible for "right-wing repression
and a military establishment that plagued Greek politics through much of its
postwar history."[24]

We are not convinced by these claims. The Greek communists formed, and
continued to form a minority. This minority was determined to seize power
by force of arms, set up a dictatorship, and liquidate opponents. In order to
achieve these objects, the KKE was willing to fight a protracted and bloody
struggle. It could not have done so without privileged sanctuaries in Yugoslavia and Bulgaria, and without continued aid from the Eastern bloc. The
KKE did not gain much support among urban workers in the course of a
revolt that never reached the cities. It alienated the bulk of the population
by terror, by promising "autonomy" to Greek Macedonia, by the forceful
conscription of youth, by the abduction of children – in short by methods that
led to the creation of a national Greek government in September 1947. The
Greek communists were not "nationalists." (The bulk of the KKE repudiated
Tito, and later backed Moscow against Beijing.) Whatever the failings of
Greek postwar governments, Greece became a freer and more prosperous
country than any of its communist-ruled neighbors. The brutality of communist tactics were not an invention of anti-communist propagandists. Had
the communists won, and even had they, by some unlikely twist, later broken

---

[23] Heinz Richter, *British Intervention in Greece: From Varkiza to Civil War. February 1945 to August 1946*. London, Merlin Press, 1985, p. 536. As regards popular support, the communist-dominated EDA (United Democratic Left, formed in 1951) gained a maximum of 24.4 percent of the votes cast in 1958, dropping to 11.8 percent in 1964.

[24] Thomas G. Paterson, *Meeting the Communist Threat: Truman to Reagan*. Oxford, Oxford University Press, 1988, p. x, p. 50.

with Moscow, Greece would have shared the fate of Yugoslavia at best, or Albania at worst. British, and later US, intervention, and the victory of the Greek army were an unmixed blessing for Greece.

The failure of the Greek communists may also have persuaded the Italian communists to tread a more cautious path than their comrades. The outcome was decided when Tito broke with the Soviets in 1948, and withdrew his support from the Greek insurgents. Fighting dragged on until 1949 in a civil war marked by village vendettas and countless atrocities. Thereafter, communist resistance collapsed: it was the first of many Western victories against revolutionary partisan forces in countries as far afield as Greece, Malaya, and the Philippines, successes that denied the myth of the ever-victorious guerrilla.[25]

Palestine was the only break in the British successs story. The Palestinian conundrum was also the first major issue, that for a time, cut across the East–West cleavage in the Cold War. The Arabs had never accepted the Balfour Declaration (1917) by which Great Britain had promised a "national home" in Palestine to the Jews. The British increasingly veered toward the Arab side, a shift which continued under Labour, despite the general sympathy that Zionists enjoyed world-wide among the democratic left until about the late 1960s. The Americans proved no more than lukewarm toward Zionism during and immediately after World War II. But the US (and to a lesser extent countries such as Canada, Australia, and Brazil) unwittingly strengthened Zionism by their unwillingness to admit the massive immigration of Jewish survivors left in displaced person camps or in the shattered Jewish remnant communities in Eastern Europe. In the past, convinced Zionists, willing to settle in the Holy Land, had formed but a small minority among European Jews. Uprooted and distraught after the war, large numbers would have preferred to start life again in the New World, preferably in the US. As things turned out, however, many European Jews looked upon Palestine as their only hope, while the bulk of American Jewry began to support the Zionist cause toward which they had previously been indifferent.

Stalin's attitude over this issue was double-edged. On being naively asked by Roosevelt during the Yalta Conference whether he was a Zionist, Stalin had replied "in principle, but I recognize the difficulty."[26] The chief difficulty was his persecution of Zionism in the Soviet Union and its dependencies. But Stalin was always flexible in his tactics. In 1947, the British, unable to resolve the Jewish–Arab dispute in Palestine, turned the matter over to the UN. To the world's amazement, the Soviet spokesmen at the UN declared their support for the partition of Palestine and the creation of both an independent Jewish and an Arab state. In 1948 the Soviet Union was one of the first to extend diplomatic recognition to Israel.[27] Later, the Soviets switched again toward

---

[25]See for instance, L. H. Gann, *Guerrillas in History*. Stanford, Hoover Institution Press, 1971.

[26]Evan M. Wilson, *Decision on Palestine: How the US Came To Recognize Israel*. Stanford, Hoover Institution Press, 1979, p. 50.

[27]Nadav Safran, "The Soviet Union and Israel, 1947–1969," in Ivo J. Lederer and Wayne S.

the Arabs. Anti-Zionism, and anti-semitism marketed under the anti-Zionist label, henceforth became major issues in the Cold War. As Israel became increasingly dependent on American support, Arab and Soviet propagandists alike associated Zionists with US imperialists, though anti-Zionists could not always agree which of their enemies were the puppets and which the puppeteers.[28]

Given the ongoing decline of British power and the extent of her financial problems, US intervention became necessary. And the British played the main role in getting the US to come back to Europe and the Middle East. By 1946 the Americans had already departed from the ostentatious neutrality displayed over Middle Eastern matters two years earlier. In retrospect therefore, the enunciation of the so-called Truman doctrine did not come in as dramatic a fashion as it appeared at the time. But matters came to a head on February 24, 1947, when Bevin decided on a gamble that shocked his own chiefs of staff nearly as much as the Americans. British Ambassador Lord Inverchapel was told to see Secretary of State Marshall and inform him that, unless the US agreed to give financial aid to the Greek armed forces, no further assistance would come to them from Great Britain. Having obtained agreement from the congressional leaders, Truman announced on November 12, 1945, the Truman doctrine: "I believe it must be the policy of the United States to support free people who are resisting attempted subjugation by armed minorities or by outside pressures."[29]

Truman was as good as his word. The Americans thereafter gave help to Greece, and the Greeks weathered the storm. In addition, the Americans strengthened their naval forces in the Mediterranean, and provided assistance to Turkey. The Soviets allowed their territorial claims on Turkey to lapse, and instead turned to attack Turkey's American connection. The US once more became fully involved in Europe. The Truman doctrine came to form a historical watershed, and ended America's return to semi-isolationism and primary concern for the Pacific Basin. The US became a global power with global concerns and had to build new institutions and agencies to handle these responsibilities.

MARSHALL PLAN AND BERLIN BLOCKADE

The Truman doctrine met its most ominous challenge in occupied Germany. The Soviets themselves appear to have been undecided about future policy. Their objects diverged: above all they wished to prevent the emergence of a united and revanchist-minded Germany, but they also wished to extract as

---

Vucinich, eds, *The Soviet Union and the Middle East: The Postwar Era*. Stanford, Hoover Institution Press, 1974.

[28]For a more detailed discussion of the historical connection between Nazi anti-semitism and modern anti-Zionism, see for instance, Robert Wistrich, *Hitler's Apocalypse: Jews and the Nazi Legacy*. New York, St Martin's Press, 1985.

[29]Barker, *The British Between the Superpowers*, p. 82.

much reparation as possible from their defeated enemy. The possibility of creating a united communist Germany must have appeared a dazzling prospect – but one in the distant future.

The available evidence suggests that the Soviets preferred at the time to consolidate communist rule in their own occupation zone, and to wait for a more propitious time – a day when the "internal contradictions" of global capitalism would become more acute, and when the Western zones would be beset by unemployment, economic chaos, and discontent, especially among the millions of refugees who had fled to West Germany. Such assumptions seemed perfectly realistic at a time when many Western economists were still making most pessimistic forecasts. Stalin may have assumed that in the event of a new world crisis the financial burden of maintaining the occupation in Germany would become too heavy for the Western powers to bear. Disillusioned, the Americans would pull out of Europe, as they had indeed announced they would toward the end of the war. Britain would then follow suit, and Soviet power would become predominant throughout Europe.

Occupied Germany formed the most important of all diplomatic battlefields. Attempts to run occupied Germany by four-power consent soon broke down, first of all over the matter of reparations. Since the Russians refused to account for their exactions in their own zone, the Western commanders in turn refused to continue deliveries to the Soviets from their respective zones. In the Spring of 1946 the deliveries were stopped; the punitive phase of Western occupation in Germany ended. At the same time, the Americans initiated the Marshall Plan (announced by General George C. Marshall, the US Secretary of State, in his speech at Harvard on June 5, 1947). Marshall had been deeply shocked by what he saw and heard in Europe during his visit there and on his return convinced Truman that aid must be given to Europe to save it from a Soviet takeover. Truman agreed but suggested that it be called the Marshall Plan so as to get it through Congress.

The Marshall Plan (officially called the European Recovery Plan, ERP) was largely drafted by George F. Kennan, head of state's policy planning staff, William L. Clayton, assistant secretary of state, and Dean Acheson, under secretary of state. Kennan's memorandum to Secretary of State Marshall did not cite communist activities as the cause of Europe's troubles but rather the disruptive effects of the war, and the destruction of plant and transportation systems, combined with the loss of morale and spiritual vigor of the people. This crisis was however exploited by local communist parties. And Truman's message to Congress asking for the Marshall Plan to be approved stressed that the purpose of the ERP was to allow Europe to recover from the devastation of war and to maintain Western civilization, "in which the American way of life is rooted."

Arnold Toynbee, the British historian, said that the concern of the world's most privileged people for the less privileged was embodied in Point IV aid and the Marshall Plan. He foresaw that this aid initiative would be recalled as the most generous act in diplomatic history and the most important achievement of the American people.

The ERP met much opposition from Republicans in Congress, but Senator Arthur H. Vandenberg's skill guided the Bill through, aided significantly by the communist coup in Czechoslavakia in February of 1948 and the tragic death of Jan Masaryk. The bill was passed soon after, on April 3, 1948. The psychological effect on Europe was profound; people began to hope, plan, and rebuild even before the first aid arrived, while the assurance of continuing US assistance was a welcome booster to morale. The Marshall Plan helped Europe to recover economically and to become stabilized politically. It also marked a political watershed for the US, symbolizing American commitment to Europe, and belief in the virtues of inter-European collaboration. It also projected overseas the ideals of the New Deal and Keynesianism. The Marshall Plan constituted an irreversible defeat for the Germanophobe segment within the American bureaucracy, for men such as Henry Morgenthau as opposed to the advocates of conciliation – Henry Stimson, John J. McCloy, James V. Forrestal, and others.

The Marshall Plan has been called "the crucial margin," the "spark" that fired the engine of economic recovery. An historian of the Plan, Michael Hogan, has argued that "It facilitated essential imports, eased production bottlenecks, encouraged higher rates of capital formation and helped to suppress inflation, all of which led to gains in productivity, improvement in trade, and an era of social peace and prosperity more durable than any other in modern European history."

Robert J. Donavan in The Second Victory: The Marshall Plan and the Postwar Revival of Europe *(1987) sums up the achievements of the Marshall Plan as a "success in terms of its own fulfilled objectives: revival of European production, a higher standard of living, progress toward industrial organization and economic integration, restoration of multilateral trade, political stabilization, integration of West Germany into the European community, containment of communism and lastly peace."*

The Marshall Plan therefore was more than just a reaction to the Cold War and Soviet aggression. It was in part a product of American idealism and generosity, and in part a neo-capitalist, Keynesian effort to reform and integrate Europe's economy, promote self-help, liberalize trade, modernize agriculture and introduce American-style democracy to Europe. The Cold War led Marshall planners to organize NATO and to seek to create stronger, more united European political and economic institutions, able to contain the Soviets and to help sustain American and European economic prosperity. The plan worked well, thanks mostly to the confidence it gave Europe's leaders, as well as the resources ($13 billion – or $90 billion in today's dollars) it made available to Europeans to enable them to reconstruct their societies. This they did largely on their own aided by technology teams, but the Americans were crucial in restoring confidence, providing money, food, fuel, and machinery and in pushing Europe toward shared defense, economic integration and the Common Market. The Europeans resisted some reforms and only partially liberalized their trade with each other but not with the external world. (They also resisted total economic integration until the early 1980s.)

The Soviet Union meanwhile came to regard the Marshall Plan as a major threat. Marshall had originally been willing to include the Eastern bloc countries among the plan's beneficiaries – a risky proposal that the US Congress would have been unlikely to accept. But Stalin gratuitously relieved Marshall of possible embarrassment. As Adam Ulam puts it in a classic work, Stalin by that time had already become subject to fears and delusions that led within a year to his break with Yugoslavia, to renewed purges inside the Soviet Union, and to the persecution of Soviet Jews.[30]

To Stalin, the Marshall Plan was a dangerous challenge, not merely because it would help to stabilize Western Europe, and extend the markets for US goods, but also because it would extend US economic influence into Eastern Europe. The Czechs received orders to abstain from participation. At the same time, Moscow's anti-Western propaganda went into top gear, marked by a degree of mendacity that astonished Westerners. (The Americans, for instance, were accused of plotting to ruin the West German potato crop by spreading destructive bugs.) At the same time, the division between Eastern and Western occupation zones in Germany hardened. In October 1947, Moscow formed the Cominform (which included the communist parties of France and Italy, as well as those of the Soviet bloc).[31] In its first manifesto, the Cominform accused Britain and the US of having fought World War II for the sole purpose of wiping out German and Japanese competition on the world markets, a charge strangely advanced at the very time when the US had begun to take an active part in helping its competitors to rebuild.

Shortly afterwards, in February 1948, the Czech communists staged a coup in Prague. Eduard Benés was driven from the Czech presidency; Jan Masaryk, his most prominent minister, jumped, or was pushed, out of a window to his death. The Czech coup destroyed the hopes of those who had imagined that the Czech communists were somehow different, and that the Soviet Union might be content to tolerate within its sphere a bourgeois democracy linked to Moscow through ties of friendship, and shared fears of a revival in a revanchist Germany. In March 1948, the Soviet representatives left the Inter-Allied Control Council for Germany. On June 20, 1948, West Germany's new currency reform went into effect as a separate endeavor, independent from financial policy in East Germany. West Germany's economic recovery had begun.

Four days later, on June 24, 1948, the Soviets began their blockade of West Berlin, designed to drive the Western Allies out of their portion of what became a beleaguered city. Historians again can only guess why the Soviets should have chosen this moment. From the Kremlin's standpoint, communist

[30]Adam B. Ulam, *Expansion and Coexistence: Soviet Foreign Policy, 1917–1973*. New York, Praeger, 1974, p. 434.

[31]Alfred Grosser, *Geschichte Deutschlands seit 1945*. Munich, Deutscher Taschenbuch Verlag, 1974, p. 108.

prospects in those parts of Europe beyond their direct control had declined. The Italian and French communist parties had been excluded from the governments of their respective countries. Communist attempts to seize power through guerrilla offensives were failing. In Spain, the communists had attempted to carry out protracted partisan warfare against the Franco regime (1945–8) but to no effect.[32] Guerrilla struggles ground on in Greece; but victory eluded the communists, and the long campaign merely left a residue of hatred. To make matters worse for Moscow, Stalin failed to subdue Tito. Yugoslavia, which was formally excluded from the Cominform on July 28, 1948, became the first communist country to free itself from Muscovite hegemony.

Under these circumstances, the Kremlin required a political success. If the Soviets could coerce the West into withdrawing from West Berlin, Moscow would surely improve its standing in the world. Encouragement would come to every communist party in Europe, with this demonstration of the full extent of Soviet strength. Moscow would be able to add West Berlin's substantial industries to those of the Soviet-occupied zone, and Berlin would become a city united under Soviet hegemony. Europe would see the end of the last democratic bastion East of the Elbe. Furthermore, West Berlin's demise would eliminate a dangerous example to its neighbors, a city moreover where the hated SPD formed by far the strongest political party. West Berlin appeared an easy target; the city seemed to depend entirely on its hinterland; the Western Allies had failed to assure for themselves internationally recognized corridors linking West Germany to West Berlin, and their communication by land remained at the Soviets' mercy. Faced with a continued blockade and endless negotiations, the Americans would surely withdraw, and their Allies follow suit. The Western powers moreover faced domestic troubles. The US was in the midst of a heated election campaign. Britain and France were in serious economic difficulties. The moment seemed to have come for a dexterous exercise in blackmail.

The American commander, General Lucius Clay, and his advisers favored calling what they regarded as a Soviet bluff by armed action to break the blockade. No one can now be sure how the Soviets would have responded, at a time when the US army in West Germany was numerically insignificant, and organizationally in disarray. (Although the draft was reinstituted in June 1948, few of the newly enlisted conscripts actually went to Europe.)[33] The crisis, however, was resolved in a way that none had expected. US and British planes successfully supplied the city that the Western air forces had devastated just a few years earlier. The Berlin blockade provided the occasion both for an unparalleled display of Western airpower, and the unanticipated ability of air

[32]Enrique Lister, "Guerrilla warfare in Spain, 1939–1951," in William J. Pomeroy, ed., *Guerrilla Warfare and Marxism from Karl Marx to the Present: Armed Struggles for Liberation and for Socialism.* New York, International Publishers, 1968.
[33]Harry G. Summers, "United States armed forces: Europe," in L. H. Gann, ed., *The Defence of Western Europe.* London, Croom Helm, 1987, pp. 286–309.

transport to supply a large metropolitan community. The Soviets made no attempt to interfere with these flights. The West Berliners made do with short rations, and gave overwhelming political support to their occupiers. (During the 1948 Berlin elections, the Berlin branch of the SED called for a boycott. Nevertheless, 86.3 percent of the electors went to the polls; of these 65.5 percent voted for the SPD, 19.4 percent for the CDU, 16.1 percent for the Free Democrats.)[34] The blockade was finally lifted in May 1949.

A balance sheet on the Berlin crisis is not easy to draw up. In the days of Metternich, the problem would have been solved by a territorial exchange that would have allotted West Berlin to East Germany, in exchange for territorial compensations to West Germany in western Thuringia or western Brandenburg. Such a deal, however, had become inconceivable by 1949, at a time when West Berliners had so fully committed themselves to the Western side. The Western powers remained stuck with an indefensible enclave; they failed moreover to gain new concessions as regards future access to their "island." They had once again demonstrated their unwillingness to risk a direct military confrontation with the Soviet Union. On the other hand, the Soviet attempt to drive its former allies out of Berlin had failed. The US had become more, rather than less, willing to engage its power in Western Europe.

The Berlin blockade also went a long way to rehabilitate the German people

---

JOHN J. MCCLOY

John J. McCloy, lawyer, banker, proconsul, was widely regarded as the very embodiment of the east coast's inner circle – the "Chairman of the Board of the American Establishment" (Walter Isaacson and Evan Thomas, The Wise Men: Six Friends and the World They Made). *McCloy filled every possible slot. He was a partner in a great New York law firm, Milbank, Tweed, Hadley, and McCloy. He served as chairman of Chase Manhattan Bank and as director of various important companies. He was for a time director of the Rockefeller Foundation and then chairman of the Ford Foundation. He sat on collegiate boards of trustees. He participated in presidential advisory commissions. He held numerous prestige jobs such as the chairmanship of the Council of Foreign Relations. He raised a family; he wrote books. He also occupied many high positions in government. Yet he had been born in a drab working-class neighborhood in Philadelphia and his very career illustrated the way in which poor people could rise to the top at a time when a select establishment was said to rule supreme.*

After World War II, McCloy was President of the International Bank for Reconstruction and Development, from 1945 to 1947. Thereafter he took over as US military governor and high commissioner for Germany, 1949 to 1952, during the crucial first years of the German Federal Republic. McCloy established a close personal relationship with Adenauer. The two made a strange pair, the buoyant, athletic American, and the elderly, restrained German. Yet McCloy listened closely to Adenauer, so much so that some wags began to call the German Chancellor the "real McCloy."

---

[34]Entry for "Berlin" in *DDR Handbuch*. Köln, Verlag Wissenschaft und Politik, 1985, v. 1.

in American eyes. Berliners, with their tough, cynical humor, their capacity for hard work, and pro-Western convictions, turned into model allies. Their city ceased to be tarnished with the shame of the Third Reich; instead, West Berlin now stood as a bastion of democracy. All Germans somehow gained from Berlin's record of resistance, an advantage that Adenauer was not slow to use. Pro-German feeling in the US gained further support from millions of German-Americans, most of them naturally delighted at the political rehabilitation of their kinsfolk in Europe. Pro-German feelings were also strong among the many American servicemen who had served or continued to serve in West Germany; marriages and liaisons between GIs and German women further cemented these bonds. To use their own language, the Germans had once again become *hoffähig* (fit to be presented at court).

THE WEST CONSOLIDATES

The Berlin blockade also had the unintended effect of strengthening US military commitments to the defense of Europe. Recent works on the origins of the North Atlantic Treaty Organization (NATO) dispose of revisionist interpretations according to which NATO was somehow imposed on its European allies by a bellicose America obsessed with Cold War fantasies.[35] Considerable opposition in fact remained at the time within the US governmental machinery towards permanent European commitments. Many Americans would have been content to give no more than general support to the Brussels Treaty (signed on March 17, 1947 between Britain, France, and the Benelux countries). But on their own, the forces of the resultant "Western Union" alliance would clearly have been inadequate.

Western Union moreover placed a disproportionately heavy burden of defense on an ailing Great Britain. Bevin, in consequence, saw the Brussels Treaty and Western Union as "a sprat to catch a whale" – "a device to lure the Americans into giving Western Europe full military backing ... in much the same way as the joint West European response to the Marshall offer had procured US economic aid."[36] According to Paul-Henri Spaak, the Belgian Foreign Minister at the time, and another of NATO's architects, the new Washington treaty would become on the Atlantic scale what the Brussels Treaty, that is to say Western Union, was on the European scale.[37] Skillful

[35]Sir Nicholas Henderson, *The Birth of NATO*. Boulder, Col., Westview Press, 1983. Nicholas Sherwen, ed., *NATO's Anxious Birth: The Prophetic Visions of the 1940's*. New York, St Martin's Press, 1985. Alfred Grosser, *The Western Alliance: European-American Relations Since 1945*. New York, Continuum, 1980. Barker, *The British Between the Superpowers 1945–1950*. Donald Abenheim, *Reforging the Iron Cross: The Search for Tradition in the West German Armed Forces*. Princeton, Princeton University Press, 1988.

[36]Barker, *The British Between the Superpowers*, p. 127.

[37]Alfred Cahen, "Relaunching Western European union: implications for the Atlantic Alliance," *NATO Review*, no. 4, August 1986, pp. 6–12.

British, Canadian, and Benelux diplomacy thus played a major part in getting the US to commit herself to an Atlantic alliance.

> *NATO was founded in 1949, but had no teeth until Truman got Congress to provide $1 billion for a mutual defense assistance program. When China entered the Korean war in November of 1950, the US feared Stalin would invade Western Europe so Truman sent four more divisions to Europe in 1951 to reassure America's allies. NATO's infrastructure was then developed under General Eisenhower whom Truman had brought out of retirement. Henceforth economic aid to Europe was cut and military assistance increased.*

Once Truman had been re-elected in 1948, hesitation within the US administration ended. A number of additional hurdles were overcome. (For instance, Norway rejected a Swedish offer to join a neutral Scandinavian bloc.) The Soviets gave additional impetus by their blockade of Berlin and by crude attempts to intimidate Norway. NATO formally came into being on April 4, 1949 — a date that few students could nowadays identify. It is worth remembering, for NATO formed, and continued to form, the most successful peacetime venture in Western cooperation. We shall refer to its military aspects in another chapter. Suffice it to say here that the alliance lasted much longer, and developed into a more integrated political and military organization than its architects had anticipated. Not that NATO lacked blemishes. It shared all the weaknesses that have traditionally beset alliances: "Jealousies inevitably spring up. Disputes engender disputes. Every confederate is tempted to throw on others some part of the burden which he ought to bear himself. Scarcely one furnishes the promised contingent."[38] But such deficiencies were at least partially balanced by the fact that the NATO partners freely cooperated in a common endeavor — unlike those of the Eastern bloc consolidated through the formation of Comecon (Council for Mutual Economic Assistance, set up on June 25, 1949, and the Warsaw Pact, concluded on May 14, 1955).

> *The preamble to the North Atlantic Treaty Oganization in 1949 stated that the Atlantic community was determined "to safeguard the freedom, common heritage and civilization of their people founded on the principles of democracy, individual liberty and the rule of law." According to Raymond Aron, alliances either evolve towards communities or else dissolve altogether.*

Of all the obstacles encountered in the Cold War, the Soviets regarded NATO as the most serious. NATO's dissolution henceforth formed their primary long-term objective. As the communists saw it, NATO formed an aggressive imperialistic pact. It was aimed, in the first instance, against the socialist states, secondarily against the Asian, African, and Latin countries engaged in the struggle to defend their independence, thirdly against the

[38]Thomas Babington Macaulay, *The History of England From the Accession of James II*. Chicago, Belford, Clarke, 1867, v. 4, p. 123.

national liberation movements in the colonial countries and, last but not least, against the democratic forces within the NATO member states themselves.[39]

In fact NATO was a purely defensive alliance to protect Central Europe and was not able or willing to project its power anywhere else. (Initially, the Allies had planned for a withdrawal behind the Rhine; once the West Germans were admitted, NATO switched to "forward defense" that would avoid surrendering the bulk of the Federal Republic to the invaders.) NATO was also defensive in the purely political sense. It lacked a propaganda or political warfare branch, and was not framed to exploit what Lenin would have called "internal contradictions." There were many of these within the Soviet empire – the contradictions between the needs of rigid central planning and growing consumer demands, between the hegemonial power of the Soviet Union and the dependent communist regimes, between the ethnic groups within the Soviet Union, between the regnant Marxist-Leninist philosophy and popular religious beliefs. NATO policy makers did not try to embarrass the Soviet Union politically, say, by calling for the independence of the Baltic republics, former sovereign states and members of the League of Nations, but now absorbed by the Soviet Union. They were content with "containment." Even containment came under fire, as George F. Kennan, the man who first coined the phrase, spent much of his subsequent career criticizing his brainchild as being too militaristic in its implementation, when he had called for the political containment of communism. From the political warfare perspective, Western policy remained reactive. The troubles experienced by the Soviet Union within its own sphere remained uncovenanted benefits, apples that dropped from a tree which NATO policy makers proved reluctant to shake.

GEORGE CATLETT MARSHALL (1880–1959)

A group of distinguished people comprising a British editor, a cabinet member, and a historian, as well as an American diplomat, and a foreign correspondent, once met in a London club to discuss who were the truly great men of the twentieth century. The chosen had to be great in strength of character, foresight, achievement, and nobility of purpose. The five agreed only on two names: Winston Churchill and George Marshall.

Their choice of Marshall is not hard to justify. His achievements need no boosting. He served as the US Army's chief of staff, 1939 to 1945, during the most critical period of US military history. Right from the start, he determined to build – not an elite force of the kind advocated by armored warfare enthusiasts, and by influential journalists such as Walter Lippmann – but an army of continental size that would defeat the Wehrmacht in the field. He built up an army from a small force, inferior at the outbreak of World War II to Belgium's or Bulgaria's. He expanded the army at an incredible pace – at a time when the US faced two of the finest fighting forces in history, those of the Third Reich, and those of imperial Japan. He was the organizer of victory, as Carnot had been in revolutionary France. Later on, as secretary of state (1945–7), he made his mark on

---

[39] *Militärlexikon*. East Berlin, Militärverlag der Deutschen Demokratischen Republik, 1985, pp. 110–11.

global diplomacy. He gave his name to the Marshall Plan that played a decisive part in the reconstruction of Europe. His was a quietly powerful personality. (He thought that his own greatest contribution to victory consisted in standing up to Churchill's egocentric genius.)

Like de Gaulle, Marshall was also a general with a social conscience. Some of his critics indeed used to call him a New Deal general. This was hardly fair because Marshall was the very opposite of a political soldier. But, as Eric Larrabee puts it in Commander in Chief: Franklin Delano Roosevelt, His Lieutenants and Their War, *New York, Harper and Row, 1987, Marshall had a better understanding than most military men of the conditions with which Roosevelt was trying to cope on assuming the presidency. When Marshall was posted to Chicago in 1936 as senior instructor in the Illinois national guard, the city was in the throes of the depression. Marshall was one of the few officers who threw himself into the task of running the civilian conservation corps to get jobless young men out of the cities into the countryside, to work on conservation and reforestation. Marshall called this "the most instructive service I have ever had, and the most interesting." The lesson stuck with him all his life. It is not surprising that Marshall became the only general ever to receive the Nobel Peace Prize. None was a worthier laureate.*

The formation of NATO nevertheless represented a turning point in the history of the US, and of the North Atlantic powers as a whole. For the first time in its history, the US had engaged in a permanent alliance linking it to Western Europe in both a military and a political sense. Opposition to NATO continued, from old-style isolationists, pacifists, the pro-Communist left, and later on from the new right.[40] But NATO's foundations were solidly laid. President Truman, at a critical time, found himself well served by a team of loyal civilian advisers (Acheson, Bohlen, Harriman, Kennan, Lovett, McCloy), men who had gone to expensive prep schools, to prestigious eastern universities, who believed in public service, and who felt convinced that America had a duty to serve the world.[41] Equally important was the new group of soldier-statesmen and soldier-viceroys – especially generals MacArthur, Marshall, Lucius Clay (military governor in Germany 1947–9), and on the British side, Sir Gerald Templer (first director of civil affairs and military government in the British zone). Clay and Templer between them can rightly claim to be counted among the unacknowledged founding fathers of the German Federal Republic.[42]

The success attained by American policy makers went beyond merely personal factors – the statesmanship shown by Truman and his advisers, and the solidity evinced by the so-called eastern establishment – they drew on a mood of profound national confidence, at the time when a victorious US dominated

[40]For the latter, see for instance Melvyn Krauss, *How NATO Weakens the West.* New York, Simon and Schuster, 1986.

[41]Walter Isaacson and Evan Thomas, *The Wise Men: Six Friends and the World They Made: Acheson, Bohlen, Harriman, Kennan, Lovett, McCloy.* New York, Simon and Schuster, 1986. David Mayers, *George Kennan and the Dilemmas of US Foreign Policy.* Oxford, Oxford University Press, 1986.

[42]See, for instance, John H. Backer, *Winds of History: The German Years of Lucius DuBignon Clay.* New York, Van Nostrand Reinhold, 1983. John Cloake, *Templer: Tiger of Malaya.* London, Harrap, 1984.

the world militarily, politically and economically. On the European side, there was also widespread commitment, especially among veterans and college-educated youth, the very group most widely inclined to criticize NATO a generation later. To those who had experienced war and its aftermath, the creation of trans-national institutions represented a challenge, to many especially welcome in contrast to traditional chauvinist slogans.

> *After the North Atlantic Treaty was signed (1949) the British held a conference in London in 1950 which laid out the basic policy objectives for Great Britain: the need to sustain the country's position as a great power, albeit of the second rank; the higher direction of the Cold War; the necessity to develop and extend Atlantic rather than European institutions of cooperation between Western states; and the transformation of the "special relationship" into a more effective partnership with the US. (See "The London conference: Anglo-American relations and the Cold War," Strategy, January–June 1950, series II, vol. II, 1987.)*

NATO had other unintended consequences. Notably, the "special relationship" between Britain and the US declined. It had depended on the success of the wartime alliance, on Churchill's personal prestige, on the skill displayed by British diplomacy in creating for a time the illusion of Britain's enduring great power status after World War II. The relationship was sustained also by ties of personal friendship. (For example, Bevin and Marshall, an incongruous pair, got on extremely well together.) In a profounder sense, it was supported by a common cultural heritage that linked many British and US diplomats, senior civil servants, and some establishment politicians. A number of highly placed Americans had studied at Oxford – Senator J. William Fullbright, for example, had attended Pembroke College as a Rhodes Scholar. (In fact, Oxford University had earlier created its own version of the Ph.D., known in Oxford as the D.Phil., specifically to meet the needs of American postgraduates.) A good many Britons, for their part, had trans-Atlantic family connections and felt at home in the US.[43] These ties did not disappear. But within the framework of NATO's high command, Britain counted for less than she had done during World War II in SHAEF (Supreme Headquarters, Allied Expeditionary Forces). By the beginning of the 1950s, there was an end to serious discussions concerning an English-speaking union that would comprise the US, Britain, and the "white" British dominions. By contrast, NATO was a political boon to West Germany and Italy. For both of them, membership in NATO and other trans-national bodies meant a new acceptance abroad, and a new political legitimacy.

[43]Ritchie Ovendale, *The English-Speaking Alliance: Britain, the United States, the Dominions, and the Cold War 1945–1951.* London, Allen and Unwin, 1985, pp. 282–3.

THE SHAKY BALANCE

The communists responded with a series of vigorous counter-offensives that blended diplomacy, propaganda, and disinformation in the accustomed fashion. The Soviets detonated their first atomic bomb (announced August 29, 1949), thereby breaking the US nuclear monopoly much more quickly than American experts had anticipated. At the same time, Cominform called for massive efforts from its associate parties to strive against Western rearmament, and to strengthen the communist position in Western trade unions, youth organizations, women's leagues, and other bodies. Yet, the communists' political effort in Western Europe did not fare well. Communist strategists had assumed that a series of economic crises and strikes would make Western Europe increasingly vulnerable politically. Instead these economies expanded at startling speed, so that the Western communist parties increasingly found themselves mere bystanders in a drama that failed to conform to the Marxist-Leninist script.

> *The Soviets built up and equipped the North Korean military and supported, if not directed, the North's "unprovoked act of aggression" in attacking South Korea. The US and the UN stopped communist expansionism and allowed the democratic modernizing South Korea to develop. (See Max Hastings,* The Korean War, *New York, Simon and Schuster, 1987).*

Above all the communists failed in their primary endeavor – to prevent West Germany's integration into NATO. West German rearmament at first proceeded slowly. The process began in May 1950, when Adenauer created the *Zentrale für Heimatdienst* as a secret think tank to study rearmament. (In a strictly legal sense, the Allies could still have punished its members with life imprisonment for engaging in clandestine military preparations.) In the same month, however, North Korean forces invaded South Korea. The US suddenly found itself involved in a major war, and became an ardent advocate of German rearmament.

Truman finally opted for a wider strategy in 1950, after reading a National Security Council Report (NSC-68) about a Soviet atomic weapon explosion in September 1949. This, coupled with Mao's victory in China, led to a new global strategy for the US. The Soviets were seen to have become more than a political menace, for atomic weapons made them a military threat, having the power to conquer the world by piecemeal aggression. The "domino theory" was developed, requiring the US to resist all communist adventures. When the North Koreans attacked in 1950, the US rallied the United Nations to oppose this aggression. NATO's military wing was organized and armed; General Eisenhower became the supreme commander in Europe. Stalin died on March 26, 1953; two days later the North Koreans agreed to the Neutral Nations Repatriation Commission. Stalin's death, war weariness and the threat of US nuclear weapons brought the Chinese and the Russians to Panmunjom, as Max Hastings shows in *The Korean War* (1987). Another scholar of that war, Callum MacDonald, claims in *The War Before Vietnam* (1988), that the US made a great mistake in using the UN to defend Korea, because this harmed that body's role as a peacekeeping force. We would argue quite the contrary; it exposed communist bloc expansionism, showed the resolve and effectiveness of resisting aggression by collective action, and thereby strengthened the hand of world peace through the UN, rather than through national alliances.

To counter West Germany's addition to Western power, Stalin had replied in what appears, at first sight, an ambivalent fashion. The Soviets strengthened the communist regime in their own zone by creating the *Kasernierte Volkspolizei*, an armed force composed of regulars (later the nucleus of the *Nationale Volksarmee*, the East German Army). They also tightened control over the captive "bourgeois" parties within their zone, the *National-Demokratische Partei Deutschlands* (specially designed to appeal to former Nazis), the *Liberal-Demokratische Partei Deutschlands*, and the *Christliche-Demokratische Union Deutschlands*, all of which were linked to the SED in an unequal alliance. In apparent contradiction to this policy, Stalin made a new offer to the Western powers in 1952. Moscow abandoned its insistence on the disarmament of Germany, and proposed that Germany be reunified, that Germany be allowed to have its own defense forces, but commit itself to permanent neutrality.

According to Adenauer's critics, Germany lost a unique chance by failing to accept this offer.[44] Adenauer's reply was indeed uncompromising. He rejected neutralization; he refused to negotiate on the basis of the Oder–Neisse line; he demanded "reunification in freedom." But even if Adenauer had followed a more conciliatory course, the neutralization of Germany on the Soviet pattern could not have worked. Germany could not have turned into a super-Sweden or a super-Switzerland. "Unification in freedom" would have required the dismantling of the communist apparatus in East Germany. Stalin could not have made such a sacrifice. Its impact on the other Soviet satellites would have been incalculable. Such a settlement moreover would have contradicted the essentials of "peaceful coexistence" as expounded by communist theoreticians. As Erich Honecker later put it (at the Ninth Party Congress of the SED) "peaceful coexistence signifies neither the preservation of the socioeconomic status quo nor ideological coexistence." On the contrary, "peaceful coexistence" can only operate between different nation states and must facilitate the "revolutionary world process."[45] There can thus be no "peaceful coexistence" between the competing social systems of communism and capitalism, and Stalin's offer was a non-starter.

In a purely technical sense the East–West exchanges hinged on the precise timetable for the proposed German elections. The Western powers insisted

---

[44]See for instance, Klaus Erdmenger, *Das Folgenschwere Missverständnis: Bonn und die Sowjetische Deutschlands-Politik, 1949–1955*. Freiburg im Breisgau, Rombach, 1964. Joseph Forschepth, ed., *Kalter Krieg und Deutsche Frage: Deutschland im Wiederstreit der Mächte 1945–1952*. Vandenhoek und Ruprecht, 1985. Peter Calvorcessi, *Survey of International Affairs 1952*. Oxford, Oxford University Press, 1955, pp. 56–7, pp. 88–90, pp. 109–12.

[45]Cited in entry for "Friedliche Koexistenz," in *DDR Handbuch*, v. 1.

that these must be held throughout Germany before the country's future was decided. But genuinely free elections in East Germany would have reduced the SED to a powerless minority. Its unpopularity was extreme. Hundreds of thousands of East Germans were "voting with their feet" to seek refuge in West Germany; to counter this movement, East Germany from 1950 onward enforced a series of laws that made *Republikflucht* (flight from the republic) into a criminal offense – this at a time when East German propaganda was emphasizing the merits of reunification.[46] All in all, East Germany lost about 3,000,000 through a migration that only ended when the zonal boundary was finally secured by barbed-wire entanglements, mine-fields, and *Schiessbefehl* (the order to fire at would-be defectors). More seriously still, widespread rioting broke out in East Germany in 1953, requiring Soviet intervention. The SED's regime rested, and would continue to rest, on Soviet bayonets.

The Soviets thus insisted that the electoral timetable be reversed, and also that West German voters be free to vote in conditions that would prevent "pressure on the voters on the part of the great monopolies." Both East and West German representatives should participate in the requisite negotiations; the East German and the West German governments should enjoy equal status. The Soviets stuck to these conditions, even though East Germany comprised only a minority of Germany's population, and the SED embraced only a small minority of East Germans. Soviet strategy in this respect paralleled the Soviet approach to the creation of the SED in East Germany in 1946. The enforced fusion between the *Kommunistische Partei Deutschlands* (*KPD*) and the SPD in East Germany had likewise been effected on the basis of equality between the two parties, though the KPD commanded an infinitely smaller following than the SPD. The unequal fusion had resulted in the annihilation of the SPD, and straightforward communist dictatorship. An all-German state founded on similar principles, with the East German power structure left intact, would have been equally unworkable. Not surprisingly, Stalin's offer failed. Two years later, in October 1954, the Federal German Republic formally joined the Western Union, and NATO, and in 1955 opened official diplomatic relations with the USSR.

After Stalin died the Soviet Union experienced a brief "thaw" that culminated in Khrushchev's denunciation of the Stalin regime in 1956. The Cominform was dissolved (1956) as the Kremlin prepared for a Soviet–Yugoslav *rapprochement*. The Soviet Union and the Western Allies concluded the Austrian "State Treaty" (1955). As we have previously pointed out, this instrument assured Austria's permanent neutrality, and benefited both partners. The West gained by ensuring for Austria a democratic regime. The Warsaw Pact profited by driving a neutral wedge between the northern and southern segments of NATO. There was a brief lull in the Cold War, soon broken by the Soviet repression of the Hungarian rising (1956), and by their new use of "atomic diplomacy" against Britain and France during the Suez crisis. (In 1956

---

[46]For details of the legislation see entry for *Republikflucht,* in *DDR Handbuch.* Köln, Verlag Wissenschaft und Politik, 1985, v. 2.

Britain and France cooperated with Israel in an attempt to seize the Suez canal, a venture that failed when the US sided with the Arabs and the Soviet Union against their Western allies.)

Few American secretaries of state have aroused as much controversy as John Foster Dulles (US secretary of state 1953–9). Sir Alexander Cadogan, a veteran British diplomat, called him "the woolliest type of pontificating American." Sir Anthony Eden described him as "tortuous as a wounded snake, with much less excuse." But Konrad Adenauer looked to Dulles as a personal friend and statesman. The difference in these judgements was not coincidental. Dulles and Adenauer had been trained in law. Both were convinced that the Soviet Union presented an ideological as well as a political danger to the West, that the Federal German Republic should be firmly aligned with the West, that a neutralized Germany would ultimately fall under Soviet influence. For Dulles, the West Germans were repentant democrats.

But Dulles did not feel at ease with British Tories. A Princetonian by education, a Presbyterian by religion, a Wilsonian liberal in politics, Dulles stood for a moralistic and legalistic approach that widely characterized American diplomacy in general. It did not go down well with the British. Eden and his colleagues believed that Dulles had misled them in the Suez crisis, and then turned against them – all with that peculiar blend of sanctimoniousness and hypocrisy once commonly ascribed by high Anglican Tories both to British nonconformist Protestants and Yankees. (As Disraeli had gibed at Gladstone, "I don't mind that the Honorable gentleman always pulls an ace from his sleeve. I do object when he insists that the Almighty had put it there.")

The British did not understand Dulles's intense anti-colonial commitment, one shared by Eisenhower and much of the US at large. As Dulles saw it, the British had colluded secretly with France and Israel in attacking Egypt. In so doing they had reverted to their evil ways of imperial pride and clandestine diplomacy. The British move had come at the very moment (in 1956) when the Hungarians were in revolt against their colonial masters, the Soviets. Dulles's anti-colonial rhetoric was bitterly resented, not only by British Tories, but also by many Labourites still proud of Britain's imperial record. For a time, the NATO alliance was shaken; the "special relationship" between the US and Great Britain never quite recovered; the Americans' previous trust in the UN diminished. But the Suez crisis had the unanticipated result of speeding Franco-German rapprochement.

Dulles might engage in fanciful rhetoric concerning a "roll back" of Soviet power, but in fact he took no action over Hungary; the US lacked the resources to do anything effective. Dulles would not even consider the possibility of recognizing a Hungarian "government in exile," that might have incommoded the Soviet Union in a diplomatic sense. It was rather British power that was "rolled back"; the British retreat in turn created new opportunities for the Soviet Union in the Middle East.

Dulles had at first believed in accommodation with the Soviet Union, but by 1952 he feared a dynamic Soviet communism and felt containment was too passive a policy to combat their militarism. He saw the need to win more cooperation from the Europeans and to organize regional pacts to restrain the Soviets but soon recognized that the US had limited resources to sustain global hegemony. He developed with President Eisenhower and the National Security Council a new grand strategy of massive retaliation to aggression. (Later

Dulles was to give up all desire for such retaliation after being told by Gerald Smith of the vast number of casualities nuclear weapons could inflict.)

NATO was pressured to assume more burdens. Although the US took on more and more foreign responsibilities, Eisenhower cut the military budget for conventional arms and decided to depend for deterrence on nuclear weapons. In this the US yielded to pressure from its NATO allies, who did not want to spend large sums on conventional weaponry instead of on welfare programs. The North Atlantic Council met in Boston in 1952. Although it called for the build-up of conventional forces, it was obliged to recognize that these forces could not be paid for and chose to rely on the US nuclear deterrent to supplement the expanding NATO land forces.

Dulles and his brother, Allen, who headed the CIA, expanded covert operations and intervention in Europe, Asia and Latin America. These covert operations hurt American integrity and prestige and entailed a high-risk policy. Overall Dulles had some successes and some failures as secretary of state. He kept the US out of Indochina. He was sensitive to Third World anti-colonialism and supported self-determination and nationalism everywhere. But as secretary of state he had too much to do and lacked the time, stamina and experience to arrive at more than a shallow analysis of many global problems. Still, it must be recognized that the US, in its new global, interventionist stance, faced numerous crises, most of which it solved. NATO-like regional pacts (begun by Acheson in 1951 with ANZUS to protect the Pacific Basin), as well as CENTRO (Central Treaty Organization with Turkey, Iran and Pakistan, 1959) and SEATO (South East Asian Treaty Organization, 1957). But when the US failed to counter the Soviet suppression of Hungary in 1956, Dulles's policy lost much credibility.

The world had become far too complicated for one man to master all its problems. Dulles was best in Europe, weakest in Latin America, and strong on the Middle East, except in moments of crisis. (At a conference on Dulles held at the Woodrow Wilson Center, Princeton University in 1988, many scholars felt that in spite of his flaws, Dulles was the smartest, most experienced, and sophisticated secretary of state of the twentieth century. He knew more about international affairs, law and the art of negotiation than anyone else in or out of government, according to Ambassador George Kennan – a strong statement coming from a man unjustly fired by Dulles. The Princeton conference also revealed Dulles as a close observer of people who consulted experts systematically and read avidly. He became the most traveled secretary – and the first to have traveled in jet aircraft – up to that time.) Dulles and Eisenhower worked well together, and most policies were hammered out jointly. But there was never any doubt that the president was in charge and that the policies were his, though he shared the making of them with Dulles. When Dulles died, Eisenhower said it was the saddest day of his life.

The Soviets after Suez vigorously continued their "peace" diplomacy, aimed at Western disarmament, a task in which they greatly benefited from Western "peace" groups. As Adam Ulam put it, in these disarmament talks "all the advantages belonged to the Soviet side, at least outwardly. The USSR could speak publicly with one voice... It could improvise the most far-reaching proposals and then reap the propaganda harvest of a rejection or an 'if' and 'but' by the West..." while there would always be Westerners willing to seize on the Soviet proposals, and then reproach their own governments for not taking the golden opportunity for banishing the nuclear nightmare forever.[47] Overall, Soviet Cold War strategists displayed a new sense of optimism, as Khrushchev genuinely believed that their economy would, in the foreseeable future, equal and then overtake the economy of the US. The Soviet Union developed its nuclear potential, and impressed the world by launching *Sputnik* (1957), a major victory both for its arms industry and for Soviet propaganda. Claims for the alleged superiority of their economic system found wide acceptance in Western universities, whereas sceptics such as economist Warren Nutter, experienced much difficulty in finding a publisher for their critiques of the Soviets' economic performance.

In addition, Soviet policy makers showed a new adaptability in their dealings with the Afro-Asian world. The Bandung Conference (1955) helped to persuade Moscow that the newly independent states of the Third World merited more diplomatic courtship than they had hitherto received. The "bourgeois" leaders in charge of the new countries could no longer simply be written off as "imperialist lackeys." A man such as Gandhi could no longer be described as an apostle of reaction. In 1956 the CPSU conceded that national independence in Africa might be won under African bourgeois leadership. The Soviets welcomed the independence of Ghana (1957), and may even have been surprised by the speed of decolonization in the rest of sub-Saharan Africa. The new countries rapidly increased their voting strength in the UN, and the Soviet Union found new allies in the General Assembly over issues concerned with Western imperialism and its sundry misdeeds, committed or alleged.

Soviet theoreticians at the same time elaborated on the doctrine of "neo-colonialism." Though granting nominal independence to their former colonies, Western financial magnates, according to this interpretation, continued to maintain the domination of alien capital in the new states, and thereby impeded their prosperity and independence. The Soviet Union determined to break the remaining links between the Western states and their former colonies, and to expand Moscow's own influence by means of friendship treaties, scholarships, economic aid, propaganda, disinformation, and support for guerrillas operating against the remaining Western bastions in Africa. The Soviet Union began its African involvement with the same exaggerated optimism that characterized contemporary attitudes in the United States.[48] The Cold War henceforth extended into the new and fragile states of Africa, many of them run by "ramshackle regimes of highly personal rule ... severely deficient in institutional authority and organisational capability," dependent on the

---

[47]Ulam, *Expansion and Coexistence*, p. 612.

[48]L. H. Gann, "The Soviet Union and sub-Saharan Africa," in Dennis L. Bark, ed., *The Red Orchestra: The Case of Africa*. Stanford, Hoover Institution Press, c. 1988.

international community for the recognition of their unstable sovereignties.[49]

At the same time, the Soviet Union renewed its diplomatic assault in Europe. In 1957 Nikolai Bulganin, the Soviet foreign minister, endorsed the Rapacki Plan, a proposal initiated by Polish foreign minister Adam Rapacki. The plan called for a "nuclear free" zone in central Europe. In 1958, Bulganin followed this suggestion by proposing an end to nuclear tests, the outlawing of nuclear weapons, and the acceptance of the Rapacki Plan. Eisenhower refused the Soviet proposal. He insisted that it omitted all essentials – particularly a means for inspecting nuclear stock piles, and for verifying their actual elimination in future. According to former Secretary of State Acheson, the plan was a trick to eliminate the American presence from Europe while leaving the Soviets free to interfere with a divided Germany.

The alliance's difficulties increased by reason of divided counsel within the West, especially during the temporary despondency engendered by the Suez venture and the Soviets' success in launching *Sputnik*. Particularly serious was George Kennan's apparent change of heart. Kennan could not be written off as a fellow-traveler or one of Lenin's "useful idiots." He had been one of the architects of containment, NATO, and the Marshall Plan. His career in the US foreign service had culminated in his appointment as US ambassador to the Soviet Union (1952–3), and he had later made his name in the academic world, including Princeton and Oxford. Kennan opposed West German rearmament; and later abandoned his original theory of containment. According to him, the US should explore the possibility of withdrawing its troops from Central Europe. He objected to NATO's employment of tactical nuclear weapons, and also attacked its conventional force posture. As Kennan saw it, NATO's conventional defenses were designed to meet only the least likely of all possible perils – an outright Soviet attack. The real danger from the Soviet Union was political rather than military, and the best defense against this threat was to set up paramilitary units designed to fight civil resistance movements. Kennan's views were influential; he derived support from men such as Erich Ollenhauer, the German Social Democratic leader, from numerous Labour politicians in Britain, and from academics all over the Western world.

Acheson and others, however, launched a vigorous counter-attack in a debate that continued to be of immediate relevance for many years to come.[50] The US would have to maintain both strong conventional and nuclear forces according to Acheson. Basic agreements requiring mutual trust could hardly be concluded until a further process of evolution had taken place within the Soviet Union. If the US were to withdraw its forces from Western Europe, the

---

[49]Robert H. Jackson and Carl G. Rosberg, "Sovereignty and underdevelopment: juridical statehood in the African crisis," *The Journal of Modern African Studies.* March 1986, v. 24, no. 1, p. 1. For Soviet doctrinal changes, see, for instance, L. H. Gann and Peter Duignan, *Burden of Empire: An Appraisal of Western Colonialism in Africa South of the Sahara.* Stanford, Hoover Institution, 1977, pp. 55–71; 103–32.

[50]Douglas Brinkley, "Kennan–Acheson: the disengagement debate," *The Atlantic Community Quarterly*, Winter 1987–8, pp. 413–25. George Kennan, *Russia, The Atom, and the West.* New York, Harper, 1958.

Soviets would be left with an overwhelming preponderance. More specifically, Acheson said, Kennan had failed to grasp the realities of power. The Soviets would not necessarily have to invade Western Europe; their purposes could be accomplished by intimidation – with the lesson of Hungary ever-present. Acheson rejected Kennan's personal assurance that there was no threat of a Soviet military invasion of Western Europe. Such a guarantee could only rest on "divine revelation," for Kennan could provide no evidence to support his case.

> *World War II had shown the need to coordinate closely foreign policy and military policy and led after the war to the formation of the national security council, the Central Intelligence Agency, and the joint chiefs of staffs to shape and coordinate US foreign policy during the Cold War. Truman originated agency cooperation and Eisenhower elaborated on it, but there was basically continuity in policies under both presidents. Although he consulted with Dulles and others Eisenhower was squarely at the center of the national security program. Both Truman and Eisenhower wished to control and to limit nuclear weaponry. But Eisenhower as a military man was prepared to use "nukes" as a weapon of military strategy; the air force chose 1,000 Soviet targets for destruction by about 3,500 weapons.*
>
> *By 1959 even Eisenhower was appalled at this world-wide planned destruction and the rapid growth of nuclear weapons. Yet he agreed to the "Single Integrated Operational Plan," by which the air force sought to enable strikes at all Soviet missile sites, command and control bases and important urban complexes. Overkill had been achieved! While "Ike" created US national security policy in the 1950s, he did not spell out national interests or relate US military power to national resources and diplomatic goals. This may have led to major problems for the US in the Middle East and Vietnam according to scholars writing in* The National Security: Its Theory and Practices, 1945– 1960, *(1986)*.

The Kennan–Acheson debate brought the word "disengagement" into public use. The debate also raised fundamental issues that remain disputed to this day. We ourselves reluctantly side with Acheson. Indeed Acheson might have strengthened his case by placing additional emphasis on two particular points: the "closed" nature of the Soviet system, and the Soviets' interpretation of peaceful coexistence. Western archives remained open – Soviet archives were closed. Westerners debated openly; Soviet scholars and statesmen toed the party line. Above all, the Soviet Union as a state remained the 'secular arm' of the CPSU; and the CPSU in turn stayed committed to the international class struggle, a conflict that could end only with the global victory of socialism. This essential argument, Kennan and his followers failed to understand. All too many of them preferred to stick to the illusion, succinctly expressed in a 1944 issue of the *New York Times*, and repeated innumerable times, that "Marxian thinking in the Soviet Union is out."[51]

The NATO connection was later subjected to many other critiques. Out-

[51]Richard A. Melanson and David Mayers, eds, *Reevaluating Eisenhower, American Foreign Policy in the Fifties*. Urbanna, University of Illinois Press, 1987.

standing among these is a work by historian Paul Kennedy, *The Rise and Fall of the Great Powers: Economic Change and Military Conflict from 1500 to 2000*. This purports to be more than a work of history; the past, Kennedy says, contains lessons for the present. According to Kennedy, the US commitment to NATO and other alliances all over the world made some sense just after World War II, when the US was indisputably the world's first economic power. But afterwards, as other countries recovered, the relative position of the US necessarily diminished, and the Americans should have cut their cloth accordingly. Instead they stuck to, and indeed enlarged their foreign commitments, thereby repeating the mistake made by many great powers before. By overextending their obligations the Americans contributed to their own economic decline – as Spain had done under the Habsburgs, and France under the Bourbons. Kennedy and like-minded policy makers therefore called for a new foreign policy that would accept the fact of relative decline, and permit the erosion of the US position in the world to proceed smoothly, without engendering crises at home or abroad.[52]

We remain unconvinced by these arguments. We see no moral or political equivalence between the US and the USSR, Kennedy's strictures notwithstanding. Nor do we regard the NATO alliance as the equivalent of an American empire. The European members of NATO are US allies by choice, not by coercion. Unlike the dependencies of *bona fide* empires – Melos in the ancient Athenian League, Hungary in the Soviet empire – the Western European members of NATO are free to withdraw from the alliance should they so desire, as indeed France did. Kennedy also oversimplified the relation between arms expenditure and economic development. This is an error of ancient standing. During the 1930s, leftists had widely assumed that global capitalism was in a state of crisis. How could capitalism escape from its contradictions? Only by pushing rearmament! Fifty years later, the argument was reversed. Global capitalism was in a state of crisis. How could it escape from its contradictions? Only by cutting down on arms expenditure! In fact there is no necessary link between low arms expenditure and a high rate of economic development on the one hand, or high arms expenditure and a low economic growth rate on the other. For example, Spain, after World War II, had one of the lowest rates of military spending and one of the lowest economic growth rates in Europe. By contrast, the US, between 1948 and 1973, experienced a higher rate of economic development than during the following 15 years. Yet in those 25 years of prosperity the rate of defense expenditure was substantially higher. This is not to say that any country can forever spend limitless sums on armaments. (British arms expenditure in World War II certainly reached the point of overstretch.) But the US position was, and remains, quite different. NATO therefore seems to us to have been one of the

[52]Paul Kennedy, *The Rise and Fall of the Great Powers: Economic Change and Military Conflict from 1500 to 2000*. New York, Random House, 1987, p. 371. For an excellent discussion of the Kennedy book, see for instance, Owen Harries, "The rise of American decline," *Commentary*, v. 85, May 1988, p. 32–6.

soundest political and military investments ever made; albeit that in today's world Kennan and Kennedy may be right and the US should now lessen its military commitments in Europe.

6

Western European Association and the Atlantic Community

The dream of a United States of Europe is an ancient one. In the Middle Ages, the Catholic Church had provided for Europe a common religious and spiritual framework; a scholar knowledgeable in Latin and philosophy found himself equally at home in universities as different as Paris, Padua, and Salamanca. The Reformation shattered Europe's religious unity; the emergent nation states fought for supremacy; Napoleon's France and Hitler's Germany strove to unify Europe by armed force. But neither wholly discredited schemes for a European federation. The interwar period was particularly fertile in such projects. (The most serious of them derived from Aristide Briand, a former French prime minister.)[1]

All these schemes, whether authored by statesmen or crackpots, contained flaws. Before World War II, the pan-European idea lacked mass support. Misconceptions concerning other nationalities remained rife at a time when foreign travel in peacetime largely remained a privilege of the wealthy – a state of affairs that only really began to change in the early 1950s. National symbolisms remained tightly defined. (No bandmaster in the British Army would have imagined during the 1940s that his men would ever play *La Sambre-et-Meuse* or *Preussens Gloria* as part of their routine, whereas 40 years later these tunes had become an accepted part of the repertoire for a British regiment.)

As regards attitudes towards specific countries, Anglophilia on the Continent was most widespread among upper-class folk who widely identified England with jockeys, butlers, nannies, governesses, bootmakers, and tailors. Fashionable ladies and progressive intellectuals, by contrast, were more likely to look to Paris, until its position as the world's fashion and intellectual capital was

[1]Carl H. Pegg, *Evolution of the European Idea, 1914–1932*. Chapel Hill, University of North Carolina Press, 1983. René Albrecht-Carrié, *One Europe: The Historical Background of European Unity*. Garden City, NY, Doubleday, 1965. Raymond Poidevin, ed., *Origins of The European Integration, March 1948–May 1950*, Brussels, E. Bruylant, 1986. Sergio Pistone, "The posthumous writings of Walter Lipgens on the history of European unification," *Federalist*, v. xxx, no. 2, 1988, pp. 85–100. Roger Morgan and Carolyne Bray, eds, *Partners and Rivals in Western Europe: Britain, France and Germany*. Aldershot, Gower, 1986.

challenged by Weimar Berlin. Germany had traditionally aroused respect from academics, technicians, youth movement enthusiasts, and – during the era of the Third Reich – from racists of every kind. After the war, European attitudes toward Germany remained ambivalent; memories of German rule and concentration camps died hard; at the same time Germany still enjoyed acclaim as the land of efficiency. Pro-Americanism was most widespread among scientists and technocrats, and among the friends and relatives of emigrants who had settled beyond the Atlantic. Of the major Western European countries, Britain was perhaps the most isolationist of all, a country where the Continent was widely (though not of course universally) associated with political reaction.

Pan-European projects had another failing. Their objectives diverged – to defend the values of conservative elites or to hasten progress, to expand free trade or to set up restrictive cartels; to promote German hegemony in Europe or to prevent German predominance; to make Europe self-sufficient in defense or to depend on the US; to preach Christianity or to spread the culture of nudists, vegetarians, and cold-shower enthusiasts. Many pan-Europeanists feared the Soviet Union above all. Others derided the United States, the famed land of vacuum cleaners, jazz bands, conveyor belts, sky scrapers, and soulless efficiency. (Few European – or indeed American – intellectuals understood the depth of American religiosity, or the central place of the hard-luck story in American political culture and folklore.)

In addition to federalist designs, there were more successful attempts at trans-national cooperation on functional lines. From the second part of the nineteenth century, European states had signed an ever-increasing number of pacts for cooperation with regard to railways, canals, tariffs, river transport, and similar services. A network of great banking and industrial enterprises extended over Europe. After World War I, the League of Nations created a variety of useful technical bodies, though none was as distinguished and comprehensive as the International Postal Union (established 1875).

In 1945 the victors created the UNO (United Nations Organization). The UN had its seat in New York, and derived much of its inspiration from the US in its new-found internationalist mood. The US became the mainstay and the principal financial resource of the UN. It used the UN for diplomatic purposes, during the successive crises that erupted over Palestine, Korea, and the Suez. The US played a major part in committing the UN – at least in theory – to the cause of human rights. It largely paid for the UN's relief and rehabilitation work, and helped in setting up bodies such as the International Atomic Energy Commission. The UN, however, disappointed its makers. It proved only slightly more effective than the League of Nations in maintaining peace; while its subordinate bodies far exceeded the League's in number, expense, and ineffectiveness.

The US also turned into a powerful protagonist for the cause of a united Europe. On the face of it, there seemed no obvious advantage for the US in setting up a rival that one day might exceed it in terms both of population and economic strength. But the Americans were convinced that their own federal experiment could stand as an example for Europe, and that a united

Europe would serve world peace better than a congerie of quarreling states. Initially the Americans were reluctant to commit themselves permanently in Western Europe. It took Truman's and Marshall's visions as well as British pressure to secure a lasting US involvement in Western Europe. But from 1947 onward, the US became the principal lobbyist in the cause of European unity. It was the Americans' new "Cold War internationalism" that created the Marshall Plan and the Truman doctrine. America helped promote a united Europe, though the new Europe failed to correspond fully to American ideas.

EARLY ATTEMPTS

The movement toward a united Europe only began to gain momentum in World War II. The majority of European states for a time lost their independence, except for Britain, Sweden, Spain, Switzerland and Portugal. In the formerly occupied countries, the resistance movements were much concerned with European unification. As Luigi Enaudi later put it (in 1947) two successive world wars had originated in the crisis of the European nation state. This crisis had in turn derived from the contradiction between the increasingly supranational character of productive processes on the one hand, and the national character of existing European states on the other. The contradiction could be resolved either with the sword of Satan (that is to say Hitler's bloody conquest) or with the sword of God (through union achieved politically). These ideas found wide acceptance. Even Hitler, at the height of his power, claimed to stand for a united Europe, however fraudulently. There was widespread commitment to change the supremacy of the nation state and to prevent the repetition of events that had led to two world wars and bloody dictatorships. The Soviet Union loomed as an external military threat, and as an internal menace through its links with local communist parties. For a time, the Soviet Union also seemed impressive in its economic development. (As late as 1960, the Soviet Union still out-produced the European Economic Community, with a total gross national product of 223 billion dollars, as against 191 billion dollars. Thereafter its relative economic power declined, with a GNP of 435 billion dollars as against the EEC's 480 billion dollars in 1970, and 1,230 billion dollars as against the EEC's 2,765 billion dollars in 1980.)[2]

Walter Lipgens has written the definitive volumes on European unification: Documents on the History of Integration, *2 volumes and* 45 Jahre um die Europäische Verfassung. *The European unity movement was basically born out of the experiences of the two world wars in the twentieth century, which showed that only unity could end the intra-European fighting and nation state rivalry. The desire for a peaceful unification of Europe was widespread in Europe after World War I, but had little or no success until after World War II, when American pressure was added.*

[2]Werner Obst, "Die Allchillesferse der Sowjetunion Abstieg zur Ökonomischen Mittelmacht,' *Criticón,* no. 97, 1986, pp. 215–17.

> *World War II revealed three guidelines as to how unity was to be achieved: the confederal approach, though through intergovernmental agencies (Churchill); the functionalist approach of supranational authorities under technocrats (Monnet); and the federalist approach (favored by resistance groups and later by France, Italy and West Germany). By the end of the 1950s, the essential characteristics of the community had been built. These were: direct elections to the European parliament, gradual strengthening of majority voting in the Council of Ministers, application of Community legislation and case law. (See Sergio Pistone in* The Federalist, a Critical Review, *39, 1988, no. 2.)*

By the end of the war, moreover, allied politicians, trade unionists, soldiers and civil servants had learned how to cooperate with their opposite numbers in other governments. The new breed of international administrators was represented by Jean Monnet (born 1888), a brilliant and versatile man who had done almost everything under the sun – from selling brandy to Eskimos to buying aircraft from Americans. Monnet was unimpressive in appearance. (Anthony Sampson, a British journalist, likened him to Hercule Poirot, the Belgian sleuth of British detective fiction.) Monnet's political views and life experience set him apart from his fellow Frenchmen. (De Gaulle jestingly referred to him as a great American.) He was nevertheless an impressive personality, a pragmatist who believed that great and apparently insoluble problems could only be solved by changing their context. Monnet had first made his name in World War I as an official in the French Board of Trade; he rose to be Deputy Secretary-General of the League of Nations; later he made money in international business, and during World War II was appointed chairman of the Franco-British Committee for Economic Coordination. In this capacity he went to the US, where he played an important part in devising Roosevelt's "victory program" for the production of aircraft. Monnet subsequently rose high in de Gaulle's French National Liberation Committee, and in 1946 was appointed France's first *Commissaire au Plan*, charged with the postwar modernization of France.[3]

Churchill, while in opposition, lent his political prestige and oratorical skill to the movement for a United Europe. Pan-European ideals also appealed to many Catholics and socialists – both professing creeds that transcended the frontiers of nation states. (Particularly noteworthy among the Catholics were men such as Adenauer and de Gasperi.) Above all, the resistance movements strengthened common links between Europeans of different nationalities, as did the pan-European experience of oppression, deprivation, and hunger. European federalism henceforth became a cause worthy of commitment for many former resistance members, and for bodies such as the *Union Européenne des Fédéralistes*, pledged to defend Europe's liberty against "totalitarianism of whatever kind."[4]

In addition, there were new designs for linking the states of Europe through

---

[3] Sir Richard Mayne, *The Recovery of Europe: From Devastation to Unity*. New York, Harper and Row, 1970, p. 170ff.

[4] James D. Wilkinson, *The Intellectual Resistance in Europe*. Cambridge, Mass., Harvard University Press, 1981, pp. 190–1.

federal arrangements. Such schemes met with wide approval at a time when the "European idea" still evoked support from gifted intellectuals as different as Albert Einstein, Ignazio Silone, Albert Camus, George Orwell, Raymond Aron, and Winston Churchill. Federalism was in the air, though it meant different things to different people. Schemes for a federal Europe appealed to planners and efficiency experts, as well as to private businessmen. They appeared particularly desirable to the defeated Germans and Italians because a united Europe would give their countries a way back into the comity of nations.

The pioneers in trans-national cooperation of the practical kind were the people of the Low Countries. In 1944, while still exiled in London, the governments of Belgium, Netherlands, and Luxemburg created Benelux (ratified in 1947). Benelux was a customs union, an association of the weak who had learned the merits of cooperation under duress. Benelux was a pioneering venture; it provided both an inspiration to its neighbors and, unintentionally, a reservoir of public servants – multilingual, honest, and experienced in transnational cooperation – many of whom later lent their talents to other international organizations.

Equally compelling seemed the arguments for trans-national organizations of a more limited kind, especially between France and Great Britain. Both had deeply embedded democratic traditions; both stood committed to a planned economy and a welfare state; each still commanded a great colonial empire that aroused both Soviet and American disfavor. Properly managed, the British and French economies were in part complementary; the British would supply fuel and the French food. Britons and Frenchmen each had a profound pride in their national tradition.

The French attitude toward Britain was, however, ambivalent. In World War II, the heaviest losses suffered by the French navy had been inflicted not by the Germans or Italians but by the British (in the engagement at Oran, Algeria, in 1940, fought by the British to prevent a possible handover of the French fleet to the Germans). Supported by the Free French, Britain in 1941 had seized Syria and the Lebanon from the Vichy government, and thereafter levered the French out of the Middle East – a serious error on the part of a power that, while still resolved to maintain its own empire, failed to understand the colonial powers' common stake in maintaining colonialism. Anglophobia was widespread both in the French navy and among the former supporters of Vichy. Such feeling was also to be found among some Gaullists, whose leaders (including de Gaulle himself) had spent their wartime in London as exiles and supplicants. France emerged from World War II as a second-rate power downcast by a sense of inferiority, determined to reassert rather than restrict its national sovereignty.

Had Stalin played his cards wisely, he might have altered the fate of Europe by flattering de Gaulle and cultivating the French. France for a time was governed by a left-wing government in which communists participated. The French and Soviets both had a stake, or thought they did, in keeping Germany weak and divided, a milch cow from which to extract the maximum reparations.

But the Soviets, far from supporting France to the hilt over questions such as the Saar territory, inclined to treat France as a dependent of Anglo-American monopolists. A special relationship between France and the US seemed equally unlikely. The French depended on US support in a variety of ways – in equipping their army, in sustaining a war in Indochina, in coping with the ever-present "dollar gap" – but dependence also bred distrust. US and French power seemed overly disparate; de Gaulle himself had all too often been crossed by the Americans in wartime. Most French intellectuals knew little about the US and cared less. Only Britain for a time seemed to fit the role of ally, an ally specially acceptable to the moderate left, including the MRP and the socialists. A Franco-British marriage would not be one of love, but one of convenience.

For the British, however, even the convenience was not apparent. Wartime experience had isolated Britain from Europe in a psychological sense; in 1940 only the "white dominions" and the US had proved reliable allies (blessed moreover with the ability to speak English with moderately acceptable accents). A Franco-British understanding would not solve Britain's financial problems. Rather than make adequate provision for re-equipping antiquated industries, the British had committed themselves to building a welfare state, to subsidizing derelict areas at the expense of growth industries. In doing so, they could expect no help from France, a half-bankrupt country with a national production much lower than Britain's. (Few Britons could have imagined then that French national output would considerably exceed Britain's 30 years later.) Help was more obviously to be expected from the Sterling Area. (This association was largely co-existensive with the British Commonwealth and empire, with the exclusion of Canada. Its members pooled most of their dollar resources in a manner that penalized dollar-earning members, and favored dollar-importers.)

Above all, the British depended heavily on the US which, in 1946, loaned Britain a total of $3,750,000,000; this was the era when experts thought that the "dollar gap" would last in perpetuity. But the US insisted that the British should make their pound sterling freely convertible into gold or dollars a year later, at anyone's demand. When the British had to meet their promise, there was a rush of merchants and bankers all over the world demanding that their pounds be cashed for gold or dollars; at this point the British broke their promise and made sterling inconvertible again to avoid bankruptcy. By 1946, Britain's position had deteriorated further. This time the crisis could only be stopped by devaluing the pound and offering it at such low cost that the world's traders would be tempted to seek pounds for their cheapness. Devaluation left the British convinced that they must continue to look to the Sterling Area. (Its cohesion was demonstrated in 1949 when all members except Pakistan followed Britain's lead in devaluing by 30.5 percent.)

Britain's financial crisis further shook her faith in Europe. The final devaluation of sterling had been forced on the British against their will. Throughout 1949, European firms holding pounds had offered them to any buyer at any reasonable price, and thereby cut the pound's value before the British had done so officially. Such proceedings were of course illegal. At the deliberations of the OEEC (Organization for European Economic Cooperation, a Marshall Plan agency), the European ministers of finance and foreign affairs threw up their hands in horror at their own merchants' black marketeering. But their governments lacked both the will and the means to stop such practices; and the British became convinced that any understanding with Europe was impossible if it involved common controls. A European union might be all right for Europeans – but not for Britons.[5] No British government, however, European-minded, could have persuaded the electorate at that time to join a European union.

The British were confirmed in what they regarded as an Anglo-American special relationship, proven in commerce and in war. According to now dated Whitehall cant, the British would act as the Greeks in the new Roman Empire, tempering American might with British diplomacy. (British phrasemongers forgot the contempt felt by the Romans of antiquity for the *Graeculi*, the "little Greeks," hired tutors and artists.) The British did participate in a variety of European arrangements, but only to a modest extent.[6] In 1947 Britain and France concluded the Dunkirk treaty, aimed against a resurgence of German aggression (not a likely contingency since Germany lay prostrate). The Dunkirk treaty, however, provided the foundation for the Brussels treaty (signed in 1948 by Britain, France, and the Benelux countries), and in 1949, the Brussels Treaty Organization (BTO) in turn linked with the US, and with Canada, Portugal, Iceland, Norway, Italy, and Denmark to form NATO (enlarged by the addition of Turkey and Greece in 1951, and the German Federal Republic in 1955).

OEEC, EPU, AND MARSHALL PLAN

The proceedings of international organizations rarely make good reading. Their protocols tend to feature convoluted language and inordinate prolixity. They are seldom conclusive. At first sight, the Organization for European Economic Cooperation (OEEC) shared these characteristics. Founded in 1948 to coordinate the Marshall Plan, OEEC was described by a senior British civil servant as "a perpetual international conference."[7] Its membership and structure kept changing. (OEEC had originally been known as the Committee for European Economic Cooperation, CEEC, and was again restyled in 1960, as the Organization for Economic Cooperation and Development, OECD.) Its composition was so variegated as to make effective cooperation almost impossible.

[5]Theodore H. White, *Fire in the Ashes: Europe in Mid-Century*. New York, Sloane, 1953, pp. 337–9.
[6]See, for instance, Richard Ovendale, *The English-Speaking Alliance: Britain, the United States, the Dominions and the Cold War, 1945–1951*. New York, Greenwood Press, 1986.
[7]Mayne, *The Recovery of Europe: From Devastation to Unity*, p. 118.

> *Secretary of State Marshall did not impose his plan on the Europeans. He and his planners wanted certain things: more economic integration, more supranational organizations to achieve integration, more liberal trade policies such as operated in the United States. But Marshall and Harriman asked the Europeans what they wanted to do. This daunting task was undertaken by the Committee for European Economic Cooperation, the precursor of the Organization for Economic Cooperation and Development (OECD). The Soviets called the Marshall Plan an imperialist plot of Wall Street to enslave Europe; US opponents named it "operation rathole," and "share the American wealth plan." American officials were pragmatic and tried to export the American way: management, technology, labor relations, corporatism – that is, getting business to work with labor and government in order to increase prosperity.*

At the start, OEEC contained 16 members (Austria, Belgium, Denmark, France, Greece, Iceland, Ireland, Italy, Luxemburg, the Netherlands, Norway, Portugal, Sweden, Switzerland, Turkey, and the United Kingdom). Between them, these countries spanned a huge area – from the North Cape to Sicily, from the Atlantic to the Black Sea. Some had constitutional and others authoritarian governments; some were underdeveloped and based on agriculture, while others were highly industrialized. Some still had major empires, others had never owned colonies; some were wedded to strict planning, others to *laissez-faire*. Some looked primarily overseas for their trade and investment, others were mainly linked to Europe. Most were minor powers, in contrast to Britain and France which still commanded important military forces. Germany, economically the most important country in Western Europe, was not represented at the conference, and Austria, which was, remained an occupied country.[8] This was hardly a prescription for success; yet the OEEC was to perform remarkably well.

In creating this instrument, the participants – the US and its Western European allies – had partly divergent purposes. All had a common stake in successful reconstruction. But they differed over the question of how to achieve it. The US looked upon the Marshall Plan as a kind of New Deal, projected abroad with domestic bipartisan support. At the same time the Americans had a wider political commitment. They hoped to create a united, free-trade Europe, convinced that their own experience might form a paradigm. To be more specific, the state department wanted the European conference to form the basis of an economic association with, in turn, would lead to a federal union. Instead of handing out aid to individual countries, the Americans preferred to deal with the OEEC as a whole; the OEEC would prepare a program, submit a schedule for assistance, and decide on how to allocate aid between its various members.[9] By doing so, the Europeans would ultimately

[8] A. W. de Porte, *Europe Between the Superpowers: The Enduring Balance*. New Haven, Yale University Press, 1979, p. 135.

[9] Alan S. Milward, *The Reconstruction of Western Europe 1945–1951*. Berkeley, University of California Press, 1984. Also Charles L. Mee, *The Marshall Plan: The Launching of the Pax Americana*. New York, Simon and Schuster, 1984. John Gimbel, *The Origins of the Marshall Plan*. Stanford, Cal., Stanford University Press, 1976. Alan R. Raucher, *Paul G. Hoffman: Architect of Foreign Aid*.

create a market of continental size, and at the same time save their continent from an economic collapse that would benefit none but the communists.

The Europeans had other priorities. They were concerned above all to cope with economic problems of an immediate kind, to gain the best possible terms for their respective countries, and to safeguard their national sovereignties. In this they succeeded. The very constitution finally adopted by the OEEC raised formidable barriers against the American design for modifying the European state system, whose complexity and internal divisions Americans were apt to ignore. (According to a favorite story told by Professor Walter Hallstein, later President of the Common Market Commission, an American business magnate was flying over Europe for the first time. "That's France down below," said his assistant. "Don't bother me with details," was the reply.) The OEEC did not unify Western Europe, but merely acted as an organization for registering international agreements made elsewhere – a body highly bureaucratized, with regular ministerial meetings and a permanent staff of 1,100 officials. The OEEC managed to allocate aid on a supra-national basis through special expert committees – in itself a remarkable achievement. But there was no full-scale economic union of the kind that the Americans would have liked.

Nevertheless, the Marshall Plan was an unparalleled achievement. President Reagan, in a speech given 40 years later, dwelt on the sheer size of the project. It cost the US treasury $13.3 billion, which is to say $90 billion in today's money. In the words of Lincoln Gordon, an economist who had worked at its Paris headquarters, the plan was "the only large-scale government program of any kind, foreign or domestic, which accomplished more, in less time, at less cost, than projected." (The European Recovery Program was officially terminated in 1951, by which time all planned targets had been reached, instead of 1952; considerably less had been spent than the $17 billion originally anticipated.) According to its admirers, it was the Marshall Plan that had initiated the European *Wirtschaftswunder*. The Marshall Plan thereafter became a model for advocates of foreign aid to the Third World.

Critics of the Marshall Plan have arrived at very different assessments. Objections came both on political and economic grounds. US revisionists, for example, questioned the Americans' sincerity in offering to extend assistance

Lexington, University of Kentucky Press, 1985. Michael J. Hogan. *The Marshall Plan: America, Britain, and the Reconstruction of Western Europe, 1947–1952*. Cambridge, Cambridge University Press, 1987. Imanuel Wexler, *The Marshall Plan Revisited: The European Recovery Program in Economic Perspective*. Westport, Conn., Greenwood Press, 1983. Othmar N. Haberl and Lutz Niethammer, eds, *Der Marshall-Plan und die Europäische Linke*. Frankfurt, Europäische Verlagsanstalt, 1986. Forrest C. Pogue, *George Marshall: Statesman, 1945–1959*. 4 vols, New York, Viking Press, 1987. Charles Kindleberger, *Marshall Plan Days*. Boston, Allen and Unwin, 1987. Robert Everett Wood, *From Marshall Plan to Debt Crisis*. Berkeley, University of California Press, 1986. Stanley Hoffman and Charles Maier, eds, *The Marshall Plan: A Retrospective*. Boulder, Col., Westview Press, 1984. Robert John Donovan, *The Second Victory: The Marshall Plan and the Postwar Revival of Europe*. New York, Madison Books, 1987. Robert Marjolin, *Le Travail D' Une Vie: Memoires, 1911–1986*. Paris, Editions Robert Laffor, 1986, and Lincoln Gordon "Recollections of a Marshall planner," *Journal of International Affairs*, vol. 41, no. 2, Summer, 1988. James L. Gormly, *The Collapse of the Grand Alliance 1945–1948*. Baton Rouge, Louisiana State University Press, 1987.

to the Soviet Union. The US had actually anticipated a Soviet rejection; the offer had been more than a cynical ploy. But Vyacheslav Molotov, speaking for Stalin in 1947, had no doubt that the offer had been meant seriously. It was the Americans' motives that were offensive. As Molotov saw it, the plan's true object was to subvert the independence of the various European countries, and to set them one against the other. The plan merely served US capitalism by extending US trade and investments overseas. It was a plot against socialist planning in Western Europe. In addition, the Marshall planners found critics among committed advocates of a free market economy and orthodox finance, including US isolationists. Objections also came from traditionally minded Europeans who took issue with the Marshall Plan experts' commitment to Keynesian economics. For instance, Henry J. Tasca, a senior US official in Rome, opposed Luigi Einaudi's deflationary policy for Italy, and Einaudi's resolve to maintain a balanced budget. Yet, as John Harper puts it in an important study, Einaudi had grasped what Tasca and his colleagues had failed to understand. "There were no political quick-fixed or technical panaceas at hand to ease the pain of a long-delayed financial stabilization."[10]

More recently, scholars have played down the importance of the plan in promoting European recovery. The plan did not solve the Europeans' balance-of-payment problems, which continued for many years. It did not, in itself, initiate the Europeans' economic revival – as argued in Alan S. Milward's *The Reconstruction of Western Europe*. Far from facing general economic collapse, Western Europe at the time was already in the midst of an investment boom sustained by the massive import of US investment goods. It was the very speed of the recovery that caused, or at least accentuated, the dollar problem. The Marshall Plan was not without value; but its primary effect was to enable the European governments to continue their ambitious domestic plans. Moreover, the speed and extent of recovery in the various Western European countries was determined far more by indigenous factors than by the amounts of assistance received. (West Germany made the most spectacular progress. Yet West Germany received less than half the aid given respectively to France and Britain, recipients of the lion's share, as indicated in table 6.1.)

We ourselves believe in the epochal importance of the plan. The offer to the Soviet Union was seriously meant. As George Kennan, director of the policy planning staff at the time, put it: "I can testify as the person in whose mind this feature of the Marshall Plan originated ... that ... the offer was made in good faith."[11] The Marshall Plan experts were quite unable to impose their own views in the teeth of opposition. Even in as poverty-stricken a country as Italy, though the US could cajole or threaten, as Harper shows, the last word lay with Italian policy makers. The Marshall planners moreover

[10] John Lamberton Harper, *America and the Reconstruction of Italy, 1945–1948*. Cambridge, Cambridge University Press, 1986, p. 158. James Edward Miller, *The United States and Italy, 1940–1950: The Politics and Diplomacy of Stabilization*. Chapel Hill, NC, University of North Carolina Press, 1986.

[11] George Kennan, "The Marshall Plan and the future of Europe," in *Transatlantic Perspectives*, Winter 1988, no. 17, p. 5.

TABLE 6.1   *Marshall Aid to European countries, up to 1954 (in million dollars)*

	Amounts of aid received	Amount received per head of population
United Kingdom	3,641	72
France	3,104	72
Italy	1,578	33
West Germany and West Berlin	1,473	29
Netherlands	980	93
Austria	726	104
Belgium and Luxemburg	557	63
Greece	264	33

Source: *Presse und Informationsdienst der Bundesregierung*, Wiesbaden. *Deutschland Heute*, Wiesbadener Graphische Betriebe GMBH, 1954, p. 308.

made no attempt to interfere with national planning. Far from it. "Virtually no attention was paid by the OEEC or the United States missions to the functioning of the market for labor or capital."[12]

> *Most US officials were not really hopeful of creating a United States of Europe by economic unification and worked primarily to revive Europe's separate economies, to push economic cooperation and to reduce trade barriers. Their aim was to reconcile France and Germany then to let the economy grow by providing aid and Keynesian management.*

Why did the Marshall Plan attain such an extraordinary and unanticipated success? For one thing, it gained widespread political acceptance in the US – this alone was an astonishing achievement. Marshall himself inspired universal respect; he evinced no political ambition; he knew how to delegate authority. (His sole instruction to Kennan on forming the planning staff was "avoid trivia.") More generally, the plan appealed to progressive trade unionists and progressive capitalists alike. (James B. Carey, secretary-general of the CIO, served alongside prominent businessmen on the Harriman Committee which played a crucial part in mobilizing public opinion in the plan's favor.) The plan met with enthusiastic welcome from New Dealers within the Democratic Party. But it was acceptable also to the bulk of Republicans who controlled Congress after the elections of November 1948.

Paul G. Hoffman, the plan's chief administrator, admirably represented the new welfare capitalism – confident, committed to rising productivity, rising wages, expanding markets, and good labor relations. Hoffman was a man of irrepressible energy, cheerful, optimistic – a "regular guy" fond of golf and poker. He was also a competent businessman who had rescued the Studebaker

[12]Charles P. Kindleberger, *A Financial History of Western Europe*. London, Allen and Unwin, 1984, p. 435.

Corporation from disaster, expanded sales, and worked his way to the company presidency. In politics, Hoffman was a progressive Republican, and a personal friend of Eisenhower. (Hoffman's defense of foreign aid, labor unions, and civil liberties during the McCarthy era later earned him the wrath of the far right.) His collaborators included Averell Harriman, banker and diplomat, who represented the US at the OEEC's headquarters in Paris. Harriman's mission chiefs in Europe in turn consisted of establishment persons *par excellence*: David K. E. Bruce, a former associate of the W. A. Harriman Company (France); Thomas Finletter, a Wall Street lawyer from Philadelphia (Britain); Norman Collisson, formerly an industrial engineer (West Germany); and James Zellerbach (of the Crown Zellerbach pulp and paper company, in Italy). Such men had impeccable social and financial connections; they believed that welfare and profit went hand in hand. They understood business; they were invulnerable to the then deadly charge of being "do-gooders" or "one-worlders."

> *Marshall Plan officials such as Lincoln Gordon were full of idealism, dedicated to public service and confident that Keynesian economics could control and direct the revival of Europe. A new agency was created to disburse aid (the European Cooperation Administration); a central coordinating office was established in Paris (the Office of Special Representative in Europe), these were special missions in each country and a coordinating organization of Europeans to decide how aid was to be dispersed (the Committee for European Economic Cooperation, later to become the OEEC). It was Harriman as special representative in Europe who suggested that the Europeans should decide who got what. Hence Europeans had to negotiate together and transcend national interest. The skill of the secretary-general of the OEEC, Robert Marjolen, was crucial in getting the cooperation of the various national delegates.*

Hence the wider impact of the plan was staggering. In political terms, the US had committed itself to being a great international power; isolationism would not revive as a major force for many years to come. There were also profound psychological consequences in Western Europe. Confidence revived (in this sense the plan constituted "the most successful American foreign policy initiative since World War II").[13] On the whole, the plan was well run; there were no scandals, and no massive diversion of funds into the pockets of bureaucratic and political racketeers. OEEC was more effective than the League of Nations. Whereas earlier loans made under league auspices had gone purely for financial stabilization, Marshall Plan assistance, supplemented by private US charities on an impressive scale, provided help in a much more all-embracing fashion. (In the first year of the program, half of all Marshall Aid imports into Europe consisted of food; by 1951 only one-quarter, the rest comprised machinery, vehicles, semi-finished products, fertilizers, and feed.) The expenditure involved was astronomical by the standards of the time. The ERP provided about $13.6 billion in appropriations until 1952. In addition,

[13]Charles Maier, "Why was the Marshall Plan successful?," *Transatlantic Perspectives*, Winter 1988, no. 17, p. 22.

the US spent about $11 billion in UNRRA (United Nations Relief and Rehabilitation Administration), and supplied about $9 billion to Austria and Germany through the Government Aid and Relief in Occupied Areas (GARIOLA) funds. From 1945 to 1952, the US furnished $37.6 billion in net foreign assistance – the largest voluntary transfer of resources in history. This practical generosity to former enemies (Austria and Germany in particular) had no parallels in European history, where victors had customarily imposed reparations on the defeated. (The only exception was a British relief program for the defeated Boer Republics at the end of the South African war, 1899–1902.)

> *The United States bore most of the burden for stopgap relief through the United Nations Relief and Rehabilitation Administration (UNRRA) from 1943 to 1947 around the world. American citizens also sent quantities of packages of food and clothing to hungry Europeans through CARE (Cooperation for American Remittances to Europe). After 1948, the US allowed more immigration from Europe – over 200,000 people per year.*

Milward believes that the Marshall Plan did not, by itself, initiate the Western European recovery. But it did make a great difference. The grants and loans made through the European Recovery Program amounted to a substantial percentage of the gross domestic capital formation of key European

TABLE 6.2   *Selected economic indicators for the OEEC countries: (1938 = 100)*

	%
Exports, value	215
Imports, value	188
Industrial production: general index	125
Agricultural production: general index	106
GNP at current prices and exchange rates	152

Source: J. Frederick Dewhurst et al., *Europe's Needs and Resources*. New York, Twentieth Century Fund, 1961, p. 15.

countries (see table 6.2). Without the Marshall Plan, the dollar crisis would have persisted with even greater severity. Austerity would have been prolonged and the pace of reconstruction slower. As it was, the plan allowed the Western European governments more scope in following their national priorities – for example, the modernization of French industries, and the elaboration of the British Welfare state. Moreover the Marshall Plan gave internationally usable dollar credits to the Western European countries in a multilateral fashion. This helped to revive both trade within Western Europe, and trade between it and the rest of the world.

The plan involved large-scale transfer of US expertise. Itinerant American engineers, industrial chemists, and executives preached productivity; they argued in favor of decentralized management, of breaking cartels, of the elimination of quotas and customs, and of labor-saving technologies. For example, at the Doboelman soap works in Holland, American experts showed the Dutch how to cut processing time from five days to two hours with a new machine. In Norway, fishermen used a new type of net made from yarn spun in Italy. In Offenbach in West Germany, Marshall Plan leather revived the handbag industry; in Lille, Marshall Plan coal kept a steel factory in business; and in Roubaix, Marshall Plan wool maintained one of the world's largest textile mills. In 1945 only 25,000 tractors were in use on French farms; two years later Marshall Plan aid had put another 100,000 tractors in the field.[14] Overall, American investment in Western Europe grew apace, and more and more US patents found customers abroad. Americans had good reason for talking about "the American century."

Economic cooperation went with the liberalization of trade. In prewar days, the various European countries had tried to protect themselves against the effects of the slump by bilateral barter deals and an elaborate game of "beggar-my-neighbor." Tariffs, import controls, and similar devices had multiplied. After World War II the Western Allies switched direction. At the Bretton Woods Conference in 1944, the Allied powers, chief among them the US, agreed to set up the International Monetary Fund (IMF). This fund was designed to make gold and scarce currencies (in effect dollars) available to its members, and thus to facilitate international trade. The same conference set up the Bank for Reconstruction and Development, for the purpose of making development loans. In 1947, the General Agreement on Tariffs and Trade (GATT) succeeded in reducing tariffs below the level of prewar years both in the US and Western Europe.

> *GATT was signed by 23 countries on October 30, 1947 in Geneva. It was designed to regulate trade and international competition as regards restrictive business practices, investments, employment and trade in commodities. It was one of three institutions (with the World Bank and the IMF) set up to control the economic order in the postwar era. The Americans never ratified GATT, but it worked, liberalizing international trade, and bringing a new prosperity to much of the world.*

OEEC went a good deal further. In 1949 it agreed to remove quantitative restrictions on at least 50 percent of total imports on private account (that is to say all but state trading). In 1950 it agreed on a "code of liberalization." The OEEC signatories continued to remove restrictions from selected products. Foreign trade expanded at a rate even faster than industrial production; five years after the end of the war, the economies of the OEEC countries had become vastly more productive than before the war (see table 6.2).

The liberalization of tariffs also involved the liberalization of exchange controls. Lacking gold and dollars, each European country had earlier tried to earn these scarce resources by pushing its exports and restricting its imports.

[14]Mee, Jr, *The Marshall Plan: The Launching of the Pax Americana*, pp. 250–2.

Having first embarked on a number of piecemeal reforms, the OEEC countries in 1950 set up a multilateral clearance system through the European Payments Union (EPU). The US provided the initial capital fund of $350 million. The EPU's accounts and assets were managed by the Bank for International Settlement in Switzerland (not by the IMF). The dollar turned into the key international currency, serving both as the accepted medium of international exchange and as the anchor for the domestic price levels of the Western European economies. This dollar-based system immediately succeeded in unblocking intra-European payments, and there was a dramatic surge in trade, as the various Western countries began to remove numerous quotas and tariffs that had previously hampered commerce between them.[15]

The Americans, of course, did not have it all their own way. In the negotiations over the EPU's creation, the US had to acknowledge the relative strength of Britain's position, for without the inclusion of sterling, EPU was unworkable. The British (and not only the British) resolutely opposed any merger of sovereignties. Hence the Americans had to relinquish their aim of using EPU as an instrument for creating a monetary and political union. But EPU did succeed in preserving the achievements of Bretton Woods. "Together with the other common endeavors within the OEEC, but perhaps more effectively, the EPU fostered a type of common cooperation and common standards of thought and behavior" that might aptly be compared to the attitude of members of the same club.[16]

The cause of European cooperation gained in many ways. Increased trade went with increased tourist and business travel. The English language consolidated its position as Europe's main tongue of international intercourse, displacing German and French. European cooperation became intellectually respectable in a way that had been unthinkable in the 1930s. In 1949, for instance, the College of Europe opened its doors in Bruges – the first and perhaps the best-known center offering programs specifically oriented towards European cooperation in the fields of administration, economics, law, and related subjects. Thousands of American students and scholars studied and carried out research in Western Europe. Western European Studies expanded on American campuses. The Fulbright Program of exchange scholarships brought thousands to and from Europe; American cultural centers and studies centers sprang up throughout Europe.

[15]We are much indebted to comments by Ronald I. McKinnon. See also his book *Money in International Exchange: The Convertible Currency System*, Oxford, Oxford University Press, 1979. EPU was only dissolved in 1958. By finally accepting article VIII of the Bretton Woods agreement, the Western European currencies became finally convertible on current account, ending discrimination against payments for imports from outside Europe.

[16]J. Frederick Dewhurst et al., *Europe's Needs and Resources*. New York, Twentieth Century Fund, 1961, p. 696.

COUNCIL OF EUROPE, AND EUROPEAN COAL AND STEEL COMMUNITY
(ECSC)

Political cooperation improved in Western Europe during this period – though to nothing like the same extent as economic collaboration. New political institutions included the Council of Europe (CE), set up in 1949 as a consultative body. The council had its headquarters in Strasbourg. The choice of location was symbolic, Strasbourg being a city half German and half French, situated in Alsace, a French region whose ownership had been disputed for centuries between France and Germany. The initial enthusiasm for the council soon evaporated; its deliberations proved of interest to only a handful of Europeans. Nevertheless, it continued to enlarge its membership (by the early 1960s, it included Austria, Belgium, Cyprus, Denmark, France, the Federal German Republic, Greece, Ireland, Italy, Luxemburg, Malta, the Netherlands, Norway, Sweden, Switzerland, Turkey, and the United Kingdom). Endowed with an elaborate organization (complete with a consultative assembly, a secretariat, committees, commissions, and a ministerial council), the council became unwieldy and top heavy. Decisions rested with the committee of ministers and unanimity was required in matters of substance. Hence any member country could use its veto to block a decision – the same arrangement that prevailed in the UN security council. The parliamentary assembly served as a purely consultative body, devoid of legislative powers. The council, however, was not totally useless. In 1950, a European Commission became empowered to investigate charges made by states (and sometimes by individuals) that human rights and fundamental freedoms had been violated.[17] The European idea at least stayed alive.

While Europe's political unification languished, functional cooperation proved a more viable alternative – especially over matters of economic concern. The most important of these new departures concerned heavy industry. The postwar generation's preoccupation with coal, iron, and steel became hard to appreciate 40 years later, by which time the "smoke stack" enterprises had become a byword for inefficiency throughout much of the Atlantic economy. Energy consumption from oil and nuclear installations had by then vastly increased over coal; fiber glass, plastic, aluminum had made great inroads into the customary supremacy of steel; trucks, cars, and planes had taken over much of the railways' former position; "high tech" seemed the key to future progress.

But at the end of the war, the heavy industries still seemed crucial in public estimation. During World War II, countries such as South Africa and Southern Rhodesia had built up their own steel industries. The reconstruction of houses, factories, railways, and mines after the end of hostilities further enhanced the demand for steel. (Between 1947 and 1951, the CEEC members' combined

[17]Anthony Sharp, "Principal Western organizations: Council of Europe," in Mayne, ed., *Western Europe*. Oxford, Facts on File Publications, 1986, p. 561.

steel output in Europe rose from 26,186,000 tons to to 41,185,000 tons.)[18] At the same time, coal remained in short supply, especially during the grim winter of 1947. Planners assumed that the fuel shortage would continue for many years to come; few imagined that by the late 1950s there would be a glut of coal and steel in Western Europe. Ecological considerations played little part in the thinking of a generation that equated clear, smoke-free skies with wartime hunger. More importantly, community and capitalist planner alike continued to regard railways, coal mines, and steel mills as the commanding heights of the economy. Railwaymen, miners, and steel workers were as the working-class elite. Given these assumptions, nothing seemed more reasonable than to build European unity on a foundation of coal and steel.

The main initiative derived from France – from men such as Monnet, a brilliant promoter and public relations expert, as well as from technocrats, and from MRP leaders such as Bidault and Schuman, liberal Catholics, schooled in the resistance. After the end of World War II, the French had reverted to a punitive line toward Germany, reminiscent of their policy immediately after World War I. But relations between French and German steel magnates had always been friendly (as evinced by the International Steel Cartel formed after World War I). Their ties survived wars and occupations. France was moreover less Germanophobe in 1945 than she had been in 1918. By the end of World War II the two countries had shared common experiences of defeat, disgrace, foreign occupation, and striking diminution in national status. As the American economic historian John Gillingham has shown, Schuman, and especially Bidault, between them played a decisive part in persuading French public opinion that traditional hostility toward *les boches* would no longer serve their interests. (The so-called Schuman plan might more aptly have been named the Bidault plan.)[19]

The French came to understand that their country must henceforth cooperate with Germany, and that France could not expect existing controls on German production to continue indefinitely, especially at a time when the Korean war (1950–3) had placed further emphasis on the production of steel. French and German heavy industries were interdependent. (West Germany, for instance, was by far the most important supplier of coke for the French steel mills; France was Germany's largest market for coal exports.) From the French standpoint, it was better to negotiate at a time when the West German state was still in a state of semi-tutelage, and before the German Federal Republic was fully admitted into a Western military alliance. The French had everything to gain from an arrangement that would do away with discriminatory German railway rates, assure access to German coal and steel, secure German goodwill, and thereby guarantee the success of French mobi-

[18]Milward, *The Reconstruction of Western Europe*, p. 363.
[19]John Gillingham, "Zur Vorgeschichte der Montan-Union: Westeuropas Kohle and Stahl in Depression und Krieg," *Vierteljahrshefte für Zeitgeschichte*, Heft 3, 1986, pp. 381–405. We are indebted to John Gillingham for showing us two papers "Solving the Ruhr problem: German heavy industry and the Schuman plan," and "Die Französische Ruhrpolitik und der Ursprung des Schuman Plans."

lization plans. The German production units in the Ruhr generally exceeded their French competitors in size; hence the French looked to a compact that would break up the integrated Ruhr firms by international arrangement.

Italy and the Benelux countries also joined. The Italian government did not in principle object to the partial surrender of their sovereignty to an international body, partly because of the relatively small size of Italian heavy industries at the time, and partly because the Christian Democrats generally saw eye to eye with MRP and CDU policy makers on ideological grounds. The Italians bargained hard in order to mitigate the removal of protection from steel industry, and succeeded in gaining a number of significant concessions. Belgium made various initial objections, but also received substantial favors. Belgium's industrial economy in 1950 still centered largely on coal and steel, it therefore remained too dependent on ECSC markets to take an independent line. As regards the Netherlands, its steel industries were highly competitive, and the ecnomic advantages of cooperation for the Dutch steel manufacturers appeared indisputable, despite Dutch hostility to Germany on political grounds. Given Holland's position as the major European freight carrier, with large ports and a solid infrastructure, European integration was likely to benefit Dutch commerce and give a boost to efforts to speed industrialization.

The Germans had their own agenda. Like their Western neighbors, they relied heavily on foreign trade and wanted an expansion of their export markets – they had largely been cut off from traditional outlets in Eastern Europe. Moreover, the Adenauer government looked to European integration to wipe out the disrepute which Germany had incurred during the Third Reich. Adenauer, a Francophile from the Catholic Rhineland, was particularly anxious to end the historic Franco-German dispute, a sentiment warmly shared by Frenchmen such as Schuman (a Lorrainer who had served in the Imperial German Army in World War I). the Germans also wished to put an end to the dismantling of selected industrial installations under the guise of reparations, and wanted to terminate the surviving allied controls on the German economy, especially those that limited the resurgence of their steel industries. They were intent on doing away with tariff barriers impeding the export of West German coal. They looked to an international coal and steel authority as an instrument for removing post-World War II controls established by France over the Saar territory (Saarland). (In 1948, the Saar had briefly joined France in an economic union; nine years later the territory reverted to the Federal German Republic.)

In addition, the Adenaeur government strove mightily to prevent the breaking up of cartels within German heavy industries, a policy advocated both by German trade unionists, and by the Americans (the latter inspired by the Keynesians' long-standing opposition to cartels and trusts). American business methods had some impact in West Germany, but overall this was less than might have been expected – given their relative post-war situations.[20] In

---

[20]For a detailed discussion, see Volker R. Berghahn, *The Americanisation of West German Industry, 1945–1973.* Cambridge, Cambridge University Press, 1986.

the end, Adenauer won over the German trade unions by offering them a form of *Mitbestimmung* (codetermination, a share in the control over major enterprises) and a variety of economic concessions. German industry as a whole agreed to help heavy industry by an investment aid law (*Investitionshilfsgesetz*, 1951) that gave powerful support for modernizing the heavy industries. There was no more talk of nationalizing them – a solution favored by German Social Democrats and British Labourites. The Ruhr reverted to its accustomed position as West Germany's main industrial center. But the new power-sharing arrangement entailed a greater degree of public control and social responsibility than had been acceptable in prewar days, and as a result a much greater measure of public confidence. West Germany had once more become a powerful negotiating partner, fully able to look after her own interests.

> *British prime ministers after World War II were opposed to joining any European organization working for a united Europe. Anthony Eden both as foreign secretary and as prime minister was adamant about staying aloof from Europe; he even talked Churchill into agreeing with him. Eden stressed Britain's link to the Commonwealth and her "special relationship with the US." Eden tried to break up Europe's effort to unite and refused all efforts to get Britain into the Common Market. Later de Gaulle was to vote against admitting Britain to the Common Market, largely because of Britain's earlier efforts to hinder the organization. Possibly, Britain might have been better off without a "special relationship" with the US and would have joined the European Economic Community earlier.*

The British, by contrast, stood aloof at a time when their position was still relatively strong, and when they could have gained extensive concessions. British policy makers favored economic and military cooperation with Western Europe. But they were preoccupied with an apparently insoluble dollar problem; they dreaded the economic consequences of full integration on the Sterling area and its payments mechanism. British steel producers did not anticipate a threat to their own position at a time when Western Europe purchased less than 5 percent of British steel exports. The British National Coal Board had no interest in joining an arrangement whereby the high authority would have the power to reallocate output, close pits, and control investment policies. The British government wanted no limitations on its unfettered authority. British unionists thought that, in joining the ECSC, steel workers might lose productivity-related wage benefits which then prevailed in the British industry. The British public as a whole remained opposed to any designs for a British union with Europe. (This hostility continued to the 1980s,[21] but thereafter rapidly diminished.) The ECSC therefore remained in spirit a Continentals' club.

In 1952 the governments of West Germany, France, Italy, and the Benelux

---

[21] Jean-Claude Deheneffe, *Europe as Seen by Europeans: European Polling 1973–1986*. Luxembourg, Office for Official Publications of the European Community, 1986, p. 32.

countries ratified the treaty establishing the European Coal and Steel Community (widely known as the Schuman plan). The treaty served as a customs union for coal, iron, and steel. The pact imposed common tariff rates on coal and steel products from other countries (not put into operation until 1958). It provided for the elimination of measures likely to distort competition – for example subsidies, double pricing and discriminatory transport schedules. In addition, it gave to the high authority, the ECSC's executive organ, the power to fix price limits as well as production and trade quotas during periods of "manifest crisis." The high authority had the right to be consulted on all major investment programs of enterprises within its purview and it was empowered to issue loans, and to contribute to investments it regarded as desirable. The ECSC thus established a single market for coal, iron, and steel, eliminated (at least in theory) all European barriers to competitive trading and all forms of price discrimination, including those in transport. The ECSC derived revenue by levies on enterprises within its sphere of operation. (In 1953 the high authority imposed contributions on coal and steel production – the first European tax in history.) These funds served to finance the ECSC's working expenses, build reserves, guarantee its loans, and finance a readaptation fund (providing grants to workers thrown out of employment by the conversion of their enterprises).

The ECSC was run by the high authority, an executive agency with supranational powers. (Decisions rendered by it, backed by a majority vote, were binding on enterprises within the member states.) The nine members of the high authority were prohibited from accepting directions from the member governments, so that they might act only in a supranational interest. The ECSC's council of ministers provided the required liaison between the Community and member states, and in certain cases, had a right of veto on the high authority's decisions. The council had the right to issue ordinances on matters directly affecting coal, iron, and steel, in conjunction with the high authority. The common assembly lacked legislative powers, but was empowered to force the resignation of the entire high authority by a vote of censure. The assembly's members were elected by their respective parliaments, but seated according to their political alignments. The Court of Justice settled disputes between members, while a consultative committee (representing producers', workers', and consumer organizations) assisted in an advisory capacity.

There were many critics. The ECSC represented a partial defeat for the US. For all the current rhetoric concerning the "American empire," the Americans could not make their views prevail. Some of them would have liked to see an integrated Western Europe – complete with a customs union and a central bank, a trans-Atlantic version of the US with all the advantages of a large and unrestricted market enjoyed by American entrepreneurs at home, and run on New Deal principles. But it was the ECSC, not the OEEC, that formed the precursor of the European Economic Community. American objections to the European solution were plentiful. US steel producers complained, with some justice, at being faced with a government-backed European steel cartel from which they were largely excluded. Advocates of free trade objected that the

ECSC represented no more than a super cartel. The "High Authority," despite its splendid title, seldom behaved as a supranational government; its strength rested on its independence rather than on effective power, and it sought the council of ministers' advice more often than was legally required. Hence, it did not by any means succeed in eliminating all protectionist devices or in wiping out the less obvious subsidies extended to their own industries by member governments. Trade in commodities such as iron ore, scrap iron, steel products, coal, and coke certainly increased within the ECSC countries during the 1950s, but this expansion occurred at a time when demands kept rising, and transnational commerce would probably have expanded in any case.[22]

The ECSC met with criticisms on other grounds. ECSC was "Europe incorporated," a restorationist venture that maintained the captains of industry in their accustomed splendor. It created a huge and unwieldy bureaucracy, remote in its Luxemburg (later Brussels) headquarters from the affairs of ordinary citizens. Finally, said critics blessed with hindsight, the founders of the ECSC had backed the wrong horse, in the sense of supporting huge industrial complexes when coal, iron, and steel were destined soon to lose much of their former importance, giving way to "high tech," industries pioneered by Americans and Japanese, rather than by Europeans.

On the credit side, however, the ECSC made substantial advances toward developing a European economic community. Its founders had to deal with problems as they existed at the time, not those that were yet in the future. The ECSC was a pioneer venture that put an end to the long-enduring hostility between France and Germany. It transcended the bonds of a simple alliance, and provided a formalized structure of economic interdependence. "International regulation of the economy was institutionalized as the alternative to the formal diplomatic resolution of major ... political conflict."[23] The ECSC created for itself a host of new lobbies with a stake in intra-European collaboration, and provided a pattern for trans-national collaboration in wider fields.

Politically, the ECSC represented a compromise between Catholics, liberals, and socialists; between capital, labor, and the state. It was run by "good Europeans," people with drive and conviction. Paul-Henri Spaak, the Belgian foreign minister, chaired the Common Assembly; Massimo Pilotti, a distinguished Italian jurist, presided over the Court of Justice. Monnet took charge of the high authority, whose remaining members included men as different as Léon Daum, a French businessman and steel expert; Heinz Potthoff, a former steel worker from Germany; Paul Finet, a Belgian and former foundry worker, who had served as first President of the International Confederation of Free Trade Unions; Albert Coppé, a Fleming, who had been Belgium's minister of economic affairs. Different in temperament, background and political conviction, they nevertheless cooperated well under Monnet's guidance,

[22]See table 19–3, Dewhurst, *Europe's Needs and Resources*, p. 607.
[23]Milward, *The Reconstruction of Western Europe*, p. 418.

and quickly acquired the habit of seeing the Community's problems as a whole.[24]

In economic terms, the ECSC became a world power. (By 1959, less than 15 years after the end of World War II, the ECSC countries accounted for 20.9 percent of the world's crude steel production, compared to 28.1 percent for the US, 19.9 percent for the Soviet Union, and 6.8 percent for Great Britain.) In a political sense, the ECSC solved the Ruhr problem in a manner that permitted the fragile new democracy in West Germany to survive and prosper. West Germany was integrated into Western Europe, and Western Europe itself became a thriving concern that belied gloomy postwar prophecies. The ECSC's founding fathers could not have asked for more.

THE EUROPEAN ECONOMIC COMMUNITY (EEC)

The ECSC's architects regarded their achievement as a mere stepping stone toward the creation of a Western Europe united in a military and political, as well as in an economic sense. The builders of such a community were ageing men in a hurry. De Gasperi, Monnet, Schuman, and Spaak were all in their sixties and seventies, Adenauer even older.[25] They had lived as grown men through two great wars that had devastated their countries. They were determined to save what they could from the wreckage, to prevent a new war, and – if necessary – make national sacrifices to achieve these aims. They felt that time was running out, that the ideal mood of the immediate postwar years was waning, and that swift action alone would secure their aim.

Their discomfiture increased when North Korea attacked South Korea in 1950; this assault heightened fears of Soviet aggression in Western Europe, and strengthened those who wanted West Germany to rearm. German rearmament, however, was to be strictly controlled. Plans for a European Defense Community (EDC), put forward in 1950 by René Pleven, the French premier, looked toward restraining Germany almost as much as the Soviet Union. French policy indeed appeared to aim at squaring the circle. As coffee-house conversation went, France wanted a German army larger than the Soviet Union's, but smaller than France's; and also a European army for Germany and a French army for France and its colonies.

The EDC design, adopted in 1952, thus provided for a limited merger of the armed forces of the ECSC countries. A new European army would be

---

[24]Mayne, *The Recovery of Europe: From Devastation to Unity*, p. 208.

[25]Anthony J. C. Kerr, *The Common Market and How it Works*. Oxford, Pergamon Press, 1977, p. 174. Other works include, in addition to those cited earlier, Walter Hallstein, *Die Europäische Gemeinschaft*. Düsseldorf, Econ Verlag, 1979, Hanns Jürgen Küsters. *Die Gründung der Europäischen Wirtschaftgemeinschaft*. Baden-Baden, Nomis, 1982. Klaus-Dieter Borchardt, *European Unification: The Origins and Growth of the European Community*. Luxembourg, Office for Official Publications of the European Communities, 1986. For Schuman's role in particular, see Raymond Poidevein, *Robert Schuman, Homme d'état*. Paris, Imprimene Nationale, 1986. René Lejeune, *Robert Schuman Une aim pour l'Europe*. Paris, Sain Paul, 1986.

jointly equipped and financed by the member states, with national contingents incorporated at the level of the smallest practicable unit, then thought to be the battalion. At the same time, member states would be able to keep national forces of their own, and even supplement them in case of need by withdrawing some of their European units – a concession considered necessary to enable France and Britain to maintain their overseas empires. Those states with least to lose – the Benelux countries and West Germany – ratified the EDC treaty. But there was widespread opposition in Italy, and particularly in France where right-wingers and communists, pacifists and jingoists rallied against the project. Politicians and generals as diverse in outlook as Pietro Nenni, Marshal Alphonse Juin, the Comte de Paris, and Kurt Schumacher joined the opposition. Above all, Great Britain continued to stand aloof. EDC finally broke down when, in 1954, the French National Assembly voted against the projects, and the deputies joyfully burst into singing the *Marseillaise*. The noes included communists, the bulk of the Gaullists (although Pleven himself had stood high in de Gaulle's wartime counsel), and most radicals and socialists.

The demise of the EDC project seemed a further setback for the Americans, who had backed it, as well as for Monnet and his fellow "Europeans." In fact, EDC could not have worked. A European army, made up of a mosaic of national contingents numbering no more than 800 to 1,200 men, could not have operated efficiently. Its components would have lacked color, ritual, and tradition – those vital elements of morale that Eurocrats of every hue seemed unable to understand. Cohesion would have been hard to maintain in such a heterogeneous army. NATO – based on solid national forces, proved a sounder solution. After the collapse of EDC, West Germany joined NATO and the Western Union. Projects for a European Political Community (EPC), a more ambitious step toward political union, were shelved, and the campaign for European unity for the moment reached an impasse.

Monnet and his coadjutors, however, proved formidable protagonists. In 1955 Monnet resigned the presidency of the ECSC high authority so as to devote himself fully to campaigning for European unity. In the same year, a foreign ministers' conference, representing the ECSC powers, met at Messina, Italy. (The participants included distinguished "Europeans" such as Gaetano Martino, host, Italian foreign minister at the time, and rector of Messina University; as well as Walter Hallstein from West Germany, a former law professor, who became foreign minister, and later wrote a standard work on the European Economic Community.

WALTER HALLSTEIN (1901–)

The ordinary reader is usually familiar with Germans such as Erwin Rommel or Karl Dönitz – one a general, the other an admiral of the German Wehrmacht, who had suffered disaster. Few know of Hallstein, a German architect of success. Hallstein was born in 1901 in Mainz, hometown of several prominent German liberals. He studied law, later taught at several universities, and made his name in the field of commercial and comparative jurisprudence. During World War II, he was conscripted into the Wehrmacht, *and captured by the Americans. He spent the rest of the war in Louisiana, where he organized a prison camp "university," and was nearly murdered for his pains by Nazi fellow captives.*

The experience of war and of his enforced stay in the US turned Hallstein into an ardent Europeanist. In 1946 he played a leading part in reopening the University of Frankfurt (traditionally a liberal institution within the German context). He thereafter visited the US as a guest professor. In 1950 Adenauer appointed Hallstein to head the German delegation in the negotiations that led to the European Coal and Steel Community. Hallstein looked and acted the typical professor – aloof, courteous, bespectacled, very much the proper Rektor *of his university. But he was a hard bargainer, a lawyer familiar with every legal complexity. Hallstein took a leading part in the creation of the European Economic Community, and in 1958 became its first president.*

Hallstein's career was controversial. He was responsible for the so-called Hallstein doctrine (put forward in an official statement in 1955). The Federal German Republic, according to this policy, would refuse to maintain diplomatic relations with any foreign state that gave official recognition to the German Democratic Republic. Only the Soviet Union was exempt from this provision. (In 1957 the Federal German Republic broke relations with Yugoslavia, and in 1963 with Cuba). But the doctrine was afterwards abandoned. (In 1968 the Federal German Republic resumed relations with Yugoslavia.) Hallstein was much more conciliatory toward the European Free Trade Association (EFTA), which he described as a necessary supplement to the EEC. Within the EEC he aroused de Gaulle's wrath, when the latter insisted on the right of France to veto majority decisions reached by the EEC.

In 1967 Hallstein resigned, and later was elected to the Bundestag *to represent the CDU. He continued to advocate the "European idea," with a remarkable degree of success.*

The conference appointed a committee under Spaak to look further into the prospects for integration. In 1956 the Spaak Committee presented its report. This formed the basis for the negotiations that created the European Economic Community (EEC) and the European Atomic Community (Euratom). The resultant treaties were signed by the Six in March 1957, and came into force on January 1958, an important date in modern European history. The agreements represented the political compromise between advocates (especially West German proponents) of an unfettered market economy, and spokesmen for a market economy modified by national planning and governmental intervention *à la française*. The treaties likewise constituted an accommodation between those who favored integration on "intergovernmental" lines and those who pleaded for "supranational" unification.

The EEC's founding fathers were superb parliamentarians, and attained a remarkable degree of success within their respective national assemblies – albeit for diverse reasons. The German *Bundestag* approved the treaties by an overwhelming majority that comprised not only the right-wing parties, but also the SPD. The Social Democrats, having bitterly opposed the EDC, German rearmament, and Germany's adhesion to NATO, now supported the EEC, and adhered to a new consensus regarding foreign policy. (Only the Free Democrats stood aloof, seeing themselves as the last representatives of a sternly national interest). The German vote reflected West Germany's new found position of strength, as the Federal Republic, during the 1950s, had expanded its exports at a faster rate than any other Western European country, and had one of the highest percentages of world exports. The Germans looked to the EEC to accelerate this process by broadening their European trade markets, bringing the expansion of their investments, and perpetuating that prosperity on which the Federal Republic's foundation seemed to rest. (In 1986 West Germany became the world leader in exports – a position previously held by the US since 1921.)

The French National Assembly likewise assented to the treaties by a great majority. In fact, the EEC's proponents gained more support than they had anticipated – France having traditionally been one of Europe's most protectionist countries. The opposition, however, remained badly divided; it included a heterogeneous collection of communists, Gaullists, Poujadistes (a right-wing group of tax protestors); and a faction within the Radical Socialist Party led by Pierre Mendès-France (a former prime minister of great personal distinction). In France, unlike West Germany, the size of the parliamentary majority reflected weakness rather than confidence. France now found herself in a difficult position as a result of the Suez defeat, and a creeping war in Algeria. On the other hand, French industrialists looked toward modernization, and were now prepared to accept those sacrifices entailed by the liberalization of trade and the resultant growth of foreign competition.

The Italian chamber likewise approved the EEC treaties with a striking majority. (Only the communists consistently voted against the treaties, whereas the Nenni socialists supported the Euratom treaty, while abstaining from the vote concerning the EEC). As the Italians saw it, the EEC would provide access to capital, markets, and other resources deemed essential for the modernization of their industries, the development of the South, for reducing widespread unemployment, and providing new markets for farmers. The Benelux countries supported the treaties with even more enthusiasm, as the EEC seemed to extend Benelux to Western Europe as a whole.[26]

Outside Western Europe, the EEC's international reception was far from favorable. Only the US unreservedly backed the design – though at a time when US exports still competed successfully in every part of the globe, and when the US still maintained a most favorable trade balance. Of the smaller powers, Denmark and Austria alone welcomed the EEC, and indeed expressed an interest in joining. The Soviets, by contrast, bitterly opposed the new association which they stigmatized as a device to strengthen the forces of West German monopoly capitalism, a line followed by Muscovite communist parties throughout the world. Switzerland, Portugal, and Spain remained aloof, for differing reasons. The Japanese feared for their exports; the Indians remained critical – the more so when some European enthusiasts with colonial leanings fantasized about a great "Euro-African" bloc.

---

[26]For details concerning the votes in the various parliaments, see Küsters, *Die Gründung der Europäischen Wirtschaftsgemeinschaft*, pp. 472–83.

Above all, the British would not join – even when they might have exerted considerable influence in shaping the new association to their interest. The British had hoped to create a European free trade area that would involve no sacrifice of national sovereignty, and that would not force British urban consumers to subsidize European farmers. The British responded to the EEC challenge by founding the European Free Trade Association (EFTA) in 1960. This comprised Britain, Norway, Sweden, Denmark, Austria, Portugal, Iceland, and Switzerland, with Finland as an associate member – an association founded purely for economic purposes, working with a minimum of bureaucratic encumbrances. Tied to the Commonwealth, hoping still for a special relationship with the US, the British continued to stand aloof, though the growing EEC market offered a fresh opportunity to expand export markets. (During the 1960s, the British were to find that they had made the wrong choice and, after two unsuccessful attempts, finally joined the EEC in 1973.)

Broadly speaking, the EEC treaty provided for common policies on trade, agriculture, transport, and competition, and for "coordination" as regards economic, social, and monetary policies, with the dividing lines between them drawn loosely so as to facilitate further integration. The Community rested on a customs union that would provide for the gradual elimination of internal tariffs and other barriers, as well as the gradual creation of a common external tariff. In addition, the EEC architects looked to a common market in which labor and capital would move freely, with uniform antitrust regulations, and the "harmonization" of wider economic policies.

In order to assure these objectives, the EEC's founding fathers set up a complex structure that drew heavily on the ECSC's design. The EEC was run by a Commission of nine members chosen by the national governments, but pledged to independence. The Commission made its decisions by majority voting through a very complex method; it applied the treaty provisions, and initiated proposals. (Subsequently the EEC Commission, the Euratom Commission, and the ECSC high authority merged into a single Commission, assisted by a secretary-general, a legal service, and specialized director-general. Their officials were divided between Brussels and Luxembourg.) The Council played a more powerful part than its equivalent in the ECSC; it was responsible for coordinating Community and national policies. In theory, the Council could decide issues by a majority vote; in practice, however, majority voting was rarely used, as the French in particular refused to subordinate what they regarded as vital national interests to a majority. (The dispute was partially settled in 1966 by the so-called Luxemburg compromise, that in practice amounted to unanimity over major issues.)

The ECSC Assembly was converted into a European parliament, with proportional membership chosen by the national parliaments. (Direct voting was only introduced in 1979.) The Assembly members were to serve as individuals, not as national representatives. Members were grouped, not by nations, but by parties. The parliament bore responsibility alike for the ECSC, Euratom, and EEC; but parliament's powers over the Community executive remained restricted, with the effect that the European parliamentarians tended to come from their respective countries "second teams." A new Court of Justice served all three communities; and heard suits by Community members, individual firms and private persons. It interpreted treaties and the actions of member states in regard to these arrangements, and also developed a "community law" code that overall tended to benefit the welfare state. The court's exact powers remained a matter of dispute, for though it could tell a member state that it was disobeying Community law, it had no means of imposing punishments. While member states usually accepted court rulings, they could of course raise legal or technical objections. The court's powers thus remained moral, but nevertheless, by no means inconsequential.

In addition, the Council chose an economic and social committee with advisory functions, representing different economic and social groups. A European Investment Bank came into being to finance development in depressed regions of the community. An equally complex structure served Euratom – with the result that the EEC turned into a bureaucrats' paradise. (By 1986, the Community employed some 17,000 civil servants as opposed to 71 serving EFTA.[27])

A EUROCRAT

Wyth us ther was a sometime EUROCRATTE.
His face was ruddy and his boddie fatte.
Ful well he knew the wynes of fair Fraunce;
Their claret did his ruddye look enhaunce.
In Brussel had he woned many a yeare
And Europ's golde had swolen his coffere.
A Swynkynge man from Wales he seyde he was,
But list'ning to the way he spoke his R's
I judged he was a wealthy Englishmanne.
His three companeyouns who with him ranne
Together praughte Social Democracie,
But naught had they to seyne of policie.

(David Thompson)

This verse is from a weekend competition set to describe a contemporary pilgrim for Chaucer's medieval Canterbury Tales, *in the* New Statesman *(London), 12 February 1982.*

How much has the EEC achieved? The record is mixed. There was bureaucratic growth and confusion – made worse by the geographic dispersion of the European Community's main institutions between Strasbourg, Brussels, and Luxemburg, with bitter rivalry between the three cities for the honor of hosting the various bodies concerned. The founders' fame did not live – unlike the fame of the American Founding Fathers. Thirty years later, few Europeans would be able to identify Monnet or the Messina Conference. Overall, the EEC failed to develop fully a new sense of European loyalty. The EEC and

[27]*Economist,* 6 December 1986, p. 62.

its associated bodies were created and staffed by a small elite, "stateless technocrats," as de Gaulle called them, and it was, to some extent, an elite of outsiders.

> *The EEC's progress toward a "Europe without frontiers" began in 1957. It was slow, but steady. In the late 1980s, the Eurocrats hoped to set aside all economic frontiers by 1992, 34 years after the initial treaties had been signed. Nevertheless, as the* Economist, *a leading British journal, pointed out (9–15 July 1988), the complications were still legion: "West Germany has extremely strict gun controls; France has an American-like right to bear arms. Denmark insists upon maintaining a passport-free arrangement with the Nordic countries, so someone flying into London from Copenhagen could be a Dane, or a Swede, or a blonde alien let into Sweden from elsewhere. Britain, with its sea frontiers, finds it convenient to check its people only at frontier ports; it eschews identity cards. France, with unpoliceable land frontiers, cares less about border posts and monitors its people from within. Entirely different patterns of government snoopiness have developed around such facts of geography. They will not be discarded this century."*

For all these deficiencies, the EEC accomplished a great deal. European commerce would surely have fared worse had it never come into being. Not merely the Europeans, but the Americans gained in the balance.[28] The EEC citizen's personal income, on average, doubled within a quarter of a century after the EEC's creation.[29] The EEC represented a remarkable achievement – a compact of moderates, especially moderate Catholics and moderate socialists – arrayed against the extreme nationalists and militant left-wingers in European politics.

The United States acted alike as a lobbyist for Western unification and as a guarantor for its security. This was a considerable departure. During the twentieth century, the US has repeatedly swung between isolationism and internationalism – the isolationism of the Midwest, of small towns, and of emigrants tired of Europe, as opposed to the internationalism of the eastern establishment, the Federal bureaucracy, Anglophile private schools, prestige universities, and international corporations. It had required strong presidential leadership and the eastern establishment to get the US to intervene in Europe during World War I. Thereafter, it drew back. After World War II, the same pattern might easily have been repeated. Initially, the US would have preferred to leave the responsibility for looking after Western Europe to Great Britain, while it looked to the Pacific Rim and Latin America. It required Stalin's mistakes, British pressure, and Truman's and Marshall's visions to prevent yet another US retreat from Western Europe, and persuade the American taxpayer to help revive a major trade competitor. Events in 1946 and 1947 convinced American politicians and officials to reverse their course. Their efforts were

---

[28]Laurence B. Krause, *European Economic Integration and the United States.* Washington, DC, Brookings Institution, 1968.

[29]Between 1960 and 1983, the per capita gross domestic product (GDP), expressed in purchasing power standards (PPS), at 1980 prices, went up from 4,286 to 8,074. A slight dip occurred in 1973, and again in 1980. See table in Klaus-Dieter Borchardt, *European Unification*, p. 30.

unwittingly aided by an army of businessmen, salesmen, moviemakers and entertainers who were continually traveling back and forth across the Atlantic – assisted by the continued decline in the price of airfares. Wartime alliances were renewed. Former enemies were reconciled. NATO came into being, and with it a multitude of other new trans-national organizations that forged a new Atlantic partnership.

7

The North Atlantic Treaty Organization (NATO)

When World War II ended, the US and its Allies had mobilized the greatest armed force in history – something like 18,000,000 men. (Of these, approximately 12,500,000 were American and 5,000,000 British.) The Western forces outnumbered the Soviet – the latter's wartime strength may have been about 12,000,000 in all. The Western alliance moreover possessed a decisive superiority at sea and in the air, as well as a temporary nuclear monopoly, and an industrial and agricultural potential vastly greater than the Soviet Union's. All the cards were stacked in the West's favor. Their military superiority did not, however, last for long. At the end of hostilities, the Soviet Union and the Anglo-Saxon countries demobilized, but the British and Americans did so far more rapidly than the Soviets. In so far as a military imbalance developed it was largely created by the West's partial disarmament.

What was the extent of the imbalance? Estimates at the time differed widely, but it is clear that in terms of manpower the disparity was never as great as the pessimists assumed. A British War Office appraisal, issued in 1951, gave a Soviet ground strength of 3,200,000, an air force of 800,000, and a navy of 600,000 men, and over 1,000,000 men for Moscow's Eastern European satellites. The NATO member states in 1950 had a combined armed strength of 4,000,000.

Manpower figures of course do not tell the whole story. The bulk of the Soviet force was stationed within the Soviet Union; substantial numbers were designed to keep down Eastern Europe. Moscow could not take for granted the loyalty of the satellite forces. There is no evidence that Stalin ever considered a lightning invasion of Western Europe although his military staff planned for one. He preferred to use military power as a potential threat, in what he regarded as a protracted political struggle; he was anxious to get the European communist parties to enter into coalitions with bourgeois governments so as to obstruct anti-Soviet policies within those countries, and to prepare for communist takeover in the long haul.

The Western European powers had problems of their own. The British and French each retained considerable commitments in their imperial possessions. The bulk of the American forces were stationed at home. The Americans in particular had initially placed their trust in the United Nations organizations (UN), whose moralistic and legalistic outlook corresponded to American liberal sentiments. Roosevelt had hoped that the US, the USSR, Great Britain, and China, the "four policemen" would cooperate to maintain world peace and that there was no need to prepare for Western military defense in Europe.[1]

Roosevelt's hopes foundered, but as relations worsened between the USSR and the West, the latter's strength – in terms of combat-ready divisions – remained negligible. (In 1949, the Western powers had no more than 12 ill-equipped divisions readily available in Europe – seven French, two British, two American, and one Belgian, in addition to small Dutch, Italian, and Norwegian forces, mostly unsuited for service in the line.) The bulk of the US, British, and French divisions were fit only for occupation duties, neither equipped, trained, nor deployed for war; most of their soldiers were anxious to get out of uniform. The Soviets, by contrast, maintained about 22 divisions in East Germany on a war footing. Overall, the Soviet ground divisions were said to number 175, in varying degrees of readiness.

Until 1949 only the US possessed a nuclear first-strike capacity, and the world might count itself fortunate that it was Washington, rather than Moscow, that briefly enjoyed such an extraordinary advantage. Between them, the US Navy and the Royal Navy possessed an overwhelming superiority in every ship-class, especially aircraft carriers, the new capital ship. But on land there was a striking imbalance. Whereas the US enjoyed complete invulnerability at home, the bulk of Western Europe lay exposed to Soviet armies. This was a remark-able asset for the Soviet Union in the Cold War, and one that Moscow had not enjoyed during the brief period of peaceful coexistence between Nazi Germany and the Soviet Union, 1939–41. But Western inferiority derived from the chosen deployment of their forces, and their unwillingness to translate manpower strength into combat-worthy divisions. The Western sense of inferiority vis à vis the Soviets was complicated by other factors. Many Western Europeans remained as frightened of a German revival as of a Soviet assault. The European Continental countries – France, Italy, the Low Countries, as well as Germany – all retained the psychological legacy of a shattering military defeat. There was widespread British reluctance to become permanently embroiled in Continental affairs. Above all, the Americans had no commitment to maintain military forces in Europe for any length of time. Isolationism remained strong among pacifists, backwoods Republicans, adherents of the extreme left, and those who put their hopes for a peaceful future in the UN. Far from being a yoke imposed by the bellicose and Russophobe Americans on a reluctant Europe, NATO mainly grew from European initiatives.[2]

NATO's immediate origin stemmed from the failure of the Council of

[1]William Park, *Defending the West: A History of NATO*. Boulder, Col., Westview Press, 1986, pp. 21–6. For an excellent survey of the position in 1945, see Alan Bullock, *Ernest Bevin: Foreign Secretary*. New York, W. W. Norton, 1983, "The world in the Summer of 1945," pp. 3–48.

[2]Lawrence S. Kaplan, *The United States and NATO: The Formative Years*. Lexington, University Press of Kentucky, 1984. Sir Nicolas Henderson, *The Birth of NATO*. London, Weidenfeld and Nicolson, 1982.

Foreign Ministers at the end of 1947 to reach agreement on the German question. The Soviets mistakenly believed that they would continue to get their way, without reciprocal concessions on their part. But Moscow's hard line merely strengthened Western resistance and promoted Western collaboration. The first and foremost advocate of a trans-Atlantic alliance was Winston Churchill. Though dismissed from Number Ten Downing Street in 1945, Churchill – as leader of the opposition – kept himself extremely well informed about the Soviet's military strength and about their political intentions. He was on close personal terms with President Truman, whom he had first met at Potsdam and whom he liked immensely. In March 1946, it was Truman who escorted Churchill to Fulton, Missouri, where Churchill delivered the famous "iron curtain" speech that defined his view of the nature of the Soviet threat. The Fulton speech was not popular at the time – Churchill had expressed himself too bluntly. But the Soviets' own conduct justified his assessment. Thus thought Attlee, and also Ernest Bevin, the British foreign secretary.

Anglo-American collaboration was fundamental to the Western alliance. There was indeed "a special relationship" between the two countries. No other Western European state had collaborated with the US on terms remotely as close as Great Britain. During World War II, the British and Americans had quarreled. But overall, there was the closest of links between British and American admirals, nuclear scientists, economic planners, businessmen, and intelligence agents. The British and Americans spoke the same language, and read the same books. In US Gallup polls, only Canada exceeded Great Britain in popularity – a state of affairs that would continue for many years.[3] There was constant interchange between British and American academics, journalists, and entertainers. For Americans, there was also the bond of snob appeal. In the US Britain commanded respect from both Anglophile members of the eastern establishment, and from intellectuals with social democratic sympathies. To most Americans, a British accent sounded better than any foreign brogue. In terms of *realpolitik*, Britain during the 1940s and the 1950s remained the most powerful of US allies. Not surprisingly, NATO was initially built round an Anglo-American core, a fact both recognized and resented by de Gaulle.

On the Western European Continent, Britain commanded a wartime legacy of goodwill, having served as the headquarters of expatriate governments such as the Dutch and the Free French. Bevin thus found an able supporter among a former resistant such as Georges Bidault, his counterpart in the French ministry of foreign affairs. Both were assisted, among others, by the Canadian leaders, especially Louis S. St Lourent, the Canadian prime minister, and leader of the Liberal Party, and by Lester B. Pearson, the Canadian secretary for external affairs, whose diplomacy profited from Canada's dual connection to North America and the British Commonwealth. Canada's adherence to the

[3]In 1989, 95 percent of US respondents favored the US, 92 percent Canada, 86 percent Britain, 59 percent Israel. *Gallup Report* no. 24, May 1989, p. 6.

alliance, as well as Iceland's, helped to persuade wavering US isolationists that NATO was not merely a European alliance in disguise, but also served American needs in the Atlantic. This was the view of statesmen such as Dean Acheson, a brilliant lawyer trained at Yale and Harvard Law School, who helped to guide US policy at this crucial point. (Acheson served as undersecretary of state 1945–7, and secretary of state from 1949 to 1953.)[4]

It was an uphill struggle to overcome US resistance. For instance ex-president Herbert Hoover advised his countrymen to build "fortress America," and avoid European entanglements. Truman managed to obtain massive bipartisan support. His coadjutators included Senator Arthur H. Vandenberg, a former isolationist converted to interventionism, whose "Vandenberg resolution" in the Senate opened the way to US adherence to NATO. There were other legal complications. Later on the Western European host countries, for example, received the right to try American servicemen charged with crimes against local citizens in the host countries' courts and under their own laws – a major political issue in the US at the time. It required courage both on the part of the Truman and later of the Eisenhower administration to resist US hostility to accords that would have been inconceivable, had they been applied in a comparable manner to Soviet citizens stationed in Eastern Europe. Even after NATO's formation (April 4, 1949), the new structure was by no means solid. (In fact, US military strength in Western Europe actually declined between 1949 and 1950.) It was the Korean war that unexpectedly and unintendedly cemented the Western alliance.

US policy makers considered that the North Korean assault formed a global test of Western steadfastness, and that West Germany might be endangered if the communists were not resisted in South Korea. Such beliefs were not unreasonable at a time when the USSR and the People's Republic of China were closely allied. Stalin had equipped and trained the North Korean army. He had installed Kim Il Sung in Pyongyang in 1945. And Soviet pilots flew some of the North Korean aircraft during the sneak attack. CIA estimates held that there was a real threat of war. In contrast to the West, the Soviet leadership could act secretly and decisively, unencumbered by public opinion and parliamentary restraints. Moscow operated on the premise that a permanent conflict with the West was inevitable, that its immediate object was to divide the West, but that its own military position was so strong as to permit the Soviet Union to initiate hostilities with little warning. As Walter Laqueur, a modern historian, puts it, "any reader of *Pravda* or of Stalin's speeches was bound to come to similar conclusions."[5] Hence the US determined at the same time both to fight in Korea and to strengthen Europe's defense.

[4]Dean Acheson, *Present at the Creation: My Years in the State Department*. New York, W. W. Norton, 1969.

[5]For a detailed study see L. H. Gann, *The Defense of Western Europe*. London, Croom Helm and Dover, Auburn House Publishing Co., 1987. For a sociological assessment, see Morris Janowitz, *The Professional Soldier: A Social and Political Portrait*. Glencoe, Ill., The Free Press, 1960. For US intelligence estimates at the time, see Walter Laqueur, *A World of Secrets: The Uses and Limits of Intelligence*. New York, Basic Books, 1985, pp. 117–21.

> *"Americans and Europeans must recognize that neither is defending a particular country, but that the ensemble is defending a common civilization." Jean Monnet*

The transformation of US policy was paralleled by changes in Western Europe, where the sense of apprehension was if anything even stronger. As Thucydides put it more than two millennia before, a successful alliance must rest on "a certain like-mindedness" between the partners, and above all, "an equality of mutual fear," a sentiment that formed "the only safe guarantee for a stable league," for then the party that wants to break faith is deterred by the thought that the odds will not be on his side.[6] It was this well founded dread that caused the individual partners to strengthen or rebuild those national forces on which their joint safety would ultimately depend.

NATIONAL COMPONENTS

Great Britain

In 1940, the British had saved themselves and placed the world in their debt by their successful defense of the British Isles and Egypt. They had also given the lie to those pacifist intellectuals who had asserted during prewar days that preparation for war was useless, and that surrender was better than war. Pacifism was of small account in British postwar politics, and the British continued to do their best to maintain the balance of power in Europe. They did so at a time when their own strength was visibly declining. In June 1944 the British empire troops deployed in Normandy had equalled those of the North Americans; by March 1945 only about one-quarter of General Eisenhower's forces were British. British power waned at a time when Roosevelt increasingly became convinced that the US and the USSR between them could solve the world's problems, that world peace required the liquidation of Western (above all British) colonialism, and the elimination of British imperial trade preferences. British intervention in Greece and its support of Turkey had played a major part in preventing these countries from falling under Soviet hegemony, an aim that should have delighted the American president, yet did not.

The first British Labour government, in all essentials, continued Churchill's policy. The British kept the draft, maintained a relatively large force (about 800,000 men and women in uniform in 1951), and spent about 10 percent of their GNP on defense (as opposed to 3 percent in prewar days). This was a remarkable effort at a time when the British continued to be beset by shortages, rationing, and all manner of economic difficulties. Not only were the British forces relatively numerous – they were efficient, and thoroughly integrated into national life. The British army weaved no plots, never aspired to become

---

[6]Thucydides, *History of the Peloponnesian War*, trans. Rex Warner. Baltimore, Maryland, Penguin Books, 1967 edn, p. 167.

the "school for the nation," despised neither politicians nor parliament, trusted its generals, and lacked collective political ambition and that *raison d'armée* that had affected so many other national armies. The British armed forces (like the Dutch but unlike those of France and Portugal) remained unaffected in their loyalty to their own government during the trauma of decolonization. As John Keegan, a highly qualified observer, put it, "Britain's army may . . . be judged one of the country's most successful institutions," clearly "among the most successful in Europe, if not the world."[7]

What was the secret of British military success? It was not their supposed willingness to pawn their economic recovery for the sake of maintaining a large military and imperial establishment. (In 1955, the British still had the highest per capita GNP in Western Europe.) Nor did British strength derive from its imperial links. The "white" dominions did not continue their close military partnership with Great Britain once the war had ended; instead they all greatly reduced their forces and concentrated on home defense. British forces withdrew from the Indian subcontinent, from Burma and Malaya, and later on from Palestine. The African empire was held by small local forces. (To give just one example, the Federation of Rhodesia and Nyasaland during the 1950s maintained no more than about 4,000 men under arms, as against 41,000 in Zimbabwe, 14,000 in Zambia, and 5,000 in Malawi after independence.)

Nevertheless, Britain's remaining imperial commitments placed it, like France, on the horns of an age-old dilemma. Should Britain prepare for a conventional war in Europe, or concentrate on imperial policing? A difficult choice, as each option required an entirely distinctive military mode. And if Britain were to concentrate on a European role, should she stress air and naval defense, or land warfare? Alternatively, should Britain build up a nuclear deterrent, or rely only on conventional means?

The nuclear option was adopted unequivocally, and without public discussion. British scientists (including German-speaking refugees) had taken an important part in early US preparations for nuclear warfare. But the US McMahon Act of 1946 categorically forbade the exchange of atomic information with foreign countries, and thereby encouraged rather than impeded nuclear proliferation within the Atlantic community. The first British Labour government resolved to go on with existing designs for providing Britain with an independent nuclear deterrent. Even though the cabinet realized that the country might have to face economic crisis, Britain could not allow herself to lag behind in a field of major importance in industrial as well as the military field. Any "false economy" would prevent Britain from dealing with the US on equal terms. The British went ahead with nuclear weapon development, and in 1952 tested their first atomic bomb – three years after the Soviet Union.

The British decision to make nuclear weapons was political rather than strategic in nature. The British built the bomb, not because senior military

[7]John Keegan, "Western Europe and its armies 1945–1985," in Gann, ed., *The Defense of Western Europe*, p. 9.

officers had lobbied for the new weaponry, or because planners had integrated nuclear weapons into a well-thought-out strategy, but solely in order to retain their status as a great power. They succeeded in this for a brief period without, however, being able to check the long-term decline of British power world-wide.

British nuclear development went with striking inventiveness in other military fields. Whatever critics of her industrial performance might say, Britain, after 1945 "continued to lead the way in a rather broader field of defense-related devices than is generally appreciated."[8] As befits a major technological power, the British also continued to maintain a substantial air force, including tactical forces, and a strategic bomber force. In terms of military manpower, the air force came to rank second after the army, leaving the Royal Navy, the Senior Service, in third place. The Royal Navy continued to be the mainstay of what later became NATO's eastern Atlantic command. Its world-wide role declined, however, as decolonization steadily diminished the available overseas bases. Increasingly, it was becoming a small-ship fleet suited for anti-submarine warfare, composed primarily of submarines, frigates, patrol craft, and the like. But this was not the whole story, for Admiral Lord Mountbatten's appointment as First Sea Lord (1955–9) proved as decisive as Admiral Sir John Fisher's appointment had been for the reform of the navy before World War I. Mountbatten promoted the development of the nuclear-powered submarine, abolished cruisers, introduced helicopters for a variety of purposes, and provided anti-ship and anti-aircraft missiles. The strike carrier, for the time being, remained the heart of the fleet. Mountbatten forced the three armed services to collaborate with an effectiveness attained at the time by no other nation. His influence on the British armed forces in the second half of the twentieth century was unrivalled.[9] And so was the Royal Navy's high morale, practical experience, and operational excellence.

It was nevertheless the army that continued to account for the major part of British military manpower.[10] During the immediate postwar period, it formed the core of what land defenses were available in Western Europe. (In 1949, it consisted of 380,000 men, organized into 30 armored regiments, 69 artillery regiments, 77 British and 8 Gurkha battalions.) It was the army that formed by far the most important component of Britain's commitment to Europe. As Sir Anthony Eden, the British foreign secretary, put it in 1954, "the United Kingdom will continue to maintain on the mainland of Europe, including Germany, the effective strength now assigned to SACEUR [Supreme

---

[8]For a selective list see Roger Beaumont, "The British armed forces since 1945," in Gann, ed., *The Defense of Western Europe*, p. 53.

[9]Field Marshal Lord Carver, *Twentieth Century Warriors: The Development of the Armed Forces of the Major Military Nations in the Twentieth Century*. New York, Weidenfeld and Nicolson, 1987, pp. 37–9.

[10]By 1958 the army's strength stood at 323,900, as against 184,900 in the Royal Air Force, and 105,400 in the Royal Navy.) For detailed figures for Britain and other powers see Institute for Strategic Studies, *The Soviet Union and the NATO Powers: The Military Balance*. London, The Institute, 1959.

Allied Commander in Europe, under NATO] – four divisions and the tactical air force – or whatever SACEUR regards as equivalent."[11] (A promise subsequently only kept in part.)

For many years after the war, the British armed forces continued to rely on conscription (extended to two years in 1950), which provided the army with about half its men. The draft had many advantages. Men entered the army from every walk of life; the draft was fairly applied; it met with acceptance from the majority of citizens. (According to a public opinion poll taken in the early 1950s, 57 percent of the respondents considered that the draft should continue, and only 33 percent thought it should end.) Conscription allowed the armed forces to expand in times of need. (By 1953, at the end of the Korean war, the army stood at 440,000 men.) Not that the servicemen particularly enjoyed themselves; discipline was often tougher than during the war, because there was more time for drill parades and inspections.[12] But the servicemen accepted the draft as an inescapable duty and a good many of them were able to travel abroad.

The army's cohesion rested on three pillars. It relied on social consensus. It was integrated into British life. And it was a law-abiding army, as befitted a law-abiding country with a low crime rate. Sergeants would yell at their men on the barracks square, but physical violence against recruits was rare and harshly punished. The infantry relied on a strong regimental spirit, as every region and every major city had its own local infantry regiment, proud of its real or alleged traditions, convinced that its own glories outshone those of any other regiment.

Above all, the army maintained a high standard in its officer corps. (Only half the applicants managed to be accepted.) Despite ongoing changes in its social composition, the officer corps remained one of the socially most conservative institutions in British life. The great public schools had traditionally provided the largest reservoir of applicants. Catholic boarding schools attained increasing importance, as they gained a reputation for endowing their graduates with that public spirit and discipline particularly desired by the REB (Regular Commissions Board). In addition, the army found recruits among university graduates, and its own "sixth form" (Standard 12) college at Welbeck.

The officer's central training institution was the Royal Military Academy Sandhurst (established in 1947 by the merger of the Royal Military College at Sandhurst, and the Royal Military Academy at Woolwich, the latter having specialized in the training of engineer and artillery officers). Recruitment to Sandhurst was somewhat democratized when the Labour government abolished the old distinction between gentlemen cadets (largely public school boys whose fathers paid for their training) and army cadets who had risen through

---

[11]Cited in Alfred F. Havighurst. *Britain in Transition: The Twentieth Century*. Chicago, University of Chicago Press, 1985 edn, p. 450.

[12]Henry Stanhope, *The Soldiers: An Anatomy of the British Army*. London, Hamish Hamilton, 1979, p. 16.

the ranks. Henceforth all officer cadets were paid by the army, not financed by their families. Nevertheless, the officer corps retained its old flavor, with the emphasis on "good form" and good manners, respectful both of the army, and of those civilian organizations that employed them once the ex-officers had doffed their uniforms.

Overall, the army became more technologically minded, and contained a larger administrative component than in prewar days. The infantry which had absorbed about half the army's strength before World War II, thereafter accounted for only about one-fifth. The less glamorous corps which supplied the fighting men with food, fuel, and ammunition, henceforth took about 40 percent of the soldiers. Headquarters and depots also accounted for substantial resources, because of the need to train and organize the conscripts.[13]

The British army of the late 1940s and the 1950s remained in many ways a World War II army, equipped with World War II weapons. Given its many limitations, this army proved surprisingly versatile. Alone among Western armies, the British scored an unbroken series of successes against guerrillas – Chinese communists in Malaya, Mau Mau in Kenya, EOKA in Cyprus, Indonesians in North Borneo. A British Commonwealth division likewise performed extremely well in Korea, in a conventional conflict.

The British (and their French allies), however, did not come up to their own expectations in the Suez campaign of 1956. Not that Britain would have been unable to defeat the Egyptians, given time. But the British were unable to strike swiftly. Fearing a repetition of the Arnhem disaster in World War II (purely an airborne operation), the British high command insisted on massive landings by sea, a time-consuming operation that left no scope for surprise. For this task, the British lacked the gift for rapid improvisation; they wavered in their objectives and, unlike the Israelis, did not have a clearly defined political purpose. Britain, for the first time faced opposition both from the USSR and the US and public opinion became bitterly divided, as lifelong friends and even members of the same family split over the war. In the end, the British withdrew from Suez, and Britain's traditional standing in the Middle East declined. So did her relative position within NATO, as West German armament proceeded, and West Germany during the 1960s turned into NATO's main European pillar.

Suez demonstrated British weaknesses in other ways. There was a rapid decline in the country's foreign currency reserves, as Indians, Middle East-erners, and Chinese withdrew funds from British banks, and as US speculators and the Federal Reserve Bank tried to get rid of their sterling. The Suez war left a legacy of acrimony in Britain with regard to the US, which had done all in its power to impede its ally's invasion. Above all, the British establishment became convinced that Britain could no longer exercise world power, and pro-European sentiments became increasingly respectable. But the establishment itself increasingly came under attack from intellectuals, as British writers struck

---

[13]Stanhope, *The Soldiers: An Anatomy of the British Army,* p. 15.

a new and sourer note (exemplified by John Osborne's play *Look Back in Anger*
which opened in 1956).[14]

The British decided to drop conscription for political and economic reasons
rather than on military grounds. (The services would have preferred national
service to continue.[15] In 1957, after the Suez debacle, Harold Macmillan
succeeded Anthony Eden as prime minister, and he chose as his defense
secretary Duncan Sandys ("shifting Sandys" according to some of the service
chiefs). The new team imposed a new solution. They resolved to rely on
"massive retaliation" and on an all-professional force – efficient, well-trained,
the kind of army that field officers best liked to command. Under the new
plan, the army would be reduced from 385,000 in 1957, to an all-regular force
of 180,000 by 1963. Great Britain henceforth everted to the prewar pattern,
the only major European power to rely on an all-professional military establishment. As the Argentinians found to their cost during the Falklands war,
the British armed forces still remained capable of fighting a successful campaign
thousands of miles from their home base. But overall, the British relinquished
their stake in Asia and Africa.

France

France's army is Europe's oldest and the most renowned. Her navy had
likewise played a major part in European history. (At the beginning of World
War II, it had formed the most modern of the world's great fleets, and was
far better prepared for war than either the army or the air force.) Despite the
disasters of World War II, the French army remained numerically the largest
in Western Europe during the immediate postwar years. (In 1950, the army
had 456,000 men under arms, the air force 68,000, and the navy 54,000. As a
result of the Algerian war and general rearmament, the corresponding figures
ten years later respectively stood at 834,000 (including 63,000 in the *gendarmerie*), 139,000 in the air force; and 76,000 in the navy.) But unlike the British
armed forces, the French military had for long felt alienated within their own
country – not surprising in a land long marked by "the absence of a clear and
abiding public attachment to a stable constitutional framework."[16]

The French armed forces had been loyal enough to the Third Republic as
long as the Republic ruled with firmness. But since the fall of France in 1940,
the fighting services vacillated between two poles, nostalgia for *la gloire* and

[14]Chester Cooper, *The Lion's Last Roar: Suez 1956*. New York, Harper and Row, 1976, passim.

[15]Martin S. Navias, "Terminating Conscription? The British National Service Controversy,"
Journal of Contemporary History, v. 24, no. 2, April 1989, pp. 195–208.

[16]John Stewart Ambler, *The French Army in Politics, 1945–1962*. Colombus, Ohio State Univer-
sity, 1966, p. 374. Also see George Armstrong Kelly, *Lost Soldiers: the French Army and Empire in
Crisis, 1947–1962*. Cambridge, Mass., MIT Press, 1965. Raoul Giradet, *La Société Militaire dans
La France Contemporaine, 1815–1939*. Paris, Plon, 1953. Paul-Marie de la Gorce, *The French Army,
A Military-Political History*. New York, George Braziller, 1963. Peter Paret, *French Revolutionary
Warfare from Indochina to Algeria: The Analysis of a Political and Military Doctrine*. New York,
Praeger, 1964.

the *crise de conscience* over loyalties. *La gloire* was real enough. Even during the disastrous 1940 campaign, many units – though out-generalled at every turn – had fought well; their casualties had been considerable, given the brief duration of the battle. But even more in evidence was the *crise de conscience*, that reflected the wider cleavages in French society and politics.

La crise de conscience had struck most heavily at the navy. Under the Third Republic, naval officers had been even more alienated from the Republic than the commissioned ranks in the army. For this state of affairs there were many reasons – personnel deployment far from home; the post-World War I inflation that had gnawed away the purchasing power of military and naval salaries; the extensive recruitment of officers from naval (frequently aristocratic) families that intermarried and looked askance at plebeians; and a nostalgic monarchism that caused many officers to regard the Republic with contempt.[17] This disdain was ungrateful because between 1922 and 1940, the Republic spent more on the navy than it had done during the preceding 55 years. Nevertheless, in the face of defeat, the admirals' ingratitude toward the Republic outdid the politicians'. (Ten admirals served Vichy in cabinet or sub-cabinet posts; Vichy was often referred to as the "government of admirals.") Anglophobia in the navy worsened when the British in 1940 destroyed a major part of the French fleet at Oran, Algeria, so as to prevent their falling under German control. Only a few ships and a single admiral had adhered to de Gaulle.

> In 1946, the French fleet numbered 3 battleships, 2 fleet aircraft carriers, 9 cruisers, 30 destroyers, and 30 submarines – reduced to 3 aircraft carriers, 3 cruisers, 66 destroyers and frigates, and 22 submarines by 1960. The Royal Navy in 1960 numbered 8 aircraft carriers, 175 destroyers and frigates, and 42 submarines.

During the postwar trials against real or suspected collaborators, naval officers formed the largest single bloc of defendants. Numerically, the French remained Western Europe's second navy – far from insignificant, despite wartime losses, and after changes and reductions that transformed it into a mainly small-ship fleet. But the admiral's gold braid ceased to be an asset for political advancement. Promotion within the navy was slow, favoring mainly the former Free French officers. Not surprisingly, the atmosphere in French wardrooms remained tense for many years afterwards.

The generals were held in only slightly better regard than the admirals. The *blitzkrieg* had discredited those who had led France in 1940 and had prepared for the wrong war. Army men also had played an important part in the Vichy regime, led by a French marshal. And these military officers, and the small force they continued to command under the terms of the armistice regime, later came to share Vichy's general discredit. Defeat caused the first of many *crises de conscience* within the army. Should a patriot obey what appeared the legal government in France? Or should he defy the marshal, despite the

---

[17]Ronald Chalmers Hood, *Royal Republicans: The French Naval Dynasties Between the World Wars.* Baton Rouge, Louisiana State University Press, 1985.

personal oath of allegiance that all military personnel had been made to swear to Pétain?

World War II was indeed a time of agonizing personal decisions, when an officer's career and reputation all too often depended on his ability to bet on the right horse. As General Boyer de la Tour recalled, "in 1942, at the time of the American landing in North Africa ... I received orders to march against the Americans. I refused. If the landing had not succeeded, I would have been a rebel." Boyer de la Tour had done the right thing. Not so General Dentz who had fought against the British and Free French in Syria in 1941. Following the liberation of France, Dentz was put on trial. He pleaded that he had obeyed orders – only to be told by the public prosecutor that "at the grade you hold, and in the functions you fulfill, one is the judge of the orders one receives." The French army long remembered the lesson.[18]

The army's problem of loyalty toward the civil power became all the more complicated during the immediate postwar period. The officer corps was purged of active or suspected Vichyites – by 1947, almost 3,000 officers had been dismissed for collaboration or for failing to join the resistance. De Gaulle faced, and solved, the supremely difficult task of amalgamating four disparate elements – the Free French forces, the army of Africa, the regular army, and the underground forces. Each had a character of its own, none was conducive to old-fashioned discipline.

The Free French who had joined de Gaulle in the early days were mostly young officers, little known before the war – keen, adventurous, contemptuous of those who refused to join what to most had seemed a hopeless cause smacking of subversion. The Free French had gained battle honors at places such as Bir-Hakeim and Kufra; they were the first on de Gaulle's promotion list. Then there was the African army that joined de Gaulle during and after the Allied conquest of French North Africa. The army of Africa had always evinced a spirit of independence; the French colonial conquests had owed much to "autonomous," often unauthorized, action on the army's part. They were not easy men to deal with from the standpoint of Paris politicians, and resented the preference given by de Gaulle to the Free French. Nevertheless, the officers in both factions had a similar background and education. Those who had exchanged shots at Dakar and in Syria, soon made their peace and fought as brothers in arms as far afield as Tunisia, Italy, the Rhône and the Rhine. Purges among the African army, (unlike those in the home army), were limited to the most senior cadres. The remainder redeemed themselves in battle. Given the relatively large size of the colonial forces, the African army came to make up the central core of the French army until the Indochinese war.[19]

Finally, the army had to absorb the resistance fighters. Whatever their party loyalties, they were apt to be leftist in outlook, impatient of discipline, used to unconventional methods and unconventional war. Many of them had fought

[18]Cited in Ambler, *The French Army*, p. 71.
[19]Paul-Marie de la Gorce, *The French Army*, p. 344.

tough little battles against German pockets of resistance, and had done so hampered by lack of weapons and equipment, but led by adventurous, dynamic men, disdainful of military bureaucracy. Much to the experts' surprise, they were successfully amalgamated into the French forces that liberated France. This task was achieved largely by General Jean Lattre de Tassigny, himself a brilliant and unconventional officer. (His First French Army, at the moment of landing, comprised 250,000 men, strengthened by the subsequent incorporation of 137,000 men drawn from the *Forces Françaises de l'Intérieur*.) The army that helped to liberate France and conquer Germany looked ragged and unfamilar in their uniforms heterogeneously derived from British and American stocks. Their *matériel* was entirely of foreign (mainly American) manufacture. But they knew how to fight. Foul-ups there were aplenty, but for a brief moment, *la gloire* outweighed any *crise de conscience*.

Then came peace, and the glory tarnished. There was some small satisfaction entailed in *la petite revanche* (the little vengeance), entailed by the occupation of the French zone in Germany. Generals lived in splendor and colonels in state, with formal parades and fine receptions. Frenchmen brought their families to Germany where they made up for the hardships of occupation by unaccustomed luxury. Such pleasures, however, could not make up for the evils of a "peace to corrupt no less than war to waste."[20] De Gaulle departed from office. Civilian planners such as Monnet had no interest in the armed forces, and thought above all of modernizing the French economy. Military salaries were further diminished in purchasing power by inflation. French officers were poor men within the world's military profession. (In 1953, a major in the French army received 95,000 francs a month, as against 120,000 francs paid to his colleague of equivalent rank in the British army, 220,000 in the Soviet army, and 280,000 in the US army). The French officers' privileges of rank counted for little when measured against those of professors and civil servants within the *dirigiste* state, in which a customs director (second class) earned more money than a lieutenant-colonel with a long and distinguished fighting career.

The temper of the French officers was worsened by many other grievances – the impact of political patronage of a kind unknown in the British and US forces, a pervasive housing shortage, difficulties of personal adjustment after long service overseas (*le mal jaune*), a sense of social isolation in a nation that no longer valued the army as of old, and a lack of modern equipment, together with large-scale personnel reductions among officers and noncommissioned officers (the feared and hated *dégagement des cadres*). Not surprisingly, the social level of the French officer corps dropped, as many highly qualified men left to take up jobs in business, administration, or the professions, and as upper-class and middle-class parents became increasingly reluctant to send their sons to Saint-Cyr (the renowned military school).

Given these obstacles, the army did amazingly well. It retained a small number of dedicated officers with a fine fighting record and a broad general

---

[20] John Milton, *Paradise Lost*, 1. 779.

culture, who gained an influential position within the military establishment. The army provided military, as well as social, advancement to numerous noncommissioned officers. The officers retained a strong *esprit de corps,* and soldiers' sons continued to become soldiers. (Among the Saint-Cyr cadets in the mid-1950s, fully 58 percent of cadets counted a father or a grandfather who had been a career soldier. Among the officers trained at the *école spéciale militaire inter-armes,* which prepared NCOs for commissions, 50.5 percent were soldiers' sons.)[21]

Frenchmen bore the burden of national service without much complaint, albeit without much enthusiasm. There were few conscientious objectors, despite the high proportion of men annually conscripted (300,000 out of 400,000 for all three services).[22] The army's equipment was gradually brought up to date, and its dependence on foreign *matériel* lessened as home industries expanded, and French manufacturers and arms exporters gained a reputation for excellence in many advanced fields – including the production of tanks, helicopters, and jet planes. (By 1950, the French army could boast, for instance, of the 15-ton light tank AMX, the EBR Panhard armored car, the ground-to-ground missiles SS10 and SS11, all indicative of an astonishing industrial revival.) Training methods improved, and so did the army's tactical doctrine. (The French pioneered the modern light division (later brigades) – mobile, trained for independent movement, with superior firepower, prepared to operate on a battlefield where atomic weapons might be used.) Traditional hostility toward Germany waned. From 1949, the French army, traditionally anti-communist in outlook, readily took to its new NATO role, and would probably have remained sullenly loyal to the Fourth Republic – but for the Republic's colonial entanglements.

The first of these derived from the French resolve to reoccupy Indochina after the end of the war. The resultant war against the Indochinese communists faced the French with extraordinary difficulties. They had to conduct hostilities thousands of miles away from their homeland against an enemy supported from nearby China, a foe well equipped and (at the end of the struggle) superior in numbers. They faced an enemy who skillfully camouflaged his political objectives. The Indochinese communists (the Viet Minh) and their leader Ho Chi Minh at first vigorously denied communist connections.[23] The French moreover faced an insoluble political dilemma: soldiers might risk their lives to maintain French sovereignty in Indochina, but few were willing to die for an independent Vietnam. Vietnamese, by the same token, might be willing to be shot at in a struggle against a communist dictatorship, but few were willing to perish for the French *tricolore.*

Indochina became a harsh test. The war was in no sense simply a guerrilla

---

[21]Douglas Porch, "The French defense and the Gaullist legacy," in Gann, ed., *The Defense of Western Europe,* p. 189.

[22]John Keegan, "France," in John Keegan, ed., *World Armies.* New York, Facts on File, 1979, p. 229. Conscientious objection was, however, only legalized in 1968.

[23]Robert F. Turner, *Vietnamese Communism, Its Origins and Development.* Stanford, Cal. Hoover Institution Press, 1975, pp. 69–72.

war, as partisan operations were extended into conventional campaigns that mutually reinforced one another. The communists maintained a balance between partisan and conventional operations, and created a situation in which "free zones" became interlaced with enemy-held areas. The French, by contrast, could not appeal to the mass of the people. They experienced great difficulties in freeing themselves from the shackles of conventional logistics. Motor trucks and motorized infantry could not easily move through trackless jungle, whereas Viet Minh carriers managed to negotiate the most difficult country, and foot slogging fighting squads achieved great mobility. The French tried to fight too far from their bases. Strategically audacious, their tactics were marked by road-bound movements and conventional hedgehog defense. All too often they would strike deep into enemy country without adequately safeguarding their own lines of communication and supply. The French commanders in Indochina in fact committed many of the mistakes made by Napoleon's generals in Spain. They neglected the essential principle that effective counter-guerrilla operations depend on a combination of close territorial control with effective striking forces. In the end, their grip weakened in disastrous fashion, and they began to suffer defeats in major, as well as minor battles. The communists, for their part, mastered the art of positional as well as of mobile warfare, and in 1954 brought off a spectacular victory at Dien Bien Phu.[24]

Dien Bien Phu did not crush the French army in Indochina; only a small proportion of its forces had been involved. During the battle, the communist ground forces had outnumbered their opponents by about ten to one, they enjoyed great superiority in *matériel* and firepower and communist casualties greatly outnumbered those of the French. But Dien Bien Phu constituted an enormous political defeat; the French were by now thoroughly tired of *la sale guerre*, the "dirty war" without fronts. In 1954 a peace conference at Geneva divided Indochina into two states, the communist Democratic Republic of Vietnam in the north, and the Republic of Vietnam, headed by Ngo Dinh Diem. The peace settlement by no means constituted a total communist victory but it was a brief respite – destined ultimately to end in a tyranny far more bloodstained than French rule at its worst.

The immediate impact of the Indochinese war on the French army was profound. The professional soldiers felt deserted by the Republic, and also ashamed of having abandoned those Vietnamese who had fought for the French cause. French military theoreticians had been radicalized by the encounter with the Viet Minh, and their new combination of Marx, marksmanship, and murder. In response, military intellectuals developed half-baked theories of their own concerning *la guerre révolutionaire*, a mode of warfare that run-of-the-mill politicians supposedly could not comprehend. To make matters worse, the army's confidence in the Republic was further shaken shortly after by the

---

[24]Peter Paret and John W. Shy, *Guerrillas in the 1960s*. New York, Frederick A. Praeger, 1962, pp. 41–2.

abortive project for a European Defense Community (EDC), a design that seemed to threaten the army's very existence.

Immediately after came the war for Algeria (1954–62), a conflict that the French army was determined not to lose. Algeria legally formed part of France and contained a substantial European minority (about 10 percent of the population), as well as numerous Arabs willing to put on French uniform. The French cultural impact in Algeria had been infinitely greater than in Indochina, and its importance for France outweighed Indochina's (the latter being a strategic irrelevancy for the metropole).

The French won in a purely military sense. There were no Dien Bien Phus. The Algerian guerrillas never built up conventional forces capable of beating the French in a major battle. By the early 1960s, the French controlled the bulk of Algeria after a fashion, but they had failed politically and psychologically. They could only have continued to hold Algeria by armed force. They had moreover drawn the wrong conclusions from the Indochinese war. The Algerian conflict was not a confrontation with world communism – no matter what French propaganda might assert. (The Algerian guerrillas, organized in the FLN (*Front de Libération Nationale*), successfully insisted throughout that communists could only join the FLN ranks as individuals, not as party members.) The war instead pitted Algerian nationalism against French nationalism, and Islam against Western creeds, both Christian and Marxist-Leninist, in a country that the French had been unable to assimilate culturally, as they had absorbed German-speaking Alsace.

The Algerian war proved even more divisive for France than the Indochinese conflict. It arrayed France against her allies, who did little to support her in what French law and army perceived as defense of the national territory. The war split the army from the politicians; it also caused cleavages within the army itself, between the conscripts and elite units such as the paratroopers and the Foreign Legion who gained such publicity and glory as the war would afford. Even more serious was the moral divide within the army. The FLN engaged in merciless terror as part of a wider strategy. It was terror totally distinct from the variety encountered by British soldiers fighting Irish or Palestinian Jewish guerrillas – only the tactics of the Mau Mau provide a parallel. The French responded savagely. France was not the world's only country where many police officers believed that "putting the boot in" went with the job. But the French now deliberately employed torture. Admittedly, this counter-terror was reactive and selective, as against the FLN's initiatory and comprehensive kind. But torture practiced by the French divided the army morally between those who approved and those who felt ashamed. Counter-terror also deepened the split between the army and the bulk of French intellectuals, apt – like their colleagues in other Western countries – to see the mote in the compatriot's eye, but not the beam in the enemy's.

The Algerian war set planners against planners. The counter-guerrilla operations required an old-style army, fit for massive deployment of infantry overseas. "Europeanists" such as de Gaulle, by contrast, looked for a modern mechanized army that would restore France as a great nation in Europe.[25] For these modernizers, Algeria was an encumbrance. In 1958 de Gaulle returned to power, ostensibly determined to maintain French sovereignty in Algeria. But with regal duplicity he proceeded to disappoint both the army and the French settlers who had helped to put him in power. As de Gaulle privately put it in succinct, though inelegant fashion: "L'Afrique est foutue et l'Algérie avec." (Africa is screwed, and along with it, Algeria.) By a strange irony, de Gaulle – a Catholic conservative and a soldier's soldier – once more became the far right's most dangerous opponent, as he had been for the men of Vichy. The Evian agreement summarily ended France's involvement in Algeria. Something like 1,300,000 people (mostly, but not all, Europeans) fled. Tens, and perhaps hundreds, of thousands of Algerians who had fought or worked with the French, were left behind and massacred. Algeria was left in ruins, a country dispirited and corrupt. And the French army stood divided between those who regarded de Gaulle as a king and those who accounted him a traitor. The Fourth Republic collapsed. But the colonial burden had gone.

Given its political experiences, the French army might then have turned into a praetorian force of the Latin American variety, politically ambitious, militarily of small account. This did not happen. The French took due precaution to guard against future plots. They kept up a large paramilitary police force, the *gendarmerie nationale*, used primarily to maintain internal order (under control of the ministry of the interior). Officers henceforth were allowed to serve for only a limited number of years with the paratroopers. French governments sought to assure the political neutrality of the army by imposing upon it the structural divisions of the political establishment, and creating a system of checks and balances.[26] While never living up to its ill-merited reputation of being *la grande muette* (the great silent one), the French army remained loyal to civilian authority, and never again turned king-maker. Even to the most conservative-minded officers, the Republic ceased to be a slut.

The French armed services remained militarily efficient, despite their unpromising legacy. Operationally, they were eventually organized into three major sections – the *forces de manoeuvre*, kept almost to full war strength; the *forces d'intervention* (paratroopers and amphibious units used for "brushfire" wars overseas), and the *forces du territoire* (motorized and armored units for home defense). The main striking force resided in the First Army, divided into three corps consisting mainly of armored divisions (one corps located in eastern France, another in West Germany, the third in northern France). French armored divisions were smaller than their US counterparts, but highly mobile, well armed, and well equipped with anti-tank weapons. The French moreover built up their own nuclear force. The Achilles heel remained the

---

[25]The best general account of the Algerian war in English still is Alistair Horne, *A Savage War of Peace: Algeria 1954–1962.* London, Macmillion, 1977. See also by the same author, *The French Army in Politics.* New York, Peter Brodrick Books, 1984.

[26]John Keegan, "Western Europe and its armies, 1945–1985," in Gann, ed., *The Defense of Western Europe,* p. 7.

reserve organization. Upon mobilization, many line units would be doubled in size with the addition of reservists. Most of these latter were assigned to logistical and rear-area roles; but on paper large and unwieldy reserve units remained which the government, in the event of war, would be hard pressed to equip.[27] For all these deficiencies, de Gaulle achieved what he set out to do – France once more became a military power in Europe.

The German Federal Republic

Nie wieder Krieg (war – never again) ran a pacifist slogan that echoed throughout Germany after the collapse of the Third Reich. *Nie wieder Sieg* (victory – never again) was the title chosen for a book by General Wolf Count von Baudissin, a Wehrmacht veteran.[28] War and victories alike had lost their glamor in post-World War II Germany. Soldiers had seen their generals sent by fellow-Germans to concentration camps and firing squads. The experience of defeat had done its work, as had war crimes tribunals and Allied re-education offices. The German politicians who prepared the Basic Law for the new Federal Republic all believed at the time that, for the foreseeable future, West Germany's security would rest with the occupying powers.[29] After 1945, there were no great lobbies in Germany clamoring for rearmament – a striking difference from the aftermath of World War I. The great German arms manufacturers successfully switched to peacetime production. Many officers (especially staff officers) had found well-paid positions in industry and commerce, where their talents and specialized knowledge were at a premium. *Ohne Mich* (without me) was a phrase widely current among veterans demobilized or released from prisoner-of-war camps. The majority of Germans at the time would have been only too glad to see their country turn into a giant Liechtenstein. Even the bulk of surviving *Waffen SS* veterans wanted nothing

[27]For a detailed breakdown and evaluation, see Douglas Porch, "French Defense and the Gaullist Legacy," in Gann, ed., *The Defense of Western Europe*, pp. 188–211.

[28]Wolf Graf von Baudissin, *Nie Wieder Sieg: Programmatische Schriften.* Munich, Piper, 1982.

[29]For a history of German rearmament in its various aspects see Donald Abenheim, *Reforging the Iron Cross: The Search for Tradition in the West German Armed Forces.* Princeton, Princeton University Press, 1988, heavily drawn on in this chapter. See also Dennis E. Showalter, "The Bundeswehr and the Federal Republic of Germany," in Gann, ed., *The Defense of Western Europe*, pp. 212–54. Major German works include Gerhard Wettig, *Entmilitarisierung und Wiederbewaffnung in Deutschland 1943–1955. Internationale Auseinandersetzungen um die Rolle der Deutschen in Europa.* Munich, R. Oldenbourg, 1967. Roland G. Foerster et al., *Anfänge Westdeutscher Sicherheitspolitik, 1945–1956. Von der Kapitulation bis zum Pleven Plan,* v. 1. Munich, R. Oldenbourg, 1982. Militärgeschichtliches Forschungsamt ed., *Aspekte der deutschen Wiederbewaffnung bis 1955.* Boppard, 1975. Julian Lider, *Problems of Military Policy in the Konrad Adenauer Era, 1949–1966.* Stockholm, Swedish Institute of International affairs, 1984. Detlef Bald, *Vom Kaiserheer zur Bundeswehr Sozialstruktur des Militärs. Politische Rekrutierung von Offizieren und Unteroffizieren.* Frankfurt, Peter D. Lang, 1981.

better than to forget the past – as witnessed by their general unwillingness to join the ex-SS combatants' association.[30]

The main impetus for rearmament came from outside. The Berlin crisis was followed by the detonation of the first Soviet atomic bomb; the US nuclear monopoly was ended. Even more disquieting was North Korea's attack on South Korea in 1950, widely misinterpreted as a trial run for a Soviet offensive in Western Europe. In the event of such an assault, the Americans foresaw a withdrawal from Central Europe, a series of nuclear ripostes, followed by a reenactment of the Allied landings in Europe in 1944 – a grim prospect for Europeans of every political stripe. A growing number of European and US policy makers therefore began to argue in favor of a "forward defense" of Western Europe, a strategy inconceivable without German assistance.

Adenauer, for his part, had no love for uniforms. He regarded rearmament as an instrument for gaining political concessions from the Allies and strengthening Germany's precarious sovereignty. Adenauer was the first German Chancellor to regard generals as mere specialists, in no wise superior to the heads of police or fire departments. Right from the start, he was determined to impose his will on the military and to insist on civilian supremacy. The new army would not follow in the footsteps of Hitler's *Wehrmacht*, or of the Weimar Republic's *Reichswehr*, much less of the Kaiser's army, that had looked askance at both political Catholics and socialists. Adenauer moreover realized that the new German army could not simply serve as his own party's household guard. Rather, it would also have to appeal to the Social Democrats, as well as to those professional officers from the *Wehrmacht* willing to contribute their skills and experience to the new army. Whereas the *Kasernierte Volkspolizei* (the barracks-based people's police) in East Germany was designed as a political instrument to serve the SED, the West German defense force would support a democratic state. Adenauer was determined to break with many of Germany's earlier military traditions, much as the Prussian military reformers had attempted to do after the defeats inflicted by Napoleon upon the Hohenzollern dynasty, in 1806.

The Kasernierte Volkspolizei *served as an East German armed force under that title from 1952 to 1956. Then it was renamed* Nationale Volksarmee *(National People's Army, NVA). See entry in* DDR Handbuch, *Köln, Verlag Wissenschaft und Politik, 1985, v. 1.*

---

[30]Out of roughly 500,000 *Waffen SS* survivors, only 20,000 joined *HIAG* (an association of ex-*Waffen SS* soldiers, formed as an SS lobby in 1950 with the innocuous title *Hilfsgemeinschaft auf Gegenseitigkeit*, a mutual aid society). When the *Bundeswehr* was formed, former *Waffen SS* colonels and generals were excluded from its ranks. Eligible lower ranks were subjected to strict scrutiny. By 1956 fewer than 3 percent of 1,310 applications from former *Waffen SS* officers had been accepted, and about 20 percent of 1,524 applications from non-commissioned officers. See David Clay Large, "Reckoning without the past: the *HIAG* of the *Waffen SS* and the politics of rehabilitation in the Bonn Republic, 1950–1961," *Journal of Modern History*, v. 59, no. 1, March 1987, pp. 79–113.

Adenauer initially intended to offer German troops to a new European army, to be formed within the framework of the European Defense Community (EDC). He assembled a small group of former *Wehrmacht* officers several of whom had been identified with the resistance against Hitler. Most of them bore names that for generations had graced the *Gotha Almanach* (the German aristocracy's *Who's Who*) – Counts Gerhard von Schwerin, Johann Adolf von Kielmansegg, Wolf von Baudissin, and Axel von dem Bussche. In a strictly legal sense, the gathering was a criminal venture; the Allies could still have punished the participants with life imprisonment for secretly engaging in military preparations. With this peril much in mind, they met secretly in 1950 at Abbey Himmerod, and produced the so-called Himmerod Memorandum, later described by Schwerin as the *Bundeswehr's* Magna Carta. The new army's founding fathers eschewed both a militia on Swiss lines and an all-professional force on the *Reichswehr* model. Instead, the memorandum proposed the creation of a citizens' army, with 12 divisions of armor to be integrated within a supranational coalition, and to serve as a mobile enveloping force near the inter-zonal border. The new force would include a tactical air arm and a coastal defense navy; their purpose would be forward defense; there would be no more talk of an Allied withdrawal behind the Rhine.

Under the new dispensation, supreme leadership would be unified. There would be an end to control by separate chiefs of staff for each of the fighting services. Nor would the command structure duplicate Hitler's crazy wartime division of power between the OKH (*Oberkommando des Heeres*) and OKW (*Oberkommando der Wehrmacht*). The new force would be strictly answerable to civilian authority. (Initially, the Federal German president was designated as commander in chief. Later on, supreme control in peacetime passed to the minister of defense, answerable to the *Bundestag*. In times of emergency and war, the chancellor would assume direction.) The new army would serve as a "school for Europe;" it would develop a new ethos of civic responsibility, and an inner-directed discipline (*Innere Führung*) for the new citizen in uniform.

Planning for the new force thereafter passed to the innocuously named *Dienststelle Blank*, headed by Theodor Blank, a Christian Democrat trade unionist who had served as a junior officer in World War II. The new office proposed a committee to screen applicants for senior posts, from men adjudged to be loyal to the democratic order.[31] The committee's task was far from enviable. According to the Allies' postwar stereotype, Germans – a militaristic lot – would rush to the colors at the trumpet's first sound. In fact, the new army's foremost difficulty for the next 15 years was shortage of permanent personnel. There was full employment; there was plenty of money to be made in civilian life; the officers' social prestige had gravely diminished. There was widespread opposition to the new army from pacifists, socialists, and also from

---

[31]Later on two bodies came into existence. The first was the *Personalgutachtungsausschuss* or PGA in the *Bundestag*, appointed to choose colonels and generals, while the *Annahmeorganisation* took care of the rest. See Abenheim, *Reforging the Iron Cross, passim*, for these and many other details.

hard-liners, former officers convinced that *Innere Führung* would never work, that no army would fight without proper respect for its national traditions, and that the "joiners" were mere careerists who used convenient political connections to further their ambitions.

There were more profound questions that hinged on the soldiers' fundamental motivation to fight. According to a joke of Wilhelminian vintage, a young keen lieutenant conducts a civics class *Instruktionsstunde* in his company. "Grenadier Cohen," sternly asks the officer, "why should a German soldier gladly sacrifice his life for His Imperial Majesty the Kaiser, His Royal Majesty the King of Prussia, and the beloved Fatherland?" Replies the Jewish soldier, "With respect, Sir; lieutenant, Sir; you are absolutely right, Sir. Why should he?"[32] Why indeed? And even more, why should a German serve in a European army that Germans did not control? Why should Germany become a manpower reservoir for the West? Why should Germans fight alongside Westerners who, until so recently, had defamed all Germany's military tradition? Could the Westerners be relied upon as allies? Did they deserve support, given the more unsavory aspects of foreign occupation, with its due quota of looting, rape, and murder? Was there any point even in thinking about a war involving nuclear devastation? Could the Soviet armies be resisted in a conventional war, given their numerical superiority? Why should Germany have to learn military skills from the West? The Western armies indeed met with censure both from Germans who wanted a true people's army, free from antiquated drill, and from those who hoped for the return of yesteryear's stern discipline. "Your British drill sergeants are even worse than ours were," a *Wehrmacht* veteran assured one of us, while we were watching a battalion of Royal Fusiliers being drilled on a barrack square. "The GIs are too undisciplined – their methods won't work for us" went the contrary complaint.

Other critiques derived from political sociology. As Donald Abenheim, an American historian points out, the social background of the officers preparing the new army differed little from those who had run the German army before World War II. They tended to be Protestants, drawn from northern Germany, trained in the traditions of the German general staff, with many aristocrats among their number. (Of the 174 professional officers serving in the *Dienstelle Blank* in 1952, 142 were Lutherans, and 134 were from northern Germany. Only 40 were southern Germans, of whom 32 were Catholics. Ninety-eight officers had belonged to the general staff or to subordinate troops' staffs, though most of them were the product of the rapid staff training courses initiated in World War II.) Surely, said the critics, the new republic would founder, if its defense were once more entrusted to the old guard.[33]

---

[32] A variant is reprinted from *Simplizissimus* in Henry Wassermann, "Jews in Jugenstil: the *Simplicissimus* 1896–1914," *Leo Baeck Institute Yearbook, 1986*. London, Secker and Warburg, 1986, facing p. 86.

[33] For details see Reinhard Stumpf, "Die Wiederverwendung von Generalen und die Neubildung Militärischer Eliten in Deutschland und Österreich nach 1945," in Militärgeschichtliches Forschungsamt, ed., *Militärgeschichte: Probleme – Thesen – Wege*. Stuttgart, Deutsche Verlagsanstalt, 1982, pp. 478–99. Both the East German Army and the *Bundeswehr* employed former *Wehrmacht*

This was not all. The design for a European Defense Community faltered, and the Germans henceforth were able to build an army of their own, albeit without its own general staff, prohibited from making its own nuclear, chemical and biological weapons, and integrated into NATO – in fact the most NATO-oriented of Western defense forces. The initial obstacles, however, seemed almost insurmountable. The first volunteers joined the *Bundeswehr* in 1955. In 1956 the Border Guard (set up by Adenauer in 1950) troops augmented the first cadres of the *Bundeswehr*. In 1957 the first 10,000 conscripts joined the ranks. But the new army was off to a bad start, given the pressure from West Germany's allies for the creation of big battalions in double-quick time. (Initial plans foresaw 90,000 men in uniform in the first year, 250,000 at the end of the second, and 500,000 at the end of the third – a rate of expansion that would exceed the *Wehrmacht*'s between 1933 and 1939.) This feat was to be accomplished under the direction of field officers commissioned in wartime, with little or no experience in training troops.

The *Bundeswehr* was at first poorly equipped. The soldiers' clothing and housing remained inadequate; their basic conditions of service – including pay, health insurance, and family allowances by 1956 were still uncertain. Most barracks and bases had been taken over by NATO allies or domestic relief agencies. The new army's first winter indeed reminded many veterans of conditions in the Russian campaign. These difficulties were slowly overcome, but others remained. The army was plagued by bitter disputes over its historical traditions – not surprising in a country where legitimacy had so often been shattered. (Admiral Ruge, one of the founders of the new defense force, named his autobiography *In Four Fleets*, referring successively to the maritime forces of the Kaiser, the Weimar Republic, the *Führer*, and the Federal German Republic, each with its own distinctive flag.)[34] The *Bundeswehr* would make a fresh start – or perhaps unconsciously revert to the stark functionalism of the *Wehrmacht* in the last stages of the war. It would become an *Armee ohne Pathos*, an army bereft of dramatics. It thus dropped much (though not all) of the colorful ceremonial in which Germans had traditionally rejoiced. Uniforms became plain and drab while the soldiers received permission to wear civilian clothes as often as possible. The *Bundeswehr* deliberately tried to set itself apart from the *Wehrmacht* – in contrast to the East German army, that continued to dress and goosestep in the old style.

Debates concerning the merits of *Innere Führung*, the new discipline, continued to arouse dissension, ranging from metaphysical arguments drawn

---

generals. Of these, seven were serving in the East German *Kasernierte Volkspolizei* in 1953, in a body that at that time was much more heavily armed than the West German *Bundesgrenzschutz*. The *Bundeswehr*, by 1957, by contrast, employed 44 generals and admirals from the former *Wehrmacht*. These ex-*Wehrmacht* generals tended to be slightly younger than their East German colleagues, and contained a much larger percentage of former general staff officers. Of 39 generals and admirals for whom details are available, 17 were the sons of officials, 13 of officers, 5 of estate owners or farmers, 3 of professional men, 1 of a factory owner. Eight were noblemen.

[34]Fredrich Ruge, *In Vier Marinen: Lebenserinnerungen als Beitrag zur Zeitgeschichte*. Munich, Berhard und Graefe, 1979.

from classical German philosophy, to ribald comment on the barrack square. According to the reformers, moral autonomy and personal initiative had always formed part of Germany's best military tradition. In two world wars, German junior officers, sergeants, and even privates had shown exceptional ability to act on their own initiative in ever-shifting combat conditions. But, said the critics, these standards derived from sentiments of honor and duty incompatible with the hedonistic values adopted by the *Bundesrepublik*. In any case, theory bore scant resemblance to practice. Whatever the intentions of reformers such as von Baudissin, one of its principal architects, the *Bundeswehr* still evinced the features that, in varying measure, have plagued all armies from time immemorial – bullying, boredom, whoring and (above all) drunkenness. The *Bundeswehr* was the *Saufschule der Nation*, the nation's "academy of inebriation," according to a newspaper taunt.[35] Conscription proved far from popular, especially among the *Abiturienten*, the formally best educated recruits. ("They drink less, but they cry more.") Prosperous West Germany lacked the old commitment to military values. Well qualified technicians had no need to join the army; hence the *Bundeswehr* had considerable trouble in securing specialists with marketable qualifications, and a relatively high proportion of the West Germany army's permanent cadres consisted of refugees from the East.

The *Bundeswehr*, like many armies, was further handicapped by the military establishment's transformation into a pressure group functioning on bureaucratic lines, involved in a constant struggle for resources and influence – a fight exacerbated by arguments that military spending adversely affected domestic prosperity and welfare rights. Bureaucratization of the *Bundeswehr* was aggravated by the extent of its integration with NATO, with its internecine conflicts, in which the briefcase proved weightier than the sword.

There were graver problems to come. The Allies had concluded no formal peace treaty with Germany. West German rearmament proceeded according to strict conditions. The Federal Republic was barred from manufacturing atomic, biological, and chemical (ABC) weapons. The *Bundeswehr* lacked a general staff of its own, and was fully integrated into the NATO command – unlike the British, French, and US armies. If war were to break out, West German soldiers would be involved in a fratricidal war against East German soldiers: Hessians would fire at Thuringians, and vice versa. In such a war, Germany would become the main theater of operations. The country would be destroyed – even in the unlikely event that no nuclear weapons were used on the battlefield.

This was not a scenario to inspire even the most enthusiastic volunteer. And yet, given its many difficulties, the *Bundeswehr*'s achievements were remarkable. Initially, the new officer corps was widely suspected of undemocratic leanings. It did, after all, contain many *Wehrmacht* officers (especially former field officers), including many *Spätheimkehrer* (men belatedly released from captivity, with none but military skills to sell). But to the critics' surprise, the new officer corps gave no political trouble. In fact the *Bundeswehr* officers turned out to be

---

[35]"Bundeswehr: Saufschule der Nation?," *Der Spiegel*, 25 June 1979.

more sympathetic to the anti-Hitler resistance during the Third Reich, and more committed to democratic values in the sense of valuing the role of opposition parties, than the population at large.[36] At the same time, the officer corps became more democratic in its composition than the old armies had been, with nearly one-third of the *Bundeswehr* officers drawn from the ranks of skilled workers, artisans, and clerks.[37]

The new army accordingly gained political acceptance. The bulk of the Social Democrats rallied to give at least restrained support to the *Bundeswehr*. (During the 1950s, the SPD's main commitment was to German reunification, whereas West German rearmament was widely regarded as an immovable obstacle to that goal. The disastrous *Bundestag* election of 1957 caused the SPD to rethink its position, and during the early 1960s, it became an advocate of full participation in NATO.)[38] The bulk of German electors had confidence in the army – as indicated by successive public opinion polls. Conscripts might not feel enthusiastic about serving *beim Bund* (in the federal forces), but there were no mutinies, few major breaches of discipline, and military performance rapidly improved, as evinced by the high marks the *Bundeswehr* won at joint NATO maneuvers.

At the same time, the *Bundeswehr* placed increasing emphasis on high quality *matériel*, a course that came easily to Europe's most highly industrialized country. Franz Joseph Strauss, Adenauer's minister of defense from 1956 to 1962, insisted on using more and more German-made equipment, that would free the *Bundeswehr* from dependence on American-designed weapons. By the early 1970s, West Germany had become almost self-sufficient in arms, with high-grade weaponry manufactured by firms such as Krauss-Maffei, Thyssen Henschel, Hanomag, Messerschmidt-Bölkow-Blohm, Carl Walther, Heckler und Koch producing a great variety of high-quality tanks, missiles, and other implements of war. High-grade weaponry in turn required an increasing number of permanent cadres to work the weapons to their best effect. (By the early 1970s, 55 percent of the *Bundeswehr* men were *Zeitsoldaten*, men who had signed on for a specified number of years, while basic military training for conscripts was shortened from 18 to 15 months.) The right of conscientious objection (claimed mainly by the well-educated) was preserved, but until the late 1960s did not much interfere with the draft – a tribute to the Federal Republic's political stability.

In a manner unforeseen by the signatories of the Himmerod memorandum, the Federal Republic grew into the strongest military power in Western

---

[36]By the 1960s, 70 percent of the population and 81.4 percent of the officers had a favorable view regarding the opposition to Hitler; 58.6 percent of the population and 95.5 percent of the officers had a positive attitude to the role of opposition parties. See tables in Stanley Rothman, *European Society and Politics*. Indianapolis, Bobbs-Merril, 1970, pp. 718–19.

[37]Twenty-three percent skilled workers and artisans; 9 percent white-collar workers; 37 percent civil servants and professional people; 10 percent self-employed businessmen; 7 percent farmers; 12 percent professional soldiers. Rothman, *European Society*, table on p. 717.

[38]Stephen J. Artner, *A Change of Course: The West German Social Democrats and NATO*. Westport, Conn., Greenwood Press, 1985.

Europe. It was also the power most committed to NATO, the only member to commit the lion's share of its combat forces to the alliance. Rearmament proceeded apace. By the late 1950s the *Bundeswehr* comprised 206,000 men with seven complete divisions at NATO's disposal. Later on it expanded to a peacetime strength of 490,000 men, with a wartime establishment of 1,250,000. The field army was organized into three corps, with a total of 12 divisions, grouped into 36 brigades (mainly armored, and armored infantry) designed for mobile operations and rapid counter-thrusts. The force was supported by a professional *Grenzschutz* (border defence force). In addition West Germany built up a large territorial defense based on a regional organization, designed for rearward defense, integrated into the *Bundeswehr* but under the West German, as opposed to NATO, command. Thirty-five years after its creation, the *Bundeswehr* provided 50 percent of NATO's land forces in Central Europe, 30 percent of its combat aircraft, and 70 percent of its naval forces in the Baltic.[39] Militarily as well as economically, the Federal Republic had become NATO's cornerstone in Europe.

Italy and the smaller European countries

During and after World War II, tales concerning the Italians' military failings became part of a transnational folklore. "How should a world army be put together to repel an extra-terrestrial invasion?" ran a German barrack-room story. "We Germans shall supply the armor, the Russians the infantry, the British the air force, the Americans the engineers, and the Italians the regimental band." In fact many Italians had given an excellent account of themselves both as regular soldiers and as guerrillas – despite poor equipment, inadequate supplies, poor political leadership, defective staff work, the unpopularity of Mussolini's war, and the political divisions within Italian society.[40] Italians had campaigned as far afield as Russia and North Africa. They had moreover served on both sides – at first aligned with the Third Reich, and from 1943 on the side of the Western Allies. Some had fought toward the end of the war for Mussolini's last "republic" in northern Italy. By contrast, about 400,000 men had been reformed as a new army under the royal government that had thrown in its lot with the Allies. Sociologically however, the officers who served in the two opposing armies remained homogeneous; they were career officers with a technical and professional cast of mind, many of them drawn from the ranks. Officers from both armies later joined Italy's peacetime forces.[41]

The Italian forces that emerged from World War II were in poor shape. The naval and air forces were largely destroyed or rendered inoperative. A

---

[39]Klaus Franke, "Europe's share of the burden," *Atlantic Community News,* January–February 1985, pp. 1 and 4. For a detailed description of its organization, see "German Federal Republic," in John Keegan, ed., *World Armies,* pp. 242–54.

[40]James J. Sadkovitch, "Understanding defeat: reappraising Italy's role in World War II," *Journal of Contemporary History,* v. 24, no. 1, January 1989, p. 51.

[41]Virgilio Ilari, *Le Forze Armate tra Politica e Potere, 1943–1976.* Firenze, Vallecchi, 1978, p. 16.

substantial number of officers left the armed forces, in part as a result of *defascistizzazione* – including 43 generals, 440 senior, and 5,300 junior officers. By 1945, the remnants of the Italian army, apart from the *carabinieri*, numbered 320,000 men.[42] Approximately 50,000 of them made up five combat groups, mainly British-equipped. Another 200,000 men were organized into five divisions and minor units, mainly deployed for logistic duties with the Fifth US and the Eighth British Armies. The remainder of the land forces were directly under Italian control, employed largely in security operations on the islands of Sardinia and Sicily where unrest was rife. In addition, there were numerous partisan formations that were gradually demobilized. The Allies at first placed far-reaching restrictions on Italian armed forces.

In 1949, however, Italy became one of NATO's founder members, and existing limits on the forces largely disappeared. Surprising as it may sound, Italy ten years later provided, at any rate in organizational terms, more divisions to NATO in Europe than West Germany, Britain, and France combined – at a time when the British Army of the Rhine (BAOR) was being reduced, and the bulk of the French army was stationed in Algeria.[43] Rebuilding Italy's military strength was a hard task. The army and navy had both experienced defeats. The army had traditionally been unpopular as an instrument of Piedmontese domination and centralization; it had been used in the past for industrial repression. The politicans who guided Italy out of the postwar disaster were not much concerned with military questions and military grievances; hence funds remained short.

Military spending increased in absolute terms; but so did the proportion of the military budget devoted to expenditure on personnel, as opposed to equipment. In theory, Italian conscripts came cheap; in practice direct and indirect personnel costs kept rising. (Indeed, some Italian conservatives feared that the communists might at some future time neutralize the army simply by raising salaries, and by multiplying jobs, all at the expense of buying arms.) At the same time Italian military expenditure declined as a percentage of the total budget.[44] The Italian armed forces and the arms industry moreover could no more cut loose from the political patronage system, with its competing *feudi* (fiefs) and dependent retainers, than could any other major institution in the state. (In the late 1950s, 66,000 military and dependent civilian families in Rome owed their livelihood to the ministry of defense.) There were also wider

---

[42]Vittorfranco S. Pisano, "The Italian armed forces," in Gann, ed., *The Defense of Western Europe*, pp. 158–87. Major works in Italian include Enea Cerquetti, *Le Forze Armate Italiane dal 1945 al 1975*. Milano, Feltrinelli, 1975. Roberto Cicciomessere, *L'Italia Armata*, Milano, Gammalibri, 1982.

[43]The Italian army then comprised 10 infantry divisions, 3 armored divisions, 5 mountain brigades, as against 7 West German divisions (3 motorized, 2 armored, 1 airborne, 1 mountain), 3 British divisions in Germany, and 2 French. See Institute for Strategic Studies, *The Soviet Union and the NATO Powers: The Military Balance*. London, The Institute, 1959.

[44]Between 1948–9 and 1958–9, military expenditure rose from 235.4 to 606.1 billion lire. Between 1953–4 and 1958–9, military expenditure declined as a percentage of the budget from 19.39 to 16.90 percent (dropping to 11.45 in 1972.) Between 1950–1 and 1958–9 military expenditure devoted to personnel costs rose from 37.2 to 54.2 percent. See Illari, *Le Forze Armate*, p. 214.

problems of a strategic kind, as Italy's geographic position imposed on the country two divergent tasks – naval and air defense in the Mediterranean, as well as safeguarding the land border in the Northeast against possible incursions on the part of Warsaw Pact forces.

Italy still had some valuable assets. Except for a small number of dedicated royalists, the great majority of officers remained in the armed forces upon the monarchy's demise, and swore allegiance to the Republic. Conscription might be unpopular, but did not meet with serious or widespread opposition. Left-wingers in fact had no wish to reduce the army to a highly paid career service that might be used against the left-wing parties in some future political crisis. Hence the 1947 constitution imposed the duty to serve in the military on all fit Italian men. Then, Italy's economic recovery, the improvement and diversification of her industries, increasingly provided high quality weapons of domestic provenance to supplement imported (mainly American) ones.

The fleet was rebuilt as a small-ship navy, generally respected for its efficiency. (By the end of the 1940s, the navy comprised 3 cruisers, 47 destroyers and frigates, and 6 submarines.) The army (organized in the main on the US model) was divided into three corps for operational missions, and seven military regions to take part in rearward defense. Brigades (mechanized, armored, alpine, and airborne) formed the basic combat units. The corps were mainly stationed along the northeastern border, designed for operational missions; separate territorial commands looked after the security of the rear areas.

The Italian army faced three major problems. The first, and as John Keegan opines, the least important, concerned its political reliability.[45] On the one hand, the army contained many communist conscripts, whom conservatives widely suspected of disloyalty. In theory, this should have been a serious issue. On the other hand, the army was widely accused by left-wingers of praetorian ambitions and a penchant for repression. It's reputation as a political instrument in part derived from the fact that two Italian security forces, the *carabinieri*, and the secret service, administratively formed part of the armed forces. The *carabinieri* were a regular elite formation. They combined the duties of military police with those of a professional force designed to cope with bandits, subversives and, if necessary, hostile partisans. Comparable to the French *gendarmerie nationale,* the *carabinieri* were more military in character, and were organized – like the Italian army as a whole – into an operational (or mobile) branch, and a territorial branch. In addition to the *carabinieri*, legally part of the army only during wartime, there were other police forces that uneasily balanced each other in a political sense. (These included the public security police, commonly known as *celere*, used to put down public disorder, and correspondingly unpopular with the left.)

Despite pessimistic predictions, the amed services experienced no mutinies, nor did they ever attempt a *coup d'état* in the Spanish fashion. None of the military or paramilitary bodies attempted to wipe out Italian democracy.

[45]Keegan, ed., *World Armies,* pp. 372–80.

Instead, the armed forces remained firmly under civilian control. (The president of the Republic acted as the nominal commander in chief, with the council of ministers answerable for defense in general, and the minister of defense responsible for specific political and technical supervision.)

The second major military problem concerned the size and efficiency of the army. Experts became increasingly convinced that too much was spent on personnel and too little on new equipment. Planners therefore decided to diminish both the number of reservists called up for national service, and to cut down on the number of brigades. The alpine and parachute brigades (the best in the army, and the units most popular with conscripts) remained exempt from this reduction. Thirdly there were wider questions concerning the army's role. Though committed to NATO, and forming NATO's largest component on the southern flank, the Italian army lacked the mobility to operate *en masse* outside its own territory, and much of its equipment remained obsolete. But despite its weaknesses and internal tensions, Italy stayed committed to NATO, and remained NATO's cornerstone in the Mediterranean – the Italians' fidelity to the alliance reflecting the electorate's continued suspicion of the Soviet Union, as against the US.[46] All things considered, the Italian Republic's defensive preparations were not unimpressive, and in the end were certainly more effective than Mussolini's much-heralded military establishment.

Belgium and the Netherlands have traditionally formed the cockpit of Europe. They share a long tradition of prosperity, a civilian ethos, parliamentary government adorned by monarchical institutions, and untroubled by fears of military intervention. Both have built and lost large colonial empires. (Holland was forced to grant independence to Indonesia, the former Dutch East India, in 1949; Belgium relinquished sovereignty over the Belgian Congo in 1960.) Both countries had unsuccessfully tried to stay neutral in World War II; and both had the same sorrowful experience of rapid military defeat and Nazi occupation. Their exile governments in London had each built up small forces, trained and equipped on the British model; these had taken a minor but honorable part in the liberation of their respective countries. Both sought security within a wider Western alliance. In terms of manpower, their respective contributions to Western defense were about equal (250,000 men for both countries combined at the end of the 1950s, a force far from negligible). They relied on a mixture of conscripts and regulars. But there were of course important differences. Holland has a single language, whereas Belgium is ethnically split between Walloons and Flemings. Belgium moreover was at that time much more industrialized than Holland, and better fitted to produce arms. Holland looked more to the sea than Belgium, and devoted more resources to naval defense.

At the time of liberation, both countries' military assets were small. The

---

[46]By 1986, 9 percent of Italians believed that Soviet values were similar or somewhat similar to their own, as compared with 14 percent of the British, 8 percent of the Germans, 4 percent of French. See Ben J. Wattenberg, "Bad Marx: how the world sees the Soviets," *Public Opinion*, March–April 1987, p. 10.

Belgians' renowned "liberation brigade" (a motorized formation that had participated in the Normandy landing) units, expanded by 1946 into three small divisions with a total of 24,000 men. The Belgian forces were subsequently integrated into NATO, and divided into *la force d'intervention*, an army corps assigned to NATO, as well as land forces for home defense (*les forces d'intérieur*), and a small *corps d'élite* consisting of paratroopers.[47]

Belgium had traditionally depended on conscripts. Increasingly however, the armed forces began to rely on regulars who, by the late 1960s, made up nearly half the army's strength.[48] The Belgian career officers derived from a much wider social spectrum than their French colleagues, and were much less likely to have been raised in military families; hence the armed forces continued to serve as an avenue for social advancement.[49] The officers were well-educated in a formal sense – not surprising in a country where diplomas had always formed passports for social advancement. But the Belgian forces had their problems. For instance, they could no more escape the tensions derived from the country's linguistic divisions than any other national institution. (Candidates for promotion had to fit into a 50:50 allocation scheme to ensure ethnic balance; there were Flemish speaking and French speaking brigades.) Fortunately, these divisions failed seriously to affect the Belgian military's hard-earned reputation for efficiency.

Belgium's language rift has been a cause of political instability – since 1946 there have been 33 governments, in part because of language problems. As a malicious French jingle goes, in Holland they work, in Belgium they quarrel:

En Hollande on travaille,
En Belgique on se chamaille.

Holland's military development was somewhat different. The Dutch con tinued to maintain a substantial navy, larger than West Germany's.[50] Their army also relied on conscripts, backed by an increasing proportion of regulars (about one-third of the army's establishment). A substantial number of these professionals had served in the Dutch East Indies, and thereafter took service in Holland where the East Indian element for a time remained strong in the

---

[47]By the end of the 1950s, the Belgian armed forces consisted of 120,000 men. 2 divisions (one infantry, one armored) were at NATO's disposal. See Institute for Strategic Studies, *The Soviet Union and the NATO powers*, p. 8.

[48]For details see Brigadier-General John H. Skinner, "Belgium," in Keegan, ed., *World Armies*, pp. 55–64. John H. Skinner, "The defense forces of the Low Countries," in Gann, ed., *The Defense of Western Europe*, pp. 255–309.

[49]See Guy van Gorp, *Le Recrutement et la formation des candidats officier de carrière à l'armée belge.* Louvain, Université Catholique de Louvain, 1969, Nouv. série, no. 56. Between 1945 and 1958, 50.3 percent of the students at the Belgian *École Royale Militaire* were sons of workmen, artisans, and clerks, as opposed to 6.5 percent in France's Saint-Cyr; 19.1 percent of the *École Royale Militaire* cadets were sons of regular soldiers, as opposed to 40 percent in Saint-Cyr.

[50]The Dutch fleet, by the end of the 1950s, comprised an aircraft carrier, 2 light cruisers, 34 destroyers and frigates, 10 submarines, and 68 other craft.

army. In 1951 the Dutch embarked on a rearmament program, increased the period of conscription from 12 to 18 months, and built up a substantial reserve. One small army corps eventually became available to NATO, but most of its formations were stationed in Holland; hence most officers and men spent the longest part of their service there. The Dutch, more than the Belgians, relaxed traditional discipline during the troubled 1960s. Jokes about Holland's "[long] hair force" became common – to which the Dutch would respond with Biblical references to Samson whose hirsute appearance had not prevented him from slaying countless philistines. Irrespective of such real or assumed military deficiencies, the Dutch built up a force that Brigadier General John Skinner, a British expert, would later describe as "small, modern, and excellently equipped."[51]

Denmark and Norway shared Holland's lack of a militaristic tradition and a relatively egalitarian society, in which military officers did not constitute a separate social class but merely a specialized profession. For all its ancient military splendor, Denmark had not fought a war since 1864 – and that a disaster. The country lacked natural defenses. Danes, like Dutchmen, moreover remained suspicious of their German neighbors. Pacifist sentiments had long been powerful. (The Progressive Party in Denmark indeed proposed in the early 1970s to replace the armed forces by an automatic telephone system, programmed to say in Russian "we surrender.") Denmark maintained the draft, but relied to a much greater extent than Norway on regular cadres, highly competent men. The Danish forces were divided into a field force, designed to cooperate with NATO, and local defense forces – an arrangement that enabled the kingdom to put one division into the field by the end of the 1950s.

Norway's position was even more exposed than Denmark's, being the only NATO member to share a common border with the USSR, except for Turkey. Like Denmark, Norway would not permit foreign forces to be stationed on its soil in peacetime, an arrangement that reflected the Scandinavians' long neutralist tradition. All the same, the Norwegians had certain advantages. Their men were hardy and well-trained, especially for winter warfare. Their small navy enjoyed a high reputation. Norwegians accepted the draft with far fewer complaints than their Danish neighbors. While NATO's northern flank remained dangerously exposed, it was not left undefended.

The Iberian Peninsula, by contrast, remained the most backward part of Western Europe. The Portuguese and Spanish armed forces, like Portuguese and Spanish society as a whole, were marked by social distinctions long since banished in Northern Europe. Both countries relied on conscription and in theory – could field large armies, but poorly equipped, and without much experience in mechanized warfare. Spain and Portugal had for generations been plagued by military coups, but in both countries the ruling dictatorships had firmly reduced the army to obedience, by varying means.

---

[51]Skinner, "The defense of the Low Countries," in Gann, ed., *The Defense of Western Europe*, p. 270.

The Portuguese armed forces amounted to no more than about 50,000 men, but were capable of rapid expansion – as shown during the long colonial wars that were to pre-empt Portugal's military resources from 1961 to 1974. In Portugal, the Salazar dictatorship operated through a tight network that linked church, army, major financial corporations, leading civil servants and the governing party through ties of friendship, marriage, and interest. But Salazar was a civilian to the core. He made sure that the army's ambitions did not extend beyond the barrack square; he gave patronage to the military but never took it.[52]

The Spanish armed forces were relatively large (some 400,000 men, including paramilitary forces such as the civil guard). Spaniards had gained plenty of military experience during the bloody civil war of the 1930s. The so-called Blue Division had also seen service in Russia where Spaniards fought on the *Wehrmacht*'s side. The Spanish forces – though praised to the sky in sermons, editorials and banquet speeches – remained starved for cash, over-officered and underpaid. This state of affairs slowly began to change from 1953 when the US, in return for military bases, began to give military aid on a large scale ($60,000,000 between 1953 and 1964). As long as she remained under the Franco dictatorship, Spain was unacceptable to NATO as a potential member. The US, however, arrived at a separate military link with Spain, establishing a relationship that in itself served as a conduit for American weapons, technology, and ideas.

In any event, the Spanish army remained much more important as a defense against rebels at home than against invaders from abroad. Spain remained a heavily policed country, with the civil guard (*guardia civil*) forming a more repressive counterpart to the Italian *carabinieri*. Spain's development of a modernized military – like her modern industrial development – only began in the 1960s. Conscription had, however, served as a school for the nation in one peculiar sense; it was the only institution in which Spaniards of every regional background and social class were forced to mingle for a time; the "mere imposition of propinquity on the sons of former enemies was a healing act."[53]

The North Americans: US and Canada

North Americans have rarely been comfortable in a military role. At the end of World War I, the US had emerged as the world's strongest industrial and financial power. But it only accepted this supremacy with reluctance. Americans moreover have traditionally viewed their military through two pairs of eyeglasses – one rose-colored, the other tinted black. They have always honored military valor and were traditionally much more willing than Britons or Canadians to accept soldiers in politics. (George Washington, Ulysses S. Grant,

[52]Matthew Midlane, "The Spanish and Portuguese defense forces," in Gann, ed., *The Defense of Western Europe*, pp. 126–57.
[53]Keegan, "Spain," in *World Armies*, p. 646.

Dwight D. Eisenhower all advanced from the officers' mess to the White House.) At the same time, they have always criticized their soldiers in relentless fashion. Countless cartoons presented generals as beer-bellied oafs; innumerable movies depicted fighting men as black sheep, bumblers, or thugs. Politicians have widely regarded the military as nature's own squanderers. (Congressional committees have traditionally concentrated on real or alleged waste, rather than on rewarding efficiency.) Even the best of US sociology remains replete with strictures that derided the soldiers' "unanticipated militarism," or adjured the military to seek a "constabulary" role rather than victory. Public opinion polls at the time accorded some prestige to men in uniform. (According to a 1955 study, officers ranked behind physicians, scientists, college professors, lawyers, clergymen, and teachers in that order; however the military's prestige improved in subsequent decades.)[54] But in the popular esteem of the mid-1950s, enlisted men came behind garage mechanics and just ahead of truckdrivers, though many an enlisted man would have envied a trucker's pay. And yet from the end of World War II, the US armed forces were the most powerful in the Western world. It was their presence in Europe that provided the ultimate backing for the Europeans' defense.

The core of the US armed forces, like those of its allies, consisted of regulars. The enlisted men and the non-commissioned officers traditionally derived from the ranks of lower-level white-collar, and from blue-collar workers; the US army was never an army drawn from the underclass, common misconceptions notwithstanding.[55] According to other widespread stereotypes, the professional officers were WASPS, either privileged graduates from expensive private schools, or small town Southerners of lower-middle-class origin – Babbitts in uniform. The stereotype contained just enough half truths to make such taunts almost deserved. According to Morris Janowitz, doyen of US military sociology, far more military than civilian leaders came from a rural background. A substantial, though a declining, number of officers derived from the South. Army leaders overwhelmingly had middle-class parents. The lower-middle classes supplied an increasing share of officers, most for the air force, least for the navy. Military leaders were overwhelmingly Protestant, of Northern European descent. They were far more likely than businessmen to have grown up in families whose fathers worked as professional men or in managerial occupations.[56] In a political sense, the military leaders mainly

[54]Morris Janowitz, *Sociology and the Military Establishment*. New York, Russel Sage Foundation, 1959, p. 97. Morris Janowitz, *The Professional Soldier: A Social and Political Portrait*. Glencoe, Ill., Free Press, 1960, p. 418; p. 227. Samuel P. Huntington, *The Soldier and the State: The Theory and Politics of Civil Military Relations*. Cambridge, Belknap Press of Harvard University Press, 1957.

[55]Sue Berryman, "National service and military service: will they fit one another?," Hoover Institution conference on National Service, September 8–9, and, by the same author, *Who Serves? The Persistent Myth of the Underclass Army.*, Boulder, Col., Westview Press, 1988.

[56]Janowitz, *The Professional Soldier*, p. 79–101. In 1950, 66 percent of military leaders in the army, 56 percent in the navy, and 70 percent in the air force were drawn from rural backgrounds, as opposed to 26 percent of business leaders (1952). Of navy leaders 61 percent were drawn from upper- and upper-middle-class families, compared to 50 percent of army leaders, and 30 percent of air force leaders. Corresponding figures for lower-middle-class officers were 34, 45, and 62

classed themselves as "somewhat conservative", followed by "conservative", with "somewhat liberal" in third place.[57]

Contrary to the stereotypes, however, the US military leaders were highly motivated, and well educated both professionally and technically. Far from being hidebound militarists, they did well in civilian occupations after retirement, especially in industrial corporations, and government service (including education and public welfare). Far from being a self-perpetuating elite, American officers were much less likely than their German or French colleagues to be "army brats." By 1950 the percentage of "self-recruited" officers in the army was no more than 11 percent, in the navy 7 percent, in the air force 5 percent – a tribute to the fluidity of the social structure, and the successful manner in which Americans had managed to integrate their officer corps into civilian society.[58] Civilian links were further strengthened by the military's willingness to draw on the American tradition of voluntary part-time service, represented by the army reserve and the national guards (the latter operated throughout the 50 states of the union).[59]

If anything, civilians exercised excessive influence. The US forces were heavily bureaucratized, enmeshed in an interlocking system of bureaucratic networks. To give just one example, the army chief of staff complained at the end of the 1950s that he had 19 civilian layers between himself and the president. Civilian control operated in a great variety of ways, through congressional control and the resultant policy changes that subjected procurement agencies to successive budgetary feasts and famines, and through the impact of industrial, governmental, and publicity lobbies. There was the growing influence of "defense intellectuals," many of them without any military experience, but increasingly influential in think-tanks and government departments.[60] Early nineteenth-century reformers in Prussia had already remarked on the natural conflict between *Federbüsche* and *Federfüchse*, between "plumed helmets" and "pen pushers," that is to say, warriors and military bureaucrats. As time went on, this contrast became intensified in the US to the pen pushers' advantage.

Bureaucratization accelerated for a variety of reasons – the complexities of the US alliance structure, the impact of the civil rights struggle in which the armed forces served as pioneers of integration, and the increasing respect paid

---

percent. As regards fathers' occupations, 44 percent of military leaders derived from professional and managerial background, as opposed to 29 percent of business leaders. And 90 percent of navy leaders, 89 percent of army leaders, and 84 percent of airforce leaders were Protestants, with a large Episcopalian component.

[57] Janowitz, *The Professional Soldier,* pp. 125–50 for details of graduates and non-graduates of academics and war colleges.

[58] For details see Janowitz, *The Professional Soldier,* especially pp. 93–5.

[59] For a detailed breakdown, see Keegan, "The United States of America," in *World Armies,* pp. 763–80.

[60] For a general history, see for instance Allan R. Millett and Peter Maslowski, *For the Common Defense: A Military History of the United States of America.* New York, Free Press, 1984. Robert Leckie, *The Wars of America.* New York, Harper and Row, 1981.

> *The president served as commander-in-chief of the three services. After numerous changes, the Americans adopted a system whereby the president was advised by the national security council, and directed policy through the secretary of defense and his department (the Pentagon), with its many agencies. The joint chiefs of staff (chaired in turn by a soldier, a sailor, and an airman), served as the secretary's executive, directly controlling the unified commands of the American forces. The staffs of the three services remained separate.*

to diplomas and paper credentials both in the armed forces and in American society. Greater still were the problems of strategic planning. US planners faced an infinitely greater range of options than those besetting their colleagues in countries such as West Germany or Israel. The armed forces also had to cope with bitter inter-service rivalries; these were so great that the American military might appear to outsiders as no more than a quarrelsome confederation uneasily coordinated through civilian – above all presidential – authority.

The American forces relied heavily for their manpower on the draft (introduced in 1941, reorganized in 1951 after the outbreak of the Korean war, through the Universal Military Training and Service Act, and finally abolished in 1971). The draft operated in a selective manner that favored university students, and thus the middle class, which supplied a larger percentage of college men than the workers. The draft supplied only part of the armed forces (by the end of the 1950s already, the majority of service men were volunteers). However, it did ensure a permanent supply of peacetime conscripts who, between them, possessed an immense and proliferating number of skills.[61] It was these skills and the leadership qualities of the American officer corps that gave the US forces a degree of adaptability, an ability to survive shifts and changes, that would probably have disorganized any other army in the world.

Overall, the US was also in good shape as regards national morale – as opposed to the poor morale of individual units subjected to the throes of rapid demobilization, rapid expansion, or sudden switches from constabulary to combat function. The strength of morale came to be underplayed when a small number of US prisoners in North Korean and Chinese captivity became turncoats, or signed confessions of atrocities. The Americans' conduct supposedly contrasted with that of their allegedly braver Turkish comrades in arms. These widely publicized comparisons overlooked the fact that the communists – possessing no interpreters able to speak Turkish – naturally concentrated on the Americans. Critiques of US soldiers also failed fully to consider the extraordinary pressure to which American (as well as allied) captives were exposed. (Only 3,800 American prisoners returned; at least 1,000 were murdered; many died of hunger or deprivation endured under unspeakable conditions.) In fact, the bulk of the US prisoners – barbers, truckdrivers, car salesmen, and so on in civilian life – bore their fate with

---

[61]By the time of the Korean war 10.7 percent of the enlisted personnel derived from technical and scientific occupations, 19.2 percent, administrative and clerical, 16.9 percent skilled mechanic, maintenance, etc. 11.5 service workers, 8.6 percent operatives and laborers, 33.1 military occupations. Janowitz, *The Professional Soldier*, p. 65.

fortitude. Nevertheless, many academics and journalists in the West saw fit to praise or exculpate the communists, while themselves leading comfortable and secure lives, and enjoying easy access to the facts.[62] From the standpoint of morale, the real significance of the war lay in the huge number of prisoners from the People's Republic of China and from North Korea who opted not to be repatriated to their respective countries under communist rule. Such a decision was inconceivable to all but a tiny handful of American soldiers (21 in all) who chose to stay in China (and most later returned to the US).

The Americans were at first reluctant to make a permanent military commitment in Europe. When the war ended, the US had 69 ground divisions with over 2,000,000 men. By 1948 this imposing force had shrunk to 91,749 men, less than one-third of the peacetime effectiveness maintained by Yugoslavia, a medium-size Balkan state. Even the open challenge to the Western powers extended in 1948 by the USSR through the Berlin blockade, and the Soviets' first explosion of an atomic bomb in 1949 did not at first prevent a steady decline in the number of American servicemen stationed in Europe. By 1950, the US forces there numbered no more than 79,495 – at a time when the US, according to its critics, was fomenting the Cold War.[63] The American ground forces in Europe were even weaker than mere figures would indicate; they could field no more than a single division and a few regiments; their morale was poor as the military suffered increasingly from "a sense of its own irrelevance."[64] To the extent that they considered the Soviets a military threat, the Americans relied on their assumed atomic monopoly. Even this was more of a potential than an actual threat to the Soviet Union. The Americans by 1949 could have assembled fewer than 200 atomic bombs. Not until 1948 did the air force have a single team capable of assembling a droppable bomb, and when General Curtis E. LeMay, the Strategic Air Command's (SAC's) new commander tested his force, he found that not a single crew could place a weapon on target in conditions approaching wartime circumstances.[65]

It was the Korean war that triggered US rearmament, more than an adherence to the NATO alliance. In 1949 Congress approved of the administration's Mutual Defense Assistance Act which provided $1.3 billion in military equipment and services for NATO. A new NATO defense committee in the same year approved of its first integrated defense program, but this plan did little more than ratify the status quo. The US would mainly provide strategic nuclear air forces and naval forces to protect NATO's shipping lanes. And even Europeans well disposed toward the US complained that on land the Americans would only fight to the last European.

[62]For details see, for instance David Caute, *The Fellow Travellers: A Postscript to the Enlightenment*. London, Weidenfeld and Nicolson, 1973, *passim*.
[63]For detailed figures, see Daniel J. Nelson, *A History of US Military Forces in Germany*. Boulder, Col., Westview Press, 1987, p. 45.
[64]Russell F. Weigley, *History of the United States Army*. New York, Macmillan, 1967, p. 501. For a general overview from 1945 to the 1980s, see Harry G. Summers, "United States armed forces in Europe," in Gann, ed., *The Defense of Western Europe*, pp. 286–309.
[65]Millett and Maslowski, *For the Common Defense*, p. 477.

But on June 25, 1950, North Korean forces invaded South Korea, and for a while it seemed that it would quickly fall to the communist assault. The communists' sudden blow came as a complete surprise to Truman's administration; the resultant dismay created a mood of crisis, reminding Americans of Nazi aggression during the 1930s, and the failure of the Western democracies to resist Hitler's challenge. The US at the same time mobilized for a limited war in Asia, and rearmed to deter another great war in Europe. As a result of the Korean conflict, the American army turned from a barracks to a field army. American intervention prevented the threatened conquest of South Korea. By the time the Korean war ended in 1953, the United States had tripled the size of its armed forces, tripled the number of men deployed in Europe (352,644 men in 1954), and quadrupled its defense budget. By 1958, the US maintained by far the largest military establishment in the Western world (850,000 men in the army, 825,000 in the air force, 600,000 men in the navy, 160,000 men in the marine corps).

There was also a power shift in the European balance. Henceforth NATO armament proceeded apace. By 1953 the US Seventh Army in Germany comprised six divisions. The Americans at the same time modernized their armored divisions, mounted their infantry in armored carriers, extended the use of military helicopters, and vastly expanded both their soldiers' firepower and mobility. By the late 1950s and early 1960s, the forces were logistically supported by a communications zone in France, with protected supply lines, reinforced by a tactical air force based in Britain and the Continent, supplied with a new generation of tanks, personnel carriers, and guns – the US Seventh Army was in great shape. "Fully equipped, highly disciplined and highly motivated, the United States armed forces in Europe were maintained at a high level of readiness, their battlefield skills honed by rigorous training and frequent field exercises."[66]

At the same time, US military morale in Europe revived, as did the Europeans' confidence in their ally. (By 1951, 58 percent of German respondents in a poll believed that the US military presence in Germany safeguarded their security; only 22 percent wanted the Americans to withdraw. Fifty-five percent of the respondents said the behavior of US troops was good, 20 percent called it fair, only 8 percent thought it was bad.)[67] Alarmist estimates notwithstanding, NATO's overall position strikingly improved. (By 1953, NATO, even without the Germans, could field 25 active divisions, 15 of them in Central Europe, supported by 5,200 aircraft dispersed to around 100 airfields.) NATO might not be able to contend in numerical terms with the Soviet Union's vast reserves. But within two years, "NATO had at least become equal to the Soviet forces deployed in East Germany."[68] To this array, Canada made a useful contribution. It had played a major part in the negotiations that persuaded the US to join NATO, and maintained a small but well trained force of regulars

[66]Summers, "US armed forces in Europe," p. 299.
[67]Nelson, *A History of US Military Forces in Germany*, p. 55.
[68]Millett and Maslowski, *For the Common Defense*, p. 496.

(120,000 in all by 1958, with an army of 48,000 men, comprising three brigade groups stationed in Canada, and one in Europe).

The US still remained by far the world's greatest naval power – at this time the Red Fleet had not yet embarked on the spectacular expansion of the 1960s and 1970s.[69] It also maintained the greatest air force. NATO ruled the waves and most of the world's airspace. Above all, the US – like the Soviet Union – kept expanding its nuclear and ballistic arsenal whose projected use and dilemmas we shall discuss at greater length in a subsequent chapter. The alliance, admittedly, continued to display many flaws, as did its US component. But overall, Western Europe by the end of the 1950s was a good deal more secure from Soviet threats than a decade earlier. US military planners in particular had reason for moderate self-praise.

ORGANIZATION AND STRATEGY

"NATO is an organisation of sovereign nations equal in status" proclaims its handbook.[70] A more inaccurate statement would be hard to find even in official handouts. From its beginnings, NATO was characterized by the diversity of its membership. (The founding states comprised Belgium, Canada, Denmark, France, Iceland, Italy, Luxemburg, the Netherlands, Norway, Portugal, the United Kingdom, and the United States – joined in 1952 by Greece and Turkey, two mutually hostile allies, and in 1954 by the Federal German Republic.) There was an enormous disparity of power and status between the members, with the US at one extreme of the spectrum, and Norway and Iceland at the other. Critics of the alliance were fond of censuring it as a facade that concealed an "American protectorate in Europe."[71] In fact, the European NATO countries' allegiance was purely voluntary. Even a small country in NATO could freely determine whether or not it wanted allied forces stationed on its soil. But critics of the alliance were perfectly justified in stressing the inequalities of power between its members: West Germany was of much greater account than, say, Denmark; the US remained immeasurably superior to the rest in nuclear weaponry and economic strength. (By 1953, the 176,000,000 North Americans still accounted for a total economic output about three times that attained by the 208,000,000 citizens of the European NATO states.) The US moreover made great sacrifices in resisting communist aggression in Korea. (The US forces incurred 157,000 casualties, about 95 percent of those suffered

[69]By 1958, the US navy – including its "moth-balled" vessels – comprised 103 aircraft carriers, 68 cruisers, 421 destroyers, 390 escort and other vessels, 125 submarines, including 6 operative nuclear powered submarines. The airforce consisted of 105 wings – each wing had 45 planes in the case of bomber formations, 75 in the case of fighters and fighter bombers. See Institute for Strategic Studies, *The Soviet Union and the NATO Powers: The Strategic Balance*. London, 1959, pp. 10–11.
[70]NATO *Handbook*, Brussels, NATO Information Service, 1983, p. 31.
[71]David P. Calleo, *Atlantic Fantasy, The United States, NATO, and Europe*. Johns Hopkins Press, 1970, pp. 27–8.

by the 16 participating members, South Korea not being a UN member at the time.) Thirty-three thousand American soldiers died for a country that most of them would hardly have been able to locate on a map before the fighting started. More than 15 billion dollars were spent by the US on the war. These sacrifices were soon forgotten. (The most enduring film memorial to the war turned out to be MASH, a semi-facetious TV series, distinguished by its anti-war mood and its refusal to contemplate the consequences of a possible communist victory in Korea.) But the US at any rate had demonstrated its willingness to support a threatened ally.

The US moreover dominated the NATO alliance by reason of its economic strength. It was the size, variety, and strength of what Eisenhower disparagingly called the US military-industrial complex which made NATO as effective as it was. As Colonel Harry Summers, the American military writer points out, the president would have been better advised to stick to the World War II term "arsenal of democracy." Nevertheless, NATO – unlike the Warsaw Pact – rested on its members' free consent, even that of the weakest. Thus Norway, as we have mentioned above, successfully insisted on keeping nuclear weapons from its soil, a reservation unimaginable for Poland or East Germany. Even Iceland's wishes met with respect. In 1956 an Icelandic coalition of progressives, social democrats and communists won an election by calling for the withdrawal of US troops. The giant prepared to submit to tiny Iceland's wishes. In the end, the US troops stayed – not because Washington had threatened reprisals, but because of the impression made on Iceland by the Soviet invasion of Hungary, and because of the economic consequences that Iceland would have faced from the departure of US dollars.[72] It was NATO's character as a voluntary association that constituted alike its weakness and its strength. None of its European members wanted to experience once more the agonies either of occupation or of liberation. The NATO alliance might not engender enthusiasm; but it did rest on popular support.

NATO's supreme command inevitably passed to the Americans. (Indeed NATO's very foundation implied a steady decline in the "special relationship" that had hitherto existed between Britain and the US). In 1950 Eisenhower became the first supreme allied commander (1950–2); it was his personality and prestige that dominated NATO during its first crucial years. Eisenhower, like his coadjutors in NATO and his opponents in the Warsaw Pact headquarters, continued to think of the World War II experience. He himself was personally acquainted with most of NATO's leading officers. He also profited from the organizational structure set up for the military under European Union's auspices. (Its commanders-in-chief defense committee had formed the first instance of continuous military cooperation and planning in Western Europe in peacetime. But the committee had been beset by bitter rivalry between Lord Montgomery, the chairman, and General Lattre de Tassigny,

[72]Lawrence S. Kaplan, *The United States and NATO: The Formative Years*. Lexington, The University Press of Kentucky, 1984, p. 183. Josef Joffe, *The Limited Partnership: Europe, The United States and the Burden of Alliance*. Cambridge, Mass., Ballinger, 1987.

both brilliant, vainglorious men, with fine war records, and both national heroes.)[73] The Western European headquarters at Fontainebleau became the model for Eisenhower's supreme headquarters (SHAPE). In a like manner, the Western European military supply board was absorbed into NATO's military production and supply board; the Western European finance and economic committee became the core of NATO's financial and economic board.

NATO's formation created a host of new problems that paralleled those faced in the creation of a Western European association. According to the facetious calculations in *Parkinson's Law* (a best seller of the 1950s), the number of enemies killed by an army varies inversely with the number of its own generals.[74] If Parkinson were right, NATO's killing ability should have been small – given the high proportion of senior officers in NATO's command structure, given also its bureaucratic intricacies. According to its French critics, NATO moreover was dominated by the "Anglo-Saxons." (Its very designation, "North Atlantic Treaty Organization," took no account of its Mediterranean members.) English became NATO's unofficial language, replete with dissonant acronyms. Traditional national jurisdictions had to be modified through complex standardization agreements that allowed aircraft, trucks, pipelines, and various communications systems to cross national borders without hindrance. The allies had to coordinate policies and strategy through a supranational organization.

To meet these problems, the allies set up an organization of considerable complexity. The Council served as the supreme organ of the alliance, with permanent representation from each member government. The Council was responsible for implementing the provisions of the treaty; its work was organized by the secretary-general who directed its Secretariat and its five divisions: political affairs, defense planning and policy, defense support, infrastructure, logistics and Council operations, scientific affairs. The Council's chief administrative officer was the secretary-general. The first incumbent was Lord Ismay, a British general who had made his reputation as chief of staff to the British minister of defence during World War II; Ismay held the post until 1957 when he was succeeded by Paul-Henri Spaak, like Eisenhower, a chairman to the manner born.

The Council was assisted by a host of specialized committees and agencies that dealt with matters as diverse as the press services and economics. NATO's military direction lay with the military committee composed of the chief-of-staff of each member state. Subordinate to the military committee were the major commands and planning groups: Supreme Command Europe (SACEUR); Supreme Allied Commander Atlantic (SACLANT); Allied Commander-in-chief Channel (CINCHAN); Canada-US Regional Planning Group (CUSRPG); and a number of other military agencies. Supreme headquarters

[73]Brigadier General A. N. Breitemey, "A second home in France," in T. E. B. Howarth, *Monty at Close Quarters*. New York, Hippocrene Books, 1985, pp. 112–13.
[74]C. Northcote Parkinson, *Parkinson's Law and Other Studies in Administration*. New York, Ballantine Books, 1964, p. ii.

were in Paris, and later shifted to Brussels. (Here NATO's impact, however, was much smaller than the EEC's. By 1987 there were still fewer than 2,300 NATO officials in Brussels, as opposed to 14,000 Eurocrats.) Subordinate agencies were located in Paris, Bonn, and Rome.

NATO remained an association of sovereign nation states; its members could leave the alliance as they pleased. (In 1966 France withdrew from the military command though it continued to cooperate with the alliance.) Individual members remained free to decide the percentage of their GNP, or the size and composition of the forces, to be contributed to the alliance.[75] NATO's strength would continue to depend on the power of its national components. Its sphere of action remained confined to Western Europe and its strategic role remained defensive. Threats to the alliance that might emerge elsewhere, in Africa, the Middle East or the Caribbean, would still have to be dealt with by its individual members – an arrangement initially welcomed and later regretted by the Americans. NATO possessed no coordinated intelligence service; the intelligence services of the individual countries would continue to operate in an uneasy, and often mutually hostile fraternity.

NATO did not possess a propaganda organization capable of rivalling the Soviet propaganda machine in Western Europe. It likewise lacked an agency for political warfare. In this regard, the allies differed among themselves and even individual member states (including the US) pursued no consistent policy. In 1953, for example, John Foster Dulles talked at length about the need to liberate Eastern Europe.[76] But when the Hungarians revolted in 1956, the US would not even withdraw diplomatic recognition from the resultant puppet regime, much less recognize a Hungarian government in exile. The want of a coordinated political strategy became all the more obvious during the later 1950s when the Soviets became more skillful in their foreign policy, increasingly used "peace" slogans on their own behalf, and resolved to make their weight felt in the Third World. The NATO powers, by contrast, were apt to underplay the political dimension of the struggle. Not for them the sound advice given to the Spartans by Alcibiades, most illustrious of Athenian exiles: "The surest way of harming an enemy is to find out certainly what form of attack he is most frightened of and then to employ it against him."[77]

There were other problems. NATO proved much less adapt at standardizing its equipment than the Warsaw Pact. Its command structure was so complex as to be certain of being superseded in the event of war. In fact NATO continued to be troubled by all those weaknesses that have traditionally beset all alliances, described in a different context by Lord Macaulay nearly a century and a half before. "Jealousies inevitably spring up. Disputes engender disputes. Every confederate is tempted to throw on others some part of the burden

---

[75]By 1958, the European members' defensive expenditure as a percentage of their gross domestic product ranged from 7 for Britain, 6.8 for France, 4.7 for the Netherlands, 3.7 for Belgium, 3 for West Germany, and 2.9 for Denmark.

[76]Lawrence S. Kaplan and Robert W. Clawson, eds, *NATO After Thirty Years*. Wilmington, Delaware, SRI, 1981, p. 104.

[77]Thucydides, *The Peloponnesian War,* p. 424.

PLATE 29   *Cartoon on Churchill's party defeat in 1945.*
(Credit: Library of Congress)

PLATE 30   UNRRA head, Mayor of New York Fiorello La Guardia with Eleanor Roosevelt.
(Credit: Library of Congress)

PLATE 31   Generals Eisenhower, Murphy, and Clay, Berlin 1946.
(Credit: Hoover Institution Archives)

PLATE 32   *Senator Arthur Vandenberg who got Republicans to support Truman's policy of*
containment and aid to Europe.
(*Credit: Library of Congress*)

PLATE 33   *Prime Minister MacKenzie King, of Canada.*
(*Credit: Library of Congress*)

UNCLASSIFIED

UNCLASSIFIED

(058/-/47)

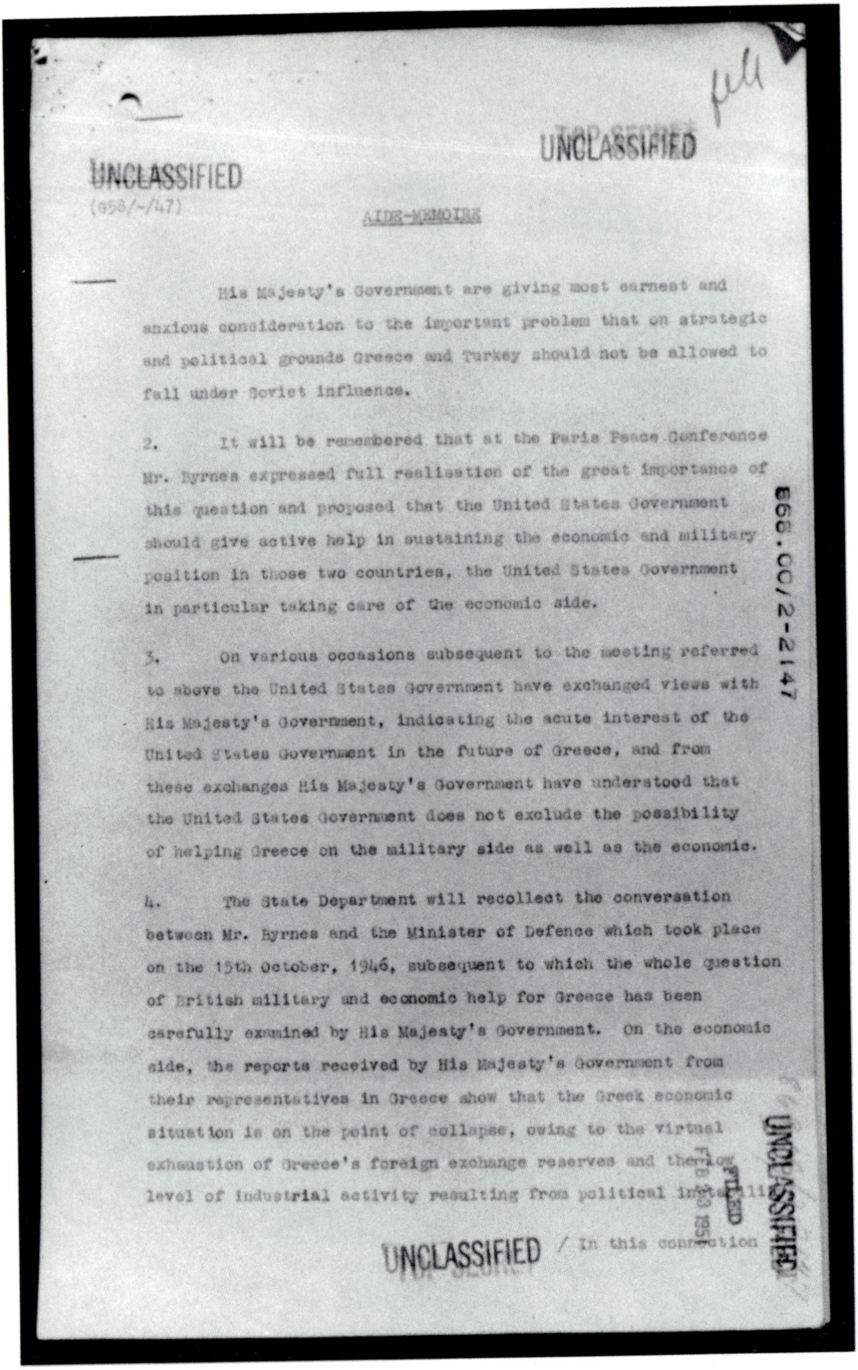

AIDE-MEMOIRE

His Majesty's Government are giving most earnest and anxious consideration to the important problem that on strategic and political grounds Greece and Turkey should not be allowed to fall under Soviet influence.

2. It will be remembered that at the Paris Peace Conference Mr. Byrnes expressed full realisation of the great importance of this question and proposed that the United States Government should give active help in sustaining the economic and military position in those two countries, the United States Government in particular taking care of the economic side.

3. On various occasions subsequent to the meeting referred to above the United States Government have exchanged views with His Majesty's Government, indicating the acute interest of the United States Government in the future of Greece, and from these exchanges His Majesty's Government have understood that the United States Government does not exclude the possibility of helping Greece on the military side as well as the economic.

4. The State Department will recollect the conversation between Mr. Byrnes and the Minister of Defence which took place on the 15th October, 1946, subsequent to which the whole question of British military and economic help for Greece has been carefully examined by His Majesty's Government. On the economic side, the reports received by His Majesty's Government from their representatives in Greece show that the Greek economic situation is on the point of collapse, owing to the virtual exhaustion of Greece's foreign exchange reserves and the low level of industrial activity resulting from political instabili

UNCLASSIFIED / In this connection

868.00/2-2147

UNCLASSIFIED

PLATE 34 *British aide memoire that contributed to the Truman Doctrine.*
(Credit: The National Archives)

PLATE 35   *President Truman notifying Congress of the Truman Doctrine, March 12, 1947.*

PLATE 36   *Currency reform of June 20, 1948, which replaced old marks for new ones and initiated rapid economic growth in Germany.*
(Credit: GIC)

PLATE 37   *Germany's reconstruction government with Konrad Adenauer.*
(Credit: GIC)

PLATE 40 *Marshall Plan aid for West Germany.*
(*Credit: GIC*)

PLATE 41 *Rebuilding with American aid.*
(*Credit: GIC*)

PLATE 42   *Pre-war Hanover.*
(*Credit: Archiv für Städtebau Konstanz Gutschow, Hamburg*)

PLATE 43   *Hanover, 1945, with rubble cleared.*
(*Credit: Archiv für Städtebau Konstanz Gutschow, Hamburg*)

PLATE 44   *Reconstruction of Hanover as of 1952.*
(*Credit: Archiv für Städtebau Konstanz Gutschow, Hamburg*)

PLATE 45   *Italian Communist Party members and railway workers striking over signing of Atlantic Pact, Milan, 1949.*
(*Credit: The National Archives*)

PLATE 46   *Public housing, Rome.*
(*Credit: Italian Cultural Center*)

PLATE 49   *Berlin airlift, April 1 to May 8, 1949.*
(*Credit: The National Archives*)

THE NEW YORK SUN, TUESDAY, JULY 22, 1947.

PEACE TODAY.   By Rube Goldberg

ATOMIC BOMB

WORLD CONTROL

WORLD DESTRUCTION

PLATE 50   *Peace Today.*
(*Credit: Library of Congress*)

PLATE 51 *War surplus tanks near Detroit, destined for NATO, 1949.*

PLATE 52 *Senators Arthur N. Vandenberg and Tom Connally conferring with Secretary of State Marshall (center) on European Recovery Plan.*
(Credit: Agency for International Development)

PLATE 53   *Drafters of the Marshall Plan: George F. Kennan and William L. Clayton.*
(*Credit: The National Archives*)

PLATE 54   *First shipment of wheat for European Recovery Plan.*
(*Credit: The National Archives*)

PLATE 55   *ECA-financed hydroelectric dam in France.*
(*Credit: The National Archives*)

PLATE 56   *British Prime Minister Anthony Eden campaigning.*
(*Credit: Library of Congress*)

PLATE 57   *Cartoon on Marshall Plan.*
(*Credit: Library of Congress*)

which he himself ought to bear. Scarcely one honestly furnishes the promised contingent. Scarcely one observes the appointed day."[78] But at least the alliance was in place.

NATO's military planners, like their opposite numbers in the Warsaw Pact, continued to think of a future conflict in terms of World War II where they had gained experience, honors, and victory. (Their preoccupation with World War II was shared by the reading public on both sides of the iron curtain, which continued with enthusiasm to buy war books of every kind.) NATO strategists in particular drew heavily on the air strategy of World War II, now rendered more potent by nuclear arms. As Montgomery, then deputy NATO supreme allied commander in Europe, said in 1954, if NATO were attacked by the Soviet Union, it would first have to assure for itself mastery in the air and on the oceans, while preventing the enemy land forces from overrunning the Western bases. In those days before Western Germany had rearmed, NATO planned to retreat to the Rhine and defend the river line. During the second phase, possibly one concurrent with the first, the enemy's land forces would be destroyed in battles made more dreadful by the extensive use of nuclear weapons delivered by aircraft. The third phase, the "bargaining phase" would witness air assaults directed against the enemy's homeland, until Moscow would accept NATO's terms.[79]

Up to the late 1950s Soviet military planners believed war was inevitable between capitalism and socialism, and they prepared for it accordingly. The main objective was to defeat NATO and to draw the US out of Europe. This could only be done if they had overwhelming offensive superiority and the resources to launch a surprise attack. The political arm of the Soviet system preached the same doctrine.

The West had to counter this threat, and the fear of a Soviet invasion shaped East–West relocation for the next 40 years and provided the justification for the policy of deterrence.

To the Soviets and Soviet sympathizers, NATO represented "the newest form of aggressive capitalism that could only perpetuate itself by embarking on new and ever more threatening imperialist ventures."[80] The Soviet Union was supposedly being encircled by a world-wide system of air bases; Soviet strategy was essentially defensive; NATO's strategy allegedly heightened those perils that it wished to avoid. We see no justice in these claims. Moscow's policy toward the West was not of the kind befitting a weaker power fearing assault. Soviet strategy put its trust in a sustained offensive that emphasized deception, speed, surprise, and the unremitting use of the strategic initiative. Soviet propaganda, far from conciliatory toward the West, took recourse in unbridled mendacity. The Soviets continued to call for the destruction of

---

[78]Thomas Babington Macaulay, *The History of England from the Accession of James II.* Chicago, Belfore, Clarke, 1867, v. 4, p. 123.

[79]Field Marshal Lord Carver, *A Policy for Peace.* London, Faber and Faber, 1982, pp. 32–3.

[80]Robert W. Clawson and Glenn E. Wilson, "The Warsaw Pact, USSR, and NATO, perceptions from the East," in Kaplan and Clawson, eds, *NATO After Thirty Years,* p. 114.

capitalism world-wide. They unhesitatingly challenged the Allies' position in West Berlin, and openly supported North Korean aggression. Soviet policy toward the West during the 1950s strikingly contrasted with Stalin's during the two years preceding the German attack against Russia when the Soviets had genuinely feared German aggression, and had genuinely attempted a policy of peaceful coexistence with the Third Reich.

NATO strategy based on "massive retaliation" also incurred criticisms of a more technical kind. How would it deal with minor assaults, say a pre-emptive Soviet occupation of West Berlin? Could the Americans actually be relied upon to use their nuclear arsenal in a limited conflict? They had not after all done so in Korea, even when the battle seemed most desparate. A strategy that involved abandoning most of West Germany made no sense, once the Germans had begun to contribute conventional forces to NATO. Massive retaliation (though later also accepted in Britain), was above all an American strategy, depending on the might of the US strategic air command. A massive force of supercarriers deployed in the Atlantic, the Mediterranean, and the Western Pacific competed with the strategic air command in deterring Soviet might. (In 1951, US navy carriers acquired their first nuclear-capable aircraft. In 1958 the US laid down the first nuclear-powered aircraft carrier, the USS *Enterprise*. In addition, the US pioneered the first nuclear-powered submarine, the *Nautilus*, launched in 1954.)[81] Massive retaliation thus seemed assured – but this assumed that the USSR would long remain inferior in nuclear weaponry, and that the US could remain invulnerable to Soviet assaults.

Such assumptions proved mistaken. In 1953 the Soviet Union exploded its first hydrogen bomb; in 1957 it launched *Sputnik*, thereby demonstrating its ability not merely to put a satellite into the sky, but also to strike at any US city. The Soviet success stimulated US counter-measures. Nuclear warfare henceforth threatened to become an artillery duel of global dimensions and inconceivable destructiveness. Such duels could not be tested in maneuvers; their strategy could not be derived from previous military history. They became the preserve of a new generation of civilian analysts who used wargames as a substitute for real conflict. Their wargaming became an abstract exercise; their nuclear strategy perforce became remote from reality, a disembodied realm in which quantification ruled supreme, and "the bomb" turned into the ultimate weapon. Nuclear controversies in the West all too often were carried out in a vacuum that took little account of Soviet thinking in this regard; such controversies increasingly resembled "the theological debates of past centuries."[82]

Above all, NATO consistently underestimated its capacity for conventional

---

[81] John Keegan, *The Price of Admiralty: The Evolution of Naval Warfare*. New York, Viking, 1988, pp. 268–9.

[82] The phrase comes from Amos Perlmutter, "The unmaking of a classic," *Orbis* v. 31, no. 4, Winter 1987, pp. 731–41, an excessively harsh review of the excellent collection by Peter Paret and Gordon Craig, eds, *Makers of Modern Strategy from Macchiavelli to the Nuclear Age*. Princeton, Princeton University Press, 1986. Foremost among the new works on nuclear strategy was Herman Kahn, *On Thermonuclear War*, Princeton, Princeton University Press, 1960.

defense, an easy mistake to make – especially at a time when the People's Republic of China was allied to the Soviet Union. The Korean war had created a great deal of uneasiness. The draft had operated in a seemingly unfair fashion. All too many men had secured exemptions for some reason or another. The sons of professors and pastors were less likely to serve in the front line than the sons of truckdrivers or steel workers. Moreover, in Korea, the US, the world's first technological and economic power, had been compelled to wage a traditional war of infantry and artillery against an opponent with vastly greater manpower resources. All three US armed services therefore began planning to employ nuclear weapons on the battlefield, and they did so in mutual rivalry. According to a widespread orthodoxy, the defense of Western Europe during the 1950s depended on nothing but the deterrent effect of the US strategic air force.

But in assessing Soviet strength on land, Western experts may have over-estimated the difficulties that the Soviets would have faced in suddenly con-centrating huge forces for a surprise assault, or the problems of maneuvering huge mechanized forces through highly built up areas on a narrow front.[83] How would generals fight battles with dozens of armored and mechanized divisions, with roads clogged, traffic jams of gargantuan proportions, essential spare parts for complex equipment gone astray. Even if nuclear weapons were only used tactically, would tank crews and infantry not be shocked beyond endurance, even if they survived nuclear blasts? Would nuclear weapons not destroy the very battlefield, reducing every major battle to total chaos? Western planners, benumbed by headcounts, were also apt to overrate the value of non-Soviet divisions within the Warsaw Pact, many of which might have proved highly unreliable in the event of conflict. Hence, as William Park, a British student of strategy, put it, "NATO was born with an inferiority complex regarding its conventional force capabilities, unwarranted even in the early years."[84]

On the American side the sense of inferiority went with the widespread conviction that NATO was weak, and that the NATO allies were somehow unwilling to pull their weight. Neither assumption appears justified. By 1958, the NATO powers had 23 divisions available for service in Western Europe, with another 18 in Italy, as well as substantial forces in southeast Europe (22 in Turkey, 12 in Greece). These could be reinforced by substantial reserves. The forces varied in composition and quality, but would surely have given a good account of themselves in a defensive campaign.

Nor was it true that the Europeans failed to pull their weight. In 1952–3, the United Kingdom and France were each spending an estimated 10 percent or more of their respective GNP on defense. By 1953 the NATO Council was able to report that defense expenditure by NATO countries as a whole

---

[83]Brian Bond, *War and Society in Europe, 1870–1970.* Oxford, Oxford University Press, 1986, p. 208.

[84]William Park, *Defending the West: A History of NATO.* Boulder, Col., Westview Press, 1986, p. 26.

was 3.5 times higher than it had been in 1949.) NATO forces were further strengthened from 1953 onward by a great array of tactical nuclear weapons. By the end of the 1950s, forward defense along West Germany's eastern border had ceased to be a chimera. No one, of course, can be sure what would have been the outcome of a war that was never fought. Nevertheless, Western Europe, by the end of the 1950s, was a great deal safer from Soviet attack than the policy makers imagined. In retrospect, General Lyman L. Lemnitzer, (supreme allied commander in Europe, 1964–9) had good reason for his confident assertion that during the three decades that followed NATO's creation "there has been more stability in Europe than that Continent has experienced in over a century."[85]

And yet, NATO's critics have been legion. They number within their ranks right-wingers, left-wingers, neutralists, isolationists, pacifists secular, and pacifists religious. We would point out that NATO's achievement is unparalleled in history. Its members joined the alliance voluntarily, and remained of their own free will. The alliance would have astonished its founders by its longevity. Military cooperation facilitated economic and political collaboration. War-battered Europe regained confidence. The links between North America and Western Europe tightened rather than weakened. No trans-national endeavor in the past achieved greater success.

[85]Cited from a presentation at a conference on "NATO after thirty years," 16 April 1980, Centre for NATO Studies, Kentucky State University, in Kaplan and Clawson, *NATO After Thirty Years,* frontispiece.

8

Cultural, Diplomatic, and Organizational Aspects of International Relations

THE SENTIMENTS OF NATIONS

The success of trans-national associations in the postwar era depended, in the last instance, on the changing sentiments of the Western nations. At the end of World War II, these should have been at their most negative, under the effects of a legacy of suffering and dreadful memories. War had also accelerated the relative decline of the Western European countries in the international arena. Britain, France, and Germany had ceased to be great powers. All Western European countries found themselves reduced to the status of lesser partners in an alliance dominated by the US. Naturally, cooperation between these unequal partners met with many difficulties. From their country's beginning, Americans had seen themselves as a new nation, with new laws, and a new and freer polity. The French observer Crèvecoeur had long ago insisted in his *Letters from an American Farmer* (1782), that America had transformed Europeans into new men, unburdened by respect for dukes, counts, or bishops of an established church. Not all Americans shared his optimism. Indeed a good many intellectuals continued to feel that they lived in a cultural wilderness that lacked Europe's great past. For culture and tradition, educated Americans had widely looked to Europe, and many had crossed the Atlantic to find inspiration and a more sophisticated way of life.

The American mood of cultural deference underwent a sea change during and after World War II. Only the US and the Soviet Union (and to a lesser extent Great Britain) had ended as winners. All other belligerent powers on the Continent had suffered defeat. America's newfound leadership of the Atlantic Community, and the economic and cultural achievements of US artists, writers, scholars, scientists and engineers, brought confidence and pride in the "American way." The US thereafter sought to shape Europe in the image of America. Some tried to create a free-trade United States of Europe, and make government more democratic and participatory. For example, the US model influenced the new constitutions of Italy and Germany. There was also an attempt to develop the economies of Europe using American models and practices. The Marshall Plan brought foreign aid, new techniques and machinery to a tired Europe. The US saw itself as a rich, strong, efficient, and practical democracy, fit for global leadership.

This was clearly a post-isolationist America. From George Washington on, American leaders had warned against foreign entanglements; yet in 1917 and 1941 the US had been pulled into Europe to restore the balance of power. After 1945 the US briefly attempted to return to isolationism – but thanks to British persuasion and Soviet militancy, it did not. World War II and its immediate aftermath therefore formed a watershed in American history. Instead of seeking to isolate itself from supposed foreign contamination, the US embarked on an interventionist course. It sought to build an Atlantic alliance able to resist Soviet pressure. It took steps to feed the hungry and helped Western Europe to recover economically. It dominated NATO, while pushing for free trade within Western Europe. It promoted cultural exchanges; assisted anti-communist bodies such as the congress for cultural freedom and created groups such as the international federation of free trade unions to counter communist labor fronts. Some of Europe's leaders resented America's leadership role, especially the French. Naturally Europeans were upset that they had lost their pre-eminence, and that their continent was divided between the two superpowers. To some came a feeling of impotence and inferiority. But the United States persisted, helping Western Europe to stabilize, and taking the lead in creating an Atlantic community that functioned through complex reciprocal relationships.[1]

Not surprisingly, there were fears concerning the threatened "Americanization of Europe." Such anxieties were not new. After World War I, American tourists, expatriates, music and movies had flooded Europe. Later American soldiers and business people were to serve as missionaries for American life styles and products. Americans saw themselves as harbingers of modernity, of mass production and mass consumption (many European intellectuals shared this assessment). "Skyscrapers," Jean-Paul Sartre reflected, "were the architecture of the future, just as the cinema was the art and jazz the music of the future."[2] In the first decade after World War II American influence intensified – and so did European apprehensions concerning their trans-Atlantic ally.

The US had originally aroused admiration among many of Europe's greatest minds. Goethe, in a poem entitled *Amerika du hastes besser* had half-jokingly praised the US for lacking ancient castles, and ancient memories of quarrels best forgotten. According to Karl Marx, the American War of Independence had initiated the new era of ascendancy for the bourgeoisie and the American civil war would do the same for the working classes. But other intellectual giants expressed their contempt. Heinrich Heine and Jakob Burckhardt had

---

[1] See Rob Kroes, "The image of Europe in America," in A. Rijksbaron, W. H. Roobol, M. Weisglas, eds, *Europe From a Cultural Perspective: Historiography and Perceptions*. The Hague, Nijgh and Van Ditmar Universitair, 1987, pp. 121–30.

[2] Cited by Frank Costiglolia, *Awkward Dominion: American Political, Economic, and Cultural Relations with Europe, 1919–1933*. Ithaca, Cornell University Press, 1984, p. 178.

taken America to task for a great variety of real or imagined ills that offended romantics and advocates of status-bound societies. Indeed "most of the typical stereotypes concerning America and American society had already been formed before 1860," long before American hegemony had even seemed conceivable.[3] According to its critics, America was an artificial society; it lacked roots; it had failed to evolve into a true state, it was materialistic, greedy, crude, anarchic, childishly optimistic, devoid of tragic imagination and high culture. Americans were uncivilized. (Carl Schurz, the German-American statesman and soldier, related with relish the story of an American visitor who was challenged to a duel by a Prussian nobleman. The American chose Bowie knives for weapons. The Prussian indignantly pronounced the suggestion barbarous, and refused to fight.) Anti-Americanism of the romantic kind often reflected class prejudice. As Charles Francis Adams, the US minister in London during the civil war had said: "the great body of the aristocracy and the commercial classes are anxious to see the United States go to pieces, while the middle and lower classes sympathize with us."[4]

From the end of the nineteenth century, traditionalist critics of America were joined by those from the left, who often took over the anti-mercantile prejudices of the traditional nobility. The left widely, though by no means universally, reviled the US for alleged capitalist exploitation, and for its failure to develop an effective working-class party or an indigenous revolutionary movement. These charges were reinforced after World War II by a coordinated disinformation campaign launched by the Soviet Union, its allies in both East and West Europe and their network of front organizations and fellow-travelers. According to the communists and their friends, the US was guilty of every conceivable offense – from exploiting the world's proletariat to using germ warfare in Korea.

Anti-Americanism in Europe had many components: deep-seated resentment among right-wingers of the transfer of world power from Berlin, London, and Paris to Washington. The dread of American economic penetration has matched the left-wing hostility to America as the bastion of world capitalism. The anti-Americanism of the Old Right was also sometimes anti-semitic – Americans were governed by Jews, or they were like Jews – plebeian hucksters. For the left, anti-Americanism likewise became at times a scapegoat ideology that blamed these alien miscreants for all the ills of modern urban society, and its assumed rootlessness and greed. A good deal of such feeling moreover was made in America. American anti-Americanism went hand-in-hand with disdain for the work ethic among dissenters who mistakenly identified it with the ills of capitalism. Books such as C. Wright Mills, *The Power Elite*; David Riesman, *The Lonely Crowd*; Sloan Wilson, *The Man in the Gray*

[3] J. W. Schulte Nordholt, "Anti-Americanism in European culture: its early manifestations," in Rob Kroes and Maarten van Rossem, *Anti-Americanism in Europe*. Amsterdam, Holland, Free Press, 1986, p. 16.
[4] James M. McPherson, *Battle Cry of Freedom, The Civil War Era*. Oxford, Oxford University Press, 1988, p. 549.

Flannel Suit; William H. Whyte, *The Organization Man*; Vance Packard, *The Hidden Persuaders* (all published in the 1950s) stood on the shelves of all major (including USA) libraries in Europe. As one British socialist put it, "I always turn to American sources when I wish to indict American capitalism."[5] By contrast, American studies remained grossly neglected. (Forty years after the inauguration of the Marshall Plan, Paris could boast of British, German, Latin-American and Spanish institutes, with an Arab institute to follow – but there was still no American institute.)

There was also anti-Americanism of the practical kind. Allied soldiers resented the "Yanks'" superior pay, their superior airs, and their success with women – gained unfairly, it was believed, through gifts of nylon stockings, Bourbon and chocolate. European officers resented taking orders from Americans within the NATO alliance. (There were also particular national grudges; Dutch naval officers for instance, had to watch their fleet being reduced to a minor auxiliary force without an oceanic role.) European civilians resented American business people and tourists – sometimes ill-mannered, loud-mouthed, and inclined to over-tip. (In their capacity as the archetypal *nouveaux riches*, Americans were later joined by *Bundesdeutsche* – cigar-smoking West Germans wearing plus-fours.)

Much more serious was the resentment of traditional power elites concerning the American part in the anti-colonialism campaign. Dutch colonials were shocked at the support given by the US to the Indonesian independence movement. The British were furious at American anti-colonialism, and Eisenhower's harsh words to the British over their invasion of Suez (1956) almost broke up the alliance. The French complained of US support for the Algerians. The CIA, for example, had taken an early option on Algerian independence, and between 1958 and 1962 organized secretly vouchered educational grants for Algerian students expelled from French universities for Algerian nationalist activities. Yet, at the same time, the CIA was accused in French newspapers of backing French right-wing causes, and of plotting the overthrow of the Republic.[6]

The US moreover was widely associated with racism. Black American soldiers (occasionally known as 'tan Yanks" in Britain) met with much less racial prejudice in Western Europe than they did at home. (According to the apocryphal remarks attributed to a British farmer, the "tan Yanks" only had one bad quality; they *would* bring those awful white men along.) Hard-line critics said the US was frozen into an oppressive hierarchy of color. (Inconceivable during the 1940s and 1950s was the notion that by the late 1980s, the average income of Japanese-Americans, Chinese-Americans, Filipino-Americans, and second-generation black West Indian Americans would exceed

[5]Stephen Hasler, *Anti-Americanism: Steps on a Dangerous Path*. London, Institute for European Defence and Strategic Studies, 1986. Max Beloff, *Europe and the Europeans*. London, Chatto and Windus, 1957.

[6]Rhodri Jeffrey-Jones, "The CIA and the demise of anti-anti-Americanism, some evidence and reflections," in Kroes and van Rossen, *Anti-Americanism in Europe*, p. 130.

the average family incomes of US whites). Yet the US also incurred censure on the part of European racists for proclaiming racial equality, and corrupting the world with "Negroid" jazz. Many Europeans imagined the US the world's most crime-ridden country, with murder and mayhem at every street corner; Americans in general were thought to lack culture and *savoir-faire* – a belief fostered by US movies and thrillers.

Above all there was the ambivalent impact of the Cold War. Initially, the Americans incurred censure not for interventionism but for their reluctance to get permanently involved in Europe. Once the isolationist tide was reversed in the US, the anti-American feeling changed tack in Europe. American "cold warriors" lacked the insight and finesse supposedly associated with European diplomacy; driven by McCarthyite hysteria, they were accused of needlessly worsening relations between Western Europe and the USSR. The latter was widely judged among committed left-wingers by a different standard. The Soviet Union might have its faults; but at least the foundations of socialism stood undamaged; and socialism was man's last best hope. All would be well if only the Americans would depart – a sentiment later expressed by graffiti on the Berlin Wall saying "Ami [Yankee] go home."

Anti-Americanism in Europe was paralleled to a lesser extent by anti-Europeanism in the US. From its beginnings, the American Republic had looked askance at Europe for its social prejudice and snobbery; the US, by contrast, was supposedly a city built on a hill, free from the corruption of the Old World. The immigrant, or the immigrant-descended American, tended to regard himself as being as well-born as the most distinguished European. (When asked, during World War II, why he did not change his name, one Sergeant Hitler, US marines, replied, "let the other guy change his.")[7] There was also in the US a powerful tradition of nativism. Not all foreigners of course incurred equal dislike. The British were liked most in US public opinion surveys; reciprocal sentiments occurred in Britain, whose people generally felt themselves closer to Americans than to Europeans, a conviction held also by Churchill, himself half-American. In popularity, the Germans ranked second in the US – not surprising in a country where so many claimed German ancestry. (The cartoon image of the typical German changed from the wartime stereotype of the Prussian, tall, monocled, and mean, to the jolly, rotund Bavarian in *lederhosen* – both quite unlike the real Germans whom GIs met in the streets of Munich and West Berlin.) The US as a country was also often kind to people of mixed ethnic origin, a group very much more numerous there than in Europe. The French reactionaries' hatred of *métèques* (persons of mixed ethnic descent) could not flourish in a country where most citizens remembered ancestors from several different countries.[8]

[7] Ted Morgan, *On Becoming American*. New York, Paragon House, 1988, p. 93.
[8] Definitions of ethnicity are murky in the US. According to the 1980 census, 50,000,000 listed their ancestry as "English," but more than half of these also linked other ethnic origins. Some 49,000,000 described themselves as "German", but three-fifths of these also reported other ancestries, and 40,000,000 stated that they were "Irish," but three-quarters also reported other

Even so, there remained in the US even by 1960 a substantial minority of citizens who indicated in a poll that they would disapprove of a marriage between foreigners and members of their own family. (Twenty-three percent of Americans polled in one particular survey would have objected to British in-laws, 34 percent to German in-laws – Jewish Americans, black Americans, and Southerners were most likely to be anti-German, 35 percent disapproved of the French, 40 percent to Italians, and 58 percent to Russians.)[9] There was also ambivalence toward their respective countries of origin among millions of European immigrants who had left home because of poverty, political discontent, religious or racial persecution. Organizers of international festivals at high school, or teachers of ethnic studies might rejoice in the razzle-dazzle of tartans, bagpipes, zithers, dajikis, and pan pipes; cooks might adapt any kind of foreign cuisine to American taste; musicians might draw on foreign tunes. But the great majority of immigrants did little or nothing to pass on their ancestral language and culture to their children and children's children. Western Europe and the US were divided also in other and more fundamental ways. In so far as opinion polls can be trusted, Americans overall remained more patriotic than Western Europeans at large – a finding that would have surprised European conservatives of yesteryear.[10]

Given the extent of such differences, it is a wonder that the Atlantic Community should have worked in the first place. In fact, the alliance underwent many crises – the Berlin airlift, the Suez incident of 1956, Vietnam in the 1960s, the "new neutralism" in Western Europe that gained in intensity during the 1970s. Nevertheless it has persisted, an astonishing achievement, given the troubled history of every alliance ever made. Among the mass of Europeans, the US remained reasonably popular, even in a country such as the Netherlands where neutralist sentiments had greatly increased.[11] Anti-Americanism might be strong among the intellectuals of the left and with the extreme right; but the great majority belonged to neither category. Whatever friction might arise between US soldiers and Europeans, the average GI was an ambassador of good will. Europeans (especially the Germans) certainly preferred the Americans to the Soviets. American values were widely adopted in a country where the very mendacity of Nazi propaganda had backfired.[12]

---

ancestries. See Nathan Glazer, "The structure of ethnicity," *Public Opinion*, v. 7, no. 5, October–November 1984, pp. 2–5.

[9]M. Koch-Hillebrand, *Das Deutschenbild: Gegenwart, Geschichte, Psychologie.* Munich, C. H. Beck, 1977, table on p. 67.

[10]For the intensity of expressed US patriotism, see for instance *Public Opinion*, June–July 1981, especially pp. 24–5. 80 percent of US respondents in a 1980 poll stated that they were extremely proud to belong to their own country; 18 percent said they were somewhat proud.

[11]According to a Dutch poll in 1981, Dutch respondents proclaimed a "positive" attitude towards foreign countries in the following order (in percentages) Belgium 51, Sweden 48, Switzerland 46, US 45, Austria 43, England 43; Denmark 42, France 41, West Germany 40, Soviet Union 6. Cited in Koen Koch, "Anti-Americanism and the Dutch peace movement," in Kroes and van Rossem, *Anti-Americanism in Europe*, pp. 108–9.

[12]Marlis Steinert, *Hitlers Krieg und die Deutschen.* Düsseldorf, Econ Verlag, 1970, p. 592 for the changing German image of the Americans.

The US moreover held a special appeal for lower-middle and working-class people all over Europe. The real workers preferred an American Hitchcock movie to the finest Soviet films made by Eisenstein. It was Irving Berlin, the son of a poverty-stricken immigrant from Siberia, raised in a tenement in New York City, who was a true son of the proletariat, not the self-conscious adherents of *Proletkult*. (The US remained for many years a magnet for Europeans: 2,981,000 legal immigrants moved from Europe to the US between 1950 and 1960; between 1960 and 1970 3,932,000 more came.) To those who left Europe after 1945, the US appeared a land of opportunity and new beginnings, where shops were full, food was plentiful, and where a knock at the door signified the arrival of a friend, rather than a *milicien*, a Gestapo or KGB agent. To the average immigrant intellectual, the US was a land where jobs, grants, and access to laboratory and library facilities were easier to attain than at home. To the craftsman, this was a country where a man might set up his own shop without guild interference (a contrast with Germany, for instance, where an electrician, a butcher, or a tailor needed to pass the *Meisterprüfung*, a guild master's exam, before he could start his own enterprise). To a businessman, the US seemed a treasure house; to a worker, it was a land of high wages. To movie-goers, old and young, the US was the home of G-men, cowboys, and sheriffs forever chasing evil-doers, or of Mickey Mouse and Donald Duck. To the lover of modern music, it was the land of swing, jazz, and stunning musicals, that European artists imitated, but could not equal.

In a wider sense, America was, and continued to be, many Europeans' hope of a better future. For immigrants and refugees it meant escape from poverty, from the sight of rubble-strewn cities, from the hatred stirred by persecution and war, from the unwelcome attentions of bureaucrats, informers, policemen or commissars. American war movies that juxtaposed in the same infantry platoon enlisted men with names as varied as O'Hara, Schmidt, Cohen, Manzini, and Kirilenko might exaggerate the success of the melting pot; but compared to Europe's ethnic and religious quarrels, America's seemed of small account. Then, to the member of a Protestant mainline church, the US was a country where a much larger proportion of men and women attended divine service than in any other major nation, while to a sectarian, it was a land of open religious dissent. It was the home of one of the world's largest, most confident, and influential Catholic communities (containing, for example, far more citizens of Irish descent than Ireland itself). To a Jew also, the US – more even than Israel – represented the world's greatest refuge, where his people flourished as nowhere else. The US stood out as a country little touched by anti-clericalism. To an old-style European liberal, the US was the bastion of free enterprise. And to a social reformer, it was the land of the New Deal. To all of them – including British Labourites such as Clement Attlee and Ernest Bevin – the US was a free country, the "arsenal of democracy" and the defender of Europe after the war.

Yet the US was a difficult country to understand. For many European intellectuals, including immigrants, it was a cultural backwater or worse – a desert. As George Bernard Shaw had commented, the US was the only country in the world that had gone from barbarism to decadence without an intervening period of civilization. This image, however, bore no relation to reality. The US had certainly come to influence popular culture, through films, jazz, musicals, toys (the teddy bear), cartoons, and advertising techniques. It had created musicals and modern fairy tales concerned with subjects such as the heroic cowboy, raised to the status of a mythical figure. But in addition, the US continued to develop its own "high culture" in a variety of ways – through amateur dramatics, church choirs, and through professional bodies, including numerous symphony orchestras and musical groups. US academic institutions multiplied and played a predominant part in the world of scholarship, and American academics began to make more of the major contributions to science, history, art , literature, and the social sciences. By the end of World War II, American provincialism was a thing of the past, and a cultural revival was about to begin.

America also surprised foreigners in other ways. To the committed socialist, for example, the US appeared inexplicable – the most advanced capitalist state in the world, and yet one that had failed to develop an independent socialist or working-class party. Irish trade unionists, Jewish *Bundists* from Eastern Europe, German Social Democrats, Finnish Marxists, Italian anarchists had all in the past gained some prominence in the organization of militant working-class groups. But the bulk of the immigrants, from whatever country, had not the slightest desire to overthrow the established political order.[13] The newcomers had all left their respective home countries for some good reason – economic, social, racial, or religious. The choice to migrate had entailed a decision in favour of individual betterment, rather than a commitment to improving the world through rebellion. They saw no need to submit to the leadership of a self-appointed elite of party functionaries, who felt that they alone were fitted to guide the backward masses on the road to a classless society. By comparison with their homelands, the immigrants found relatively little class conflict, or indeed class awareness in the United States.

The great majority of newcomers liked what they saw. America might not be the Jews' legendary *goldene medinah* (the golden state), or the Germans' *Land der unbegrenzten Möglichkeiten* (the land of unlimited opportunities), but it was, on the whole, preferable to home, and the overwhelming majority of immigrants stayed. According to a European stereotype that remained current on both sides of the iron curtain, the immigrants remembered their old country with nostalgia. In fact, they remained highly ambivalent; love for the former homeland widely mingled with resentment – an element in US national psychology hard for Europeans to comprehend.[14] The newcomers over-

---

[13]We have dealt with this at greater length in L. H. Gann and Peter Duignan, *The Hispanics in the United States: A History*. Boulder, Col., Westview Press, 1986.

[14]For a recent expression of this customary stereotype see for instance the report by Burchard Brentjes, a visiting professor from Halle in the DDR, on the Germans whom he met in the US in *Neue Heimat: Journal aus der Deutschen Demokratischen Republik*, no. 2, 1988.

whelmingly accepted, as did native-born Americans, the Constitution and the Bill of Rights; these documents provided for the citizens the equivalent of kingship by divine right. Politicians might be inept or corrupt; but the principles of governance stood unchallenged. In the same way, the immigrants admired a country without an established church, and without a state-imposed church tax (such as the German *Kirchensteuer*); they looked with approval on a country that lacked a hereditary aristocracy, and that stood committed, at least in theory, to the proposition that all persons were created free and equal. The immigrants, in the main, welcomed the opportunities provided by a country that left newcomers alone, that required no work permits (of the type needed, say, by immigrants to Great Britain or France), a land that offered the opportunities of a continent, and judged a man by what he did more than by his speech or dress. They remained in touch with their friends and relatives in Europe, so that letters and visits from expatriates provided Europeans with a private source of news concerning the United States, information of a more practical and often more accurate kind than what was purveyed by official bodies. There was no way in which anti-Americanism – however soph- isticated – could counter such appeals. During the Stalin era, the Soviet Union lost the battle for European public opinion; the Americans won.

The impact of war and its aftermath helped to produce equally striking changes in the sentiments of Western Europeans toward one another. Such psychological shifts are hard to measure. Documentary accounts – books, newspaper articles, personal letters and diaries – in the last instance only reflect their authors' views. Public opinion polls are subject to other disabilities. Much depends on the way in which questions are framed, and much on the respondents' own culture. The French and Italians are traditionally less willing to give public expression to private sentiments than British or Americans. Respondents moreover may be influenced in their answers by what they consciously or unconsciously imagine to be socially acceptable. (A cruel West German cartoon shows a middle-aged householder in conversation with a poll taker. "Let me fill in your questionnaire first," says the German; "and then I will tell you what I really think about the Jews.") National images that Europeans held with regard to one another have moreover traditionally ex- pressed particular cultural or political as much as genuinely ethnic preferences. In many European countries, for example, the higher bourgeoisie was traditionally Anglophile; the lower-middle classes were frequently pro-German; liberal intellectuals pro-Jewish and pro-French – irrespective of their personal experi- ences with English, German, French, or Jewish people.[15]

Nevertheless, certain generalizations are in order. World War I had begun with an orgy of hatred intensified by propaganda. The mood of World War II was more subdued, as ideological hostilities often overlaid older national enmities. The changes were particularly striking in Germany where nationalist fervor had been cultivated by the Nazis to a degree unparalleled elsewhere.

[15]For a discussion, see John A Lukacs, *The Last European War, September 1939–December 1941*. Garden City, New York, Anchor Press, 1976, p. 383ff.

German collective psychology was particularly complicated, for the Germans had a long tradition of national self-hatred, as well as of self-exaltation. "I know full well that we Germans are, and will remain beasts and mad animals – as our neighbors call us, and as we well deserve,"[16] Martin Luther had written this four centuries before. Nietzsche, Thomas Mann, and even Konrad Adenauer later gave expression to similar sentiments, that would have been almost in conceivable to an Englishman about his own nation. Guilt concerning the Nazi record, and the shattering experience of defeat weakened German nationalist sentiment far more than Allied attempts at "re-education." War also disabused Germans of the assumption that all German-speakers ought to be united in a single empire (an assumption not shared for their own countries by English-speakers in Scotland, Ireland, England, Australia, and the US, or by French-speakers in France, Belgium, Switzerland, and Quebec).

The French ceased to be the *Erbfeind*, the hereditary enemy. (During World War II, Goebbels had felt obliged to combat Francophile sentiments rife in Germany after 1940, when many Germans had identified Marshal Pétain with their own Hindenburg, both of them defeated generals temporarily raised to national leadership.) After World War II, Francophobia in Germany did not regain political currency. German sentiments toward Britain were equally complex. In the past, Britain had incurred hatred among right-wing intellectuals as the "new Carthage" and anti-British hostilities had deepened as a result of the bombing campaign. On the other hand, the British had also aroused a good deal of reluctant admiration for their patriotism and their imperial splendor. After World War II, the British army of occupation generally commanded respect; so did the British Labour government, particularly within the ranks of German Social Democrats.

It was the British, rather than the Germans, who felt most inclined to stand aloof from Western Europe. The British on the whole preferred to look to the US and toward their own dominions, a sentiment deepened by wartime experience and by massive postwar emigration to the US and other English-speaking countries overseas. The British had always been conscious of their geographical separation. ("Continent cut off by channel gale" supposedly ran a British newspaper headline.) "If I ever have to choose between Europe and the open sea, I shall always choose the open sea," Churchill had explained to de Gaulle.[17] According to Bevin, the Council of Europe was a "possible Pandora's Box ... filled with Trojan Horses." In British academia, "European studies" did not truly come into their own until the 1960s. For British politicians there were many Europes: the Europe of NATO for collective security; the Europe of history that included the Eastern sector and Russia; the Europe of trans-national organizations that assured "non-integrated" cooperation. The British wanted collaboration – but not a merger.

British attitudes toward particular European countries were equally ambiva-

[16]Cited by Koch-Hillebrecht, *Das Deutschenbild*, initial unnumbered page.
[17]See Roger Morgan, "Perceptions of Europe in Great Britain since 1945," in Rijksbaron et al., *Europe From a Cultural Perspective*, p. 105.

lent, especially with regard to Germany. Whereas humanitarians and inter-nationalists in Britain had pitied the Germans after World War I as the victims of a harsh and unjust peace, anti-Germanism had become intellectually respectable in the wake of World War II. Anti-Germanism was sanctioned by distinguished historians such as Sir Lewis Namier and A. J. P. Taylor. Indeed the very speed of West German recovery seemed ominous to those who suspected the Germans of planning for World War III. But there was also in Britain a long tradition of respect for the "earnest" "hardworking" Teuton. (These sentiments were particularly strong perhaps among working-class people, and among soldiers stationed in Germany.) Anti-Germanism in Britain was too diffuse to serve as a political rallying cry, and it weakened during the 1950s.

French attitudes were even more complex, toward Europe generally and toward their German neighbors. France had once dominated Europe under Napoleon; thereafter French influence receded. The Franco-Russian *entente* of 1891 marked a further retreat, in that henceforth France relied on alliances to protect herself against an overweening Germany. These measures had failed to keep the enemy from the gate. In World War II, as in World War I, the German occupiers had engendered fear and hatred; but the hatred was far from universal, and after the war soon diminished among the educated. According to public opinion studies in the 1960s, the most anti-German person in France was likely to be an elderly peasant woman residing in a village or a small town, endowed with no more than an elementary education. (In the US, by comparison, anti-German sentiments were most likely to be current among blacks, Jews – who had been pro-German during World War I – Southerners, and people along the eastern seaboard.)[18] French opinion leaders were inclined to be pro-German, and most pro-German of all were likely to be university graduates living in Paris, aged between 20 and 34. For them, hating the Germans had ceased to be chic. Anglophobia, of the visceral kind had also ceased to be acceptable (as it had once been among the French ultra-right and the navy). After World War II the Pétain regime had become discredited, and with it the Anglophobe propaganda in which Vichy had excelled. Moreover, a number of Free French (as well as Dutch, Belgian, Norwegian, and other) expatriates had served in Britain during World War II. No reasonable French-man or woman still seriously believed that Britain was France's sworn enemy.

During the 1950s, national stereotypes within Western Europe were modi-fied further by scholarly exchanges, American economic penetration, mass tourism, and the emergence of a trans-national youth-culture with its universal affection for movies, music and jeans. British children at festive school occasions, British Conservative delegates at party conferences might still lustily apostrophize their homeland with *Land of Hope and Glory*:

---

[18]Koch-Hillebrecht, *Das Deutschenbild*, pp. 72–3.

Wider still and wider, may thy banner spread,
God who made thee mighty, make thee mightier yet.

But no Briton, no Frenchman, no Italian could any longer conceive of a new war among Western Europeans. Overall, the sentiment of nations toward one another had changed greatly for the better.

CULTURAL DIPLOMACY

During the eighteenth century Catherine the Great had gained a reputation for cultural diplomacy as the "Semiramis of the North" (the mythical Assyrian queen noted for her beauty and wisdom) by flattering Parisian *philosophes* and greasing their palms. Frederick the Great followed a similar policy; Voltaire's presence at Potsdam was as useful to the Prussian king as Diderot's to the Russian empress at St Petersburg, for the purpose of projecting an image of enlightenment among foreign intellectuals. During the nineteenth century, cultural diplomacy ceased to be personal. Its appeal widened and its methods changed. Nation states increasingly tried to impress foreigners through a variety of expedients – exhibitions, decorations and honors for deserving writers and artists, government-subsidized schools abroad, and so on. Mission work, once devoted to the task of spreading a religious faith, became secularized – symbolized by the French claim for a *mission civilisatrice*. Bureaucrats stepped in to spread culture and, hopefully, political and economic influence at large.

It was the French who pioneered cultural diplomacy of the modern kind. They did so in part to rehabilitate their national glory after the defeat suffered in the Franco–German war of 1870–1. Newly founded institutions included the *Alliance Française* (set up in 1883 to teach French in the colonies and abroad), as well as institutes later created at foreign universities.[20] The Germans and Italians followed suit with private organizations designed to teach their languages in foreign lands. During World War I, government-inspired propaganda, and government-supported cultural ventures acquired even greater importance as a means of making friends and blackening the enemy – an art in which the British were (however mistakenly) believed superior to all competitors. For a time money grew scarce, but during the 1930s the pace once again quickened. In 1932 the Germans founded the Goethe Institute (recreated in 1952), and from 1933, the Nazi government placed a new emphasis on pushing *kultur* abroad – while tarnishing it at home. The British set up the British Council (which from 1935 received a small government subsidy).[21] The Americans, by contrast, left the promotion of culture to private enterprise –

---

[20] J. M. Mitchell, *International Cultural Relations.* London, Allen and Unwin, 1986.
[21] Mitchell, *International Cultural Relations*, appendix C. Frank A. Ninkovitch, *The Diplomacy of Ideas: US Foreign Policy and Cultural Relations, 1938–1950.* Cambridge, Cambridge University Press, 1981. Richard F. Staar, ed., *Public Diplomacy: USA Versus the USSR.* Stanford, Hoover Institution Press, 1986.

to publishers, jazz musicians, journalists, film producers, and to the labor of immigrants, whose enthusiastic letters to friends and relatives in the "old country" did more for America's reputation in Europe than all government-sponsored publicity.

This state of affairs fundamentally changed during and after World War II, especially with the Cold War. All belligerents used culture for propaganda purposes. The early British color film *Henry V* stirringly presented Shakespeare's drama to glorify British valor; *Alexander Nevski*, a great Soviet movie, reminded Soviet citizens and foreigners alike that German invaders had been defeated by the Russians in the past, and would assuredly be beaten again. After the end of World War II, the Soviets made an even greater effort that linked diplomacy, propaganda, and cultural exchanges. So did the Americans' publicity campaign abroad, which soon outdid that of their allies. (For example, between 1950 and 1960, the estimated programming of hours per week of foreign broadcasting increased as follows: US 497 to 1,495; Soviet Union 553 to 1,015; Great Britain 598 to 643; France 198 to 326.) Cultural diplomacy operated through a great array of institutions, private, semi-private, governmental, trans-national, such as the Committee for Cultural Cooperation of the Council of Europe.[22]

The objects of cultural diplomacy varied enormously. It served as an instrument of the Cold War – but only in part. The Western Europeans especially were more concerned with influencing neutrals and, above all, their own allies than with converting their enemies. Cultural diplomacy was said by its defenders both to serve peace and defend national interests, since it would, it was believed, impress allies, conciliate neutrals, and convert opponents. Cultural diplomacy supposedly would also lubricate international trade, and spread enlightenment. It would correct those unfavourable national stereotypes that people have held about their neighbors since the days of St Paul, when he had rebuked the Cretans for being "always liars, evil beasts, sour bellies."[23] It would support conventional diplomacy and provide opportunities for artists and writers to show their nation's culture, and was intended to spread usage of the cultural diplomat's own tongue abroad – an important economic as well as cultural consideration. Cultural diplomacy moreover furnished careers for a new breed of administrators and facilitators, college-educated men and women who either worked within the framework of traditional diplomatic services, or in those numerous semi-official and trans-national organizations that multiplied after World War II. Cultural lobbying turned into a bureaucratic art.

The means of cultural diplomacy were as diverse as its ends. Its instruments included Arts Councils and friendship societies; the "twinning" of native and foreign cities; support for cultural congresses, scientific conventions, opera and drama; poetry readings, orchestras, and art exhibitions, the awarding of

---

[22]Anthony Haigh, *Cultural Mission of the Council of Europe*. Strasbourg, Council for Cultural Cooperation, Council of Europe, 1971.
[23]Epistle to Titus 1: 12.

prizes; and teacher and student exchanges. Aid was provided for the estab-lishment abroad of libraries, colleges, and cultural centers (such as the most successful British *Brücken* and the US *Amerikahäuser* set up in occupied Germany after World War II). Overall, the new cultural diplomacy was more urbane in tone than that of World War II and the stormy 1930s. There was an end to straightforward hate propaganda, and also to obvious absurdities (such as the Italian medic's wartime claim that the allegedly poor fighting qualities of British troops derived from the practice of tonsillectomy, a muti-lation that left victims easily frightened and confused).[24] But the main inspi-ration for cultural diplomacy remained nationalistic, however courteous the presentation.

Nowhere was cultural diplomacy taken more seriously than in France, even before André Malraux, a distinguished writer who was appointed minister of state for cultural affairs (1959) under the Fifth Republic. It seemed particularly important to the French, given the relative decline of their power, and of their language, in international communication; the adoption of English as a first foreign language in most European (including French) schools; the place assumed by American movies and films in French entertainment; and the penetration of English words into French. The French thus waged an official campaign to replace loanwords such as "computer" by French neologisms such as *ordinateur* – a policy avoided by the Germans, who experienced comparable inanities under the Nazis when, for example, the alien *Telefon* had turned into a *Fernsprecher* (far-speaker).

The French effort was impressive. Untold numbers of visitors, for instance, attended art exhibitions; and French continued to be taught throughout most of the world, despite the by now relatively limited role played by France in world diplomacy or commerce. But cultural diplomacy was costly in financial terms, while the linkage between bureaucracy and the art world sometimes had ludicrous results. (For example, the New York Museum of Modern Art, by the 1960s, had bought more than 200 pictures painted by Jean Dubuffet, a French modernist who helped to invent "pop art," while the French Museum of Modern Art had early on refused to buy his controversial works. Dubuffet retaliated by refusing to exhibit in French official museums and agreed in 1961 to participate in an important "retrospective" at the Musée des Arts Décoratifs, a private body. When the news came out Dubuffet was promised a Legion of Honor if he would only donate some of his works to the Paris Museum of Modern Art, and the Musée des Arts Décoratifs was menaced with eviction from its government-owned buildings in the Louvre – a threat not, however, made good.[25]

Italy followed the French model, though in a less thorough and confident fashion. Italian was not used nearly as widely abroad as French. The Italians also had to live down the memory of Fascism. But they had a well-publicized record of anti-Fascist resistance, and their Fascism had never been remotely

---

[24]Mitchell, *International Relations*, p. 31.
[25]Sanche de Gramont, *The French: Portrait of a People*. New York, Putnam, 1969, p. 359.

as savage as Nazism. They, like the French, instituted a directorate-general of cultural relations within their foreign ministry; this coordinated Italy's cultural diplomacy and collaborated with the ministry of education in supporting Italian schools and institutions abroad. The Dante Alighieri Society (first established in 1889) continued its work. The Italians profited from the presence of countless emigrants in countries as far afield as the US, Argentina, and Brazil, as well as from the mass of foreign tourists visiting Italy. They maintained 80 institutes abroad by the early 1970s, and ten Italian universities ran courses for foreigners (the University of Perugia having pioneered this work in 1925). A less publicized aspect of Italian cultural diplomacy hinged on the continued Italianization of the German-speaking populations in South Tyrole whose grievances in this regard went unsupported by the Second Austrian Republic.

The Germans moved even more cautiously than the Italians. German cultural propaganda had been discredited by organizations such as the *Verein für das Deutschum im Ausland* during the Nazi era. The West German foreign ministry maintained an important cultural relations department (*Kulturabteilung*) responsible for formal arrangements such as cultural conventions; relations with international organizations; the activities of cultural attaches in West German embassies in foreign countries; subsidies for schools abroad; international art events, and so on. In addition, the Germans left much scope to unofficial agencies such as the Goethe Institute (with its headquarters in Munich, West Germany's true cultural capital) and the *Deutsche Akademische Austauschdienst (DAAD)*, a German academic exchange service. The DAAD was re-established in 1950, with the goal of promoting international relations between institutions of higher education. Branch offices were opened in Paris, London, New York, and elsewhere.

As always, the Germans paid special attention to schools. By the 1980s, Germany maintained abroad 507 schools and colleges (of which 284 were part-time) as against 373 for Italy, and 361 for France.[26] Educational institutions ranged all the way from full-time *Gymnasien* (secondary school) to *Sonnabendschulen* (Saturday morning schools), which relied mainly on the talent of volunteers who gave German courses to youngsters, and received some financial backing from German consulates. Other bodies included schools for the children of German experts abroad; schools founded without official support by German residents overseas; "European schools" for the children of officials of member countries serving the European Community; or *Begegnungsschulen* (encounter schools, designed for German and local children abroad, with counterparts in West Germany). The Germans likewise promoted events such as book fairs (including the Frankfurt bookfair, a major annual event): the "German month" in major foreign cities (combining book exhibitions and art festivals), as well as cultural conventions (the latter in part designed to attract foreigners to isolated West Berlin as a new *Kongresstadt* (or conference city).

Overall, Germans seemed to feel much less defensive about the place in the world of their own language than the French; Germans were much more ready

---

[26]Mitchell, *International Cultural Relations*, p. 193.

to use English or French as a medium of instruction abroad than the French were willing to employ foreign tongues. Such confidence in this respect reflected the continued importance of German as the most widely spoken language in Europe, save Russian; German moreover was the only idiom extensively used by native-speakers on both sides of the Iron Curtain. The West German cultural effort differed, however, from that of other Western nations in that the Federal Republic worked in competition with the German Democratic Republic, a rival state that labored to project abroad a dual image, both socialist and German. In this competition, the East German communists found themselves in a difficult position, for East Germans could pick up radio broadcasts and television programs originating in West Germany, Austria, and Switzerland; thus East Germany could never isolate itself in a cultural sense, while foreigners generally continued to identify West Germany with Germany as a whole.

Whereas the Germans followed a mixed system, the British mainly relied on the British Council, an independent agency, separate from the publicity division of the British foreign office, and on other non-official bodies such as the BBC, and the Inter-University Council (merged with the British Council in 1980). The Inter-University Council played a vital part in assisting the new universities to set up in the British colonial countries after World War II. The British Council served as a maid-of-all-work, providing lectures, libraries, exhibitions, film shows, concerts, and so on. The British Council, like the BBC, was governed by its own board, on which its funding organizations – the foreign office and commonwealth relations office, and the overseas development administration – were represented, but did not dictate policy. The Council stood outside the civil service, yet its most senior representatives abroad enjoyed diplomatic status as cultural attachés. It was a system that went well with that informal "old boy network" which continued to play such an important part in British life.

The Council's work curiously reflected therefore both the strengths and weaknesses of British diplomacy in general. The British did not make full use of those many opportunities open to them in Western Europe after the war. During the war, Britain had offered a haven to countless foreign nationals who had come as political refugees, as members of Allied forces, or as employees of governments in exile. British political prestige stood high after the war. So did her cultural reputation, which benefited from events such as the Festival of Britain in 1951; from the efflorescence of British film-making during the 1950s; the vigor of British dramatic performances; the important role played by British academics in staffing existing and new universities in the commonwealth; the reputation of the BBC as a source of news; the enduring splendor of the British monarchy; and the country's continued reputation for political sanity. But laboring under severe financial constraints, the British initially reduced the British Council's grant from the foreign office (from £2,700,000 in 1946–7 to £1,625,000 in 1953–4); thereafter funding improved, reaching £3,391,000 in 1960–1 – but even this sum amounted to no more than a small fraction of the £42.9 million spent on the foreign service, foreign office grants, and associated expenditure.[27]

Jokes about the British Council were many. But overall, the British Council, the BBC, the Arts Council, and collegiate bodies such as the British Institute at Florence gave good value for money. The British Council (like the United States Information Agency) maintained libraries overseas (important especially in countries such as Italy and France where public libraries left much to be desired, and where readers found a convenient access to English-language books and journals in reading rooms maintained by British and US tax payers). The Council also gave courses in English, promoted art exhibitions, facilitated scientific exchanges, provided information about Britain in general, encouraged drama tours, and even labored to get business sponsorships for art exports.

It was, however, the Americans who made the largest investment in officially funded diplomacy in the Western world. In this, as in so many other respects, the Americans were latecomers. American cultural influence throughout the world was enormous – many a foreigner who had never heard of Thomas Jefferson or Walt Whitman knew all about Benny Goodman, Thomas Edison, and Irving Berlin, not to speak of Wrigley's chewing gum, Coca Cola, Ford cars, and Hollywood. But the US did not engage in officially funded cultural relations until 1938 – by which time Nazi propaganda extended all the way to Latin America and the US. As regards cultural diplomacy, the Americans possessed both great weaknesses and strength. Among left-wing intellectuals and upper-class conservatives alike, the Americans had to contend with the stereotyped image of the US as a bastion of provincialism, materialism, greed, and selfishness. Isolationism remained a powerful force, and so did popular suspicion of official propaganda. On the other hand America was widely admired abroad especially by working-class people impressed by American freedom and high living standards. Unlike the European countries, the US had an immense reservoir of foreign-born or foreign-descended citizens representing almost every one of the world's languages. Countless Americans moreover had lived abroad, as soldiers, missionaries, businessmen, teachers, and experts. This huge potential only needed to be mobilized.

Official work began when in 1938 a division of cultural relations was created in the department of state, with responsibility for a broad range of activities including academic exchanges, cooperation in the fields of music, art, and literature, broadcasts, and the like. The department of state appointed cultural affairs officers to embassies and legations – first of all in the Americas, later also in various European countries. The US supported cultural institutes founded jointly by American and local citizens, mainly with the object of teaching English to indigenous people, and the local language to Americans. (By 1956 there were 27 cultural centers in the rest of the world, as well as 300 schools operating in other republics in the New World.)

After the attack on Pearl Harbor, the State Department cooperated with

[27]*Whitaker's Almanack*, London., 1962, p. 598.

the office of war information to set up Voice of America (which started to broadcast overseas in 1942). In 1946 moreover Senator Fulbright persuaded Congress to fund an impressive program of educational exchanges, a cultural Marshall Plan, the Fulbright-Hays Program. But compared with the massive effort made abroad by the Soviet Union and its foreign supporters, the US effort at first remained small in scope. The office of war information dissolved in 1945, and Voice of America struggled on a scanty budget. Cultural relations in the main were left to private enterprise.

Change came with the intensification of the Cold War. Radio Free Europe came into existence in 1950 for broadcasts to Eastern Europe, and Radio Liberty in 1953 for broadcasting to various linguistic groups in the Soviet Union – both organizations centered in Munich. The Central Intelligence Agency (CIA) gave surreptitious and circuitous support to various anti-communist organizations abroad. In 1953 moreover the United States Information Agency (USIA) was set up as an independent body reporting to the president through the national security council. USIA had a hard furrow to plow. Its directors changed frequently; and so did its officially allotted functions. It was excluded from educational exchanges (such as the Fulbright program) and from overseas cultural presentation programs; these were left to the more prestigious state department, lest educational and cultural work be tainted with the smear of propaganda. USIA was badly mauled during the last stages of the McCarthy campaign – so much so that it became difficult to recruit competent people for the broadcasting services.[28]

Despite these problems, USIA gradually expanded into an empire – with a budget exceeding that of many an independent African country. (By the early 1980s, the agency's annual expenditure stood at $433,000,000 – not much admittedly, compared with the $2,225,000,000 that went to the international development cooperation agency, and the $2,094,000,000 to the department of state). The scope of the agency's work was immense. A list of its functions alone would fill several pages. To give just a few examples: it built a huge library service, comprising (by 1981) some 200 libraries in 95 countries, a marvelous resource for foreigners wishing to learn more about American culture and politics, in addition to maintaining a major library at its own headquarters. It had a massive overseas publication program with journals such as *Dialogue* (a quarterly, offering opinion and analysis on subjects of current intellectual interest in the US) and *Problems of Communism* (a leading scholarly journal). The agency maintained an American studies program abroad, as well as "Arts America" (designed to encourage private-sector involvement and assist qualified artists and performers on foreign tours). The agency advised foreign publishers on US copyright law, acquired and produced video tape programs and films for distribution. It maintained press centers

---

[28]Mitchell, *International Relations*, pp. 56–7. For a detailed description of functions, see Matthew Lesko, *Information USA*. New York, Viking, 1983, pp. 641–6. USIA later became for a time the International Communication Agency before reassuming its original name. Also see Frank A. Ninkovitch, *The Diplomacy of Ideas*.

to provide foreign journalists in the US with background information. It administered a large program of fellowships, grants, and educational exchanges, and helped with career counselling, as well as conducting research for various other government departments. Without embarrassment, the agency might have chosen for its departmental motto the Latin tag *nihil humanum mihi alienum est* (nothing human is alien to me).

After World War II, German affairs took up much of US concern over Western Europe, with Germany a divided country and West Berlin a threatened outpost. Instead of France, West Germany now became the keystone of Washington's strategy in Western Europe. There were many good reasons for this shift. More Americans worked in the Federal German Republic than in any other European country. (By the 1980s, American soldiers and dependents in the FRG amounted to around 400,000; businessmen, traders, scholars, students, another 400,000; tourists included about 5,000,000 Americans a year.) West Germany became America's leading trade partner in Europe, and over 750 major American businesses maintained subsidiaries there. About 1,500 major German companies sold their products in the US. West Germany came to invest some $10 billion in the US; US investments in West Germany were about the same. There were other links – ties between German and American cities, joint exchanges, cultural societies – not surprisingly, since an estimated 49 percent of Americans claimed to trace at least one ancestor to Germany. By contrast, German studies in the US had always been modest in extent. About 24 percent of college students took German in 1960, but thereafter the decline in language training and German studies was severe and only one in 50 US high-school students studied German in 1987, though one in ten did Spanish, and one in 20 did French. Few North Americans now do advanced degree work in German studies (about 0.6 percent over a 20 year period, 1965–86). German language training may have been the worst hit in a general decline in language training in the US since 1960. However, the defense language institute in Monterey, California, kept up its wartime intensive language instruction; there German continued to be the third most taught language. About 60 percent of colleges and universities in the 1980s still had German language programs and German history was widely studied.

Western European studies programs or centers also developed after the war, but few gave Ph.Ds or MAs; they mostly provided undergraduate teaching and faculty research on Europe or its nation states. Cultural interchange and foreign affairs programmes were promoted also through a host of semi-official and private organizations, some of them influential. These included such groups as the World Affairs Councils in the US, and the Royal International Institute in Great Britain. (The Institute published an annual *Survey of International Affairs*, and also acted as a forum where important visitors from abroad would air their views.) Throughout Western Europe and the US, new institutes sprang up to study contemporary history and politics, and international affairs; for example the Belgian Royal Institute for International Relations was founded in 1947. It organized studies and research committees as well as conferences, and maintained its own library and publication program (journal, newsletter and conference proceedings). But it was in the United States that the academic response was greatest. International studies programs, Russian studies programs, and European studies programs developed in major universities. The Carnegie, Ford, and Rockefeller foundations largely supported all the work until 1957, when the US government passed the National Defense Education Act to stimulate language studies. In a different context, the US film industry played a major part in spreading American ideas overseas, a fact recognized by politicians such as Senator William Benton who called for a "Marshall Plan of ideas."

In addition, there was a broad range of new trans-national institutions. These included bodies such as the International Council of Scientific Unions (set up in 1931) and the European Science Foundation (ESF), established in 1983 at Strasbourg to promote cooperation in fundamental research, the free movement of research workers, and the harmonization of research programs.) The International Association of Universities came into being in 1950, with its headquarters at Paris. The European Community created its own Standing Conference on University Problems. The Organization for Economic Cooperation and Development (OEDC) maintained a Center for Educational Research and Innovation.

Of much wider scope was UNESCO (founded in 1945 as a specialized agency of the UN). UNESCO was administered by a director-general and its own international civil service, subject to direction from an executive board elected by the General Assembly. UNESCO in turn developed an extensive bureaucracy (with over 1,500 personnel by the 1960s). Its publications were numerous, including directories, handbooks, bulletins, and statistics (see, for example, its *Statistical Yearbook*). UNESCO promoted professional conferences, seminars and symposia, and particularly attempted to give assistance to Third World countries in fields such as librarianship and education. It stimulated many other ventures, including a massive cultural history of mankind, and a variety of technical assistance projects; but its achievement overall fell far behind its professed objects. The Western countries, especially the US, provided the greater part of the funds, though their political influence lessened with the expansion of the UN's membership. (The UN had started with 44 members in 1945 – by 1967 membership had tripled; the new Afro-Asian members to some extent shared the Soviet bloc's hostility to "Western imperialism," a bias that became ever more apparent in UNESCO's international proceedings.)[29]

To sum up, informal cultural diplomacy has been practiced since the days of King Solomon, whose calculated display of wealth and wisdom had rendered speechless the visiting Queen of Sheba. Cultural diplomacy of the bureaucratic kind, however, is of twentieth century origin. It has turned out to be costly, and deepened the suspicions of those who disparaged "official" culture as an instrument of class or national politics. It was also subject to strict limitations;

[29]Walter H. C. Laves and Charles A. Thompson, *UNESCO: Purpose, Progress, Prospects*. Bloomington, Indiana University Press, 1957.

to give just one example, the Soviets, for all their great efforts, never succeeded in turning Russian into the lingua franca of Eastern Europe or in greatly enhancing Russian cultural prestige. By contrast, the reputation achieved abroad by German universities during the nineteenth century, and their ability to attract thousands of US students and professors, had predated modern cultural diplomacy and had depended on the free market of ideas and on free institutional competition.

In trying to project a favorable national image abroad, cultural diplomats faced many difficulties. What was England – the land of Cromwell or of King Charles I? What was Germany – the land of Marx or of Bismarck? At its best, cultural diplomacy did contribute to cultural interchange, and supplemented that wider informal network of cultural relationships which included countless enterprises: publishing, scholarship, librarianship, film-making, television, tourism, migration, the marketing of music, and even the toy industry. Nevertheless, cultural diplomacy became institutionalized, a permanent feature on the international landscape. In a minor way, it helped to solidify the Atlantic Community. As Willy Brandt put it (with some exaggeration) in his capacity as West German foreign minister, cultural relations had by the 1960s become the third pillar of foreign policy.

AMERICA'S RESPONSE TO WORLD LEADERSHIP

America faced many challenges as a result of its world leadership during and after World War II. Before the war, the US had largely been an insular, isolationist country, a land of immigrants. Except for Latin America, the US had as yet only marginally concerned itself with international affairs. The state department was small; US universities took scant interest in other lands, languages or peoples, except for Western Europe and Latin America. The US would probably have returned to "fortress America" after the war, but for the decline of British power in Europe and the Middle East, and the resultant power vacuum, and, most importantly, because of the threat to Europe posed by communist militancy.

The US had to find and carry out a clear, coherent, consistent and balanced national strategy for its global responsibilities. New foreign affairs bureaucracies came into being. In wartime, the US had to build up its foreign language skills and to train a cadre of experts to plan the war and to administer captured territories. After the war, the US had to enhance the business community's abilities to work in Europe and Asia; train additional cadres for international posts and educate students and adults in foreign affairs. This complicated process has continued for over 45 years, and although not everywhere successful, the US has done better than might have been expected.

Public servants and academics concerned with foreign affairs increased their expertise. US businessmen learned to cope in Europe and Asia. Travel increased; and hundreds of thousands of scholars and students, tourists and businessmen went to Europe or came to the US from Europe. (The Fulbright program by 1988 had sent 54,000 Americans abroad and brought in 100,000 foreigners.) Students from around the world flocked to US schools (in 1988 there were 343,000 foreign students in the country). Europe's scientists became accustomed to studying and working with American scientists.

Foreign affairs bureaucracies

In the wartime and postwar periods the US had to rebuild its foreign affairs machinery and shape new agencies to carry out its role as a global power. The state department lost its monopoly to speak on foreign affairs; instead a multitude of new bureaucracies developed to share in the formation of foreign policy.[30] The new machinery expanded first in international, multilateral organizations: the United Nations, the World Bank, and the International Monetary Fund. Thereafter the US had to create aid machinery to carry out the Truman doctrine and the Marshall Plan. In 1949 Truman announced the Point Four Program of technical assistance to developing countries. In the same year the US joined the North Atlantic Treaty Organization (NATO). The resultant new agencies were not under the state department. The Economic Cooperation Administration (1947) dealt with the Truman doctrine and the Marshall Plan. A Technical Cooperation Administration operated the Point Four Program. In 1947 the National Security Act set up the Central Intelligence Agency (CIA), and the national security council, which also brought the Pentagon into foreign affairs.

Several factors entered into the relative decline of the state department. These included the reluctance of the department itself to shoulder some of the new functions; congressional intervention; the department's deficiencies in carrying out certain of the new tasks thrust upon it; President Roosevelt's own distrust of "State"; the wartime growth of bureaucracy as a whole, and the bureaucratic ambitions of other departments. As a result, something like 90 percent of the civilian officials dealing with foreign affairs in one way or another between 1939 and 1944 had not been members of the state department.[31] Essentially, "State" lost control over economic programs, and information and intelligence before the end of the war. In 1949 the Hoover Commission recommended that the state should not run specific programs but should "concentrate on policy formulation and coordination."

From 1945 to 1953 the state department had taken charge of information and educational exchange programs, but gave up its information duties when the United States Information Agency was formed (1953). The department also lost out to the CIA in intelligence gathering; the CIA operated under the executive office of the president, not under the state department. Part of its mission was to collect and evalute foreign intelligence relating to national security, including foreign political, economic, scientific, technical, military,

[30]This section is largely based on David D. Newsom, "The US foreign affairs structure in a changing world," *The Washington Quarterly*, Summer, 1987, v. 10, no. 3, pp. 203–11.
[31]Ibid., p. 205.

geographic, and sociological intelligence – an immense assignment employing many intellectuals who might otherwise have sought academic posts. In addition, the CIA was charged with counter-intelligence outside the US, and with coordinating such operations run abroad by other bodies, within what was euphemistically called the American intelligence community.

We have made no attempt to tell the story in detail. The published sources are plentiful, but widely tainted by the deceptive use of evidence, hidden agendas, and sensationalism. Many archival records naturally are not available to scholars, or are made accessible only in a selective and misleading fashion. A few generalizations must therefore suffice. The major European states had a long tradition of maintaining intelligence services. Of these, the British service was probably the most efficient – despite postwar revelations about defections and the real and alleged infiltration of Soviet spies. The Americans were relative newcomers to the game. (Failure to predict the outbreak of the Korean war, for instance, led to reforms in the CIA under Walter Bedell Smith. With the appointment of Allen Welsh Dulles as director (1953–61) the CIA was strengthened and became more aggressive.)

Intelligence in general was widely distorted by the media, and also by the agents themselves. The overwhelming majority of intelligence work is office work, code-breaking and library research, which has little to do with the secret agents of fiction – be they curvaceous and seductive ladies, or strong, lantern-jawed gentlemen. Intelligence operatives of all nations naturally pay special attention to the activities of their competitors, both in their own and in the opposing camp. In doing so, analysts may lose sight of the main duty incumbent on an intelligence organization – to provide reliable situation assessments for the use of their own governments. In this respect, the relative efficiencies of the various competing intelligence organizations is hard to assess. To do so would require comparative case histories. How did the US, the British, the French, the Soviet, the Chinese intelligence communities judge, say, the prospects of the incumbent South African regime at a time of the Sharpeville riots in 1960, when professional scholars and journalists widely forecast a rapid breakdown? How many intelligence organizations in any country predicted at the time that South Africa, in the subsequent two decades, would actually increase its gross domestic product by more than 11 times? The answer almost certainly is – none!

Such questions, unfortunately, are easier to pose than to answer. As regards the CIA, it soon acquired an extraordinary reputation for the most improbable deeds of derring-do, sophisticated intrigue, and outright villainy. This image derived from thrillers, yellow journalism, real or alleged revelations on the part of turncoats, and anti-American propaganda. Between them, these produced the unintended effect of making the orgnization seem more efficient and ruthless than it could possibly have been – an unsolicited boon for the CIA's successive directors and staff.

As regards the state department, Dean Acheson later criticized its record in his autobiographical account *Present at the Creation*. He claims "State" muffed both information and intelligence gathering responsibilities because of gross stupidity and lack of imagination. Nevertheless, postwar policy was reasonably conducted to achieve peace settlements, the reconstruction and recovery of Europe, and the building of NATO and regional pacts such as CENTO and SEATO. Strong-willed secretaries of state (Acheson and Dulles) and strong-willed presidents (Truman and Eisenhower) saw to that, and "State" acted as coordinator. But the White House became the real leader of the foreign policy establishment through the National Security Council (made up of the vice-president, the secretaries of state and defense, and a small staff). The decisions of the NSC were then conveyed to other agencies and departments.

Foreign policy agencies included, partly as a result of pressure from Congress and the public, the foreign agricultural services, set up in 1954 to increase the sales of US agricultural products abroad. But the resultant bureaucratic expansion led to new problems. There were quarrels over turf and operating procedures among the Central Intelligence Agency, the Defense Intelligence Agency, the intelligence agencies serving each of the armed services, and the National Security Agency. The divisions within the executive branch meant the US seldom spoke with a united voice. There were repeated calls for better policy planning. Priorities were, however, hard to establish. Although the US had global responsibilities it had limited resources. How best to use these resources occasioned heated debate in every administration. The machinery was constantly challenged and amended; every four years after a presidential election thousands of new officials were brought in.

Nevertheless, the US, by the end of the 1950s, had developed the apparatus needed to lead the Western world and to deter the Communist one. Western Europe and Japan had recovered from the war and had become thriving democratic countries. NATO had built a shield to defend Western Europe against the communist bloc. The US had cooperated with, and used, the UN for peacekeeping purposes; the Soviets had been contained in Iran and Greece; North Korea had been defeated. The CIA had built the world's best intelligence organization. The Voice of America spread hope for communized Eastern Europe, and the USIA practiced a much expanded kind of cultural diplomacy.

The US academic and philanthropic institutions

World War II had a profound impact on the social sciences in the United States. American think-tanks, colleges and universities had been traditionally oriented toward Europe in their courses. But European studies were subject to serious limitations. Whereas individual scholars and teachers often displayed much expertise, there were few centers of European studies. (Even Columbia University has only had a European Institute since the late 1940s.) Worse still, American schools – with few exceptions – either neglected non-Western areas completely or limited their research and teaching in these regions to classical languages, ancient history, and literature. As a result, universities, defense agencies, government, business, and many professions found themselves increasingly handicapped during and after the war by a shortage of specialists with competence or experience in Asia, Africa, the Middle East, and Eastern Europe. War, however, broke long-standing habits of intellectual isolation. Millions of Americans put on uniforms, learned foreign languages, and for a time lived and fought in countries that previously they would hardly have been able to identify on a map. War also affected the social sciences in other ways. The army research branch, interested in the various aspects of a fighting man's life, helped to pioneer new survey techniques, and caused the department of defense to sponsor research in the behavioral sciences. The research and analysis branch of the OSS provided jobs to numerous American and emigre scholars, schooled them in team work, and acquainted them with new problems. This branch played a major part in promoting area studies, assembling research data and documents; its work was one of those factors that helped make American scholarship in area studies predominant in the world.[32]

As America's responsibilities and interests around the world grew, it developed a foreign affairs constituency anxious to know about the new states and regions, so as to influence the public debate on important international issues. There were bitter controversies on the question of who had "lost" China to the communists. (Almost all the best-known US scholars in the Far Eastern field believed that Mao Tse-tung's victory had been both inevitable and beneficial.) There were equally heated disputes over Yalta. By and large, however, a broad consensus developed after 1947 on Western European affairs; this helped the president in checking Soviet might, aiding the US allies, and protecting the Western world.

Private foundations expanded greatly after World War II because of the heavy increase in federal corporation tax and the excess profit tax. Sixty percent of company-sponsored foundations came into existence between 1949 and 1959. International affairs grants increased thereafter, but were still a small proportion of the money given away (only 8 percent for the largest foundations). Exchanges of personnel, economic aid, and technical assistance also received much support from foundations.

In 1941, the US government had only 20 employees doing research on the Soviet Union; only about 20 colleges taught Russian and about 30 had courses in Russian history. (It was much better supplied with specialists on Western Europe and its languages, because European history and languages had long been an important part of college and university education.) The US therefore had to build up its language and area expertise during and after World War II. After the war, government stopped funding these programs for a while, but major foundations stepped in. In 1946 the Rockefeller Foundation funded the Russian Institute at Columbia University, and the Carnegie Corporation established a Russian research center at Harvard University. By 1951 there were four Russian area studies programs supported by the foundations. The Ford Foundation from 1952 on took the lead in funding graduate student education in area studies (Eastern Europe, Latin America, Middle East, East

---

[32]Robin W. Winks, *Cloak and Gown: Scholars in the Secret War, 1939–1961*. New York, Quill, William Morrow, 1987, p. 111.

Asia, Southeast Asia, Africa). The Ford Foundation paid for 44.3 percent of area specialists' training, and when the federal government returned to aiding language and area studies (1958), the government's share rose to 54.2 percent. (There was little government support, however, for Western European studies.)

The need for language and area specialists grew, as the Soviets achieved their triumph with *Sputnik*, as decolonization created many new states in Asia, Africa and the Middle East, and as the US government pushed through the National Defense Education Act (1958). (The act provided a $295 million loan fund to lend college students $1,000 each at 3 percent interest over 10 years, with a 50 percent reduction if the student later taught at an elementary or secondary school. In addition, $280 million was voted for grants to state schools for facilities in sciences or modern foreign languages, roughly $28 million for language studies in higher institutions; funds were also set aside for graduate students planning to go into college or university teaching.) Initially, the government mainly supported the research of scholars studying the Soviet Union and Eastern Europe, but after 1958 also provided funds for training experts in the non-Western world.[33]

The international studies programs that developed in the major American universities were coordination centers which promoted teaching and research. Columbia University's school of international affairs (1947), and Princeton's Woodrow Wilson center for international relations (1948), attained international fame. Indiana University developed a Western European Studies program and awarded a Master's degree. (Title VI or NDEA 1957 excluded Western European studies support until 1972. Afterwards four centers were established and awarded about 15 fellowships a year; Eastern European and Soviet Union centers numbered 13.)

Even the limited support for European studies, however, began to decline from about 1960. Western Europe now prospered; its affairs no longer dominated the headlines to the same extent. By contrast, many new African states appeared on the global scene, providing new challenges for researchers. Area studies absorbed more and more student and faculty interest. Fewer people applied for fellowships to study Western Europe; fewer doctoral dissertations were written on European subjects; fewer students studied European languages. (European studies steadily declined until 1970 when Columbia University established a council for European studies to improve graduate training, stimulate collaboration between American and European scholars, and facilitate research.

Fortunately, this was not the entire story. The major universities did at least cover the history, literature, and languages of Europe. There were also new kinds of institutional support. The office of education in the department of health, education and welfare funded universities and individual scholars. The

---

[33]See Richard Lambert, "The educational challenge of internationalization," *The Washington Quarterly*, v. 10, no. 3, pp. 163–82, and in the same issue, Dorothy Atkinson, "Understanding the Soviets: the development of US experts in the USSR," pp. 183–202.

National Science Foundation, the Ford Foundation, the Rockefeller Foundation, the Guggenheim Foundation and Fulbright-Hays financed faculty research programs. Additional backing came through the Institute of International Education, a private agency with some money from government, and the American Council of Learned Societies and the Social Science Research Council with money from the Ford Foundation. Western Europe and Eastern Europe studies programs got most support early on, as did Latin American studies, a traditional area of US interest. Up to the mid-1950s, the Carnegie, Rockefeller, and Ford Foundations were the main support of international affairs institutes and area studies in the United States, though the government also came in to support non-Western studies. From 1953 onward, the Carnegie Corporation began to direct its attention to the British Commonwealth and its colonial empire, especially Britain's African dependencies.

Although interest in foreign affairs kept growing in the US after the war, there were only a few foreign affairs journals before the 1970s. The leading international relations journal was *Foreign Affairs*, published since 1922 by the Council on Foreign Relations, New York. After World War II, some universities also began to put out influential journals, for example, Columbia University's school of international affairs issued the *Journal of International Affairs* (1947); Princeton University's Woodrow Wilson center for international relations published *World Politics* (1948), and the University of Pennsylvania's foreign policy research institute put out *Orbis* (1955). The Foreign Policy Association of New York expanded its *Great Decisions* or *Headline* series (1918). All played a part in informing the general public about crisis areas or issues. In addition, world affairs' councils sprang up around the country in the 1940s and 1950s. They offered lectures, seminars, conferences and library facilities largely to middle-class, liberal audiences concerned with foreign affairs. Research institutes further expanded, especially after 1957 (the launch of *Sputnik*); from 1958 area language and culture programs were established across the country and dealt with almost every part of the world.[34] (By 1988 there were over 1,200 public policy research institutes concerned with foreign affairs in the US and many of them had publishing programs and journals.) The US had ceased to be a provincial, isolationist country, and henceforth played a leading part in the world of international scholarship and cultural diplomacy.

[34]See Ousa Sananikone, "The world of journals: international affairs journals," *The Washington Quarterly*, v. 11, no. 2, Spring, 1988, pp. 209–14.

9

Decolonization

As the Western European states recovered at home, they lost their colonies abroad. In retrospect, decolonization takes on an air of inevitability, and of a single drama. Pressured alike by the Soviet Union and the US, pushed by indigenous independence movements, the powers of Western Europe came to realize that colonial commitments had to end, that Kipling's "great game" was up. Within a little over two decades the flags of Great Britain, France, Belgium, and Holland were hauled down. The colonial powers failed to cooperate with one another in a common defense of empire. The imperial cause no longer appealed to the mass of the people in the metropolitan countries – especially since a long and bloody world war had recently been fought in the causes of freedom, self-government, and hostility to racism. The ideological initiative during and after World War II passed to the critics of colonialism and to Asian and African nationalists, who were supported (with differing motives) by both the United States and the Soviet Union. The colonial rulers encountered bitter and sustained criticism in the metropolitan parliaments, the media, the universities, the churches, and even within the ranks of their own colonial services. In consequence, these warlords became increasingly apologetic. They compromised, and each reform and concession led to fresh demands.

The imperial powers faced more practical considerations, also. Empire, it was realized, did not pay, either militarily or economically. But the European powers were not forced out of Africa by economic imperatives. On the contrary, decolonization came just at the time when the African colonies were beginning to show some economic return for the imperial countries.[1] But the costs of empire increased vastly – both in political and military terms. The British and French recognized this first, the Portuguese last. The French came to see that they were compounding their wartime losses by expensive colonial campaigns. The war in Indochina imposed great sacrifices on their country, and no sooner were they rid of that commitment than they found themselves

---

[1]David Fieldhouse, *Black Africa, 1945–1980: Economic Decolonization and Arrested Development.* London, Allen and Unwin, 1986, *passim*.

faced with a serious struggle in Algeria that weakened France in Europe. The loss of Indochina in 1954, moreover, in no way injured the French economy. Contrary to predictions made by diehard colonialists the French got over the disappearance of their East Asia empire just as quickly as the Dutch recovered from the loss of their possessions and investments in Indonesia. Imperialist might was apparently incompatible either with a balanced budget or with true grandeur on the European continent. The rulers lost the will to rule (with the exception of the Portuguese, who hung on in Africa until 1975, the white Rhodesians, who gave up in 1980, and the white South Africans who continued to hang on thereafter).

THE OVERSEAS BACKGROUND

President Roosevelt, and advisers such as Harry Hopkins, opposed Western colonialism. Roosevelt regarded the British system of imperial preferences as an obstacle to world prosperity and the British empire as a potential threat to peace. The state department looked to a policy of accelerated reform whereby the colonial regimes would become accountable to an international authority in which the US would have a predominant voice. American pressure was far from negligible in its effects. The colonizers, especially the British, became more defensive; reformers could point to the American stance to help win improved conditions for the colonies. (The Colonial Development and Welfare Acts, passed by the British parliament, were, in part, designed as a reply to American criticism of British colonial rule.)

But Roosevelt's successors, preoccupied with the Cold War, became much less interested in colonial issues. The anti-colonial cause certainly continued to appeal to the liberal conscience. Jewish-Americans became concerned with the Palestinian issue, but otherwise there were no powerful ethnic lobbies. Black Americans, during the two decades following World War II, were – for the most part – too much preoccupied with their own emancipation to take an active interest in countries such as the Gold Coast and Uganda, of which they knew little and, in general, cared less.[2]

The Soviet Union's role in decolonization was likewise marginal; despite its incessant denunciation of Western imperialism. According to Soviet theoreticians, Western imperialism was the bane of the twentieth century – a judgement that would one day return to haunt them when Soviet nations came to style the Soviet Union itself an oppressive empire. But, in practice, Stalin was concerned above all to solidify Soviet power in Eastern Europe. He had scant respect for indigenous independence leaders such as Kwame Nkrumah of the Gold Coast. The Soviet Union at the time lacked a powerful fleet and

[2]Peter Duignan and L. H. Gann, *The United States and Africa: A History*. Cambridge, Cambridge University Press, 1984, pp. 284–93. Thomas J. Noer, *Cold War and Black Liberation: The United States and White Rule in Africa 1948–1968*. Columbia, University of Missouri Press, 1985, for a contrary interpretation.

its air force was in no condition to transport men and material over great distances. The communist parties in Africa and the Middle East counted for little. Many of their most active members derived from the ranks of ethnic minorities (Jewish and British-descended people in South Africa, European settlers in Algeria and Morocco, Levantines in Egypt). The Communist Party of India was in no better shape. (During the years following Indian independence, its membership fell from 89,000 in 1948 to 20,000 in 1950 – a negligible number, given India's huge population.)[3]

The Soviets somewhat improved their position from the mid-1950s onwards, when they modified their stance toward the newly independent countries. For instance, Angolan communists, supported by the Portuguese Communist Party, in 1955 founded the Communist Party of Angola which later joined with other groups to form the Popular Movement for the Liberation of Angola (MPLA). World-wide, however, the communist movement was badly divided by the Sino–Soviet split. Moscow propagandists shared with the West's intelligence officers a taste for exaggerating the power of communist subversion. But in truth, communist influence on the various independence movements in Asia and Africa remained of small account, except in Indochina, and later in the Portuguese African possessions.

Of much greater immediate importance was the United Nations. From its inception, in San Francisco in 1945, the United Nations took an anti-colonial stance that "provoked deep forebodings in delegates representing colonial interests" – this despite the leading part taken in the UN's foundations by such men as General J. C. Smuts, the South African prime minister.[4] Nationalist China and the Soviet Union used the UN as a forum to express their anti-colonial views; so did the Arab states; so did an Australian delegation; so did many Latin American republics. The UN charter established a Trusteeship Council with more extensive powers of supervision over former League of Nations mandated territories, and a membership much more hostile toward the colonial powers than the League of Nations had ever been. The council heard oral petitioners from nationalist organizations in dependent Western territories, and these bodies now found at their disposal a global lectern and pulpit. Whereas the former German territories had simply been parcelled out among the victors after World War I in the form of League mandates, the Italian colonies after World War II received independence (Libya in 1951), or

[3]See the relevant entries on individual countries in Witold S. Sworakowski, ed., *World Communism: A Handbook 1918–1965*. Stanford, Cal., Hoover Institution Press, 1973, including Peter Duignan, "Subsaharan Africa;" L. H. Gann, "Lesotho," "Nigeria," "Sudan," "South Africa;" Morton Schwartz, "India." For the connection between Soviet domestic and foreign policy, see Helen Desfosses Cohn, *Soviet Policy Toward Black Africa: The Focus on National Integration.* New York, Praeger, 1972.

[4]Crawford Young, "Decolonization in Africa," in L. H. Gann and Peter Duignan, *The History and Politics of Colonialism*, v. 2. Cambridge, Cambridge University Press, 1970, pp. 450–502, especially p. 456. Also see Crawford Young, *Ideology and Development in Africa.* New Haven, Conn., Yale University Press, 1982. Prosser Gifford and Wm Roger Louis, eds, *Decolonization and Independence: The Transfer of Power, 1960–1980.* New Haven, Conn., Yale University Press, 1980. William Jackson, *Withdrawal from Empire: A Military View.* New York, St Martin's Press, 1986.

were attached to an independent African state (Eritrea, joined to Ethiopia), or returned to Italy with a firm deadline for self-government (Somalia, linked to British Somaliland in 1960, became independent as the Somali Republic later in the year).

The UN professed to give expression to what became known as world opinion. In fact, though not in theory, this opinion was identified with the views of a new elite of academics, radio commentators, journalists, clergymen – members of a diploma-bearing salariat who widely, though far from universally looked upon themselves as a new progressive vanguard. This vanguard took pride in its assumed freedom from those trammels of bigotry, class interest, and false consciousness that supposedly afflicted unenlightened philistines. They were an influential group; they were well educated; they had strong moral commitment; they stood resolved to reshape the Third World on humanitarian and democratic lines.

The new vanguard helped to bring about a remarkable shift in metropolitan opinion. During the heyday of colonialism, it had been the advocates of empire who had held the moral initiative. Men such as Kipling had imbued empire with a moral mission. His much misquoted poem "The White Man's Burden" had called upon the empire builders – not to enrich themselves – but "to fill the mouth of Famine, and bid the sickness cease," in other words to extend a paternalistic social service state to the antipodes.

After World War II, the commanding heights of morality were occupied by the critics of Western colonialism. They used the means of publicity developed by Victorian domestic reformers – meetings, petitions, editorials, demonstrations – to pursue their overseas objectives. According to world opinion as henceforth defined, colonialism was accounted a Western sin, associated with sea-borne, rather than with landlocked empires, concerned with Belgian, British, Dutch, French and Portuguese oceanic expansion, rather than with Soviet or Chinese conquests made by land. Anti-colonialism acquired both the optimism and moral fervor once associated with the anti-slavery movement, or the anti-Corn Law league in Britain during the earlier part of the nineteenth century, or subsequent opposition to the "unspeakable Turk." Anti-colonialism widely went with sympathy for the oppressed; use of a pseudo-scientific vocabulary replete with question-begging terms such as "national liberation," "take-off," "modernization," "mass mobilization," and the like; as well as an unjustified faith in the assumed moral superiority of the colonized. Anti-colonialism went with an extraordinary and ill-founded optimism concerning the post-colonial future in erstwhile imperial possessions. It also entailed far-reaching changes in the direction of scholarly research, as anthropologists, economists, political scientists and historians increasingly became concerned with the fate of the ruled rather than the rulers. The very vocabulary of scholarship changed, as terms drawn from the European experience with the Third Reich – "collaboration," "resistance" – became part and parcel of the new scholarly terminology, and thereby enhanced its political appeal.

How effective were these opinion makers? Defenders of the old order were apt to overestimate the reformers' immediate influence. They were by no means united in their view. For instance John Kenneth Galbraith, a liberals' liberal, praised the British record in India, where the British, in his view, had come as liberators, and where their rule had been "a model of compassion and concern for the masses as compared with the despotism and anarchy that it replaced."[5] In the metropolitan countries – not to mention the colonies themselves – established patterns of racial discrimination passed but slowly. (The British army lagged fully two decades behind the US armed forces in the integration of their ranks. As late as the 1960s, "coloured" (that is to say non-European) recruits in the British army were "excluded from the Household Cavalry, Footguards, Highland and Lowland Brigades, RMP [Royal Military Police], the Military Provost Staff, and Intelligence Corps" – this at a time when the British earnestly censured white Rhodesians for similar practices.[6]

The anti-colonialists could not on their own have overthrown imperial rule. But they did manage to create a new orthodoxy regarding both the assumed desirability and inevitability of decolonization. This orthodoxy varied from country to country. Its most influential version for the time being was the British – strangely blended of Fabian Society tracts, editorials in the *Manchester Guardian*, and novels, such as E. M. Forster's long-dated *A Passage to India* (first published in 1924) and Doris Lessing's tales of white decadence in the Rhodesian backveld. The new orthodoxy impugned not only the colonial system itself, but even more its local agents and allies – Indian princes, European settlers, Arab sheiks. Even convinced defenders of empire, such as Ernest Bevin – according to Churchill, "a working class John Bull" – became convinced that Britain must henceforth switch its support and back peasants against pashas.

Within the British dependencies, there was a long-term shift of equal consequence. Before and immediately after World War I, the British had been apt to encourage immigrant minorities successful in the economic field – Jews in Palestine, white settlers in the two Rhodesias and in Kenya, Chinese in Malaya, and to a minor extent, Indians in East Africa. From the 1930s onwards there was a slow and fitful reappraisal. In 1930, for instance, Lord Passfield (formerly Sidney Webb, the British colonial secretary in the Labour government) issued the so-called "Passfield memorandum," reaffirming the "paramountcy of native interests" in East Africa. In the 1930s, the British imposed restrictions on Jewish immigration into Palestine – part of the same long-term shift.

This change of policy particularly affected the intelligentsia's outlook towards white settlers in Africa. In Victorian and Edwardian days, both academic and popular literature had widely praised the European expatriate

[5] John Kenneth Galbraith, *A View From the Stands: Of People, Politics, Military Power and the Arts*. Boston, Houghton and Mifflin, 1986, pp. 191–3.
[6] House of Commons defense committee session, 1986–7. *Ethnic Monitoring and the Armed Forces*. London, HMSO, 1987, p. 3. The quota system and similar restrictions were abolished only in 1969.

as empire-builders, the representatives of imperial power, middle-class values, and private enterprise in Darkest Africa. This interpretation was in fact wide of the mark, though it accorded with the self-congratulatory mood of British, French, and Portuguese imperialism. By the late 1950s, the prevailing intellectual opinion had become unrecognizable. The settler's past identification with the metropolitan ruling strata now turned to his discredit. All too often the white settlers became identified with the "guilty men" of British Labour mythology in the 1930s – hardened, conscienceless reactionaries. The clean-cut, square-jawed adventures of imperial imagination turned into the "new Bourbons" of Africa, who changed only to move yet further to the right.[7]

At the same time, the leftist intelligentsia in the US and Western Europe increasingly shifted their enthusiasm from the Soviet Union and Eastern Europe to countries further afield – Algeria, Cuba, Rhodesia, and South Africa. The Soviets' own revelations about Stalin's crimes led to disillusionment. So did the Soviet invasion of Hungary in 1956. So did re-evaluations of Marxist-Leninism undertaken by ex-communists such as Milovan Djilas. By the late 1950s, it had become unthinkable for left-wing Oxford students to volunteer for work on projects such as the Yugoslav Youth Railway, popular among leftists in the late 1940s. Far from promising a radiant future, the Eastern European states had become inconvenient reminders of the problems that beset "real existing" socialism. The Third World peasant took the place of the First World proletarian as the leftist intelligentsia's culture hero. The cause of decolonization thereby acquired increasing ideological momentum in the West itself.

Decolonization in general was marked by the inability or unwillingness of the various colonial powers to cooperate. The British, as we have seen, played a major role in levering the French out of the Middle East, and were responsible for expelling the Italians from Africa. The EEC did not concern itself with colonial affairs. French, British, Dutch, Belgian, and Portuguese policy makers in the colonies had little in common, knew little of one another's problems, and failed to collaborate either in mending or ending their respective regimes. Neither was there a response to suggestions that the development of Africa, for example, should turn into an all-European task (an idea put forward many years earlier by Diedrich Westermann, a noted German Africanist). Far from demanding increased white immigration to their respective countries, white settlers in Algeria, Kenya, and Southern Rhodesia overwhelmingly called for restrictions on massive white immigration to their territories, and thereby contributed more to keeping down their own numbers and political influence than all their metropolitan critics combined.

The colonial establishments moreover were neither uniform in composition

[7]The phrase "new Bourbons" derives from Patrick Keatley, *The Politics of Partnership: The Federation of Rhodesia and Nyasaland.* Harmondsworth, Penguin Books, 1963, p. 219. See also L. H. Gann, "The white settler: a changing image," *Race*, May 1961, no. 2, pp. 28–40. L. H. Gann, "Changing patterns of a white elite: Rhodesian and other settlers," in L. H. Gann and Peter Duignan, eds, *The History and Politics of Colonialism in Africa, 1914–1960*, pp. 92–170.

nor isolated from the changing climate of opinion at home. As colonial governments became more complex, increasing numbers of technical officers joined their ranks – archivists, agronomists, irrigation engineers, demographers, and others, people familiar with anti-colonial critiques put forward by professors such as Harold Laski, or writers such as Leonard Woolf or George Orwell. Even in Victorian days no British governor would have got far had he chosen to ignore the influence of the press and the power of parliamentary debates at home.

Moreover, British colonial rule had its own institutional forms of self-criticism. This found expression, for instance, in those huge multi-volume reports, issued by colonial commissions of enquiry or command papers, that later provided evidence for historians (just as Victorian commissions of enquiry had furnished material for Marx's and Engels's attacks on British capitalism). In addition, the colonial service contained its own dissidents, men like that mythical district officer, Boanerges Blitzen, satirized in a Kipling poem: "Certainly he scored it, bold, and black and firm, / In that Indian paper – made his seniors squirm, / Quoted office scandals, wrote the tactless truth – / Was there ever known a more misguided youth?"[8]

Even in Kipling's days, Blitzen was not dismissed – merely posted to the worst districts. But other Blitzens rose high in the service. By the postwar era they had advanced into senior positions in the very centers of imperial power, in the British colonial office, the India office, and their European Continental equivalents – men such as Sir Andrew Cohen in the British, Robert Delavignette in the French, or Pierre Ryckmans in the Belgian, colonial establishments?[9]

Above all, there were profound sociological changes within the colonies themselves. Colonial governance in its heyday had rested on a coercive apparatus remarkably small in size. (The Dutch military establishment in the Dutch East Indies in 1939 had deployed a colonial army numbering no more than 38,000 men to control some 40,000,000 Indonesians. At that time, the British army on the Indian subcontinent comprised 57,000 British troops and 157,000 Indian regulars to police some 389,000,000 Indians. The British military establishment in Africa was even smaller – in peacetime, the Northern Rhodesian defense force consisted of one African battalion with just over 800 men – this to serve a protectorate more than three times the size of Britain.) The civilian establishments within the colonies were equally limited in size and function.

After the end of World War II colonial rule became increasingly hard to

---

[8]"The man who could write," *Rudyard Kipling's Verse: Definitive Edition.* Garden City, New York, Doubleday, 1939, pp. 16–17.

[9]For appraisals of these rulers, see, for instance, Philip Woodruff (Philip Mason), *The Men who Ruled India.* London, Jonathan Cape, 1954, 2 vols, L. H. Gann and Peter Duignan, *The Rulers of British Africa, 1870–1914.* Stanford, Cal., Stanford University Press, 1978. L. H. Gann and Peter Duignan, eds, *African Proconsuls: European Governors in Africa.* New York, Free Press, 1978. L. H. Gann and Peter Duignan, *Burden of Empire: An Appraisal of Western Colonialism in Africa South of the Sahara.* Stanford, Hoover Institution, 1977.

maintain, as more and more Africans and Asians acquired a Western education, and strove to step into the rulers' shoes. Men such as Shri Jawaharlal Nehru, or Kwame Nkrumah gained positions of leadership. They drew support from a new class of Western educated professional and semi-professional people – teachers, civil servants, clerks, welfare officers. The new class expressed widespread popular grievances, and at times managed to arouse almost millenarian expectations among the unlettered concerning the assumed benefits of freedom to come. It also created a network of new organizations, congresses and parties whose very names – United National Independence Party (in Zambia), *Partai Nasional Indonesia, Rassemblement Démocratique Africain* – reflected Western inspiration. These parties gained widespread popular support at home, and at the same time communicated with the anti-colonial vanguard abroad in a way that would have been impossible for tribal chiefs and *mahdis* of an earlier generation.

Although the British and Dutch had initially been badly defeated by the Japanese in World War II, the former had not lost their military skill. By the end of the war, the British had regained all their possessions in South East Asia. The Dutch too returned to the East Indies after the war, attacked the local insurgents, and by 1949 had largely reconquered Indonesia. After a lengthy guerrilla war in Algeria, the French, by 1958, had won back military control over the bulk of that territory. But continuing colonial rule would have entailed a massive military deployment of the kind that the powers were neither willing nor able to maintain. The Belgians, for example, faced in 1960 with an African ultimatum – abdicate or fight – abdicated.

THE BASTIONS FALL

Decolonization in Africa began as a result of an intra-imperial struggle. Ethiopia was liberated from Italian rule by one of the most brilliant campaigns in British military history; in 1941 the last Italian forces surrendered, and the emperor Haile Selassie subsequently regained his throne. In Libya, it was the British Eighth Army that overthrew Italian rule. In Asia, decolonization in a formal sense began in 1946 when the US, at long last, granted independence to the Philippines. India followed a year later through the Indian Independence Act of 1947. The devolution of imperial power was part of a process that had begun after World War I, and thereafter accelerated. After World War I, India had imposed protective tariffs against British-imported textiles; Indians had advanced into the prestigious Indian civil service. It was in no sense true that the surrender of Singapore to the Japanese had forever destroyed British prestige in the Far East; the British later made a magnificent comeback, and inflicted the greatest military defeats sustained by Japan in any single land campaign. The Indian army had proved overwhelmingly loyal; the Japanese could only persuade a small percentage of Indian prisoners to serve on the Japanese side, while some 2,500,000 Indian soldiers fought in the imperial cause. The early defeat and conquest of Europe's Asian colonies by the

Japanese had aroused Asian nationalism, and it was not stifled by later victories of the Allies.

Once the war ended however, British power in India rapidly decayed. The British demobilized the bulk of their own forces; independence became a popular cause, one that the British had already accepted in principle. They were unable to contain the bitter ethno-religious contentions that divided the sub-continent; the break-up of the empire in India in certain respects paralleled the dissolution of the Austro-Hungarian empire after World War I. In agreeing to divide the subcontinent into two states – India and Pakistan – the British bowed to forces they could not resist. In the end, independence was negotiated with the new political class, British-educated, dedicated at least in theory to British principles of parliamentary governance. The princes were abandoned. The Indian military was not consulted. The minority sects, and castes such as the Untouchables, were left aside. The major territorial problems connected with provinces such as the Punjab, Bengal, Kashmir, and the northwestern frontier were left for resolution to Britain's imperial successors. Lord Louis Mountbatten, the last British Viceroy, had a genius for public relations. He insisted on a speedy resolution that would win him personal renown. His brilliance in this respect helped to hide the realities of what became a bloody catastrophe, involving the murder of hundreds of thousands, and the enforced migration of tens of millions. These expulsions paralleled in extent the mass expulsions of German, Hungarian, Polish, and other ethnic minorities carried out in Central and Eastern Europe after 1945. It was "an ignominious end" to two centuries of highly successful rule.[10]

Nevertheless, India and Pakistan, the two imperial successor states, thereafter consolidated themselves. Their relations with the erstwhile imperial power remained friendly. The Anglicized Indians' "colonial complex" faded. (An Indian student facetiously commented to his London landlady, "Thank God, we are no longer bloody natives, we are now bloody foreigners.") English remained the official language of communication – as it did in nearly all other former British possessions. British civil servants from India and other former colonies easily found new jobs at a time when the Western economies were booming. The former colonial powers were not plagued – as Austria and Germany had been after World War I – by a host of unemployed and discontented military officers and ex-imperial administrators. Instead, ex-colonial officials secured employment in academia, business, or government agencies, where their technical qualifications and administrative experience stood them in good stead. (An overseas settlement department, set up in London to help returning officials, found few clients for its services.) India and Pakistan alike moreover remained members of the Commonwealth, a loose and ill-defined association that sweetened for imperialists the bitter pill of decolonization.

Far more serious in its domestic implications for the erstwhile rulers, was

---

[10]Paul Johnson, *Modern Times: The World from the Twenties to the Eighties.* New York, Harper and Row, 1985, p. 474.

decolonization in South East Asia. In Indonesia, Dutch rule had been shattered by the Japanese occupation of the Dutch East Indies in World War II. There were futile attempts in 1946 to create a Netherlands-Indonesia union. But fighting thereafter broke out between the Dutch and Indonesians; the Netherlands, under heavy US and UN pressure, agreed to negotiate. In 1949 complete sovereignty was transferred to the Republic of the United States of Indonesia. A loose association briefly remained in existence between the two countries, but in 1956, Indonesia abrogated both the union and the Indonesian debt to the Netherlands. The Dutch-speaking elite lost all influence. Several hundred thousand Dutch residents and Indonesians, many of Euro-Asian descent, emigrated to the Netherlands, and Dutch almost entirely ceased to be spoken in Indonesia. The US (followed by Japan) now became the former colony's chief trade partner. Dutch colonialism became a footnote in history that most Indonesians and also most Dutch people thereafter preferred to forget. Holland was enriched by the immigration of energetic new citizens (for example, the Dutch army absorbed many veterans from the East Indies), among them Asians and Eurasians. On the other hand, there remained in Holland a residual hostility toward the US, aroused in part by the Americans' part in the dissolution of the empire.[11]

We have already dealt with French decolonization in Indochina and North Africa in the chapter on the French army, but one or two points merit recapitulation or elaboration. It had been the Japanese invasion of 1940 that broke the French hold on Indochina. In 1945 the Japanese proclaimed Indochina's independence and allowed the communist-led Vietminh to seize power. In their own interest, the French might have conceded independence so as to consolidate their hold on North Africa, a region geographically much closer, and far more important to French trade than Indochina. After initial hesitation, the French preferred to fight; the war continued from 1946 to end in 1954, under exceedingly unfavorable conditions for the French.

Whereas the British had successfully defeated guerrilla movements in isolated areas such as Kenya, Cyprus, and Malaya, the French waged war in Indochina, a country neighboring on China, a major power willing to give unstinting support to the Vietminh. The task proved beyond French resources, In 1954 a peace conference at Geneva in effect divided Indochina into two separate countries, the Republic of Vietnam in the South, and the Democratic Republic of Vietnam in the North. Economically, the South did better than the North. But militarily, the North was much superior; politically, it was centralized under the harsh rule of the Workers' Party of Vietnam, an orthodox communist body that killed, jailed, or expelled all domestic opponents, and resolved to take over the southern state as well.

The Indochinese war was followed in 1954 by another bloody conflict in Algeria. After a savage war the French finally gave way; in 1962 Algeria

---

[11]For a general history, see David Joel Steinberg, ed., *In Search of Southeast Asia: A Modern History*. New York, Praeger, 1971, and the extensive bibliography therein.

emerged as a sovereign state, the last of the French colonial possessions in the Muslim world to gain independence.

Once again independence resulted in a massive population shift, quite unforeseen by the peace-makers. More than 1,500,000 refugees made their way to France (1,000,000 from Algeria, 250,000 from Morocco, 175,000 from Tunisia – as against only 300,000 from Indonesia). These exiles, mostly Frenchmen (or their offspring by indigenous women), or French citizens of Spanish, Maltese, Italian, or Jewish descent, proved an economic asset to France, which benefited from their "energy, organizational skill, and love of risk."[12] For instance, in the Languedoc they were credited with raising agricultural output by superior supervision and organization of the labor force, and by more efficient marketing techniques. In the Aude, they introduced new machinery, fertilizers, and modern dairy equipment. In Corsica, the *pieds noirs* (white settlers) mainly went to urban centres where they expanded the hotel and restaurant business, among other ventures. The large influx of North African Jews revitalized the French Jewish community (which increased from 300,000 to 500,000), thereby partially undoing the demographic effects of Nazi and Vichy persecution in World War II.

From the colonizers' standpoint, conditions appeared very different in the Middle East and in sub-Saharan Africa. At the end of World War II, British influence seemed more firmly established in the Middle East than ever. The British controlled Transjordan, Iraq, and Palestine; they had taken Libya from Mussolini and Rommel. They were ensconced in Iran, where the southern oil fields and the refinery at Abadan constituted an economic enclave producing more oil than all the Arab countries combined.[13] The Anglo-Iranian oil company possessed its own fleet, hospitals, schools, and its own world-wide distribution organization. The Suez Canal formed another British-controlled enclave, stretching from the Mediterranean to the Red Sea, and westward three-quarters of the way to Cairo, with a network of roads, railways, harbors, airfields, supply depots, and barracks. "Black Africa" – down to the Zambezi – remained under the sway respectively of British, Belgian, French, and Portuguese administration; self-government for these colonies appeared but a distant prospect. Southern Rhodesia was run by European-descended minorities. Far from looking to the end of empire, the various ruling powers stood committed to imperial development.

The British imperial chain in the Middle East first snapped in Palestine, the often promised land, holy alike to Jews, Christians, and Muslims. Palestine for centuries had formed part of the Ottoman monarchy. During World War I the British had conquered it, defeating the Turks, and (through the Balfour declaration, 1917) promised to set up a national home in Palestine for the Jews while fully protecting Muslim and Christian rights. The British gradually

[12]William B. Cohen, "Legacy of empire: the Algerian connection," *Journal of Contemporary History*, v. 15, 1980, pp. 97–123, especially p. 100.

[13]Wm Roger Louis, *The British Empire in the Middle East 1945–1951: Arab Nationalism, The United States, and Postwar Imperialism*. Oxford, Clarendon Press, 1984 – the definitive work.

modified this self-appointed obligation. In 1923, they separated Transjordan from Palestine, and turned Transjordan into a dependent kingdom – Jordan. In addition, they imposed limits on Jewish immigration – a restriction that appeared all the more onerous to the Jews after Hitler was handed on a platter dictatorial power in Germany.

Britain's pro-Arab tilt continued during and after World War II. Ernest Bevin, the British foreign secretary in the postwar Labour government, was not anti-semitic – despite bitter charges made against him. He was convinced, however, that the Jewish question could only be solved in the Jews' homelands rather than in Palestine. The British could not afford to alienate the Arabs – for without Arab support, the British could neither stem future Soviet expansion in the Middle East, nor rely on secure oil supplies. Bevin placed much of the blame for the Palestinian imbroglio on Washington. According to him, it was sheer hypocrisy on Washington's part to call for increased Jewish immigration into Palestine at a time when the Americans were unwilling to increase their own immigration quotas for would-be newcomers from Eastern and Central Europe. Bevin and his advisers felt Palestine should become a binational state, allied to Britain, with a constitution that would recognize the Arabs as a majority, while respecting Jewish minority rights.

This solution might have worked – but only if the Jews in Europe had been successfully integrated into their respective homelands. In fact this was only accomplished in the Western democracies. Few American, British, or French Jews ever chose to go to Palestine, but the position was very different in Central and Eastern Europe. The Nazis' war against the Jews had left the survivors traumatized and uprooted. The communist regimes in the Soviet Union, Poland, and Romania differed in their attitudes; but overall the Jews continued to suffer from many *de facto* disabilities that prevented their successful integration. Whereas Americans had no difficulty in describing their Jewish fellow citizens as Jewish-Americans, few Poles – however tolerant – could have conceived of a Jewish-Pole; few Russians could have envisaged a Jewish-Russian.

From the Arabs' point of view, Palestine was, or should have been both an Arab and a Muslim country. (There was at the time no sense of a "Palestinian" nationality.) Jews and Christians alike, being "scriptural peoples," deserved toleration. It was, however, intolerable that the Jews should create a national state of their own in Palestine, lord it over true believers, and rule over the Muslims' holy sites in Jerusalem. Zionism clashed both with the Arabs' political aspirations (strong especially among the Western-educated), and their religious convictions (powerful chiefly among the masses). Whereas the Zionists stood ever ready to compromise, the Arabs – to their own loss – invariably insisted on the whole loaf. The Arabs at this time would accept neither partition, nor even a cantonal arrangement that would give local autonomy to Jews in specially designated areas.

The Jewish case likewise blended religious and secular arguments. Practicing Jews regarded Palestine as the land promised to them by God. This belief had also been shared by Lord Balfour, a practicing Christian, though it was unintelligible to secularists such as Bevin. To many, though not all, Jewish believers, and to some non-Jewish supporters of Zionism, Hitler appeared the modern Haman – his murder campaign could be reconciled to the divine purpose if it could be shown to have contributed in some sense to the restoration of Zion. The Jews moreover claimed Palestine by right of achievement. Jewish agricultural colonization and Jewish industrial enterprise had proved successful beyond the boldest expectations held by the founding fathers of Zionism.[14]

Both Jews and Arabs moreover consistently misinterpreted one another. Zionists, especially the socialists within their ranks, widely imagined that Arab opposition to Zionism stemmed only from Arab pashas supported by British intrigue. The Arab "masses" might be persuaded to cooperate with their Jewish fellow workers against their common oppressors. Arab nationalists, in an equally mistaken manner, associated Zionism with the interests of British – later of American – imperialists, though Arab theoreticians could not always agree which of their assumed enemies were the puppets and which the puppet masters.

As for the British, they might have played the Jewish rather than the Arab card, a solution favored by Churchill. By doing so, the British would have gained a client state dependent on them for arms. The British would also have gained the support of the Jewish American lobby, and cashed in on the good will already won from Jews all the world over through the Balfour declaration. The Jews already enjoyed local military superiority in Palestine by reason of a well-organized underground army, a large reservoir of military and technical skills, and the efficiency of a "para-state" developed during the mandatory era. The Jews moreover enjoyed a source of support that the Arabs lacked, a large body of supporters within the US who variously justified the cause of Zionism on the grounds of historical justice, material progress, democracy, or Biblical prophecy. Jewish and Arab aspirations proved irreconcilable and there was widespread violence in Palestine. To all intents and purposes Palestine became an ungovernable country.

The British handed over the issue to the UN early in 1948, convinced that they would be able to reckon on a pro-Arab majority within that international forum. But much to the British policy makers' consternation, the Soviet Union and the US for once cooperated. Moscow, despite its long-standing hostility to Zionism, was concerned above all to disrupt the British Empire. Washington backed the Zionists partly for humanitarian reasons and partly for domestic expediency. The Israelis inflicted a shattering defeat on the Arabs, and in 1948 Israel declared its independence, the first Jewish state since the Romans had taken Palestine.

Thereafter, Britain's power in the Near East quickly disintegrated. The

---

[14]For a good general history, see Howard M. Sachar, *A History of Israel: From the Rise of Zionism to Our Time*. New York, Alfred Knopf, 1978. The classical case for Arab nationalism is expressed in George Antonius, *The Arab Awakening: The Story of the Arab National Movement*. Philadelphia, J. B. Lippincott, 1939.

British had hoped to keep their hold over the Suez Canal through an Anglo-Egyptian alliance. This design, however, soon came to nothing. Faced with solid Egyptian opposition, the British decided to withdraw from the Suez canal whence the last British troops departed in 1956. Egypt nationalized the Canal soon afterwards. The British then tried to reassert their position by reoccupying it in cooperation with France and Israel. But British policy makers were thoroughly confused: while colluding with Israel, Britain nearly slithered into a war with Israel in order to meet treaty obligations to Jordan. (In October 1956, the Israelis carried out a mechanized raid on a Jordanian border post and the British took preliminary steps toward the implementation of a war plan against Israel code-named "Cordage.")[15]

By participating in the Suez venture, the British failed in their twin aims – to regain control of the canal, and to oust the Nasser regime. Instead, the British drew upon themselves the joint anger of the Soviet Union and the US thereby destroying what remained of Britain's former position as a great power in the Middle East. The British policy also aroused universal Arab hostility and, even more importantly, passionate opposition from many British voters who opposed the Suez venture on moral, political, and strategic grounds. Though militarily successful, the British had to withdraw in 1956. British power in the Middle East thereafter collapsed. The victors of El Alamein were reduced to political insignificance in a region they had once dominated and had done much to develop.

Sub-Saharan Africa for the time being, seemed quiescent. But on October 15, 1945, shortly after the end of World War II, a pan-African congress met at Chorlton Town Hall in Manchester, England. Delegates included a brains' trust of future prime ministers, such as Kwame Nkrumah and Hastings Kamuzu Banda, both graduates of American academic institutions. The congress, in retrospect, stood out as a landmark in modern African history though at the time few Englishmen and fewer Africans ever heard of it. Delegates proclaimed a policy of reformist socialism; they vigorously denounced imperial rule and called for independence as a cure for the ills of Africa. By the standards of subsequent generations, the demands of the congress were moderate. At the time however, its program seemed almost utopian.[16]

Except for the defeated Italians, the Western empires in Africa appeared to have emerged from the war almost unscathed. There were, at the end of World War II, only three black-ruled countries in existence, Liberia and Ethiopia in Africa, and Haiti in the Caribbean, all widely stigmatized as examples of the

---

[15]Anthony Gorst, "31 years after: a survey of cabinet discussion: October–December 1956," *Contemporary Record*, Summer 1988, p. 61.

[16]For African decolonization, see Wm Roger Louis, *Imperialism at Bay*. Oxford, Oxford University Press, 1978. Rudolf von Albertini, *Decolonization: The Administration and Future of the Colonies 1919–1960*. New York, Africana Publishing Co, 1982. Gann and Duignan, *Burden of Empire*. Crawford Young, "Decolonization in Africa," in L. H. Gann and Peter Duignan, eds, *The History and Politics of Colonialism, 1914–1960*. Cambridge, Cambridge University Press, 1970, v. 2, p. 45–502. J. D. Hargreaves, *Decolonisation in Africa*. New York, Longman, 1988. Franz Ansprenger, *The Dissolution of Colonial Empires*. New York, Routledge, 1989.

blacks' supposed incapacity for successful self-government. The French and Belgian empires in Black Africa had served as bastions of France's and Belgium's resistance to Germany during World War II. Far from planning to dismantle their respective African empires, the European colonial powers all looked to strengthening their hold through a blend of economic development and cautious political reform.

To some extent the colonial powers initially succeeded in these aims. The last two decades of colonial rule saw economic expansion on an impressive scale in many parts of Africa. Health services and schools expanded; more dams, more roads, more airfields came into existence. A number of new university colleges opened their doors. But at the same time, political consciousness spread among ex-servicemen and educated Africans, especially those who served the imperial power in subordinate capacities as teachers, clerks, welfare officers, junior civil servants, and interpreters.

There was also a shift in metropolitan attitudes – especially among the British. Under the stewardship of Arthur Creech Jones, Labour's colonial secretary, the British switched their support from traditional or pseudo-traditional chiefs to the "new Africans," from rural to urban interests. Indirect rule through "native authorities" went by the board around 1947. Instead local government developed through elected bodies. The new ethos was best represented by Sir Andrew Cohen (assistant secretary of state in charge of Africa, later governor of Uganda.) Cohen, a Cambridge man of leftish convictions, believed that the African territories were bound to reach independence within a generation, and that this development should proceed in well-planned stages in cooperation with the African intelligentsia, and ongoing economic development, linked to massive state intervention.

The decisive break came in the Gold Coast (later Ghana). The Gold Coast was to British reformers a model colony *par excellence*. There were no immigrant European or Indian communities to complicate the situation. There were no white-owned plantations. The country enjoyed a modest degree of prosperity, based on the enterprise of small cultivators and extensive cocoa exports. New political parties came into existence, including the United Gold Coast Convention, with Kwame Nkrumah as its organizing secretary. But in 1948 rioting broke out in the colony. By the standards of inter-communal violence in India, the Gold Coast riots were insignificant. But they convinced the colonial office that reforms must be speeded up, and – after a series of constitutional shifts and turns – Ghana became an independent member of the Commonwealth in 1957.

Ghana's initial prospects looked bright. The newly independent country enjoyed many advantages that Africans of a later generation might have envied – a balanced budget and a healthy balance of trade, a small army (8,000 men) and a limited bureaucracy that the country could afford, a stable currency and a bearable public debt (amounting to less than half the country's annual revenue), a solid infrastructure (including the British-built harbour at Takoradi), an ample supply of foods, as well as cash crops for export. Parliamentary democracy, however, failed to prosper. Nkrumah turned out to be the first in a new generation of African dictators.

But independence granted to Ghana could not now be denied to Nigeria or the other British colonies. Decolonization, according to its defenders, would strengthen the West in the Cold War by relieving it of a moral burden, while creating new states that would defend their own independence. Decolonization would entail economic development, and the spread of Western parliamentary institutions, as well as diminishing Western military responsibilities. Decolonization would please alike anti-colonial Americans, and humanitarian lobbies in Western Europe. (The concept of a "civilizing mission" thus disappeared from the terminology of newly emerging academic disciplines concerning Africa.) Decolonization also pleased those British Tories who wanted to close the door to Asian and African immigrants, an object achieved in part through the 1962 Commonwealth Immigration Act. There was also the international demonstration effect, as concessions made to Ghanaians influenced political development throughout British, and later also in Francophone, Africa. Nkrumah led the drive against colonialism by training African nationalists and by verbal assaults in the UN; his motto "Seek ye first the political kingdom" encouraged black nationalists everywhere. In 1960 alone 15 African states became independent.

Not that tides went all one way. Southern Rhodesia (later Rhodesia, then Zimbabwe) was a "self-governing colony" run by the local Europeans. In Northern Rhodesia (now Zambia), white settlers exercised considerable power in what remained a British colonial possession ruled from London. In 1953, the British united the two Rhodesias and Nyasaland (now Malawi) in the Federation of Rhodesia and Nyasaland (1953–63). The new state was a loose association, uneasily balanced between imperial and settler power. Ostensibly, the federation rested on a partnership between blacks. In fact, the settlers held a predominant position, in uneasy partnership with London. The federation was designed for several complementary purposes. It was to create a larger and more stable economic unit than its three separate components had been. It would promote alike British investment and local industrial expansion, and politically, it would provide a British bastion against Afrikaner-ruled South Africa, and the emerging black states alike. But the Federation of Rhodesia and Nyasaland was short-lived. Zambia and Malawi achieved independence in 1964; Rhodesia issued a declaration of unilateral independence (UDI) in 1965, and thereafter remained effectively under white rule until 1980. Within little more than a decade of Ghana's independence, the Union Jack had disappeared from Africa.

To sum up, decolonization in India and most of Sub-Saharan Africa did not come through an armed struggle, nor was it carefully planned. The main cost of decolonization was not born by the great metropolitan companies, which mostly managed to adjust to the new regimes. The principal costs fell on the colonizers' erstwhile local allies – white settlers, African chiefs, Indian princes, those many unhappy Muslim soldiers who had fought in the French army in Algeria, and their like. In most of "black Africa" – as opposed to Algeria and

Rhodesia – the door to self-government was unlocked for African nationalists to push it open. The British arrived at this policy "not in response to, but in anticipation of [African] nationalist pressure by a freakish concatenation of American anticolonialism, Indian nationalism, British economic need, and moral utopianism."[17] The colonialists turned out to have been the unwitting state builders of a new Africa – its political map drawn by and legitimized through the European empires. Their demise aroused immense expectations that the successor states failed to meet. Africans of a subsequent generation had cause to remember the witticism current in France after the fall of Napoleon III – "how fair was the Republic under the Empire." With the burden of empire removed, all ex-colonialist nations prospered – to the shock of those Marxist theoreticians who had held that only colonial super-profits kept capitalism from collapsing. The end of empire altered the global map, but spelled neither the end of capitalism nor victory for the socialist cause.

[17]Ronald Robinson, "Sir Andrew Cohen: proconsul of African nationalism," in L. H. Gann and Peter Duignan, eds, *African Proconsuls European Governors in Africa*. New York, Free Press, 1978, p. 380.

PART IV

The Shaping of Society

10

Economic Development

When World War II drew to its close, Europe seemed to face catastrophe. There was hunger and devastation. There was the specter of civil strife. Prophets of doom abounded. Recalling the dread experiences of the Mexican and Russian revolutions, Karl Brandt, an agricultural expert not addicted to bloodcurdling speculations, foresaw new insurrections in liberated Europe; desperately hungry city folk would requisition food from farmers; farmers would resist; farmsteads would go up in flames, herds would be slaughtered, haystacks burned, grain elevators wrecked, and mass starvation become inevitable.[1] The dollar shortage, to take another failed prediction, was widely thought to be incurable. (Only a few brave souls such as Sir John Hicks and Milton Friedman continued to challenge this assumption.)

None of these disasters occurred. The world economy recovered at a speed none had dared to predict. The 30 years following the end of the war saw economic expansion all over the world, a period of growth and prosperity rarely if ever equalled in world history.[2] All Western European countries shared in this remarkable success story – one that strikingly differentiated Western from Soviet occupied Eastern Europe. At a time when socialism's intellectual appeal in the West was perhaps at its strongest, Western economies proved far superior to the socialist ones of the East – a proposition easily tested by setting against one another the respective postwar performances of West Germany and East Germany, or Austria and Czechoslovakia, countries comparable in their general development at the end of World War II. For intellectuals, poets, novelists, and playwrights, the postwar era commonly seemed an age of anxiety, partly because of the Cold War and the atomic bomb. By contrast, for the overwhelming majority of their fellow citizens, the postwar era was one of hope and accomplishment, and an increase in day-to-day well-being for Europeans, with the elimination of scourges such as polio,

---

[1]Karl Brandt, *The Reconstruction of World Agriculture*. New York, W. W. Norton, 1945, pp. 179–80.

[2]See, for instance, Herman Van Der Wee, *Prosperity and Upheaval: The World Economy 1945–1980*. Berkeley, University of California Press, 1986.

and remarkable creativity in science and technology (also in the social sciences, history, archaeology, and other intellectual fields). North America and Western Europe between them became again the world's powerhouse of industrial and scientific innovation.

AN OVERVIEW

During the 30 years following World War II, the Western countries both augmented and diversified their respective economies, aided in this by the US and by the closer economic association of Western Europe. The political creativity of an era that produced a host of able statesmen such as Attlee, Truman, Adenauer, de Gaulle, and de Gasperi was reflected also in the economic field. Admittedly, the Western European countries did not all recover at the same speed. (West Germany had the highest and Great Britain the lowest growth rate.)[3] Patterns of international trade shifted in Britain's disfavor in regions as far afield as Latin America, South Africa, and Australasia, where the British had once held a dominant position. The US took Britain's place as the world's largest exporter, with its biggest markets in Canada, Western Europe, and Japan.

The dollar became the world's main reserve currency. US policy makers aimed, not at an American "empire," but at free trade, financial stability, and the elimination of all obstacles in the way of free convertibility. The Americans could not enforce measures such as the devaluation of the French franc in 1948 and of the British pound in 1949. But they applauded devaluation as a step toward realism, and as a prerequisite for convertibility in Europe. For this purpose the US were willing to use aid, diplomacy, and unofficial persuasion within the newly emergent trans-Atlantic elite. Similarly the Americans played a major part in the negotiations that culminated in the European Payments Union, designed to do away with cumbersome bilateral agreements. This is not to say that other currencies, especially the pound, lost international significance. But the sterling area steadily loosened, and the dollar stood supreme.

Prosperity, of course, was far from universal in the West. (By the end of the 1950s, there were in Italy more jobless people than at the height of the Depression, if official statistics are to be trusted.) But overall, there was a striking increase in economic well-being. Full employment, and increasing material wealth came almost to be taken for granted in the democratic states.[4]

---

[3]The indexes of GNPs (at 1954 prices and exchange rates, with 1950 ranking as 100) stood as follows in 1958: West Germany 177; Austria 161; Italty 154; France 142; Great Britain 118. J. Frederic Dewhurst et al., *Europe's Needs and Resources: Trends and Prospects in Eighteen Countries.* New York, Twentieth Century Fund, 1961, p. 17.

[4]At the height of the Depression, Germany had 5,576,000 unemployed, down to 683,000 in 1958. Comparable figures for Britain 2,829,000 and 501,000; for Italy 1,006,000 and 1,759,000. Norman Luxenburg, *Europe Since World War II: The Big Change.* Carbondale, Southern Illinois University Press, 1979, p. 218.

Their prosperity rested on multiple foundations. Above all, Western countries enjoyed political stability – freedom alike from foreign invasion and domestic disorder. In every major Western country except Spain, parliamentary democracy functioned without serious challenge to its legitimacy. The political armies of the 1930s – with their colored shirts, flags, marching songs, and brass knuckles – disappeared from the streets of Europe, together with the hunger marchers, and the dejected army of men who had once stood in line for the dole.

The psychic energy that had gone into war was now transmuted – sometimes in strange forms. Hanna Reitsch, a woman flying ace of World War II became a flying instructor. She received VIP treatment in the US where, in Arizona, she received the international character award with the name of "Supersonic Sue."[5] Her countrywoman, Beate Uhse, another famed wartime flier, built up a great chain of sex shops thereafter. Still the husband-headed family remained the norm. Even an unskilled laborer gained prestige merely by his ability to maintain his wife and children. His job did not have to turn into a "career" to win him esteem. There was social stability, in the sense that rates of crime, abortion, suicide, drug addiction, and divorce everywhere lagged far behind those later attained during the 1960s and 1970s. Not that the postwar era was free of labor unrest: there were strikes aplenty. But jobs were prized at a time when men and women alike still remembered the depression and mass unemployment, while the discipline enforced in the military remained an unconscious legacy from World War II. Former military officers and resistance leaders alike turned from warlike to pacific pursuits – doing well in the bargain. (The crack SS division *Das Reich*, for instance, had a bloody record in suppressing French partisans when the division advanced to the Normandy battle in 1944 and suffered enormous casualties. The surviving SS officers, later interviewed by Max Hastings, a British military historian, turned out to have built prosperous careers once the war had ended. So had the Resistance survivors who had fought against the SS *Panzergrenadiers*.)[6] Peace, in other words, released immense energies that were henceforth applied to economic reconstruction.

Within the Western world, it was the free enterprise economy of the US that formed the mainspring of global prosperity. We have previously referred to US economic predominance in the world in this period. The Americans continued to lead in most fields of economic endeavor – the manufacture of steel, the production of coal, oil and automobiles, agriculture and the use of tractors on the land, or the ordinary workers' take-home pay.[7] Americans

[5] Judy Lomax, Hanna Reitsch: *Flying for the Fatherland*. London, John Murray, 1988, p. 183.
[6] Max Hastings, *Das Reich: Resistance and The March of the 2nd SS Panzer Division Through France June 1944*. New York, Holt, Rinehart and Winston, 1983, p. 235.
[7] In 1965 steel production (in million tonnes) stood at 119 in the US, 41 in Japan, 37 in West Germany, 27 in Britain, 20 in France. By 1967, the number of tractors (in thousands) stood as follows: 4,822 in the US; 1,257 in West Germany; 1,107 in France. By 1966, the number of students in higher education (in thousands) stood at 6,390 in the US; 537 in France; 407 in West Germany; 311 in England and Wales. By 1969, the average take-home pay of individual workers with a wife and two dependents (in US dollars) amounted to 460 in the US; 209 in West Germany; 199 in

owned most of the world's cars, radios and TV sets. They had the world's highest living standards, as American workers on the average worked shorter hours and produced more than their competitors.[8]

> *"By easing balance-of-payments constraints and freeing key bottlenecks for specific goods, American aid allowed the European economies to generate their own capital more freely certainly without returning to the deflationary competition of the 1930s. US aid served, in a sense, like the lubricant in an engine – not the fuel – allowing a machine to run that would otherwise buckle and bind." (Charles S.* Maier, In Search of Stability, Cambridge, Cambridge University Press, 1987, p. 173.*

America also dominated foreign lending. (The book value of all US investments abroad rose from $7.2 billion in 1946 to $11.79 billion in 1950, and later to $31.82 billion, by which time US corporations accounted for more than half of the aggregate book value of all foreign investments in the world.)[9] No expert during this period could have conceived of the situation which obtained in the late 1980s, by which time the US had reverted to its nineteenth-century position of being a net debtor nation. Americans took the major share in the multinational corporations that further linked the US to Western Europe in what appears to us an altogether beneficial manner. For a time the US dominated the world of finance – a position that would radically change a generation later when most of the word's greatest banks had become Japanese, and when these huge organizations attained incomes larger than those of entire countries.[10] Overall, US lenders shifted their foreign investments from mining, smelting, trade, and the like, into technically more complex enterprises such as petroleum-linked industries and manufacturing. (Between 1950 and 1967, the US stake in European manufacturing industries grew more than tenfold. About 50 percent went to the EEC, and a further 40 percent to Great Britain.) Western Europe by comparison, lagged behind in this respect – not a single trans-European company of note was formed after the establishment of the Common Market.

The multinational corporations differed greatly in size, makeup, function,

---

Great Britain; 189 in France. See Luxenburg, *Europe Since World War II*, pp. 196, 238, 222, 211, 230.

[8]By 1965 the number of radio sets (in hundred thousands) stood as follows: 240 in the US; 26 in West Germany; 16.2 in Great Britain; 15.3 in France. Corresponding numbers for TV sets in 1967 (in hundred thousands) amounted to 78 in the US; 13.8 in West Germany; 14.5 in Great Britain; 8.3 in France. Electric production (in million kilowatts) by 1964 stood at 1,084 in the US; 180 in Japan; 183 in Great Britain; 161 in West Germany; 94 in France; 77 in Italy. Luxenburg, *Europe Since World War II*, pp. 201, 197, 228, 165.

[9]Lewis D. Solomon, *Multinational Corporations and the Emerging World Order*. Port Washington, NY, National University Publications, Kennikat Press, 1978, pp. 9–12.

[10]The *Economist*, 25 July 1987, p. 64. The biggest company by that time was NTT with a market capitalization of $333 billion, more than six times the total GNP of Denmark, a sovereign country, and a prosperous one to boot. For general works, see Christopher Tugenhat, *The Multinationals*. London, Spottiswoode, 1971. Michael Z. Brooke and H. Lee Remmers, *The Strategy of Multinational Enterprise: Organisation and Finance*. Harlow, Longman, 1970. Raymond Vernon, *Sovereignty at Bay, The Multinational Spread of US Enterprises*. London, Longman, 1971.

and structure. Their products ranged from soap to cornflakes, from auto-mobiles to oil tankers. But all had certain characteristics in common. They had their headquarters in one country, with at least one subsidiary abroad. They created their own modes of management, their own hierarchies, their own architectural image of concrete-and-plate-glass efficiency, complete with outside fountains to suggest art and conventionally abstract sculptures to suggest originality. The multinationals depended on a great fund of specialized knowledge in research, finance and marketing. They diffused managerial and technical expertise. They created trans-national bonds of a personal kind. They were usually run more efficiently than state agencies. But they developed huge bureaucratic structures of their own that in turn created new and unforeseen vulnerabilities. To friends and enemies alike, they seemed characteristically "American," just as the organization of modern general staff techniques had once seemed characteristically "Prussian" to the world at large.

> *In 1958 The Institute Européen d'Administration des Affaires (INSEAD) was established at Fontainbleu, France, to educate European business managers from Western Europe. Later, other business schools, modeled on the American, were set up in Barcelona, Delft, Geneva, Lausanne, London and Manchester. INSEAD however became the most prestigious and influential, its graduates fiercely recruited by multinationals and national firms.*

The Americans tried to show the Europeans: how to run their companies; how to move in other markets; how to react to politics; how to become more free-market oriented and less dependent on cartels, monopolies and tariffs. American management techniques met with much resistance but did finally triumph. German managers especially opposed American efforts to demo-cratize industry. While the Germans took to free trade, free markets and internationalism, they opposed efforts to end cartels and monopolies.

US interests in Europe were best served by political stability, free trade, a free market ideology, mass production, and consumerism, all of which increased American market shares and profits. Nevertheless, Europeans also gained as the new ideas assisted their recovery and democratization. They did not fully adopt the American model; indigenous European styles and organizations survived. (Under Allied pressure the giant *IG Farben* concern was broken up after the war into four separate enterprises. Heavy industry was divided into 26 enterprises, but these were partially reintegrated within the framework of the European Coal and Steel Community. The huge banking concerns – *Deutsche Bank, Dresdner Bank*, and *Commerzbank* – were broken up, but later reintegrated.) But Europe was partially Americanized by adopting American business and management techniques and by developing free trade within the European economic community. The American "invasion," as it was perceived by some, aroused fears of technological dependence on the US, a dread of US industrial predominance; and alarm at losing control of national planning. These concerns would later create a form of economic Gaullism in Europe. Few foresaw that the tide would turn during the late 1970s and 1980s, when

Europeans bought up US affiliates overseas, established their own affiliates in North America, and once more became major investors in the US economy.

After World War II, the terms of trade for Europe were stable, but fell in 1948, 1949, and 1950. Trade terms steadily, albeit slowly, improved after mid-1951. The UK suffered a continuous decline however in the 1950s and 1960s as it lost commercial predominance in its colonies and dominions. Britain never made up that gap in trade, even after joining the European Common Market. The EEC has achieved its greatest success in encouraging commerce. Trade (mostly in industrial goods) has been concentrated within the common market, with protective barriers limiting imports from non-EEC countries. West Germany supplied the majority of industrial goods to Europe, and Britain the least. West Germany, Great Britain and France remained the major markets for the other European states.

> The European Recovery Program (1948–51) and Mutual Security help gave American credits to make up for Europe's dollar deficit. The European Payments Union restored currency convertibility; the Marshall Plan and the ECSC thus revived welfare capitalism. (Charles S. Maier, In Search of Stability, p. 178.)

To summarize, the postwar period benefited from the rapid pace of economic development, industrialization and the modernization of Western Europe and the formation of two regional groups (each having a population of almost 350,000,000 people). There was extensive trade within each group and between each group. Exports to Eastern Europe have grown by almost 11 percent each year since 1955, while imports from Eastern to Western Europe averaged almost 9 percent per year. Trade within Western Europe in turn grew by about 10 percent a year. Trade with the East was usually discouraged by the US, especially in advanced industrial equipment with military uses. But the Europeans resisted this pressure, and in the 1970s the resultant disputes became a major source of disagreement within the Atlantic Community. Willy Brandt's Ostpolitik especially irritated the Americans, and when Western Europe chose to finance oil and gas development in the Soviet Union the alliance was severely strained. From the mid-1960s, the volume of inter-European trade continued to rise and the US share of trade with Europe steadily declined. The US in effect helped create and develop in the postwar period its two greatest rivals for exports: the EEC and Japan.

European trade assumed certain characteristics: it became mainly an exchange of manufactured goods; most countries exported and imported similar items; commerce expanded most for capital goods, less for consumer products; and trade was largely conducted between countries at similar levels of economic development. Most members of the EEC came to converge in their economic structures. Factor endowment seemed to play a less important role in European trade than had previously been imagined. The British, French, and Germans accounted for about 55 percent of the EEC's trade with other regions.

Since 1945, thanks to American pressure, a more open trading system has been in effect. The US led the way and the Europeans and the Japanese followed. The system worked for almost 30 years, then began to tighten up. Trade had grown at a rate of 5.7 percent a year from 1960 on, with GATT primarily responsible for decreasing tariffs after World War II. (In 1947 the average tariff on manufactured goods was 40 percent; by 1970 it had dropped to below 10 percent.) Unfortunately, agricultural products were not included in GATT so they received subsidies and protection. Textiles were also not included and became an expensive and foolish exception to open-trading. (The Multifiber Arrangement (MFA) started in 1961, was in effect restrictionist and protectionist and hurt Third World producers.)

Between 1950 and 1960 trade between the US and Western Europe changed dramatically. It was to alter even more between 1960 and 1970. In 1950 Europe exported only 40 percent as much as the US did to Europe; the figure rose to 58 percent in 1960 and 78 percent in 1970. US trade with Europe was dominant only in "high tech" goods, and lost ground after the 1950s in standardized products such as cars, TVs, textiles, and so on. The US percentage of trade decreased for several reasons: EEC protectionism and development, an over-valued dollar, and American multinationals locating affiliates in Europe. Still, after World War II, the US steadily increased its share of exports to Third World markets. While exports to the US increased, Europe's share of exports to third parties decreased – mostly because the US exports were concentrated in agricultural products and capital goods.

Capital movements in the postwar period were at first dominated by US government aid, assistance and relief programs, mostly in grants rather than loans as after World War I. For immediate relief in 1946 and 1947 the US transferred about 2 billion dollars to Western Europe. In 1948 the OEEC was set up; humanitarian aid shifted to economic aid, and Western European economic development was structured for the next 20 years. The European Recovery Program (Marshall Plan) of grants from the US continued until 1951 – about 13.3 billion dollars were transferred. (The Eastern European countries did not participate and the division of Europe agreed to at Teheran and Yalta was confirmed by the Marshall Plan. Eastern Europe developed its own Council of Mutual Economic Assistance.) In spite of recessions between 1950 and 1952 caused largely by the Korean war, 1953 was a banner year for Western European recovery. Rapid economic growth continued steadily thereafter until 1973.

Major flows of capital out of Western Europe began in 1950. The European Payments Union controlled the flow of money; and late in the 1950s the US balance of payments went into surplus. The continued economic growth in Western Europe and the establishment of the EEC in 1957 attracted more US investment, but in 1950 Western Europe had more invested in the US (5.3 billion) than the US had invested in Western Europe (3.1 billion). Since the nineteenth century the US had been an importer of capital, but this began to change after World War II. It increased its investments in Western Europe between 1950 and 1958 with direct investment at around 24.5 billion, while the Europeans' direct investment was just under 10 billion and portfolio investment around 24.5 billion.

The US continued to expand investments in Western Europe for many reasons: to avoid, after 1958, the Common Market tariffs; to find lower labor and transportation costs; to make use of opportunities in Europe's rapidly expanding economy. Also American multinationals sought new markets, higher profits and growth in the Atlantic Community. Multinationals frightened some European governments and companies (a fear vividly expressed in Servan-Schreiber's book, *The American Challenge*, 1960), but were initially welcomed. Western Europe also increased its stake in the US market, especially between 1958 and 1965. In spite of some doubts over American invesment, Europeans sought American partners for their capital, technology, management skills and "know how."

Not that the US economy was without flaw. Americans had traditionally shown supreme skill at rapidly applying scientific discoveries (including those made abroad) for industrial use. (Penicillin, discovered in Britain, was first mass-produced in the US.) But during the 1950s new competitors arose on the world market, especially Japan, which rapidly expanded its industrial production in the wake of the Korean war. The Japanese not only raised the quality of their products, but also proved particularly good at putting theoretical knowledge gained abroad to practical use. (American scientists, including Nobel Prize winner William Shockley, invented the solid state transistor. In 1953 Western Electric licensed this technology to Sony, who made dramatic improvements to it and launched many new electronic products that successfully competed with American-made merchandise.)[11] Japanese manufacturers in the twentieth century went through the same cycle as German manufacturers had done in the nineteenth, a transformation that turned the appellation "made in Germany," or "made in Japan," from a stigma indicating a low-quality product into an industrial badge of honor.

There were other danger signals for the US. In the past, it had led the race for improving worker productivity,[12] but during the 1950s, began to fall behind in this respect compared with competitors such as West Germany and France.[13] Nevertheless, overall US productivity continued to expand, and the US remained at the same time a less regulated, and a less litigious country than it was to become in the 1960s and after.[14] There was a striking sense of confidence (expressed for instance in the size and luxury of American cars –

[11]Robert B. Reich, "The rise of techno-nationalism," in *The Atlantic Monthly*, May 1987, pp. 63–9.
[12]Between 1929 and 1950, growth rates of output for employee stood at 1.7 in the US, 1.2 in Germany, 1.1 in Great Britain and 0.3 in France. Between 1950 to 1960 the corresponding figures stood at 2.1, 5.9, 2.0, 4.6. Rothman, *European Society*, p. 167.
[13]Theodore H. White, *Fire in the Ashes: Europe in Mid-Century*. New York, William Sloane Associates, 1953, pp. 64, 366.
[14]The annual rate of civil law suits increased in the US from 2.2 during 1950–60; 3.9: 1960–70; 6.8: 1970–80; 10.5: 1980–86. See Warren T. Brookes, "Biggest threat to productivity and competitiveness in US," *San Francisco Chronicle*, 29 April 1987.

commodious vehicles, designed to serve families, and safer than smaller foreign imports). There remained in the US a conviction, long since on the wane in Great Britain, that the makers of cars, soapflakes, and breakfast food contributed as much or more to human happiness and dignity as preachers, teachers, or bureaucrats. Germans might justifiably talk about their *Wirtschaftswunder*; but it was the American economic miracle that helped shape the world and produced what historian William L. O'Neill called "the American high."

Western Europe benefited from the US connection in countless ways – through the provision of food and Marshall Aid, expanding markets, the adaptation of US marketing and managerial methods, the transfer of technology (including the use of patents). Europe had in part fallen into arrears in the industrial sphere. The gap between American and European productive methods had greatly increased since the end of the previous century. For instance, when the Marshall Plan began to operate in 1948, there was not one single continuous strip steel mill in Continental Europe – compared with over 20 such mills in the US. Cheap strip steel and sheet metal meant cheap refrigerators, automobiles, food cans, wash basins, and sinks. Hence Europeans had to pay more for such amenities than Americans. This was not the fault of European technicians who were as skilled as their US counterparts. But in all too many fields, Europe was fettered by two many cartels, too many trusts, too many small, family-owned companies, and too many conservative habits. America provided not merely aid, but new methods of production, management, and skills. A new breed of European came into being, known in France as *Il n'y a qu'à*. This was a specialist who had visited the US and who returned with the belief that "all we have to do," was to copy the Americans, from installing a new forklift to designing a new flowchart.[15]

Technology, science, information techniques, managerial skills of course cut across national boundaries, through universities, research laboratories, multinational corporations and defense programs. The 1930s and early 1940s had produced a host of innovations – radar, television, the electron microscope, nylon, the jet engine and the jet airliner, penicillin, and plastics. The late 1940s witnessed the development of the computer and the transistor. Between them, these inventions changed the world economy, as they were adapted to mass markets. Such innovations transcended national boundaries; the US pioneered many technical advances, but profited in a reciprocal fashion from European technological and scientific skill. (Non-US designers pioneered front-wheel drive, disc brakes, fuel injection, rotary and diesel engines in automobile design.)[16]

Above all, Europe continued to provide for the US an army of immigrants (nearly 3,000,000 people between 1941 and 1960). Overwhelmingly, they did well in the new country, their life experiences contrasting with the supposed

[15]White, *Fire in the Ashes: Europe in Mid-Century*, pp. 64, 366.
[16]Kenneth T. Jackson, *Crabgrass Frontier: The Suburbanization of the United States*. Oxford, Oxford University Press, 1985, pp. 246–71.

evils of rootlessness and alienation that intellectuals had traditionally associated with migration. "Cling to the fatherland, the dearest," Schiller had adjured his fellow citizens: "Hier sind die starken Wurzeln deiner Kraft / Dort in der fremden Welt stehst du allein, / Ein schwankes Rohr." (Here are the deepest roots that give you strength; there, in the alien world you stand alone, a feeble reed.) The immigrants gave the lie to such rhetorical animadversions. Having once settled down, the newcomers did better, on the average, after ten years than native-born Americans (an achievement traced at length by Barry R. Chiswick, an American economist).[17]

The traffic across the Atlantic of course went both ways. After the war, Americans came to Europe by the hundreds of thousands as diplomats, USIS officials, tourists, soldiers, scholars, students, journalists, aid administrators, technicians, businessmen, and entertainers. American TV, movies and records dominated Europe's popular culture. Western Europe was – and remained – the most important US export market. Contrary to legend, Europe was also the greatest recipient of US capital, having absorbed by 1970 more US investment than Africa, Asia, and Latin America put together.[18] In addition, Western Europe once more became a world supplier of capital in its own right. Europeans also invested heavily in the US. (Whereas US placements in Europe increased by $5 billion between 1949 and 1955, the value of Europe's claims on the US went up by $9 billion during the same period, with $4 billion in long-term investments.) Britain and France, and to a lesser extent West Germany and the Benelux countries, also exported substantial amounts of capital to the rest of the world, assisting global recovery. London once more resumed its position as one of the world's financial capitals; as did Swiss cities such as Basel and Zurich.

Initially, commerce within this network was impeded by the "dollar gap." Its cause was bitterly disputed. British observers blamed the dollar shortage on periodic US recessions. American free enterprise economists censured Europeans for lack of competition, excessive consumption and lack of investment, for trying to peg the exchange rates at undervalued levels. Whatever the rights and wrongs of this debate, Europeans encountered great difficulties in purchasing food, machinery and raw materials from the US at a time when Europe was still suffering from the after-effects of war. Savings were scarce, the gap in applied technology had widened between Europe and the US, and capital goods were dear. (A certain make of washing machine could be bought in New York for the equivalent of eight working hours – 500 labor hours were needed to acquire the same machine in Paris.)

---

[17]Barry R. Chiswick, "The economic progress of immigrants: some apparently universal patterns," in William Fellner, ed., *Contemporary Economic Problems*. Washington, DC, American Enterprise Institute, 1979. See also his *The Employment of Immigrants in the United States*. Washington, DC, American Enterprise Institute, 1982.

[18]See table in L. H. Gann, *Neo-Colonialism, Imperialism, and the "New Class."* Menlo Park, Cal., Institute for Humane Studies, 1975, p. 6. By 1970, total US investments stood as follows (in thousands of US dollars): Europe: 24,471; Canada: 22,801; Third World (Asia, Africa, Latin America): 21,290.

Charles P. Kindelberger, an economist who served with the Marshall Plan cadre, disagrees with the thesis of the threatening economic collapse or a communist takeover in Western Europe. Maier and Milward have argued that economic recovery had started before the US sent aid. Kindelberger, and others, show how important the promise of US aid and support was to morale and the starting of the recovery process before aid arrived. Furthermore American aid was for the recovery of Europe, not its development beyond prewar levels. The state department did not control the plan so as to seek to regain its power over American foreign policy. Keynesians had more to say than did diplomats about the Marshall Plan's operations. In any case, there was no one dominant voice or leader for the Marshall Plan. Pragmatism dominated and each state was treated differently and in accordance with its own wishes, rather than those of the American aid administrators; Italy was treated differently from Germany, or France. But the aid officials believed that Germany's economic recovery was essential for Europe's recovery and that was what they worked for by easing reconstruction in German industry.

The Americans hoped to solve this problem by a combination of aid, liberally applied, and trade, duly liberalized. Aid was channelled through the Marshall Plan. The Marshall Plan, unlike previous peace settlements, did not distinguish between victors and vanquished. It blended both idealism (in its willingness to rebuild Europe as a potential competitor) and enlightened self-interest (in the sense of benefiting a variety of bureaucratic, agricultural, and industrial lobbies in the US). The liberalization of commerce was promoted by the Bretton Woods conference of 1944. This resulted in the creation of the International Monetary Fund (IMF) and the International Bank for Reconstruction (the World Bank). The IMF (operative from 1947) originally looked to a system of orthodox finance. Its charter assigned to it limited authority to promote fixed international currency rates. It received powers to acquire monetary reserves through contributions from its members to lend cash to countries experiencing *temporary* balance of payment deficits. Countries experiencing *fundamental* disequilibrium were pledged by the rules either to reform their domestic policies or – everything else failing – to devalue their currencies. Fixed, predictable exchange rates were seen as an instrument for the promotion of world trade. In 1952 the IMF issued a statement declaring that loan recipients were expected to repay their debt within three to five years at the most.

Established in 1944, the IMF and the World Bank were designed to cope with imminent risks to the world economy in the immediate postwar era. Before World War II, the world economy had been sunk in depression. The international trade system had broken down; trading partners had become fearful of accepting payment in one another's currency. The IMF was erected to firm up the trading system by organizing an arrangement of fixed exchange rates for member states – thereby assuring that currencies were truly "convertible." The World Bank, for its part, was to address the problem of capital flows. It was to assist in attracting private investment to regions devastated by war or embarking on decolonization – where business confidence might be unreasonably low.

In the quarter century following World War II, the world economy performed remarkably well. Europe and Japan not only recovered, but prospered.

The system worked until the early 1970s, thereafter the major countries allowed their currencies to float; many loan recipients (especially Latin American and African countries) built up huge debts that in practice would never be repaid. The IMF granted loans to countries whose problems were of a permanent kind; the rules of conservative finance went out of the window, and the IMF's character altered in a radical fashion.[19] During the first two postwar decades, however, the IMF system of pegged exchange rates operated reasonably well. The Europeans, above all the Germans, saved a great deal of money, and on the whole invested their funds wisely. (By 1955 Western Europe was placing more than 14 percent of its GNP in new plants, equipment, commercial buildings, and public works.) The Europeans' propensity to save reflected a mood of confidence and other intangibles of a psychological kind. (These perhaps found sartorial expression in trans-Atlantic men's fashions that favored broad, padded shoulders, military hair styles, and the almost compulsory wearing of hats – the latter brought to an end by fashion leaders such as President John F. Kennedy, much to the hatters' distress.)

Whilst Western Europe and North America drew more closely together, the artificially imposed gap between the two Europes widened. Stalin was convinced that socialism could only be created in isolation, by closing off the Soviet Union and its satellites to Western "corruption." Hence Moscow in 1947 rejected proffered Marshall Aid both for itself and its satellites, just as in 1946 it had refused the offer of a billion dollar US loan and the chance of joining the World Bank and the IMF.[20] The Western European countries, especially West Germany, Austria, and Italy, were largely (though not entirely) cut off from their former trade partners in Central and Eastern Europe, and became even more dependent than before on their links with North America.

The US and Western Europe had much in common. For instance both shared in the growing power of the state in the economy. Generalizations in this regard are hard to make, for there were many cross currents. American planners put their trust in monetary manipulation, and deficit spending and public regulation, rather than public ownership. Even in the field of public hydroelectric power, the Americans relied on a system that blended public and private ownership.[21] By contrast, Europeans – especially the British, French, and Italians – nationalized a number of major industries after the war. But the tide of nationalization soon ebbed, giving way to government controls of a more indirect kind, controls that henceforth required of businessmen a

[19]Geoffrey E. Nunn and David L. Shapiro, "Is it time to phase out the IMF?," *Los Angeles Times*, 22 May 1983. The standard book is Charles P. Kindleberger, *A Financial History of Western Europe*. London, Allen and Unwin, 1984. Edward S. Mason and R. E. Asher, *The World Bank Since Bretton Woods*. Washington, DC, Brookings, 1973. M. de Vries, *The International Monetary Fund in a Changing World, 1945–1985*. Washington, IMF, 1986.

[20]Walter LaFeber, *America, Russia, and the Cold War, 1945–1975*. New York, John Wiley, 1976 edn p. 40. For a recent study of the period, see also Hugh Thomas, *Armed Truce: The Beginnings of the Cold War, 1945–1946*. New York, Atheneum, 1987, and the literature cited in the section on the Cold War.

[21]David L. Shapiro, *Public Power in the Pacific North West: A Failed Policy or a Policy Failure?* San Francisco, Cal., Cato Institute and University Press of America, 1989.

thorough knowledge of bureaucratic procedures and contacts. At the same time, the existing responsibilities of the state for its citizens widened. The state increasingly took over functions once left to churches, private bodies, or extended family networks. State power grew in a great variety of fields such as public health, maternal and child welfare, unemployment, old-age security, childcare, and subsidized public housing.

This revolution put new powers into the hands of planners. Critics such as John Jewkes, an Oxford economist, bitterly complained of what he called this new "species," whose members shared similar vices. They simplified the nature of economic problems; they failed to realize that poverty had been man's perennial state; they mistakenly regarded particular industries as homogeneous in character; they derided the consumer and consumer values; they held the distributive trades in unjustified contempt.[22] Jewkes might have lengthened the charge sheet. The planners – like so many generals – were apt to plan for the crises of yesteryear. They were preoccupied with existing shortages of food and raw materials; they failed to look ahead to the declining birthrate; they did not understand the trends that were leading to better designed bridges and cars with less metal in their makeup, or more "knowledge intensive" products with a lower raw material content. They failed to plan for the coming age of high technology: the era of microelectronics, biotechnology, photonics, and ceramics lay beyond their predictive abilities. They tended to prefer statutory public monopolies to unrestricted competition, and large to small enterprises. All too often, moreover, the planners' efforts at redistributing the national wealth benefited the new diploma-bearing salariat in public services, and the middle class more than the working class.

There was among planners a widespread (though far from universal) contempt for the private entrepreneur, especially for those small entrepreneurs who were destined to play a large part in technological innovation. Equally widespread was a snobbish disdain for the petty bourgeoisie – for grocers and their sons and daughters – as common at the time among economists as among poets. The petty bourgeoisie, in the general view, was bound for economic extinction, since small firms could not compete against large corporations backed by great resources of capital, managerial ability, and technological expertise. This generalization was, however, true only in part. Old-fashioned tinkers, tailors, and candle-stick makers indeed could not prevail over factories turning out mass-produced merchandise. But on the other hand industrial expansion gave great scope to all manner of new businesses. These included repair shops of every kind, garages, restaurants, and a host of other enterprises that provided personal services. There was new scope for contractors and sub-contractors who took orders for specialized work from large corporations. Small firms, unhampered by top-heavy bureaucracies, took a major part in research and development – for instance in high technology electronics. So from the mid-1970s smaller firms, having lost some ground, once more began to increase their relative stake in the US economy – in a manner that no

[22]John Jewkes, *Ordeal by Planning*. London, Macmillan, 1948, pp. 104–27.

economist or political scientist had predicted a generation earlier.

Planners of whatever kind rarely managed to foresee the wider consequences of their efforts at social engineering. (To give just one instance, "slum clearance" enthusiasts who rehoused the poor in high-rise apartment buildings, surrounded by green spaces, were invariably taken by surprise at the resultant rise in juvenile delinquency, crime, and drug abuse. Amongst other things, mothers living on the tenth floor of a huge block could no longer keep an eye on their youngsters getting into mischief down below, and granny had ceased to live round the corner, as in the old days.) Planning in its worst and most authoritarian sense found architectural expression in pseudo-monumental building styles and in monstrosities such as Charles Le Corbusier's *Unité d'Habitation* at Marseille or in the *Märkische Viertel* in West Berlin, built without the slightest regard for the occupants' own preferences (and invariably avoided by their respective architects for their personal residences).

The fact remains that planners enjoyed enormous popular respect after the war. In the English-speaking countries, this feeling went hand-in-hand with the intellectual prestige accorded to John Maynard Keynes. In his world view, employment and the gross national income were determined by the total level of spending. Since taxation only affected disposable consumer income and private spending, any decline in private spending might be offset when a government spent its tax revenues. Shortfalls in private investment could be cured by government spending to take up the slack, an assumption that put immense trust in the beneficial role of the state, its functionaries and agents. Given their assumption about the role of taxation, Keynesians had no difficulty in supporting redistributive taxation. They could even argue that progressive taxation would actually stimulate economic growth since the poor overall have a higher propensity to consume than the rich. Keynesian economics thus provided a powerful intellectual justification for policies that, in any case, commanded widespread public approval.

Government expansion necessarily entailed national planning, often linked to the nationalization of key industries, another solution enjoying widespread support at the time. (For instance, in Great Britain the call for privatization only made a wide appeal from 1980 onward, despite Britain's long experience with the ills that beset so many nationalized industries.)[23] The planners understood neither the extent of the expanding "second economy," nor its untaxed wealth, uncounted by official statisticians. The planners predictive record – like the forecasting record of intelligence agencies and academic futurologists – proved no better than the forecasting capacity of astrologists who had served seventeenth-century princes. But the planners' confidence was itself infectious and their popular respect lasted throughout the early postwar period.

Equally popular was the welfare revolution. Middle-class and working-class

---

[23]In Great Britain in 1964, 28 percent of respondents in a poll wanted more nationalization, 51 percent no change, only 21 percent more privatization. By 1983, the corresponding figures stood at 18 percent, 40 percent and 42 percent. Dennis Kavanagh, *Thatcherism and British Politics: The End of Consensus?* Oxford, Oxford University Press, 1987, p. 293.

people alike shared the expectation for welfare services paid for from public funds. Calls for the conciliation of trades unions proved likewise irresistible; labor was powerful at a time when conditions were good and labor scarce.

The bulk of voters and of academic and state planners shared certain conscious or unconscious assumptions. They looked upon the government as guardian and guarantor of prosperity – after all had not capitalism failed in the depression? They tended to prefer inflation to deflation (a generalization not applicable to West Germany and Switzerland). They dreaded unemployment as the greatest of all evils. Government took over the function of saving for many citizens, who came to accept state-provided old-age pensions and medical insurance as a matter of right, and therefore felt free to spend more of their current income. Taxes began to rise, though not at the same rate. Nevertheless, the expansion of government was kept in bounds. It was only from about 1960 onward that government spending in the major Western countries began to exceed 30 percent of the estimated GNP (see table 10.1).

TABLE 10.1   *Percentage of government spending to GNP*

	West Germany	*Sweden*	*United Kingdom*	*United States*
1940	12[a]	12	23[b]	18
1960	15	24	30	27
1980	43	57	42	33

[a] 1935 [b] 1938
Source: Edwin S. Mills, *The Burden of Government*. Stanford, Cal. Hoover Institution Press, 1986, p. 12.

Overall, Western Europe and the US went through an extended boom after 1948 – albeit one marked by great regional disparities. This boom had many components. The population rose, as Western Europe and North America augmented their respective numbers through migration and relatively high birthrates. Most economies in Continental Europe continued to benefit from rural reserves of labor, as countrymen and women continued to flock into cities – a process that would reach world-wide dimensions. Farming became increasingly mechanized and increasingly productive. (In Germany, the labor force was further swelled by millions of refugees from the Soviet zone, and from the former German regions now ceded to Poland and Czechoslovakia.) New factories were continually being built; the industrial output grew apace. (Agriculture, forestry, and fisheries, played a much smaller part than manufactures in the great Western European boom.) Public demand for durable consumer goods kept rising. Europeans at least managed to eliminate by stages the backlog of unexploited technology. War itself had contributed to industrial innovation. The aftermath of war intensified this process, and further disrupted earlier restraints, including many antiquated trade restrictions and cartel arrangements. A generation of professional managers and technocrats, reliant on new machinery and new methods, undertook to produce a broad range of new products. In retrospect, it was a period of remarkable achievement.

ECONOMY AND GOVERNMENT

It is not by the intermeddling ... of the omniscient and omnipotent State, but by the prudence and energy of the people, that England has hitherto been carried forward in civilisation; and it is to the same prudence and the same energy that we now look with comfort and good hope. Our rulers will best promote the improvement of the nation by strictly confining themselves to their own legitimate duties, by leaving capital to find its most lucrative course, commodities their fair price, industry and intelligence their natural reward, idleness and folly their natural punishment, by maintaining peace, by defending property, by diminishing the price of law, and by observing strict economy in every department of the state. Let the government do this: the People will assuredly do the rest.[24]

When Macaulay penned these lines in 1830, most British and American (and a substantial number of Continental European) readers, agreed with him. After the end of World War II, few would have done so. The state had extended its functions until they touched on almost every human activity. It owned and managed airlines, mines, railways, and many banks and industries, directed investments and engaged in national planning. It provided education, health services, and unemployment insurance. It patronized the arts – in place of the olden-time magnates and patricians. It engaged in foreign espionage on a scale unknown in the past. It defined the nature of pornography and in some countries licenced streetwalkers. An encyclopedia would be needed to do justice to all its activities.

The state also wielded immense prestige (the precise extent of this varied, of course, from country to country). The subjects of Protestant monarchies in Northern Europe – above all Swedes and British – had the most trust in their state, Italians the least. But overall, the reputation of the democratic state was in the ascendant. The role of religious traditions and the family were played down. Postwar literature took little account of the manner in which family networks had always helped their members to cope with the perils of emigration, expulsion, hunger, and deracination. Not that ample information on the subject had not long been available. (To mention just one example, medical officers investigating the health of poverty-stricken Londoners in pre-World War I London had pointed to the low infant mortality of Jewish slum dwellers and the superior health of Jewish schoolchildren, attributing this

---

[24]Lord Macaulay, "Southey's colloquies on society," in *Critical and Historical Essays Contributed to the Edinburgh Review*. New York, Armstrong and Sons, 1880, p. 121.

to a high incidence of breast feeding, the low incidence of extra-domestic employment of Jewish women, and the absence of venereal diseases and alcoholism.[25] But national planners were apt to take inadequate account of such social complexities.

The planners, without exception, agreed on what they regarded as the inherent failings of an uncontrolled market economy. Its reputation had been tainted by the great slump and resultant unemployment. World War II had seen apparently successful intervention by the state into the economy on a grand scale. Untold numbers of present and future policy makers had served the state. They had done so either in the armed forces, or in civilian agencies where the exercise of power gave a sense of mission and accomplishment to senior incumbents (such as economists John Maynard Keynes or John Kenneth Galbraith, once an administrator in the US Office of Price Administration). British Labourites and paternalistic Tories, German Social Democrats, French Catholic democrats might disagree among themselves on many issues – but none questioned the beneficent nature of state intervention. Indeed "all the major modern ideologies – conservatism, liberalism, socialism .. had a hand in the expansion of state activity" in Western Europe.[26]

> "Nobody in Europe believes in the American way of life – that is, in private enterprise ..." A. J. P. Taylor, British historian broadcasting on the BBC in November, 1945.

State power was equally on the rise in the US. To its European critics and admirers alike, the US might appear as the world's bastion of free enterprise. But whereas Europe was supposedly being Americanized, the US underwent a process of partial Europeanization in the sense of acquiring an enormous state apparatus. (Between 1947 and 1957, the governmental payrolls nearly doubled, from $1,109 million to $2,533 million – including all local, state, and federal agencies.) The economics of "public choice" as yet remained in their infancy. Instead, the 2,000 young economists and administrators who staffed the European recovery offices administering the Marshall Plan overwhelmingly adhered to Keynesian economics. They, and their seniors were apt to be impatient with Continental European advocates of free enterprise, men such as Luigi Enaudi, Ludwig Ehrhard, or Walter Eucken whose works remained unread in English-speaking countries. Far from resisting the trend toward state planning, US advisers in Europe actively promoted it. (When World War II ended, the US thus made aid to Italy dependent on the creation of an economic plan, and sent experts of their own to collaborate with the Italian authorities to this purpose.)[27]

---

[25] J. M. Winter, *The Great War and the British People*. London, Macmillan, 1985, pp. 15–16.
[26] Neil Elder, "The functions of the modern state," in Jack Hayward and R. N. Berki, eds, *State and Society in Contemporary Europe*. Oxford, Martin Robertson, 1979, p. 60. Claude Andrien, *Les Nationalisations de La Libération*. Paris, Presses de la Foundation Nationales des Science Politiques, 1987.
[27] Sergio Ricossa, "Italy," in Carlo M. Cipolla, ed., *The Fontana Economic History of Europe*. Glasgow, Fontana Books, 1978, v. 1, p. 307.

Charles S. Maier in In Search of Stability *(Cambridge, Cambridge University Press, 1987), concludes that American postwar policy in Germany (and Japan) was a great success. The Americans were able to put economics over politics, to insist on the primacy of questions about output and efficiency and not about ideology. The "politics of productivity" won out in the postwar years, and Europe and Japan recovered magnificently and served as engines of growth for the world economy. The 1950s became the great epoch of "stabilized growth capitalism" for the West and of centrist political governance.*

There were, however, limits to America's power and its ability to restructure Europe, even though European leaders accepted US leadership as a kind of "consensual hegemony" and "gentlemanly persuasion." The system worked because it did increase productivity, open up trade and make Europe's industries and businessmen more efficient in a relatively frictionless economic Atlantic Community, led by the US.

State interventionism not only appealed to bureaucrats and experts, but rested on widespread, almost universal, popular consent. Businessmen during World War II had widely become associated with regulatory agencies, and served the state as temporary civil servants. Many great firms looked to the state for favors of every kind. As John Kenneth Galbraith put it in mordant fashion, "socialism in our time comes not from socialists but from the heads of large corporations when they learn from their bankers that resort must be had to the government, and fast."[28] Trade unionists looked to the state, and so did the poor who expected the state to rectify social inequities.

The bureaucratic state had powerful allies in the legal profession, and even more so in the universities that supplied it with graduate recruits and highly trained advisers. Some professors also had material incentives. As Craig Roberts, a US economist, put it in a critique,

private enterprise does not provide the research grants that are the bread and butter of influential social scientists. [In the US] these grants come from the National Science Foundation, the National Endowment for the Humanities, the US Department of Labor, and so forth. Neither can private enteprise provide the positions of power which academics enjoy as cabinet ministers and Presidential advisers. Any social scientist who can discover a social problem than can be parlayed into a new federal program is set for life.[29]

But the widespread commitment to state intervention in academia rested on far more than just material temptation. There was a striking, though often naive trust in the social sciences whose terminology shaped the very vocabulary of public political discourse. Plans might go awry – but planning became a praise word.

It was therefore with almost universal approbation that governments kept growing in size, complexity, and function. Table 10.2, which illustrates the

---

[28] John Kenneth Galbraith, *A View from the Stands: Of People, Politics, Military Power and the Arts*. Boston, Houghton Mifflin Co., 1986, p. 172.
[29] Craig Roberts, "The political economy of bureaucratic imperialism," *The Intercollegiate Review*, Fall, 1976, pp. 1–15.

rise in government expenditure during the years 1947 to 1957, the era of recovery, speaks for itself. The data may be crude, since they take no account of differential inflation rates. Neither do they include the rising disbursement of *Länder*, cantons, municipalities, county councils, and other local governments. But the figures do point in an impressionistic fashion to a transnational trend. In all Western countries, save only conservative Switzerland, government spending went up significantly. And thereafter, the expansion of official expenditure would continue to accelerate.[30] Many streams merged into this current. Fear of communist popular fronts produced welfare capitalism; there were rising expectations – the mere fact that each new generation felt no gratitude to the past, but took its own living standard for granted; the popularization of "relative poverty" concepts; the interest of "spending" ministries, and "spending" lobbies; the enhanced influence of the mass media; plus the social spenders' assumed moral superiority. All contributed to an exponential process which, if unchecked, would negate the assumptions of Lord Macaulay. Whatever their political convictions, the planners also placed implicit trust in the officials' managerial skill, personal honesty, and work ethic – a trust not necessarily justified as the Victorian work ethic declined, and state power grew apace.

The state and planning

Keynesianism came to dominate government policies in most of the Atlantic Community during and after World War II. His "Tract on monetary reform" for example called for managed money and postulated the doctrine that budgetary and monetary management could achieve and support economic growth. Keynes's *The General Theory of Employment, Interest and Money* (1936) became the bible for the postwar mixed economies of the Atlantic Community. Europe's leaders, remembering the crises and depressions after World War I, sought to avoid them by establishing Keynesian monetary arrangements. Governments therefore undertook economic and financial management of the market, money supply and the budget.

During the war "accommodative finance" set up Lend Lease by the US to give war supplies to Britain and Russia without requiring repayment later on. All told, the US provided about 30 billion dollars to its Allies. (Britain, however, had to use what resources it had in gold reserves and foreign investments as well and had to cut back on its exports.) Wartime planning in Britain had helped to prepare for a Keynesian international financial system; full employment was the goal, to be assisted by establishing variable currency values. The US wanted to end trade restrictions, autarchy and trade discrimination, and to limit international credit so as not to overburden itself.

---

[30]For tables see David Marquand, *The Unprincipled Society: New Demands and Old Politics*. London, Jonathan Cape, 1988, appendix, table v. The rate of increase varied from country to country. But for the OECD states as a whole, public spending as a percentage of the gross domestic product went up from 28.5 (1955–7) to 44.0 (1977–9).

TABLE 10.2 Total central government expenditure (in millions)

	Belgium (francs)	Denmark (kroner)	France (francs)	West Germany (marks)	Italy (lire)	Netherlands (guilders)	Norway (kroner)
1947	76,456	1,883	2,357 (1950)	11,613 (1950)	1,215	5,095	2,936
1957	108,422	4,496	5,649	31,822	3,069	8,893	4,765

	Portugal (escudos)	Spain (pesetas)	Sweden (kronor)	Switzerland (francs)	United Kingdom (pounds)	US (dollars)
1947	5,694	13,533	4,108	1,947	3,354	39,032
1957	8,230	42,932	13,024	2,238	5,218	69,433

Source: B. R. Mitchell, *European Historical Statistics*, London, Macmillan, 1980, pp. 736–9.
US Department of Commerce, Bureau of the Census. *Historical Statistics of the United States: Colonial Times to 1957*, Washington DC, 1960, pp. 736–7.

The Bretton Woods agreement in 1944 was a compromise between British and US wishes. There was fixity (gold standard of the US dollar at $35 per ounce) and flexibility (changeable parity rates in currency as Keynes wished). Bretton Woods also established an international credit pool (the IMF) to finance temporary balance of payments difficulties. This too was a Keynesian plan. The IMF provided for currency convertibility and prohibited discriminatory currency practices.

Europe recovered and grew remarkably because the Marshall Plan promoted a rapid increase in agricultural productivity (helped by tractors, seeds and fertilizers), that in turn released labor for industry and established efficient investment programs. Rigorous monetary stabilization helped Germany and Italy; wage restraints especially in Germany, Holland, and Italy allowed speedy reconstruction and new American management techniques; and technology spurred entrepreneurship. Peace, stability and improved morale of people and government led to enormous capital formation – Germany 27 percent, France and Italy 20 percent, Great Britain 16 percent.

American labor and business leaders wanted to see social democratic unions, the purging of communists from union federations, at least in Britain and Germany, and cooperation with elements of the non-communist left. CIO and AFL leaders at first refused to play an anti-communist role, but reacted to communist obstructionism in unions and in the world federation of trade unions in 1946–8. American unionists then worked with Europeans to form the ICFTU, thus splitting the European trade union movement and hurting socialist parties.

There were then three essentials for the postwar financial system: balance of payments financing, convertibility of currencies, and limited exchange adjustment. Keynes saw the flaws in the system – there were no provisions for a transitional period to rebuild the economy and to do away with years of accumulation of trade and exchange restrictions. He had to accept the American parts of the plan which, he felt, would fail; but he reassured himself and other government officials by saying the IMF weaknesses would be rectified, the US having committed itself to take responsibility, if anything were to go wrong.

Europe, however, fell into economic disarray in 1946–7. There were fuel shortages, strikes, and a severe winter, the pound fell and the US responded first with the Marshall Plan, and then with greatly increased credits, grants, and loans to Europe. US pressure contributed to the devaluation of Europe's currencies, and worked to reduce trade restrictions and quotas within the OEEC. Currency transferability became common within the European Payments Union; as a result Europe's financial strength grew steadily. By 1959 the postwar transition was over; currencies were convertible, trade restrictions on all but agricultural goods were largely ended, and the European currencies were in balance with the US dollar. (In the 1960s a dramatic change was to occur as Western Europe and Japan challenged the US dominance of the world economic order.)

Planning for the postwar period began before the war ended, probably because the Allies had not considered carefully enough what to do after World War I, resulting in an unholy mess. Reparations were the main concern – who was to get what. The other motive for planning was to ensure a weak, unmilitaristic Germany. The Soviets were most interested in reparations; while the British and the US wanted to guarantee a Europe free from the German menace.

Both sides wanted Germany to pay for some of the damage she had caused, so factories were dismantled, especially in the Russian sector. But Britain and the US soon realized that a Germany stripped of manufacturing capabilities would hurt the whole of Western Europe. Humanitarian concerns also led them to help feed Germany and to restore her productivity, so she could pay for reparations and play a part in rebuilding the economies of Western Europe.

One of the most important financial reforms took place in West Germany in June 1948 under minister of the economy Ludwig Ehrhard, who abolished most price controls, ended rationing, and greatly reduced the scope of state regulation. During the same year, the Western Allies introduced a comprehensive currency reform that once more provided West Germans with a stable mark, and put an end to the unofficial currency based on cigarettes and similar merchandise. The reform was inequitable in application. Owners of bank accounts and insurance policies were penalized. Owners of homes, farms, and factories, by contrast, gained in an indirect fashion. The currency reform in fact amounted to an unplanned method of redistributing property. Nevertheless, the reforms did serve their purpose: between them, helped along by the Marshall Plan, they set the stage for the German economic miracle.

By contrast, most European states had to devalue their currencies in 1949, only to find that the US started stockpiling primary goods and minerals to fight the Korean war. Retail prices increased by 50 percent and wholesale by as much as 40 percent. A recession came in 1952; prices for primary goods declined to 1948 levels and remained stable for five years, showing how interdependent the members of the Atlantic Community were. Inflation, however, remained moderate through the rest of the 1950s and the 1960s.

Government planning became the norm in Europe after 1945. The Soviet Union had led the field after 1919, but Western European countries had followed suit in some fashion during the depression, and especially during World War II. Better statistics were kept to allow for sound planning. Wartime controls had been extensive, and after the war government expanded, and economists provided techniques (national income accounting) and theories (Keynes) for central planning.

Two systems came to dominate. The Soviet model of planning prevailed in all of Eastern Europe (direct controls, quotas and targets set by a central organization characterized this). Western Europe used several different planning modes that were all essentially Keynesian. The Keynesians did not use direct control but let the market produce the goods, while planners concerned themselves with monetary policy, government tax and spending levels, to ensure full employment. Britain planned least, the Soviet Union most. Rather than rely on a plan, such as the French developed, the Labor government had three goals: to manage total demand, to achieve full employment, and to redistribute wealth by the tax system, in order to achieve equality, with some nationalization of key industries. But no central planning group was established by any British government in the postwar period. Overall, these Keynesian policies did not meet the planners' expectations. Western Europe became disillusioned with the nationalization of the postwar years; income redistribution widely helped the middle class, and budget and monetary control may have caused destabilization as often as stabilization.

After the war, when the US took an interventionist posture as opposed to its traditional isolationism, Keynes was exported back to Europe with America's aid programs, especially the Marshall Plan which gave US administrators some power over economic planning in Europe. Albert O. Hirschman, an aid official himself and now an Emeritus Professor at the Institute for Advanced Study, Princeton, documents how the Keynesian revolution was re-exported to Europe. Hirschman shows how the Marshall Plan helped create les trente ans glorieuses, *the 30 glorious postwar years that were "the most sustained and dynamic period of economic expansion in human history."*

Keynesianism helped the US achieve international hegemony by leading the world's economic recovery, though the Keynesians were not as dominant in West Germany or Japan, where the military held sway, assisted by non-Keynesian businessmen, bankers and lawyers, as they were in Britain, France, and Italy, where American aid officials had more influence.

Keynes's model purported to show how government deficit spending might stimulate the economy and thereby engender full employment while restraining inflation through government controls. While the Keynesians triumphed in Europe their influence declined in the US. The British returned to the demand control management and deficit spending that Keynes preferred to coercive physical control. The French chose indicative planning, which was basically an extension of Keynes's view of the economic role of the state. US advisers had less success in Italy because the Italians preferred to build up their currency reserves and left plants and labor underused. Italian monetarists clashed with American Keynesians. In Hirschman's view the Keynesians not only helped revive the economies of Western Europe but also brought a civic culture and a sense of public service to a Europe which had lost much of its public spirit during the war. They laid the basis for the economics of growth, so popular in the 1950s and 1960s, by using ideas "of the multiplier, the marginal efficiency of capital, the propensity to save ... which made some economists believe they knew how to control economic growth." Keynes thus spurred the whole field of development economics which did so much harm to the colonial and decolonized world and Latin America. Even as Keynes's theory stimulated dedication to public service, it also made economists arrogant and too confident that government could control and direct the economy.

Planning required a whole new set of economic tools. Hence another major figure associated with Western planning was Jan Tinbergen, a Dutch economist. He developed econometric models to measure alternative plans and supply and demand figures. Tinbergen worked on plan models for the Dutch economy from 1950 on. The French plan ("indicative planning") emerged from government efforts to reconstruct an economy ravaged by

World War II. It aimed at recovery by developing key sectors (power, steel, transport, etc.) through direct planned investment in certain areas, and through consultation with business and labor leaders. The French economy did grow; the structure of the economy was changed, and investor confidence was restored.

Centralized political bargaining extended throughout the Atlantic Community for the purpose of securing agreement between business, government, and labor concerning price and wage changes. But this system widely broke down as a result of inflation in the 1960s. All the planning complexes of West Europe converged into a single system of monetary and fiscal policies, price and wage controls, foreign trade control, limited direct control with some spending on key sectors.

Bureaucratic ascendancy

"State power" is a widely used term. It is of course always an abstraction – shorthand designating the work of countless salaried career officials. These men and women differ enormously in function, training, and power. In theory, bureaucracies operate according to rational and generalized rules set out in writing, and their roles are specialized and differentiated, with strictly defined spheres of competence, and well demarcated lines of authority. Within the organization, recruitment and promotion are based on achievement. Its officials are protected from arbitrary dismissal, and can be disciplined only according to specified procedures. Coordination is achieved by a hierarchical form of organization. Officials are answerable to the public through their respective ministers, servants not masters of the commonwealth.

So much for the generalizations of great scholars such as Max Weber.[31] But in fact these only applied to the bureaucracies developed by the "law-and-order" states of yesteryear, with restricted tasks. As civil service machines kept expanding in size and function, they departed to an even greater extent from the Weberian model. Bureaucracies in the Western countries nevertheless had many common characteristics.[32] Their structure roughly resembled that of a three-layered cake – with a college-trained elite of decision makers at the top (in Great Britain, the "administrative" class), recruited mainly from the ranks of the upper-middle and middle classes; in the second layer stood a corps

---

[31] Hans H. Gerth and C. Wright Mills, eds, *From Max Weber: Essays in Sociology*. Oxford, Oxford University Press, 1958, pp. 196–244.

[32] The literature is extensive. See, for instance, John A. Armstrong, *The European Administrative Elite*. Princeton, Princeton University Press, 1973. Richard Rose, ed., *Public Employment in Western Nations*. Cambridge, Cambridge University Press, 1985. Brian Chapman, *Profession of Government: The Public Service in Europe*. London, Allen and Unwin, 1959. Henry Jacoby, *The Bureaucratization of the World*. Berkeley, Cal., University of California Press, 1973. Paul P. van Riper, *History of the United States Civil Service*. Evanston, Ill., Peterson, 1958. For the relations between big business and the state, and business bureaucracies, see for instance, David Granick, *The European Executive*. Garden City, NY, Anchor Books, 1962. Raymond Vernon, ed., *Big Business and the State: Changing Relations in Western Europe*. Cambridge, Mass., Harvard University Press, 1974. Douglas E. Ashford, *The Emergence of the Welfare State*. New York, Basil Blackwell, 1987.

of executive officials (the British "executive" class), and at the bottom a host of clerical and other lower-ranking employees (the British "clerical" class), corresponding to skilled workers in industry. As time went on these differences became attenuated, and bureaucratic expansion offered new opportunities for functional and social advancement. Bureaucratic empire building went on apace, especially in Canada after 1944; an ever-growing body of high school and college trained men and women found employment; there was a striking expansion in the number of clerks and specialists – archivists, engineers, meteorologists, soil conservation experts, and so forth – commonly organized in separate bodies with their own career structure.

Bureaucratic expansion had many unforeseen aspects. The cost of compliance rose, as regulations became ever more complex, forms became more difficult to fill out, regulations multiplied, and private firms and public corporations alike increasingly had to draw on the services of lawyers and chartered accountants to keep up with the demands of the state. Few civil service machines attempted to engage in "birth control" of documentation, or insisted, as a matter of policy, on the issue of "user-friendly" forms. (The US National Archives' "records management" program did help in this regard.) The expansion of state bureaucracies also contributed to the proliferation of private bureaucracies – this at the small entrepreneur's expense. For instance, in the past, a Jewish or Sicilian immigrant in New York, having accumulated some savings, had been able to open a small shop without further ado. Under the new dispensation, his or her job became much more difficult. The modern shopkeeper had to be experienced in the art of filling out forms, the intricacies of withholding tax, and a host of other skills not usually available to newcomers, such as the Puerto Ricans who flocked to New York in the wake of World War II.[33]

On every level the bureaucracies' paperwork increased as reporting procedures became more involved, and official hierarchies more intricate. Civil servants and legislators all over the world proceeded on the assumption that the citizen's time was of no value in their dealings with government offices. The flood of official documents became a torrent. As the state extended its functions, offices required information on an ever-increasing range of matters, and produced, collected and accumulated more and more written papers. This process was accelerated by changes in administrative techniques. The invention of the typewriter had ushered in the mechanization of the office. Then came accounting machines, devised for the rapid multiplication of letters, reports, forms and memos, and finally the installation of electronic equipment. The most trivial transaction could now be recorded and find its way into a specific file; hence the mass of records often came to exceed the administrators' ability to assimilate the information contained in the files, to trace transactions, and dispose of them efficiently. (In the US, for example, the federal records alone increased from 4 million to 18.5 million cubic feet between 1937 and 1947 –

[33]L. H. Gann and Peter Duignan, *The Hispanics in the United States: A History*. Boulder, Col., Westview Press, 1986, pp. 85–7.

and this was only a start.)[34] The mass production of records could lead to administrative amnesia – a widespread complaint.

For all their deficiencies, bureaucracies proved adaptable, powerful, and effective provided they were not overloaded. Corruption in the higher levels was relatively rare, compared with what had been customary in Europe before the end of the eighteenth century or with practices common after decolonization in most Third World countries in the twentieth century. Scandals there were – but the administrative machine never ground to a halt. Bureaucrats in general did best when their functions were clearly prescribed and predictable. (For example, an archivist or a meteorologist each had strictly defined tasks that even the most ambitious of bureaucratic empire building department heads could not expand. A commissioner for race relations, by contrast, had an open-ended brief; the scope for improving race relations seemed infinite, and so was his bureau's potential for growth.)

Apart from these general similarities the various bureaucracies in Western Europe continued to bear their respective national stamp. It was perhaps this combination of national and trans-national qualities that made them relatively effective and facilitated popular approval for their rapid growth. In all the main Western countries, bureaucracies had for long learned from one another – as had industries and universities. The various German states, especially Prussia, had been heavily indebted to the French example, and French bureaucratic efficiency had helped to make the Teutonic version (for instance in the field of financial administration). The British had in turn been influenced by the German example in the field of social welfare; the Germans had benefited from British experience in the field of local government; the Austro-Hungarian empire had left its stamp on Northern Italy – and so the story continued.[35]

In modern times, the French continue to provide an excellent professional training to their top-level civil servants through the *grandes écoles*. They also profit from the manner in which civil servants at the highest level combine legal, financial, and technical expertise in one person. Professionalism was strengthened by bodies such as the École Nationale d'Administration, founded in 1946, with its emphasis on the social sciences. The ENA continued to send out successive waves of "self-confident and mutually acquainted peer groups" who made their way through the entire administrative system and also provided a powerful contingent for the EEC and the European parliament. The Gallic approach went with a long tradition of planning, and *étatiste* mind that induced French officials to see themselves as the true guardians of the national interests, and gave them a liking for centralized, comprehensive codified solutions to political problems. France, with its belief in comprehensive national planning and an elitist bureaucracy, in turn exercised a considerable influence on its neighbours. By the early 1960s, Belgium Norway, Britain, and Italy each had

[34]L. H. Gann, "Archives and the study of society," *Rhodes-Livingstone Institute Journal*, no. 16, 1954, pp. 47–67.
[35]For the interpenetration of civil service traditions, see Ernest Barker, *The Development of Public Services in Western Europe 1660–1930*. Oxford, Oxford University Press, 1945.

to some extent adopted the French approach, with adaptations to their own national setting.[36]

The German civil service shared the French professionalism. The German tradition, like the French, derived from Roman law, and was characterized by a legalistic cast of mind; added to this there was among the Prussian civil servants of old a long legacy of estate, as well as state management. While legal studies remained the gateway to the higher levels of an administrative career in Germany, law courses were by no means narrow in scope, and included economics, social insurance, and labor law, as well as public finance. The same held true for the curricula of the higher school of administrative studies, set up at Speyer in 1947. West Germany, of all the major powers, however, had been the keenest to keep economic planning to the minimum – partly as a reaction against the centralized tyranny of the Third Reich, and the regimented command economy created in East Germany. (It was only from the mid-1960s that the emphasis began to change, with an increased stress on state regulation justified on social and economic grounds.)

Austria, on the other hand, adopted a highly centralized approach, one that merged the *étatiste* traditions of the Habsburg dynasty with the precepts of Austro-Marxism. Austria had produced many of the greatest free enterprise economists of the twentieth century. It also produced some of the leading socialist thinkers, and engaged in the most extensive nationalization ventures in non-communist Europe; hence it became after World War II, "the country with the largest non-private economic sector in the Western world,"[37] In this respect, it was Austria, rather than better known Britain or Sweden, that took the lead.

Italy's bureaucratic structure reflected the deep-seated differences between the North – in many ways a part of Central Europe – and the South, a Mediterranean land. Italy adhered to Roman law, like France and Germany; her bureaucratic apparatus, developed in the original kingdom of Piedmont, was *étatiste* and centralizing in temper. But this machine proved less well adapted to the functions of a modern state than the civil services of her northern neighbors. The Italian civil servants' pay was low – a state of affairs that was only partially remedied by reforms introduced in 1973. Inadequate remuneration encouraged venality. Italian officials, like Italian university lecturers, had to take on outside work to make ends meet. Partly as a result of modest pay, the Italian bureaucracy recruited a disproportionate number of southerners, thereby contributing a pre-industrial flavor to the operations of the bureaucracy. There was a spirit of narrow legalism. Training facilities lagged behind those provided by other major industrial countries, as witnessed by the tardy establishment at Caserta of a higher school of public administration. There was a chaotic conglomerate of agencies, poorly coordinated.

---

[36]See Elder, "The functions of the modern state," p. 65, and Vernon, *Big Business and the State*, pp. 8–9.
[37]Eduard März, "Austria's economic development, 1945–1978," in Kurt Steiner, ed., *Modern Austria*. Palo Alto, Society for the Promotion of Science and Scholarship, 1981, p. 128.

On the other hand, there were also islands of efficiency, such as the *Banca d'Italia*, known for the probity and competence of its personnel.

Britain's civil service contrasted strikingly with the rest. The British continued to put their trust in well-educated gentlemen, amateurs, preferably educated at Oxford or Cambridge. Officials were well paid, honest, and commanded high prestige. The British civil service had been excellently adapted to the needs of the old-time "constabulary state" that had avoided interference in the economy. The British had proved to be great administrators of empire. Even anti-colonial scholars in modern Africa later reluctantly came to praise the British empire builders' "patriotism and probity ... self discipline and other remarkable ideals of public duty and responsibility as now remain, unfortunately, yet to be learned and emulated by succeeding generations of indigenous African leaders."[38] But the British civil service proved less adept at economic planning, and at solving the immense tasks set by the ever-growing demands made on the state by economic interventionism. This generalization continued to hold true, despite the increasing trend toward professionalism since the issue of the Plowden report in 1961.

The US civil service remains much harder to classify. Bureaucracy of this kind in the US is of relatively recent origins (it was only in 1883 that a civil service commission came into being). Expansion was rapid from the new deal era onward. But administrative responsibilities remained divided among an ill-coordinated federation of departments, agencies, and commissions, with enormous differences in their respective performances. The central government departments were created by acts of Congress, each headed by a political official who changed with each administration. The US was too huge in size, too varied in ethnic and cultural terms, to produce mandarins comparable to senior British civil servants, with a common culture rooted in Oxbridge, or to the French *énarche*. In the US, lawyers wielded enormous power in public administration, as they did in so many other departments of public life. The US civil service was much derided in public – as was the authority of the state in general. But it also had its strong suites. Many highly qualified men and women were attracted to its ranks; it was also "more broadly representative of the population as a whole than that of any ... European country, with the possible exception of the Soviet Union."[39]

Taken together, these large bureaucratic machines, and those of the various smaller countries, came to form an immensely powerful establishment. Public service became one of the major industries in the Western world, and the state one of the largest individual employers. By 1955 public treasuries of various kinds in Western Europe spent an estimated $62 billion (excluding operating expenditures of government enterprises and publicly owned corporations).

[38] Johnson U. J. Asiegbu, *Nigeria and Its British Invaders 1851–1920*. New York, Nok Publishers, 1984, p. xxix. For a more detailed discussion, see L. H. Gann and Peter Duignan, *The Rulers of British Africa, 1870–1914*. Stanford, Cal., Stanford University Press, 1978.
[39] Stanley Rothman, *European Society and Politics*. Indiannapolis, Bobbs-Merrill, 1970, p. 668.

This represented 28 percent of Western Europe's gross national product.[40] The impact of government expenditure varied considerably from country to country. (The "high" spending countries, in descending order were Luxembourg, Sweden, Great Britain, France and Belgium. The "upper-middle" countries comprised Norway, West Germany, Switzerland, Denmark, and the Netherlands. The "lower-middle" countries included Austria, Ireland, and Italy – with Greece, Spain, and Portugal at the bottom.[41] But all Western states spent much more than in prewar years. Governments also accounted for a substantial part of national capital accumulation as a percentage of public and private fixed capital formation. Again the percentages differed widely. (By 1955 Sweden and Spain stood at the top, with 30.1 percent, and 27.4 percent respectively. The United Kingdom accounted for 9.5 percent, West Germany 13.3 percent, France 13 percent, Belgium 11.2 percent, Italy 10.1 percent, and Norway 8.8 percent.)

Such figures, of course, lend themselves to contrasting interpretations. Statistics differed widely in quality and coverage, both from agency to agency, and from country to country. Statistics did not reflect the workings of the "second economy." And statistics could provide no indication of the relative efficiency with which information was supplied, collected, and evaluated in different countries. (A charming one-act comedy from Mexico showed how a census taker and the members of a slum family collaborated in mutually convenient fables that would permit each of them to conceal their respective lives.)[42] The statistical evidence, is, however, incontrovertible in one respect. Administrative growth and official expenditure during the late 1940s and 1950s reached nothing like the extent attained in the subsequent two decades. Nevertheless, the national and international bureaucracies had become major economic powers. Their strengths and foibles would help to shape the economic future of the West.

The state as entrepreneur

The entrepreneurial role of the state in Europe is of ancient standing. Princely governments had run a variety of public enterprises during the mercantilist era. Parliamentary governments followed suit, especially during the years before World War II, when the predecessors of the Anglo-Iranian Oil Company in Britain, *Compagnie Française des Pétroles* in France, *Ente Nazionale Idrocarburi* in Italy, and *Volkswagen* in Germany had been wholly or partly acquired by the government. After the war the trend toward nationalization accelerated – but without a consistent pattern, and for different reasons. Socialists wished

[40]The breakdown was as follows (in percentages): goods and services: 50.4, civil functions: 32.1, transfers: 30.5, subsidies: 4.3, interest on public debt: 6.7, capital formation: 8.1, defense: 18.3. J. Frederick Dewhurst, *Europe's Needs and Resources: Trends and Prospects in Eighteen Countries.* New York, Twentieth Century Fund, 1961, p. 406.
[41]Dewhurst, *Europe's Needs*, detailed table on p. 467.
[42]Emilio Carballido, "El censo," in Frank Dauster and Leon F. Lyday, eds. *En un Acto: Nueve Piezas Hispanoamericanas.* New York, Van Nostrand, 1974, pp. 5–20.

to control what they regarded as the commanding heights of the economy; patriots wanted to punish wartime collaborators; planners desired to salvage concerns, or develop backward regions; technologists looked to the state for the purpose of creating new industrial arts. The state acquired vast power through its ability to direct – or misdirect – enormous resources, to create new industries, or to keep alive enterprises that had long ceased to merit support on economic grounds.

This transformation occurred at a time of increasing prosperity in the West. The various European economies all recovered, albeit at different speeds. By 1960 the dollar gap had closed, and Europeans removed most import quotas on dollar goods. Trade flourished. During the two decades following 1950, production expanded at an average compound rate of 5.5 percent per year, compared with 5 percent in the world as a whole. The Western Europeans gained substantial ground on the US, their gross domestic product growing twice as fast, although the output of the average American was still over twice that of the average European. The Americans still remained powerful; their multinational companies had invested heavily in Europe; the dollar remained the principal international currency, but the Americans' advantage was partly offset after 1958 by the EEC's larger volume of external trade and faster growth rate.[43]

By the mid-1950s the state in Western Europe controlled all postal communications, telephone services, nearly all radio and television stations, the central banks, the railways, more than half of the scheduled airlines, most of Europe's electricity generation and distribution, as well as large segments of the mining and steel industries. The state accounted for 100 percent of coal mining in Britain and Italy; 98 percent in France, 60 percent in Holland, but only 26 percent in West Germany. In Austria, government owned 95 percent of the iron and steel industry, in Norway 66 percent. The Italian state oversaw 80 percent of pig iron, and 50 percent of steel production. West Germany, by contrast had only 5 percent of industry in state ownership, while Great Britain veered to and fro. (The steel industry was nationalized by Labour in 1951, denationalized by the Tories in 1953, and re-nationalized by Labour in 1967.) Governments likewise held a considerable stake in the Western European metal processing industries, and in the production of crude oil. The state had also acquired a minor share in manufacturing industries, for instance in the making of electrical equipment (in Austria and Italy), transport equipment (Italy and France), and automobiles (France).[44] Overall, the planners insisted on what they regarded as national priorities for the purpose of securing "stability, growth and balance" within their own borders.[45]

How far did the state contribute to, or retard Western Europe's astonishing recovery? The answer is hard to give, for many reasons. Economics is not an

[43]John Pinder, "Europe in the world economy," in Cipolla, *The Fontana Economic History of Europe*, v. 1, pp. 343–53.

[44]Dewhurst, *Europe's Needs and Resources*, table on p. 439 for detailed percentages.

[45]Vernon, *Big Business and the State*, p. 8.

exact science. Economists – like historians, political scientists, and anthropologists – are good at giving *ex post facto* explanations: but economists are no better than their colleagues in other disciplines at short-term or long-term forecasting – either as regards the fate of individual industries or of entire countries. If it were otherwise, good economists would be multibillionaires, having successfully applied their predictive skills to the operations of the stock exchange, instead of lecturing to students at moderate salaries. The economists' inability to turn their discipline into an exact science is not surprising given the complexity of their subjects matter, and – in a wider sense – the complexity of human motivation. No economist can create controlled laboratory conditions. Nowhere in the West did the free market work without let or hindrance; conversely, state enterprise always worked within a wider setting influenced by market factors both in the official and also in the "second economy." Large private corporations worked hand in glove with ministries. State-owned enterprises sometimes functioned like efficient private firms, given a competitive market situation. Throughout Western Europe a variety of mixed economies operated, with many common features.

The record is thus mixed. State intervention was uniformly benign whenever the state succeeded in stabilizing the monetary exchange rate regime – and malign when the state failed to do so. States, overall, did less well when they turned into entrepreneurs, and directly ran economic enterprises. No European state planner, for example, understood the future importance of the computer industry, despite the pioneering work done in Britain in designing complex machines to break German codes during World War II. The development of the computer industry during the 1960s turned out to be essentially an achievement of American private enterprise.[46] The steel industry, a key institution from the planners' perspective, had a very different history. All major Western countries substantially increased their steel output during the two decades that followed World War II. In this sense they were all successful, no matter what system of ownership they chose to adopt. On the other hand, the Westerners' relative share in world production diminished during this period.[47] The exceptions – apart from Japan – were West Germany, which almost managed to hold its own, together with the Benelux countries, and Italy which registered a small increase. (The Italian success was attained in part through a state corporation, *Istituto per la Ricostruzione Industriale* in that body's most creative period.) The Austrian state was a major entrepreneur. Nevertheless, Austria could replicate cost of the advantages of competition, because it was linked to a larger West European market at fixed exchange rates with free trade. As long as the Austrians avoided subsidies to loss-making industries, as

---

[46]Nicolas Jéquier, "Computers," in Vernon, ed., *Big Business and the State*, pp. 195–228.

[47]Total steel production, in thousand tonnes, in 1952 stood as follows: US: 84,522, West Germany: 18,629, Britain: 16,681, France: 10,867, Benelux: 8,753, Japan: 6,988, Italy: 3,535. Between 1952 and 1972, the US share of world production dropped from 39.7 to 19.3 per cent. West Germany: 8.8 to 7.0 percent. Britain 7.8 to 4.1 percent. France 5.1 to 3.8 percent. Benelux stayed at 4.1 percent. Italy rose from 1.7 to 3.1 percent and Japan from 3.3 to 15.5 percent. J. E. S. Hayward, "Steel," in Vernon, ed., *Big Business and the State*, p. 256.

long as decision making in their state-owned enterprises remained decentralized and disciplined by the world market, they did quite well. The Benelux countries relied on privately owned firms. They encouraged mergers between these corporations to such an extent that each country's steel production came to be dominated by a single firm. The Germans stuck to private enterprise, heavily dependent on major banks, and for a time did well. So did France which – by dint of generous state aid to the steel industry – secured massive concentration and modernization without state ownership.[48] A part of the French motor car industry passed into public ownership, but nationalized factories had to compete with private enterprise – with the effect that both Renault and Citroen turned out cars of high quality.

Great Britain did not do nearly as well in comparative terms. State intervention failed to cure the existing ills of the steel industry, and the British kept falling behind. (The financial losses incurred by the nationalized coal industry and railways derived in part from the government's commitment to keep down prices as part of an anti-inflationary program.) But even Britain's competitors on the European Continent came to face serious problems. Market restriction agreements tended to perpetuate unprofitable and under-used capacity at the expense of the most efficient firms. Direct and indirect involvement of government in industry reinforced the tendency to prevent market forces from operating – the more so since public servants were even more likely to see themselves as champions of an assumed national interest than those traditional family firms that had once provided Europe's great steel masters.

Overall, public enterprise thus failed to come up to expectations, and by the early 1960s the first postwar wave of nationalizations in Europe had come to an end. Nationalization of this type had largely involved taking entire sectors into public ownership or trying to salvage failing concerns in the private sector. Many of these nationalized firms had failed to show profits at all, or at least profits in any way comparable to those secured in the private sector. The substitution of public for private ownership had not improved worker-management relations, and had not inspired what so many nationalizers had hoped for – a new ethos in the operation of public enterprise.[49]

Government also took a hand in regional development. This entailed the use of official funds for three separate tasks: to promote a new prosperity in overseas colonies (as envisaged for instance in the British Colonial Development and Welfare Acts passed from 1940 onward); to support new industries in depressed areas at home (advocated in Britain by the Barlow report, 1941); and to revive entire regions such as Corsica, Sardinia, and the Italian South along Europe's own backward agricultural periphery.

After World II, both France and Belgium embarked on massive state investment in their African colonies for the purpose of developing their respective possessions, and shoring up colonial rule, as did the British. In

---

[48] J. E. S. Hayward, "Steel," in Vernon, ed., *Big Business and the State*, p. 257.
[49] Stuart Holland, "Europe's new public enterprises," in Vernon, ed., *Big Business and the State*, p. 25.

1947, for example, the British started an extensive official project to grow peanuts ('groundnuts' in British terms) in Tanganyika (now Tanzania). The Labour government then in power thereby hoped to provide Britain with ample supplies of fats and oil at a time when these commodities were scarce all over the world. The project also owed a great deal to an intense commitment to colonial development, by now a secular doctrine of improvement that had absorbed all the moral fervor that had once gone into the evangelization of Africa.

Other considerations influenced the project. These included respect for the supposed triumphs of Soviet mechanized agriculture on collectivized farms; a widespread though ill-founded contempt for the assumed inefficiency of small-scale agricultural enterprise; a commitment to the massive use of outside capital for the purpose of breaking the cycle of poverty that supposedly kept backward countries in perpetual misery. There was also the legacy of wartime experience of large-scale planning, and mechanization. The massive deployment of tractors would win the battle against hunger, just as the massive deployment of British tanks had vanquished the Germans in the battle of El Alamein.

Money was no object, and by 1949 some £20,000,000 had been spent. The project produced many official jobs, but few nuts; by 1950 the planners realized that mechanized production on the scale envisaged would not pay. Had the British simply improved transport facilities, and offered adequate monetary incentives alike to white planters and African cultivators, they would have been able to purchase all the nuts they wanted – a safe assumption, given previous experience with groundnut crops in Africa. But the prestige of government-initiated enterprise was by now so firmly established that even the great losses incurred by the British Overseas Food Corporation could not dim the reputation of publicly financed enteprise.[50]

Much more successful was the so-called Gezira scheme in what was then the Anglo-Egyptian Sudan. Originating in 1925, this project rested on the state and private tenants, and embraced an area of roughly 1,000,000 acres. The state provided irrigation works; the Sudan Gezira Board (originally a private syndicate nationalized in 1950) supervised transport, cotton ginning, and marketing. The proceeds were divided between the board (which obtained 20 percent, the state (which received 40 percent), and the tenants (who likewise got 40 percent). The tenants (29,000 by 1952) boasted of a much higher living standard than most of their neighbors; they also had some stake in managing their own affairs through village councils and a tenants organization elected by the project participants.

The project did well financially, but it was not without flaws. As Lord Hailey, one of the great proconsular scholars of the British empire, pointed

[50]For a summary, see L. H. Gann and Peter Duignan, *Burden of Empire: An Appraisal of Western Colonialism in Africa South of the Sahara*. Stanford Cal., Hoover Institution Press, 1967, pp. 268–9, and for details Alan Wood, *The Groundnut Affair*. London, The Bodley Head, 1950. For a general pespective, see Peter Duignan and L. H. Gann, eds, *The Economics of Colonialism*. Cambridge, Cambridge University Press, 1975.

out "the tenantry seem to have lacked that sense of ownership which can create so powerful a personal interest in the improvement of the land. The necessity of concentrating on the efficiency of the economic crop has to some extent prevented the emergence of a body of self-reliant peasant farmers with a balanced husbandry."[51] Contrary to a widespread misapprehension, moreover, relative economic prosperity did not inhibit political radicalism. On the contrary, it was precisely among the Gezira tenants that the Sudanese Communist Party found some of its most loyal adherents.

Far more important still were the efforts made by the Italians to use state agencies for the purpose of developing the Italian South (paralleled on a smaller scale by French projects for the development of regions such as Corsica and Britanny). In 1951 Italy set up the *Cassa per il Mezzogiorno* (Fund for the South) with a capital of 1,2880 billion lire equalling about $2 billion at current exchange rates, to be spent for the period 1950 to 1962. Italian planners thereby hoped to reduce unemployment in the South, provide jobs for new entries into the labor force, and reduce the enormous economic gap that divided North from South. Money went into a great variety of projects. These included investment in enterprises in which the government had traditionally taken an important part – schools, public utilities, and the like. In addition the state tried to improve agriculture by land reform, irrigation projects, soil reclamation, road building, the construction of water works and similar improvements. It promoted railway building, electrical undertakings, and a variety of associated enterprises. Up to 1957, the planners mainly stressed farming. Thereafter they gave much more emphasis to manufacturing through so-called industrial "growth points." There was heavy state investment in oil, natural gas petrochemical industries, steel, and other ventures.

Again it is not easy to draw up a balance sheet. Overall, the Italian economy did superbly well. (Between 1950 and 1959, the Italian gross national product rose by 65 percent; Italians could pride themselves on a growth rate exceeded only by Japan (103 percent), and West Germany (81 percent). State intervention was kept in bounds as long as liberals such as Luigi Enaudi had a say in politics. Italian state enterprise – unlike most other state-run ventures in Western Europe – entered a wide range of service and manufacturing industries, as well as basic industries. But Italian planners did not intend to eliminate the market mechanism; state holding companies did not necessarily hold a majority of the stock within the corporations that the state helped to finance. Public corporations aimed at making profits.

Luigi Enaudi (1874–1961) was one of modern Italy's most important economic theoreticians. His liberal economic assumptions attacked both fascism and communism and in 1943 he fled from Italy to Switzerland. After Mussolini's fall, he returned, and became president of the Banca d'Italia. A Liberal member of the constituent assembly in 1956, he served as deputy premier, under Alcide de Gasperi, and in this capacity

[51]Lord Hailey, *African Survey: A Study of Problems Arising in Africa South of the Sahara*, revised 1956. Oxford, Oxford University Press, 1957, p. 1013.

> *stabilized the lira. He was elected president of the Republic in 1948, and at the expiration of his term returned to academic life. In 1960 he published the first of his monumental eight-volume series* Cronache Economiche e Politiche di un Trentennio *(1960–1965).*

Nevertheless, there were many problems. The state kept expanding its hold – especially in the 1960s. (The share of public investment in the South rose from 27 percent between 1959 and 1962 to 56 percent in 1972.) Public enterprise aroused innumerable complaints: inadequate control of investment projects, failure properly to evaluate management efficiency, recurrent deficits. Managerial recruitment became subject to political patronage, as jobs tended to go to militants within the major political parties. The result was a "bureau-cratized entrepreneurship ill suited to technical innovation."[52] State control of public enterprises suffered because the administration as a whole was slow. Public enterprise came to serve as an instrument for financing political parties through an elaborate system of local contracts and favors – all the more so since Italian parties lacked adequate revenue of their own (except for the Italian Communist Party). Given the weaknesses of the Italian state, public corporations dealt with the central administration from a position of excessive strength. In fact the Italians would have done better to reform the existing state machine, instead of further adding to its tasks – a failing not confined to Italy.

To sum up, there was progress in the South – both in the "official" and the "second" economy. But the much discussed imbalance between North and South continued. Far from declining, labor migration from South to North accelerated. Many reasons contributed to the planners' comparative failure. The Italian South was no more a homogeneous region than were the other parts of Italy. (There were considerable differences between Calabria on the one hand and Sicily on the other; Sicily itself had sub-regional distinctions.) State planning was ill-suited to take account of varied local conditions. Nor could it cope with psychological factors, with "pre-industrial" attitudes that continued to beset the South – including widespread upper-class disdain for technicians, merchants, and manual laborers. Well-meaning reforms moreover, as always, had unintended consequences. The land reforms of the 1950s benefited small farmers and increased their numerical and electoral strength in a manner welcome to the Christian Democratic Party. But small farmers often failed to modernize their methods – all the more so since protectionist tariffs tended to favor the inefficient. Whatever its real and supposed achievements, state intervention failed to achieve what the planners had aimed for – the

[52]Giselle Podbielski, *Italy: Development and Crisis in the Post-War Economy.* Oxford, Clarendon Press, 1971, pp. 132–53. Also see Epicarmo Corbino, *Cinquant' Anni di Vita Economia Italiana, 1915–1965.* v. 2. Naples, Edizione Scientifiche Italiane, 1966. Fabio Luca Cavazza and Stephen R. Graubard, *Il Caso Italiano.* Milan, Garzanti, 1974. For comparative studies, see Kevin Allen and M. C. Maclennan, *Regional Problems and Policies in Italy and France.* London, Allen and Unwin, 1970. Josselyn Hennessy, Vera Lutz, Guiseppe Scimone, *Economic 'Miracles:' Studies in the Resurgence of the French, German and Italian Economies Since the Second World War.* London, André Deutsch, 1964.

economic unification of Italy and the modernization of the South. These changes would have to wait until the 1980s, by which time Italy had turned into one of the great economic powerhouses of Europe.

Government, science, and technology

After World War II, the states of the Atlantic Community all came to believe that public and private funding should be invested in scientific education and research. The successes of wartime research in providing military weapons had convinced planners that science and technology could produce a rational world and guarantee material well-being for all citizens – at least of the developed countries. Scientific and technological progress, it was widely believed, would lead to economic development. (Similar optimism had prevailed after World War I.)

In World War II enormous sums had been spent for research and development – not just by government, but also by private concerns. Science was mobilized; government and industry cooperated on a massive scale, and the results were staggering. Not only did the US and Great Britain provide most of the equipment to fight the war and to feed the Allied nations, but fundamental discoveries were made in antibiotics, radar, computers, atomic weaponry, chemicals, plastics, and so on. Government and science and technology had triumphed. The leaders of the postwar era believed that such cooperation would also bring economic development. National science planners were in power, and worked not only with governments but with a host of new international organizations such as FAO, OECD, UNESCO, and WHO.

The reconstruction of Europe took about five years before real economic growth was possible. But starting in 1950, new techniques offered the chance to expand the economy. Different countries chose different priorities. The Germans and Italians concentrated on chemical, electrical and engineering industries; the British and French worked on aerospace, computers and nuclear power. Universities and research institutes at government insistence expanded and produced more graduate students. Scores of new discoveries were made in almost all fields, perhaps most dramatically in agriculture, medicine, and electronics. National science boards were established in all industrialized states. Government intervened mostly through controls, grants, manpower planning, and nationalization. The goal was better health and an increase in material well-being for the populace. The ten years from 1950 to 1960 saw great developments, stimulated at first in the US by the Korean war (1950–3). Research budgets grew from 15 to 20 percent each year in the United States. Such efforts stimulated West Europe to follow suit.

The dreams of the 1950s were not fully realized. Industrial investment, manpower plans, and government plans were often simplistic. Government intervention failed to improve things in many cases, and plans and nationalization seldom brought much economic development; nor did big government research budgets for science and technology produce sustained economic progress. Private industries continued to invent and to develop more than did universities and government research. Planning did best in France and worst in Great Britain. The research and development programs too often concentrated on failing industries; government never seemed to understand the major role that management must play in successful economic innovations.

While scientists and technologists had certainly gained more prestige and power during the war and after, they also began in the 1960s to be held accountable for their discoveries. Public skepticism grew; many thought scientific planning had failed. The belief that rational scientific organization of knowledge would lead to perfect societies where economic benefits would be equitably shared was ended. Government still provided vast sums for universities and research institutes for theoretical and applied research. But hope declined that science and technology would dominate society for the better.

Britain and Germany: a case study

What of the most important question of all, the state's performance as planner and entrepreneur with regard to national economies as a whole? The answer is not easy to give. All Western European states – and, to a minor extent, even the US – had become mixed economies, though the power of the state varied considerably from one to another. All had planning mechanisms of some kind. No Western state, on the other hand, possessed a fully planned economy – not even France where indicative planning, in one critic's view, turned into a "euphemism for self-fulfilling prophecy," and where practice never conformed to theory.[53]

Trans-national comparisons moreover are difficult to make, for many reasons. The accuracy and comprehensiveness of statistics differ from country to country.[54] Global statistics conceal differential performance between different sectors of the economy, and within them. There are special problems involved in looking at different national economies as if they were horses in a race, their relative speed being assessed by their respective growth. One of the difficulties bears on simple arithmetic, often ignored in comparisons between the growth rates of large and small economies. An imaginary example may illustrate the point. The empire of Bigland – for the sake of argument – has a gross national product of 1,000 gold barrels. The principality of Tinyland has a gross national product of only 100 gold barrels. The difference between their respective gross national products thus amounts to 900 gold barrels. Bigland's gross national product, over a given period grows by 100 percent, reaching 2,000 gold barrels. Tinyland's gross national product, by contrast, augments at a rate of 400 percent, attaining a total of 400 gold barrels at the end of our period. The differences between Bigland's and Tinyland's gross national product now amounts to 1,600 gold barrels instead of 900 gold barrels. In statistical terms, the gap between Bigland's and Tinyland's economy has

[53]Sanche de Gramont, *The French: Portrait of a People*. New York, Putnam, 1969, p. 441.
[54]See for instance P. T. Bauer, *Dissent on Development: Studies and Debates in Development Economics*; Cambridge, Mass., Harvard University Press, 1972, *passim*.

actually increased, despite Tinyland's far more spectacular development. This simple arithmetical consideration should be kept in mind by those who claim that the gap between rich and poor countries keeps increasing at the poor nations' expense.

Despite such difficulties, it is possible to make comparisons of a rough and ready kind between countries of approximately equal size and economic status. West Germany and Great Britain may serve as convenient examples. Their economic assumptions were dissimilar, but their physical structure had much in common. West Germany had put its trust after World War II in *Soziale Markwirtschaft* based on a modified form of *laissez-faire*, inspired by the Freiburg school of economics. Britain relied on Keynesian economics that allotted a much greater role to the state. The two countries resembled one another in physical size, population, the number of persons in the total labor force, and the percentage of workers in industry. They had reached comparable levels of economic development. How did they fare?

> *West Germany's area was 95,700 square miles, Britain's 93,000. West Germany's population in 1961 was 53.5 million; Britain's 52.75 million. The working population respectively stood at 21.3 million and 24.9 million (1962). The percentage of workers in industry amounted to 37 percent in both countries. For a detailed comparison, see Hennessy, Lutz, Scimone,* Economic Miracles, *especially pp. 16–17.*

In theory, all advantages lay with Britain. By the mid-1950s, she still boasted Western Europe's largest gross national product, and also the highest gross national product per capita ($1,152 in 1955, at European relative price weight, compared with $975 in West Germany, $969 in France, $464 in Italy, though $2,310 in the US.) True enough, the British advantage may not have been as great as these figures indicate. Comparative gross national product figures contain many flaws. Even a casual traveller in Europe during the mid-1950s was struck by the way in which British austerity continued to contrast with the apparent prosperity of Western Germany and France. Nevertheless, the British were still in the front rank. Britain's public services commanded respect; her political system enjoyed a much greater degree of legitimacy than West Germany, France, or Italy – burdened respectively by memories of the Third Reich, of Vichy, or Fascism. The "second economy" was probably smaller than in any other major European country. Britain had received more Marshall aid than any other country in the world. British cities had endured much less damage in World War II than the cities of Germany. Above all, Britain had emerged as a victor from World War II. It is difficult even to imagine how Britain would have fared had she lost – as Germany did – one-third of her total territory, if the remainder had been separated by a zonal boundary, and if a southern British rump state had been forced to cope with millions of penniless refugees into the bargain. In the event, Britain during the 1950s had one of the lowest growth rates in Western Europe, much lower than West Germany's. She continually lagged behind West Germany in the rise of productivity per head of working population and in a variety of other economic indicators.[55]

Britain's comparable failure was not a matter of public disquiet when "the low growth rate was a matter of concern only to sophists, calculators, and economists."[56] After all the gross national product continued to augment until the mid-1970s, a point all too easily ignored by those who spoke of the "British disease."[57] Many privately owned British industries remained efficient – including agriculture, banking, retailing, insurance. Even public enterprise did well in some sectors (for instance in the subsequent exploitation of North Sea oil). Nevertheless, the British had the lowest growth rate among the major industrial countries. The consequences were far-reaching. There was a striking shift in Western Europe's balance of power, the most important change in Western European economic history since World War II. Britain's relative decline continued until by the 1980s her gross national product ranged well behind that of West Germany and France, destined to slip into fourth place behind Italy. The British mood of confidence gave way to a widespread sense of despondency, first of all expressed in the literature produced by the "angry young men" of the 1950s, and later in economic studies with titles such as *The Economic Decline of Britain, The British Disease, The Stagnant Society,* and even *Suicide of a Nation.*[58]

What had gone wrong? Some explanations hinge on Britain's historical legacy. According to this interpretation, Great Britain had already experienced a lengthy decline both in industrial, managerial, and military terms ever since the end of the last century. By World War I, when the Royal Navy still ruled the seas, the British fleet had become inferior in tactics and technology to the Kaiser's *Hochseeflotte*; its commanding admiral wielded a "flawed cutlass." Britain's naval troubles merely reflected more deep-seated problems affecting industries, scientific education, and military leadership as a whole – thus the thesis in Correlli Barnett's fascinating book *The Swordbearers* and other works.[59] After World War II the British politicians, Labour and Tory alike, merely took over a decaying firm.

The argument, however, seriously overstates Britain's weaknesses. The

[55]For a detailed tabulation, see Hennessy, Lutz, Scimone, *Economic Miracles,* ibid.

[56]Samuel Brittan, "How English is the English sickness?" in *Washington Quarterly,* v. 3, no, 4, Autumn 1980 p. 151.

[57]For a detailed appraisal, see "The British economy since 1945," *Economic Progress Report,* no. 100, London, July 1978. Alec Cairncross, *Years of Recovery: British Economic Policy 1945–1951.* New York, Methuen, 1985.

[58]David Coates and John Hilliard, eds, *The Economic Decline of Britain: The Debate between Left and Right.* Brighton, Wheatsheaf, 1986. G. C. Allen, *The British Disease.* London, Institute for Economic Affairs, 1976, Michael Shanks, *The Stagnant Society.* Harmondsworth, Penguin Books, 1972. Arthur Koestler, *Suicide of a Nation: An Enquiry into the State of Britain Today.* New York, Macmillan, 1964, W. Beckerman, ed., *Slow Growth in Britain: Causes and Consequences.* Oxford, Clarendon Press, 1979. Alan Sked, Britain's *Decline: Problems and Perspectives.* New York, Basil Blackwell, 1987.

[59]Correlli Barnett, *The Swordbearers.* New York, Morrow, 1964; *The Collapse of British Power.* New York, Morrow, 1972; *The Pride and the Fall.* New York, Free Press, 1987.

British economy grew at a remarkable pace during the three decades preceding World War I (albeit more slowly than the US and German economies, which started later and operated from a larger base). British production of coal, iron, and steel rapidly expanded; so did British manufacturers.[60] The Royal Navy learned from its mistakes and it had been the Kaiser's prized fleet that fell prey to boredom, a sense of defeat, and ultimate mutiny, not the Royal Navy. Britain emerged from World War I as the world's greatest and most modern military power, with the largest tank force (pioneered by Britain), the largest air force, and the most powerful navy. The greatest victories in World War I had been those won by Britain in 1918.[61] Far from being economically decadent, Britain made important technical and industrial advances during the 1920s and 1930s, the supposed locust years of Labourite folklore.[62] After World War II Britain continued to occupy an important place as an industrial and scientific leader and, in theory, should have achieved a predominant role in Western Europe.

One explanation for Britain's troubles hinges on what might be called the inevitability of "rustbelt degeneration." Regions that take the lead in traditional industries such as steel and coal are supposedly bound to suffer as once-successful enterprises become obsolescent over time. Britain – especially Northern England and Scotland – having pioneered these older industries, was likely to slide economically as steelmaking, coal mining, and similar ventures were overtaken by industrial old age. This argument again is open to doubt. Of all European countries, the Grand Duchy of Luxemburg had concentrated most heavily on traditional heavy industries. But by the latter part of the 1980s Luxemburg had successfully readjusted and presented to the world a minor miracle – a small country with negligible unemployment, the only balanced budget within the EEC, a stable currency, and not a cent of foreign debt.[63] Luxemburg had successfully switched to an economy dominated by trade and services. So, in a somewhat different fashion, did the state of Massachusetts in the US – in short, there is nothing inevitable about "rustbelt decline."

Other critics blamed aspects of the class system in Great Britain – a supposedly archaic military–diplomatic establishment, the civil servants, the workers. Britain, for example, carried a much heavier burden of armaments than West Germany: hence she fell behind in the economic race. But there was no necessary correlation between the level of defense expenditure and the relative economic progress made by the various Western countries. Britain

[60]According to figures cited by A. J. P. Taylor, *The Struggle for Mastery in Europe 1848–1981*. Oxford, Clarendon Press, 1954, pp. xxix–xxxiii, the increases between 1880 and 1914 (in million tons) was as follows: coal: 149 to 268, pig iron: 7.8 to 11, steel: 1.3 to 6.5. Between 1880 and 1913, manufacturing producton went up from 54 to 100 (1913 being 100).

[61]For a discussion of war myths, see John Terraine, *The Smoke and the Fire: Myths and Anti-Myths of War, 1861–1945*. London, Sidgwick and Jackson, 1980.

[62]Sidney Pollard and David Crossley, *The Wealth of Britain*. London, Batsford, 1968, pp. 249–72.

[63]*Europe*, June 1987, pp. 9–10.

was indeed the highest military spender. In 1955, 8.2 percent of the British gross national product went on defense. By contrast, Spain at the time devoted only 2.2 percent of its gross national product to the military and naval establishment – yet Spain did least well in economic terms.

Other critics have cited the ineffectiveness of the British senior civil servants. Gentlemen educated at Oxford and Cambridge, untutored in economics or technology, addicted to classical studies, the cult of the amateur, and the pleasures of clubmanship, were supposedly unfitted to administer a modern economy. But these same civil servants were highly efficient in running Hong Kong, a colony that achieved an extraordinary degree of economic success through a competitive market economy based on free trade – under the most unfavorable physical conditions imaginable. (Hong Kong was without any kind of natural resources, an already overcrowded island that absorbed untold numbers of refugees from the Chinese mainland into the bargain.) Neither should all the blame be laid at the British workers' doorstep. According to superannuated Tory clubmen, it was the working man – idle, prone to strike at the shop steward's slightest nod – who was to blame for Britain's ills. But during the crucial 1950s, Britain did not suffer particularly from labor disturbances, when compared to the US or other major industrial countries of Western Europe.

What of the argument that West Germany started almost from scratch in 1945; hence, unlike Britain, the Germans had no way to go but up? This proposition is arguable up to 1955, by which time West Germany had recovered. But thereafter the West German economy continued to grow at a much faster rate than Britain's. An alternative explanation points to the huge number of refugees and expellees (13,000,000 in all flocked into West Germany between 1945 and 1960). These men and women supposedly supplied West Germany with docile, cheap, skilled and unskilled labor, and thereby permitted industry to pull ahead. It is true that they were an economic asset, but they were also an economic burden. They required housing, care, and social services; had no refugees come to West Germany the Federal Republic might have been able to devote more funds to improving its industrial equipment and the conditions of its indigenous work force. (In 1950, the refugees received 41 percent of all social security benefits – more than twice their share relative to population.)

Neither is it correct to say that the German workers were more exploited than their British confrères, or that their trade unions were weaker than British unions. (By 1954, West Germany actually spent more on social security benefits than Britain.) The German trade unions had become more powerful than they had been under the Weimar Republic. (During the republican era, there had been some 200 trade unions; after World War II, they united in the *Deutsche Gerwerkschaftsbund* (*DGB*) which included most German workers, except the clerical employees and civil servants. The workers received important con cessions, including the right of co-management in the iron and steel industry.)

What, then, did go wrong in Britain? As we see it, Britain's relative weakness derived from two separate, though not unrelated, sources: an accumulation of existing flaws, and the general policy. Overall, the Germans were superior in technical education. (In 1957, for example, the University of Manchester rejected a proposal for a chair in machine tool technology; a similar chair had been created in Germany as early as 1904, but Manchester nevertheless felt that the subject had not yet proved its academic respectability. A chair was only created in 1961, and filled with a refugee from Germany.)[64] Even more seriously perhaps, the British lagged behind the Germans in the technical education of managers, and of foremen and supervisors – the non-commissioned officers within the industrial army. British trade unionists were more restrictionist and did not work as hard as their German comrades; the unions were more divided, far more likely to engage in demarcational disputes, and more frightened of technological change that might bring job losses. The British made a major investment in council (public) housing with controlled rents; such tenants were more reluctant to move from one city to another in search of jobs, and the labor force was less flexible as a result. Entrepreneurial talent overall enjoyed less esteem in Britain than in Germany. (An outstanding British civil servant or academic was far more likely to gain a knighthood or similar honor than a successful manufacturer or trader.)

But far more important, in our opinion, was the role of the state. The British were more highly taxed than the Germans. (During the 1960s, income tax provided over half of Britain's revenue, compared to only about one third of West Germany's.)[65] Government expenditure per head of the popuation was much higher (in 1955 per capita expenditure amounted to $302 in Britain, $272 in France, $216 in West Germay, $110 in Italy). The British saved less. The gross domestic capital formation was much lower as a percentage of the gross national product in Great Britain than in her major competitors.

Above all, British nationalized (as well as numerous privately managed) industries failed to meet the planners' expectations. The country went through several phases of nationalization. All were pursued for reasons of domestic policy; all were taken up without regard for the experience of Continental countries such as Austria or Sweden. The British maintained loss-making industries; they sporadically resorted to wage and price control. They subsidized firms willing to start factories in decaying rustbelts. The nationalization policies lacked insistency; they created a climate of uncertainty. Public management left much to be desired, as did management in many privately owned enterprises. Britain thereby contrasted not only with West Germany, but also with social democratic Sweden. The Swedes developed an elaborate system of welfare benefits supported by high taxes on personal income and on personal consumption. But the Swedes kept their hands off the industrial machine; ownership and control was left in private hands, subject to the discipline of

[64]Wolfgang Mock, *Technische Intelligenz im Exil: Vertreibung und Emigration Deutschsprachiger Ingenieure nach Grossbritannien 1933 bis 1945*. Düsseldorf, Verlag, 1986, p. 157.

[65]In 1955 gross domestic capital formation in Britain stood at 16.3 per cent of the gross national product. Corresponding figures were as follows in other major industrial countries (in percent): France: 17.7, Italy: 21.6, West Germany: 25.7. Dewhurst, *Europe's Needs*, table on p. 472. For government expenditure per capita and distribution, see Dewhurst, table on p. 407.

free competition. Nor did the Swedes devote much money to the support of loss-making industries – at least until the late 1970s. Sweden remained an industrial state of world class – Volvo cars stood out as international status symbols of excellence. A substantial share of Swedish welfare state expenditure moreover went into an excellent system of general and technical education. British planners would have been well advised to learn from the Swedish example.

To sum up, in attempting to account for Britain's relative decline, we primarily blame the misplaced role of the state. Not that the state did universally badly as an entrepreneur, but far too much was expected of it, both at home and abroad. Having been trained in the classics rather than in modern languages, British policy makers cannot justly be censured for failing to read in the original the works of foreign economists such as Ehrhard, Eucken, or Enaudi. They might however have profited from a more detailed study of their own greatest economic thinker, Adam Smith, whose magisterial observations on state planning and state enterprise may serve as a caution:

> Princes, however, have frequently engaged in many other mercantile projects, and have been willing, like private persons, to mend their fortunes by becoming adventurers in the common branches of trade. They have scarce ever succeeded. The profusion with which the affairs of princes are always managed, renders it almost impossible that they should. The agents of a prince regard the wealth of their master as inexhaustible; are careless at which price they buy; are careless at what price they sell; are careless at what expense they transport his goods from one place to another. Those agents frequently live with the profusion of princes, and sometimes too, in spite of that profusion, and by a proper method of making up their accounts, acquire the fortunes of princes.[66]

ENERGY AND INDUSTRY

Coal, iron, and steel formed the tripod that had sustained industrial might since the eighteenth century until oil largely replaced coal in the late 1950s. Between them the colliery, the steel mill, and the railway marshalling yard symbolized industrial greatness. Such had been the assumptions shared alike by Alfred Krupp and Lenin. Such were the assumptions that widely continued to guide planners after World War II. Coal mining, the steel industry, and great steel-consuming manufacturers such as shipyards and car factories employed great numbers of workmen, were tempting to unionize, and easy to control on a national scale. Their place in industrial history, and in its future, was apt to be overestimated accordingly. From the beginnings of the industrial

[66]Adam Smith, *An Inquiry into the Nature and Causes of the Wealth of Nations*. New York, Modern Library, 1937, p. 771.

revolution, the light industries and the services, such as banking, wholesaling, retailing, transport and insurance, played an essential part, but the importance of heavy industry was all too easily forgotten by the 1980s, when the heavy industries in the Western world had largely become the politicians' headache and the ecologists' despair.

Fuels

The postwar Atlantic Community became a massive user of oil, gas and coal as industrial development expanded and as people became able to afford better heating, electric household conveniences such as refrigerators and air conditioning, electric washers and dryers. But in the rush to increase farm yields much harm was done to the land, rivers and sea coasts of the world. Coal dust blackened cities; car fumes created smog; fertilizers harmed the soil; pesticides poisoned good bugs as well as bad, water sources and wildlife.

The fight against environmental degradation was not, of course, new. The struggle had begun in the middle of the last century, when Victorian "improvers" and their opposite numbers on the Continent began to engage the state in campaigns for the amelioration of municipal health and sanitation. (The first law to deal with air pollution was the Smoke Nuisance (Metropolis) Act of 1853.) The Americans pioneered the creation of national parks. (Yellowstone National Park opened in 1872; thereafter the movement spread to all major industrial countries in the Western world.) From the turn of the present century, the German *Länder* had initiated legislation for the "protection of nature" (*Naturschutz*). The first comprehensive *Reich* law, oddly enough, centered on the protection of birds (*Reichsvogelschutzgesetz*, 1908.) Initially, the environmental lobbies had derived their main support from the traditional right (the "huntin', shootin', fishin'" set in Britain), and from rural romantics (including the youth movement in Germany). From the 1960s environmental issues became linked, above all, to progressive politics – symbolized in 1962 by the publication of *Silent Spring* by Rachel Carson, a book as influential for the environmental movement in the US as *Uncle Tom's Cabin* had been for the anti-slavery movement. In the US and Western Europe public authorities led the way, supported by private industries with a stake in pollution control devices, and urged on by a network of unofficial organizations (such as the World Wildlife Fund, 1961 – later renamed the World Wide Fund for Nature). There were new efforts to use the resources of industrial technology and science to repair the ravages wrought by industrial technology and science. There were new methods to conserve and restore lands, regulate the disposal of waste and chemicals – albeit only with partial success. The push for economic growth in the 1950s helped to heighten the environmental concerns of the 1960s. Ecology, pollution, conservation, and land-use studies became common terms in the public battle to save the environment and to improve the quality of life in industrial societies.

One of the crucial materials in energy production was coal. Coal (among other uses) forms raw material for a variety of industrial processes. It supplied fuel for fireplaces and furnaces, and power for steam engines. Of course, it had many disadvantages. The conversion of coal into power is by its very nature an inefficient, wasteful, and pollutant process by the standards of more advanced technologies. It was a nonrenewable resource that became progressively harder to exploit. (From the mid-1920s, Western Europe – once a great coal exporter – had begun to develop steadily growing deficits in its energy account.) Coal deposits were unevenly distributed geographically. Coal mining depended on natural conditions to a much greater extent than any manufacturing industry. These conditions varied from coal field to coal field and from colliery to colliery, as seams differed greatly in extent, thickness, cleavage, faulting, inclination, and location relative to existing urban centers or ports. In contrast to oil, coal was expensive to mine and expensive to move.

Coal mining was also a dangerous occupation that threatened the miners' health and lives. Mining created new social cleavages, as miners tended to form isolated communities with their own local cultures; mine workers inclined toward political militance; their work was grim – the kind that traditionally attracted the least favored of immigrants (for instance Polish workers in the collieries of the Ruhr and of Pennsylvania). The use of coal entailed widespread pollution of water and air – an ancient not a modern problem. As a mid-Victorian lament had put it:

> The AIRE below is doubly dyed and damned
> The AIR above, with lurid smoke is crammed
> The ONE flows steaming foul as Charon's Styx
> Its poisonous vapours in the other mix.
> The sable twins the murky town invest –
> By them the skin's begrimed, the lungs oppressed.
> How dear the penalty thus paid for wealth
> Obtained through wasted life and broken health.[67]

The London pea soup fogs that lent romance to old Sherlock Holmes movies were in large measure a product of coal furnaces and coal fires now, for the most part, happily superseded in Great Britain. (In December 1952, London had an infamous fog attack that killed about 4,000 people.) From its beginning, the image of industrial civilization was blackened in the eyes of intellectuals by coal dust.

As industrial skills advanced during the twentieth century, coal encountered competitors – oil, natural gas, and hydroelectric power. (Between 1920 and 1955 the production of solid mineral fuels increased by about 28 percent in Western Europe, whereas the output of hydroelectricity, oil and gas rose by more than 1,000 percent.) From the 1950s onward, nuclear power also entered the lists – greeted at the time with enormous enthusiasm by the advocates of progress, of no matter what political orientation. Nevertheless, coal continued

[67]William Osburn, "A poem read before members of the Leeds Philosophical and Literary Society (1847)," cited in Asa Briggs, *Victorian Cities*. Evanston, Ill., Harper and Row, 1970, p. 139.

to dominate Western Europe's energy supply – so much so that by the mid-1950s even radical changes in the production of other fuels, and the rapid expansion of hydroelectric power, had only slightly lessened its supremacy. As late as 1955, lignite, oil, natural gas, peat, wood, and hydroelectricity between them furnished no more than 16 percent of Western Europe's primary energy production, measured calorifically.[68]

The period after 1955 saw Western Europe switch from coal to oil as the primary source of power. (By 1960, oil provided 32 per cent of Europe's energy needs.) The inability of the European coal industry to supply enough cheap coal for postwar reconstruction hastened the change to oil. Economic development is closely tied to energy supplies and cost. The amount of energy consumption in turn is linked to higher standards of living. Since 1945 Europe has been concerned to ensure a safe, stable supply of power for its people and industry. When coal failed, imported crude oil became the major source of energy. The switch from coal to oil is easily explained – lower prices, and ease of production. Cheap prices meant cheap power, which meant more rapid economic development. Cheap oil then was to spur Europe's rapid growth until 1973.

But coal remained king between 1945 and 1955 though World War II had gravely diminished European coal production. There were shortages everywhere – mine workers had been killed or injured, or had sought less unpleasant jobs. Strikes were common after the war. Pitprops were often unavailable, spare parts hard to get; machinery was run down, and transport widely in disarray. As a result, European coal production outside the Soviet Union had, by 1945, dropped to about two-fifths of its prewar level.[69] (The Ruhr, Europe's greatest coal producer, which had once produced 400,000 tons of coal a day, turned out no more than 25,000 tons.)

The Europeans' overriding problem initially hinged on shortages. During their long autumns and winters, Europeans shivered in poorly heated or unheated homes. Coal-burning electric power plants and locomotives lacked fuel. Industry faced an acute production crisis, made worse by European interdependence on coal. (For instance, the French iron and steel industry heavily relied on German imports, and thus found itself in severe trouble during the harsh winter of 1946–7.) Pessimism was rife. (When the French government formally accepted its great "modernization plan," the prime minister, Félix Gouin, explained that even if the French coal output were to reach its target of 65,000,000 tons in 1950, France would still have to cope with a shortfall of between 20 and 30 million tons a year, if the needs of the "basic" sectors were to be met.)[70]

Europe was saved in part by American coal, even though in terms of

[68]J. Frederick Dewhurst et al., *Europe's Needs and Resources: Trends and Prospects in Eighteen Countries.* New York, Twentieth Century Fund, 1961, pp. 571–2.
[69]Richard Mayne, *The Recovery of Europe: From Devastation to Unity.* New York, Harper and Row, 1970, pp. 31–2.
[70]Alan S. Milward, *The Reconstruction of Western Europe 1945–1951.* London, Methuen, 1984, p. 132.

national income, mining after World War II dropped to a negligible proportion of the US total production. (By 1957, mining accounted for $6.2 billion out of a total $364 billion at current prices, little more than one-tenth of the value allotted to wholesale and retail trade.) Nevertheless, American coal miners played a crucial part in Europe's economic recovery. At the end of World War II US coal miners had the world's highest productivity (5.9 tonnes per man shift in 1948, as against 3 in Canada, and 1.5 in Great Britain.[71] In Europe coal cost $12–15 a ton to produce; in the US, $4–5). American coal exports rapidly increased, reaching a total of 80,000,000 tonnes in 1957.

A great deal of Marshall Plan money went into equipment and modernization of plant, including coal plants. Methods of production improved in a variety of ways, through the large-scale use of loading machinery underground (in which the US led the world), through the introduction of haulage trucks with a higher capacity than had formerly been considered practical, through the use of coal pipelines carrying a mixture of coal and water, and a host of other devices.

As a result, the production of coal kept expanding – even in the US where petroleum rapidly surpassed bituminous coal and lignite in dollar value.[72] Production increases in Western Europe were even more impressive, as Western Europeans during the 1950s invested heavily in coal production.[73] (Between 1952 and 1956, investment in the coal industry in EEC countries amounted to $250 million a year, or $1 for each tonne produced.) By 1955 the EEC countries produced more coal than the US; one out of every three tonnes of coal produced in the world derived from Western Europe. By the late 1950s, the booming economies of Western Europe had completely outstripped the coal industry's ability to produce power. As Europeans became more prosperous, they became increasingly reluctant to work down the mine shafts. Coal mining costs continued to rise, as large-scale investments failed to bring corresponding increases in production. In short, coal mining became unprofitable and oil became cheaper and more readily available.

Coal mining – a major industry with a huge labor force – particularly appealed to those who looked for a solution to industrial problems through public ownership. But year after year, the National Coal Board in Great Britain, the operating agency for the industry nationalized in 1946, continued to lose money, despite substantial new investments. (For instance, high-cost mines continued to operate in South Wales and Scotland, whereas the British should have concentrated on the richer coal mining areas of the Eastern Midlands.

[71]Norman Luxenburg, *Europe Since World War II: The Big Change*. Carbondale, Ill., Southern Illinois University Press, 1979, p. 132.

[72]In 1945, the value of production of bituminous coal, lignite, and Pennsylvania anthracite stood (in million dollars) at 2,092 and the value of petroleum at 2,094. By 1956 corresponding figures amounted to 2,649 and 7,297 respectively. US department of commerce, *Historical Statistics*, p. 350.

[73]World production at the time amounted (in thousands of tonnes) US: 447,577, Great Britain: 225,157, West Germany: 131,811, France (plus the Saar territory): 72,664, Belgium: 29,978, Netherlands: 11,895.

Cross-subsidization at the expense of efficient mines wasted capital, a mistake repeated by the British with regard to other decaying industries such as the Clydeside shipyards.) In France, the annual reports of the *Charbonnages de France*, the government-owned corporation that operated the mining industry, told a similar story. Not that private enterprise did much better. In Germany the greater part of the coal mining industry remained in private hands, but German mines also mostly operated at a loss.

Europe instead became increasingly dependent on imported oil, especially oil produced at first in the US, then in the Middle East, and oil refining turned into a major European industry. The increased use of oil had far-reaching consequences. Industry no longer had to be sited near coal-bearing areas. Energy costs were lower so development was faster. Oil, like coal, provided an essential raw material for many chemical industries; it provided fuel for power plants, automobiles, planes, and ships. Oil encouraged the shipbuilding industry by its need for tankers – a major consideration at a time when shipbuilding remained an important industry both in Western Europe and the US. Oil production in the US increased enormously, and so (oddly enough) did the estimates of proved reserves. (The production of crude oil rose from 1,713,765, in thousands of 42-gallon barrels, in 1945, to 2,617,233 in 1956, while estimated proved reserves went up from 20,826,813 to 30,434,649.) Railways increasingly became electrified or used diesel oil. The use of nuclear power slowly expanded. Coal output, by contrast, declined in every major European country during the 1960s.[74]

Blaming the EEC planners now seems easy in retrospect. They had devoted huge investments to an ageing industry, at a time when oil was making further inroads into the energy markets of the coal producing countries, and when atomic power had become practical for industrial use. (The world's first large-scale atomic power station, Calder Hall in England, began to generate electricity in 1956 – at its peak it could turn out 90,000 kilowatts.) In theory, European planners should have foreseen the impending decline in demand for coal production. In practice, they did not – but neither did academicians such as J. D. Bernal, a leading Marxist-Leninist scientist in Britain, who predicted at the end of the 1950s that coal would be needed on an increasing scale for several decades to come.

European planners could have dismantled the huge apparatus of state direction over the so-called commanding heights of the economy. But the public would never have permitted such a radical solution at the time. (Friedrich von Hayek, one of the great free enterprise theoreticians, was loudly booed when he tried to explain his principles to Austrian industrialists on a visit to his homeland.)[75] The planners were expected to plan, and they did. Their most pressing problems after the war hinged not on the conundrums of

[74]Brian R. Mitchell, *European Historical Statistics: 1750–1975*. London, Macmillan, 1981, pp. 434–6.
[75]Personal information from Kurt Leube, editor (with Chaki Nishiyama) of *The Essence of Hayek*. Stanford, Cal., Hoover Institution Press, 1984.

subsequent abundance but on ever-present shortages. And this problem they solved for a time with remarkable success.

As was stated earlier, the insufficiency of coal supplies in the early 1950s slowed the reconstruction of Europe. The OEEC in carrying out the Marshall Plan sought to solve the problem. Numerous official reports (e.g. the British Harley report, 1956) recognized that although coal was important to Europe, oil imports would have to be increased. As oil and its costs were down, imports kept increasing and Europe's GNP expanded greatly, as did the material well-being of citizens in the Atlantic Community. The increased energy production and use unfortunately led to environmental problems of smoke, pollution and the deterioration of the cities. These were early recognized and at least for coal pollution solved after 1955 – by building higher chimneys, burning cleaner coal and using diesel oil instead. The pollution problems relating to cars and water were not so easily dealt with.

Iron and steel

The story of the iron and steel industry in many ways replicates that of coal. Iron and steel have traditionally enjoyed enormous industrial prestige. *Stahlhart* (steel-hard) turned into a German praise word; "cold steel" came to symbolize the British soldier's prowess with the bayonet. Prince Otto von Bismarck had been proud to be known as the "Iron Chancellor." Josif Dzhugashvili called himself Stalin, the man of steel. A nation's industrial strength could supposedly be measured in terms of its ability to turn out steel ingots – a superstition that made a mistaken and costly appeal to many Third World countries during the age of decolonization. Iron and steel nevertheless formed essential materials whose production – like that of coal – had been dominated by Europe a century ago. Europe, at the end of World War II, suffered from pervasive steel shortages.

Western European steel production recovered however to an astonishing extent. New investment poured into the industry, and as late as 1959 Western Europe once more figured as the world's greatest steel producer, turning out more ingots than either the US or the Soviet Union.[76] The bulk of the European steel industry passed under public ownership, or became subject to an extensive measure of public control – a policy facilitated by the extensive private cartelization undergone by the industry from earlier days, when the ownership of steel mills had already been widely linked to the ownership of coal mines and other associated industries. (Iron and steel became virtually a government monopoly in Austria. It was more than half government owned in Italy, Norway, and Sweden. The British steel industry, nationalized by Labour, was returned to private ownership by a Conservative government in 1953, but still

---

[76]In 1959 production of crude steel, in millions of tons, stood as follows: world total: 302.0, Western Europe: 91.8 (EEC: 63.1, United Kingdom: 20.5. Of the EEC countries West Germany including Saar produced 30.6, France: 15.2) US: 84.8, USSR: 60.0. Dewhurst, *Europe's Needs*, p. 603.

retained a measure of government control. In France and West Germany, the bulk of the industry remained privately owned, but governments wielded considerable influence on steel policies, and public funds were extensively used for development.)[77]

The publicly owned industries nevertheless were but islands within a sea of private enterprise. It was only during the 1970s that state-owned companies gained a truly significant share in manufacturing in Western Europe. The great bulk of investment continued to go into private rather than nationalized firms.[78] The nationalized industries had to compete with suppliers of rival products. Publicly owned corporations had to order machinery, spare parts, services, and supplies from private firms. Moreover nationalized industries remained exposed to public scrutiny – often hostile – in press and parliament. Hence coal and steel were used, and continued to be used, far more effectively in Britain, West Germany, France, and Switzerland than in the Soviet Union and its Warsaw Pact allies.[79] The major steel industries in Western Europe continued to expand their output which went on rising until the late 1960s and early 1970s.

By this time, the traditional steel producers were beginning to lose their accustomed supremacy. For instance, the basic oxygen furnace, first commercially used in Austria, revolutionized production costs. Within Europe, the Netherlands, and, more importantly, Japan outside Europe, promptly installed the more efficient furnace. The US, and to a lesser extent Britain and West Germany, had invested heavily in open-hearth furnaces and were reluctant to scrap existing equipment for the sake of modernization. They lost in the bargain, and by 1964 Japan had become the world's third largest steel producer. Overall, the Western coal, iron, and steel industries fell further and further behind.

Liberal and socialist critics in the past had blamed the private cartels of the coal, iron, and steel industries as a major source of European economic inflexibility. Government intervention, however, did little to correct the resultant faults. While the ECSC arrangements contained provisions for maintaining competition, the national governments wielded sufficient influence to evade the high authority's declared policy. Hence the iron and steel industry, long noted for administering its activities in concert, took in its stride "the existence

---

[77]In West Germany, the federal government, *Länder*, and municipalities between them owned the following percentages of national production: coal: 18, crude iron and steel: 22, lead and zinc: 44, iron ore: 55, electricity: 62, aluminium: 70, gas: 91. Josselyn Hennessey, Vera Lutz, Giuseppe Scimone, *Economic Miracles: Studies in the Resurgence of the French, German and Italian Economies Since the Second World War*. London, André Deutsch, 1964, pp. 38–9. See also R. Joseph Mousen and Kenneth D. Walker, *Nationalized Companies*. New York, McGraw-Hill, 1983.

[78]In 1956, for example, investments within the EEC were distributed as follows (in percentages of the gross national product) West Germany: public: 2,9, private: 19.7. France: 2.1 and 16.0. Italy: 3.2 and 17.6. Netherlands: 3 and 22.2. Belgium: 4.4 and 12.8. *Communauté Economique Européenne, Conferénce Européenne: Progrètechnique et Marché Commun*. Brussels, CEE, 1960, v. 1, p. 248.

[79]For detailed figures see Paul Kennedy, "What Gorbachev is up against," *The Atlantic Monthly*, June 1987, p. 33.

of the new [ECSC] organization and its professed objectives to competition."[80]

In the long run, both European taxpayers and consumers paid a heavy price for policies that all too often resulted in great bureaucratic fiefs, distinguished by excessive productive capacities, excessive public power, and extensive subsidization. The policy makers of the late 1940s and 1950s had of necessity, however, looked at the world through very different spectacles. They initially faced a world beset by shortages. Then came an unparalleled industrial boom that created huge additional demands for coal and steel, which lasted for about a quarter of a century. Industrial prosperity admittedly was uneven in its impact.[81] West Germany and Italy had the highest growth rate, Britain one of the lowest. Nevertheless, in every Western country, manufactures increased to a remarkable extent, accounting for about one-third of the gross national product both of Western Europe and the US.

Consumer goods

The great boom brought a new consumer revolution, that deepened the split between Western and Eastern Europe. In the East consumption remained restricted, linked overwhelmingly to the political requirements of the *nomenclatura* (higher ranks of the party, state, military, and cultural bureaucracy). The consumer revolution depended mainly, though not entirely, on private enterprise. Most of the merchandise that made life easier or more convenient originated from privately owned factories. These operated to meet a large and long pent-up demand. A European or an American, born at the start of World War I, and who survived World War II, would have reached the age of 40 by the mid-1950s. He or she was likely to have married, started a family, and perhaps shouldered a mortgage. He or she would have experienced the shock of the Great Depression, grown up in age of relative austerity, valued a job, and would also have acquired new expectations, both material and psychological.

Markets expanded for all manner of consumer goods, including clothing, the Western European shopper's largest item of expenditure after food. The textile industry was diversified in many ways, for instance through the extensive use of artificial fibers, a field in which European countries, especially Germany, had done much of the pioneer work. Durables compromised a great variety of goods, washing machines, refrigerators, driers, typewriters, cameras, radios and television sets – products requiring considerable skill in their manufacture, yet designed as standardized items for the masses. The pace of the consumer revolution varied widely from one country to the next. The US had long provided a huge market where customers broadly shared similar tastes. European countries varied more widely in their respective national styles, in shoes,

---

[80]Dewhurst, *Europe's Needs*, p. 607.

[81]Between 1950 and 1957, production rose (1950 equalling 100 percent as follows: West Germany: 210, Italy: 177, France: 169, Netherlands: 144, Belgium: 136, United Kingdom: 124, Sweden: 122, Ireland: 110. Ibid., p. 23.

clothes, or good furniture. But as regards durables, goods valued for their utility more than their appearance, consumer resistance in Europe was no greater than in the US – with the difference that a European worker during the early 1950s received on average only about half the pay of an American worker, so could not buy as much.

The most important of the new durables was the motor car. Between them, the Volkswagen "beetle," the British Morris Minor, Volvos, Renaults, Citroens, and Fiats helped to change European life styles and patterns of production and consumption – just as Fords, Chevrolets and Studebakers had done in the US. The automobile industry remained in the hands of private enterprise to a greater extent than coal, iron, and steel. (However, the Volkswagen company in Germany was operated by the state. The Renault works in France formed another important exception – they were nationalized because Louis Renault, their owner, had been charged with collaboration during World War II.) In France and Germany, however, state-owned or state-run enterprises had to compete with rival products and were managed as efficiently as private firms.

The effect of the car on life style was enormous, on both sides of the Atlantic. Americans might speak of car hoods, Britons of bonnets, Spaniards of *cubiertas*, and Portuguese of *capotas*, but in a deeper sense drivers talked the same lanuage where cars were concerned. Gaullists might extol *l'Europe des patries* (the Europe of fatherlands), but the car increasingly linked Europe through new modes of tourism, consumer credit facilities, and consumption patterns. The car made the various European countries look smaller from a driver's perspective, and made them look more alike.

Cars both created and destroyed. They added to pollution, and to the annual toll of accident victims. They crowded the streets of ancient cities, and deprived them of some of their charm. Later, expressways were driven through slums and robbed poor people of their homes. Expressways routed through historic cities caused many beautiful buildings to be torn down. Cars gave new opportunities to criminals – not only because of car stealing, but because they facilitated robberies and allowed speedier getaways. Cars also became a favored weapon of terrorists. On the other hand, they provided the peaceful majority with new opportunities for travel and recreation. Cars created new industries and new institutions – for instance the motel, in North America. (The word "motel" had first been used by a San Luis Obispo proprietor in 1926; for long motels were regarded as dens of vice, fit only for the "hot pillow trade." After World War II, their reputation improved, motels attracted workers and middle-class families, and by 1960, 60,000 motels were in operation in the US.) Cars created mobile home parks, and facilitated the decentralization of factories and offices and the growth of suburbs. Cars required the construction of huge, publicly supported highway systems; and a privately owned infrastructure to service them and feed the occupants; they allowed greater freedom for workers.

Cars resulted in new highway lobbies, supported by automobile manufacturers, road builders, manufacturers of oil, rubber, and asphalt, by construction industries, home builders, and labor unions. Trucks, cars, and buses fundamentally changed existing patterns of transport and residence, and put many a railroad and street car out of business as well. Cars facilitated shopping in new centers and supermarkets, and enabled suburban housewives to take their children to ballet lessons and tennis lessons; they also made teenagers more independent of parental control. There was a profound influence on the layout of cities – the car speeded the growth of suburbia. These aggregations were much disliked by poets and intellectuals. But suburban homeowners now enjoyed privileges once available only to the rich – the availability of personal credit, ownership of a personal carriage, and of fenced-in grounds. There was now access to the great national and state parks. The car created huge industrial complexes, such as GM, Fiat and Volkswagen, and the automobile industry indirectly developed a great number of subordinate manufacturing and distribution networks. The industry gave employment to armies of technicians, designers, and operators, and created a niche for a host of small entrepreneurs who ran gas stations, garages and parts shops. Cars became new status symbols; as a British journal put it, "when a person has become a motor car owner .. he has attained a feeling of social liberation."[82]

In Europe, as in the US, cars became big business. By 1958 an estimated 39,000,000 motorized vehicles crowded the roads of Western Europe, including about 18,000,000 motor cycles, scooters, and so on. By 1958 about 4.5 million passenger cars and commercial vehicles came off the Western European assembly lines (as opposed to about 6,220,000 vehicles in the US in 1957), and European models had become popular abroad. At the same time, there was a shift in the industrial balance of power. During the 1930s, the British car industry had been the largest in Europe. But British pioneers, such as Herbert Austin and William Morris, had been practical men in the tradition of the Victorian workshop. Austin had no patience with university graduates; the British lagged behind in the employment of those highly trained specialists who dominated the middle levels of German and American management.[83] By 1957 West Germany had already become Europe's top producer, with an output of 1.5 million units, followed by Great Britain with 1.4 million, France 1.1 million, and Italy 400,000. The British share continued to decline. The domestic market share also diminished as factories at Dagenham, Longbridge, and Cowley became bywords for strikes and labor disputes. (From 1968 to

[82]"The unfinished revolution," the *Economist*, 25 January 1986, pp. 12–13. For a history, see for instance, Jean-Pierre Bardou, Jean-Jacques Chanaron, Patrick Fridenson, and James M. Laux, *The Automobile Revolution: The Impact of an Industry*. Chapel Hill, NC, University of North Carolina Press, 1982. Kenneth T. Jackson, *Crabgrass Frontier: The Suburbanization of the United States*. Oxford, Oxford University Press, 1985, especially pp. 187–9. Paul C. Wilson, *Chrome Dreams: Automobile Styling Since 1893*. Radnor, Pa, Chilton Books, 1976. Scott L. Bottles, *Los Angeles and the Automobile: The Making of the Modern City*. Berkeley, University of California Press, 1987. For the automobile industries of particular countries, Michael Sedgwick, *Fiat*. New York, Arco Publishing Co, 1974. Walter Henry Nelson, *Small Wonder: The Amazing Story of the Volkswagen*. Boston, Little Brown, 1965. Shotaro Kamiya, *My Life with Toyota*. Tokyo, Toyota Motor Sales, 1976. John B. Rae, *The American Automobile Industry*. Boston, Twayne Publishers, 1984. See also Peter Collier and David Horowitz, *The Fords: An American Epic*. New York, Summit Books, 1987.

[83]Jonathan Wood, *Wheels of Misfortune: The Rise and Fall of the British Motor Industry*. London, Sidgwick and Jackson, 1988.

1987, the domestic market share of British car manufacturers fell disastrously from 40.6 percent to 15.5 percent.)

Europeans specialized in small cars that began to invade US markets in large numbers during the late 1940s. They were economical in fuel, and conveniently served as second cars for the growing number of two-car households in the US. European cars changed much less in style and appearance from one year's model to the next than automobiles made in America, and European imports were apt to appeal to particular groups. For instance, the Volvo pleased liberal sophisticates. The Volkswagen was apt to be avoided by Jewish Americans, but otherwise was liked by purchasers who wanted fuel economy, an air-cooled engine, and ease of parking, in a relatively low-priced product. Fiats were more likely to sell as second cars and to the trendy. The much more highly priced British Jaguars were bought by the smart set and the wealthy.

In the 1950s, Americans swooned over Elvis and rocked around the clock – boys wore grease in their hair and girls wore poodle cuts and poodle skirts. Fast food and fast cars were the new entertainment as drive-ins sprang up everywhere.

It was no secret – girls liked boys with cars. A guy in a '57 Chevy Bel Air convertible was a real catch. Long, low, sleek, and hot – the car with the flashing smile offered endless promises of top-down fun under the sun. Never before had the freedom and joy of a whole generation been so keenly captured in a single car. The '57 Chevy had the world on a string as America's love affair with cars blossomed. "Sweet, smooth and sassy" the Chevy convertible had an optional 283 cubic inch fuel injector V-8 engine, which was the best engine in history for a popular car. It was loaded with chrome and styling. (Adapted from advertising for the '57 Chevy)

But the large American car continued to attract purchasers, though more wasteful of space and materials. The big "gas guzzler" began to meet real trouble only in the early 1970s, when gasoline prices suddenly rose, and when the US government intruded by insisting on new safety standards that made these cars excessively heavy, more expensive to manufacture, and with heavier fuel consumption. But large or small, the motor car came to symbolize the twentieth century just as the railway engine had symbolized the nineteenth.

High technology

The industrial scene underwent further modification as a result of new inventions perfected during World War II and immediately after. Many were inventions of obvious military purpose – radar, the atomic bomb (produced by the combined skills of US and immigrant European scientists, and with US technology), rockets (pioneered mainly by the Germans) and jet fighters (the prototypes originating through German and British ingenuity, later developed into jet airliners by the Americans and British). There were also many pharmaceutical products such as DDT, penicillin, and streptomycin. There were plastics (originated in prewar days in the US, Britain, and Germany, though the US took the lead in production after the war.)[84] Another major wartime innovation was the computer, pioneered by the British for the purpose of decoding German messages in World War II, and later perfected in the US, like so many other new inventions. (In 1944, Howard Aitken of Harvard completed his "Harvard Mark 1" – a machine superseded within two years by the electronic computers, ENIAC, installed at the University of Pennsylvania, and EDSAC, devised by Dr M. V. Wilkes at Cambridge University.

> *Economically the 1950s and 1960s were a time of solid economic growth and prosperity in both Europe and the US. The high rates of growth were partly due to the Europeans' ability to close the technology gap that separated Western Europe from the US, as well as a plentiful labor supply. Growth and abundant labor were also stimulated by major agricultural changes, which began in the US and then spread to Europe and to the Third World through the "green revolution."*

Electronics soon developed to an astounding extent. The British had pioneered radar; radar in turn gave an impetus to the invention of transmitters and detectors capable of dealing with wavelengths far shorter than those previously used in radio. War also accelerated the development of "servomotors," small power units which could instantly respond to signals. The combination of electronic instruments and servomotors then helped to perfect the techniques of automation and cybernetics.[85]

The years following World War II witnessed the application of nuclear power to industrial use, the invention of the transistor, of solar-powered batteries, and of long-paying micro-groove records, all developments fraught with far-reaching economic or social consequences. Television had begun before World War II. (The BBC established its first service as early as 1936.) But after World War II, television became the most important channel of mass entertainment in the US, and US movies continued to dominate abroad.

The social impact of these new industries was immense. Tourism grew as air travel became speedier and relatively cheaper – no longer a privilege for the few, but a convenience for all classes. (The mass immigration of Puerto Ricans into New York, for example, began after World War II, when the price of air fares dropped substantially, and in 1951 the phrase "the jet set" denoted the wealthy who flew off to Europe at a moment's notice.) Every owner of a television set or of a record player acquired a movie theater, an opera house, and a concert hall in their own living room. The rate of technological change continued to gain momentum.

The new technology affected national economies in a variety of ways.

---

[84]By 1958, the US produced 2,000,000 tons out of a world production of 4,000,000 tons. Germany turned out 600,000 tons, Britain 471,000 tons, France 170,000 tons. Dewhurst, *Europe's Needs*, p. 805ff.

[85]The standard history for the first half of the present century is Trevor I. Williams, *A History of Technology: The Twentieth Century c. 1900 to 1950*. Oxford, Clarendon Press, 1978, p. 607. The earlier period is covered in Charles Joseph Singer et al., *A History of Technology: The Late Nineteenth Century c. 1850–1900*. Oxford, Clarendon Press, 1958.

(According to a rough estimate, the US production in 1956 of television sets, civilian jet aircraft, and computers – three kinds of merchandise not available in 1945 – added up to no more than one-fifteenth of the total output of the US, the world's industrially most advanced country at the time.)[86] Overall, the new industrial revolutions were as uneven in their international impact as the old industrial revolutions had been. The late 1950s and the 1960s produced a bulky technical literature concerned with the real or supposed technology gaps that divided the East from the West, or Western Europe from the US. The Soviet Union aroused both anxiety and admiration by putting *Sputnik* into space, by the large number of engineers that graduated each year from Soviet universities, and also because of the Soviets' alleged advantage in being able to automate their industries much more rapidly than the capitalist countries (who were tied to immediate profitability). The Soviets loudly claimed that in time they would overtake the West. So effectively was their case presented that scholars such as Warren Nutter faced great difficulty in finding an audience in American academia sympathetic to his critiques of Soviet performance.[87]

The Soviets and their allies did indeed rapidly expand their basic industries.[88] Urbanization proceeded apace in Eastern, as well as in Western, Europe. Soviet engineers at their best proved a match for their rivals anywhere in the world. The Soviets excelled in certain technical fields – especially those concerned with the military and with space research. Here they had to compete with Westerners, though their customers – that is Soviet generals and space explorers – were always right. But the Soviet system was wasteful in machinery, materials, and men; while the ordinary consumer continued to be short-changed. Marxist-Leninist forecasts notwithstanding, scientific and technological creativity continued to center in the West.

Within the Western world, the predominance of the US aroused almost equal anxiety. Hence academicians took a great deal of time to explain, deplore, or correct the "technology gap," the resultant "American challenge," *le défi Américain*.[89] The US clearly enjoyed many advantages, some of which were later lost. It had a large market, a large reservoir of home-bred or immigrant scientists and technologists, and the world's most productive workforce. As mentioned earlier, Germany never recovered the scientific pre-eminence which it had held before Hitler ravaged German science, unwittingly benefiting America. In the postwar period, almost every young German scientist wanted

[86]The Atlantic institute, *The Technology Gap: The US and Europe*. New York, Praeger, 1970, p. 114.

[87]G. Warren Nutter, et al., *Growth of Industrial Production in the Soviet Union*. Princeton, NJ, Princeton University Press, 1962. A British Marxist scientist J. D. Bernal, *World Without War*. New York, Monthly Review Press, 1958, p. 57 praised the Soviet system among other things, for being able to push automation faster than the US.

[88]For statistics, see Luxemburg, *Europe Since World War II*, p. 281ff.

[89]See, for instance, the Atlantic institute, *The Technology Gap: US and Europe*. Stanley Woods, *Western Europe: Technology and the Future*. London, Croom Helm, 1987. Edward F. Denison and Jean-Pierre Poullier, *Why Growth Rates Differ: Postwar Experience in Nine Western Countries*. Washington, DC, The Brookings Institute, 1967. A. Kramish, *Europe's Enigmatic Gap*. Santa Monica, Cal., The Rand Corporation, 1967.

to study and conduct research in the US – reversing a historical trend of Americans studying in Germany. That tendency diminished in the 1960s, but the German government continued to support and pay for visits to the US and even provided funds for American scientists to come to Germany.

The US possessed freedom from many traditional restraints that continued to beset European industrialists. It pioneered new management techniques, and organizational innovations. For example, during World War II the US developed federal research and development contracts which linked government, industry, and the universities in pursuit of new scientific and technological goals. Systems analysis, originally developed to cope with problems besetting the military and industrial complex, began to be applied in industry during the late 1950s, and thereafter in the civilian branches of government.[90] Overall, the US continued to spend much more on research and development than the Europeans, though less than the Japanese.

The Americans also tended to put new technologies to use more quickly than Europeans. US trade unionists were more likely to accept automation than their European confrères, and concentrated on collective bargaining for the best deals, in terms of wages and fringe benefits for their members. The US benefited from a close connection between universities and modern industry – as evidenced by new industrial complexes that developed near academic institutions, for instance along Route 128 outside the Massachusetts Institute of Technology (MIT), and in Silicon Valley, California, close to Stanford University. The US led in semiconductors, electronics, and computers (the first business computer was sold in 1954, only ten years after the first electronic data processing system had become operational). This led to solid state microcircuitry, satellite communications, and a variety of advanced products.

The Americans benefited from superior patent laws that offered more protection to their owners than European codes. In Europe there was less cooperation between universities and business (except in West Germany) and less collaboration between business and government. European governments on the whole were more apt to penalize through their fiscal policies the more efficient firms – in effect rewarding their less productive competitors. As long as a European manager felt reasonably sure that the government would step in to prevent his firm from going under, he had little incentive to meet the risk and expense of adopting the latest techniques – especially when any extra profits would be heavily taxed. Also European business and industry was often less competitive than its rivals, preferring to share a market rather than to dominate and risk alienating fellow entrepreneurs.

The American advantages, however, should not be exaggerated – and none of them were destined to be permanent. The new technologies depended on discoveries and inventions derived from a new trans-Atlantic internationale that comprised both Americans and Europeans, from men and women who

[90]Victor Basiuk, *Technology and World Power*. New York, Foreign Policy Association, 1970, pp. 19–20.

frequently had multiple loyalties. Should Einstein be regarded primarily as a German, a Swiss, a Jew, or an American? Einstein himself had joked on the subject. The new knowledge was internationalized in a great variety of ways, through the migration of people (the "brain drain"), and corporations (multinationals), and the migration of capital, techniques, patents and licences, the US being the main originator in the latter.

Investment in electronic gadgetry did not necessarily increase performance. Offices, banks and post offices came to install a great deal of electronic equipment; but bank depositors did not gain quicker or more efficient access to their balance sheets. Postal services declined rather than improved. (During the 1950s, the average airmail letter from Britain took five days to reach its destination in the US; 30 years later, the time had doubled and sometimes tripled.) Technological predominance moreover only affected certain sectors of particular industries in any given country. There was no uniform level of technology in any specific country, neither in the US nor in Europe. Considerable differences remained between plants in any industrial field – regardless of the size of the plant, or whether it belonged to a capital-intensive or a labor-intensive industry. Overall the US continued to lead in many high-tech enterprises.

The publicity given to advances made along the high-tech frontier rather obscured innovations made in more established industries, in enterprises that continued to produce the bulk of national incomes. In many of these, Europeans did very well. Britain, for instance, excelled in the float glass process for producing smooth plate glass. The British also established an initial lead in the use of nuclear power for industry. Sweden and Switzerland pioneered the transmission of electrical energy at very high voltages. The Germans continued to excel in machine tool industries, chemical industries, and optics. The European car industry as a whole made numerous innovations – and so on.

Initial backwardness in specific industries moreover might be compensated by unexpected subsequent "jumps." France, for example, was slow to modernize its telephone system. (As late as 1973 France ranked behind poorer countries such as Spain and Greece in the number of telephone lines per capita.) The French sytem was known for its inefficiency, but failure to invest in telecommunications did not derive from lack of technical knowledge, but from cultural predispositions that continued to play an important part in economic history. From its introduction in France during the 1900s, the telephone had been regarded with suspicion. Old-fashioned Frenchmen regarded the domestic telephone as an instrument that would enable a married woman to make amorous assignations behind her husband's back. It would enable social climbers to bypass hierarchies and the etiquette of leaving cards. De Gaulle himself hated the intrusiveness of the telephone and would not permit one by the side of his near-regal person. In allowing telecommunications to languish, he was also following long-standing French tradition that set great store by government control of information. During the 1970s, however, the French changed their policy. Telecommunications then made a greater leap within a single decade then any sector in the economy since World War II.

The French also pioneered a new computerized system, "Minitel," which provided ordinary people with a way of communicating anonymously with a huge number of correspondents, thereby stimulating both the French economy and in some cases the erotic imagination.[91]

Technological predominance, in other words, was apt to shift and change. Technological advance was not a zero-sum game, in which one party's gain was necessarily another's loss. As the Atlantic Institute soberly concluded in a report prepared at the end of the 1960s, "the overall US technological lead has neither widened, nor affected Europe's economic growth, its export performance, or its scientific and technical abilities."

Workers and unions

In the years preceding World War I and through World War II, trade unions through most of Europe had been reduced to a parlous condition. During the 1930s unemployment had been widespread, and the unions' bargaining position had weakened accordingly. The Fascists and Nazis, and their allies had smashed all free trade unions in the countries under dictatorial rule. During World War II, Britain, Sweden, and Switzerland had been the only European countries that could still boast of independent trade unions. After the war, however, trade unionism revived. Collective bargaining worked well in Britain and Sweden, though unionists during 1945 to 1958 were not equally successful in France, West Germany, and Italy. Nevertheless, there was a striking rise in the average wage in manufacturing industries from 1950 to 1955. The increase was highest in France (14.8 percent), and lowest in Italy (5.8 percent). In Britain there was an 8.7 growth and in Germany 7.8. Britain, while experiencing a relatively high wage rise, had a low increase in labor productivity; hence retail prices went up.

> *Important changes in the world economy modified Keynesian economies. Wage-bargaining became the major cause of inflation from the 1950s on, with annual negotiations.*
>
> *Technological change increased enormously after World War II. From the 1970s, many people had to retrain several times during their working life. New skills were needed, new locations developed, older industries contracted, and whole areas went into decline. More mobility (both of firms and of employees) was needed in post-industrial societies, but mobility was often impeded by housing shortages, by lack of a policy of locating businesses, and by the welfare state. Wage and cost inflation in the 1970s forced policy makers to rethink what government should do.*

In the postwar years the status of workers in the US and Western Europe improved significantly and unemployment was almost abolished in the US, except among blacks and Puerto Ricans. Millions of men came into the workforce, drawn by higher wages and better working conditions. The old no longer risked penury upon retirement; social security and pension plans

[91] Justine de Lacy, "France: the sexy computer," *The Atlantic*, July 1987, pp. 18–26.

cared for the needs of most elderly people who lived longer and retired younger than at any time before. Housing improved everywhere in West Europe and the US; comprehensive health schemes and social welfare programs expanded. By 1970 the citizens of the West were the most prosperous and well-cared-for people in history. The improved status of citizens and workers was linked to economic development, government intervention, and the massive growth in transfer payments and high rates of taxation. (People had better housing after World War II – almost all houses in urban Western Europe and the US had inside plumbing and flush toilets. By 1970, a car, a TV set, refrigerator, washer, and drier were common goods in 90 to 95 percent of homes in the Atlantic community except for parts of Spain, Portugal, and Italy.) Hours of work had decreased from 45–49 hours a week in 1945 to 42–45 hours a week in Western Europe by 1970 (40 hours a week in the US were standard in industry by 1950). Paid vacations and days off increased; health care programs and retirement schemes were universal in industry and government. Retirement benefits equalled 60–70 percent of final earnings and unemployment benefits were 30–90 percent of earnings. The welfare state, supported by labor, therefore produced a greater equality in income distribution.

> *The European Recovery Program (ERP) did not split the European labor movement and did not revolutionize it by the "gospel of productivity" opines* Anthony Carew in Labour under the Marshall Plan, *Manchester, Manchester University Press, 1987. European labor was badly divided, before the Marshall Plan, between communist and non-communist unions. The Americans wanted to increase productivity and introduce a labor partnership with business. American union leaders helped depoliticize the union movement in Europe by stressing higher wages over influence in management. European labor leaders did "study tours" in the US and became familiar with American management methods but did not fully embrace the "productivity message." There were national productivity centers in Britain, France, West Germany, and Italy, but none controlled labor unions. In fact, the AFL and CIO both felt they had little or no influence on the ERP and became disenchanted with the Economic Cooperation Administration (ECA). US labor leaders felt the ERP's labor division had been too large, too idle, and concerned more with fighting the communist unions than with promoting productivity. Carew's thesis shows the limits of America's influence and cautions against corporatist explanations that labor and business were in full partnership in the postwar decade.*

OEEC countries saw the price indexes of government expenditures rise to an average annual rate of 5.1 percent from 1950 on. High wages were an element in this increased cost of government. While government share increased, consumption goods and prices averaged a 3 percent rise. The biggest share of government expenditure went to health, social security and education. With the growth of the economy, people also saved more. "Engles' law" came into play – that is, budget share on food declined with rising income, although nations varied in the percentage of budget that they allocated to comestibles. Spain, France, Italy, and Sweden spent more than did Germany, Norway, Britain, or Denmark, while the Irish spent almost as much money on alcohol as on food. Housing, clothes, and durable goods all showed an increase in budget share in the postwar period. Eastern European countries, on the other hand, ranked far behind Western Europe in availability of consumer goods, fresh vegetables and meat, housing, and so on. Only East Germany came close to the Western European average.

By 1950 economic life in Western Europe had returned at least to prewar levels, and unemployment was not a serious problem. But inflation was. Collective bargaining replaced political activity as the *modus operandi* for improving wages and conditions of work. Although socialist parties grew in strength, and in a few countries ruled the state, they did not engage in political warfare against the capitalists or the employers. National productivity increased greatly, making it easier to satisfy the workers and to establish good industrial relations. Real wages more than doubled between 1950 and 1970, whereas they had fallen in the interwar period. (This was perhaps caused by the move toward more collective bargaining, as had been the rule in the US.) No longer suffering from severe unemployment, northern Europe, after 1955, had a shortage of labor, and later had to import millions of migrant workers from Portugal, Spain, Sicily, Yugoslavia, and Turkey.

Full employment strengthened the bargaining power of the trade unions – indeed the late 1940s, the 1950s, and the 1960s in retrospect seem the unions' golden age. Workers' representatives were admitted to the councils of major industries (including the European coal and steel community.) On the national level, the most successful workers' organization on the European Continent was the Federation of Trade Unions in West Germany (*Deutscher Gewerkschaftsbund, DGB*). By 1955 this had attained a membership of 6,000,000 (comprising 35 percent of all wage earners, 12 percent of white-collar employees, and – remarkably – 41 percent of civil servants). The confederation was dominated by the large-wage-earners unions; it stood for a policy of moderation and compromise that stressed the common interests between wage earners and white-collar workers. The member unions were organized on industrial lines, *IG Metall* accounting for 25 percent of the entire confederation. The DGB contained Catholics, as well as social democrats; it could not lean as openly toward the SPD as in the Weimar era. But no West German government could possibly ignore union influence. (At the end of the 1950s, about 40 percent of the *Bundestag* members were union members, about 30 percent of them in the ranks of the SPD.)

Even more powerful was the Trades Union Congress (TUC) in Great Britain. (In 1955, there were 9,600,000 trade unionists in Great Britain; by 1970 their number had risen to 11,000,000, or 43 percent of the British labor force, the great majority of them linked to the TUC.) The TUC was affiliated to the Labour Party and dominated its councils. Like the DGB and other European trade unions, the TUC played a vital part in the expansion of the welfare state, though it is far from certain that workers were its main beneficiaries. In terms of membership, and in terms of workers' loyalty, the TUC's power was enormous. Nevertheless, its internal problems were many, and it was highly bureaucratized. (David Low, the famed cartoonist, represented the TUC as a huge, lumbering, ungainly horse.) The TUC had little control over affiliates and national unions had little control over local enterprise unions. Because of overlapping jurisdictions and failure to organize sound branch unions, shop stewards gained excessive power. A great many stewards' positions later were held by communists or Trotskyites, and the result was a radicalization of the British trade union movement. The Labour Party needed a strong charismatic leadership to link the government, the political parties and the unions – leadership such as it had possessed after World War II.

Trade unions also played a significant part in the US. The American labor union was the largest in the Western world, with about 18,000,000 members in 1955. Of these, 10,000,000 belonged to the American Federation of Labor, AFL, and 5,200,000 in the Congress of Industrial Organization, CIO. (By far the largest union within the AFL was the International Brotherhood of Teamsters, followed by the International Association of Machinists. The biggest organizations within the CIO were the United Steelworkers of America and the United Automobile Workers of America.) In addition there were numerous independent unions, including the United Mine Workers of America. The US unionists were therefore divided; they lacked their British colleagues' political clout. (The Labor-Management Relations Act, 1947, known as the Taft-Hartley Act, for instance, made the closed shop illegal, forbade unions to apply secondary boycotts, and imposed a variety of other organizational and political restrictions on the unions.) American unions also suffered from criminality and graft to a much greater extent than British or German unions. Nevertheless the American unionists' industrial power was immense, and it was only in the 1960s and 1970s that unions began to experience a striking decline in membership and public esteem.

The communist-dominated unions on the European continent fared much worse by comparison. French workers were militant and class conscious, ready to strike, but far more reluctant to pay trade union dues. They were also politically divided. The principal French union was the *Conféderation Générale du Travail (CGT)*. The CGT fell under communist domination, with the result that dissident moderates split from the movement in 1947, and founded their own organization the *CGT Force Ouvrière*. The results were disastrous for the CGT. Its membership declined from 6,000,000 in 1946 to little over 1,000,000 in 1965 (the CGT itself still claiming 1,700,000). Collective bargaining developed more slowly in France than in Britain, because the communists were more interested in the CGT as a political instrument than as a means to gain higher wages and improved benefits for their members. In Italy, the communists again ran the largest trade union, the *Confederazione Generale Italiana del Lavoro (CGIL)*, with about 3,500,000 members. In addition there were separate Christian Democratic and socialist unions.

Despite these divisions and the numerous resultant weaknesses, trade unions occupied a position of great strength in Western Europe. They were accepted as the workers' legitimate representatives (Britons even spoke of the union movement as a new "estate of the realm"). Unions had political power, especially as far as the communist and socialist parties were concerned. Communist-dominated unions were a powerful political tool for the French Communist Party in the struggle to create a communist-dominated society.

Even more contentious was the relation between trade unions and technical innovation. At the beginning of the industrial revolution in Europe, angry mobs had destroyed machinery. Furious bargemen had hurled stones at the first steamers plying along the Rhine river. As workers acquired a greater stake in industry, attitudes changed, albeit slowly. The problem was particularly acute for craft unions designed to protect their members specialized skills. (In Britain, for instance, there were more than 600 unions by the 1950s, many of them craft unions – unlike the Transport and General Workers Union, the Amalgamated Engineering Union, and the Electrical Trade Union, that were organized, like American unions, by industry.) Especially in Britain, the craft unions with their tradtional pride of status defended their members' rights in bitter demarcation disputes that pitted worker against worker, sometimes to the point of absurdity. Hence the British found problems of innovation and automation harder to solve than the Americans. In the US, "industrial unions" operated on a plant basis; they tried to assure for their members "fair shares" derived from enhanced productivity; the Americans could more easily retrain and reassign to new jobs workers displaced by automated methods. Americans were more mobile, both geographically and socially, for immigrant laborers had already changed their life styles in the process of coming to a new country (an experience shared by the millions of East German refugees in West Germany). By and large, automation and other forms of innovation proved easiest in specialized industries – chemicals, electronics, plastics, and cars. (For instance, in France, the state-controlled Renault company was the first auto-manufacturing company in Europe to adopt an automation program, completed with locally made equipment.)[92]

Management

Management as an identifiable profession had its origins in the US, and the 1950s were the golden years of American management. The chief executive officer (CEO) ran everything, and his word was law. There was relatively little foreign competition, and "raiding" was as yet rare. The CEOs planned strategy and operated plants. Management moreover was academically respectable. (It had become a subject of academic study as early as 1881 at the University of Pennsylvania.) The US pioneered the great business schools; in addition big companies set up their own schools. The management schools soon spread to Europe. Indeed the "managerial revolution" (a term popularized by James Burnham) came to fascinate social scientists preoccupied with the growth of a new group of managers who did not personally own the companies that they administered. The managerial revolution went with changes in industry that turned many family firms into join stock companies, run by impersonal bureaucracies. The new managerial elite improved its relative status *vis à vis* the traditional professions in the armed services, the

[92] J. Frederick Dewhurst et al., *Europe's Needs and Resources*, p. 789.

Church, schools, and universities. It was the managers of large companies who drew the biggest salaries, occupied the largest offices, and drove the most splendid cars – complete with company expense accounts. The new management acquired trans-national ties – so much so that traditionalists began to complain of the new *copinage technocratique*, the old boys' network of the technocratic kind.

The extent of this transformation should not, of course, be exaggerated. Managers did not turn into a single cohesive class. They varied enormously in training, power and income. There was a world of difference (and not just in scale) between the salaried supervisor of a small store and the executive director of a huge multinational concern. The small family firm did not die out – on the contrary, there were countless new opportunities for small enterprises in the various new service industries, and in contracting and sub contracting businesses. Family connections continued to play an important part in economic organization and in politics. (Sir Harold Macmillan's cabinet contained five members to whom he was related.) Dynasties remained important in big business, though to make one's way it no longer sufficed of course to be "daddy's boy." The great family firms insisted that members destined for highly placed positions should acquire a thorough professional training, and this ensured their survival. In West Germany, for example, the Krupp dynasty outlived the Hohenzollerns, the Weimar Republic, the Third Reich, and the Allied occupation. in France, the Berçot family continued to control interlocking companies that included Michelin (for tyres), Citroen (cars), and Berliet (trucks). In Britain, the Pilkingtons ran Pilkington's glass; Sachers and Sieff directed Marks and Spencer. In Italy there were Pesenti (for cement), Pirelli (tyres), Olivetti (typewriters), Marzotto (textiles), Zanussi and Borghi (refrigerators). In social-democratic Sweden, of all countries, the old industrial oligarchy was if anything even more influential. By the late 1960s, 15 great families, headed by the Wallenbergs, the Kempes, and others, controlled one-fifth of Swedish private industry.[93]

Friedrich Krupp (1787–1826) had founded a steel foundry in Essen in 1811, at a time when Napoleon's Continental blockade had cut off Germany from British steel imports. His son Alfred (1812–87) profited from the opening of the South German market through the creation of the Prussian-dominated German customs league. He pioneered new methods of steel making, new forms of mass production, became a major manufacturer of railroad equipment, and the greatest armament manufacturer. After the death of his son, Friedrich Alfred (1854–1902), a friend of the Emperor William II's, the firm was turned into a joint stock company run by Friedrich Alfred's daughter Bertha (1886–1957) and her husband Gustav Krupp von Bohlen und Halbach (1870–1950). By that time the Krupp fortune had become the greatest in Germany. Gustav's son Alfred (1907–67), who collaborated with the Nazis, succeeded in restoring the firm as a family concern. The Krupp works were badly damaged by Allied bombardment; Alfred was sentenced by an American military court to 12 years imprisonment, but released in 1951. Alfred

---

[93]Anthony Sampson, *Anatomy of Europe*. New York, Harper and Row, 1968, p. 109.

rebuilt the Krupp enterprise, but finally had to give up personal direction and shortly before his death the firm was turned into a foundation (Stiftung). Alfred's only son Knut relinquished his inheritance for a cash settlement. See Biographisches Wörterbuch zur Deutschen Geschichte, *Munich Francke Verlag, 1974, v. 2. pp. 1557–61, including bibliography.*

Nevertheless, professional management experts achieved increasing prominence. They included men such as Eric Woodroofe, chairman of Unilever Limited, a huge Anglo-Dutch combine specializing in the manufacture of margarine, soap, and related products. Woodroofe was the product of neither a public school nor of Oxbridge. He had been educated at a provincial high school and Leeds University; he was a scientist who had worked his way up in research at Unilever, but combined scientific ability with expertise in marketing. Overall, the professional managers tended to come from middle-class or upper-middle-class backgrounds. They were normally university graduates, usually with an advanced technical training. (Many of them were trained in American business schools, or multinational corporations, in prestigious European schools such as Sankt Gallen in Switzerland, or in the European business institute set up in Fontainebleau outside Paris in 1959). They were familiar with the same technical terminology, read similar trade journals, moved in the same world of luxury hotels, first-class air travel, diplomatic parties, and select seminars. They profited from growing markets, rising incomes, expanding consumer demand. After the privations of World War II, most Europeans wanted an American-style consumer society, and were willing to work and save accordingly. Hence managers of large firms had to readjust accustomed attitudes. They had to think in terms of great trans-national markets. They had to deal with state bureaucracies engaged in national planning. Professionally trained technocrats dropped the paternalistic attitudes of bygone generations. They became attuned to dealing with great trade union bureaucracies, with mass advertising, with mass markets. Small and medium-sized firms continued to play an important part, but they faced serious problems – the growing complexity of labor laws, safety regulations, interference from labor unions and the state. The widening markets of Western Europe put a new premium on skills, competitiveness, and marketing experience, all of which the new breed of manager could provide. Management styles varied from country to country, but increasingly "American" ways of doing business spread throughout the Western world.

AGRICULTURE

Farming is the most diversified of economic pursuits. Pastoralists, wine growers, and wheat producers employ different methods for their different products. Irrespective of economic specialization, farmers differ in social conditions – there is little in common between, say, the manager of a California agro-business, a well-to-do English tenant farmer, and a French *métayer* (share cropper). Agriculturists also vary in the techniques that they employ, in the nature of their capital equipment, and of course in politics and life style.

At the end of World War II, regional and national differences were, if anything, more noticeable than a generation later. In terms of yields from animals and land, Britain, Denmark, and the Netherlands stood out as the most efficient producers, concentrating on meat, milk, butter, and cheese. Southern Europe (especially isolated regions such as Corsica and Sicily) were much more backward – so much so that scholars spoke of "the underdeveloped areas within the Common Market."[94] In an economic sense, livestock played a secondary part, and Southern Europe's agricultural output was apt to take a more direct and simpler path from the field to the kitchen – without the intervening stage of turning fodder into meat or milk.

But whether a farmer bred goats or cows, whether he spoke the Sicilian dialect of Italian, the Rhenish variant of German, or the Scottish version of English, whether he had learned his skills from father and grandfather or at an agricultural college, he always had to wrest his living from the land. He lived in relative isolation. He faced the perils of animal and plant diseases. He depended on the weather, and could never be certain of a good crop. Townsmen talked about the weather insofar as it affected their vacation plans; to farmers, rain and sun at the right times were a matter of survival. Even minute local differences of climate and soil could be of tremendous importance. Hence farming, of all industries, was and remains unsuitable for national planning on the grand scale – a fact widely ignored by town-bred theoreticians.

Farming has always been one of Europe's main industries. (By the mid 1950s 38.1 percent of the total land area in Western Europe as a whole and 60.3 percent of EEC land was devoted to agriculture, though there were great regional differences). About 31,000,000 Western European and nearly 5,000,000 Americans were employed in farming. The value of the farmers' gross output was staggering. (In 1955 the value of the gross output of agriculture in Western Europe alone stood at approximately $30 billion at domestic farm-gate prices, including the direct subsidies paid by governments to farmers. In the US, during the same year, the joint output of farming, forestry, and fisheries amounted to 16.1 billion dollars.)[95]

During and after World War II, farmers appeared both as the stepchildren of their national economies and as members of a specially favored lobby. In Continental Europe (though not in the US, Great Britain, or European countries such as Denmark, exempt from the direct ravages of war) farmers had suffered tremendously from the impact of military operations. Farmers had been strictly regulated in the production of crops and their distribution, often to their disadvantage. They had lost most of their draft animals, and at this

---

[94]See Sergio Barzanti, *The Underdeveloped Areas Within the Common Market*. Princeton, Princeton University Press, 1965.

[95]For statistical details, see J. Frederic Dewhurst et al., *Europe's Needs and Resources: Trends and Prospects in Eighteen Countries*. New York, Twentieth Century Fund, 1961, pp. 479–519. US department of commerce, *Historical Statistics of the United States: Colonial Times to 1957*. Washington, DC, bureau of the census, 1960, pp. 257–304.

time horses still played a key role. (The German armies that invaded Russia in 1941 actually used more horses than had served the Kaiser's troops in World War I.) Farmers generally were regarded with some ambivalence by their urban compatriots. During World War II and its aftermath, farmers had been heavily involved in, and supposedly had illegitimately profited from the "second economy" without which Europeans would, no doubt, have gone hungry even more often than they did. As a British Fabian pamphlet put the matter:

> The people, especially the farmers, were sick of controls. They fed themselves, their families, and their workers before they sold anything off the farm. They began rebuilding their livestock, a slow process dependent mainly on supplies of feed. They sold in the black market rather than through the controlled channels. Such conduct was doubtless unpatriotic, but it was not unnatural. Most countries were suffering more or less from inflation and shops were bare of anything farmers wanted to buy. Why then part with his harvest for worthless *francs* or *drachmae* when by holding it he could live well and have a couple of cows in two years time? In the *long term* interest of European food and agriculture it is not so certain that he was wrong.[96]

A working farmer could not have put the case better than this committed adherent of national planning. Hungry townsmen, however, were not likely to see things the same way – especially given the strength of traditional urban prejudice. (Every European tongue is full of derisory epithets at the farmers' expense – they are "hayseeds" and "rednecks". *Dumm wie'n Bauer* (stupid as a farmer) says the Berliner. *Boeren* in Dutch means both to farm and to belch.) It was not only Marx who spoke of the idiocy of rural life.

In other ways, however, farming enjoyed special esteem. During and after World War II, hunger had been a common experience in Continental Europe. Even in Britain, food was short. "During the author's eight months' stay in England in 1948," wrote an American scholar, "his eleven year-old daughter, in excellent physical condition at the time of departure from the United States ... developed anemia as a result of protein shortage ... despite the fact that her diet was ... reinforced at times with food imports from America which were not available to English children."[97] The food shortage made a profound psychological impression. It was widely expected to last for a long time. The farming industry thus seemed to merit special support for strategic reasons, and also for the purpose of coping with those difficulties that faced Europeans in achieving a reasonable balance in their international trade and payment accounts. Planners insisted that their countries should increase agricultural production – even at excessive cost – in order to save foreign exchange that

[96]Margaret Digby, *Tomorrow's Food: A Study of the World's Food Situation*. London, Fabian Publications, 1946, p. 18.
[97]R. A. Brady, *Crisis in Britain: Plans and Achievements of the Labour Government*. Berkeley, University of California Press, 1950, fn. 10 on p. 448.

might be used for the purpose of importing capital equipment.

Domestic politics played an equally important role. Agricultural interests were generally over-represented in the legislatures of Europe and the US. (Farm lobbies were important; farm blocs were commonplace in parliaments. Agriculturists played a specially important part in many of Europe's ruling parties such as the CDU in West Germany, and the Christian Democratic Party in Italy). The farmers' friends did not, of course, necessarily act in the farmers' long-term interest when supporting protection for the farmers' income in the form of price support for major crops, tariff duties, import quotas, subsidies and dumping of surpluses. But the economic deficiencies of such measures were not widely understood until later. (By 1986–7 farmers in the EEC were receiving $45 billion in subsidies.) From 1960 on diplomatic relations between Western Europe and the US (a great exporter of foodstuffs) became acrimonious over the question of free trade in agriculture.

Equally important were cultural considerations of a more intangible kind. Nationalists of every hue were apt to identify the national virtues of their respective peoples with the farmers' weal. In fact, peasants, speaking local dialects and rooted in local folkways, had been the last to participate in those national cultures promoted by urban educators, politicians, and bureaucrats. Peasants had been among the last to be turned into Italians or into Frenchmen by agencies such as the schools, the army, or later on by political parties and welfare offices.[98] But in theory at least, peasants occupied a special place in the scale of national virtue. Such sentiments were not confined to members of rural lobbies, but were also expressed by parliamentarians who wished to be accounted supporters of peasant individualism, friends of the family farm, admirers of village life, with its real or supposed charms.

In Western Europe (as opposed to communist-dominated Eastern Europe) agriculture recovered at a much faster pace than the most optimistic of forecasters had imagined. No Western European government was foolish enough to nationalize farms and subject them to the proven inefficiency of socialist planning and management. Agricultural recovery went with reconstruction in general. Farmers benefited, as well as townsmen, as railways resumed their operations, bridges were repaired, factories and hydroelectric plants once more set to work. By 1949 or 1950, farming output in all European countries, except Germany, Austria, and Greece at least equalled prewar levels. By the mid-1950s, nearly every crop that could be grown under European climatic conditions was produced in larger quantities than before World War II. Malthus and his followers once again turned out to be mistaken in their forecasts. Western European farm production during this period grew more than twice as fast as the population. (By 1958–9, the index of agricultural production of the OEEC member countries combined stood at 140, as against

---

[98]The phrase derives from the title of Eugen Weber, *Peasants into Frenchmen: The Modernization of Rural France, 1870–1914*. Stanford, Cal., Stanford University Press, 1976. Also see Gordon Wright, *Rural Revolution in France: The Peasantry in the Twentieth Century*. Stanford, Cal., Stanford University Press, 1964, *passim*.

100 for the years 1935–8. The US record was, if anything, even more impressive, with a corresponding figure of about 148.) Less than half the number of Americans earned their living in agriculture yet production increased two or threefold.

These quantitative changes were accompanied by qualitative changes in the patterns of land usage. Permanent grasslands, land temporarily under grass, orchards, vineyards and industrial crops (particularly sugar beet) expanded, while the areas devoted to cereals or potatoes contracted. Overall, about 60 percent of Western Europe's farm production came from livestock, and 40 percent from crops. More and more European housewives were able to serve protein-rich food to their families – milk, cheese, butter, meat, instead of carbohydrates such as bread and potatoes, the poor man's traditional fare.

Statistics of this kind must, of course, be treated with caution. They come from census-takers who may employ differing methodologies and whose findings are not always reliable. Official statistics can take no account of the "second economy" or of the citizen's reluctance to give accurate answers. National figures may conceal enormous regional differences, which of course remained as important during the long period of Western European prosperity as they ever had been. Life continued to be much harder, for example, in some picturesque Apulian village in southern Italy – its streets flanked by whitewashed, low-roofed houses, its uncobbled roads ready to turn into quagmires in the rain, far from any major industries – than, say, in a trim little rural community in Essex, near the London markets, prosperous, and supplied with every amenity. Agricultural advances taking place during the 1940s and 1950s, were uneven, not merely from country to country and region to region, but even from farm to farm.

Yet progress there was on an impressive scale. New varieties of cereals and other grasses, with careful seed selection, increased yields per acre and permitted particular crops to be grown over wider areas than before. Specialized breeding of cattle and hogs, and improved feeding practices, resulted in higher yields of milk and meat.[99] The "green revolution" began in the 1950s and further increased yields, especially of corn, rice, and wheat. Farmers did particularly well with crops that responded to high levels of fertilizers (nitrogens, phosphates, and potash). Pesticides, water pumps, and high priced machinery were part of the system. The green revolution raised grain production from 620 million tonnes in 1950 to almost 1.7 billion in 1985. But progress brought problems: higher costs, and more weeds and insects, resulting in the use of more fungicides, herbicides, and insecticides. More water was needed to help the land to absorb the chemicals. Excessive pumping led to a fall in water tables. As a result the costs of farming went up steadily and more and more land was over-worked or became salt-encrusted. But the public and

---

[99] The index of agricultural production in the OEEC member states between 1935 and 1938 (= 100) rose as follows by 1956–7: all commodities 131, livestock 129, all cereals 129, potatoes 127, sugar beets 162, fruits and nuts 184, vegetables 137, all meats 129, milk 123, eggs 135. Dewhurst, *Europe's Needs*, p. 494.

policy makers dreaded hunger more than long-term ecological deterioration, hence little was done. Moreover, the rapid rise in oil prices in 1973 was disastrous to farmers who depended so heavily on oil-based chemicals such as nitrogen fertilizer. Farms failed; land values plummeted. High-cost farming began to decline, and low-cost farming prospered (with relatively low inputs of chemicals, diversified crops, and smaller acreages).

As impressive in its effects as the green revolution was the heightened pace of mechanization. In this respect the Americans at first enjoyed a commanding lead. This is not to say that all American farmers were among the most progressive. There were still backward regions in the South and in the Appalachians, where cultivators from remote parts of the Balkans would have felt themselves at home. But overall there were striking changes. The efficiency of farming operations greatly improved. (Between 1945 and 1957 the index man hours of labor for farm work declined from 112 to 79, if figures for 1947–9 are 100.) The number of farms in operation diminished (from 5,967,000 to 4,857,000); the average size of farms increased. Wage rates went up (from an average of $101 to $168 per month). The nature of work changed as more and more machines came into use – tractors, trucks, grain combines, corn pickers, milking machines, pickup balers, field forage harvesters, and so on. (Overall the value of farm implements and machinery nearly tripled, from 6,291 to 17,300 million dollars.)[100]

Change in Western Europe was almost equally striking. In prewar days, farmers on the European Continent had mainly depended, like their forefathers, on the power of human and animal muscle. Even many city-bred youngsters would then have been familiar with the ringing sound of scythes being sharpened, the sight of peasants plowing the land with horses, or the pungent smell of manure spread on open fields. Villagers, say in rural Germany, would make a rigid distinction between "cow peasants" and "horse peasants" (the latter owning their own horses). A good deal of the farmers' conversation had been horse talk – about horses used for work, horses for ceremonial occasions, horses for breeding, horses for war.

The modern farmer, by contrast, became an expert mechanic, skilled in the maintenance and care of machines. (Between the immediate prewar years and 1957, the number of tractors employed on Western European farms grew more than tenfold, from 206,900 to 2,377,800. The largest increases occurred in West Germany – from 33,000 to 600,000; in France – from 36,000 to 535,000; and in Britain – from 50,000 to 450,000.) European agriculture followed the pattern in the US and the number of tractors used on farms rose, between 1937 and 1957, from 1,370,000 to 4,600,000. (The Marshall Plan brought over 200,000 tractors to French farmers alone.) Farmers now depended on imported gasoline, a nonrenewable source of power. Tractors – unlike horses – do not provide manure; hence farmers had to rely more than in the past on artificial fertilizers, whose correct usage requires great expertise to

---

[100]For detailed statistics see bureau of the census, *Historical Statistics of the United States: Colonial Times to 1957*. Washington, DC, US Government Printing Office, 1960, pp. 257–304.

prevent deleterious ecological consequences. On the other hand, tractors do not need fodder; hence more land became available for alternative crops.

The effects of the gasoline engine were immense. The motor truck helped to facilitate commerce, to move bulky goods to remote parts of the countryside not served by railways, and to end rural isolation. The new tractors became to many farmers not merely instruments for making a living, but also a source of prestige and pleasure. And farmers acquired many other kinds of mechanical implements, for instance, machinery for milking. (According to estimates for the major industrial countries, outlays for all other machinery approximately equalled expenditure for tractors.)

Changes in farming techniques also owed much to government-promoted research, education, and advisory services. (For these purposes, the Netherlands spent most per male worker employed in agriculture, followed in descending order by Great Britain, Norway, and Sweden, with France, Italy, and Greece at the bottom.) Colleges and universities, including such respected institutions as the University of California at Davis, or the University of Reading in England, taught student farmers, and carried out basic research in all aspects of agriculture, including soils, seeds and fertilizers, plant and animal genetics. A variety of official bodies and cooperative organizations promoted training, and disseminated information. As well as these training programs and field advisory services, the representatives of private farm equipment and fertilizer firms helped to spread new techniques into the remotest areas. Throughout the Atlantic Community, farmers increasingly adopted techniques that were primarily associated with the US.

Governments intervened in many ways, through direct and indirect subsidization of farming, through price support designed to give farmers a steady income or to raise the efficiency of farming operations, through quotas, tariffs, and a host of regulations. Not all governments committed themselves to such policies to the same extent. For instance, Dutch policies proved sufficiently flexible to keep the prices of most products close to those prevailing internationally. Denmark, too, assisted its farmers in many ways, but without supporting particular prices wih public funds. As a result, Danish prices for agricultural crops remained fully competitive in the international market. Yet the Netherlands and Denmark actually increased their agricultural production more than Western Europe as a whole.

Nor did national policies designed to keep prices above the international levels succeed in improving the farmers' income in comparison to that of industrial workers. "High price policies have contributed indirectly to a disparity between farm and non-farm incomes ... [High price policies] kept too many people on farms, while labor shortages in the cities ... produced successful claims for higher wages. More ex-farmers in the towns would have improved farm incomes for those remaining in agriculture ... Better incomes for fewer farmers would probably have lessened the pressure for higher farm prices," thereby lessening the urban workers' demand for wage increases to meet the "increased cost of living."[101]

[101]Ibid., p. 517.

But whatever mistakes governments may have made, farming continued to undergo remarkable changes. Output rose, as fewer farmers produced more crops. The average farmer's income rose, though in a highly disparate fashion, and not (overall) at the same pace as the wages of city folk. The exodus from village to city accelerated, especially in West Germany, the US, and France.[102] (Excluding Greece, Italy, and Spain, whose statistics were unreliable, agricultural employment for Western Europe decreased by about 11 percent per year during 1950–5, as about 1.8 million people left the land.) Labor was thus released to other sectors of the economy to spur economic growth and urbanization. Farmers spent more on city-made products – machinery, fertilizers, vehicles, and fuel. Urban amenities increasingly came to be taken for granted on farms; electrification spread through the countryside, enabling farmers to purchase washing machines, radios, and television sets. Farming, in certain respects, became more like other industries – though with great local variation.

All over Europe, the rural population diminished, and there were great regional shifts. Large numbers of French people continued to depart from western and southeastern France to the north and northeast, as southern Italians migrated from Sicily and Calabria to Lombardy and Tuscany. Spaniards, Portuguese, and Italians went to Germany, the Irish to England, American southerners to the northern and northeastern parts of the US. In addition there was a striking increase in local travel, as rural people got jobs at nearby factories or building sites, taking a bus in the morning and returning to the village at night.

The effects of this rural exodus varied a great deal from region to region, but its overall impact was immense. By the early 1960s, a traveler, say, in the Massif Central in France might wander into an abandoned village and walk through the hushed streets without meeting a soul. Doors and windows were boarded up. The stranger could pick his fill from the laden peach or cherry trees standing untended in the orchards of deserted farms. No dog would bark. The village church might still stand, picturesque, but disused and empty. The decline of a village from full life to perhaps total abandonment would, of course, take many decades. The local nobility or bourgeoisie would be the first to go. Then more people would depart to seek work in the towns. Later, only a few elderly people would be left. On occasion, whole villages would simply vanish, and nature would regain her own.

The effects of this transformation were felt far beyond the villages. Country-bred men and women continued to provide secondary and tertiary industries with workers and with customers – thereby contributing to the industrial recovery. Traditional occupations declined, as rural shoemakers, harness makers, knife grinders, and tailors found ever fewer customers. Fewer women

---

[102]Between 1930 and 1960, the percentage of the work force engaged in agriculture declined as follows: Great Britain from 8 percent to 6 percent; France 34 to 21; West Germany 30 to 11; US 19 to 7. Stanley Rothman, *European Society and Politics*. Indianapolis and New York, Bobbs-Merrill, 1970, p. 146.

than before went into domestic service – traditional employment for village girls anxious to earn money before marriage. Middle-class women in the cities accordingly bought more washing machines, and more driers, and employed babysitters to look after their children.

The gradual disappearance of the peasant-born servant maid alone had far-reaching cultural consequences. It had been the labor of servant maids and of cooks that had enabled middle-class people in cities to be free of the drudgery of housework, to go out to theaters and concerts, to give stylish receptions and grand dinners, and to entertain scholars or artists in their drawing room. As domestic assistance became scarcer, the middle and upper-middle classes had to change their life styles. Village-born servant maids had played an important part in transmitting folkways to the cities. The maids had taught the children how to speak the local dialect, and had taken their young charges for a visit to the home farm. Maids had related folktales or never-to-be-forgotten ballads like the one of how little Marie sat upon a stone – and had her throat slit by a wicked lover. Forty years later, such lore had widely been replaced by television and horror comics.

The social consequences of the rural exodus went very much further. According to ancient and continuing traditions of social criticism, the results of such depopulation were deplorable. English schoolchildren of yesteryear used to memorize Oliver Goldsmith's famous lines (from his poem "The Deserted Village") ... a bold peasantry, their country's pride / When once destroy'd, can never be supplied.

Much indeed was lost – innumerable traditions, an entire way of life. It is difficult moreover to visualize nowadays how beautiful the countryside looked in those distant days before World War II, before freeways and traffic jams had become a commonplace even in fairly remote parts of Germany or England, when rivers such as the Rhine were free from pollution and safe for the careful swimmer. For farmers had not only produced crops; they had played an essential (and rarely recognized) role in maintaining the beauty of the land by tending hedges, keeping fields free from weeds, and so on. European literature moreover is full of allusions to the happiness of traditional peasant life, to the peasant's love for the land, and his sorrow at being uprooted from the native soil. Life on the family farm was said to be sweet, with its simple pleasures and accustomed pieties.

Such encomiums of rural felicity, in truth, usually derived from the city, from men and women who themselves had never cleaned a cowshed, fed a pig, or laboriously ground by hand oil cakes for fodder. Genuine country people widely lacked such sentimental attachments. "La terre est ingrate," as French farmers put it, "the earth is ungrateful." Traditional rural society in Europe had been nothing like as stable as its admirers assumed. Land owner-ship, for instance, had fluctuated a great deal even in the old days, and farms and estates would change hands. Slow emigration to the cities had gone on for centuries. (According to a case study on newcomers to Marseille during the nineteenth century, it had been precisely the most enterprising, the most energetic countrymen who had made their way to the port – certainly not the disoriented, uprooted, alienated countryfolk of romantic fiction.[103]

By the middle of the twentieth century, the majority of people in rural France clearly wanted to get away from the villages. According to French opinion surveys, they regarded life on the farm as harder than in the city. They wanted a better education for their children and more opportunities of the kind that only urban life could offer. Work in town offered a steadier income; there was more comfort and culture and more personal liberty. Over 50 percent of the respondents said that they would leave the farm if they could; only 38 percent indicated that they would like to remain; and only one-fifth wanted their children to stay. And few wives wanted their daughters to marry farmers.[104]

The agricultural transformation also had implications unforeseen immediately after World War II. The threatened food shortage became instead a surplus, subsidized at the general taxpayer's expense. By about 1960, the markets of Western Europe were frequently oversupplied with dairy products, mainly in the form of butter. There were periodic surpluses of pork, eggs, beef, and wheat. The US, in similar manner, was grappling with excess supplies of grain, dairy products, and cotton. The progress accomplished by European agriculturalists in raising efficiency and output was not matched by comparable advances in farm incomes. Food consumption increased much less quickly than demand for other merchandise, and as the production of other sectors rose, the share of agriculture in the national income diminished.[105] Rural prosperity was far from universal. In Italy and France especially, expensive public projects, designed to raise living standards in the backward periphery, in regions such as Sicily and Corsica, had failed to meet the planners' expectations. But when all is said and done, the progress that had been achieved was immense. Food became more widely available and better quality than ever before. Europeans and Americans alike had good cause to prefer the problems of abundance to those occasioned by scarcity and hunger in the Communist bloc. But, overall, agricultural politics in Western Europe had become highly nationalistic and protectionist.

The EEC (founded 1957) did not solve these difficulties, it worsened them. Whereas some countries (the Netherlands and Denmark) were aggressively for free trade; others (Germany, Belgium and Great Britain) were protectionist. The Common Agriculture Policy (CAP) aimed to rationalize all agricultural policies. But politics intruded and protectionism and subsidies took over after 1960, ironically at a time when European farmers became highly productive and least in need of protectionism. Under protection and guaranteed prices as high or higher than 50 percent above world prices, farmers produced mountains of surplus grain, butter and beef, and tensions increased among the states

---

[103]William H. Sewell, *Structure and Mobility: The Men and Women of Marseilles 1820–1870.* Cambridge, Cambridge University Press, 1985, *passim.*

[104]Colin Dyer, *Population and Society in Twentieth Century France.* New York, Holmes and Meier, 1978, pp. 200–2.

[105]Michael Tracy, *Agriculture in Western Europe: Challenge and Response 1880–1980.* London, Granada, 1982, pp. 232–3.

of the EEC as well as with the outside world. In the Treaty of Rome, 1957, the Stresa conference in 1958, and later in 1960, the EEC agreed on internal free trade, commodity preference in foreign trade, and financial solidarity in European agriculture. A complex bureaucratic system developed after 1960 to handle and to regulate agriculture – 95 percent of EEC regulations came to deal with agriculture. The key weakness of the EEC system was its price policy, which encouraged a massive rise in production of unnecessary farm products. These problems became even more acute after the 1960s, as did the difficulties derived from the association of the "overseas territories" of EEC members with the Treaty of Rome – tackled in part by the Treaty of Jaunde in 1962. Nevertheless, Western Europeans felt they were a great deal better off having to worry about "butter mountains" and "wine lakes" than the food shortages of the recent past.

PRIVATE SERVICES AND THE CONSUMER REVOLUTION

The distributive occupations have never enjoyed a good name among intellectuals, and nor have those who work in them. Marxist-Leninists of whatever kind do not regard distributive enterprises as wealth-producing bodies. German right-wingers used to fill many a dreary tome in unfavorably contrasting *Händler und Helden* (hawkers and heroes) or *raffendes und schaffendes Kapital* (predatory, as against creative capital). These attitudes exist today in academia, and in international or national organizations that profess to give aid to backward countries. Such attitudes in fact have no justification. Distributors contribute to the national wealth as much as producers. This much is obvious to any ordinary Soviet housewife who must stand in a long line outside a Soviet state store – a dowdy shop, poorly run, poorly supplied, a firm where the customer is always wrong.[106]

Prejudice against the distributive trades is linked in particular to a dual and linked bias against white-collar workers on the one hand and shopkeepers on the other. White-collar workers have increased in number and diversity during the last century; between them they command an extraordinary range of skills – adjustors, auditors, bank tellers, bookkeepers, buyers, cashiers, computer programmers, credit agents, collectors – the list is endless. But white-collar workers have never been accorded the same respect given, say, to laborers, miners and foundrymen, preferred recruits for the revolutionary guards of the proletarian army. Clerical employees are supposedly a dull lot, and the virtues in which they most excel – punctuality, accuracy, competence – neither make the headlines nor appeal to the literary intelligentsia.

Shopkeepers have had an even worse press, more so in Europe than the

---

[106]David K. Willis, *Klass: How Russians Really Live*, New York, St Martin's Press, 1985, gives a popular account.

US, and nowhere more than in Great Britain. Better a wicked baron than a virtuous grocer — thus the common consent among many educated people. The alleged deficiencies of the petty bourgeoisie are many and variegated. It is supposedly a class marked by philistinism and moral cowardice; it is also assumed to be in a state of social decay. Hence non-Marxist and Marxist scholars alike "have in large measure avoided dealing with the *Kleinbürgertum* [the lower middle class] . . . because they approvingly prophesied its extinction."[107]

Such beliefs lack justification on both historical and economic grounds. The petty bourgeoisie was never among history's chosen cowards. In Germany, the popular word for a petty bourgeois philistine is *Spiesser*, originally meaning "pikeman" — that is to say a burgher equipped to defend his city with a pike. In Britain, Oliver Cromwell's New Model Army in the seventeenth century, the finest fighting force of the time, had been recruited from the ranks of shopkeepers and tradesmen. A large proportion of the British tankers who conquered at El Alamein had been born in semi-detached houses with names like "Belleview" or "Mon Repos," situated in the suburban heart of Great Britain that so many intellectuals affect to despise. Much, if not most of the great music and art in the Western world was created by the offspring of the petty bourgeoisie. (The "aristocratic" music of the eighteenth century was largely composed by men whom Marx would have classed as petty bourgeois. Knights, barons, and their ladies danced to the splendid minuets and sarabandes written by humbly born geniuses like Haydn and Mozart.)

Antipathy to the petty bourgeoisie, especially the shopkeepers, on economic grounds, are equally ill conceived. More than two centuries ago, Adam Smith observed: "the prejudices of some political writers against shopkeepers and tradesmen are altogether without foundation. So far from it being necessary to tax them, or to restrict their numbers . . . they can never be multiplied so as to hurt the publick, though they may so as to hurt one another."[108]

Neither is the petty bourgeoisie on the road to economic extinction. In the Western world, especially in the most advanced countries, the distributive trades are thriving. Far from declining, white-collar workers have grown in numbers during the postwar years, in comparison with blue-collar workers. The growth of the distributive sector has occurred both in absolute and relative terms. By the early 1950s commerce, banking, insurance, and finance in Western Europe already accounted for $28.2 billion, that is to say, 14.7 percent of the gross domestic product, and 11.4 percent of the labor force. These white-collar occupations alone produced a larger portion of the gross domestic product than agriculture, forestry, and fishing between them ($23.9 billion, or 12.4 percent.)[109] In the US, the service sector was even larger; within this

[107]Arno J. Mayer, "The lower middle class as a historical problem." *Journal of Modern History*, v. 47, no. 11, March 1975, p. 409.

[108]Adam Smith, *An Inquiry into the Nature and Causes of the Wealth of Nations*. New York, The Modern Library, 1937, p. 342.

[109]for detailed statistics, see J. Frederick Dewhurst et al., *Europe's Needs and Resources: Trends and Prospects in Eighteen Countries*. New York, Twentieth Century Fund, 1961, pp. 130-1. US department of commerce, bureau of the census, *Historical Statistics of the United States: Colonial Times to 1957*. Washington, DC, US Government Printing Office, 1960, p. 140.

sector commerce occupied the biggest place; and within the commercial sector retailing was the most significant occupation – almost twice as important as the wholesale trade.[110] Far from becoming extinct, small enterprises managed to hold their own despite the increase in large-scale organizations.

Generalizations are difficult of course, for the distributive trades were marked by enormous variety in the size, wealth, and nature of the organizations engaged therein. The largest firms included, for instance, great department stores (such as *Kaufhof* in Germany, Marks and Spencer in Great Britain, Macy's and Federated Department Stores in the US). Department stores had opened in the US in the nineteenth century, and greatly extended their scope thereafter. They operated in cities, where customers were many, and where the volume of trade was large. In terms of organization these stores delegated authority to subordinate executives with each department head responsible for purchasing a related stock of goods and supervising their sale in distinct sections of the store. Department stores offered many advantages, including low fixed prices, and a wide assortment of goods (made possible by a large turnover). They gave customers a sense of status, of impersonal service, different from the relationship prevailing between a customer and a tailor or storekeeper in a London or Paris shop where a purchase might involve a lengthy, and sometimes unwelcome conversation about the weather, the crops, or a neighbor's alleged marital infidelities. They also furnished an opportunity for shoppers to buy under one roof anything their family might need, without the necessity of running around to several speciality shops. Department stores offered a sense of restrained luxury that a small retailer could not provide. Shopping in such a store became for many housewives an enjoyable pastime, as well as an economic pursuit.

Other distributive enterprises comprised cooperatives (favored by moderate social reformers) and also chain stores. (The latter are separate shops under common ownership, each with a similar organization, and similar appearance.) Chain stores concentrated on selling highly standardized goods such as groceries that consumers buy on a day-to-day basis. Chains benefited from economies in sales promotion and advertising, through standardization of operating procedures, from spreading risks, and from their ability to purchase goods on a large scale. Chain stores came later to Western Europe than to the United States but their number expanded greatly after 1950.

The latest addition to the list are supermarkets, developed in the US during the 1930s, and greatly expanded after World War II. Supermarkets offered many advantages, including lower prices, free parking, and self-service, so that purchasers could inspect and choose goods without the sometimes unwelcome attentions of sales staff. Supermarkets therefore relied on the art of displaying

---

[110]In 1957, the national income from the major service industries in the US was distributed as follows (in million dollars): retail trade and automotive services: 38,693, wholesale trade: 20,929, business services not elsewhere classified: 4,841, personal services: 4,019, engineering and other professional services: 1,952, miscellaneous repair services and trade services: 1,488. *Historical Statistics of the United States: Colonial Times to 1957*, p. 518.

and packaging goods; they provided a great variety of merchandise. Self-service stores spread rapidly in Western Europe from the mid-1950s. Supermarkets especially brought about far-reaching changes in purchasing habits, and were particularly popular in the suburbs, where they widely replaced the old neighborhood store. The spread of supermarkets went with motorization and the availability of refrigeration. Henceforth housewives and house-husbands would only have to go to the supermarket once or twice a week to load the family station wagon with merchandise – a far cry from the old days when mother or the maid had walked daily to the nearest shops, and carried home her meat and vegetables in a shopping basket.[111]

In theory, the small shopkeeper should have disappeared in the face of such formidable competition. In practice, this did not happen. Though retailing – like agriculture – had long been an overcrowded industry, "independents" continued to account for a large share of the retail turnover in the US, and for the greater proportion in Western Europe. (Percentages varied greatly from country to country, from 96 percent of the total in Italy in the early 1950s, to 51 percent in Great Britain, a country distinguished by the efficient management of the retail trade.)

Small shopkeepers, however, had to change their methods. In the past, the village store had dealt in almost every conceivable merchandise, buying and selling in small quantities, an occupation that necessarily entailed a great deal of man (and woman) power, often the labor of poor relations. As cities grew and demand expanded, independent storekeepers survived, for instance by developing specialized skills. A family-run store in a suburb, unless favorably located, had a hard time competing against a supermarket – but not as a specialist outlet in women's clothing, sports goods, or gourmet foods. A shoemaker's hand-made shoes could rarely prevail against mass-produced footwear sold in a big store. But there were plenty of orders for a cobbler who mended shoes, for a TV store that would service and repair television sets, or for an electrician to put right those broken appliances that defied their owners' skills. (A sign outside a London electrician's shop read "do it yourself – then bring it to us.") Small entrepreneurs survived in many ways – by providing special services such as home deliveries, or by concentrating in luxury goods, or in specific "ethnic" markets in American cities. A small speciality shop might obtain a lease in a new or refurbished center with pseudo-rural designations – "barn," "village," and such like – used to attract customers.

Overall, shopkeepers played as large, perhaps even a larger share in the customer revolution than large enterprises – a matter that still remains to be investigated. But wherever they did their shopping, Western Europeans and Americans continued to spend more and more. They also shifted their demands, devoting a larger portion of their incomes to clothing, furniture,

[111]Commission of the European Communities. *Changes in the Structure of the Retail Trade in Europe*. Luxembourg, Office for Official Publications, 1982. Harold Barger, *Distribution's Place in the American Economy Since 1869*. Princeton, NJ, Princeton University Press, 1955. Delbert J. Duncan and Charles F. Phillips, *Retailing: Principles and Methods*. Homewood, Ill., Irwin, 1959.

and appliances than to food. Small shops staked out for themselves a large portion of this expanding trade – so much so that the greater part of all manufactured clothing, for example, was sold through small stores individually owned.[112] Family grocers also learned new techniques. Over 70 percent of the housewives in Austria, Germany, Italy, and Norway continued to patronize their local grocer, who began to stock frozen and pre-packaged foods as well as the customary fresh fruit and vegetables.

The resultant consumer revolution had far-reaching effects. Early nineteenth-century writers had hoped or feared that the poor, propelled by hunger, would overthrow the social order and all established intellectual values. As Heinrich Heine had put it

> A silent stockfish, well fried in butter
> Does more to convince the reds in the gutter
> Than a brilliant thinker like Mirabeau
> And all the debaters since Cicero.

But far from enduring immiseration, as Heine, Marx, and other intellectuals had predicted, the masses continued to improve their living standards. This process accelerated at the end of World War II. As wartime and postwar shortages ended, consumers became more discriminating. (Germans jokingly said, "nach der Fresswelle kam die Edelfresswelle." This might be roughly rendered "after the years of hunger had ended, we were first content just to guzzle; then we insisted on guzzling delicacies.") Traditional social distinctions in dress and consumption patterns diminished. (There was, at the same time, a decline in the prestige of what might be called the minor uniform-wearing occupations. In the old days, postmen, fire fighters, railway conductors and policemen – people with steady jobs wearing a standardized service dress – had been envied by workers in insecure employment; after the war prestige patterns within the working class began to shift.) Under the old dispensation, rich or even moderately rich people could afford to have their boots and jackets made to measure by craftsmen. (A successful parliamentarian in London during the early 1950s, for example, might still have availed himself of such services.) As the consumer revolution went on, even the rich turned to buying their clothes off the racks in the stores like everyone else. On the other hand, perfumes, deodorants, and quality soaps ceased to be the prerogative of the well-to-do, even relatively poor people could now afford to be well groomed.

Just before World War I, George Bernard Shaw had published one of his great comedies, *Pygmalion* (popularized later through the musical *My Fair Lady*). Shaw's play hinges on an "incredible" transformation when a snobbish professor of phonetics and a kindly colonel join forces to turn Eliza Doolittle, a poor flower girl, into a duchess. They accomplish this miracle by teaching her cleanliness, manners, dress sense, and English elocution. Two generations later, such a feat would have been much less noteworthy. Flower girls and duchesses by that time wore similar frocks (though duchesses could afford

---

[112]Dewhurst, *Europe's Needs*, pp. 252, 196.

more original designs). They watched the same movies and the same TV programs; and a flower girl desirous of changing a Cockney accent into a BBC accent could do so through a self-study course in English pronunciation with gramophone records. An ambitious modern flower girl could have surprised society ladies in other ways, for instance by acquiring a broad musical culture. This she could do not by buying expensive opera and concert tickets, but by regularly listening to the BBC's Third Programme (provided by public enterprise), or more effectively still by purchasing classical records (produced by private enterprise).

Some moralists deprecated this process. "Admass" became a fashionable term at the time to decry the real or supposed evils of mass culture and advertising. The hostility to "Admass" had many springs – elitism, rural nostalgia, social snobbery, disappointment at socialist revolutions gone awry. "Admass" was widely linked with the loss of rural simplicity. But the village of former days was not as happy a place as the romantics believed. The agricultural laborers especially hated their labor. It was hard to get up at dawn, rain or shine, summer and winter, weekday or holiday, to till the land or tend the beasts.[113] Work in a warm factory or shop, with regular shifts, and opportunities for shopping in good stores made a greater appeal. "Admass," may not have added to human happiness in the abstract. But the desire for higher living standards, for the benefits that mass production could bestow on consumers, had certainly not been imposed on working-class people by a "false consciousness" created by the advertiser's art. To give one example, an anarchist congress held in Spain in 1898 had portrayed the ideal society that was to emerge from the great revolutionary upheaval of the future. Workers would live in great apartment houses, lit by electricity, serviced by automated elevators and rubbish disposers; they would become leisured supervisors of machines; and in this new society iron would replace wood, and tokens take the place of money.[114] Such had been the dreams of the genuinely poverty-stricken – and the consumer society went a long way toward fulfilling such fantasies, with credit cards in part taking the role of tokens. "Admass" certainly contributed to consumer choice, and to the levelling (downwards and upwards) of society. (Western Europe's rural periphery, Italy's "deep South," and the remoter parts of Ireland, Spain and Portugal, were again left behind in this respect.)

Consumerism in turn was linked to advertising. Advertising is an ancient trade, and one that has been impugned for centuries. As Dr Johnson, the English writer and lexicographer, wrote more than 200 years before:

Advertisements are now so numerous that they are very negligently perused, and it is therefore necessary to gain attention by magnificence of promise, and by eloquence sometimes sublime and sometime pathetic ... The trade of advertising is now so near perfection that it is not easy

[113]For the study of an East Anglian rural community, see Ronald Blythe, *Akenfield, Portrait of an English Village*. New York, Dell Publishing Co, 1973.
[114]Raymond Carr, *Spain 1808–1975*. Oxford, Clarendon Press, 1982, p. 455.

to propose it as a moral question to the public ear, whether they do not sometimes play too wantonly with our passions.[115]

Dr Johnson's strictures have since been frequently extended, though not stylistically improved, in social critiques with question-begging titles such as *Partners in Plunder, The Hidden Persuaders,* and *Der Manipulierte Mensch.*[116]

Intellectual complaints should, however, be seen in perspective. As long as shoppers bought only staple necessities, such as bread and potatoes, there was no need for advertising. Nor was there a place for advertisers as long as the working class bought only secondhand clothes and a frock-coat, or as long as a fine cane was passed on from father to son as an heirloom. New products such as electric shavers, frozen food, and air conditioners, produced in great quantities, by contrast, required a new informational network. This the advertisers supplied, and advertising soon turned into a major industry. (Between 1945 and 1957 alone, the volume of advertising in the US more than tripled, from $2,874.5 million to $10,310.6 million.)

Advertising became ubiquitous – it was on radio, TV, and billboards, in newspapers and magazines. Advertisements helped to finance television programs. At its worst advertising became a public eyesore, and at its best a minor form of art. Advertisers were loathed by the intelligentsia, who imputed to them mysterious powers of manipulating the masses. But despite their reputation, advertisers could not coerce customers into buying unwanted goods. Nor could they create market monopolies for a particular brand. The small European car, and later the Japanese car, for example, did not make inroads on the US market because foreign automobile producers were better at advertising than the giants of Detroit – they succeeded because they created the type of cars that American consumers wanted to buy.

The travel agent, motel manager, and holiday camp supervisor likewise played an important part in furthering the consumer revolution. Europeans and Americans had always traveled a great deal. An eighteenth-century wayfarer might have met all kinds and conditions of men, journeymen in search of employment, vagrants, ditch diggers, tinkers, street musicians, highwaymen, pilgrims, harlots, as well as respectable travelers, merchants and their like. But rich or poor, most of them were on the move by necessity – the Grand Tour of the Continent, undertaken for instruction or pleasure, was reserved for the very rich. During the nineteenth century well-to-do people came to patronize hotels in larger numbers, including fashionable establishments at places such as Interlaken or St Mortiz in Switzerland, or along the French Riviera.

---

[115]Dr Samuel Johnson, cited in Will and Ariel Durant, *Rousseau and Revolution*, New York, Simon and Schuster, 1967, p. 786.

[116]Joseph Brown Matthews and R. E. Shellcross, *Partners in Plunder: The Cost of Business Dictatorship.* Washington, NJ Consumers' Research, 1935. Vance Oakley Packard, *The Hidden Persuaders.* New York, Pocket Books, 1970. Herbert W. Franke, *Der Manipulierte Mensch: Grundlagen der Werbung und der Meinungsbildung.* Brockhaus, Wiesbaden, 1964. For a contrary interpretation, see Dean Amory Worcester, *Welfare Gains From Advertising: The Problem of Regulation.* Washington, DC, American Enterprise Institute for Public Policy Research, 1978.

From mid-twentieth century onwards tourism was for the masses, for people who took part in conducted tours, camping, youth hosteling, journeys by air, train, bus and car, and other comparatively cheap means of travel. The accent began to shift from lengthy sojourns to shorter ones, taken more frequently. These changes were brought about by rising incomes, by improvement in air travel, by the extending ownership of family cars, and by the decline in parochial prejudice and xenophobia. Tourism during the 1950s became a mass industry. (By 1955, hotels, local transport enterprises, and shops in Western Europe received about $2.1 billion from foreign tourists. More than half this sum was paid out by tourists from other European countries; Americans spent about $460 million, and other non-European tourists about $500 million.) The number of people involved was astronomical. Arrivals in all Western European countries combined in 1957 amounted to 34,502,000 – 19,258,000 in the EEC alone.[117] For better or worse, the elite who had once patronized the Orient Express were outnumbered now by ordinary folk in economy class.

The private insurance agent rarely figures in literature as a principal architect of the social service society. Insurance companies nevertheless have helped to change the modern citizen's life. Eliza Doolittle carried no insurance. Had she remained a flower girl in pre-World War I London, she would have depended in emergencies on her drunken father, and on friends and relatives. Half a century later, she would have been able to afford the services, not merely of well-publicized state agencies, but also of private insurance companies, to protect herself against every conceivable kind of risk – ill health, fire, burglary, accident, a pension for her old age, and a life premium payable to her dependents in the event of her death. Though public insurance expanded so did private insurance – becoming an enterprise of enormous size and complexity. (In the US for example, the total assets of all private life insurance companies alone amounted, in 1957, to $101,309 million, compared to the total assets or liabilities of all US banks, reckoned at $242,629 million.) The value of hospital insurance, to give another example, stood at $121,432 million. Both figures reflected a striking increase over those of 1945 – $44,797 million, and $32,685 million respectively.

In Europe, insurance was also important, and it accounted for a substantial amount of foreign business (especially for Britain and Switzerland). Despite the growth of government-provided social services, private insurance continued to play a major part in protecting people against unforeseen mishaps. Sickness insurance, for example, in the late 1950s was "mostly still in the hands of autonomous, privately organized and operated insurance funds or societies."[118] Companies operating on both sides of the Atlantic were able to provide wider coverage and gained the advantage of more widely pooled risks both by the federation or amalgamation of smaller companies, and also by the pooling of funds previously differentiated between different occupational groups.

The influence of insurance societies and pension funds went even wider.

[117]Dewhurst, *Europe's Needs*, pp. 281, 661.
[118]Ibid., p. 381.

Private pension and deferred profit sharing plans became a major part of the economy through investments in every form of enterprise. Through their pension, trade union, and other private insurance funds, working people thus acquired a major stake in the means of production, so much so that Peter Drucker, a US social scientist, was able to speak by the 1970s of an "unseen revolution" designated by the term "pension fund socialism."[119] According to his calculations, employees in American business owned through their pension funds at least 25 per cent of its equity capital; while the pension funds of the self-employed, public employees, schools and universities between them owned at least another 10 per cent. Eliza Doolittle's descendants had come a long way.

[119]Peter Ferdinand Drucker, *The Unseen Revolution: How Pension Fund Socialism Came to America.* New York, Harper and Row, 1976, p. 1.

I I

Social Development in the Atlantic Community

Few statistical calculations arouse greater anxiety among the learned than those connected with demography. At the end of the eighteenth century, when Western Europe experienced a striking growth of population, Thomas Malthus demonstrated to his own satisfaction that natural population growth – if unchecked – would always exceed the means of subsistence. Chaste living therefore furnished "the only virtuous means of avoiding the vice and misery which results from the principles of population."[1] Given the preachers' and prophets' scant success over the millennia in persuading men and women to practice sexual continence, Malthus's conclusion was indeed pessimistic.

But during the twentieth century Western birthrates declined. Thus the center of anxiety began to shift, and fear of overpopulation gave way to fear of depopulation. League of Nations experts made gloomy forecasts that seemed to bear out predictions made earlier in the century by Oswald Spengler, a German philosopher, of the demise of the West (*Untergang des Abendlandes*). During the 1930s, *L'Illustration*, a respectable French journal, went even further in its pessimism, prophesying that within half a century the French people would cease to exist.[2] Such apprehensions did not seem totally unjustified, given the declining size of families in Western (though not Southern and Eastern) Europe, together with the dread of war and the demographic disasters it would bring.

POPULATION, HEALTH CARE, AND MIGRATION

The effects of war were certainly grim enough. But the demographers' foreboding proved unjustified. World War I had been followed by a striking fall in birthrates (ranging from 25 percent in Britain, 1913–17, to 50 percent in

[1]Cited in essay on "Malthus" in Palgrave's *Dictionary of Political Economy*, ed., Henry Higgs. London, Macmillan, 1926, v. 2, p. 670.
[2]Colin Dyer, *Population and Society in Twentieth Century France*. London, Hodder and Stoughton, 1978, p. 176.

Belgium and Germany). During World War II, by contrast, marriage and birthrate increased in both belligerent and neutral countries.[3] The upswing in birthrates continued during the postwar years when returning servicemen got married and started families. The resultant "baby boom" had not been predicted by any demographer, sociologist, or economist. Their inability to forecast the demographic rejuvenation of an ageing country such as France during and after World War II renders questionable other attempts to forecast the long-term demographic future of Western society. The psychological causes of the baby boom are still not well understood, and nor are the causes for its differential impact on Western countries. (The population of the Netherlands rose most strikingly; Belgium's population grew little.) But both Western Europe and the US experienced demographic growth (as demonstrated in table 11.1). It was only during the 1960s that birthrates in North America and Western Europe once more began to drop.

The effects of the baby boom were indeed far-reaching. There was a new demand for schools, housing, kindergartens, playgrounds, and for goods such as baby carriages, strollers, and playpens. France especially experienced a demographic rebirth: a country that had been ruled by ageing men, that was prone to pessimism and a constant search for security, it developed a new sense of confidence and enterprise. The "fossils" who had led the French army disappeared, as did the "mental sclerosis" that had pervaded French industry. (France also adopted the most generous family allowance plan of any European country, and made generous provisions for maternity and child care – though the long-term success of these in increasing the birthrate are in doubt.)

Demographic rejuvenation also had· consequences of a less direct kind. During World War II many young men (and some young women) had rapidly advanced into positions of responsibility. (To give an example, E. T. (later Sir Edgar) Williams, an Oxford historian, rose to be Montgomery's chief intelligence officer in North Africa at the age of 30 and became a brigadier general at a time of life when a peacetime officer would hardly have reached the rank of major. In his tutorials Williams would often refer to an eighteenth-century toast in British officers' messes that called for "a sickly season and a bloody war" to speed up promotion.) This unusual mobility now continued in peacetime, when economic expansion, and the development of private business and public enterprise provided many new jobs. More importantly, demographic growth of itself created new customers and thereby contributed toward economic prosperity. More youngsters enrolled in schools and universities. The "youth market" expanded, as more young workers than ever before brought home substantial pay packets. Demobilized GIs, British,

---

[3]Between 1938 and 1944 the birthrate (in percentages) rose approximately as follows: France: 11, Netherlands: 17, Britain: 18, Switzerland: 29, Sweden: 34, Spain: 36. Only Germany and Italy experienced a striking decline, Germany: − 22, Italy: − 23. For a comparative table see J. Frederic Dewhurst, et al., *Europe's Needs and Resources: Trends and Prospects in Eighteen Countries*. New York, Twentieth Century Fund, 1961, p. 43. For a complete rundown of demographic statistics, country by country, see B. R. Mitchell, *European Historical Statistics, 1750–1975*. New York, Facts on File, 1980, pp. 27–158.

TABLE 11.1   *Population of selected countries: 1939–1959 (in millions)*

Western Europe	1939	1959
Austria	6.7	7.0
Belgium	8.4	8.6
Denmark	3.8	4.6
France	41.3	45.2
Great Britain	47.8	52.0
Republic of Ireland	2.0	2.8
Italy	44.3	49.4
Netherlands	8.9	11.2
Norway	3.0	3.6
Spain	25.5	30.1
Sweden	6.3	7.5
Switzerland	4.2	5.3
West Germany	49.2 (1949)	54.9

US and British dominions		
Australia	6.6 (1933)	10.3 (1960)
Canada	11.5 (1941)	18.0 (1960)
New Zealand	1.5 (1936)	2.4 (1961)
South Africa (whites)	2.0 (1936)	3.0 (1961)
US	131.0 (1939)	179.3 (1957)

German, and French veterans in college no longer felt that they were gaining qualifications merely to face subsequent unemployment. (The Canadian government expanded its bureaucracy by 40 percent during the war to take care of veterans.) There was a striking decline in the youth cult that had gained so much popularity both among left-wing and right-wing intellectuals in prewar days. The world had become for the young a distinctly better place.

The population growth after World War II had many facets. More children were born. More children survived. There was a sharp fall in infant mortality – a marvellous boon.[4] There was an equally remarkable rise in average life expectancy. Population ageing only began to affect the labor force in many countries from the late 1950s on, and migrant workers then made up for the labor shortages in Western Europe. Better quality food became available to the poor; medical services became more widely available; new housing was built. Ten years after the end of one of the most destructive wars in history, Europeans and Americans were generally better fed and housed than ever before.

[4]Between 1938 and 1955 death rates for children between one and four dropped as follows: in Austria: 5.7 to 2.1, Belgium: 6.4 to 1.8, Denmark: 2.4 to 1.3, France: 5.6 to 1.9, Germany: 5.4 to 1.8, Italy: 14.1 to 4.5, Netherlands: 3.5 to 1.4, Norway: 2.9 to 1.5, Portugal: 22.2 to 10.5, Sweden: 3.4 to 1.2, England and Wales, 4.9 to 1, Scotland: 7 to 1.4, Dewhurst, *Europe's Needs,* p. 38.

The war years and the postwar years also proved a golden age in medicine – one that no longer centered on Germany, France, and Britain, but on the English-speaking world, with the US in first place. For example, in 1941, Dr Selman Waksman isolated streptomycin. The US developed the large-scale production of penicillin, first discovered by Alexander Fleming, and originally developed by Howard Florey and Ernest Chain in England. Blood transfusions became an established part of surgical practice. In 1949, Macfarlane Burnet, an Australian, showed that animal tissues and organs could be successfully transplanted from one individual to another, provided certain conditions were met; these findings, tested by Peter Medawar and others, became the basis of human organ transplants (the first kidney transplant from a cadaver to a patient was performed in Chicago in 1950). In 1953 Dr Jonas Salk, an American, announced the success of the first clinical trials of a vaccine against polio. In the same year Francis Crick, an Englishman, and James Watson, an American, published their findings on the "double helix" structure of deoxyribonucleic acid (DNA), the substance that transmits hereditary characteristics. In elaborating their theories regarding this chemical code of life, Crick and Watson helped to open up the new field of molecular biology. Similar advances occurred in many other fields of medicine and biology, with far-reaching effects for the future. As a result of these and other discoveries many infectious diseases were conquered or controlled, including scarlet fever, diphtheria, measles, whooping cough, and polio. Vaccinations and new drugs kept down the death rate for small pox, cholera, malaria, and a host of other afflictions. Not that gains were made on every front. There were more deaths from cancer and heart trouble – diseases that tend to strike harder at urban than at rural people; and deaths from road accidents increased dramatically as car ownership became ever more widespread. Nevertheless, the overall gain was remarkable.

There was too, a general advance in human health, due to a combination of factors – improved living standards, improvements in the private and public provisions of health care facilities, and in public health regulations. By 1960, all of Europe had elaborate systems of health control, and agencies to enforce the regulations. International cooperation over health matters increased. (For instance the World Health Organization (WHO) came into being in 1948, and did good work in helping to fight diseases such as cholera, malaria, and tuberculosis.) Standards of sanitation generally improved, and the modern state gave greater priority to public health matters such as vaccination, inoculation, quarantine, control of communicable diseases, control of purity of water and food. The state regulated sanitation; it licenced providers of health care; it regulated hospitals and medicines. All governments became concerned to a greater or lesser extent with the battle against disease.[5]

The new era of health-consciousness saw a striking increase in the number of physicians. (Between 1927 and 1956, the number of physicians in Western Europe grew by 91 percent. The figure for people per physician in France

[5]See in Milos Macura, "Population in Europe 1920–1970," in Carlo M. Cipolla, ed., *The Fontana Economic History of Europe. The Twentieth Century,* part I. London, Collins/Fontana Books, 1976.

declined from 1,500 in 1938, to 1,100 in 1954. There was a comparable growth in the number of dentists. Nursing enjoyed high prestige. As a popular British encyclopedia put it, in terms quaint or offensive to subsequent generations, "nursing ranks high as a profession for women, since it has an essentially feminine appeal" – at this time far fewer women were able to gain medical degrees than 30 years later.[6] More hospital beds became available than in prewar years. Piped water supplies and sewerage were extended. There were further improvements in industrial health care, and in facilities for school-children. Between 1930 and 1954 expenditure on medical care for national insurance schemes almost quadrupled in Western Europe – from $1,171 million to $4,493 million (at constant prices). Health insurance systems brought medical services to everyone, rich or poor. The cost of medical care continued to rise, however, hurting those who had no health insurance, and costing taxpayers dearly.

Whereas most Western countries had provided accident and sickness insurance before World War II, national health schemes began to be developed after 1945. The first in force was the British National Health Insurance set up in 1946 (but not put into effect until 1948). Thereafter, compulsory health insurance spread to most of the rest of Europe. The British also pioneered the National Health Service (NHS) which operated side by side with private services. The National Health Service did suffer from numerous deficiencies that became more and more obvious to subsequent generations: costs expanded and complaints regarding the standard of services increased. Nevertheless, the NHS was immensely popular at the start – one of the first postwar Labour government's most spectacular achievements, and one that no subsequent administration dared dismantle.

By the mid-1950s, health care accounted for a total of about 3 percent of Western Europe's gross national product – albeit with striking variations between the rich and poor countries.[7] These figures are not easy to evaluate, for there is no precise correlation between public health and public health expenditure. The Luxemburgers' well-being was not superior to that of the Swiss, although Luxemburg spent a good deal more in proportionate terms than Switzerland. But overall, the money was well spent, and Western Euro-peans, on the average, were healthier and better fed than their ancestors had ever been – infant mortality declined to 15 per 1,000, and life expectancy increased to over 70 years.

Migration

The postwar era was also an age of migration *par excellence*

---

[6]*Everyman's Encyclopedia.* London, J. Dent and Sons, 1961, v. 9, p. 352.
[7]In 1954, France, West Germany, and Britain spent 3.6 percent of their GNP on total medical care and health related cash benefits. Other countries' percentages: Sweden: 3.1, Switzerland: 2.6, Italy: 2, Portugal: 1.4, Spain: 0.3, Luxemburg: 3.9. Dewhurst, p. 383.

Es, es, est und es
Es ist ein harter Schluss
Weil, weil, weil und weil
Weil ich aus Frankfurt muss.

"It is a hard end, but I have to leave Frankfurt, and seek my fortune elsewhere" went the opening lines of a traditional German folk song whose cheerful marching rhythm defied its melancholy lyrics. The singer, in his own words, departed from his native city because he no longer liked his master's work, and his mistress's cooking. During and after World War II, there were far worse reasons why men and women left home. As we have seen, some 9,000,000 Germans were expelled from formerly German regions taken over by Poland and the Soviet Union; 3,000,000 were forced out of Czechoslovakia, and about an equal number fled from the Soviet occupied zone. The bulk of the remaining Jewish population of Eastern Europe joined the exodus, as did numerous Poles, Croats, Serbs, and others.

There was also a massive outflow of Europeans overseas – especially to the United States and to the British dominions.[8] These countries acquired a more cosmopolitan air, as Greeks, Poles, Germans, Italians, as well as English, Welsh, Scots, and Irish, settled as far afield as New York, Chicago, Sydney, Johannesburg, Auckland, Toronto, and Montreal. Australia, for the first time in its history, acquired a large non-British component. The white population of South Africa and Southern Rhodesia grew apace. Israel absorbed Jews from all over the world, first of all from Eastern and Central Europe, later from the Middle East.

But by far the most important beneficiary was the US, which between 1945 and 1957 alone, received more than 2,500,000 immigrants from all parts of Europe (about 75 percent of all immigrants went to the US.) The emigrants were generally young, and likely to have skills or professions. If they were lucky, they would get some help from expatriate kinsmen, friends, or fellow church members. But in the main the newcomers had to rely on their own efforts to find employment, or housing, to choose a doctor or dentist for their families. They tended to be individualists in outlook – militant class consciousness did not travel well across the ocean. Historically, these migrants formed part of the last great movement of Europeans overseas.

Equally important were the additional and overlapping population shifts. These included the move from the countryside to the city; the migration from Europe's agricultural periphery (Southern Italy, Spain, Portugal, Greece, and Turkey) into the industrial heartland; and a new movement from the former imperial possessions – from Algeria, the West Indies, the Indian subcontinent, and elsewhere – into Europe. In the US, these population movements were paralleled by the exodus of rural Southerners (especially black people) into the cities of the North and West, and by the immigration of Hispanic people

---

[8]The estimated number of emigrants, 1941 to 1961 (in thousands) was as follows: Great Britain: 2,209, Germany: 1,490, Italy: 1,325, Spain: 709, Netherlands: 416, Portugal: 415. Mitchell, *European Historical Statistics*, p. 145.

(above all Mexicans, but also Puerto Ricans, later Cubans, Dominicans, Central Americans) to the US mainland.

The shift from the countryside into the cities, as we have indicated before, formed part of a long-term trend that entailed a transformation in agricultural methods and employment. Cities continued to grow in size. (By the mid-1950s, Western Europe comprised 41 cities with over 500,000 inhabitants, including 13 cities with more than 1,000,000.) The average European or American was employed in offices, factories, and workshops, and was no longer familiar with life on the farm, as his or her ancestors had been.[9] The average child could no longer tell the difference between a Friesian and Jersey cow, or between a wheat and a rye stalk; much of Europe's traditional folklore ceased to have relevance. City children instead picked up new kinds of knowledge, about cars, metros, and traffic signs. City lore and city slang took the place of traditional folklore and rural speech. What changed after World War II was not just the extent of the movement from village to town, but its acceptance as a fact of life – no longer as a menace to national culture or even national integrity. As prosperity spread, an increasing number of city people bought, or rented homes in the suburbs, or in housing projects favored by town planners to relieve real or perceived overcrowding. Accustomed neighborhoods changed their characters as, say, Jewish Londoners moved from Whitechapel to Golders Green. The new exodus, however, also had the unintended effect of weakening traditional urban cores, diminishing their tax base, and leaving them more open to crime than before.

Migration from Europe's agricultural periphery into the industrial heartlands had also gone on for centuries. In seventeenth-century Holland, many of the hardest and most poorly paid jobs had been performed by German *Hollandgänger*. Later, Poles had joined the trek and migrated into those German Rhenish provinces that had once furnished workmen for Holland, but had subsequently themselves experienced industrialization. By the middle of the twentieth century inter-European migration had greatly accelerated. Reconstruction and industrial development had produced widespread labor shortages; aggravated by an ageing population, the raising of the school leaving age, the wider availability of early retirement, and the diminution in industrialized countries of the agricultural population that had once provided an indigenous labor reserve. After the 1950s large-scale emigration from Europe ended and immigration rose – in 1960 there was a net immigration of 1.7 million people. By 1971, something like 8.5 to 9 million newcomers had made their way to Northern and Western Europe in search of jobs. Some were Irish people, who constantly moved to England (about 350,000 came between 1946 and 1950), and many more – about half the total – were from the Mediterranean basin, that is Portugal, Spain, Italy, and Greece. Turkey and Yugoslavia were also a

---

[9]Between 1930–44 and 1967, the percentage of workers in agriculture had changed as follows: Great Britain: 8 to 4, United States: 23 to 6, Sweden: 36 to 12, Germany: 18 to 11, France: 33 to 18, Austria: 31 to 20, Italy: 49 to 25, Spain: 56 to 34. Norman Luxenburg, *Europe Since World War II: The Big Change*. Carbondale, Ill., Southern Illinois Press, 1973, p. 221.

source of migrants (beginning in the early 1960s, then in increasing numbers). The "guest workers" tended to stay for a short time and then return home; they were mostly young men. This profile changed in the 1970s when married men and their families began to arrive in increasing numbers.

Migrants were difficult to integrate, especially socially. Unskilled or semi-skilled laborers from abroad universally became the butt of hostile jokes. These were always similar though their target changed from country to country – the "dumb Pole" in the US, the Irishman in Britain, the Finn in Sweden, the Portuguese in Brazil, the Belgian in Holland. Many of these foreign-born migrants, unable to communicate well in the host country's language, lived in isolated enclaves, in ethnic ghettos. They desired to save money, and this led them to accept poor housing conditions, sometimes malnutrition, and social isolation. The local people widely rejected the newcomers; there was talk of *Überfremdung* (of being overrun by foreigners). European attitudes resembled US attitudes concerning illegal aliens, who were accused of stealing jobs from the American poor, or of illegitimately benefiting from US welfare facilities.

The experience of mass migration in many ways added to the Americanization of Western Europe – whatever his political convictions, the average European worker was far more familiar with Groucho than with Karl Marx. Overall, American society coped much more readily with alien incomers than the various European societies. The US had begun as a land of immigrants; aliens were expected to take out naturalization certificates and become US citizens – and so they did in large numbers. Such traditions of course were not totally absent in Europe. France, for instance, had absorbed many immigrants in the past, and continued to do so during the postwar years. But by and large a naturalized American was accounted an American, whereas a Sicilian or a Serb naturalized in France did not thereby become a Frenchman.

During the 1950s and 1960s, immigrants came to Western Europe from ever further afield. They included returning settlers from Algeria, Morocco, Indonesia, and elsewhere, many of whom were professional people. Expatriate intellectuals and white South Africans such as S. Herbert Frankel, Meyer Fortes, and Max Gluckman enriched African studies in Great Britain. In addition, Western Europe, for the first time experienced a fairly substantial immigration of black and brown peoples – West Indians, West Africans, Indians, and Pakistanis. (Britain had taken 650,000 Indians, Pakistanis and West Indians by 1960.) Not that black people had been absent from Western Europe. They had come for centuries in small numbers as domestic workers, sailors, and soldiers (for instance in the French forces that had occupied the Rhineland after World War I, and in the US forces in World War II). Black people had also made their way to Western Europe (especially Britain and France) as students and teachers. But the average European rarely saw a black person except in the movies. A black woman student from the US recalled with surprise and amusement how she was followed in remote Austrian villages by admiring crowds of small children who wanted to touch her strange-looking skin, and enquired whether the color would come off in the bath tub.

In the course of the 1950s, and even more during the 1960s, the number of black and brown immigrants grew greatly – especially in Great Britain, despite British attempts to restrict immigration by devices such as the Commonwealth Immigration Act 1962. According to the 1951 census, the "colored" people born overseas numbered only 75,000. By 1966, the "colored" population in England and Wales amounted to 929,000 of whom 213,000 had been born in Britain.[10] Afro-Britons and Indo-Britons became a new component of the population, as did Algerians or Moroccans in France, and Indonesians in Holland. Contrary to the stereotype, these men and women were not all unskilled or semi-skilled workers. They included scholars, such as A. W. (later Sir Arthur) Lewis, a West Indian economist. They comprised physicians (many of them employed in National Health Service hospitals), technicians, and shopkeepers (including numerous Indian expatriates from East Africa). But a substantial proportion performed some of the least desirable jobs; they crowded into the poorest accommodation of the inner cities; they complained, as did black Americans, of being the last to be hired and the first to be fired – though unemployment only became a problem in the 1970s. In this respect, as in so many others, Europeans had to learn how to cope with problems that had first beset the US.

HOUSING, CITIES, AND PLANNING

World War II had seen the destruction of buildings on a tremendous scale. Whole cities had been razed. Few additional houses had been constructed during the war; those that survived had not been repaired. There were also long-term problems. Most of Europe's older houses, built more than a century before with traditional craftsmanship, were durable enough, but they did not conform to the standards of modern hygiene. The prewar *Altstadt* (old city) in towns such as Cologne or Frankfurt in Germany seemed to tourists like a stage setting, with its narrow, winding lanes, antique fountains, and ornamental façades. But no family with money to spend actually wanted to live in an *Altstadt*, for most were picturesque slums. Overcrowding was rife in Europe, as in many parts of the US. (Contrary to a widespread misconception, in countries such as Germany, Switzerland, and the Netherlands the problem in villages was actually as bad, or worse than, in the city.)

Standards of hygiene left much to be desired. In this, as in many respects, notions of acceptability differed widely from country to country. (In the early 1950s, less than 11 percent of domestic dwellings in France, Belgium, Italy, Austria, Spain, Portugal, and Greece were equipped with baths or showers).[11] Europeans in general did not in those days share the conviction – later diffused by television advertisements for soap and deodorants – that a daily bath was a civic duty, or that for a person to sweat was a supreme social offense; this became a new cultural norm that went with the decline of heavy manual labor,

[10]Alfred F. Havighurst, *Britain in Transition: The Twentieth Century*. Chicago, University of Chicago Press, 1985, p. 527.

[11]Dewhurst, *Europe's Needs*, p. 213–45 for detailed statistics on all aspects of housing and hygiene.

and expansion of office employment. Nevertheless, social expectations grew as living standards improved, and with this came the demand for better housing.

Within a remarkably short period, most Western Europeans came to be better housed than in the past. At the end of the war, there had been a great housing shortage. Many houses had been destroyed altogether (25 percent in Germany, 7.6 in France, 6.5 in Britain); even more were badly damaged, and repairs had been delayed during wartime. Thereafter, the pace of reconstruction accelerated. By 1950 the number of houses built in Western Europe already exceeded the number for the best prewar years. Up to 1957 the annual volume of construction rose by another 80 percent, and in that year nearly 1.9 million new buildings were finished – 6.4 units per 1,000 inhabitants, closely approximating the rate in the US. The total number of dwellings completed in Western Europe was almost double the number attained in 1937 – a triumph for the (largely private) building industry, aided by substantial government subsidies. (More than half the buildings completed in Western Europe received some form of official aid.)

The reconstruction of badly bombed cities such as Hamburg, Rotterdam, and Coventry provided new opportunities for city planning. These were not, however, widely utilized, given the constraints under which planners had to work. Money was short; so was skilled labor and building materials. Housing was an immediate priority; the homeless had to be accommodated quickly. Strict limits were set by the existing facilities for sewage, transportation, and power. The modernizers could not totally obliterate existing city patterns, even though radicals such as Corbusier would have liked to do so. The public at large wanted familiar urban sights restored, while planners largely drew on the experiences gathered during two world wars in repairing damage and clearing rubble. Reconstruction conformed to existing institutions, laws, and accepted notions concerning urban zoning that separated industrial areas, shopping districts, and residential quarters.[12] The growth of suburbia continued to segregate classes residentially – a sharp break from the older urban pattern where classes had, so to speak, been segregated vertically, with maids and cooks living in the attics of great houses, and working "below stairs" in kitchens and basements, while their employers, *die Herrschaft*, the lordlings, had dwelt on the ground and first floors. Success in reconstruction was quantitative more than qualitative, but success there was. In less than a single decade the rubble had been cleared, the gaunt wartime ruins had disappeared, and Europeans – on average – lived more comfortably than ever before.

Much was due to the enterprise of the private contractors, who built nearly all the new houses in the US, and a large proportion of those in Europe. The scale of operations varied – some contractors were petty entrepreneurs; others ran huge companies capable of constructing great housing estates. Private

[12]We are indebted to a paper by Jeffrey M. Diefendorf "Urban reconstruction in Europe after World War II." His edited volume *Rebuilding Europe's Bombed Cities* was published in 1990 (London, Macmillan, and New York, St Martin's Press).

contractors incurred widespread censure from theoreticians for a number of reasons – for example, their real or alleged inability to engage in research, or to profit from the most advanced methods, and for submitting to the mass taste for "gingerbread" designs (in other words, giving the supposedly unenlightened buyers what they wanted). It became almost an article of faith among experts that the building industry was inefficient, or that it was marked by "low productivity," deprived in part from "the small size of the average firm or establishment."[13] Despite these charges, construction costs from about 1950 onward rose less rapidly in Europe than the average hourly earnings of industrial workers. Hence the builders' performance was presumably better than its reputation.

The level of a nation's housing cannot be assessed solely in statistical terms, according to the number of new constructions or the number of rooms per dwelling. The majority of British people had baths in their houses, whereas most French townspeople preferred to visit municipal baths, but this did not mean that British people were cleaner. In the Netherlands and in the British Isles, householders liked to work in their own yards. Apartment dwellers on the Continent lacked gardens of their own, or they cultivated little *Schrebergärten* (small gardens set apart in contiguous areas specially designated for the purpose in German cities). This did not necessarily imply that dwellers in German apartments derived less satisfaction from their lives than Dutch owners of small houses. Many of the contrasts in accommodation observable in Europe derived from social and historical factors as much as from differences in living standards. But despite these national variations, there was a general drift into suburbs, as residence in a *Villenviertel* (a district set aside for villas) ceased to be the preserve of the well-to-do.

The move into the suburbs was at its most striking in the US. Here, there was plenty of space; more families owned cars, and the US led the world in the construction of bridges and freeways; this was a country of "fix it" and "do-it-yourself," where manual skills were on the average more widely diffused among ordinary homeowners, and more widely honored than in Europe. Out in the suburbs the noise from neighbors was less obvious, suburbanites could indulge their taste for working on their own houses and land; there was a greater sense of independence.

This preference found striking expression in the statistics of urban demography. In 1900 the central cities had comprised 61.9 percent of the US metropolitan area, the suburban and fringe portions only 38.1 percent. By 1960, the picture had radically altered, as central cities claimed barely half the population of metropolitan areas.[14] Existing ethnic enclaves changed their composition, as those Germans, Jews, Italians, and others who could afford it bought homes in the suburbs, and new immigrants – especially black and Hispanic people – moved into the inner city.

The new suburbanites tended to be youthful, married, reasonably well educated, and keen to raise families. Despite beliefs to the contrary, sub-

---

[13]Dewhurst, *Europe's Needs,* p. 223.
[14]William M. Dobrincer, *Class in Suburbia.* Englewood Cliffs, NJ, Prentice-Hall, 1963, p. 143.

urbanites varied greatly in social and ethnic composition. By 1960 Levittown (a suburb investigated by Willian M. Dobriner, an American sociologist) contained nearly as many foremen, craftsmen, skilled and semi-skilled workers as people with office jobs. Suburbanites nevertheless had a bad press. They were reviled in books such as *The Organization Man*,[15] and pitied for their supposed alienation and self-destructive ethic. They were accused of philistinism, selfishness, and bigotry. They were caricatured on television shows. They were investigated without mercy by itinerant sociologists, so much so that one exasperated victim cried "when you eggheads run out of surveys to take and the dust begins to settle, we will [once more] be able to enjoy the life we have always known and feel content with."[16] For all the disapproval of the erudite, the people in the suburbs liked their houses, and found life in general improved – despite such disadvantages as lengthy commuting and lack of some cultural amenities.

The shift to the suburbs had far-reaching consequences. Especially in the US, the railways lost much of their former importance to trucks and cars. Oil, electricity, and natural gas increasingly replaced the direct use of coal as a fuel. The construction industries boomed, with huge demands for freeways, airports, supermarkets, and schools. The construction of new infrastructures entailed enormous capital investments, and expansion of credit. Urban expansion also taxed the planners' ingenuity in other ways. Planning of some kind was adopted in every European country in their need to rebuild bombed cities (especially heavily damaged city cores); control the spread of great conurbations; safeguard agricultural land; preserve green belts; clear slums; and generally balance the rival claims of farming, housing developers, and industry. (Next to Great Britain, the Netherlands developed the most comprehensive planning system in Western Europe.) The planners, however, bitterly disagreed among themselves. Should a rubble-strewn city center, for instance, simply be rebuilt in the traditional manner? Or should it be totally recast in accordance with modern town planning notions? The Germans, in general, chose the former, wanting to see the ancient town hall, the ducal castle, and the old streets restored to their former splendor.

Exact reconstruction, however, proved impossible. Mainz, to give an example, became part of a larger conurbation centering on Frankfurt, efficiently linked to other centers by suburban trains. Mainz increasingly became a well-to-do suburb, a university town, and, in part, a dormitory. The *Altstadt* was gentrified and housing there became the preserve of well-to-do people rather than the poor. In other towns there were new and imaginative departures. For example, Coventry, an English city heavily bombed during the war, was rebuilt with a new city center including a traffic-free shopping precinct with linked rooftop parking – a solution with great advantage to citizens and adopted in many other towns.

[15]William H. Whyte, *The Organization Man*. New York, Simon and Schuster, 1956.
[16]Peter Binzen, *Whitetown USA: A First-Hand Study of How the "Silent Majority" Lives, Learns, Works, and Thinks*. New York, Vintage Books, 1970, p. 5.

Walter Gropius revolutionized design in the twentieth century. He came to the US in 1937 after founding the famous Bauhaus *school in Germany and chaired the architecture department at Harvard University. He and his followers pioneered the development of prefabricated building, tubular steel furniture, integrated floor plans for private homes and much more. Gropius built box-like simplified buildings; they were to be mass-produced, have stark, undecorated surfaces with flat roofs, and much glass and glass brick to let light and sunshine into the interior of his buildings. His style was not popular at the time and has not grown in the public affections.*

There were many problems. For example, how to deal with the challenge of the automobile. The car gave a great degree of personal freedom to its owner, but it also made huge territorial demands on cities. Cars require expressways and freeways. Shopping centers, factories, barracks, places of entertainment, and apartment blocks all needed huge parking lots. There was an expanded need for junk yards. Cars also contributed to, though they did not cause, urban spread. Some planners favored the solution proposed by the Swiss architect Le Corbusier (pseudonym of Charles Edouard Jeanneret). Le Corbusier was at the height of his fame during the postwar years. He prepared plans for cities as far afield as Moscow, Bogotá, Algiers, and Ismir. He designed huge apartment blocks, built according to his doctrine that a house was "a machine for living in." These great concrete slabs were to be equipped with their own shops, and other community facilities and were to be surrounded by ample green spaces. High density construction, according to its proponents, had many advantages. High density living would reduce journeys to work, save valuable farming land, and create new community structures. Moreover, it could hardly be avoided in a city such as West Berlin, an isolated enclave.

But the new "slab blocks" lacked the intimacy of earlier designs built on the courtyard pattern, with enclosed spaces where children could play safely, and where mothers could watch their offspring from above, making sure that they would not get into trouble. Slab constructions, such as the *Märckische Viertel* in West Berlin, turned out to be architectural monstrosities. Slum clearance created new social problems, as old neighborhoods were broken up, and existing social bonds snapped, and houses were torn down that were still architecturally sound, and might have been repaired for much less than the massive expenditure required for urban renewal projects.

Advocates of dispersal, by contrast, insisted that apartment living appealed only to a minority of city dwellers; that high-rise blocks were costly in construction and upkeep; that they did not in fact save much land; and that urban gardeners both produced a surprisingly large amount of food, and beautified the urban landscape at no cost to the taxpayer. Above all, dispersed living affording greater consumer satisfaction, with a degree of personal pride and personal choice of a kind incompatible with Le Corbusier's gigantic living machines. However, dispersal itself engendered controversy. Should the suburban layout be left to the operation of the free market? Should there be zoning? Should suburbia be planned through the creation of new garden cities, free from soulless ribbon development, "organic" communities that would form new social entities, with their people firmly rooted into integrated communities?

The spokesmen of a free market generally got short shrift in the postwar years – notwithstanding previous American experience in this regard. For instance, Houston, Texas, managed to get by with minimal planning, and yet developed into a prosperous, progressive city, well supplied with every kind of cultural facility – grand opera, professional theaters, chamber music groups of distinction, museums, colleges, and a world-famous medical center financed by oil and cotton philanthropists. Houston followed an older tradition, derived from the nineteenth century, when most pioneer settlements had been unplanned, yet many turned out well. The planners did not necessarily do any better. For example, the high-rise buildings as we have pointed out before invited neither pride nor loyalty among the flat dwellers; they frequently turned into slums, disfigured by graffiti and rubbish, criminality and drugs.

The British made a remarkable effort in building New Towns (by the early 1960s there were 15 of them – eight in the London region). But they also encountered problems. They afforded only a limited number of dwellings (80,000 by 1961). Overall, they failed to come up to the postwar planners' idealistic expectations: "the evidence . . . shows how limited the opportunities, how provincial the life and how deprived the culture is of new towns." Moreover, by any rational cost benefit analysis, or reasonable forecasts of the future requirements of society, the "New Towns" would be seen now as follies "too expensive for a country such as Britain to build without some prior economic need." Planning for New Towns moreover encountered additional snags. "What if mobility is more important to the person or family than rootedness? What if various new services (e.g. more books, clothes, new TV, record collection, home freezers) are disproportionately valued by some while these total sources are being allocated? Are these things to be declared uneconomical?"[17]

Similar problems arose with regard to housing finance. Should the allocation of housing be planned or left to the free market? One side argued that, appearances to the contrary notwithstanding, free competition would do the best job. To take a case, a millionaire might build a fine mansion and later vacate this residence, to buy a town house; the mansion might be bought by a successful professional man who in turn would sell his suburban home to a small contractor, the small contractor's modest residence in the inner city would go to a chauffeur, the chauffeur's condominium to a semi-skilled worker, and the semi-skilled worker's dwelling to an unskilled laborer glad to escape from an inner-city slum. Down the line, every purchaser would benefit in the end, exercise personal choice, rely on personal initiative, with every incentive to improve his or her own property – all without costing the taxpayer a penny. The free market moreover had performed well – not merely in times of

[17]Nathan Silver, "Urbanism and special pleading," *Encounter*, September 1970, v. xxxv, no. 3, pp. 78–84, especially p. 83.

prosperity, but even in times of despair. (Exposed to innumerable air raids, Berliners, for example, had relied to a great extent on their own initiative to repair their damaged homes, to turn basements and sheds into makeshift habitations, or to find new accommodation, at a time when the German state machinery had been breaking down.)

The advocates of control, on the other hand, pleaded that the state should interfere as a matter of equity, that only public intervention would ensure "fair shares for all" (a popular British slogan at the time). As in so many other respects, Europeans and Americans alike settled on a compromise: private initiative and public direction or enterprise functioned side by side in a manner that makes their respective contributions or deficiencies hard to disentangle. Rent control had operated in many European countries ever since World War I, despite many obvious disadvantages. (In France, for instance, rent control after World War I, had contributed to a widespread housing shortage by diminishing financial incentives for the construction of rental accommodation.) Rent control continued in various forms after World War II, and the consequences were always similar, though their impact varied. It created a stratified market; tenants in rent-controlled apartments paid artificially low rents, while those obliged to find accommodation in uncontrolled apartments had to pay more. Where inflation was serious (especially so in France and Italy) the cost of repairs soon came to exceed the frozen rents and landlords could no longer afford even minimum maintenance; hence the housing stock deteriorated.

The position became particularly serious in American cities such as New York, where crime was rife. In stricken areas, many owners of slum properties ceased to maintain their property or even to collect the rent. In extreme cases the landlord actually turned to arson to rid himself of a well-insured albatross. As buildings were abandoned or burned out, neighborhoods became even less desirable; the exodus accelerated; and the tax base further weakened, especially since it was the most skilled and affluent people who were the first to leave. Slum streets in cities such as New York or Cleveland came to look as if they had been attacked by enemy bombers. Gradually becoming aware of the problems, many European governments by the end of the 1950s either modified rent control or ended it altogether (a policy initiated by Belgium in 1957), though it expanded in the US.

Less destructive was the provision of public aid for new housing. In the US, the federal housing administration (FHA, created in 1934 as part of the New Deal) had for many years provided housing loans on liberal terms. Faced with the return of some 12,000,000 demobilized ex-servicemen the Americans greatly expanded FHA facilities after World War II ("GI loans"). In addition, accumulated savings provided mortgage funds; by the end of the 1950s about 1,000,000 units were being constructed every year, with a peak of 1,400,000 during one year. Of the dwellings completed in Western Europe in 1957, nearly 58 percent received some form of financial aid requiring the disbursement of public funds. The overall effect of public aid remains hard to judge. Only one safe generalization can be made – there was no correlation between the extent of public assistance, and the ability of any particular country to cope with the citizens' housing needs. Switzerland provided little public aid, Britain a great deal, yet Swiss families were certainly no more badly housed than the British.[18]

In addition, public authorities put up housing of their own. The extent of public housing, the style and methods employed, the success attained, again differed a great deal from country to country. (By 1957, public bodies supplied 58.1 percent of all new dwellings completed in Great Britain, 38.8 in France, 30.1 in Sweden, 27.3 in the Netherlands; only 2.5 in West Germany, and 2.1 in Switzerland.)[19] Some of these projects (for instance those in Copenhagen) were extremely well run, others turned out to be sinks of misery. Their fate depended to a large extent on the tenants' social culture – hard-working, law-abiding families would maintain their apartment and its surroundings; the *Lumpenproletariat* would allow an apartment block to deteriorate. Housing projects on their own could not change tenants' life styles. Nor was there any correlation between the extent of public intervention and the relative success of any country's housing effort.

The British relied heavily on the efforts of municipal governments that specially favored council houses (small dwellings for rent). Council houses on the whole, though not universally, contrasted favorably with the large council estates where the poor were accommodated in apartments, that sometimes degenerated into places of crime and misery. But even council housing was far from popular; housing allocations gave preference to long-standing residents at the expense of recent immigrants; allocation of scarce resources often went with political or personal favoritism. Council housing contributed to the relative inflexibility of the British labor force, with residents fearing to leave their homes to find new jobs in other cities in case they lost their existing entitlements to a low rent. Council houses moreover proved unpopular in the long run – so that prime minister Margaret Thatcher's policy to sell council houses to their occupants during the 1980s turned out to be one of the most attractive features of her electoral platform. Nevertheless, public housing did make a genuine contribution to what was, overall, a success story in Western Europe.

Architectural and town planning, unlike most municipal decison-making, also raised aesthetic questions. In a democratic society, no adult is compelled to read any particular kind of poetry, listen to any special form of music, or look at pictures painted in any peculiar mode. But citizens cannot avoid being affected by the style of the apartment blocks that they occupy, the public buildings in which they do business, or the churches where they worship. Such buildings necessarily reflect their designers' cultural, sometimes even their political, outlook. Hence styles varied to such an extent that generalizations are difficult to make. Buildings put up after World War II differed enormously –

---

[18]New dwellings receiving public aid, as percentage of all new dwellings completed in 1957, varied as follows: Switzerland: 7, Italy: 21, West Germany: 52, Great Britain: 58, Austria: 65, Spain and Norway: 66, Denmark: 85, France: 91, Netherlands: 95, Sweden and Ireland: 97. Dewhurst, *Europe's Needs*, p. 231.

[19]Ibid, p. 237 for a complete table.

from "gingerbread," pseudo-Tudor, and neo-Victorian, to starkest modernism.

> *Coventry, an English city badly damaged in World War II, offers an architectural success story. Coventry cathedral was splendidly rebuilt according to a design by Sir Basil Spence. Work began in 1954, and the new cathedral successfully blended old and new, as the damaged fourteenth-century cathedral was incorporated into the modern building. The cathedral gained splendor from Sir Jacob Epstein's bronze group of St Michael and the Devil; from the magnificent windows in colored glass representing on one side man's progress through life, and on the other side God's revelation in history; and from a magnificent tapestry designed by Graham Sutherland. Coventry cathedral pleased not only the critics, but also its own worshippers, and represented perhaps the last great architectural expression of Anglican piety.*

The great English architect Sir Basil Spence at Coventry blended contemporary and traditional designs. But far more influential were the uncompromising modernists. They included famed architects such as Frank Lloyd Wright, Walter Gropius, Mies van der Rohe, and Le Corbusier, whose styles dominated most of the Western world during the late 1940s and the 1950s. All these artists shared a common outlook "which might be termed liberal, left, and slightly authoritarian."[20] They drew on a common legacy, much of it derived from the German *Bauhaus* school. The *Bauhaus* pioneers during the Weimar Republic had wanted to get away from the so-called *kitsch* of the Victorian and Wilhelminian age, from architecture studded with a profusion of nymphs, goddesses, sword-wielding maidens, lions, and unicorns. Modernists called for honesty in the use of material, for plain designs that would eschew ornamentation, and that would cause structural design to follow function.[21] They insisted on stark, angular regularity; they wanted to reform public taste; they were not afraid to shock. They took pride in challenging philistines and in stigmatizing the public's assumed obscurantism.

Unfortunately, the reformers' achievements all too often turned into new clichés, more unimaginative than the worst of Wilhelminian art. Huge concrete-and-glass structures multiplied all over the world. Many of them were graceless edifices – hard to maintain, heavily dependent on energy, difficult and expensive to heat in winter and hard to keep cool in summer, shoddily constructed, built with complete indifference to the users' real needs, bereft of the sensitivity required to blend the new with the old, or with the existing environment, designed to please official selection boards, academic seminars, and architectural reviewers rather than the public. One of these buildings (just one of many) was Yale University's art and architecture center,

---

[20]Charles Jencks, "The modern fragmentation: architecture and politics," *Encounter,* v. xxxv, no. 3, September 1970, p. 73.

[21]For a brilliant account that sets the *Bauhaus* school in the wider cultural context, see Peter Gay, *Weimar Culture: The Outsider as Insider.* New York, Harper and Row, 1970. For a popular critique, see Tom Wolfe, *From Bauhaus to Our House.* New York, Farrar, Straus, Giroux, 1981.

designed by Paul Rudolph, and completed in 1963. As a critic put it, in words on which we cannot improve:

> Despite all the talk of functionalism, the building's most distinguishing mark is its disregard, even scorn, for the interests of its users. The site is ringed with high concrete walls and its entrance is hard even to locate. Forget about being welcomed. Once inside, one encounters a maze constructed entirely of unfinished concrete that looks as if the owner ran out of money before the wall surfaces could be applied. The elevator, stair, and airflow systems are inadequate. The structure leaks badly, it is dusty, and poorly heated and cooled. Visible deterioration is rampant.
>
> The building has been disliked by Yale's New Haven neighbors from the start and has unquestionably contributed its bit to strained university–city relations. As such it nicely illustrates the central conflict that has dogged avant-garde architecture until recent years – namely the use of public buildings by elites to make philosophical statements without regard to the concerns or needs of the recipient public.[22]

Early American settlers, ignorant of academic architecture, had done a great deal better when they put up state houses in Virginia and Massachusetts, giving their constructions both comfort and simple classical dignity. But edifices like the art and architecture building at Yale, or the new Congress Hall in West Berlin (completed by Hugh Stubbins in 1957, and known to resentful West Berliners as "the pregnant oyster"), might be styled the public planners' art *par excellence*. Its legacy remained to disfigure cities all over the world.

WOMEN, MARRIAGE, AND THE FAMILY

Marriage customs on both sides of the Atlantic historically followed similar patterns. During the nineteenth century as a result of urbanization these patterns were subjected to all manner of changes which were, on the whole, even more far-reaching in the US than in Europe. On the US frontier women were always far fewer in number than men. Here an unmarried woman could find a new man friend or husband much more easily than in a settled region. American frontier women had therefore always been known for their independent spirit. The same applied to women immigrants who came from Europe to great industrial centers such as New York. They found new job opportunities, while at the same time accustomed social controls weakened perhaps to an even greater extent than in Europe, friends, neighbors, and relatives having been left in the "old country." New responsibilities were thrust on immigrant working-class wives. The domineering Jewish mother or Italian mother of fiction was truly American. Overall, marriage in the New World developed into a more voluntary bond, much less influenced by parents

---

[22]Karl Zinsmeiter, "The revolt against alienation," *Policy Review*, Summer 1987, p. 63.

than in Europe. In the twentieth century marriage mores began to grow more alike on the two sides of the Atlantic, but Americans still tended to wed earlier than in Western Europe; they were also more independent of family and less bound to ethnicity or religion. If European travelers are to be believed Americans have traditionally tended to marry more for love and personal satisfaction than for family or generational concerns.

There was all over the Western world a sharp lowering of the average marriage age after World War II, which was not reversed until the 1960s. Young people in all industrial societies attained increasing freedom to marry at whatever age they wished, and whomever they chose. The same relaxation occurred over divorce, except for Catholics. People came to expect and demand more of marriage. And the Atlantic Community, in spite of rising divorce rates and the incidence of cohabitation, has remained committed to marriage as a key institution. Allowances were gradually made over the age at which suitors had customarily been expected to marry, and over legitimizing trial marriages; though these changes did not occur on a large scale until the 1960s. Parents have continued to preach the merits of marriage, and the state has continued to promote the growth of the nuclear family through tax benefits, subsidies to home ownership, and to suburban development after World War II.

The postwar era, then, ushered in revolutionary social changes. Young people had a wider range of choices than ever before. Divorce became more acceptable throughout all industrial societies, even Catholic ones.[23] Divorce rates went up (at least after 1957); marriage rates dropped; people married later, and cohabitation before marriage became more acceptable. Births out of wedlock have steadily increased, especially among the black population (in 1940 the rate was 4 percent; in 1985 it was 20 percent for all races and 62 percent for blacks).

These changes were partly caused by a shift in priorities and by increased opportunities for women in the work place. Women's attitudes to marriage changed profoundly. The postwar baby boom of 1945 to 1952 saw people marrying early, and having three or four children. Suburbs expanded; new schools sprang up; the economy was growing, and prosperity promoted stability in marriage. Parents brought up in the depression era had low, but attainable, aspirations. But from 1955 on the pace of social change quickened and the institution of marriage altered with it.

During the war, great numbers of men and women had postponed marriage. Their lovers might have gone to find new work far away, or donned uniform and gone abroad – the future seemed far from certain. Once the war ended, demobilized servicemen wanted to have families. The result was a high rate of early marriage, and the baby boom which produced the largest youth cohort in the history of the world, with major consequences for Western societies.

[23]See John Modell, "Historical reflections on marriage," in Kingsley Davis and Amyra Crossboard-Schechtman, eds, *Contemporary Marriage: Comparative Perspectives on a Changing Institution,* New York, Russell Sage Foundation, 1985, ch. 4.

As Europe recovered its prosperity and the US economy continued to prosper, early marriage, early childbearing and high birthrates were encouraged. The mores and morals of the postwar epoch disapproved of sex without marriage. Nevertheless, premarital sex increased in the 1950s (and spectacularly in the 1960s and 1970s) as birth control methods improved and society took a somewhat more permissive attitude toward the young. Abortion became more available and acceptable, at least for Protestants. But for most people, marriage still appeared the only acceptable way to have sexual intimacy on a continuing basis; cohabitation became for some (roughly 15 percent), a socially sanctioned alternative only after the 1950s.

There was an increase in single-parent families in the US, starting in 1954 for blacks, and in the 1960s for whites.[24] Statistically, single parents tend to be less educated than "dual" parents, and are more likely to be unemployed or have lower incomes; they rent rather than own a home. Whereas in 1959–60 only 9 percent of children lived with just one parent, by 1986 25 percent did so. In 1960 three-quarters of black children lived with both parents, by 1986 only 40 percent did so. After 1960 the proportion of people who never married doubled. (See US census bureau, *Marital States and Living Arrangements*, March 1986, Washington, DC, GPO, 1986.) According to George Gilder, the female-headed family created a chain of problems, as many children from such families later disrupted classrooms, filled the jails, thronged the welfare rolls, and took to dope.

In theory, the breakup of traditional family structures should have accelerated after the war. Sociologists have identified two long-term trends. The first might be styled the "maternalization" of authority within the nuclear family. As father no longer worked at home, the task of disciplining the children increasingly devolved to the mother. The second shift entailed the "privatization of the nuclear family." This implied the severing of extended family ties, and a transformation from an economic unit in which every member had an allotted place to a mere partnership freely entered into by a man and a woman for emotional support, sexual satisfaction, and childcare.[25]

Generalizations are difficult to make since many contradictory trends were at work. A caution is nevertheless in order. Though the traditional, or supposedly traditional, family was subject to change, social commentators have consistently overstated the extent to which family ties have weakened in the West. Two centuries ago Oliver Goldsmith had deplored

> That independence Britons prize so high
> Keeps man from man, and breaks the social tie;

[24]See for instance Graham B. Spanier, "Cohabitation in the 1960s: recent changes in the United States," Davis and Grossbard-Shechtman, eds, *Contemporary Marriage,* ch. 3.

[25]See for instance Edward Shorter, *The Making of the Modern Family.* New York, Basic Books, 1975. Sar A. Levitan and Richard Belous, *What's Happening to the American Family.* Baltimore, Johns Hopkins University Press, 1981. And the review article by Andrew Hacker, "Farewell to the family?," *The New York Review of Books,* 18 March 1982, pp. 37–44. See also entries on "Marriage" in *International Encyclopedia of the Social Sciences.* New York, Macmillan and Free Press, 1968, v. 10, pp. 1–22.

The self-dependent lordlings stand alone
All claims that bind and sweeten life unknown.

Goldsmith exaggerated, however, as have twentieth-century social scientists in the US – a point made with some force by a group of scholars during the 1970s who looked at life in Muncie, Indiana, first made famous in the 1920s as "Middletown" in studies by Robert and Helen Lynd.[26] Recent sociological findings, statistical data, and common-sense observations alike support those who stress the resilience of family institutions in the US and in Western Europe. In Germany the family endured as a bastion that enabled society to cope with the extraordinary stress brought about by the Nazi dictatorship, defeat, and enormous population displacements. (The West German illegitimacy rate in 1950 amounted to only 9.5 percent, a surprisingly low figure, given the instability brought about by mass migrations.) Contrary to widespread misconception, for example, the migration of Mexican newcomers to the US actually strengthened family solidarity, as the decision to move across the border was much influenced by the economic support and help offered by their relatives.[27] Again, most elderly Americans during the 1980s lived at home or were cared for by their relatives; only a small percentage of the aged were confined to nursing homes. Indeed an anthropologist would probably be surprised at the value of goods and services that continued to be exchanged, say, between the members of an extended Norwegian-American family in Oregon, or an Italian-American family in New Jersey.

Nevertheless, there were striking changes after World War II – both for better and for worse. Life became easier for many home makers, especially women who worked for wages during the day and still had to keep house at night. Their labor was lightened through the advent of refrigerators, washing machines, and frozen foods. Car ownership spread, especially in the US, and, to a lesser extent, in Great Britain. Suburbanites created for themselves a whole range of new institutions linked to the church or the temple, to the local library, to local education authorities. They joined private associations, supported and participated in team sports or chess clubs, symphony orchestras, athletics clubs, adult classes in music, foreign languages, psychology, and so on. Suburbia was far from the cultural wasteland that some imagined. In the US especially and to a lesser extent in Great Britain, returning veterans received modest benefits for study at university, insurance and health care, and loans for housing that helped in setting up families. Television sets, radios, record players brought entertainment into the home, and at the same time satisfied long pent up consumer demand.

All over the Western world, while the rural population declined, and the

<hr>

[26]Theodore Caplow, Howard M. Bahr, Bruce A. Chadwick, Reuben Hill, and Margaret Holmes Williamson, *Middletown Families, Fifty Years of Change and Continuity.* Minneapolis, University of Minnesota Press, 1982.

[27]Robert R. Alvarez, *Familia: Migration and Adaptation in Baja and Alta California, 1800–1975.* University of California, 1987. Christian Graf von Krockow, *Die Deutschen in ihrem* Jahrhundert: 1890–1990. Hamburg; Rowohet Verlag, 1990, p. 276.

birthrate dropped after 1955, cities and suburbs grew and women left traditional forms of employment such as domestic service. The proportion of women in the salaried labor force increased – most of all in Sweden, followed by the US, least in the Netherlands, Spain, and Portugal.[28] Statistics in this regard must of course be treated with care. They are heavily biased in favor of workers who receive cash wages, as against men and women who labor without monetary remuneration on family farms or in family-run stores. Statistics are also difficult to compare between countries, given differing national census procedures. But overall, the available figures permit of some broad generalizations.

Western Europeans on the average still worked longer hours than Americans during the postwar decade (46 hours compared to 42), and a higher proportion of Western Europeans were at work.[29] All over Western Europe, but especially in the more highly developed countries, women were moving into paid employment as typists, sales staff, assemblers, and supervisors. The average of women in employment went up; female child labor declined on farms in less developed countries such as Spain, Portugal, and even Austria; more young girls went to school, and women's educational standards continued to rise. But college was widely seen as preparatory to marriage not to a profession or job. (In Western Europe as a whole, women, by 1955, constituted about a quarter of the paid labor force.) In addition, manufacturers increasingly gave attention to the "female market," to women's tastes in personal adornment, household furnishings, furniture, appliances, or the body size and upholstery in automobiles.

There were other changes in marital mores. In the old days, young mothers had relied for child-rearing advice on older relatives, the clergy, or perhaps a respected neighbor. But migration uprooted young families from their relatives. City-bred middle-class women, therefore increasingly turned to books written by specialists such as Dr Benjamin Spock and Arnold Gesell, whose books began to gain widespread popularity in the US after World War II.[30] The fame of these "baby doctors" went with more permissive and more child-centered attitudes than had been customary in the past – and at this time the vocabulary drawn from Freudian psychology began to gain popular

[28]The proportion of women in the labor force stood as follows in 1960 (percent): Sweden: 56, US: 42.8, West Germany and France: 45.1, Great Britain: 40.4, Italy: 32.4, Belgium: 25.1, Netherlands: 17.2, Spain: 16.2, Portugal: 15.9. T. Paul Schultz, "The value of time in high-income countries: implications for fertility," In Kingsley Davis, Mikhail Bernstam, Rita Ricardo-Campbell, eds, *Below-Replacement Fertility in Industrial Societies: Causes, Consequences, Policies*. NY Population Council, Cambridge University Press, 1987. Table p. 96. For a complete breakdown of statistics concerning population, births, deaths, marriages, divorces, life expectancy etc. world-wide see United Nations, *Demographic Yearbook 1959*. New York, United Nations, 1959.

[29]By 1950 the "activity rate," that is to say the proportion of both sexes at work in the US stood at 42 percent of the US, as against a Western European average of 46 percent. Dewhurst, *Europe's Needs*, p. 63.

[30]Benjamine McLane Spock, *The Common Sense Book of Baby and Child Care*. New York, Duell, Sloan, and Pearce, 1946. Arnold Lucius Gesell, *Studies in Child Development*. New York, Harper, 1948, and *The Child from Five to Ten*, New York, Harper, 1946.

currency. Europeans and Americans alike continued to have relatively large families. But married couples took more care to plan their families, as mechanical means of birth control became more widely available and more acceptable than before; traditional methods such as "withdrawal" (*coitus interruptus*) were used less frequently. (It was not until 1960 that the "pill," the oral contraceptive, first developed by doctors Gregory Pincus and John Rock, began to be sold commercially.)

Cohabitation – live-in arrangements between unmarried couples – had in former times mainly been confined to dissidents who stood apart from the lower-middle and middle classes. They were likely to stem from the very poor at the bottom of the social scale, and the Bohemians, the literary intelligentsia, and the aristocracy at the top. In the 1960s, aristocratic and Bohemian privilege in this regard began, so to speak, to be democratized. During the 1950s, however, traditional family values still commanded almost universal popular approval – as revealed by popular movies, literature, and song.[31] This was true even in the US, mistakenly thought by Europeans to be a Mecca for divorcees. To be exact, divorce in the US had shown a drop during the Depression of the 1930s, followed by a huge peak in 1946, and a subsequent decline to a plateau, with a figure of 9.2 per 1,000 married women of 15 years and over in the year 1960, as against 8 per 1,000 in 1920.[32] Compared with the divorce figures of the 1960s and 1970s, those during most of the 1950s were moderate. (The rapid rise in the US divorce rate began in 1957, and by 1979, was 27 percent higher than it had been at the peak of 1946.) But during the 1940s and 1950s, families were generally more stable. The average couple expected to remain wedded for life; their children assumed that the family bonds would endure. Relatively few children grew up with that sense of insecurity likely to follow a divorce. Few marriages as yet faced the dual pull of a separate professional career for each parent.

Even then, the consequences of divorce were far from negligible. In the US and elsewhere, divorced couples on average did less well economically and psychologically than their married friends; family disorganization often led to juvenile delinquency as a single mother struggled to keep her children from the temptations of the street. These problems were not yet particularly prevalent among black American families. According to the 1950 census figures, 78 percent of black families then consisted of husband-and-wife households, as against 88 percent of white families. The figures for both population groups had changed little from before World War II. The decline for black families began in the early 1950s; during the 1960s, conditions for both whites and blacks rapidly changed for the worse.

The full story goes beyond the scope of this book. We shall content ourselves by briefly referring to some standard explanations for this apparent disaster.

[31]Charles Murray, *Losing Ground: American Social Policy 1950–1980*. New York, Basic Books, 1984, pp. 131–2.
[32]Clifford Kirkpatrick, "Family: disorganization and dissolution," *International Encyclopedia of the Social Sciences*. New York, Macmillan and Free Press, 1968, v. 5, p. 316.

According to some critics of US society, the problems of the black family essentially derived from unemployment among black unskilled and semi-skilled men. Finding themselves without work, or even without the hope of securing a job, these men could not afford to assume the traditional role of family heads. Hence young black women chose to raise children on their own. Unemployment in turn sprang from causes beyond poor people's control – the mechanization of US industry which reduced the need for semi-skilled and unskilled workers; the prevalence of racism in the US; and also those assumed contradictions within the capitalist system that rendered periodic crises inevitable. Other analysts stress the exodus of black middle-class and professional people from formerly black segregated townships. As residential apartheid waned from the late 1950s, prosperous and well-educated blacks were able to move into the suburbs, as their European forerunners had already done. Hence the black underclass was left to its own devices, lacking middle-class role models.

Conservatives, by contrast, put more emphasis on "law-and-order," or rather the lack of it, in the slums. Crime discourages legitimate enterprises. So do urban riots – foolishly lauded by militant intellectuals for voicing the workers' wrath. In truth, riots hurt the poor, not the rich. Riots caused shopkeepers and tradesmen in the slums to sell their businesses, thereby diminishing available services to the black underclass, and the chances for local employment. Ill-designed social welfare policies only worsened the problems of the black family by putting a premium on single motherhood. Another explanation hinges on cultural factors. The *Lumpenproletariat*, of whatever racial ancestry, despises regular work. So do romantic literati who regard punctuality, courtesy, obedience to lawfully constituted authority, and application to steady labor as the hallmark of the philistine. During the 1960s, the values of the underclass and of the progressive intelligentsia fused; they were popularized through broadcasts, novels, movies, and television shows. The easy availability of drugs, and of easy employment in the illegal economy linked to drugs, only worsened the situation. But men who live either by the values of the underclass or the progressive intelligentsia, unfortunately, do not make steady husbands. Nor do they make reliable employees in jobs that require attentive and disciplined labor. Hence more mothers preferred to raise their children alone.

These explanations all have some value. They are not mutually incompatible. But they are not all of equal importance. Unemployment was not the main reason for the growing number of female-headed households. Rates of illegitimacy increased, no matter whether jobs were relatively plentiful (as they were in the 1960s), or whether jobs grew scarce (as they did in the late 1970s). The exodus of the black middle class from what were once segregated or semi-segregated black townships certainly changed for the worse the social composition of these areas. But the same factor affected other ethnic groups (Italians, Armenians, Poles) who did not experience the disruption of traditional family values to the same extent as blacks. Urban rioting and crime proved a disaster for the poor of whatever racial ancestry, but again, not all poor people were affected to the same extent. Arguments that hinge on the vulnerability of capitalism to crises do not explain why the disruption of traditional family values should have been less noticeable during the great slump of the early 1930s. No sociologist will ever be able to arrive at an unchallenged conclusion in this matter. But we ourselves put special blame on the rejection of traditional values, especially the contempt for hard work, punctuality, and fidelity in marriage, shared alike by many highly educated people and street-corner thugs. In our view, these changes in cultural values have hurt the poor more than the rich.

Whatever the explanations for the crisis, the symptoms were indisputable. In 1959, the majority of low-income blacks had lived in families very much like those of white families, while 30 percent resided in households headed by single women. By 1985 the latter percentage had almost doubled, and the one-parent family had become far more prevalent among poor blacks than among poor whites. Conditions in Hispanic families closely paralleled those of blacks. The feminization of black poverty had advanced to a degree that would have seemed unimaginable during the 1950s, before the full development of the US welfare state. By 1987, 61 percent of black children were born out of wedlock; and 53 percent of black mothers never married.

In Western Europe too, the divorce rate rose sharply immediately after World War II, but dropped thereafter.[33] Cross-cultural comparisons are hard to make, for in Catholic countries such as Ireland, Spain, and Italy, divorce remained illegal. A man might take a mistress, but could not cast aside his wife. The percentage of illegitimate births also varied considerably from country to country. They were highest for Austria and Sweden (for very different reasons), followed by West Germany, France, then Britain.[34] Again, it is hard to generalize. Illegitimacy did not necessarily imply social instability in all countries. Villagers in Austria and Bavaria did not feel quite so strongly about young women who had borne children out of wedlock; the priest and relatives insisted only that the young lovers must marry. Austria thus had a high illegitimacy ratio, yet much family stability. By contrast, the illegitimacy ratio was negligible in Ireland, another staunchly Catholic country, and also in the Protestant Netherlands.

In every Western country, Catholic or Protestant, the significant rise in the illegitimacy rate only began in the 1960s. In Sweden the rate grew in particularly startling fashion; between 1955–60 and 1983, the percentage of illegitimate births went up from 10.4 to 43.7 as more and more unmarried couples lived together without the stigma of social disapproval. In the US the illegitimacy rate tripled between 1940 and 1960 alone. As we have said, illegitimacy struck particularly at blacks and Hispanics (especially Puerto Ricans). The

[33]Between 1956 and 1960, illegitimate births per 100 live births stood at 13.3 in Austria, 10.4 in Sweden, 6.9 in West Germany, 6.2 in France, 4.7 in Great Britain, 3.6 in Norway, 2.9 in Spain, 1.3 in the Netherlands. See table in Jean Bourgeois-Pichat, "The unprecedented shortage of births in Europe," in Davis et al., *Below Replacement*, p. 15. The US figure for 1960 was 5 percent.
[34]Bourgeois-Pichat, table on p. 11.

causes determining ethnic differentiation in the illegitimacy rate are hard to disentangle, but joblessness among black men was probably not a major factor, even with rising unemployment among black youths from 1954 onward. Swedes, and US blacks both have a high illegitimacy ratio (and men are not unemployed in Sweden at a high rate), but then both have a very high proportion of young women who never marry.

In the postwar period, most women married at a younger age (in their late teens or early twenties), than was the case 30 years later – at a time in their lives when they were physically fittest, best able to bear children, and cope with the stress of looking after babies. Abortions became somewhat more available and accepted, at least for Protestants and nonbelievers. Adoptions as yet were comparatively rare – even in the US, where the adoption rate had always been highest. (In England, by contrast, adoption had been inadmissible under common law, and was only recognized by statute in 1926.) Throughout the Western world, the husband-and-wife family, with legitimate offspring born in a marriage sanctioned by law – and often also by the church, chapel or synagogue – remained the accepted norm.

A visitor from Mars, interested in studying the marriage and childbearing patterns of the postwar world, might well assume that women born in the years of the Great Depression and its aftermath would be reluctant to have large families. But he would be mistaken. It was precisely the women born in the late 1920s and early 1930s who were most eager to bear children. Why should these women have found traditional marriage and child-bearing so much more attractive than their descendants, born 25 years later during an extended period of prosperity? Sociological explanations are necessarily tentative, since the intimate behavior of millions of people scattered over many different countries cannot be reduced to hard-and-fast rules, but some generalizations may be put forward. Firstly, marriage and children offered a sense of psychological security to the untold numbers of European women who had undergone air raids, hunger, persecution, or expulsion. Women lost to their own kin wanted to create new families. Then, the bonds of traditional marriage might appear restrictive to university-trained women who expected interesting jobs in management or academia, but the number of women with high professional aspirations remained small after World War II, even in the US. The prospect of becoming a full-time homemaker seemed attractive to many women who worked on family farms, or who had made their living during the war in factories, shipyards, and workshops, where work was hard, repetitive, and sometimes dangerous. By comparison, the job of a housewife might well seem more attractive – at least for a woman with a husband who did not chase girls, gamble, or return drunk on a Saturday night, in a mood to beat his spouse, but instead brought home a regular paycheck. At a time when the social security system was relatively undeveloped, marriage still offered women security; children were an economic investment as their parents' support in old age, as well as a source of emotional satisfaction and fulfillment.

The impact of war on women differed considerably from country to country. Great Britain had been the only country in the world to draft women as well as men. British women had served in auxiliary organizations such as the ATS (Auxiliary Territorial Service); women in khaki had not merely tended the wounded or drove trucks, but had served as gunners in anti-aircraft batteries. In Nazi Germany the shift had been smaller than in the Allied countries. In fact the Nazis' ideological commitment to keeping women at home had contributed to the defeat of the Third Reich. Even in 1943, when the Reich belatedly turned to "total war" and attempted to increase war production at all costs, the number of women in employment had not substantially increased. There had indeed occurred a slight shift from farm and domestic labor to office work. But the overall employment statistics changed little. (In September 1944, there were 14,897,000 women in paid jobs as against 14,262,000 women in May 1939.)[35] When the war ended, women had to take the place of millions of men killed, crippled, or captured. Women performed the heaviest of labor. (A common sight had been women at work to clear the rubble in bombed cities – the so-called *Trümmerfrauen*.) But the decisive transformation in the labor market for German women did not occur until the 1960s – not as a product of defeat but of prosperity. Only then did German women begin to approach the percentage of British and American women in paid employment.

In the US women made up the largest female labor force in the Western world. Unlike in Britain, there had been no conscription of women in World War II. American women had taken jobs in an economy that left the allocation of labor to market forces. Women had migrated to distant cities in large numbers – either to accompany husbands or men friends, or to take up posts on their own in factories, especially war-related plants. (During the first three and a half years of war, over 7,000,000 women had changed their county of residence, and a third of these joined the labor force.) This migration had caused a host of new problems – delinquency soared among young women and teenage runaways. At the same time, women had acquired new skills in jobs as varied as welding hatches, riveting gun emplacements, binding keels, typing letters, keeping files, or driving trucks. (During World War II, the proportion of women in employment had risen from just over 25 percent to 36 percent – an increase greater than during the preceding four decades. By 1946, the female labor force had increased by 57 percent. Nearly 20,000,000 women were in paid employment – 35 percent of all workers, as against 25 percent in 1940. Manufacturing took the largest number – 2,500,000, and an additional 2,000,000 took up office jobs.)

Black women especially benefited from increased occupational mobility. (During the war, the proportion of black women employed as servants dropped from 72 to 48 percent and the proportion occupied on farms went down from 20 to 7 percent.) More important still, there was a striking shift in the age and marital status of all women in employment. (The share of married women in employment went up from 15.2 percent in 1940 to more than 24 percent by 1945, by which time wives, for the first time, came to compose almost a

[35]Dörte Winkler, *Frauenarbeit im "Dritten Reich"*, Hamburg, Hoffman und Campe, 1977, p. 201.

majority of women workers.)[36] Women joined labor unions; women's wages increased; women's expectations began to change. It had become acceptable for married women to work.

Nevertheless, differentiation based on sex widely remained the rule – especially in business and the professions. (For instance, the US army refused to commission women doctors until 1943.) Women remained excluded from most top policy-making bodies. They were usually paid less than men for the same work. They found promotion harder to achieve than men. There was a widespread lack of child care facilities. And when the veterans came back from the war, they also expected to return to their accustomed jobs, given widespread prejudices against working women, together with deep-seated fears concerning future unemployment. As war plants were reconverted to peacetime production women workers were the first to be fired. Feminists failed in their endeavor to secure adoption of an Equal Rights Amendment to the Constitution. The *New York Times* praised a hostile vote in the Senate in 1946 on the grounds that "motherhood cannot be amended."[37]

Nevertheless, a considerable number of gains remained. By 1949, the female labor force had increased by over 5.25 million, compared with the 1940 figures. Far more married women continued to work. (By 1952, some 10.4 million wives held jobs, almost three times the number employed in 1940.) Older women especially stayed on the payroll. (By 1950 women between 35 and 54 constituted 40 percent of all women at work.) Work for women became an increasingly accepted part of middle-class life, especially for wives with grown-up children. A number of professional barriers disappeared. For instance, school boards that had barred married women from employment now permitted them to stay. Medical schools accepted more women students than before. Women henceforth were to dominate the secretarial and teaching professions. Though economic equality as yet remained a distant goal, "the decade of the 1950s marked a turning point in the history of American women."[38] And by and large, the New World proved a model for the Old World to follow.

The extent of these changes at the time should not be exaggerated, and for many women on both sides of the Atlantic the full-time housewife's lot as yet seemed more agreeable than the factory worker's. Marriage offered security; woman's place was still widely supposed to be at home as long as she had young children. It was only in subsequent decades that US attitudes began to undergo fundamental change. According to a California poll in 1947, men had primarily prized their wives for being good housekeepers. Men also had rated

---

[36]William H. Chafe, *The American Woman: Her Changing Social, Economic and Political Roles, 1920–1970*. Oxford, Oxford University Press, 1972, p. 148, *passim*. Jean Bethke Elshtain, *Women and War*. New York, Basic Books, 1987.

[37]Ibid., p. 188.

[38]Mikhail S. Bernstam, "Competitive human markets, interfamily transfers, and below replacement fertility," in Davis et al., *Below-Replacement Fertility*, p. 11; p. 136. D'Ann Campbell, *Women at War with America: Private Lives in a Patriotic Era*. Cambridge, Mass., Harvard University Press, 1984.

highly wives who had a good disposition, cooked well, and stayed at home. Forty years later, a similar poll found that married men and women alike stressed fidelity and the bond of common interests – important considerations at a time when both partners were likely to work outside the home. (By that time, respondents also placed a high value on sharing household chores: cooperation in domestic tasks was thought to be even more significant for a good marriage than an active sex life, and much more important than having children.)

During and after World War II, traditional family values went unchallenged by the media. American movies followed a strict code of prescribed decency; television producers took good care not to put programs on the air that would offend the average subscriber to *Reader's Digest*. But even then there was an incipient sense of restlessness among the formally educated. This found expression in works such as Simone de Beauvoir's *The Second Sex*, published in the US in 1953.[39] (Though de Beauvoir did not in fact live up to her declared principles, but permitted herself to be exploited by her philandering lover, Jean-Paul Sartre, in a manner that would have shocked a Victorian matron.) Male discontent with traditional family life was reflected, too, in books by Jack Kerouac and William Whyte, both products of the 1950s. Even more important was the work of Alfred C. Kinsey, a man "outwardly formal and old-fashioned" yet "one of the great social revolutionaries of our time."[40] Kinsey considered himself a proponent of value-free science, a rationalist. He criticized traditional morality, and confronted what he regarded as public hypocrisy regarding homosexual behavior, masturbation, and the sexuality of women; he was a scholar at war with every doctrine that inhibited sexual pleasure. Kinsey's books found a wide readership, but the so-called liberated values as yet mainly appealed to specialized groups. These included the disaffected urban underclass, jet-setters, artists, would-be artists, students, and academics. There was an increase in cohabitation among young unmarried people over a wide spectrum – even in Europe where traditional marriage patterns had delayed both formal and informal unions. Partners in such live-in arrangements included all kinds of people – soldiers stationed abroad who lived with local women, and also civilians, who tended to be youthful, well-educated, city-bred, far away from their parents, and without religious ties. Irregular unions for such people in no way, however, precluded subsequent marriage and an ascent to ironclad respectability.

[39]Simone de Beauvoir, *The Second Sex*. New York, Knopf, 1953, originally published in 1949 as *Le Deuxième Sexe*. Betty Friedan, *The Feminine Mystique*. New York, Norton, 1963. Jack Kerouac, *On the Road*. New York, Viking Press, 1957. William H. Whyte, *The Organization Man*. New York, Simon and Schuster, 1956.

[40]William L. O'Neill, *American High: The Years of Confidence 1945–1960*. New York, Free Press, 1986, p. 48. Alfred C. Kinsey, *Sexual Behavior in the Human Male*, Philadelphia, W. B. Saunders, 1948. *Sexual Behavior in the Human Female*. New York, Pocket Books, 1965, first published 1953. Charles Murray, *Losing Ground: American Social Policy 1950–1980*, New York, Basic Books, 1984.

CRIME, DRUGS, AND DRINK

Relative marital stability during the postwar decade went with what, in retrospect, appears a remarkably low crime rate. Statistical evidence on a comparative basis is hard to assess, given the striking variations in the availability of relevant figures and the manner in which they are collected. Crime is ever-present in all societies; every occupation – banking, insurance, professional sports, even academia – has its seamy underside. Like an army, crime depends not merely on professional cadres, that is to say habitual criminals, but on available reserves of potential recruits, and on supply and support services. These too vary according to the social structure of any given country, making comparison difficult. The US, for example, always had a much higher crime rate than Great Britain, and Mexico a much higher rate than the US. (In 1958, seven and a half times as many homicides were committed per head of the population in the US, as in Great Britain, and more than seven times as many in Mexico as in the US. The Uniform Crime Reports (UCR) issued annually by the federal bureau of investigation moreover seriously underestimate actual crime rates because citizens fail to report an estimated 50 percent of all crimes.)

Circumstances in Britain have always differed greatly from the US however. For one thing Britain is an island, its people are tried by a common culture, and are relatively homogeneous in an ethnic sense. Britain has never engaged in that naive and perilous attempt at social engineering entailed in American prohibition (1920–33). Prohibition had been designed in part to force Americanization on foreign immigrants, especially working-class immigrants, and in part to impose a moral standard on an entire nation. Instead it promoted new forms of criminal organization, and new ways of corrupting public authority, in turn creating enormous new funds that were reinvested in other sections of the underground economy – gambling, prostitution, and the drugs trade. Prohibition had encouraged crime as a corporate enterprise. The US, moreover, remained a continent of immigrants. Given its national and racial diversity, its youthfulness, social and economic cleavages, its size, the easy mobility of motor cars, the availability of firearms, sociologists should wonder at the stability of US society rather than at the size of its crime figures.

Generally, crime was not nearly as widespread after World War II as it became during and after the 1960s. During World War II there had indeed been a widespread fear that returning servicemen, schooled in the art of killing, would commit all manner of outrages. Surprisingly enough, the first decade of the postwar period witnessed a falling off in crime (murder, rape, armed robbery, theft) in the US, and in the Western European countries, though the decline was not equally pronounced in all of them. In fact, demobilized veterans were infinitely more likely to be starting families than robbing their neighbors. Crime there was, but a resident of a run-down neighborhood such as Chorlton-on-Medlock in Manchester, England, a haunt of prostitutes at night, could walk the streets in darkness without a thought that he or his wife might be assaulted. Violence was more prevalent in American cities, where the crime rate climbed after the war.[41] But even so, old-timers of every ethnic derivation agree that during the 1950s life and property even in big-city slums were much safer than a generation later – an impression borne out by published statistics on the rise of crime in the US.[42]

What accounts for these relatively low crime figures? Above all, in Europe there was an end to public crime committed by political armies that had plagued the Weimar Republic and, to a smaller extent, other Western European countries during the 1930s – these were uniformed, disciplined forces, led by experienced combat soldiers, ready to march in the streets, with banners flying, and bands playing, and ready to beat or murder their opponents. That military style never regained political currency after the war. The militant demonstrators of the 1960s instead adopted a freer and more spontaneous mode – a change that oddly reflected a similar transformation in dancing, from the formal tangoes, waltzes, and Schottisches of old, to the freestyle beat of rock and roll. The returning veterans of World War II had worn uniforms at a time in their lives when (statistically) they were most crime-prone. When they came out of the service, they were largely past the "crime age." They returned to their studies, married, and took jobs. Crime and criminality mainly appeal to young men, the unemployed, those with low IQs, those afflicted with parental criminality and disruptive family situations. For a great number of reasons, family cohesion loosened for many blacks in the US from the early 1950s and for whites during the 1960s – at the very time when new drugs and a new youth culture contributed to a rise in crime.

After 1954 blacks became six or seven times more likely to end up serving time in prison; they entered mental hospitals at twice the rate of whites and had double the incidence of whites for diabetes, nephritis, and hypertension. Black citizens were four times more likely to be killed than whites. About 30 percent of blacks lived as an underclass, their lives full of stress, feeling resented, feared, and despised as inferior. It is no wonder many suffered low self-esteem and took to a career of crime and drugs – just as poverty-stricken young Irish immigrants were among the most crime-prone in nineteenth-century American slums.

Exhaustive explanations for the rising incidence of private crime are, however, hard to give, and are apt to reflect the political and moral assumptions of their respective proponents. According to many traditionalists, crime derives from the current permissiveness of society. A clique of soft-hearted and soft-

---

[41]The number of major offenses in cities with more than 25,000 people known to the police went up from 322,190 in 1945 to 457,370 in 1957, though figures for murder and non-negligent homicide varied little, from 2,361 in 1945 to 2.533 in 1957. Bureau of the census, *Historical Statistics of the United States: Colonial Times to 1957*. Washington, DC, Government Printing Office, 1960, p. 218.

[42]Between 1950 and 1985 the total number of federal and state prisoners in the US tripled – from 166,123 to 483,053. Bureau of the census, *Statistical Abstract of the United States, 1988*, p. 175. For the crime problem in general, see, for instance "Crime and punishment," in L. H. Gann and Peter Duignan, *The Hispanics in the United States: A History*. Boulder, Col., Westview Press, 1986, pp. 293–313.

headed politicians, psychiatrists, and literary intellectuals, abetted by liberal judges and bureaucrats, supposedly were conspiring to coddle criminals at the expense of law-abiding Americans. Respect for the law and law-enforcement declined; crime figures accordingly rose. But countries such as Norway and Denmark were more, not less, permissive in cultural attitudes than the US – yet had far lower crime figures. No scholar, moreover, has as yet arrived at a full explanation for the high crime rate among black Americans. (Although blacks have long represented only about 10 to 12 percent of the population they are, year in year out, charged with 48 percent or so of crimes for murder, 46 percent of rape, and 62 percent of robberies. Black crime rates are overall about four times that of whites.) And Mexico – a country not troubled by permissiveness – had a higher rate than the US. What matters in controlling crime is not so much the severity of punishment, as its certainty; and in this respect the US lagged far behind Western Europe.

There were other explanations for the striking rise of crime in the US after the 1950s. Some sociologists saw crime as a covert form of class or race warfare. But the victims of white murderers were almost always whites, the victims of blacks mostly blacks. Until drugs became a factor, crime was committed by the poor against the poor, rather than against the rich – a generalization that had been as true in eighteenth-century London as in twentieth-century New York. Other explanations derive from open or concealed racist assumptions. "Latins have a quick smile and a quick knife" say the bar-room patriots. "Blacks are violent by nature." Such unwarranted generalizations take no account of changing social circumstances. Puerto Rican and black New Yorkers do indeed have to contend with high crime rates. But when Puerto Ricans first arrived in New York, they were remarkably law-abiding and rarely took drugs. Black rural Southerners had always been pacific people who had rarely fallen foul of the law. Even among urban blacks in big city slums, crime had been much less pervasive in the 1940s than a generation later. We have already alluded to these changes in the chapter on the family; but some points bear repeating. The rise in black lawlessness was linked, at least in part, to that great exodus from the South and the subsequent removal of the great majority of middle-class whites from the cities and of middle-class blacks from communities such as New York or "Bronzeville" in "Black metropolis" (a Chicago ghetto study by J. C. St Clair Drake and H. Clayton in the 1940s).[43] It was this shift, made possible by the weakening of residential segregation, that deprived black people of their natural elite, and left the local underclass to their own devices.[44]

Advocates of a free market economy are more inclined to blame the welfare state for rising crime rates. By disrupting family cohesion and diminishing or eliminating internal authority within the family through welfare devices, such

[43] J. C. St Clair Drake and Horace R. Clayton, *Black Metropolis: A Study of Negro Life in a Northern City*. New York, Harper and Row, 1962 (original version published 1945), 2 vols.

[44] Nicholas Leman, "The origins of the underclass," *The Atlantic Monthly*, June 1986, pp. 31–54; July 1986, p. 54–68.

as aid to dependent children, the public philanthropists unwittingly eroded the work ethic. Minimum wage laws, the argument continues, reduced employment opportunities for unskilled youngsters, and have had similar effects. Street people of whatever race, untrained or unwilling to take low-status jobs, unaccustomed to punctuality, to habits of saving, to courteous behavior toward customers and respect toward supervisors, do not do well on the labor market. Hence, according to this theory, delinquency predicts socioeconomic status better than socioeconomic status predicts delinquency.[45] New York City, for instance, experienced rapidly rising crime rates at the same time as the city was making large-scale expansions in its welfare services. But many other factors must be entered in the equation. For instance, not all welfare states had a high crime rate: Sweden, with its all-embracing system, had a much lower crime rate than the US. Above all, most welfare recipients do not turn to crime; the majority of slum dwellers are law-abiding people – victims rather than perpetrators of violence.

Other arguments emphasize demographic factors in accounting for the smaller crime rates of the 1940s and the 1950s, and their subsequent rise. Mugging, rape, murder, and robbery are crimes for the fit and young, especially for men between the ages of 13 and 25. Thus, it was the baby boom after 1945 that was a major cause of the subsequent rise in crime, simply because there were more young people than at any time in history. The more youths there are, the more crimes they will commit. But the demographic explanations on their own no more account for the rising crime rate than those that emphasize poverty, class divisions, disparities in income, lack of social services, or migrancy. For instance, Portuguese labor migrants in Western Europe or Mexican illegals in the US, most of them single, young men without money in their pockets, had a remarkably low crime rate. Victorian England, to mention an even more striking example, had a youthful population and a high birthrate. Poverty was pervasive; Victorian slums shocked even the most hard-bitten visitors; class divisions ran deep; social services as yet remained in their infancy. Yet Victorian England, between 1850 and 1890, experienced a sharp drop in crime.

Similar objections apply to other single-cause explanations, including those that stress the impact of drugs. Drug abuse certainly leads to crime. Crime in turn worsens poverty, for muggers mainly rob the poor or neighborhood stores which serve the poor. Drug usage during the 1940s and 1950s was less widespread than later; it grew during the 1960s, like crime. But the increasing popularity of drugs in itself requires an explanation. Drug addiction cannot simply be linked to the prevalence of unemployment or poverty; both had been far more widely spread during the Great Depression, at a time when drugs were known, but not widely used.

[45]For a detailed study of crime from the free market standpoint see, for instance, James Q. Wilson, ed., *Crime and Public Policy*. San Francisco, ICS Press, Institute for Contemporary Studies, 1983. James Q. Wilson and Richard J. Herrnstein, *Crime and Human Nature*. New York, Simon and Schuster, 1985.

Crime therefore has no single cause. Like other social afflictions, it derives from a conjunction of many circumstances – religious, social, economic, and demographic – that vary from country to country. The US was more prone to crime than its allies, in part because its society was more heterogeneous, youthful, and mobile. Crime, like sport, entertainment, and industry, was subject to ethnic succession. Poverty-stricken immigrants and their sons tended to start at the bottom of the economic ladder, and perform unskilled and semi-skilled work in industry. If athletically inclined, they took up tough sports such as boxing or playing football in city lots. Once they got on in life, workmen or their sons would advance to skilled, supervisory, or managerial jobs; popular entertainers would be succeeded by classical performers, pugil-ists, and baseball players by professionals in tennis, golf, or swimming – sports that required expensive capital equipment.

A similar process was at work in crime. The unlettered and criminally disposed turned to mugging or petty robbery, employment that required little expertise, and inexpensive equipment – perhaps a brass knuckle or a blackjack – and yielded scant profit. Advancement in crime entailed doing highly skilled jobs, such as safe breaking, or promotion to supervisory or managerial pos-itions in criminal syndicates. The most highly educated criminals turned to white-collar crime requiring much expertise – embezzlement, fraud, tax evasion – offences committed by the well-to-do, not the poor. Every ethnic community, whether Irish, Jewish, Italian, or black, experienced this form of succession both in legitimate and criminal employment.

By comparison, Western Europe had less crime, and Western European crime patterns differed largely from those in the US. There was indeed a relatively higher rate of violence among immigrant Irishmen in Britain, and among Corsicans and Algerians in mainland France. But ethnic succession in crime was less marked in Western Europe than in the US, not because immigration in the former was insignificant, but because it experienced less inter-ethnic mobility than the US, both in criminal and legitimate enterprises. Family life was more stable in Europe; families had fewer children and a lower divorce rate than the US. Unemployment rates were also lower, at least up to the late 1970s.

The US and Western Europe also differed strikingly in vulnerability to drug abuse. (Drug usage owed a great deal to the medical profession. Opium had been widely used by physicians, by a number of literary artists, by people with money and eccentric life styles. Sherlock Holmes had been addicted to his opium-laced "7 percent solution," but the worthy Dr Watson never used narcotics.) During the twentieth century, the scope of narcotics widened as medical men and psychiatrists were the first to experiment with or dispense dangerous drugs such as heroin and LSD. For reasons not well understood, Americans took to drugs to a much greater extent than Europeans – especially after World War II. During the 1950s, estimates for habitual drug users in the US varied between 50,000 and 100,000, but there are no accurate figures. No European country remotely attained these levels. (According to estimates published in 1961 West Germany supposedly contained well under 5,000 drug addicts, Britain between 350 and 400 users; nor was drug abuse as yet a problem in France, Italy, or the Scandinavian countries – all of which were to register striking increases in usage during subsequent years.)[46]

The first drug users had comprised many middle-class whites, somewhat detached from conventional society, who frequented or resided in urban areas where illegal drugs could be purchased easily. During the early 1950s, new immigrants from the southeastern parts of the US, Puerto Rico, and Mexico moved into urban districts where illicit drugs had long been available. A high proportion of drug users (mainly of heroin and marijuana) came from urban slums where they had been introduced to drugs by their peers in street-corner society. Addicts at that time were mostly black youths who tended to come from disturbed families and lived in bad environments. Later Hispanics too began drug taking. Those who became drug users were widely prone to pessimism and futility and a low sense of worth. The need for money to buy drugs led to criminality; larceny and theft were the usual crimes of drug users. Drug addiction, of course, worsened the users' situation and physical health, and often led to unemployment or irregular employment as well as imprisonment (among regular drug users, entertainers, and physicians were best able to continue their employment).

The US focused its efforts on stopping the illicit trade in drugs. Great Britain, on the other hand, decriminalized drug taking and offered free drugs through physicians. Britain neither stigmatized nor imprisoned the narcotics user; hence fewer addicts took to crime to obtain drugs. The US continually stepped up its arrest of drug peddlers and users. By 1961 the narcotics offenders in the prison population had doubled, but drug consumption continued to rise during the following decades. During the 1960s, new hallucinogenics and other drugs came on the market; they were widely bought by young people and intellectuals, a different profile from heroin users. Thrill seeking, experiments at consciousness raising, a spirit of rebellion, helped to promote the habit. The resultant addiction to various drugs remains hard to cure. (Less than 3 percent of addicts treated in New York hospitals between 1953 and 1955 remained drug free after five years.)

The general health hazards of drugs of course should not be exaggerated. In statistical terms, the perils posed to human life were actually much less than those of drinking and cigarette smoking; these habits remained socially acceptable during the postwar years, promoted by advertising, and by peer-group pressure, as symbols of emancipation for women and the young. Estimates concerning drug abuse moreover were purely conjectural; usage fluctuated, and users did not necessarily become addicts. Nevertheless, the perils of the drug culture were bad enough, affecting the users' minds, health, social habits, and crime patterns. The drugs trade came to mirror legitimate commerce with its complex marketing, advertising, and financial operations. Drug dependency supported gangsters and prostitution. All efforts to reduce

---

[46]See John A. Clausen, "Drug addiction: social aspects," in *International Encyclopedia of the Social Sciences,* v. 4, pp. 298–303.

drug usage failed – only ageing of individuals seemed to diminish its use.

Overall, alcoholism remained a much greater social evil than drug addiction. It was a long-standing menace to health and family stability, a contributor to traffic accidents and personal violence. The cause and overall impact of alcoholism still remains only partly understood. Comparative research on the drinking patterns of, say, Jewish and Irish Americans were instructive in showing that popular stereotypes were not necessarily mistaken, and that Jews did drink much less than Irish people. Alcoholism is apparently linked to specific cultural assumptions – especially those that link manliness with the ability to drink large quantities. The bar-room culture is especially influential among communities made up of young males, be they men in slums, Marines in lonely outstations, or miners in remote compounds. Even so, patterns of addiction varied greatly between different countries. An international comparison of rates of alcoholics made in 1958 placed France at the top of the list.[47] The US came second (with an estimated 4,447,000 alcoholics, according to a 1962 estimate). Down the list (in descending order) came Sweden, Switzerland, Denmark, Canada, Norway, England and Wales, with Italy at the bottom – but even in England or Italy, the indirect effects of alcoholism were enormous, and its victims were to be found on Skid Row, among middle classes, and the rich.

THE WELFARE STATE AND SOCIETY

Kinder, Küche, Kirche (kids, kitchen, church) in theory at least described woman's proper role in traditional Germany. All over Europe, *Kinder, Küche, Kirche* were also the traditional providers of social welfare. Children were supposed to look after their aged parents in a predominantly agricultural society. Needy and aged kinsmen shared a meal in the kitchen of a well-to-do farmer with the rest of the family. The Church provided all manner of social services, including poor relief and education. It was not for nothing that poor peasants in Catholic Spain had fought with desperate intensity for their church against the Napoleonic invaders. The nineteenth century introduced far-reaching changes through the spread of towns, the diffusion of industry, and in Catholic countries the growing power of anti-clerical parties resolved to curb the power of the Church. Between them, commercial enterprise and the state largely, though not entirely, replaced the Church as a provider of welfare services.

Private insurance turned into a major business enterprise. The well-to-do began to take out policies designed to cover all manner of risks. Large firms increasingly made special arrangements for their employees, either through collective agreements between workers and employers, or through the personnel and public relations policies of individual corporations. In addition, protection against a wide range of social risks to individual citizens was offered

[47] Judson Brown, "Drinking and alcoholism: social aspects," in *International Encyclopedia of the Social Sciences*, v. 4, pp. 268–75.

by religious institutions, friendly societies, trade unions, and sometimes in Europe through political parties. The role of private enterprise in social welfare varied enormously from state to state. The literature on the subject, however, remains relatively scanty. As the standard work much used in this chapter put it in 1961, "information on these various private schemes, extensive though they are believed to be in some countries, is virtually non-existent."[48]

Even more important was the state as a provider of social welfare. Bismarck's social security legislation, initiated in 1883 in Imperial Germany had stood out as a pioneering venture. Its purpose had been to weaken the Social Democrats and to give the workers a stake in the imperial order. Bismarck's example found many imitators and the role of the state kept widening – the more so as men and women increasingly moved away from their accustomed neighborhoods where the Church and extended family had provided support. The extent of these changes should not be exaggerated. Even after World War II, a large proportion of the population in Western Europe and America continued to live and work in the communities where they had been born, or returned to native towns and villages after demobilization – a fact all too easily ignored by academics who themselves belong to a particularly mobile profession.

Nevertheless, there was after World War II more social and geographical mobility than in the past; hence demands on state aid kept growing. Social security took three distinct forms: social insurance (usually financed through contributions from employers, employees, and often also the state); public assistance (a much older form of welfare by which needy individuals, widows, orphans, the disabled, and others were given aid in cash or kind); and public services (that provided specific benefits to any qualified members of the community, regardless of individual need, or contribution to an insurance scheme). Welfare provisions were bewildering in their diversity; the welfare state grew in haphazard fashion, until it resembled a giant centipede – unsightly, slow, hard to understand in its legwork, but capable of getting across enormous obstacles.

Welfare eventually embraced all manner of benefits: public housing, health insurance, worker's compensation, medical insurance, pensions and funeral benefits, unemployment benefits, family allowances. Following the Great Depression, expenditure on these and other services continually expanded in all Western European countries.[49] The disruption brought about by World War II might have been expected to retard this growth, but civil service organizations proved incredibly tough; they outlasted the call-up of personnel, the disorganization due to destruction of records in air raids, and the evacuation of offices. Far from diminishing, the administrative structure continued to grow after the war, as did the demand for welfare services.

[48]Dewhurst et al., *Europe's Needs*, p. 393.
[49]Taken together, public expenditure in Belgium, Denmark, Finland, France, Great Britain, Italy, Netherlands, Spain, Sweden, and Switzerland (at 1954 prices) between 1930 and 1954 increased at the following percentages: Total: 291, health: 284, pensions: 359, family allowances: 1,763, other: 275. Only unemployment benefits diminished by 22 percent – itself an indicator of prosperity, ibid., p. 400.

Many lobbyists combined to further this expansion – aristocrats driven by a sense of *noblesse oblige*; egalitarians who saw in the welfare state an instrument for redistributing national wealth; believers in efficiency who resented poverty as an obstacle to the creation of a powerful state reliant on productive factories and powerful armies manned by well-fed, well-educated, and healthy recruits; religious believers who regarded the relief of poverty as a sacred duty; politicians of every stripe who hoped to attract voters through the provision of statutory benefits; bureaucrats eager both to help their fellow citizens and, at the same time, to increase the scope and power of their respective departments; intellectuals resolved to improve humanity's lot; private firms who looked to the state as a purchaser of their merchandise – the list would fill many pages. Above all, there was at the end of World War II a general sense of optimism, a spirit of confidence that looked to the eradication of poverty and disease as an achievable and expected aim of government. Citizens felt they were entitled to aid from the state; bureaucrats and politicians agreed with them.

> *New standards of sanitation and quarantine were developed. Governments everywhere became increasingly concerned with prevention and control of diseases, and with improving life expectancy. Only a few states considered it part of their responsibility to interfere in issues of fertility or migration. The state generally supervised standards of public health, vaccination and inoculation, quarantine, control of communicable diseases, control of the purity of water and food. It regulated the licensing of members of the medical and health care professions. It also regulated sanitation, the operation of hospitals, distribution of medicines and drugs, and protection of the worker in the workplace. Many private and public health insurance schemes were established throughout the Atlantic Community. There were improvements in the registration of vital events and in the supervision of international health conventions.*

With the diversity of its inspiration, and the economic disparities between the Western European countries, the advent of the welfare state differed greatly in its impact.[50] The Iberian Peninsula, the most backward part of Western Europe in an economic sense, also lagged far behind in the provision of public welfare. By the end of the 1950s, both Spain and Portugal operated a number of official and semi-official projects for health care, unemployment benefit, pensions, family allowances, and so on. These were organized on corporate lines, but only for a small number of occupations. They were financed to a considerable extent by employers and offered a very limited range of services. Their effectiveness and extent bore little relation to the propagandistic slogans that the Franco and Salazar dictatorships promoted at home and abroad.

[50]Adrian Woodbridge, "Has the welfare state gone wrong?" in the *Times Literary Supplement*, 5 June 1987, p. 600. The literature is enormous and includes Douglas E. Ashford, *The Emergence of the Welfare State*. Oxford, Blackwell, 1987, Malcolm Wicks, *A Future for All: Do We Need the Welfare State?* Harmondsworth, Penguin Books, 1987. Peter Taylor-Gooby, *Public Opinion, Ideology, and the Welfare State*. Boston, Routledge, Kegan Paul, 1985. Shmuel N. Eisenstadt and Ora Ahimeir, eds, *The Welfare State and Its Aftermath*. London, Croom Helm, 1985. Howard Glennerster, *Paying for Welfare*. Oxford, Blackwell, 1985. The fundamental work is William H. Beveridge, *Full Employment in a Free Society*. New York, W. W. Norton, 1945.

The welfare state developed to a much greater extent first in Scandinavian countries (1920s), then in the Netherlands, Belgium, Switzerland, West Germany, and Austria, with Ireland and Italy gradually catching up with their more prosperous neighbors. France, in theory, introduced one of the world's most comprehensive social security schemes in 1946. On paper, it applied to every French citizen, wage earner or not. In practice, there were numerous rejections from farmers, artisans, and shopkeepers who preferred their own professional organizations. Nevertheless, the French scheme was unusual in that it covered every aspect of social security (health, accidents at work, retirement pensions, family allowances) and all was planned with Gallic rigor, though it was less effective in fact than in design.

Overall, the various Western European states built elaborate mixed systems that embraced private firms, friendly societies, and other cooperative insurance agencies, as well as the state. The state then extended the range of social insurance, to pay family allowances, and similar benefits. Insured workers became entitled to a wide range of social security allowances. Their extent varied from country to country, with West Germany, France, the Netherlands, and Sweden in the vanguard, and the poorer states (including Austria, Ireland, and Italy) in the rear. Entire categories of the population as yet remained uncovered by official or semi-official schemes, and depended on such voluntary arrangements as individual families chose or were able to make.

The United States was a special case. Americans had traditionally put their trust in private enterprise and private benevolence on the part of churches, welfare societies, and ethnic associations. A great deal of scope was left to individual states and cities – especially to great conurbations such as New York that built municipal welfare states of their own. For the US as a whole, it was Roosevelt's New Deal that laid the foundations of a social service state that would – in terms of dollars and cents – develop ultimately into the most highly funded (but not the most comprehensive) welfare machine in history. The New Deal introduced four lasting changes. These comprised social security, aid to families with dependent children (AFDC), workmen's compensation, and unemployment insurance. Social security and workmen's compensations would take care of those who could not or should not have to work; unemployment insurance would look after workers thrown out of their jobs for reasons beyond their control; AFDC would lighten the lot of single parents and small children. In each instance, help would go to upstanding citizens who had fallen on evil days, or were too old or too sick to support themselves. The bulk of this expenditure derived from cash grants. But the New Deal was in no sense designed to provide help merely because a person was poor, or labored under some social disadvantage.[51]

[51]Charles Murray, *Losing Ground: American Social Policy 1850–1980*. New York, Basic Books, 1984, p. 17, written from the free enterprise standpoint. Other critiques of the welfare state include Morton Paglin, *Poverty and Transfers in Kind*. Stanford, Cal., Hoover Institution Press, 1980. Martin Anderson, *Welfare: The Political Economy of Welfare Reform*. Stanford, Cal., Hoover Institution Press, 1978. For contrary interpretations, see James T. Patterson, *America's Struggle Against Poverty, 1900–1980*. Cambridge, Mass., Harvard University Press, 1981. Michael B. Katz, *In the Shadow of the Poorhouse: A Social History of Welfare in America*. New York, Basic Books, 1986.

World War II had accelerated the welfare revolution in the US. The federal government grew dramatically. (Between 1940 and 1946 the federal budget grew sixfold – from $9 billion in 1940 to $64 billion in 1946). Welfare services expanded though at nothing like the same rate as they did in Britain, Scandinavia, or even West Germany. In the US they were not aimed at the poor, but at veterans, who were perceived to have sacrificed much.[52] Veterans' benefits were greatly increased, from $610 million in 1942 to $5,728 million in 1952. The government concentrated aid for veterans on health, housing, and above all on education. During its 12 years of existence, the GI Bill provided educational assistance for 7.8 million veterans in what turned out to be the greatest project of its kind in history. The majority of the Bill's beneficiaries were trained in technical schools or on the job. In addition 2.2 million went to colleges or universities – far more than had been expected. The total spent for education and training amounted to $14.5 billion; in addition, the veterans' administration guaranteed or insured nearly $16.5 billion in loans for homes, farms, or businesses.

There were many other welfare advances.[53] The US made a start on public housing – this with approval from Senator Robert Taft, an avowed conservative who happened to agree with liberals on this particular aspect of social policy. A postwar Housing Act provided for 356,000 units to be built during a period of 15 years, though many of them were of shoddy construction and soon became slums. Truman also submitted an extensive federal health care program involving a national health insurance scheme, but he was unable to gain congressional approval for his design. By the time the Korean war erupted the president's Fair Deal was practically over, given the absence of a liberal majority in Congress. Reformers and would-be reformers during the 1950s settled for increases in limited categories of welfare. But growth was impressive in some of those fields. For example, the number of beneficiaries in the old-age, survivor and disability program quadrupled between 1950 and 1960 (from 3.5 million to 14.8 million).[54] But the most spectacular expansion in the welfare system only occurred during the 1960s under the Kennedy and Johnson presidencies' war on poverty, thanks to new and potent coalitions of welfare lobbyists, social workers, civil rights activists, social scientists, progressive educators, clerics with a social mission, reform-minded civil servants, and lawyers – the latter uniquely American in the strength of their numbers and prestige.[55]

[52]Patterson, *America's War Against Poverty*, p. 85.

[53]William L. O'Neill, *American High: The Years of Confidence: 1945–60*. New York, Free Press, 1986, p. 10.

[54]Rita Ricardo Campbell, *Social Security: Promise and Reality*. Stanford, Cal., Hoover Institution Press, 1977, p. 20. By 1975 the number of beneficiaries had grown to 31.9 million from 3.5 million in 1950. Annual cash benefits grew from $1 billion in 1950 to $11 billion in 1960, to $67 billion in 1975.

[55]Between 1952 and 1972 national expenditure on defense increased by 12 percent; expenditure on total domestic services (including education, income maintenance, health services of all kinds, etc.) rose by 80 percent. For a breakdown, see Roger A. Freeman, *The Growth of American Government: A Morphology of the Welfare State*. Stanford, Cal., Hoover Institution Press, 1975, p. 7.

How much did the welfare planners achieve? The answer is not easy to give. Social expenditure differed considerably from country to country in kind and extent. More importantly, there were striking disparities in national priorities. These reflected historical traditions and anxieties, rather than designed plans. For instance the French and, to a lesser extent, the Italians, spent a great deal on family allowances. The British, plagued by long and bitter memories of joblessness, took care to cover a larger part of their labor force by unemployment insurance than any other Western European state. The Germans concentrated on pension payments and on social insurance programs, a form of welfare that they had historically pioneered. The Scandinavian countries developed extensive pension and family allowance programs; these were organized by the state and administered through local boards, while unemployment insurance remained the responsibility of trade unions and other nongovernmental bodies. Sweden especially developed a far-reaching system that provided not only for general medical care, and sickness insurance, but also for birth, marriage, and funeral grants, home services for the bedridden and for working mothers, psychologists at child guidance clinics, convalescent homes for recovering psychiatric patients, retraining for the unemployed, services for the blind, paralysed, and so on.

Whatever system or systems were adopted by the various Western European countries, expenditure grew all round, as did the proportion of insured persons in every country. (By 1957, 100 percent of the population in Great Britain, Sweden, and Norway, more than 80 percent in West Germany, more than 60 percent in Italy, Switzerland, and Austria, were eligible for some form of national sickness insurance program, with Belgium, France, the Netherlands, Spain, and Portugal lagging behind in descending order.) The greater part of the labor force in Great Britain, Belgium, Norway, and West Germany were entitled to unemployment insurance; there were widespread arrangements for old-age pensions, invalids, and family allowances.[56]

It is hard to know how much was accomplished. Obviously, the countries with more highly developed economies were able to spend proportionately more on social security. But given a roughly equal degree of economic development, there was no obvious correlation between any given country's expenditure for social security programs as a part of its gross national product, and that country's general well-being. The Saar Territory (*Saarland*) topped the list of spenders in terms of GNP percentages, as against Switzerland's relatively modest outlay, but it is difficult to argue that the Saarlanders were better off than the Swiss. Even national ideology did not matter as much as

---

[56]The following percentage of the labor force in 1955 was covered by unemployment insurance: Great Britain: 84, Belgium: 57, Ireland: 55, West Germany: 54, Austria: 44, Sweden: 40, Denmark: 31, Switzerland: 28, Italy: 26. Expenditure for pension payments under social insurance programs as part of the 1954 gross national product stood as follows: Western Europe: 3.9, West Germany: 6.1, Austria: 5.3, Belgium: 4.8, Sweden: 4.3, Italy: 3.8, France: 3.7, Great Britain: 3.2, Norway: 2.5, Portugal: 1.3, Spain: 0.6. Expenditure on family allowances as a percent of the 1954 GNP stood as follows: France: 4.2, Italy: 2.4, Belgium: 2.1, Netherlands: 1.6, Great Britain: 0.6, West Germany: 0.2. See Dewhurst, *Europe's Needs*, pp. 385, 391, 393 for statistical tables.

was assumed both by the proponents and opponents of the welfare state. Common misconceptions notwithstanding, the British, for example, spent a good deal less as a percentage of their gross national income on social services than the West Germans – despite Britain's commitment to the welfare state, and West Germany's dedication to a free market economy.[57]

The same consideration applies to health services. All Western countries without exception experienced a decline in mortality after World War II, part of a long-term trend that had begun more than a century earlier. During the nineteenth century a married woman could expect as a matter of course that one or several of her babies might die in early infancy. Infectious diseases had once taken a heavy toll of children of pre-school age. By the late 1950s, however, the death rate for infants and young children had dropped in a startling fashion.[58] Older people likewise had a much better chance of surviving to a ripe old age than their ancestors. Bismarck's social security legislation had set the pensionable age at 65; but relatively few retired workers had lived long enough to make much use of the benefits to which they were entitled. Two generations later, there were far more pensioners, and the labor force as a whole had become older. The biblical life span of "three score and ten" had become the norm for Sweden, the US, France, and Britain, while all over the Western world the crude death rate had diminished since the start of World War II (from 10.6 per thousand in 1939 to 9.4 in 1958 in the US, and from 13.7 to 10.2 in Western Europe). The crude death rate of course understated the drop in mortality because the population as a whole was getting older.

The decline in the death rate constituted the most remarkable achievement in the social sphere, given man's propensity to value a long life more than any other secular benefit. The longer life expectancy had many causes – above all the great reduction in deaths from infective and parasitic diseases as a result of anti-microbial therapy.[59] However, there is no straightforward correlation between the diminution in mortality and the expansion of the welfare state after World War II. Mortality declined at about the same rate in Great Britain and the US, even though the British built a comprehensive National Health Service, whereas the Americans did not. The decline was even more striking in Spain, where public welfare services remained deficient.[60]

---

[57]In 1954 total social expenditure as a percentage of the gross national product stood as follows: Western Europe: 10.9, Saar: 19.6, West Germany: 14.0, France: 13.5, Belgium: 12.6, Italy: 11.5, Sweden: 10.6, Great Britain: 9.3, Netherlands: 7.5, Norway: 7.4, Switzerland: 6.6, Portugal: 4.6, Spain: 1.3. Dewhurst, *Europe's Needs*, p. 399.

[58]In Germany the death rate for infants under one year of age per 1,000 live births dropped as follows: 1901–10: 186, 1939: 72, 1958: 36, in Great Britain: 1891–1910: 153, 1939: 54, 1958: 54. Corresponding figures for France were: 164, 68, 32; for Italy: 175, 97, 48. For tables see Dewhurst, *Europe's Needs*, pp. 37 and 38.

[59]Iwao M. Moriyma, "Mortality", in David L. Sills, ed., *International Encyclopedia of the Social Sciences*, v. 10, p. 500.

[60]Between 1949 and 1958 the British crude death rate per 1,000 went down from 10.7 to 9.5. The Spanish death rate diminished from 11.6 to 8.7 (if the published statistics may be trusted). For a comparative table see UN *Demographic Yearbook 1959*. New York, United Nations, 1959, pp. 552–3.

The welfare state had inbuilt limitations. Benefits kept expanding in a variety of ways as welfare families received aid in kind as well as in cash – clothing, school lunches, and free milk, as well as help with rent, school fees, and the like. These provisions were no doubt beneficial for the recipients. Nevertheless, we ourselves adhere to the old-fashioned proposition that the most effective welfare system was the traditional husband-and-wife family, especially a family where mother stayed at home to look after her young children. The traditional family may have been romaticized by its defenders, but nevertheless their arguments seem to be borne out by subsequent US statistics concerning crime and other social problems faced by single-parent as opposed to two-parent families.

Despite the extension of the welfare state, moreover, large pockets of poverty continued to exist through the years of recovery – the traditional deprivation of remote villages in Calabria, Co. Galway, or the Appalachians, and the misery of urban slums. Class differences softened, but did not disappear. Even in Britain, supposedly the classical exponent of the welfare state "the welfare measures of the labour Government did not, of themselves, produce a more egalitarian or open society. The profile of the class struggle, or even simply of the distribution of wealth, showed relatively little change between 1945 and 1951."[61]

Whatever its achievements, the welfare state certainly did not live up to all the many expectations of its founders and their optimistic trust in their own ability to change society. There were also numerous unanticipated effects. For example, no US planner foresaw that aid for dependent children (AFDC) would help to break up common law marriages among the poor. AFDC went to mothers who reared children without the breadwinner's support. It thus had the unintended consequence of shifting economic power within the family from the man to the woman, a bitter pill to swallow for white, black, or Hispanic men wedded to traditional concepts of male dominance. AFDC moreover created anomalies: a poorly paid laborer might actually benefit his common law wife and children by leaving home, and thus making the woman eligible for aid. Desertion – so to speak – might become a form of chivalry.

AFDC was a peculiarly American solution; its administration was based on US middle-class notions of propriety. But the welfare state all over the world created other unexpected problems – an expanding and expensive bureaucracy, new temptations for graft, and a growing tax burden that came to weigh heavily on workers as well as the well-to-do. Welfare benefits did not necessarily all go to the needy; on the contrary middle-class people also received substantial aid, especially as regarded benefits in kind such as the free health service in Britain, free secondary school places, and food subsidies. Indeed the very extent and cost of the welfare state after 1945 meant that many of the new social reforms were financed by transfers of income within lower-income groups themselves, an observation applicable to other countries besides Britain.

---

[61]Kenneth O. Morgan, *Labour in Power 1945–1951*. Oxford, Oxford University Press, 1985, p. 185.

In the US the middle class, more than the working class, especially benefited from a free college and university education.

Not surprisingly, there were many problems as time went on. Critiques of the welfare state went with censure of the intellectual assumptions held by its makers. It had owed an enormous debt to the social scientists, mostly optimistic heirs of the enlightenment, who believed that human nature was almost infinitely malleable, capable of being fundamentally changed through proper understanding of human behavior. The social sciences looked to great new breakthroughs, comparable to the marvellous discoveries made by seventeenth- and eighteenth-century astronomers. The reformers moreover had come almost universally from the ranks of middle-class people, and all too often assumed unquestioningly that the poor could be converted to middle-class standards merely by being placed in a middle-class environment. This proved harder to achieve in practice than in theory, belying the social engineers' assumptions, and exposing their unexpectedly poor record of prediction, together with their "inability to discern, separate, and measure the multitudinous interacting influences on social behavior."[62]

Despite these shortfalls, the welfare state at the time proved immensely popular. Its expansion was due, not just to the efforts of Keynesian professors and bureaucrats, but to the overwhelming force of public opinion. The growth of the welfare state went with a new prosperity, and a new sense of social entitlement that affected every nation in the West – even Switzerland, most conservative of European countries. Gradually, almost every citizen with an officially recognized identity number became not merely a contributor to but also a beneficiary of the welfare state. Overall, the lot of the old and poor improved, as did people's general health. A number of educational and training programs attained considerable success. The welfare state neither abolished poverty nor assured for its beneficiaries freedom from welfare dependency (known as "transmitted deprivation" in British literature). Contrary to all predictions, Switzerland, the least welfare-conscious country in Europe, also turned out to be one of its most prosperous, and least troubled by those social ills that beset so many other societies.[63]

Still, the welfare state commanded – and went on to command – almost universal approval. Social Democrats and Christian Democrats, British Labourites and Tories, US Democrats and Republicans all collaborated in its extension. This applied not merely to Western Europe, but also to the United States where private enterprise continued to be honored more than in the Old World. Everett Carll Ladd's and Seymour Martin Lipset's assessment of US public opinion during the late 1970s applied equally to every Western country: "When asked whether the federal or state governments should cut back on spending for public services, the public today overwhelmingly favor sustaining or

[62]Tom Alexander, "The social engineers retreat under fire," in *Fortune,* October 1972, p. 134.
[63]Ralph Segalman, *The Swiss Way of Welfare: Lessons for the Western World.* New York, Praeger, 1986.

increasing public spending."[64] Whatever its critics might say, no party or government at the time could have resisted the trend toward entitlement.

Commitment to the welfare state then was almost universal. By contrast, there was scant public concern for ecological issues. Experts worried over questions such as soil conservation, but these issues rarely made the headlines. In the rush to repair the ravages of war, increase material well-being, exploit natural resources, and increase farm yields, much harm was done to the land, rivers, and sea coasts of the Western world. Coal dust blackened cities, car fumes created smog, fertilizers harmed the land, and pesticides poisoned not only bugs but also water sources and wildlife. We have referred to the growing ecological concerns of the era in another chapter. We shall here limit ourselves by pointing out that the battle against the pollution of land, water, and skies had been waged for many years, but that ecological campaigns did not become a major political movement until the 1960s. In this battle the state led the way, but private groups played an important part – universities, civic organizations, and bodies such as the World Wildlife Fund (1961, later renamed the World Wide Fund for Nature). They pushed for conservation, land restoration, and the regulation of waste disposal and chemicals. It was the economic growth of the 1950s that helped to make the environmental concerns of the 1960s into a popular cause.

[64]Everett Carll Ladd Jr and Seymour Martin Lipset, "Public opinion and public policy," in Peter Duignan and Alvin Rabushka, eds, *The United States in the 1980s*. Stanford, Cal., Hoover Institution Press, 1980, p. 63.

PART V

Thought and Culture

Education

After the hard years of war, there was in the Western world a new hunger for instruction and knowledge. In every Western country educational expansion was unparalleled in terms of expenditure, construction, admissions, research and professional manpower deployed in schools and colleges. (In the US alone, educational expenditure between 1945 and 1956 more than tripled – from $3,393 million to $12,334 million – as compared to a total expenditure of $5,312 million for the whole of Western Europe in 1955.) Education was regarded as a universal good by liberals and Marxists alike, by the religious-minded and freethinkers. Schools and universities were expected to perform an increasing number of tasks – to teach literacy and numeracy, transmit high culture, inspire patriotism, promote equality and social mobility, further international understanding, save souls, turn out good citizens, train efficient workers, produce knowledgeable specialists, achieve psychological adjustment, deepen aesthetic sensibility, and so on.

AN OVERVIEW

At the end of World War II, continued expansion of education on an enormous scale could hardly have been predicted. More children entered the schools than ever before, because of rising birthrates, while the educational profession on both sides of the Atlantic faced a daunting array of problems. In Europe, many school and university buildings had been damaged or destroyed; many teachers had been killed; students had forgotten what they had once learned. There was also a sense of disorientation brought about by roller-coaster politics. The effects of political instability on education are of course hard to gauge. (For instance, a case study of a Catholic elementary school in a North German village emphasizes how relatively little did actually change as regards syllabus and teaching methods during the Nazi and postwar years.)[1] Nevertheless

[1]Manfred Köhler, *Die Volksschule Harsum im Dritten Reich: Wiederstand and Anpassung einer Katholischen Dorfschule.* Hildesheim, August Lax, 1985.

education had suffered, and in German occupied Europe it had been degraded by Nazism.

There was also a pervasive sense of instability and relativism. A French teacher of middle age during his or her career would have had to come to terms with the Third Republic, Vichy, liberation, and the Fourth Republic. Even more difficult was the problem of education in West Germany, where the denazification process was seen by many US educators as a noble venture in remodelling the entire German national psyche. (The French and Russians, and to a lesser extent the British, were more cynical in this regard.) We have discussed denazification in other contexts, and shall recapitulate on just a few major points.

Denazification was eye-wash, said one group of critics. It failed to make any fundamental changes in Germany. All too many Nazis simply went under ground. The educational establishment was particularly resilient; its members played along for a time until the occupiers found more urgent tasks, or withdrew altogether.[2] The Allies lacked resources, and a consistent plan. They differed among themselves and were capricious and inconsistent in the manner in which they applied their policies. Allied officers generally knew little about Germany. Few of them spoke good German; hence they resorted to government by interpreters and paramours. Alternatively, they conceded too much influence to émigrés whose psychological clock regarding Germany had stopped at the moment when they went into exile. In any case, the Allies were not liked by the Germans. How then could foreigners serve as role models for reluctant subjects?

At the same time, the Allies incurred censure for going too far. They failed to differentiate between true criminals and harmless citizens unfortunate enough to get ensnared in Nazi officialdom. The so-called *Persilschein* (the document certifying its bearer to have been denazified) was a bureaucratic travesty. (By 1959, almost every German in the US zone had filled in a questionnaire. Something like 3,000,000 charges were handled by 22,000 employees. Some 900,000 sentences were meted out – many of them nominal.) The Germans were denazified not so much by Allied intervention, as by their own disastrous experience with the Third Reich.

Our own assessment is more positive. Despite their many failings, the Allies restored the German educational system with remarkable speed. In the British zone, for instance, most children immediately went back to school – despite staggering wartime casualties among German teachers, and the destruction of school buildings.[3] The Allies instituted exchange visits and exchange programs

[2]Peter Merkl, "The impact of the US occupation on the domestic development of Western Germany," Conference on US occupation policies, Hoover Institution, Stanford, May 1986. James F. Trent, *Mission on the Rhine: Reeducation and Denazification in American Occupied Germany*. Chicago University of Chicago Press, 1982. Constantine Fitzgibbon, *Denazification*. London, Michael Joseph, 1969. Edward N. Peterson, *The American Occupation of Germany: Retreat to Victory*. Detroit, Wayne State University Press, 1977.

[3]D. C. Watt, *Britain Looks to Germany: British Opinion and Policy Toward Germany Since 1945*. London, O. Wolff, 1956, pp. 68–98 for the British occupation.

(through agencies such as the British-instituted *Brücke*). They set up libraries and issued new textbooks. (Already by October 1945, the Americans had printed over 5,000,000 textbooks.)[4] In this respect alone, the gain was enormous – Nazi textbooks had enjoined young boys to die for the *Führer*, and young girls to bear certifiably Aryan children for the Fatherland.

Even more important perhaps were the indirect effects of education. When all is said and done about the looting ("liberating") done by Allied soldiers, rape, and the temporary confiscation of private houses for Allied use, countless Germans also had good experiences. Many returned from British and US prison camps with a favorable outlook toward democracy (74 percent in the case of a large US sample).[5] And many Allied administrators earned respect as individuals – from General Lucius D. Clay down to local commandants or advisers whose friendly regard for their little bailiwicks was long remembered. There were also friendly individual contacts between Allied soldiers and Germans, ranging from love affairs and marriages to informal little discussion circles. (One of the two co-authors, then a British sergeant, still fondly remembers lengthy sessions with German veterans in which he, by origin a German Jew, answered with some difficulty a host of earnest questions about the Jewish religion – set against the travesties that had once filled *Der Stürmer*, *Das Schwarze Korps*, and other Nazi papers.) It was education in an indirect and non-quantifiable sense.

Not that this lightened ordinary teachers' tasks. They were often shaken in their confidence, and indiscipline resulted from the impact of foreign occupation, a pervasive black market, and political strife. Even British education, not affected by enemy occupation, had such problems. (A former British officer found that while he had easily handled feuding Pathani warriors serving under his command in the British Indian Army he could not master British slum children in an East London school.) In general, the teaching profession was not well paid, nor did it command much prestige. (Among 11 ranked professions in selected countries in the West, doctors and lawyers consistently came out on top during the early 1950s. Secondary school teachers – the field officers in the army of education – occupied the highest place in the prestige ladder in Norway, and third place in both Spain and Switzerland. But elsewhere they only made fifth or sixth place; in the US they came seventh, below hospital nurses.)[6] The golden years of teacher recruitment had been in the Great Depression, when many first-class candidates had been glad to find jobs in teaching which offered social advancement for working-class men and women. During the 1950s, by contrast, many more graduates found jobs in business and government, while the teaching profession in the Western countries suffered from an exodus of trained scientists and mathematicians who went

[4] Review by Marshall Knapper of Roy Willis, *The French in Germany, 1945–1949*, Stanford, Stanford University Press, 1962, in *Journal of Modern History*, September 1962, v. xxxlv, p. 367.

[5] Arnold Krammer, *Nazi Prisoners of War in America*. New York, Stein and Day, 1979.

[6] For table see J. Frederick Dewhurst et al., *Europe's Needs and Resources: Trends and Prospects in Eighteen Countries*. New York, Twentieth Century Fund, 1961, pp. 338–9 for comparative salaries and status.

into industries where salaries were higher and where qualified people enjoyed higher status than in the classroom.

Yet teachers at the same time had to cope with both the old difficulties, and the new demands on education. In France and Belgium, the struggle continued between clerical as against secular education. Rising birthrates during and after World War II produced a new generation of "baby boomers" who crowded into schools and later into colleges. There were new calls to end class privileges in education, to admit more working-class children to secondary schools, and to update curricula. (The Canadians expanded their government bureaucracy threefold to give employment to returning veterans after the war.)

The sense of dislocation also extended to the US, albeit for different reasons. Seen from the perspective of the 1930s, traditional US education all too easily appears in a romantic light, not apparent to contemporaries at the time. Education in America, unlike Britain, was plagued by Red hunters, cultists, and eccentrics – all of whom mistakenly assumed that by purging the schools they would purge the nation. American, unlike European, schools faced bitter battles for racial integration (resolved at least in law and on paper through the historic *Brown versus Board of Education* decision, 1954).

There were also bitter struggles over broader issues of educational philosophy. As a *New York Times* writer put it in 1947: "America's public school system is confronted with the most serious crisis in its history."[7] After a six-month tour across the US, he reported that since 1940, 350,000 teachers had left the public school for better jobs; one in seven teachers held substandard qualifications, that 70,000 teaching posts went unfilled. The average teacher's salary was less than a garbage collector's, truck driver's or bartender's; the teachers' morale was low, and overcrowding rife; strikes were numerous; many school buildings were in a deplorable state. The sense of crisis extended to larger questions too, with disagreement on the purpose of education, finance, the role of private as against public education, accessibility, standards, curricula, disicipline and juvenile delinquency, and, above all, the ever-rising expectations of the public. These expectations were hard to meet, given the profound differences in resources available to educators in different parts of the country. The southern US school districts were especially poor. Salaries for white and black teachers were low – around $900 and $600 a year. (About half of the teachers had no college training.) The education establishment looked to the federal government for aid, but got little help until 1965.

America's educational debate hinged to a significant degree on the pros and cons of progressive education.[8] The struggle was between those who championed the traditional school (subject oriented, supposedly rigid, and authoritarian), and those who championed the modern school (child-centered, supposedly flexible, and progressive.) The progressives wanted education for all, not just for the academically able; they played down mastery of subject

---

[7]See Diane Ravitch, *The Troubled Crusade: American Education 1945–1980*. New York, Basic Books, 1983, p. 6.

[8]Ibid., chs 2, 4, 5.

matter, and opposed competitive grading, drill, and memorizing. They tried to replace total reliance on reading by experimentation and projects, teacher control by teacher–student cooperation; they wanted a child-centered core curriculum rather than traditional courses. Students should "live effectively," rather than pile up knowledge. The progressives wanted the core curriculum to deal with family, life, and community problems, not with French, geometry or history.

There were many misconceptions on the subject, and progressive education aroused bitter resistance in the US. Criticisms dating from the 1950s sound as if they had been written yesterday,[9] (It was in 1955 that Rudolf Flesch published *Why Johnny Can't Read*. Nearly three decades later, he put out *Why Johnny Still Can't Read*. Originally a refugee from Vienna, Flesch himself had learned English as a second language.) Schools of education met with strident censures.[10] The US, said the censors, had developed a dual academic system that provided teacher training through separate departments or schools of education which developed their own methods and mystique. Even courses in the teaching of specific subjects fell mainly to educationalists, not mathematicians or historians or scholars in English literature. The former devised their own advanced degrees, such as the D.Ed., described by Arthur Bestor, a leading US educator, as a doctorate with its teeth pulled. The doctors of education imposed their anti-intellectual agenda through a dubious credentialling system and bureaucratic control that would have horrified British or French headmasters. (In postwar Britain, secondary school teachers required a good university degree in the subject that they taught. The Diploma of Education, obtained after one year's postgraduate study, was often optional; indeed some headteachers would not employ teachers who had acquired this qualification.) British headteachers were indeed rulers in a way inconceivable to the principal of a US public school, harried probably by a powerful educational bureaucracy, and by parental pressure.

Criticism against the US public schools gained additional force from long-standing deficiencies in educational philosophy. Educational theorists on both sides of the Atlantic had inclined consistently to undervalue the parents' and the religious community's part in education. They ignored the extent to which children profited from their parents' comments, conversation, and help with homework. It was the unofficial part taken by parents that linked education to class, more than money. It also helped to make or mar new syllabuses. (For instance, the "new math" once touted in schools, had no hope of success given parental ignorance of the newly amended subject.)

Fortunately, however, this was not the whole story. For all the complaints,

[9] Arthur E. Bestor, *Educational Wastelands: The Retreat from Learning in Our Public Schools*. Urbana, Ill., University of Illinois Press, 1953, p. 67, and n. 8 on p. 212.

[10] Arthur Bestor, *The Restoration of Learning: A Program for Redeeming the Unfulfilled Promise of American Education*. New York, Knopf, 1955, p. 172. For more recent critiques see E. D. Hirsch, *Cultural Literacy: What Every American Needs to Know*, Boston, Houghton Mifflin, 1987. Allan Bloom, *The Closing of the American Mind: How Higher Education Has Failed Democracy and Impoverished the Souls of Today's Students*. New York, Simon and Schuster, 1987.

the postwar years in many ways became a golden age for education. The baby boom filled the schools, creating a demand for new teachers and new schools. Unemployment ceased to haunt the teaching profession. Colleges and universities revived from wartime torpor. Professors in the US, Britain, Germany, and France all agreed on one point – returning veterans made excellent students. They wanted to make up for lost time; they had been starved of intellectual fare; they had matured in the armed services, learned the merit of discipline, and worked hard. Moreover, they came in large numbers, especially to colleges and universities in the US. The postwar students were of a more varied social composition than their predecessors. (The number of US veterans who would probably not have obtained a higher education without the GI Bill amounted to between one-fifth and one-fourth of all ex-servicemen who went to college. The British had a similar, though less generous, scheme for ex-servicemen.) Their presence in the universities generally raised standards. On US campuses, the GI Bill undoubtedly contributed to the advances made in science, technology, and economic enterprise after the war, and "broke the genteel cocoon in which much of higher education had been wrapped."[11] (The percentage of US adults with a college degree increased from 4.6 in 1940 to 6.2 in 1950 and 7.7 in 1960. By 1985 the figure was 19.4.)

Schools and universities enjoyed other less tangible advantages. In the US and Western Europe alike, many able men and women became teachers and did excellent work, no matter what the merits or demerits of the methods by which they had been trained. There was a widespread sense of purpose and mission, shared by the much-derided Allied re-education officers in occupied Germany, by German students who shivered in unheated lecture rooms, and by their opposite numbers in Britain or the US who pursued their studies in more comfortable conditions, but with equal earnestness. Education was harder to get for these men than for their descendants – and was accordingly more highly prized.

There was also that impalpable, yet impressive, legacy derived from the past through widely shared cultural traditions. Progressives suffered from a widespread misapprehension that popular education in the bad old days had served merely to sustain class privilege, favor the elites, and provide the poor with "the necessary but scanty equipment."[12] In fact, the educational outlook was more favorable at the end of World War II. For one thing, illiteracy had largely been eliminated in northern Europe and the US, albeit not in southern Europe. (The illiteracy rate in 1950 amounted to 3.2 percent in the US, 3.3 in France and Belgium, 14.4 in Italy (mainly the South), 17.3 in Spain, and 44.1 in Portugal.)

[11]Ravitch, *The Troubled Crusade*, p. 14. For education in Britain, France, and Germany, and a comparative perspective with the US, see Fritz K. Ringer, *Education and Society in Modern Europe*. Bloomington, Indiana University Press, 1979. Ulrich Littman, "Academic exchange and its impact," in Karl Kaiser and Hans Peter Schwarz, eds, *America and Western Europe: Problems and Prospects*. Lexington, Mass., D. C. Heath and Co, 1977, pp. 62–984.
[12]François Bedarida, *A Social History of England*. London, Methuen, 1979, p. 157.

Old fashioned or "primary" illiteracy moreover had strikingly differed from the new "secondary" illiteracy of high school students. "Primary illiteracy" had not necessarily implied lack of verbal comprehension or deficient literary taste. To give an example, an illiterate Irish soldier who had left a remote village in World War II to join the British Army could still entertain a barrack room audience by reciting lengthy ballads dealing with mournful subjects such as one legendary Private McCuffery's feat in slaying a wicked British officer. This entailed a linguistic ability and a trained memory not enjoyed by many a high school graduate a generation later.

A good deal of credit for this "hidden" education belonged to the family, church, and temple. Youngsters who had regularly attended church may or may not have profited spiritually. They did, however, benefit in a literary sense from singing hymns, listening to sermons and Bible lessons, reciting the Lord's Prayer and the Apostle's Creed, studying the catechism, reading the Book of Common Prayer, the King James Bible, or their equivalents in other denominations. Provided they were literate, men and women without much formal schooling would read works that all too often proved inaccessible to their well-qualified descendants. (At the turn of the last century enlisted British soldiers in the army in India, supposedly the dregs of British society, would find Dumas, Dickens, and Balzac on their regimental library shelves. "As for the *Decameron* of Boccaccio," recalls a former British private, "every soldier in the British Forces in India who could read had read this volume from cover to cover. It was considered very hot stuff.")[13] Many ordinary people also wrote well. It was not for nothing that private manuscript collections in European and American archives contained many nineteenth- and early twentieth-century diaries and letters written by poorly schooled soldiers, sergeants, trail bosses, miners, artisans, servants housewives who wrote copiously and well – with a stylistic verve not conveyed by modern textbooks or rock and roll lyrics.

Popular education had also gained, for instance, through private enterprise in the publishing industry. Publishing companies placed on the market inexpensive series such as *World Classics* and *Everyman's Library* in England, the *Reclam* editions in Germany, and the *Modern Library* in the US. There were the efforts made by the Workers' Educational Association in England, by working men's clubs in Germany, the Educational Alliance and night schools in the US – all inspired by a similar spirit of earnestness, uplift, and working-class solidarity. To give an example, the International Ladies' Garment Worker's Union (ILGWU,) a labor union that had formerly been mainly comprised of Jewish workers, gave courses in economics, history and philosophy. The Jewish labor movement promoted popular culture in many other ways, through sustaining a Yiddish labor press and encouraging a "proletarian" literature in Yiddish. "The Jewish labor movement and its institutions became the secular substitute for the old community" that the immigrants had left

[13]Byron Farwell, *Mr Kipling's Army: All the Queen's Men*. New York, W. W. Norton, 1981, p. 198.

behind.[14] The Jewish workers' efforts in this regard found parallels in many other countries. At a time when this legacy still existed, when there was still a hunger for education, it was both a difficult and a marvellous time to be a teacher.

ELEMENTARY, TECHNICAL, AND SECONDARY SCHOOLS

Few institutions in the Western world were more bewildering in their variety than the school systems. The mode of public control differed – from strict centralization in France, devolution of power to the *Länder* in Germany, and to local authorities in Britain and the US. There were public schools and private schools, the latter divided between church schools and institutions run under secular auspices. (During the early 1950s, as many as 71.2 percent of all primary school students in the Netherlands went to private, mainly religious, schools; 52.6 percent in Belgium; 25 percent in England and Wales; 23.5 in Spain.) The confessional factor in school politics continued to play a major part, for instance in France where "far from establishing unity, the . . . elimination of God from the civic manuals divided the country profoundly, and exacerbated the clash of Church and republic."[15]

For all this diversity in structure, there was a certain uniformity in the sense that education remained partially, but not wholly, linked to social class (though least so in the US and Norway). The various national systems of education were apt to resemble a three-layered cake. All children of whatever social origin went to elementary schools; middle-class children, and also a working-class contingent drawn from the able or the fortunate, continued their education in secondary schools – grammar schools, *Gymnasien, lycées*. These secondary schools again differed in status. The most obvious distinction arose in Britain between the public schools and the best of grammar schools on the one hand, and the run-of-the-mill state secondary schools on the other. The former were frequented mainly, though not entirely, by the upper-middle class – an impecunious clergyman or military officer might scrimp and save to send his son to Eton. There was an additional rift between the grammar schools and the modern secondary schools, the latter emphasizing technical education, and therefore occupying a lesser place in the British social hierarchy. Continental secondary schools were more egalitarian at least on paper. In fact there was a world of difference between a renowned institution such as *Louis le Grand* in Paris, and an obscure *lycée* in a provincial city. After World War II, all European countries tried to extend educational opportunities, and extend the school age (the British for example through the Education Act, 1944). The Americans aimed at secondary education for all, but had only partial success. (In 1940, 24.5 percent of adults had a high school diploma, by 1950 34.3 per-

---

[14]Lucy Dawidowicz, "The Jewishness of the American Jewish labor movement," in *The Jewish Presence: Essays on Identity and History*. New York, Harcourt Brace Jovanovich, 1977, p. 122.
[15]Theodore Zeldin, *France 1848–1945*. Oxford, Oxford University Press, 1973, v. 1, p. 626.

cent had one, and by 1960, 41.1 percent had graduated. The figure rose to 73.9 by 1985.)

In terms of expenditure and buildings, primary schooling was every nation's stepchild. Many schools had been built in the nineteenth century. (In Britain, over half the schools in use in 1956 had been built before 1900; the proportion was much larger in countries such as Spain, and even France.) The position in fact worsened for a while after World War II when rising birthrates, shortage of accommodation and staff created special difficulties; classes became even larger than before, and classrooms were often too full. School construction, however, went at a rapid pace, especially in the wealthier countries – the US, West Germany, Britain, and the Scandinavian states. The construction campaign benefited schoolchildren in many ways, but also had the unintended consequence of raising consumer expectations. In the remoter villages, young students would unfavorably contrast the splendid new school buildings with their own, often harsh, domestic circumstances. New school construction may have played some part in promoting the consumer revolution.

School building in fact became big business. In Britain postwar school building centered on a tightly-knit group of progressive architects, committed to central planning, scientific management, and mass production methods, especially prefabrication. Prefabrication provided a means of building cheaply at a time when men, materials and money were scarce. In addition, postwar architects such as Stirral Johnson-Marshall were believers in the child-centered education that many of them had experienced in progressive boarding schools. These architects – unlike so many public planners – did not, however, simply impose their views on a reluctant public; instead they made sure of public support; they concentrated on everyday detail such as child-sized furniture and toilet facilities, as well as striking murals and color schemes, improved lighting and layout that appealed to all. These socialist architects gained their first major success in the Tory-controlled county council of Herefordshire; thereafter they employed similar methods in many other parts of England, with conspicuous success in standardizing new techniques that were later applied to many other projects.[16]

The various Western countries all increased their educational expenditure, though not yet to anything like the level attained during the 1960s and 1970s. (By 1955 education accounted for 2.4 percent of the gross national product in Western Europe, and in the US 4.8 percent by 1960.) School enrollment went up most of all in the Northern European countries, least of all in the rural regions of Southern Europe, where compulsory school attendance was far from universally observed, and where many young children continued to help on the farm.

At the same time, the school leaving age generally rose, most of all in the US. (By 1960 five states required attendance to the age of 18 or high school graduation; five insisted on education up to the age of 17, and the remainder

[16]Andrew Saint, *Towards a Social Architecture: The Role of School Building in Post-War England.* New Haven, Yale University Press, 1987.

up to 16.) In Western Europe, the differences were more striking. (By 1955, 15.9 percent of the youngsters between the ages of 15 and 19 were enrolled in full-time secondary schools – 9.2 in general and 6.7 in technical courses.)[17] The Scandinavian countries ranged at the top of the European list, Belgium, France, and Switzerland came second, Britain and West Germany only third – West Germany's poor record in this respect belied the assumptions of those who saw a direct link between the accessibility of secondary education and economic success. Spain and Portugal were at the bottom. Nevertheless, the proportional number of youngsters at school continued to go up all over the Western world. So did the time spent at school, as family farms diminished in number, and changing methods of production ended the need for child labor. (In 1959, for example, de Gaulle raised the French school leaving age to 16.)

There were other improvements. Textbooks and other teaching materials became more easily available than before. Relatively more men and women entered the teaching profession. Classes diminished in size, though striking differences remained in this respect between the richer and the poorer countries. (In the mid-1950s, a primary school teacher in Portugal or Spain had to supervise classes averaging 40 or more children; the average in West Germany stood at about 35, in France, Britain, and Italy at about 30. Sweden easily led the rest, with just over 20, as against nearly 35 in Denmark.)

The teacher–pupil ratio in secondary schools was considerably better – 20 students to one class on the average. In this respect, Denmark, Austria, and the Netherlands were in the lead, with an average of about 15. The educational significance of these figures is hard to measure. There is no evidence that Danish elementary schoolchildren received a better education than their contemporaries in Sweden; nor were youngsters in Austrian secondary schools conspicuously more successful than their opposite numbers in West Germany, even though Austria had the lower teacher–student ratio.

How much did the students learn? A satisfactory answer is hard to supply, given the enormous differences that existed between the various high schools in the various Western countries. A strikingly high percentage of European youngsters went to private rather than public schools (100 percent in the Republic of Ireland, 62.3 in the Netherlands, 56.2 in Belgium, 42.1 in France, 24.7 in Italy; 12.6 in England and Wales; 11.9 in West Germany, 10.8 in Switzerland, 8.2 in Sweden). Parents sent their children to private schools for a large number of reasons: because they wished them to be brought up as Catholics (for instance in the US, Britain, and France); or because of the private schools' superior discipline and academic orientation; or because fathers wanted for their sons (and often also their daughters) those special social advantages that went with a prestigious boarding school, most of all in Britain. (Public schools, far from withering away under successive Labour

[17]The percentages in 1955 for the individual countries stood as follows, as regards education for the ages 14–19; Sweden: 35.3, Denmark: 29.7, Belgium: 27.8, France: 25, Netherlands: 21.9, Germany: 18.2, Italy: 9.8, Spain: 6.5. Dewhurst, p. 315.

governments, emerged stronger than ever, with 20 percent more pupils than before the war.[18]

Much depended also on the way in which pupils were selected for high schools. Unlike the Americans, the Europeans stuck to highly selective procedures. West Germany during the 1950s lagged behind the US and many European states in providing high school education: 18 percent in Germany, 31 percent in France, 66 percent in the US. The British, for example, for many years, enforced the "eleven plus" system that attempted to sort out the academically minded from the rest by the time children reached the age of 11. But the system was far from satisfactory; according to expert opinion, about one-third of the children picked for grammar schools turned out to be unsuited, whereas many children kept out under the system would have profited by being allowed to go to grammar schools. From the late 1950s onward, the British tried to resolve this difficulty by instituting "comprehensive" schools for all, but still failed to root out inequality. (Public schools survived, with their upper-class clientele, while many first-class grammar schools, which had provided a ladder for advancement to working-class children, went by the board.)

The Germans and French differentiated in other ways. Their secondary schools specialized into schools with a classical syllabus (*Gymnasien* or *lycées*) and those with a "modern" orientation that emphasized modern languages, mathematics, and sciences (*Oberrealschulen* and *collèges*). Overall, the Europeans, again unlike the US, insisted on advanced diplomas awarded upon examination (the school certificate and the higher school certificate in Britain, the *Abitur* in Germany, the dreaded *baccalauréat* in France.) The Europeans stood resolved to produce a high school elite; the Americans believed in an egalitarian system. But in fact the quality of US high schools varied to such an extent that the proportion of American students receiving a first-class education in high schools may not have differed much from the average proportions in Europe.

Overall, the problems of American education seemed even more multifarious than those in Europe. During World War II, racial integration had advanced in industry, and after the war desegregation came to the US armed forces. At the same time, the NAACP and other liberal bodies were continuing their efforts to end apartheid in schools. Success came in 1954 when the supreme court in the *Brown* decision declared unconstitutional all state-imposed racial segregation in the public schools. This was a monumental step at a time when 40 percent of US schoolchildren attended segregated schools. *Brown II* (a second court case resolved in 1955) left the implementation of desegregation to local authorities, which slowed the pace of change; but the victory over such racial inequality was largely complete after the courts in 1968 demanded total compliance.

Some southern cities desegregated quickly and peacefully; most did not, and many whites fled to the suburbs or enrolled their children in private

[18]Anthony Sampson, *Anatomy of Britain Today*. New York, Harper and Row, 1965, p. 198. Dewhurst, p. 315. Roy Lowe, *Education in the Post-War Years*. London, Routledge, 1988.

schools. Southern politicians issued the 'southern manifesto' stating that they intended to resist by legal means enforced integration. State legislatures passed new laws, but all in vain; the federal government was determined to end segregation in schools. In 1956 Eisenhower created a civil rights commision within the department of justice, a division to take charge of federal protections for civil rights. The riots at Little Rock, Arkansas, followed in 1956; federal troops intervened; the battle, while not over, had been largely won with regard to desegregation in schools. It took until the 1960s, however, to extend civil rights throughout the South for all citizens.

> *Schools of education stressed training on how to teach, they largely ignored the question of what to teach, according to E. D. Hirsch (author of* Cultural Literacy: What Every American Needs to Know*). The decline in American schools started in the 1940s and 1950s when professional educators gained control of schools and textbooks, but it was not until after 1965 that SAT scores began to fall because of poor teaching and the lack of a standard core of knowledge, Hirsch believes.*

Equally contentious were the problems hinging on progressive education – that is to say on the very purpose of schooling in a heterogeneous society. Progressive education had grown out of the progressive movement of the early twentieth century. Jacob Dus, Jane Adams, John Dewey, and William James were its pioneers. Their philosophy had lost influence in politics, but lived on in progressive education, centering on schools of education, especially Columbia University's teachers' college. One of the most important advocates of the new education was William Heard Kilpatrick, a doyen of teachers' college. Kilpatrick was a power in the land; he taught over 35,000 students in his lifetime. "Projects" were his talisman. The ideas of teachers' college spread through the US. The Progressive Education Association propagandized the new secular religion, and it gained further support in 1944 from the US office of education's division of vocational education in the "Prosser resolution" which helped spread progressive education after the war. Regional conferences avidly endorsed the mandate for progressive education and life adjustment schooling. By the mid-1950s, 55 percent of public high schools taught no foreign languages and little history.

There were many critics, especially after 1949. Mortimer Smith, Mortimer Adler, Albert Lynd, Arthur Bestor, and Paul Woodring pointed to all manner of educational foolishness. Smith's book *And Madly They Teach*, for instance, excoriated teachers, though more especially administrators and schools of education, for stressing life adjustment courses, and for allotting more importance to hairdressing than history. Vocational courses were lambasted by scholars and laymen alike. Progressive education was particularly unpopular during the McCarthy period, when its proponents were denounced as communists. By the end of the 1950s the red scare was over and, ironically, American schools emerged from the period with better safeguards for free speech and association, and the removal of state imposed restrictions on academic freedom, according to Ravitch (*The Troubled Crusade*).

PLATE 58   *Nixon and Eisenhower on Republican election night, 1952.*
(Credit: Library of Congress)

PLATE 59   *Eden, Dulles, Churchill, and Nixon, Washington DC, 1953.*
(*Credit: Library of Congress*)

PLATE 60   *Secretary of State Dulles in his office, 1956, press conference.*
(*Credit: Library of Congress*)

PLATE 61   *Secretary of State John F. Dulles with German Foreign Minister Heinrich von Brentano, President Eisenhower, and Chancellor Adenauer.*
(Credit: Library of Congress)

PLATE 62   *Aerial view of the Pentagon in Washington DC.*
(*Credit: Library of Congress*)

PLATE 63   *Supreme Court, Washington DC.*
(*Credit: Library of Congress*)

PLATE 64   *Federal Marshal reading injunction against school picketing in Clinton, Tennessee,*
1956.
(Credit: Library of Congress)

PLATE 65   *Integrated high school.*
(*Credit: Library of Congress*)

PLATE 66   *Segregated bus terminal, Atlanta, Georgia.*
(*Credit: Library of Congress*)

PLATE 67   *America's "Dream Machine", the 1957 Chevrolet Bel Air.*

PLATE 68 *John L. Lewis, the flamboyant head of the United Mine Workers of America,* *1952.*
(*Credit: Library of Congress*)

PLATE 69 *George Meany, head of the AFL-CIO, testifying before Senate Committee Investigating Labor, 1957.*
(Credit: Library of Congress)

PLATE 70 *Walter Reuter, head of the United Automobile Workers of America.*
(Credit: Library of Congress)

PLATE 71 *Senator J. W. Fulbright of Arkansas.*

PLATE 72 *Senator Pat McCarran (of McCarran–Walters Act, 1943, designed to keep out subversives) screening merchant seamen.*
(*Credit: Library of Congress*)

PLATE 73   *Senator Joseph McCarthy on last day of Army–McCarthy hearings, June 1954.*
(*Credit: Library of Congress*)

PLATE 74   *French Foreign Minister Georges Bidault addresses conference on Marshall Plan,*
July 1947.
(*Credit: The National Archives*)

PLATE 75   *Stepping stones to European Recovery.*
(*Credit: Library of Congress*)

PLATE 76   *Signing of the Pact of Brussels, March 17, 1948. Belgian Prime Minister Paul
Henri Spaak addressing Assembly.*
(*Credit: The National Archives*)

PLATE 77   *Atlantic Pact Parley, May 14, 1949, in London: Spaak with French, Belgian,
and Luxemburg foreign ministers.*
(*Credit: The National Archives*)

PLATE 78   *Launching the European Coal and Steel Union, Paris, April 18, 1951.*
(*Credit: GIC*)

PLATE 79   *Anthony Eden, Konrad Adenauer, Dean Acheson, and Robert Schuman.*
(*Credit: GIC*)

PLATE 80 *Aachen, 1945.*
(Credit: Hans Konig)

PLATE 81 *Aachen, 1970.*
(Credit: Gerhard Thomalla)

The Soviets' success in 1957 in sending their satellite *Sputnik* into orbit, came as an uncovenanted boon to traditionalists in US education. The prestige of progressive education somewhat declined, and subject-oriented courses once more came into fashion. Progressive education suddenly seemed out of joint with the needs of a technological society. (Congress in 1958 passed the National Defense Education Act to encourage the study of science, mathematics and foreign languages.) American educational theory shifted again, though the sciences profited more than the humanities. Thereafter the pendulum continued to swing between a "soft," child-centered education on the one hand, and a "hard," subject-centered education on the other. But progressive education continued to maintain its hold on the pedagogic imagination.

US schools, critics claimed, saw further decline from 1965 on – from first grade through high school. Not only did SATs (Scholastic Aptitude Tests) fall in standard, but general literacy and math skills also declined, while drop-out rates increased, especially among blacks and Hispanics. American students continually scored poorly in international comparisons, especially from the 1970s on, even though the US spent three or four times more per capita on students than any other nation. Students worked less, knew less, and did less homework, although some minorities stayed in school at a higher rate than previously. The child-centered, trivialized curriculum, effective living courses and social utility concerns robbed school of competition, the learning of important facts, and memorization. Subject content widely decayed – not Shakespeare but sport novels became required reading. Textbooks grew blander as publishers were reluctant to offend vocal lobbies.

The teachers' authority was further weakened by the 1960s assault on traditional standards. In West Germany, leftist attacks on accustomed family values derived a special edge from the assumption that Nazism had found psychological inspiration from the authoritarian structure of the German family. Such theories were disseminated in academia during the 1950s, and later percolated down to the schools. They failed to recognize that *Hitlerjugend* leaders had themselves supported revolt against reactionary elders – *Kalkkisten*, "calcification chests," was the *Hitlerjugend* word. Neither did theories concerning the "authoritarian personality" explain why patriarchical congregations of old-fashioned Scottish Calvinists, or Old Amish in the US should have failed to turn out little Fascists.

Overall, progressive education contributed to the reduction of course requirements. Foreign languages, mathematics, and science widely dropped from the US curriculum except for the college-bound. Teachers felt insecure about what to teach; a debilitating form of relativism took over the schools – truth and values were regarded as relative, hence any subject was supposedly as good as any other, and student interest fell. Progressive education failed in the US because it was not relevant to the needs of the country; it did not pass the test of pragmatism, and left too many students uneducated, untrained, and semi-literate. The lucky ones were those who had taken college preparatory courses. Many features of American progressive education were adopted by

European school systems in the 1960s – curriculum reform, comprehensive schools, child-centered schools, teacher training colleges – at a time when the movement had come under severe intellectual assault in the US itself.

The problems of education worsened as a result of weakening family structures. As we have pointed out elsewhere, black families proved particularly vulnerable from the late 1950s, but they were not alone. Divorce, and illegitimacy figures rose and instability in family life increased. As James S. Coleman noted in his 1966 report, school achievement, and test scores correlate with socioeconomic status. Faced with children from difficult home backgrounds and waves of new immigrants, the schools asked less of the students and all too often produced poorly educated graduates.[19]

Nevertheless, the tapestry was full of bright patches. The US was also a land of educational opportunity – more so than any other country in the world. There were in effect three different school systems, each with a different orientation, audience, and achievement level. The public school system (elementary, secondary, and college), served as society's intended tool to overcome differences of birth and wealth and to produce an egalitarian culture. There were also two sorts of private school system: religion-based schools working with a religious community of parents and students, and secular private schools. Both kinds of private school did better than the public school in almost all aspects. They were more academic, had fewer vocational courses, and involved parents to a greater extent. Again, according to Coleman, students in private schools scored higher in verbal and mathematical tests and had lower drop-out rates. Academic success did not necessarily derive from the students' social class, it could stem from their and their parents' sense of religious community. Catholic schools had traditionally done better in raising the academic standards of minorities and lower socioeconomic groups, be they Irish, Italian, black or Hispanic. In spite of the traditionally lower status of their students, Catholic school graduates went on to college at a higher rate than public school leavers. The Catholic school students had fewer disciplinary problems, and higher achievement levels, and graduates subsequently became more successful as a result of family cohesion. This may also have been behind their educational success in the postwar period.[20]

The Catholic Church, dominated by the Irish and Irish-Americans, was a building church. By 1960 there were over 14,000 Catholic educational institutions and 10,500 were elementary schools. About one child in eight in the US went to a Catholic elementary school; one in 12 were in Catholic high schools. Some 207,000 priests, brothers, sisters and lay persons taught in Catholic schools though the number of lay teachers increased four times as fast as religious in the 1950s. In 1950 Catholic colleges had 112,765 students, two-thirds of whom were male.

Of course not all Catholic schools were good; much depended on the amount

[19]Myron Magnet "How to smarten up the schools," *Fortune*, February 1 1988, pp. 86–94.
[20]See Luther B. Otto, "Choice and consequences in education," *Science*, 11 September 1987, pp. 1357–8.

of aid from the bishop's office, or on the school's location. In some areas – largely the South – Catholic schools were inferior to the public schools, but in northern cities Catholic high schools were better than most public high schools. Overall Catholic schools scored better in tests. This owed much to the discipline of Catholic schools and their allegiance to traditional schooling. Stable family life and a sense of religious community also contribute to the success of Catholic, and also of Lutheran, and other religious private schools. Religious schools moreover could harshly discipline or expel the persistently idle or the trouble-makers – unlike public schools which had to put up with hell-raisers in the classroom to everyone else's detriment. Religious schools were therefore particularly fitted as ladders for the social advancement of the church-going working class, and most Catholic high schools were college preparatories.

Generalizations with regard to curricula and performance in the schools of the Atlantic Community are hard to make. The curricula differed strikingly in content from one country to the next. (Belgium and Switzerland, for example, insisted on a thorough knowledge of their respective national tongues, the Scandinavian countries, Holland and West Germany emphasized English.) Americans were less likely to be proficient in foreign languages and the geography of foreign countries than their opposite numbers in Europe, but made up for these deficiencies by greater practical skills. For all their many and widely publicized weaknesses, the American high schools, with their insistence on education for all, may for a time have made Americans the most productive workers on earth. If published statistics are to be trusted, American high schools in the 1950s, also did well in turning out citizens who were politically literate. Forty-four percent of the population read newspapers regularly for political information and 12 percent did so often by 1960. (The comparative figures for France were 18 percent and 10 percent respectively in 1958.)[21] Overall, American schoolteachers during the 1940s and 1950s, therefore, often did better by their students than critics believed.

Europeans and Americans both improved their technical education, albeit through different means. Two-year junior colleges, or community colleges, were peculiarly American institutions. The Europeans paid more attention to apprenticeship and training – especially the Germans, whose industrial efficiency owed a great deal to the excellent training of skilled workers and foremen. (By the mid-1950s, 31.3 percent of youngsters between the ages of 15 and 19 served as apprentices in West Germany, 25.3 percent in Switzerland, only 10 percent in France.)[22] More money was spent than ever before on trade schools, senior technical schools, and polytechnics; their overall enrollment increased – so much so that by 1955 more than 1.5 million students attended junior and senior technical schools in Western Europe.

Educational facilities strikingly increased all over the Western world, but in quality and method education continued to differ greatly from country to

[21]Stanley Rothman, *European Society and Politics*. Indianapolis, Bobbs-Merrill, 1970, p. 354.
[22]Dewhurst, p. 328.

country, and within each country. National traditions proved tenacious. (The Americans, for example, did not succeed in their zone of occupation in Germany in setting up a system of comprehensive education modelled on their own high schools. Nor did they do much to promote social studies on American lines, or to diminish the autocracy of the *Ordinarius* or full professor within his own department or research institute at German universities. Changes in this direction only came much later, and not as a result of American pressure.) The academic attainments of secondary students during the late 1940s and the 1950s exceeded, on average, those of their successors in the late 1970s and 1980s – despite the extraordinary investment made in education all over the Western world. (In the US, for example, the percentage of GNP devoted to education between 1950 and 1985 increased from 3.4 in 1950 to 6.6 in 1985; expenditure on primary and secondary school education went up from $3 billion to $149 billion. Yet during the same period, the average combined mathematics and verbal score on the scholastic aptitude test diminished from 970 to 906.)[23]

Functional illiteracy was to remain a widespread problem, and one not confined to the US. During the 1980s, the French prime minister, François Mitterand, shocked the world by announcing that there could be 8,000,000 illiterate Frenchmen (an astonishing display of candor since no French prime minister in living memory had ever admitted in public that the French were deficient in anything).[24] His mood of self-censure, however, was not unique, to judge from the popularity attained by books with titles such as *La France paresseuse* (Lazy France), with harsh criticism of France's educational and industrial performance.

During the late 1940s and the 1950s, the links between class and education continued. But the tie weakened as secondary schools produced a growing "meritocracy," a diploma-bearing elite whose members did not necessarily owe their position to family connections, class, or inherited wealth, who aspired to careers that would lead to influential positions by way of university, the armed services, or corporate employment. This elite had certain characteristics in common. Its members were less likely to be familiar with Latin, Greek, and Roman history than their predecessors. They mainly used English as a language of international communications, though the victory of English was of course by no means absolute. (French, for instance, remained important as a second language within the EEC and in the Mediterranean countries; German continued to be much used in Holland and also in Eastern Europe.) But overall English became to the postwar meritocracy what Latin had been to the literate classes of medieval Europe – the principal language of international communications, as well as a prestige symbol. (The use of English spread

---

[23]Terry Hartle, "Education reform: we have a lot to learn," in *Public Opinion*, September to October 1987, p. 48.

[24]Denys P. Doyle, "Educational turmoil in Japan, Britain, and at home," in *Public Opinion*, September to October 1987, p. 45. Victor Sherrer, *La France Paresseuse*. Paris, Editions du Seuil, 1987, is a critique of French industrial and labor performance.

through textbooks, teacher exchanges, student travel, tourism, imported films and jazz, and through English terminology in international organizations, trade, banking, aviation, maritime communications, and the military. It also dominated in the social sciences, scientific and technological publications.) The members of the meritocracy, sporting their hard-earned diplomas, were well-educated, confident, and public spirited up to a point, but tended like all elites to confuse their own wealth with the nation's.

HIGHER EDUCATION

The nature and quality of higher education varied equally throughout the Atlantic Community, and included an immense range of institutions: *grandes écoles*, universities, research institutes, and technical universities (such as the *Technische Hochschulen* in Germany and the great institutes of technology in the US – MIT, Cal-Tech, etc.); law and medical schools (usually separated from universities in Europe;) schools of business; seminaries for clergymen; academies of fine art, military science, veterinary science, librarianship, and so on. The goals set for higher education varied equally. For example, universities such as Oxford and Cambridge had originally been designed to turn undergraduates into gentlemen firmly grounded in the classics and the Christian faith, as had also been the inspiration of early American foundations such as Harvard and Yale. German universities in the nineteenth century had been the first to emphasize specialized scholarship and independent research, based on *Lehrfreiheit* (freedom to teach) and *Lernfreiheit* (freedom to learn.) This German model had been adopted in the US to develop postgraduate education, and had introduced a new spirit of professionalism. The Europeans were organized on a chair–faculty basis however, while the US adopted the department–college system.

> *There was no single system of university education in the Atlantic Community. Each nation had a system based on its own cultural history and degree of government control and funding. In Europe (and Canada) government has traditionally served as the prime employer of graduates, but this is not true of the United States, with its strong private school system and its large private economic sector. In Germany and in France, the teacher is usually a civil servant.*
>
> *Italy has a unified national system of public universities, France has three divisions – the grandes écoles, the universities, and the research units. The United States has the largest (over 3,000 establishments) and most complex system with at least six divisions – public and private (secular and religious) universities, 4–5 year colleges, technical and arts schools, and two-year colleges.*

Higher education varied too in its social purpose, as Churchill once said scathingly of a dessert "this pudding has no theme." In the US especially, universities have been expected at various times to serve almost every conceivable end – to promote learning, create an elite, preach citizenship, spread religion, strengthen morality, lighten the lot of the downtrodden, serve as ladders for social advancement, and to foster the arts, to the extent of providing facilities for poets and artists in residence. No wonder that some began to speak of the "multiversity." Institutions of higher learning varied in range, quality, and reputation, but throughout the Western world had one feature in common: an expansion in size and numbers after World War II. Growth took place at an accelerating rate, even more during the 1960s and 1970s than in the 1950s.

The US was in the vanguard of commitment to higher education, in which respect it had always surprised foreign travelers. During the 1860s, Sir Charles Dilke, a British visitor, had expressed his astonishment thus: "Teaching, high and low, is a fashion in the West, and each of these young States has established a university of the highest order, and placed in every township not only schools, but public libraries, supported from the rates, and managed by the people. Not only have the appropriations for education purposes by each State been large, but those of the Federal government have been upon the most splendid scale."[25]

This commitment showed undiminished vigor after World War II. In the US, as in Western Europe, the postwar demand for university expansion stemmed from the public more than the professors (who in subsequent decades widely incurred blame for having unwisely advocated the multiplication of academic facilities for selfish career purposes). It was the public who correctly equated college training with a chance of class mobility and a professional career. Many other factors contributed to academic growth, including civic pride in state universities and local community colleges, and the American tradition of self-help and voluntary giving that rewarded with public prestige the donors to private colleges or universities.

This tradition was not uniquely American. The British had civic universities sustained by municipal pride, as well as an extensive system of adult education that went back for well over a century, sustained in part by the trade unions and other voluntary bodies. But nowhere was the tradition more highly developed than in the US. Had Leland Stanford, a late nineteenth-century railway king and multimillionaire, been the Kaiser's subject in Imperial Germany, he would no doubt have striven for the pseudo-bureaucratic title of *Geheimer Kommerzienrat* (privy commercial councillor), perhaps even *Wirklicher Geheimer Kommerzienrat* (truly privy commercial councillor). In France, he would have aimed at the legion of honor, in Britain for a knighthood or peerage. (Lord Nuffield founded Nuffield College, Oxford, and became a peer.) The super-rich Stanford, however, used his money to found his own university. American private and public benevolence toward academic institutions continued after World War II, aiding the remarkable expansion of American university education. (To be exact, in 1950 there were 1,851 institutions of higher learning in the US; by 1960 their number had grown to 2,008 and by

[25]Charles Wentwork Dilke, *Greater Britain: A Record of Travel in English-Speaking Countries During 1866–7*. Philadelphia, J. B. Lippincott, 1869, p. 78.

1970 to 2,556.[26] Numerical comparisons with Europe are difficult, given institutional diversity, and differences in organization, but the total was a fraction of the US figure.

In Western Europe after World War II, the growth of universities did not proceed on the same scale, but was nevertheless impressive. Institutions everywhere benefited by a new influx of students, most of them veterans. The British took the lead in expansion – not surprising given Labour's belief in enlightenment and education as an instrument for human betterment, plus the considerable proportion of dons (professors) in politics. The most significant period of British university expansion did not occur until the 1960s, when a number of new universities were built (known as "plate-glass" universities because of their architectural style). But during the late 1940s and 1950s, academic facilities did begin to expand. Universities' charters, for example, were granted to colleges already in existence: Nottingham 1948; Southampton 1952; Hull 1954; Exeter 1955; Leicester 1957. These "redbrick" universities lacked the ancient traditions and social prestige associated with Oxford or Cambridge, but had certain advantages. Some developed proud indigenous traditions (for instance Manchester, an older civic university, where distinguished scholars such as Sir Lewis Namier, a historian, and Max Gluckman, an anthropologist, held chairs). The "redbrick" universities drew their students mainly from their own localities, and thus developed a civic tradition of their own. They also offered some courses that were designed to meet the needs of local industry. (For example, the Manchester College of Science and Technology, founded in 1956). But overall, the British continued to lag behind Germany and the US in providing higher education, especially in technological teaching, which did not command the same prestige in Britain as elsewhere. (Before World War II there were about 50,000 students at various British universities; by 1960 this figure had only grown to 100,000, though it increased more in the 1960s and after.)

In addition, the British (as well as the Belgians and French) expanded higher education in the colonies, where universities were regarded as instruments for "nation building," as well as agencies for diffusing knowledge. (Existing colleges were raised to university status at Ibadan in Nigeria in 1948, at Makerere in Uganda in 1949, and at Khartoum in 1951. A new institution, the University College of Rhodesia and Nyasaland was founded in 1955.) Initially these new institutions were linked to British universities (principally London.) They awarded British degrees and thereby provided their graduates with an academic "currency" desperately desired by educated Africans at the time, valid not only in the local, but also in the international job market.

There was considerable academic expansion on the European Continent. The European unity movement found expression in a number of new schools (the College of Europe, founded at Bruges in Belgium in 1959, the University Institute of European Studies at Turin in 1952, and later the European

[26]Lionel S. Lewis, *Scaling The Ivory Tower; Merit and Its Limits in Academic Careers.* Baltimore, Johns Hopkins University Press, 1975, p. 14.

University Institute at Florence, formed in 1972 by the EEC member states.) These institutions did not enjoy the prestige and influence wielded by old-fashioned national universities such as the Sorbonne or Göttingen or Leiden, but they did create their own networks of professors and graduates, new interests and intellectual friendships, which helped to sustain the movement toward closer political association in Western Europe.

"National" schools also grew in numbers. For example, in 1945, the French founded the *Ecole Nationale d'Administration*, the latest of their *grandes écoles* whose importance we have already noted. In addition, the French promoted university building as part of their *mission civilisatrice* in occupied Germany. The University of Mainz was set up with French help in 1946; two years later the French-supported University of the Saarland opened its doors. Neither institution subsequently met the French backers' expectations by becoming centers for the diffusion of Gallic culture. After World War II, the French similarly expanded their work in their West African Colonies through the *Institut Français d'Afrique Noire* (IFAN), research centers, and the *Université de Dakar*.

Even more unexpected was the development of the Free University of Berlin (set up with American assistance in West Berlin in 1948). The Free University was designed to provide a haven for refugee professors and students from the communist-controlled University of Berlin located in the city's Eastern sector. But far from turning into an anti-communist bastion, the Free University later attracted many leftists, including students unwilling to do military service in West Germany, and during the 1960s acquired a well-merited reputation for Marxist, quasi-Marxist, and pseudo-Marxist militancy.

In purely quantitative terms, the effect of this academic boom was astonishing. In 1930, students in European universities had formed a negligible proportion of the population. Then their numbers began to rise, and during the 1950s nearly, and in some places more than, doubled.[27] There was an equally striking increase in the ratio of students in institutions of higher learning to the total population. Admittedly, no European country in this respect could equal the US. Nevertheless, even in Europe, a university education ceased to be the prerogative of a tiny minority. (In 1956 the ratio of students in institutions of higher education per 10,000 in the general population was 34 in France, 32 in Sweden, 28 in the Netherlands, 26 in West Germany, 23 in Switzerland – of course such figures have little bearing on true educational standing.) The proportion of women at college went up, as did the percentage of university graduates trained in science and technology. Contrary to widespread beliefs there was, however, no direct correlation between this percentage and the economic success attained by individual countries. Britain,

---

[27]The number of students in higher education (in thousands) rose as follows for the years, respectively, 1930, 1950, 1960: England and Wales: 46; 107; 177 (1961). Sweden: 8; 17; 37. Austria: 16; 25; 39. Germany: 113; 123; 265. France: 74; 140; 272. Italy: 45; 145; 192. US 972; 2,297; 3,583. Norman Luxenburg, *Europe Since World II: The Big Change*. Carbondale, Southern Illinois University, 1979. Table 33, p. 211. On countries, see *The World of Learning*, London, Europa Publications.

widely censured for its addiction to classical studies and snobbish disdain for "practical" subjects, in fact stood near the top of the Western European list for percentage of graduates in science and technology, outdone only by Portugal, Switzerland, and Norway.[28]

Qualitative judgements, unfortunately, are infinitely harder to make than quantitative assessments. Much first-rate work was done both in the sciences and the humanities on both sides of the Atlantic. Discrimination against religious and ethnic minorities declined. (In Germany and Great Britain, as in the US, Catholics had found themselves at a disadvantage in higher education before the war, but in West Germany, for example, Catholic students gradually increased in numbers, from 29 percent in 1950 to 44 percent in the 1970s – a figure roughly equal to their proportion in the population. In the US, Catholics advanced into prestigious teaching positions from which they had previously been widely excluded. Jewish academics, who had also experienced discrimination at prestige universities, gained prominence in American higher learning.)

The Germans rebuilt their universities, at first on conservative lines. As Wolfgang J. Mommsen, a German historian, put it, "those scholars who represented the political left [during the Weimar era] had either emigrated or died; the liberal center had been morally compromised by its general collaboration with the National Socialist regime, if often for opportunistic reasons. Only conservatives had a relatively clean record; for the most part they had kept aloof from politics of any kind."[29] German universities initially reverted to the rule of the *Ordinarien* (full professors) endowed with great power, and treated with extraordinary respect. (Their dominance was ended only during the 1960s.) Traditional standards were rebuilt. Learned bodies such as the Max Planck Society resumed work in earnest, and so did foundations linked to major political parties, such as the Friedrich-Ebert-Stiftung. A handful of émigrés returned, including prominent thinkers such as Golo Mann, the historian, and Richard Löwenthal, a political scientist.

THE MAX PLANCK SOCIETY

The basic idea for a research university was developed by Wilhelm von Humboldt in the nineteenth century. German scientists desiring to be free of administrative and teaching chores organized the Kaiser-Wilhelm Gesellschaft in 1911 for basic research. In 1948 this insititute became the Max Planck Society (named for the German physicist). Over the years the MPS has developed an extensive network of independent research institutes,

---

[28]In 1954, the number of graduates in science and technology as a percentage of all graduates stood as follows: Portugal: 37, Switzerland: 33, Norway: 32, Great Britain: 31, Sweden: 30, Netherlands: 30, France: 30, Germany: 26, Italy: 23, Denmark: 21, Belgium: 21, Ireland: 20, Spain: 17, Austria: 19, Finland: 14, See Dewhurst, p. 329.

[29]Wolfgang J. Momsen, "The academic profession in the Federal Republic of Germany," in Burton R. Clark, ed., *The Academic Profession: National, Disciplinary, and Institutional Settings.* Berkeley, University of California Press, 1987, p. 68.

and receives substantial public funding although it has scientific and administrative autonomy. With an annual budget of about $500 million a year (shared between the federal and state governments) the society and its 60 research institutes has acquired great prestige (and 23 Nobel prizes). Members form part of an elite, and are expected to succeed. The MPS has clearly helped German Länder *develop scientifically and economically much as Stanford Research Institute did for California. Tension soon developed between Planck institute and universities however. The universities were jealous of the researchers' freedom, level of funding and lack of teaching or administrative duties.*

But Germany and Austria did not recover their former scientific primacy. Vienna and Berlin, once among the leading centers of Western thought, reverted to provincial status after the Jews had departed, and the Third Reich had done its worst. West Berlin turned into an island split from the surrounding province of Brandenburg and East Berlin. Vienna (like the port of Trieste in northeastern Italy) was separated from its former hinterland in communist-ruled southeastern Europe. (Vienna's drift to provincial condition was apparent even in fashion, as many Viennese began to wear rural clothing taken from Austria's Alpine province – so much so that returning émigrés imagined their native city taken over by countryfolk.) Berlin and Vienna still put on fine musical performances, and served as international conference centers, but the old spark had gone. Paris remained livelier. But the city had also suffered much, and for all the excellent work done by French academics, Paris was no longer *la ville lumière*, the city of light. Great Britain continued to be a major centre of intellectual innovation (in terms of Nobel prizes in the sciences, the British continued to hold second place during the new "American" era, just as they had done in the "German" era, pre-1933). Fine work continued to be done in countries such as Sweden and Switzerland whose universities had escaped the impact of Fascism, Nazism, or foreign occupation.

It was the United States that now became the world's main academic, scientific and technological center, and the greatest source of inventions and patents. The Americans had more money than Europeans to spend on research institutes, laboratories and libraries. (Among the great university libraries, Harvard University library, for example, had nearly 11,000,000 volumes in 1986; the Bodleian library at Oxford nearly 5,000,000 volumes; the *bibliothèque de la Sorbonne* at Paris and the *Niedersächsische Staats-und Universitätsbibliothek* at Göttingen each had just over 3,000,000.)

The US government, learning from its World War II experience, poured vast sums into research and development programs through contract research, the National Science Foundation, and similar programs. The Europeans followed suit. America was now attracting many of the best brains from Europe and the rest of the world. During the two decades that followed the end of World War II, scientists in Europe developed closer ties with the US than with any European country, and many preferred to publish their work in American, rather than European, journals.

Trans-atlantic collaboration was a strong force for cross-cultural cooperation and scientific progress. A 1987 survey by the Commission of the European

Communities in Brussels documented this fruitful interchange. Forty percent of European respondents had collaborated with US scientists. (The French claimed the highest percentage, 48 percent, while only 25 percent reported collaboration with West German or British scientists. Half the scientists in the survey had been trained in the US; it had become essential for success to have done work in the US.) After World War II, European leaders widely considered that sending their own nationals to the US for advanced training was the fastest way to restore their scientific cadres. Many Europeans did not go back. The resultant brain drain from Europe to the US during the two decades following World War II may have appeared small in percentages (2 to 3 percent a year), but in terms of quality it was significant. (For example, the number of British-born scientists who were members of the Royal Society and came to the US tripled within 20 years.)[30]

As regards the social sciences and humanities, Western Europe soon recovered from the Iron Age brought about by Nazism and Nazi occupation. Again, we can only give a few tentative examples. For instance, the Germans began to examine their recent past. During the Nazi period and its immediate aftermath, German history had moved to the Anglo-Saxon world. Most serious work on German history had been done by Britons such as Alan Bullock and Sir John Wheeler-Bennett, by Americans such as Gordon Craig, and by German émigrés naturalized in the US, such as Hajo Holborn, Peter Gay, Peter Paret, George Mosse, and many others. Henceforth no German or Austrian could write the history of his own country without knowing the English literature. But German scholarship recovered as intellectuals began to look to the West. (In 1949 the *Institut für Zeitgeschichte* opened its doors in Munich.) There was a painfully long interval until consideration of the Third Reich and the "final solution" became *salonfähig* (socially acceptable) in teaching institutions; bitter disputes continued (such as the *Historikerstreit* of the 1980s, the battle of historians concerning the uniqueness or otherwise of Nazi persecution of the Jews). But German scholars did make serious efforts to come to terms with their own history. Germany was, above all, spared a revival of intellectual Nazism, complete with *Rassenkunde* (racial science) and pseudo-heroes.

The French, as in former times, excelled in social history. (In 1948 they created, for example, the *Institut Français d'Histoire Sociale*, in Paris.) British scholarship retained its excellence and well-deserved reputation for narrative style. Nevertheless, many lacunae remained, for instance, with regard to the study of the US, a relatively neglected subject in Europe. (London University set up an Institute for Germanic Studies in 1950, an Institute for Commonwealth Studies in 1955, but an Institute for US Studies only in 1965.)

In the US, however, there was striking expansion, and expenditure in higher education went from $3 billion in 1950 to $76 billion in 1960.[31] An important part of the great success story of higher education in the postwar years was

---

[30]"America's seductive charms," *Science*, v. 237, 4 September 1988, p. 1,107.
[31]Ravitch, *The Troubled Crusade: American Education, 1945–1980*, p. xii.

the GI Bill that gave all veterans the opportunity to further their education. The GI Bill provided tuition, book fees and a monthly subsistence allowance for veterans, and millions took advantage of it. In 1945 only some 88,000 veterans returned to school, but by 1946, 1,013,000 had enrolled, and the college population almost doubled. Not everyone was pleased. Robert M. Hutchins, head of the University of Chicago and James B. Conant, president of Harvard University, for example, thought academic standards would be lowered. The critics were wrong; the veterans proved to be some of the best students schools had ever seen.

Campus life changed dramatically; the traditional "college man" was overwhelmed. Many veterans were married, lived in Quonset huts, studied hard, and ignored college pranks and customs. The GI Bill, Diane Ravitch concluded, was the most ambitious and successful effort in mass education ever attempted by any society. Between 1945 and 1952 7.8 million veterans went back to school (universities, college, high school, trade schools, training programs); over 2,323,000 went to college. Equality of opportunity in education was attained at least for veterans; perhaps 450,000 to 550,000 went to university who would not otherwise have gone. Veterans certainly promoted the expansion of American education, science and technology, opened up higher education and forced the founding of more colleges. Federal aid through the GI Bill has been called "the most important educational and social transformation in American history."[32]

This college and university growth took place amid copious complaints regarding the quality of US academic endeavor. American universities, said critics, lacked a moral purpose and common design, and even at their best were no more than intellectual supermarkets.[33] In expanding the universities so greatly, the Americans had merely succeeded in lowering academic quality – more meant worse. American professors supposedly promoted permissiveness, but also "repressive tolerance." The professors stood accused of spreading elitism, secularism, and an arid cult of credentials, but were also censured for defending naively populist values. Subject to grim principle of "publish or perish," professors were likened to bees, producing enormous quantities of books and articles that rested unread in library stacks. Yet they also incurred blame for writing too little and talking too much. On the one hand professors supposedly labored too hard to make their education "relevant", on the other they were accused of having their heads in the clouds, remote from the ordinary citizen's concerns. American higher education was blamed at one and the same time for promoting ethnocentricity and "one worldism," for being too formalistic and too faddish. Above all, many critics of all political persuasions agreed, American higher education had deteriorated, and was continuing to

---

[32]Ibid., p. 15.

[33]See for instance Jacques Barzun, *The House of Intellect*. New York, Harper, 1959, and *The American University*. New York, Harper and Row, 1968. Theodore Caplow and Reece J. McGee, *The Academic Marketplace*. New York, Basic Books, 1960. Pierre van den Berghe, *Academic Gamesmanship*. New York, Abelard-Schuman, 1970.

deteriorate in comparison with those happier days when true learning and a broad classical culture had still been prized. In addition, they said, American education suffered from a persuasive worship of novelty. Academics all too often forgot that nothing blunts more quickly than the cutting edge.

Some of these charges were no doubt true; all were of ancient standing. An academic mass education certainly implied diminished quality. A British grammar school student working for higher school certificate was expected in the late 1940s to read Goethe in his German class, and Racine in his French class; in this he or she was equal or superior in learning to an American college graduate. It was these qualitative differences that made statistical comparisons difficult between, say, British and US students receiving higher education. American higher education moreover had always been down-to-earth. "In special and selected studies, Michigan is as merely practical as Swift's University of Brobdingnag," Sir Charles Dilke reported with surprise during the 1860s. Courses varied from "criticism, arts of design," to "fine arts, history, ethics, Oriental languages." Americans have always sought applied skills: "the war with crime, the war with sin, the war with death – Law, Theology, Medicine ... to these, accordingly, the university applies her chiefest care." American education moreover had always been permissive. "The only one of the common charges brought against America ... that is thoroughly true is the statement that American children, as a rule, are 'forward, ill mannered and immoral'."[34]

More to the point were the charges with regard to the liberal-left tilt in the social sciences and humanities at the prestige universities, a trend that dated at least from the 1930s and that continued during the 1950s – at a time when US academe was beset by McCarthyism.[35] The Cold War brought questions of loyalty and internal security to the American society. Government conducted hearings; the media and schools suffered the most. Subversives were sought out in the department of state, in radio, TV, and journalism, in Hollywood, and in high schools and colleges. Many who had joined the Communist Party in the 1930s, either because of the failures of capitalism or because of the threat of Fascism, were especially vulnerable. Fellow-travelers and communist sympathizers were rooted out of schools and the media.

The most notorious loyalty investigations were conducted by Senator Joseph McCarthy of Wisconsin. The house committee on un-American activities was especially active in seeking "subversives" in education. State committees held hearings. The University of Washington, under pressure, fired 31 professors, and the University of California in 1949 demanded a loyalty oath of its faculty to avert an investigation of state universities. The University of Chicago, however, did not bow to political interference. Many called before the various committees "took the Fifth" so as not to be compelled to give the

---

[34]Dilke, *Greater Britain,* pp. 76, 72, 211.

[35]See for instance Seymour Martin Lipset, *Political Man: The Social Bases of Politics.* New York, Doubleday, 1960. For a detailed survey of a later date, see Carl Ladd, *Professors, Unions, and American Higher Education.* Berkeley, Carnegie commission on higher education, 1973.

names of people who were involved with the Communist Party, or to avoid answers to any questions that would incriminate themselves. Academics were deeply divided about whether membership of the Communist Party disqualified one from teaching, but the public had no doubts; 90 per cent said in a Gallop poll that they believed communists should be barred from teaching.

The impact of McCarthyism, however, may easily be exaggerated, as we have pointed out in our chapter on the Cold War. Leftists did not experience exclusion as a group from teaching posts in any academic discipline. (In this respect, their experience during the 1950s was quite different from that of conservatives during the 1960s, and 1980s; by that time conservatives were *de facto* deemed ineligible for teaching positions at prestige universities in new fields such as black studies, ethnic studies, women's studies, African studies, and Chicano studies.) There were moreover relatively few committed socialists among the American professoriat; in this respect, the US differed from France and Britain. American professors also did not wield the social prestige commanded by their German colleagues in their capacity as scholars and as senior civil servants. American professors were more likely to see themselves as a moral elite. There clung to much of the professoriat a peculiar piousness, a sense of being among the righteous, chosen to set the moral agenda for the nation – a sense of election no doubt inherited from those Calvinist, Baptist, Lutheran, and Methodist pastors who had founded so many American universities.

US professors in the humanities and social sciences tended to be relativists, rather than absolutists. They widely disliked capitalists and millionaires. Academics such as C. Van Woodward, John Garraty, and Thomas Bailey, men famed and influential for their scholarship – united in censuring the American "robber barons" for their ruthlessness in the jungle of big business. The bulk of liberal-minded professors were apt to overlook the way in which Andrew Carnegie or John D. Rockefeller and their ilk had improved the material well-being of the working class because they lowered production costs, and introduced more efficient methods than their competitors. It was these entrepreneurs who helped the US assume world industrial leadership.[36] Such interpretations, however, were not widely presented in the standard US textbooks.

Nevertheless these weaknesses were balanced by great strengths – often obscured by the Americans' own capacity for cultural self-criticism, and also by that snobbish and unjustified contempt for American scholarship and culture always widespread in Europe. At the turn of the century Fritz Haber, one of the great German-Jewish scientists, had scathingly referred to "the caricature of the American who tirelessly runs after the dollar and who, because of his wish for self enrichment loses all sense for law and order as well as the interest in any kind of intellectual culture."[37] This caricature remained alive

[36]For an exception, see for instance Robbert Hessen, *Steel Titan: The Life of Charles M. Schwab.* Oxford, Oxford University Press, 1975.

[37]Cited in Fritz Stern, *Dreams and Delusions: The Drama of German History.* New York, Knopf, 1987, p. 59.

and well after World War II; its popularity with second-raters among the European intelligentsia remained undiminished. The possessor of a German *Abitur*, or of a French *baccalauréat* might indeed know more than an American high school graduate. But on coming to the university, German and French students were more tempted to rest from their labors than their American counterparts who, at a good American university, would be expected to work in a more systematic fashion. American academia at its best was distinguished by its trans-national outlook, inter-disciplinary approach, and attention to social issues. It was Americans who pioneered economics, immigrant history, area studies, frontier history, and so on. Academic diversity, adaptability, receptivity to new ideas, and global outreach contrasted favorably with the Europeans' more nationalistic orientation. (A history student at Oxford during the late 1940s could take a first-class honors degree knowing nothing of the history of Russia, China or the US; his contemporary at Harvard would not have succeeded with a similarly narrow orientation.)

There were many more religious colleges and universities in the US than in Europe; their impact should be acknowledged. Protestant affiliated colleges declined in number in the 1950s and 1960s – in order to get state and federal aid, church-run schools had to give up control. But Catholic colleges retained their religious affiliation. The Jesuits and Dominicans dominated Catholic religious higher education in the US. By 1950, there were 25 Jesuit colleges educating 42 percent of male students in Catholic institutions. Jesuit colleges such as Georgetown, Holy Cross, Fordham, St Louis and the University of San Francisco had earned reputations as excellent undergraduate schools (and as sports powers). However, although the Jesuits and Dominicans had strong traditions of scholarship in Europe they failed to live up to that in the US. Perhaps this was inevitable in an immigrant church dominated by the Irish, who were more concerned with religious and secular training than with scholarship. For the Jesuits in any case it was a conscious policy to educate an elite of community leaders (lawyers, businessmen, teachers), rather than scholars. Catholic colleges were also often deficient with regard to a well-trained faculty, library facilities, laboratories, and so on.

Graduate programs did not develop in Catholic colleges until after World War II (except for Catholic University which concentrated on priests and the religious). The leading Catholic school after 1950 was Notre Dame, run by the Congregation of the Holy Cross. Its famous football team was augmented by high academic achievement under the leadership of Father John V. Cavanaugh (1946–52) and later by Father Theodore M. Hesburgh. The 1950s saw a fierce debate over the quality of Catholic education and intellectual life, and the paucity of achievement of scholars in Catholic schools. Father John Tracy Ellis, an historian, asserted that he could not find any major graduates in science from Catholic colleges, and that he would not rank any Catholic college in the 50 best colleges or universities in the country. Catholic schools supposedly failed to develop "enquiring minds," and promoted authoritarian certitude. (Similar criticisms were made regarding colleges run by other denominations. Lutheran schools provided their students with a good education, but made no great contribution to Lutheran theology, unlike theological faculties at some German universities.) Such charges were particularly embarrassing because American Catholics had the biggest and wealthiest school system of any religious group in the world.

Nevertheless Catholicism emerged in the 1950s more confident and more certain than ever before of its rising status in American society, with a better educated, more mobile, priesthood and laity. Catholic parish priests and the hierarchy, teachers and trade unionists, were militantly anti-communist, even though movements like the Catholic Workers were led by socialists such as Dorothy Day and Michael Harrington. Catholics, as well as Protestants, benefited from the religious revival of the 1950s. As Father Dolan noted in *The American Catholic Experience*, there was a new found pride and sense of achievement; there were new churches and schools; there was a record number of priests and religious, led by the new Pope John XXIII (1958).

The US traditionally had been more open to foreign scholars than Europe (or Canada). The impact of these newcomers varied considerably. Those French intellectuals who had found a refuge in New York mostly went home again after their country had been liberated. Spanish refugee professors were more likely to seek jobs in Latin America than the US. British expatriates, by contrast, made a major contribution in fields such as anthropology, geography, British and British empire studies, and English literature. The "special relationship" obtained between British and American academics, in the sense that books in English circulated freely on both sides of the Atlantic, and that there was an easy interchange between British and American scholars. Equally important were the German academic refugees who contributed to fields as varied as art history, physics, mathematics, history, musicology, sociology, philosophy, the natural sciences, and others. These men and women profited from the peculiar openness of American academic institutions to outsiders.

At times, this openness went to extraordinary lengths. During World War II, for example, many German Marxist émigrés, among them Franz Neumann and Herbert Marcuse, all leading theoreticians of the Frankfurt school of sociology, worked in the research and analysis branch of the Office of Strategic Services. More German-born professors labored for the OSS than for the German *Abwehr*.[38] The American establishment may not have been well advised to rely overly on the Frankfurters' analysis, given the previous inability of these expatriates to predict during the Weimar era either the impending fate of their own native Germany, or of European Jewry. But the Americans at least deserved commendation for their willingness to employ outsiders in a manner that would have been inconceivable either to the British MI5, the French *Sureté*, or the Soviet KGB.

Given their openness, given the extent of their resources, given the solid foundations of their own native scholarship, the Americans did supremely well after World War II. They excelled in academic pursuits, including practically

---

[38]Barry M. Katz, "The Criticism of arms: the Frankfurt school goes to war," *Journal of Modern History*, v. 59, no. 3, September 1987, pp. 439–78.

all the fields in which Europeans had hitherto held a commanding lead. Science, engineering, economics, sociology, Soviet studies, African studies, Far Eastern studies, Western European studies – all were grist to the American academic mill – the folklore of peasants in nineteenth-century France, the development of Jewish religion, the roots of the Enlightenment, the social significance of grand opera, the structure of English feudalism, the evolution of African kinship, the origins of the Cold War – the list goes on.[39] The US contribution to the study of European history, culture, and politics remained immeasurably greater than Europe's contribution to the US. Indeed American studies remained a stepchild of European academia. (Of all history courses given at West German universities between 1949 and 1989, only 2 percent were devoted to US history. Forty years after the creation of NATO, only one in 9 German universities offered American history as a subject – a serious matter for the new German elites in government, politics, and education.)[40]

Despite such omissions, academic links between Europe and the US tightened in a variety of ways, through conferences, lecture tours, guest programs, long-term visits, exchanges of students and teachers arranged through bodies such as the Fulbright Commission, or the German academic exchange service (DAAD). (By 1955 Western European scholars in the US made up 43 percent of all foreign scholars; American scholars in Western Europe amounted to 54 percent of all foreign scholars.) No European academic worth his or her salt could henceforth ignore American intellectual achievements. As Henry Rosovsky, a former Harvard dean, put it without false modesty in the 1980s: "between two-thirds and three-quarters of the world's best universities are located in the United States. . . . In higher education 'made in America' still is the finest label."[41]

[39]For a general review of US historiography after World War II, see for instance Michael Kammen, ed., *The Past before us: Contemporary Historical Writing in the United States*. Ithaca, Cornell University Press, 1980.

[40]Memorandum by German University Professors, German studies association newsletter, v. xiv, no. 1, Spring 1989, pp. 12–13.

[41]Henry Rosovsky, "Highest education," *New Republic*, 13–20 July 1987, pp. 13–14.

13

Science and Technology

For science, the twentieth century was the best of times and the worst of times. Science stood against millenarians who fought for the total transformation of mankind, and the annihilation of all obstacles in their way. The Nazis did not wipe out German science, but they degraded it through pseudo-disciplines such as *Rassenkunde* (racial lore) represented by learned charlatans such as Hans Günther, and by diploma-bearing criminals who committed murder in the guise of medical experiments. The flight of German-Jewish scientists impoverished German science. The Soviets under Stalin liquidated real or assumed dissidents, while encouraging cranks such as Trofim Lysenko, a plant breeder patronized by Stalin, but later demoted under Khrushchev. The West produced its own anti-scientific contingents. These included fundamentalist Christians and militant Freudians who – like the master himself – would not argue with their critics, but dismissed them on the grounds that they were themselves unstable people in need of conversion or psychotherapy. As Freud said, "my inclination is to treat those colleagues who offer resistance exactly as we treat patients in the same situation."[1]

But the twentieth century was also a magnificently creative age. It revolutionized every science – mathematics, chemistry, biology, astronomy, medicine, archaeology, and above all, physics. The epochal work of men such as J. J. Thomson (discoverer of the electron), Wilhelm Roentgen (pioneer of X-ray research), Max Planck (originator of the quantum theory), Werner Heisenberg (the uncertainty principle) and Albert Einstein (originator of the special and general theories of relativity) profoundly affected the arts and philosophy as well as the natural and physical sciences by shattering commonsense certainties inherited from an earlier past. By the end of World War II, their discoveries had begun to change the world in a manner that no prophet would have been able to predict. Research into the properties of the electron,

[1] Cited by Paul Johnson, *Modern Times: The World from the Twenties to the Eighties*. New York, Harper and Row, 1983, p. 6.

carried out by Thomson and Hendrik A. Lorentz had become the basis of great industries. Electromagnetic waves, forecast by James Clerk Maxwell and discovered by Heinrich Hertz, had made near instantaneous communications practicable around the globe. The X-rays discovered by Wilhelm Roentgen had helped to revolutionize medicine, as had the Curies' work on radium. Einstein's explanation of the photoelectric effect had helped to prod television from experiment to reality.[2] At the same time, the great team of scientists assembled to make an atomic bomb through the "Manhattan project" had made warfare destructive to a degree that would have shocked even Attila the Hun and Genghis Khan. It had been Einstein's famous equation $E = MC^2$ (energy = mass times the square of the velocity of light) that provided the theoretical foundation for the production of the atomic bomb. Initially, in 1939, Einstein had used his prestige in writing to President Roosevelt to warn of the Germans' assumed ability to produce atomic weapons; this and other warnings led to the establishment of the Manhattan project. After the war, Einstein and other scientists worked to stop nuclear bomb proliferation, but by this time the genie was out of the bottle and could never be put back.

The scientific and technological revolutions derived from these and other discoveries spanned the world, but the centers of achievement had shifted. At the beginning of the twentieth century, the scientific strongholds had been in Britain, France, and especially the German-speaking parts of Central Europe. When Albert Einstein jokingly remarked after World I that only a dozen men really understood relativity, Einstein's colleague, Walther Nernst, could still facetiously reply, "and eight of them live in Berlin!"[3] But from the 1930s on, the scientific balance of power underwent major shifts. The English-speaking world proved far more hospitable to refugees from the European dictatorships than any other part of the globe. Niels Bohr, a Danish physicist, escaped to the US in 1943 and advised on the atomic bomb. Italy, by now under Fascist tyranny, was the birthplace of the refugee physicists Emilio Segré and Enrico Fermi. Even more important were the lands once included within the Austro-Hungarian empire, whose intellectual and social turbulence had produced a great scholarly tradition long since decayed. A substantial number of scholars from the former Habsburg empire found new homes in Britain, one of the traditional leaders in science. (The Cavendish laboratory in Cambridge, the great physicist Lord Rutherford's former home, had alone produced no fewer than 14 Nobel prize winners by the early 1970s.) Illustrious refugees to Britain included Freud, von Hayek, a leader of the Austrian School of free enterprise economics, Karl (later Sir Karl) Popper; Bronislaw Malinowski, a founder of modern anthropology with its emphasis on fieldwork, Ludwig Wittgenstein, the philosopher-mathematician, and P. T. Bauer (later Lord Bauer) who made his name both in African studies and development economics. These voluntary and enforced exiles were joined by numerous Jews born in Germany, including physicists Max Born, Rudolf (later Sir Rudolf) Peierls, and mathematician

---

[2] Ronald W. Clark, *Einstein: The Life and Times.* New York, Avon Publishers, 1984, p. 661.
[3] Ibid., p. 214.

Bernhard Neumann. Overall, Britain owed five of her Nobel prize winners – Born, Ernst Chain, Sir Bernard Katz, Max Preutz, and Hans Krebs – to prewar escapees from Hitler. Later, no fewer than 41 out of the 700 members of the Royal Society were Jewish immigrants.[4]

But the greatest intellectual migration was across the Atlantic. (And most made their homes in the US, rather than Canada or Latin America, which were inclined to keep out brilliant foreigners in misguided attempts to protect their own academics from competition, and safeguard their national cultures.) The new arrivals included voluntary immigrants (such as French-born André F. Cournand, a physiologist and a Nobel laureate, and Canadians such as Charles P. Huggins who won a Nobel prize for his work on cancer research). More British scientists came to work in the US (including an entire team who crossed the Atlantic in World War II to work on the Manhattan project). But the great majority of newcomers were driven from their homelands by the Nazis.[5] Most were Jews, but by no means all. (For instance, Victor Hess chose emigration because of his Jewish wife, and Erwin Schrödinger left Germany because he disliked Nazism, particularly its racial policies.) The impact on Germany was devastating, especially in the fields of chemistry, medicine and physics. Before 1933, Germany had been more strongly represented in nuclear physics than any other country. (More than 30 percent of the 46 Nobel laureates between 1901 and 1939 had their roots in German culture.) Foreign physicists would learn German almost as a matter of course. Thereafter the US gained an unquestioned lead, and Germany dropped to the rank of a secondary power in the world of science. Refugee scientists included many Austrians and Germans such as Einstein, the Newton of the twentieth century, as well as a remarkably large number of Hungarian Jews, able to speak German, trained in the German tradition, and scarcely distinguishable in exile from German and Austrian Jews. Among them were luminaries such as Eugene Wigner, Leo Szilard, Edward Teller, and John von Neumann.

As we have pointed out before, these émigrés did not directly bring about the scientific predominance of the US; the foundations had been laid before. In physics, the US had made important advances from the 1920s onward (Robert Andrew Millikan, for instance, was awarded the Nobel prize for physics in 1923). Although ambitious students still found much value in a period of study in Europe, most of the new PhD graduates were American-trained. By the 1940s, American physicists such as Ernest O. Lawrence, Edwin M. McMillan, J. Robert Oppenheimer, Glenn Seaborg, and J. H. van Vleck, had gained world-wide renown.[6] The European refugees now found a warm academic reception, popular acclaim (Einstein, seen as the archetype of the

[4]Anthony Sampson, *The New Anatomy of Britain.* New York, Stein and Day, 1973, p. 332.

[5]Donald Fleming and Bernard Bailyn, eds, *The Intellectual Migration: Europe and America, 1930–1960.* Cambridge, Mass., Harvard University Press, 1969. Bernt Engelmann, *Germany Without Jews.* New York, Bantam Books, 1984, especially pp. 1979–80. H. Stuart Hughes, *The Sea Change: The Migration of Social Thought, 1930–1965.* New York, Harper and Row, 1975.

[6]Daniel J. Kevles, *The Physicists: The History of a Scientific Community in Modern America.* New York, Knopf, 1977.

kindly, eccentric, and brilliant professor, received movie-star treatment, much to his embarrassment), financial support, and employment of a kind not available to them in lesser centers such as Toronto, Istanbul, Jerusalem, and Buenos Aires, where a handful of exiles had also sought refuge.

The US had other advantages. Americans were less reverential of established ways than Europeans. The US had a large number of public and private institutions. College professors, however – as many refugees noted to their regret – did not enjoy the same social prestige as their opposite numbers in Europe. But foreigners gained professorships more easily than in many European countries (where professors widely counted as civil servants, and were often required to hold the citizenship of the respective countries in which they taught). Scientists moreover spoke an international language; they found acceptance more easily than poets and novelists, rooted by necessity in their own native tongues.

After the war the United States became the center of the science world, especially for Western Europe. For the next 20 years scientists in European countries developed closer ties with the US than with any of their neighbors. Trans-Atlantic collaboration was a strong force for cross-cultural experiences and encouraged cooperation and scientific progress. Large numbers of European scientists were trained in the US and to have worked there was a prerequisite for success. Europe's postwar leaders saw that this was the fastest way to restore their scientific cadre. For two decades or so there was a major brain drain to the United States. In proportion it may appear small – 2–3 percent a year – but it was significant, for many of the best scientists went.[7] This intellectual migration solidified the overall supremacy of the US in the world of science (with Britain as the most important center outside the US, linked by the easy movement of English-speaking academics across the Atlantic).

The traffic, of course, went both ways. The part taken by Werner von Braun and other German rocket scientists and engineers in US rocket development is well known. But the plan under which these Germans were brought to the US, "Project Paperclip" was only part of a more comprehensive program of "intellectual reparations." As Allied armies advanced into Germany, teams of American and British experts visited hundreds of targeted German research institutions, colleges, and industrial firms. They interviewed personnel, examined products and processes, blueprints, research reports, and so on. In effect, they indulged in industrial and technological plunder in virtually every area of German expertise, including wind tunnels, tape recorders, synthetic fuels and rubber, color films, textiles, machine tools, heavy equipment, ceramics, optics, dyes, and electronic microscopes. Ostensibly, the information gathered would be made available to the rest of the world. In practice, much was

---

[7]See "America's seductive charms," *Science*, v. 237, 4 September 1987, p. 1107. For Germany's scientific reparations, we are indebted to John Gimble, *Science, Technology and Reparations: Exploitation and Plunder in Postwar Germany*. Stanford, Stanford University Press, 1990, and private information from the author.

transferred by scientific consultants and document-screeners to their own firms.

This story was not told until the appearance of John Gimble's meticulous account (see footnote 7). According to his estimates, the total value of patents and other technological knowledge appropriated by the Americans and British may have amounted to about ten billion dollars, the figure mentioned by the Soviet Union at the Moscow meeting of the Council of Foreign Ministers in 1947 – a figure dismissed at the time by the US state department as "fantastic."

General Lucius D. Clay, then the American military governor in Germany, later shut down the program in the interests of German economic recovery, but failed in his efforts to have a monetary evaluation made to establish a credit for Germany's reparation account. The Americans and British (unlike the Soviets) did not physically remove German research records, but merely used them for their own purposes. Nevertheless, the popular belief that the US took no reparations from Germany needs to be drastically modified. The exploitation program had a negative effect both on the early resumption of German postwar research and on its economic recovery. In the long run, however, the Allied exploitation furthered an extensive network of American–German scientific, business, and industrial collaboration. The program contributed indirectly to the American climate of opinion that ensured West Germany's inclusion in the Marshall Plan.

War and its aftermath created further changes. Many sciences, including many branches of physics, now merged with government. This new cooperation was due in part to the cost and complexity of the new scientific tools. Pioneers of Western science such as Galileo had worked with equipment on a par with an artisan's. The plant needed for the Curies' research in physics at the beginning of the twentieth century would have been affordable to any small firm. But as time went on, many of the sciences required a capital investment in complex instruments whose cost would beggar all but multinational corporations or governments. Of the new scientific complexes, the Manhattan project, leading to the construction of the atom bomb, was the best known. Another was the MIT radiation laboratory which developed radar techniques essential both for campaigns in the air, and at sea (against submarines).

SCIENTIFIC AND TECHNOLOGICAL ADVICE TO THE PRESIDENT AND CONGRESS

The Soviet Union developed its atomic bomb; then Mao Tse-tung spent two months visiting Stalin, during which time the pair proclaimed the Sino-Soviet bloc's continued hostility to capitalism. Just a few months after Mao returned to China, the Korean war broke out. The public naturally felt threatened by this aggressive, militaristic communist bloc and later President Eisenhower sought scientific and technological advice on how to counter the communists. A technological capabilities panel was formed, which recommended developing the intercontinental ballistic missile, the sea-based Polaris missile, and the U-2 reconnaissance plane. After Sputnik *(1957), Eisenhower appointed a science adviser*

(James R. Killian, Jr, of MIT), and a president's science advisory commission. The latter dealt mostly with military affairs and greatly influenced presidential policies up to the mid-1960s; later it had less influence.

As part of this great war effort, President Roosevelt in 1941 established the Office for Scientific Research and Development (OSRD) which developed into "a central organization for all the estates of science," funded by the taxpayer, with billion dollar expenditures. (After the war, the work of OSRD devolved into a research and development board to coordinate military research, the Office of Naval Research, a civilian Atomic Energy Commission set up in 1946, and separate provision for basic research promoted by the National Science Foundation (NSF) created in 1950.)[8] The US government also helped to change engineering education: before 1940 this discipline had stressed pragmatic training in mathematics, physics, and science, as well as construction, production methods, design, and drafting. Few engineering professors had a doctoral degree; they came from industry. In the postwar period engineers became more like scientists, paying less attention to design and production. Graduate study was emphasized. Government and industry encouraged this development; scientist-engineers increasingly replaced design engineers – mathematics won out over design courses. The federal government continued to fund science and engineering training as part of national defense, and the NSF financed changes in engineering to make it more scientific, especially in grants for space and defense. Government support for research at universities greatly increased and it aimed for the scientist-engineer, as did research offices in the armed services (the Air Force Office of Scientific Research, the Office of Naval Research, the Army Research Office). Hence the generalist, the pragmatist, the design engineer largely disappeared in universities. Engineers continued to accomplish great things, but in certain respects, the relative decline of American engineering had begun.[9]

The Office of Naval Research founded in 1946 was the base from which government-supported research and development came in the postwar years. The ONR was a major contributor to the postwar science scene thanks to its breadth of vision, its flexibility, and its outreach to the scientific community. Government influence in research increased enormously and federal funds doubled threefold in the first 40 years after the war.

European science encountered comparable changes. Government became increasingly important; great scientific-governmental complexes were extended through agencies such as CERN (the research station of the European Council for Nuclear Research set up at Geneva), the National Research and Develop-

[8]A. Hunter Dupree, *Science in the Federal Government: A History of Policies and Activities*. Washington DC, Johns Hopkins University Press, 1986, pp. 371–5.
[9]See Arnold D. Ken and R. Byron Pepes "Why we need hands-on engineering education," *Technology Review*, October 1987, pp. 36–42. Harvey Brooks, "National science policy and technological innovation," in Ralph Landau and Nathan Rosenberg, eds, *The Positive Sum Strategy, Harnessing Technology for Economic Growth*. Washington DC, National Academy Press, 1986.

ment Corporation in Great Britain, and the *Centre National de la Recherche Scientifique* (*CNRS*) – all of these drew on US experience. (US innovations included the research contract, whereby government farmed out research and development to private enterprise institutions, with the government bearing all costs, including those of administration and infrastructure, on a reimbursable basis, generally with no profits or loss to either individuals or institutions.) Under the new dispensation, scientists enjoyed a new and unaccustomed status. The "boffins" (British military slang for scientific experts) came into their own, and science offered a new ladder of social advancement. In Britain, Oxford and Cambridge ceased to be dominated by a handful of interlocking academic families; the Royal Society became largely an association of self-made men. Scientists rose to high honors, and important official appointments. For instance C. P. Snow was knighted in 1957 and created baron in 1964. A physicist, Snow had an active career in academia and government. He served as technical director of the ministry of labour (1940–4) and was civil service commissioner from 1945 to 1960. He then served as parliamentary secretary to the ministry of technology (1961–6). Snow was a gifted novelist too, and lectured and wrote widely on science and society.

> *The military-physics complex directed much of scientific research in wartime and in postwar America. It was military funding that enabled Stanford University's electronic engineers and physicists to make it one of the leading universities in the world. Other universities had similar success, obtaining contracts from the Atomic Energy Commission, or the Office of Naval Research. From 1946 the American military and the AEC became the major sources of funds for physics research in the US, displacing private foundations. Research came to require vast funding; government had the wherewithal; the military wanted specific projects developed. Their patronage profoundly affected research and the quality of life of researchers; things became hectic and more bureaucratic; managerial skills took precedence over research skills for project managers. The military determined what direction research would take, supporting and funding for example solid state physics and work on quantum electrons. Research also became less concerned with new undertakings than with refining techniques and instrumentalism in all aspects of physics (see Science for the year 1987).*

At the top of the new academic totem pole, experts in the hard sciences (especially physics) obtained a far greater share of official funding than scholars in other disciplines. Overall, they were a confident lot. The advent of nuclear warfare shocked some of those physicists who had helped to bring about the transformation; the prospect of a nuclear apocalypse also frightened many intellectuals and literary people. But the mass of scientists and the general population were not much affected by such terrors. On the contrary, there was a general and ill-founded mood of optimism that caused forecasters to look for a new age of plenty in the field of energy. This mood found expression in those "atoms-for-peace" programs by which the Americans and, to a lesser extent, the British and French, helped to diffuse nuclear technology abroad. The scientific community overall remained confident and complacent, reluctant to "ask awkward questions or to upset the arrangements by which esoteric research involving the construction and use of massive and expensive machinery, was supported without the need for extensive public debate."[10]

Science had indeed become expensive. Its costs could only have been acceptable to a public marvelously impressed by the new discoveries, and with the concept of science as an endless frontier that would revolutionize ordinary life. Between 1945 and 1967, the US experienced a period of steady growth in public research and development – expenditures increased on average up to 15 percent a year in real terms, supplemented by a substantial growth in private expenditure. (Public spending only levelled off in 1967, during the Vietnam war; private investment began to exceed public outlay from the late 1970s.) Money went to fund rising salaries for scientists and on expensive equipment. The traditional structure of academic prestige was thus overturned; classicists and philologists – the most revered scholars in nineteenth-century Europe – now came at the bottom of the pyramid; while the physical scientists, yesteryears' outsiders, moved to the top.

The US continued to hold a striking lead in most scientific and technological developments – in nuclear physics, biochemistry, chemistry, medicine, biotechnology, and electronics. The US became a Mecca for postgraduate students from Europe and later from the Third World. Far more graduates were produced, both in the pure and the applied sciences and engineering, than in all other Western countries combined. Only the USSR could compete in numbers, though not in qualitative terms (see table 13.1).

The US led in the number of scientific patents registered and exported, and in

TABLE 13.1   *Graduates in pure and applied sciences: 1956*

Country	Pure sciences		Applied sciences	
	Total	Per 1,000,000 inhabitants	Total	Per 1,000,000 inhabitants
USSR	12,000	56	60,000	280
United States	23,500	144	22,500	137
Great Britain	5,200	105	2,800	57
France	1,760	41	2,988	70
West Germany	3,450	67	4,450	86
Switzerland	215	44	399	82
Italy	2,436	51	2,200	45

Source: J. Frederick Dewhurst et al., *Europe's Needs and Resources; Trends and Prospects in Eighteen Countries.* New York, Twentieth Century Fund, 1961, p. 816.

[10] Jeffrey Marsh, "Science and society," *Commentary*, April 1978, p. 101.

the number of scientific books and papers published. It came near to or exceeded the rest of the world in the total number of Nobel prizes awarded in the "hard sciences," physics, chemistry, medicine, and physiology. The US and Britain between them gained far more Nobel prizes than all other countries combined. To be exact, between 1945 and 1967, US scientists won 54 Nobel prizes (14 of the winners were foreign-born), as against 68 for the rest of the world. (Of the latter, 24 went to Britain, 10 to Germany, seven to the USSR. Only Britain came close to the US in the number gained in one particular science, receiving 11 prizes in chemistry, as against 12 won by US scientists.)[11] While France was poorly represented in the Nobel awards French scholars did well in being awarded five of the 30 Field medals given since 1932. (The Field medal, granted by the International Mathematics Congress, is equivalent to the Nobel prize.)

The US continued also to invest more than any other country in research and development. This lead lessened somewhat during the late 1970s.[12] Nevertheless, since World War II, it has spent the most, and accomplished most, in absolute terms. The accomplishments of course entailed no US monopoly in any major branch of science of technology; it was an international rather than an American century. But overall, since 1945, US scientific and technological predominance paralleled the US global lead in military, industrial, and financial enterprises.

What of the wider impact of science? The new partnership between big research, big government, big business, big grant-giving bodies, raised difficult moral issues about the use to which science should be put, the scientists' responsibility for their work, and the secrecy or otherwise to be maintained over scientific information. Scientists such as Snow scathingly criticized the separation that existed between the world of arts and humanities and the world of science. But in truth, such divisions were quite arbitrary. The logics employed in computer programs had already preoccupied scholastic philosophers; Einstein's quest for an intelligible universe cannot be separated from the Judeo-Christian religious heritage. Moreover the world of science was itself profoundly divided. Modern physics fragmented into several sub-fields such as solid-state physics, plasma physics, and low-energy physics. Each sub-field produced revolutionary developments, for example from solid-state physics came electronics (the transistor and microcircuitry). This process was complicated and ambivalent. On the one hand, there were many new cross-disciplinary sciences such as cermetics (created through the fusion of ceramics and metallurgy), biochemistry, astrophysics, and radio-biology. On the other hand, the division of scientific labor became so marked that the average biologist could no longer talk to the average physicist or mathematician about

---

[11]For a detailed table, see *Encyclopaedia Britannica*. Chicago, William Benton, 1968, v. 16, pp. 549–55.

[12]In 1969, the US spent $25.6 billion on research and development; West Germany, France, and Britain $8.3 billion, Japan $3 billion. By 1979, corresponding figures stood at £25.3 billion; $19.3 billion; $11.4 billion. Stephen Bechtel, "Technology and its role in modern society," in Landau and Rosenberg, eds, *The Positive Sum*, p. 138.

his or her own speciality. Even individual disciplines became increasingly fragmented, so that one investigator might spend a lifetime on a minor problem hardly comprehensible even to his colleagues.

Under such circumstances, a broader scientific world view was hard to obtain and harder still to communicate to the layman. Indeed, the messages of science were widely misunderstood. Thus Einstein's theory of relativity sometimes came to be mistakenly equated with moral relativism, or with the belief that the world is ruled by chance. In fact Einstein's unsuccessful search for a unified field theory was inspired by his profound belief that God does not play dice with the universe, and that there were absolute laws governing nature and the universe. Relativism in science had actually come rather by way of Heisenberg's "indeterminacy principle." Heisenberg, father of quantum mechanics and the famous "uncertainty principle" (or indeterminacy) had overturned traditional physics and influenced other fields and disciplines as well. The "uncertainty principle" stated that it is impossible to determine accurately both the position and momentum of a subatomic particle such as the electron. These findings seemed to put an end to those absolute certainties for which physics had searched. Essayists such as Joseph Wood Krutch then mistakenly used the "indeterminacy principle," to show that men had free will and could not be treated as mechanical, deterministic beings subject to absolute regularity and control, as was assumed by the behaviorist psychology propounded by B. F. Skinner and others.

Between them, the various sciences in fact seemed to be sending mixed messages to the layman. As Harold J. Morowitz, a leading scholar in the field of molecular biophysics and biochemistry, put it, scientists appeared to contradict one another's fundamental assumptions. Biologists, who had once postulated a privileged role for the human mind in nature's hierarchy, moved relentlessly towards the rigid materialism that had characterized nineteenth-century physics. By contrast physicists, faced with compelling experimental evidence, shifted from strictly mechanical models of the universe to others in which the mind played an integral role in all physical events. It appeared as if the two disciplines were fast-moving trains going in opposite directions.[13] Even the mathematicians sounded an uncertain note, as the work of the mathematician Kurt Gödel and others brought to light what appeared to be irresolvable paradoxes and showed the futility of trying to set up complete systems based on the formalizations of mathematics.[14]

This is not to say that science degenerated into solipsism (the view which asserts that only the self is knowable). Even in the subatomic world there are objective features that exist independently of any observer. Thus every single electron observed by scientists to date has always revealed the exact same value for its electrical charges. No matter who has made the measurement, or

---

[13]Harold J. Morowitz, "Rediscovering the mind," *Psychology Today*, August 1980, p. 12.

[14]Philip J. Davis and Reuben Hersh, *The Mathematical Experience*. Boston, Houghton Mifflin Co., 1981, pp. 162, 228.

how it was made, the result has always turned out essentially the same.[15] Nevertheless, the advances made in physics and mathematics shattered accustomed notions of space and time – at least for intellectuals. Most ordinary citizens continued to feel at home in a Newtonian universe.

Human beings moreover suddenly realized that they could "see" a great deal more than ever before. The human eye, unaided, can provide access to only a small segment of the known world. But the world open to human understanding is so much greater. At one end of the invisible spectrum there are cosmic rays, a trillionth of a centimeter in wavelength; at the other, there exist infrared waves, heat radiation, and very long wavelengths used for radio, radar, and television – all invisible to the naked eye. The landscape seen with human eyes is dramatically different, yet no more real, than the same scene captured on an infrared plate, and showing a mass of detail beyond our vision. The same goes for the strange images captured by photographs made with the aid of high-powered microscopes and telescopes, for televised images derived from space research, or from complex tools that provide researchers with millions of detailed photos of subatomic collisions. The stark pictures that poured forth from such devices were reminiscent of abstract expressionist painting.[16] Images drawn from crystallography resembled the work of cubists. Just as science gave a new inspiration to modern art, so modern art both presaged and paralleled the new world of science. They conveyed a similar message – that the universe is infinitely more mysterious and harder to understand and to control than the pioneers of traditional mechanistic science had ever imagined.

REVOLUTIONARY APPLICATIONS

Il n' existe pas des sciences appliquées, mais seulement l'application des sciences.[17] (There are no applied sciences, only applications of science, Louis Pasteur once explained to a great agricultural congress.) Theory and practice can never be divorced – nevertheless there are great gradations between scientific research whose ultimate practical utility cannot be foreseen at the time, and investigations that serve immediately known ends. The postwar period was one of brilliant achievement in both fields, mostly in direct continuation of work done in wartime and in the prewar years. During this era, nuclear physics was widely regarded as the queen of sciences (a status later awarded to biology, as was presaged by Szilard's postwar switch from physics to biology). A student interested in the details of scientific advance in the field of physics must turn to comprehensive studies, such as Isaac Asimov's history of physics, written

[15]Michael Riordan, *The Hunting of the Quark: A True Story of Modern Physics.* New York, Simon and Schuster, 1987, p. 40.

[16]Ibid., p. 23.

[17]Cited from a speech at Lyons, at the Congrès viticole et sériocole, 9–14 September 1872 in the *Oxford Dictionary of Quotations.* Oxford, Oxford University Press, 1979, p. 369.

for laymen with some grounding in mathematics.[18] Equally valuable and more entertaining are works on individual scientists such as Enrico Fermi or Otto Hahn, a field of scientific biography that remains to be more thoroughly plowed.[19] Here we can only touch on a few major developments.

Some of the most important advances hinged on research on subatomic particles. During the 1930s, scientists had only known three elementary particles – the proton, photon, and electron.[20] These were visualized in a relatively simple fashion. The electron, for instance, was seen as a tiny, inert ball surrounded by an electric and magnetic field, with lines radiating from it like rigid spokes. This relatively simple world soon changed in a fundamental fashion, and with far-reaching results. By the early 1950s, quantum electrodynamics could account for the electromagnetic interactions of electrons, positrons, and photons to an amazing degree of accuracy. Scientists also attempted to explain the "strong" force that governed the interaction of neutrons and protons. This strong force, however, turned out to be much more difficult to understand than scientists had anticipated, and whole new families of particles emerged in the search for an underlying order.

Their study depended on complex new machines, which were pioneered in the US by Ernest O. Lawrence, inventor of the cyclotron. High-energy physics got into its stride from the late 1940s as newly built particle accelerators became capable of delivering uniform, controlled beams of high-energy electrons, protons, and pions. The accelerators were ideal research tools for producing new particles and their properties by smashing one into another. Research in these fields was pioneered at Berkeley radio laboratory where Lawrence taught many of the world's leading accelerator physicists, including Luis W. Alvarez, M. Stanley Livingston, Edwin McMillan, Robert R. Wilson, and others. In addition, work proceeded abroad, including the Soviet Union. A new "synchrotron," developed by a consortium of Eastern universities in the US, allowed proton bunches to travel in fixed orbits inside a circular vacuum pipe. Whereas the old cyclotrons had been limited by the size of the magnet pole faces that could be manufactured, the new machines were limited only by space and funds. The newly organized Atomic Energy Commission provided the funds for the Brookhaven National Laboratory and its powerful "cosmotron" (started 1952). In 1955 Berkeley completed its "bevatron" that would surpass the "cosmotron", used in the search for antiprotons. Thereafter the construction of larger and more powerful accelerators became an international preoccupation. The Soviets in 1957 took the energy lead by building their "synchro-phastotron;" Western Europe joined the race by constructing CERN, and the US in 1961 created the "alternating gradient synchrotron" at

[18]Issac Asimov, *The History of Physics*, New York, Walker and Co., 1983. Thomas S. Kuhn, *The Structure of Scientific Revolutions*. Chicago, Chicago University Press, 1970. Edward Harrison, *Masks of the Universe*. New York, Macmillan, 1985. C. P. Snow, *The Physicists*. Boston, Little, Brown, 1981.

[19]Laura Fermi, *Atoms in the Family*. Chicago, University of Chicago Press, 1954. Otto Hahn, *A Scientific Autobiography*. New York, Scribner, 1966. Clark, ibid.

[20]Richard Rhodes, *The Making of the Atomic Bomb*. New York, Simon and Schuster, 1988, *passim*.

Brookhaven, and thereafter SLAC, the "Stanford linear accelerator." These large accelerators came to extend over whole city blocks – the scientific colosseums of the twentieth century.

The resultant discoveries kept changing man's concept of the universe. As early as 1932, Carl O. Anderson, an American at Cal. Tech had discovered a new particle in a shower of cosmic rays. This particle was the electron with a positive, instead of a negative charge, a "positron," the first indication that the universe consisted not only of matter but also of anti-matter. Even more important was the discovery of the anti-proton by a team led by Owen Chamberlain and Emilio Segré at Berkeley's radiation laboratory. The anti-proton was a negatively charged particle with exactly the same proton mass. The new science interpreted the subatomic world as divided into particles and anti-particles; when they meet, they produce a state of pure energy that can create in turn other anti-particles and particles. These included one of a wholly peculiar kind, the neutrino, detected in 1956 by Clyde Cowan and Frederick Reines of the Los Alamos Laboratory. The neutrino proved particularly difficult to understand; it had neither mass nor electric charge, and had virtually no interaction with other known particles. As a result of these and other studies, scientists by 1959 had classified 30 known sub-particles, and the number kept increasing. "In their attempt to understand the forces holding together the nuclei, and tearing them apart, these scientists had broken open a veritable Pandora's Box."[21]

Equally important was the development of lasers, developed in the Soviet Union by Nikolai G. Basov and Aleksandr M. Prochorov, and in the US by (among others) Charles H. Townes, like his Soviet colleagues a Nobel laureate. As Townes records, "the laser was born one beautiful spring morning (in 1951) on a park bench in Washington, DC. As I sat in Franklin Square, musing and admiring the azaleas, an idea came to me for a practical way to obtain a very pure form of electromagnetic waves from molecules. I had been doggedly searching for new ways to produce radio waves at very high frequencies, too high for the vacuum tubes of the day to generate. This shortwave length radiation, I felt, would permit extremely accurate measurements and analysis, giving new insights into physics and chemistry."[22] Townes realized that if man were to obtain wavelengths shorter than those that could be produced by vacuum tubes, scientists must use the ready-made small devices known as atoms and molecules. Later discussions with students at Columbia University over lunch produced a new vocabulary. "Laser" came to stand for light amplification; "maser" for microwave amplification by stimulated emission of radiation.

The first device was an ammonia maser, completed in the mid-1950s, built round ammonia gas, since the ammonia molecule was known to interact more strongly than any other with microwaves. In 1957 Townes turned to the application of light waves, almost 10,000 times higher in frequency than

[21]Riordan, The Hunting of the Quark, p. 69, and passim, much used in this section.
[22]Charles H. Townes, "Harnessing light," Science 84, November 1984, pp. 153–5.

microwaves. There were many practical problems to be resolved, but in 1960 Theodore H. Maiman, a physicist with Hughes Aircraft Company demonstrated the first operating laser, while Ali Javan, William R. Bennett Jr, and Donald R. Herriott at Bell Labs built a second, and completely different type. As Towne explains, the new devices had far-reaching and indeed unforeseen consequences. Masers came to be used to communicate to space over long distances and pick up radio waves from distant galaxies. Astrophysicists later discovered natural masers in interstellar space that generate enormous microwave intensity from excited molecules. Hydrogen masers made possible the construction of an atomic clock accurate to one part in 100 trillion. Laser beams had even more far-reaching application. The beam of a one-watt laser directed at the moon, for instance, could be seen by television equipment on the lunar surface when the lights of the greatest cities on earth were undetectable. More powerful pulsed lasers could deliver energy over a very short period to fantastically high levels. This made them suitable for an enormous variety of scientific, medical, and industrial uses, as they were capable of melting or tearing apart any substance, even the atoms themselves. By the end of the 1960s, most new lasers were being designed in industrial laboratories. In addition, lasers had revolutionary applications in the field of communications. A single light beam can, in principle, carry all the radio and TV emissions and all telephone calls in the world without any one of them interfering with another.

There were equally striking discoveries in the field of astronomy. In 1929 Edwin Hubble, using the newly completed 100-inch reflecting telescope on Mount Wilson in southern California, posited a universe in a state of regular expansion. Hubble's crucial observations pointed to a beginning, to a time when all matter in the universe clung together, and seemed to provide evidence for a unique primeval event that cosmologists came to call the "big bang," an unimaginable explosion that created space, time, and energy, as we know them. Or, as a traditional theologian would have put it, "And God said, Let there be light: and there was light." Twenty years later, in 1949, a 200-inch telescope on Palomar Mountain went into operation. Walter Baade of the Mount Wilson staff, working with Henrietta Swope, showed that the intergalactic distances were much greater even than Hubble had assumed. The universe must therefore be much older. By the mid-1950s, astronomers and nuclear physicists had arrived at three distinct methods for determining the age of the universe, which based on present-day knowledge is reckoned to be around 20 billion years.

The new physics and the new astronomy enormously extended the size and age of the known universe. Our own galaxy, the Milky Way, turned out to be only one among billions of others spread through space. More startling still, these galaxies were racing away from one another in a great cosmic expansion. No previous generation had ever had to contemplate a universe of such unimaginable extent. The new discoveries in space went with new archaeological techniques (such as carbon dating, perfected by Willard F. Libby and others in 1955) that also increased the known age of mankind. These startling advances gave a boost to human imagination. All manner of fantasies gained popularity concerning UFOs (unidentified flying objects) from outer space, extraterrestrial beings, and time-travelers. In the realm of serious science, the cosmology evolved by Hubble and his successors combined with high-energy physics in the search for a new synthesis, a general unification theory that, if proved, would tie together all known fundamental forces of the universe and thereby complete Einstein's work. Should theoretical physicists succeed in this endeavor, they would change not merely the image of the physical universe, but mankind's entire philosophical outlook.[23]

In biology, one of the most striking new breakthroughs occurred through work by James D. Watson and Francis Crick on the structure of DNA, first published in 1953. As David Baltimore, another Nobel laureate, points out, previous biological research had proceeded on two separate routes. The physiological approach had envisaged living organisms as factories, and sought to understand how the machines were put together, how they worked, and how they were integrated. The genetic approach, on the other hand, asked questions about blueprints and decisions. "In the factory analogy, genetics leaves the greasy machines and goes to the executive suite, where it analyzes the planners, the decision makers, the computers, the historical records."[24] The factory, in Baltimore's imagery, is the cell. By the early 1950s, a great deal of work had been done both on genetics, and on the physiological properties of the cell, but there was no understanding of the way in which the executive suite and factory floor were linked.

After World War II, the US was for a while the world center of biochemistry, thanks partly to a flood of European biochemists fleeing the Nazis in the 1930s and partly to the progressive policies of the national institutes of health. As a result many talented American scientists emerged, although the field was still dominated by émigrés such as Carl Cori, G. Hopkins, Fritz Lipmann, and Otto Warburg. One of the few Americans to win acclaim was Arthur Kornberg, who won a Nobel prize in 1959 for his research on the biosynthesis of DNA.

Watson and Crick supplied the answer. In 1944, an experiment by Oswald Avery and his colleagues at the Rockefeller Institute had shown that the chemical transmitter of genetic information was deoxyribonucleic acid (DNA). Alfred Hershey and Martha Chase at the Cold Spring Harbor laboratory later extended their work. Watson and Crick therefore had a good idea where to look. Studying molecular structure using X-rays was a field in which British science excelled. By the early 1950s, two investigators in London, Rosalind Franklin and Maurice Wilkins had independently achieved high-resolution

---

[23]Allan Sandage, "Inventing the beginning," *Science 84*, November 84, pp. 111–13. John H. Schwarz, "Completing Einstein," *Science 85*, November 1985, pp. 60–4. Paul Davies, *Superforce: The Search for a Grand Unified Theory of Nature*. New York, Simon and Schuster, 1984.

[24]David Baltimore, "The brain of a cell," *Science 84*, November 1984, pp. 149–51. For more detailed works, see for instance James D. Watson, *The Double Helix*. London, Weidenfeld, and Nicolson, 1981.

pictures of DNA. These X-ray pictures were far from perfect. But, as Baltimore puts it, they combined "insight, hunch, and an analysis" to build a model of DNA structure that found almost immediate acceptance. Genes are constructed of four chemical units arranged along each of two complementary strands, and the units form a code of instruction necessary for an organism's growth and reproduction. The cell's brain, so to speak, is comparable to a tape reader scanning an array of information encoded in a linear sequence that is ultimately translated into three-dimensional proteins. The analogy with the computer was obvious. Using their new skills, scientists acquired ever-growing ability to decipher the coded information. Genetic engineering became for the first time a practical possibility.

These and other scientific advances were stunning in their consequences. Nuclear physics applied to war provided man with apocalyptic powers of destruction. Hans A. Bethe, one of the leading physicists involved in nuclear weapons research, said, "there is no limit, in principle, to the size of the fusion [hydrogen] bomb."[25] This was not all. The new discoveries in genetics represented "the ultimate ascendance of man to the control of all chemicals of his surroundings, including other living organisms" – powers that even Faust had not dared to ask in his pact with the devil. The new sciences progressed at an accelerating pace. They created new technologies, and these shaped new tools of research, which in turn revolutionized the sciences. This transformation went with new attempts to formulate theories that would unite the fundamental forces of nature. Biologists similarly sought to link the functioning of a cell with the questions concerning origins. According to Horace Freeland Judson, a scientist and historian of science: "The unification of developmental biology with neurobiology and these with perceptual and cognitive psychology – these three unifications span from the mature science of physics through the younger but explosively progressing science of biology to the infantile science of psychology."[26] In twentieth-century science, revolution itself ceased to be revolutionary.

SILICON VALLEY AND STANFORD UNIVERSITY

Stanford engineers and administrators are usually praised as the architects of Silicon Valley; but it was the federal government which really made the Santa Clara Valley the center of electronics, aerospace, and semiconductors. Provost Terman helped by linking the university to industry, by recruiting talented scientists ("steeples of excellence") and creating (in 1950) an industrial park for high-tech companies. Some of these were founded by Stanford faculty or graduates, through enterprises such as Varian Associates and Hewlett-Packard. Most important was the large number of government grants and

---

[25]Hans A. Bethe, "The hydrogen bomb," for *Scientific American*, in *Atomic Power*, New York, Simon and Schuster, 1955, p. 166. Abraham Pais, *Inward Bound*. Oxford, Clarendon Press, 1986.

[26]Horace Freeland Judson, "Paradoxes of prediction: the shape of science to come," *Science 85*, November 1985, p. 36. Also see Horace Freeland Judson, *The Search for Solutions*. New York, Holt, Rinehart, and Winston, 1980.

contracts awarded to the area during and after World War II. New companies sprang up everywhere in the valley; but it was the coming of William Shockley's transistor laboratory in 1955 that set off the semiconductor revolution and really founded Silicon Valley. Over 50 companies were spin-offs from Shockley's group. Terman had invited Shockley to come to Stanford's industrial park and to cooperate with the faculty but Shockley brought in his own team. He did not join the Stanford faculty or go to the industrial park until after his group broke up (Fairchild and Intel emerging as the most important spin-offs).

The transformation of science in turn accelerated warfare and industrial change, giving rise to new industries. The interplay between science and industry was of course of long standing. During World War I, chemists such as Chaim Weizmann in Britain and Fritz Haber in Germany had made a larger contribution to the military effort of their countries than any field marshal. During World War II and its aftermath, the time gap between new discoveries and their practical application narrowed. Science stimulated both public and private enterprise. The former (broadly speaking) took the main share in promoting advances useful in war. The atom bomb did not come to humanity through the efforts of private arms manufacturers once derided as "merchants of death." Instead, the Manhattan project represented US public enterprise of a kind never seen before in American history. The project "bore no relation to the industrial or social life of our country; it was a separate state, with its own airplanes and its own factories and its thousands of secrets. It had a particular sovereignty, one that could bring about the end, peacefully or violently, of all other sovereignties."[27]

Once the war ended, the Atomic Energy Act turned over to the Atomic Energy Commission a monopoly of the production and ownership of fissionable material. The Act thereby created what James R. Newman, one of its draftsmen, called "an island of socialism in a sea of private enterprise."[28] Under the terms of the subsequent Atomic Energy Act (1954), private enterprise acquired a larger share. Even so, the industry remained strictly regulated; entry needed government permission; official authority was required to construct plants or acquire raw materials and fuels; nuclear products could only be sold to the government; the industry remained subject to government regulation regarding prices to be charged or over licencing its main inventions. In Western Europe, government played an even more essential part in developing the nuclear power industry. The year 1956 proved a landmark. The first US atomic power generating plant started up at Lemont, Illinois (Calder Hall in Great Britain began to feed electricity produced by nuclear power into the British national grid in that same year). Nuclear power was also applied to a variety of other uses, for instance naval engineering. In 1954, the US launched the *USS Nautilus*, a nuclear-powered craft, followed in 1959 by *NS* (Nuclear Ship) *Savannah*, a merchant ship launched in 1959, whilst the Soviets in 1957 put into commission the *Lenin*, an icebreaker. Nevertheless, initial hopes for

[27]Herbert S. Marks, cited in Rhodes, *The Making of the Atomic Bomb*, p. 276.
[28]David F. Cavers, "The Atomic Energy Act of 1954," in *Atomic Power*, p. 117.

cheap power turned out to be misplaced and coal, oil, and hydroelectric energy remained the main workhorses of industry.

WERNER MAGNUS MAXIMILIAN VON BRAUN (1912–1977)

In 1946, a Zurich company performed a new play by the émigré German playwright Carl Zuckmayer. The play was called The Devil's General (Des Teufels General), *and hinged on the moral conundrums of a German soldier who had lent his abilities to Hitler. Zuckmayer might have written an equally fascinating play concerning Werner von Braun. Von Braun's life encompassed even more contradictions than Zuckmayer's flawed hero (based on Ernst Udet, a real-life German flying ace who committed suicide in Hitler's service). Von Braun was born in Wirsitz, East Prussia, son of a Prussian aristocrat who had reached high office in the Weimar Republic. From an early age, von Braun was fascinated by science fiction, space travel, and the romances of Jules Verne. Having presented a brilliant doctorate at the University of Berlin, he began to experiment with liquid fuel rockets. This was a subject of greatest interest to the German military, who were prevented by the Versailles Treaty from developing heavy artillery of the conventional kind. Von Braun became the German army's top rocket specialist – much to the disappointment of his father, who would have preferred his son to take up the duties of a conventional landowner. From 1937, von Braun helped to build the German rocket experimental station at Peenemünde, for a time the world's leading center of rocketry. Von Braun developed numerous weapons, including the V2. (His career later became the subject of a laudatory movie "I aim for the stars," which prompted a comedian to add, "but I hit London." Braun himself reportedly commented that his rocket had worked perfectly, except for landing on the wrong planet.)*

Fortunately for the Allies, the V2 came too late to affect the fortunes of war, and when hostilities ended, von Braun transferred his services to the US under "operation paperclip," a project for rounding up leading German military technicians and scientists. (The Soviets had a similar policy, though according to von Braun they only picked up the lower-ranking members of his team.) Von Braun became a US citizen; his three children from the marriage with his youthful second cousin Maria Louise von Quistrop were born in the US. His ability gained him rapid promotion, and in 1956 he became the director of the development operations division, Army Ballistic Agency. If he had had his own way, von Braun could have succeeded in orbiting a satellite before Sputnik, but he was eventually given the go-ahead for Explorer I, *launched by* Jupiter-C *in 1958. Explorer I was the first satellite to make a major scientific discovery, revealing the Van Allen belts encircling the earth. In 1958 von Braun and his team were transferred to the newly created NASA, a civilian agency, and von Braun became director of the agency's George C. Marshall space flight center at Huntsville, Alabama, which built the Saturn 5 rocket for the Apollo project. The Americans reached the moon; thereafter Congressional and public interest declined; NASA's budget diminished. Von Braun resigned from NASA in 1972, and joined Fairchild Industries as vice-president for engineering development. It was an astonishing transformation – from Prussian junker's son, and engineer for the Nazis, to US technocrat, who built the American space engines.*

Governments also promoted rocket-technology – initially for military purposes, later also for space research and communications. The Germans had been the most successful pioneers. The Treaty of Versailles at the end of World

War I had forbidden heavy artillery to Germany; hence German planners decided that rockets might fill the gap in the Reich's armory. The Germans built the first guided rockets, used to attack London: German scientists and engineers later helped both the USSR and the US in their rocket research. In 1957 the Soviets fired *Sputnik* into orbit. In 1958 the US responded by creating the National Aeronautic and Space Administration (NASA), a civilian body designed to promote and coordinate space exploration in a race with the Soviet Union conducted for military advantage, scientific information, and national prestige. In that same year the US also launched the first of its major space enterprises, the *Explorer* and *Vanguard I* missions, both of considerable value to astronomers.[29]

War also played an essential part in the development of the jet plane. The British pioneer was Sir Frank Whittle, an RAF officer, whose single-engine Gloster experimental jet fighter first flew in 1941. The Germans launched the Messerschmitt-262 in 1942, and in 1944 the Americans brought out the highly successful Lockheed Shooting Star or F-80. With their great speed, rate of climb, and operational ceilings, jet fighters quickly replaced piston-engine aircraft in the postwar air forces. Later on, the jet-propelled bomber came into its own, followed by the jet-propelled civilian airliner. Its development began in the West in 1956, when engineers from the Royal Aircraft establishment at Farnborough began to discuss the possibilities of a supersonic passenger plane. Owing to the anticipated expense, the British decided that they could only build the plan in partnership with another country; hence France and Britain agreed in 1962 to construct the Concorde (operational in 1969, one year after the Soviets had first flown their Tupolev 14). The Americans, however, retained leadership in military and commercial aviation. Whereas only 10 percent of the adult US population had ever traveled in an airliner during the late 1940s, 63 percent had done so by 1977, and the figure kept increasing. The jet aircraft in turn had far-reaching consequences. It tied the deep South, the South West, and the Far West more effectively to the rest of the country than before. The US came to be more closely linked with Canada, the Caribbean, and above all with Western Europe. There were other changes. The jet plane required large airports situated well away from city centers, and thus speeded the process of urban decentralization begun by suburban trains and motor cars. Great airports all over the world began to look alike and to provide similar services.

The calculations needed for building nuclear weapons and nuclear power stations or for putting spacecraft into orbit required a speed of operation and complex computations that could only be obtained from machines of immense efficiency. The British once again did important pioneering work during World War II, when they built the first rudimentary computers for use in decoding

---

[29]Ronald W. Clark, *Works of Man*. New York, Viking, 1985, p. 312. Roger E. Bilstein, *Flight in America 1900–1983*. Washington DC, Johns Hopkins University Press, 1984, p. 205. Carl Solberg, *Conquest of the Skies: A History of Commercial Aviation in America*. Boston, Little Brown, 1979.

intercepted German messages. The Americans began independent work on ENIAC, the "electronic numerical integrator and computer" used to calculate gun trajectories. It was von Neumann who created the first truly programmable electronic computer in 1947.[30] However, the cost of the sophisticated electronics was so high that industry at first had to make do with simpler machines, laboring under serious technical limitations. These were overcome with remarkable speed, mainly through the efforts of scientists employed at universities and private firms such as the Bell Telephone Laboratories. In this, as in many other "high-tech" developments, the Americans largely dominated the field.

By 1959 the industry had advanced a long way. Its progress was symbolized by a conference of computer experts held in Paris in 1959 under UNESCO's auspices. The meeting had attracted some 2,000 specialists, drawn from 37 countries, and already representing by that time something like 100,000 experts the world over. The machines discussed at Paris were already a million times faster in their respective operations than the computers of 12 years earlier, and a thousand times faster than those in operation three years before. They had ceased to be "computers" in the true sense of the word. They were not merely capable of great speed; they had already become capable of associating ideas, of translating (albeit imperfectly) from one language to another; they had acquired prodigious memories; they were able both to act on judgements fed in by their programmers, and to arrive at judgements not anticipated by their designers. In science, computers could store data, assist in statistical analysis, carry out complex calculations, simulate intricate concatenations of circumstances. The computer became as revolutionary a new device for scientific enquiry in the late twentieth century as the telescope and microscope had been in the seventeenth century.

The application of computers was equally important in war, space research, banking, librarianship, commerce, and industry throughout the Atlantic Community. Computers would affect the operations of every collective enterprise. They could perform routine clerical labor such as writing circular letters, and keeping track of pay rolls or stock inventories. But they could also do much, much more. By the late 1950s, for example, there were already control machines – computers that could direct and supervise machine processes. (For example, the Fairey-Ferranti 3D machine could operate cutting tools to the precision of one-thousandth of an inch, in three dimensions, and simultaneously carve a one-piece section of a supersonic aircraft.[31] The age of the computer had entailed revolutionary changes in the storage and transmittal of information. (By the early 1980s, there were in existence more than 1,350 different computerized "databases" containing almost inconceivable amounts of information.)[32] By now, computers could carry out an immense number of

[30]Susan West, "Beyond the one-track mind,", *Science 85,* November 1985, pp. 102–5.
[31]Dewhurst, *Europe's Needs,* pp. 804–5.
[32]Alfred Glossbrenner, *The Complete Handbook of Personal Computer Communications.* New York, St Martin's Press, 1983, p. 7. Heinz R. Pagels, *The Dreams of Reason: The Computer and the Rise of the Sciences of Complexity.* New York, Simon and Schuster, 1988.

jobs, many of them boring or unpleasant, previously done by human beings. A whole range of industrial and managerial operations became automated. Computers kept becoming smaller and cheaper to buy. At the same time, there were new and unanticipated perils – computer errors or failures, computer infiltration crimes committed for personal gain, and much more frightening "viruses" (destructive commands maliciously implanted into a computer for the purpose of sabotage motivated by political, military, or personal considerations). In a more abstract sense, computer users might fall victim to the computer's inbuilt weaknesses, its inability to transcend a simply binary mode of operation. Nevertheless, the computer revolution could not be reversed.

Computer development depended on other revolutionary changes in associated fields, especially in transistors and integrated circuits. The World War II ENIAC had depended on some 18,000 valves, all of them bulky by modern standards. Each demanded considerable quantities of electricity, and became inconveniently hot in use. In 1948, William Bradford Shockley made several major discoveries with regard to semiconductors. Semiconductors have peculiar properties. Their resistance decreases with rising temperatures and the presence of certain impurities. They also allow an electric current to pass much more easily in one direction than another; hence they can act as 'rectifiers.' Shockley discovered that germanium crystals containing specific impurities not only served well as rectifiers, but also that they can be used to amplify currents. So operations that once had taken place inside the glass-enclosed vacuum of a valve were now made to occur inside a germanium crystal. Not only was the crystal minute in size compared with a valve; it also did its job without creating the heat of a valve and was virtually immune to shock and vibration.[33]

During the 1950s, a whole range of solid state devices came into use ("solid state" because the movements of the electric current took place in a solid crystal rather than the vacuum of a valve). Pioneers such as Shockley, John Bardeen, and Walter Brattain working at Bell Telephone Laboratories perfected the transistor which largely replaced the cumbersome valve. Thousands of transistors, each designed to perform a specific electronic function, could easily be incorporated into a computer. The integrated circuit later enabled designers to build a large number of transistors and their associated circuitry into a small chip cut from a thin wafer of silicon. Computer development accelerated with the discovery of small, integrated circuits (chips) in 1957 by Jack Kilby of Texas Instruments in Dallas. Kilby noted that integrated circuits could be produced in one single silicon chip or slice, that contained capacitors, distributed capacitor, resistors, and transistors. A year later, Robert Noyce, a physicist at Fairchild Semiconductors, independently came to the same conclusion and made it work. Both men received credit for inventing the integrated circuit and the second industrial revolution was underway. Yet neither man is known by the public at large.[34] "Starting in the 1960s, the number of circuit

[33]Clark, *Works of Man*, p. 287.
[34]See Samuel C. Florman "Anonymous heroes," *Technology Review*, January 1988, p. 20.

components that can be built into one chip has doubled almost every year, until now [1984] the number has approached a million – yet the cost of the chip, even in inflated dollars, has remained about the same."[35]

As Bardeen said in an interview at the time of Shockley's death in 1989, the transistor was one of the world's greatest inventions, and it changed all our lives.[36] Radios, television sets, and computers had shrunk in size and cost, while increasing in efficiency. All manner of new breakthroughs became possible – from "invisible" hearing aids to new electronic equipment light enough to be lifted into space by satellite. A whole range of industries came into being, with new industrial concentrations – from "Silicon Valley" in northern California, to "Silicon Glen" in Scotland.

These advances were paralleled in many other fields, for instance in chemistry and pharmacy. As mentioned earlier, US private manufacturers perfected the mass production of penicillin discovered in Britain by Alexander Fleming, Howard W. Florey, and Ernst Chain. Major advances occurred in the study of antibodies. (For instance, during the 1950s, MacFarlane Burnet and others showed that individual white blood cells can be primed by foreign substances to produce a specific type of antibody.) Chemists perfected their knowledge of the sulfa drugs; psychotropic agents (including LSD: first used by physicians, not drug addicts), insecticides such as DDT; birth control pills, and new vaccines (particularly the polio vaccine developed by Jonas E. Salk in 1954). New man-made substances revolutionized industry, including plastics and fibers tailor-made for specific tasks – artificial rubber, fiberglas, nylon, and a host of others. For technologists and scientists, the 1940s and 1950s were indeed a heroic age.

Between them, these scientific and technological advances created a new internationale of experts trans-Atlantic in orientation, as familiar with Harvard and Berkeley in the US as with Cambridge in England. In this world, the US predominated, but did not enjoy a monopoly in any one of the new disciplines. Indeed from the mid-1960s, its lead began to diminish. (For example, its share of foreign patents in other countries declined from 65 per cent in 1971 to 59 percent in 1981.) Even so, performance remained impressive. The US spent more on research than its competitors, and got better results per dollar of expenditure than comparable European institutions; Americans published more, and continued to receive more Nobel prizes; the GNP per employed civilian worker in the US (when properly adjusted for relative purchasing power), remained the world's highest.[37] Americans continued to play the primary role in diffusing the new technology world wide.

The Americans' remarkable part in new industries such as electronics mainly derived from efforts made by private enterprise – including firms such as IBM (computers), AT and T (telecommunications), and Boeing (commercial jet

[35] John Bardeen, "To a solid state," *Science 84,* November 1984, p. 145.
[36] *Peninsula Times Tribune* (Palo Alto), 14 August 1989, p. A6.
[37] Harvey Brooks, "National science policy and technological innovation," in Landau and Rosenberg, eds, *The Positive Sum Strategy*, pp. 139–45.

liners). The main, though not the only, exceptions were found in defense and space research. Private industry in turn depended on a partnership between a few powerful, innovative giant firms, and a vast body of smaller entrepreneurs who excelled in innovating and developing new markets.[38] Forecasts made earlier by socialists, predicting the demise of small entrepreneurs, turned out to be wholly mistaken. On the contrary, the free enterprise system possessed a remarkable capacity for self-regeneration. Technological innovation in turn, however, depended on a broad range of social skills that went far beyond scientific and technical brilliance – administrative and marketing abilities, a capacity for managing personnel, and so on. Contrary to popular assumptions, "the notion that innovation is initiated by research is wrong most of the time."[39]

[38] James D. Marver, "Trends in financing innovation," in Landau and Rosenberg, *The Positive Sum Strategy*, p. 473–8.
[39] Stephen J. Kline and Nathan Rosenberg, "An overview of innovation," in Landau and Rosenberg, *The Positive Sum Strategy*, p. 288.

14

The Arts

AN OVERVIEW

Few professional groups have gained more from the industrial revolution and the development of a market economy than musicians, writers, and artists. Three centuries ago, poets, dramatists, and musicians of the higher rank depended on the patronage of Church and aristocracy. In return for their favors, the great lords expected and received abject flattery. (The great Haydn was well treated at the princely court of the Esterhazy family. But as *Vize-kapellmeister* he still hardly ranked higher than a senior domestic.) Liberation from aristocratic thralldom and usually from material poverty came with the advent of the industrial revolution, a mass public, and a mass market.

During the nineteenth century, and even more during the twentieth, this market rapidly expanded. So did the number of and remuneration of musicians, writers, and artists, and of that under-appreciated army of music and art teachers, editors, secretaries, and marketing experts who provided essential support. The social position of writers, artists, and musicians greatly improved, as the descendants of Grub Street hacks became well-paid journalists and the grandsons of itinerant fiddlers were professional musicians.[1] At the same time, the cultural markets became more and more specialized. Writers, for example, now served an immense number of customers with the most varied tastes. Their readers desired above all to be entertained; many also wished for practical instruction in almost every subject under the sun. The demand for books, journals, and manuals greatly increased, and so did the demand for specialists of every description – editors, technical writers, speech writers, script writers for radio and television, and translators (the latter a crucial contingent given their importance in diplomacy, international organizations, and in the world-wide diffusion of science, technology, and popular culture).

The resultant mass production of printed matter, art, and music (and of

---

[1]For a study of one particular German-Jewish musical family, see Günter Wagner, *Die Musikerfamilie Ganz aus Weisenau Ein Beitrag zur Musikgeschichte der Juden am Mittelrhein*. Mainz, Schott's Söhne, 1974.

phonograph records) was linked in turn to improvements in recording, printing, photocopying, photography, and other means of duplication; the creation of new outlets for books and monographs (public libraries, book clubs, mail-order houses, etc.); new kinds of popular publications (magazines and comics); new entertainment industries (pop concerts and television); and growth of the advertising industry which both promoted books and records and gave employment to writers, musicians, and artists; the mass diffusion of do-it-yourself books, reproductions of great artists, popular encyclopedias, and other reference works; changes in the techniques of the book trade (for instance through the sale of magazines and paperbacks in supermarkets); and, above all, the worldwide growth of the publishing and record industries.[2]

Particularly noteworthy in this regard was the production of paperback books. Publications in paperbacks (printed on cheap paper, with pages uncut) had long been the norm in France, and Reclam's *Universal-Bibliothek* had provided the masses with cheap editions of the classics ever since the Kaiser's days. In Great Britain, Allen (later Sir Allen) Lane launched Penguin in 1935. Toward the end of the 1930s expansion on an even larger scale began in the US with the founding of Pocket Books Inc. By 1956 the total number of paperbacks issued by British publishers was estimated in hundreds of millions, and in the US was reckoned at 1,000,000,000. Book sales, especially paperback sales obtained an enormous boost from the growing markets of college students, graduates, and professors who accounted for much of the so-called quality trade. Publishing turned into a highly specialized business that included a huge array of enterprises – commercial, university, and government presses, each with specialized techniques and clientele.

GASTON GALLIMARD (1881–1975)

According to Karl Marx, ideology forms nothing but the superstructure of class interests. The bourgeoisie, like any other class, will throw up individual dissidents. But collectively, the bourgeois will always look after their friends, and strike at their enemies. The publishing business provides no support for this thesis. Left-wing authors of real or assumed ability had no more trouble in finding publishers than right-wing authors. There were entrepreneurs who published left-wing works from a sense of personal conviction – Victor Gollancz, a Labour Party supporter in Britain, Giangiacomo Feltrinelli, a communist sympathizer in Italy, were both heads of publishing empires. Others were more catholic in their tastes. One of the most important of such publishers was Gaston Gallimard, head of the most influential and prestigious publishing house in France.

Gallimard's catalogues look like collegiate reading lists. Everybody who was anybody in French literature published through Gallimard – left-wingers such as Louis Aragon and Jean-Paul Sartre, right-wingers like Louis-Ferdinand Celine and Jean Cocteau. Gallimard did not seek out authors; authors sought out Gallimard. As head of Editions Gallimard and Nouvelle revue française, Gallimard could make or break reputations;

---

[2]See entry under "Publishing" in *Everyman's Encyclopaedia*. London, Readers Union, J. M. Dent and Sons, 1961, v. 10, p. 310.

he was more powerful in French cultural life than any cabinet minister in French politics. He was adaptable. During the German occupation in World War II, Gallimard conformed to Nazi censorship, and rubbed shoulders with Nazi sophisticates. But he was also a master of political reinsurance. While taking care not to offend the new order, he closed his eyes when members of his staff maintained links with the French underground. After liberation, Céline, a collaborator, had to flee the country for fear of retribution. But Gallimard was defended by Aragon, Sartre, and André Malraux, men who had nothing in common except that their names all figured prominently in Gallimard's catalogues.

Gallimard's career also illustrated the dynastic principle that continued to prevail in many French firms. Gaston's son Claude (born 1914) entered his father's business in 1966, by which time Gaston was in his seventies. Claude became directeur général adjoint, *and then years later assumed the magisterial title of* président-directeur général. *Like his father, Claude had been educated at the prestigious Lycée Condorcet in Paris. Like his father, he was a member of the select Automobile Club. And like his father, he was driven by the desire, not only for profit, but for literary and social prestige; both men achieved power in their land. As Pierre Assouline, Gaston Gallimard's biographer commented (in* Gaston Gallimard: A Half Century of French Publishing*), "writers die, but publishers remain."*

The number of new titles printed went up in an astounding fashion. During the first half of the eighteenth century, the estimated number had been only 93 a year in Great Britain, and 600 during the first quarter of the nineteenth century. By 1963 the British figure had reached over 20,000, as compared to 19,000 in the US. Thereafter the US rapidly pulled ahead, with over 56,000 in 1966, as compared to nearly 29,000 in Britain, 24,000 in France, 23,000 in West Germany. Only a relatively small proportion of these titles, roughly one-fourth in the US, just over one-third in Great Britain, were "literature." Even so, the overall literary output was enormous.[3]

In theory, men of letters and artists should have rejoiced in the financial and social progress achieved by their profession. No longer were they reliant on patrons, and likely to be shown the door through having offended some proud earl, bishop, or baron. In practice, the literary intelligentsia's unease remained. Indeed, a good many intellectuals adopted that disdain for common workers or tradesmen that had once distinguished writers with high-born patrons. A shopkeeper could not possibly be a hero, nor could a clerk. As Sartre wrote, "whether he identifies himself with the Good and with divine Perfection, with the Beautiful or the True, a clerk is always on the side of the oppressor."[4] (Michael Collins, a real-life post-office clerk, and later a hero of the Irish independence struggle, would assuredly have smiled at the Frenchman's effrontery.) Sartre's value judgement nevertheless became part of an established literary convention throughout much of the Western world. To be an "outsider" aloof from bourgeois convention became a much desired honor.[5] The

[3]For a detailed breakdown see UNESCO *Statistical Handbook 1968, United Nations,* Paris, 1961, p. 759.

[4]Jean-Paul Sartre, "The 'Situation' in Literature," in Stanley Hoffman and Paschalis Kitromilides, eds, *Culture and Society in Contemporary Europe, A Casebook.* London, Allen and Unwin, 1981, p. 53.

[5]For a discussion, see Colin Wilson, *The Outsider.* Boston, Houghton and Mifflin, 1956.

common reader's taste supposedly stood beneath contempt – and not merely according to the literary intelligentsia. As the *World Almanac and Book of Facts* sadly noted in an annual review of US publications: "Best-sellers demonstrate anew that readers sought entertainment rather than literary merit. The suspense of criminal adventure and variations on themes of sexual behavior were popular. The 20 year battle against grammar, syntax, and academic writing, resulted in a spate of bad writing.[6]

The literary intellectuals' sense of unease had many sources. There were the existentialists, full of gloom. There were Marxists, quasi-Marxists, and pseudo-Marxists who contrasted the miseries of existing capitalist democracies with the imagined splendors of socialist societies present or future. There were many cultivated persons whose reaction toward the common reader varied from mild disdain to the stridency of Herman Marcuse and his friends, who despised "repressive tolerance" and opposed free speech for all whom they styled reactionaries.[7] But the dissatisfaction went much deeper. The old patron might have been capricious and disdainful, but he was at least a recognizable person, with quirks and foibles well understood. A mass public, by contrast, was immensely varied, and hard to know.

> *Since World War II, intellectual alienation in the United States has produced an adversarial culture that condemns American society root and branch. Its adherents see America as flawed and corrupt, imperialist and capitalistic. Bruno Bettelheim finds many of these people psychologically disturbed, estranged from the world they live in and angry at themselves, their parents and their society. Their alienation is projected against the American way of life. In general, radical critics have expected too much of Western, capitalist societies and believed naively in the perfectibility of man and society. Since they then set unrealistically high standards for the US (but not for the USSR) it is easy to attack its social system. (See Paul Hollander, "Alienation and adversary culture,"* Society, May-June 1988, pp. 41–8.

Not that intellectuals were bad at self-advertisement. As Macauley had scathingly observed a century and a half before, "we expect some reserve, some decent pride in our hatters and our bootmakers. But no artifice by which notoriety can be obtained is thought too abject for a man of letters."[8] Artists, musicians, and literary men and women nevertheless disliked a task that falls naturally to any other entrepreneur. Literary people moreover faced the difficult task of serving a great variety of markets. (In German-speaking Central Europe, for example, the classic division had been between the habitués of the coffee house and the regulars assembled at a *Stammtisch*, the special table set aside for them at an inn or public house.) The markets grew ever larger, more varied, and unpredictable, divided by ideology, taste, and social class. The

[6]*The World Almanac and Book of Facts.* New York, New World Telegram, 1959, p. 766.

[7]Robert Paul Wolff, Barrington Moore, and Herbert Marcuse, *A Critique of Pure Tolerance.* New York, Beacon Press, 1965.

[8]Thomas Babington Macaulay, "Mr Robert Montgomery," in *Critical, Historical, and Miscellaneous Essays, and Poems.* Chicago, Belfort, Clarke, and Co., 1887, v. 1, p. 518.

latter remained a subject of peculiar preoccupation in Great Britain, where even some left-wingers remained as hidebound as the most "true-blue" Tories. As a reviewer in the leftist *New Statesman* described a Cuban revolutionary, without a trace of irony or embarrassment, "although of working-class background ... he evidently showed early signs of a penetrating and reflective mind."[9]

The distinction between these many markets was of course by no means rigid. Some truly great literature retained an appeal that transcended social class, notably the Bible. There was also constant interchange between the various literary "cultures." For example, the vocabulary created by Sigmund Freud in part became the intellectual property of every reader or movie-goer; it is hard nowadays to imagine earlier ages unfamiliar with terms such as "repression," "super-ego" and "guilt complex." (Freud himself was turned by a popular movie into a sabre-swinging man of action in *The Nine Percent Solution*, a movie that would have pleased the Viennese master more than the best book review.) By contrast, words once known only to black musicians and street people – "rock and roll," "cool," "hip," "groovy," – went up in the world during the 1940s and 1950s. Certain forms of art or quasi-art – advertising, posters, cartoons, jazz, and the humorous movies made by the Marx brothers or Danny Kaye appealed to poor and rich alike. But individual authors rarely commanded a national appeal. At the end of the nineteenth century, Benito Pérez Galdos in Spain, Victor Hugo in France, Dostoevsky in Russia had still received public burials attended by enormous crowds drawn from every social class.[10] In the second part of the twentieth century such mass demonstrations of grief over the death of a writer as a national figure became the exception. (Sartre's public funeral in Paris was perhaps the last such occasion.) By and large, the various literary and artistic markets followed broad class divisions ably classified by Herbert J. Gans, an American sociologist.[11] These division were not of course rigid. An admirer of Keats's poetry might also enjoy reading comics; a Bach lover might also be a Beatles *aficionado*. But Gans's categories do have a descriptive value.

"High culture" was produced for restricted audiences, the well-educated in a formal sense; the culture of "serious" musicians, artists, and writers. This culture differed from all others in that its users widely accepted the standards and perspectives of the creators. The makers of high culture prided themselves on their small but discerning public; their products were commonly subsidized through public agencies, foundations, universities, private benefactors, or commercial businesses willing to take losses for reasons of prestige. (This form of subvention largely replaced the subsidy usually paid in former times to impecunious lecturers, *Privatdozenten*, rabbinical scholars, and men of letters by wealthy fathers-in-law.) Practitioners of high culture widely disliked the

[9]Mervyn Jones, "Power and pistols," *New Statesman*, 19 October 1984, p. 30.

[10]C. P. Snow, *The Realists: Eight Portraits*. New York, Colliers, 1987, p. 255.

[11]Herbert J. Gans, *Popular Culture and High Culture: An Analysis and Evaluation of Taste*. New York, Basic Books, 1974.

world of commerce and industry that supposedly turned the intellectual into an "accomplice of a large industrial complex which depends for its survival on him, as he depends on it for his own."[12] Ordinary men and women, especially members of oppressed ethnic minorities, were commonly assumed to lead meaningless lives and to perform meaningless labor, in a condition of helpless alienation. This supposition had no foundation in facts; nevertheless the common man's assumed alienation widely became part of the "high culture's" accepted orthodoxy.[13] Heirs to the romantic movement, the practitioners of high culture were apt to glorify the artist as rebel and role model.

Modernism was the most influential cultural movement among intellectuals before and after World War II. It loved novelty, fads, and new fashions in art and literature. But it was destructive of Western values, traditions, and artistic forms; in fact many critics will argue it was destructive of literature and art as such (George Lukács). Rather than concern itself with shared cultural values, morals, and beliefs, modernism glorified the individual, the unique, and the subjective and personal. Modernism left a number of its followers confused and at war with society, as Roland Strombley has noted.[14]

The ordinary literate public could no longer understand the modernist artist musician or writer. Only the avant-garde could understand (or claim to understand) the modernists. While the intelligentsia wanted the new and the different, preferred the pessimistic to the optimistic, the individual to the shared view, the general public rejected modernism and became disenchanted and confused. Most listeners, for example, could not decide whether atonal music was ridiculous or significant – there was no question, in our view, about it being unpleasant to listen to. Then modernism, having destroyed the comprehensibility of Western culture, took as its theme that men were unable to communicate and all things were relative and fragmented. Even science was attacked. Some braver intellectuals counter-attacked and asserted that there must be clear, shared standards, not relativism and subjectivism; that Western man had evolved ethical values and artistic standards that were universal and comprehended by most literate people.

The majority of practitioners of high culture were cultural relativists, having learned from Marx that supposedly absolute values were linked to the material interests of specific social classes, and from Freud that deeply held moral convictions might merely reflect drives sprung from an opaque unconsciousness. The complexities of modern physics contributed to what John

---

[12]Hans Magnus Enzenberger, "The industrialization of the mind," in Hoffman and Kitromilides, *Culture and Society,* p. 104.

[13]See, for instance, L. H. Gann and Peter Duignan, *The Hispanics in the United States: A History.* Boulder, Col., Westview Press, 1986, pp. 320–5. A market survey published in 1981 showed that 59 percent of Hispanic respondents disagreed with the statement "I don't get much pleasure from my work; work is just what I do to earn a living." Only 28 percent of respondents agreed with the statement "Many people are puzzled by the changing values in this country." Respondents overwhelmingly wanted to make their way in the world and acquire material wealth.

[14]See Roland N. Strombley, *After Everything: Western Intellectual History Since 1945.* New York, St Martin's Press, *passim.*

Archibald Wheeler, one of Niels Bohr's collaborators, had called an "observer-created universe, in which things supposedly 'exist' only after they have been seen or measured."[15] High culture had other characteristics: widespread disdain for the business world, for the bourgeoisie and – above all – the petty bourgeoisie, a contempt adopted by avant-garde intellectuals from the gentry and would-be gentry of former times. Anti-bourgeois prejudice mingled with feelings of disorientation and disintegration, a conviction that "things fall apart, the center cannot hold." The twentieth century had seen the growth among many intellectuals of scepticism, narcissism, irrationalism, and relativism. Benedetto Croce, an Italian philosopher of history, had sought to overcome scepticism and provide a framework for "responsible humanism" through historicism. He constructed a new kind of liberalism and offered a system of truth and value in a world of relativism and totalitarian systems.[16] But his impact was limited.

Writers such as Ernest Hemingway tried to simplify English prose style; in our opinion, they paid for their endeavor by a curious flatness, a loss of those rhetorical qualities prized by the Victorians. Authors such as Heinrich Böll were concerned with reflection rather than action. Leading academic modernist poets after 1950 seem to have lost the traditional voice of poetry – love and simplicity were largely dismissed, as were politics and a social sense, or a commitment to anything other than poetry itself. American poetry acquired more sophistication, but suffered from a note of social isolation, philosophical unease, and anger. Lacking the cleverness and neatness of British poetry, American verse nevertheless seemed to some critics to speak louder, to be more exciting. However, most of those responsible for high culture looked askance at harmony and melody in music and plots in novels. "Rocking horse" rhythm widely fell into disrepute; this is one of the reasons why schoolchildren ceased to learn verses by heart, as their forebears had done. Practitioners of high culture tended to be introspective, and much preoccupied with writing about one another (Walter Benjamin, Sartre, Georg Lukács, Michel Crozier, and many others). They seemed to believe that quality went with exclusiveness, failing to realize that quality or its opposite may inhere in any art form.

"Upper-middle" culture, by contrast, appealed to a much wider public, including the college-educated professionals, executives, and managers. This clientele prized art of a less abstract and experimental kind. Fiction such as the stories by Herman Wouk, Nevil Shute or J. B. Priestley stressed plots more than mood. Their fictional heroes were more concerned with winning a struggle with other men or nature, rather than with their own alienation. Upper-middle readers also had a taste for popular history, written by non-academics such as Winston Churchill. Upper-middle almost imperceptibly merged into "lower-middle" culture, which mainly appealed to the members

---

[15]Michael Riordan, *The Hunting of the Quark: A True Story of Modern Physics.* New York, Simon and Schuster, 1987, p. 40.

[16]See David D. Roberts, *Benedetto Croce and the Uses of Historicism.* Berkeley, Cal., University of California Press, 1987.

of lower-status professions such as accountancy and other white-collar occupations. This public was interested in stories whose heroes were ordinary people (as in the best-selling novels of Arthur Hailey) and preferred plots that accepted the validity of traditional virtues, religion, and romantic love. The size of this public was great, making possible the mass circulation of *Life, Reader's Digest, Cosmopolitan,* and similar magazines.

"Low" culture was enjoyed mainly, though by no means entirely, by the young and by people with little formal education. This public liked action, melodrama, and morality plays. Clark Gable, Kirk Douglas, Gary Cooper, and John Wayne were among their screen heroes; Milton Berle, Lucille Ball, Bob Hope, and Red Skelton among their most popular TV comedy artists. Low culture also provided a mass public for comics, and for a new professional group whose cultural history as yet remains to be written – the journalist-counsellors, (known as "agony aunts" in the UK). These ladies ("Dear Abby") gave sensible advice for readers facing those real-life moral problems that many churchmen began to shun. Such counsellors made their appearance even in the Third World. ("Tell me, Josephine," wrote a young woman to Dear Abby's equivalent in Zambia, "I have two boyfriends, both miners. One is a truly kind man. The other is marvellous at loving. Whom should I marry?" – "Wed the kind man [went the answer] and teach him how to be marvellous at loving.")[17]

Low culture, all the world over, was strongly influenced by American example through films, TV, jazz, records, musicals, clothing, toys, cartoons, and advertising. Materialism, the lust for consumer goods thought to be peculiar to Americans, also spurred Europe's recovery and made possible the enormous rise in the material well-being of most Europeans.

These cultural categories were by no means mutually exclusive. There was constant interchange between them; audiences and readership fluctuated; no culture consumer ever fitted neatly into a single pattern. For example, many of Churchill's great oratorical phrases passed into ordinary speech, and many intellectuals liked to read detective stories and comics, surreptitiously or otherwise. Crime, love, and war – the three great epic themes from time immemorial – continued to attract readers and viewers from all educational backgrounds. Jazz and blues had made their impact in the 1920s and continued their hold on popular culture in the US and in Western Europe. After 1955 rock and roll began to attract the young from every social class. The cultural market place, so derided by Marcuse and others, continued to provide almost infinite choice. The failures of Western artists, whatever they were, did not derive from lack of opportunity.

Intellectual and cultural life thrived after the war. New libraries, exhibition halls, art galleries, and museums were built. Universities expanded at an extraordinary rate with the coming of mass college education. (To give one example, the US had fewer than 1,000 colleges before 1945; by 1985 there were over 3,100.) Indeed universities took an increasingly important part in

---

[17]Barbara Hall, ed., *Tell me, Josephine.* New York, Simon and Schuster, 1964.

the nation's intellectual and artistic life, as independent artists and writers were appointed as salaried artists or poets "in residence." Political controversies, once debated in independent journals, were transferred to the senior common room of major colleges. Exhibitions, music festivals, scholarly conferences all increased international exchanges. And although national style continued there did develop an international style in cultural affairs. European intellectuals were freed from the pall of Nazism and Fascism and responded with a great creativity. Transactions across the Atlantic increased enormously not only in government relationships (NATO, USAID, USIS), but also individual relationships (student and scholar exchanges), tourism, and business.

The cultural reconstruction of Europe had actually begun during the resistance to Fascism and (except for the existentialists) produced a literature of hope and a call for the revival of humanist traditions in Western civilization. For example, the Italian Ignazio Silone (*Bread and Wine,* 1939) and Carlo Levi (*Christ Stopped at Eboli,* 1947) dealt with the Fascists' exploitation of the peasants in the south of Italy. François Mauriac, a committed Catholic of sardonic disposition, a giant on the French literary scene, already a sexagenarian at the end of the war, further added to his reputation. (The first volume of his *Cahiers noirs* had been published underground during the occupation.) Writers who had directly come out of the resistance were Jean Bruller "Vercors" (*The Silence of the Sea*) and Algerian-born Albert Camus (*The Stranger,* 1942 and *The Plague,* 1947). In Italy, Eduardo de Felippo, Ugo Betti, and Diego Fabbri called for a renewal of values and honesty. The end of Nazism and Fascism meant for many liberation and a period of creativity seldom matched in world history. Many intellectuals, of course, especially the existentialists, refused to admit any progress in the face of capitalism, and the dread of nuclear warfare hanging over society. Yet there was a renaissance within the Atlantic Community which contrasted with a dark age for the countries that fell under communist control.[18]

Europe's cultural recovery was amazing. War had devastated the intellectual class and its high culture. Thousands of Europe's leading scholars and artists had emigrated during the 1930s, and many left after the war. These refugees helped to shift the heart of intellectual and artistic life to the United States. New York and, to a lesser extent, Los Angeles, became the main centers of expatriate Weimer culture. One of the most unusual escape plans to get Jewish intellectuals out of Europe was mounted in New York. Varian Fry, an American, was sent to Vichy, in France, to organize the program. One of its chief agents, an academic turned wartime document forger and black marketeer *par excellence* was "Albert Hermant" (his real name was Albert Hirschman, a German, later a famous economist in the US). Hermant operated from Marseilles and brought out a distinguished group of luminaries: Hannah Arendt, André Breton, Marc Chagall, Marcel Duchamp, Max Ernst, Jacques Lipschitz,

[18]See H. Stuart Hughes, *Contemporary Europe: A History.* Englewood Cliffs, NJ, Prentice-Hall, 1961, pp. 407–14.

and Heinrich Mann. Hirschman not only saved artists but also smuggled out socialist and liberal political leaders.[19]

> *For many intellectuals, the postwar era was an age of anxiety. W. H. Auden saw depravity in all; Graham Green proclaimed the total corruption of mankind, while Samuel Beckett's plays sought to show man's inability to communicate at all. Intellectuals, especially on the non-communist left, were frustrated and disenchanted; they feared atomic warfare and political catastrophe. In contrast, ordinary people, while sober and realistic about the problems that had to be overcome, once the Marshall Plan started to make Europe more productive, became more hopeful. They were, on the whole, satisfied with the material well-being they enjoyed, the increased opportunities in education for their children and the promise of peace in Europe behind the American nuclear shield and NATO. In fact, for most Americans and Europeans the 1950s were one of the best decades in history.*

The intellectual immigrants to the US also comprised a large number of British people, practitioners of high and middle, as well as low culture. Thousands of British expatriate artists, performers, and scholars have contributed since the 1920s to cross-cultural collaboration with the US in a variety of arts. Movie stars, the most popular group of all, included British-born Charlie Chaplin, Cary Grant, Boris Karloff, David Niven, Michael Caine, Michael York, and the great movie director Alfred Hitchcock. The invasion of British popular musicians began with George Shearing, followed by the Beatles, the Rolling Stones, and the Kinks, and later by Boy George, and others.

New York replaced Paris and Berlin as the Western world's main art and literary center, for Hitler's coming to power had caused many German artists to flee: Max Beckmann, Max Ernst, Lyonel Feiniger, George Grosz, Raoul Hausmann, Wassily Kandinsky, Oskar Kokoschka, Kurt Schwitters, and the Swiss Paul Klee who had been living in Germany and died in 1940. Art, architecture, music, both popular and classical, films and TV became the leading fields of US cultural dominance. Artists of all kinds moved freely between the US and Western Europe, and established a pattern of reciprocal relationships and influences within the Atlantic Community, and the US came to play a major part in both popular and elite culture. The worldwide counter-culture of the 1960s had its beginnings in the US during the late 1950s – complete with blue jeans, rock and roll, James Dean, Marlon Brando, irreverence, skepticism, *Mad* magazine, and drugs. It was known as the "Beat generation."

The reconstruction of Europe and the building boom in the US called forth a group of brilliant architects and builders, mainly Americans or refugees living in the US. Engineering, in which the US dominated, became more important, as did design. Italians excelled in industrial design and the use of reinforced concrete (especially Piero Luigi Nervi), but the Americans and British were almost as good in prefabricated building and product design.

---

[19]See Robert Kuttner's essay on Hirschman in *The New Republic*, 23 November, 1987, p. 48.

World War II had a revolutionary effect on design and furniture, building materials, and "prefab" production methods. It was wartime research which developed plastic, strong new adhesives, and nylon. The mass production of ships, aircraft, houses, in the US and Britain, paved the way for peacetime mass production of schools and other buildings, furniture, TVs, cars, and new roads. Industrial design, advances in chemistry, engineering, and manufacturing during the war created new opportunities in Europe and the US in housing, urban and suburban development, road building. Good new designing in the US, particularly of household and electrical items, rapidly spread throughout the Atlantic Community. The need to rebuild the means of transport, cities, houses, and schools, forced the change to inexpensive, quick construction. An international style developed in public housing (large blocks, regular, monotonous, and depersonalizing), and in uniform office blocks made of prefabricated, reinforced concrete slabs, glass, or plastic cinder blocks.

> *Product design first became a profession in the United States during the 1930s. Men such as Henry Dreyfus, Raymond Loewy, and Walter Teague dominated the field, and turned out classic designs like the Cold Spot refrigerator of Sears Roebuck and Co., and the Brownie camera. After World War II American leadership continued, but with increasing competition from the Italians and the Japanese from the 1970s onward.*

American architecture came of age in the 1950s, in a movement directed by Europeans (Walter Gropius, Ludwig Mies van der Rohe, Le Corbusier) and the native-born (Eero Saarinen, Paul Rudolph, and the firm of Skidmore, Owings, and Merrill). Their designs, especially of high-rise office buildings, came to dominate world architecture. In postwar Europe Le Corbusier was the dominant architect. In Great Britain rough concrete became the most popular material, but produced heavy depressing buildings. In the US, Mies van der Rohe (more influential than Le Corbusier) created the steel-framed, glass-walled apartments and office towers for the urban building boom. The style soon spread to Europe. The original *Bauhaus* architects in the Weimar Republic had stressed quality and honesty in design. But all too often, their heirs turned out dull, gloomy buildings that disfigured cities throughout the Western world – repetitive, unimaginative, with leaking roofs and air conditioning of poor design, caging workers in tiny, plain cubicles where they either roasted or froze behind glass walls. Such was the charge made by Tom Wolfe in *From Bauhaus to Our House* (1981).

> *Since the 1920s the Germans had been in the vanguard of architecture and design. The Bauhaus School of Design members fled from Dessau to the US and Britain when Hitler attacked them as socialists and internationalists in 1933. Abroad, the Bauhaus school developed the cult of design modernism – that is that form must follow function – a style that, in our opinion, impoverished architecture for the next 40 years or so. Le Corbusier, Mies van der Rohe, and Walter Gropius brought modernism to the United States, where Philip Johnson became its leading practitioner until the 1980s when he led the way to post-modernist architecture.*

LITERATURE AND THE THEATER

Literature

Western literature of the postwar era was both copious and diverse, as noted in a monumental reference work by Martin Seymour-Smith: *New Guide to Modern World Literature.*[20] High Culture, in general, as we have said, displayed a somber mood; writers and artists widely saw the world reduced to moral squalor as a result of Fascism. A future historian using as his or her only source the literature of high culture produced during the middle of the twentieth century would remain unaware that the three postwar decades were years of striking economic recovery, declining poverty, and rising living standards, a period of political reconciliation and democratic consolidation in Western Europe – a time of heroic endeavor and of unpredicted success.

Some poets, novelists, and dramatists preferred darker themes – not without justification. Continental Europeans had recently undergone a terrible war, hunger, persecution, a holocaust, and foreign occupation. Nazi rule had struck like a plague; the image of pestilence figured largely in literature. In Alberto Moravia's novel *The Epidemic* (*L'Epedemia*, 1941) or Albert Camus's *The Plague* (*La Peste,* 1947) whole societies are perverted by disease. These writers were anything but poseurs, their hopelessness was authentic – far more so than the literary disillusionment of the early twentieth century had been. It was not surprising that Existentialism became the most celebrated philosophy among Western intellectuals after World War II. Existentialists at times blended their protest against man's imperfection and their sense of tragedy with ill-concealed snobbery. They felt convinced that the world held neither divine law nor salvation; in their view, man stands alone in a featureless, measureless void. Man nevertheless has freedom of action; his actions can influence other human beings – an insight borne out by the resistance movements in World War II. Existentialists were not necessarily unbelievers. According to Sartre an Existentialist might be a Christian just as well as an atheist. But in practice, Existentialism was full of "dread, despair and death."

Novels dominated the literary scene; "engaged literature," realism or neo-realism infused most writing. The themes centered on the poor and the oppressed, the harsh world of war and class-ridden society. In France, André Gide and Camus were pre-eminent. In the US, J. D. Salinger's *The Catcher in the Rye* (1951) and Ralph Ellison's *Invisible Man,* (1952), were acclaimed. Ernest Hemingway, a favorite American author, won a Nobel prize in 1954 with his *The Old Man and the Sea.* Norman Mailer proclaimed the pointlessness of war to Americans in his first (and some would say his only good) novel *The Naked and the Dead* (1948). In Britain, Evelyn Waugh's trilogy of the 1950s: *Men at Arms, Officers and Gentlemen,* and *Unconditional Surrender* blended satire, British preoccupation with social class, and a black sense of incongruity.

American literature gained international status. The United States had begun

---

[20]Martin Seymour-Smith, *The New Guide to Modern World Literature.* New York, Peter Bedrick Books, 1985.

American literature gained international status. The United States had begun as a cultural dependency of Great Britain and Europe; many nineteenth-century Americans had tended to look upon their own literature as an inferior cousin of British literature. "The Americans as a whole were slow to recognize their own native geniuses" yet "American self-discovery developed into a major world literature, and New York in time replaced London as the cultural capital of the English-speaking world."[21] American literature benefited from a variety of regional and ethnic strains (including British, Irish, Jewish, black, German, Hispanic, and southern). Americans were less concerned with social class than the British; they lacked the preoccupation of Germans, Italians, and Frenchmen with the Nazi and Fascist legacies. Americans prized pragmatism, experimentation, and social criticism. After World War II, American literature at last received recognition – symbolized by the award of Nobel prizes for their earlier work to William Faulkner (1949), Ernest Hemingway (1954), and John Steinbeck (1962).

The 1950s witnessed the emergence of a new literary generation including many 'ethnic" writers whose rise to literary fame paralleled "ethnic succession" in other spheres of American life. These included J. P. Donleavy whose satirical novel *The Ginger Man* (1955) was set in Dublin, in a world of apparent insanity. Saul Bellow's heroes, by contrast, were generally Jewish intellectuals struggling to find a place for themselves in urban America. Ralph Ellison (in *Invisible Man*) dealt with the travail of black America as did Richard Wright, author of classics such as *Black Boy* (an autobiography, 1945), and James Baldwin (*Go Tell It on the Mountains*, 1953). Vladimir Nobokov, a Russian exile, made his name with *Lolita* (1955), a book popular for its hero's erotic obsession with a young girl. In addition, there was, from the late 1950s, among the avant garde a new preoccupation with anarchic violence. Nazi intellectuals and their predecessors had glorified an assorted crew of old-time pirates, mercenaries (*Landsknechte*), and other Germanic cut-throats. In the US some writers turned instead for their inspiration to the black *lumpenproletariat* in modern US cities (for instance, Norman Mailer, *The White Negro*, 1957). By literary sleight-of-hand, the streetwise hipster turned into a David ready to slay Goliath of the philistines. The cult of the violent outsider came into full flower during the 1960s, complete with worship of self-fulfilment, self-advertisement, and self-pity that Mailer and others helped to popularize. The Spartan virtues were not for them.

European writers meanwhile were still trying either to come to terms with the grim legacy of Nazism and Fascism, or to forget the war and collaboration. They could not forget. Everywhere people wanted to tell *their* story. Realism and neo-realism dominated literature and films. Rebirth ideologies dominated – there was little looking back to the inglorious Fascist pasts. The terms varied according to language but basically meant a rebirth: *Kahlschlag* in German, *renaissance* in French, *rinascita* in Italian, all grew to mean reconstruction. Reconstruction meant not just the rebuilding of Europe's cities and roads, but

[21]Ibid., p. 25.

also its political and cultural unity. The United States was seen as a liberating force by the common people, though some politicians and intellectuals were concerned about the dangers of nuclear war. There were also fears that US imperialistic capitalism would take over Europe's empires and that national identities would be submerged by Americanization. Some intellectuals, in particular, railed against Americanization, but many ordinary Europeans welcomed it.

German writers were now repelled by the heroic Nazi epithets of icy-cold (*eiskalt*) and steely-hard (*stahlhart*). There was almost a complete cessation of those lugubrious tracts that used to juxtapose decadent Western *Zivilisation* to creative German *Kultur*. Some even questioned whether poetry should, or could, still be written after the horrors of Auschwitz – forgetting the shattering verses composed by Jeremiah in what had been, for ancient Judaea, an age of total war and unimagined horror. German writers now stressed the falsity of Nazi values, and the sufferings of human beings under extreme stress. Especially noteworthy were Ernest Wiechert's *The Forest of the Dead* (1940), and Eugen Kogon's *The Theory and Practice of Hell* (1950). Authors such as Theodor Plivier stressed war's terrors. Heinrich Böll emphasized its pointlessness. So, in popular form, did Hans Helmut Kirst, whose novels reached an enormous public. Some German writers like Günther Grass, Heinrich Böll, Hans Magnus Enzensberger, and Martin Walser, sought to play a political role through their work, and felt writers in other countries should follow their lead.[22] Like-minded young men joined in the influential *Gruppe 47*, whose members later criticized the philistinism, the materialism, the careerism, and the moral insensitivity associated in their minds with the German Federal Republic and the *Wirtschaftswunder*. But the pioneers of *Gruppe 47* themselves became part of a new, left-leaning literary establishment, firmly entrenched in the publishing industry, television, and radio.

There was a revival too, of German writers who had gained fame during the Weimar Republic, and thereafter gone into either "internal" or foreign exile. It was admittedly a selective renaissance. For instance, Ricarda Huch, a liberal Catholic, a gifted historian and novelist, and personally a most courageous woman, never regained the fame that was her due. But others did, including Stefan Zweig (posthumously, as he had committed suicide), Lion Feuchtwanger (an erstwhile Stalinist who wisely chose to go to the US), Bertold Brecht (who went back to East Berlin), and Alfred Döblin (who returned to Germany as an officer in the French army). The writers of the immediate postwar period were naturally preoccupied with Nazism, its political and psychological mainsprings, and its effects. Nazism was particularly hard to confront for German intellectuals, given the extent to which it had appealed to the educated classes, especially students. As a group, students had been the

[22]See K. Stuart Parkes, *Writers and Politics in West Germany*. New York, St Martin's Press, 1986. Ralf Schnell, *Die Literatur des Bundesrepublik, Autoren, Geschichte, Literaturbetrieb*. Stuttgart, J. B. Metzlersche Verlagsbuchhandlung, 1986.

most pro-Nazi in Weimar Germany, and had formed the most anti-semitic social set in the Wilhelminian Reich; a Jew then would have been much more likely to have been excluded from a student association than from a *Stammtisch* (a table reserved for a certain group of intimates, say, in a coffee-house), a glee club, an athletics league, or a veterans' lodge.[23] Not that German intellectuals were unique in this respect. As the Franco-Jewish intellectual Bernard Henri Levy was later to point out, proto-Fascist forms of racism had widely appealed to French men of letters; he even called it "the French ideology."[24] Yet the European student estate subsequently managed to make out a special claim to anti-Fascist credentials in a manner that would have astonished even Felix Krull, the con-man of a celebrated novel by Thomas Mann (*The Confessions of Felix Krull, Confidence Man*, translated 1955).

Works dealing with Nazism in a critical fashion could only be produced during the era of the Third Reich by Germans living in internal or external exile, or in jail. It was only after the war ended that such literature came to be widely known in Germany. (In this respect, German literature played a particularly important part, German being the only language widely spoken on both sides of the Iron Curtain.) One of the most striking German poets of the twentieth century was Albrecht Haushofer (a member of the resistance executed just before the war ended). His *Moabiter Sonette* written in jail on toilet paper and smuggled out by a friend, stands out as a masterpiece of German literature. Another writer, once proscribed, was Nelly Sachs (Nobel laureate of 1965), whose work tried to interpret the Jewish fate in religious terms, perceiving in the wandering Jews representatives of all mankind's tragic fate. Günter Grass (*The Tin Drum*, 1957) tried to mix satire with surrealism, while one of the most popular books of the postwar period was by a former Free Corps fighter Ernst Von Salomon, *The Questionnaire* (1951), which dealt smugly with "the farce of denazification."[25]

The greatest German writer of the century was Thomas Mann. Mann's work was marked by a profoundly Germanic ambivalence – he suffered from love–hatred concerning his own class, the *Bildungsbürgertum* (the formally well-educated bourgeoisie) concerning his status as an honored but uprooted émigré and, above all, concerning his native Germany. His postwar work included *Doctor Faustus: The Life of the German Composer Adrian Leverkuehn as Told by a Friend* (translated into English 1949). Mann was a pessimist, profoundly concerned with decadence. His *Doctor Faustus* attempted to bring up to date the Faust legend, with its self-destructive diabolical pact that mirrored Germany's surrender to Hitler. One of the greatest writers of his generation, Mann was lionized in the US where he completed his great series of novels on the Biblical

---

[23]For student anti-semitism, see for instance, Nobert Kampe, "Jews and anti-semites at universities in Imperial Germany ..." *Leo Baeck Institute Year Book*. London, Secker and Warburg, 1987, v. 32, pp. 43–101.

[24]Cited in Paul Johnson, *Modern Times: The World From the Twenties to the Eighties*. New York, Harper and Row, 1983, p. 576.

[25]Hughes, *Contemporary Europe*, p. 412.

theme concerning Joseph and his brothers. But Mann never liked the US. He had few dealings with real-life Americans, not even German-Americans, a group whose successful adaptation to a democratic culture might have been of interest to a writer so preoccupied with the German condition. Mann's disdain for the US sprang from contempt for its mass culture, fear of McCarthyism, and a regret for the old anti-Fascist days, when the enemy had been clearly defined and when (one should add) the expatriate writers had depended for their lives on the country that had given them shelter. On leaving the US in 1953, Mann denounced what he called the Americans' barbarous infantilism, and the deficiencies of a land fit for grabbers, fools, and gangsters.

Mann's views were widely shared by numerous intellectuals, including sociologists such as Marcuse, who stayed in the US, and Theodor W. Adorno and Max Horkheimer, who returned to West Germany where they were showered with honors, but continued to feel as alienated as they had in the US. Their dislike was not of course shared by the bulk of expatriate intellectuals in the US – certainly not by giants such as Sir Karl Popper (one of the foremost political philosphers of the twentieth century) or Max Weinreich (the world's leading Yiddish literary scholar). Nor was it shared by the great mass of ordinary German and Austrian refugees. They had read neither Marx nor Marcuse, and they prized the land of their adoption, and its values. (In fact, the most successful refugee scholars in the fields of sociology, literary studies, and history, mainly derived from the second generation trained at American and British universities. These included, among others, Peter Gay, Hannah Green, Peter Paret, George Mosse, Werner Angress, and Henry Pachter in the US; Peter Ganz and Sir Geoffrey Elton in Britain – all of them conservatives by Horkheimer's or Marcuse's standards.)

Mann, like so many other expatriates was determined to be fair to the Soviet Union – despite the fact that some 70 percent of the German-speaking intellectuals who had taken refuge there during the Stalin era had been arrested, and many of them had perished.[26] Mann's use of a double standard regarding Stalin's Soviet Union on the one hand and Truman's US on the other, persisted among many European and American intellectuals – and was sharply commented on by critics such as Sidney Hook and Arnold Beichman. Indeed Miklos Haraszti's strictures concerning the role of fellow intellectuals in his native Hungary had wider relevance. "After World War II, writers and artists became the builders of a directed culture because of their prior commitment to a planned society."[27] Not much duress was needed to bring them into line because of their commitment to a new order that promised to end both the intellectual's moral alienation and the workers' physical misery. The list of

[26] Anthony Heilbutt, *Exiled in Paradise: German Refugee Artists and Intellectuals in America from the 1930s to the Present.* New York, Viking, 1983. For a critical review see Peter Shaw, "Critics of society," *Commentary,* December 1983, pp. 88–92. For the standard work on the German intellectuals in the Soviet Union see David Pike, *German Writers in Soviet Exile 1933–1945.* Chapel Hill, University of North Carolina Press, 1982, p. 357. See also H. Stuart Hughes, *The Sea Change: The Migration of Social Thought, 1930–1965.* New York, Harper and Row, 1975.

[27] Miklos Haraszti, "The seduction of censorship," *The New Republic,* 25 November 1987, p. 33.

pro-communist or Marxist intellectuals was equally long in Western Europe, especially in France, and also in Latin America.[28] (Pablo Neruda, the Chilean Nobel laureate, almost matched in his sycophancy of Stalin the East German court poet Johannes Becher. Becher, however, outdid Neruda in poor taste by honoring the Soviet dictator in verse, rhyming *Bodensee* (Lake Constance) with *Reh* (deer), and *Monument* with *Student.*)

At the same time, the communist challenge aroused committed literary opposition. There was a new literature of Soviet prison-camp experience, including Helmut Gollwitzer, (*Und führe wohin du nicht willst. Bericht einer Gefangenschaft*), and Menachem Begin (*White Nights*) which presaged Solzhenitsyn's *One Day in the Life of Ivan Denisovich*, and *The Gulag Archipelago*. Raymond Aron, the very model of a French literary mandarin, one of the leading philosophers, sociologists, and literary critics in his country, published *The Opium of the Intellectuals* (English translation 1957). This was a brilliant critique of Marxists and *marxisants* that still deserves to be read today. Many disappointed ex-communists entered the lists, including Arthur Koestler, Camus, and Ignazio Silone. Even more important was the British writer George Orwell. Orwell, though a Labour supporter, disliked what he called the "pansy left" for their uncritical admiration of the Soviet Union, intellectual snobbery, and lack of patriotism. Orwell's masterpieces, *Animal Farm* (1945) and *Nineteen Eighty-Four* (1949) reflect his hatred of tyranny of any kind – Nazi or Soviet. The books also were a prophetic warning in that Orwell foresaw the evils of state control and a variety of new techniques of imposing it. According to Orwell, the ultimate danger to human freedom does not come from the reactionary right, but from the new aristocracy of ideologues, bureaucrats, scientists, publicity managers, sociologists, teachers, journalists, and politicians determined to reshape humanity in their own unpleasant image.

Orwell's writing was not without flaws. But *Nineteen Eighty-Four*, for example, is full of a fury that may have helped the general public to resist totalitarian manipulation – as evidenced later by the widespread disillusionment with Marxism-Leninism in the Soviet Union, and even more so in Eastern Europe, where the regnant philosophy produced popular unrest. Orwell's powerful pen and intellectual courage made him one of the most distinguished writers of the century though scorned by leftist intellectuals.[29] (By the early 1980s, 12,000,000 copies had been sold of *Nineteen Eighty-Four*.) Orwell coined new phrases that passed into popular speech such as "Big Brother," "doublethink" "proles," and "Thought Police."

There were also the war historians, both participants and professionals. Some of them wrote extremely well, dealing with the real world where decision counted, and where victory or defeat would shape the fate of nations. War historians, especially those involved in command, such as Dwight D. Eisen-

---

[28]David Caute, *Communism and the French Intellectuals: 1914–1960*. London, Macmillan, 1964.
[29]Peter Stansky and William Abrahams, *Orwell: The Transformation*. New York, Knopf, 1980, and *The Unknown Orwell*. New York, Knopf, 1972. George Woodcock, *The Crystal Spirit: A Study of George Orwell*. New York, Schocken, 1984.

hower (*Crusade in Europe*, 1948) and Bernard L. Montgomery (*Normandy and the Baltic*, 1948) commanded a huge readership. As regards appeal and skill, Winston Churchill, a brilliant amateur historian, undoubtedly stood at the top of the list with his monumental six volumes on World War II, with their short, forceful titles such as *Their Finest Hour, Triumph and Tragedy*. Indeed Churchill was perhaps the last of the great statesman-writers like Bismarck, Disraeli, Gladstone, Theodore Roosevelt, Woodrow Wilson, and de Gaulle. All too many public men later preferred to give employment to a new kind of professional, the ghost writer (who in turn might hire sub-ghosts), for the task of polishing the named author's reputation.

A substantial number of war historians of the period also deserve to be mentioned as literary artists with a wide readership. They include B. H. Liddell Hart, Correlli Barnett, John Keegan, Hubert Essame (the latter a professional soldier whose verve and pungency gave distinction to his work). Equally distinguished as stylists were outstanding historians whose work had a wider scope than war – men such as A. J. P. Taylor, Gordon Craig, Robert Conquest, Sir John Wheeler-Bennett, and Golo Mann, each of whom deserve a literary review essay of their own. It might be noted that British historians maintained, on the whole, the world's highest literary standards within their profession, and this applies to Marxists as much as to their political opponents. Christopher Hill, Eric Hobsbawm, George Rudé, and E. P. Thompson all, at one time, belonged to the British Communist Party historians' group, until they became disillusioned. Outstanding among philosophers was Bertrand Russell, whose *History of Western Philosophy* (1945), witty, urbane, and skeptical, deserves also to be read as a work of literature.

Western literature was also enriched by the effects of colonial emancipation – by works mostly in English and French by African and Caribbean authors but mirroring growing anti-colonial sentiments among the European-trained elite. These included Léopold Sedar Senghor, a Senegalese poet-politician. Senghor was culturally a Frenchman, but deeply influenced by German romantic thought. He also owed much to the philosophy of Maurice Barrès, a French nationalist who had proclaimed the values of inherited folk traditions and of French provincial life, as against the supposedly soulless metropolis, and who wrote of the unbreakable bonds between the living and the dead. Senghor proclaimed the gospel of *negritude* (blackness) and of African spirituality, as did Aimé Césaire, a black West Indian. Outstanding Anglophone African writers included Chinua Achebe, an Ibo, whose splendid novel *Things Fall About* (1958) blended stylistic verve with sociological insight. Another prominent Nigerian was Cyprian Ekwensi who had begun his career writing for the local pulp market, then graduated to serious literature.

The theater

Serious theater during the war lay dormant in Germany and Italy, though not in occupied France. Afterwards, national theater revived in much of Europe, with government help. High culture was increasingly funded by those ordinary taxpayers whom the avant garde thought of as philistines. State subsidy of the theater, as of concert halls and art galleries, created a market in which artists competed for the favors of a new cultural bureaucracy more sympathetic to modern art than the public at large. But it was not modern art alone that profited. Amid the ruins of Berlin the great German classics were played again. It was in an ear-shattering silence that Lessing's Jewish sage Nathan der Weise walked again on the stage, and the fanatic's terrible line rang through the theater, "der Jude wird verbrannt" (let the Jew be burned). It was amid a similar silence that the prisoners emerged from their dungeon in Beethoven's *Fidelio*. The stage was never to seem so real again in the later years of affluence. At the same time, there was a new modern and international art of the theater, and American musicals became popular in Europe.[30]

During the war and after, French theater was dominated by Claudel, Sartre, and Anouilh, and the absurdists. Jean Anouilh was France's most popular dramatist before 1950, and Sartre's *No Exit*, and Camus's *Caligula* enjoyed great success. French theater was well supported by the state. (There were two national theaters – the Comédié Française and the Odéon.) The most important figure in the postwar period was Barrault, the actor-producer at the Théâtre Marigny (1946–56) where many great productions were mounted. While the Comédié Française declined after the war, the Théâtre National Populaire under Jean Vilar became one of the best companies in Paris. A major development in the postwar era was the growth of regional theaters in France. (Décentralisation Dramatique set up seven Centres Dramatique around France.) These regional theaters ran permanent touring companies as well (1946–61). In 1959 when André Malraux was minister of culture the national theaters were reorganized and a new Théâtre Récamier was set up under Barrault.

The 1950s were dominated by the theater of the absurd, represented by Eugene Ionesco (a Rumanian living in France) and by a dour, minimalist writer, the Irishman, Samuel Beckett. His *Waiting for Godot* (1953, London 1955, the US 1956) was called by some the most original play of the 1950s, but was not well received in New York – it was confusing and irritating to most Americans. Beckett and others were nihilists, so concerned with the absurdity, the starkness, and the inanity of the human condition, that they in effect sought to destroy conventional theater. Beckett portrayed a world in which humanity had no place, was incapable of action or understanding or indeed even of effective communication.[31] Another important writer was Jean Genêt, a criminal, homosexual, and a living embodiment of existentialism. He wrote many disturbing and nasty plays, with great stylistic power. His best play may have been *The Balcony* (1956) about life in a brothel, where politicians fornicate while a revolution shakes the outside world.

British theater, helped by government subsidies, revived after the wartime

---

[30]See entries for France, England, Germany, Italy, and the US in *Oxford Companion to the Theater*. Oxford, Oxford University Press, 1983.
[31]See Beckett entry, *The Oxford Companion to the Theater*.

closures. For the first time the British government began to assist the arts through the Council for the Encouragement of Music and the Arts (later simply called the Arts Council). Several touring companies were formed, the Bristol Old Vic was opened, and repertory theater in London was supported. High quality British and European plays were put on at the Art Theatre (1942–1953), by writers such as Peter Ustinov, Terence Rattigan, J. B. Priestley, and Christopher Fry. In the 1950s a group of "angry young men" arrived on the scene, to censure the welfare state, mass culture, the atomic bomb, class values, imperialism, patriotism, and mothers-in-law.

These new young men included Kingsley Amis (*Lucky Jim*, 1954), John Braine (*Room at the Top*, 1957), Alan Sillitoe (*Saturday Night and Sunday Morning*, 1958). Their plays and novels were provincial, full of thwarted fury, and deeply concerned with class. Much postwar writing shared the same tired cynicism or stark despair. Overall, the quality of British literature during the middle of the twentieth century bore no comparison with the work produced in the much derided Victorian era – any more than French literature of the period could equal in vigor and quality the work accomplished during the reign of Louis-Philippe. Nor is there much evidence that such literarure mirrored the mood of the British people at large.

---

*Cabarets were the first entertainment to revive in German cities after 1945, performing in the little arts (*Kleinkunst*) of song, dance, pantomime, and magic. Cabaret could take on a political and satirical tone to cover all shades of the political spectrum.*

The theater did not easily recover in war-torn, divided Germany; it was in Switzerland that German-speaking playwrights first made their names after the war. With the theaters destroyed, many actors dead or imprisoned, and the public disoriented, German-speaking Central Europe faced a terrible sociological loss. The once-great cultures of Vienna, Berlin, and Frankfurt had been sustained in the past by a vigorous bourgeoisie – well-educated merchants, manufacturers, and professional men with cultural aspirations, many of them Jewish by religion or descent, or linked to Jews through ties of friendship or marriage. These men had filled their bookshelves with the works of Lessing, Schiller, Goethe, and Heine. They had bought the latest novels, patronized the theater, opera, and art galleries for reasons of social prestige as well as artistic enjoyment. They had entertained artists at home, and supported them financially. This liberal bourgeoisie was now extinguished by war, persecution, and murder. Their place was never quite filled again. State intervention, state subsidies, and bureaucratic enterprise could not, on their own, restore to Vienna or West Berlin the intellectual and artistic primacy they had once enjoyed, despite the lavish scale on which institutions such as the Viennese state opera were supported by public funds. Neither could the communists in East Berlin recreate the intellectual vigor that had once characterized Germany's former capital. Brecht held sway in East Berlin; and the Berliner Ensemble had some impact in the West. But within a few years literature in

East Germany, as in Eastern Europe as a whole, mostly conformed to "socialist realism," – except for manuscripts hidden in desk drawers or smuggled abroad. Since prewar German theater had largely centered on Berlin, and since Berlin was now both divided and geographically separated from West Germany, substitutes had to be found. The federal and state governments supported the theater, and Hamburg and Bremen became hubs of theatrical endeavor.

> *After the war, the Italian and French governments made an agreement to limit the number of films completed from Hollywood and subsidized the making of films* in situ. *But American films proved more popular and Hollywood moved to France and Italy to make many of their pictures, thus circumventing the quota system.*

In Italy the government also subsidized the theater, and movies which replaced drama as the more popular medium there. Their movies gained an international reputation and the major film directors such as Zeffirelli moved back and forth between opera, movies, and theater. Cinecetta gave the Italian film industry the economic base required to compete with Hollywood and to launch a neo-realist school in movies and the theater – with great international influence. Major cities set up permanent companies (*teatro stabile*) to offer security to actors and to present regular performances of Italian and international plays.

In the US theater mainly meant New York, given the slow growth of regional, civic, and university theater in the 1930s and 1940s. (No regional theater gained national prominence even in the 1950s.) Comedies and musicals had carried New York through the war years, but dramatic theater remained in a depression in the 1950s. Television took away middle-class customers until the late 1950s and theaters were lost in favor of productions for the small screen. Production costs were high (for instance, union rates for actors and musicians were sometimes prohibitive). Talent was scarce (or perhaps inhibited by the Cold War atmosphere and the house committee on un-American activities). Tennessee Williams's and Arthur Miller's somber plays dominated, and there was a revival of Eugene O'Neill in the 1950s. Some new talent appeared (William Inge, Paddy Chayefsky, William Gibson), but except for Williams, Wilder, Miller, and O'Neill, American plays – unlike musicals – did not often run in Europe.

An off-Broadway theater sprang up in the postwar period. For example, the Phoenix Theater Company (formed in 1953) put on many European classics, and the Living Theater (1947) became recognized for innovative productions in New York and Europe. The Living Theater performed Brecht's and Weill's *The Threepenny Opera* (1955) which ran for a record 2,600 performances. But government and foundation money did not come to aid the dramatic arts in America until the late 1950s, in contrast to earlier and more generous support in Europe.

Themes varied widely, but some American playwrights now made a reputation as connoisseurs of decadence. They included Tennessee Williams, a

Southerner, whose play *Glass Menagerie* (1945) agonized over the alienation of "violent and crippled eccentrics, homosexuals, madmen, sex-driven women." *Streetcar Named Desire* is set in a pathological world that drives the heroine into madness. Other decadents included Truman Capote, another Southerner with a taste for decay; Kurt Vonnegut, a satirist steeped in literary pessimism; Jack Kerouac, praise singer of drunks, beats, and bums; and Henry Miller, a man obsessed with orgasms and phony prophets. Arthur Miller created a tragic hero, in *Death of a Salesman* (1949): Willy Loman is a salesman whose professed values clash with his real conduct, and who finally commits suicide.[32] His experience was not common among real-life salesmen, whose children were made to read the play in high school for their educational improvement.

America's greatest achievements in the theater were in musical comedies or musicals, especially after World War II, when tours, records, tapes, and movies based on musicals brought this American genre to most of Europe. US composers and librettists (Allen Jay Lerner, Frederick Loewe, Cole Porter, Rogers and Hammerstein) dominated the world of musicals. Almost every year a successful new musical opened on Broadway, to be quickly followed by a London season. (For example, *Brigadoon*, 1947, London, 1949; *Kiss Me Kate*, 1948, London 1951; *South Pacific*, 1949, London, 1951; and the biggest of them all *My Fair Lady*, 1956, London, 1958.) American musicals seemed to decline in the 1960s. British musicals, their only rivals, had a modest revival after the war and a few made it to Broadway for example (*The Boy Friend*, London, 1955, New York, 1959), but it was not until 1960 that the English had a great hit *Oliver!*

How much of an impact was made by the world of letters and the theater? Their productions bore little resemblance to the lives of those ordinary Americans (or Europeans) who raised families, bought a home in suburbia, participated in the deliberations of their local PTA, joined the Elks, the Lions, or the Knights of Columbus, contributed to the Red Cross. They did not exploit women in the manner of Bertold Brecht, Jean-Paul Sartre, or Ernest Hemingway. Nor did ordinary people share the literary cult of alienation, rather they felt a justifiable sense of achievement. What did such people listen to, or read? From the mid-1950s on they tended to read less and watch more TV. Published best-seller lists help to elucidate public taste. Magazines and works such as *Life, Look, Saturday Evening Post, Better Homes and Gardens, The General Foods Kitchen Cook Book, Better Homes and Gardens Decorating Ideas*, made a tremendous appeal to married couples in suburban homes. So did works of popular history, such as William L. Shirer, *The Rise and Fall of the Third Reich*, or conservative politics such as Barry Goldwater, *The Conscience of a Conservative*, and Allen Drury, *Advise and Consent* (all at the top of the 1960 best-seller list of non-fiction). Popular works of fiction included imaginary history such as Leon Uris, *Mila 18*, James Michener, *Hawaii*, and Gladys Schmitt, *Rembrandt*. "Serious" literature was represented by works such as John Steinbeck, *The Winter of our Discontent*, Harper Lee, *To Kill a Mocking Bird*, Giuseppe di

[32]Seymour-Smith, *The New Guide to Modern World Literature, passim.*

Lampedusa, *The Leopard* (a work of fictionalized history), and Henry Miller, *Tropic of Cancer* (popular for its erotic interest at a time when ordinary readers were still inclined to read straight pornography in a surreptitious fashion).[33]

In addition, there was, on both sides of the Atlantic, an enormous market for traditional genre – tales of knight errantry. The modern knight errant came to dominate modern literature, with the same mission that had fallen to him in the past.

> Nought is more honorable to a knight
> No better doth beseem have chivalry,
> Then to defend the feeble in their right,
> And wrong redress in such as wend awry.[34]

The new knight errant came in three main guises – as a detective fighting crime, as a Western hero battling against assorted crews of villains, and as a secret agent who ferreted out clandestine machinations of Nazis, communists and mysterious global syndicates. The detectives descended from Sherlock Holmes, whose enormous literary progeny by now included priests, rabbis, and maiden ladies. Authors of thrillers such as Earl Gardener, Georges Simenon, and Dorothy Sayers remained household names on both sides of the Atlantic, as did many writers of spy fiction. Ever since R. Rider Haggard, Rudyard Kipling, John Buchan, the British had dominated the spy novel. Subsequent British masters of the genre included Eric Ambler, Graham Greene, and John Le Carré. Their tales satisfied fantasies of invisibility and secret power, linked to exploits of the most improbable kind. The most outrageous of these were found in Ian Fleming's James Bond novels (the first being *Casino Royale*, 1953) in which the hero fought and fornicated his way to an inevitably victorious conclusion.

AGATHA CHRISTIE (MARY CLARISSA MILLER) (1890–1976)

Agatha Christie was the most famous writer of detective stories of her time, with a huge readership on both sides of the Atlantic. (She was in fact half American, her father had been a well-to-do New Yorker, her mother English.) Her spread of knowledge was enormous. She was a qualified pharmacist; she had done wartime nursing; she was a capable archaeological worker, a gifted singer, and a successful gardener. She was twice married, and at the end of her life became a grandmother. She was twice titled (as the wife, in her second marriage, of Sir Max Mallowan, she could choose to be called either Lady Mallowan or, in her own right, Dame Agatha). Her capacity for work was prodigious. During her life she turned out more than 100 books, psychological novels, short stories, plays, verse, and above all mysteries. These gained enormous circulation in paperback as well as hardback editions, selling hundreds of millions of copies.

As a writer of popular fiction, she – so to speak – broadened the social circle of British

[33] *The Bowker Annual of Library and Book Trade Information.* New York, Bowker, 1962, pp. 69–70, listing best-sellers of 1960s including books published in the late 1950s.
[34] Cited in Carolly Erickson, *Great Harry: The Extravagant Life of Henry VIII.* New York, Summit Books, 1981, p. 165.

> *detectives. Sherlock Holmes had been a man. Tommy and Tuppence Beresford, two of Agatha Christie's sleuths, made up an early husband-and-wife team, but they were of course young, handsome, and impeccably upper class. Miss Marple, a later creation, was an elderly spinster, indubitably well brought up, but conservative in tastes and ideas, not the kind of person often invited to a fashionable party. Even more eccentric was Hercule Poirot, her favorite detective – a portly Belgian, grandly mustachioed, egotistical, and very, very un-British. Agatha Christie's critics complained that her plots were bloodless parlor games, crossword puzzles cast in prose, lacking in depth. Nevertheless, her books gave an enormous amount of pleasure to one of the largest reading publics in the world.*

The Americans (especially Zane Grey and Max Brand) had created the Western hero who symbolized a part-mythical past. The most productive of many Western writers was Louis L'Amour. His output was truly phenomenal: by 1987 he had sold nearly 160,000,000 books around the world, and over 30 novels were made into movies and television dramas.[35] Together with Harold Robbins and Irving Wallace, he was one of the three best-selling novelists in the US. His stories were fast-moving; his style was simple; his heroes were hard-working, self-educated, lonely, and unbelievably brave. His stereotypes were applied without reference to race or gender. His Indians were either heroes or villains, as were his white ranchers, gamblers, and gun-slingers. High culture might prize the anti-hero; but the public at large took a more optimistic view of life, on both sides of the Atlantic.

RADIO AND TV

Art through the ages depended on direct experience – the ordinary person's access to works of art was largely limited to churches and public squares (paintings tended to be in private homes or churches, but sculpture was often public). An eighteenth-century German village lad, for instance, had three ways of hearing professional musicians. He might hear a band play at a village fair or wedding; he might sing at church accompanied by an organist; and if pressed into the army, he would march to the tune of a regimental band. During the twentieth century came a striking and irreversible change. Professionally produced music became accessible to ordinary people almost anywhere. It could be reproduced easily and sent long distances over the air, or it could be played at home on a record player.

Radio was one of the key inventions. It played a decisive role in politics and in the popular arts during the 1930s and 1940s, and thereafter maintained considerable, though somewhat diminishing, importance. Roosevelt, Hitler, and Churchill had one thing in common: each in his own way was a magnificent radio performer. Major politicians by this time depended to a much greater extent on the radio than on public meetings in order to reach a nationwide audience. World War II was fought and experienced over the radio, as well as

---

[35]See the review essay by Louis Erdrich on Louis L'Amour in *New York Times Book Review*, 7 November 1987.

on the battlefield. War also enhanced the role of radio as a cultural medium; it formed a portable concert hall enabling ordinary soldiers and workers to listen to serious as well as light programs. There was classical music as well as swing, instructional talks as well as propaganda. In Britain and the US especially radio drama became a serious art form. As sets improved in quality and dropped in price, the radio became commonplace in most Western households. (At the end of the 1950s, Western Europeans still owned more than eight times as many radios as television sets.)[36] It was the radio that linked the remotest farm to urban centers. Radio stations continued to increase in the 1950s.[37] The advent of television diminished the relative importance of radio in homes in the industrial world, but did not eliminate it as the major means of communication in the workplace and in less developed regions.

The first public demonstrations of television in the US date from the early 1920s. In 1928 General Electric's experimental station broadcast television's first live drama, "The Queen's Messenger." In 1936 the BBC established its first regular television service. During World War II, television development languished in Europe, and the Americans pulled ahead, as in many other industries. (The first US television star was not a person but a doll – Felix the cat.) In 1939 television reached another milestone when Andrew Geller's shoe store initiated commercial sponsorship of a television program. By 1945 the American Broadcasting Company (ABC) was able to put together extensive programs with such stars as Henry Morgan and Bing Crosby. Just three years later 37 television stations were operating in the US, centering mainly on East Coast cities, with four major networks (NBC, CBS, ABC, and Du Mont Television Network). At the time of Pearl Harbor (1941) there were only a few hundred sets in the country; by 1948 the number had risen to a quarter of a million.[38]

In retrospect the "golden age" of television appears to have begun then. (Great dramas included *Marty*, *Requiem for a Heavyweight*, *The Miracle Worker*, and *The Days of Wine and Roses*.) New York became the center of quality production adjusted to the tastes of what was as yet a relatively small middle-class audience able to purchase expensive sets. This was an era of pioneer work in entertainment. Television gave employment to a host of well-known and lesser-known radio performers, as well as actors and actresses from the movies and the stage. Live television drama flourished, with programs such as "Philco playhouse," "Playhouse 90," "Studio One," "Hallmark Hall of Fame," "Armstrong Circle Theater," "Kraft Television Theater," all taken seriously by the

[36]Between 1938 and 1957, the number of radios in Western Europe increased (in thousands) from 27,538 to 66,733. The proportion of radio sets per 100 inhabitants rose from 10.6 in 1938 to 22.4 in 1957. The percentage by country in 1957 varied from 34.3 in Britain to 6.7 in Portugal. J. Frederick Dewhurst, et al., *Europe's Needs and Resources: Trends and Prospects in Eighteen Countries*, New York, Twentieth Century Fund, 1961, p. 265.

[37]Between 1937 and 1957, the number of transmitting stations in the US grew from 734 to 3,717. United Nations, *Statistical Yearbook, 1958*, p. 576.

[38]Michael Winship, *Television*. New York, Random House, 1988. Rick Marshall. *The History of Television*. New York, Gallery Books, 1986.

actors, writers, producers, and sponsors' advertising agencies (many of which set up their own creative departments). Equally popular was television comedy, with brilliant performers such as Groucho Marx, Milton Berle, Jack Benny, and Red Skelton. "Sitcoms" (situation comedies) were the most popular programs all through the 1950s. Many were simply transferred from radio, such as Burns and Allen and Jack Benny, but TV also developed its own programs like the "Honeymooners," and "I Love Lucy" (the most populat sitcom ever). Family comedies were also popular in the postwar decade – "Ozzie and Harriet," "Make Room for Daddy," "Father Knows Best" showed idealized family life with no real problems. When exported these were well received in Great Britain. Westerns were also a staple; "The Lone Ranger" brought to the small screen a romanticized version of the American West. In the late 1950s Hollywood made films for TV, and about 30 a week were shown in prime time. Western series such as "Gunsmoke" and "Bonanza" also became popular in Europe.

Talk shows and game shows filled up TV's fringe time (that is before and after prime time, 8 to 11 pm). Talk show hosts Steve Allen, Jack Parr, Johnny Carson became folk heroes and quiz shows were also very popular – "The Price is Right," "The $64,000 Question," "What's My Line?"). Variety shows (comic and musical) absorbed much prime time. Successful singers like Perry Como, Dinah Shore, Kate Smith, Andy Williams, and Nat King Cole had their own shows. Variety shows faded out in the 1970s with "The Sonny and Cher Comedy Hour" being the last successful musical variety show (1973–4). Mini-series and docudramas evolved from the golden age of American TV and from British traditions of drama. Sport has been part of the staple TV fare since the beginning; roller derbies, hockey, wrestling, baseball, and basketball were the most popular through the 1950s in the US.

Before 1948, news came from newspapers, radio, and theater newsreels. After that people got their news largely from television. "Douglas Edwards with the news" was the most popular news progam in history – over 38,000,000 viewers. No newspaper or magazine had ever approached that figure. The marriage of TV news and politics was consummated during the 1948 presidential convention. Ed Murrow's "See It Now" began an era of hard-hitting TV journalism, investigative reporting and discussion of controversial issues. By the end of the 1950s TV stations numbered almost 500. "The Huntley-Brinkley Report," begun in 1956, soon became the most successful television news team in history.

There was hardly anything that television could not do – animal shows with dolphins and dogs as actors (Rin-Tin-Tin, Lassie), classical concerts, detective stories, sermons, lectures, sportscasts, gangster series (for instance "The Untouchables"). Television also became a powerful force in politics. (As early as 1952, Walter Cronkite's program "Pick the Winner" provided a forum for political candidates to present their views on national and international issues.) Overall, television emphasized traditional values, with shows such as "Life with Father," "Leave it to Beaver," in which the suburban father figure ran the household in a sensible yet kindly fashion. American television, then as now, enthralled viewers by its great diversity and high technical standards.

By the end of the 1950s, television had undergone profound changes. Improved mass production meant that television sets became affordable for the bulk of the population. The number of TV stations had increased enormously. (Between 1949 and 1959, the number of private television stations in the US went up from 69 to 566.) The number of households with sets rose from 940,000 in 1949 to 44,000,000 in 1959 – almost three times as many as in the whole of Western Europe. Yesteryear's elite viewing circles turned into mass audiences. (During the commercial breaks of runaway hits such as "I Love Lucy" water pressure in large cities would fall as viewers dashed into their bathrooms and kitchens.)[39] Television ratings played an ever increasing role in shaping commercial programs; ratings picked up as pop shows came to dominate the screen. Quizzes, for example, abounded – cheap and easy to make, and designed to appeal to the lowest common denominator. Inventions such as the magnetic tape helped to bring about the demise of live TV drama, as did the pressure of huge budgets and the ratings game. Quality declined and shows were produced for a mass audience, assumed to have the IQ of an 11 year old. There were also changes in the labor force of the entertainment industry – by the end of the 1950s, TV stars began their careers on TV itself rather than on radio or in the movies.

After a brief time lag, television became quite as popular in Western Europe as in the US. (Between 1953 and 1958 the number of television sets in Western Europe rose from 2,240,000 to 14,350,000.) Great Britain was the first country to accept the new medium on a grand scale. The state-owned BBC broadcast BBC1, and, later, BBC2 channels, and commercial television started up in the 1950s. By 1958, more than half the television sets in Western Europe (8,899,000) were owned by the British.[40] Television thereafter spread to every country in the world. In Europe, as in the US, television sets were first owned by well-to-do people, particularly the upper-grade liberal professions, followed by salaried employees, and urban wage earners, with farmers bringing up the rear. But in Europe and the US ownership broadened, until the "telly" came to be regarded almost as a domestic necessity, like a stove or a fridge. At that date programs were mostly bought from the US and the programs other stations produced were usually imitations of what was seen on American TV.

The organization of the radio and television industry varied greatly. In the US, the bulk of the industry was privately run and owned (though there were also "public" stations financed by local bodies, often with support from subscribing viewers or commercial enterprise). In Europe, ownership and control mainly rested with the state, though with important exceptions (for instance Radio Luxemburg). Television literally spanned the world. In 1962, AT and T (American Telephone and Telegraph Company) for the first time transmitted experimental programs from the US to Britain and France via its

[39]William L. O'Neill, *American High: The Years of Confidence 1945–1960*. New York, Free Press, 1986, p. 83.
[40]Dewhurst, *Europe's Needs*, p. 265, 267.

artificial satellite *Telstar*. Irrespective of ownership and control, radio and especially television turned into a powerful economic force. Television came to be used in a variety of high-tech industrial processes. The manufacture of television sets itself turned into a mammoth enterprise (dominated first by the US, later by Japan, then South Korea). TV advertising enhanced the size and variety of the mass market by creating, or at least by stressing, new wants. Television easily crossed national boundaries. (Queen Elizabeth II's coronation in Britain in 1953 was watched with fascination by viewers in many different countries, especially in the US.) For better or worse, the small screen helped to link and to transform the postwar world.[41]

American television dominated the European market throughout the postwar period. This was not only because of technical excellence or expensive productions, it was also Europe's fascination with the US, its people and culture (or lack of it). America's wealth, size, and diversity, and especially its Western past, as well as crime, violence, and sexuality were all part of it. US television programs were also escapist and action-packed, which was what many Europeans wanted. Adventure and detective series sold well but most popular were comedy and variety shows, and later series dealing with the rich and powerful. In 1955 the top shows were:

> Jackie Gleason
> Toast of the Town (Ed Sullivan)
> I Love Lucy
> Milton Berle
> Dragnet (detective series)
> Disneyland
> Martha Raye
> Groucho Marx
> Jack Benny

Even in the 1980s, American TV programs remained cheaper to buy from the US than to produce in Europe, despite greater production expenses. By 1988 US program exports earned about $500,000,000. Western European states could buy for $2,500 a program that would have cost them $250,000 to produce at home; hence they kept buying American TV shows. European ideas about America and its people were unfortunately too often shaped by these TV and movie productions, which gave views not always flattering or accurate.

Britain has been the chief rival of the US as an exporter of TV film (and movies); but British TV tended to be only shown on public television (or in art theaters) and therefore only reached small audiences. (This was true even of a highly successful British series "Upstairs, Downstairs," the story of an Edwardian noble family and their servants. The program was watched with fascination all over the world, including the Soviet Union, but never made

---

[41]For cultural critiques, see for instance, Horace Newcomb, ed. *Television: The Critical View.* Oxford, Oxford University Press, 1986.

commercial channels in the US.) In general, Americans have been bored by British cultural series – the characters talk in strange accents and things move slowly. US imports on the other hand have always been popular in Britain (and Western Europe) because they are escapist, filled with action, violence, sex, and adventure. American advertising on TV revolutionized the way merchandise was sold, and increased sales dramatically. Commercials became technical works of art and were intended to induce people to buy by entertaining or amazing viewers. The "Marlboro man," the rugged outdoorsman, sold and sold cigarettes, and that style was imitated in Western Europe.[42]

Television in general has not had a good press among people of culture. According to many critics, it creates a dream world for the poor, and manipulates the masses by turning statesmen into public entertainers. It is thought to be detrimental to education, as children watch the silvery screen instead of doing their homework; indeed television violence, some believe, promotes juvenile delinquency. Television in fact causes a general decline in civilized values – so the charge sheet continues.

We are not so sure. The rise of the television industry did not inhibit serious reading; on the contrary, the number of serious books published, bought, and sold has continued to rise. Tyrants had manipulated the masses long before television was invented; Hitler and Stalin had reigned before there was a TV set in any household. Educational standards have declined in many respects; but many factors have contributed to this cultural loss. The link between violence on the screen and violence in real life is tenuous at best.[43] If television's cultural consequences were indeed as evil as the critics allege, South Africa in the 1950s and 60s should have been in better cultural condition than other industrialized countries. There, the advent of television was artificially delayed because the ruling National Party long feared that it would both erode customary moral standards, and promote the use of English over Afrikaans. There is however no evidence that South Africa was in better cultural shape than the other Western nations at that time. Many television programs were, and indeed remain, poor in quality and taste. But television has also widened the audience for serious talk shows, plays, ballet, and music. Television has given legitimate pleasure to countless viewers, families as well as lonely people, the sick, widowed, aged, or deserted. We hesitate therefore to emulate Mr Pecksniff, in Charles Dickens's *Martin Chuzzlewit*, in deriding our fellow citizens' cultural preferences.

THE MOVIES

The postwar period saw a film renaissance in Western Europe and the United States. War had turned films inward; national production became simpler and

---

[42] Jeffrey Hart, *When the Going Was Good*. New York, Crown Publishers, 1982, pp. 35–6.

[43] See for instance J. D. Halloran, R. L. Brown, and D. C. Chaney, *Television and Delinquency*. Leicester, Leicester University Press, 1970, p. 8.

more realistic for the Europeans who lacked studios, equipment, and actors, and for about ten years after the war they concentrated on small-scale pictures. The Americans dominated the mass market and produced big, flashy movies with technical innovations such as stereophonic sound, cinema-scope, and 3D. Many of Europe's best directors and actors went to Hollywood but from the 1960s Hollywood began to go to Europe to cut costs and to take advantage of French and Italian government subsidies for locally made films.

The US challenge was hard to meet. The vast size of its home market made for economies of scale that immensely benefited film makers in foreign export drives. The state department supported this offensive by vigorously battling for free trade. The US had an immense reservoir of talent, to which countless European expatriates had contributed. Traditionalists among European governments tried to fight the influx of US films with subsidies to their own industries, and by tariffs, import quotas, and political manipulation. But the US film industry also had powerful allies in Europe, including European corporations that sought to profit by joint production agreements with American companies. In addition there was political support from unexpected quarters. For instance the Christian Democrats in Italy limited only slightly the massive influx of movies – not just to please the US State Department, but also because the Hollywood style went with the CDs' own conservative values. And the US Hays Code (enforcing standards of decency) was strict enough to please European as well as American traditionalists.

The US film industry itself owed an enormous debt to film moghuls of immigrant stock who had worked their way up from poverty. These included men such as Louis B. Mayer, a Russian-born Jew, who had begun his working life in his father's ship-salvaging and scrap-iron business, and ended as czar of the Metro-Goldwyn-Mayer empire. As Mayer put his policy on films with his own mother-wit, "messages are for Western Union." He saw his role as an entertainer, a view that appealed to American and European mass audiences. US film makers excelled not merely in a technical sense. They created a style that transcended the boundaries of class, ethnicity, and nationality, and it proved a resounding success in Europe as well as America.[44]

Film costs kept rising and quality began to decline much as in television. American commercial movies made for profit overwhelmed artistic films (mostly made in Europe), although Europeans produced many excellent films. Realistic motion pictures dominated in Italy: Roberto Rossellini's *Open City* (1944), *Paisa* (1946), Vittorio de Sica's *Shoe-Shine* (1946), and *Bicycle Thieves* (1948), became film classics dealing with war-torn Italy, using the outdoors and ordinary people. In the 1950s, British, French, and Swedish films were the best. In the *Seventh Seal* and *Wild Strawberries* Ingmar Bergman, a Swedish director, showed himself the greatest film maker of the period, his poetic but austere vision brought to life by a company of outstanding actors. A "new wave" of film makers (Roger Vadim, Louis Malle, Jean-Luc Godard, François

[44] Victoria de Grazia, "Mass culture and sovereignty: the American challenge to European cinemas, 1920–1960,' *The Journal of Modern History*, v. 61, no. 1, March 1989, pp. 53–87.

Truffaut) emerged in France. These film makers stressed amorality, rather than morality as in prewar films.

In the US, the most popular themes remained Westerns, crime, espionage, war, and musicals. More violence and sex appeared on screen. For Brigitte Bardot and Marilyn Monroe, Gina Lollabrigida and Mamie Van Doren, breasts and buttocks sometimes became more important than acting skill, despite their indisputable talent. One writer boldly opined that Monroe and Bardot had "a blatant, child-whorish sex appeal."[45] Still, there was more to US film acting than the sensuousness and self-indulgence of the sex-kittens – Grace Kelly and Audrey Hepburn projected aristocratic, reserved, elegant, and refined images. But overall, popular culture became more sexually explicit, more like the sexual freedom during wartime. Hugh Hefner began publishing *Playboy* in 1953, and the centerfold became part of the new sexual freedom obtained in movies, TV, and novels. *Peyton Place* as a movie (1956), later (1962) as a TV series, codified the newfound interest in sex in small town America.

Just as musicals dominated American theater after World War II, so they dominated the film industry, and became America's leading cultural export. Richard Altman's *The American Film Musical* (1987) distinguishes three major types. "Fairy-tale musicals" grew out of the European operetta tradition, Americanized as a story of romance between the ordinary male and the disdainful female; the "show musical" has a show within a show; while "folk musicals" often deal with small town life, barn dances, and family sing-alongs. Professionally and technically the "folk musical," Altman claims, was the most advanced American art form and kept alive the tradition of folk entertainment until replaced by TV, records, and rock and roll.

"GROUCHO" (JULIUS HENRY) MARX

George Bernard Shaw, no mean exponent of histrionics, called Groucho "the world's greatest living actor" with good reason. Groucho was a superb performer. His art appealed to all, company presidents and clerks, suburban housewives and intellectual sophisticates. Audiences on both sides during the Spanish civil war, ferociously divided by politics and ideology, alike roared with laughter as they watched Groucho on the screen – a comic opera dictator who looked oddly like a conventional Spanish politician. (His Excellency reads a long official document. "A child of four could understand this," says the great leader, "get me a child of four!")

What was Groucho's secret? he lacked the social graces and turned personal offensiveness into an art form, in his private life as well as on the stage. He publicly cultivated the air of a leering satyr, a pose not hard to assume for a man who went through three divorces, and thereafter traveled with a "secretary companion." He defied the mighty. ("I would horsewhip you, if I had a horse.") He lacked a formal education. He was born in a New York tenement, the son of a poverty-stricken immigrant Jewish tailor. He worked in a grocery store, and later joined an itinerant vaudeville group together with his brothers, all as crazily named as himself. (Harpo was named from his instrument, the harp; Gummo

---

[45]Hart, *When the Going Was Good*, p. 51.

from his gumshoes; Chico from his reputation as a ladykiller; Zeppo from Zippo, star
of a chimpanzee act.)

    Groucho's was a remarkable success story. His group advanced to Broadway, and then
into movies. Gummo and Zeppo later left the ensemble to become theatrical agents; then
Chico and Harpo died. Groucho, now alone, created a new identity for himself through
"You Bet Your Life," a radio–television show begun in 1947. He had thus succeeded in
every medium of the entertainment business.

    Groucho was a master of the unexpected twist, the outrageous insult, of crazily inverted
logic. He wedded chutzpah to surrealism. He always stuck up for himself. (When his
daughter Melinda was prevented from swimming in a pool with friends at a country club
that excluded Jews, Groucho wrote a highly publicized letter to the club president: "Since
my little daughter is only half-Jewish, would it be all right if she went into the pool only
to her waist?") In one sense, Groucho was as much a social critic as his namesake Karl,
who was surprisingly capable of Groucho-like wit ("The Emperor Napoleon III," Karl
Marx wrote, "worships only one trinity – infantry, cavalry, artillery.") In his comedy
acts, Groucho would put down the proudest magnates and the grandest of grandes dames.
What is more, he could also put down his audiences, an even more difficult feat. (When
a contestant at his quiz show was asked her age, she replied "approaching 40." "From
which direction?" he queried.) Groucho was not merely a clever comedian, but a moralist
who taught people how to laugh at themselves.

Hollywood continued to tower over the film industry worldwide. It enjoyed enormous advantages – a tradition of technical competence, a huge domestic market, a wealth of artistic ability. Clark Gable, Walt Disney, Danny Kaye, Gregory Peck, Charlton Heston, Marilyn Monroe, Cary Grant, Marlon Brando, the Marx brothers, and many more, became household names everywhere. Hollywood's film magnates were the world's greatest; Hollywood studios the most highly capitalized. The American film industry moreover drew heavily on foreign talent. Englishmen such as Alfred Hitchcock and Charlie Chaplin felt at home in the US. So did Swedes like Ingrid Bergman, or Italians like Sophia Loren. So too did Germans and Hungarians – particularly those exiles who came to the US to escape Nazi persecution. (According to a refugee joke, a German at a film studio overheard a group of Hungarians speaking Hungarian. "Hey you guys," said the German, "Don't you know that this is Hollywood? Speak German!")

It was thus American film makers who were the first to confront the postwar crisis. From as early as the late 1940s, film audiences started to decline in a striking fashion, and cinemas began to close. (Between 1945 and 1951, 51 shut their doors in New York, 64 in Chicago, and 134 in southern California, the film industry's very heartland.[46] British film audiences soon dropped likewise. (In the late 1940s more than three-quarters of the British population had gone to the cinema at least once a year. Forty years later three quarters of the British population did not go to the cinema at all.) In France the slump in movie-going occurred somewhat later. (Between 1957 and 1966 annual attendance

---

[46]Michael Pye, "New channels for movies," in Lloyd, *Movies of the Fifties,* p. 3. David Docherty, David Morrison, and Michael Tracey, *The Last Picture Show? Britain's Changing Film Audiences.* London, BFI, 1987.

plummeted from 411,000,000 to 232,000,000.) But in every major industrial country, the story was similar; more and more families stayed at home to watch television; fewer and fewer stood in line outside the local picture house. (During the 1980s the trend did begin to reverse, as new style movie theaters offered a choice of several films, and acquired a cultural, as well as popular appeal.)

American film moghuls at first blamed television, and responded with all kinds of gimmicks, "3D" viewing, and ever more stunning film spectacle. But the crisis in movie production had causes more profound than merely competition from a sister industry. The old-time Gaumont or Odeon, with its velvet-covered seats, electric organ, and colored lighting, had offered not merely entertainment, but a sense of luxury to families living in overcrowded, under-heated apartments, a place where a young couple might cuddle in the balcony, and their elders find relaxation from the stress of wartime and postwar hardship. As living standards rose, television sets became more easily accessible for everyone; but so did cars, espresso cafes, amateur theater, local glee clubs, restaurants, and holidays abroad. Homes became much more comfortable. The move to suburbia also affected the movie industry – the big cinemas usually had been built in downtown areas, while the new suburban affluence meant that a family outing on a Saturday night became less of an event that it had been during the Depression, the war, and immediate postwar years. It is a fact that film attendance in the US had actually started to decline from 1947, long before the average American owned a TV set.

THE SILVER SCREEN

The movie screen creates its own world. An actor or actress able to project a particular image on screen can rise to fame and fortune. (Such social ascent commonly went with a name change.) Great movie personalities created their own stereotypes of morality, social class, and nationality – these in turn influenced worldwide audiences. Mary Pickford, a pioneer acress in the talkies, turned into "America's sweetheart," full of sweetness and virtue. Marilyn Monroe became a sex symbol in a more permissive era. (In fact, Mary Pickford had reputedly begun her career by selling sex; Marilyn Monroe prided herself on giving it away.)

The screen also influenced national stereotypes. Leslie Howard, once a London clerk, was transformed into the beau idéal of the English gentleman, brave, quiet, and honorable. (This, in fact, was precisely what he was.) He died tragically in World War II, when the plane taking him to the US was shot down by the Germans, who believed the aircraft was carrying a passenger of supreme importance. Howard was succeeded as the archetypal English gentleman by David Niven. Niven was unusual in that he was what his screen image presented, a former British officer trained at Sandhurst. (He had earned a living at various times as a whisky salesman, laundry delivery man, journalist, and racing promoter.)

Erich von Stroheim, Hollywood's archetypal junker (Prussian), came from a very different background. He owed his patent of nobility to his own inventiveness (having never risen beyond the rank of noncommissioned officer in the old Austro-Hungarian army).

Von Stroheim came to Hollywood as a refugee from Nazi Germany. His accent was for him, as for so many other foreign artists, both a burden and an opportunity. Few actors with foreign accents could make it into straight roles in Hollywood at the time. (There were a few exceptions, mostly beautiful blondes such as Greta Garbo, Ingrid Bergman, Marlene Dietrich.) Foreign accents in the American audience's imagination were likely to go with exotic oomph (Carmen Miranda); exotic wickedness (Peter Lorre); exotic wisdom (the "Charlie Chan" movies); or exotic military nobility. Von Stroheim, driven into heavily Germanic roles against his will, took on a new persona – monocled, stiff, courageous – more Prussian than the genuine von Quitzows, von Bredows, and von Bülows whose names had once filled the Royal Prussian Army lists.

Even more astonishing was the career of Kirk Douglas, whose life is truly a rags-to-riches tale. Douglas (born Issu Danielovitch, of Jewish parents, like Howard and von Stroheim) grew up as the local ragman's son in a small upstate New York mill town. He managed to get a student loan and attended college, then served in the US navy in World War II, and thereafter achieved fame as an all-American symbol of toughness and virility – in the role of army officer, boxing champion, or gladiator fighting for liberty (in Spartacus). Douglas was indeed a courageous athlete, and one of the few tough-guy actors who needed no stuntman to take his place in fast-paced action scenes. The ragman's son, became the all-American hero.

Between 1948 and 1959 film studios had to sell their theater chains because of anti-trust laws. They could no longer force theaters to take all their films, good or bad. Film companies then turned to hit films as opposed to mass production. Hollywood began to use TV as an outlet, first to rerun old hits and then as a medium for inexpensive films. So Hollywood survived, but in a different form.

MUSIC

Music, like other art forms, underwent major changes in the twentieth century. In part, these came about through new technologies in electronic sound-making. There were new instruments (the electric guitar, the cinema organ, and others), which added greatly to the varieties of sound that musicians could employ. The new devices also contributed to raising acceptable noise levels in music, and introduced a new class division between those who enjoyed the blare of stereos, and those who hated the raucous noise. For the ordinary music lover, one of the most striking changes came through the long-playing record (LP). In 1948 Columbia introduced a fine-groove record made of clear vinylite, one of the new plastic substances. This record rotated at 33.3 rpm (as opposed to 78) and had a maximum playing time of 30 minutes. The LP made an enormous contribution to consumer choice, dominating the music market for something like 40 years, until it was increasingly replaced by cassettes and compact discs. The LP was produced by, and distributed by, private enterprise. Pioneer-businessmen included people such as Russ Solomon, founder of Tower Records, a small store in Sacramento, California, that expanded into a great chain. In these musical supermarkets buyers could find almost anything, from jazz and traditional folk music to the most obscure classics. Ordinary householders henceforth could build up collections, and arrange their own programs in a manner previously unavailable to music lovers. Amateur listeners became more like professional musicians in being able to play the same music over and over again. Long-playing records opened vast new markets for every kind of music. Not only the well-known classics became readily available, but work that had previously been neglected – be it the Mannheim school of the eighteenth century, or works written during the Renaissance and the Middle Ages. There was a market for jazz, for the blues, for ethno-music, for the modern music produced by composers such as Arnold Schoenberg and Aaron Copland.

By dint of spreading musical knowledge, the long-playing record in turn gave a boost to the number of people who attended concerts given by professional and amateur musicians. Especially in the US, there was a striking growth in the number of professional orchestras as well as private groups. Far from declining into an age of "Admass," classical music spread more widely than ever before, thanks to scores of European conductors (Arturo Toscanini, Otto Klemperer, Serge Koussevitsky, George Szell, Bruno Walters) and musicians, and teacher-composers (Gregor Piatagorsky, Darius Milhaud, Arnold Schoenberg) who came to the United States. According to the traditionalists, the twentieth century produced no musical giants – and no one knows why. If money and the availability of technical resources could produce musical genius, the twentieth century should have exceeded the age of Haydn, Mozart, and Beethoven. If ideological uniformity could have brought about towering ability, the Soviet Union should have by far surpassed czarist Russia in creativity. If religious faith alone could have created great music, Ireland should have excelled. Had the secret lain in a sense of national well being and security, New Zealand should have filled the bill. In fact, the twentieth century was an age in which access to great music became available to the ordinary citizen throughout the Atlantic community; and modern atonal music appealed to few. The US led in the production of popular music while the British dominated the classical field.

During and after World War II, the US became the world's principal music center. In this respect again, it benefited from the influx of refugees from Nazi Germany and the Soviet Union. (The Nazis not only persecuted Jewish composers, but also stigmatized modernists of whatever ethnic ancestry as "cultural Bolsheviks." The Soviets called such people "bourgeois formalists," but meant the same.) Hindemith, the great German classical composer, taught at Yale from 1940 to 1953, before returning to Europe. Arnold Schoenberg, the Austrian pioneer of atonal music and the twelve-tone scale, ended his days in Los Angeles. The Americans were tolerant of dissenters; they had money; they also had creativity. By the 1970s, the US was pre-eminent in popular music, opera, orchestras (at least in New York, Boston, Philadelphia, Chicago, and Cleveland); and jazz, country and blues, and rock and roll became major cultural exports. American musical sophistication achieved new heights thanks to radio, TV, records, and tapes, and the LP introduced a musical revolution.[47] Thousands of children's bands and orchestras sprang up after the war in the new suburban schools.

> *Before World War II professional music groups were largely concentrated on the East Coast and in a few big cities. During the postwar epoch musical life expanded and was dispersed throughout the country. New symphony orchestras and opera companies, chamber music and vocal groups were launched. By 1960 the US had 42 professional orchestras (25 of them major); growth was mainly in the Southeast, the Southwest, and the West. (By 1988, there were 166 professional orchestras, 30 of them major ones. Opera companies also proliferated throughout the US from just a few cities: by the 1960s there were 27, by 1987 there were 154.) As population shifted from the Northeast and Middle West they brought a demand for good music and helped to establish orchestras, opera companies, and chamber groups where they settled. The large immigrant group from Europe played a major part in creating a demand for classical music. Later the music division of the national endowment for the humanities committed itself to regional dispersion of musical groups, and corporate sponsorship also promoted regional culture groups.*

Classical music remained divided into many different schools. Composers such as Jean Sibelius in Finland, Ildebrando Pizzetti in Italy, or Benjamin Britten in England, followed more traditional modes. So did Aaron Copland, who drew on indigenous American, especially black American, traditions. Hindemith remained indebted to great nineteenth-century German masters such as Bruckner. Others tried to strike out along entirely new paths, and among these innovators was Schoenberg and his pupils, Alban Berg and Anton Webern. Schoenberg, like Wittgenstein, Freud, and many other cultural iconoclasts, was Viennese, a child of the Austro-Hungarian monarchy and its turmoils. He was brilliant; he was also arrogant, intolerant of criticism, contemptuous of the public, unable and unwilling to communicate to mass audiences. Schoenberg had little use for Hindemith's aim, to write *Gebrauchsmusik* (music for use). Not surprisingly, Schoenberg's music failed to find popular acceptance, even though sympathetic conductors would sandwich his dissonant pieces among others of more traditional appeal. By contrast, great Soviet musicians – Prokoviev, Shostakovitch, Kachaturian, and others – did acquire a popular appeal. The old and the new music alike became international, as records and air travel allowed rapid, frequent interchange between Europe and the US. European conductors and musicians moved to and fro, conducting or playing in Berlin, London, Vienna, New York, and San Francisco. Most conductors of major American orchestras were European.

As regards public performances London, for most of the postwar era, remained the center of classical music. London had more good orchestras (five) and more great conductors than any other city. The city's pre-eminence was also built on the work of the two best recording orchestras of the day:

[47]Richard Altman, *The American Film Musical.* Bloomington, Indiana University Press, 1987, *passim.*

the Royal Philharmonic Orchestra and the Philharmonia, led by Sir Thomas Beecham and Herbert von Karajan respectively. British dominance ended in the 1960s with the death of Klemperer; concert attendance and record sales declined and did not revive until the 1980s, after the introduction of the compact disc (CD). Music repertoires for recording expanded and new groups sprang up to present programs ranging from Beethoven to Dowland and folk music. Another development equally noteworthy was the performances by small groups. For example the Academy of St Martin in the Fields from the later 1950s often played with only 15 or fewer musicians. (The Academy developed three groups: ten or fewer for chamber music, 12–25 players, and full orchestra 64.) Recording made the Academy of St Martin in the Fields successful and profitable. In general, however, London musicians and conductors were less well paid and received lesser subsidies than Continental European orchestras.

> In the early 1950s a new kind of jazz came out of the West Coast. Its acknowledged leader was Dave Brubeck (and the Brubeck Quartet of Paul Desmond, Joe Dodge, and Bob Bates.) There were of course other stars – Gerry Mulligan, Chet Baker, Stan Getz – but Brubeck was "the cat." This new jazz was more intellectual, complicated, and white-oriented than previous jazz groups, although blacks were still important, especially Erroll Garner, Oscar Peterson, Art Tatum, Dizzy Gillespie, and Ella Fitzgerald. The West Coast groups were more orderly and disciplined but still stressed improvisation and a free spirit. The small combos spread out across the country into jazz clubs and supper clubs, but big bands also continued to develop, with famous names like Count Basie, Woody Herman, Duke Ellington.

In popular music, the US led the way. Jeffrey Hart in *When the Going Was Good* (1982) proclaimed 1945 to 1955 as the golden period of American popular music, which had begun in 1914 and was led by largely Jewish songwriters and composers (Irving Berlin, Jerome Kern, George Gershwin, Richard Rogers, Oscar Hammerstein, and Lorenz Hart). The postwar period saw the decline of the big band, and the rise of the star singer – Bing Crosby, Frank Sinatra, Nat King Cole, Perry Como, Pattie Page – all of whom toured Europe and sold millions of records there. The US influence spread through tours, records, tapes, film musicals. Even scores for Broadway musicals were recorded and played on radio and on home record players. Jazz was especially popular, with great names such as Errol Garner, Oscar Peterson, and Louis Armstrong. Popular singers like Sinatra and Crosby became cult heroes; Frank Sinatra's concerts caused teenaged girls to go into swooning hysterics. New York and Hollywood dominated in that decade but with the coming of rock and roll music in the mid-1950s, initiatives and performers spread to the Midwest and South.

The move to northern cities of southern blacks transformed American popular music throughout the Atlantic community. Jazz was of black inspiration, pioneered by itinerant black bands, and by great masters such as Duke Ellington. At the start of the 1930s, black bands – barred from the fashionable restaurants and hotels – moved from one small town to another to play at local dances. Later this music gained status as well-known ensembles went on regular tours, traveling in expensive coaches, and playing for wealthy audiences. Detroit, Chicago Southside, and East St Louis were especially important as blacks from the Mississippi delta began playing their folk music with electric guitars; urban blues were the result. With its strong rhythm it became the music of a youthful sexual rebellion against parents and society; it was slyly or crudely sexual music. (Rock and roll, in black slang, meant having sex.) The titles too were blatantly sexual: "Rock Around the Clock", "Rock Me All Night Long." Rock and roll was also distinguished by "the insistent, heavy beat with guitars and drums dominating the melody, the shouted rather than sung lyrics, the repetitive phrasing, the ear-splitting electronic amplification ... the atmosphere of feverish excitement ... blurred sounds ... nasal twangs."[48]

The explicit sexual lyrics – "Baby Let Me Bang Your Box," "Drill Daddy Drill" reached their ultimate practitioner in Elvis Presley, who was catapulted on to the national scene after TV appearances on the Ed Sullivan show in 1955–6. Presley looked like a high school principal's ideal of a wholesome young man; yet his music also symbolized rebellion against traditional proprieties. Buddy Holly (and the "Crickets") from Lubbock, Texas, was an earlier white founder of rock and roll, but his style had none of Presley's smoldering sexuality. Holly, critics claim, was a better musician and innovator than Presley and was more popular in Britain and Europe than in the US. Unfortunately Holly died (along with a Hispanic rock and roll musician Richie Valens) in a plane crash in 1959. Elvis was conscripted into the army, and when he got out in 1960, had little more to contribute to rock and roll. The dynamics passed to Liverpool, England, and the Beatles, who graphically showed the richness of the reciprocal influences of relations between the US and Europe. The Beatles, after appearing on "Toast of the Town" in 1960, brought a revived, more complex variety of rock and roll to the US.[49]

But it was black musicians – Fats Waller, Bo Diddley, Chuck Berry, and B. B. Williams who laid the foundations for rock and roll. Because they were black they were not accepted as country and western singers. Berry played at the Cosmopolitan Club in East St Louis, Illinois, and added an occasional country and western tune to his Nat King Cole selections. It proved danceable, and whites came to hear him. His songs were basic to the rock and roll revolution; they were sly and sexy, and appealed to the young. Berry influenced American musicians greatly; and he had even more impact on the Beatles and the Rolling Stones in Britain.[50] But white audiences in those days preferred white singers who sounded like blacks. So Bill Haley's "Rock Around the

[48]Hart, *When the Going Was Good,* p. 132.

[49]Ibid, pp. 134–5.

[50]See Chuck Berry: *Chuck Berry: The Autobiography.* New York, Harmony Books, 1987. For the history of rock and roll see John Tobler and Pete Frame, *Rock 'n' Roll: The First 25 Years.* New York, Exeter Books, 1980, *passim.*

Clock" was seventh on the charts in 1955. And it was Holly and Presley who really took black songs and sounds and created rock and roll for white audiences. Presley had the most hits – 8 in the top 40 and three number ones in the US and in the UK. (His biggest hits were "Heartbreak Hotel," "I Need You, I Love You," "Hound Dog," "Love Me Tender.") They live on and have become American classics.

ART

In the 1940s intellectuals such as Norman Podhoretz claimed American culture had no status. Many European and American people believed him: Americans were thought to be vulgar yet innocent, materialistic and provincial. America's culture, such as it was, was felt to be purely derivative of Europe's; her art and literature were widely regarded as inferior. In the postwar world this view was shattered.

America became the friend, protector, and developer of Europe after the war, when the US led the world politically, economically, and militarily. There developed a "newfound pride in the American way of life and American culture flourished."[51] Artists felt this new confidence and tried to articulate it by paying special attention to American life and popular culture. This new art reflected both their country's postwar affluence, its technological and scientific dominance, and also its consumerism, commercialization, civil unrest, and the anxieties engendered by the Cold War. The new art ran counter to European style by turning first to abstract expressionism. New ways of expression such as pop art followed, as American artists focused on the industrial system of mass production and mass communication.

America itself became the subject matter of pop art. This followed on from abstract expressionism (itself an extension of European modernism) that sought to build an American form of art. The abstract expressionist artists had wanted to show that American art was different from, and superior to, European art. The exhibition "School of New York" in 1951 made the comparison explicit in its title. Some critics chose to interpret abstract expressionism as uniquely American and distinct from expressionism. Others saw it as individualistic and alienated from American society and its vulgarity and industrialism.[52] Whatever the truth, American artists succeeded in creating a new art, abstract, controversial, but wholly American.

---

[51]Sidra Stich, *Made in USA: An Americanization in Modern Art. The 50s and 60s*. Berkeley, University Art Museum, University of California Press, 1987, p. 6.
[52]Ibid., p. 7.

PABLO RUIZ PICASSO (1881–1973)

Picasso's entry in the British Who's Who *barely fills 23 lines, a fraction of the space devoted to many other worthies now forgotten. Even a casual review should fill many pages. For everything about Picasso was impressive – the number of his pictures, his styles, his exhibitions, his friends, his enemies, and his love affairs. His very name was sonorous (he was christened Pablo Nepomuceno Crispiano de las Santisima Trinidad Ruiz y Picasso). He was the best-known artist of his age. Students who have never heard of Giotto know about Picasso; television watchers who care not a whit for modern art are delighted by commercials that use Picasso's techniques. Picasso represented – like no other artist – the revolution in modern art from naturalism (in which he also excelled), to cubism and surrealism. All was grist to his mill – sculpture, portraits, posters.*

He apparently defied all. A native-born Spaniard, he made his name in France. He denounced Fascism (especially in his world-famous picture Guernica*) at a time when Fascism seemed a winning cause. A one-time communist, he painted a portrait of Stalin at the Soviet leader's death, which caused a furore, since the Soviets had previously locked up a great collection of Picasso's early works in the basement of Leningrad's Hermitage museum. Picasso's comment was that everyone had a right to react to his pictures in their own way – forgetting the ordinary Soviet citizens' right to see what they pleased.*

*Picasso stood for more than novelty in art. His success embodied the advance of the leftish avant garde into the new establishment, and he was judged a prophet in political matters. His success moreover was of the tangible kind that figured on a balance sheet. According to the romantic image of the nineteenth century, the true artist starved in a garret. Picasso was wealthier than many of those whom he affected to despise. An obituary (*New York Times, *April 9, 1973) discreetly commented, "Picasso's works fetched enormous prices at auctions, in the hundreds of thousands of dollars. By sales through his dealers, the artist himself became wealthy, although the precise size of his estate is not known." He was a unique artist; he was also a new kind of entrepreneur, protestor turned millionaire.*

Paris had continued to dominate the fine arts after the war, primarily because Matisse, Picasso, Rouault, Braque, Léger, and Dufy were finally perceived as great modern painters. But other cities challenged Paris's leadership as a marketplace for art (New York, Zürich, and Düsseldorf) or as an innovative source (New York and London). War had given inspiration to British painters and sculptors, especially those officially commissioned as war artists. They included Henry Moore, one of the most notable modern sculptors since Rodin. During the war, Moore produced a famous series of drawings that interpreted the grim world of London air raid shelters improvised in underground stations, with their mood of mixed anxiety, stoicism, and courage. Moore's main work consisted of wood and stone carvings that stressed truth to the material used and to inherent content rather than verisimilitude. In general now, art became more international, and new American painters came to the fore, abandoning realistic, and impressionistic art and seeking not surface reality but hidden reality.

> *German art had a hard time recovering from Nazism. American art acted as a catalyst in the 1950s, esepcially the two major exhibitions sponsored in Berlin in 1958 by the Museum of Modern Art, New York – "New American painting" and "Jackson Pollock: 1912–1956." Abstract expressionist art appealed to young German painters and provided a stimulus for the next two decades.*

The US in the postwar period went through three important art movements: abstract expressionism (AE), pop art, and minimalism. Abstract expressionism made New York the center of the art world for a time. None of America's modern painters had previously had much influence on Europe, nor were they highly respected. AE in a sense represented a revolt against European art conventions. The leaders of the new movement were Jackson Pollock, Clifford Still, Franz Kline, and second in importance only to Pollock, Willem de Kooning. By 1950–1, theirs was the pre-eminent movement in American art (it began to decline in 1960–1). Representational art was regarded as reactionary by the abstract artists; freedom, impulsiveness, spontaneity, the unconscious and the formless were sought instead.

Pollock became famous for his "drip" paintings of 1947–51. (He has been compared by some critics to Cézanne and Picasso in originality.) Pollock lived and died in the same frenetic style which characterizes his paintings. De Kooning, who led the abstract expressionist movement from 1951 to 1960 painted many of the most beautiful paintings of the abstractionists (notably *Gansevort*, 1949).

> *Pop-art caught on well with the media, museums, collectors and gallery dealers in the late 1950s and the 1960s. The term "pop art" was coined by a British critic, Laurence Alloway, to describe the work of British artists who were following the popular culture imagery of American artists.*

Pop art involved a kind of super realism, honoring the commonplace of everyday life – a Campbell's soup can, Dick Tracy, urinals, and shopping carts. It was pioneered by Marcel Duchamp during his stay in the US. The most important pop artists in the US were Robert Rauschenberg, Jasper Johns, Andy Warhol, and Roy Lichtenstein; in Great Britain David Hockney and Richard Hamilton were best known. Pop art declined in the late 1960s and by that time it had restored representational art to respectability (even though the successor movement – minimalism – was not realistic). Artists became more interested in balance, color, and design, but in realistic portrayal. At the same time, relativism replaced absolutism; standards were overturned, individual vision and intuition replaced reason and community.

Many critics wondered if pop art could really be classed as art at all, since it dealt with the banal material of daily life. But that was the essence of the new art; it aimed to reproduce for closer inspection the ordinary, the mass products and imagery of everyday. Some critics even saw popular art as a patriotic response to the Cold War – American flags were widely depicted. In any case American art, after a period of abstract expressionism, focused on all aspects of American mass culture, not just high culture. Pop art by the late 1950s had replaced abstract expressionism.

As a result of America's new role of leadership in the world, artists and intellectuals had become more interested in the history of American culture. Postwar confidence led to the founding of numerous American studies programs (ASPs). (In 1944 there were 29 ASPs, in 1956 there were 82, in the US.)[53] Books and articles on all aspects of American history and culture rolled off the presses. American art was re-examined, exhibited, honored. The Metropolitan Museum of Art in 1954 had an exhibit of "Two Centuries of American Art" and in 1957 opened eight permanent galleries of American painting. Then in 1958 "Art: USA: 58" opened in Madison Square Garden, displaying 1,540 paintings and 300 sculptures.

American intellectuals in the 1950s thus not only began to take pride in their heritage but also to throw off their sense of cultural inferiority to Europe. *Partisan Review* asked 24 respected thinkers to write about "Our Country and Our Culture." America was seen by the contributors as the defender of Western culture and successor to a failing Europe: the US was the most powerful and wealthy nation in the world, therefore its culture should also be valued. Many felt less alienated or exiled in this new America, where artists and writers were more highly prized.

The *Partisan Review* authors still feared the mass culture which prevailed in the US. "Admass" consumerism, conformity, Coca-Cola, TV, comics, *Time*, *Life*, and many other items of popular culture were to be deplored. *Kitsch* no, the avant garde yes. Nevertheless, mass culture's power and appeal had to be recognized. As the postwar period wore on, American society became more and more middle class in its goals, values, and standards of material well-being. Goods and services, popular culture, advertising, all were targeted toward this large and growing middle class. Nationwide firms sprang up, the interstate highways bound the country more closely together, the mass media provided for readers, listeners, and viewers standardized information and entertainment. The country became more homogeneous, and regionalism declined; an all-American popular culture was born: "As a hybrid form of democracy crossed with free-market capitalism, mass culture seemed peculiarly American, a rebuff of European aristocratic traditions and communist economics."[54]

To conclude, American culture and folkways were studied, written, and spoken of in a new light. Artists became more interested in the American way of life, and less concerned with European images and iconography. The mood was upbeat and affirmative; there was vitality, and appreciation, for example, of the machine-made – the result being a cultural boom during the 1950s. There were more book exhibits, new museums flourished. The museums themselves became more open, less elitist; they ran lectures, bookshops, res-

[53]Ibid., p. 8, see also Diana Crane. *The Transformation of the Avant-Garde: The New York Art World, 1940–1985.* Chicago, University of Chicago Press, 1987.

[54]Stich, *Made in USA*, p. 9.

taurants, film programs, and larger exhibitions. Artists in the past had often seen themselves as alienated, impoverished outsiders in US society. By the 1950s, many had ceased to feel this. Some at least became celebrities; others advanced to the faculties of great universities and commanded high prices for their work.

The Cold War and the special relationship with Europe brought America out of its isolationism and involved it deeply in international affairs. The effects of the rebuilding of Europe, the Marshall Plan, and foreign and cultural diplomacy, led to the exporting of American technology, goods, and popular culture. The American way of life became known throughout the world. Foreigners compared America's freedom, free enterprise economy, consumerism, material well-being, and cultural achievements with the record of the communist world, especially the Soviet Union. Americans themselves felt their country was superior in most fields; artists and writers became proud of being American.

15

Religion

God's death has been proclaimed many times. For two centuries, a succession
of great Western thinkers – d'Holbach, Marx, Nietzsche, Freud – had gloried
in intellectual deicide. All great religions were subjected to a harsh reduc-
tionism at different times. According to Hitler, they could be reduced to the
quirks of racial consciousness; for Stalin, they represented only the concealed
interests of particular social classes; according to Freud, they merely gave
voice to unconscious drives and fears. All that remained was to give God a
decent burial. Even for many believers, the prospects of religion seemed dim
after World War II. The churches in liberated Europe stood accused of
pusillanimity, or worse, for having failed adequately to resist the Nazi menace;
many churches found themselves beset by a sense of guilt. This found
expression, for instance, in the German Protestants' *Evangelische Selbstprüfung,*
a conference report issued after the war, shaped by the thoughts of Karl Barth
(a German theologian removed by the Nazis from his professorship, as was
his colleague, Paul Tillich, another Protestant theologian influential after
World War II).

Eastern Europe remained occupied by the Soviet Union. Professing Christians and Jews met with widespread persecution within the Soviet sphere. In
the West, there was no oppression, but the churches did have to cope with
opposition of a less bloody kind: amused skepticism, unsure eclecticism,
secularism or materialism, sullen indifference, or despair. In the Catholic
countries there was also a strong anti-clerical tradition. (In the US, anti-
clericalism was in a way replaced by the liberals' keen and often snobbish
dislike for old-fashioned Protestantism.) Religious skepticism was reflected,
for example, in Bertrand Russell's influential *History of Western Philosophy,* and
Will Durant's multi-volume *Story of Civilization.* Durant, like Russell, wrote
wittily and well and was deservedly influential, though much underrated by
professional historians, most of whom (unlike Durant) failed to make either
the Book of the Month Club, or gain a wide readership. An uncertain eclecticism marked Arnold Toynbee's massive *Study of History* – erudite, full of

gloomy generalizations and portentous forecasts, much translated and even abridged after World War II, but thereafter almost forgotten.[1] Even more discouraging for committed believers was widespread indifference, linked not to "a frenzied search for pleasure after the restrictions and horrors of war but rather, among the young [to] a need and a demand for morose and cynical enjoyment, and among older people a need for an unquiet repose."[2]

Indifference all too easily tipped into despair, an oppressive sense of absurdity. For many the universe seemed senseless; there was no purpose in human existence; man was but a tiny spark doomed to everlasting extinction. Religious beliefs of the traditional kind had supposedly been swept into the dustbin of history. The writings of Jean-Paul Sartre, Max Frisch, Cesare Pavese, Graham Greene, the plays of Samuel Beckett and Jean Anouilh, the verse of Jacques Prévert, all expressed in different ways a conviction that faith, hope, and charity, as understood by St Paul, were illusions. Moreover, ignorance was rife even among professed believers. (In the US, a land of self-proclaimed Bible readers, only 34 percent of the respondents in a 1954 poll could identify the author of the Sermon on the Mount, and only 46 percent could name all four Evangelists.)[3] Above all, the holocaust, war, and tyranny, as experienced in the twentieth century, had once more raised in its most poignant form Job's ancient question as to why an all-good, all-wise, and all-powerful God should have allowed the wickedness that had destroyed innocents in their millions.

There was also the burden of guilt. Had the churches done enough to oppose the horrors of Nazism and Fascism, especially the persecution of the Jews? Had Christians in fact played a more honorable part than non-believers? A relatively small number of German officers and soldiers, for example, had refused to participate in the execution of innocents – Jews, gypsies, and other unarmed civilians, as well as Soviet prisoners of war. These courageous Germans had included professing Christians, but most of them seem to have been inspired by secular motives – a sense of honor, professional duty, or commitment to legal process. (Contrary to a widespread assumption, the "refusers" had even included fully fledged Nazi party members.)[4] In any case, in Germany and the rest of occupied Europe, the Good Samaritan was as much a rarity as in the days of the New Testament.

Doubt and skepticism played a part in lowering church attendance after World War II; so did the great shifts of population that broke up traditional

[1]William James Durant. *The Story of Civilization*. New York, Simon and Schuster, 1935–75, seven vols, Arnold Joseph Toynbee, *A Study of History*. Oxford, Oxford University Press, 1934–61, 12 vols, Bertrand Russell, *History of Western Philosophy*. New York, Simon and Schuster, 1972.

[2]G. Naidenoff SJ, "The present state and the problems of mission of the Catholic Church," in Waldemar Gurian and M. A. Fitzsimons, eds, *The Catholic Church in World Affairs*. Notre Dame, University of Notre Dame Press, 1954, p. 193.

[3]*Religion in America*. Gallup report, no. 236, May 1985. See also article on religion in *International Encyclopedia of the Social Sciences*. New York, Free Press, 1968, pp. 421–8. H. Stuart Hughes, *Contemporary Europe*, pp. 420–1.

[4]David H. Kitterman, "Those who said 'No!' Germans who refused to execute civilians during World War II," *German Studies Review*, v. I, no. 2, May 1988, pp. 241–54 for individual case histories.

congregations; so did the growth of the entertainment industries. On a Sunday, the average English worker was more likely to take his family to a film show at the nearby Odeon than to church. The same applied to most Catholic countries; by the 1950s, only between 10 and 15 percent of Italian and French Catholics regularly went to mass. The churches in Europe had also lost in many other ways. The war had occasioned enormous physical damage – cathedrals and chapels bombed, meeting halls gutted, property looted, funds confiscated or stolen. Worse still were the human losses: clergymen killed in battle, air raids, or murdered in concentration camps; their parishioners decimated. (To give one example, practically half of the 20,000 students of a federation of Catholic *Gymnasium* in Germany died in combat in World War II.)

Generalizations, of course, are difficult to make. Church attendance and congregational loyalty varied enormously from country to country, from region to region, from class to class, and between the genders. In Italy and France, for instance, women traditionally went to mass more often than their fathers and husbands. Peasants in Normandy were more likely to be solid churchgoers than rural people in Provence. By contrast, urban workers, teachers, and college professors were more likely to be anti-clerical than rural gentry or army and naval officers. In Britain, there was a long-standing split between the Anglicans, associated traditionally with rural England and with the establishment, and the nonconformists, powerful especially in Scotland and Wales, well represented also among skilled workers and shopkeepers in the industrial cities. These traditional distinctions were on the decline. But they were strong enough to add a faintly confessional touch to politics, as nonconformists were more likely to vote for Labour than the Tory Party. In France the position, in a sense, was reversed, and the Protestants formed a small minority. But this minority held an extraordinarily influential position in the highest reaches of state administration, higher education, and finance. (*HFP* – *haute finance protestante* – was a widely used term expressing alike reluctant admiration and guarded disapproval.) The US, by contrast, was the only major country in the world where adherents of Protestant sects (as opposed to members of an established Protestant church) made up the great majority of the population. Among these Protestants, Sectarians, Episcopalians, Congregationalists, Unitarians, and Methodists were more likely to be well off and well connected than Lutherans, Baptists (and Catholics). Churchgoing overall was much more popular in the US than in Europe, but even so professional people were less likely to attend services regularly than workers. (In the 1950s, 34 percent of the Protestant workers regularly attended church, whereas 47 percent of professional people did so.) Given these manifold differences, it is not surprising that the churches could not speak with a united voice. In fact differences of opinion within each church were probably as great as the divergencies between them.

Nevertheless, the prospects for religion were better than pessimists assumed. War had indeed brought nihilism and despair, enmity and betrayal; it had also engendered innumerable acts of courage and compassion. There were martyrdoms, and there was also a holiness disguised as routine. For instance, a German estate owner's wife was sent an assignment of slave laborers from a nearby concentration camp. Shocked at the men's condition, she established secret communications with resistance leaders inside the camp in order to organize an escape. To her surprise, she received a request from an imprisoned priest for hosts (the bread used in the Catholic communion) complete with precise instructions on how to bake it. She regularly prepared the bread. As the workers (mostly Jews) returned to camp each night, they would, at fantastic risk, conceal the bread in their clothes. The German woman was at first convinced that the bread would never get to the priest, because the emaciated and famished men would eat it. But every piece was duly delivered.[5]

War had changed the spiritual scene in other ways. Nazism had been a great challenge to Christianity. Nazi theoreticians such as Alfred Rosenberg had denigrated St Paul for being a Jew and for pleading world Jewry's cause.[6] German Protestant churches in particular had ingloriously capitulated to the Nazis in excluding non-Aryans from the pastorate and congregation. As distinguished a philosopher as Martin Heidegger had sung the Nazis' praise in 1933 in terms that blended obscurantism and servility. After the war, churchmen, like laymen, fell over themselves to disclaim any links they might have had with the Nazi party. The Jewish religion, persecuted and vilified by the Nazis, later dismissed even by Toynbee as a "fossil," did not die. On the contrary, its three main groupings, Orthodox, Conservative, and Reform Judaism, all regained vigor, especially in the US and in Israel – the latter becoming the main center of Jewish religious activity in the world.

Christianity, far from declining, also expanded. Religious statistics are difficult to gather, and harder still to evaluate. But by the middle of the twentieth century, about one third of the world's population called themselves Christians. An estimated 900,000,000 in all (including some 450,000,000 Catholics, 150,000,000 Greek Orthodox, 300,000,000 Protestants of many different nominations, and members of various national churches – Armenian, Ethiopian, and so forth). The disasters of war had created anguish and skepticism, but had also occasioned a revival of belief among many of the stricken. Once the fighting ended, a new crop of dedicated and able men and women (including numerous veterans) decided to train as priests and pastors, nuns, and brothers. The immediate postwar years in fact became a golden age of ecclesiastical, as well as of academic recruitment. The Catholic Church in the US particularly benefited; it was only in the late 1950s that the number of applications for the religious life gravely diminished and the pastorate began to age. Statistics in this regard vary greatly from country to country. (In 1950, Europe had an estimated 215,000 priests 53,000 of them Frenchmen, the most numerous national clergy in the world. Latin America, supposedly a stronghold of

[5]Wendelgard von Staden, *Nacht über dem Tal, Eine Jugend in Deutschland*. Dusseldorf, Eugen Diederichs Verlag, 1979, p. 85.

[6]Alfred Rosenberg, *Der Mythus des 20. Jahrhunderts: Eine Wertung der Seelisch-Geistigen Gestaltenkämpfe unserer Zeit*. Munich, Hoheneichenverlag, 1934, pp. 75, 235, 457, 480, 605.

Catholicism, lagged behind with 24,500 priests. The US and Canada, by contrast, had over 53,000 secular and regular priests, an impressive figure nearly three times as great as for the Church of England.) The Catholics maintained a major missionary enterprise. (Between the early 1930s and the early 1950s, the number of Catholic missionaries doubled worldwide, with Ireland supplying proportionately the largest number of missionary priests, followed by the Low Countries.)[7]

> *Throughout Western Europe and the US, secularization grew during the 1950s. In Catholic countries the Church lost influence on issues such as divorce, abortion, birth control, and marriage. In the first year after the war, church attendance was high – in Italy 75 percent of the people went to church regularly but then the figure declined to about 35 percent by 1980. Thanks to wider use of birth control devices the birthrate declined steadily from the late 1950s on, even in Catholic countries where artificial birth control was forbidden.*

Overall, the Catholic Church in Europe had emerged from the war with heightened prestige and influence, especially in countries where Christian Democratic parties predominated. Many churchmen had played an honorable part in the various resistance movements. The Catholic Church had made all kinds of political compromises with Nazism and Fascism, but had never reneged on its spiritual principles. No doubt the Church could have done more to condemn Hitler's murder campaign against the Jews, as well as Nazi atrocities against Poles, Russians, gypsies, and a score of others, but according to Hungarian scholar Istvan Deák, "no other institution produced a greater number of heroes in the years before and during the Holocaust: Polish, German, Italian, and French nuns, monks, priests and lay priests, who gave their lives or suffered imprisonment for the sake of Jews."[8] The Church for many years had tried to defend the workers and the poor through Papal encyclicals *Rerum Novarum* (1891) and *Quadragesimo Anno* (1931). Worker-priests sought to win back workers to the Church and to defend workers against exploitation. The movement began in 1946 when priests donned work clothes and went into the factories; by 1951 there were more than 90 worker-priests in France alone. Some became communists, more became socialists, and some got married, and left the Church. The Vatican forbade any more priests to go to the factories and sharply restricted the activities of worker-priests. In 1959 the Church ended the experiment completely, saying working in factories was not compatible with being a priest. (Worker-priests cropped

---

[7]According to the *New Catholic Encyclopedia*, New York, McGraw Hill, 1967–71, entries under "missions," there were 61,859 missionaries in 1932 and about 125,000 missionaries a generation hence. Of these, 55,000 were natives of the countries in which they worked. The missionaries included 45,000 priests, 12,000 brothers, 75,000 sisters. There were as many mission priests from Ireland as there were priests inside Ireland. One out of every three priests in Holland was a missionary, one out of every four in Belgium, one out of every 11 in France, and 1 out of every 17 in the US.

[8]Istvan Deák, "The incomprehensible holocaust," *The New York Review of Books*, v. xxxvl, no. 14, 28 September 1989, p. 66.

up again in a sense in revolutionary theology in Latin America in the 1970s.)

American Christianity indeed came to occupy a particularly important place on the world's religious stage. The US became the world's foremost Catholic, as well as Protestant and Jewish, country. Faith, of course, cannot be measured in statistics. The application of Gallup polling techniques to the measurement of religious belief would probably have been regarded by both St Thomas Aquinas and Martin Luther as devils' work, or at least a numerological superstition. Nevertheless, statistics have some illustrative value, and all polls agree that a much higher proportion of Americans than Europeans (except the Irish) went to church, and believed in the existence of God, heaven and hell – or at least in life after death, perhaps the most essential component of a religious outlook.

In this regard, there was an extraordinary difference between the US and Western Europe.[9] A century and a half before, American religiosity had struck Alexis de Toqueville on his visit to the US, and it had surprised many foreign visitors thereafter. Immigrants had built their own churches and schools; and there was a connection, however tenuous, between church membership and ethnicity. There was, however, no institutional link between church and state; ecclesiastical vigor profited from private endeavor in the religious field, just as material prosperity benefited from private enterprise in the economic sphere. Clergymen moreover had always acted as cultural pioneers on the open frontier; they had built churches, schools, colleges, universities, and imprinted their stamp on American culture.

According to the American historian Arthur M. Schlesinger, intolerance toward Catholics was the nation's oldest prejudice. Hyphenated Americans, especially Catholic ones, were regularly criticized in the press and textbooks and from the pulpit and the lectern. Catholics' loyalty and commitment to American values was doubted. Catholic schools were said to be inferior and divisive. Nativistic anti-Cathjolic prejudice waned after World War II (except over the question of federal aid to Catholic schools). No new Paul Blanshards took up the pen or microphone to attack Catholics on the national scene. Non-Catholic Americans continued distrustful of the Church in Rome but not at home – as witnessed by the election of John F. Kennedy to the presidency in 1960. The traditional division between Protestants, Catholics, and Jews began to soften. Increasing energy instead went into organizations with a political focus, right or left, such as the National Council of Churches, Christian Law Association, National Federation for Decency, Americans for God, or into organizations to assure disarmament, relieve world hunger, or help the divorced. These bodies split, not on denominational lines, but between liberals and conservatives.

In addition, there was another rift and one of much older standing. It

---

[9]According to a 1980 comparison, the percentage of respondents who stated that they believed in life after death stood as follows: Republic of Ireland: 76, Northern Ireland: 72, US: 71, Spain: 55, Italy: 47, Great Britain: 45, Norway: 44, Netherlands: 42, West Germany: 39, Belgium: 37, France: 35, Denmark: 26. *Religion in America,* Gallup report no. 259, April 1987, p. 54.

was the division between traditional churches and so-called cults outside the framework of established congregations. The latter displayed the American penchant for religious experimentation, especially on the frontier. Far from appealing only to the downtrodden and to outsiders, such dissident groups, with strong leaders and apparently bizarre theological systems, had much wider appeal. As Sir Charles Dilke, a well-bred Englishman, had noted with polite contempt on visiting the western United States during the 1860s, "There is a strange turning toward the supernatural among this people." It affected, not "the uneducated Irish," but rather "the strong-minded, half educated Western man, shrewd and keen in trade, brave in war, material and cold in faith, but credulous to folly . . . when the supernatural of the present day is set before them . . ."[10] Bodies such as the Church of Scientology (developed during the 1950s by L. Ron Hubbard, a former naval officer and a successful science fiction writer) followed in this tradition with their search for the true self, their missionary fervor, and their tendency to fragment.

America's religious vigor persisted after World War II, not merely on the farm, but also in suburbia, in "Middletown."[11] Conservative Protestants (divided into Fundamentalists, Evangelicals, and Charismatics) retained, and even widened their appeal, particularly among the white and black poor. The US turned into the world's main reservoir of Christian missionary labor, and the main source of the Catholic Church and missionary funding.[12] American economic and technological expansion abroad was replicated by US religious influence. Except in China, missionary churches expanded all over the world – in Africa, South East Asia, Latin America. Churches continued to operate both above ground, and underground in the communist-ruled parts of the globe.

Christianity throughout the world remained a powerful, though discordant force, and enjoyed other advantages. Rancor between its various denominations declined – as did old-style anti-clericalism – even in France, once the heartland of anti-clerical feeling. As an American Jesuit noted with surprise, "as a Catholic priest always wearing the characteristic soutane, I have travelled over the last 10 years between 60,000 to 70,000 miles in every direction without ever having heard anyone in France mock or insult me."[13] There was increased cooperation between the various churches in a variety of other ways. In 1948, for example, the World Council of Churches (WCC) convened for the first

[10]Charles Wentworth Dilke, *Greater Britain: A Record of Travel in English-Speaking Countries During 1866–7*. Philadelphia, J. B. Lipincott, 1869, v. 1, p. 139.

[11]Theodore Caplow, "Religion in Middletown," *The Public Interest*, no. 68, Summer 1982, pp. 78–87.

[12]Peter Duignan and L. H. Gann, *The United States and Africa: A History*. Cambridge, Cambridge University Press, 1984, p. 359.

[13]Naidenhoff, "The present state and problems of the missions of the Catholic church," in Gurian and Fitzsimons, eds, *The Catholic Church in World Affairs*, p. 194. The fathers' findings were borne out by statistics. According to 1959 polls, 61.8 percent of non-believers stated that they felt tolerant or favorable toward Catholics; 63 percent of Catholics had similar attitudes towards non-believers. See also Stanley Rothman, *European Society and Politics*. Indiannapolis and New York, Bobbs-Merrill, 1970, p. 200

time at Amsterdam, including most of the Protestant denominations in the world, as well as the Greek Orthodox and old Catholic Churches.

The WCC was not considered an unmixed blessing. The Catholic and Russian Orthodox Churches went unrepresented, as did the growing army of Evangelical Christians, and other dissident groups such as the Ethiopian, and Zionist black churches in South Africa. These latter particularly appealed to the unlettered, and all of them continued to increase their relative strength within the Protestant world. For all its shortcomings, the WCC, between 1948 and the early 1970s, gained increasing prestige, and stood committed to Western democracy. (Thereafter the council adopted an increasingly radical and anti-Western stance that found expression in the Nairobi Assembly in 1975.) In the US, the National Council of Churches was formed in 1950 to strengthen divided Protestantism and work for ecumenicalism. But overall the era of Protestant predominance in American history was over, except in the South. (The Southern Baptists were the largest of the Protestant churches, active especially in the rural South among less educated people.)

In the Jewish world at large, American Jewry from the late 1930s onward attained that intellectual dominance once held by German-speaking Jewry. American Jews steadily improved their position in business and industry, the public services, and academia. They largely, though not entirely, left the ranks of the working class. Prejudice against Jewish-Americans steadily diminished.[14] Among them were many of the world's leading Jewish academics, and the bulk of Jewish Nobel prize winners. (In this respect, American Jews became far more influential than British Jews, not merely in absolute but also in relative numbers. The US had offered broader educational facilities to the children of poverty-stricken immigrants than had Britain, where access to grammar schools and universities was more restricted.)

At the same time, American Jews became the main source of help for less-favored coreligionists overseas. (Jewish private aid in this regard paralleled the work done by American Catholics and Lutherans for their fellows in Western Europe and elsewhere.) American Jewry also became the principal foreign support for Israel. It had not always been thus. Before the war, Zionism had found its most numerous backers among Jewish lower middle-class people and intellectuals in Eastern Europe. The bulk of Eastern European Jewish workers had stood aloof, as had the majority of the Jewish upper class both in Western Europe and North America. But after World War II, support for Israel did transcend the differences between the various branches of Judaism, and became equally widespread among the secular and the religious – except for militant socialists on the one hand, and the ultra-orthodox on the other.

To sum up, the various churches remained divided over a great array of social, political, and theological issues. Nevertheless, it was during the twentieth century that Christianity acquired a strong foothold on every continent.

---

[14]Charles E. Silberman, *A Certain People: American Jews and Their Lives Today*. New York, Summit Books, 1985.

Contrary to earlier predictions, faith did not perish. As Paul Kurtz, a secular humanist, later concluded with regret:

> In the late nineteenth century, it was widely believed by the leading intellectuals that superstitious religions would decline and that, with increased education, improved standards of health, and economic well-being, the classical religious orthodoxies would be replaced by a humanist civilization based upon reason and science. But, although the technological revolution has made great progress, shrinking the globe, facilitating travel and communications between peoples and raising the standards of living and education worldwide, ... religious loyalties have persisted.[15]

CHURCHES IN POLITICS AND SOCIETY

A great many present-day students of sociology, history, political science, and even religion interpret the world in terms of social class as the main determinant of social behavior. Religion, all too often, gets short shrift – an omission that may reflect the religious skepticism widespread in academia more than social realities. The US provides a convenient example. Jewish Americans, since the days of Franklin Roosevelt, have mainly voted for the Democratic Party, particularly its liberal wing, even though the Jews rapidly rose in terms of social class, and should therefore have sided increasingly with the Republicans. "Jews live like Anglos and vote like Puerto Ricans" – this crude generalization has some justification.

An even more striking example can be found in Germany. According to a widespread orthodoxy, the German petty bourgeoisie during the early 1930s was ground between two millstones – monopoly capital at the top, organized labor at the bottom. Frightened of sinking into the ranks of the proletariat, the German petty bourgeoisie cast their votes for the Nazis and thereby enabled Hitler to gain power. The stereotype involved here reflects the intense dislike of the petty bourgeoisie that characterized so many intellectuals (including those many intellectuals ashamed of their own lower middle-class origins). In fact, the German petty bourgeoisie during the 1930s was badly split. This was particularly true of the farmers, an important section of the German petty bourgeoisie at the time. As Richard F. Hamilton has shown in a pioneering work, Protestant farmers tended to vote for the Nazis, but Catholic farmers were far more likely not to.[16] Religious or cultural affiliation widely transcended social class.

The postwar years witnessed a number of striking changes in the social and

[15]Paul Kurtz, "The growth of Fundamentalism world wide: a humanist response," *Free Enquiry,* Winter 1986–7, p. 18. For detailed statistical appraisals, see *World Christian Encyclopedia: A Comparative Survey of Churches and Religions in the Modern World,* ed., David Barrett, Oxford, Oxford University Press, 1982.

[16]Richard F. Hamilton, *Who Voted for Hitler.* Princeton, Princeton University Press, 1982.

religious landscape of the West. Within the Atlantic Community as a whole (including the US, Canada, and Western Europe) Catholics slightly out-numbered Protestants (nominal church members being included on both sides). By and large, and with many exceptions, Catholics, however, lagged behind Protestants in terms of material success. The period following World War II witnessed an overall improvement in the Catholic condition, an improvement that no sociologist had foreseen. The Catholic Church, far from declining, played an important, though indirect part in Western politics.[17] Both in the US and Western Europe the Catholic Church became more liberal, and accepting of democratic values. It encouraged Catholics to support Christian Democratic parties in West Germany, France, and Italy. Throughout the Atlantic Com-munity Catholics increased their social and political influence as they became better educated and moved into the middle class. Catholics in West Germany gained the most, as they formed almost half the population in a divided Germany; they sent more of their children to high school and university than previously, and benefited more from the economic recovery than did Protestants. Catholic Flanders in Belgium moved from being one of the most backward, to the most economically advanced, part of Belgium. Dutch Catholics also made demographic, economic, and social gains. English Cath-olics, mostly of Irish extraction, progressed from being a subculture to the mainstream of English society, as they too benefited from educational support and increasingly married non-Catholics. American Catholics moved up the social and economic ladder after the war and became more numerous in prestige professions. Anti-Catholic sentiments declined through the US except over the school aid issue. The economic condition of French Canadians in Quebec began to rise *vis à vis* their more urbanized and English-speaking countrymen.

There were also changes in thought. Already before World War II, Catholic thinkers in Europe had begun to turn from scholastic philosophy. The Jesuit houses of study at Lyon, under Henri de Lubac (Cardinal de Lubac) played a leading part in modifying church doctrine and teaching after World War II. They broke with what they regarded as the mistaken confidence of schol-asticism in its ability to explain everything to the erudite. American Catholic theologians and philosophers, by contrast, had never been much preoccupied with speculative thought, but rather concerned themselves with practical issues: buildings, church–state relations, and education. American Catholic leaders were concerned more with the task of transforming the sons and daughters of immigrants into middle-class Americans, rather than into scholars and scientists. Conservative Irish and Irish-American priests dominated the church in the US. It was not until the late 1950s and the early 1960s that neo-scholasticism was buried. (So completely was scholasticism dropped that a Jesuit seminary in the East invited Sidney Hook, a committed agnostic, to

---

[17]See Eric O. Hanson, *The Catholic Church in World Politics.* Princeton, Princeton University Press, 1987, *passim*, and review in *The New York Review of Books,* by J. M. Cameron, 5 November 1987, pp. 41–3.

lecture to novitiates on the philosophy of Thomas Aquinas.) But overall, the Catholic Church in the US, after 1945, was ready unquestioningly to accept the values of liberalism and democracy, and to assume the leadership of Catholicism in the Western world.

For the Catholic Church both in Europe and the US the war against Protestantism ended; ecumenism flourished; Catholic thinkers such as Pater Oswald von Nell-Breuning played a major part in reshaping Catholic thought on social questions (Nell-Breuning, for example, had a considerable influence on German trade unionism and the debate on "co-determination"). Vernacular language came to be accepted for the liturgy; the Index (a list of books not to be read by Catholics) was ended. Even Luther's reformation hymn *Eine feste Burg ist unser Gott*, in Carlyle's marvellous translation, was sung in Catholic churches, and the Reformation was finally accepted as a legitimate protest against corrupt church practices. There was a better attitude toward Jews; the spirit of the Catholic Church was thus enlarged and made more modern, tolerant and relevant. While church governance remained hierarchical, Catholics were enjoined to be good democrats and to be concerned for the poor and inept in society.

The greatest challenge faced by all traditional religions during the twentieth century derived from Nazism, and from Marxism-Leninism in its manifold variety. While stressing the primacy of economics, Marxism-Leninism operated in many ways as an apocalyptic religion that promised a new heaven on earth – a classless society in which all contradictions would find ultimate resolution. The churches' response was divided, ranging from uncompromising hostility to open sympathy. Avowed defenders of Stalin and his henchmen were few. They included divines such as Hewlett Johnson, an Anglican dean, an honest but misguided man who took Soviet propaganda at its face value. Accommodation was a more common response. It was an obvious choice in Soviet-occupied Europe where churchmen, determined to keep religious institutions at work, desisted from provoking the new rulers. There seemed much sense in the African proverb "do not insult the crocodile until you have crossed the river."

Accommodation was widespread also in those Western European countries where the communist parties were politically strong, especially in France and Italy. Catholic politicians in practice compromised with communists on a great variety of issues, both in central and in local governments; practical political considerations were apt to prevail over doctrine. Compromise appealed especially to those who thought that capitalism undiluted was of itself a great evil, and to those who equated unswerving hostility to the Soviet Union with Nazism, Fascism, militarism, or revanchism. Hence German Protestant theologians such as Barth and Martin Niemöller, men who had bravely resisted Hitler, chose to apply a different standard to Stalinism. The unintended effect of this policy was to play down Stalinist and Maoist horrors, a common feature of Western intellectuals and the media. In this regard, readers of a minor journal such as the *Tablet* (a British Catholic publication) were a great deal better informed than those who relied on papers such as the *Church Times*

(Anglican) or the London *Times*, or the *New York Times*. In those years it was as yet inconceivable that the day would come when (in 1989) Roy Medvedev, a Soviet historian, would explain to a meeting in Moscow that 36,000,000 36,000,000 people had fallen victim to Stalin's terror between 1927 and 1939, not counting the millions who had died in famines.[18]

But there was also committed opposition to Marxism-Leninism and to the Soviet Union's political ambitions. This opposition derived particular strength from the US, from minorities within the Protestant churches, and even more from the Catholics. American missionary bodies in particular were profoundly shocked by the persecution inflicted on Christian priests and pastors and on their Chinese converts by Mao Tse-tung after 1949. The Chinese drama entailed the American churches' first direct confrontation with communism as a ruling creed. Many Americans, especially Catholic Americans, moreover, had relatives in Eastern Europe and they entertained no doubt as to what had happened under Stalin's draconian rule. Moreover, no taint of collaboration with an occupying Nazi regime clung to the American churches, Catholic or Protestant. In the US, unlike Britain, the postwar era was one of ecclesiastical as well as secular self-confidence. (Between 1940 and 1960 the membership of churches and synagogues increased from an estimated 50 percent of the population in 1950 to almost 70 percent in 1960.)[19] While mainline Protestant churches declined, there was a religious revival for Fundamentalists and Evangelicals who stressed the Bible and faith, such as the Southern Baptists. The new Evangelicalism railed against Catholics, communists, and pornographers. *Christianity Today*, founded in 1956, was its forum and Billy Graham its voice. Conservative sectarians improved their organization and financial status. They were also among the first to use television for evangelical work, and thereby successfully made use of a new medium neglected by the mainline churches (with a few exceptions, such as Catholic Bishop Sheehan).

American churchmen had traditionally concentrated on matters of practical concern, on raising funds, building churches, and supporting schools. Religious institutions of higher learning had done well in undergraduate education; many added, after 1946, postgraduate training of a practical kind – law, business, education. After World War II, American churchmen also assumed an important role in religious theory. Catholic theologians such as John Courtney Murray and John Cronin challenged Marxism-Leninism in the ideological sphere, and did so with a degree of knowledge and sophistication that strikingly contrasted with the primitive anti-communism of the John Birch Society or Senator Joseph McCarthy. (Cronin's attitude in part reflected his long experience of anti-communist battles in the trade union field.) A change in Catholic attitudes with regard to the communist challenge came

[18]Paul Quinn-Judge, "Soviets raise count on Stalin's victims," *Christian Science Moniter,* 30 January 1989.
[19]Robert T. Handy, *A Christian America: Protestant Hopes and Historical Realities*. Oxford, Oxford University Press, 1984, p. 187.

only during the 1960s, under the pastorate of John Paul XXIII, marked by the optimism that infused the bull *Pacem in Terram*.[20]

Highly influential was Reinhold Niebuhr, a German-American by descent and cultural background, one of the leading Protestant thinkers of the time. Niebuhr considered himself a realist in the Augustinian tradition.[21] He was profoundly preoccupied, as Martin Luther had been, with Man's fallen state and original sin. Beginning as a pacifist, Niebuhr became a militant opponent of Nazism, and later of communism. He combined his contempt for tyranny with a firm commitment to social reform. He had much respect for the British Labour Party, warmly reciprocated by Labourites as diverse in outlook as Richard Crossman, Dennis Healey, and Tony Benn. In the US, Niebuhr's impact was greater still. A whole generation of liberal academics and statesmen proclaimed their debt to Niebuhr – Adlai Stevenson, Arthur Schlesinger Jr, McGeorge Bundy, Hubert Humphrey, Jimmy Carter – this despite Niebuhr's contempt for what he called "Whitehall religion," blended of political opportunism and sanctimony.

Eight European states are predominantly Catholic (France, Italy, Spain, Portugal, Luxemburg, Belgian, Poland, and Ireland). Six states of Northern Europe are Protestant, and three are divided almost equally between Catholic and Protestant (West Germany, the Netherlands, and Switzerland). As noted earlier, throughout the Atlantic community, church influence in domestic politics varied considerably. In the English-speaking countries (unlike West Germany and Italy) there was no major party that specifically claimed to be Christian. In Britain, the influence of the churches was on the decline, with falling memberships and diminished funds. (The only major exception in this respect was the Catholic Church which gained through Irish immigration, and a small but influential number of converts.) The Church of England had ceased to be a Tory stronghold. Indeed Archbishop William Temple (who died in 1944) had made his name as a supporter of Labour and of Christian social action, a course that appealed to many of the Church's generally ill-paid clergymen. The nonconformist churches, though still influential in Scotland, Wales, and Northern Ireland, had lost much of their former influence in the Liberal and Labour Parties; their political power was on the wane (as was that of the Free churches in Sweden). As a leading historian of the British Labour Party put it, "in this serious, if somewhat baffled age, the moral religion preached by the government and its unimpeachable public servants, supplied the substitute secular gospel for which the people craved."[22]

The Butler Education Act of 1944 in Great Britain had led to a great expansion of segregated Catholic secondary schools and of educational opportunities. These, in turn, allowed working-class Catholics to leave their inner-

---

[20]George Weigel, *Tranquillitas Ordinis: The Present Failure and Future Promise of American Catholic Thought on War and Peace*. Oxford, Oxford University Press, 1987, p. 207.

[21]Richard Wightman Fox, *Reinhold Niebuhr: A Biography*. New York, Pantheon Books, 1985.

[22]Kenneth O. Morgan, *Labour in Power, 1945–1951*. Oxford, Oxford University Press, 1985, p. 200.

city parishes and become socially and geographically more mobile. The English Catholics (and second generation Irish Catholics) underwent *embourgoisement* – a new, educated Catholic middle class developed as the state substantially financed the great school expansion programs of the 1950s. The clergy had wanted Catholic schools to maintain the Catholic subculture in church-controlled schools, but in this they ultimately failed.

English Catholics now number over 5.5 million. The majority traditionally voted Labour and only one-third married non-Catholics in postwar decades (though by the 1970s this proportion was up to two-thirds). English Catholics go to church more regularly than other denominations do; they outnumber worshippers at Church of England services and represent one-half of all churchgoers in England. The majority of English Catholics tended to be immigrants, Irish, and working class; in many ways they resembled Protestant nonconformists in their social situation. However in the postwar years, as the economy expanded, Catholics also experienced increased social mobility, and emerged from their subcultures. In some constituencies, the Catholic vote began to be important. (The same mobility occurred in US Catholics, but they kept their hyphenated status, that is, they called themselves Irish-American, Italian-American, or Polish-American. In England, they became Englishmen or Englishwomen with an Irish name.)

The Catholic Church in England thus broke out of its fortress-like subculture and became less hierarchical and part of the general secular English society.[23] In the United States, however, religious affiliation remained a safer guide for predicting a voter's party loyalty than income. While there was no established church, as in Britain, the religious communities – Baptists, Methodists, Calvinists, Lutherans, Unitarians, together with the Episcopalians – continued to supply the greater part of men influential in the state and the economy – such

---

As immigration from Ireland slowed, Catholics in England lost their working-class status and with more education Catholics completed the movement into the middle class. (Catholic schools supported by the state, thanks to the Education Act of 1944, educated one in 11 English children.)

As a result of education and middle-class status, Catholic views became similar to non-Catholics in divorce, contraception, and abortion. Catholics in England (as in the US) no longer always married other Catholics.

Between 1951 and 1969 Geoffrey Gorer carried out detailed surveys concerning sexual behavior in Great Britain. These showed a progressive loosening of sexual standards.

Nevertheless, by 1969, 46 percent of the men and 89 percent of women respondents were either virgins at the time of marriage, or had married the person with whom they first had sexual relations. Their behavior contrasted with the 19 year old truck driver who remarked "if it comes along, you don't turn it down," or of the 18 year old woman who replied "twice a week, if I like the boy. It depends on exams." (Arthur Marwick, Beauty in History, 1988)

---

[23]Michael P. Hornsby-Smith, *Roman Catholics in England: Studies in Social Structure Since the Second World War.* Cambridge, Cambridge University Press, 1987.

as bankers, senior civil servants (especially in the state department), presidents of great universities, office holders in the Republican Party. The Republican Party in the main continued to represent the "old stock" descended from Northern European Protestants. As Ralph W. Burgess, deputy secretary of the treasury and highly placed previously in the National City Bank, happily explained when Eisenhower gained office: "our kind of people are now in power."[24]

The Protestant establishment, however, faced several serious challenges. There was an ongoing defection of intellectuals from the Protestant ranks to secular humanist and socialist movements of the non-communist variety – a problem common to US Protestants, their coreligionists in Northern Europe, and also the Jews. Peculiar to America was the race problem. Black Americans, among the country's most committed Protestants, overwhelmingly supported the Democrats. Activist religion played a dominant role in the civil rights movement. On December 1, 1955, Mrs Rosa Parks, who was black, refused to give up her seat to a white passenger in Montgomery, Alabama. Hers was a symbolic act with tremendous repercussions. She gained overwhelming support from the churches, especially from black congregations. Martin Luther King, the famous spokesman, and later martyr, for the movement, was a black Protestant clergyman. So were many of his supporters such as Jesse Jackson. King had for long been a bitter critic of militarism and capitalism, but he managed to represent a broad coalition that united secular liberals, Jews, and Christians of many varieties – above all black Protestants. It was the black churches that formed the guards regiments of the civil rights movement. By contrast, Fundamentalists and Evangelicals of every color were more likely to withdraw from the political arena; they built their own schools, churches, clubs, and recreation centers; they saw themselves as a people apart. They only rejoined the political fray during the 1970s, by which time their ranks had been strengthened through numerous defections from the mainline churches, and the Christian Right had learned the techniques of political activism from the New Left.[25]

American Catholics mainly backed the Democratic Party, part of the New Deal coalition, although they widely voted for Eisenhower in 1952. Among their numbers were some militant dissenters who resented the establishment altogether, and the most important of these was Senator Joseph McCarthy. McCarthyism was an entirely new phenomenon in that it constituted, for the first time ever, a calculated attack on the loyalty of members of the Protestant, Anglo-Saxon establishment rather than on members of minority communities

---

[24]E. Digby Baltzell, *The Protestant Establishment: Aristocracy and Caste in America*. New York, Random House, 1964, p. 291. See also: George Marsden, ed., *Evangelicalism and Modern America*. Grand Rapids, William B. Eerdman, 1984; Robert T. Handy, *A Christian America*, 1984; Jay P. Dolan, *The American Catholic Experience*. Garden City, NJ, Doubleday, 1985; Andrew M. Greeley, *The American Catholics: A Social Portrait*. New York, Basic Books, 1977; John Cogley and Rodger Van Allen, *Catholic America*. Kansas City, Sheed and Ward, 1986.

[25]Denesh d'Souza, "Out of the wilderness: the political education of the Christian right," *Policy Review*, no. 41, Summer 1987, pp. 54–9.

such as Jews, Irish, or blacks.[26] McCarthy failed to mobilize the Evangelical Christians and Protestant millenarians. Had he succeeded in breaking down their self-chosen isolation, his thrusts at the establishment would have been more difficult to parry.

The bulk of American Catholics, however, no more sympathized with McCarthy than the majority of Protestants did. Thanks, in part, to the GI Bill, Catholics began to go to university in greater numbers and to move into positions of influence. They were active in the trade union movement (which counted many Polish-Americans, Italian-Americans, and Irish-American members). Catholic schools and universities grew in number and gained new prestige. Catholics began to advance into teaching positions in major national universities where they had previously encountered discrimination. More importantly, Catholics of Irish, Polish, and Italian descent vastly improved their economic position. By 1974, Jews ranked first in terms of the national family income average of American denominational groups (in 1974 dollars) among non-Spanish speaking whites in the northern metropolitan cities. Catholics came right behind the Jews, on average, earning more than the members of any other Christian denomination (followed in the northern cities, in descending order by Episcopalians, Presbyterians, Methodists, Lutherans, and Baptists). Catholics actually made more money than Jews when compared with those of the same educational and occupational background. Particularly successful in this regard were Irish Catholics, whose overall educational attainments came to exceed that of every Gentile white group. Polish and Italian Catholics likewise did well in terms of occupational mobility and had great financial success, though not in educational achievement or prestige positions.

The Catholic advance in this respect went counter to all academic theories that postulated a peculiar link between success and the Protestant ethos. As Andrew M. Greeley commented, "the idea of Italians being the second-richest Gentile group, and Poles and Slavs making more money in northern cities than British Protestants, will shock many."[27] But the silent revolution was unmistakable. While Catholics overall still lagged behind in terms of occupational prestige, they had achieved a powerful position. Politically, Catholics remained faithful to traditional New Deal issues in social policy. As far as the race issue was concerned, younger Catholics, on the average, turned out to be "less opposed to integration than comparable Protestants," and Irish Catholics were "right behind Jews in their support for racial integration."[28]

On the European Continent, there were also far-reaching structural changes, albeit for different reasons. Catholics comprised 49 percent of the Federal German Republic population (as against one third in the prewar *Reich*). Of the 11 *Länder* (states) four had a Catholic majority, especially Bavaria, the largest, and a stronghold of Catholic conservatism, as opposed to the more liberal Rhineland-Westphalia, with a large Catholic working class. Catholic

[26]Baltzell, *The Protestant Establishment*, p. 287.
[27]Greeley, *The American Catholic*, p. 65, for supporting statistical tables see pp. 54–6.
[28]Ibid., p. 270.

thought had influenced the new constitution (built on the assumption that there was a transcendental moral law above the sovereign state). Liberal Catholic thought had also influenced the Freiburg school of economics (centering on a traditional Catholic university). (Most of the Freiburg school's leading members – Walter Eucken, Wilhelm Röpke, Franz Böhm – were practicing Catholics.)

In West Germany, the Catholics emerged from the political ghetto that had been theirs in the Wilhelminian *Reich* and the Weimar Republic. Adenauer was a Catholic; so were most of his ministers. Protestant Prussia had disappeared from the map, and with it the erstwhile Protestant predominance. Bonn, the new capital, was mainly a Catholic city. Catholics dominated the CDU (about 74 percent of Catholics voted for the Christian Democrats), and in the Federal Republic no longer had to cope with old-fashioned anticlericalism (once popular in the SPD and, even more so, in the Nazi Party). Particularly during the Federal Republic's early days, the Catholic Church actively supported the CDU. It was only from the mid-1950s that there was a shift. This derived in part from changes within the SPD. Determined to attract more Catholic workers and salaried employees, the SPD dropped Marxism in favor of a reformist philosophy that could cite Pope John's *Mater et Magistra* in support of its position. The SPD, by contrast, retreated from its insistence on secular and interdenominational schools and welcomed Catholic voters into positions of leadership in the party.

The Protestant Church (reformed after the war as the *Evangelische Kirche in Deutschland*) found itself in unaccustomed opposition. The Protestant Church had been one of the principal supporters of the Hohenzollern establishment, and during the Weimar Republic, the clergy's position had declined both in political and economic terms. Shrinking salaries had hit a married clergy much harder than celibate Catholic priests. Many pastors had rejected the Weimar Republic. After the end of World War II, militant German nationalism became discredited within the Protestant Church. Some Protestants came to support the CDU, but many others turned to the Social Democrats. The Protestant clergy, like the Social Democrats, widely opposed West German rearmament; they advocated German reunification as an instrument of improving East–West relations; they played an important part in the legislation that legalized conscientious objection to military service; the Protestant Church Synod in 1958 condemned nuclear warfare. The Protestant pastorate increasingly shifted to left of center, toward a humanitarian reformism often mingled with pacifism – a position widely shared also by Lutherans in Scandinavia.

The Protestant bourgeoisie were suspicious of the new German state, fearing that it might become a Catholic state. This attitude was especially strong among the higher echelons of the bureaucracy, the clergy and university professors, primarily in law and theology. The Protestant ideals of state, public service, and *Kultur* were to be preserved by constitutional laws and the supreme court.

But in a certain sense, the Protestant Church in West Germany also formed part of the official establishment. Protestants, as well as Catholics, continued to rely on state support through church taxes (*Kirchensteuer*), and other forms of assistance. After the turmoil of war and its aftermath, the Protestant Church once more resumed its former character as "an official organization run according to the model of the state."[29] The German Federal Republic, moreover, continued to resemble the departed *Reich* in that Protestants continued to hold a favored position in academia, the administration, business, and the military. (Whereas Catholics made up approximately 49 percent of the population, their share in the German elites amounted to no more than 14 percent of university professors, 19 percent in business, 21 percent in mass media, 27 percent in public administration, 30 percent in non-business associations.)[30]

The Catholics' relative under-representation derived in part from geography; German (unlike American) Catholics were particularly numerous in rural regions. The social differences between Catholics and Protestants, however, did begin to change. Catholics increasingly migrated to the cities and attended university; new industries moved into Bavaria; Munich became a leading financial and industrial center and, in some ways, the intellectual and artistic capital of Western Germany – a process that paralleled the shift of new industries from the French-speaking parts of Belgium to strongly Catholic Flanders, with Antwerp an expanding port and metropolis.

The Catholics' position was equally strong in Italy where the Christian Democrats formed the ruling party. In Italy, even more than in Germany, clericalism of the old-fashioned variety weakened, "as the population shifts from country to city and from South to North were breaking up the fastnesses of Christian Democrat conservatism."[31] Overall, however, the Christian Democrats adapted more successfully to ongoing change in Italy than the communists. In France the MRP functioned as one of the leading parties of the Fourth Republic. Catholic communicants (especially women) voted heavily for the moderate parties. (Practicing Catholics formed 24 percent of those who voted for the Communist Party, 48 percent for the Socialist party, 56 percent for the Radical party, 74 percent for the UNR, and 79 percent for the MRP.) French Catholic thinkers such as Etienne Henry Gilson, one of the leading medievalists of the twentieth century, and Jacques Maritain, a neo-Thomistic philosopher, remained among the most influential intellectuals of their time.[32] It was only in Spain, still traumatized by the civil war, that the Catholic Church continued a stronghold of traditional conservatism. Clericalism was strong too in Portugal.

To sum up, the churches in Western society continued a powerful force, sustained by a network of professional, cultural and social associations. The religious divisions within the Western world remained, but lessened in inten-

---

[29]Heinz Kloppenburg, "Die evangelische Kirche von 1945 bis 1970," in Hans Dietrich Bracher, ed., *Nach 25 Jahren*. Munich, Kindler, 1970, p. 358.

[30]Rothman, *European Society and Politics*, p. 204.

[31]H. Stuart Hughes, *The United States and Italy*. Cambridge, Mass., Harvard University Press, 1965, p. 266.

[32]Maritain provided the Christian Democratic parties with a practical manifesto in his *Christianity and Democracy*, 1942.

sity. The churches in politics spoke with many voices; but they were heard. Whilst relativism and secularism in their many forms continued to be a powerful, vibrant and pervasive force, religion in the mid-twentieth century flourished in a manner that surely would have surprised Nietzsche, Freud, and Marx.

16

Conclusion

When Macaulay in 1848 introduced his great *History of England*, he promised his readers a success story. He would relate "how from the auspicious union of order and freedom sprang a prosperity of which the annals of human affairs had furnished no example." His narrative would "excite thankfulness in all religious minds, and hope in the breast of all patriots." His would be a tale of "physical, moral, and intellectual improvement."[1] Macaulay's confidence jars a modern reader. From the second part of the last century, the tide of optimism had already begun to turn. Nietzsche was a pessimist; so was Taine; so were countless *fin de siècle* artists and writers.[2] It was fear of impending decadence that caused Pierre de Coubertin to advocate in France the promotion of gymnastic and athletic exercises. It was fear of degeneration that persuaded so many intellectuals to declaim against "a rotten peace," and welcome the outbreak of World War I with a martial enthusiasm they later preferred to forget.

Gloomy foreboding remained in fashion after the peace had been signed. Men as different in outlook as Spengler and Freud cast the darkest of horoscopes for civilization. Their fears were not idle. Nazi barbarism went beyond the darkest nightmares. It was not without cause that Stefan Zweig, a civilized European, quoted in his autobiography from Shakespeare's *Julius Caesar* (V. iii. 63), "The sun of Rome is set; our day is gone. Clouds, dews and dangers come; our deeds are done."[3] In the end, Nazi tyranny collapsed; the Allies won – but at great cost. Much of Europe lay in ruins. Entire populations had been uprooted or exterminated.

To expect a rapid recovery and extended prosperity would then have appeared sheer irresponsibility. Ports were out of commission, factories bombed, whole cities razed. Hunger and sickness were rife; refugees in their

[1]Thomas Babington Macaulay, *The History of England from the Accession of James II*, Chicago, Belford, Clarke, and Co., c. 1869, v. I, pp. 13–14.
[2]Eugen Weber, *Fin de Siècle*, Cambridge, Mass., Havard University Press, 1986.
[3]Stefan Zweig, *Die Welt von Gestern: Erinnerung eines Europäers*. Vienna, Fischer Verlag, 1952, p. 354.

millions came to the West. There were deep-seated fears for the demographic future of Western Europe. Profound structural problems also beset the European economies – weaknesses derived from trade barriers, excessive cartelization, industrial obsolescence, and so on. The dollar gap (Western Europe's dollar balance-of-payments deficit *vis à vis* the US) was expected to continue indefinitely. No economist envisaged a situation in which the US 40 years later would be a debtor nation with a huge budgetary deficit. Even optimists in 1945 anticipated but a short-lived postwar boom, followed by yet another long-lasting slump, as had happened after World War I. British workers and servicemen dreaded future unemployment. British capitalists shared their fears.

This was not all. War and tyranny had left Europe with a grim psychological legacy of humiliation, pain, and betrayal. How could Europe revive when so many of its people had undergone terrors that had exceeded the surrealists' craziest nightmares? War and occupation might reasonably have been expected to have worsened national hatreds – Franco–German, Anglo–German, Italo–German, and so forth. There was also good reason to dread the return of violence to domestic politics, with uniformed columns marching in the streets, and gunmen waiting in ambush. Terror – like inflation – has its own kind of Gresham's law to the effect that bad money drives out good. War and dictatorship had habituated Europeans to violence; violence would surely continue.

Germany in particular could reasonably have expected a revival of Nazism in a country partitioned, impoverished, and demoralized to an even greater extent than after World War I. Evidence for pessimism regarding a recrudescence of Nazism was not far to seek.[4]

More immediate still was the unanticipated Soviet threat. To its admirers, the Soviet Union still represented the wave of the future. To its detractors it appeared a menace. The Soviets already dominated Eastern Europe. Their military potential was great, their determination assured, their wartime economic achievements astounding. (The Soviet Union, despite dislocation and destruction, had turned out 102,500 armored vehicles, 142,000 aircraft, and 490,000 artillery guns.)[5] If unchecked, the Soviets would surely extend their power into Western Europe by force or stealth. Who would stop them? The Europeans? They were exhausted by the war, and divided to boot. The Americans? They seemed all too likely to retreat once more from global responsibility, as they had after World War I.

Western political and economic fears were paralleled by cultural apprehensions. Religion was supposedly on the decline. Gloom and doom pervaded Sartre's philosophy, Toynbee's study of history, Orwell's counter-Utopia, Schoenberg's music, Dali's paintings and Beckett's plays. Their anxieties,

---

[4]Waler Laquer and Richard Breitman, *Breaking the Silence*. New York, Simon and Schuster, 1986, *passim*.

[5]Field Marshal Lord Carver, *Twentieth Century Warriors: The Development of the Armed Forces of the Major Military Powers in the Twentieth Century*. London, Weidenfeld and Nicolson, 1987, p. 314.

admittedly, were not shared by the mass of ordinary people who stood in line to buy tickets at the local Gaumont, Odeon, or soccer stadium. But dread of the future infused a good deal of Europe's literary and artistic world. Such fears sometimes went with a pervasive anti-Americanism, strong especially, perhaps, among French intellectuals. This anti-Americanism was of ancient standing. European intellectuals had always been ambivalent about the American Republic which, for some, seemed doomed to failure from its beginnings. As Dean Tucker had remarked, "as to the future grandeur of America, and its being a rising empire under one head ... it is one of the idlest, most visionary notions that was ever conceived even by the writers of romance."[6] But after 1945, the US was clearly the most successful of all great powers – and earned envy and admiration accordingly.

The resultant anti-Americanism in Europe affected André Malraux on the right as much as Sartre on the left. (Indeed Harold Laski, an influential intellectual in the British Labour Party, admired the Americans' vigor, equality, and adaptability.) Americans, like Jews, incurred criticism for the most contradictory reasons. They were soft – but they were also warmongers. They lacked that ruthlessness properly associated with true virility – but they also waged germ warfare. (*Ridgeway la peste*, ran the Parisian slogan referring to General Ridgeway, a US commander first in Korea, later in NATO.) The Americans sought to dominate Europe – but they would also leave her in the lurch. They were attacked as the world's parvenus, global purveyors of cultural rubbish. Antipathy of this kind may of course have reflected not merely dislike of real flesh-and-blood Americans, but also fear of modernization developing within Europe's own cultures. Germans might complain, for example, at the Americanized appearance of their new cities – all glass and concrete, without realizing it was their own *Bauhaus* style, transmogrified beyond the Atlantic, and returned to the Fatherland.

Americans proved no more immune from cultural pessimism than Europeans. It was true that the US was prosperous and afforded a haven for countless immigrants. It was also true that poverty overall declined, and America's material wealth visibly increased. Fewer American than French or Italian intellectuals believed in the reputed workers' paradise in the Soviet Union. Nevertheless, widespread apprehensions persisted among many US intellectuals concerning their country. This malaise had many springs. For instance, adherents of *realpolitik* questioned US ability to continue as the world's leading military and economic power in the long term.[7] More thorough-going pessimists dreaded ultimate ecological catastrophe. For many, technology had turned into a monster that would destroy its maker.

Profoundest of all were anxieties concerning atomic warfare, the Cold War, and the threatened manipulation of man's innermost being. Such dreads were

[6]Cited in Dale Van Every, *Ark of Empire, The American Frontier 1784–1803*. New York, Quill, William Morrow, 1963 (1988 edn, p. viii).
[7]Paul Kennedy, *The Rise and Fall of the Great Powers: Economic Change and Military Conflict from 1500 to 2000*. New York, Random House, 1987.

often associated with a fear of anonymous manipulatory powers associated with modernity. The old-fashioned caricature of the capitalist had at least been straightforward. "Hoggenheimer," the old cartoon figure of South Africa, had been a potbellied, top-hatted scoundrel, complete with cigar, diamond ring, hooked nose, and a mansion in London's West End. Hoggenheimer was hateful, but at least he was identifiable, perhaps even to be envied. Far more fearsome were the new, anonymous figures of power – the "hidden persuaders" of high-powered marketing, who covertly pushed the masses into consumerism, and destroyed their moral fiber. Indeed the superfluity of good things available to ordinary shoppers in supermarkets now seemed as dreadful to some intellectuals as poverty had appeared to their predecessors. Mass consumption *à l'américaine* would wipe out the cultural splendors of the past. (A Spanish cartoon, drawn by Juan Belleta, shows a medieval king who smilingly points to his great castle, and says to his little son "one day, all this will be yours." The castle bears a huge sign, "Burger King.") A few even feared that consumerism, new advertising techniques, and the cult of television would destroy men's souls. "The race has given up on the ideals of individual attainment and is slipping backward into an oceanic state of mass passivity."[8] It was a far cry from Macaulay's early-Victorian confidence.

Such fears proved exaggerated on both sides of the Atlantic. Western Europe after 1945 experienced an extraordinary recovery. Millions of refugees settled down in new or rebuilt homes, and became productive citizens. Millions of veterans readjusted to civilian life. The ingenuity and dedication that had gone into the preparation for battle and combat was turned to peaceful pursuits. European cities and industries were rebuilt and modernized. Savings increased and new capital was invested. Within five years of the end of the war, the gross national product of all Western European countries exceeded that of 1938. By the end of the 1950s, economic expansion had further accelerated, albeit at different rates for different countries. (Between 1950 and 1959 the index of GNP, at 1954 prices and exchange rates, with 1950 as 100, rose as follows: West Germany: 187, Austria: 168, Italy: 164, Netherlands: 151, France: 145, Belgium: 132, Norway: 132, Portugal: 132, Sweden: 132, United Kingdom: 121.)[9] Equally impressive was the economic achievement of the US whose GNP at current prices doubled between 1945 and 1957 (from 201 billion dollars to 402.6 billion dollars).

Statistical methods differed from country to country. Official statistics also failed to cover, or at least undervalued, certain activities. Almost by definition, these included all those black market transactions that helped to keep going the European economies during the immediate postwar period. Statisticians moreover have traditionally paid more attention to the output of goods than to the provision of services. (This preference stems in part from an ancient

---

[8] Sven Bikkert, Review of Mark Crispin Miller's, *Boxed in the Culture of TV*, in *The Atlantic*, September 1988, p. 94.

[9] J. Frederic Dewhurst et al., *Europe's Needs and Resources: Trends and Prospects in Eighteen Countries*. New York, Twentieth Century Fund, 1961, p. 17.

but vulgar prejudice against services, as against "real" industries.) Moreover, services are particularly hard to measure since so many are rendered by small firms, or by individuals ill trained or reluctant to keep books. But no matter how experts evaluate the statistics, there was impressive growth. There was also diversification. Old industries underwent improvement and new ones came into being. Thanks to the Marshall Plan agriculture enhanced its output – so much so that the prevailing preoccupation with shortages soon gave way to apprehension concerning surpluses.

Change of course was uneven. US long-term growth was slower than West Germany's or Japan's – a fact that would later lead to much self-searching. But starting from a huge base, even slow growth in the US was bound to be large in absolute numbers. Moreover, it was Washington's declared policy after World War II to help rebuild former enemy countries, and to reduce the economic gap between the US and its existing and new allies. The Americans could not reasonably complain, therafter, that they had succeeded in their aim. Western Europe's and Japan's successes were particularly impressive. The United Kingdom, Western Europe's leading country at the end of World War II, gradually fell behind the rest in absolute terms, but even their economy continued to expand. West Germany's *Wirtschaftswunder* restored it as Western Europe's principal economic power. Italy's equally remarkable recovery presaged a long-term shift in which the backward Mediterranean countries increasingly improved their relative position *vis à vis* the countries of Northern and Western Europe. A similar process was afoot in the US where the deep South and the West made striking advances.

Overall, recovery proceeded far more quickly in the capitalist countries west of the Iron Curtain than in the socialist countries to the East – an elementary truth more obvious to millions of German "border-crossers' than to the left-wing academics and journalists of the time. There was a plethora of *real existierend* or "real existing" communist models – Soviet, East German, Polish, Albanian, North Korean – as opposed to the utopian variety. But none of them succeeded in creating "socialism with a human face." For all their conviction about the moral and economic superiority of their own system, the communists could never equal Western enterprise and creativity. (Though conditions were roughly comparable, East Germany developed more slowly than West Germany, Czechoslovakia more slowly than Austria, North Korea more slowly than South Korea; Shanghai and Canton more slowly than Hong Kong.) Culturally, the various communist countries seemed at best to remain frozen following an initial period of growth after World War II. The Soviet Union's cultural and technological impact on Eastern Europe was infinitely less than America's on Western Europe. Few Eastern Europeans learned Russian well; many Western Europeans, by contrast, studied and became fluent in English. Goods flowed from America to Western Europe; in the East goods went to the USSR.

These Western achievements later lost much of their glamor. This is not surprising for material prosperity, once attained, is soon taken for granted. Young German radicals of the 1960s and the 1970s, for instance, would sneer at their elders, members of the *Wiederaufbaugeneration*, the *Verdienergeneration* (the rebuilder's generation, the profiteers' generation), with their taste for consumerism. These views strike us as neither novel nor appropriate. In the past, noblemen and priests were wont to decry the common people's taste for luxuries – supposedly unfitting for their station in life, and tending to make them both proud and slothful. In modern times, many secular intellectuals have adapted and embellished these prejudices. The intellectual's contempt for "meretricious" merchandise should be recognized for what it is, an untoward claim to social, or moral superiority on the part of a privileged, diploma-bearing elite.[10]

Not that all progress was necessarily good, or came without a price-tag, both in a technical and a cultural sense. For instance, the planners of the postwar period naturally concentrated on the immediate problems, rather than those of the future. At a time when food, steel, and coal were all in desperately short supply, policy makers were concerned above all with increasing the output of farms, steels mills, and coal mines. (As late as 1957, the so-called Wise Men's Report, issued by OEEC experts concluded that the EEC would continue to face a long-term shortage of energy.) Such assumptions, of course, made no sense later on, when Western Europeans had to worry about excessive steelmaking and shipbuilding capacity, and food surpluses. But postwar achievements must be seen in context, and at the time they were indeed impressive. The European economies all advanced and diversified; they developed closer links with each other, and with North America.

At the same time, the long-term shift continued from village to city, out of agriculture into industry, and from industry into service occupations (except in West Germany). This was a transformation for which the Jews of Europe had, so to speak, provided an earlier model widely held to their discredit.[11] For centuries, thinkers and statesmen had deplored this shift. Western literature is full of philippics against *Landflucht* (flight from the land), and calls for *le retour à la terre* (return to the land). The continued decline of village life did indeed shatter time-honored customs. Urbanization and the flight from the land at the same time reduced the cultural distance between different geographical regions, and between town and countryside generally. It is, however, all too easy to indulge in pointless nostalgia. Life in the traditional village was neither romantic, nor necessarily peaceful. Rural violence was common in the preindustrial world. Nor was traditional village life healthy in the physical sense. Cheap soap, underclothing, shoes, and shirts were unavailable, vermin abounded in thatched roofs, sanitation was primitive, and drinking water often contaminated. As late as 1950, only 8 percent of the communes had clean,

[10]Toyin Falola, ed., *Britain and Nigeria: Exploitation or Development*. London and Highlands, New Jersey, Zed Books, 1986.

[11]See, for instance, Ezra Mendelsohn, *The Jews of East Central Europe Between the World Wars*. Bloomington, Indiana University Press, 1983. During the interwar period, very backward parts of Eastern Europe, such as Ruthenia in Czechoslovakia still had a substantial Jewish farming sector, but this was declining, as had the farming components among Jewish populations everywhere else.

piped drinking water in Indre-et-Loire, upriver from Angers in France.)[12]

Nostalgia is an equally unreliable guide with regard to customary kinship systems. Traditional families, or what were later thought of as traditional families, had indeed commanded fierce loyalties. They had also possessed their dark side – greed, envy, fear of the future, with rigid limits on individual decision making, and bitter, sometimes deadly, quarrels – as is made obvious by surviving court records and testimonies.[13]

Changes in family structure should not, of course, be exaggerated during the postwar years. As we have seen, earlier long-standing fears concerning the demographic decline of Western Europe proved quite misplaced. Improvements in medicine and hygiene continued to extend the human lifespan. A Mozart aria had praised *una donna di quindici anni*; (a lady of 15); Balzac had surprised the world by asserting that there could be great beauty in *une femme de trente ans* (a woman of 30). By the 1950s, a lady in her forties or fifties might still be svelte and *sportive* to a degree that would have startled her grandmother. Western birthrates once again went up. Indeed France underwent a remarkable demographic rejuvenation. These were the years of the "baby boom," when returning servicemen married and started families. The great majority of these families were still husband-headed. (More and more women were coming into paid employment, but the average mother was either a full-time homemaker, or only had a part-time job.) The mother-headed family was comparatively rare, as was the two-income, no-children family. Women had not yet made much of an advance into the more highly paid managerial or professional posts. For many women marriage offered social advancement. A nurse would consider a physician a good catch; a company secretary would similarly regard the branch manager. Later, as women's liberation proceeded, marriage may have declined as an avenue of social promotion, a subject that remains to be investigated.

There can be no doubt that marriages throughout the Western world (particularly in the US) were more stable in the 1950s than later on. The average child grew up with the security of both a mother and a father in the home. The various Western nations overall became younger, and demographic growth increased both the size of the available labor force and the size and nature of the available markets.

What was the reason for this phoenix-like revival? No single explanation will suffice. War, defeat, and their leaders' infamous conduct had discredited both Nazism and Fascism. Their cause no longer appeared – as it had during the 1930s – the cause of youth, and of a banner-waving future. Instead, the US and Britain had out-produced, out-organized, out-thought, and out-fought the Axis powers. All over Western Europe, democracy was now accepted in

---

[12]Weber, *Fin de Siècle*, p. 56.

[13]A mine of unused information for Rhodesian whites, including minority groups such as Afrikaners, Sephardic as well as Ashkenazic Jews and Greeks are the records of the Master of the High Court in the National Archives of Zimbabwe. Some of the surviving wills would have furnished the material for many a Balzac novel.

public as the only legitimate form of government. The bulk of Western voters had had enough of political violence. Soviet communism now began to earn successive discredit, through the Prague coup of 1948, the East German rising of 1953, the abortive Hungarian revolution of 1956, and Khrushchev's revelations concerning Stalin's crimes in the Soviet Union itself. The communists maintained some support among Western intellectuals, and continued to enjoy a considerable following among the French and Italian electorates; but in every Western country, they remained a minority.

Government was held in the hands of moderates, whether of the left or the right – Labour, Social Democrats, Christian Democrats, and Tories. The Old Right, ultra-patriotic, unyielding, often anti-semitic, did not disappear, but steadily weakened. The new conservatives were yesterday's liberals and centrists – an enormous change for the better. The various Western economies operated through a combination of private enterprise, nationalized enterprise, and public welfarism. There was agreement on the principle; only the terms of the compromise would vary. It was the moderates moreover who labored for Western European integration, and equated it with future prosperity and a new understanding between Europe's feuding nation states. (The Schuman declaration of 1950 that had originally proposed the ECSC began with the assertion that only new creative efforts would safeguard world peace.) The cause of European integration owed a great deal to Catholics such as de Gasperi, Adenauer, and Schuman; but the integrationists also included Protestants such as Walter Hallstein, and socialists such as Paul-Henri Spaak, and Paul Finet (the latter first president of the International Confederation of Free Trade Unions, later head of the ECSC High Authority). Indeed, an English trade unionist stressed that Continental labor unions had, in most cases, been "the keenest and most consistent supporters of integration projects in Western Europe," and had largely been responsible for their broadly based support.[14] This is not to say that Europeans suddenly turned into Europeanists. The Luxemburgers' national motto "Mir woelle bleiwe was mer sin" (we wish to remain what we are) might have appealed to Europeans on both sides of the Iron Curtain. But at least there was now a widespread willingness to accept trans-national economic cooperation and moderate politics. (Incredible as it would have appeared to the French in 1948, 40 years later the remains of Jean Monnet were transferred in state to the *Panthéon*, shrine of French nationalism, bedecked with European flags of blue and gold.)

The moderates' success is easier to chronicle than to explain. The currency of political morality had grossly depreciated during the years of war, occupation, and terror; now it re-stabilized. The rule of law ceased to be identified with the rule of mediocrity; the *Rechtsstaat* ceased to be regarded with contempt by men and women who had experienced its demise and the new Basic Law steadily won legitimacy in the FRG. France, under its reconstituted republic, revived from the misery of Vichy. Italy, under its new republic, recovered from Mussolini's tinsel glory. Henceforth Italian politics

---

[14]Richard Mayne, *The Community of Europe*. New York, W. W. Norton, 1963, p. 51.

remained untroubled by irredentism or dreams of conquest.

The moderates' triumph was even greater in West Germany. German nationalism had held the center of the stage for more than a century. The cause of German unification had been dear to free trade liberals and Marxists, to adherents of *realpolitik* and romantics. Prusso-German nationalism had dominated German historiography. But suddenly the martial splendor crumbled. The *Reich* lay shattered. Translated into American terms, it was as if the US had lost all its western and southwestern states, as if their populations had been expelled, as if the remainder of the US had been divided, and separated by a rigid artificial border drawn across the map, as if both rump states had been subjected to foreign occupation, and the smaller of the two to communist dictatorship. Contrary to all reasonable expectations, however, the Germans adjusted. They did so with such remarkable rapidity as to occasion some doubts with regard to the strength of that German national feeling once taken for granted. But the new West German state, helped by the Americans, quickly and unexpectedly established for itself political legitimacy; Bonn was not Weimar. The aged Adenauer turned out to be Germany's greatest twentieth-century statesman, who performed the seemingly impossible. The Soviet threat was contained. NATO, for all its weaknesses, served its purpose; it reintegrated West Germany and Italy into Western Europe and it provided a shield against communist militarism.

The citizens of Western Europe and North America were indeed fortunate at the time in finding guidance from a remarkable number of able personalities. The democracies had often been derided in the past for their supposed inability to produce first-rate leaders – in contrast to the *Führer*, *duci*, *vozhdi*, *conducatori*, and *verzérek* of the dictatorial kind. In fact, the list of able democratic statesman was long, and included Churchill, de Gaulle, Adenauer, de Gasperi, Truman, and Eisenhower. Overall, they served their respective countries well. But even the best of them could have accomplished little without that remarkable shift that caused the US to abandon isolationism after World War II, and assume leadership of the Free World.

It was a great time to be American. During World War II, it was the US that had served as the arsenal of democracy. It was the US that underwrote bodies such as UNRRA (United Nations Relief and Rehabilitation Administration, 1943), GATT (General Agreement on Tariffs and Trade, 1947), the Marshall Plan (1947), and NATO (1949). It was the US that supplied much of the inspiration for a united Europe, and even the symbolism. (The Council of Europe's flag displayed golden stars arranged in a circle on a blue ground, and resembled early US flags that used stars for the purpose of designating a new constellation.) It was the US that in the Korean war played the decisive part in stopping for the first time armed communist aggression. (The Soviet Union had supplied North Korea with fighter plans and Soviet pilots, heavy artillery and T 34 tanks, whereas the US had withheld heavy equipment from the South Korean president, Syngman Rhee, fearing his aggressive intentions.) It was also the US that supplied the military assistance required to stabilize Western Europe against the Soviet threat. From this time on, it was the US that provided the world's greatest number of Nobel laureates, just as it supplied most of the new patents, industrial, and managerial skills. It was the US that led in the productivity of labor, that rightly prided itself on having the highest living standards; and it was the US that supplied much of the vision and pressure required for closer association between the European states.

Western Europe and North America became an Atlantic Community more closely linked than ever before, politically, militarily, but also culturally. Not that the flow was one way – a truth often forgotten by American bar-room patriots and by Europeans frightened of *le défi americain*, the American challenge. European-born artists and professors found new audiences in the US. Americans in Europe learned foreign tongues, acquired a liking for foreign cookery and wines, and sometimes married Europeans. Talent and technology moved from Europe to the US (in the car industry, most postwar inventions such as the disc-brake derived from Europe). But American influence overseas was even more important, and books in English were translated far more widely into foreign tongues than books written in any other language.[15] Henceforth the US made a major contribution to the high culture of the Western world through works of art, music, literature, and scholarship.

The US also dominated the popular arts. The Lone Ranger became the world's modern Siegfried or Beowulf. In popular music, performing artists such as Duke Ellington, and composers such as Irving Berlin personified American vigor, optimism, and the success story of legend. Berlin was not merely the son of poverty-stricken immigrants, the poor man who made good. He was also the "primitive" artist whom so many European romantics praised in theory, and derided in practice. He respected the public – unlike Europeans such as Schoenberg and Stravinsky who despised them. Irving Berlin was in some ways like the old itinerant fiddler who had gone from fair to fair. He lacked formal training, could not read scores, and required a mechanical device on his piano to make key changes. Yet the vigor and charm of his music, his tremendous output, his enormous public appeal, made him the archetypal American of popular imagination.

It was this confident American personality that played the major part in constructing and shaping the Atlantic Community. To denounce the US of the 1940s and 1950s became a fashionable pursuit for American academics during the 1960s and 1970s. Critics called it a scoundrel time, an age of philistinism. We see no merit in such interpretations. We agree rather with William O'Neill who entitled his book on the era *American High: The Years of Confidence, 1945–1960* and with John Patrick Diggins who wrote *The Proud Decades: America in War and Peace, 1941–1960*.

This feeling of confidence spilled back into Western Europe. American influence on the old world had of course been of long standing. From its beginnings, the US had accommodated far more European emigrants than any other country in the world. (To this day well over four fifths of Americans

---

[15]Robert Deutsch, "A cross-cultural history of international relations: books, translations in the twentieth century," *Quantum: Historical and Social Research*, no. 36, October 1985, pp. 3–41.

trace all or most of their ancestors to Europe, including many Hispanics.) The US continued to influence Europe in a variety of ways, through her example as an individualist society wedded to private enterprise, and as a haven for European emigrants and capital.

An even more thorough penetration of American mores into Europe began at the turn of the present century. "German children began to dress as cowboys and Indians ... to celebrate *Fasching*, while French children dressed as cowboys and Indians to celebrate Mardi Gras."[16] The tide of American influence rose through movies, jazz, comics – no *Proletkult* art could compete with Hollywood for the loyalty of the masses. The US became the beneficiary of the greatest ever intellectual migration from Europe. US constitutional liberty was triumphantly vindicated at a time when orthodox Marxists felt convinced that all advanced capitalist societies must ultimately perish from their internal contradictions, and submit to Fascism. In retrospect, it is clear that neither native nor foreign critics gave sufficient credit to the US for its enormous achievement in preventing that variegated country from becoming a Lebanon, a Cyprus, or a Northern Ireland of continental proportions.

Instead, the US became a world role model, and World War II greatly contributed to this process. The war threw 3,500,000 Americans into Europe. Thereafter several hundreds of thousands Americans stayed, as servicemen and their dependents. Europeans saw in action American techniques of mass production, bridge building, blood-transfusion, airport direction, sanitation, car maintenance, and so on. Theodore White said, in a now half-forgotten classic "The United States Armed Forces Network ... had for a while the largest listening audience in Europe, and probably taught more Continentals the use of idiomatic English than all the schoolhouses of the Continent."[17] Thereafter, Europe experienced a new influx of US businessmen and multinationals, managerial consultants, aid administrators, engineers, academics, tourists, bankers, journalists, performers, technicians, teachers, and communications experts. These men and women, with their twangy accents and forward manner, did not always gain for themselves the popularity they deserved in their own estimation. But overall, NATO and the Marshall Plan were a beneficient invasion.

In March 1948, Britain, France, Belgium, the Netherlands, and Luxemburg, fearing an aggressive Moscow in league with local communist parties, signed the Brussels Treaty to come to each other's aid if attacked. Washington supported such regional security agreements and asked to be included in the pact (though the Soviets claimed the US was weakening the UN and was creating an aggressive bloc). In spite of opposition the US and its allies (Canada, Britain, France, Italy, Belgium, the Netherlands, Luxemburg, Norway, Denmark, Ireland, and Portugal) signed on April 4, 1949 the North Atlantic treaty creating NATO. The signatories agreed that an attack on one

[16]Theodore H. White, *Fire in the Ashes: Europe in Mid-Century.* New York, William Sloane Associates, 1953, p. 363.
[17]Ibid., p. 363.

was an attack on all, and implied a moral if not a legal responsibility on the part of the US to come to Europe's aid. The US thus gave up nonentanglement. Having twice been drawn to Europe's rescue, the US now decided it was best to warn an aggressor beforehand, that the Americans would protect their allies.

North America now had its first large peacetime military budget and first peacetime conscription. Thanks in part to British guidance, a corps of able American politicians and officials, and a perceived Soviet threat, the US decided to stay in Europe, to help in rebuilding, and in the containment of communism.

What did the Marshall Plan actually do? Although scholars disagree on the exact importance of the plan to European recovery, most agree that it played a major role. Concretely, the ERP provided food, fuel, raw materials, housing, machinery, and means of land reclamation. The Marshall Plan dealt with the repair of infrastructures (roads, railways, canals, bridges) and replacement of ships; it stimulated industrial production by unclogging bottlenecks, and agricultural production by supplying tractors, seeds, improved methods of farming and stock raising. The dollar gap was bridged, facilitating loans to small businesses. Western Europe was rebuilt and became prosperous. The largest share of ERP money went to Britain, then to France, Italy, and West Germany, in that order. The Marshall Plan spent $13.5 billion (about $90 billion in 1988 dollar values).

The Marshall Plan also nurtured the OEEC, and the European Coal and Steel Community in 1952 (Schuman plan) whereby the French and German coal and steel industries were under the ECSC with other nations participating. The Marshall Plan achieved in spectacular fashion its goal of increasing industrial and agricultural productivity (30 percent gain in industrial production, 15 percent in agricultural output and the GNP rose by 32.5 percent by 1951). Europe had recovered and had reached a stage of self-sustaining growth when the ERP ended in 1952.

The Economic Cooperation Administration (ECA, staffed by enthusiasts, many of them Keynesians, from the US) modernized Europe's industries and agriculture and provided technical assistance. Over 210 production teams visited the US to learn American manufacturing techniques, methods of smelting, foundry practices, and so on. Over 1,000 workers, managers, and agricultural experts came in 1950 alone. The US in turn sent out 372 experts to lecture on engineering, marketing, research methods, and standardization. ERP had over 2,000 full-time administrators in Europe and 200,000 tractors a year were sold to Europe, structurally transforming agriculture, increasing production above prewar standards and freeing millions of farm laborers and farmers for work in towns in industry and construction.

History will show that the Marshall Plan not only rebuilt Europe but also helped to create the Atlantic Community (NATO, ECSC, EEC), bringing the US out of its isolationism to cooperate with Europeans for the benefit of peoples on both sides of the Atlantic. The Marshall Plan was one of the greatest economic success stories of modern times and helped to make Western Europe by 1960 the second most important industrial and trading center in the world. After 1951 the Marshall Plan continued in other guises and names: the ECA became the Mutual Security Agency and in 1953 the Foreign Operations Administration was first renamed the International Cooperation Administration, then in 1961 called the Agency for International Development (AID).

Since the Marshall Plan's inception the US has been an internationalist state, a global power willing to project its power and influence over the entire non-communist world, first in Western Europe and Japan, then to the impoverished Third World. And although American planners did not succeed in creating a United States of Europe then, they did lay the foundation for such a policy and achieved partial success with the creation of the European Economic Community and the Common Market by the Treaty of Rome, signed on March 25, 1957. If all goes as planned in 1992, a United States of Europe will have been achieved, as a proportion of American officialdom has wished.

The emergent Atlantic order achieved what to earlier generations would have appeared a Utopia. Old national enmities ebbed and democratic governments won the loyalty of their citizens. A new war between France and Britain, France and Germany, France and Italy, Germany and Britain or Norway, now appeared as improbable as a war between those former ancient enemies, England and Scotland. Material living standards rose. Immense advances were made in science, health care, and technology. Racial, national, and religious prejudice diminished in intensity. To measure the extent of their decline is hard, for public opinion surveys do not necessarily tell the whole truth. But there is no doubt that social mobility improved after World War II for all minorities – for Catholics in mainly Protestant countries such as Britain, Holland, West Germany, and the US, as for blacks and Jews in the US. Antisemitism ceased to be a major force in the politics of the Atlantic states; its political impact remained confined to the Soviet bloc and the Muslim world. Anti-Catholicism waned too, except in enclaves such as Northern Ireland. The major religions all made their peace with the democratic order – not surprisingly when the US had become the world's most important Protestant, Catholic, and Jewish country.

The postwar era saw the rise of Catholics to higher social and economic power and political influence in Belgium, Britain, Holland, West Germany, and the United States. This upward mobility was spurred on by Catholic resistance to Fascism, and their wartime record in Britain and the US. The opening of higher education and the professions to Catholics in Europe and the US saw the end of ghettos and working-class status. The GI Bill educated hundreds of thousands of Catholic Americans to the highest level and prestige professions (scholars, doctors, scientists, teachers, engineers, lawyers) were entered by Catholics in much greater numbers than before.

And religion did not disappear. Marx, Freud, and Lenin had all believed that the days of the great religions were numbered. Their assumptions were shared by many religious people, who imagined that faith, strong two centuries beforehand, had declined ever since. No such thing happened. In fact many churches may have been in better spiritual condition in the twentieth than in the eighteenth century – when King Louis XVI had grumbled at a proposed high appointment on the grounds that "at least the archbishop of Paris should believe in God," and when an English newspaper had carried advertisements such as the following: "wanted, a curacy in a good sporting county, where the duty is light, and the neighbourhood convivial."[18]

None of the great postwar achievements came without cost. Yesterday's solutions became tomorrow's problems. The planners' optimism turned into the euphoria of the 1960s, the age of the "new frontier," the "great society," and the "war against poverty." For a brief spell all seemed possible to the Keynesian planners. But in fact, the welfare state and foreign aid, greeted with so much hope at its inception, occasioned new troubles of its own – rising costs, a burgeoning bureaucracy, unrealistic expectations, and unintended consequences. The public consensus waned. The left later demonstrated that the welfare state did not in fact produce social equality, and that the middle classes may have been the chief beneficiaries of the free public services in general, and free educational services in particular. Conservatives pointed out that unchecked expansion of welfare expenditure would overload the economy, and overburden the taxpayer. Many of the welfare planners' basic assumptions were seen to be questionable. According to the new liberal dispensation there should be no limit to the scope and power of government. But as the state's powers expanded, its administrative efficiency seemed to contract.

In education, for example, experts had widely taken for granted that increased expenditure on schools and teachers would necessarily raise educational standards. These in turn would create a better educated workforce, and thereby enhance productivity. Greater social equality supposedly could be produced by administrative fiat. Money certainly counts in education, but excellence cannot be bought by cash alone. Standards are also influenced by intangible cultural factors – the particular ethos of a school, the force of religion, of social custom, and above all, the decisive part played by parents. (It is significant that Antony Flew, a British expert, entitled his critique of British education, *Power to the Parents: Reversing Education Decline*, London, Sherwood, 1987.) Flaws in the educationists' agenda were matched by flaws in the Keynesian and welfare planners' agenda in general.

Traditional kinship bonds and ties of cultural allegiance now weakened or snapped, under a new malaise that came with prosperity – again its extent is hard to measure. (The great majority of respondents in public opinion polls continued to declare themselves happy with their lot.) But discontent there was, especially among intellectuals. Demands once met created new demands; visions of social utopias kept receding into the future.

But for all these travails, the postwar years were marvellous, "thirty golden years" of achievement anticipated by few. Western Europe and North America became more closely linked than ever before, to their great mutual benefit. The debt owed by the New World to the Old was repaid in full. Had Macaulay

---

[18]George Rudé, *Europe in the Eighteenth Century: Aristocracy and Bourgeoisie*. Cambridge, Mass., Harvard University Press, 1985, pp. 126–7.

returned to survey the postwar scene in the West, he would have felt vindicated in his optimism.

To conclude, Europe's renaissance after 1945 was to a considerable extent initiated, supported, and guided by American generosity, values, and methods. Western Europe not only recovered, it prospered economically, spiritually, and militarily more than anyone could have dreamed at the end of the war. It was rebuilt by th Marshall Plan and defended by the American-initiated NATO, although some of Europe's leaders and especially its intellectuals failed to appreciate the American achievement or to accept the Americanization of Europe. Americans descended on Europe by the thousands; they came as relief officials, as diplomats and soldiers, as businessmen and analysts, as students and scholars. The Americans brought new forms of constitutional democracy, science and technology, popular culture, the consumer society, and multi-nationals. Their life style, customs, foods, clothing, music, and movies intensified the partial Americanization of Europe which had begun after World War I. It was a process that many deplored, few would reverse, and none could end.

Maps

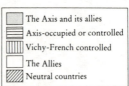

The Axis and its allies
Axis-occupied or controlled
Vichy-French controlled
The Allies
Neutral countries

MAP I *Axis expansion in Europe, 1942*

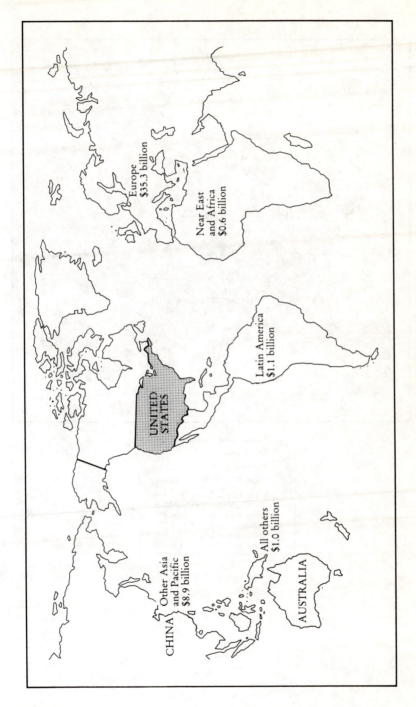

MAP 2   *US foreign aid, military and economic, 1945–54*

ICELAND

NORWAY FINLAND

ATLANTIC SWEDEN

SOVIET UNION

DENMARK
NETHER-
LANDS
IRELAND GREAT
BRITAIN

OCEAN GER.
DEM POLAND
REP
BELGIUM GER.
FED. CZECHOSLOVAKIA
REP.
AUSTRIA HUNGARY
FRANCE SWIT. RUMANIA BLACK SEA
YUGOSLAVIA BULGARIA
ITALY ALBANIA TURKEY
PORTUGAL SPAIN GREECE

MEDITERRANEAN SEA

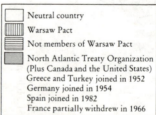

☐ Neutral country

▥ Warsaw Pact

☰ Not members of Warsaw Pact

▨ North Atlantic Treaty Organization
(Plus Canada and the United States)
Greece and Turkey joined in 1952
Germany joined in 1954
Spain joined in 1982
France partially withdrew in 1966

MAP 3 *Europe in the Cold War*

MAP 4 *The six EEC members 1958*